Life-Span Human Development

Fifth Edition

Carol K. Sigelman
The George Washington University

Elizabeth A. Rider
Elizabethtown College

Australia • Canada • Mexico • Singapore • Spain • United Kingdom • United States

Publisher: Vicki Knight
Acquisitions Editor: Michele Sordi
Developmental Editor: Kristin Makarewycz
Technology Project Manager: Erik Fortier
Assistant Editor: Jennifer Wilkinson
Editorial Assistant: Jessica Kim
Marketing Manager: Dory Schaeffer
Marketing Assistant: Nicole Morinon
Advertising Project Manager: Tami Strang
Art Director: Vernon Boes
Project Manager, Editorial Production: Paul Wells
Print/Media Buyer: Barbara Britton
Permissions Editor: Chelsea Junget

Printed in Canada
1 2 3 4 5 6 7 09 08 07 06

For more information about our products, contact us at:
Thomson Learning Academic Resource Center
1-800-423-0563
For permission to use material from this text or product, submit a request online at http://www.thomsonrights.com.
Any additional questions about permissions can be submitted by email to thomsonrights@thomson.com.

Library of Congress Control Number: 2004116829

Student's Edition ISBN: 0-534-55381-8
Instructor's Edition ISBN: 0-495-03015-5
International Student Edition ISBN: 0-495-00682-3

Production Editor: Denise DeLancey, Graphic World Publishing Services
Text Design: Jennifer Dunn
Cover Design: Larry Didona
Photo Researcher: Terri Wright
Illustration: Graphic World Illustration Studios
Cover Images: (center image) © Banana Stock/age fotostock (clockwise from top) © Patrick Sheandell/age fotostock; © Digital Vision/Getty; © Stockbyte Gold/Getty Images; © Photodisc; © Ben Welsh/age fotostock; © Banana Stock/age fotostock; (leaf) © Royalty-free/CORBIS; (daisies) © Royalty-free/CORBIS
Cover Printer: Transcontinental Printing/Interglobe
Compositor: Graphic World, Inc.
Printer: Transcontinental Printing/Interglobe

Thomson Higher Education
10 Davis Drive
Belmont, CA 94002-3098
USA

Asia (including India)
Thomson Learning
5 Shenton Way
#01-01 UIC Building
Singapore 068808

Australia/New Zealand
Thomson Learning Australia
102 Dodds Street
Southbank, Victoria 3006
Australia

Canada
Thomson Nelson
1120 Birchmount Road
Toronto, Ontario M1K 5G4
Canada

UK/Europe/Middle East/Africa
Thomson Learning
High Holborn House
50–51 Bedford Road
London WC1R 4LR
United Kingdom

Latin America
Thomson Learning
Seneca, 53
Colonia Polanco
11560 Mexico
D.F. Mexico

Spain (including Portugal)
Thomson Paraninfo
Calle Magallanes, 25
28015 Madrid, Spain

To the students who have inspired us

Brief Contents

Contents

CHAPTER 6

CHAPTER 7

CHAPTER 11
Self and Personality 286

CHAPTER 12
Gender Roles and Sexuality 322

Preface

Welcome to the fifth edition of *Life-Span Human Development.* This new edition has many exciting changes, yet it retains the core features valued by students and instructors over the years. We remain firmly committed to our unique integrated topical–chronological approach and to a presentation that is both research-oriented and relevant to the "real world." However, we cast an even brighter light on the all-important nature–nurture issue, offer stronger and more up-to-date coverage of key topics and controversies in life-span human development, and add new pedagogical features and supplements to enhance the teaching–learning process.

A Topical and Chronological Approach

The most distinctive feature of this book is its unique *integrated topical–chronological approach.* Almost all other life-span development textbooks adopt a chronological or "age–stage" approach, carving the life span into age ranges and describing the prominent characteristics of individuals within each age range. In contrast, we use a topical approach for the overall organization of the book blended with a chronological approach within chapters. Each chapter focuses on a domain of development such as physical growth, cognition, or personality and traces developmental trends and influences in that domain from infancy to old age. Each chapter calls attention to age groups through major sections on infancy, childhood, adolescence, and adulthood.

Why Topical?

Why have we fought the tide? Like many other instructors, we have typically favored topically organized textbooks when teaching child, adolescent, or adult development courses. As a result, it seemed natural to use that topical approach in introducing students to the whole life span. Besides, chronologically organized texts often have to repeat themselves as they remind readers of where development left off in an earlier age period (covered several chapters ago).

More importantly, a topic-by-topic organization conveys the flow of development in each area—the systematic, and often dramatic, transformations that take place and the developmental continuities. The topical approach also helps us emphasize developmental *processes*—how nature and nurture interact over the life span to bring change.

Finally, a predominantly topical approach is more compatible with a *life-span perspective,* which views any period of life in relation to what comes before and what is yet to come. In chronologically organized textbooks, many topics are described only in connection with the age group to which they seem most relevant—for example, attachment in relation to infancy or sexuality in relation to adolescence and adulthood. A topical organization makes readers ask intriguing questions that they might otherwise not ask, such as these about attachment relationships:

- What do infants' attachments to their parents have in common with, and how do they differ from, attachments between childhood friends or between adult romantic partners?
- Do securely attached infants later have a greater capacity to form and sustain friendships or romantic partnerships than infants whose early social experiences are less favorable?
- What are the consequences at different points in the life span of lacking someone to be closely attached to?

Attachments are important throughout the life span, and a topical organization helps make that clear.

Why Chronological?

We adopted a topical approach because we consider it the best way to introduce the how and why of human development. We also appreciate the strengths of the chronological approach, particularly its ability to portray the whole person in each period of the life span. For this reason, we integrated the age–stage approach with the topical organization, aiming to have the best of both worlds.

Each topical chapter contains major sections on infancy, childhood, adolescence, and adulthood. The existence of these sections is proof that the chapters consider development in each of the domains covered across the *whole* life span. These age–stage sections call attention to the distinctive qualities of each phase of life and make it easier for students to find material on an age period of particular interest to them. Our degree of emphasis on each period of the life span varies depending on the topic.

We believe that our integrated topical–chronological approach allows us to convey the flow of life-span development in particular areas and the factors influencing it while highlighting the major physical, cognitive, and psychosocial developments within any particular developmental period.

Adaptability of the Integrated Topical–Chronological Approach

Even though links among chapters are noted throughout the book, instructors who are teaching short courses or who are otherwise pressed for time can omit a chapter without fear of rendering other chapters incomprehensible. For example:

- A cognitively oriented course might omit one or more of the socially oriented chapters (Chapters 11, 12, and 14–17).
- A socially oriented course might omit one or more of the cognitive chapters (Chapters 6–10).

Moreover, this approach allows instructors enough flexibility to cover infancy, childhood, and adolescence in the first portion of the course, if they prefer, and to save the material on adulthood for the end.

Research-Oriented and Real Coverage

Why has *Life-Span Human Development* continued to receive high praise from both faculty and students over the years? We think it is because we have worked to create a text that is rigorous yet readable and research-oriented yet "real" to students. The fifth edition of *Life-Span Human Development* continues in this tradition, tackling complex theoretical controversies and presenting the best of both classic and contemporary research from multiple disciplines in a way that is accessible and relevant to students' experiences.

We believe that it is critical for students to understand how we know what we know about development—to appreciate the research process. With that in mind, we describe illustrative studies and present their data in graphs and tables, and we cite the authors and dates of publication for a large number of books and articles, all fully referenced in the bibliography at the end of the book. Some students may wonder why they are there. It is because we are committed to the value of systematic research, because we are bound to give credit where credit is due, and because we want students and their professors to have the resources they need to pursue their interests in human development during and after the course.

We also appreciate that solid scholarship is of little good to students unless they want to read it and can understand it. We maintain that even the most complex issues in human development can be made understandable through clear and organized writing.

To make the material more "real," we clarify developmental concepts through examples and analogies, connect topics in the text to topics in the news, and highlight implications for everyday functioning. We also incorporate material relevant to students' current and future roles as parents, teachers, psychologists, nurses, day care workers, and other human service professionals. And we help students see that major theories of human development do not just guide researchers but can help anyone analyze issues that we all face—including such practical matters as raising children, working with troubled adolescents, or coping with Alzheimer's disease in the family.

Organization of the Text

Core Concepts: Chapters 1 to 4

The book begins by orienting students to the life-span perspective on human development and to approaches to the scientific study of development (Chapter 1), as well as to the central issues and theoretical perspectives that have dominated the field (Chapter 2). It then explores developmental processes in some depth, examining genetic influences (Chapter 3) and early environmental influences (Chapter 4) on development. These chapters show how genes contribute to typical changes and individual differences throughout the life span and how people are products of their prenatal and postnatal environments.

Development of Basic Human Capacities: Chapters 5 to 10

Chapters on the growth and aging of the body and nervous system (Chapter 5) and on the development of sensory and perceptual capacities (Chapter 6) launch our examination of the development of basic human capacities. Chapter 7 covers Jean Piaget's perspective on cognitive development and the quite different perspective offered by Lev Vygotsky; Chapter 8 views memory and problem solving from an information-processing perspective; Chapter 9 highlights the psychometric approach to cognition, exploring individual differences in intelligence and creativity; and Chapter 10 explores language development and the roles of language and cognition in educational achievement.

Development of Self in Society: Chapters 11 to 17

The next three chapters concern the development of the self: changes in self-conceptions and personality, including vocational identity (Chapter 11); in gender roles and sexuality (Chapter 12); and in social cognition and morality (Chapter 13). The self is set more squarely in a social context as we trace life-span changes in attachment relationships (Chapter 14) and in roles and relationships within the family (Chapter 15). Finally, we offer a life-span perspective on developmental problems and disorders (Chapter 16) and examine why people die and how they cope with death (Chapter 17).

Big Picture Perspective: Epilogue

As in previous editions, we end with an epilogue that summarizes major developments in each of seven periods of the life span and broad themes in life-span development that are emphasized throughout the book. This conclusion focuses attention on the whole person and serves as a handy reference throughout the course for students who want the big picture. Some instructors assign this at the beginning of their courses to help ground students; others use it both to start the course and to stimulate discussion at the end.

New to This Edition

In this edition, we put the nature–nurture issue on center stage, introduce "Summing Up" sections within chapters, and bring to life several new topics and research findings.

Highlighting the Nature–Nurture Issue

If students gain nothing else from their study of human development, we hope they gain a deeper understanding of the nature–nurture issue and of the many interacting forces acting on, and being acted on by, the developing person. We want students to understand that human development is an incredibly complex process that grows out of transactions between a changing person and a changing world and out of dynamic relationships among biological, psychological, and social influences. No contributor to development—a gene, a temperament, a parent, a culture—acts alone and is unaffected by other influences on development.

In this edition, we introduce the nature–nurture issue in Chapter 1. Each subsequent chapter includes one or more illustration of the intertwined contributions of nature and nurture to development. These topics are listed for easy reference in the theme index that appears on the book's endpapers. Along the way, we describe some exciting studies involving molecular genetics that compare individuals with and without particular genes and with and without particular life experiences to bring home what it means to say that genes and environment interact to influence development. For example, it becomes clear in Chapter 3 that the odds of depression become high only when a person is at genetic risk for depression and experiences multiple stressful events. In the process of writing these nature–nurture segments—which cover topics ranging from physical growth and the effects of prenatal alcohol exposure, to temperament and theory of mind, to autism and aging—we expanded coverage of evolution, genes, hormones, and other biological forces in development, enriched descriptions of social and cultural influences on development, and, most importantly, illuminated the complex interrelationships between biological and environmental influences that are at the heart of the developmental process.

Summing Up

Another feature new to this edition is "Summing Up" paragraphs at the end of each major section of each chapter to supplement the "Summary Points" at the conclusion of each chapter. We believe that these internal summaries will help students consolidate what they are learning when they read a chapter and when they review the material afterward.

Understanding the Data: Exercises on the Web

To reinforce students' understanding of current research data, these interactive online exercises link the text's research-oriented figures and tables to critical thinking exercises on the Book Companion Website (http://psychology.wadsworth.com/sigelman_rider5e). Icons next to selected figure and table captions in the text, and prompts at the end of each chapter, guide students to online exercises for specific figures and tables.

Keeping Current

As always, the book has been thoroughly updated from start to finish; it conveys the most recent discoveries and insights developmentalists have to offer. We take pride in having written a well-researched and well-referenced book that professors and students can use as a resource. We added some exciting new topics and greatly expanded and updated coverage of other topics. A sampling follows.

Chapter 1. Understanding Life-Span Human Development

- New section, "Framing the Nature–Nurture Issue," to put this all-important issue in a starring role from the start of the book
- Concrete illustration of research methods with a study that uses verbal report, behavioral observation, and physiological measures
- Inclusion of Urie Bronfenbrenner's bioecological model in the first chapter to call attention to issues in understanding diversity in human development

Chapter 2. Theories of Human Development

- New coverage of Gilbert Gottlieb's evolutionary–epigenetic systems perspective, including material on ethology
- New twists on this chapter's attempt to show how each major theorist would explain teenage pregnancy

Chapter 3. Genes, Environment, and Development

- The latest from the Human Genome Project and the potentials of new molecular genetics research
- New emphasis on how genes turn on and off over the course of development partly in response to environmental influences
- New evidence of social class differences in the heritability of intelligence
- Descriptions of both the contributions and the limitations of behavioral genetics

Chapter 4. Prenatal Development and Birth

- The latest research on prenatal development and teratogens
- Expanded coverage of birthing practices
- New reproductive technologies

Chapter 5. The Physical Self

- More material on early and later brain development, including a separate section that covers brain plasticity
- A dynamic systems perspective on the emergence of motor skills
- Adolescent risk taking in relation to brain development during adolescence
- The latest research on teens and sleep

Chapter 6. Perception

- Issues in assessing hearing impairment across the life span
- Reorganized and updated coverage of the perceptual capacities of adults
- Interventions for both infants and elderly adults with hearing impairments

Chapter 7. Cognition

- New research on the infant's mastery of object permanence
- Expanded coverage of Vygotsky's perspective, including a comparison of his theory with that of Piaget
- Cognitive development in relation to children's humor and belief in Santa Claus

Chapter 8. Memory and Information Processing

- A sharper focus on developments in memory and information processing
- Coverage of autobiographical memory with references to scripts and eyewitness memory
- A description of what is "normal" forgetfulness in old age and what is not

Chapter 9. Intelligence and Creativity

- Information on modern intelligence tests including the Kaufman Assessment Battery for Children and Reuven Feuerstein's Learning Potential Assessment Device
- Historical changes in average intelligence quotient (IQ) scores
- The effectiveness of early intervention programs for preschool children and IQ training for elderly adults

Chapter 10. Language and Education

- Relationships between language skills, reading, and academic achievement
- Trends in science and mathematics education
- A section on integrating school and work during adolescence
- Integrated description of the educational implications of the theories and research in Chapters 6 through 9

Chapter 11. Self and Personality

- Clarification of links between early temperament and later personality
- Continued emphasis on the concept of goodness of fit between person and environment in relation to both personality development and vocational development
- New information on nature, nurture, and personality in different cultures
- Coverage of the controversy over the degree of continuity in adult personality

Chapter 12. Gender Roles and Sexuality

- Clarification of which gender differences are not substantiated by research
- The latest research on gender-role development including the contributions of biology and environment

Chapter 13. Social Cognition and Moral Development

- The roles of biology and culture in the development of a theory of mind
- The importance of a mutually responsive orientation between parent and child in the early development of conscience
- In-depth coverage of the multiple roots of youth violence and a new integrative model of influences on aggression

Chapter 14. Attachment and Social Relationships

- Coverage of a major National Institute of Child Health and Human Development study of the effects of day care
- Emphasis on connections between attachment and emotional regulation
- New research on the effects of early social deprivation on the quality of later relationships and social development
- New findings concerning the emotional lives of older adults

Chapter 15. The Family

- Trends in family life and the issue of whether the family is in decline
- Contributions of nature and nurture to differences between mothers and fathers
- New research linking attachment styles to adjustment during the transition to new parenthood
- A new empowerment approach to preventing abuse

Chapter 16. Developmental Psychopathology

- Expanded coverage of the developmental psychopathology perspective
- New illustrations of the diathesis–stress model of psychopathology
- Leading hypotheses about the core problem in autism, including the extreme male brain hypothesis
- The latest breakthroughs in understanding of attention deficit hyperactivity disorder, anorexia nervosa, depression, and Alzheimer's disease

Chapter 17. The Final Challenge: Death and Dying

- Controversies over whether aging and death are genetically programmed or are the result of haphazard damage

- The dying experience in different cultures
- The latest challenges to traditional assumptions about how people grieve
- The latest in the quest to extend life and questions about the merits of that quest

Epilogue. Fitting the Pieces Together

- Summary of major developments in each of seven periods of the life span
- Integration of physical, cognitive, personal, and social aspects of the whole person
- Reinforcement of the book's messages about life-span development

Chapter Organization

The chapters of this book use a consistent format and contain the following:

A *chapter outline* orients students to what lies ahead.

Introductory material stimulates interest, lays out the plan for the chapter, and introduces key concepts, theories, and issues relevant to the area of development to be explored.

Developmental sections (Chapters 5–17) describe key changes and continuities, as well as the mechanisms underlying them, during four developmental periods: infancy, childhood, adolescence, and adulthood.

"*Explorations*" *boxed features* allow more in-depth investigation of research on a topic (for example, perception and the performance of aging drivers, adolescent brain development and adolescent risk taking, language acquisition among deaf children, the big fish–little pond effect on academic self-concept, ethnic identity, genetic and cultural influences on parenting styles, and issues surrounding euthanasia).

"*Applications*" *boxed features* examine how knowledge has been used to optimize development in a domain of development (for instance, to treat genetic defects, promote lifelong health, improve cognitive functioning across the life span, combat the effects of stereotypes of aging on the self-perceptions of older adults, treat aggressive youth, help social isolates, prevent family violence, and lengthen life).

The "*Summing Up*" sections within and the "*Summary Points*" section at the end of each chapter give an overview of the chapter's main themes to facilitate student learning and review of the material.

The new "*Understanding the Data: Exercises on the Web*" test students' comprehension of current research data with online critical thinking exercises based on select figures and tables in the text.

"*Critical Thinking*" questions challenge students to think about or apply the chapter material in new ways.

The "*Key Terms*" section lists the new terms introduced in the chapter in the order in which they were introduced and (new to this edition) with the page number on which they were introduced. The terms are printed in boldface, defined when they are first presented in a chapter, and included in the glossary at the end of the book.

The "*Media Resources*" section describes selected websites that offer further information about chapter topics and are accessible from the book's website at *http://psychology.wadsworth.com/sigelman_rider5e.* Students are also directed to the other resources available at that site, on the Wadsworth Psychology website *(http://psychology.wadsworth.com),* and on the Wadsworth Life-Span CD-ROM.

Supplements

The fifth edition of *Life-Span Human Development* is accompanied by a better array of supplements prepared for both the instructor and the student to create the best learning environment inside and outside the classroom. All the continuing supplements have been thoroughly revised and updated, and several are new to this edition. Especially noteworthy are the new media and Internet-based supplements. We invite instructors and students to examine and take advantage of the teaching and learning tools available.

For the Instructor

Instructor's Manual with Test Bank. Revised by Bradley Caskey, University of Wisconsin, River Falls. This manual contains chapter-specific outlines; a list of print, video, and online resources; and student learning objectives. The manual has a special emphasis on active learning with suggested student activities and projects for each chapter. The test bank, in both print and computerized form, consists of 135 multiple-choice, 20 true or false, 20 fill-in-the-blank, and 10 essay questions for each chapter, all with page references. Each multiple-choice item is categorized based on type (factual or conceptual).

ExamView® Computerized Testing. Create, deliver, and customize printed and online tests and study guides in minutes with this easy-to-use assessment and tutorial system. ExamView includes a Quick Test Wizard and an Online Test Wizard to guide instructors step by step through the process of creating tests. The test appears on screen exactly as it will print or display online. Using ExamView's complete word-processing capabilities, instructors can enter an unlimited number of new questions or edit questions included with ExamView.

Multimedia Manager Instructor's Resource CD-ROM. With the one-stop digital library and presentation tool, instructors can assemble, edit, and present custom lectures with this

Microsoft PowerPoint tool. The Multimedia Manager contains lecture outlines for each chapter of the fifth edition of *Life-Span Human Development,* figures and tables from the text, and animations. Instructors can use the material or add their own material for a truly customized lecture presentation. This CD-ROM also contains the electronic *Instructor's Manual with Test Bank* files.

***CNN Today* Life-Span Development Video Series, Volumes 3–4.** Illustrate the relevance of developmental psychology to everyday life with this exclusive series of videos for the life-span course. Jointly created by Wadsworth and CNN, each video consists of approximately 45 minutes of footage originally broadcast on CNN and specifically selected to illustrate important developmental psychology concepts. The videos are divided into short 2- to 7-minute segments, perfect for use as lecture launchers or as illustrations of key developmental psychology concepts. Special adoption conditions apply.

Wadsworth Developmental Psychology Video Library. Bring developmental psychology concepts to life with videos from Wadsworth's Developmental Psychology Video Library, which includes thought-provoking offerings from Films for Humanities and other excellent educational video sources. This extensive collection illustrates important developmental psychology concepts covered in many life-span courses. Certain adoption conditions apply.

For the Student

Study Guide. Written by coauthor Elizabeth A. Rider of Elizabethtown College, the study guide is designed to promote active learning through a guided review of the important principles and concepts in the text. The study materials for each chapter include a comprehensive multiple-choice self-test and exercises that challenge students to think about and to apply what they have learned.

Life-Span: A Multimedia Introduction to Human Development (CD-ROM). This comprehensive CD-ROM explores the major developmental milestones from conception to death through seven interactive learning modules:

- Prenatal Development, Birth, and the Newborn
- Infancy and Toddlerhood
- Early and Middle Childhood
- Adolescence
- Early and Middle Adulthood
- Late Adulthood
- Death, Dying, and Bereavement

Each learning module explores physical and cognitive development, language development, learning, personality development, social–emotional development, and moral development. Each learning module features narrated concept overviews, explanatory art and videos, critical-thinking applications, drag-and-drop games for the review of key terms and concepts, section quizzes, and a final test. *Life-Span* also features a video selector, a multimedia glossary, and links to the Internet for further study.

Current Perspectives: Readings from InfoTrac® College Edition. Compiled by Gabriela Martorell, Portland State University. This new reader includes at least one article per chapter exploring the Nature/Nurture debate discussed throughout the text. Each article is followed by 2 to 3 critical thinking questions for class discussion or homework assignments.

Internet-Based Supplements

WebTutor™ Advantage on WebCT and Blackboard. This web-based software for students and instructors takes a course beyond the classroom to an anywhere, anytime environment. Students gain access to a full array of study tools, including chapter outlines, chapter-specific quizzing material, interactive games, and videos. With WebTutor Advantage, instructors can provide virtual office hours, post syllabi, track student progress with the quizzing material, and even customize content to meet students' needs. Instructors can also use the communication tools to set up threaded discussions and conduct real-time chats. "Out of the box" or customized, WebTutor Advantage provides a powerful tool for instructors and students alike. The software is also available with an eBook on WebTutor Advantage+ on WebCT and Blackboard.

InfoTrac College Edition. With InfoTrac College Edition, instructors can stimulate discussions and supplement lectures with the latest developments in developmental psychology. Available as a free option with newly purchased texts, InfoTrac College Edition gives instructors and students 4 months of free access to an extensive database of reliable, full-length articles (not just abstracts) from hundreds of top academic journals and popular periodicals.

Wadsworth Psychology Website at http://psychology.wadsworth.com. This website provides instructors and students with a wealth of free information and resources, such as the following:

- Journals
- Associations
- Conference listings
- Psych-in-the-News
- Hot topics
- Book-specific student resources including practice quiz questions, Understanding the Data exercises, interactive activities, Internet links, critical-thinking exercises, and discussion forums, at this book's website *(http://psychology.wadsworth.com/sigelman_rider5e)*

Additional instructor resources include the following:

- Research and Teaching showcase
- Resources for Instructors archives
- Book-specific instructor resources

Developmental PsychologyNow. This interactive, online student learning tool uses diagnostic Pre- and Post-Tests, along with media-rich Personalized Study Plans (which include Integrated Learning Modules, text pages, weblinks, and videos), to help students identify those topics in the text that they need to review. Although any student can use Developmental PsychologyNow without any instructor setup or involvement, an Instructor Grade Book is available to monitor student progress. FREE when ordered with a new copy of the text.

Acknowledgments

We are very grateful to five "cohorts" of reviewers for the constructive criticism and useful suggestions that have helped us make each edition of this book better than the one before.

Reviewers of the first edition were Fredda Blanchard-Fields of Louisiana State University, Janet Fritz of Colorado State University, John Klein of Castleton State College, Rosanne Lorden of Eastern Kentucky University, Robin Palkovitz of the University of Delaware, Suzanne Pasch of the University of Wisconsin at Milwaukee, and Katherine Van Giffen of California State University at Long Beach.

Reviewers of the second edition were David Beach of the University of Wisconsin–Parkside, Charles Harris of James Madison University, Malia Huchendorf of Normandale Community College, Vivian Jenkins of the University of Southern Indiana, Nancy Macdonald of the University of South Carolina–Sumter, Jim O'Neill of Wayne State University, Marjorie Reed of Oregon State University, and Ruth Wilson of Idaho State University.

Reviewers of the third edition were Bob Bornstein, Miami University–Oxford; Donna Brent, Hartwick College; Mary Ann Bush, Western Michigan University; Shelley Drazen, Binghamton University (SUNY); Suzanne Krinsky, University of Southern Colorado; Becky White Loewy, San Francisco State University; Russell Miars, Portland State University; Elizabeth A. Rider, Elizabethtown College; Eileen Rogers, University of Texas at San Antonio; Timothy Shearon, Albertson College of Idaho; Polly Trnavsky, Appalachian State University; and Catherine Weir, Colorado College. Catherine Weir also deserves thanks for her substantive contributions to the revision of several chapters.

Reviewers of the fourth edition were Denise Ann Bodman of Arizona State University, Kim G. Brenneman of Eastern Mennonite University, Mary Ann Bush of Western Michigan University, Yiwei Chen of Bowling Green State University, Michelle R. Dunlap of Connecticut College, Marion Eppler of East Carolina University, Dan Florell of Eastern Kentucky University, James N. Forbes of Angelo State University, Claire Ford of Bridgewater State College, Charles Harris of James Madison University, Karen Hartlep of California State University at Bakersfield, Debra L. Hollister of Valencia Community College, Stephen Hoyer of Pittsburg State University, David P. Hurford of Pittsburg State University, Wayne G. Joosse of Calvin College, Bridget C. Kelsey of the University of Oklahoma, Brett Laursen of Florida Atlantic University, Sherry Loch of Paradise Valley Community College, Becky White Loewy of San Francisco State University, Ann K. Mullis of Florida State University, Ronald L. Mullis of Florida State University, Robert F. Marcus of the University of Maryland, Mark Rafter of College of the Canyons, Mark Runco of California State University at Fullerton, Timothy Shearon of Albertson College of Idaho, and Luis Terrazas of California State University at San Marcos.

Reviewers of the fifth edition were Howard Bierenbaum of the College of William & Mary, Cheryl Bluestone of Queensborough Community College, Elaine H. Cassel of Lord Fairfax Community College, Jody S. Fournier of Capital University, Rebecca J. Glover of University of North Texas, Cheryl Hale of Jefferson College, Linda Jones of Blinn College, Susan Magun-Jackson of the University of Memphis, Gabriela A. Martorell of Portland State University, Bridget C. Murphy-Kelsey of University of Oklahoma, Susan L. O'Donnell of George Fox University, Shirley M. Ogletree of Southwest Texas State University, Rob Palkovitz of University of Delaware, Louise Perry of Florida Atlantic University, Pamela Schuetze of Buffalo State College, and Robin Yaure of Penn State Mont Alto.

We would like to thank David Shaffer of the University of Georgia for all that his work did to make the first and second editions of this book a success. And for all that they did to assist with the preparation of this edition, we are appreciative of our student assistants James Bach, Aaron Dusso, and Victoria Indivero.

Credit for excellent supplementary materials goes to Bradley Caskey, who revised the *Instructor's Manual* and Test Bank; coauthor Elizabeth Rider, who wrote the *Student Guide;* Cheryl Hale, who wrote the critical thinking questions for Understanding the Data: Exercises on the Web; Jori Reijonen, who wrote the Pre- and Post-tests for Developmental PsychologyNow; and Kathy Trotter and Michie Swartwood, who wrote the material for the *Life-Span* CD-ROM that accompanies this book.

Producing this book required the joint efforts of Wadsworth and Graphic World Publishing Services. We thank our editor, Michele Sordi, for her capable leadership of the project, and Kristin Makarewycz, the development editor, for helping make this edition the most visually appealing and pedagogically effective edition yet. We thank Denise DeLancey and her assistants Sara Blackwell and Nicole Sneed at Graphic World for outstanding management of the book's production; Cheryl Whitley, Kelly Hinch, Craig Beffa, Linda Balestreri, Jackie Favazza, and Sandy Brown at Graphic World for composition of the book; Jennifer Dunn for her creative work on the graphic design; and Terri Wright and Austin MacRae for photo research. All of these pros were a joy to work with, and the book is much better because of them. We are grateful, as well, for the able assistance of Paul Wells, production project manager; Vernon Boes, art director; Erik Fortier, technology project manager; Jennifer Wilkinson, assistant editor; and Jessica Kim, editorial assistant. We also appreciate the strong support of Tami Strang, advertising project manager; Dory Schaeffer, marketing manager; and Nicole Morinon, marketing assistant.

We remain deeply indebted to sponsoring editors past—to C. Deborah Laughton, who insisted that this project be undertaken, and to Vicki Knight, who skillfully shepherded the first edition through its final stages and oversaw the second edition. Finally, Lee Sigelman has coped superbly again with a distracted and unamusing partner, and Corby Rider has learned creative ways to help rather than hinder his mom's work.

About the Authors

CAROL K. SIGELMAN is associate vice president for research and graduate studies and professor of psychology at the George Washington University. She has also been on the faculty at Texas Tech University, Eastern Kentucky University (where she won her college's Outstanding Teacher Award), and the University of Arizona. She has taught courses in child, adolescent, adult, and life-span development and has published research on such topics as the communication skills of individuals with developmental disabilities, the development of stigmatizing reactions to children and adolescents who are different, and children's emerging understandings of diseases and psychological disorders. Through a grant from the National Institute of Child Health and Human Development, she studied children's intuitive theories of AIDS and developed and evaluated a curriculum to correct their misconceptions and convey the facts of HIV infection. Through a grant from the National Institute on Drug Abuse, she and her colleagues have conducted similar research on how well children and adolescents of different ages understand the effects of alcohol and drugs on body, brain, and behavior and how to change their understandings. For fun, she bikes with her husband and walks her cat, Doughy.

ELIZABETH A. RIDER is professor of psychology and Registrar at Elizabethtown College in Pennsylvania. She has also been on the faculty at University of North Carolina at Asheville. She earned her undergraduate degree from Gettysburg College and her doctorate from Vanderbilt University. She has taught courses on child and life-span development, women and gender issues, applied developmental psychology, and genetic and environmental influences on development. She has published research on children's and adults' spatial perception, orientation, and ability to find their way. Through a grant from the Pennsylvania State System for Higher Education, she studied factors associated with academic success. The second edition of her text on the psychology of women, *Our Voices,* was published by John Wiley & Sons in 2005. When she is not working, her life revolves around her son and a fun-loving springer spaniel.

CHAPTER one

Understanding Life-Span Human Development

© Joel Gordon

WHEN ROBERT DOLE RAN for president in 1996 at age 73, Ella Miller, nearing age 116, did not think he was too old. Although she voted for Bill Clinton, she figured age was an advantage for Dole: "I think he's just beginning to be a man. I've learned more since I've become old" (Tousignant, 1996).

Born in Tennessee in 1880—15 years after the Civil War, 2 years before Franklin Delano Roosevelt was born, and years before the automobile, much less the Internet—Mrs. Miller was the eldest daughter of former slaves. She had only two dresses as a child, and she recalls seeing her first airplane and thinking it was going to fall on her (Tousignant, 1995). She received no formal education. She married but had no children. After her husband, Isaac, died at age 70, she worked as a domestic helper for two elderly women until she retired (at age 107!). One of the growing number of **centenarians** (people age 100 or older) in the United States, Mrs. Miller spent her last years with her niece, remained active in church, spoke to elementary school children about life in the late 1800s, and stocked up on candy and cookies whenever she went grocery shopping. She became a celebrity, hosting Martin Luther King Jr. in her home, meeting Presidents Bush (Sr.) and Clinton, and talking to Oprah Winfrey and Bill Cosby on the phone (Frost, 2000).

Mrs. Miller attributed her long life to never worrying: "I try to make life more jolly than sad" (Tousignant, 1996). She was pleased to share her rules of living: "Be on time, save your money, care about one another, love life, love people and have a desire to be somebody. All living is about love. Joy is in helping others" (Frost, 2000). Just entering her third century, she died in 2000 of heart failure at age 119, as old as humans get ("Ella Galbraith Miller," 2000).

© James A. Parcell/*The Washington Post*

Centenarian Ella Miller, daughter of former slaves, at age 115.

This book is about the development of humans like Ella Miller—and you—from conception to death. Among the fascinating and important questions it addresses are these: What does the world look like to newborn infants? Does the divorce of a child's parents have lasting effects on the child's personality or later relationships with the other sex? Why do some college students have more trouble than others deciding on a major or committing themselves to a serious relationship? Do most adults really experience a midlife crisis in which they question what they have done with their lives? How do people typically change as they age, and how does retirement affect them? It also takes on more fundamental questions: How does a single fertilized egg cell evolve into an adult human being? How do genetic and environmental influences shape human development? How can we optimize development?

Do any of these questions intrigue you? Probably so, because we are all developing persons interested in ourselves and the other developing people around us. Most college students want to understand how they and those they know have been affected by their experiences, how they have changed over the years, and where they may be headed. Many students also have practical motivations for learning about human development—for example, a desire to be a better parent or to work more effectively as a psychologist, nurse, teacher, or other human services professional.

This introductory chapter lays the groundwork for the remainder of the book by addressing some of these basic questions about the nature of life-span human development and describing ways to study it.

How Should We Think about Development?

We begin by asking what it means to say that humans "develop" over the life span, how we can conceptualize the life span, and how we can approach the single biggest issue in the study of development, the nature–nurture issue.

Defining Development

Development can be defined as systematic changes and continuities in the individual that occur between conception and death, or from "womb to tomb." Development entails many changes; by describing these changes as systematic, we imply that they are orderly, patterned, and relatively enduring—not fleeting and unpredictable like mood swings. Development also involves continuities, ways in which we remain the same or continue to reflect our pasts.

The systematic changes and continuities of interest to students of human development fall into three broad domains:

1. *Physical development.* The growth of the body and its organs, the functioning of physiological systems, the appearance of physical signs of aging, the changes in motor abilities, and so on.

2. *Cognitive development.* The changes and continuities in perception, language, learning, memory, problem solving, and other mental processes.
3. *Psychosocial development.* The changes and carryover in personal and interpersonal aspects of development, such as motives, emotions, personality traits, interpersonal skills and relationships, and roles played in the family and in the larger society.

Even though developmentalists often specialize in one of these three aspects of development, they appreciate that humans are whole beings and that changes in one area affect the others. The baby who develops the ability to crawl, for example, has new opportunities to develop her mind by exploring the contents of shelves and cabinets and to hone her social skills by trailing her parents from room to room.

How do you picture typical changes from birth to old age? Many people picture tremendous positive gains in capacity from infancy to young adulthood, little change during early adulthood and middle age, and loss of capacities in the later years. This stereotyped view of the life span is largely, although not entirely, false. Nevertheless, it has some truth with respect to biological development, for example. Traditionally, biologists have defined **growth** as the physical changes that occur from conception to maturity. We indeed become biologically mature and physically competent during the early part of the life span. **Biological aging** is the deterioration of organisms (including humans) that leads inevitably to their death. Biologically, then, development involves growth in early life, stability in early and middle adulthood, and declines associated with aging in later life.

Most modern developmental scientists have rejected this simple model of the life span, however. They recognize that developmental change at any age involves both gains and losses. They appreciate, too, that people do not always improve or worsen but instead become different (as when a child who once feared loud noises comes to fear hairy monsters under the bed instead). Development clearly means more than positive growth during infancy, childhood, and adolescence. And **aging** involves more than biological aging; it refers to a range of changes, *positive and negative,* in the mature organism. Because both positive and negative changes—gains and losses—occur in every phase of the life span, we should not associate child development only with gains (Baltes, Lindenberger, & Staudinger, 1998). For example, adults are more competent in many ways than children, but they are also more prone to depression (Gotlib & Hammen, 1992). Nor should we associate aging only with loss: expertise and wisdom often grow from early adulthood to middle and later adulthood (Baltes, Lindenberger, & Staudinger, 1998), and adults age 60 and older score higher on vocabulary tests than adults ages 18 to 30 (Verhaeghen, 2003). The common view is that in later life, "We fall apart and there's nothing to be done about it" (Cruikshank, 2003, p. 2). This is simply not true; for many, ". . . old age is a time of ripening, of becoming most ourselves" (Cruikshank, 2003, p. 203). In short, development involves gains, losses, neutral changes, and continuities in each phase of the life span.

© Ariel Skelley/CORBIS

The child is not the only developing person in this photo. Younger members of the family contribute to the ongoing development of their older relatives.

Conceptualizing the Life Span

What periods of the life span do you distinguish? Table 1.1 lists the periods that many of today's developmentalists regard as distinct. You will want to keep them in mind as you read this book, because we will constantly be speaking of infants, preschoolers, school-age children, adolescents, and young, middle-aged, and older adults. Note, however, that the given ages are only approximate. Age is only a rough indicator of level of development, and there are many differences among individuals of the same age. This is especially true of elderly adults, whom some people stereotype as "all alike" when they are probably more diverse than the members of any other age group (Andrews, Clark, & Luszcz, 2002).

Table 1.1 represents only one view of the periods of the life span. Age—like gender, race, and other significant human characteristics—means different things in different societies. Each society has its own ways of dividing the life span and of treating the people who fall into different age groups. Each socially defined age group in a society—called an **age grade** or age stratum—is assigned different statuses, roles, privileges,

Period of Life	Age Range
Prenatal period	Conception to birth
Infancy	First 2 years of life
Preschool period	2 to 5 or 6 years (some prefer to describe as *toddlers* children who have begun to walk and are age 1 to 3)
Middle childhood	6 to about 12 (until the onset of puberty)
Adolescence	Approximately 12 to 20 (when the individual is relatively independent of parents and assumes adult roles)
Early adulthood	20 to 40 years
Middle adulthood	40 to 65 years
Late adulthood	65 years and older

Table 1.1 An Overview of Periods of the Life Span

© AP/Wide World Photos

Each January 15 in Japan, 20-year-olds are officially pronounced adults in a national celebration and enter a new age grade. Young women receive kimonos, young men receive suits, and all are reminded of their responsibilities to society. Young adults also gain the right to drink, smoke, and vote. The modern ceremony grew out of an ancient one in which young samurai became recognized as warriors (Reid, 1993). The age-grading system in Japanese culture clearly marks the beginning of adulthood.

and responsibilities. We, for example, grant "adults" (18-year-olds by law in the United States) a voting privilege not granted to children and give retail discounts to older adults but not to young or middle-aged adults. We also segregate children into grades in school based on age. Just as high schools have "elite" seniors and "lowly" freshmen, whole societies are layered into age grades.

Different societies have their own ways of dividing the life span into socially meaningful periods, or age grades (Fry, 1999). In Western industrialized societies, the life span is often visualized as a straight line extending from birth to death. In some cultures, however, the recognized phases include a period before birth and an afterlife, or the life span may be pictured as a circle that includes reincarnation or some other way of being "recycled" and born again (Fry, 1985; Kojima 2003). The St. Lawrence Eskimo simply distinguish between boys and men (or girls and women), whereas the Arusha people of East Africa have six socially meaningful ages for males: youths, junior warriors, senior warriors, junior elders, senior elders, and retired elders (Keith, 1985).

Once a society has established age grades, each society defines what people should and should not be doing at different points in the life span. According to Bernice Neugarten and her colleagues (Neugarten, Moore, & Lowe, 1965), these expectations, or **age norms**, are society's way of telling people how to act their age. In our culture, for example, most people agree that 6-year-olds are too young to date or drink beer but are old enough to attend school. We also agree that adults should leave home between the ages of 18 and 25, marry around age 25, and retire around age 65 (Neugarten, Moore, & Lowe, 1965; Settersten, 1998). In less-industrialized countries, where couples typically have children in their teens and often become ill, disabled, and unable to work in middle age, age norms typically call for earlier achievement of such milestones (Shanahan, 2000).

Why are age norms important? First, they influence people's decisions about how to lead their lives. They are the basis for what Neugarten (1968) termed the **social clock**—a sense of when things should be done and when a person is ahead of or behind the schedule dictated by age norms. Prompted by the social clock, for example, an unmarried 25-year-old may feel that he should get married before it is too late, or a childless 35-year-old might fear that she will miss her chance at parenthood unless she has a baby soon. Second, age norms affect how easily people adjust to life transitions. Normal life events such as having children typically affect us more negatively when they occur "off time" than when they occur "on time," at socially appropriate ages (McLanahan & Sorensen, 1985). It can be challenging indeed to experience puberty as either an 8-year-old or an 18-year-old or to become a new parent at 13 or 48.

Like age grades, age norms and the meaning of age differ not only from culture to culture but also from subculture to subculture. Our own society is diverse socioeconomically, racially, and ethnically, and African American, Hispanic American, Native American, Asian American, and European American children are likely to have different developmental experiences. Within each of these broad racial and ethnic groups there are immense variations associated with such factors as specific national origin, length of time in North America, degree of integration into mainstream society, language usage, and socioeconomic status. Generally, individuals from lower-income families in this society tend to reach milestones of adulthood such as starting work, marrying, and having children earlier than individuals from middle-income families do (Shanahan, 2000).

Consider one example: Linda Burton (1996a) studied age norms in a low-income African American community and found it is considered appropriate for a young woman to become a mother at 16 and a grandmother at 34—earlier than in most middle-class communities, white or black. Teenage mothers in this community looked to their own mothers and, especially, their grandmothers to help them care for their children. Similar norms prevail among low-income European Americans in rural Appalachia. It may seem unusual from a middle-class perspective for children to be born to mothers so young and then to be raised largely by people other than their mothers and fathers. Yet it is not unusual in cultures around the world for child care responsibilities to be shared like this with grandmothers and other relatives (Rogoff, 2003). Nor is there evidence that such care is damaging to development.

As the Explorations box on page 6 illustrates, the meanings of childhood, adolescence, and adulthood have also changed from historical period to historical period. Not until the 17th and 18th centuries in Western cultures were children viewed as innocents to be protected rather than as potential workers who should grow up quickly; not until the late 19th century was adolescence recognized as a distinct phase of the life span; and not until the 20th century has our society defined a period of middle age in which the nest is emptied of children and a period of old age characterized by retirement.

The broader message is clear: We must view development in its historical, cultural, and subcultural context. We must bear in mind that each social group settles on its own definitions of the life span, the age grades within it, and the norms appropriate to each age range, and that each grade experiences its own set of life events. We must appreciate that the major periods of the life span recognized today—adolescence, middle age, and so on—have not always been considered distinct and that they bring with them different experiences in different cultures. One of the most fascinating challenges in the study of human development is to understand which aspects of development are universal and which aspects vary from social context to social context.

Framing the Nature–Nurture Issue

Developmental scientists want to understand the processes that shape human development, which means grappling with the **nature–nurture issue,** or the question of how biological forces and environmental forces act and interact to make us what we are. We highlight this central issue in development throughout the book.

On the *nature* side of the debate are those who emphasize the influence of individual heredity, universal maturational processes guided by the genes, biologically based predispositions produced by evolution, and biological influences such as hormones and brain growth spurts. To those who emphasize nature, development is largely a process of **maturation,** the biological unfolding of the individual according to a plan contained in the **genes** (the hereditary material passed from parents to child at conception). Just as seeds turn into mature plants through a predictable process, humans "unfold" within the womb (assuming that they receive the necessary nourishment from their environment). Their genetic program then makes it likely that they will walk and utter their first words at about 1 year of age, achieve sexual maturity between 12 and 14, and gray in their 40s and 50s. Maturational changes in the brain contribute to cognitive changes such as increased memory skills and to psychosocial changes such as increased understanding of other people's feelings. Genetically influenced maturational processes guide all of us through many of the same developmental changes at about the same points in our lives.

On the *nurture* side of the nature–nurture debate are those who emphasize change in response to **environment**—all the external physical and social conditions and events that can affect us, from crowded living quarters and polluted air, to social interactions with family members, peers, and teachers, to the broader cultural context in which we develop. Rather than seeing maturation as the process behind development, those on the nurture side of the nature–nurture debate emphasize **learning**—the process through which experience (an aspect of environment) brings about relatively permanent changes in thoughts, feelings, or behavior. A certain degree of physical maturation is clearly necessary before a child can dribble a basketball, but careful instruction and long, hard hours of practice are just as clearly required if the child is to excel in basketball.

If nature is important in development, we would expect all children to achieve similar developmental milestones at similar times because of maturation, and we would expect differences among individuals to be largely caused by differences in genetic makeup. If nurture or environment is important in development, we would expect humans to be alike if their environments are alike but also expect human development to take different forms depending on the individual's life experiences. As you will see repeatedly in this book, developmental changes are generally the products of a complex interplay between nature (genetic endowment, biological influences, and maturation) and nurture (environmental influences, experiences, and learning). It is not nature *or* nurture; it is nature *and* nurture. To make matters more complex, it is nature affecting nurture and nurture affecting nature. Much of the excitement of developmental research comes from trying to determine how these two forces combine to make us what we are (for example, see Ge, Donnellan, & Harper, 2003).

Ponder this sample nature–nurture question. In the United States, there is consistent evidence that, on average, boys are more likely than girls to engage in physically aggressive behavior and men commit more violent crimes than women (Hyde, 1984; Knight, Fabes, & Higgins, 1996). Does this sex difference reflect nature (biological differences between the sexes, such as different hormone balances) or nurture (for example, a tendency of parents to tolerate or even encourage aggression in boys but to suppress it in girls)? How might you try to answer this nature–nurture question?

One approach is to find out whether sex differences in physical aggression are evident in different societies. This is what prompted Robert Munroe and his colleagues (2000) to study aggression among 3- to 9-year-old children in four nonindustrialized societies from diverse parts of the globe: Belize, Kenya, Nepal, and American Samoa. In each society, 24 girls and 24 boys were studied. Residents of the communities studied were trained to observe children's social behavior, includ-

Historical Changes in Periods of the Life Span

Every human lives and develops in a historical context. Being a developing person today, therefore, differs from being a developing person in other times. Moreover, the quick historical tour that you are about to take should convince you that the phases of the life span recognized today were not always perceived as distinct and may not always be perceived as distinct.

Childhood

Phillippe Ariès (1962) conducted an ambitious historical analysis and concluded that, before 1600, European societies had little concept of childhood as we know it. Until then, he believed, children were viewed as miniature adults. In medieval Europe (A.D. 500–1500), for example, 6-year-olds were dressed in miniature versions of adult clothing and expected to work alongside adults at home, at a shop, or in the fields (Ariès, 1962). Moreover, a 10-year-old convicted of stealing could be hanged (Kean, 1937).

Henry Lillie Pierce Fund, Courtesy Museum of Fine Arts, Boston

☾ Although medieval children were pressured to abandon their childish ways as soon as possible and were dressed like miniature adults, it is doubtful that they were really viewed as miniature adults.

It is now clear that it is an exaggeration to say that pre–17th-century adults held a miniature-adult view of childhood (Cunningham, 1996; Hanawalt, 2003). Parents throughout history seem to have recognized that children are different from adults. Nevertheless, before the 17th and 18th centuries, people in Western societies pressured children to grow up, adopt adult roles, and contribute economically to the family's survival as soon as possible. During the 17th and 18th centuries, the modern concept of childhood gradually came into being. Children came to be seen as more distinctly childlike—as innocent beings who should be protected, given a proper moral and religious education, and taught skills such as reading and writing so that they would eventually become good workers (Cunningham, 1996).

The historical context of child development continues to change. Some observers argue that modern society has been reverting to a medieval view of childhood—asking children to grow up quickly and to cope with terrorists, drugs dealers, gun violence, and other social ills (Elkind, 1992; Koops, 2003). Others note that parents are more anxious than ever before about how to raise children and less confident of their abilities, given the challenges of modern life (Stearns, 2003). Might we be exposing children to too many "adult" issues and situations too early in life? Maybe, but consider that children in colonial America often slept in the same room with their parents and probably learned a bit about human sexuality in the process, or consider that the age of consent for sexual relations was 12 or younger as late as the end of the 19th century (Coontz, 2000b). Historians have discovered that the experience of childhood is not clearly better or worse than it was in past eras; it is merely different. In all eras, it seems, parents have tried to be good parents—but they have often treated their children badly (Colón, 2001).

Adolescence

If the modern concept of childhood arose only during the 17th and 18th centuries, perhaps it is not surprising that **adolescence**—the transitional period between childhood and adulthood that begins with puberty and ends when the individual has acquired adult competencies and responsibilities—came to be viewed as a distinct period of the life span in Western societies only at the end of the 19th century and beginning of the 20th century (Hine, 1999; Kett, 1977). Before the industrial revolution, work took place within the family household; families farmed, built furniture, or engaged in other trades at home. Children contributed as they became able; age mattered little (Gillis, 2003). Early in the industrial revolution, factories needed cheap labor. At first they could make do with children; later they used immigrants. But as industry advanced, it needed an educated labor force, so laws were passed restricting child labor and making schooling compulsory. By the middle of the 20th century, adolescence had become a distinct life stage in which youths spent their days in school—separated from the adult world, living in their own peer culture, and subject to stronger peer influence (Furstenberg, 2000).

As adolescents began to attend college in large numbers after World War II, the age of entry into the adult world was postponed further (Furstenberg, 2000; Keniston, 1970). Today, many "emerging" adults spend years taking steps forward and steps backward (for example, leaving their parents' home only to return to it) before they finally become autonomous with respect to such key markers of adulthood as completing an education, leaving the nest, making a living, and forming a romantic relationship (Cohen et al., 2003).

Adulthood

Adulthood is also different today than it was in past eras. In ancient Rome, the average age of death was 20 to 30 years old; in the late 17th century, it was 35 to 40 years (Dublin & Lotka, 1936). These figures, which are *averages,* are low mainly because so many more infants died in the past. However, even those lucky enough to make it through early childhood had relatively low odds, by modern standards, of living to be 65 or older. The average life expectancy has continued to increase dramatically during this century in many countries—at first because more babies survived infancy and early childhood and more recently because more people are living into old age (National Research Council, 2001). In 1900, the average life expectancy for a newborn born in the United States was about 47 years. By 2001, the life expectancy had climbed to 77 years overall—80 for a white female, 75 for a black female, 75 for a white male, and 69 for a black male (Freid et al., 2003).

© Lewis W. Hine/CORBIS

☾ How might your childhood have been different if you had worked in the coal mines like these boys?

The makeup of the U.S. population also changed significantly in the 20th century. In 1900, about 4% of the population was 65 and older. By the mid-1990s, the percentage was close to 13% and climbing (Hobbs, 2001). Census takers are closely watching the **baby boom generation**—the huge number of people born between 1946 and 1964—move into middle age. By 2030, when most baby boomers will have retired from work, an estimated 20% of the U.S. population—one of five Americans—will be 65 or older (Hobbs, 2001). No wonder we hear a lot about the challenges to society that an aging population will present.

What are some implications of these changes? As 20th-century parents began to bear fewer children and live long enough to see their children empty the nest, Western societies began to recognize middle age as a distinct period between early adulthood and old age (Moen & Wethington, 1999). Interestingly, middle age has been stereotyped as either a time of midlife crisis and turmoil or a time of stability and little developmental change. It is now understood to be a time of good health, stable relationships, many responsibilities, and high satisfaction for most people. It is also a time when people cope successfully with changes such as menopause and other signs of aging and achieve peak levels of cognitive functioning (Squires, 1999; Willis & Schaie, 1999).

The experience of old age also changed during the 20th century, with the introduction of Social Security, Medicare, and other such programs for the elderly (Cole, 1992). In earlier centuries, people who survived to old age literally worked until they dropped; now they retire in their 60s. As a result, we have come to define old age as the retirement phase of life. Today's elderly adults also have fewer chronic diseases and disabilities, and are less affected by the ones they have, than elderly adults even a century ago (Costa, 2002). Kenneth Manton estimated that today's 85-year-old is about as healthy as a 65-year-old just 25 years ago (Trafford, 1996).

In sum, age—whether it is 7, 17, or 70—has meant something different in each historical era. And most likely, the experience of being 7, 17, or 70 will be different in the 21st century than it was in the 20th.

ing their aggressive behavior. Aggressive behavior was defined as assaulting (hitting, kicking, or otherwise attacking someone), horseplay (roughhousing), and symbolic aggression (making insulting or threatening gestures or statements).

As Figure 1.1 shows, boys exhibited more aggression than girls in all four societies studied. Overall, about 10% of boys' social behaviors, compared with 6% of girls' behaviors, were aggressive. Boys, and girls too, were especially likely to behave aggressively when they were in a group with a relatively large number of boys. Munroe and his colleagues noted that male play groups in which young males compete for dominance are observed in primate species other than human beings. Establishing dominance in the peer group gives males an edge in competing for mates and reproducing. As a result, genes that predispose males to be aggressive may have been built into the human genetic code over the course of evolution (Barash, 2002).The evidence in support of nature in Munroe's study is not strong, but it hints that genes could contribute to gender differences in aggression.

However, cultural differences in aggression—as well as in the extent of gender differences in aggression—were also evident in this study. The two most patrilineal cultures (cultures in which families are organized around male kin groups) were Kenya and Nepal. These proved to be the cultures in which aggressive behavior was most frequent (10–11% of social acts, as opposed to 4–6% in Belize and American Samoa). Moreover, sex differences in aggression were sharpest in these patrilineal cultures. The Black Carib of Belize, by contrast, are known as a nonviolent people; they proved to be the least aggressive group of children studied and the group in which boys and girls differed least. As is often the case when we ask whether nature or nurture is more important in development, these findings, like those of other studies, suggest that both nature and nurture contribute to gender differences in aggression—and make us want to conduct more research, including studies examining both biological and cultural differences between the sexes, to understand more fully why males, especially in some cultural contexts, are more aggressive than females.

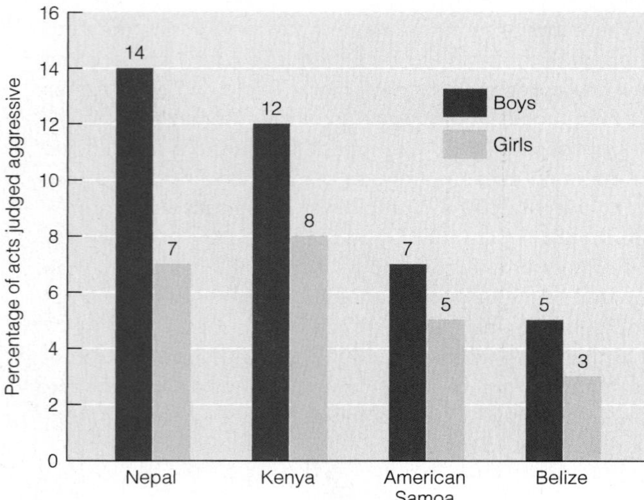

Figure 1.1 Aggression among children in four cultures.
Source: Based on means reported in Munroe et al. (2000)

Summing Up

Development is systematic changes and continuities over the life span, involving gains, losses, and neutral changes in physical, cognitive, and psychosocial functioning; it is more than growth in childhood and biological aging in adulthood. It takes place in an historical and cultural context and is influenced by age grades, age norms, and social clocks. Concepts of the life span and its distinctive periods have changed over history and differ from culture to culture. In the 17th and 18th centuries, children came to be seen as innocents; in the late 19th century, adolescence emerged as a distinct phase; and only in the 20th century have we recognized a middle-aged "empty nest" period and an old age characterized by retirement. Finally, development is brought about by the interaction of nature (biology and maturation) and nurture (environment and learning). ■

What Is the Science of Life-Span Development?

If development consists of systematic changes and continuities from conception to death, the science of development consists of the study of those changes and continuities. In this section we consider the goals of the science of life-span development, its origins, and the modern life-span perspective on development.

Goals of Study

Three broad goals guide the study of life-span development: the description, explanation, and optimization of development (Baltes, Reese, & Lipsitt, 1980). To achieve the goal of *description,* developmental scholars characterize the behavior of humans of different ages and trace how that behavior changes with age. They describe both normal development and individual differences, or variations, in development. Although average trends in human development across the life span can be described, it is clear that no two people (even identical twins) develop along precisely the same pathways. Some babies are considerably more alert and active than others. Some 80-year-olds are out on the dance floor; others are home in bed.

Description is the starting point in any science, but scientists want to achieve their second goal, *explanation.* Developmentalists seek to understand why humans develop as they typically do and why some individuals develop differently than others. To do so, developmentalists study the contributions of nature and nurture to development.

The third goal is *optimization* of human development. How can humans be helped to develop in positive directions? How can their capacities be enhanced, how can developmental difficulties be prevented, and how can any developmental problems that emerge be overcome? Pursuing the goal of optimizing development might involve evaluating ways to stimulate intellectual growth in preschool programs, to prevent alcohol abuse among college students, or to support elderly adults after the death of a spouse.

The Modern Life-Span Perspective

Some early pioneers of the study of human development, the subject of the Explorations box on page 10, viewed all phases of the life span as worthy of study. However, the science of human development began to break into age-group specialty areas during the 20th century. Some researchers focused on infant or child development, others specialized in adolescence, and still others formed the specialization called **gerontology,** the study of aging and old age. In the 1960s and 1970s, however, a true **life-span perspective** on human development began to reemerge. Paul Baltes (1987) has laid out seven key assumptions of the life-span perspective (see Baltes, Lindenberger, & Staudinger, 1998, for an elaboration). These are tremendously important themes that you will see echoed throughout this book.

1. *Development is a lifelong process.* Today's developmentalists appreciate that human development is not just "kid stuff," that we change throughout the life span. They also believe that development in any period of life is best seen in the context of the whole life span. For instance, our understanding of adolescent career choices is bound to be richer if we concern ourselves with formative influences in childhood and the implications of such choices for adult development.

2. *Development is multidirectional.* To many pioneers of its study, development was a universal process leading toward more "mature" functioning. Today's developmentalists recognize that humans of any age can be experiencing growth in one set of capacities, decline in another set, and no change in still another.

3. *Development involves both gain and loss.* As noted earlier, development at every age involves both growth and decline. Gaining a capacity for logical thought as a school-age child may mean losing some capacity for fanciful, imaginative thinking the child had as a preschooler, for example.

4. *Development is characterized by lifelong plasticity.* **Plasticity** refers to the capacity to change in response to positive or negative experiences. Developmental scholars have long known that child development can be damaged by a deprived environment and optimized by an enriched one. It is now understood that this plasticity continues into later life—that the aging process can be altered considerably depending on the individual's experiences. For example, elderly adults who have been losing intellectual abilities can, with special training and practice, regain some of those abilities (Baltes, Lindenberger, & Staudinger, 1998). What is more, older adults who regularly engage in mentally stimulating activities such as playing chess, playing a musical instrument, and dancing (the dancer has to think about the steps) are less likely than their mentally inactive peers to develop Alzheimer's disease and other forms of dementia (Verghese et al., 2003). Studies of animals tell us this may be because mental stimulation forms new connections among neurons in the brain, even an aging brain.

5. *Development is shaped by its historical–cultural context.* This theme, which has been introduced already, is illustrated well by the pioneering work of Glen Elder and his colleagues on how the Great Depression of the 1930s affected the later life courses and development of the era's children and adolescents (Elder, 1998; Elder, Liker, & Cross, 1984). A few years after the stock market crashed in 1929, one of three workers was unemployed and many families were tossed into poverty (Rogler, 2002). Although many families survived the hardships of the Great Depression nicely, this economic crisis was harder on children than on adolescents, especially if their out-of-work and demoralized fathers became less affectionate and less consistent in disciplining them. When this was the case, children displayed behavior problems and had low aspirations and poor records in school. As adults, the men had erratic careers and unstable marriages, and the women were seen by their own children as ill tempered. Clearly the trajectories our lives take can be affected for years by the social context in which we grow up.

6. *Development is multiply influenced.* Pioneers of the study of development believed that development is caused by genetically programmed maturational processes. Learning theorists have argued just as strongly that how we develop is the result of our unique learning experiences. It may be human nature to look for simple explanations of complex phenomena. For example, many of us try to explain inexplicable events such as school shootings in terms of one cause, whether it is a gene for aggression, permissive parenting, the availability of guns, or too much violence in the media (Wachs, 2000). Development is not so simple. Today's developmental scientists appreciate that human development is the product of many interacting causes—both inside and outside the person, both biological and environmental. It is the often-unpredictable outcome of ongoing interactions between a changing person and her changing world.

7. *Understanding development requires multiple disciplines.* Because human development is influenced by everything from biochemical reactions to historical events, it is impossible for

The plasticity of the brain is evident even in old age if people remain intellectually active.

Explorations

Pioneers of the Study of Life-Span Development

Just as human development has changed through the ages, attempts to understand development have evolved over time. Although philosophers have long expressed their views on the nature of humans and the proper methods of raising children, it was not until the late 19th century that the first scientific investigations of development were undertaken. Several scholars began to carefully observe the growth and development of their own children and to publish their findings in the form of **baby biographies.** Perhaps the most influential baby biographer was Charles Darwin (1809–1882), who made daily records of his son's development (Darwin, 1877; see also Charlesworth, 1992). Darwin's curiosity about child development stemmed from his interest in evolution. Quite simply, he believed that infants share many characteristics with their nonhuman ancestors and that understanding the development of the individual embryo and child can offer insights into the evolution of the species. Darwin's evolutionary perspective strongly influenced early theories of human development, which emphasized universal, biologically based maturational changes (Cairns, 1998; Parke et al., 1994).

Baby biographies left much to be desired as works of science, however. Because different baby biographers emphasized different aspects of their children's behavior, baby biographies were difficult to compare. Moreover, parents are not entirely objective observers of their own children, and early baby biographers may have let their assumptions about evolution and development bias their observations. Finally, each baby biography was based on a single child—often the child of a distinguished family. The **case study method**—an in-depth examination of an individual that often involves compiling and analyzing information from a variety of sources, such as observation, testing, and interviewing the person or people who know her—is still used today. The case study method can provide rich information about the complexities of an individual's development and the influences on it. It is particularly useful in studying people with rare conditions and disorders, when it is simply not possible to assemble a large sample of people to study, and it can be a good source of hypotheses that can be examined further in larger-scale studies. The main limitation of case studies is that conclusions based on a single case may not hold true for other individuals; researchers cannot necessarily generalize beyond the single case.

We can give Darwin and other eminent baby biographers much credit for making human development a legitimate topic of study and influencing early views of it. Still, the man most

G. Stanley Hall is widely recognized as the founder of the scientific study of human development.

one discipline to have all the answers. A full understanding of human development will come only when many disciplines, each with its own perspectives and tools of study, join forces. Anthropologists, biologists, historians, psychologists, sociologists, and many others have something to contribute. Some universities have established interdisciplinary human development programs that bring members of different disciplines together to forge more integrated perspectives on development.

Summing Up

The study of life-span development, guided by the goals of description, explanation, and optimization, began with the baby biographies written by Charles Darwin and others. Through his use of surveys and his attention to all phases of the life span, including the storm and stress of adolescence, American psychologist G. Stanley Hall came to be regarded as the founder of developmental psychology. By adopting the modern life-span perspective on human development set forth by Baltes, we assume that development (1) occurs throughout the life span, (2) can take many different directions, (3) involves gains and losses at every age, (4) is characterized by plasticity, (5) is affected by its historical and cultural context, (6) is influenced by multiple interacting causal factors, and (7) can best be understood if scholars from multiple disciplines join forces to understand it. ■

often cited as the founder of developmental psychology is G. Stanley Hall (1846–1924), the first president of the American Psychological Association. Well aware of the shortcomings of baby biographies, Hall attempted to collect more objective data on large samples of individuals. He developed a now all-too-familiar research tool, the questionnaire, to explore "the contents of children's minds" (Hall, 1891). By asking children questions about every conceivable topic, he discovered that children's understanding of the world grows rapidly during childhood and that the "logic" of young children is often not logical.

Hall went on to write an influential book, *Adolescence* (1904). Strongly influenced by Darwin's evolutionary theory, Hall drew parallels between adolescence and the turbulent period in the evolution of human society during which barbarism gave way to modern civilization. Adolescence, then, was a tempestuous period of the life span, a time of emotional ups and downs and rapid changes—a time of what Hall called **storm and stress.** Thus it is Hall we have to thank for the notion that most teenagers are emotionally unstable—a largely inaccurate notion, as it turns out (Arnett, 1999). Yet as Chapter 5 and other parts of this book will reveal, Hall may have been right to mark adolescence as a time of dramatic changes because substantial changes in the brain and in cognitive functioning take place during this period.

Hall capped his remarkable career by turning his attention to the end of the life span in *Senescence* (1922), an analysis of how society treats (or, really, mistreats) its older members. Although his methods were limited by modern standards, and although his ideas about evolution and its relation to periods of human development were flawed, he deserves much credit for stimulating scientific research on the entire human life span and for raising many important questions about it (Cairns, 1998).

How Is Developmental Research Conducted?

How do developmental scholars gain understanding of the complexities of life-span development? Through the scientific method used in any physical or social science. Let us review for you, briefly, some basic concepts of scientific research and then turn to research strategies devised specifically for describing, explaining, and optimizing development.

The Scientific Method

There is nothing mysterious about the **scientific method.** It is both a method and an attitude—a belief that investigators should allow their systematic observations (or data) to determine the merits of their thinking. For example, for every "expert" who believes that psychological differences between males and females are largely biological in origin, there is likely to be another expert who just as firmly insists that boys and girls differ because they are raised differently. Whom should we believe? It is in the spirit of the scientific method to believe the data—that is, the findings of research. The scientist is willing to abandon a pet theory if the data contradict it. Ultimately, then, the scientific method can help the scientific community and society at large weed out flawed ideas.

The scientific method involves a process of generating ideas and testing them by making observations. Often, preliminary observations provide ideas for a **theory**—a set of concepts and propositions intended to describe and explain some aspect of experience. Jean Piaget, for instance, observed his own children's development and used these observations as the basis for his influential theory of cognitive development (see Chapter 7).

Theories generate specific predictions, or **hypotheses,** regarding a particular set of observations. Consider, for example, a theory claiming that psychological differences between the sexes are largely caused by differences in the ways that parents and other adults treat boys and girls. Based on this theory, a researcher might hypothesize that if parents grant boys and girls the same freedoms, the two sexes will be similarly independent, whereas if parents let boys do more things than they let girls do, boys will be more independent than girls. Suppose that the study designed to test this hypothesis indicates that boys are more independent than girls no matter how their parents treat them. Then the hypothesis would be disconfirmed by the findings, and the researcher would want to rethink this theory of sex-linked differences. If other hypotheses based on this theory were inconsistent with the facts, the theory would have to be significantly revised or abandoned in favor of a better theory.

This, then, is the heart of the scientific method: Theories generate hypotheses tested through observation of behavior, and new observations indicate which theories are worth keeping and which are not (see Figure 1.2).

Sample Selection

Any study of development focuses on a particular research **sample** (the group of individuals studied) with the intention of generalizing to a larger **population** from which the sample is drawn (a well-defined group such as premature infants, American high school students, or Chinese elders). Although it is probably advocated more than it is used, the best approach is to study a **random sample** of the population of interest—a sample formed by identifying all members of the larger population and then, by a random means (such as

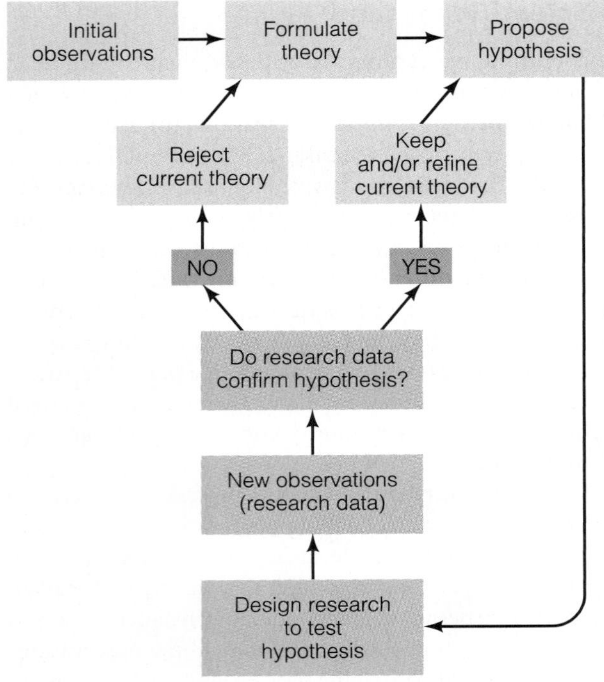

Figure 1.2 The scientific method in action.

drawing names blindly), selecting a portion of that population to study. Random sampling increases confidence that the sample studied is representative of the larger population of interest and therefore that conclusions based on studying the sample will be true of the whole population.

In practice, developmentalists often draw their samples—sometimes random, sometimes not—from their local communities. Thus, researchers might survey a random sample of students at local high schools about their drug use but then be unable to make statements about American teenagers in general if, for example, the school is in a suburb where drug-use patterns are different than they might be in an inner-city area. They would certainly be unable to generalize about Kenyan or Brazilian high school students. As a result, researchers must be careful to describe the characteristics of the sample they studied and to avoid overgeneralizing their findings to populations that might be socioeconomically or culturally different from the research sample (Rogoff, 2003).

Data Collection

No matter what aspect of human development we are interested in—such as the formation of bonds between infants and their parents, adolescent drug use, or memory skills in elderly adults—we must find appropriate ways to measure what interests us. Look briefly at some pros and cons of three major methods of data collection used by developmental researchers: self-report measures, behavioral observations, and physiological measurements. We illustrate them with a study by Julie Hubbard and her colleagues (2002) that used all three approaches. Hubbard was interested in the relationship between anger and two styles of aggression among 8-year-olds, as determined by teachers' responses to questions about children's behavior in the classroom: a "hot" kind of aggression in which children hit, pinch, and otherwise abuse other children when provoked, and a cooler, more calculating style of aggression in which children use aggression to get what they want. The researchers expected aggressive children of the first type to be more likely than aggressive children of the second type to become angry in a laboratory situation in which another child (a confederate of the researchers) cheated shamelessly in a board game about astronauts and won.

Obviously the researchers needed a way to measure anger in the anger-provoking situation. How would you measure it?

Verbal Reports

Interviews, written questionnaires or surveys, and tests and scales designed to measure abilities or personality traits all involve asking people questions either about themselves (self-report measures) or about someone else (for example, child behavior as reported by parents or teachers). These verbal report measures are often standardized, meaning that they ask the same questions in precisely the same order for everyone so that the responses of different individuals can be directly compared.

Hubbard's research team used a verbal report measurement to assess anger. The researchers had the children in the study watch a videotape of all the turns in the game they played with the cheating confederate, stopped the tape at each turn, and asked each child, "How angry did you feel now?" The child responded on a four-point scale ranging from 1 (not at all) to 4 (a lot). The researchers were able to use these ratings to calculate for each child an average degree of self-reported anger over the entire game and to look at changes in degree of anger as the game progressed.

Although self-report and other verbal report methods are widely used to study human development, they have shortcomings. First, self-report measures typically cannot be used with infants, young children, or other individuals who cannot read or understand speech well. Informant surveys, questionnaires, or interviews are often used in these situations instead. Second, because individuals of different ages may not understand questions in the same way, age differences in responses may reflect age differences in comprehension or interpretation rather than age differences in the quality of interest to the researcher. Developmental researchers always face the challenge of ensuring that their data-gathering tools measure the same thing at all ages they intend to study. Finally, respondents may try to present themselves (or those they are providing information about) in a positive or socially desirable light.

Behavioral Observations

Naturalistic observation involves observing people in their common, everyday (that is, natural) surroundings (Pellegrini, 1996). Ongoing behavior is observed in homes, schools, playgrounds, workplaces, nursing homes, or wherever people are going about their lives. Naturalistic observation has been used to study child development more often than adult development, largely because infants and young children often cannot be studied through self-report techniques that demand verbal skills. The greatest advantage of naturalistic observation is that it is the only technique that can tell what children or adults do in everyday life.

Yet naturalistic observation has its limitations. First, some behaviors (for example, heroic efforts to help other people) occur too infrequently and unexpectedly to be observed in this manner. Second, it is difficult to pinpoint the causes of the behavior, or of any developmental trends in the behavior, because in a natural setting many events are usually happening at the same time, any of which may be affecting behavior. Finally, the mere presence of an observer can sometimes make people behave differently than they otherwise would. Children may "ham it up" when they have an audience; parents may be on their best behavior. Therefore, researchers sometimes videotape the proceedings from a hidden location or spend time in the setting before they collect their "real" data so that the individuals they are observing become used to their presence and behave more naturally.

To achieve greater control over the conditions under which they gather behavioral data, researchers often use **structured observation;** that is, they create special conditions designed to elicit the behavior of interest. Hubbard used structured observation by setting up the astronaut game situation and having the confederate cheat to provoke children's anger. The confederate was carefully trained to behave exactly the same with each of the 272 participants in the study. Sessions were videotaped; Hubbard then trained graduate and undergraduate students to code second by second whether the participants' facial expressions were angry, sad, happy, or neutral and whether they showed nonverbal signs of anger (for example, slamming game pieces on the table). Pairs of observers coded some of the same videotapes to ensure that they would come to similar conclusions about what facial emotion or nonverbal behavior was being expressed. (Some other studies of emotional expression use coding systems that measure discrete movements of parts of the face.)

Structured observation permits the study of behaviors rarely observable in natural settings. By exposing all research participants to the same stimuli, this approach also increases the investigator's ability to compare the effect of a stimulus on different individuals. Concerns about this method center on whether conclusions based on behavior in specially designed settings will generalize to behavior in natural settings.

Physiological Measurements

Finally, developmental scientists sometimes take physiological measurements to assess variables of interest to them; for example, they use brain scanning techniques to measure the activity in particular parts of the brain while individuals engage in learning tasks, chart changes in hormone levels in menopausal women, or collect measurements of heart rate and other signs of arousal to assess emotions.

Hubbard's team collected data on two physiological measures of anger by attaching electrodes to children's hands and chests (after convincing the children that astronauts frequently wear sensors when they go into space!). Emotionally aroused people, including angry ones, often have sweaty palms and show low skin conductance, or electrical resistance of the skin, as measured by electrodes attached to the hand. Their emotional arousal is also given away by a high heart rate, measured through electrodes on the chest.

Physiological measurements have the advantage of being hard to fake; the person who tells you she is not angry may be aroused, and the adolescent who claims not to take drugs may be given away by a blood test. Physiological measurements are also particularly useful in the study of infants because infants cannot tell us verbally what they are thinking or feeling. The main limitation of physiological measurements is that it is not always clear what they are assessing. In Hubbard's study, for example, skin conductance was related to the other measures of anger as expected but heart rate was not. The researchers noted that individuals' heart rates slow when they are interested in something, so in the Hubbard study a slow heart rate may have meant either high interest or low anger, making its meaning ambiguous.

These, then, are the most commonly used techniques of collecting data about human development: verbal report measures (interviews, questionnaires, and tests), behavioral observation (both naturalistic and structured), and physiological measures. Because each method has its limitations, knowledge is advanced the most when *multiple* methods are used to study the same aspect of human development and these different methods lead to similar conclusions. In the Hubbard study, the use of multiple methods of assessing anger allowed the researchers to distinguish between children showing "hot" and "cool" types of aggression, but only on some scales (especially, the structured observations of nonverbal behavior and the physiological skin conductance measurement).

The Experimental and Correlational Methods

Once developmental scientists have formulated hypotheses, chosen a sample, and figured out what they want to measure

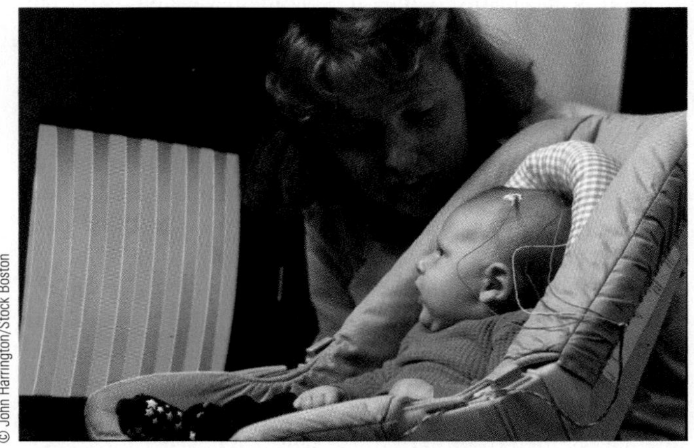

Physiological measurement techniques include measuring brain activity through electrodes attached to the scalp as infants respond to different stimuli.

and how to measure it, they can test their hypotheses. The most powerful research method for explaining behavior and identifying the causes of developmental changes in behavior is the experiment. When experiments cannot be conducted, correlational research techniques may suggest answers to important *why* questions.

The Experimental Method

In an **experiment,** an investigator manipulates or alters some aspect of the environment to see how this affects the behavior of the sample of individuals studied. Consider an experiment conducted by Lynette Friedrich and Aletha Stein (1973) some years ago to study how different kinds of television programs affect the social behavior of preschool children. These researchers divided children in a nursery school into three groups: one group was exposed to violent cartoons such as *Superman* and *Batman* (aggressive treatment condition), another group watched episodes of *Mister Rogers' Neighborhood* portraying many helpful and cooperative acts (prosocial treatment condition), and a third group saw programs featuring circuses and farm scenes with neither aggressive nor altruistic themes (neutral control condition).

The goal of an experiment is to see whether the different treatments that form the **independent variable**—the variable manipulated so that its causal effects can be assessed—have differing effects on the behavior expected to be affected, the **dependent variable** in the experiment. The independent variable in Friedrich and Stein's experiment was the type of television children watched—a variable with three possible values in their study: aggressive, prosocial, or neutral. One dependent variable that Friedrich and Stein chose to study was aggressive behavior. Any variable represents one specific way of measuring a concept of interest. Friedrich and Stein chose to use a complicated naturalistic observation system to count several types of aggression actions toward classmates in the nursery school. Behavior was observed before each child spent a month watching daily episodes of one of the three kinds of television programs and was recorded again after that period to see if it had changed. The independent variable is the hypothesized cause, and the dependent variable is the effect, when cause–effect relationships are studied. Similarly, if researchers were testing drugs to improve memory function in elderly adults with Alzheimer's disease, the type of drug administered (for example, a new drug versus a placebo with no active ingredients) would be the independent variable and performance on a memory test battery would be the dependent variable.

So, did the number of aggressive behaviors observed "depend on" the independent variable, the type of television watched? Children who watched violent programs became more aggressive than children who watched prosocial or neutral programs—but only if they were already relatively aggressive. Thus, this experiment demonstrated a clear cause–effect relationship, although only for some children, between the kind of behavior children watched on television and their own subsequent behavior.

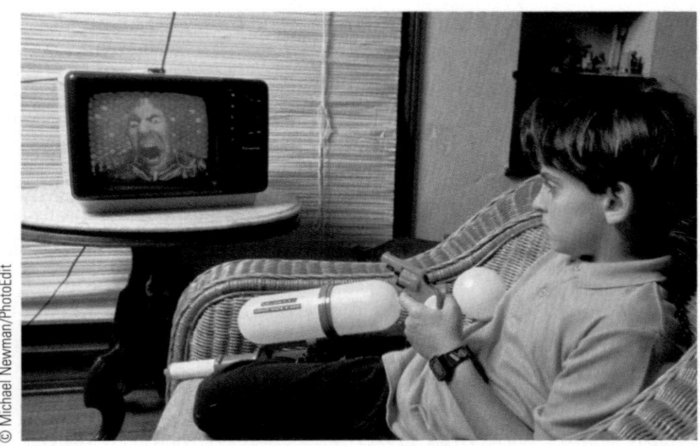

© Michael Newman/PhotoEdit

Many studies demonstrate that observational learning of aggression occurs among children who watch a lot of violence on television.

This study has the three critical features shared by any true experiment:

1. *Manipulation of the independent variable.* Investigators must arrange for different groups to have different experiences so that the effects of those experiences can be assessed. If investigators merely compare children who already watch a lot of violent television and children who watch little, they cannot establish that violent television watching *causes* increased aggression.

2. *Random assignment of individuals to treatment conditions.* **Random assignment** of participants to experimental conditions (for example, by drawing names from a jar) is a way of ensuring that the treatment groups are similar in all respects at the outset (in previous tendencies to be aggressive or helpful, in socioeconomic status, and in all other individual characteristics that could affect social behavior). Only if experimental groups are similar in all respects initially can researchers be confident that differences among groups at the end of the experiment were caused by differences in the experimental treatments they received.

3. *Experimental control.* In a true experiment with proper **experimental control,** all factors other than the independent variable are controlled or held constant so that they cannot contribute to differences among the treatment groups. Friedrich and Stein ensured that children in the three treatment conditions were treated similarly except for the type of television they watched. It would have ruined the experiment, for example, if the children exposed to violent programs had to watch them in a small, crowded room where tempers might flare but the children in the other two groups watched in larger, less crowded rooms. The variable of interest, the type of TV watched, would then be confounded, or entangled, with the degree of crowding in the room, and the researchers would have been unable to separate the effects of one from those of the other.

The greatest strength of the experimental method is its ability to establish unambiguously that one thing causes another—that manipulating the independent variable causes a change in the dependent variable. When experiments are properly conducted, they contribute to our ability to *explain* human development and sometimes help us to *optimize* it.

Does the experimental method have limitations? Absolutely! First, the findings of laboratory experiments do not always hold true in the real world, especially if the situations created in laboratory experiments are artificial and unlike the situations that people encounter in everyday life. Urie Bronfenbrenner (1979), who has been critical because so many developmental studies are contrived experiments, once charged that developmental psychology had become "the science of the strange behavior of children in strange situations with strange adults" (p. 19). Experiments often show what can cause development but not necessarily what *does* most strongly shape development in natural settings (McCall, 1977).

A second limitation of the experimental method is that it cannot be used to address many significant questions about human development for ethical reasons. How would you conduct a true experiment to determine how older women are affected by their husbands' deaths, for example? You would need to identify a sample of elderly women, randomly assign them to either the experimental group or the control group, then manipulate the independent variable by leaving the control group participants alone but killing the husband of each woman in the experimental group. Ethical principles obviously demand that developmentalists use methods other than true experimental ones to study questions about the effect of widowhood—and many other important questions about development.

Researchers sometimes study how a program or intervention affects development through a **quasi experiment**—an experiment-like study that evaluates the effects of different treatments but does not randomly assign individuals to treatment groups. A gerontologist, for example, might conduct a quasi experiment to compare the adjustment of widows who choose to participate in a support group for widows and those who do not. When individuals are not randomly assigned to treatment groups, however, uncontrolled differences among the groups studied could influence the results (for example, the widows who seek help might be more sociable than those who do not). As a result, the researcher is not able to make strong statements about what caused what, as in a true experiment.

The Correlational Method

Largely because of ethical issues, most developmental research today is correlational rather than experimental. The **correlational method** generally involves determining whether two or more variables are related in a systematic way. Researchers do not randomly assign participants to treatment conditions, manipulate the independent variable, or control other factors, as in an experiment. Instead, researchers take people as they are and attempt to determine whether there are relationships among their experiences, characteristics, and developmental outcomes.

How might a correlational study of the effects of television on children's aggressive behavior differ from Friedrich and Stein's experiment on this topic? In a well-designed correlational study, L. Rowell Huesmann and his colleagues (2003) correlated elementary school children's TV viewing with their aggressive behavior as adults 15 years later. Children picked their favorites from lists of TV programs and indicated how often they watched so that a self-report measure of the amount of violent TV watched could be created. The researchers then correlated the TV-watching measure with a measure of adult aggressive behavior that combined in one index criminal behavior, traffic violations, spouse abuse, physical aggression, and other such behavior.

Huesmann and his colleagues were then able to determine the strength of the relationship between these two variables by calculating a **correlation coefficient**—a measurement of the extent to which individuals' scores on one variable are systematically associated with their scores on another variable. A correlation coefficient (symbolized as r) can range in value from $+1.00$ to -1.00. A positive correlation between TV viewing and aggression would indicate that as the number of hours of TV children watch increases, so does the number of aggressive acts they commit (see Figure 1.3, Panel A). A positive correlation of $r = +0.90$ indicates a stronger, more predictable positive relationship than a smaller positive correlation such as $r = +0.30$. A negative correlation would result if the heaviest TV viewers were consistently the least aggressive children and the lightest viewers were the most aggressive children (see Panel B). A correlation near 0.00 would be obtained if there was no relationship between the two variables—if it was impossible to predict how aggressive children would be based on their TV-viewing habits (see Panel C).

Huesmann's team found the positive relationship they predicted between watching violent TV as a child and engaging in aggressive and antisocial behavior as an adult. People who watched a great deal of violent TV as children, whether they were male or female, had higher composite aggression scores as adults than did people who had watched less violence as children. But does this correlational study firmly establish that watching action-packed programs causes children to become more aggressive? Or can you think of alternative explanations for the correlation between watching TV and aggression?

One possibility in correlational studies is that *the direction of the cause–effect relationship is reversed.* That is, exposure to violent TV may not cause children to become aggressive, but aggressive children may be more likely than other children to seek blood and gore on TV. However, this problem of determining the directionality of causation was not as bothersome in Huesmann's study as it is in correlational studies that measure both variables of interest at the same time. It is difficult to argue that aggression in adulthood caused violent TV watching in childhood. Moreover, Huesmann collected data on how aggressive children in his sample were during childhood. He was then able to demonstrate that, although more aggressive children watch more violent TV than other children do, watching violent TV predicts becoming an aggressive adult even controlling for how aggressive these adults were as children.

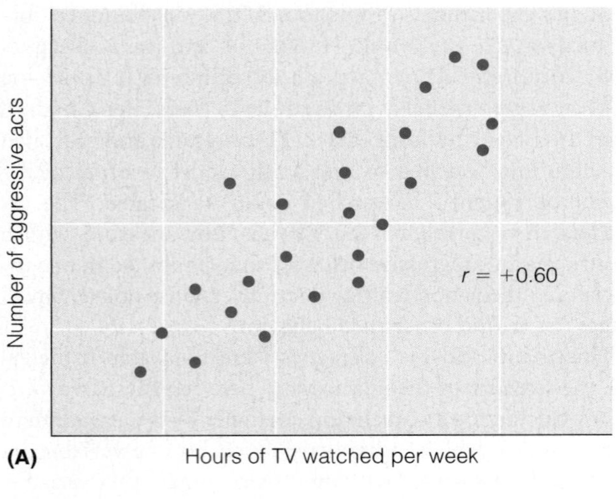

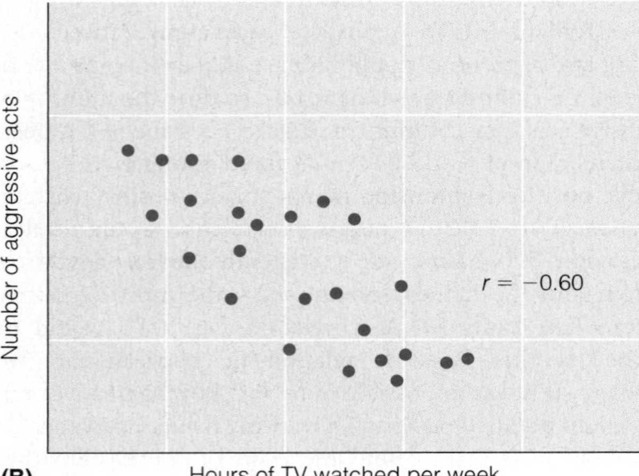

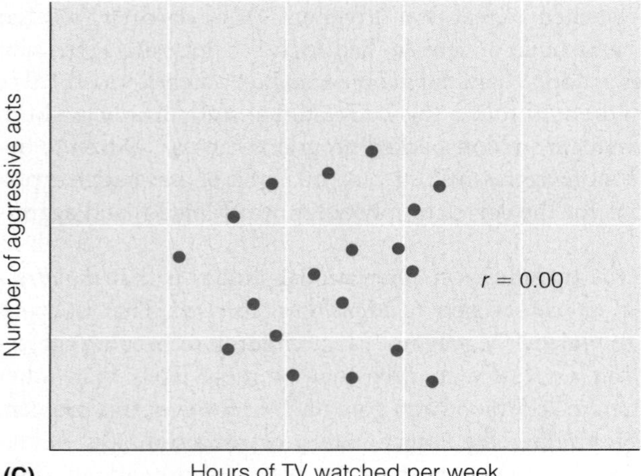

Figure 1.3 Plots of hypothetical correlations between the amount of TV children watch and the number of aggressive acts they display. Each dot represents a specific child who watches a high, medium, or low amount of TV and commits a high, medium, or low number of aggressive acts. Panel A shows a positive correlation between television watching and aggression: the more TV children watch, the more aggressive they are. Panel B shows a negative correlation: the more TV children watch, the less aggressive they are. Finally, Panel C shows zero correlation: the amount of TV watched is unrelated to the amount of aggression displayed.

A second possibility in correlational studies is that *the association between the two variables is caused by some third variable.* An example of such a third variable might be parental rejection. Some children might have parents who are harsh and rejecting, and they might watch more TV than most children to avoid unpleasant interactions with their parents. They may be aggressive because they are angry and upset about being rejected. If so, watching TV did not cause these children to become more aggressive than their peers. Rather, a third variable—parental rejection—may have caused both their aggressive ways and their TV-viewing habits.

Thus, the correlational method has one major limitation: it cannot unambiguously establish a causal relationship between one variable and another the way an experiment can. Correlational studies can *suggest* that a causal relationship exists, however. Indeed, Huesmann's team used complex statistical techniques in which a correlation is corrected for the influence of other variables to show that watching violent television in childhood probably contributed to aggression in adulthood. Several potential third variables, including parental rejection, low socioeconomic status, and low intelligence quotient (IQ)—all correlated with both watching violent TV and aggression—were ruled out as explanations of the relationship between TV viewing and aggression. Still, despite all their efforts to establish that the direction of the cause–effect relationship is from watching violent TV to aggression rather than vice versa, and to rule out possible third variables that could explain the TV–aggression relationship, Huesmann's team could not establish a definite cause–effect link because of the correlational nature of the study.

Despite this key limitation, the correlational method is extremely valuable. First, as already noted, many problems can be addressed only through the correlational method (or through quasi experiments) because it would be unethical to conduct certain experiments. Second, correlational studies allow researchers to learn about how multiple factors operating in the "real world" conspire to influence development. Because life-span development is influenced by multiple factors rather than one factor at a time, experiments are not enough. Today's developmental researchers rely on complex correlational designs and statistical methods to understand relationships among potential causal factors such as life experiences and personal characteristics and to understand their joint contributions to good or poor developmental outcomes (Wachs, 2000). See Table 1.2 for a comparison of experimental and correlational methods.

Overall, the ability to understand why humans develop as they do is advanced the most when the results of different kinds of studies *converge*—when experiments demonstrate a clear cause–effect relationship under controlled conditions and correlational studies reveal that the same relationship seems to be operating in everyday life, even in the context of other possible causes. The results of multiple studies addressing the same question can be synthesized to produce overall conclusions through the research method of **meta-analysis** (Glass, McGaw, & Smith, 1981; Lipsey & Wilson, 2001). As one meta-analysis of research on the link between watching vio-

Table 1.2 A Comparison of the Experimental Method and the Correlational Method

Experimental Method	Correlational Method
Manipulation of an independent variable (investigator exposes participants to different experiences)	Study of people who have already had different experiences
Random assignment to treatment groups to ensure similarity of group	Assignment by "nature" to groups (groups may not be similar in all respects)
Experimental control of extraneous variables	Lack of control over extraneous variables
Can establish a cause–effect relationship between independent variable and dependent variable	Can suggest but not firmly establish that one variable causes another
May not be possible for ethical reasons	Can be used to study issues that cannot be studied experimentally for ethical reasons
May be artificial (findings from contrived experimental settings may not generalize well to the "real world")	Can study multiple influences operating in natural settings (findings may generalize better to the "real world")

lence on television and behaving aggressively showed, there was a reliable relationship between the two (Anderson & Bushman, 2002; Bushman & Anderson, 2001). The magnitude of the correlation is usually between +0.10 and +0.30. That may seem small, but it is larger than the average correlation between calcium intake and bone mass or between time spent doing homework and academic achievement (Bushman & Anderson, 2001). Moreover, the relationship shows up in studies using the correlational method and in studies using the experimental method and in both laboratory and naturalistic settings.

Developmental Research Designs

Along with the experimental and correlational methods used by all kinds of researchers to study relationships between variables, developmental researchers need specialized research designs to study how people change and remain the same as they get older. To achieve the goal of describing development, researchers have relied extensively on two types of research designs: the cross-sectional design and the longitudinal design. A third type of design, the sequential study, has come into use in an attempt to overcome the limitations of the other two techniques. First look at three influences on the outcomes of developmental studies, then explore the strengths and weaknesses of the cross-sectional and longitudinal designs.

Age, Cohort, and Time of Measurement Effects

Developmental studies can be influenced by three factors: age effects, cohort effects, and time of measurement effects. **Age effects** are the effects of getting older. What interests researchers in any developmental study is the relationship between age and an aspect of development. **Cohort effects** are the effects of being born in a particular historical context. Any **cohort** is a group of people born at the same time, either in the same year or within a specified span of years (that is, as part of a particular generation). People who are in their 80s today not only are older than people in their 50s and 20s but also belong to a different cohort or generation and have had different formative experiences.

Finally, **time of measurement effects** in developmental research are the effects of historical events and trends occurring when the data are collected (for example, effects of 9/11 or of the creation of the World Wide Web). Time of measurement effects are not unique to a particular cohort but can affect anyone alive at the time. Once you are aware that age, cohort, and time of measurement can all influence developmental research findings, you can appreciate that both the cross-sectional and the longitudinal designs have their limitations.

Cross-Sectional and Longitudinal Designs

In a **cross-sectional design,** the performances of people of different age groups, or cohorts, are compared. A researcher interested in the development of vocabulary might gather samples of speech from several 2-, 3-, and 4-year-olds; calculate the mean (or average) number of distinct words used per child for each age group; and compare these means to describe how the vocabulary sizes of children age 2, 3, and 4 differ. The cross-sectional study provides information about *age differences.* By seeing how different age groups differ, researchers can attempt to draw conclusions about how performance changes with age.

In a **longitudinal design,** the performance of one cohort of individuals is assessed repeatedly over time. The language development study just described would be longitudinal rather than cross-sectional if a researcher identified a group of 2-year-olds, measured their vocabulary sizes, waited a year until they were age 3 and measured their vocabularies again, did the same thing a year later when they were age 4, then compared the mean scores of these same children at the three ages. In any longitudinal study, whether it covers only a few months in infancy or 50 years, the same individuals are studied as they develop. Thus, the longitudinal design provides information about *age changes* rather than age differences.

Now, does it matter whether researchers choose the cross-sectional or the longitudinal design to describe development? Suppose a team of researchers was interested in whether attitudes about the roles of men and women in society typically become more traditional or more liberated over the adult years. Suppose they conducted a longitudinal study by administering the gender-role questionnaire three times to a group of men and women: in 1960 (when the men and women were 30); in 1980 (when they were 50), and in 2000 (when they were 70). But in 2000, another research team conducted a cross-sectional study of this same question, comparing the gender-role attitudes of adults 30, 50, and 70 years old at that time. Figure 1.4 illustrates these two designs, and Figure 1.5 portrays the hypothetical age trends they might generate.

What is going on in Figure 1.5? The cross-sectional study seems to say that as people get older, their attitudes about gender roles become more traditional. The longitudinal study suggests precisely the opposite: as people get older, their attitudes about gender roles seem to become more liberated. How could a cross-sectional study and a longitudinal study on the same topic lead to such different conclusions?

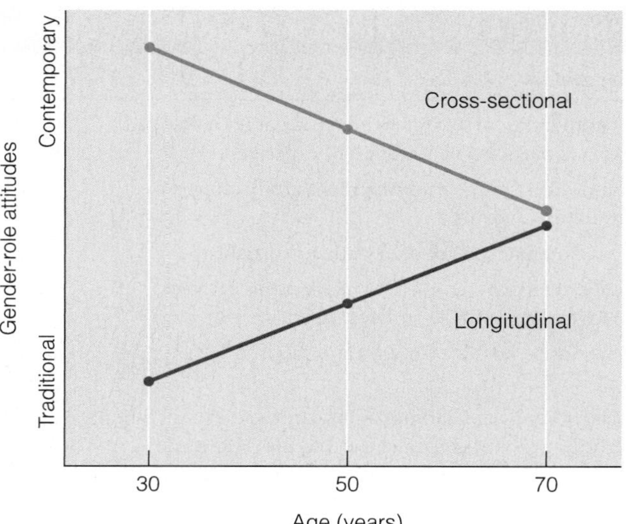

Figure 1.5 Conflicting findings of hypothetical cross-sectional and longitudinal studies of gender-role attitudes. How could the two studies produce different age trends?

Strengths and Weaknesses of the Cross-Sectional Design

In the cross-sectional study of gender attitudes, the three age groups being compared represent three cohorts of people. The 70-year-olds were born in 1930, the 50-year-olds in 1950, and the 30-year-olds in 1970. The cross-sectional study tells how people of different ages (cohorts) differ, and this can be useful information. But the cross-sectional technique does not necessarily tell how people develop as they get older. Do 70-year-olds hold more conservative gender-role attitudes than 30-year-olds because they are older or because they are members of a different cohort raised in a more traditional period when women mainly stayed home and raised children? We cannot tell. *Age effects and cohort effects are confounded, or entangled.*

Possibly, then, older adults' unliberated responses to the questionnaire in 2000 reflect views they learned early in life and maintained for the rest of their lives. Perhaps their views did not become more traditional as they got older. And perhaps the 30-year-old cohort, which grew up when the women's movement was in full swing, formed liberated gender-role attitudes early in life and retained those liberated attitudes as they grew older. Perhaps, then, what initially looked like a developmental trend toward greater traditionalism (an age effect) is actually a cohort effect resulting from differences in the formative experiences of the different generations studied.

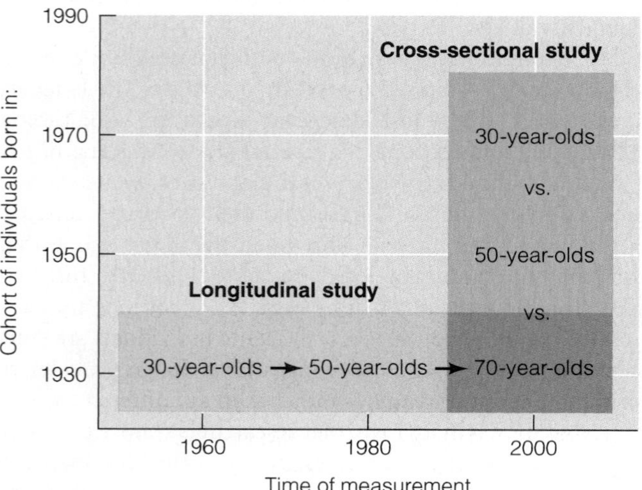

Figure 1.4 Cross-sectional and longitudinal studies of development from age 30 to age 70.

The problem of cohort effects is the central problem in cross-sectional research. As you will see in Chapter 9, cross-sectional studies of performance on intelligence tests once appeared to indicate that people experience significant declines in intellectual functioning starting in middle age. Yet the older adults in these studies grew up in a time when many people did not graduate from high school. Subsequent studies have shown that these older people probably did not lose intellectual abilities in old age (a true developmental or age effect); they merely performed less well than younger cohorts because they received less education in their youth (a cohort effect).

Despite this central problem, developmentalists still commonly use the cross-sectional design. Why? Because it has the great advantage of being quick and easy: researchers can go out this year, sample individuals of different ages, and be done with it. Moreover, this design should yield valid conclusions if the cohorts studied are likely to have had similar growing-up experiences—as when 3- and 4-year-olds rather than 30- and 40-year-olds are compared. It is when researchers attempt to make inferences about development over the span of many years that cohort effects become a serious problem.

The second major limitation of the cross-sectional design is that, because each person is observed at only one point, researchers learn nothing about how each person changes with age. They cannot see, for example, whether different people show divergent patterns of change in their gender-role attitudes over time or whether individuals especially liberated in their attitudes as 30-year-olds are also especially liberated at 70. To address issues like these, they need longitudinal research.

© Bettman/CORBIS

For baby boomers growing up in the 1950s, sex roles were more traditional than they are now.

Strengths and Weaknesses of the Longitudinal Design

Because the longitudinal design traces changes in individuals as they age, it can tell whether most people change in the same direction or whether different individuals travel different developmental paths. It can indicate whether the characteristics and behaviors measured remain consistent over time—for example, whether the bright, aggressive, or dependent young person retains those same traits in later life. And it can tell whether experiences early in life predict traits and behaviors later in life. The cross-sectional design can do none of these.

What, then, are the limitations of the longitudinal design? In the hypothetical longitudinal study of gender-role attitudes, adults were first assessed at age 30, then reassessed at age 50 and age 70. The study centered on *one cohort* of individuals: members of the 1930 birth cohort. These people were raised in a historical context in which gender-role attitudes were traditional and then saw the women's movement change many of those attitudes considerably. Their responses in 2000 may have been more liberal than their responses in 1960 not because gender-role attitudes typically become more liberal as people get older but because major societal changes occurred from one time of measurement to the next during the time frame of the study. In the longitudinal study, then, *age effects and time of measurement effects are confounded.* The researchers would not be able to tell for sure whether the age-related changes observed are true developmental trends or whether they reflect historical events occurring at a particular point of assessment or between assessments during the study.

The problem, then, is that researchers may not be able to generalize what they find in a longitudinal study to people developing in eras different than the ones in the study. Gender-role attitudes became more liberal in the United States from the 1970s to the 1990s. For example, in 1977, more than half of respondents to a survey said it was more important for a wife to help her husband's career than to have her own; by 1996, only about one in five agreed (Brewster & Padavic, 2000). But perhaps we would obtain different "developmental" trends if we did a hypothetical longitudinal study in an era in which sexism suddenly became popular again.

The longitudinal design has other disadvantages. One is fairly obvious: this approach is costly and time-consuming, particularly if it is used to trace development over a long span and at many points in time. Second, because knowledge is constantly changing, measurement methods that seemed good at the start of the study may seem dated or incomplete by the end. Third, participants drop out of long-term studies; they may move, lose interest, or, especially in studies of aging, die during the course of the study. The result is a smaller and often less representative sample on which to base conclusions. Finally, there may be effects of repeated testing; sometimes simply taking a test improves performance on that test the next time around.

Are both the cross-sectional and the longitudinal designs hopelessly flawed, then? That would be overstating their weaknesses. Cross-sectional studies are very efficient and informative, especially when the cohorts studied are not widely different in age or formative experiences. Meanwhile, longitudinal studies are extremely valuable for what they can reveal about changes in performance that occur as individuals get older—even though it must be recognized that the cohort studied may not develop in precisely the same way that an earlier or later cohort does. Still, in an attempt to overcome the limitations of both cross-sectional and longitudinal designs, developmentalists have devised a more powerful method of describing developmental change: the sequential design.

Sequential Designs: The Best of Both Worlds

A **sequential design** combines the cross-sectional approach and the longitudinal approach in a single study (Schaie, 1994). A sequential study of gender-role attitudes might begin as a cross-sectional study comparing the attitudes of different age groups of adults (say groups of 30-, 40-, and 50-year-olds in 1980). It might then repeatedly assess the attitudes of the individuals in these cohorts as they age (for example, in 1990 and 2000). As shown in Figure 1.6, researchers would then have three longitudinal studies of three cohorts, as well as three cross-sectional studies of different age groups, to analyze.

Sequential designs, by combining the cross-sectional and longitudinal approaches, improve on both. They can tell researchers (1) which age-related trends are truly developmental in nature and reflect how most people, regardless of cohort, can be expected to change over time (age effects);

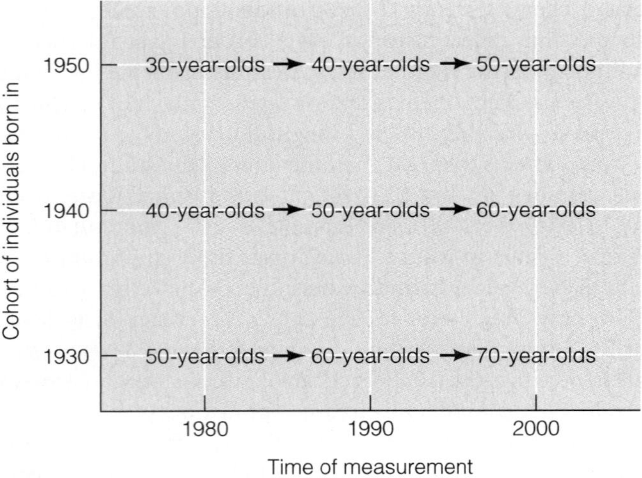

Figure 1.6 A sequential research design combines the cross-sectional and longitudinal approaches. This design starts with a cross-sectional study in 1980 and reassesses the same people every 10 years.

(2) which age trends differ from cohort to cohort and suggest that each generation is affected by its distinct growing-up experiences (cohort effects); and (3) which trends suggest that events during a specific period similarly affect all cohorts alive at the time (time of measurement effects). In short, sequential designs can begin to untangle the effects of age, cohort, and time of measurement and to indicate which age trends are truly developmental in nature. Yet they are extremely complex and expensive and are not always able to provide definitive answers. See Table 1.3 for a summary of the three basic developmental designs.

Summing Up

The scientific method involves formulating theories and testing hypotheses by conducting research with a sample (ideally a random sample) from a larger population. Common data collection methods include verbal reports, behavioral observations, and physiological measures. The goal of explaining development is best achieved through experiments; in correlational studies, it is difficult to determine the direction of influence and to rule out third variables. Developmental research designs seek to describe age effects on development. Cross-sectional studies compare different age groups but confound age effects and cohort effects. Longitudinal studies confound age effects and time of measurement effects. Sequential studies combine the cross-sectional and longitudinal approaches. ■

How Do We Protect the Rights of Research Participants?

Developmental researchers must be sensitive to issues involving **research ethics**—the standards of conduct that investigators are ethically bound to honor to protect their research participants from physical or psychological harm (Sales & Folkman, 2000). Remember the study by Hubbard and colleagues (2002) described earlier in this chapter, in which 8-year-olds were deliberately provoked to become angry after witnessing another child cheat them and win a board game

Table 1.3 Cross-Sectional, Longitudinal, and Sequential Developmental Designs

	Cross-Sectional Method	Longitudinal Method	Sequential Method
Procedure	Observe people of different cohorts at one point in time	Observe people of one age group repeatedly over time	Combine cross-sectional and longitudinal approaches; observe different cohorts on multiple occasions
Information Gained	Describes age differences	Describes age changes	Describes age differences and age changes
Advantages	Demonstrates age differences in behavior and hints at developmental trends Takes little time to conduct and is inexpensive	Indicates how individuals are alike and different in the way they change over time Can reveal links between early behavior or experiences and later behavior	Helps separate the effects of age, cohort, and time of measurement Indicates whether developmental changes experienced by one generation or cohort are similar to those experienced by other cohorts
Disadvantages	Age trends may reflect cohort effects rather than true developmental change Provides no information about change in individuals over time	Age trends may reflect time of measurement effects during the study rather than true developmental change Relatively time-consuming and expensive Measures may later prove inadequate Participants drop out Participants can be affected by repeated testing	Complex and time-consuming Despite being the strongest method, may leave questions about whether a developmental change can be generalized

unfairly? The researchers recognized that their study raised ethical issues. As a result, they arranged for the following: (1) children's parents observed the session through a one-way mirror so that they could call a halt to it if they thought their child was becoming too upset; (2) so that children would not leave with bad feelings about losing, they played another game with the confederate that was rigged so that they would win; (3) children were debriefed about the real purposes of the study; and (4) children enjoyed snack and play time with the confederate (who, by the way, was concerned that the participants would leave thinking that he or she was a cheater).

Many such ethical issues arise. For example, is it ethical to tell children that they performed poorly on a test to create a temporary sense of failure? Is it an invasion of a family's privacy to ask adolescents questions about conversations they have had with their parents about sex? Should a study of how a hormone replacement pill affects menopausal women be halted if it appears that the drug is having harmful effects? If a drug to treat memory loss in elderly adults with Alzheimer's disease appears to be working, should it be withheld from the control group in the study?

Such issues have led the federal government (through the Office of Human Research Protections), the American Psychological Association (1982), the Society for Research in Child Development (1990), and other organizations and agencies to establish guidelines for ethical research with humans. Federal regulations require universities and other organizations that conduct research with humans to have institutional review boards that determine whether proposed research projects conform to ethical standards and to approve the projects only if they comply. The federal government has tightened its oversight of research in recent years as a result of past abuses (Fisher, 1999; Sales & Folkman, 2000).

Deciding whether a proposed study is on safe ethical ground involves weighing the possible benefits of the research (gains in knowledge and potential benefits to humanity or to the participants) against the potential risks to participants. If the potential benefits greatly outweigh the potential risks, and if there are no other, less risky procedures that could produce these same benefits, the investigation is likely to be viewed as ethical. The investigator's ethical responsibilities boil down to respecting the rights of research participants by (1) allowing them to make informed and uncoerced decisions about taking part in research, (2) debriefing them afterward (especially if they are not told everything in advance or are deceived), (3) protecting them from harm, and (4) treating any information they provide as confidential.

1. *Informed consent.* Researchers generally should inform potential participants of all aspects of the research that might affect their decision to participate so that they can make a voluntary decision based on knowledge of what the research involves. But are young children or mentally impaired children or adults capable of understanding what they are being asked to do and of giving their *informed* consent? Probably not. Therefore, researchers who study such "vulnerable" populations should obtain informed consent both from the individual (if possible) and from someone who can decide on the individual's behalf—for example, the parent or guardian of a child or the legal representative of a nursing home resident. Investigators must not pressure anyone to participate and must respect participants' right to refuse to participate, to drop out during the study, and to refuse to have their data used by the investigator.

2. *Debriefing.* Researchers generally tell participants about the purposes of the study in advance, but in some cases doing so would ruin the study. If you told college students in advance that you were studying cheating and then gave them an opportunity to cheat on a test, do you think anyone would cheat? Instead, you might set up a situation in which students believe they can cheat without being detected and then debrief them afterward, explaining the true purpose of the study. You would also have an obligation to make sure that participants do not leave feeling upset about cheating.

3. *Protection from harm.* Researchers are bound not to harm research participants either physically or psychologically. Infants may cry if they are left in a room with a stranger, adolescents may be embarrassed if they are asked personal questions, and investigators must try to anticipate such consequences (Koocher & Keith-Spiegel, 1994). If harm to the participants seems likely, the researcher should consider another way of answering the research question. If participants become upset or are harmed, the researcher must take steps to undo the damage.

4. *Confidentiality.* Researchers also have an ethical responsibility to keep confidential the information they collect. It would be unacceptable, for example, to tell a child's teacher that the child performed poorly on an intelligence test or to tell an adult's employer that a drinking problem was revealed in an interview. The confidentiality of medical records concerning a person's physical and mental health is now particularly well protected by the Health Insurance Portability and Accountability Act of 1996, or HIPPA (Gostin, 2001). Only if participants give explicit permission to have information about them shared with someone else, or in rare cases in which the law requires disclosure of information (such as when child abuse is suspected), can that information be passed on.

Summing Up

Researchers must adhere to standards of ethical research practice, with attention to ensuring informed consent, debriefing individuals from whom information has been withheld, protecting research participants from harm, and maintaining confidentiality of data. ■

How Do We Understand Development in Its Ecological Context?

We conclude this chapter by bringing up an issue that will concern you throughout this book. If we take seriously the idea that human development occurs in a cultural and historical context, our studies of development must be sensitive to the ecology of human development (Rogoff, 2003). To help you think about what this really means, consider an influential conceptual model of development formulated by American psychologist Urie Bronfenbrenner. Many years ago, he became disturbed that many developmentalists studied human development out of context, expecting it to be universal and failing to appreciate how much it could vary from culture to culture, from neighborhood to neighborhood, and from home to home. Bronfenbrenner formulated an ecological model, later renamed a **bioecological model,** of development in an attempt to portray how nature and nurture interact to produce development (Bronfenbrenner, 1979, 1989; Bronfenbrenner & Evans, 2000; Bronfenbrenner & Morris, 1998).

In Bronfenbrenner's view, the developing person, with his biological and psychological characteristics, is embedded in a series of environmental systems that interact with one another and with the individual over time to influence development. Bronfenbrenner described four environmental systems that influence, and are influenced by, the developing person, as shown in Figure 1.7.

1. The **microsystem** is the immediate environment in which the person functions. The primary microsystem for a firstborn infant is likely to be the family—perhaps infant, mother, and father, all reciprocally influencing one another. The developing child may also experience other microsystems such as a day care center or grandmother's house. We have much evidence that the family environment is an important influence on child development and are coming to appreciate the importance of peer groups, schools, and neighborhood environments.

2. The **mesosystem** consists of the interrelationships or linkages between two or more microsystems. For example, a marital conflict in the family (one microsystem) could make a child withdraw from staff members and other children at the day care center (a second microsystem) so that her experience there becomes less intellectually stimulating. A loving home environment, by contrast, is likely to allow an individual to benefit more from experiences in the day care center or later in the classroom or at work.

3. The **exosystem** consists of linkages involving social settings that individuals do not experience directly but that can still influence their development. For example, children interacting with their parents at home can be affected by their parents' work experiences and their parents' social relationships outside the home (such as a distant but critical mother-in-law or an accepting and helpful best friend).

4. The **macrosystem** is the larger cultural context in which the microsystem, mesosystem, and exosystem are embedded. The shared understandings and ways of life that we call **culture** include beliefs and practices concerning the na-

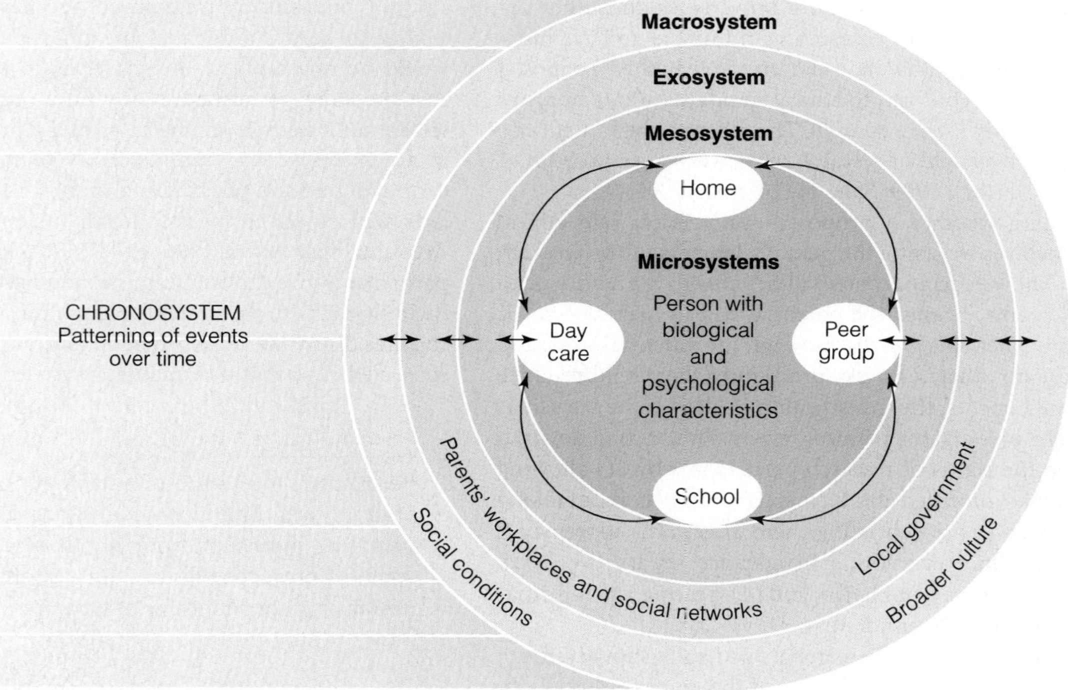

Figure 1.7 Urie Bronfenbrenner's bioecological model of development pictures environment as a series of nested structures. The microsystem refers to relations between the developing person and her immediate environment, the mesosystem to connections among microsystems, the exosystem to settings that affect but do not contain the individual, the macrosystem to the broader cultural context of development, and the chronosystem to the patterning over time of historical and life events. Researchers face many challenges in studying the developing person in context.

SOURCE: Adapted from Kopp & Krakow (1982)

ture of humans in different phases of the life span, what children need to be taught to function in society, and how people should lead their lives as adults.

In addition, Bronfenbrenner introduced the concept of the **chronosystem** to capture the idea that changes in people and their environments occur in a time frame and unfold in particular patterns or sequences over a person's lifetime. We cannot study development by taking snapshots; we must use a movie camera and understand how one event leads to another. Thus conflict between husband and wife leads to divorce and to changes in family members and their relationships, or societal events such as economic depressions, wars, and technological breakthroughs alter individual development while individuals affect the course of history (Modell & Elder, 2002). Each of us functions in particular microsystems linked through the mesosystem and embedded in the larger contexts of the exosystem and the macrosystem, all in continual flux.

What does the bioecological model imply for the study of human development? First, it suggests the need for complex longitudinal and sequential designs and complex statistical techniques capable of assessing the many interacting influences on development portrayed in Bronfenbrenner's model. When there is reciprocal or mutual influence operating—for example, between parent and child—it is not meaningful to think only of the one-directional influence of an independent variable on a dependent variable.

Second, Bronfenbrenner's model points to the need to study samples of developing persons from a variety of ecological settings, not just white middle-class America. A particularly important aspect of the ecology of human development is **socioeconomic status (SES)**, the status in society of an individual or family based on such indicators as occupational prestige, education, and income. We know that the developmental experiences and trajectories of children are significantly affected by whether they grow up in poverty or affluence. On average, although there are many exceptions, parents high in socioeconomic status tend to provide more stimulating and supportive home environments for their children than low–socioeconomic status (low–SES) parents do. The result is higher academic achievement, better adjustment, and other positive outcomes (Bornstein & Bradley, 2003).

In one especially well-designed experimental study, families living in low-income housing projects were randomly assigned to move to middle-income neighborhoods, move to other low-income neighborhoods, or stay in their low-income housing projects. Both parents and children who moved to the higher–SES neighborhoods benefited, as shown by measures of their physical and emotional health and levels of achievement (Leventhal & Brooks-Gunn, 2003). Similarly, aging tends to be a more positive experience for affluent adults than for adults living in poverty, who are disproportionately females and minority group members (Cruikshank, 2003). And, as we have already explained, it is important to study different national, racial, and ethnic groups to understand how their developmental experiences differ.

Third, the bioecological model highlights the importance of using culturally sensitive research methods and measurements. Ensuring that questionnaire and interview questions and testing and observation procedures mean the same thing in different cultures can be extremely challenging (Rogoff, 2003). To illustrate, when one organization translated a survey into 63 languages and then had the questions translated back into English, strange things happened: "married or living with a partner" was translated as "married but have a girlfriend," and "American ideas and customs" became "the ideology of America and border guards" (Morin, 2003). When another team sought to conduct a cross-cultural study of caregiver–infant interactions, they faced a dilemma about whether to observe such interactions when the caregiver and infant were alone (typical in American homes) or when the caregiver and infant were in a group (typical in Micronesia). They settled on observing in both social contexts to avoid findings that might be biased toward one group or the other (Sostek et al., 1981).

Finally, researchers who attempt to study cultural influences on development or racial, ethnic, and socioeconomic differences must work hard to keep their own cultural values from biasing their perceptions of other groups. Too often, for example, researchers in the United States have judged minority group children and adults according to white middle-class standards and have labeled them "deficient" when they would better be described as "different" (Ogbu, 1981; Phinney, 2000). More and more developmentalists today appreciate the importance of understanding human development in its ecological context, but doing so is a tremendous challenge.

Clearly, developmental researchers have some serious issues to weigh if they want their research to be not only well designed but also ethically responsible and culturally sensitive. Understanding life-span human development and the complexities of interactions between nature and nurture is an incredibly complex undertaking. It would be impossible if researchers merely conducted study after study without guiding ideas. Theories of human development provide those guiding ideas; they are the subject of Chapter 2.

Developmental findings established through the study of a sample of middle-class European American children may not hold true for these Bedoin nomad children living in the Egyptian desert.

Summing Up

Developmental researchers have more awareness than ever of the need to appreciate and study the influences of the ecological context of development, as portrayed in Bronfenbrenner's bioecological model in which the individual (including his or her biological characteristics) interacts with environmental systems called the microsystem, mesosystem, exosystem, and macrosystem over time (chronosystem). Researchers must use complex, longitudinal research designs; study samples from diverse populations (for example, groups differing in ethnicity and socioeconomic status); develop culturally sensitive methods and measures; and keep their own cultural values from biasing their conclusions. ■

Summary Points

1. Life-span human development involves systematic changes and continuities between conception and death. Developmental changes involve growth and aging and gains, losses, and neutral changes in the physical, cognitive, and psychosocial domains. They are the result of both nature and nurture.

2. Concepts of the life span and its distinctive periods (or age grades and their corresponding age norms and social clocks) have changed greatly over history and differ greatly from culture to culture today.

3. The science of life-span development has three goals: the description, explanation, and optimization of development. It started in the late 19th century with baby biographies and G. Stanley Hall's questionnaires; it is now guided by Paul Baltes's life-span perspective.

4. The scientific method involves formulating theories based on observations, using theories to generate specific hypotheses, testing hypotheses by collecting new observations, and using the data so obtained to evaluate the worth of theories.

5. Researchers study a sample, ideally a random sample, from a population, using data collection techniques such as verbal report measures (interviews, questionnaires, and tests), behavioral observations (naturalistic or structured), and physiological measurements.

6. To explain development, researchers rely on experiments with the manipulation of an independent variable, random assignment, and experimental control. In the correlational method, it is more difficult to determine the direction of causal influence and to rule out third variables.

7. Developmental researchers rely principally on cross-sectional designs (with cohort effects) and longitudinal designs (with historical effects) to describe development, or they combine the two approaches in more powerful sequential designs.

8. Developmental researchers must adhere to standards of ethical research practice with attention to informed consent, debriefing, protection from harm, and confidentiality.

9. Developmental researchers face issues in appreciating the importance of and in the study of the ecological context of development, as captured in Urie Bronfenbrenner's bioecological model.

Critical Thinking

1. Given the age grades and age norms that prevail in our society, how would you compare the advantages and disadvantages of being (a) an adolescent as opposed to a young adult, or (b) an elderly adult as opposed to a young adult?

2. You are interested in developmental changes in moodiness from age 12 to age 20. Design both a cross-sectional and a longitudinal study of this question, and weigh the advantages and disadvantages of the two designs. Also, using the material on verbal report, observational, and physiological measurements, develop two distinct approaches to measuring moodiness for use in your research.

3. Does the adequacy of the nutrition a child receives during the prenatal period affect the child's IQ test performance at age 5? Suggest both an experimental design and a correlational design to study this question. What features make the two designs different, and what are their pros and cons? Hint: Do not forget to consider ethical issues.

4. You want to interview elderly women shortly after the death of their husbands about their emotional reactions to widowhood. Based on the material on ethical issues in developmental research, what ethical issues would you be concerned about? What steps would you take to make your study as ethical as possible?

5. Using Bronfenbrenner's bioecological model, characterize the environmental systems in which you are developing.

Key Terms

centenarian, 2
development, 2
growth, 3
biological aging, 3
aging, 3
age grade, 3
age norms, 4
social clock, 4
nature–nurture issue, 5
maturation, 5
genes, 5
environment, 5
learning, 5
adolescence, 6
baby boom generation, 7
gerontology, 9
life-span perspective, 9
plasticity, 9
baby biographies, 10
case study method, 10
storm and stress, 11
scientific method, 11
theory, 11
hypothesis, 11
sample, 11
population, 11
random sample, 11
naturalistic observation, 12
structured observation, 13
experiment, 14
independent variable, 14
dependent variable, 14
random assignment, 14
experimental control, 14
quasi experiment, 15
correlational method, 15
correlation coefficient, 15
meta-analysis, 16

age effects, 17
cohort effects, 17
cohort, 17
time of measurement effects, 17
cross-sectional design, 17
longitudinal design, 17
sequential design, 19
research ethics, 20
bioecological model, 22
microsystem, 22
mesosystem, 22
exosystem, 22
macrosystem, 22
culture, 22
chronosystem, 23
socioeconomic status (SES), 23

Media Resources

Websites to Explore

Visit Our Website

For a chapter tutorial quiz and other useful features, visit the book's companion website at *http://psychology.wadsworth.com/sigelman_rider5e*. You can also connect directly to the following sites:

Census Data
The website of the U.S. Census Bureau provides a wealth of statistical information about the population of the United States, including information about different age groups.

Resources in Life-Span Developmental Psychology
Child and Adolescent Development
For a large menu of resources on life-span human development and child and adolescent development, explore the "Developmental Psychology Links" on the Social Psychology Network, maintained by Scott Plous of Wesleyan University. This web page links you to professional organizations such as the Society for Research in Child Development and to journals in the field, as well as to selected web resources on infancy and childhood, adolescence, and aging.

Gerontology Resources
For a comprehensive directory of web resources on statistics, professional organizations, and literature on aging, Alzheimer's disease, and death and dying, try exploring the "Gerontology Resources" links listed on the InfoQuest! Information Services gerontology page.

Bronfenbrenner
Urie Bronfenbrenner, emeritus professor at Cornell University and developer of the bioecological model, maintains a website, in which he outlines his current interests and lists his recent publications. His recent interests range from the "growing chaos" in children's environments today to developmental processes in middle adulthood and old age.

Understanding the Data: Exercises on the Web

For additional insight on the data presented in this chapter, try out the exercises for these figures at *http://psychology.wadsworth.com/sigelman_rider5e:*

Figure 1.1 Aggression among children in four cultures

Figure 1.5 Conflicting findings of hypothetical cross-sectional and longitudinal studies of gender-role attitudes

Life-Span CD-ROM

Go to the Wadsworth Life-Span CD-ROM for further study of the concepts in this chapter. The CD-ROM includes narrated concept overviews, video clips, a multimedia glossary, and additional activities to expand your learning experience.

DEVELOPMENTAL PsychologyNow™

Developmental PsychologyNow is a web-based, intelligent study system that provides a complete package of diagnostic quizzes, a personalized study plan, integrated multimedia elements, and learning modules. Check it out at *http://psychology.wadsworth.com/sigelman_rider5e/now.*

CHAPTER two

Theories of Human Development

SHERRY IS AN ATTRACTIVE 15-year-old whose relationship with Robert has become the center of her life. She gets by in school, but most of what goes on in the classroom bores her. Her relationship with her parents has been strained, partly because her mother does not want her to spend so much time with Robert. Robert, age 16, is also struggling at school and juggling his part-time job, family responsibilities, and time with Sherry. And these two teenagers have a more serious problem: Sherry is pregnant. The sex "just happened" one night after a party and continued thereafter. Neither Sherry nor Robert wanted a baby; neither used a contraceptive.

Having children is a normal part of human development during the adult years, but how can we explain unwanted pregnancies during adolescence from a developmental perspective? What is your theory of the developmental origins of this particular teenage pregnancy? What explanations might the leading theories of human development offer? More practically, what can be done to reduce the high rate of teenage pregnancy in U.S. society? We attempt to answer these questions in this chapter to illustrate that different theories of human development offer different lenses through which to view the same events.

Teenage pregnancy is one of many facts of human development.

Developmental Theories and the Issues They Raise

As noted in Chapter 1, a theory is a set of ideas proposed to describe and explain certain phenomena—in this book, of human development. In science, it is not enough simply to catalog facts without organizing this information around some set of concepts and propositions. Researchers would soon be swamped by meaningless data and become trivia experts who lack "the big picture." A theory of human development provides needed organization, offering a lens through which researchers can interpret any number of specific facts or observations. A theory also guides the collection of new facts or observations, making clear (1) what is most important to study, (2) what can be hypothesized or predicted about it, and (3) how it should be studied. Because different theorists often have different views on these critical matters, what is learned in any science greatly depends on which theoretical perspectives become dominant, which rests on how well they account for the facts.

All of us hold some basic beliefs about human development—for example, about the importance of genes versus good parenting in healthy development. Reading this chapter should make you more aware of your own assumptions about human development and how they compare with those of the major theorists. Scientific theories are expected to be more rigorous than our everyday theories, however. A good developmental theory should be the following:

- *Internally consistent.* Its different parts and propositions should tie together and should not generate contradictory hypotheses or predictions.
- *Falsifiable.* It can be proved wrong; that is, it can generate specific, testable hypotheses that can be studied and either supported or not supported by data. If a theory is vague or generates contradictory or ambiguous hypotheses, it cannot guide research, cannot be tested, and therefore will not be useful in advancing knowledge.
- *Supported by data.* A good theory should help us better describe, predict, and explain human development; its predictions should be confirmed by research results.

Theories that fail to meet these evaluation criteria—theories that are not internally consistent, falsifiable, and supported by data—need to be revised or discarded.

In this chapter, we examine four major theoretical viewpoints:

1. The *psychoanalytic* viewpoint developed by Sigmund Freud and revised by Erik Erikson and other followers
2. The *learning* perspective developed by B. F. Skinner, Albert Bandura, and others
3. The *cognitive developmental* viewpoint associated with Jean Piaget
4. The emerging *contextual–systems* approach, exemplified by Urie Bronfenbrenner (see Chapter 1), Lev Vygotsky, and Gilbert Gottlieb

Each theory makes particular assumptions or statements about the nature of human development.

To aid comparison of these theories, we outline five key developmental issues on which theorists—and people in general—often disagree (P. H. Miller, 2002; Parke et al., 1994): nature and nurture, the goodness and badness of human nature, activity and passivity, continuity and discontinuity, and universality and context specificity. We invite you to clarify your stands on these issues by completing the brief questionnaire in the Explorations box on this page. Later in the chapter, Table 2.4 on page 52 indicates how the major developmental theorists might answer the questions, so you can compare your assumptions with theirs. In Explorations boxes throughout this chapter, we pretend to speak for the theorists, imagining what each might say about the causes of teenage pregnancy. We suggest that you predict what each theorist will say before you read each of these boxes to see whether you can successfully apply the theories to a specific problem. It is our hope that as you grasp the major theories, you will be in a position to draw on their concepts and propositions to make sense of your own and other people's development.

Nature and Nurture

Is development primarily the product of nature (biological forces) or nurture (environmental forces)? As you saw in Chapter 1, the nature–nurture issue is the most important and most complex issue in the study of human development. A strong believer in nature—in individual genetic makeup, universal maturational processes guided by genes, biologically based predispositions built into genes over the course of evolution, and other biological influences—would claim that all normal children achieve the same developmental milestones at similar times because of maturational forces, that major changes in functioning in late adulthood are biologically based, and that differences among children or adults are largely because of differences in genetic makeup and physiology. By contrast, a strong believer in nurture would emphasize environment—the range of influences outside the

Explorations

Where Do You Stand on Major Developmental Issues?

Choose one option for each statement, and write down the corresponding letter or fill it in at the end of the box. Compare your results with those in Table 2.4 on page 52.

1. Biological influences (heredity and maturational forces) and environmental influences (culture, parenting styles, and learning experiences) are thought to contribute to development. Overall,
   a. biological factors contribute far more than environmental factors.
   b. biological factors contribute somewhat more than environmental factors.
   c. biological and environmental factors are equally important.
   d. environmental factors contribute somewhat more than biological factors.
   e. environmental factors contribute far more than biological factors.
2. Children are innately
   a. mostly bad; they are born with basically negative, selfish impulses.
   b. neither good nor bad; they are tabula rasae (blank slates).
   c. both good and bad; they are born with predispositions that are both positive and negative.
   d. mostly good; they are born with many positive tendencies.
3. People are basically
   a. active beings who are the prime determiners of their own abilities and traits.
   b. passive beings whose characteristics are molded either by social influences (parents, other significant people, and outside events) or by biological changes beyond their control.
4. Development proceeds
   a. through stages so that the individual changes rather abruptly into a different kind of person than she was in an earlier stage.
   b. in a variety of ways—some stagelike and some gradual or continuous.
   c. continuously—in small increments without abrupt changes or distinct stages.
5. When you compare the development of different individuals, you see
   a. many similarities; children and adults develop along universal paths and experience similar changes at similar ages.
   b. many differences; different people often undergo different sequences of change and have widely different timetables of development.

	Statement				
	1	2	3	4	5
Your pattern of choices:					

person. Nurture includes influences not only of the physical environment but also of learning experiences, child-rearing methods, societal changes, and the cultural context in which the person develops. Like the English philosopher John Locke (1632–1704), a strong believer in nurture would argue that human development can take many forms depending on the individual's experiences over a lifetime.

The Goodness and Badness of Human Nature

Are people inherently good, inherently bad, or neither? Well before modern theories of human development were proposed, philosophers of the 17th and 18th centuries were taking stands on the nature of humans. Thomas Hobbes (1588–1679), for one, portrayed children as inherently selfish and bad and believed that it was society's responsibility to teach them to behave in civilized ways. By contrast, Jean Jacques Rousseau (1712–1778) argued that children were innately good, that they were born with an intuitive understanding of right and wrong, and that they would develop in positive directions as long as society did not interfere with their natural tendencies. In the middle was Locke, who maintained that infants are **tabula rasae,** or "blank slates," waiting to be written on by their experiences. That is, children were neither innately good nor innately bad but could develop in any direction depending on their experiences.

These different visions of human nature are all represented in one or more modern theories of development and have radically different implications for how people should raise children (Pinker, 2002). In teaching children to share, for example, should people assume that their innate selfish tendencies must be battled at every step, that they are predisposed by nature to be helpful and caring, or that they have the potential to become either selfish beasts or selfless wonders depending on how they are brought up?

Activity and Passivity

Are people active in their own development, or are they passively shaped by forces outside themselves? With respect to this **activity–passivity issue,** some theorists believe that humans are curious, active creatures who orchestrate their own development by exploring the world around them and shaping their own environments. The girl who asks her mother for dolls at the toy store and the boy who clamors instead for toy trucks are actively contributing to their own gender-role development.

Other theorists view humans as passive beings largely the products of forces beyond their control—usually environmental influences but possibly strong biological forces. From this vantage point, children's academic failings might be blamed on the failure of their parents and teachers to provide them with the proper learning experiences, and the problems of socially isolated older adults might be attributed to societal neglect of the elderly rather than to deficiencies within the individual. Theorists disagree about how active individuals are in creating and influencing their own environments and, in the process, in producing their own development.

Continuity and Discontinuity

Do you believe that humans change gradually, in ways that leave them similar to the ways they were before, or do you believe they change abruptly and dramatically? One aspect of the **continuity–discontinuity issue** concerns whether the changes people undergo over the life span are gradual or abrupt. Continuity theorists view human development as a process that occurs in small steps, without sudden changes. In contrast, discontinuity theorists picture the course of development as more like a series of stairsteps, each of which elevates the individual to a new (and often more advanced) level of functioning. When an adolescent boy rapidly shoots up 6 inches in height, gains a bass voice, and grows a beard, the change seems discontinuous (see Figure 2.1).

A second aspect of the continuity–discontinuity issue concerns whether changes are quantitative or qualitative in nature. Quantitative changes are changes in *degree* and indicate continuity: a person gains wrinkles, grows taller, knows more vocabulary words, or interacts with friends more or less frequently. By contrast, qualitative changes are changes in *kind* and suggest discontinuity. They are changes that make the individual fundamentally different in some way. The transformations of a caterpillar into a butterfly rather than just a bigger or smarter caterpillar, of a nonverbal infant into a speaking toddler, and of a prepubertal child into a sexually mature adolescent are examples of qualitative changes.

So, continuity theorists typically hold that developmental changes are gradual and quantitative, whereas discontinuity theorists hold that they are more abrupt and qualitative. Discontinuity theorists often propose that people progress through **developmental stages.** A stage is a distinct phase of the life cycle characterized by a particular set of abilities, motives, emotions, or behaviors that form a coherent pattern. Each stage is viewed as qualitatively different from the stage before or the stage after. Thus, the preschool child may be said to solve problems in a different manner than that of the infant, adolescent, or adult.

Figure 2.1 Is development continuous (A) or discontinuous (B)? That is, do people change quantitatively, becoming different in degree (as shown in Panel A with size), or do they change qualitatively, becoming different in kind (as shown in Panel B when a tadpole becomes a frog)?

Universality and Context Specificity

Finally, developmental theorists often disagree on the **universality–context-specificity issue**—on the extent to which developmental changes are common to all humans (universal) or different from person to person (context specific). Stage theorists typically believe that the stages they propose are universal. For example, a stage theorist might claim that virtually all children enter a new stage in their intellectual development as they enter adolescence or that most adults, sometime around age 40, experience a midlife crisis in which they raise major questions about their lives. From this perspective, development proceeds in certain universal directions.

But other theorists believe that human development is far more varied. Paths of development followed in one culture may be different from paths followed in another culture. For example, preschool children in the United States sometimes believe that dreams are real but give up this belief as they age. By contrast, children raised in the Atayal culture of Taiwan have been observed to become more convinced with age that dreams are real, most likely because that is what adults in their culture believe (Kohlberg, 1966b). Even within a single culture, sequences of developmental change may differ from subcultural group to subcultural group, from family to family, or from individual to individual.

Now that you are familiar with some major issues of human development that different theories resolve in different ways (see Table 2.1), we will begin our survey of the theories, starting with Freud's well-known psychoanalytic perspective.

Summing Up

Theories are concepts and propositions that organize and explain the facts of human development. They are adequate to the extent that they are internally consistent, falsifiable, and supported by data. The five major issues in the study of human development confronted by developmental theorists are nature and nurture, the goodness and badness of human nature, activity and passivity, continuity and discontinuity, and universality and context specificity. ■

Freud: Psychoanalytic Theory

It is difficult to think of a theorist who has had a greater effect on Western thought than Sigmund Freud, the Viennese physician who lived from 1856 to 1939. This revolutionary thinker challenged prevailing notions of human nature and human development by proposing that people are driven by motives and emotions of which they are largely unaware and that they are shaped by their earliest experiences in life (Hall, 1954). His **psychoanalytic theory** continues to influence thinking about human development, even though it is far less influential today than it once was. Because you have undoubtedly been introduced to this theory before, we cover it only briefly.

Instincts and Unconscious Motives

Central to Freudian psychoanalytic theory is the notion that humans have basic biological urges or drives that must be satisfied. Freud viewed the newborn as a "seething cauldron," an inherently selfish creature "driven" by **instincts,** or inborn biological forces that motivate behavior. These biological instincts are the source of the psychic (or mental) energy that fuels human behavior and that is channeled in new directions over the course of human development.

Freud strongly believed in **unconscious motivation**—the power of instincts and other inner forces to influence behavior without awareness. A teenage boy, for example, may not realize that his devotion to body building could be a way of channeling his sexual or aggressive urges. So, you immediately see that Freud's theory emphasizes the nature side of the nature–nurture issue: biological instincts—forces that often provide an unconscious motivation for actions—are said to guide human development.

Id, Ego, and Superego

According to Freud (1933), each individual has a fixed amount of psychic energy that can be used to satisfy basic urges or instincts and to grow psychologically. As a child de-

Table 2.1 Issues in Human Development

Issue	Description
1. Nature–Nurture	Is development primarily the product of genes, biology, and maturation—or of experience, learning, and social influences?
2. Goodness–Badness of Human Nature	Are humans innately good, innately bad, neither (tabula rasae), or both?
3. Activity–Passivity	Do humans actively shape their own environments and contribute to their own development—or are they passively shaped by forces beyond their control?
4. Continuity–Discontinuity	Do humans change gradually and in quantitative ways—or do they progress through qualitatively different stages and change dramatically into different beings?
5. Universality–Context Specificity	Is development similar from person to person and from culture to culture—or do pathways of development vary considerably depending on the social contexts?

© UPI-Bettmann/CORBIS

Sigmund Freud's psychoanalytic theory was one of the first, and one of the most influential, theories of how the personality develops from childhood to adulthood.

velops, this psychic energy is divided among three components of the personality: the id, the ego, and the superego. At birth, all psychic energy resides in the **id**—the impulsive, irrational part of the personality whose mission is to satisfy the instincts. It seeks immediate gratification, even when biological needs cannot be realistically or appropriately met. If you think about it, young infants do seem to be all id in some ways. When they are hungry or wet, they fuss and cry until their needs are met. They are not known for their patience.

The second component of the personality is the **ego,** the rational side of the individual that tries to find realistic ways of gratifying the instincts. According to Freud (1933), the ego begins to emerge during infancy when psychic energy is diverted from the id to energize cognitive processes such as perception, learning, and problem solving. The hungry toddler may be able to do more than merely cry when she is hungry; she may be able to draw on the resources of the ego to hunt down Dad, lead him to the kitchen, and say "cookie." However, toddlers' egos are still relatively immature; they want what they want *now.* As the ego matures further, children become more capable of postponing their pleasures until a more appropriate time and of devising logical and realistic strategies for meeting their needs.

The third part of the Freudian personality is the **superego,** the individual's internalized moral standards. The superego develops from the ego as 3- to 6-year-old children internalize (take on as their own) the moral standards and values of their parents. Once the superego emerges, children have a parental voice in their heads that keeps them from violating society's rules and makes them feel guilty or ashamed if they do. The superego insists that people find socially acceptable or ethical outlets for the id's undesirable impulses.

Conflict among the id, ego, and superego is inevitable, Freud said. In the mature, healthy personality, a dynamic balance operates: the id communicates its basic needs, the ego restrains the impulsive id long enough to find realistic ways to satisfy these needs, and the superego decides whether the ego's problem-solving strategies are morally acceptable. The ego must strike a balance between the opposing demands of the id and the superego while accommodating the realities of environment.

According to Freud (1964), psychological problems often arise when the individual's limited amount of psychic energy is unevenly distributed among the id, the ego, and the superego. For example, a person diagnosed as an antisocial personality, or sociopath, who routinely lies and cheats to get his way, may have a weak superego, whereas a married woman who cannot undress in front of her husband may have an overly strong superego, perhaps because she was made to feel deeply ashamed about any interest she took in her body as a young girl. Through analysis of the dynamics operating among the three parts of the personality, Freud and his followers attempted to describe and understand individual differences in personality and origins of psychological disorders.

Psychosexual Development

Freud (1964) maintained that as the child matures biologically, the psychic energy of the sex instinct, which he called **libido,** shifts from one part of the body to another, seeking to gratify different biological needs. In the process, as outlined in Table 2.2, the child moves through five **psychosexual stages:** oral, anal, phallic, latent, and genital.

Freud emphasized the role of nature over that of nurture in development, maintaining that inborn biological instincts drive behavior and that biological maturation guides all children through the five psychosexual stages. Yet he also viewed nurture—especially early experiences within the family—as an important contributor to individual differences in adult personality. At each psychosexual stage, the id's impulses and social demands come into conflict. Harsh child-rearing methods can heighten this conflict and the child's anxiety.

To defend itself against anxiety, the ego adopts unconscious coping devices called **defense mechanisms** (Freud, 1964). Consider the defense mechanism of **fixation**—arrested development in which part of the libido remains tied to an early stage. A baby boy who was rarely allowed to linger at the breast, was screamed at for mouthing and chewing paychecks and other fascinating objects left lying around the house, or was otherwise deprived of oral gratification might become fixated at the oral stage. He would then seek to satisfy unmet oral needs and to avoid the potentially more agonizing conflicts of the anal stage. He might display this oral fixation by becoming a chronic thumb sucker and, later in life, by chain-smoking, talking incessantly (as college professors are prone to do), or depending too much on other people.

Similarly, the 3-year-old who is harshly punished for toileting accidents may become fixated at the anal stage and turn into an inhibited or stingy adult. Or she may deal with her anxiety through another defense mechanism, **regression,**

Table 2.2 The Stage Theories of Freud and Erikson

Freud's Psychosexual Theory		Erikson's Psychosocial Theory	
Stage (Age Range)	**Description**	**Stage (Age Range)**	**Description**
Oral stage (birth to 1 year)	Libido is focused on the mouth as a source of pleasure. Obtaining oral gratification from a mother figure is critical to later development.	Trust vs. mistrust (birth to 1 year)	Infants must learn to trust their caregivers to meet their needs. Responsive parenting is critical.
Anal stage (1 to 3 years)	Libido is focused on the anus, and toilet training creates conflicts between the child's biological urges and the society's demands.	Autonomy vs. shame and doubt (1 to 3 years)	Children must learn to be autonomous—to assert their wills and do things for themselves—or they will doubt their abilities.
Phallic stage (3 to 6 years)	Libido centers on the genitals. Resolution of the Oedipus or the Electra complex results in identification with the same-sex parent and development of the superego.	Initiative vs. guilt (3 to 6 years)	Preschoolers develop initiative by devising and carrying out bold plans, but they must learn not to impinge on the rights of others.
Latent period (6 to 12 years)	Libido is quiet; psychic energy is invested in schoolwork and play with same-sex friends.	Industry vs. inferiority (6 to 12 years)	Children must master important social and academic skills and keep up with their peers; otherwise, they will feel inferior.
Genital stage (12 years and older)	Puberty reawakens the sexual instincts as youths seek to establish mature sexual relationships and pursue the biological goal of reproduction.	Identity vs. role confusion (12 to 20 years)	Adolescents ask who they are and must establish social and vocational identities; otherwise, they will remain confused about the roles they should play as adults.
		Intimacy vs. isolation (20 to 40 years)	Young adults seek to form a shared identity with another person but may fear intimacy and experience loneliness and isolation.
		Generativity vs. stagnation (40 to 65 years)	Middle-aged adults must feel that they are producing something that will outlive them, either as parents or as workers; otherwise, they will become stagnant and self-centered.
		Integrity vs. despair (65 years and older)	Older adults must come to view their lives as meaningful to face death without worries and regrets.

which involves retreating to an earlier, less traumatic stage of development. She may revert to infantile behavior—cooing like a baby and demanding juice from a baby bottle. Similarly, the man who has had a terrible day at work may want his wife to act like his mother and "baby" him. In this way, Freud argued, early experiences may have long-term effects on personality development.

The phallic stage from age 3 to age 6 is an especially treacherous time, according to Freud. Youngsters develop an incestuous desire for the parent of the other sex. (The boy's Oedipus complex and the girl's Electra complex are explained in Chapter 12.). If all goes well, they resolve the emotional conflict they experience by identifying with the same-sex parent and in the process incorporating that parent's values into the superego. After the lull of the latent period, during which sexual urges are tame and 6- to 12-year-olds invest psychic energy in schoolwork and play, adolescents experience new psychic conflicts as they reach puberty and enter the final stage of psychosexual development, the genital stage. They may have difficulty accepting their new sexuality, may reexperience some conflicting feelings toward their parents that they felt during the phallic stage, and may distance themselves from their parents to defend themselves against these anxiety-producing feelings. During adulthood, people may develop a greater capacity to love and typically satisfy the mature sex instinct by having children. However, Freud believed that psychosexual development stops with adolescence and that the individual remains in the genital stage throughout adulthood.

In the Explorations box on page 33, we imagine what Freud might have said about the causes of teenage pregnancy and about the case of Sherry and Robert described at the start of the chapter. What might you say if you were Freud?

Strengths and Weaknesses

Many developmentalists fault Freud for proposing a theory that is ambiguous, internally inconsistent, difficult to pin down and test, and therefore not easily falsifiable (Fonagy &

Explorations

Freud on Teenage Pregnancy

I welcome this opportunity to return to life to comment on the problem of teenage pregnancy. As you know, I was always fascinated by sex! We must realize that teenagers experience intense emotional conflicts during the genital stage of psychosexual development. Their new sexual urges are anxiety-provoking and may reawaken the sexual conflicts of earlier psychosexual stages.

I would need to find out more about the early childhood experiences and psychic conflicts of Sherry and Robert to pinpoint the specific causes of their risky sexual behavior, but basically I and other psychoanalytic theorists would tend to view teenage pregnancy as an expression of the adolescent's emotional needs or psychological problems (Farber, 2003). For example, stressful experiences in the family in early childhood have been found to contribute to teenage pregnancy (Russell, 2002). Teenagers who engage in risky sex may not have strong enough egos and superegos to keep their selfish ids in check (Babikian & Goldman, 1971; Hart & Hilton, 1988). Perhaps Sherry and Robert sought immediate gratification of their sexual urges with no thought of future consequences and no sense of guilt. Possibly these teenagers were motivated by inner conflicts that had their roots in infancy or the preschool years. For instance, girls from homes without fathers are more likely than other girls to get pregnant (Ellis et al., 2003). Perhaps Sherry never fully resolved her phallic stage issues and was unconsciously seeking to possess her father by possessing Robert. Robert might have been seeking to gratify his unconscious desire for his mother through Sherry. These reawakened feelings of love for the other-sex parent are common and often cause adolescents to distance themselves from their parents. Teenagers are especially likely to engage in risky sex, though, if they have significant psychological problems (Lavan & Johnson, 2002).

In short, teenage pregnancy is likely to result from difficulty managing sexual urges because of personality problems rooted in early childhood experiences.

Target, 2000). Testing hypotheses that require studying unconscious motivations and the workings of the unseen id, ego, and superego has been challenging. Freud himself offered little hard evidence to support his theory. Moreover, when the theory has been tested, many of its specific ideas have not been supported (Crews, 1996; Fisher & Greenberg, 1977). As a result, one critic called it "a theory in search of some facts" (Macmillan, 1991, p. 548).

To illustrate, Freud initially uncovered evidence that many of his patients had been sexually or physically abused during childhood. Because he could not believe it, he said that children in the phallic stage wished for and fantasized about, but did not experience, seduction by their parents (Gleaves & Hernandez, 1999; Masson, 1984). This claim has received little support (Crews, 1996). We now know that child sexual abuse is widespread and can contribute to lasting psychological difficulties (see Chapter 12).

Although many of Freud's specific ideas have been difficult to test or have not been supported by research, many of his general insights have stood up well and have profoundly influenced theories of human development and psychotherapy (Fonagy & Target, 2000). First, Freud called attention to *unconscious processes* underlying human behavior; some of his insights in this area are supported by modern neuropsychological research (Guterl, 2002). Second, he was one of the first to highlight the importance for later development of *early experiences* in the family. Finally, he pointed out the important role of *emotions* in development. Developmentalists have often slighted emotional development, focusing instead on observable behavior or on rational thought processes.

Summing Up

Freud's psychoanalytic theory characterizes humans as irrational beings largely driven by inborn biological instincts of which they are largely unconscious; partitions the personality into the id, ego, and superego (which emerge in that order); and proposes that libido is rechanneled across five psychosexual stages: oral, anal, phallic, latent, and genital. Each stage involves conflicts that create the need for defense mechanisms and have lasting effects on personality. Parents significantly affect a child's success in dealing with these conflicts, usually by being overly restrictive. Although Freud called attention to the unconscious, early experiences in the family, and emotional development, his theory is not easily falsifiable and many of its specifics lack support. ■

Erikson: Neo-Freudian Psychoanalytic Theory

Another sign of Freud's immense influence is that he inspired so many disciples and descendants to contribute to the understanding of human development. Among these well-known neo-Freudians were Alfred Adler, who suggested that siblings (and rivalries among siblings) are significant in development; Carl Jung, a pioneer in the study of adult development who claimed that adults experience a kind of midlife crisis (see Chapter 11) then become freer to express both the "masculine" and the "feminine" sides of their personalities; Karen Horney, who challenged Freud's ideas about sex differences; Harry Stack Sullivan, who argued that close friendships in childhood set the stage for intimate relationships later in life (see Chapter 14); and Freud's daughter Anna, who developed techniques of psychoanalysis appropriate for children.

But the neo-Freudian who most influenced thinking about life-span development was Erik Erikson (1902–1994; see Chapter 11 for more detail). Erikson studied with Anna Freud and emigrated from Germany to the United States when Hitler rose to power (Friedman, 1999). Like Sigmund Freud, Erikson (1963, 1968, 1982) concerned himself with the inner dynamics of personality and proposed that the personality evolves through systematic stages. However, Erikson's point of view differed from Freud's in the following ways:

- Erikson placed less emphasis on sexual urges as the drivers of development and more emphasis on social influences such as peers, teachers, schools, and broader culture.
- Erikson placed less emphasis on the irrational, selfish id and more on the rational ego and its adaptive powers.
- Erikson held a more positive view of human nature, seeing people as active in their development, largely rational, and able to overcome the effects of harmful early experiences.
- Erikson maintained that human development continues during adulthood.

Psychosocial Stages

Erikson believed that humans everywhere experience eight major **psychosocial stages,** or conflicts, during their lives.

© UPI-Bettmann/CORBIS

Erik Erikson built on Freudian theory and proposed that people experience eight psychosexual crises over their life span.

(Erikson's psychosocial stages are next to Freud's in Table 2.2.) Whether the conflict of a particular stage is successfully resolved or not, the individual is pushed by both biological maturation and social demands into the next stage. However, the unsuccessful resolution of a conflict will influence how subsequent stages play out.

For example, the first conflict, trust versus mistrust, revolves around whether or not infants become able to rely on other people to be responsive to their needs. To develop a sense of trust, infants must be able to count on their primary caregivers to feed them, relieve their discomfort, come when beckoned, and return their smiles and babbles. Whereas Freud focused on the significance of the caregiver's feeding practices, Erikson believed that the caregiver's general responsiveness was critical to later development. If caregivers neglect, reject, or respond inconsistently to infants, the infants will mistrust others. A healthy balance between the terms of the conflict must be struck for development to proceed optimally. Trust should outweigh mistrust, but an element of skepticism is also needed: an overindulged infant may become too trusting (a gullible "sucker").

So it goes for the remaining stages of childhood. If all goes well as children confront and resolve each conflict, they will gain a sense of self and learn to be autonomous, develop the initiative that allows them to plan and tackle big projects, and acquire the sense of industry that will result in mastering important academic and social skills. This will position adolescents to successfully resolve the conflict for which Erikson (1968) is best known, identity versus role confusion. Erikson characterized adolescence as a time of "identity crisis" in which humans attempt to define who they are (in terms of career, religion, sexual identity, and so on), where they are heading, and how they fit into society. As part of their search, they often change their minds and experiment with new looks, new majors, new relationships, and new group memberships.

Whereas Freud's stages stopped with adolescence, Erikson believed that psychosocial growth continues during the adult years. Successfully resolving the adolescent conflict of identity versus role confusion paves the way for resolving the early adulthood conflict of intimacy versus isolation and for becoming ready to participate in a committed, long-term relationship. Successful resolution of the middle age conflict of generativity versus stagnation involves individuals gaining a sense that they have produced something that will outlive them, whether by successfully raising children or by doing something meaningful through work or volunteer activities. Finally, elderly adults who resolve the psychosocial conflict of integrity versus despair find a sense of meaning in their lives that will help them face death.

Erikson clearly did not agree with Freud that the personality is essentially "set in stone" during the first 5 years of life. Yet he, like Freud and other psychoanalytic theorists, believed that people everywhere progress through systematic stages of development, undergoing similar personality changes at similar ages. Individual differences in personality presumably reflect the different experiences individuals have as they struggle to cope with the challenges of each life stage. Both biological maturation and demands of the social environment influence the individual's progress through Erikson's sequence of psychosocial stages. As an illustration, the Explorations box on this page expresses what Erikson might have said about teenage pregnancy.

Strengths and Weaknesses

Many people find Erikson's emphasis on our rational, adaptive nature and on an interaction of biological and social influences easier to accept than Freud's emphasis on unconscious, irrational motivations based in biological needs. Erikson also seems to have captured some central developmental issues in his eight stages. He has had an especially great effect on thought about and research on adolescent identity formation and changes during adulthood (see Chapter 11). Still, Erikson's theory has many of the same shortcomings as Freud's. It is sometimes vague and difficult to test. And although it provides a useful *description* of human personality development, it does not provide an adequate *explanation* of how this development comes about. Important psychoanalytic theorists such as Erikson continue to shape understanding of human development (Austrian, 2002), but many developmentalists have rejected the psychoanalytic perspective in favor of theories that are more precise and testable.

Summing Up

Neo-Freudian Erikson adopted much of Freud's thinking but emphasized biological urges less and social influences more; emphasized id less and ego more; held a more optimistic view of human nature and people's ability to overcome early problems; and theorized about the life span. According to Erikson, development proceeds through eight psychosocial stages involving issues of trust, autonomy, initiative, industry, identity, intimacy, generativity, and integrity. Parents, peers, and the larger culture influence how conflicts are resolved. The theories of both Freud and Erikson have been influential but are difficult to test and tend to describe development better than they explain it. ■

Learning Theories

> Give me a dozen healthy infants, well formed, and my own specified world to bring them up in, and I'll guarantee to take any one at random and train him to become any type of specialist I might select—doctor, lawyer, artist, merchant, chief, and yes, even beggar-man and thief, regardless of his talents, penchants, tendencies, abilities, vocations, and race of his ancestors. (Watson, 1925, p. 82)

There is a bold statement. It reflects a belief that nurture is everything and that nature, or genetic endowment, counts for nothing. It was made by John B. Watson, a strong believer in the importance of learning in human development and a pioneer of learning theory perspectives on human develop-

Explorations

Erikson on Teenage Pregnancy

I am not as obsessed by sex as my inspiration, Dr. Freud, but I can agree with him on some things. I agree that emotional conflicts rooted in early experience can affect later behavior. For example, if either Robert or Sherry had unresponsive caregivers when they were infants, they could have had difficulty resolving the psychosocial conflict of trust versus mistrust. Adolescents who never developed a strong sense of trust in other people may fear being abandoned and may try to use sex to keep that from happening.

Ah, but why focus on infancy? I agree with Dr. Freud that accepting one's self as a sexual being is an important task of adolescence, but that's just one aspect of the broader adolescent psychosocial conflict of identity versus role confusion. Adolescents change rapidly, physically and cognitively, and they are asked by society to establish who they are as individuals and as members of society. Many adolescents seek a sense of identity by experimenting with different roles and behaviors to see what suits them. They try drugs, dye their hair orange, join radical groups, change majors every semester, and yes, have sex—all to forge a firm sense of identity. I should know: I was the tall, blond stepson of a Jewish doctor and wandered all over Europe after high school, trying out a career as an artist and several other possibilities before I ended up studying child psychoanalysis under Anna Freud and finally found my calling in my mid-20s (Friedman, 1999).

So, perhaps Sherry and Robert were simply searching for their identities when they began their sexual relationship. Or maybe they tried to find an easy resolution to their role confusion by latching prematurely onto an identity as the other's boyfriend or girlfriend rather than going through the hard work of experimenting to find out who they are (Erikson, 1968). If this is the case, I must be pessimistic about their future. I maintain—and research bears me out—that one must know oneself before one can love someone else; that is, one must find one's true identity and end role confusion before one can resolve the conflict between intimacy and isolation (Orlofsky, 1993).

ment. Early learning theorists emphasized that human behavior changes in direct response to environmental stimuli; later learning theorists grant humans a more active and cognitive role in their own development but still believe that their development can take different directions depending on their experiences.

Watson: Classical Conditioning

Watson's (1913) **behaviorism** rested on his belief that conclusions about human development and functioning should be based on observations of overt behavior rather than on speculations about unobservable cognitive and emotional processes. Watson rejected psychoanalytic theory and devoted a good deal of his time to trying to explain Freud's fascinating discoveries about humans in terms of basic learning principles (Rilling, 2000). He maintained that learned associations between external stimuli and observable responses are the building blocks of both normal and abnormal human development. Like John Locke, Watson believed that children have no inborn tendencies and that how they turn out depends entirely on the environment in which they grow up and the ways in which their parents and other significant people in their lives treat them.

John B. Watson was the father of behaviorism.

To make his point, Watson and colleague Rosalie Raynor (1920) set out to demonstrate that fears can be learned—that they are not necessarily inborn as was commonly thought. They used the principles of **classical conditioning,** a simple form of learning in which a stimulus that initially had no effect on the individual comes to elicit a response through its association with a stimulus that already elicits the response. The Russian physiologist Ivan Pavlov called attention to classical conditioning. In a famous experiment, he demonstrated how dogs, who have an innate (unlearned) tendency to salivate at the sight of food, could learn to salivate at the sound of a bell if, during a training period, the bell was regularly sounded just before they were given food.

Watson and Raynor presented a gentle white rat to a now-famous infant named Albert, who showed no fear of it. However, every time the rat was presented, Watson would slip behind Albert and bang a steel rod with a hammer. The loud noise served as an **unconditioned stimulus** (**UCS**)—that is, an unlearned stimulus for fear—which in turn is an automatic, unlearned, or **unconditioned response** (**UCR**)to loud noises (babies are naturally upset by them). During conditioning, the stimuli of the white rat and the loud noise were presented together several times. Afterward, Watson presented the white rat to Albert without banging the steel rod. Albert now whimpered and cried in response to the white rat alone. His behavior had changed as a result of his experience. Specifically, an initially neutral stimulus, the white rat, had become a **conditioned stimulus** (CS) for a **conditioned response** (**CR**), fear, as shown in Figure 2.2. This learned response generalized to other furry items such as a rabbit and a Santa Claus mask. By today's standards, Watson's experiment would be viewed as unethical, but he had made his point: emotional responses can be learned. Fortunately, fears learned through classical conditioning can be unlearned if the feared stimulus is paired with an unconditioned stimulus for happy emotions (Jones, 1924).

Classical conditioning is undoubtedly involved when infants learn to love their parents, who at first may be neutral stimuli but who become associated with the positive sensations of receiving milk, being rocked, and being comforted. And classical conditioning helps explain why adults find certain songs on the radio, scents, or articles of clothing "turn them on." A range of emotional associations and attitudes are acquired through classical conditioning.

According to the learning theory perspective, then, it is a mistake to assume that children advance through a series of distinct stages guided by biological maturation, as Freud, Erikson, and other stage theorists have argued. Instead, learning theorists view development as nothing more than learning. It is a continuous process of behavior change that is context specific and can differ enormously from person to person. Watson's basic view was advanced by B. F. Skinner.

Skinner: Operant Conditioning

Skinner (1905–1990), whose name is as well known as that of any American psychologist, had a long, distinguished career at Harvard University. Through his research with animals, Skinner (1953) gained understanding of another important form of learning, **operant** (or instrumental) **conditioning,** in which a learner's behavior becomes either more or less probable depending on the consequences it produces. A learner first behaves in some way then comes to associate this action with the positive or negative consequences that follow it. The basic principle behind operant conditioning makes sense: people tend to repeat behaviors that have pleasant consequences and cut down on behaviors that have unpleasant con-

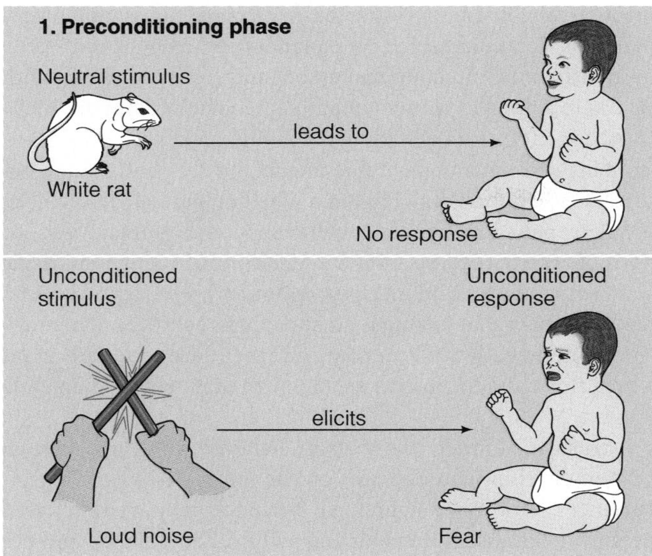

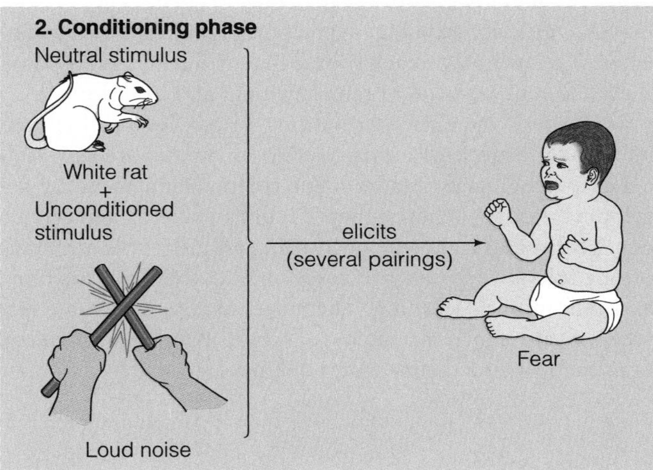

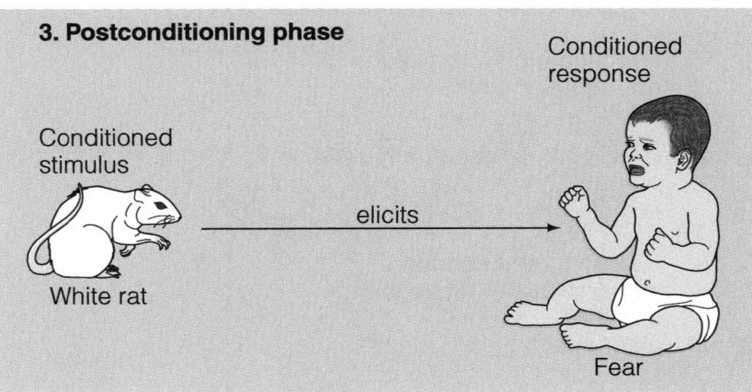

Figure 2.2 The three phases of classical conditioning.

sequences. Through operant conditioning, individuals learn new skills and a range of habits, both good and bad.

In the language of operant conditioning, **reinforcement** occurs when a consequence strengthens a response, or makes it more likely to reoccur. If a preschool child cleans his room, receives a hug, then cleans his room more frequently, the hug provided **positive reinforcement** for room cleaning. *Positive* here means that something has been added to the situation, and *reinforcement* means that the behavior is strengthened. Thus a positive reinforcer is an event that, when introduced following a behavior, makes that behavior more probable. (Note that the effect on the child's behavior defines a consequence as reinforcing, not the belief that the child might find a hug reinforcing.)

Behaviorists have found that it is best to provide continuous positive reinforcement when a new skill or habit is first being learned, reinforcing every occurrence. Then, to maintain the behavior, it is best to shift to a partial reinforcement schedule in which only some occurrences of the behavior are reinforced and the pattern is unpredictable. Then the learner is likely to continue performing even if reinforcement stops.

Negative reinforcement (which is *not* a fancy term for punishment) occurs when a behavioral tendency is strengthened because something negative or unpleasant is removed from the situation, or is escaped or avoided, after the behavior occurs. Have you been in a car in which an obnoxious buzzer sounds until you fasten your seat belt? The idea is that your "buckling up" behavior will become a habit through negative reinforcement: buckling your seat belt allows you to escape the unpleasant buzzer. No candy or hugs follow the action, so negative rather than positive reinforcement makes you likely to buckle your seat belt. Many bad habits allow people to escape or avoid unpleasantness and were learned through negative reinforcement. Teenagers may learn to lie to avoid long lectures from their parents or to drink because it allows them to escape feelings of anxiety at parties. In each case, a behavior is strengthened through negative reinforcement—through the removal or elimination of something unpleasant.

Contrast reinforcement, whether it is positive or negative, with punishment: Whereas reinforcement increases the strength of the behavior that preceded it, **punishment** decreases the strength of, or weakens, that behavior. Two forms of punishment parallel the two forms of reinforcement. **Positive punishment** occurs when an unpleasant event is

B.F. Skinner's operant conditioning theory emphasized the role of environment in controlling behavior.

added to the situation following a behavior (for example, a cashier is criticized for coming up short of cash at the end of the day). **Negative punishment** occurs when something pleasant is removed from the situation following the behavior (the amount she was short is deducted from her pay). Both positive and negative punishment decrease the likelihood that the punished behavior will be repeated.

The four possible consequences of a behavior are summarized in Figure 2.3. In addition, some behavior has no consequence. Behavior that is ignored, or no longer reinforced, tends to become less frequent through a process called **extinction.** Indeed, a good alternative to punishing a child's misbehavior is ignoring it and reinforcing desirable behavior incompatible with it. Too often, the well-behaved child is ignored and the misbehaving child gets the attention—attention that serves as positive reinforcement for the misbehavior.

Skinner and other behavioral theorists have emphasized the power of positive reinforcement and have generally discouraged the use of physical punishment in child rearing. By contrast, many parents believe that physical punishment of bad behavior is necessary in raising children; indeed, 80% of American adults believe that children sometimes need a "good, hard spanking" (Flynn, 1994). What does research say about who is right?

Although it is generally best to use more positive approaches before resorting to punishment, punishment makes children comply with parents' demands in the short run (Benjet & Kazdin, 2003). Spanking or another form of physical punishment can be effective in changing behavior in the longer run if it (1) is administered immediately after the act (not hours later when the child is being an angel), (2) is administered consistently after each offense, (3) is not overly harsh, (4) is accompanied by explanations, (5) is administered by an otherwise affectionate person, and (6) is combined with efforts to reinforce more acceptable behavior (Domjan, 1993; Gershoff, 2002; Perry & Parke, 1975). Frequent physical punishment can have undesirable effects, however. Although researchers cannot always be sure whether punishment causes problem behavior, problem behavior causes punishment, or both, research suggests that physical punishment may make children resentful and anxious and may breed aggression by teaching them that hitting is an appropriate way to solve problems. The negative effects of punishment are especially clear when the child punished is older than 6 years (Benjet & Kazdin, 2003).

In sum, Skinner, like Watson, believed that the course of human development depends on the individual's learning experiences. One boy's aggressive behavior may be reinforced over time because he gets his way with other children and because his parents encourage his "macho" behavior. Another boy may quickly learn that aggression is prohibited and punished. The two may develop in different directions based on their different histories of reinforcement and punishment.

Skinner's operant conditioning principles can help explain many aspects of human development and are still studied by psychologists (Staddon & Cerutti, 2003). Yet some developmentalists believe that Skinner placed too much emphasis on a single type of learning and too little emphasis on the role of cognitive processes such as attention, memory, and reflection in learning. Therefore, today's developmental scholars are more attracted to Albert Bandura's cognitive brand of learning theory than to Skinner's.

	PLEASANT STIMULUS	UNPLEASANT STIMULUS
ADMINISTERED	**Positive reinforcement, adding a pleasant stimulus** (strengthens the behavior) Dad gives in to the whining and lets Moosie play Nintendo, making whining more likely in the future.	**Positive punishment, adding an unpleasant stimulus** (weakens the behavior) Dad calls Moosie a "baby." Moosie does not like this at all and is less likely to whine in the future.
WITHDRAWN	**Negative punishment, withdrawing a pleasant stimulus** (weakens the behavior) Dad confiscates Moosie's favorite Nintendo game to discourage whining in the future.	**Negative reinforcement, withdrawing an unpleasant stimulus** (strengthens the behavior) Dad stops joking with Lulu. Moosie gets very jealous when Dad pays attention to Lulu, so his whining enables him to bring this unpleasant state of affairs to an end.

Figure 2.3 Possible consequences of whining behavior. Moosie comes into the TV room and sees his father talking and joking with his sister, Lulu, as the two watch a football game. Soon Moosie begins to whine, louder and louder, that he wants them to turn off the television so he can play Nintendo games. If you were Moosie's father, how would you react? Here are four possible consequences of Moosie's behavior. Consider both the type of consequence—whether it is a pleasant or aversive stimulus—and whether it is administered ("added to" the situation) or withdrawn. Notice that reinforcers strengthen whining behavior, or make it more likely in the future, whereas punishers weaken it.

Bandura: Social Cognitive Theory

In his **social cognitive theory** (formerly called social learning theory), Stanford psychologist Bandura (1977, 1986, 1989, 2000) claimed that humans are cognitive beings whose active processing of information plays a critical role in their learning, behavior, and development. Bandura argues that human learning is very different from rat learning because humans have far more sophisticated cognitive capabilities. He agrees with Skinner that operant conditioning is an important type of learning, but he notes that people think about the connections between their behavior and its consequences, anticipate the consequences likely to follow from their behavior, and often are more affected by what they believe will happen than by the consequences they actually encounter. Individuals also reinforce or punish themselves with mental pats on the back and self-criticism, and these cognitions affect behavior. More generally, Bandura wanted his position to be called *social cognitive theory* rather than *social learning theory* for a reason: to distance himself from some early, behavioral learning theories and to emphasize that his theory was about the motivating and self-regulating role of cognition in human behavior (Bandura, 1986).

Bandura's cognitive emphasis was clear when he called attention to observational learning as the most important mechanism through which human behavior changes. **Observational learning** is simply learning by observing the behavior of other people (called *models*). By imitating other people, a child may learn how to speak a language and tackle math problems, as well as how to swear, snack between meals, and smoke. Observational learning is regarded as a more cognitive form of learning than conditioning because learners must pay attention, construct and remember mental representations (images and verbal summaries) of what they saw, retrieve these representations from memory later, and use them to guide behavior. It is an especially important form of learning in less industrialized societies, where children learn not in schools where they are segregated from adults and given formal instruction but through participation in everyday activities in which they actively observe and listen to their elders and learn skills such as weaving and hunting without adults intentionally teaching them (Rogoff et al., 2003).

In a classic experiment, Bandura (1965) set out to demonstrate that children could learn a response neither elicited by a conditioned stimulus (as in classical conditioning) nor performed and then strengthened by a reinforcer (as in operant conditioning). He had nursery school children watch a short film in which an adult model attacked an inflatable "Bobo" doll: hitting the doll with a mallet while shouting "Sockeroo," throwing rubber balls at the doll while shouting "Bang, bang, bang," and so on. Some children saw the model praised, others saw him punished, and still others saw no consequences follow his violent attack. After the film ended, children were observed in a playroom with the Bobo doll and many of the props the model had used to work Bobo over.

What did the children learn? The children who saw the model rewarded and the children in the no-consequences condition imitated more of the model's aggressive acts than did the children who had seen the model punished. But interestingly, when the children who had seen the model punished were asked to reproduce all of the model's behavior they could remember, they showed that they had learned just as much as the other children. Apparently, then, children can learn from observation without necessarily imitating (performing) the learned responses. Whether they will perform what they learn depends partly on the process of **vicarious reinforcement** in which learners become more or less likely to perform a behavior based on the consequences experienced by the model they observe.

In recent years, Bandura (2000) has called attention to the concept of **human agency,** ways in which people deliberately exercise cognitive control over their environments and lives.

A person is never too old to learn by observing others.

Albert Bandura highlighted the role of cognition in human learning. He is on the faculty at Stanford University.

People form intentions, foresee what will happen, evaluate and regulate their actions as they pursue plans, and reflect on their functioning. These cognitions play a real causal role in influencing behavior. Most importantly, individuals develop a high or low sense of self-efficacy about their ability to control themselves and their environments in different areas of life. Whether you undertake an action such as going on a diet or studying for a test and whether you succeed depend greatly on whether you have a sense of self-efficacy with respect to that behavior.

Watson and Skinner may have believed that people are passively shaped by environment to become whatever those around them groom them to be, but Bandura does not. Because he views humans as active, cognitive beings, he holds that human development occurs through a continuous reciprocal interaction among the person (the person's biological and psychological characteristics and cognitions), the person's behavior, and the environment—a perspective he calls **reciprocal determinism.** As Bandura sees it, environment does not rule, as it did in Skinner's thinking: people choose, build, and change their environments; they are not just shaped by them. Nor does biology rule; genetic influences on human behavior are evident, but cultural forces also change human environments. This influences biological evolution by influencing which traits increase the odds of survival (Bandura, 2000). People's personal characteristics and behaviors affect the people around them, just as these people are influencing their personal characteristics and future behaviors.

Like Watson and Skinner, Bandura doubts that there are universal stages of human development. He maintains that development is context specific and can proceed along many paths. It is also continuous, occurring gradually through a lifetime of learning. Bandura acknowledges that children's cognitive capacities mature, so they can remember more about what they have seen and can imitate a greater variety of novel behaviors. Yet he also believes that children of the same age will be dissimilar if their learning experiences have differed considerably.

Obviously there is a fundamental disagreement between stage theorists such as Freud and Erikson and learning theorists such as Bandura. Learning theorists do not give a general description of the normal course of human development because they insist that there is no such description to give. Instead, they offer a rich account of the mechanisms through which behavior can change. They ask people to use principles of learning that are universal in their applicability to understand how each individual changes with age in unique ways (Goldhaber, 2000). These learning principles can certainly help you understand teenage pregnancy; we imagine what Bandura would say about it in the Explorations box on this page.

Strengths and Weaknesses

Watson's and Skinner's behavioral learning theories and Bandura's modern social cognitive theory have contributed immensely to the understanding of development and con-

Explorations

Bandura on Teenage Pregnancy

Let me begin by building on the work of a learning theorist who preceded me. B. F. Skinner would undoubtedly get right to the heart of it and say that teenagers have sex because sex is reinforcing—and that they become pregnant because using a contraceptive is not! One team of researchers put it well: "It is quite likely that if teenagers had to take a pill to become pregnant, early childbearing would quickly vanish as a social problem" (Furstenberg, Lincoln, & Menken, 1981).

This is true enough, but my social cognitive brand of learning theory offers additional insights into teenage pregnancy. Sherry and Robert have been discovering a great deal about sexual behavior through observational learning. Today's adolescents live in a social world filled with messages about sex from their peers, the media, and to a lesser extent, their parents. They actively process this information for future use. If they learn that their friends are sexually active, and if they think that their friends find sex more reinforcing than costly, they are likely to do what their friends are doing (Benda & DiBlasio, 1994). Having sexually active or pregnant older siblings also increases an adolescent's risk of pregnancy (B. C. Miller, 2002). Adolescents also watch sex on TV all the time—often exploitive sex with hardly a mention of birth control or such consequences as HIV infection or the stresses of teenage parenthood.

Finally, let me emphasize that people's expectations about the consequences of their actions are often more important than the reinforcers and punishers actually operating in their lives. If Robert, for example, believes that using a condom will decrease his sexual enjoyment, or if Sherry believes that Robert will get mad if she asks him to use a condom, those beliefs will surely decrease the chances that they will use protection. In subcultures in which adolescents believe that early parenthood has many positive and few negative effects on their lives, we should not be surprised to see many young parents (Unger, Molina, & Teran, 2000).

tinue to be influential. Learning theories are precise and testable. Carefully controlled experiments have shown how people might learn everything from altruism to alcoholism. Moreover, learning principles operate across the life span and can be used to understand behavior at any age. Finally, learning theories have practical applications; they have been the basis for many highly effective techniques for optimizing development and treating developmental problems.

Still, learning theories, even Bandura's social cognitive theory, leave something to be desired as explanations of human development. Consider the following demonstration. Paul Weisberg (1963) reinforced 3-month-old infants with smiles and gentle rubs on the chin whenever they happened to make babbling sounds such as "bababa." He found that these infants babbled more often than did infants who received the same social stimulation randomly rather than only after each babbling sound they made. But does this mean that infants normally begin to babble *because* babbling is reinforced by their caregivers? Not necessarily. All normal infants, even deaf ones, babble around 4 months of age. Moreover, no matter what experiences are provided to newborns, they will not be maturationally ready to babble. We must suspect, then, that the maturation of the neural and muscular control required for babbling has more than a little to do with the onset of babbling during infancy.

This example highlights two criticisms of learning theories as theories of human development. First, learning theorists rarely demonstrate that learning is responsible for commonly observed developmental changes; they show through their experiments only that learning might have resulted in developmental change. Some critics wish that learning theorists would provide a fuller account of normal changes across the life span. Second, early learning theorists, and even Bandura, probably put too little emphasis on biological influences on development such as genetic endowment and maturational processes that affect how people respond to learning experiences. We may learn to fear snakes, for example. However, probably because snakes were a threat to our ancestors, we have evolved so that we learn to fear snakes more easily than we learn to fear bunnies or flowers (Ohman & Mineka, 2003).

Summing Up

Learning theorists maintain that humans change gradually and can develop in many directions depending on environmental influences. Behaviorist Watson focused on the role of classical conditioning in the learning of emotional responses; Skinner highlighted operant conditioning and the roles of reinforcement and punishment. Bandura's social cognitive theory emphasizes the importance of cognitive processes in observational learning, human agency, self-efficacy, and reciprocal determinism among a person, his behavior, and his environment. Learning theories are well supported and applicable across the life span, but they do not necessarily explain normal developmental changes and they underemphasize biological influences on development. ■

Cognitive Developmental Theory

After behavioral learning theories dominated the study of development in the 1950s and 1960s, many developmentalists began to look for a theory that was both more cognitive and more clearly developmental. They found what they wanted in the remarkable work of Jean Piaget. No theorist has contributed more to the understanding of children's minds than Piaget (1896–1980), a Swiss scholar who began to study children's intellectual development during the 1920s. This remarkable man developed quickly himself, publishing his first scientific work (a letter to the editor about an albino sparrow) at age 11. Eventually, Piaget blended his interest in zoology and the adaptation of animals to their environments with his interest in philosophy. He then devoted his career to the study of how humans acquire knowledge and use it to adapt to their world.

Piaget's lifelong interest in cognitive development emerged while he worked at the Alfred Binet laboratories in Paris on the first standardized IQ test. IQ tests estimate individuals' intelligence based on the number and types of questions they answer correctly. Piaget soon became interested in children's wrong answers and noticed that children of about the same age gave the same kinds of wrong answers. By questioning them to find out how they were thinking about the problems presented to them, he began to realize that young children do not simply know less than older children do; instead, they think in a qualitatively different way. Eventually Piaget developed a full-blown theory to account for changes in thinking from infancy to adolescence.

Piaget: Constructivism

Influenced by his background in biology, Piaget (1950) viewed intelligence as a process that helps an organism adapt to its environment. The infant who grasps a cookie and brings it to

Swiss psychologist Jean Piaget revolutionized the field of human development with his theory of cognitive growth.

her mouth is behaving adaptively, as is the adolescent who solves algebra problems or the mechanic who fixes cars. As humans mature, they acquire ever more complex cognitive structures, or organized patterns of thought or action, that aid them in adapting to their environments.

Piaget insisted that children are not born with innate ideas about reality, as some philosophers claim. Nor are they simply filled with information by adults, as learning theorists tend to claim. Instead, Piaget took a position called **constructivism,** claiming that children actively construct new understandings of the world based on their experiences. Some preschool children, for example, develop on their own the idea that the Sun is alive because it moves across the sky, that children may get diseases if they tell lies or otherwise misbehave, and that babies come from the baby store.

How do children construct more accurate understandings of the world? By being curious and active explorers: watching what is going on around them, seeing what happens when they experiment on the objects they encounter, and recognizing instances in which their current understandings are inadequate to explain events. Children use their current understandings of the world to help them solve problems, but they also revise their understandings to make them fit reality better (Piaget, 1952). The *interaction* between biological maturation (most importantly, a developing brain) and experience (especially discrepancies between the child's understanding and reality) is responsible for the child's progress from one stage of cognitive development to a new, qualitatively different, stage.

Jean Piaget believed that children are naturally curious explorers who try to make sense of their surroundings.

Stages of Cognitive Development

Piaget proposed four major periods of cognitive development: the sensorimotor stage (birth to age 2), the preoperational stage (ages 2 to 7), the concrete operations stage (ages 7 to 11), and the formal operations stage (ages 11 to 12 or older). These stages form what Piaget called an *invariant sequence;* that is, all children progress through the stages in the order they are listed without skipping stages or regressing to earlier stages. The ages given are only guidelines.

The key features of each stage are summarized in Table 2.3; we will describe them in depth in Chapter 7. The core message is that humans of different ages think in qualitatively different ways (Inhelder & Piaget, 1958).

Infants in the **sensorimotor stage** deal with the world directly through their perceptions (senses) and actions (motor

Table 2.3 Jean Piaget's Four Stages of Cognitive Development

Stage (Age Range)	Description
Sensorimotor (birth to 2 years)	Infants use their senses and motor actions to explore and understand the world. At the start they have only innate reflexes, but they develop increasingly "intelligent" actions. By the end, they are capable of symbolic thought using images or words and can therefore plan solutions to problems mentally.
Preoperational (2 to 7 years)	Preschoolers use their capacity for symbolic thought to develop language, engage in pretend play, and solve problems. But their thinking is not yet logical; they are egocentric (unable to take others' perspectives) and are easily fooled by perceptions because they cannot rely on logical operations.
Concrete operations (7 to 11 years)	School-age children acquire concrete logical operations that allow them to mentally classify, add, and otherwise act on concrete objects in their heads. They can solve practical, real-world problems through a trial-and-error approach but have difficulty with hypothetical and abstract problems.
Formal operations (11 to 12 years or older)	Adolescents can think about abstract concepts and purely hypothetical possibilities and can trace the long-range consequences of possible actions. With age and experience, they can form hypotheses and systematically test them using the scientific method.

abilities). They are unable to use symbols (gestures, images, or words representing real objects and events) to help them solve problems mentally. However, they learn a great deal about the world by exploring it, and they acquire tools for solving problems through their sensory and motor experiences.

The preschooler who has entered the **preoperational stage** of cognitive development has the capacity for symbolic thought but is not yet capable of logical problem solving. The 4- or 5-year-old can use words as symbols to talk about a problem and can mentally imagine doing something before actually doing it. However, lacking the tools of logical thought, preoperational children must rely on their perceptions and as a result are easily fooled by appearances. For example, they tend to think that large objects will sink in water, even if they are lightweight. According to Piaget, preschool children are also egocentric thinkers who have difficulty adopting perspectives other than their own. As a result, they may cling to incorrect ideas simply because they want them to be true.

School-age children who have advanced to the **concrete operations stage** are more logical than preschoolers. They use a trial-and-error approach to problem solving and do well on problems that involve thinking about concrete objects. These children can perform many important logical actions, or operations, in their heads on concrete objects (hence, the term *concrete operations*). For example, they can mentally categorize or add and subtract objects. They can also draw sound, general conclusions based on their observations. However, they have difficulty dealing with abstract and hypothetical problems.

Adolescents who have reached the **formal operations stage** are able to think more abstractly and hypothetically than school-age children. They can define *justice* abstractly, in terms of fairness, rather than concretely, in terms of the cop on the corner or the judge in the courtroom. They can formulate hypotheses or predictions in their heads, plan how to systematically test their ideas experimentally, and imagine the consequences of their tests. It often takes some years before adolescents can adopt a thoroughly systematic and scientific method of solving problems and can think logically about the implications of purely hypothetical ideas. Then they may be able to devise grand theories about what is wrong with parents, the school system, or the federal government.

Obviously, children's cognitive capacities change dramatically between infancy and adolescence as they progress through Piaget's four stages of cognitive development. Young children simply do not think as adults do. And even adolescents do not always use their cognitive capacities, as illustrated in the Explorations box on this page, where we imagine what Piaget might say about teenage pregnancy.

Strengths and Weaknesses

Like Freud, Piaget was a true pioneer whose work has left a deep and lasting imprint on thinking about human development. You will see his influence throughout this text, for the mind that "constructs" understanding of the physical world also comes, with age, to understand sex differences, moral values, emotions, death, and a range of other important aspects of the human experience. Piaget's cognitive developmental perspective dominated the study of child development for 2 or 3 decades, until the information-processing approach to

Explorations

Piaget on Teenage Pregnancy

Teenagers must decide whether or not to have sex and whether or not to use a contraceptive. These decisions demand cognitive abilities, and that, of course, is where my theory comes in. Now, you might think that an adolescent who has reached my stage of formal operations would be ready to consider all the possible consequences of his or her actions and make sound decisions. That is true. However, different children achieve formal-operational thinking at different rates. Sherry and Robert are not doing well in school and may be slow developers still functioning in the stage of concrete operations. Or they may have begun to show early signs of formal-operational thought but do not yet have the more advanced cognitive skills required to consider all the long-term implications of the alternatives they face.

Adolescents may also get in trouble because they don't use the cognitive abilities they have or because their understandings are inaccurate. Studies show that many teenagers fail to anticipate that they will need a contraceptive, act impulsively without thinking about the consequences of their behavior, misunderstand their risks of becoming pregnant, and have many misconceptions (pardon the pun!) about sex and contraception (Aarons & Jenkins, 2002; Cobliner, 1974; Morrison, 1985). In one study, 13- to 15-year-olds averaged only 40% correct on a test about reproduction, contraception, and sexually transmitted diseases; more than 60% did not know that urinating after sex will not prevent pregnancy, for example (Carrera et al., 2000).

I conclude, then, that the cognitive limitations, failures to think ahead, and knowledge gaps of many teenagers have much to do with today's high rate of teenage pregnancy. These adolescents are not necessarily in the throes of personality conflicts, as Dr. Freud would have you believe. Nor are they deprived of the proper learning experiences, as Drs. Skinner and Bandura argue. They may simply be cognitively immature and uninformed.

studying cognition took command in the 1980s (P. H. Miller, 2002). This approach emphasizes processes such as attention, memory, decision making, and the like. It will be the focus of Chapter 8 and has guided research on gender, social cognition, and other topics addressed in this book. More recently, the sociocultural perspective on cognitive development offered by a contemporary of Piaget, Lev Vygotsky, has received a good deal of attention, as you will see next in the section on contextual–systems perspectives on development.

Despite the rise of rival theories, most developmentalists today accept Piaget's basic beliefs that thinking changes in qualitative ways during childhood, that children are active in their own development, and that development occurs through an interaction of nature and nurture. Piaget's description of intellectual development has been tested and has been largely, although not wholly, supported. Finally, Piaget's ideas have influenced education and child rearing by encouraging teachers and parents to pitch their educational programs to children's level of understanding and to stimulate children to discover new concepts through their own firsthand experiences.

Still, Piaget has had his share of criticism (Lourenco & Machado, 1996; also see Chapter 7). For example, critics fault him for saying too little about the influences of motivation and emotion on thought processes. Based on research evidence, they also question whether Piaget's stages really hang together as coherent modes of thinking applied to a range of problems; instead, specific cognitive skills seem to be acquired at different rates. Critics also conclude that Piaget underestimated the cognitive abilities of young children. And they challenge the idea that all humans in every culture develop through the same stages toward the same endpoints. As a result, developmentalists began to seek theoretical perspectives that allowed more diversity in the pathways that human development could take but retained Piaget's theme that nature and nurture interact to produce developmental change.

Summing Up

Piaget's cognitive developmental perspective holds that intelligence is an adaptive process in which humans create new understandings of the world through their active interactions with it (constructivism). The interaction of biological maturation and experience causes children to progress through four universal, invariant, and qualitatively different stages of thinking (sensorimotor, preoperational, concrete operational, and formal operational). Despite Piaget's immense influence, developmentalists question whether development is as stagelike and universal as he claimed. ■

Contextual–Systems Theories

Contextual–systems theories of development (some are called contextual theories, some systems theories) generally hold that changes over the life span arise from the ongoing transactions between a changing organism and a changing world (see, for example, Li, 2003; Riegel, 1979; Wachs, 2000). Changes in the person produce changes in his environment; changes in the environment produce changes in the person. The individual and the physical and social contexts with which he interacts are part of a larger system. Moreover, development does not always leads in one direction toward some mature endpoint like formal-operational thought, as stage theorists tend to believe. It can proceed in a variety of directions and take a variety of forms depending on the complex dynamics between biological and environmental influences.

Urie Bronfenbrenner's bioecological model, introduced in Chapter 1, illustrates a systems perspective on development; the individual is embedded in and interacts with four environmental systems. Here, consider two different theorists who emphasize the importance of the context in which development takes place and the idea that development grows out of systems of interacting influences: Lev Vygotsky, who highlighted influences of the sociocultural environment on cognitive development, and Gilbert Gottlieb, who emphasizes that development takes place in the context of our evolutionary history as a species and arises from ongoing interactions between biological and environmental influences.

Vygotsky: A Sociocultural Perspective

Vygotsky (1962, 1978) was a Russian psychologist who was an active scholar when Piaget was formulating his theory and who took issue with some of Piaget's views. He died before he could fully develop his own theory, but his perspective has attracted much interest among developmental scientists in the past 2 decades, especially among those looking for alternatives to Piaget's theory.

Lev Vygotsky.

Vygotsky challenged Piaget's view that humans develop through universal stages of cognitive development. Instead, his **sociocultural perspective** maintains that cognitive development is shaped by the sociocultural context in which it occurs and grows out of children's interactions with members of their culture. Each culture provides its members with certain tools of thought—most notably a language, but also tools such as pencils, art media, mathematical systems, and computers. The ways in which people in a particular culture approach and solve problems are passed from generation to generation through oral and written communication. Hence culture, especially as it is embodied in language, shapes thought. As a result, cognitive development is not the same universally; it varies across social and historical contexts depending on the tools of thinking the culture makes available.

In Vygotsky's view, then, cognitive development is a social process. Piaget tended to see children as independent explorers developing their minds through their experiments with the world of objects. Vygotsky saw them as social beings who develop their minds through their interactions with parents, teachers, and other knowledgeable members of the culture. If, for example, Mom coaches Ben on how to fold paper to make a paper airplane, Ben may repeat her words to himself later when he tries to construct a plane. Through such social dialogues, children learn how skilled problem solvers in their society go about tackling problems and gradually internalize the language used by their mentors so that it becomes part of their own thinking. Adults continue to learn this way—through dialogues between themselves and other members of their culture.

Notice that the socialization process of interest to Vygotsky is similar to Bandura's observational learning. But in Vygotsky's view, children do not just imitate models. Instead, they and their social partners are true partners in development. They *coconstruct* knowledge as they collaborate on problem-solving tasks. In the process, what begins as social interaction using the tool of language becomes individual thought. As you will see when we return to Piaget and Vygotsky in Chapter 7, Vygotsky's ideas have had a strong effect on education, serving as a basis for educational approaches in which children are tutored or coached by more knowledgeable mentors. Yet Vygotsky may have been so intrigued by social processes in development that he paid too little attention to biological influences and to differences among individuals who develop within the same cultural context. Gilbert Gottlieb's evolutionary–epigenetic systems perspective gives both biological and environmental influences their due.

Gottlieb: An Evolutionary–Epigenetic Systems View

Gottlieb's perspective on development grew out of earlier work by evolutionary biologists, psychologists, and psychobiologists attempting to look at human development in the context of evolutionary theory (Bjorklund & Pellegrini, 2002; Gottlieb, 2000, 2002, 2003; Li, 2003). In his influential theory of evolution, Charles Darwin (1859) maintained that genes that aid their bearers in adapting to their environment will be passed on to future generations more frequently than genes that do not. Evolutionary theory therefore makes us ask how the characteristics and behaviors we commonly observe in humans today may have helped our ancestors adapt to their environment and may therefore have become part of the shared genetic endowment of our species.

Inspired by Darwin, the field of **ethology** arose and took as its mission the task of understanding the evolved behavior of various species in their natural environments (J. Archer, 1992; Hinde, 1983). Noted ethologists Konrad Lorenz and Niko Tinbergen asked how many apparently innate animal behaviors might be adaptive in the sense that they contribute to species survival. Because behavior is adaptive only in relation to a particular environment, ethologists have used naturalistic observation as a method of study. So, for example, they have recorded birdsongs in the wild, analyzed their features carefully, explored how male birds learn the songs characteristic of their species, and attempted to understand how songs aid birds in reproduction and survival.

Ethologists suggest that humans, too, display species-specific behaviors that are the products of evolutionary history. In Chapter 3, you will look at the basics of Darwinian evolutionary theory, and in Chapter 14, you will encounter attachment theory, an influential ethological theory that views the formation of close relationships between human infants and their caregivers as evolved behavior that increases the odds that the young will survive.

While some researchers have been examining the evolutionary roots of human behavior, others have been studying in elaborate detail how products of evolution such as genes and hormones interact with environmental factors to guide the course of an individual's development (Gottlieb, Wahlsten, &

Gilbert Gottlieb seeks to understand how biology and environment interact to produce development.

☾ Similarities between animals and humans make us suspect that many aspects of human development are the product of evolution.

Lickliter, 1998; Lickliter & Honeycutt, 2003). Developmental biologist Gilbert Gottlieb (1992, 2000, 2002; Gottlieb, Wahlsten, & Lickliter, 1998) is one, and he has put forth a modern **evolutionary–epigenetic systems perspective** on development. According to this perspective, development is the product of complex interplays between nature and nurture—that is, between interacting biological and environmental forces that form a larger system. Researchers can focus on the interplay of nature and nurture both at the level of the species interacting with its environment over the course of evolution and at the level of the individual, with her unique genetic makeup, interacting with her unique environment over the course of a lifetime (Li, 2003).

The starting point in the evolutionary–epigenetic perspective is recognition that evolution has endowed us with a human genetic makeup. We do not start out as tabula rasae. Rather, we are predisposed to develop in certain directions rather than in others—for example, to develop so that we master language, use tools, display guilt, act aggressively, mate and bear children, and do the other things that humans do (Pinker, 2002). However, genes do not dictate anything; they only make certain developmental outcomes *more probable* than others. What happens in development depends on the **epigenetic process**, the process through which nature and nurture, genes and environment, jointly bring forth development in ways difficult to predict at the outset. In describing the epigenetic process, Gottlieb emphasizes mutual influences over time involving (1) the activity of genes, which turn on and off at different points during development; (2) the activity of neurons; (3) the organism's behavior; and (4) environmental influences of all kinds, as shown in Figure 2.4.

Gottlieb accuses biologists of the past of wrongly claiming that genes dictate development in a one-directional and deterministic way. They need to appreciate that environmental factors influence the activity of genes just as genes influence environment. The biochemical environment of a cell, as influenced by factors such as nutrition received, can influence whether and how the genes in that cell express themselves and, in turn, how they influence an individual's emerging traits. Sensory stimulation, gained partly through the infant's exploratory behavior, not only produces neural activity and changes the brain but also affects the activity of genes, which then influence the production of proteins that contribute to the building of the neural networks necessary for normal sensory systems (Johnston & Edwards, 2002). If an individual grows up in a typical environment that supplies normal sensory experiences, all is likely to go well in development, but if

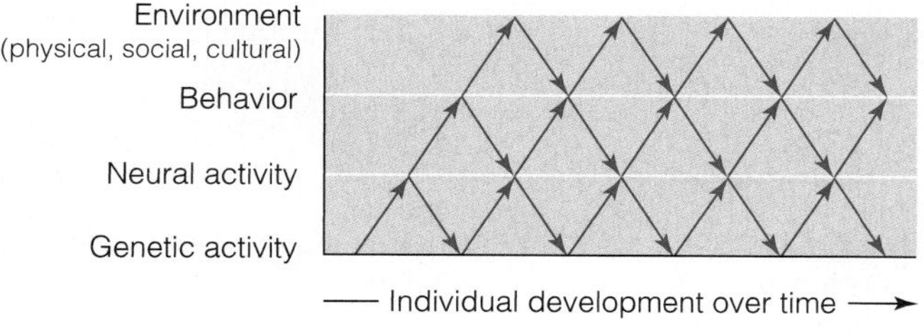

Figure 2.4 Gottlieb's model of bidirectional influences. Genes do not determine development; rather, genetic influences interact with environmental influences, the individual's behavior, and activity at the neural level to make certain developmental outcomes more or less probable in the epigenetic process. Psychologists often focus on behavior–environment interactions, and biologists on genetic–neural interactions, but ALL parts of the system influence every other part (Gottlieb, 2003). Can you think of an example of each type of influence?

SOURCE: From Gottlieb, G. (1992). *Individual development and evolution: The genesis of novel behavior.* New York: Oxford University Press, p. 186. Copyright © 1991 by Oxford University Press, Inc. Used by permission of Oxford University Press, Inc.

an individual is deprived of sensory stimulation, the outcome may be different.

Gottlieb has made his case by demonstrating that behavior that most people assume is innate or instinctive—etched in the genetic code of all members of a species in the course of evolution—may or may not express itself depending on environmental influences. He showed, for example, that the tendency of young ducks to prefer their mothers' vocal calls to those of other birds such as chickens is not as automatic as you might guess (Gottlieb, 1991). Duckling embryos that were exposed to chicken calls before they hatched, then were prevented from vocalizing at birth, came to prefer the call of a chicken to that of a mallard duck. Similarly, baby rats do not instinctively seek water when they are dehydrated. They need to have had at least one previous experience of being dehydrated and then being able to drink water (Hall, Arnold, & Myers, 2000). A behavior as basic as drinking water when thirsty, then, requires not only a biologically based sensitivity to dehydration but also specific and early learning experience that allows the organism to associate drinking with dehydration.

The message is clear: genes do not determine anything. They are partners with environment in directing organisms, including humans, along certain universal developmental pathways as well as in unique directions (Gandelman, 1992; Gottlieb, Wahlsten, & Lickliter, 1998). Even seemingly instinctive, inborn patterns of behavior will not emerge unless the individual has both normal genes and normal early experiences. And there is no point trying to figure out how much of an individual's traits and behavior is caused by nature and how much is caused by nurture because genes and environment "coact."

More recently, Gottlieb has argued that experiences during the lives of organisms can influence genetic activity in those organisms and, ultimately, the course of biological evolution in their species. Imagine that a colony of rodents used to eating soft vegetation encounters some hard, but tasty and nutritious, seeds and begins to eat them (Johnston & Gottlieb, 1990). Eating the seeds would be tough work, and the bone tissue of the mice's jaws and teeth might grow in response—a change in anatomy brought on by a change in the animals' environment and activity, not by a change in their genetic makeup. Chewing hard could also activate genes that had been dormant. Over time, if seed-eating rodents survived and reproduced more often than leaf-eating rodents, their genes would become more common in the population and the course of evolution would be affected. Thus, a change in environment and behavior in one generation could change the genetic makeup of a species over several generations. Now think about humans. We actively and deliberately change our environments by farming, urbanizing, polluting, fighting infectious diseases, and so on. As we change our environments through cultural evolution, we may change the course of biological evolution because our new environments may make different genes critical to survival. An intriguing example: a gene associated with a high tolerance of the lactose in milk is far more prevalent in human populations that have a tradition of dairy farming than in other human populations (Aoki, 1986).

Because genes only make particular developmental outcomes more or less probable in epigenesis, we cannot tell how the developmental story will end until we see what emerges from the long history of interactions among the multiple factors influencing development. We cannot easily predict the specific directions in which a particular person will develop; we must plan on being surprised. The evolutionary–epigenetic systems perspective helps us appreciate that each person's development takes place in the context of our evolutionary history as a species. That is, we share certain genes with other humans because those genes enabled our ancestors to adapt to their environments. This perspective also helps us appreciate that the development of the individual arises from complex interactions over time among genetic, neural, behavioral, and environmental influences—interactions in which genes affect environment and, importantly, environment affects the ways in which genes are expressed.

No matter how contextual–systems theorists define the forces that interact to shape development, they believe that people and their environment are in continual flux, and that changes in one inevitably produce changes in the other because they are all part of a larger system. Modern theorists cannot ignore that people develop in a changing cultural and historical context—something that Piaget and other stage theorists tended to do. Nor can they focus all of their attention on environmental influences and ignore that humans are biological organisms whose genes contribute to their development and influence the experiences they have—something that early learning theorists tended to do. Some thoughts Gottlieb might have about contributors to teenage pregnancy are presented in the Explorations box on page 48.

Strengths and Weaknesses

Contextual–systems perspectives on development are complex, but that is because life-span human development is complex. We can applaud Gottlieb, Vygotsky, Bronfenbrenner, and

Gottlieb on Teenage Pregnancy

What do mallard ducks have to do with teenage pregnancy? I'll tell you! I believe that Sherry and Robert are faced with a pregnancy because of the workings of multiple, interacting forces within themselves and their environment. According to my evolutionary–epigenetic systems theory, teenage pregnancy is unlikely to be rooted in one simple cause, such as a weak superego or delayed cognitive development. We must look at Sherry's and Robert's development from an evolutionary perspective and then analyze carefully the ongoing interactions between these changing young people (their genes, neural activity, and behavior) and the changing world in which they are developing (their physical, social, and cultural environment).

We know that sexual behavior is basic to human nature and that two basic mating strategies have evolved that optimize the chances of having children and passing on one's genes (Belsky, Steinberg, & Draper, 1991; Geary, 2000). In the parental investment strategy, both parents invest much energy in the care of a small number of children. In the mating strategy, individuals have sex with many partners, bear many children, and do not invest much energy in the care of any of them. Fathers often desert their families, for example.

Evolutionary psychologists theorize that human children notice, based on their early experiences, which mating strategy is most common and adaptive in their environment and then adopt it themselves later in life. Thus, I suspect that Sherry and Robert did not grow up with their fathers, did not receive attentive care from either parent, and observed their parents dating multiple partners. Seeing little parental investment in child rearing at home, they may have adopted the mating strategy of having sex with multiple partners starting early in life. In support of this view, father absence, especially early in a child's life, has been linked to high rates of both early sexual activity and teenage pregnancy, even when researchers hold constant other factors associated with father absence, including third variables such as low socioeconomic status (Ellis et al., 2003).

It's also worth noting that Sherry and Robert, like other adolescents, are biological beings with a genetic endowment that, in interaction with their neural activity, behavior, and environment, shapes their development. They are experiencing rapid physical, hormonal, neural, cognitive, and psychosocial change, and their environments are changing as they mature. We must consider all the possibilities for mutual influence among the many aspects of the developmental system.

For example, adolescent couples actively influence and are influenced by those around them, including each other (Corcoran, 1999). They also live in a cultural context. The United States has undergone several important social changes in recent years that have altered the adolescent experience—for example, greater sexual permissiveness and more single-parent families and working mothers (Bronfenbrenner & Morris, 1998). Consider, too, social and political controversies about whether the Food and Drug Administration should approve the morning-after contraceptive pill that has already been approved in many European countries, about whether abortion should continue to be legal, and about whether sex education should emphasize abstinence or safe sex. Sherry and Robert have undoubtedly been influenced by these social forces. Indeed, some of these factors may explain why, even though the teenage pregnancy rate in the United States has been declining for a number of years, it is still 9 times higher than rates in most Western European nations (Meschke, Bartholomae, & Zentall, 2002; Singh & Darroch, 2000). The rate is especially high among African American and Latina adolescents living in low-income urban areas where educational and vocational opportunities are limited and early motherhood is common and accepted as normal (Farber, 2003). Indeed, in some cultures early childbearing is a desired outcome rather than a problem (Davies et al., 2003).

So, a multitude of interacting factors, both biological and cultural, contribute to the high adolescent pregnancy rate. If my evolutionary–epigenetic systems perspective on development seems complex, that's because human development is complex!

like-minded theorists for emphasizing some important truths about human development. Development is the product of both biological and environmental forces interacting within a complex system. And we cannot always predict how it will turn out unless we look more closely at the ongoing transactions between the person and the environment.

This means that contextual–systems theorists can be faulted for failing to provide a clear picture of the course of human development and for being only partially formulated and tested at this point. But a more serious criticism can be made: contextual–systems perspectives may never provide any coherent developmental theory. Why? If we take seriously the idea that development can take a range of paths depending on a range of interacting influences both within and outside the person, how can we ever state generalizations about development that will hold up for most people? If change over a lifetime depends on the ongoing transactions between a unique person and a unique environment, is each life span unique? The problem is this: "For the contextualist, often the only generalization that holds is, 'It depends.'" (Goldhaber, 2000, p. 33).

In light of these concerns, some theorists propose combining contextual–systems perspectives with the best features of stage theories that propose universal paths of development (Lerner & Kauffman, 1985). Researchers might then see humans as moving in orderly directions in some aspects of their development, yet they could also try to understand how that developmental course differs in different social contexts. They might view developmental attainments such as formal-operational thinking not as inevitable achievements but as attainments that are more or less probable depending on the individual's genetic endowment and life experiences.

Summing Up

Contextual–systems theories view development as the product of ongoing transactions and mutual influence between the individual and his environment. Vygotsky's sociocultural perspective called attention to collaborations between children and mentors that allow children to internalize the tools of thinking available in their culture. Ethology asks how species-specific behaviors may have evolved, and Gottlieb's evolutionary–epigenetic systems perspective highlights mutual influences among genes, neural activity, behavior, and environment both over the course of evolution and during the epigenetic process. Contextual–systems theories are incomplete, however, and do not provide a coherent picture of human development. ■

Theories in Perspective

That completes this survey of some grand and emerging theories of human development. These theories can be grouped into even grander categories based on the broad assumptions they make about human development (Pepper, 1942; Reese & Overton, 1970; Goldhaber, 2000).

Stage theorists such as Freud, Erikson, and Piaget form one broad group and have much in common. They believe that development is guided in certain universal directions by biological–maturational forces within the individual. Humans unfold—much as a rose unfolds from its beginnings as a seed—according to a master plan carried in their genes, assuming that they grow up in a reasonably normal environment. They evolve through distinct or discontinuous stages that are universal and lead to the same final state of maturity. Parents who subscribe to the stage theory perspective on development are likely to be supportive but not pushy in their efforts to enhance their children's development. They would tend to trust their children to seek the learning opportunities they most need at a given stage in their growth. They would respond to their children's changing needs and interests but would not feel compelled to structure all their children's learning experiences.

By contrast, learning theorists such as Watson, Skinner, and Bandura emphasize the role of environment more than the role of biology in development. Parents who subscribe to a learning theory model of human development are not likely to trust genetically guided maturational forces to ensure that their children develop in healthy directions. Such parents may assume that their children will not develop (or at least will never be Harvard material) unless they are systematically exposed to particular learning experiences. These parents are likely to take deliberate steps to shape desirable behaviors and eliminate undesirable ones in their offspring.

Finally, contextual–systems theorists emphasize both biology and environment as components of a larger system. Humans contribute actively to the developmental process (as stage theorists such as Piaget maintain), but environment is also an active participant in the developmental drama (as learning theorists maintain). The potential exists for both qualitative (stagelike) change and quantitative change. Development can proceed along many paths depending on the intricate interplay of nature and nurture. Parents who adopt a contextual–systems model of development, such as Vygotsky's sociocultural perspective or Gottlieb's evolutionary–epigenetic systems view, are likely to appreciate that their children are influencing them just as much as they are influencing their children. They are likely to view themselves as partners with their children in the developmental process.

It is because different theories rest on different basic assumptions that they offer such different pictures of human development and its causes. Theorists who view the world through different lenses not only study different things but are likely to disagree even when the same "facts" are set before them because they will interpret those facts differently. This is the nature of science. Our understanding of human development has changed, and will continue to change, as one prevailing view gives way to another. From the beginning of the study of human development at the turn of the 20th century through the heyday of Freud's psychoanalytic theory, a stage theory perspective prevailed, emphasizing biological forces in development (Cairns, 1998; Parke et al., 1994). In the 1950s and 1960s, learning theories came to the fore, and attention shifted from biology toward environment and toward the view that children are blank tablets to be written on. Then, with the rising influence of cognitive psychology and Piaget's theory of cognitive development in the late 1960s and 1970s, a stage theory model emphasizing the interaction of nature and nurture gained prominence. Finally, in the 1980s and 1990s, we gained a fuller appreciation of the roles of both biological–genetic and cultural–historical influences on development.

Where are we today? The broad perspective on key developmental issues taken by contextual–systems theorists such as Vygotsky and Gottlieb is the perspective that most 21st-century developmentalists have adopted. The field has moved beyond the extreme, black-or-white positions taken by many of its pioneers. We now appreciate that humans, although not tabula rasae, have evolved so that they have the potential to develop in good and bad directions; that human development is always the product of nature and nurture; that humans and their environments are active in the developmental process; that development is both continuous and discontinuous in form; and that development has both universal aspects and

Applications

Using Developmental Theories to Prevent Teenage Pregnancy

In 1995, 49% of females and 55% of males ages 15 to 19 had had sex (U.S. Census Bureau, 2000). Although the teenage pregnancy rate has dropped since it peaked in 1991, almost 1 in 10 females ages 15 to 19 becomes pregnant each year, almost half of these pregnant teenagers give birth, and more of them than ever are not married (Farber, 2003). Although the consequences vary greatly from family to family and are not as bad as many people believe, they sometimes include an interrupted education, low income, and a difficult start for both new parent and new child (Furstenberg, 2003; Farber, 2003). Meanwhile, sexually transmitted diseases, including AIDS, are epidemic among adolescents; yet all too many continue to engage in risky sex (Hogan, Sun, & Cornwell, 2000). What practical solutions to the problem of unwanted teenage pregnancy might different developmental theorists offer?

Psychoanalytic theorists tend to locate the problem within the person. Sigmund Freud might want to identify and target for intervention teenagers who have especially strong ids and weak egos and superegos or who are experiencing extremes of anxiety and strained relationships with their parents. Erik Erikson might identify teenagers who are having significant problems resolving the crisis of identity versus role confusion. High-risk teenagers might then be treated through psychoanalysis; the aim would be to help them resolve the inner conflicts that might get them in trouble. This approach might work with teenagers who are psychologically disturbed. The only problem is that pregnant teenagers do not have much higher rates of psychopathology overall than those who do not become pregnant (Farber, 2003).

Adopting Jean Piaget's cognitive developmental perspective might make us pessimistic that young teenagers can learn to engage in long-term planning and rational decision making about sexual issues until they are solidly into the formal operations stage of cognitive development. However, if we could identify the kinds of faulty cognitive structures or misunderstandings that young adolescents have about their risks of pregnancy and about contraceptive methods, we could attempt to correct their mistaken ideas using concrete examples and simple explanations. The solution to teenage pregnancy, then, would be improved sex education programs—programs that provide teenagers with accurate information and help them think clearly about the long-term consequences of their sexual decisions. Sex education programs that are carefully designed and teach decision-making and communication skills can succeed in increasing the use of contraception and reducing pregnancy rates (Franklin & Corcoran, 2000). However, education alone is often not enough, so perhaps we need to consider solutions that locate the problem in the environment rather than in the individual's psychological weaknesses or cognitive deficiencies.

Learning theorists strongly believe that changing the environment will change the person. In support of this belief, it appears that the most effective approach to teenage pregnancy prevention is to make contraceptives readily available to teens through health clinics and to teach them how to use them (Franklin & Corcoran, 2000; Kirby, 2002). This approach reflects a Skinnerian philosophy of encouraging the desired behavior by making it more reinforcing and less punishing. Albert Bandura's social cognitive theory suggests that it might also

aspects particular to certain cultures, times, and individuals. In short, the assumptions and theories that guide the study of human development have become increasingly complex as the incredible complexity of human development has become more apparent.

As we have emphasized, a main function of theories in any science is to guide research. Thus Freud stimulated researchers to study inner personality conflicts, Skinner inspired them to analyze how behavior changes when its environmental consequences change, and Piaget inspired them to explore children's thinking about every imaginable topic. Different theories stimulate different kinds of research and yield different kinds of facts.

Theories also guide practice. As you have seen, each theory of human development represents a particular way of defining developmental issues and problems. Often, how you define a problem determines how you attempt to solve it. To illustrate, take one last look at teenage pregnancy. As you have seen, different theorists hold radically different opinions about the causes of teenage pregnancy. How do you think each would go about trying to reduce the rate of teenage pregnancy? The Applications box on this page offers some ideas.

We hope you are convinced that theories are not just useless ideas. Developmental researchers need theories to guide their work, and every parent, teacher, human services professional, and observer of humans is guided by some set of basic assumptions about how humans develop and why they develop as they do. We hope that reading this chapter will stimulate you to think about your own theory of human development. One way to start is by comparing the answers you gave to the questions in the Explorations box on page 28 with the help to provide teenagers with more role models of responsible sexual behavior. Through the right observational learning experiences, teenagers might develop more sexually responsible habits and learn that the consequences of safer sex are likely to be more desirable than the consequences of early parenthood (Unger, Molina, & Teran, 2000).

Contextual–systems theorists such as Lev Vygotsky and Gilbert Gottlieb would aim to change both the person and the environment—to change whole systems of interacting biological and environmental forces. Quick fixes are unlikely to work. The solution may require changing the broader social context in which adolescents develop, with attention to parent, peer, and partner influences on adolescents. Teenage pregnancy in poverty areas may not be reduced significantly until poor parents face fewer stresses, schools are safe and stimulating, jobs are available, and more disadvantaged young people gain hope that they can climb out of poverty if they pursue an education and postpone parenthood (Farber, 2003).

You can see, then, that the theoretical position an individual takes has a profound effect on how that person attempts to optimize development. Yet, as you have also seen, each theory may offer only a partial solution to the problem being addressed. In all likelihood, multiple approaches will be needed to address complex problems such as the high rate of teenage pregnancy—and to achieve the larger goal of understanding human development.

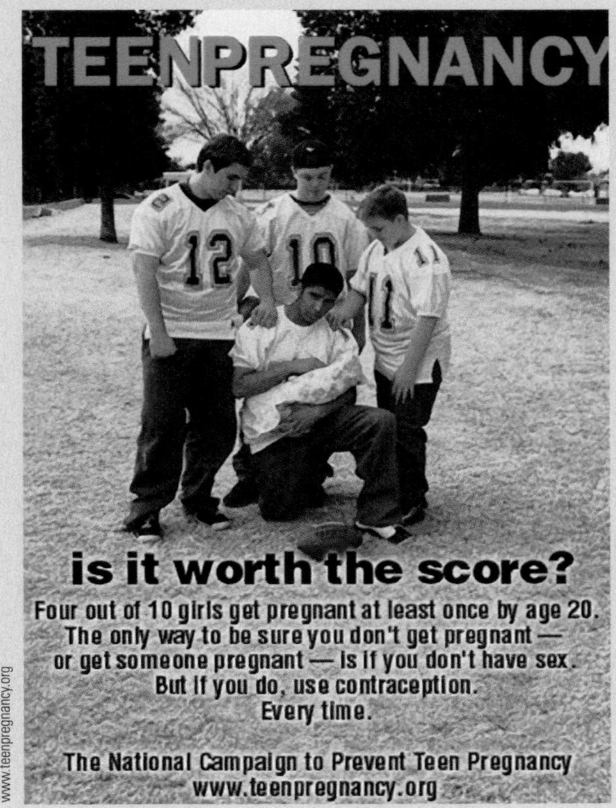

www.teenpregnancy.org

This ad is designed to prevent teenage pregnancy. Do you think it will be effective?

summary information in Table 2.4 and seeing which theorists' views are most compatible with your own.

You need not choose one theory and reject others. Because different theories often highlight different aspects of development, one may be more relevant to a particular issue or to a particular age group than another. Many developmentalists today are theoretical **eclectics** who rely on many theories, recognizing that no major theories of human development can explain everything but that each has something to contribute to our understanding. In many ways, emerging contextual–systems perspectives on development provide the broadest point of view yet proposed. There is no reason many of the insights offered by Erikson, Piaget, Bandura, and others cannot be incorporated within this perspective to help us understand changing people in their changing worlds.

Summing Up

During the 20th century, stage theories such as Freud's emphasizing biological forces gave way to learning theories emphasizing environmental influences. Piaget's cognitive developmental theory emphasized the interaction of nature and nurture, but its concept of universal stages has given way to more complex contextual–systems theories such as those of Vygotsky and Gottlieb. These theorists expect certain outcomes to be more or less probable depending on mutual influences between a person and a social context and between biological and environmental factors. Theories influence both research and practice, and many developmentalists are theoretical eclectics. ■

Table 2.4 Compare Yourself with the Theorists

In the Exploration box on page 28, you were asked to indicate your position on basic issues in human development by answering five questions. If you transcribe your answers (a, b, c, d, or e) here, you can compare your stands with those of the theorists described in this chapter (and review the theories). With whom do you seem to agree the most?

	Question 1	2	3	4	5
Your pattern of answers:					

	Theory: Theorist					
	Psychoanalytic Theory: Freud's Psychosexual Theory	**Psychoanalytic Theory: Erikson's Psychosocial Theory**	**Learning Theory: Skinner's Behavioral Theory**	**Learning Theory: Bandura's Social Cognitive Theory**	**Cognitive Developmental Theory: Piaget's Constructivism**	**Contextual Systems Theories: Vygotsky's Sociocultural and Gottlieb's Evolutionary–Epigenetic Systems Perspectives**
MESSAGE	Biologically based sexual instincts motivate behavior and steer development through five psychosexual stages, oral to genital	Humans progress through eight psychosocial conflicts, from trust vs. mistrust to integrity vs. despair	Development is the product of learning from the consequences of one's behavior through operant conditioning	Development is the product of cognition, as illustrated by observational learning and human agency	Development proceeds through four stages of cognitive development, from sensorimotor to formal operations	Development takes many directions depending on transactions between a changing person and a changing environment
NATURE–NURTURE	b. More nature (biology drives development; early experience in the family influences it, too)	c. Nature and nurture equally	e. Mostly nurture	d. More nurture	b. More nature (maturation interacting with experience guides all through the same stages)	c. Nature and nurture equally
GOODNESS–BADNESS OF HUMAN NATURE	a. Bad (selfish, aggressive urges)	d. Good (capable of growth)	b. Neither good nor bad	b. Neither good nor bad	d. Good (curious)	c. Both good and bad (people have biologically based predispositions toward both)
ACTIVITY–PASSIVITY	b. Passive (humans are influenced by forces beyond their control)	a. Active	b. Passive (humans are shaped by environment)	a. Active (humans influence their environments)	a. Active	a. Active
CONTINUITY–DISCONTINUITY	a. Discontinuous (stagelike)	a. Discontinuous (stagelike)	c. Continuous (habits gradually increase or decrease in strength)	c. Continuous	a. Discontinuous (stagelike)	b. Both continuous and discontinuous
UNIVERSALITY–CONTEXT SPECIFICITY	a. Universal	a. Universal (although stages may be expressed differently in different cultures)	b. Context specific (direction of development depends on experiences)	b. Context specific	a. Universal	b. Context specific

Summary Points

1. A theory is a set of ideas proposed to describe and explain certain phenomena; it is valuable if it is internally consistent, falsifiable, and supported by data. Theories of human development address issues concerning nature and nurture, the goodness and badness of human nature, activity and passivity, continuity and discontinuity, and universality and context specificity in development.

2. According to Sigmund Freud's psychoanalytic theory, humans are driven by inborn instincts of which they are largely unconscious and shaped by early childhood experiences as their ids, egos, and superegos conflict and they progress through five psychosexual stages.

3. According to Erik Erikson's more socially oriented, neo-Freudian version of psychoanalytic theory, development is a lifelong process involving eight psychosocial stages, beginning with trust versus mistrust and concluding with integrity versus despair.

4. Learning theorists hold that different humans develop in many different directions because of environmental influences. John B. Watson emphasized classical conditioning, B. F. Skinner focused on operant conditioning. Albert Bandura's social cognitive theory emphasizes observational learning, human agency, and reciprocal determinism.

5. Jean Piaget's cognitive developmental theory lays out four universal, invariant stages in which children actively construct increasingly complex understandings by interacting with their environments.

6. Contextual–systems perspectives on development are illustrated by Lev Vygotsky's sociocultural perspective (with its emphasis on how culture shapes thought) and Gilbert Gottlieb's evolutionary–epigenetic systems perspective (which emphasizes the evolutionary context of development and views epigenesis as the product of mutual influences among genes, neural activity, behavior, and environment).

7. During the 20th century, stage theories emphasizing forces within the person and universal maturational processes gave way to learning theories emphasizing environmental factors, which in turn gave way to Piaget's cognitive developmental stage theory and, most recently, to contextual–systems theories that emphasize the dynamic interaction between a person and an environment.

Critical Thinking

1. Jasper, age 6, has just started first grade and suddenly has a case of school phobia. Every morning he complains of headaches, tummy aches, and foot aches and begs his mother to let him stay home. His mother let him stay home almost all of last week and is trying desperately to understand why Jasper does not want to go to school. Help her out by indicating what particular psychoanalytic, learning, cognitive developmental, and contextual–systems theorists might propose as an explanation of school phobia.

2. Matilda, age 78, fell and broke her hip recently and has become overly dependent on her daughter for help ever since, even though she can get around quite well. How might particular psychoanalytic, learning, cognitive developmental, and contextual–systems theorists explain her old-age dependency?

3. Pick any two theorists from different theoretical camps and imagine what advice they might give to a room full of preschool teachers about how best to enhance the social skills of their students.

4. You have decided to become an eclectic and to take from each of the four major perspectives in this chapter (psychoanalytic, learning, cognitive developmental, and contextual–systems theory) only one truly great insight into human development. What four ideas would you choose, and why?

Key Terms

tabula rasae, 29
activity–passivity issue, 29
continuity–discontinuity issue, 29
developmental stage, 29
universality–context-specificity issue, 30
psychoanalytic theory, 30
instinct, 30
unconscious motivation, 30
id, 31
ego, 31
superego, 31
libido, 31
psychosexual stages, 31
defense mechanisms, 31
fixation, 31
regression, 31
psychosocial stages, 34
behaviorism, 36
classical conditioning, 36
unconditioned stimulus, 36
unconditioned response, 36
conditioned stimulus, 36
conditioned response, 36
operant conditioning, 36
reinforcement, 37
positive reinforcement, 37
negative reinforcement, 37
punishment, 37
positive punishment, 37
negative punishment, 38
extinction, 38
social cognitive theory, 39
observational learning, 39
vicarious reinforcement, 39
human agency, 39
reciprocal determinism, 40
constructivism, 42
sensorimotor stage, 42
preoperational stage, 43
concrete operations stage, 43
formal operations stage, 43
contextual–systems theories, 44
sociocultural perspective, 45
ethology, 45
evolutionary–epigenetic systems perspective, 45
epigenetic process, 45
eclectic, 51

Media Resources

Websites to Explore

Visit Our Website

For a chapter tutorial quiz and other useful features, visit the book's companion website at *http://psychology.wadsworth.com/sigelman_rider5e*. You can also connect directly to the following sites:

Freud

This site of the Abraham A. Brill Library of the New York Psychoanalytic Institute and Society (see especially "Sigmund Freud on the Internet") offers biographical information and excerpts from a few of the writings of the founder of psychoanalytic theory.

Piaget

The Jean Piaget Society provides biographical information, links to other Piaget resources on the web, and lists of suggested readings for those who would like to learn more about Piaget's research and writings.

B. F. Skinner
The B. F. Skinner Foundation works with Harvard University to archive Skinner's literary estate and also publishes significant works in the study of behavior. Its website contains a brief biography of the late behaviorist by his daughter, Julie S. Vargas, and a nontechnical summary of operant conditioning.

Teenage Pregnancy
For those interested in the topic of teenage pregnancy, the website for the National Campaign to Prevent Teenage Pregnancy offers a wealth of statistics and information about approaches to preventing teenage pregnancy.

Life-Span CD-ROM

Go to the Wadsworth Life-Span CD-ROM for further study of the concepts in this chapter. The CD-ROM includes narrated concept overviews, video clips, a multimedia glossary, and additional activities to expand your learning experience.

DEVELOPMENTAL
PsychologyNow™

Developmental PsychologyNow is a web-based, intelligent study system that provides a complete package of diagnostic quizzes, a personalized study plan, integrated multimedia elements, and learning modules. Check it out at *http://psychology.wadsworth.com/sigelman_rider5e/now.*

CHAPTER three

Genes, Environment, and Development

A NEWSPAPER STORY ABOUT Jim Lewis and Jim Springer inspired Thomas Bouchard Jr. and his associates (Bouchard, 1984; Bouchard et al., 1990) to undertake a study in which they reunited identical twins who had been separated soon after birth and asked them to complete a 50-hour battery of tests. Together after spending all but the first 4 weeks of their 39 years apart, Jim and Jim discovered that they had both married women named Linda—and then women named Betty. They named their first sons James Alan and James Allan, had dogs named Toy, and liked Miller Lite beer and Salem cigarettes.

Barbara Herbert and Daphne Goodship, also reunited after 39 years apart, both wore a beige dress and a brown velvet jacket when they met for the first time in London. They shared a habit of "squidging" (pushing up their noses), had fallen down the stairs at age 15, laughed more than anyone they knew, and never voted.

Yet identical twins Jessica and Rachel Wessell, despite growing up together and being close, are far from identical. One excels in math, the other in English. One has cerebral palsy, possibly because of oxygen deprivation or damage to her brain at birth, and is in a wheelchair; the other was in the marching band in high school (Helderman, 2003).

Perhaps the influence of genes on development must be taken seriously. So must the influence of environment. How do nature and nurture, heredity and environment, contribute to the shaping of physical and psychological characteristics? That is the puzzle we grapple with in this chapter. Many people are environmentalists at heart, believing that there is no such thing as a "bad seed," that proper parenting and a stimulating environment can make any child develop well, and that most of the psychological differences among people reflect their experiences over a lifetime. Reading this chapter should increase your appreciation of genetic contributions to development and give you new insights into the importance of environmental influences.

We begin with a brief look at ways in which genes make humans similar in their characteristics and development. Then the chapter turns to what each person inherits at conception and how this genetic endowment can influence traits. Then it explores research findings on how genes and environment make individuals different from one another in intelligence, personality, and other important characteristics. Finally, we draw some general conclusions about heredity and environment from a life-span perspective. We start by focusing on the characteristics all humans share.

Identical twins share some remarkable similarities, even when separated early in life, but differ as well.

Evolution and Species Heredity

Most descriptions of heredity focus on its role in creating differences among people. Some individuals inherit blue eyes, others brown eyes; some inherit blood type O, others blood type A or B. But it is remarkable that almost every one of us has two eyes and that we all have blood coursing through our veins. And virtually all of us develop in similar ways at similar ages—walking and talking around 1 year, maturing sexually from 12 to 14, watching our skin wrinkle in our 40s and 50s. Such similarities in development and aging are a product of **species heredity**—the genetic endowment that members of a species have in common, including genes that influence maturation and aging processes. Humans can feel guilty but cannot fly; birds can fly but cannot feel guilty. Each species has a distinct heredity. Species heredity is one reason certain patterns of development and aging are universal.

To understand where we got our species heredity, we must turn to evolutionary theory. We introduced Gilbert Gottlieb's modern evolutionary–epigenetic systems theory in Chapter 2, but here we go back to basics—to the path-blazing work of Charles Darwin (1809–1882). Darwin's theory of evolution sought to explain how the characteristics of a species change over time and how new species can evolve from earlier ones (Darwin, 1859). It has been and continues to be tremendously important to our understanding of why humans develop as they do. The main arguments of Darwin's theory are as follows:

1. *There is genetic variation in a species.* Some members of the species have different genes (and different genetically influenced characteristics and behaviors) from others. If all members of the species were genetically identical, there would be no way for the genetic makeup of the species to change over time.
2. *Some genes aid adaptation more than others do.* Suppose that some members of a species have genes that make

them strong and intelligent, whereas others have genes that make them weak and dull. Those with the genes for strength and intelligence would likely be better able to adapt to their environment—for example, to win fights for survival or to figure out how to obtain food.

3. *Genes that aid their bearers in adapting to their environment will be passed to future generations more frequently than genes that do not.* This is the principle of **natural selection**—the idea that nature "selects," or allows to survive and reproduce, those members of a species whose genes permit them to adapt to their environment. By contrast, genes that reduce the chances that an individual will survive and reproduce will become rarer over time because they will not be passed to many offspring. Through natural selection, then, the genetic makeup of a species can slowly change.

Consider a classic example of evolution. H. B. D. Kettlewell (1959) carefully studied moths in England. There is genetic variation among moths that makes some dark and others light. By placing light and dark moths in several sites, Kettlewell found that in rural areas light-colored moths were most likely to survive but that in industrial areas dark moths were most likely to survive. The explanation? In rural areas, light-colored moths blend in well with light-colored trees and are therefore better protected from predators. Natural selection favors them. However, in sooty industrial areas, light-colored moths are easy pickings against the darkened trees, whereas dark moths are well disguised. When industry came to England, the proportion of dark moths increased; as pollution was brought under control in some highly industrialized areas, the proportion of light-colored moths increased (Bishop & Cooke, 1975).

Notice, then, that evolution is not just about genes. It is about the *interaction between genes and environment.* A particular genetic makeup may enhance survival in one kind of environment but prove maladaptive in another. Which genes are advantageous, and therefore become more common in future generations, depends on what environments a group experiences and what traits that environment demands.

Each species has its own species heredity, the product of natural selection.

According to evolutionary theory, then, humans, like any other species, are as they are and develop as they do partly because they have a shared species heredity that evolved through natural selection. Solutions to problems faced by our ancestors thousands of years ago in such important areas as mate selection, childbearing, and parenting may have become built into the human genetic code. Not all human similarity is because of genes, however; through the process of cultural evolution, we "inherit" from previous generations a characteristically human environment and ways of adapting to it (Bjorklund & Pellegrini, 2002). The most significant legacy of biological evolution may be a powerful brain that allows humans to learn from their experiences, to find better ways of adapting to their environment or even changing it, and, with the help of language, to share what they have learned with future generations (Bjorklund & Pellegrini, 2002).

Summing Up

Humans are similar and develop similarly partly because of a shared species heredity produced by biological evolution. According to Darwinian evolutionary theory, if there is genetic variation in a species—and if some genes aid members of the species in adapting to their environment, surviving, and reproducing—those genes will become more common in the population over time through the process of natural selection. Humans are also similar because they inherit a characteristically human environment through cultural evolution. ■

Individual Heredity

To understand how genes contribute to differences among humans, you must start at **conception,** the moment when an egg is fertilized by a sperm. Once you understand what is inherited at conception, you can examine how genes influence traits.

The Genetic Code

A few hours after sperm penetrates ovum, the sperm cell begins to disintegrate, releasing its genetic material. The nucleus of the ovum releases its own genetic material, and a new cell nucleus is created from the genetic material provided by mother and father. This new cell, called a **zygote** and only the size of a pinhead, is the beginning of a human. Conception has occurred.

The genetic material contained in the new zygote consists of 46 threadlike bodies called **chromosomes,** which function as 23 pairs. Both members of a chromosome pair influence the same characteristics. Each chromosome is made up of thousands of genes, the basic units of heredity. Genetic scientists now believe a person has around 30,000 genes (Pennisi, 2003). Each is a stretch of deoxyribonucleic acid (DNA), the double helix molecule whose chemical code guides development. Specifically, genes provide instructions

Explorations

The Human Genome Project

On June 26, 2000, Francis Collins, head of the Human Genome Project within the National Institutes of Health, and J. Craig Venter, then head of Celera Genomics Corporation, a private company that launched its own furious effort to unscramble the genetic code, jointly announced the completion of a draft version of the human genome (International Human Genome Sequencing Consortium, 2001). In April 2003, they announced that the sequencing project was essentially complete, 13 years after it had begun and 50 years after James Watson and Francis Crick discovered the structure of DNA (Pennisi, 2003). What did this massive project involve, and what has it told us?

Researchers at several universities and companies in the United States and England mapped the sequence of the chemical units or "letters" that make up the strands of DNA in human chromosomes. They still needed to do a good deal of "spell checking" when they made their initial announcement, but they had a pretty good draft of the human genome (Weiss & Gillis, 2000). The drudgery of this monstrous task was done by supercomputers and robots the size of small cars working alongside human technicians. The raw material analyzed was DNA samples from a few humans of diverse racial backgrounds.

The four basic units of the genetic code are the bases A (adenine), C (cytosine), G (guanine), and T (thymine). It is now estimated that the human genome has 3.1 billion of these chemical letters. Interestingly, only about 3 to 4% of the human genome—1 inch out of an estimated 6 feet of DNA—is believed to consist of genes, each of which is a specific sequence of from 1000 to 100,000 bases (Weiss, 2000). The functions of other stretches of DNA are not entirely clear, but they appear to play a role in regulating the activity of genes, turning them on and off (Plomin et al., 2003). About 999 of 1000 bases are identical in all humans; it is the remaining 1 of 1000 that makes us different. We share most of our genes not only with humans of other races but also with other primates and even with mice (Simpson & Elias, 2003).

Once a gene associated with a disease or disorder is located on a particular chromosome amid the DNA surrounding it, much remains to be done before useful applications of this information are possible. Researchers may attempt to devise a test for the gene, study the functions of the gene's products so that they can begin to understand how the disease or disorder comes about, and only then attempt to develop new drugs and other means of preventing or curing the dysfunction associated with the gene (Hawley & Mori, 1999; Weiss, 2003b). As James Watson, codiscoverer of the double helix structure of DNA, put it, "We have the book, and now we've got to learn how to read it" (Weiss & Gillis, 2000, p. A12).

for the production of particular amino acids, which in turn form proteins, the building blocks of all bodily tissues and of essential substances such as hormones, neurotransmitters, and enzymes. Our understanding of the makeup of our 46 chromosomes has been greatly advanced by the **Human Genome Project,** a massive, government-sponsored effort to decipher the human genetic code, as the Explorations box on this page shows.

A sperm cell and an ovum contribute 23 chromosomes each to the zygote. Thus, of each chromosome pair—and of each pair of genes located on corresponding sites on a chromosome pair—one member came from the father and one member came from the mother. Sperm and ova, unlike other cells, have only 23 chromosomes because they are produced through the specialized process of cell division called **meiosis.** At the start of this process, a reproductive germ cell in the ovaries of a female or the testes of a male contains 46 chromosomes. It splits to form two 46-chromosome cells, and then these two cells split again to form four cells—but in this step each resulting cell receives only 23 chromosomes. The end product is one egg (and three nonfunctional bodies) in a female or four sperm in a male. Each resulting sperm cell or ovum thus has only one member of each of the parent's 23 pairs of chromosomes.

The single-celled zygote formed at conception becomes a multiple-celled organism through the more usual process of cell division, **mitosis.** During mitosis, a cell (and each of its 46 chromosomes) divides to produce two identical cells, each containing the same 46 chromosomes. As the zygote moves through the fallopian tube toward its prenatal home in the uterus, it first divides into two cells; then, the two then become four, the four become eight, and so on, all through mitosis. Except for sperm and ova, then, all human cells contain copies of the 46 chromosomes provided at conception. Mitosis continues throughout life, creating new cells that enable us to grow and replacing old cells that are damaged.

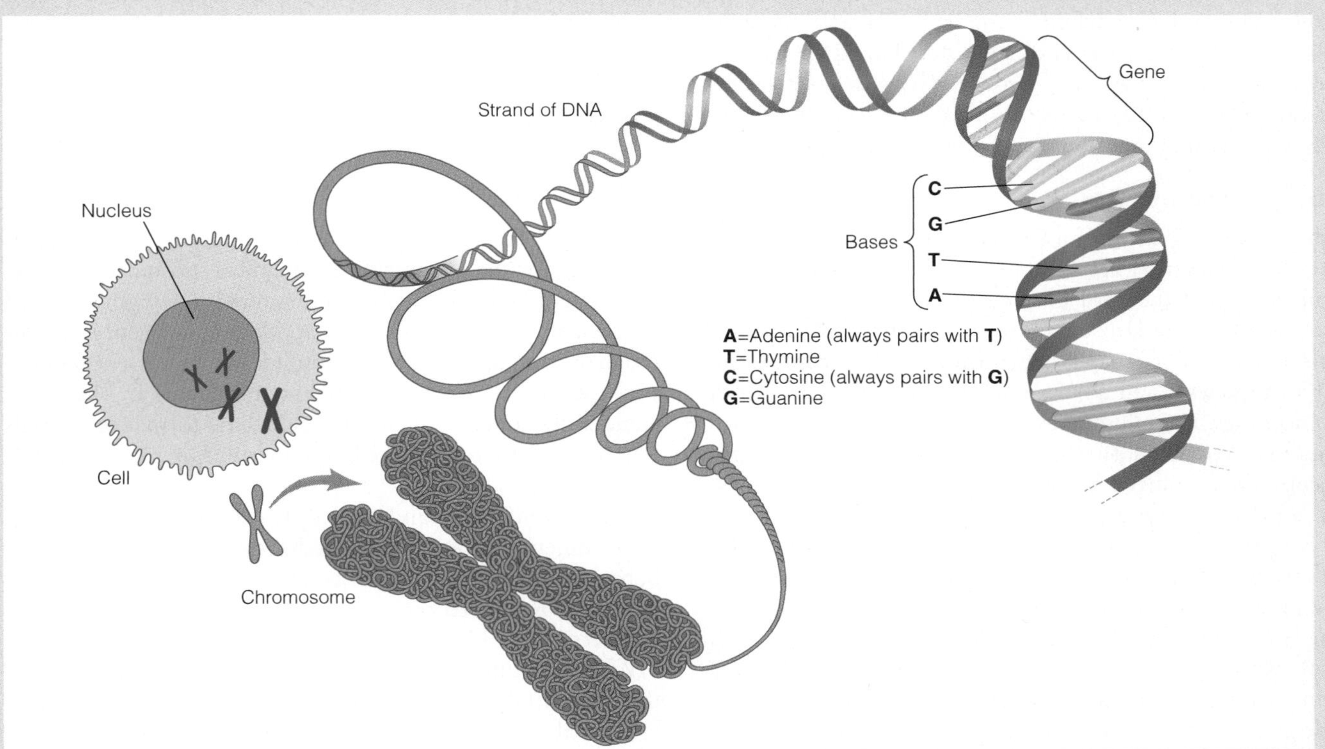

The chromosomes in each cell consist of strands of DNA made up of sequences of the bases A, T, C, and G, some of which are functional units called genes.

SOURCE: Adapted from Weiss, R. (2000, May 23). For DNA, a defining moment: With code revealed, challenge will be to find its meaning and uses. *Washington Post*, p. A16.

Genetic Uniqueness and Relatedness

To understand how people are both different from and like others genetically, consider that when a pair of parental chromosomes separates during meiosis, which of the two chromosomes will end up in a particular sperm or ovum is a matter of chance. And, because each chromosome pair separates independently of all other pairs, and because each reproductive cell contains 23 pairs of chromosomes, a single parent can produce 2^{23}—more than 8 million—different sperm or ova. Any couple could theoretically have 64 trillion babies without producing 2 children with identical genes.

The genetic uniqueness of children of the same parents is even greater than this because of a quirk of meiosis known as **crossing over.** When pairs of chromosomes line up before they separate, they cross each other and parts of them are exchanged, much as if you were to exchange a couple of fingers with a friend during a handshake. Crossing over increases the number of distinct sperm or ova that an individual can produce. In short, it is incredibly unlikely that there ever was or ever will be another human exactly like you genetically. The one exception is **identical twins** (or identical triplets, and so on), which result when one fertilized ovum divides to form two or more genetically identical individuals, as happens in about 1 of every 250 births (Plomin, 1990).

How genetically alike are parent and child or brother and sister? You and either your mother or your father have 50% of your genes in common because you received half of your chromosomes (and genes) from each parent. But if you have followed our mathematics, you will see that siblings may have many genes in common or few depending on what happens during meiosis. Because siblings receive half of their genes from the same mother and half from the same father, their genetic resemblance to each other is 50%, the same genetic resemblance as that of parent and child. The critical difference is that they share half of their genes *on the average;* some siblings share more and others fewer. Indeed, we have all known some siblings who are almost like twins and others who could not be more different if they tried.

Fraternal twins result when two ova are released at approximately the same time and each is fertilized by a different sperm, as happens in about 1 of every 125 births. Fraternal twins are no more alike genetically than brothers and sisters born at different times and need not even be of the same sex. Grandparent and grandchild, aunt or uncle and niece or nephew, and half-brothers and half-sisters have 25% of their genes in common on average. Thus, everyone except an identical twin is genetically unique, but each person also shares genes with kin that contribute to family resemblances.

Determination of Sex

Of the 23 pairs of chromosomes that each individual inherits, 22 (called *autosomes*) are similar in males and females. The chromosomes of the 23rd pair are the sex chromosomes. A male child has one long chromosome called an **X chromosome** because of its shape, and a short, stubby companion with fewer genes called a **Y chromosome.** Females have two X chromosomes. The illustration on this page shows chromosomes that have been photographed through a powerful microscope, then arranged in pairs and rephotographed in a pattern called a **karyotype.**

Because the mother has only X chromosomes and the father's sperm cell has either an X or a Y chromosome (depending on how the sex chromosomes sort out during meiosis), it is the father who determines a child's gender. If an ovum with its one X chromosome is fertilized by a sperm bearing a Y chromosome, the product is an XY zygote, a genetic male. A single gene on the Y chromosome then sets in motion the biological events that result in male sexual organs (Hawley & Mori, 1999). If a sperm carrying an X chromosome reaches the ovum first, the result is an XX zygote, a genetic female. Perhaps if these facts had been known in earlier eras, women would not have been criticized, tortured, divorced, and even beheaded for failing to bear male heirs.

So, a genetically unique boy or girl has roughly 30,000 genes on 46 chromosomes arranged in 23 pairs. How do these genes influence the individual's characteristics and development? It is still a mystery, but we have several clues to the answer.

Translation of the Genetic Code

As you have seen, genes provide instructions for development by calling for the production of chemical substances. For example, genes set in motion a process that lays a pigment called *melanin* in the iris of the eye. Some people's genes call for much of this pigment, and the result is brown eyes; other people's genes call for less of it, and the result is blue eyes. Genetically coded proteins also guide the formation of cells that become neurons in the brain, influencing potential intelligence.

Genes influence and are influenced by the biochemical environment surrounding them during development and the behavior of the developing organism (Gottlieb, 2002). As a result, a particular cell can become part of an eyeball or part of a kneecap depending on what cells are next to it during embryonic development and what they are doing. You should therefore think of the genetic "blueprint" as written in erasable pencil rather than in indelible ink and of genes as active

(A)

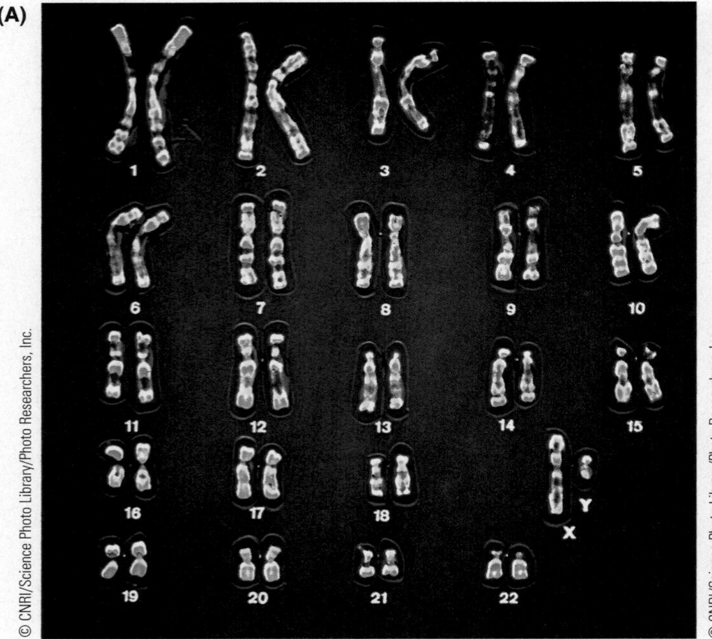

(B)

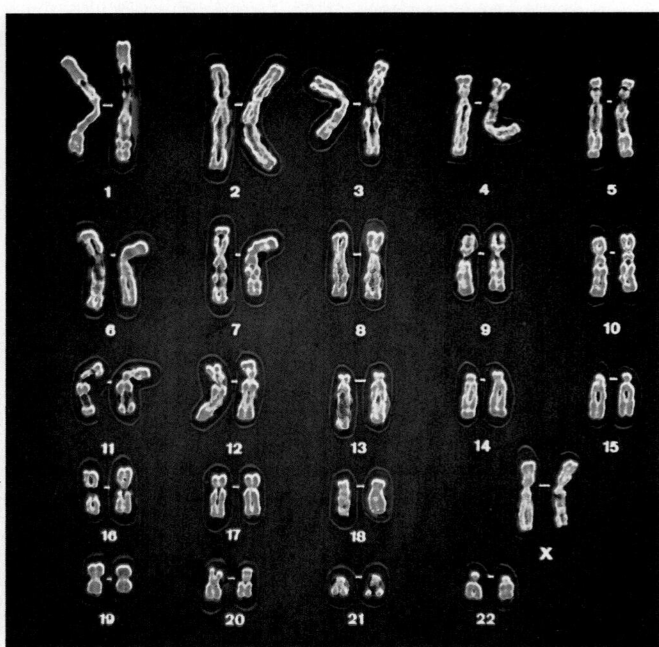

The male karyotype (A) shows the 22 pairs of autosomal chromosomes and the 2 sex chromosomes—an elongated X and a shorter Y chromosome. The photographic arrangement of a female's chromosomes (B) shows 2 X chromosomes.

forces in development throughout the life span. A multitude of environmental factors not only in the womb but also throughout life influence where and when genes are activated and how they are expressed. As a result, no one completely understands the remarkable process that transforms a single cell into millions of diverse cells—blood cells, nerve cells, skin cells, and so on—all organized into a living, behaving human.

Nor do we fully understand how genes help bring about certain developments at certain points in the life span. Current thinking is that gene pairs with specific messages to send are regulated—turned on or off—by other stretches of DNA over the course of development (Plomin et al., 2001; Plomin et al., 2003). It is becoming clearer that genes are active players in the developmental process and that having specific genes may be less important in human development than which are activated and when.

Ultimately, environmental factors have a great deal to do with which genetic potentials are translated into physical and psychological realities. Consider the genes that influence height. Some people inherit genes calling for exceptional height, and others inherit genes calling for a short stature. But **genotype,** the genetic makeup a person inherits, is different from **phenotype,** the characteristic or trait the person eventually has (for example, a height of 5 feet 8 inches). An individual whose genotype calls for exceptional height may or may not be tall. Indeed, a child who is severely malnourished from the prenatal period onward may have the genetic potential to be a basketball center but may end up too short to make the team. Environmental influences combine with genetic influences to determine how a particular genotype is translated into a particular phenotype—the way a person looks, thinks, feels, and behaves.

Mechanisms of Inheritance

Another way to approach the riddle of how genes influence people is to consider the major mechanisms of inheritance—how parents' genes influence their children's traits. There are three main mechanisms of inheritance: single gene-pair inheritance, sex-linked inheritance, and polygenic (or multiple gene) inheritance.

Single Gene-Pair Inheritance

Through **single gene-pair inheritance,** some human characteristics are influenced by only one pair of genes—one from the mother, one from the father. Although he knew nothing of genes, a 19th-century monk named Gregor Mendel contributed greatly to our knowledge of single gene-pair inheritance and earned his place as the father of genetics by crossbreeding different strains of peas and carefully observing the outcomes (Henig, 2000). He noticed a predictable pattern to the way in which two alternative characteristics would appear in the offspring of cross-breedings—for example, smooth seeds or wrinkled seeds, green pods or yellow pods. He called some characteristics (for example, smooth seeds) *dominant* because they appeared more often in later generations than their opposite traits, which he called *recessive.*

As an illustration of the principles of Mendelian heredity, consider the remarkable fact that about three-fourths of us can curl our tongues upward into a tubelike shape, whereas one-fourth of us cannot. It happens that there is a gene associated with tongue curling; it is a **dominant gene,** meaning that it will be expressed when paired with a **recessive gene,** a weaker gene that can be dominated like the one associated with the absence of tongue-curling ability.

The person who inherits one "tongue-curl" gene (label it U) and one "no-curl" gene (call it −) would be able to curl his tongue (that is, would have a tongue-curling phenotype) because the dominant, tongue-curl gene overpowers the recessive, no-curl gene. Using the photo and diagram on page 62 as a guide, you can calculate the odds that parents with different genotypes for tongue curling will have children who can or cannot curl their tongues. A father will contribute one of his two genes to a sperm, and the mother will contribute one of her two genes to an ovum. Each child inherits one of the mother's genes and one of the father's.

Dominant genes triumph over recessive genes. If a father with the genotype UU (a tongue curler) and a mother with the genotype −− (a non–tongue curler) have children, each child they produce will have one gene for tongue curling and one for a lack of tongue curling (genotype U−), and each will be a tongue curler. Because the tongue-curl gene dominates, you can say that this couple has a 100% chance of having a tongue-curling child. Notice that two different genotypes, UU and U−, both produce the same phenotype: an acrobatic tongue.

A tongue-curling man and a tongue-curling woman can surprise everyone and have a child who lacks this amazing talent. These two parents must both have the U− genotype. If the father's recessive gene and the mother's recessive gene happen to unite in the zygote, they will have a non–tongue-curling child (with the genotype −−). The chances are 25%—one out of four—that this couple will have such a child. Of course, the laws of conception are much like the laws of cards. This couple could beat the odds and have a whole family of non–tongue-curling children or could have none. Because people who cannot curl their tongues must have the −− genotype, two non–tongue-curling parents will have only non–tongue-curling (−−) children.

Table 3.1 lists several other examples of dominant and recessive traits associated with single gene-pair inheritance. Some physical characteristics in this table (such as eye color and hair color and curliness) are influenced by more than a single pair of genes. Also, in some cases, a dominant gene incompletely dominates a recessive partner gene, so the recessive gene is expressed to some extent, as when crossing red and white flowers produces pink ones—a phenomenon called **incomplete dominance.** In still other cases of single gene-pair heredity, two genes influence a trait but neither dominates the other; instead, both are expressed. This is called **codominance** because the phenotype of the person with two distinct genes in a pair is a compromise between the two genes. For example, an AB blood type is a mix of A and B blood types. Single gene-pair inheritance is more complex than it looks at first glance.

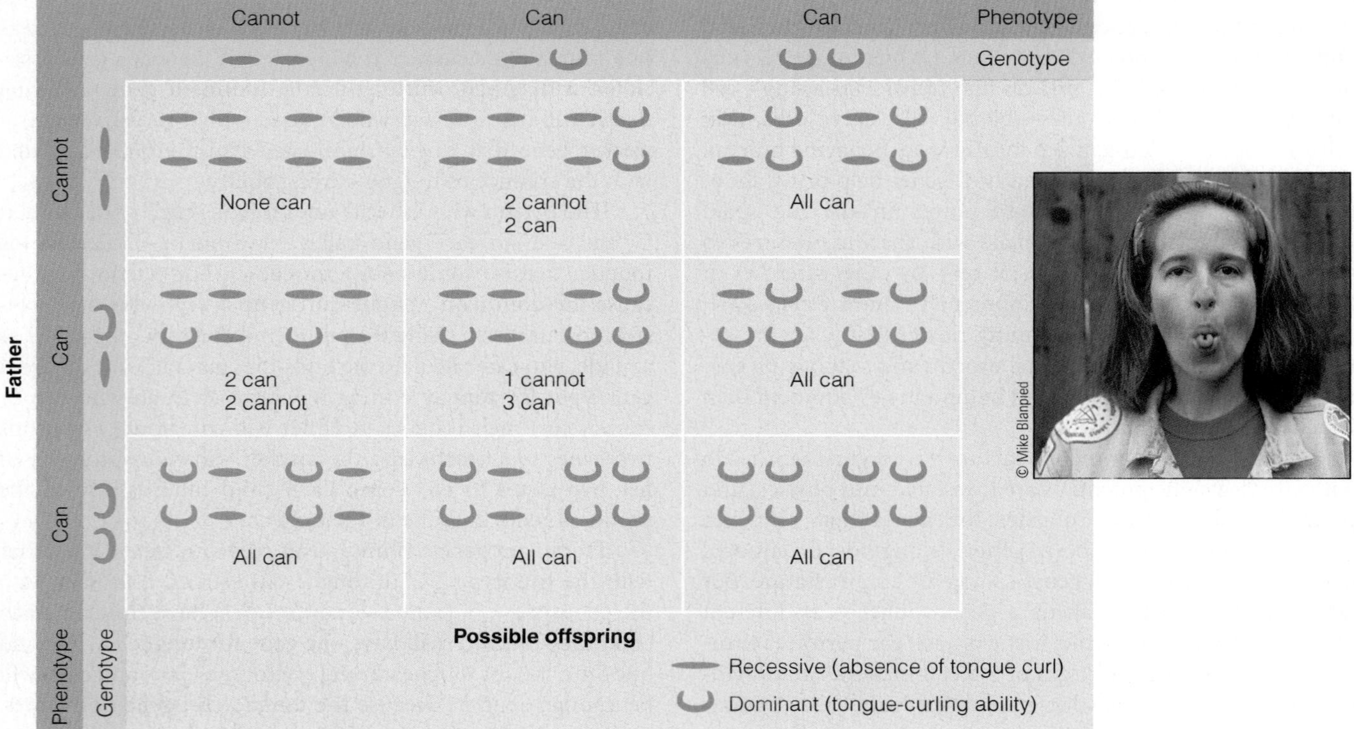

Figure 3.1 Can you curl your tongue as shown? Tongue-curling ability is determined by a dominant gene; if you can curl your tongue, then either your mother or your father can, because one of them must have the dominant might still be able to curl their tongues. All possibilities are shown in the figure; each of the nine boxes shows the gene combinations of the four possible children a particular mother and a particular father can have.

However, many genetically linked diseases and defects are entirely caused by two recessive genes, one inherited from each parent, as you will see shortly.

Sex-Linked Inheritance

Sex-linked characteristics are influenced by single genes located on the sex chromosomes rather than on the other 22 pairs of chromosomes. Indeed, you could say *X-linked* rather than *sex-linked* because most of these attributes are associated with genes located only on X chromosomes.

Why do far more males than females display red–green color blindness? The inability to distinguish red from green is caused by a recessive gene that appears only on X chromosomes. Recall that Y chromosomes are shorter than X chromosomes and have fewer genes. If a boy inherits the recessive color-blindness gene on his X chromosome, there is no color-vision gene on the Y chromosome that could dominate the color-blindness gene. He will be color blind. By contrast, a girl who inherits the gene usually has a normal color-vision gene on her other X chromosome that dominates the color-blindness gene (see Figure 3.2). She would have to inherit two of the recessive color-blindness genes (one from each parent) to be color blind. Which parent gives a boy who is color blind his color-blindness gene? Definitely his mother, for she is the source of his X chromosome. **Hemophilia,** a deficiency in the blood's ability to clot, is also far more common among males than females because it is associated with a gene on X chromosomes.

Polygenic Inheritance

So far we have considered only the influence of single genes or gene pairs on human traits. Every week, it seems, we read in the newspaper that researchers have identified "the gene" for cancer, bedwetting, happiness, or some other phenomenon. However, most important human characteristics are influenced by multiple pairs of genes, interacting with environmental factors, rather than by a single pair of genes; that is, they are **polygenic traits.** Examples of polygenic traits include height, weight, intelligence, temperament, and susceptibility to cancer and depression (Plomin et al., 2001).

When a trait is influenced by multiple genes, there are many degrees of the trait depending on which combinations of genes individuals inherit. The trait (for example, intelligence) tends to be distributed in the population according to the familiar bell-shaped or normal curve. Many people are near the mean of the distribution; fewer are at the extremes. This is the way intelligence and most other measurable human traits are distributed. At this point, we do not know how many

Table 3.1 Examples of Traits Influenced by Dominant and Recessive Genes

Dominant Trait	Recessive Trait
Brown eyes	Gray, green, hazel, or blue eyes
Dark hair	Blond hair
Nonred hair	Red hair
Curly hair	Straight hair
Normal vision	Nearsightedness
Farsightedness	Normal vision
Roman nose	Straight nose
Broad lips	Thin lips
Extra digits	Five digits
Double jointed	Normal joints
Pigmented skin	Albinism
Type A blood	Type O blood
Type B blood	Type O blood
Normal hearing	Congenital deafness
Normal blood cells	Sickle-cell disease*
Huntington's disease*	Normal physiology
Normal physiology	Cystic fibrosis*
Normal physiology	Phenylketonuria (PKU)*
Normal physiology	Tay-Sachs disease*

* Condition described in this chapter.
SOURCES: Burns & Bottino, 1989; McKusick, 1990.

gene pairs influence intelligence or other polygenic traits. What we can say is that unknown numbers of genes, interacting with environmental forces, create a range of individual differences in most important human traits.

Mutations

We have described the three major mechanisms by which the genes inherited at conception influence traits: single gene-pair, sex-linked, and polygenic inheritance. Occasionally, however, a new gene appears as if out of nowhere; it is not passed on by a parent. A **mutation** is a change in the structure or arrangement of one or more genes that produces a new phenotype. For example, experts believe that the recessive gene for the sex-linked disorder hemophilia was first introduced into the royal families of Europe by Queen Victoria. Because no cases of hemophilia could be found in the queen's ancestry, the gene may have been a mutation that she passed to her offspring (Massie & Massie, 1975). New cases of hemophilia, then, can be caused by either spontaneous mutations or sex-linked inheritance. The odds that mutations will occur are increased by environmental hazards such as radiation, toxic industrial waste, and agricultural chemicals in food (Burns & Bottino, 1989).

Some mutations have beneficial effects and become more common in a population through natural selection. The gene associated with **sickle-cell disease,** a blood disease common among African Americans in which red blood cells take on a sickle shape, is a good example (this is described further later in the chapter). It probably arose as a mutation but became more prevalent in Africa, Central America, and other tropical areas over many generations because having one of the recessive sickle-cell genes protected people from malaria and allowed them to live longer and produce more children than people without the protective gene. Unfortunately, the sickle-cell gene does more harm than good where malaria is no longer a problem. Thus, mutations can be either beneficial or harmful, depending on their nature and on the environment in which their bearers live.

Chromosome Abnormalities

Genetic endowment can also influence human characteristics through **chromosome abnormalities,** in which a child receives too many or too few chromosomes (or abnormal chromosomes) at conception. Most such abnormalities are because of errors in chromosome division during meiosis. Through an accident of nature, an ovum or sperm cell may be produced with more or fewer than the usual 23 chromosomes. In most cases, a zygote with the wrong number of chromosomes is spontaneously aborted; chromosome abnormalities are the main cause of pregnancy loss. However, around 1 child in 160 is born with more or, rarely, fewer chromosomes than the normal 46 (Simpson & Elias, 2003).

One familiar chromosome abnormality is **Down syndrome,** also known as *trisomy 21* because it is associated with three rather than two 21st chromosomes. Children with Down syndrome have distinctive eyelid folds, short stubby limbs, and thick tongues (see photo page 64). Their levels of intellectual functioning vary widely, but they are typically

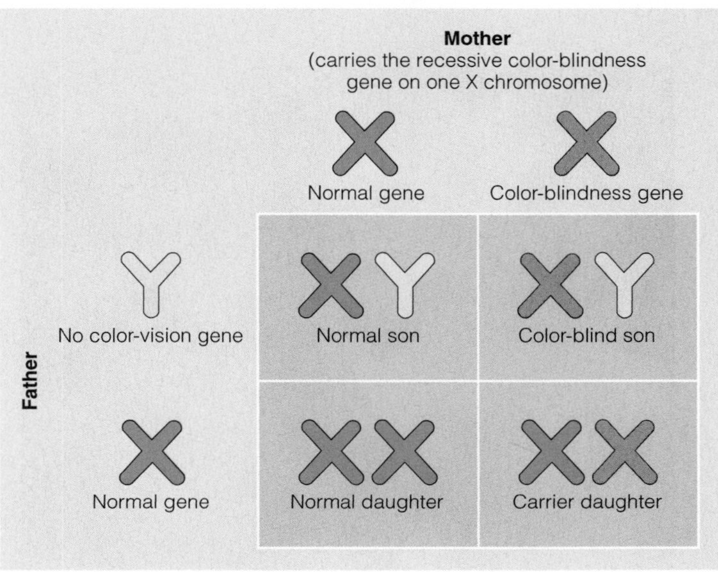

Figure 3.2 The workings of sex-linked inheritance in red–green color blindness.

mentally retarded to some degree and therefore develop and learn at a slower pace than most children. Improved medical care has lengthened their lives, and special education and other training programs have improved their functioning (Roizen & Patterson, 2003). Although they have more trouble gaining acceptance by their peers as they get older, people with Down syndrome generally have pleasant personalities and are well adapted within their families later in life (Hanson, 2003).

What determines who has a Down syndrome child and who does not? Chance, partly. The errors in meiosis responsible for Down syndrome can occur in any mother—or father. However, they are especially likely if a parent is older. The chances of having a baby with the syndrome are about 1 in 1000 for mothers under 30 but climb to about 1 in 140 for mothers age 40 or older (see Figure 3.3). A father's age has a bearing on the odds of a Down syndrome birth but not as much as the mother's age (Hawley & Mori, 1999). This is probably because ova, which begin forming during the prenatal period, have more years in which to degenerate than sperm, which do not begin to be produced until puberty, are produced continuously, and mature in only about 75 days (Hawley & Mori, 1999). Older mothers and fathers are also more likely than younger ones to have been exposed to environmental hazards that can damage ova or sperm, such as radiation, drugs, chemicals, and viruses (Strigini et al., 1990).

Most other chromosome abnormalities involve cases in which a child receives either too many or too few sex chromosomes. Like Down syndrome, these sex chromosome abnormalities can be attributed mainly to errors in meiosis that become increasingly likely in older parents and in parents whose chromosomes have been damaged by environmental hazards. One well-known example is **Turner syndrome,** in which a female (about 1 in 3000) is born with a single X chromosome (XO) in each of her cells. These girls remain small and often have stubby fingers and toes, a "webbed" neck, a broad chest, and underdeveloped breasts. They are unable to reproduce,

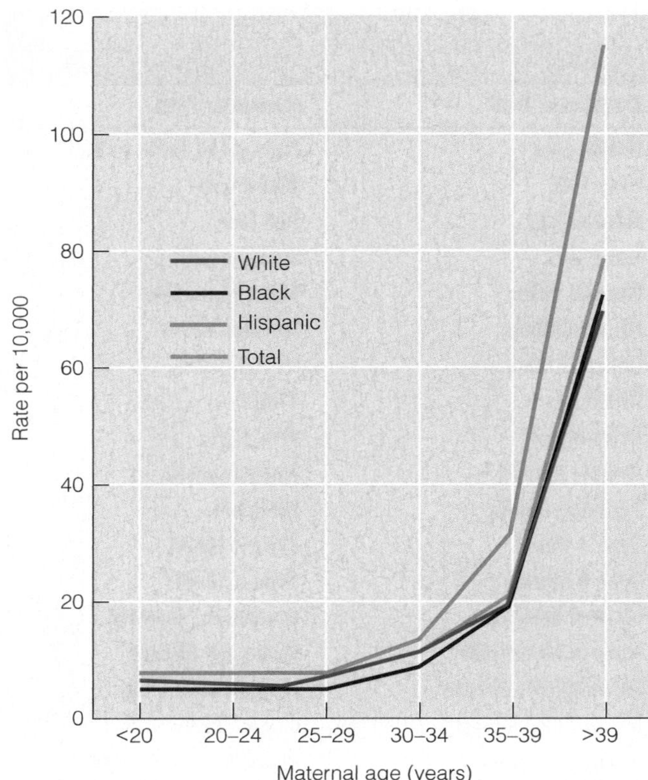

Figure 3.3 The rate of Down syndrome births increases steeply as the mother's age increases.

SOURCE: "Down Syndrome Prevalence at Birth" (1994)

Children with Down syndrome can live rich lives if they receive appropriate educational opportunities and support.

typically favor traditionally feminine activities, and often have lower-than-average spatial and mathematical reasoning abilities (Downey et al., 1991).

Another example is **Klinefelter syndrome,** in which a male (1 in 200) is born with one or more extra X chromosomes (XXY). Klinefelter males tend to be tall and generally masculine in appearance, but they are sterile and at puberty develop feminine sex characteristics such as enlarged breasts. Most have normal general intelligence test scores, but many are below average in language skills and school achievement (Mandoki et al., 1991).

Finally, **fragile X syndrome** is worth noting because it is the most common hereditary cause of mental retardation (Kingston, 2002; O'Donnell & Warren, 2002). Some affected individuals have large jaws and ears; most are mentally retarded. In this condition, one arm of the X chromosome is only barely connected to the rest of the chromosome and looks as if it is about to break off (hence the term *fragile*). The condition is caused by sex-linked inheritance and therefore is more common among males than females; in females, a normal gene on the second X chromosome overrides the recessive gene responsible for fragile X. The root of the problem is too many repeats or duplications of a sequence of three letters in the genetic code. The result is lack of a protein important to the formation of connections between neurons of the brain (O'Donnell & Warren, 2002). The number of repeats of the

DNA segment responsible for fragile X syndrome increases from generation to generation, causing more serious mental retardation in later generations.

Genetic Diagnosis and Counseling

To set parents-to-be at ease, we begin this description of genetic diagnosis and counseling by noting that 97% or more of babies will *not* be born with major birth defects (Simpson & Elias, 2003). However, there are some 5000 diseases and disorders associated with a single gene or pair of genes, many more polygene disorders, and several chromosome abnormalities that can affect human development (Brown, 2003; Simpson & Elias, 2003). **Genetic counseling** is a service that provides information on the nature, inheritance, and effects of genetic disorders and offers guidance to people who suspect or learn that they or their unborn children are at risk for some genetically based problem.

Today's genetic counselors have access to more information than ever about the nature, detection, and treatment of genetic defects. Now that it is possible to quickly and inexpensively analyze a person's DNA from a cheek swab, genetic testing is easier than ever. Hundreds of specific genetic tests—the number is growing daily—have been devised (Simpson & Elias, 2003). Within a decade or so, it may be possible to sequence a person's entire genome for less than $1000 (Guttmacher & Collins, 2003). To illustrate issues in modern genetic diagnosis and counseling, we focus on sickle-cell disease and Huntington's disease. Several other genetic diseases, including **cystic fibrosis,** hemophilia, phenylketonuria (PKU), and **Tay-Sachs disease,** are described in Table 3.2.

Table 3.2 Some Genetic Disorders

Disease	Description	Genetic Mechanism	Diagnosis and Treatment
CYSTIC FIBROSIS	Glandular problem results in mucus buildup in lungs that makes breathing difficult and shortens life; common among Caucasians	Recessive gene pair; carriers were protected from epidemics of diarrhea in Europe	DNA test can identify most carriers, but so many mutations are possible that tests for all are not feasible; hours of physical therapy and antibiotics to keep lungs clear can prolong life, and experimental gene therapy has had some success
PHENYLKETONURIA (PKU)	Lack of enzyme needed to metabolize phenylalanine in milk and many other foods results in conversion of phenylalanine into an acid that attacks the nervous system and causes mental retardation	Recessive gene pair	Routinely screened for with a blood test at birth; special diet low in phenylalanine prevents brain damage
HEMOPHILIA	Deficiency in blood's ability to clot; more common in males than in females	Sex-linked inheritance (gene on X chromosome)	DNA analysis of cells obtained through CVS or amniocentesis can detect it; blood transfusions can improve clotting and reduce the negative effects of internal bleeding
HUNTINGTON'S DISEASE	Deterioration of the nervous system in middle age, associated with dementia, jerky movements, personality changes	Dominant gene	Test enables relatives to find out whether they have the gene; preimplantation genetic diagnosis of embryonic cells may be used to assure a healthy child
SICKLE-CELL DISEASE	Blood cells are sickle-shaped rather than round, stick together, make breathing difficult, and cause painful swelling of joints; common in African Americans	Recessive gene pair; carriers were protected from malaria in Africa	Blood test can determine whether parents are carriers (newborns in the United States are screened with a blood test); antibiotics and blood transfusions relieve symptoms
TAY-SACHS DISEASE	Metabolic defect results in accumulation of fat in a child's brain, degeneration of the nervous system, and early death; common in Jewish people from Eastern Europe	Recessive gene pair	Blood test can determine whether parents are carriers, and fetal DNA analysis can determine whether a child is affected; medication may help, but most victims die in childhood

SOURCES: Davidson, 2002; Kingston, 2002; Simpson & Elias, 2003.

Explorations

Prenatal Detection of Abnormalities

Pregnant women today, especially those over 35 or 40, turn to a variety of medical techniques to tell them in advance whether their babies are likely to be normal (Simpson & Elias, 2003). The easiest and most commonly used method is **ultrasound**—the use of sound waves to scan the womb and create a visual image of the fetus on a monitor screen. Ultrasound can indicate how many fetuses are in the womb and whether they are alive, and it can detect genetic defects that produce visible physical abnormalities. Prospective parents often enjoy "meeting" their child and can find out (when the pregnancy is far enough along) whether their child is going to be a girl or a boy. Ultrasound is now widely used even when abnormalities are not suspected. It is safer than X-rays and is generally considered safe (Simpson & Elias, 2003).

To detect chromosome abnormalities such as Down syndrome and to determine whether the genes for particular single gene-pair disorders are present, **amniocentesis** is commonly used. A needle is inserted into the abdomen, and a

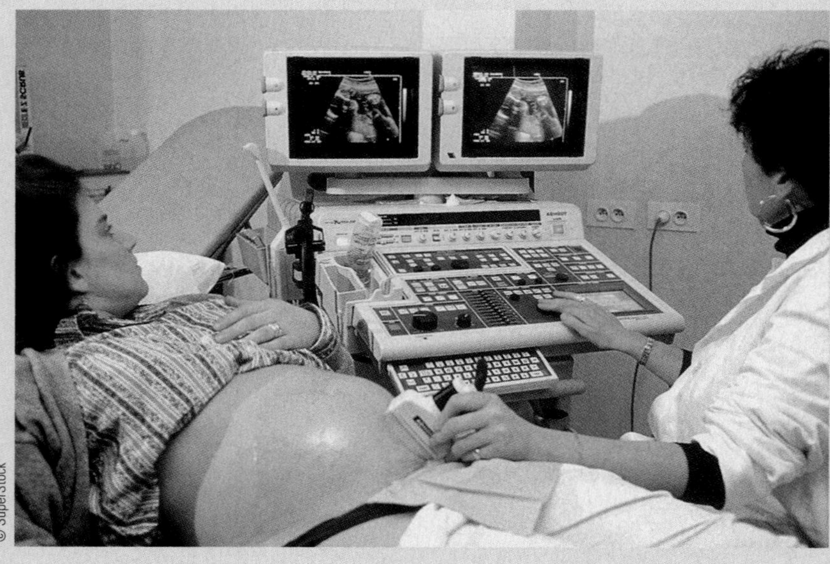

© SuperStock

Ultrasound monitoring.

If a couple concerned about a particular genetic disorder seeks the advice of a genetic counselor, the counselor might first obtain a complete family history from each partner—one that includes information about the diseases and causes of death of relatives, any previous problems in childbearing, and the countries of origin of relatives. For some defects and disorders, especially those influenced by multiple gene pairs, family histories may be the only basis for calculating the odds that a problem may occur. However, blood tests or cheek swabs can determine whether prospective parents carry the genes for countless single gene-pair and sex-linked conditions.

Suppose an African American couple learns from such a diagnostic test that they are both carriers of the recessive gene for sickle-cell disease. Individuals with this disease have sickle-shaped blood cells that tend to cluster together and distribute less oxygen through the circulatory system than normal cells do (Davidson, 2002). They have great difficulty breathing and exerting themselves, experience painful swelling of their joints, and often die early from heart or kidney failure. A genetic counselor might tell the couple that about 9% of African Americans in the United States have the genotype we will call *Ss;* they carry one dominant gene *(S)* that calls for round blood cells and one recessive gene *(s)* that calls for sickle-shaped blood cells (Thompson, 1975). Such people are called **carriers** because, although they do not have the disease, they can transmit the gene for it to their children. The child who inherits two recessive sickle-cell genes *(ss)* has sickle-cell disease. The genetic counselor would therefore explain that an *Ss* father and an *Ss* mother (two carriers) have a one-in-four, or 25%, chance of having a child with sickle-cell disease *(ss).*

This couple also has a two-in-four, or 50%, chance, of having a child who will be a carrier like themselves. This is significant, the counselor would say, because the dominant gene associated with round blood cells shows incomplete sample of amniotic fluid is withdrawn. Fetal cells that have been shed can be analyzed to determine the sex of fetus, the presence of a range of chromosomal abnormalities, and, through DNA analysis, the presence of the genes for many genetic defects. Despite a risk of miscarriage in about 1 of 200 cases, amniocentesis is considered safe and is often recommended for older mothers (Simpson & Elias, 2003; Stefos, 2002). It is not very painful, although one mother described it as feeling like "someone sticking a turkey baster through my belly button" (Hawley & Mori, 1999). Its main disadvantage is that it is not considered safe until the 15th week of pregnancy (Simpson & Elias, 2003).

Chorionic villus sampling (CVS) involves inserting a catheter through the mother's vagina and cervix (or, less commonly, through the abdomen) into the membrane called the *chorion* that surrounds the fetus, and then extracting tiny hair cells from the chorion that contain genetic material from the fetus. Sample cells can then be analyzed for the same genetic defects that can be detected using amniocentesis. The difference is that chorionic villus sampling can be performed earlier, as early as the 10th week of pregnancy, allowing parents more time to consider the pros and cons of continuing the pregnancy if an abnormality is detected (Simpson & Elias, 2003). The safety of CVS has improved to the point that it is not much riskier than amniocentesis.

Parents who have reason to believe they are at high risk to have a baby with a serious condition can minimize their risk by using new reproductive technologies (see Chapter 4 for more examples). **Preimplantation genetic diagnosis** involves fertilizing a mother's eggs with a father's sperm in the laboratory using in vitro fertilization (IVF) techniques, conducting DNA tests on the first cells that result from mitosis of each fertilized egg, and implanting in the mother's uterus only eggs that do not have chromosome abnormalities or genes associated with disorders (Simpson & Elias, 2003). Although costly, this option may appeal to couples who would not consider abortion but do not want to have a child with a serious defect. Preimplantation genetic diagnosis can now screen for more than 90% of the most common genetic disorders (Adams, 2003). It is controversial because it could be used not only to prevent disorders but to try to create "designer" children with the characteristics parents want.

Finally, **maternal blood sampling** can yield fetal cells that slipped through the placenta and can be analyzed with no risk to the fetus (Simpson & Elias, 2003; Yang, Kim, & Jung, 2002). These tests are not yet accurate enough for regular use in clinical practice, however. Fetal cells only rarely make it to the mother's bloodstream and may be hard to distinguish from fetal cells left from previous pregnancies. Still, this noninvasive method of prenatal diagnosis will probably improve and become more common (Yang, Kim, & Jung, 2002). For some time, maternal blood has been tested for the presence of abnormal levels of alpha-fetoprotein, an indicator of Down syndrome and other abnormalities of brain development, especially with other indicators (Mennuti & Driscoll, 2003).

Prenatal diagnostic techniques such as ultrasound, amniocentesis, CVS, preimplantation genetic diagnosis, and maternal blood sampling can provide tremendously important information when there is reason to suspect a problem. Yet most couples can look forward to immense relief when they are told that their babies are just fine.

dominance—that is, it does not mask all the effects of the recessive sickle-cell gene. Thus, carriers of the sickle-cell gene have many round blood cells and some sickle-shaped cells (see the photo on this page). When they are at high altitudes, are given anesthesia, or are otherwise deprived of oxygen, carriers may experience symptoms of sickle-cell disease—painful swelling of the joints and severe fatigue.

After providing the couple with this information, the genetic counselor might discuss prenatal screening procedures that can detect many genetic abnormalities prenatally. Three widely used techniques (amniocentesis, chorionic villus biopsy, and ultrasound), as well as the newer methods of preimplantation genetic diagnosis and maternal blood sampling, are described in the Explorations box on pages 66–67. For the parents whose tests reveal a normal embryo or fetus, the anxiety of undergoing the tests and waiting for the results gives way to relief. For parents who learn that their fetus has a

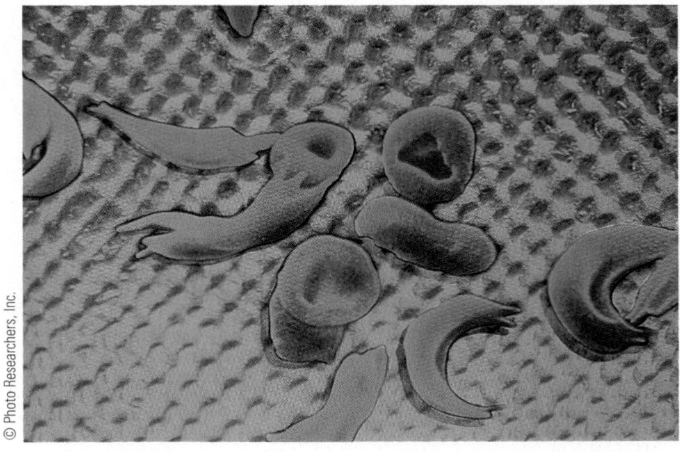

Sickle-shaped (elongated) and normal (round) blood cells from a carrier of the sickle-cell gene.

serious defect, the experience can be agonizing. The alternatives are abortion, which may be contrary to the couple's religious or personal beliefs, or the challenges of raising a child with a serious disorder. In the case of sickle-cell disease, a blood test is used to screen newborns for the disease, and affected children begin a life of treatment with blood transfusions and antibiotics to prevent infections (Davidson, 2002).

Now consider the issues surrounding **Huntington's disease,** a famous (and terrifying) example of a genetic defect associated with a single dominant gene. It typically strikes in middle age and steadily deteriorates the nervous system. Among the effects are motor disturbances such as slurred speech, an erratic and seemingly drunken walk, grimaces, and jerky movements; personality changes such as increased moodiness and irritability; and dementia or loss of cognitive abilities (Bishop & Waldholz, 1990; Sutton-Brown & Suchowersky, 2003). Any child of a parent with Huntington's disease is almost certain to develop the disease if she receives the dominant (but fortunately rare) Huntington's gene rather than its normal counterpart gene at conception; the risk for an individual who has a parent with Huntington's disease is therefore one out of two, or 50%. (You may wish to work the odds for yourself using the approach shown in Figure 3.1 on page 62)

In 1983, James Gusella and his colleagues applied emerging techniques for locating specific genes on specific chromosomes to study a large family with many cases of Huntington's disease and traced the gene for it to Chromosome 4 (Bishop & Waldholz, 1990). This discovery led to the development of a test to enable the relatives of Huntington's victims to find out whether or not they inherited the gene so that they would not have to spend a good part of their lives fearing the worst (Sutton-Brown & Suchowersky, 2003). Not all people at risk for Huntington's disease choose to take the Huntington's test, but many who do take it feel better knowing one way or the other what the future holds (Wiggins et al., 1992). Also, if one prospective parent has the gene and the couple wishes to have children, preimplantation genetic diagnosis (see page 67 of the Explorations box) can be used to test fertilized eggs for the presence of the gene, and the doctor can then implant only eggs without the gene in the mother's uterus. Unfortunately, researchers still do not understand the function of the Huntington's gene and cannot prevent brain deterioration in affected individuals. Progress in preventing and treating genetic disorders is being made rapidly, however, as you will see later. Meanwhile, we are ready to explore how heredity and environment contribute to important psychological differences among humans.

Summing Up

Each person inherits at conception a unique genetic makeup, or genotype, contained in his or her 30,000 some genes arranged along 23 pairs of chromosomes (including the sex chromosomes, XX or XY). Parent and child have 50% of their genes in common and siblings share 50% on average. The genotype influences actual traits (phenotype) through the mechanisms of single gene-pair, sex-linked, and polygenic inheritance. A few individuals are also powerfully affected by genetic mutations or by chromosome abnormalities such as Down (trisomy 21), Turner (XO), Klinefelter (XXY), and fragile X syndromes. Genetic counseling tells parents about their risks of having a child with a genetically based disorder; techniques of prenatal diagnosis include amniocentesis. ■

Studying Genetic and Environmental Influences

Behavioral genetics is the scientific study of the extent to which genetic and environmental differences among people or animals are responsible for differences in their traits (Plomin et al., 2001; Plomin et al., 2003). It is impossible to say that a given person's intelligence test score is the result of, say, 80%, 50%, or 20% heredity and the rest environment. The individual would have no intelligence without both genetic makeup and experiences. It is possible for behavioral geneticists to estimate the **heritability** of measured IQ and of other traits or behaviors. Heritability has a specific meaning: the proportion of all the variability in the trait within a large sample of people that can be linked to genetic differences among those individuals. To say that measured intelligence is *heritable,* then, is to say that differences in tested IQ within a particular group of people are to some degree attributable to the different genetic endowments of these individuals. It is critical to understand that estimates of heritability differ from study to study depending on what sample is studied and how (Maccoby, 2000).

It may seem from their title that *behavioral geneticists* tell us only about genetic contributions to development, but in fact their work tells us about the contributions of both genetic and environmental factors to differences among people. Variability in a trait that is not associated with genetic differences is associated with differences in experiences. How do behavioral geneticists gather evidence?

Experimental Breeding

To study the relative influence of genes and environment on animal behavior, behavioral geneticists sometimes design breeding experiments, much like those Gregor Mendel conducted to discover the workings of heredity in plants. For example, **selective breeding** involves attempting to breed animals for a particular trait to determine whether it is heritable. In a classic study, R. C. Tryon (1940) tested numerous rats for the ability to run a complex maze. Rats that made few errors were labeled *maze bright;* those that made many errors were termed *maze dull.* Then, across several generations, Tryon mated bright rats with bright rats and dull rats with dull rats. If differences in experience rather than differences in genetic makeup had accounted for maze performance differences in the first generation of rats studied, selective breeding would have had no effect. Instead, across generations, the differences in learning performance between the maze-bright and maze-dull groups of rats became increasingly larger. Tryon showed that maze-learning ability in rats is influenced by genetic makeup.

Selective breeding studies have also shown that genes contribute to such attributes as activity level, emotionality, aggressiveness, and sex drive in rats, mice, and chickens (Plomin et al., 2001). In recent years, researchers have been conducting experiments with animals that involve inserting a particular variant of a gene in cells or "knocking out" a normal gene and then determining the effect the gene has on functioning by comparing the manipulated animals with control animals (Wehner & Balogh, 2003). Because people do not take kindly to the idea of being selectively bred or having their genes knocked out by experimenters, such research cannot be done with humans. Instead, research on genetic influence in humans has relied primarily on determining whether the degree of genetic similarity between two people is associated with the degree of physical or psychological similarity between them.

Twin, Adoption, and Family Studies

Twins have long been recognized as important sources of evidence about the effects of heredity. A simple type of twin study involves determining whether identical twins reared together are more similar to each other in certain traits than fraternal twins reared together. If genes matter, identical twins should be more similar because they have 100% of their genes in common, whereas fraternal twins share only 50% on average.

Today, most sophisticated twin studies include not only identical and fraternal twin pairs raised together but also identical and fraternal twins reared apart—four groups in all, differing in both the extent to which they share the same genes and the extent to which they share the same home environment (Bouchard & Pedersen, 1999). Identical twins separated near birth and brought up in different environments—like the twins introduced at the beginning of the chapter—are particularly fascinating and informative because any similarities between them cannot be attributed to common family experiences.

However, the twin method has been criticized. Some have charged that identical twins are treated more similarly than fraternal twins and that their more similar environment contributes to their greater similarity. Identical twins *are* treated more similarly. However, there appears to be little relationship between how similarly twins are treated and how similar they turn out to be psychologically (Loehlin, 1992), and there is now accumulating evidence that the genetic similarity of twins causes them to be treated similarly (Reiss, 2003). Critics also charge that behavioral geneticists underestimate the role of prenatal influences and the possibility that identical twins are more psychologically similar than other siblings, even if they are separated after birth, because they shared the same womb (Devlin, Daniels, & Roeder, 1997). Finally, it has been charged that the twin method is more suited to identifying genetic influences than to identifying environmental ones. It asks whether twins who share 100% of their genes are more similar to one another than twins who share 50% of their genes, but it does not allow us to determine whether pairs of individuals who share the same environment are more similar than pairs who share 50% of their experiences (Turkheimer, 2000).

A second commonly used method is the adoption study. Are children adopted early in life similar to their biological parents, whose genes they share, or are they similar to their adoptive parents, whose environment they share? If adopted children resemble their biological parents in intelligence or personality, even though those parents did not raise them, genes must be influential. If they resemble their adoptive parents, even though they are genetically unrelated to them, a good case can be made for environmental influence. Like the twin method, the adoption method has proved useful in estimating the relative contributions of heredity and environment to individual differences, but it also has been criticized. Researchers must be careful to correct for the tendency of adoption agencies to place children in homes similar to those they were adopted from. Also, because adoptive homes are generally above-average environments, adoption studies may underestimate the effect on human differences of the full range of variation in the environments families provide for children (Stoolmiller, 1999).

Finally, more researchers are conducting complex family studies that include pairs of siblings who have different degrees of genetic similarity—for example, identical twins, fraternal twins, full biological siblings, half siblings, and unrelated siblings who live together in stepfamilies (Reiss, 2000; Segal, 2000). They are also measuring qualities of these family members' experiences to determine how similar or different the environments of siblings are. Researchers are even looking at all of this longitudinally so that they can assess the extent to which both genes and environment contribute to continuity and change in traits as individuals develop (Reiss, 2000).

Estimating Influences

Having conducted a twin, adoption, or family study, behavioral geneticists use statistical calculations to tell whether or not a trait is genetically influenced and to estimate the degree to which heredity and environment account for individual differences in the trait. When they study traits that a person either has or does not have (for example, a smoking habit or diabetes), researchers calculate and compare **concordance rates**—the percentage of pairs of people studied (for example, pairs of identical twins or adoptive parents and children) in which, if one member of a pair displays the trait, the other does, too. If concordance rates are higher for more genetically related than for less genetically related pairs of people, the trait is heritable.

Suppose researchers are interested in whether homosexuality is genetically influenced. They might locate gay men who have twins, either identical or fraternal, locate their twin siblings, and find out whether they, too, are gay. In one study of this type (Bailey & Pillard, 1991), the concordance rate for identical twins was 52% (29 of the 56 twins of gay men were also gay), whereas the concordance rate for fraternal twins was 22% (12 of 54 twins of gay men were also gay). This finding and others suggest that genetic makeup contributes to both men's and women's sexual orientation (Bailey, Dunne, & Martin, 2000). But notice that identical twins are *not* perfectly concordant. Environmental factors must also affect sexual orientation. After all, Bailey and Pillard found that, in 48% of the identical twin pairs, one twin was gay but the other was not, despite their identical genes.

When a trait can be present in varying degrees, as is true of height or intelligence, correlation coefficients rather than concordance rates are calculated (see Chapter 1). In a behavioral genetics study of IQ scores, a correlation would indicate whether the IQ score of one twin is systematically related to the IQ score of the other, such that if one twin is bright, the other is bright, and if one is not so bright, the other is not so bright. The larger the correlation for a group of twins, the closer the resemblance between members of twin pairs.

To better appreciate the logic of behavioral genetics studies, consider what Robert Plomin and his colleagues (Plomin et al., 1988) found when they assessed aspects of personality among twins in Sweden whose ages averaged 59. One of their measures assessed an aspect of emotionality—the tendency to be angry or quick tempered. The scale was given to many pairs of identical twins and fraternal twins—some pairs raised together, others separated near birth and raised apart. Correlations reflecting the degree of similarity between twins are presented in Table 3.3. From such data, behavioral geneticists can estimate the contributions of three factors to individual differences in emotionality: genes, shared environmental influences, and nonshared environmental influences.

1. *Genes.* In this example, genetic influences are clearly evident, for identical twins are consistently more similar in emotionality than fraternal twins are. The correlation of +0.33 for identical twins reared apart also testifies to the importance of genetic makeup. If identical twins grow up in different families, any similarity in their psychological traits must be caused by their genetic similarity. These data suggest that emotionality is heritable; about a third of the variation in emotionality in this sample can be linked to variations in genetic endowment.

2. *Shared environmental influences.* Individuals living in the same home environment experience **shared environmental influences,** common experiences that work to make them similar—for example, a common parenting style or exposure to the same toys, peers, schools, and neighborhood. Do you see evidence of shared environmental influences in the correlations in Table 3.3? Notice that both identical and fraternal twins are slightly more similar in emotionality if they are raised together than if they are raised apart (0.37 exceeds 0.33, 0.17 exceeds 0.09). However, these correlations tell us that shared environmental influences are weak: twins are almost as similar when they grew up in different homes as when they grew up in the same home.

3. *Nonshared environmental influences.* Experiences unique to the individual—those that are not shared by other members of the family and that work to make individuals different from each other—are referred to as **nonshared environmental influences.** Whether they involve being treated differently by parents, having different friends, undergoing different life crises, or even being affected differently by the same events, nonshared environmental influences make members of the same family different (Rowe, 1994). In Table 3.3, notice that identical twins raised together are not the same; even though they share 100% of their genes *and* the same family environment; a correlation of +0.37 is much lower than a perfect correlation of +1.00. Any differences between identical twins raised together must be either because of differences in their unique, or nonshared, experiences or because of errors in measuring the trait. Perhaps identical twins are treated differently somehow by their parents, friends, and teachers, or perhaps one twin experiences more stress than the other, and this results in differences in their degrees of emotionality. Anyone who has a brother or sister can attest that different children in the same family are not always treated identically by their parents. They do not have the same experiences outside the home, either.

Through twin, adoption, and family studies, then, researchers can learn about the contributions of genes, shared environment, and nonshared environment to similarities and differences among humans. Yet some developmentalists, because they believe that genetic and environmental influences are intertwined, fault the methods used by behavioral geneticists and their approach of trying to separate the contributions of nature and nurture (Lewontin, Rose, & Kamin, 1984; Gottlieb, 2002). We will return to these criticisms later.

Table 3.3 Correlations from a Twin Study of the Heritability of Angry Emotionality

	Raised Together	Raised Apart
Identical twin pairs	0.37	0.33
Fraternal twin pairs	0.17	0.09

By dissecting this table, you can assess the contributions of genes, shared environment, and nonshared environment to individual differences in angry emotionality.

Genes. Are identical twins more similar than fraternal twins? Yes: 0.37 is greater than 0.17, and 0.33 is greater than 0.09; therefore greater genetic similarity is associated with greater emotional similarity.

Shared environment. Are twins who grow up together more similar than twins raised apart? Only a small effect of shared environment is evident: 0.37 is slightly greater than 0.33, and 0.17 is slightly greater than 0.09.

Nonshared environment. Are identical twins raised in the same home dissimilar, despite sharing 100% of their genes and the same environment? Yes: a correlation of .37 is far less than a perfect correlation of 1.00, suggesting a good deal of nonshared environmental influence.

SOURCE: Plomin et al., 1988.

Molecular Genetics

The Human Genome Project, by providing a map of the human genome, has opened the door to exciting new approaches to studying genetic and environmental influence. **Molecular** genetics is the analysis of particular genes and their effects, including the identification of specific genes that influence particular traits and the comparison of animals or humans who have these specific genes with those who do not. Samples of DNA obtained from inside people's cheeks can be analyzed, for example, to identify how the genomes of people who have a particular condition or trait differ from the genomes of people who do not have it. Moreover, once a gene's location and role are known, it is possible to test a DNA sample for the presence of specific genes associated with a particular disease, disorder, or other trait (Kingston, 2002). As a result, researchers can study how people who have a particular variant of a gene differ from those who have different variants.

Methods based on molecular genetics are being used to identify the multiple genes that contribute to polygenic traits (Plomin et al., 2003). The goal is to say things such as "this gene accounts for 20% of the variation, and two other genes account for 10% of the variation each," in a phenotype or trait (for example, reading ability or depression). So far, analyses based on molecular genetics suggest that many genes contribute to each polygenic trait or disorder and that each gene makes only a small contribution (Plomin et al., 2003).

Much research is being done, for example, on a gene called *apolipoprotein E,* or *apoE.* One variant of apoE, apoE4, has been linked to a higher-than-normal risk of Alzheimer's disease, the most common cause of dementia in later life (Williams, 2003; also see Chapter 16). Although apoE4 is only one contributor to Alzheimer's disease and many Alzheimer's patients do not have it, researchers can now test research participants for the presence of apoE4, then study differences between individuals with the gene and individuals without it. In one such study (Hofer et al., 2002), elderly adults with the apoE4 gene showed greater memory deterioration over a 7-year period than did individuals without it, even though none of the participants had diagnosable Alzheimer's disease yet. Other researchers are finding that certain environmental factors such as head injury and a high cholesterol level increase the odds that a person with the apoE4 gene will develop Alzheimer's disease (Williams, 2003). It has not been possible to diagnose Alzheimer's disease definitively until after death. However, genetic research may soon make it possible to identify early, based on their genetic makeup and their cognitive functioning, people who will develop Alzheimer's disease and who can benefit from treatment (see Chapter 16).

Because it is possible to compare large samples of people who do or do not have particular gene variants, researchers may not need to rely as much in the future on studies of twins and adopted individuals. They will also be better able to answer questions about how specific genes and combinations of genes interact with specific environmental factors to shape development (Rowe, 2003; Hutchinson et al., 2004).

Summing Up

Behavioral genetics seeks to establish the heritability of traits (the percentage of variability in a trait that can be linked to genetic differences among individuals), as well as the contributions of shared environmental influences (forces that make individuals in the same family similar) and of the nonshared environmental influences (unique experiences that make family members different). Methods include selective breeding studies of animals and twin, adoption, and family studies of humans in which concordance rates and correlation coefficients are calculated. Today, techniques of molecular genetics are being used to analyze DNA samples to identify genes associated with particular traits and to compare people who do or do not have specific genes. ■

If you have brothers or sisters, do you think your parents treated you better or worse than they treated your sibling? If so, what might have been the effects of these nonshared environmental influences on your development?

Accounting for Individual Differences

Findings from behavioral genetics studies have dramatically changed and challenged the way people think about human development, as you will see throughout this book. We give a few examples here, drawn from studies of intellectual abilities, temperament and personality, and psychological disorders (see Plomin et al., 2001, 2003; Rowe, 1994, for reviews). Expect some surprises.

Intellectual Abilities

How do genes and environment contribute to differences in intellectual functioning, and how do their relative contributions change over the life span? Consider the average correlations between the IQ scores of different pairs of relatives presented in Table 3.4. These averages are primarily from a review by Thomas Bouchard Jr. and Matthew McGue (1981) of studies involving 526 correlations based on 113,942 pairs of children, adolescents, and adults. Clearly, these correlations increase when people are closely related genetically and are highest when they are identical twins. Overall, the heritability of IQ scores is about 0.50, meaning that genetic differences account for about 50% of the variation in IQ scores and environmental differences account for the other half of the variation in the samples studied (Plomin, 1990).

Can you detect the workings of environment? Notice that (1) pairs of family members reared together are somewhat more similar in IQ than pairs reared apart; (2) fraternal twins, who should have especially similar family experiences because they grow up at the same time, tend to be more alike than siblings born at different times; and (3) the IQs of adopted children are related to those of their adoptive parents. All of these findings suggest that *shared* environmental influences tend to make individuals who live together more alike than if they lived separately. Notice, however, that genetically identical twins reared together are not perfectly similar. This is evidence that their unique or *nonshared* experiences have made them different.

Do the contributions of genes and environment to differences in intellectual ability change over the life span? You might guess that genetic influences would decrease as people accumulate experience, but you would be wrong: genetic endowment appears to gain importance from infancy to adulthood as a source of individual differences in intellectual performance (McCartney, Harris, & Bernieri, 1990; McGue et al., 1993; Plomin & Spinath, 2004).

In a longitudinal study of identical and fraternal twins conducted by Ronald Wilson (1978, 1983), identical twins scored no more similarly than fraternal twins on a measure of infant mental development during the first year of life; thus, evidence of heritability was lacking in infancy. This may be because powerful maturational forces keep redirecting infants back to the same species-wide developmental pathway, regardless of specific genetic makeup or experiences (McCall, 1981). The influence of individual heredity began to show around 18 months of age. Identical twins even experienced more similar spurts in intellectual development than fraternal twins. The identical twins in the study stayed highly similar throughout childhood and into adolescence, the correlation between their IQ scores averaging about 0.85. Meanwhile, fraternal twins became *less* similar over the years; the correlation between their IQ scores had dropped to 0.54 by adolescence. As a result, the heritability of IQ scores increased from infancy to adolescence. The contribution of genes to individual differences in IQ remains high during adulthood and may be even greater in old age than earlier in life (Posthuma, de Geus, & Boomsma, 2003).

Table 3.4 Average Correlations between the IQ Scores of Pairs of Individuals

Family Pairs	Raised Together	Raised Apart
Identical twins	0.86	0.72
Fraternal twins	0.60	0.52
Biological siblings	0.47	0.24
Biological parent and child	0.42	0.22
Half siblings	0.31	—
Adopted siblings	0.34	—
Adoptive parent and adopted child	0.19	—
Unrelated siblings (same age, same home)	0.26	—

SOURCE: All but two of these averages were calculated by Bouchard and McGue (1981) from studies of both children and adults. The correlation for fraternal twins reared apart is based on data reported by Pedersen et al. (1985); that for unrelated children in the same home is based on data reported by Segal (2000).

Whereas the heritability of intelligence test performance increases with age, shared environmental influences become less significant with age, explaining about 30% of the variation in IQ in childhood but close to 0% in adulthood (McGue et al., 1993; Plomin & Spinath, 2004). Why might this be? Siblings may be exposed to similar (shared) learning experiences when they are young, but as they age, partly because of their different genetic makeups, they may seek and have different (nonshared) life experiences. They may elicit different reactions from their parents, join different peer groups, encounter different teachers, and so on.

Does this evidence of the heritability of IQ scores mean that we cannot improve children's intellectual development by enriching their environment? Not at all. True, the IQs of adopted children are, by adolescence, correlated more strongly with the IQs of their biological parents than with the IQs of their adoptive parents. However, the *level* of intellectual performance that adopted children reach can increase dramatically (by 20 points on an IQ test) if they are adopted into more intellectually stimulating homes than those provided by their biological parents (Scarr & Weinberg, 1978, 1983). Most likely, then, stimulating environments help children realize more fully their genetically based potentials. It is critical for parents, teachers, and others concerned with optimizing development to understand that genetically influenced qualities can still be altered.

Temperament and Personality

As parents know, different babies have different personalities. In trying to describe infant personality, researchers have focused on aspects of **temperament**—a set of tendencies to respond in predictable ways, such as sociability, activity level, and emotional reactivity, that serve as the building blocks of later personality (see Chapter 11 for a fuller description of temperament.) Behavioral genetics research indicates that genes contribute to individual differences in temperament in infancy and beyond (Ebstein, Benjamin, & Belmaker, 2003; Plomin et al., 2001).

For example, Arnold Buss and Robert Plomin (1984) reported average correlations from around 0.50 to 0.60 between

© Stockphoto.com/Richard Hirneisen

The temperament of infants is genetically influenced. (These twins look a bit wary.)

the temperament scores of identical twins. The corresponding correlations for fraternal twins were not much greater than zero. Think about that: a zero correlation is what you would expect if they were strangers living in different homes rather than fraternal twins who, on average, share half their genes, the same home, and often the same bedroom. It does not seem to matter whether researchers look at fraternal twin pairs, ordinary siblings, or unrelated children adopted into the same family; *living in the same home does not seem to make children more similar in personality* (Dunn & Plomin, 1990).

Similar conclusions have been reached about the contributions of genes and environment to adult personality (Loehlin et al., 1998; see also Chapter 11). Of all the differences among adults on major dimensions of personality, about 40% of the variation is attributable to genetic differences (Loehlin, 1985). Only 5% of the variation reflects the effects of shared family environment. Indeed, identical twins are about as similar in personality when they are raised apart as when they grow up in the same home (Bouchard et al., 1990). The remaining 55% of the variability in adult personalities is associated with nonshared environmental influences.

Herein lies a significant message: The family environment is important in personality development but usually not because it has a standard effect on all family members that makes them alike. Parents do appear to influence their children to adopt attitudes and interests similar to their own, at least while they are living at home (Eaves et al., 1997; Plomin et al., 2001). Shared environment also helps make adolescent siblings similar in the extent to which they engage in delinquent behavior (Rowe, 1994) and smoke, drink, and use other substances, more because of the influence of siblings on one another than because of parental influences (Hopfer, Crowley, & Hewitt, 2003). Yet behavioral geneticists have discovered repeatedly that environment often plays a more important role in creating differences among family members than in creating similarities among them (Reiss, 2000; Rowe, 1994). When it comes to many personality traits, unique, nonshared environmental influences rather than shared ones, along with genes, seem to be most significant.

Researchers who once assumed that parents molded all their children's personalities in similar directions are trying to figure out why brothers and sisters have such different personalities. It is increasingly clear that siblings are treated differently by their parents, experience their relationships with one another differently, and often have different experiences with peers, teachers, and other people outside the home (Dunn & Plomin, 1990; Reiss, 2000). But can researchers show that differences in experience are responsible for differences in personality? Sometimes. In one study of identical twins, for example, negative parental feelings toward and harsh discipline of one identical twin were linked to more acting out by that twin than by the twin treated more positively by parents (Asbury et al., 2003). Because identical twins have identical genes, this finding cannot be interpreted as an example of genes influencing parents' reactions to a child. These and other studies suggest the value of looking more closely at nonshared environmental influences. Developmentalists have assumed for too long that parents treat all their children much the same and steer them along similar developmental paths (Harris, 1998). Increasingly, it seems more useful to ask how genetic differences and nonshared experiences, both inside and outside the home, might explain differences in the development of brothers and sisters.

Psychological Disorders

As you will see throughout this book, both genes and environment contribute to psychological disorders across the life span—to alcohol and drug abuse, depression, attention deficit hyperactivity disorder, eating disorders, criminal behavior, and every other psychological disorder that has been studied (Plomin & McGuffin, 2003; State et al., 2000). Consider just one example. **Schizophrenia** is a serious mental illness that involves disturbances in logical thinking, emotional expression, and social behavior and that typically emerges in late adolescence or early adulthood. In the 1950s and 1960s, experts were convinced it was caused by mothers who were cold and inconsistent in their parenting style (Rowe & Jacobson, 1999). Now we know that genes contribute substantially to this disorder, although it is not yet clear which genes are most influential. The average concordance rate for schizophrenia among identical twins is 48%; that is, if one twin has the disorder, in 48% of the pairs studied, the other has it, too (Gottesman, 1991; Owen & O'Donovan, 2003). By comparison, the concordance rate for fraternal twins is only 17%. In addition, children who have at least one biological parent who is schizophrenic have an increased risk of schizophrenia *even if they are adopted away early in life* (Heston, 1970). Thus, the increased risk these children face has more to do with their genes than with being brought up by a schizophrenic adult.

It is easy to conclude, mistakenly, that any child of a schizophrenic is doomed to become a schizophrenic. But here are the facts: Whereas about 1% of people in the general population develop schizophrenia, about 13% of children who have a schizophrenic parent become schizophrenic (Gottesman, 1991; Cardno & Murray, 2003). So, although children of schizophrenics are at greater risk for schizophrenia than other children, 86 to 90% of the children of one schizophrenic parent do not develop the disorder. Even for the child of two parents with schizophrenia or for an identical twin whose twin develops the disorder, the odds of developing schizophrenia are only about one in two.

Clearly, then, environmental factors also contribute significantly to this mental illness. People do not inherit psychological disorders; they inherit *predispositions* to develop disorders. Genes and environment probably interact so that a person who has inherited a genetic susceptibility to schizophrenia will not develop the disorder unless he also has stressful experiences that trigger the illness—for example, is exposed to an infectious disease prenatally or experiences complications during delivery that result in oxygen deprivation (Cannon et al., 2003). Moreover, adopted children who have a biological parent with schizophrenia are at greater risk of developing schizophrenia if they grow up in a dysfunctional adoptive home than if they grow up in a healthy family environment (Wahlberg et al., 1997).

In short, you now know that children may inherit predispositions to develop several problems and disorders and that their experiences interact with their genetic makeup to determine how well adjusted they turn out to be. Such work also indicates that it is overly simple and often wrong to assume that any behavioral problem a child displays must be the result of bad parenting.

The Heritability of Different Traits

Although genes contribute to variation in virtually all human traits that have been studied, some traits are more heritable than others. Figure 3.4 presents some correlations obtained in the Minnesota Twin Study between the traits of identical twins raised apart and reunited later in life, and it makes our point.

Observable physical characteristics, from eye color to height, are strongly associated with individual genetic endowment. Even weight is heritable; adopted children resemble their biological parents but not their adoptive parents in weight (Grilo & Pogue-Geile, 1991). Certain aspects of physiology, such as measured brain activity and reactions to alcohol, are highly heritable, too (Lykken, Tellegen, & Iacono, 1982; Neale & Martin, 1989). In addition, genetic differences among older adults influence both levels of performance and changes in performance over time in markers of aging such as lung capacity and arterial blood pressure (Finkel et al., 2003a), and genes account for about half of the variation in susceptibility to diseases and death (Yashin, Iachine, & Harris, 1999; see also Chapter 17).

If physical and physiological characteristics are strongly heritable, general intelligence is moderately heritable. Somewhat less influenced by genes are aspects of temperament and personality and susceptibility to many psychological disorders. Genetic endowment contributes, but only modestly, to differences in attitudes and interests, which are influenced mainly by nonshared experiences (Olson et al.,

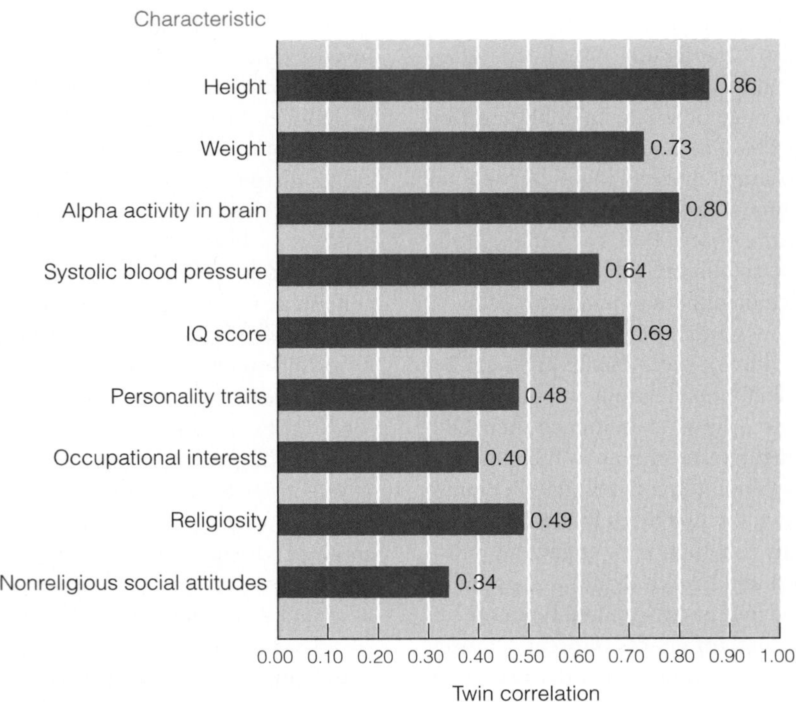

Figure 3.4 Correlations between the traits of identical twins raised apart in the Minnesota Twin Study.
SOURCE: Bouchard et al. (1990)

2001; Rowe, 1994). Finally, there is the occasional trait that does not seem to be influenced by genes. Creativity is an example. Identical twins are not much more alike than fraternal twins, so heritability is low. However, twins of both sorts are similar to one another, suggesting that the shared environment is somehow important in nurturing creativity, possibly because certain parents give their children a good deal of freedom to be inventive and others make their children color within the lines (Plomin et al., 2001; Reznikoff et al., 1973).

In sum, heredity influences physical traits more than psychological ones and influences a few traits, such as creativity, little. However, most psychological traits are heritable to some extent, with genes accounting for up to half of the variation in a group and environmental factors (shared environmental ones in childhood but more often nonshared environmental ones) accounting for the other half or more of the variation (Plomin et al., 2001; Wachs, 2000).

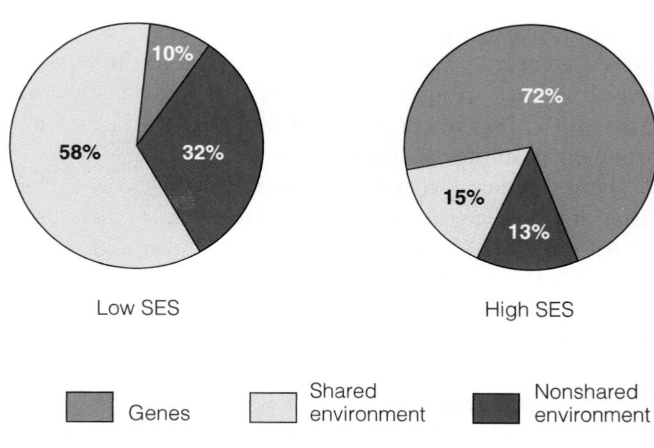

Figure 3.5 The proportions of variance in child IQ scores explained by genes, shared environment, and nonshared environment differ for children from low or high socioeconomic status (SES) environments.

SOURCE: Data are from Turkheimer et al. (2003)

Influences on Heritability

Researchers are becoming more aware that heritability is not a fixed quality; rather it varies depending on the sample studied. First, it varies in relation to the age of the sample, as you have already seen. In a particularly striking example of this, an eating disorders survey was administered to female twins who were age 11 and prepubertal, age 11 and pubertal, and age 17 and pubertal. Genes explained 54% of the variation in survey responses indicative of high risk for eating disorders among girls who had reached puberty but 0% among the 11-year-old girls who had not yet reached puberty. For prepubertal girls, shared environmental factors were the most important influence on responses (Klump, McGue, & Iacono, 2003). This study hints that genes that help trigger eating disorders in adolescence may be activated by the biochemical changes associated with puberty and may not be active before adolescence.

Second, heritability estimates differ depending on the environment of the individuals studied. Many classic twin and adoption studies involved children and adults from middle-class environments, and they showed that genetic differences among children have a lot to do with IQ differences. However, Eric Turkheimer and his colleagues (2003) recently studied the heritability of IQ in a sample that included many children from very low-income families as well as children from affluent homes. As shown in Figure 3.5, among children from wealthy families, genes accounted for 72% of the variation in IQ, whereas shared environment was not important—as in most previous studies. By contrast, genes explained only about 10% of the variation in IQ among children from poor families; instead, shared environmental influences accounted for almost 60% of the variation. One interpretation of this finding is that a deprived and unstimulating environment drags most children down, regardless of whether their genetic potential is high or low, but that some families living in poverty are able to offer a home environment that helps their children thrive despite their disadvantage. In more affluent environments, children may have more freedom to build niches that suit their genetically based predispositions and that then make them more or less intellectually inclined depending on their unique genetic makeup (Kendler, 2003). Whatever the explanation, it is clear that the heritability of a trait is not constant; it is affected by the age, socioeconomic status, and other qualities of the sample studied.

Summing Up

Behavioral genetics studies show that intellectual abilities are heritable and that the contribution of genes increases with age, whereas the contribution of shared environment decreases. Differences in infant temperament and adult personality are largely caused by genes and nonshared, but not shared, environment. Susceptibility to psychological disorders such as schizophrenia is also heritable, but it often takes a combination of genes and environmental stressors to produce a disorder. Physical and physiological characteristics are more strongly influenced by genes than are intellectual abilities and, in turn, personality and social attitudes; creativity does not seem to be heritable. Finally, heritability differs depending on the age and socioeconomic status of the sample studied. ■

Heredity and Environment Conspiring

What should you conclude overall about the influences of genes and environment and about the ways in which these two great forces in development conspire to make us what we are? Genes do not just orchestrate our growth before birth and then leave us alone. Instead, they are "turning on" and "turning off" in patterned ways throughout the life span, helping shape the attributes and behavioral patterns that we carry with us through our lives and changing their activity in response to environmental stimuli (Gottlieb, 2002). An evolved and shared species heredity makes us similar in the ways we develop and age. Unique individual genetic makeups cause us to develop and age in our own ways. No less important are environmental influences, from conception to death.

From infancy through childhood and adolescence, children's unique genetic potentials increasingly show themselves in their behavior. Identical twins start out similar and remain similar, but fraternal twins, like brothers and sisters generally, go their own ways and become increasingly dissimilar. Shared environmental influences—the forces that make children in the same family alike—are stronger early in life than they are later in life. Nonshared environmental influences—those unique experiences that make members of the family different—remain important throughout the life span. In short, as we move out of the home and into the larger world, we seem to become, increasingly, products of our unique genes and our unique experiences. But the two do not operate independently. Genes and environment are interrelated in interesting and important ways.

As you have seen throughout this chapter, behavioral geneticists try to establish how much of the variation observed in human traits such as intelligence can be attributed to individual differences in genetic makeup and how much can be attributed to individual differences in experience. Useful as that research is, it does not take you far in understanding the complex interplay between genes and environment over the life span (Turkheimer, 2000). As Ann Anastasi (1958) asserted years ago, instead of asking *how much* is because of genes and how much is because of environment, researchers should be asking *how* heredity and environment work together to make us what we are. With that in mind, consider the workings of gene–environment interactions and gene–environment correlations (Ge, Donnellan, & Harper, 2003; Rowe, 2003).

Gene–Environment Interactions

Genes do not determine anything; instead, they provide us with potentials that are realized or not depending on the quality of our experiences. Consider an interesting study using modern molecular genetics techniques. Avshalom Caspi and his colleagues (2003) sought to understand why stressful experiences cause some people but not others to become depressed. Using a large sample of New Zealanders who had been studied longitudinally, Caspi's team performed DNA analysis to determine which variants of a gene known to affect levels of the neurotransmitter serotonin in the brain each person in the sample had (serotonin has been linked to depression in previous research). They also administered surveys to measure the stressful events each person had experienced between ages 21 and 26, and whether, at age 26, each person reported a diagnosable case of depression in the past year. In Figure 3.6, you can see that genes matter (having genes that predispose a person to depression results in a slightly higher probability of depression overall than having genes that protect against depression). You also see that environment matters (overall, depression becomes more likely as the number of stressful events a person experiences increases).

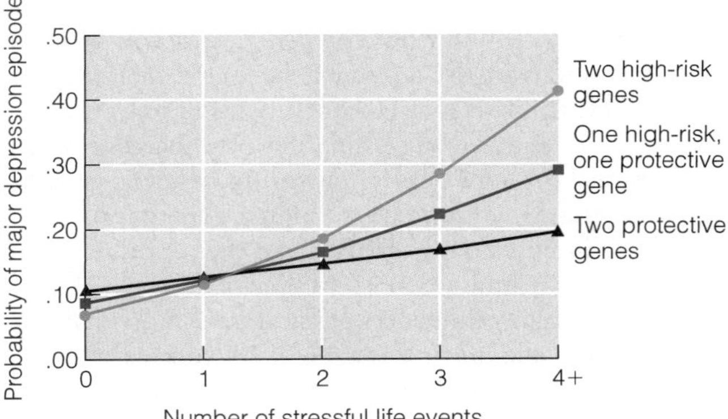

Figure 3.6 The odds of a depressive episode at age 26 are highest for individuals who: (1) inherit two genes known to increase the risk of depression rather than two genes known to protect against depression, and (2) experience four or more stressful life events between ages 21 and 26. This is an example of gene–environment interaction: the effects of genetic makeup on depression depend on how stressful a person's environment is, and the effects of stressful life events depend on the person's genotype.

SOURCE: Reprinted with permission from Caspi et al. (2003, July 18). Influences of life stress on depression. *Science, 301,* p 388, Figure 1B. Copyright © 2003 AAAS. http://www.sciencemag.org.

The real message in the figure, however, is embodied in the concept of **gene–environment interaction:** how our genotypes are expressed depends on what kind of environment we experience, and how we respond to environment depends on what kind of genes we have. In Figure 3.6, you see that individuals with two of the high-risk variants of the gene are more vulnerable to depression than people with two of the protective variants of the gene—but *only* if they experience multiple stressful events. By comparison, even multiple stressful events will not easily cause people with the protective genes to become depressed. Thus the genes people have make a difference only when an environment is stressful, and a stressful environment has an effect only on individuals with a genotype that predisposes them to depression. Genes and environment interact. It may turn out to be this way for many disorders: it may take a combination of high-risk genes and a high-risk environment to trigger problems (Caspi et al., 2003).

Gene–Environment Correlations

Each person's genetic makeup also influences the kinds of experiences she seeks and has. Sandra Scarr and Kathleen McCartney (1983), drawing on the theorizing of Robert Plomin, John DeFries, and John Loehlin (1977), have proposed three kinds of **gene–environment correlations,** or ways in which a person's genes and his environment or experiences are systematically interrelated: passive, evocative, and active. The concept of gene–environment *interactions* tells us that people with different genes react differently to the environments they encounter. By contrast, the concept of gene–environment *correlations* says that people with different genes encounter different environments (Loehlin, 1992). As an illustration, imagine children with a genetic potential to be highly sociable and other children whose genes make them shy.

Passive Gene–Environment Correlations

The kind of home environment that parents provide for their children is influenced partly by the parents' genotypes. Because parents provide children not only with a home environment but also with their genes, the rearing environments to which children are exposed are correlated with (and are likely to suit) their genotypes.

For instance, sociable parents not only transmit their "sociable" genes to their children but also, because they have "sociable" genes, create a social home environment—inviting their friends over frequently, taking their children to many social events, and so on. These children inherit genes for sociability, but they also experience an environment that matches their genes and that may make them more sociable than they would otherwise be. By contrast, the child with shy parents is likely to receive genes for shyness *and* a correlated environment—one without much social stimulation.

Evocative Gene–Environment Correlations

A child's genotype also *evokes* certain kinds of reactions from other people. The smiley, sociable baby is likely to get more smiles and social stimulation than the withdrawn, shy baby. Similarly, the sociable child may be sought more often as a playmate by other children, the sociable adolescent may be invited to more parties, and the sociable adult may be given more job assignments involving public relations. In short, genetic makeup may affect the reactions of other people to a child and, hence, the kind of social environment that the child will experience.

© Tim Pannell/CORBIS

If the son of a basketball player turns out to be a good basketball player, is it because of genetic endowment or experience? We cannot say because genes and environment are correlated. Through passive gene–environment correlation, the children of athletes not only inherit their parent's genes but also grow up in sports-oriented family environments.

Active Gene–Environment Correlations

Finally, children's genotypes influence the kinds of environments they *seek*. The individual with a genetic predisposition to be extraverted is likely to seek parties, invite friends to the house, join organizations, and otherwise build a "niche" that is highly socially stimulating. The child with genes for shyness may actively avoid large group activities and instead develop solitary interests.

Passive, evocative, and active genotype–environment correlations can all operate to influence a particular trait. However, Scarr and McCartney suggest that the balance of the three types of genotype–environment correlations shifts during development. Because infants are at home a good deal, their environment is largely influenced by their parents through passive genetic influences. Evocative influences operate throughout life; our characteristic, genetically influenced traits consistently prompt characteristic reactions in other people. Finally, as humans develop, they become increasingly able to build their own niches, so active gene–environment correlations become increasingly important.

Genetic Influences on Environment

Is there evidence supporting Scarr and McCartney's claim that people's genes are correlated with, and possibly influence, their experiences in life? Indeed. Behavioral geneticists are discovering that measures of environment are themselves heritable. What this means is that identical twins are more similar than fraternal twins, and biological siblings are more similar than adoptive siblings, in the environments they experience and in their perceptions of these environments, for example:

- Both objective and perceived aspects of parenting style, such as warmth and the quality of the parent–child relationship (Plomin & Bergeman, 1991; Reiss, 2003)
- Time spent watching television (Plomin et al., 1990)
- Number of stressful life events experienced (Kendler et al., 1993)

If our genetically influenced personality traits affect how others treat us and what experiences we seek and have, these findings make sense. For example, identical twins who are irritable and difficult could help create a conflict-ridden family environment, whereas calm and controlled children could help create a cohesive family environment, even if they are raised apart (Krueger, Markon, & Bouchard, 2003).

Such findings challenge some of our most fundamental assumptions about human development. After all, they say that what we regard as purely environmental influences on development partly reflect the workings of heredity (Reiss, 2000; Rowe, 1994). Robert Plomin (1990) suggests that we must question our assumptions. Suppose we find that parents who read to their children have brighter children than parents who do not read to their children. In the not-so-distant past, most developmentalists would have interpreted this finding rather uncritically as evidence that parents make important contributions to their children's intellectual development by reading to them. Without denying the importance of parents, suppose we offer this alternative interpretation: Parents and children whose genes predispose them to be highly intelligent are more likely to seek opportunities to read than parents and children who are less intellectually inclined. If this is the case, can we be so sure that reading to children *causes* them to be brighter? Would we be able to show that reading to children is beneficial even when the parents and children involved are genetically unrelated? One more example: If we observe that aggressive children tend to have parents who are negative and hostile toward them, can we be sure that the children's aggression is because of the experiences they have had growing up with negative parents? Is it not also possible that they inherited genes from their irritable and aggressive parents that predisposed them to be irritable and aggressive themselves (O'Connor et al., 1998)?

Perhaps the most convincing evidence of the importance of gene–environment correlations comes from an ambitious study by David Reiss, Jenae Neiderhiser, E. Mavis Hetherington, and Robert Plomin, summarized in their book, *The Relationship Code* (2000). The sample for this study consisted of 720 pairs of same-sex adolescents who differed in their degree of biological relationship from identical twins to biological siblings to unrelated stepsiblings. The researchers measured environmental factors such as parent–child and sibling–sibling interaction and adolescent adjustment variables such as self-esteem, sociability, depression, and antisocial behavior.

This major study suggested that family processes are important, but not for the reasons developmentalists have traditionally assumed. Family processes, Reiss and his colleagues argue, appear to be a mechanism through which the genetic code is expressed. Repeatedly, the study revealed that genes shared by parents and children partly or even largely accounted for relationships between children's experiences and their developmental outcomes—for example, between negative parenting tactics and antisocial behavior by adolescents. In 44 of 52 instances in which significant relationships between measures of the family environment and adolescent adjustment were detected, genes influenced both family environment and adolescent adjustment and accounted for most of the relationship between the two (Reiss & Neiderhiser, 2000).

This research suggests that genes and environment conspire to shape development. Genes influence how parents, peers, and others treat children. These environmental influences—usually nonshared ones that differ from sibling to sibling—then influence the individual's development, often working to reinforce genetically based predispositions (Lytton, 2000; Reiss, 2000). As a result, behavioral geneticists, who often emphasize the importance of genes, and socialization researchers, who stress the role of experiences in development, are both right. The practical implication is that caregivers sensitive to a child's genetically based predispositions will be in a good position to strengthen the child's adaptive tendencies and suppress or work around the maladaptive ones.

It is no surprise that identical twins look alike even as adults. Note that they often have similar facial expressions and stances.

Controversies Surrounding Genetic Research

Society will have to grapple with the complex and troubling ethical issues that have arisen as geneticists have gained the capacity to identify the carriers and potential victims of diseases and disorders, to give parents information that might prompt them to abort a pregnancy, and to experiment with techniques for altering the genetic code through gene therapy. As the Applications box on page 79 illustrates, applications of gene therapy to humans have not yet been successful but are likely to be pursued more vigorously as knowledge expands. Some observers worry about Nazi-like attempts to create a superrace of clones. For these and other reasons, genetic research is controversial and will remain so.

Likewise, behavioral genetics research is controversial among developmental scientists. On the one hand, it has provided some important insights into human development: that genes are important, that the unique experiences of siblings are more influential than those they share, that children influ-

Applications

Prevention and Treatment of Genetic Conditions

Ultimately, genetic researchers want to know how the damaging effects of genes associated with diseases and disorders can be prevented, cured, or at least minimized. One of the greatest success stories in genetic research involves **phenylketonuria (PKU),** a disorder caused by mutations in a single pair of recessive genes. Affected children lack a critical enzyme needed to metabolize phenylalanine, a component of many foods (including milk). As phenylalanine accumulates in the body, it is converted to a harmful acid that attacks the nervous system and causes children to be mentally retarded and hyperactive.

In the mid-1950s, scientists developed a special diet low in phenylalanine, and in 1961, they developed a simple blood test that could detect PKU soon after birth, before any damage had been done. Today, newborn infants are routinely screened for PKU, and affected children are immediately placed on the special (and, unfortunately, distasteful) diet (Miller, 1995). They must stay on it for their entire lives or risk deterioration in cognitive functioning (National Institutes of Health, 2000). Here, then, genetic research led to the prevention of one of the many causes of mental retardation. And here is a clear-cut example of the interaction between genes and environment: a child will develop the condition and become mentally retarded only if he inherits the PKU genes *and* eats a normal (rather than a special) diet.

Aided by information generated by the Human Genome Project, researchers are actively experimenting with **gene therapy**—interventions that involve substituting normal genes for the genes associated with a disease or disorder or otherwise altering a person's genetic makeup. In some experiments, viruses are used to carry normal replacement genes into an individual's cells (Hay, 2003; Hawley & Mori, 1999). Gene therapy experiments to treat such genetic disorders as hemophilia (through infusions of normal genes into the blood) and cystic fibrosis (using aerosol sprays to deliver normal genes to the lungs) are under way and are having some success (Driskell & Engelhardt, 2003; Hay, 2003; Walsh, 2003).

Yet progress in gene therapy has been slow because of a host of problems (Hay, 2003; Weiss, 2003a). The death of Jesse Gelsinger, a young man from Arizona who was the first person to die in a gene therapy trial, is illustrative. His immune system attacked the viruses that were to carry normal genes into his malfunctioning liver and destroyed not only the virus but his own organs (Fischer, 2000). This 1999 tragedy resulted in stricter controls on gene therapy research.

Although effective gene therapies undoubtedly will be developed, it is simpleminded to think that gene therapies will prevent or cure most diseases and disorders. Why? Because most conditions are the product of genes and environment interacting. Researchers not only must deliver the right genes to the body in sufficient number to have the desired effect but must get them to turn on and off when they should to produce normal functioning, which is influenced partly by the environment surrounding cells (Weiss, 2003a). Preventing or curing polygenic disorders such as schizophrenia will be especially hard because this will require a better understanding of how multiple genes *and* multiple environmental risk factors contribute to disorders. No "quick fix" such as the PKU diet will be possible. Still, the pace of breakthroughs in gene therapy research will increase, and societies must grapple with the ethical issues these advances raise (Petersen & Bunton, 2002).

Gene therapy experiments with mice promise to yield treatments that could benefit humans.

ence parents just as parents influence children. Nonetheless, many respected researchers continue to question the validity of some behavioral genetics research surveyed in this chapter. They believe that techniques for calculating heritability attribute too much importance to genes and too little to environment because they credit to genes some variance caused by a combination of genetic and environmental influence (McCartney, 2003; van Os & Sham, 2003). They doubt that the influences of genes and environment on individual differences can ever be cleanly separated and maintain that parents have far more important effects on their children's development than some behavioral geneticists acknowledge (Collins et al., 2000; Lerner, 2003). They also emphasize that behavioral genetics research tells us little about what we should really want to understand: the long and complex process through which genotypes are translated into phenotypes (Gottlieb, 2003).

Still, parents may be in a better position to be good parents if they understand their children's genetically based predispositions and how to respond appropriately to them. Providing children with optimal experiences depends on knowing which environments stimulate healthy development and which do not. It is fitting, then, that the next chapter takes a closer look at early environmental influences on development.

Summing Up

Both genes and environment are at work over the life span, but from infancy to adolescence genetic influences gain importance and shared environmental influences become less significant. Genes help determine not only how we respond to experiences (through gene–environment interactions) but also what experiences we have (through passive, evocative, and active gene–environment correlations). Now you can understand why today's developmentalists regard it as foolish to ask whether nature *or* nurture is responsible for human development. People are shaped by an incredibly complex interplay of genetic and environmental influences from conception to death. ■

Summary Points

1. As humans, we share a species heredity that, as Darwin's theory of evolution holds, is the product of the natural selection of traits over the course of evolution. Species heredity and cultural evolution make some aspects of development and aging universal.

2. Each human also has an individual heredity provided at conception, when sperm and ovum, each with 23 chromosomes because of meiosis, unite to form a single-cell zygote with 46 chromosomes, containing some 30,000 genes mapped by the Human Genome Project.

3. The genetic basis for development is not completely understood, but we know that genes provide a "code" that influences, with environmental factors, how cells are formed and how they function; that regulator DNA turns genes "on" and "off" throughout the life span; and that environmental factors influence how a genotype (genetic makeup) is translated into a phenotype (actual traits).

4. There are three main mechanisms of inheritance: single gene-pair inheritance, sex-linked inheritance, and polygenic (multiple gene) inheritance. Most important human traits are influenced by polygenic inheritance. Some children are also affected by noninherited changes in gene structure (mutations); others, because of errors in meiosis, have chromosome abnormalities. Genetic counseling offers information and guidance to people at risk for genetic conditions, and abnormalities can be detected prenatally through amniocentesis, chorionic villus sampling, ultrasound, and preimplantation genetic diagnosis.

5. Behavioral genetics researchers conduct twin, adoption, and other family studies that describe resemblances between pairs of people using concordance rates and correlation coefficients. They then estimate the heritability of traits and the contributions of shared and nonshared environmental influences. More recently, they are using molecular genetics to identify and study particular genes and their implications.

6. Performance on measures of intelligence is a heritable trait. Infant mental development is strongly influenced by a species-wide maturational plan, but over the course of childhood and adolescence, individual differences in mental ability more strongly reflect both individual genetic makeup and nonshared environmental influences.

7. Aspects of temperament, such as emotionality, and personality are also genetically influenced; shared environmental influences on personality are minimal. Similarly, psychological disorders such as schizophrenia have a genetic basis.

8. Overall, physical and physiological characteristics are more strongly influenced by individual genetic endowment than are intellectual abilities and, in turn, personality traits or social attitudes. In addition, certain traits such as creativity do not seem to be genetically influenced.

9. Overall, both genes and nonshared environmental influences are influential over the life span, whereas shared environmental influences become less important after childhood. Gene–environment interactions mean that environment influences how genes are expressed and that genes influence how people react to their environment. Passive, evocative, and active gene–environment correlations suggest that people experience and seek environments that match and reinforce their genetic predispositions.

Critical Thinking

1. Hairy knee syndrome (we made it up) is caused by a single dominant gene, *H*. Using diagrams such as those in Figure 3.1 and Figure 3.2, figure out the odds that Herb (who has the genotype *Hh*) and Harriet (who also has the genotype *Hh*) will have a child with hairy knee syndrome. Now repeat the exercise, but assume that hairy knee syndrome is caused by a recessive gene, *h*, and that both parents again have an *Hh* genotype.

2. Suppose you want to find out how much genetic endowment influences the shyness of adolescents. Sketch two behavioral genetics studies that could be conducted to answer this question, and indicate what they would be able to tell you about the contributions of genes, shared environment, and nonshared environment to shyness.

3. Researchers have found evidence that children who are physically punished by their parents tend to behave more aggressively around their peers than children who are not. What explanation for this finding might a social cognitive learning theorist such as Albert Bandura (Chapter 2) propose? What alternative explanations does research on behavioral genetics, including work on gene–environment correlations, suggest?

4. Alan's biological mother developed schizophrenia and was placed in a mental hospital when he was only 1 year old. He grew up with his father and stepmother (neither of whom had psychological disorders) from then on. Based on the material in this chapter, what would you tell Alan about his chances of becoming schizophrenic if you were a genetic counselor?

Key Terms

species heredity, 56
natural selection, 57
conception, 57
zygote, 57
chromosome, 57
Human Genome Project, 58
meiosis, 58
mitosis, 58
crossing over, 59
identical twins, 59
fraternal twins, 60
X chromosome, 60
Y chromosome, 60
karyotype, 60
genotype, 61
phenotype, 61
single gene-pair inheritance, 61
dominant gene, 61
recessive gene, 61
incomplete dominance, 61
codominance, 61
sex-linked characteristic, 62
hemophilia, 62
polygenic trait, 62
mutation, 63
sickle-cell disease, 63
chromosome abnormalities, 63
Down syndrome, 63
Turner syndrome, 64
Klinefelter syndrome, 64
fragile X syndrome, 64
genetic counseling, 65
cystic fibrosis, 65
Tay-Sachs disease, 65
carrier, 66
ultrasound, 66
amniocentesis, 66
chorionic villus sampling (CVS), 67
preimplantation genetic diagnosis, 67
maternal blood sampling, 67
Huntington's disease, 68
behavioral genetics, 68
heritability, 68
selective breeding, 68
concordance rate, 69
shared environmental influences, 70
nonshared environmental influences, 70
molecular genetics, 70
temperament, 72
schizophrenia, 73
gene–environment interaction, 76
gene–environment correlation, 76
phenylketonuria (PKU), 79
gene therapy, 79

Media Resources

Websites to Explore

Visit Our Website
For a chapter tutorial quiz and other useful features, visit the book's companion website at *http://psychology.wadsworth.com/sigelman_rider5e*. You can also connect directly to the following sites:

The Human Genome Project
The Human Genome Project is an international research effort aimed at characterizing the makeup of all 46 human chromosomes by mapping sequences of their DNA. For a look at how this is done, as well as the latest in efforts to understand and prevent genetic defects and diseases, check out the website for the National Human Genome Research Institute.

Genetic Education and Counseling
The Genetics Education Center at the University of Kansas Medical Center also has a website with a wealth of good materials on the Human Genome Project and on genetic disorders and conditions. It is aimed at educators and genetic counselors. Among its features are a glossary of genetic terms; a page on the ethical, legal, and social implications of genetic research; and up-to-date information about the Human Genome Project.

Cracking the Code of Life
This Public Broadcasting Service (PBS) program, originally aired on *NOVA* in April 2001, chronicles the race to complete the human genome map. You can watch the entire 2-hour program on its companion website, which contains links for learning more about DNA sequencing, exploring the issues surrounding genetic manipulation, and revisiting the nature versus nurture debate.

GeneTests
To learn about a particular disease and its diagnosis and symptoms and to find whether a test for it exists, consult GeneTests, which, although aimed at doctors, is readable. Click on "Gene Reviews" and search for a disease.

Huntington's Disease
For a closer look at this devastating and deadly disease caused by a single dominant gene, visit the website of the Huntington's Disease Advocacy Center. Stories of people who have lived with Huntington's disease, as well as recent news and research findings, are provided. Under the link to "Answers to HD Questions," the etiology of Huntington's disease is explained.

Sickle-Cell Disease
The American Sickle Cell Anemia Association's website has much information about this disease of special interest to African Americans.

Understanding the Data: Exercises on the Web

For additional insight on the data presented in this chapter, try the exercises for these figures at *http://psychology.wadsworth.com/sigelman_rider5e:*

Table 3.4 Average Correlations between the IQ Scores of Pairs of Individuals

Figure 3.5 The proportions of variance in child IQ scores explained by genes, shared environment, and nonshared environment differ for children from low or high socioeconomic status (SES) environments

Figure 3.6 The odds of a depressive episode at age 26 are highest for individuals who: (1) inherit two genes known to increase the risk of depression rather than two genes known to protect against depression, and (2) experience four or more stressful life events between ages 21 and 26. This is an example of gene–environment interaction: the effects of genetic makeup on depression depend on how stressful a person's environment is, and the effects of stressful life events depend on the person's genotype

Life-Span CD-ROM

Go to the Wadsworth Life-Span CD-ROM for further study of the concepts in this chapter. The CD-ROM includes narrated concept overviews, video clips, a multimedia glossary, and additional activities to expand your learning experience. For this chapter, check out the following clip, and others, in the video library:

VIDEO Environmental Influences on Early Brain Development

Developmental PsychologyNow is a web-based, intelligent study system that provides a complete package of diagnostic quizzes, a personalized study plan, integrated multimedia elements, and learning modules. Check it out at *http://psychology.wadsworth.com/sigelman_rider5e/now.*

CHAPTER four

Prenatal Development and Birth

Prenatal Development

Conception

Prenatal Stages

- The Germinal Period
- The Embryonic Period
- The Fetal Period

Prenatal Environment

Teratogens

- Drugs
- Diseases
- Environmental Hazards

The Mother's State

- Age
- Emotional Condition
- Nutritional Condition

The Father's State

Perinatal Environment

Possible Hazards

- Anoxia
- Complicated Delivery
- Medications

The Mother's Experience

- Cultural Factors
- Postnatal Depression

The Father's Experience

Neonatal Environment

Identifying At-Risk Newborns

Risk and Resilience

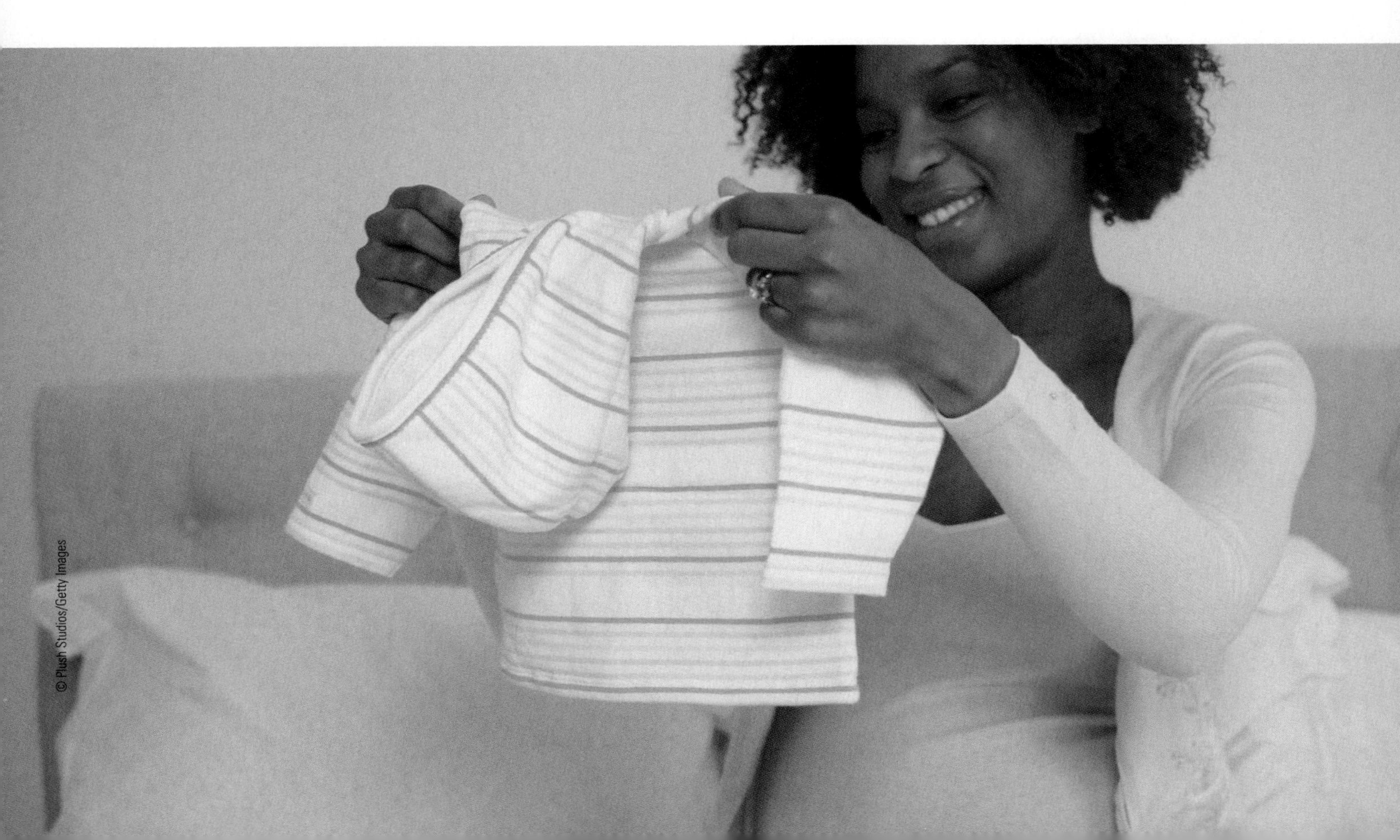

ON SEPTEMBER 11, 2001, Florence Engoran, 4 months pregnant, was stepping off the elevator on the 55th floor of the south tower of the World Trade Center when she realized something was terribly wrong. She made it down the 55 flights of stairs, the last 20 in darkness and surrounded by thick clouds of dust, following the impact of United Airlines flight 175. After reaching the street, Engoran ran alongside others trying to escape the falling debris following the collapse of the huge building until she fainted and was taken to a hospital. Despite a few contractions that day, attributed to stress and dehydration, Engoran carried her baby to term. For weeks, though, she experienced anxiety related to the events of that day.

What are the possible effects of prenatal exposure to maternal stress? How might Engoran's daughter Emily be affected by her mother's exposure to the dust, debris, and asbestos released that day? These are the sorts of questions that we address in this chapter as we explore first prenatal development and then the environment of the womb.

Prenatal Development

Perhaps at no time in the life span does development occur faster, or is environment more important, than between conception and birth. What maturational milestones normally occur during this period?

Conception

Midway through the menstrual cycle, every 28 days or so, females ovulate: An ovum (egg cell) ripens, leaves the ovary, and begins its journey through the fallopian tube to the uterus. Usually the egg disintegrates and leaves the body as part of the menstrual flow. However, if the woman has intercourse with a fertile man around the time of ovulation, the 300 million or so sperm cells in his seminal fluid swim, tadpole style, in all directions. Of the 300 to 500 sperm that survive the long, 6-hour journey into the fallopian tubes, 1 may meet and penetrate the ovum on its descent from the ovary (Sadler, 2004; see also Figure 4.1). Once this 1 sperm penetrates the egg cell, a biochemical reaction occurs that repels other sperm and keeps them from entering the already fertilized egg. As explained in

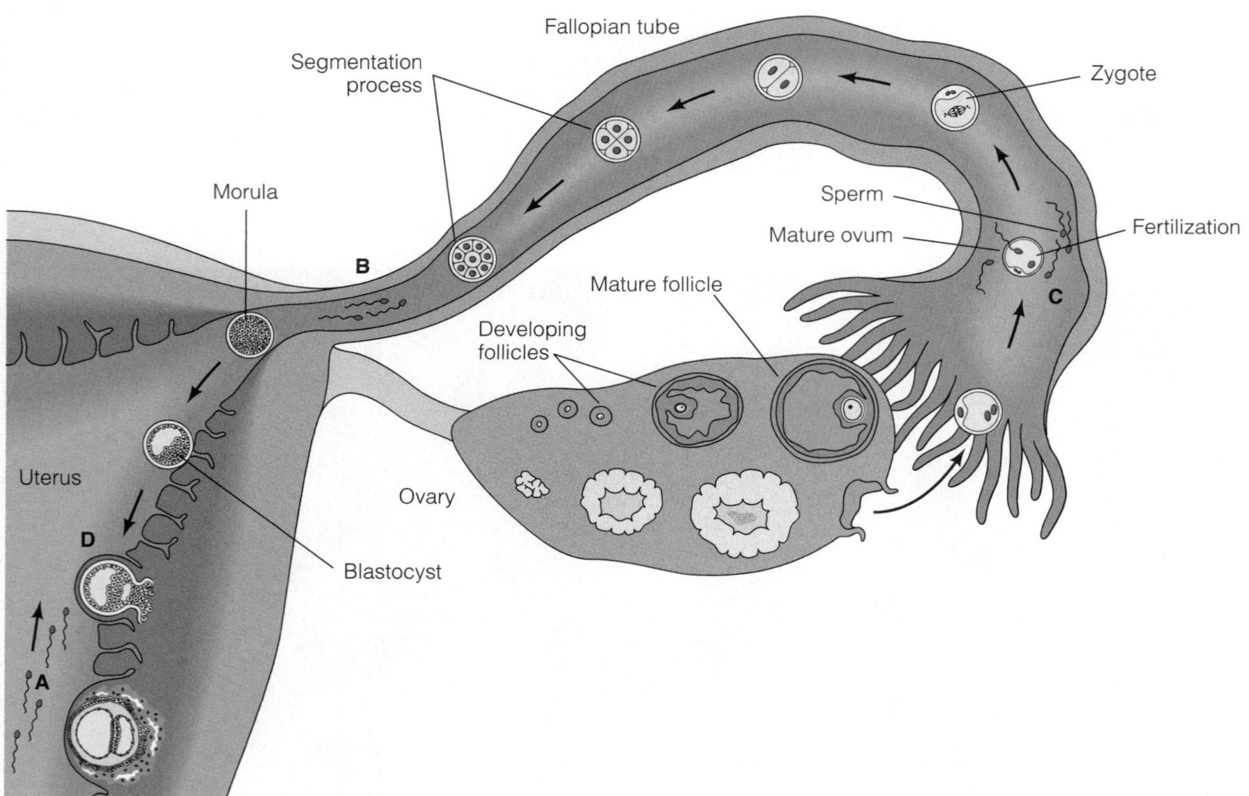

Figure 4.1 Fertilization and implantation. (A) Millions of sperm cells have entered the vagina and are finding their way into the uterus. (B) Some spermatozoa are moving up the fallopian tube (there is a similar tube on the other side) toward the ovum. (C) Fertilization occurs. The fertilized ovum drifts down the tube, dividing and forming new cells as it goes, until it implants itself in the wall of the uterus (D) by the seventh or eighth day after fertilization.

Chapter 3, conception, the beginning of life, occurs when the genetic material of the sperm and egg unite to form a single-celled zygote. The process may sound simple, but, as you can see in the Explorations box on this page, many couples cannot conceive a child, much as they want to, and seek medical help.

Prenatal Stages

The zygote contains the 46 chromosomes that are the genetic blueprint for the individual's development. It takes about 266 days (about 9 months) for the zygote to become a fetus of bil-

Explorations

Reproductive Technologies: New Conceptions of Conception

Many couples have no trouble conceiving children, but approximately 8% experience difficulties conceiving a child despite desperately wanting one. Infertility is equally likely to be traced to the man as the woman and stems from a variety of causes. For example, adolescents and adults who have contracted sexually transmitted diseases may become infertile (Steinberg et al., 1998). Many of these couples turn to **assisted reproduction technologies (ARTs)** to try to have a child. Some couples are helped in relatively simple ways. A man may be advised to wear looser pants and underwear (because an unusually high temperature in the testes interferes with sperm production). A woman may be asked to take her temperature to determine when she ovulates and is therefore most likely to become pregnant.

When simpler methods fail, some couples move on to more elaborate (and expensive) technologies. These typically start with or include prescription drugs for the woman to stimulate her ovaries to produce more eggs. Although this is the least invasive and least expensive ART, it has recently come under fire because of its connection to multiple births (Gleicher et al., 2000). Several highly visible cases of multiple births—Kenny and Bobbi McCaughey's septuplets in 1997 and Iyke Louis Udobi and Nkem Chukwu's octuplets in December 1998—resulted after the mothers had taken "fertility drugs." Chukwu's eight babies all weighed less than 2 pounds at birth (the smallest one—just over 10 ounces—died soon after birth) and racked up medical bills of about $400,000 each before going home (Nichols, 1999). Health problems are likely with such births. Two of the McCaughey children, for example, suffer from cerebral palsy. The health of Chukwu's surviving children is unknown.

To reduce the chances of such risky higher-order multiple births, many physicians suggest "selective reduction" in which some embryos are aborted to improve the outcome for the remaining embryos. Both Chukwu and the McCaugheys refused this option for personal or religious reasons. However, when Zoe Efsthatiou of Cyprus conceived 11 babies using fertility drugs, she elected to reduce the number to 4.

Another ART is **artificial insemination,** which involves injecting sperm, either from a woman's partner or from a donor, into her uterus. In **in vitro fertilization (IVF),** several eggs are removed from a woman's ovary, fertilized by sperm in a Petri dish in the laboratory, then transferred to the woman's uterus in hopes that one will implant on the wall of the uterus. The first such "test tube baby" was Baby Louise, born in England in 1978. Many variations of IVF are possible, depending on who provides the eggs and the sperm. A couple wanting to have a child (the would-be biological mother and father) could donate both eggs and sperm. At the other extreme, an infant conceived through IVF could wind up with five "parents": a sperm donor, an egg donor, a surrogate mother in whom the fertilized egg is implanted, and a caregiving mother and father (Beck, 1994). Couples who seek IVF had better bring their checkbooks; it costs at least $10,000 a try and is successful only about one time out of five (Kowalski, 2000).

What are the implications for the new family of using IVF and other reproductive technologies? Infertile couples may experience many heartbreaks in their quest for parenthood if try after try fails. But what if they succeed? To find out, Chun-Shin Hahn and Janet DiPietro (2001) compared mother–child pairs in which the children were conceived through IVF with mother–child pairs in which the children were conceived the usual way. The children were ages 3 to 7 at the time of the study, and mothers and teachers completed a variety of measures assessing developmental outcomes of the children.

The two groups of mothers were remarkably similar in their parenting behaviors, and the two groups of children were similar in their behaviors. Teachers thought that the IVF mothers were more openly affectionate with their children. And IVF mothers reported greater protectiveness toward their children, possibly because they had tried so hard and paid so much to become parents and undoubtedly wanted their children very much. In other research, parents reported caring just as much for children conceived with the help of someone else's sperm or egg (and therefore genetically unrelated to them) as for children conceived through IVF using their own sperm and egg (Golombok et al., 1995).

Thus, children conceived through today's reproductive technologies do not appear to be handicapped by their unique start in life, but they also do not seem to benefit from their parents' greater emotional involvement with them. Ultimately, how a child is conceived may be inconsequential relative to how a child is raised.

lions of cells that is ready to be born. This prenatal development is divided into three stages or periods: the germinal period, the embryonic period, and the fetal period.

The Germinal Period

The **germinal period** lasts approximately 2 weeks; the important events of this period are outlined in Table 4.1. For the first week or two, the zygote divides many times through mitosis, forming the **blastocyst,** a hollow ball of cells about 150 cells that is the size of the head of a pin. When the blastocyst reaches the uterus around day 6, it implants tendrils from its outer layer into the blood vessels of the uterine wall. This is quite an accomplishment; only about half of all fertilized ova are successfully implanted in the uterus. In addition, not all implanted embryos survive the early phases of prenatal development. Approximately 15% of recognized pregnancies end in miscarriage, and many unrecognized pregnancies—perhaps as many as 50%—are believed to terminate with miscarriage (Sadler, 2004). Many of these early losses are because of genetic defects.

The Embryonic Period

The **embryonic period** occurs from the third to the eighth week after conception. During this short time, every major organ takes shape, in at least a primitive form, in a process called **organogenesis.** The layers of the blastocyst differentiate, forming structures that sustain development. The outer layer becomes both the **amnion,** a watertight membrane that fills with fluid that cushions and protects the embryo, and the **chorion,** a membrane that surrounds the amnion and attaches rootlike extensions called *villi* to the uterine lining to gather nourishment for the embryo. The chorion eventually becomes the lining of the **placenta,** a tissue fed by blood vessels from the mother and connected to the embryo by the **umbilical cord.** Through the placenta and umbilical cord, the embryo receives oxygen and nutrients from the mother and eliminates carbon dioxide and metabolic wastes into the mother's bloodstream. A membrane called the *placental barrier* allows these small molecules to pass through, but it prevents the large blood cells of embryo and mother from mingling. It also protects the developing child from many harmful substances, but as you will see shortly, it is not infallible; some dangerous substances slip through.

Table 4.1 Events of the Germinal Period

Day	Event
1	Fertilization usually occurs within 24 hours of ovulation.
2	The single-celled zygote begins to divide 24–36 hours after fertilization.
3–4	The mass has 16 cells and is called a morula; it is traveling down the fallopian tube to the uterus.
5	An inner cell mass forms; the entire mass is called a blastocyst and is the size of a pinhead.
6–7	The blastocyst attaches to the wall of the uterus.
8–14	The blastocyst becomes fully embedded in the wall of the uterus. It now has about 250 cells.

Table 4.2 Events of the Embryonic Period

Week	Event
3	Now an embryo, the person-to-be is just 1/10 of an inch (2 mm) long. It has become elongated, and three layers emerge—the ectoderm, mesoderm, and endoderm.
4	The embryo is so curved that the two ends almost touch. The outer layer (ectoderm) folds into the neural tube. From the mesoderm, a tiny heart forms and begins to beat. The endoderm differentiates into a gastrointestinal tract and lungs. Between days 21 and 28, eyes develop.
5	Ears, mouth, and throat take shape. Arm and leg buds appear. The handplate from which fingers will emerge appears. The heart divides into two regions, and the brain differentiates into forebrain, midbrain, and hindbrain.
6–7	The embryo is almost 1 inch long. The heart divides into four chambers. Fingers emerge from the handplate, and primitive facial features are evident. The important process of sexual differentiation begins.
8	Most structures and organs are present. Ovaries and testes are evident. The embryo begins to straighten and assumes a more human appearance.

Meanwhile, the cells in the interior of the blastocyst give rise to the ectoderm, mesoderm, and endoderm. These will eventually evolve into specific tissues and organ systems, including the central nervous system (brain and spinal cord) from the ectoderm; muscle tissue, cartilage, bone, heart, arteries, kidneys, and gonads from the mesoderm; and gastrointestinal tract, lungs, and bladder from the endoderm (Sadler, 2004).

Development proceeds at a breathtaking pace (see Table 4.2). The beginnings of a brain are apparent after only 3 to 4 weeks, when the neural plate folds up to form the neural tube (see Figure 4.2). The bottom of the tube becomes the spinal cord. "Lumps" emerge at the top of the tube and form the forebrain, midbrain, and hindbrain (see Figure 4.3). The so-called primitive or lower portions of the brain develop earliest. They regulate such biological functions as digestion, respiration, and elimination; they also control sleep–wake states and permit simple motor reactions. These are the parts of the brain that make life possible.

In as many as 5 out of 1000 pregnancies, the neural tube fails to fully close (Birnbacher, Messerschmidt, & Pollak, 2002). When this happens at the bottom of the tube, it can lead to spina bifida, in which part of the spinal cord is not fully encased in the protective covering of the spinal column. Failure to close at the top of the neural tube can lead to anencephaly, in which the main portion of the brain above the brain stem fails to develop, or encephalocele, in which a por-

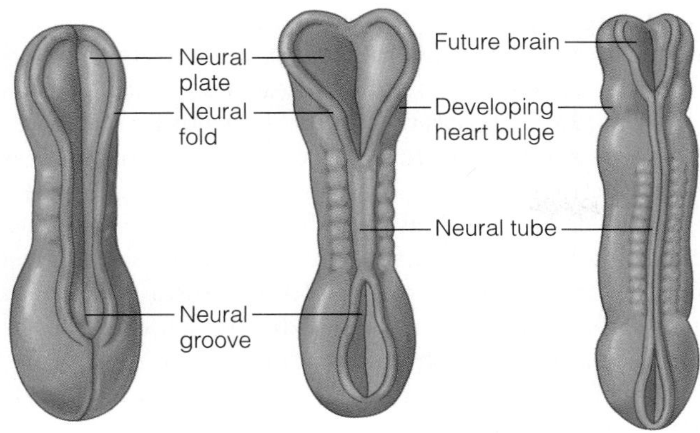

Figure 4.2 The nervous system emerges from the neural plate, which thickens and folds to form the neural groove. When the edges of the groove meet, the neural tube is formed. All of this takes place between 18 and 26 days after conception.

tion of the brain protrudes from the skull. Neural tube defects are more common when the mother is deficient in folic acid, illustrating the importance to development of good maternal nutrition (Hall, 2000). We will have more to say about nutrition in a later section.

Other critical organs are also taking shape. Just 4 weeks after conception, a tiny heart not only has formed but also has begun to beat. The eyes, ears, nose, and mouth rapidly take shape in the second month, and buds appear that will become arms and legs. During the second month, a primitive nervous system also makes newly formed muscles contract. Only 60 days after conception, at the close of the embryonic period, the organism is a little over an inch long and has a distinctly human appearance.

The important process of sexual differentiation begins during the seventh and eighth prenatal weeks. First, undifferentiated tissue becomes either male testes or female ovaries: If the embryo inherited a Y chromosome at conception, a gene on it calls for the construction of testes; in a genetic female with two X chromosomes, ovaries form instead. The testes of a male embryo secrete **testosterone,** the primary male sex hormone that stimulates the development of a male internal reproductive system, and another hormone that inhibits the development of a female internal reproductive system. In the absence of these hormones, the embryo develops the internal reproductive system of a female.

Clearly, the embryonic period is dramatic and highly important because it is when the structures that make us human evolve. Yet most pregnant women, either because they do not yet know they are pregnant or do not appreciate the value of early prenatal care, do not go to a doctor until *after* the eighth week of prenatal development, too late to prevent the damage that can be caused by an unhealthy lifestyle.

The Fetal Period

The **fetal period** lasts from the ninth week of pregnancy until birth (see Table 4.3). Proliferation of neurons continues at a

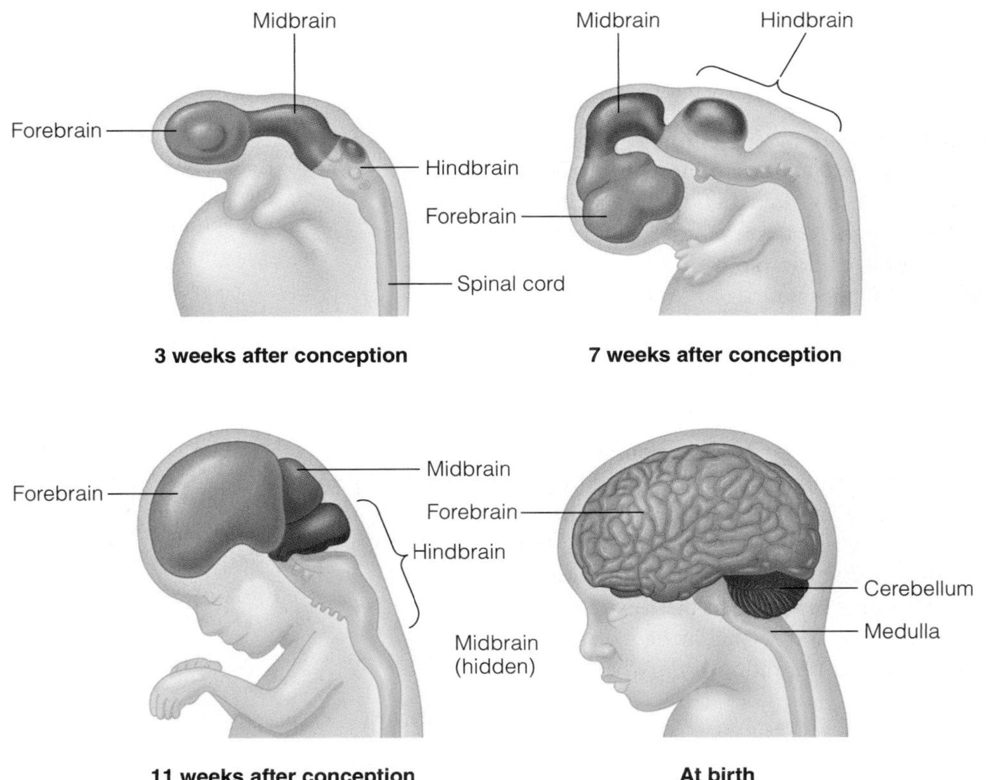

Figure 4.3 The brain at four stages of development, showing hindbrain, midbrain, and forebrain.

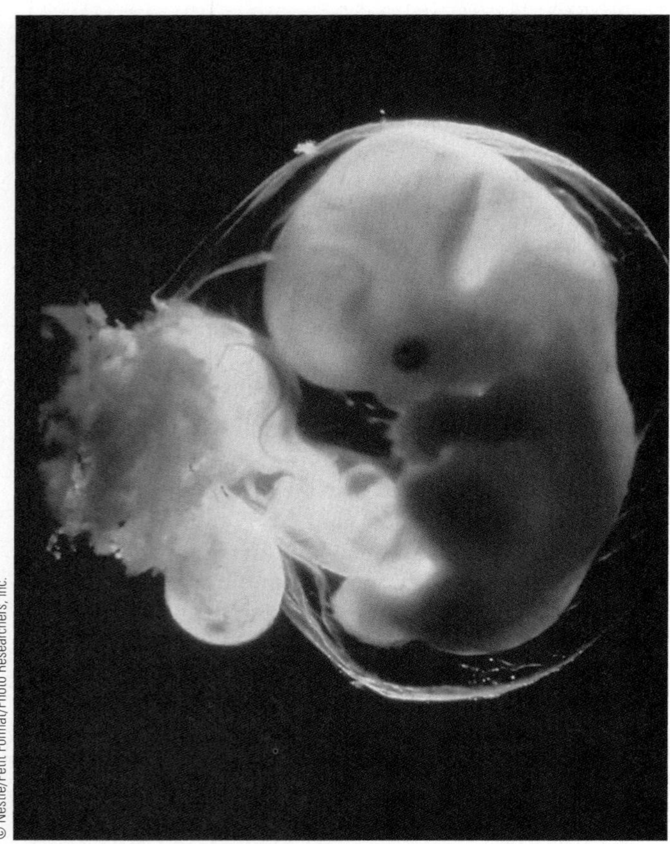
© Nestle/Petit Format/Photo Researchers, Inc.

By 5 to 6 weeks after conception, head, torso, and limbs have formed, a tiny heart has begun to beat, and the umbilical cord (lower center) has taken shape to transport nutrients. By the end of the embryonic period (8 weeks), all major organs have formed.

staggering rate during this period; by one estimate, the number of neurons increases by 250,000 every minute throughout all of pregnancy, with a concentrated period of proliferation occurring between 10 and 20 weeks after conception (Aylward, 1997). As a result of this rapid proliferation, the young infant has around 100 billion neurons. Another period of proliferation takes place after birth, but this produces an increase in glial cells, not nerve cells. Glial cells function primarily as support cells for neurons. Once formed, neurons migrate from their place of origin to particular locations within the brain where they will become part of specialized functioning units. The impetus for migration is influenced by genetic instructions and by the biochemical environment in which brain cells find themselves. Neurons travel along the surface of glial cells and detach at programmed destinations in the developing brain. Neurons migrate to the closest or innermost parts of the brain first and to the farthest or outermost parts last. Much neuronal migration occurs between 8 and 15 weeks after conception.

In addition to proliferation and migration of cells, **differentiation** is occurring. Early in development, every neuron starts with the potential to become any specific type of neuron; what it becomes—how it differentiates—depends on where it migrates. Thus, if a neuron that would normally migrate to the visual cortex of an animal's brain is transplanted into the area of the cortex that controls hearing, it will differentiate as an auditory neuron instead of a visual neuron (Johnson, 1997). These early cells that have not yet specialized are known as **stem cells.** In 1998, researchers discovered how to separate stem cells from human embryos and grow these cells in the laboratory. This procedure has been controversial because of its use of human embryos, but it shows great promise for someday treating serious diseases such as Parkinson's disease, diabetes, and Alzheimer's disease by engineering specialized cells from stem cells.

Organ systems that formed during the embryonic period continue to grow and begin to function. Harmful agents will no longer cause major malformations because organs have already formed, but they can stunt the growth of the fetus and interfere with the wiring of its rapidly developing nervous system.

In the third month of pregnancy, distinguishable external sex organs appear, the bones and muscles develop, and the fetus becomes frisky: By the end of the third month (that is, by the end of the first third of pregnancy, or *trimester*), it moves its arms, kicks its legs, makes fists, and even turns somersaults. The mother probably does not yet feel all this activity because the fetus is still only about 3 inches long. Nonetheless, this tiny being can swallow, digest food, and urinate. All this "behaving" contributes to the proper development of the nervous system, digestive system, and other systems of the body (Smotherman & Robinson, 1996).

Table 4.3 Events of the Fetal Period

Week	Event
9	Bone tissue emerges and the embryo becomes a fetus. The head of the fetus looks huge relative to the rest of the body—it takes up about half of the total length of the fetus. The fetus can open and close its mouth and turn its head.
10–12	Fingers and toes are clearly formed. External genitalia have developed. Movements have increased substantially—arms and legs kick vigorously, but the fetus is still too small for the mother to feel all these movements. The fetus also shows "breathing" movements with its chest and some reflexes.
13–16	The heartbeat should be audible with a stethoscope. Fetal movements may become apparent to the mother. The skeleton is becoming harder.
17–22	Fingernails and toenails, hair, teeth buds, and eyelashes grow. Brain development is phenomenal, and brain waves are detectable.
23–25	These weeks mark the age of viability, when the fetus has a *chance* of survival outside the womb.
26–32	The fetus gains weight, and its brain grows. The nervous system becomes better organized.
33–38	The last 6 weeks of a full-term pregnancy bring further weight gain and brain activity. The lungs mature and begin to expand and contract.

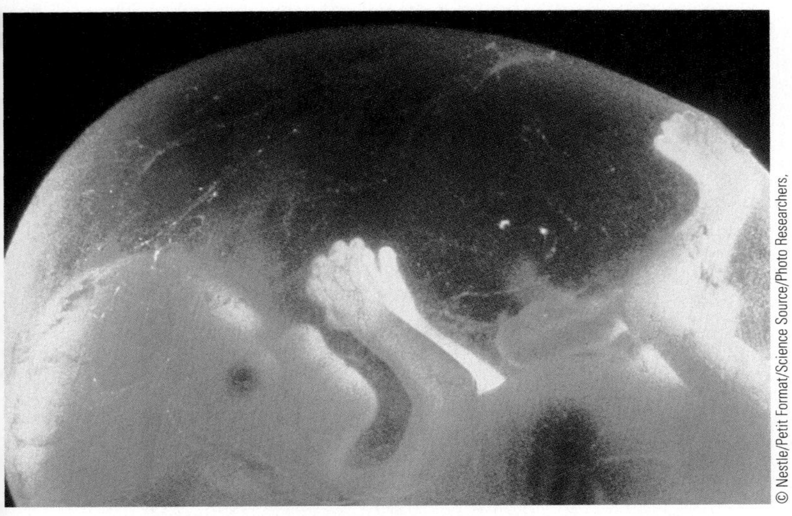
© Nestle/Petit Format/Science Source/Photo Researchers.

☾ By 16 weeks, the fetus has a distinctly human appearance.

During the *second trimester* (the fourth, fifth, and sixth months), more refined activities appear (including thumb sucking), and by the end of this period the sensory organs are functioning: Premature infants as young as 25 weeks respond to loud noises and bright lights (Allen & Capute, 1986; Sadler, 2004). At about 24 to 25 weeks after conception, midway through the fifth month, the fetus reaches the **age of viability,** when survival outside the uterus is possible *if* the brain and respiratory system are well enough developed (Lorenz, 2000). The age of viability is earlier today than at any time in the past because medical techniques for keeping fragile babies alive have improved considerably over the past few decades. Still, somewhere between 42 and 83% of infants born this early do not survive, and of those who do, many experience chronic health or neurological problems (Hack & Fanaroff, 1999).

During the *third trimester* (the seventh, eighth, and ninth months), the fetus gains weight rapidly. This time is also critical in the development of the brain, as is the entire prenatal period (see Chapter 5). Early in pregnancy, the basic architecture of the nervous system is laid down. During the second half of pregnancy, neurons not only multiply at an astonishing rate (proliferation) but they also increase in size and develop an insulating cover, **myelin,** that improves their ability to transmit signals rapidly. Most importantly, guided by both a genetic blueprint and early sensory experiences, neurons connect with one another and organize into working groups that control vision, memory, motor behavior, and other functions. For good reason, parents should be concerned about damage to the developing human during the first trimester, when the brain and other organs are forming. However, they should not overlook the significance of the second and third trimesters, which are critical to normal brain functioning and therefore to normal development (Diaz, 1997).

As the brain develops, the behavior of the fetus becomes more like the organized and adaptive behavior seen in the newborn. For example, Janet DiPietro and her colleagues (2002) assessed heart rates and activity levels in 52 fetuses at 24, 30, and 36 weeks following conception and at 2 weeks following birth.

© Photo Lennart Nilsson/Albert Bonniers Forlag AB, *A Child is Born*, Dell Publishing Company

☾ During the fetal period, growth is substantial and there is little room for the fetus to move in the womb. This 20-week-old fetus is curled into the classic "fetal position" in its tight quarters.

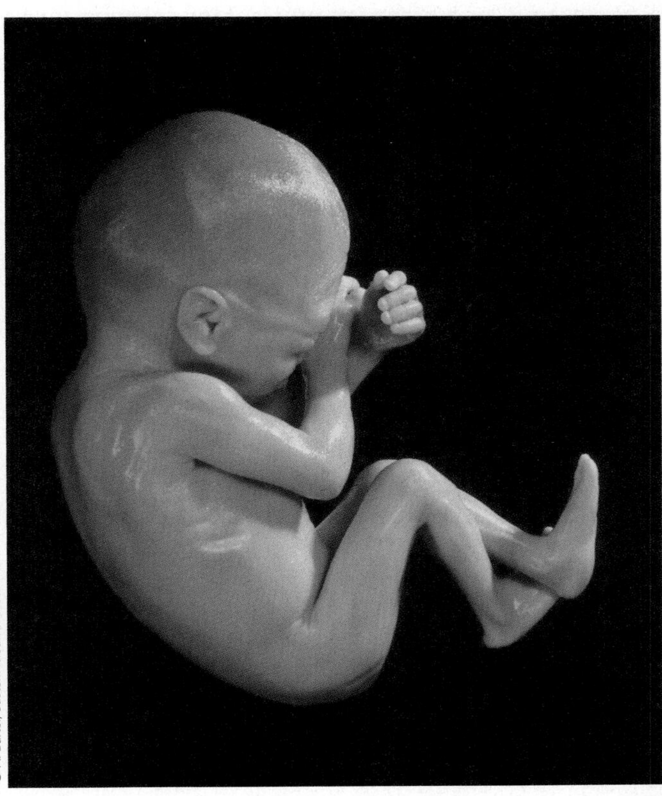
© A. Bartel/Custom Medical Stock Photo

☾ At 24 weeks of gestation, this fetus has reached the age of viability, when it might have a chance to survive outside the womb if born early.

Only at 36 weeks of gestation did heart rate activity and movement become increasingly organized into coherent patterns of waking and sleeping known as **infant states.** Fetuses whose heart rates and movements were concordant (that is, they matched) at 36 weeks showed better regulation of their behavioral states 2 weeks after birth. They were more alert, less irritable, better able to sustain their attention, and more likely to maintain control even during stressful parts of the postnatal examination.

In other research by DiPietro and her colleagues (1996b), they found that, with age, fetal heart rates become increasingly responsive to such stimuli as a vibrator placed on the mother's abdomen. Fetuses moved, on average, about once a minute and were active 20 to 30% of the time. As Figure 4.4 shows, at 20 weeks, fetuses spent only about 17% of their time in one or another organized infant state such as quiet sleep, active sleep, or active waking. By the end of the prenatal period, they were in one distinct state or another at least 85% of the time. They spent most of their time snoozing, especially in active sleep. Whereas in the 20th week of pregnancy they were almost never active and awake, by the 32nd week they spent 11 to 16% of their time in an active, waking state. The patterns detected in this and other studies suggest that important changes in the nervous system occur 28 to 32 weeks after conception, when premature infants are typically well equipped to survive. As the nervous system becomes more organized, so does behavior.

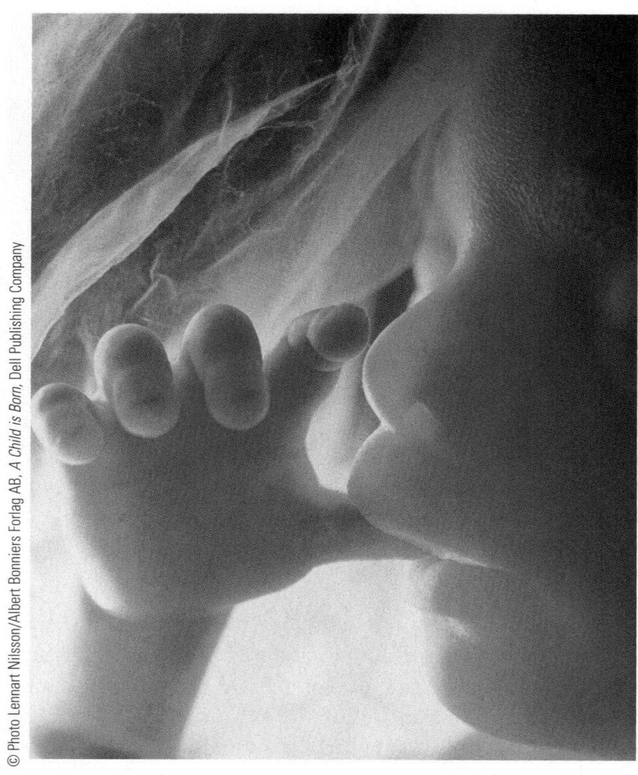

© Photo Lennart Nilsson/Albert Bonniers Forlag AB, *A Child is Born*, Dell Publishing Company

As it nears the end of the gestational period (38–40 weeks for a full-term infant), the fetus engages in many behaviors observed in newborns (here, it sucks its thumb).

Interestingly, different fetuses displayed consistent differences in their patterns of heart rate and movement, and the researchers detected correlations between measures of fetal physiology and behavior and measures of infant temperament (DiPietro et al., 1996a). For example, active fetuses tended to be active, difficult, and unpredictable babies, and fetuses whose states were better organized were also better regulated at 3 months after birth, as indicated by their waking fewer times during the night. The message is clear: Newborn behavior does not spring from nowhere; it emerges long before birth. There is a good deal of continuity between prenatal behavior and postnatal behavior.

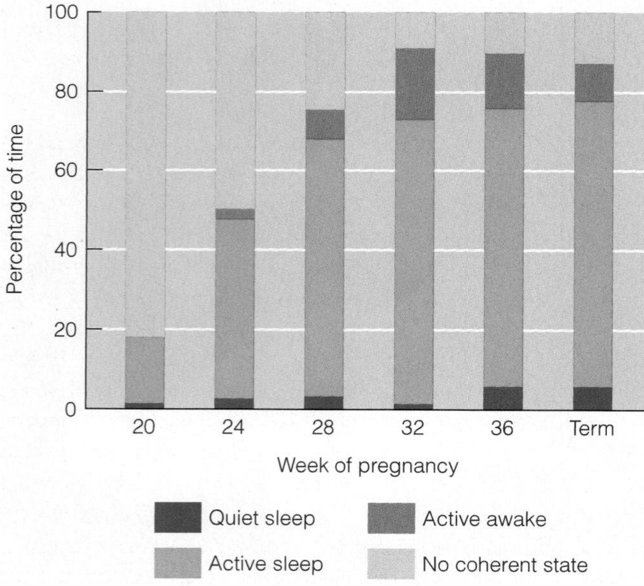

Figure 4.4 The percentage of time the fetus spends in different states from the 20th week until the end of pregnancy. Time in one coherent state or another increases with age, and most time is spent in a state of sleep.

SOURCE: From DiPietro, J. A., Hodgson, D. M., Costigan, K. A., Hilton, S. C., & Johnson, T. R. B. (1996b). Fetal neurobehavioral development. *Child Development, 67,* 2553–2567. Copyright © 1996 Society for Research in Child Development, Inc. Reprinted by permission.

By the middle of the ninth month, the fetus is so large that its most comfortable position in cramped quarters is head down with limbs curled in (the "fetal position"). The mother's uterus contracts at irregular intervals during the last month of pregnancy. When these contractions are strong, frequent, and regular, the mother is in the first stage of labor and the prenatal period is drawing to a close. Under normal circumstances, birth will occur within hours.

Summing Up

Following conception, development during the prenatal period proceeds through three stages at an astonishing rate. During the germinal stage, the zygote divides many times, forming a blastocyst, which makes its way to the uterus where it implants itself. The embryonic stage occurs from the third to the eighth week after conception. During this time, every major organ begins to take shape through the process of organogenesis. During the last stage, the fetus increases in size and undergoes tremendous brain development. ■

The Prenatal Environment

The mother's womb is the **prenatal environment** for the unborn child. Just as children are influenced by their physical and social environments, so too is the fetus affected. Physical environment includes everything from the molecules that reach the fetus's bloodstream before birth to the architecture of a home to the climate outside it. Social environment includes all the people who can influence and be influenced by the developing person and the broader culture. Although early theorists tended to view environment as a set of forces that shaped the individual, as though a person were just a lump of clay to be molded, we now know this is not the case. Recall the explanation from Chapter 2 of *reciprocal influences:* people shape their physical and social environments and are, in turn, affected by the environments they have helped create. For example, if a woman uses cocaine during pregnancy, her newborn may be extraordinarily fussy: Environment has affected development. But a fussy baby is likely to affect his environment by irritating his mother, who then expresses her tenseness in her interactions with him; this makes him fussier, which aggravates his mother even more, and her aggravation, in turn, makes him even crankier. Such transactions between person and environment begin at the moment of conception.

The developing embryo-then-fetus is a vulnerable little creature. How can its development be optimized? What hazards does it face? "Experts" throughout history have offered several odd ideas about the effects of the prenatal physical environment on growth. For example, it was once believed that pregnant women could enhance their chances of bearing sons if they ate red meat and salty snacks, whereas eating vegetables and sweet snacks would supposedly increase the likelihood of having daughters (Springen, 2004). And until the early 1940s, it was widely—and wrongly—believed that the placenta was a marvelous screen that protected the embryo and fetus from nicotine, viruses, and all kinds of other hazards. Today, we understand that transactions between the organism and its environment begin at conception. When all is right, the prenatal environment provides just the stimulation and support needed for the fetus to mature physically and to develop a repertoire of behaviors that allow it to seek more stimulation, which in turn contributes to the development of more sophisticated behavior. When the prenatal environment is abnormal, development can be steered far off track, as you will now see as we examine the influence of various substances. But just as exposure to some substances can place children at risk, other factors can enhance their developmental outcome, as you will see in later sections of this chapter.

Your main mission here is to discover the extent to which early environmental influences, interacting with genetic influences, make or break later development. The nature–nurture issue, then, is the central issue to consider to understand prenatal development and its influence on the developing person. Early environmental influences on development—bad and good—demand serious attention. Such influences interact with genetic makeup throughout the life span to make us who we are. If a common genetic heritage can make different human beings alike in some respects, so can similar environments. If unique genes make one person different from another, so do unique experiences.

Teratogens

A **teratogen** is any disease, drug, or other environmental agent that can harm a developing fetus (for example, by causing deformities, blindness, brain damage, or even death). The list of teratogens has grown frighteningly long, and the environment contains many potential teratogens whose effects on development have not yet been assessed. Before considering the effects of some major teratogens, however, let us emphasize that only 15% of newborns have *minor* problems and even fewer—perhaps 5%—have more significant anomalies (Sadler, 2004). We will start with a few generalizations about the effects of teratogens, which we will then illustrate with examples (Sadler, 2004):

- *Critical period.* The effects of a teratogenic agent are worst during the critical period when an organ system grows most rapidly.
- *Dosage and duration.* The greater the exposure and the longer the exposure to a teratogen, the more likely it is that serious damage will occur.
- *Genetic makeup.* Susceptibility to harm is determined by the unborn child's and by the mother's genetic makeup. Therefore, not all embryos and fetuses are affected, nor are they affected equally, by a teratogen.
- *Environment.* The effects of a teratogen depend on the quality of both the prenatal and the postnatal environments.

Look more closely at the first generalization, which is particularly important. A period of rapid growth is a **critical period** for an organ system—a time during which the developing organism is especially sensitive to environmental influences, positive or negative. As you will recall, organogenesis takes place during the embryonic period (weeks 3 to 8 of prenatal development). As Figure 4.5 shows, it is during this time—before many women even realize they are pregnant—that most organ systems are most vulnerable to damage. Moreover, each organ has a critical period that corresponds to its own time of most rapid development (for example, weeks 3 to 6 for the heart and 4 to 7 for the arms and fingers). Once an organ or body part is fully formed, it is usually less susceptible to damage. However, because some organ systems—above all, the nervous system—can be damaged throughout pregnancy, *sensitive periods* might be a better term than *critical periods.*

Drugs

The principles of teratology can be illustrated by surveying just a few of the many drugs—prescription, over the counter,

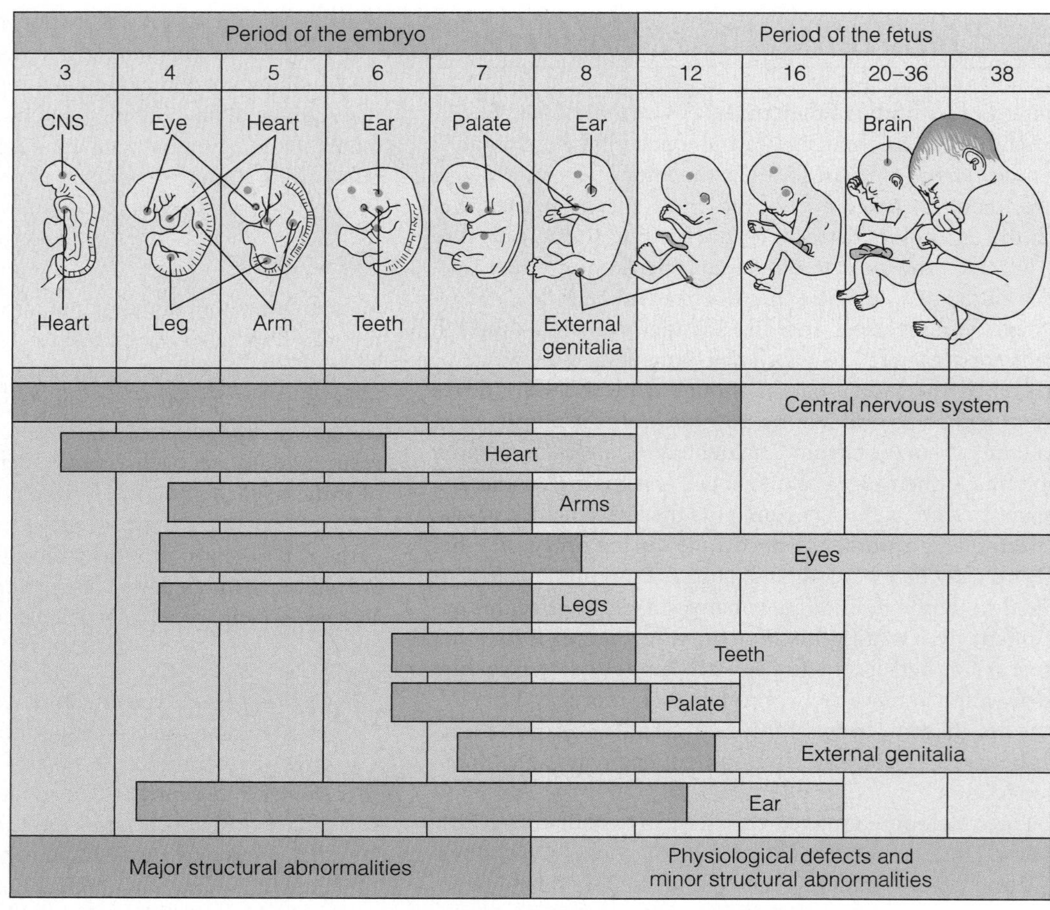

Figure 4.5 The critical periods of prenatal development. Teratogens are more likely to produce major structural abnormalities during the third through the eighth prenatal week. Note, however, that many organs and body parts remain sensitive to teratogenic agents throughout the 9-month prenatal period.

Source: Adapted from Moore, K. L. (1988). *The developing human.* Philadelphia: W. B. Saunders.

and social—that can disrupt prenatal development. More than half of pregnant women take at least one prescription or over-the-counter drug during pregnancy (Kacew, 1999). Under a doctor's close supervision, medications used to treat ailments and medical conditions are usually safe for mother and fetus. However, certain individuals exposed to certain drugs in certain doses at certain times during the prenatal period are damaged for life.

Thalidomide. In the late 1950s, a West German drug company sold large quantities of **thalidomide,** a popular tranquilizer said to relieve morning sickness (the periodic nausea many women experience during the first trimester of pregnancy). Presumably, the drug was safe; it had no ill effects in tests on pregnant rats. Tragically, however, the drug had adverse effects on humans. Indeed, more than any other drug, thalidomide alerted the world to the dangers of taking drugs during pregnancy.

Thousands of women who used thalidomide during the first 2 months of pregnancy gave birth to babies with all or parts of their limbs missing, with the feet or hands attached directly to the torso like flippers, or with deformed eyes, ears, noses, and hearts (Rodier, 2000). It soon became clear that there are critical periods for different deformities. If the mother had taken thalidomide 20 to 22 days after conception (34 to 36 days after the first day of a woman's last menstrual period), her baby was likely to be born without ears. If she had taken it 22 to 27 days after conception, the baby often had missing or small thumbs; if thalidomide was taken between 27 and 33 days after conception, the child was likely to have stunted legs or no legs. And if the mother waited until 35 or 36 days after conception before using thalidomide, her baby was usually not affected. Thus, thalidomide had specific effects on development, depending on which structures were developing when the drug was taken.

Thalidomide, banned for years, is again being prescribed by physicians, this time for treatment of conditions associated with leprosy, acquired immunodeficiency syndrome (AIDS), tuberculosis, and some forms of cancer (Wright, 2000). Given its tragic past association with birth defects, the manufacturers of thalidomide have stamped each pill with a drawing of a pregnant woman inside a circle with a diagonal line through it (the universal "no" symbol) and have included a picture of a baby with the characteristic

☾ This mother uses her leg to hug her daughter because she was born without arms. *Her* mother took the drug thalidomide early in pregnancy when arm buds were forming.

stunted limbs on the packaging accompanying the pills. Critics, however, worry that these measures will not be enough to prevent future birth defects.

Tobacco. Despite warnings on cigarette packages that smoking may damage fetuses, about 15% of pregnant women smoke during pregnancy (Pollack, Lantz, & Fruhna, 2000). Some studies report that as many as 30% of pregnant women smoke an average of 9 cigarettes per day (Wisborg et al., 2000). Women who smoke experience higher rates of miscarriage than nonsmokers (Ernst, Moolchan, & Robinson, 2001). The babies of mothers who smoke tend to grow more slowly in the womb and are likely to be born prematurely and small (Habek et al., 2002). Smoking restricts blood flow to the fetus and reduces the level of growth factors in the umbilical cord (Sagall, 2003). The more a mother smokes, the greater the growth retardation and the more significant the neurological problems (Law et al., 2003). More than half of infants born to women smoking 20 or more cigarettes a day end up in neonatal intensive care and experience some central nervous system impairment (Habek et al., 2002). "Passive smoking" may be risky as well; birth weights are lower when both parents smoke than when only mothers smoke (Haug et al., 2000). But if fathers smoke and mothers do not, the risk of low birth weight is no greater than when neither parent smokes. Often the small babies of smokers experience catch-up growth after they are born and reach normal size by late infancy, but the more their mothers smoke, the less likely it is that their growth will catch up completely (Streissguth et al., 1994). As they age, these children are at greater risk of becoming overweight (Wideroe et al., 2003).

The babies of smokers are also more susceptible than other babies to respiratory infections and breathing difficulties (Diaz, 1997). The more a woman smokes during pregnancy, the greater the odds of **sudden infant death syndrome (SIDS)**, in which a sleeping baby suddenly stops breathing and dies (Gressens, Laudenbach, & Marret, 2003). Some studies also link maternal smoking to at least mild cognitive difficulties and to behavioral problems such as impulsivity and hyperactivity (Hellstrom-Lindahl & Nordberg, 2002; Kotimaa et al., 2003). These effects appear to last at least into childhood. Finally, findings from longitudinal studies have led some researchers to conclude that chronic prenatal exposure to nicotine—a legal substance—has more negative effects on central nervous system development than sporadic exposure to the illegal drug cocaine (Frank et al., 2001; Slotkin, 1998).

In sum, maternal smoking during pregnancy is unwise because it slows fetal growth and contributes to respiratory and, possibly, cognitive difficulties. These effects may be caused not only by nicotine and other chemicals in cigarettes but also by toxic by-products of smoking, such as carbon monoxide, that reduce the flow of blood and oxygen to the fetus.

Alcohol. Alcohol consumed by the mother readily crosses the placenta, where it can directly affect fetal development and disrupt hormone functions of the placenta (Gabriel et al., 1998). Prenatal alcohol exposure disrupts the normal process of neuronal migration, leading to several outcomes depending on the severity of the effects. The most severe is a cluster of symptoms dubbed **fetal alcohol syndrome (FAS)**, with noticeable physical symptoms such as a small head and distinctive facial abnormalities (see Figure 4.6). Children with FAS are smaller and lighter than normal, and their physical growth lags behind that of their age mates (Cornelius et al., 2002; Day et al., 1999).

Children with FAS also show signs of central nervous system damage. As newborns, they are likely to display excessive irritability, hyperactivity, seizures, or tremors. Most children with FAS score well below average on IQ tests throughout childhood and adolescence, and many are mentally retarded (Korkman, Kettunen, & Autti-Rämö, 2003; Streissguth et al., 1999). Hyperactive behavior and attention deficits are also common among these children. Longitudinal research indicates that more than 90% of them have mental health problems later in life; they are likely to get into trouble at school, break the law, lose jobs, and experience drinking problems (Baer et al., 2003; Autti-Rämö, 2000; Colburn, 1996).

As many as 30% of pregnant women drink some alcohol during pregnancy; 12% admit to "risk drinking" (seven or more drinks per week or five drinks on one occasion); and up to 4% abuse alcohol (O'Connor & Whaley, 2003; Stratton, Howe, & Battaglia, 1996; Wisborg et al., 2000). As a result, 3 in 1000 babies in the United States are born with FAS and suffer its symptoms all their lives. Children who were exposed prenatally to alcohol but do not have FAS experience milder alcohol-related effects labeled either *fetal alcohol effects* or *alcohol-related neurodevelopmental disorder.* These individuals do not have all the features of FAS but have physical, behavioral, cognitive, or a combination of these problems (Hankin, 2002).

How much drinking does it take to harm an unborn baby? In keeping with the dosage principle of teratology, mothers who consume larger quantities of alcohol are at greater risk for having children with alcohol-related complications (Roccella

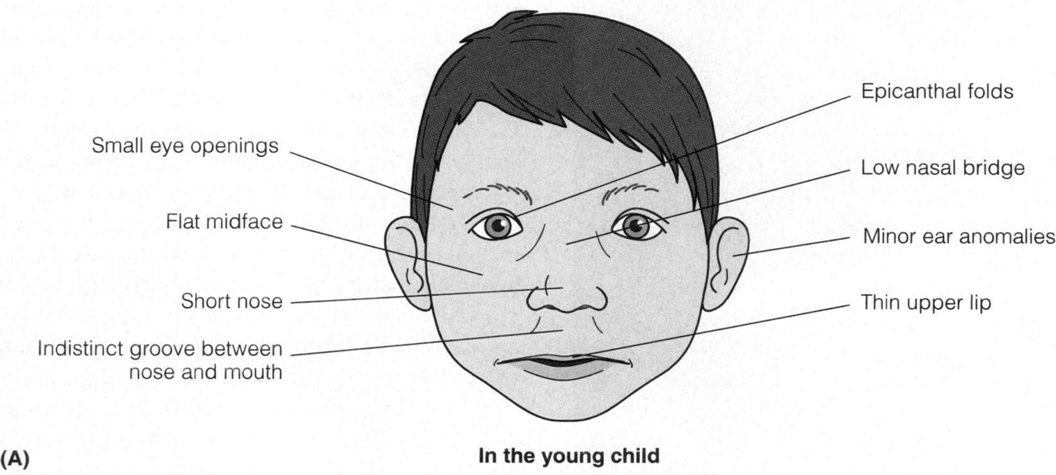

Figure 4.6 (A) Characteristic features of a child with fetal alcohol syndrome (FAS). (B) Child with FAS, illustrating many features in the drawing. Such children may also have cardiovascular and limb defects.

SOURCE: T. W. Sadler (2004, p. 156).

& Testa, 2003; Streissguth et al., 1999). The pattern of drinking is also important. Binge drinking (consuming five or more drinks during a single session) has more negative effects on fetal development than consuming the same number of drinks across multiple sessions (Jacobson & Jacobson, 1999). Consuming five drinks in one evening results in higher blood alcohol levels for both mother and fetus than consuming one drink on each of five evenings. Finally, in keeping with the critical-period principle of teratogens, the effects of alcohol depend on which systems are developing at the time of exposure. The facial abnormalities associated with FAS result from consumption during the first trimester, when the face and skull bones are forming. During the second and third trimesters, there is much fetal growth as well as rapid brain development; thus, alcohol consumption during this latter part of pregnancy is likely to stunt growth and brain development.

No amount of drinking seems to be entirely safe (Rolater, 2000). Even a mother who drinks less than an ounce a day is at risk to have a sluggish or placid newborn whose mental development is slightly below average (Jacobson et al., 1993). What is more, there is no well-defined critical period before or after which fetal alcohol effects cannot occur; drinking late in pregnancy can be as risky as drinking soon after conception (Jacobson et al., 1993).

Why do some babies of drinking mothers suffer ill effects but others do not? To answer this, you need to consider the nature–nurture issue again. First, the chances of damage depend partly on the mother's physiology—for example, on how efficiently she metabolizes alcohol and, therefore, how much is passed to the fetus (Shepard & Lemire, 2004). Complicating the situation, problem drinkers often have other problems that can aggravate the effects of alcohol on the fetus or cause damage—among them, malnutrition, use of drugs other than alcohol, cigarette smoking, and lack of prenatal care (Armstrong, 2003). In addition, consistent with the third principle of teratogenic effects, the embryo's genetic makeup and physical condition influence its ability to resist and recover from damage. So, for example, one fraternal twin may show all the physical abnormalities associated with FAS but the other twin, although exposed to the same prenatal environment, may show almost none; by contrast, identical twins respond similarly when exposed to alcohol prenatally (Streissguth & Dehaene, 1993). As the third principle of teratology states, both the child's and the mother's characteristics influence the extent to which a given teratogen proves damaging. Thus, the genetic makeup of both the mother and the child interact with environmental forces to determine the effects of alcohol on development.

Finally, note that it is not just the mother's use of alcohol that can adversely affect development. Some research indicates that a father's use of alcohol can influence fetal development. Other research, however, shows that paternal drinking does not affect fetal development but adversely affect later development through poor parenting (Leonard & Das Eiden, 2002). And fathers who abuse alcohol or drugs are often with partners who abuse alcohol or drugs, making it difficult to separate the effects of the mother's use of these substances from the father's use (Frank, Brown, et al., 2002). So researchers really do not know whether a father's consumption of alcohol causes the problems or whether the problems arise from things often associated with a father's abuse of alcohol.

Cocaine. Although there is no "cocaine syndrome" with characteristic physical abnormalities such as those associated with FAS, cocaine use can damage the fetus (Van Beveren, Little, & Spence, 2000). It can cause spontaneous abortion in the first trimester of pregnancy and premature detachment of the placenta or fetal strokes later in pregnancy (Diaz, 1997). Cocaine also contributes to fetal malnourishment, retarded growth, and low birth weight (Klitsch, 2002). At birth, a small proportion of babies born to cocaine users experience withdrawal-like symptoms such as tremors and extreme irritability and have respiratory difficulties (Diaz, 1997).

Cocaine-exposed infants show deficits on several measures of information processing (Singer et al., 1999) and sensory motor skills during their first year (Arendt et al., 1998). Fortunately, most problems caused by prenatal cocaine exposure do not persist into childhood (Frank, Jacobs, et al., 2002). For problems that persist, it is unclear whether they are caused by the prenatal exposure to cocaine or to other prenatal or postnatal risk factors affected infants may experience as the children of substance-abusing parents. For instance, many pregnant women who use cocaine also tend to smoke or drink alcohol during pregnancy (Frank, Jacobs, et al., 2002; Klitsch, 2002). Other research shows that cocaine-using mothers are less attentive to their babies and engage in fewer interactions with them at 3 and 6 months than non–drug-using mothers or mothers who use drugs other than cocaine (Mayes et al., 1997).

Table 4.4 catalogs several substances and their known or suspected effects on the child. What should you make of these findings? You now understand that drugs do not damage all fetuses exposed to them in a simple, direct way. Instead, com-

Table 4.4 Some Drugs Taken by the Mother That Affect the Fetus or Newborn

Drug	Effects
Alcohol	Results include a small head, facial abnormalities, heart defects, low birth weight, and intellectual retardation (see main text).
Antiepileptic drugs	Drugs such as Dilantin, Luminal, and Tegretol, used to treat seizures, increase the incidence of cleft lip and palate, neural tube defects, and restricted growth.
Aspirin and nonsteroidal anti-inflammatory drugs (e.g., Advil)	An occasional low dose is OK, but used in large quantities, such drugs may cause neonatal bleeding and gastrointestinal discomfort. Large amounts of these over-the-counter pain killers have been associated with low birth weight and increased risk of miscarriage (Li, Liu, & Odouli, 2003).
Chemotherapy drugs	Such drugs cross the placenta and attack rapidly dividing cells. They can increase malformations and lead to miscarriage.
Marijuana	Heavy use of marijuana has been linked to premature birth, low birth weight, and mild behavioral abnormalities such as irritability at birth, but it does not cause physical abnormalities or have long-lasting effects on most children (Fried, O'Connell, & Watkinson, 1992).
Narcotics	Addiction to heroin, codeine, methadone, or morphine increases the risk of premature delivery and low birth weight. The newborn is often addicted and experiences potentially fatal withdrawal symptoms; e.g., vomiting and convulsions. Longer-term cognitive deficits are sometimes evident.
Sex hormones	Birth control pills containing female hormones have been known to produce heart defects and cardiovascular problems, but today's pill formulas are safer. Progesterone in drugs used to prevent miscarriage may masculinize the fetus. Diethylstilbestrol, once prescribed to prevent miscarriage, increased the risk of cervical cancer and created infertility and pregnancy problems in exposed daughters (DESAction, 2000; Kaufman et al., 2000).
Stimulants	Heavy caffeine use has been linked to miscarriages (Cnattingius et al., 2000), higher heart rates (Schuetze & Zeskind, 1997), and abnormal reflexes and irritability at birth (Jacobson et al., 1984), but it does not seem to have long-lasting effects on development (Barr & Streissguth, 1991). Cocaine use can cause premature delivery, spontaneous abortion, and low birth weight, and it may result in later learning and behavioral problems (see main text). Amphetamine use has been linked to aggressive behavior and low school achievement (Billing et al., 1994).
Tobacco	Babies of smokers tend to be small and premature, have respiratory problems, and sometimes show intellectual deficits or behavioral problems later in development (see main text). Sons whose mothers smoked during their pregnancy may later have fertility problems (Storgaard et al., 2003).

SOURCES: Based partly on information from Batshaw, 2002; Diaz, 1997; Friedman & Polifka, 1996; Winn & Hobbins, 2000.

plex transactions between an individual with a certain genetic makeup and the prenatal, perinatal, and postnatal environments influence whether or not prenatal drug exposure does lasting damage (Van Beveren, Little, & Spence, 2000). Still, women who are planning to become pregnant or who are pregnant should avoid all drugs unless they are prescribed by a physician and essential to health.

Diseases

Just as drugs can jeopardize the prenatal environment, so can diseases. Here, we take a look at three diseases that illustrate principles of teratogens—rubella, syphilis, and AIDS. Table 4.5 summarizes these and other maternal conditions that may affect prenatal development.

Rubella. In the early 1940s, a doctor discovered that many infants born to women affected by **rubella** (German measles) during pregnancy had one or more of a variety of defects, including blindness, deafness, heart defects, and mental retardation. Because rubella was fairly common, there were enough cases for doctors to see that the environment of the womb leaves the fetus vulnerable to outside influences. Rubella is most dangerous during the first trimester, a critical period in which the eyes, ears, heart, and brain are rapidly forming. Yet not all babies whose mothers had rubella, even during the most critical period of prenatal development, will have problems. Birth defects occur in 60 to 85% of babies whose mothers had the disease in the first 2 months of pregnancy, in about 50% of those infected in the third month, and in only 16% of those infected in the fourth or fifth months (Kelley-Buchanan, 1988). Consistent with the critical-period principle, damage to the nervous system, eyes, and heart is most likely during that part of the first 8 weeks of pregnancy when each of these organs is forming, whereas deafness is more likely when the mother contracts rubella in weeks 6 to 13 of the pregnancy. Today, doctors stress that a woman should not try to become pregnant unless she has been immunized against rubella or has already had it. As a result of successful immunization programs, 85% of women are now immune to this previously common infection (Sadler, 2004).

Syphilis. Now consider another teratogen, the sexually transmitted disease **syphilis.** Syphilis during pregnancy can cause miscarriage or stillbirth (Genc & Ledger, 2000). Babies

Table 4.5 Maternal Diseases and Conditions That May Affect an Embryo, Fetus, or Newborn

Disease or condition	Effects
SEXUALLY TRANSMITTED DISEASES (STDs)	
Acquired immunodeficiency syndrome (AIDS)	If transmitted from mother to child, AIDS destroys defenses against disease and may lead to death. Mothers can acquire it through sexual contact or contact with contaminated blood (see main text).
Chlamydia	Chlamydia can lead to premature birth, low birth weight, eye inflammation, or pneumonia in newborns. This most common STD is easily treatable.
Gonorrhea	This STD attacks the eyes of the child during birth; blindness is prevented by administering silver nitrate eyedrops to newborns.
Herpes simplex (genital herpes)	This disease may cause eye and brain damage or death in the first trimester. Mothers with active herpes are advised to undergo cesarean deliveries to avoid infecting their babies during delivery, because 85% of infants born with herpes acquire the virus during birth.
Syphilis	Untreated, it can cause miscarriage or serious birth defects such as blindness and mental retardation (see main text).
OTHER MATERNAL CONDITIONS OR DISEASES	
Chicken pox	Chicken pox can cause spontaneous abortion, premature delivery, and slow growth, although fewer than 2% of exposed fetuses develop limb, facial, or skeletal malformations.
Cytomegalovirus	This common infection shows mild flulike symptoms in adults. About 25% of infected newborns develop hearing or vision loss, mental retardation, or other impairments, and 10% develop severe neurological problems or even die.
Influenza (flu)	The more powerful strains can cause spontaneous abortions or neural abnormalities early in pregnancy.
Rubella	Rubella may cause vision and hearing loss, mental retardation, heart defects, cerebral palsy, and microcephaly (see main text).
Toxemia	Affecting about 5% of mothers in the third trimester, its mildest form, preeclampsia, causes high blood pressure and rapid weight gain in the mother. Untreated, preeclampsia may become eclampsia and cause maternal convulsions, coma, and death of the mother, the unborn child, or both. Surviving infants may be brain damaged.
Toxoplasmosis	This illness, caused by a parasite in raw meat and cat feces, leads to blindness, deafness, and mental retardation in approximately 40% of infants born to infected mothers.

SOURCES: Based partly on information from Batshaw (2002); Ratcliffe, Byrd, & Sakornbut, (1996); Simpson & Creehan, (1996); and Winn & Hobbins (2000).

born alive to mothers who have syphilis, like those born to mothers who have rubella, often suffer blindness, deafness, heart problems, or brain damage. This shows that different teratogens—here, syphilis and rubella—can be responsible for the same problem. However, whereas rubella is most damaging in the early stage of pregnancy, syphilis is most damaging in the middle and later stages of pregnancy. This is because syphilitic organisms cannot cross the placental barrier until the 18th prenatal week, providing a window of opportunity for treating the mother-to-be who finds out she has the disease. Even with appropriate treatment—penicillin—some infants are infected or die (Genc & Ledger, 2000).

AIDS. The sexually transmitted disease of greatest concern in recent decades is **acquired immunodeficiency syndrome (AIDS)**, the life-threatening disease caused by the human immunodeficiency virus (HIV). AIDS destroys the immune system and makes victims susceptible to "opportunistic" infections that eventually kill them unless they are treated with multiple drugs. HIV-infected mothers can transmit the virus to their babies (1) prenatally, if the virus passes through the placenta; (2) perinatally, when blood may be exchanged between mother and child as the umbilical cord separates from the placenta; or (3) postnatally, if the virus is transmitted during breast-feeding. Somewhere between 15 and 35% of babies born to HIV-infected mothers are infected (Newell, 2003; Thorne & Newell, 2000). The rate is much lower if these mothers take azidothymidine, also called AZT or zidovudine, to treat the HIV or if their newborns are given a new drug called nevirapine, which helps block transmission of HIV at birth (Newell, 2003; Stringer et al., 2004). Bottle-feeding further reduces the rate of HIV transmission from affected mothers to their infants (Brown, 2000c). Infected infants now live longer than they did at the outset of the AIDS epidemic because of the development of appropriate treatments—64% are alive at age 6, and many survive into adolescence (French Pediatric HIV Infection Study Group, 1997).

Mother-to-child transmission of HIV in the United States has decreased more than 40% since peaking in 1992, (Key & DeNoon, 1998; Lindegren et al., 1999). But mother-to-child transmission continues to be a tremendous problem in Africa and other parts of the world with AIDS epidemics. In 2003, for example, about 700,000 infants became infected with HIV from their mothers and most of these cases occurred in sub-Saharan Africa (Avert, 2004).

Environmental Hazards

Radiation. A mother can control what she ingests, but sometimes she cannot avoid a hazardous external environment. After atomic bombs were dropped on Hiroshima and Nagasaki in 1945, not one pregnant woman who was within one-half mile of the blasts gave birth to a live child, and 75% of those who were within a mile and a quarter of the blasts had stillborn infants or seriously handicapped children who died soon after birth (Apgar & Beck, 1974). Surviving children of these mothers had a higher-than-normal rate of mental retardation and greater incidence of leukemia and cancers (Kodama, Mabuchi, & Shigematsu, 1996; Vorhees & Mollnow, 1987). Even clinical doses of radiation, such as those used in X-rays and cancer treatment, are capable of causing mutations, spontaneous abortions, and a variety of birth defects, especially if the mother is exposed between weeks 8 and 15 (Hill & Haffner, 2002). Therefore, expectant mothers are routinely advised to avoid X-rays unless they are essential to their own survival, and women who work with X-ray equipment must take proper precautions. Despite some concern about it, by the way, a woman who works in front of a computer screen all day does not appear to place her fetus at risk (Parazzini et al., 1993).

Pollutants. Pollutants in the air we breathe and the water we drink include "heavy metals," such as lead, which are discharged by smelting operations and other industries and may be present in paint, dust, or water pipes in old houses. Children exposed to lead prenatally show impaired intellectual functioning as infants in proportion to the amount of lead in their umbilical cords (Bellinger et al., 1987; Canfield et al., 2003; see also Figure 4.7). This finding holds true even after controlling for other differences among children, such as socioeconomic status. Lead exposure postnatally is also dangerous. It is estimated that one in four children under age 6 in the United States lives in a home with lead dust from old paint (Rogan & Ware, 2003). Even exposure to low levels of lead—lower than previously thought to be safe—is associated with IQ decreases of 4 to 7 points (Rogan & Ware, 2003).

Clearly, there is a critical need for more research aimed at identifying a huge number of chemicals, wastes, and other en-

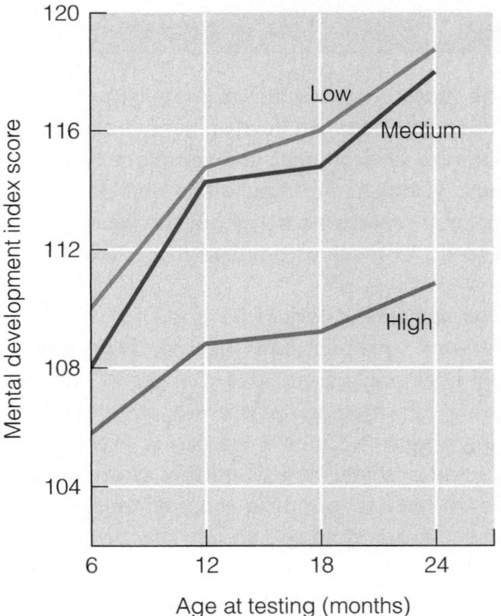

Figure 4.7 Mental development scores of infants with low, medium, or high levels of lead in their umbilical cords before birth.

SOURCE: Adapted with permission from Bellinger, D., Leviton, A., Waternaux, C., Needleman, H., & Rabinowitz, M. (1987). Longitudinal analyses of prenatal and postnatal lead exposure and early cognitive development. *New England Journal of Medicine, 316*, 1037–1043.

vironmental hazards that may affect unborn children. One expert estimates that there are 70,000 synthetic chemicals "out there" that children may be exposed to, and fewer than 20% of these have been evaluated for toxicity (Morris, 1999).

The message is unmistakable: The chemistry of the prenatal environment often determines whether an embryo or fetus survives and how it looks and functions after birth. A variety of teratogens can affect development, although as you have learned, the influence of teratogens varies. Effects are worst when organ systems are growing most rapidly; not all embryos or fetuses are equally affected by the same teratogen; harmful effects depend on the genetic makeup of both the mother and her unborn child and on the quality of the prenatal and postnatal environments; and effects are more serious with greater exposure to teratogens. By becoming familiar with the information touched on here, and by keeping up with new knowledge, parents-to-be can do much to increase the already high odds that their unborn child will be normal as it approaches its next challenge: the birth process.

The Mother's State

What can parents, especially the mother-to-be, do to sustain a healthy pregnancy? The Applications box on this page explores how parents can set the stage for a healthy pregnancy. Here, we describe three characteristics of the mother that can affect the quality of the prenatal environment—age, emotional state, and nutritional status.

Age

At one end of the age spectrum, 11- and 12-year-old girls have given birth; at the other end of the spectrum, a woman gave birth to twins just days before her 57th birthday (CNN News, 2004). These are, however, unusual cases. The safest, and more typical, time to bear a child appears to be from about age 16 to age 35 (Amini et al., 1996; Gilbert, Nesbitt, & Danielsen, 1999; Orvus et al., 1999). Very young mothers have higher-than-normal rates of birth complications, premature deliveries, and low–birth-weight babies. The reproductive system of the young teen (15 years or younger) may not be physically mature enough to sustain a fetus, making this group most vulnerable to having a low–birth-weight baby. However, the greater problem appears to be that teenagers often do not seek prenatal care, and they are more likely to face adverse socioeconomic conditions than mothers in their 20s. Unfortunately, these conditions are likely to persist after the birth, leading to increased death rates before their first birthday among infants born to mothers 15 years or younger (Phipps, Blume, & DeMonner, 2002).

As for mothers older than 35, they are twice as likely to lose a fetus—miscarry—than younger mothers (Fretts & Usher, 1997). In the past, many fetal deaths in older women

Applications

Getting Life Off to a Good Start

The more we learn about important environmental influences on human development, the better able we are to optimize environment and therefore to optimize development. Although the nature and quality of an individual's environment matters throughout the life span, it seems sensible to do as much as possible to get a baby's life off to a good start.

For starters, it would be good for babies if more of them were planned and wanted. Moreover, a woman should begin making positive changes in her lifestyle, such as giving up smoking, before she even thinks about becoming pregnant. Once a woman is pregnant, she should seek good prenatal care as quickly as possible so that she will learn how to optimize the well-being of both herself and her unborn child and so that any problems during the pregnancy can be managed appropriately. The guidelines for pregnant women are not that complicated, although they are often violated. They boil down to such practices as eating an adequate diet, protecting oneself against diseases, and avoiding drugs. Research suggests that special intervention programs, such as home visits to mothers who smoke, to encourage healthy habits and provide social support can prevent damage to their children (Olds, Henderson, & Tatelbaum, 1994).

Today, many couples also enroll in classes that prepare them for childbirth. These classes started in the 1940s to help reduce the fear and pain experienced by many women during labor and delivery. The **Lamaze method** of prepared childbirth teaches women to associate childbirth with pleasant feelings and to ready themselves for the process by learning exercises, breathing and pushing methods, and relaxation techniques that make childbirth easier (Lamaze, 1958). Parents typically attend Lamaze classes for 6 to 8 weeks before the delivery. The father or another supportive person becomes a coach who helps the mother train her muscles and perfect her breathing for the event that lies ahead. Couples who participate in childbirth preparation classes report a greater sense of control during labor and delivery, and this sense of control is associated with higher levels of satisfaction with the childbirth experience (Hart & Foster, 1997). Unfortunately, following their delivery, many women say that their prenatal classes did not go as far as they could have in providing practice with the coping strategies useful for a smooth delivery (Spiby et al., 1999).

were caused by congenital abnormalities. With today's extensive prenatal testing of women older than 35, however, fewer babies are dying from congenital problems, partly because many such fetuses are identified early and aborted. Still, fetal death rates remain higher for older women for reasons poorly understood (Fretts & Usher, 1997). Keep in mind that despite the increased risk of fetal death among older women, most older women have normal pregnancies and healthy babies.

Emotional Condition

Does it matter how the mother feels about being pregnant or how her life is going while she is pregnant? Life is filled with many stressors—both chronic (for example, poverty or ongoing anxiety about terrorist attacks) and acute (for example, evacuating the World Trade Center on September 11, 2001). Being pregnant does not make stress disappear; for some women with unintended or mistimed pregnancies, stress levels may increase. How might the fetus be affected by the mother's experience of stress?

When a women such as Florence Engoran, introduced at the beginning of the chapter, becomes emotionally aroused, her glands secrete powerful hormones such as adrenaline (also called epinephrine) that may cross the placental barrier and enter the fetus's bloodstream. At the least, these hormones temporarily increase the fetus's motor activity. A temporarily stressful experience such as falling or receiving a scare will generally not damage mother or fetus. It is only when a mother experiences *prolonged and severe* emotional stress and anxiety during her pregnancy (as a result, for example, of the death of her husband or another child or of a cancer diagnosis) that damage may be done (Hansen, Lou, & Olsen, 2001). The most likely effects are a faster and more irregular heart rate and stunted prenatal growth, which can lower birth weight; premature birth; and birth complications (Monk et al., 2000; Mulder et al., 2002). Following birth, babies whose mothers had been highly stressed during pregnancy tend to be smaller, more active, more irritable, and more prone to crying than other babies (de Weerth, van Hees, & Buitelaar, 2003). Some research shows that stress during pregnancy can also cause delays in cognitive development (Buitelaar et al., 2003).

How might maternal stress stunt fetal growth and contribute to the offspring's irritability and anxiety? The mechanisms are not yet clear. The link between stressful experiences and small, premature babies may involve stress hormones, changes in the immune system, reduced blood flow through the arteries in the uterus, or even a poor diet (see, for example, DiPietro, Costigan, & Gurewitsch, 2003; Teixeira, Fisk & Glover, 1999). Whatever the mechanism, it is clear that not all stressed mothers have babies who are small and arrive early. In one revealing study (McCubbin et al., 1996), pregnant mothers were brought to the laboratory and asked to take a stressful arithmetic test. Those whose blood pressures rose the most dramatically during this mild stress test were more likely than other women to deliver premature babies with low birth weights. Thus, the *presence* of stress in a woman's life may not be as important as her *responsiveness* to stress in determining outcomes. Other research seems to confirm this: Mothers with a positive outlook are less likely to deliver low–birth-weight babies (Lobel et al., 2000).

The link between maternal stress and active, irritable behavior in infants is also hard to explain. Hypotheses include the idea that stress directly causes behavioral problems, that the baby of an emotional mother may simply be genetically predisposed to have a "difficult" temperament, and that a mother's emotional tensions may affect her care of the baby *after* birth. Because experimentation is impossible, establishing causal links is difficult. Still, mothers who experience severe stress during pregnancy should probably seek therapeutic help. In one study, the babies of stressed mothers who received counseling weighed more at birth than the babies of stressed mothers who did not get help (Rothberg & Lits, 1991).

Stress and anxiety are not the only maternal states to consider. Maternal depression during pregnancy may lead to motor delays in newborns (Lundy et al., 1999). Depression affects levels of neurotransmitters (brain chemicals) in both mothers and their newborns. Researchers have found a connection between these changes in neurotransmitter levels and certain immature motor responses of newborns. They do not yet know, however, whether these effects persist.

Nutritional Condition

At the turn of the last century, doctors advised mothers to gain a mere 10 to 15 pounds while pregnant. With better understanding of nutrition and pregnancy, doctors now recommend a healthy, high-protein, high-calorie diet with a total weight gain 25 to 35 pounds for normal-weight women, although many women gain more than this recommended weight during their pregnancy (Olson, 2002). At the other extreme, doctors know that inadequate prenatal nutrition and lack of weight gain can be harmful. Severe maternal malnutrition, which occurs during famine, stunts prenatal growth and produces small, underweight babies (Stein et al., 1975; Susser & Stein, 1994). The effects of malnutrition depend on when it occurs. During the first trimester, malnutrition can disrupt the formation of the spinal cord, result in fewer brain cells, and even cause stillbirth (Susser & Stein, 1994). Restrictive dieting, use of diuretics, and eating disorder behaviors during the first trimester can also cause serious problems, such as neural tube defects (Carmichael et al., 2003). During the third trimester, malnutrition is most likely to result in smaller neurons, a smaller brain, and a smaller child overall.

The offspring of malnourished mothers sometimes show cognitive deficits as infants and children. Poor prenatal nutrition may also put some children at risk for certain diseases in adulthood, especially hypertension, coronary heart disease, and diabetes (Barker, 1998; Goldberg & Prentice, 1994). Some research challenges this, however, and in many cases prenatal malnutrition does not have serious long-term effects on development (Golub et al., 1996). Among women who are adequately nourished, it is difficult to establish a connection between specific nutrients and birth outcome or later behaviors (Langley-Evans & Langley-Evans, 2003; Mathews, Youngman

& Neil, 2004). One exception to this is a deficiency of folic acid, which, as mentioned earlier, has been linked to neural tube defects. Otherwise, much depends on whether a child receives an adequate diet and good care after birth (Wachs, 1995). Dietary supplements, especially when combined with stimulating day care, can go a long way toward heading off the potentially damaging effects of prenatal malnutrition. Best, of course, is good nourishment before *and* after birth.

The Father's State

What about characteristics of the fathers? Does the father's state have any influence on the quality of the prenatal environment or birth outcome? Unfortunately, there is not a lot of research on the father's contributions to prenatal development beyond his genetic contribution. But researchers know that the father's age, just like the mother's age, can influence development. We noted earlier that women older than 35 are at greater risk of miscarriage than younger mothers. This risk is even greater if the father is also older (40 years or older, according to de la Rochebrochard & Thonneau, 2002). In addition, there is a slightly elevated risk of neural tube defects, kidney problems, and Down syndrome among children born to older fathers (McIntosh, Olshan, & Baird, 1995). Like the risk of miscarriage, the likelihood of Down syndrome is greater when both mother and father are older (Fisch et al., 2003). Another study found an increased risk of congenital heart defects for children of older fathers (Olshan, Schnitzer, & Baird, 1994).

A father's exposure to environmental toxins can also affect a couple's children. A father's prolonged exposure to radiation, anesthetic gases used in operating rooms, pesticides, or other environmental toxins can damage the genetic material in his sperm and cause genetic defects in his children (Stone, 1992; Strigini et al., 1990).

Summing Up

The womb is an environment that can influence the unborn child in favorable or unfavorable ways. There are numerous teratogens, such as alcohol and diseases, that can adversely affect prenatal development. The effects of teratogens depend on several factors, including timing, dosage, genetic makeup of both the mother and her unborn child, and quality of the prenatal and postnatal environments. The mother's emotional and nutritional state can influence the unborn child, as can the age of both the mother and the father. ■

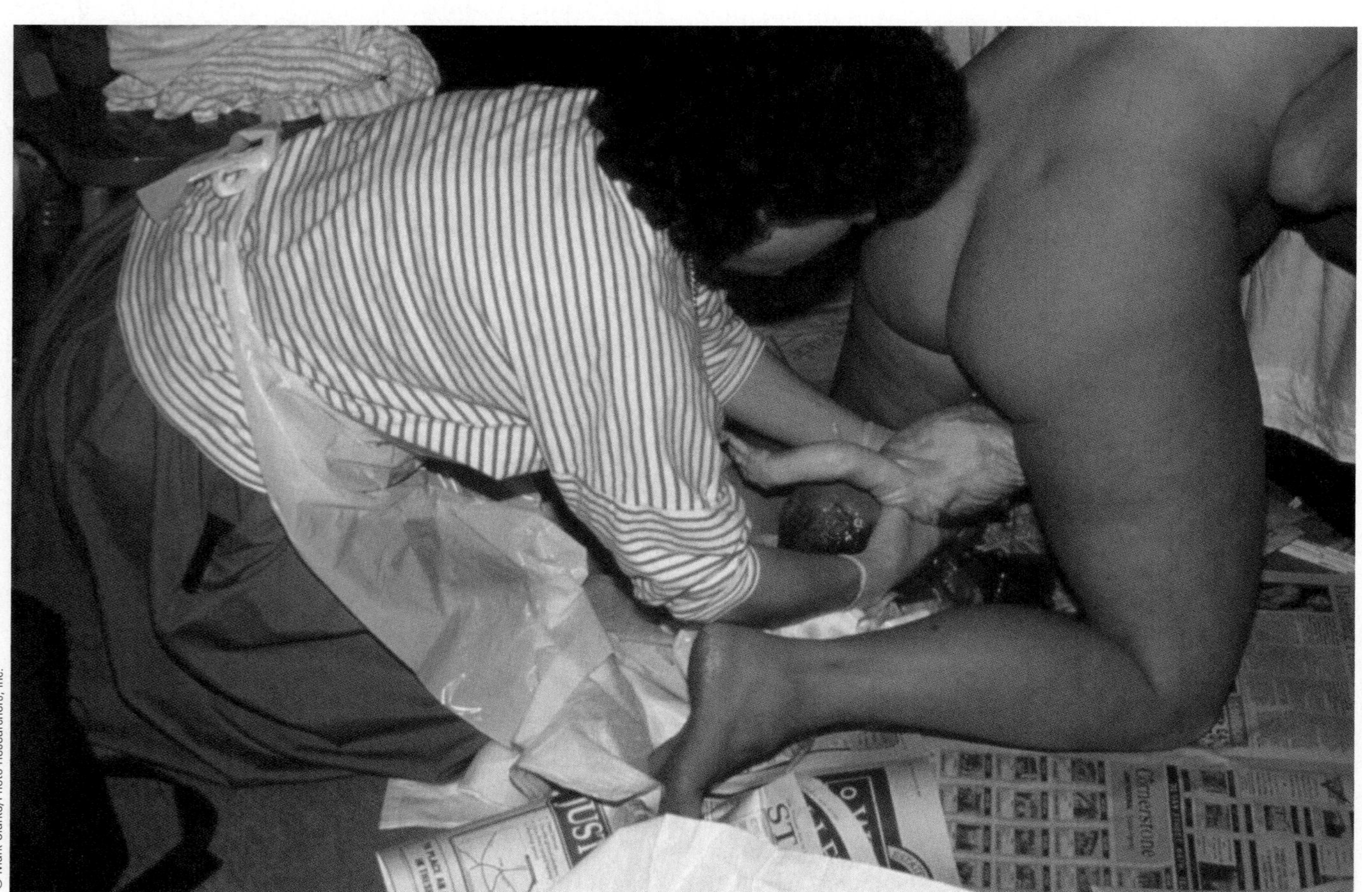

☾ Although most births in Western cultures take place in hospitals, this woman is giving birth at home.

The Perinatal Environment

The **perinatal environment** is the environment surrounding birth; it includes influences such as drugs given to the mother during labor, delivery practices, and the social environment shortly after birth. Like the prenatal environment, the perinatal environment can greatly affect human development.

In most Western cultures, there has been a dramatic shift in birthing practices. In 1930, 80% of births took place at home; by 1990, this figure had plummeted to 1% (Zander & Chamberlain, 1999). This change in birth setting was accompanied by a shift from thinking about birth as a natural family event that occurred at home to thinking that birth is a medical problem to be solved with high technology (Ackermann-Liebrich et al., 1996). Despite the medical setting of most births today, many couples want to give birth in a more relaxed atmosphere that gives them the peace of mind provided by nearby modern technology and a comfortable homelike feeling. Many hospitals have responded by restructuring their labor and delivery rooms and practices to give parents greater flexibility and control when it comes time to deliver.

Increasingly, a laboring woman has a partner, relative, or friend with her during labor and delivery; women find the support provided by this familiar person helpful and reassuring (Somers-Smith, 1999). Some women have the support of a *doula*—an individual trained to provide continuous physical and emotional support throughout the childbirth process. Such support tends to shorten labor and reduce the need for pain medication and assisted delivery such as use of forceps or vacuum (Hodnett et al., 2003; Scott, Klaus, & Klaus, 1999). Mothers with continuous labor support also report more positive feelings about the birth experience, fewer symptoms of postnatal depression, and greater likelihood of breast-feeding than nonsupported mothers (Scott, Klaus, & Klaus, 1999). Clearly, then, the context surrounding labor and delivery is important: Women who receive more support during childbirth have more positive experiences.

Childbirth is a three-stage process (see Figure 4.8). The first stage of labor begins as the mother experiences regular contractions of the uterus and ends when her cervix has fully dilated (widened) so that the fetus's head can pass through. This stage of labor lasts an average of 6 to 7 hours for firstborn children and 4 to 6 hours for later-born children, but it may last much longer depending on the individual and her circumstances (Albers, 1999; Jones & Larson, 2003). It ends when the cervix has dilated to 10 centimeters. The second stage of labor is delivery, which begins as the fetus's head passes through the cervix into the vagina and ends when the baby emerges from the mother's body. This is when the mother is often told to "bear down" (push) with each contraction to assist her baby through the birth canal. For first deliveries, this stage takes about 1 hour; for later deliveries, it can be 15 to 20 minutes (Albers, 1999; Jones & Larson, 2003). Finally, the third stage of the birth process is the delivery of the placenta, which lasts only a few minutes.

When the birth process is completed, the mother (and often the father, if he is present) is typically physically exhausted, relieved to be through the ordeal of giving birth, and exhilarated all at once. Meanwhile, the fetus has been thrust from its carefree but cramped existence into a strange new world.

Possible Hazards

In most births, the entire process goes smoothly, and parents and newborn quickly begin their relationship. Occasionally, however, problems arise.

Anoxia

One clear hazard during the birth process is **anoxia,** or oxygen shortage (also called *asphyxia*). Anoxia can occur for any number of reasons—for example, because the umbilical cord becomes pinched or tangled during birth, because sedatives given to the mother reach the fetus and interfere with the baby's breathing, because mucus lodged in the baby's throat prevents normal breathing, or even because the mother is older (Gilbert, Nesbitt, & Danielsen, 1999). Anoxia is dangerous primarily because brain cells die if they are starved of oxygen for more than a few minutes. Severe anoxia can cause mental retardation or **cerebral palsy,** a neurological disability associated with difficulty controlling muscle movements (Anslow, 1998; Carter, 1998). Milder cases of anoxia make some infants irritable at birth or delay their motor and cognitive development. However, many victims, especially those whose environments after birth are optimal, function normally later in childhood (Sameroff & Chandler, 1975). Children who experience relatively brief anoxia usually suffer no ill effects, but children with prolonged anoxia often have permanent disabilities (Sorensen & Borch, 1999).

The chances of anoxia have been greatly reduced by the use of fetal monitoring procedures during labor and delivery. Doctors are now alert to the risk of anoxia if the fetus is not positioned in the usual head-down position. If the baby is born feet or buttocks first (a **breech presentation**), delivery becomes more complex and takes longer, although most breech babies are normal. A vaginal delivery is nearly impossible for the 1 fetus in 100 lying sideways in the uterus. The fetus must be turned to assume a head-down position or be delivered by **cesarean section,** a surgical procedure in which an incision is made in the mother's abdomen and uterus so that the baby can be removed. Now, consider the potential hazards associated with delivery procedures and technologies.

Complicated Delivery

In some cases, mothers may need assistance with delivery, possibly because labor has proceeded too long with too little to show for it or because of concern about the well-being of the baby or mother. There is much debate in the medical literature about whether delivery is better assisted with forceps or with vacuum extraction (Johanson & Menon, 2000; O'Grady, Pope,

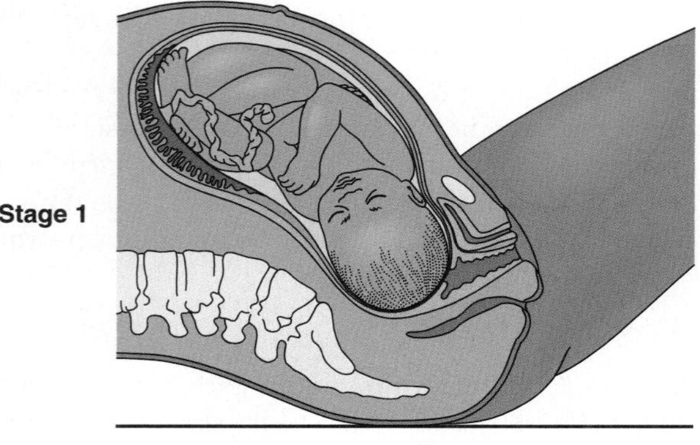

(A) Dilation of the cervix begins

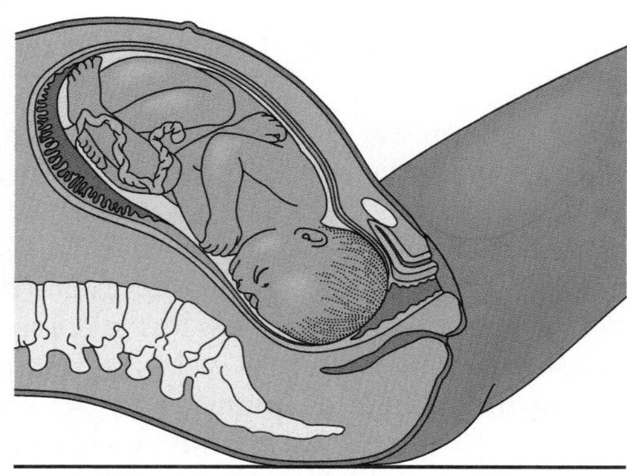

(B) Contractions are greatest and cervix opens completely

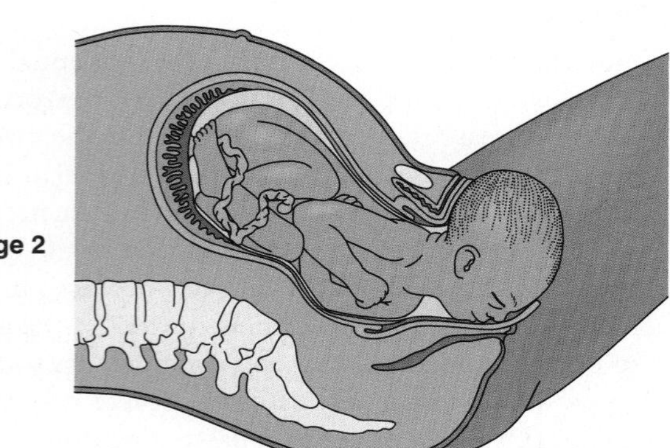

(C) Baby's head appears

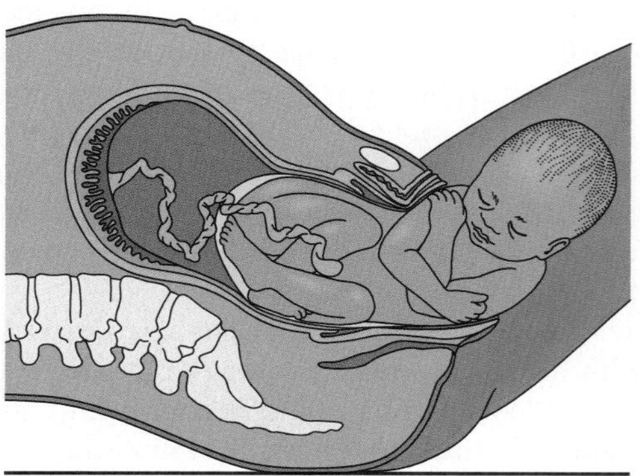

(D) Baby passes through the vagina

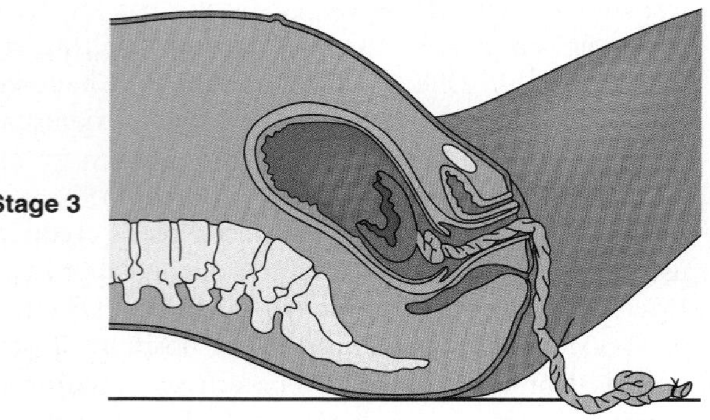

(E) Expulsion of the placenta

Figure 4.8 The three stages of labor. Stage 1: (A) Contractions of the uterus cause dilation and effacement of the cervix. (B) Transition is reached when the frequency and strength of the contractions are at their peak and the cervix opens completely. Stage 2: (C) The mother pushes with each contraction, forcing the baby down the birth canal, and the head appears. (D) Near the end of stage 2, the shoulders emerge and are followed quickly by the rest of the baby's body. Stage 3: (E) With a few final pushes, the placenta is delivered.

& Patel, 2000). For years, doctors frequently used forceps (an instrument resembling an oversized pair of salad tongs). However, forceps on the soft skull of the newborn occasionally caused serious problems, including cranial bleeding and brain damage. Alternatively, doctors may use vacuum extraction ("suction") to assist difficult deliveries. This procedure has fewer risks associated with it, although it is not risk free. In a vacuum extraction, a cup is inserted through the opening of the birth canal and attached to the baby's head. Suction is applied to make the cup adhere to the baby's scalp; during each contraction and with the mother bearing down, the doctor uses the traction created by the suction to help deliver the baby. From the mother's point of view, vacuum extraction is less traumatic than forceps (Shihadeh & Al-Najdawi, 2001). For the baby, however, there is likely to be swelling of the scalp and some marking where the cup was attached. More serious injuries are possible if the vacuum is not properly used. Unfortunately, women who deliver with vacuum assistance report less satisfaction than mothers who deliver by other methods with the overall birth experience (Schindl et al., 2003).

Cesarean sections, too, have been controversial. Use of this alternative to normal vaginal delivery has prevented the death of many babies—for example, when the baby is too large or the mother is too small to permit normal delivery, when a fetus out of position cannot be repositioned, or when fetal monitoring reveals that a birth complication is likely.

Medical advances have made cesarean sections about as safe as vaginal deliveries, and few ill effects on mothers and infants have been observed. Mothers who have "C-sections" take longer to recover from the birth process and are sometimes less positive toward and involved with their babies, at least during the first month after birth (DiMatteo et al., 1996). Nonetheless, the development of babies born by cesarean appears to be perfectly normal (Durik, Hyde, & Clark, 2000).

However, many observers have questioned why cesarean deliveries have become so much more common—to the point that they accounted for 26% of births in the United States in 2002 (Hamilton, Martin, & Sutton, 2003). The U.S. government tried to reduce the rate of cesareans in the 1990s but managed to reduce it only slightly to 21% of all deliveries before it crept back up to its current rate (Ventura et al., 2001). It is understood now that mothers who have one cesarean birth need not have all their subsequent babies by cesarean, as was believed only a short time ago (Harrington et al., 1997). Nonetheless, some obstetricians continue to rely heavily on this procedure because it protects them from the costly malpractice suits that might arise from complications in vaginal deliveries (Castro, 1999). Not only do some physicians prefer C-section deliveries, but some mothers prefer them as well. Mothers who undergo planned C-sections rate the birth experience more positively than any other group, including those who deliver by pushing the baby out vaginally (Schindl et al., 2003). Finally, C-sections generate more revenue than vaginal deliveries. On average, a cesarean delivery costs about $11,500 in the United States compared with $7000 for a vaginal delivery (March of Dimes, 2003).

In a few instances, tension between the hospital's concerns and the mother's wishes related to delivery practices can put them at odds. In 2004, a hospital sought and received permission from a judge for guardianship of a fetus so that it could force the mother to deliver her baby by cesarean section (The Associated Press, 2004). The hospital argued that a vaginal delivery would endanger the life of the child because an ultrasound showed that it was large. The mother, on the other hand, feared having a C-section because a friend had died following this surgery. Furthermore, she had successfully delivered six previous children vaginally. By the time the hospital obtained the court order for guardianship, the parents had gone to another hospital, where the mother vaginally delivered a healthy baby girl.

Overall, birth by cesarean delivery can be lifesaving in some cases and is unlikely to disrupt normal development, but it is more common than it needs to be in our society.

Medications

Concerns have been raised about medications given to mothers during the birth process—analgesics and anesthetics to reduce their pain, sedatives to relax them, and stimulants to induce or intensify uterine contractions (Simpson & Creehan, 1996). Sedative drugs that act on the entire body cross the placenta and can affect the baby. Babies whose mothers receive large doses of obstetrical medication are generally sluggish and irritable, are difficult to feed or cuddle during the first few days of life, and smile infrequently (Elbourne & Wiseman, 2000). In short, they act as though they are drugged. Think about it: Doses of medication large enough to affect mothers can have much greater effects on newborns who weigh only 7 pounds and have immature circulatory and excretory systems that cannot get rid of drugs for days or even weeks.

Regional analgesics, such as epidurals and spinal blocks, reduce sensation in specific parts of the body. Because they do not cross the placenta, they have fewer ill effects on babies and are preferred by many physicians. Epidurals are also rated by mothers as more effective for pain control than other forms of analgesics (Macario et al., 2000; Sheiner et al., 2000). But with these advantages mothers and physicians must weigh disadvantages, including longer labor times with epidurals (Halpern et al., 1998).

In sum, taking obstetric medications is not as risky a business today as it once was, but it is still a decision that requires the pros and cons to be weighed carefully. The effects depend on which drug is used, how much is taken, when it is taken, and by which mother.

Possible hazards during birth include anoxia; breech presentation; the need for assisted delivery through forceps, vacuum extraction, or cesarean section; and the use of medications for pain relief. Fortunately, most deliveries, although unique from the parents' perspective, are routine from a clinical perspective. In the next section, you will look briefly at the birth experience from a family perspective.

The Mother's Experience

What is it really like to give birth to a child? In a study of Swedish mothers (Waldenström et al., 1996), most mothers admitted that they experienced severe pain and a good deal of anxiety, including feelings of outright panic. Yet most also emerged from the delivery room feeling good about their achievement and their ability to cope ("I did it!"). Overall, 77% felt the experience was positive and only 10% said it was negative. And, despite longer labors and more medication, first-time mothers did not perceive labor and delivery much differently than experienced mothers did.

What factors influence a mother's experience? Psychological factors such as the mother's attitude toward her pregnancy, her knowledge and expectations about the birth process, her sense of control over childbirth, and the social support she receives from her partner or someone else are important determinants of her experience of delivery and of her new baby (Waldenström et al., 1996; Wilcock, Kobayashi, & Murray, 1997). Social support can be especially important. When the father, or another supportive person whose main role is to comfort the mother, is continuously present during labor and delivery, women experience less pain, use less medication, are less likely to have cesarean sections, and are more likely to feel better about the birth process (Hodnett & Osborn, 1989; Kennell et al., 1991).

Cultural Factors

The experience of childbearing is shaped by the cultural context in which it occurs. For example, different cultures have different views of the desirability of having children. In some, a large family is a status symbol, whereas in the People's Republic of China, a "one-child policy" discourages multiple childbearing in hopes of slowing population growth and raising the standard of living. As a result of this policy, the average number of children a Chinese woman bears dropped from nearly five children in 1970 to fewer than two in recent years. The ratio of boys to girls has also changed; many parents want their one child to be a boy who can support them in old age and therefore abort female fetuses identified through ultrasound tests or abandon their female babies after they are born.

Practices surrounding birth also differ widely. Among the Pokot people of Kenya, for example, cultural beliefs and rituals help ensure strong social support of the mother and a successful birth (O'Dempsey, 1988). The community celebrates the coming birth, and the father-to-be stops hunting lest he be killed by animals. As a result, he is available to support his wife. A midwife, aided by female relatives, delivers the baby. The placenta is buried in the goat enclosure, and the baby is washed in cold water and given a mixture of hot ash and boiled herbs so that it will vomit the amniotic fluid it has swallowed. Mothers are given plenty of time to recover. They go into seclusion for 1 month and devote themselves entirely to their babies for 3 months.

In Uttar Pradesh in northern India, by contrast, the blood associated with childbirth is viewed as polluting, and the whole event as shameful (Jeffery & Jeffery, 1993). A *dai,* a poorly paid attendant hired by the woman's mother-in-law, delivers the baby. The *dai* typically hates her menial, disgusting job, provides no pain relievers, discourages the mother from crying out in pain, and offers little emotional support. The mother is kept in the house for several days and in the family compound for weeks so that she will not pollute others. Because the baby is also believed to be polluted, its hair is shaved off.

Many observers charge that childbirth in highly industrialized Western societies has become too "medicalized," with women hospitalized, hooked up to monitors, and separated from most friends and family members. Should we return to more traditional ways of birthing that view delivery less like a major medical event and more like a typical life event? As the Indian example illustrates, not all "traditional" practices are in the best interests of parents and babies. Also, Western societies do a far better job than developing countries of preventing mother and infant mortality. In some areas of sub-Saharan Africa, for example, about 15% of babies die during childbirth or in the first year of life (Caldwell, 1996). In Western, industrial societies, infant mortality rates have dropped from almost 30 infants out of 1000 in 1950 to 7 infants out of 1000 in 2004 (Division of Vital Statistics, 2004). Unfortunately, infant mortality is twice as high for black infants compared with white infants (Guyer et al., 2000). The secret to a more optimal birth experience may be to blend beneficial traditional practices such as offering emotional support to new mothers with modern medical know-how.

Postnatal Depression

Some new mothers suffer from depression following the birth of their baby. As many as 60% of all new mothers report feeling tearful, irritable, moody, anxious, and depressed within the first few days after birth (Najman et al., 2000). This condition—the baby blues—is relatively mild, passes quickly, and is probably linked to the steep drops in levels of female hormones that normally occur after delivery and to the stresses associated with delivering a child and taking on the responsibilities of parenthood.

A second, and far more serious, condition is **postnatal depression**—an episode of clinical depression that lasts months rather than days in a woman who has just given birth. It affects approximately 1 in 10 new mothers (Cooper & Murray, 1998). Only rarely does a woman who has never had significant emotional problems become clinically depressed for the first time after giving birth. Most affected women have histories of depression, and many were depressed during pregnancy. Also, women vulnerable to depression are more likely to become depressed if they are experiencing other life stresses on top of the stresses of becoming a mother (Honey, Bennett, & Morgan, 2003). Lack of social support—especially a poor relationship with a partner—also increases the odds (Boyce, 2003; Heh, 2003).

Postnatal depression has significant implications for the parent–infant relationship. One study compared the children of 58 mothers who experienced postnatal depression with the children of 42 nondepressed mothers over a 5-year period (Murray et al., 1999). The children of the depressed mothers were less securely attached to their mothers during infancy and were less responsive during interactions with their mothers at age 5. They also tended to respond negatively when another child approached them in a friendly manner.

Mothers who had been postnatally depressed report greater behavioral problems by their children. At age 11, children of postnatally depressed mothers show more violent behavior even when researchers control for family characteristics and later episodes of depression (Hay et al., 2003). The violence exhibited by these children is associated with anger management problems, attention problems, and hyperactive behavior. In another study, adolescents whose mothers had been postnatally depressed showed elevated levels of cortisol, which is associated with major depression (Halligan et al., 2004). The implication of these results is that early experiences with a depressed mother might predispose these children to later depression.

How might maternal depression in the weeks and months following delivery affect children's behavior and increase their odds of developing depression? Mothers who are depressed tend to be relatively unresponsive to their babies and may even feel hostility toward them. They are tired, distracted, and often lack the energy needed to be fully engaged with their infants. Even though mothers typically recover from postnatal depression, research suggests that their early attitudes about their babies and the resulting pattern of early mother–child interactions set the stage for ongoing interaction problems that affect the child's behavior (Murray et al., 1999). The contribution of genes inherited from their depression-prone mothers and of stressful experiences before birth, after birth, or both may precipitate depression in the child (Goodman, 2002). Thus, for their own sakes and for the sakes of their infants, mothers experiencing more than a mild case of the baby blues should seek professional help in overcoming their depression.

The Father's Experience

Until the 1970s, fathers in Western culture were routinely excluded from the birth process. Today, however, many men prepare for fatherhood before delivery, attend prenatal classes with their partner, and are present for their child's birth (Gage & Kirk, 2002). Like mothers, fathers experience the birth process as a significant event in their lives that involves a mix of positive and negative emotions. Also like mothers, fathers tend to be anxious during pregnancy and birth. In several studies, new fathers admitted that they felt scared, unprepared, helpless, and frustrated during labor (Chandler & Field, 1997; Chapman, 2000; Hallgren et al., 1999). They found labor to be more work than they had expected and sometimes felt excluded as the nurses took over. For most men, attending prenatal classes with their partner improves their experience of childbirth, although for a few men, the added knowledge that comes with these classes increases their anxiety (Greenhalgh, Slade, & Spiby, 2000). Despite the stresses, negative emotions usually give way to relief, pride, and joy when the baby finally arrives (Chandler & Field, 1997). Indeed, most fathers find early contact with their babies special. As one father put it, "when my wife handed Anna to me, I was completely unprepared for the intense experience of fatherhood. I was overwhelmed by my feeling of belonging to and with this new child" (Reed, 1996, p. 52).

Summing Up

The perinatal environment, or the environment surrounding birth, influences both the child and the parents. Childbirth is a three-step process consisting of labor, delivery of the baby, and expulsion of the placenta. Despite recent concerns about overuse, cesarean sections are common. Perinatal risks to the baby include anoxia, assisted delivery (for example, forceps, vacuum extraction, and cesarean section), and the effects of medications given to the mother. ■

The Neonatal Environment

So now that parents have a baby, what do they do? Here you will look at the **neonatal** environment—the events of the first month and how parents might optimize development of young infants.

There are marked differences in how parents interact with their newborns. For example, in societies where infant mortality is high, babies may not even be named or viewed as people until they seem likely to survive (Nsamenang, 1992). The Beng, who are concentrated in small farming towns along the Ivory Coast, believe that newborns are not entirely in this world but exist in the world the babies will eventually inhabit after death (L. Gottlieb, 2000). Once their umbilical cord stump falls off between 4 and 5 days after birth, they begin to inhabit this world but still vacillate between the two worlds for another 4 to 5 years. During this time, the Beng regard their children as vulnerable. Spiritual beliefs influence their child care practices, leading to, for example, twice daily enemas for infants using a chili pepper solution.

Among the !Kung, a hunting and gathering society of the Kalahari Desert in southern Africa, babies are carried upright in slings during the day and they sleep in the same bed with their mothers at night (Konner, 1981). They are breast-fed whenever they want and may not be weaned until the ripe old age of 4. In general, infants in hunter–gatherer societies are indulged considerably, at least until their survival is assured.

Infant care practices are considerably different in modern, industrialized societies where infant mortality is lower. Babies typically sleep apart from their parents; they breastfeed, if at all, for only a few months before being switched to the bottle and then to solid food; and they generally must learn to accommodate their needs to their parents' schedules. Mayan mothers in Guatemala, who sleep in the same bed with their babies until they are toddlers, express shock at the American practice of leaving infants alone in their own bedrooms (Morelli et al., 1992).

Regardless of where they live, new parents are often uncertain about how to relate to their babies and may find the period after birth stressful. T. Berry Brazelton (1979) has devised a way to help parents appreciate their baby's competencies and feel competent themselves as parents. He developed a newborn assessment technique, the Brazelton Neonatal Behavioral Assessment Scale, that assesses the strength of infant reflexes and the infant's responses to 26 situations (for example, reac-

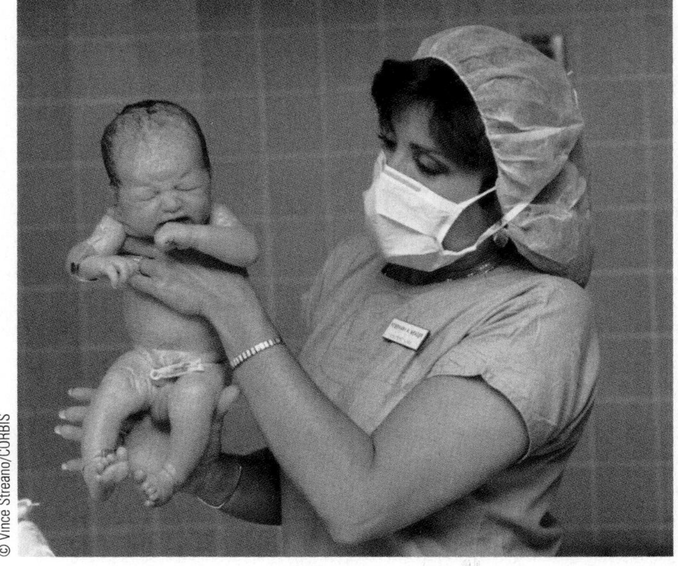

Most newborns have not yet acquired the "cuteness" of somewhat older babies. Instead, they are often red, wrinkled, and swollen in places, and they may be covered with amniotic fluid, blood, fine downy hair (lanugo), and a white greasy substance (vernix). Their heads may even be misshapen from coming through the birth canal or from the use of forceps or suction during delivery.

© Amranand/SuperStock

In many cultures, mothers keep their babies close to them all day and night to ensure their survival.

tions to cuddling, general irritability, and orienting to the examiner's face and voice). Brazelton uses this test to teach parents to understand their babies as individuals and to appreciate many of the pleasing competencies that they possess. During "Brazelton training," parents observe the test being administered and learn how to administer it themselves to elicit smiles and other heartwarming responses from their babies.

Identifying At-Risk Newborns

In the end, a few infants are considered **at risk** for either short-term or long-term problems because of genetic defects, prenatal hazards, or perinatal damage. It is essential to these infants' survival and well-being that they be identified as early as possible. Newborns are routinely screened using the **Apgar test,** which provides a quick assessment of the newborn's heart rate, respiration, color, muscle tone, and reflexes (see Table 4.6). The test has been used for more than 50 years and, despite its "low-tech" nature, is still considered a valuable diagnostic tool (Casey, McIntire, & Leveno 2001). The simple test is given immediately and 5 minutes after birth. It yields scores of 0, 1, or 2 for each of the five factors, which are then added to yield a total score that can range from 0 to 10. Infants who score 7 or higher are in good shape. Infants scoring 4 or lower are at risk—their heartbeats are sluggish or nonexistent, their muscles are limp, and their breathing, if they are breathing, is shallow and irregular. These babies will immediately experience a different postnatal environment than the normal baby experiences because they require medical intervention in intensive care units to survive, as you will see at the end of the chapter.

One particular group of at-risk babies that should be examined more closely are those with low birth weight. Approximately 8% of babies born in the United States have a low birth weight (less than 2500 grams, or 5½ pounds). Some of these babies are born at term, but many are born preterm (less than 37 weeks of gestation) and are more at risk. The survival and health of these small infants is a concern, particularly for infants born with very low birth weight—less than 1500 grams (Paneth, 1995). Although low–birth-weight infants account for about 8% of all births, they account for 65% of all infant deaths (Murphy, 2000). And according to one analysis, they account for more than 80% of the money spent on pregnancies and deliveries (Adams et al., 2003). As Table 4.7 illustrates, the younger (and smaller) babies are at birth, the lower their chances of survival.

Low birth weight is strongly linked to low socioeconomic status. According to Hughes and Simpson (1995), "women who live in poverty, who have low levels of education, who work in low-wage jobs, and who have few other social resources are more likely to suffer adverse birth outcomes than are more advantaged women" (p. 87). Most programs attempting to prevent low birth weight target the health conditions associated with poverty, such as poor nutrition and inadequate prenatal health care (Hughes & Simpson, 1995). Unfortunately, such programs have not been terribly successful because they do not address many entrenched behaviors and beliefs that accompany socioeconomic disadvantage in the United States.

Table 4.6 The Apgar Test

Factors	Score		
	0	1	2
HEART RATE	Absent	Slow (under 100 beats per minute)	Moderate (over 100 beats per minute)
RESPIRATORY EFFORT	Absent	Slow or irregular	Good; baby is crying
MUSCLE TONE	Flaccid; limp	Weak; some flexion	Strong; active motion
COLOR	Blue or pale	Body pink, extremities blue	Completely pink
REFLEX IRRITABILITY	No response	Frown, grimace, or weak cry	Vigorous cry

Table 4.7 Survival and Health of Premature Babies by Gestational Age

Factor	Results (in weeks and %)			
Number of completed weeks since last menstruation	<23 weeks	23 weeks	24 weeks	25 weeks
Percentage of babies who survive	0–15%	2–35%	17–58%	35–85%
Percentage of survivors with chronic lung disease	89%	57–70%	33–89%	16–71%
Percentage of survivors with a severe neurodevelopmental disability*	69%	30%	17–45%	12–35%

* Includes cerebral palsy, mental retardation, blindness or severe myopia, and deafness.
SOURCE: Based on data from Hack & Fanaroff, 1999.

In addition to poverty, there are many other risk factors for low birth weight, including factors that we have already described such as smoking and stress. The more risk factors experienced during pregnancy, the greater the likelihood of delivering a small baby (Rosenberg, 2001).

Low birth weight is also associated with multiple births, which have increased substantially over the past several decades largely because of increased use of ovulation-stimulating drugs to treat infertility (Guyer et al., 1999). In 1980, there were 37 higher-order multiple births (three or more) for every 100,000 births; by 1997, this figure had jumped to 173 multiples for every 100,000 births. Among single-birth infants, approximately 5% are low birth weight, but among twins, nearly half are low birth weight. Among higher-order multiples, 86% are low birth weight (Cohen et al., 1999).

The good news is that most low–birth-weight babies born since the advent of neonatal intensive care in the 1960s function within the normal range of development (Hack, Klein, & Taylor, 1995). However, compared with normal–birth-weight children, low–birth-weight children are at greater risk for blindness, deafness, cerebral palsy, poor academic achievement, autism, and health problems. Respiratory difficulties are likely because premature babies have not yet produced enough **surfactant,** a substance that prevents the air sacs of the lungs from sticking together and therefore aids breathing. The most common neurological problem for low–birth-weight infants is cerebral palsy.

Although the long-term prognosis for low–birth-weight babies is now good, many children born with a very low birth weight continue to experience neurosensory impairments and academic problems throughout their childhood and teen years (Saigal et al., 2000). The fate of premature and low–birth-weight babies depends considerably on two factors. The first is their biological condition—their health and neurological status in particular (Koller et al., 1997). The second is the quality of the postnatal environment they experience. For instance, in a study of more than 8000 infants, Dennis Hogan and Jennifer Park (2000) found that the disadvantages of low birth weight

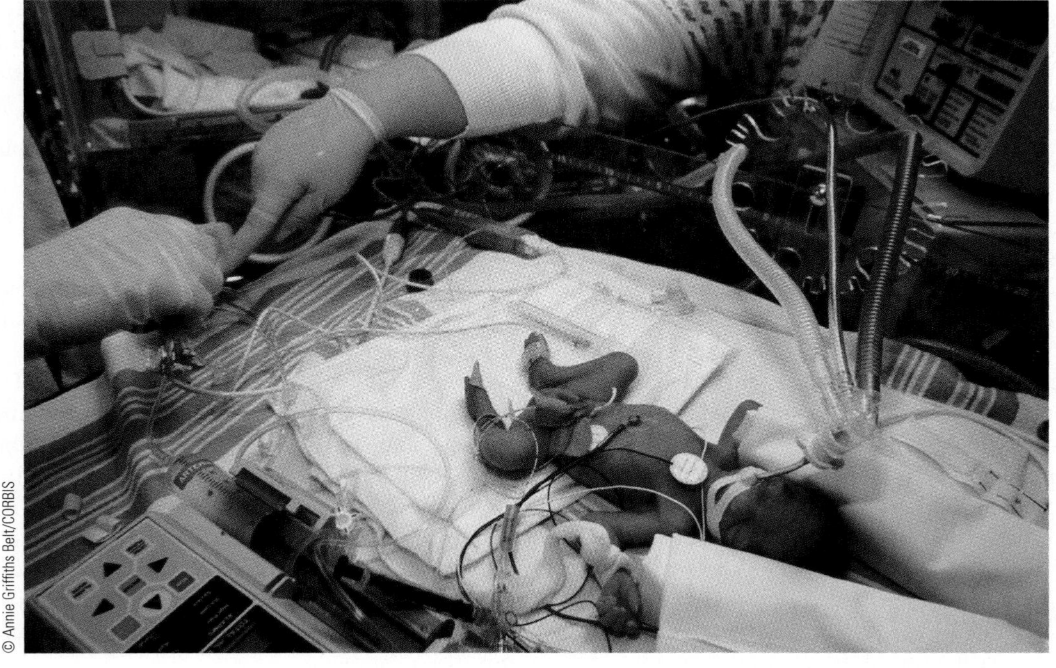

Modern technology permits the survival of younger and smaller babies, but many experts believe we have reached the lowest limits of viability between 23 and 24 weeks of gestation.

were amplified for children of minority status growing up in poverty with a single parent. In contrast, low–birth-weight babies who live with two parents and whose mother is well educated, although they start out with delays, improve and may even catch up to the average child by age 8 (Ment et al., 2003).

Other research shows that at-risk infants can benefit from programs that teach their parents how to provide responsive care and appropriate intellectual stimulation to them once they are home. Home visits to advise parents, combined with a stimulating day care program for low–birth-weight toddlers, can teach mothers how to be better teachers of their young children and stimulate these children's cognitive development. In an ambitious project called the Infant Health and Development Program, premature and low–birth-weight infants at eight sites have benefited from such early intervention (Bradley et al., 1994; Brooks-Gunn et al., 1993; McCarton et al., 1997). The program involved weekly home visits during the first year after birth and then biweekly home visits and attendance by the infant at a special day care center for half a day every day from age 1 to age 3. Mothers were given childcare education and support. The program appears to help parents provide a more growth-enhancing home environment—for example, to give their babies appropriate toys and learning materials and to interact with them in stimulating ways.

The intervention helped these at-risk babies, especially the heavier ones, achieve more cognitive growth by age 3 than they would otherwise have achieved. However, an impressive 14-point boost in IQ scores at age 3 for heavier low–birth-weight children who received the intervention had dropped to a 4-point advantage at age 8 (McCarton et al., 1997). Children who weighed 2000 grams (4 pounds 6 ounces) or less at birth did not get much benefit. Researchers have more to learn, then, about what it takes to keep the development of at-risk children on a positive track after the **perinatal period,** the period surrounding birth, comes to a close. However, everything researchers know about life-span environmental forces suggests that supportive parents and programs can do a great deal to optimize every child's development. It seems that premature, low–birth-weight babies can achieve normal levels of intellectual functioning during childhood when they live in middle-class homes, when their mothers are relatively educated, and most importantly, when their mothers, rich or poor, are attentive and responsive when interacting with them (Brooks-Gunn et al., 1993; Miceli et al., 2000).

Studies such as these raise a larger issue about the importance of early experience. Some developmentalists take seriously the concept of critical (or sensitive) periods in early development. Others stress the resilience of human beings, their ability to rebound from early disadvantages and to respond to environmental influences throughout their lives rather than only during so-called critical periods. Which is it?

Risk and Resilience

To what extent does harm done in the prenatal or perinatal period last, and to what extent can postnatal experiences make up for it? You have encountered many examples in this chapter of what can go wrong before or during birth. Some damaging effects are clearly irreversible: The thalidomide baby will never grow normal arms or legs, and the child with FAS will always be mentally retarded. Yet throughout history, many children turned out fine even though their mothers—unaware of many risk factors—smoked and drank during their pregnancies, received heavy doses of medication during delivery, or experienced serious illness. So, although many factors place a fetus at risk and increase the likelihood of problems after birth, not all at-risk infants end up with problems (Fraser, 2004). Is it also possible that some babies exposed to and clearly affected by risks recover from their deficiencies later in life?

Indeed it is, and researchers now have the results of major longitudinal studies that say so. Emmy Werner, with her colleague Ruth Smith, studied a group of babies born in 1955 on the island of Kauai in Hawaii for 40 years (Werner, 1989a, 1989b; Werner & Smith, 1982, 1992, 2001). This was a monumental undertaking. All women of Kauai who were to give birth in 1955 were interviewed in each trimester of pregnancy, and physicians noted any prenatal, perinatal, or postnatal complications. On the basis of this information, each baby was categorized as having been exposed to severe, moderate, mild, or no prenatal or perinatal stress. At ages 1, 2, 10, 18, 32, and 40 years, researchers diligently tracked down their participants and conducted interviews (initially with the mothers and later with the children), administered psychological and cognitive tests, rated the quality of the family environment, and conducted medical examinations. Remarkably, at the 40-year follow-up, the researchers still had 70%, or 489 participants, from their original group of 698 babies born in 1955.

One-third of the children classified as at risk showed considerable **resilience,** getting themselves back on a normal course of development. Through this self-righting capacity, they were able to mature into competent, successful adults with no evident learning, social, or vocational problems despite being at risk for poor outcomes. Two major findings emerge from this research:

- The effects of prenatal and perinatal complications decrease over time.
- The outcomes of early risk depend on the quality of the postnatal environment.

The postnatal environments of these successful at-risk children included two types of **protective factors** that helped the children overcome their disadvantage:

- *Personal resources.* Possibly because of their genetic makeup, some children have qualities such as intelligence, sociability, and communication skills that help them choose or create more nurturing and stimulating environments and cope with challenges. For example, parents and other observers noted that these children were agreeable, cheerful, and self-confident as infants, which elicited positive caregiving responses. They also believed that they were in control of their own fates—that through their actions, they could bring about positive outcomes.
- *Supportive postnatal environment.* Some at-risk children receive the social support they need within or outside the fam-

ily. Most importantly, they are able to find at least one person who loves them unconditionally and with whom they feel secure.

Clearly, hazards during the important prenatal and perinatal periods can leave lasting scars, and yet many children show remarkable resilience. There seem to be some points in the life span, especially early on, in which both positive and negative environmental forces have especially strong effects. Yet *environment matters throughout life.* It would be a mistake to assume that all children who have problems at birth are doomed. In short, early experience by itself can, but rarely does, make or break development; later experience counts, too, sometimes enough to turn around a negative course of development.

Summing Up

As Chapters 3 and 4 have testified, both nature and nurture contribute to life-span human development. Certain genes and early environments can have profound negative effects on development. Yet most of us come into existence with an amazingly effective genetic program to guide our development. Most of us, whether we grow up in Kenya or Japan or the United States, also receive the benefits of a normal human environment, one that joins forces with this genetic program to promote normal development. Sometimes, early insults cannot be undone; other times, only very adverse conditions over a long period can keep us from developing normally. Even then, we often show resilience if given half a chance. ■

Summary Points

1. Prenatal development begins with conception and proceeds through the germinal, embryonic, and fetal periods. Growth during the prenatal period is faster than during any other period of the life span.

2. The environment of human development includes all events or conditions outside the person that affect or are affected by the person's development, including both the physical and the social environment. A variety of teratogens, such as diseases and drugs, can significantly affect development. Four principles help researchers understand the effects of teratogens: effects are worst when organ systems are growing most rapidly, effects are more serious with greater exposure to teratogens, harmful effects depend on the genetic makeup of both the mother and her unborn child, and the effects of teratogens often depend on the quality of the prenatal and postnatal environments.

3. The perinatal environment includes the conditions surrounding birth. Childbirth consists of three stages: labor, delivery of the baby, and delivery of the placenta. Nearly 1 out of every 4 babies is delivered by cesarean section. Perinatal risks to the baby include anoxia, assisted delivery, and the effects of medications given to the mother.

4. Most new parents are anxious during labor and delivery but find the experience a positive one. Support for new mothers varies across cultures. Ways of getting human lives off to a good start today include prenatal care, Lamaze classes, alternative birth centers, neonatal intensive care units, and training for parents of at-risk infants.

5. Some problems created by prenatal and perinatal hazards are long-lasting, but many at-risk babies show remarkable resilience and outgrow their problems, especially if they have personal resources, such as sociability and intelligence, and grow up in stimulating and supportive postnatal environments where someone loves them.

Critical Thinking

1. Thinking about the material in Chapters 3 and 4, develop a plan for preventing mental retardation that involves consideration of both genetic and environmental contributors (prenatal, perinatal, and postnatal) to significantly limited intellectual development.

2. Some people argue that women who abuse alcohol or other drugs during pregnancy should be charged with abuse or attempted murder or with murder if they have a miscarriage. Using material from this chapter on teratogens and the prenatal environment, argue both sides of this issue.

3. Imagine you have been charged with speaking to a group of mothers-to-be about possible hazards influencing prenatal development. Describe for them the four principles of teratogens and illustrate each principle with an example.

4. Thinking about research on birth and the perinatal environment, arrange the perfect birth experience for you and your baby and justify its features. Where would you be, who would be there, and what would be done?

5. Write a newsletter for parents-to-be. Your goal is to describe the unborn baby's environment and compare this with the environment outside the womb after the baby is born.

6. What are the ethical concerns raised by stem cell research? If you and your partner undergo fertility treatment and subsequently have "extra" embryos frozen in a laboratory with no plans for additional children, will you donate these for stem cell research? Why or why not?

Key Terms

assisted reproduction technologies (ART), 85
artificial insemination, 85
in vitro fertilization (IVF), 85
germinal period, 86
blastocyst, 86
embryonic period, 86
organogenesis, 86
amnion, 86
chorion, 86
placenta, 86
umbilical cord, 86
testosterone, 87
fetal period, 87
differentiation, 88
stem cells, 88
age of viability, 89
myelin, 89
infant states, 90
prenatal environment, 91
teratogen, 91
critical period, 91
thalidomide, 92

sudden infant death syndrome (SIDS), 93
fetal alcohol syndrome (FAS), 93
rubella, 96
syphilis, 96
acquired immunodeficiency syndrome (AIDS), 97
Lamaze method, 98
perinatal environment, 100
anoxia, 101
cerebral palsy, 101
breech presentation, 101
cesarean section, 101
postnatal depression, 104
neonatal, 105
at risk, 106
Apgar test, 106
surfactant, 106
resilience, 108
protective factors, 108
perinatal period, 108

Media Resources

Websites to Explore

Visit Our Website

For a chapter tutorial quiz and other useful features, visit the book's companion website at *http://psychology.wadsworth.com/sigelman_rider5e.* You can also connect directly to the following sites:

The Human Embryo
The Multi-Dimensional Human Embryo project website contains photos taken with magnetic resonance imaging of every stage of prenatal development.

18 Ways to Make a Baby
Originally broadcast by PBS in October 2001, this *NOVA* program investigates the world of assisted reproduction. Its companion website contains interactive and multimedia opportunities to explore topics related to fertility and reproduction, such as human cloning and cell division.

Life's Greatest Miracle
Using the microimagery of Swedish photographer Lennart Nilsson, this PBS *NOVA* program tracks the growth of a baby from embryo to newborn. Winner of an Emmy award, it is available to watch in its entirety on the companion website. The site also provides background on the stem-cell debate and contains related multimedia resources for further exploration.

Best Bet on Pregnancy and Birth
Childbirth.org provides practical advice on a variety of pregnancy- and birth-related topics, including fertility, cesareans, *doulas,* and labor.

Stem-Cell Research
The National Institutes of Health maintains a website where it provides information about stem cells and related research.

Birth Defects
The website for the National Center on Birth Defects and Developmental Disabilities includes links to information on birth defects and disabilities, press releases, and current health news.

Understanding the Data: Exercises on the Web

For additional insight on the data presented in this chapter, try the exercises for the following figures at *http://psychology.wadsworth.com/sigelman_rider5e:*

Figure 4.4 The percentage of time the fetus spends in different states from the 20th week until the end of pregnancy. Time in one coherent state or another increases with age, and most time is spent in a state of sleep.

Table 4.7 Survival and Health of Premature Babies by Gestational Age

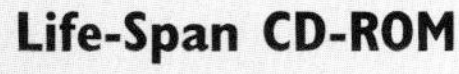

Life-Span CD-ROM

Go to the Wadsworth Life-Span CD-ROM for further study of the concepts in this chapter. The CD-ROM includes narrated concept overviews, video clips, a multimedia glossary, and additional activities to expand your learning experience. For this chapter, check out the the following clips, and others, in the video library:

VIDEO Ultrasound

VIDEO The Apgar Assessment

DEVELOPMENTAL Psychology Now™

Developmental PsychologyNow is a web-based, intelligent study system that provides a complete package of diagnostic quizzes, a personalized study plan, integrated multimedia elements, and learning modules. Check it out at *http://psychology.wadsworth.com/sigelman_rider5e/now.*

CHAPTER five

The Physical Self

"JOSH IS A 12-YEAR-OLD BOY with constitutional growth delay. Although he has grown at a normal rate throughout childhood, his height is below the 5th percentile line on the growth chart. His bone age is delayed by 2 to 3 years, so he is unlikely to reach a normal adult height. He has always been the smallest child in his class, and the size difference is getting more noticeable as some of his classmates begin their growth spurts: Josh looks more like a 4th grader than a 7th grader. He is having school problems this year, after moving into a new school. His teachers report that 'he's either a clown or a bully in class, and he just does not pay attention.' He likes sports and is good at soccer, but the coach does not want to let him try out for the team—he is afraid Josh will get hurt. The older boys at school sometimes pick him up and carry him around, calling him 'Peewee' and 'Squirt.' He has started spending a lot of time alone in his room and does not seem interested in anything. After his last visit to the doctor, he said, 'I'm sick of hearing how tall I'll be in 10 years. I'm a shrimp now, and that is all that matters.'" (Rieser & Underwood, 2004)

Josh's case illustrates the complexity as well as the significance of growth and development. Although he is growing at the normal *rate* of development, he is still markedly shorter than other boys his age. What are the processes underlying Josh's growth? And what are the psychological implications for Josh and other children, adolescents, and adults of the physical changes that occur throughout the life span?

These are the sorts of questions that we address in this chapter on the physical self. We start by examining the major physical systems that underlie human functioning, including the endocrine and nervous systems. We also look at the reproductive system as it matures during adolescence and changes during adulthood. And we watch the physical self in action, as motor skills develop during childhood and physical fitness and motor behavior change during adulthood. We identify influences on physical development and aging so that you can better understand why some children develop—and some older adults age—more rapidly than others.

Building Blocks of Growth and Development

Physical capabilities are fundamental to what people are able to do in life. A 5-year-old child is physically able to experience the world in ways markedly different from those available to a 5-month-old infant. Mariah, for example, can throw a ball with her mom, run with her dog, play hopscotch with her friends, feed and dress herself, and enjoy many of the rides at the amusement park. Changes in her brain have increased her memory abilities and capacity to think, and her language skills are astounding compared with those of the 5-month-old. Yet Mariah and other 5-year-olds are limited by their physical selves. It will be years before their brains are fully developed, allowing greater concentration and more sophisticated thought processes. Their strength and coordination on motor tasks will continue to improve, and their bodies will grow taller and heavier and will mature sexually.

Human growth and development is an incredibly complex process, occurring over years. It is influenced by both genetic and environmental factors. At certain times and for certain developments, genetic influences are greater, whereas at other times, environmental influences are more powerful. But as we explained in previous chapters, genetic and environmental forces are always working together. Consider height. The average female in the United States is about 5 feet 4 inches (162 cm) and the average male is 5 feet 9 inches (175 cm), but there is considerable variability. Sandy Allen from the state of Indiana, for instance, is considered the tallest woman in the world at 7 feet 7 inches; most women with Turner syndrome are nearly 3 feet shorter than this—4 feet 8 inches on average. Even among those considered within the average range of height, there is variability. Genes account for some of this: Tall people tend to have tall parents, whereas short people often have "short genes" hanging on their family tree. Research with identical twins confirms a fairly strong genetic component to height.

But even if you inherit the genetic propensity to be tall (or short), environment can influence the expression of those genes. If you lack adequate nutrition, for example, you may not realize your full growth potential. And consider the case of children with celiac syndrome. An abnormality with their stomach lining leaves them unable to absorb nutrients from food despite adequate consumption. Their disease leads to malnutrition, which stunts growth. As Figure 5.1 shows, however, treatment that restores absorption of nutrients leads to dramatic **catch-up growth.** This catch-up growth after a period of malnutrition or illness reflects the body's struggle to get back on the growth course it is genetically programmed to follow.

Even features of the natural environment can influence growth and development. People who live in colder climates tend to be shorter and somewhat heavier than those in warmer climates (Schell & Knutsen, 2002). This seems to be explained by the body's temperature control system—people in cold climates benefit from a smaller surface area through which body heat can be lost, and the opposite is true of people in warm climates. Moreover, children's height gain is fastest in the warm spring months and slowest in the cool fall months (Schell & Knutsen, 2002). Air pollution and noise have also been shown to slightly retard growth and development both prenatally and postnatally (Schell & Knutsen, 2002).

To understand how growth can be influenced by genes and environments, you need to consider the workings of the endocrine and nervous systems.

The Endocrine System

The endocrine, or hormonal, system consists of a group of **endocrine glands** that secrete chemicals called *hormones* directly into the bloodstream. Perhaps the most critical of the en-

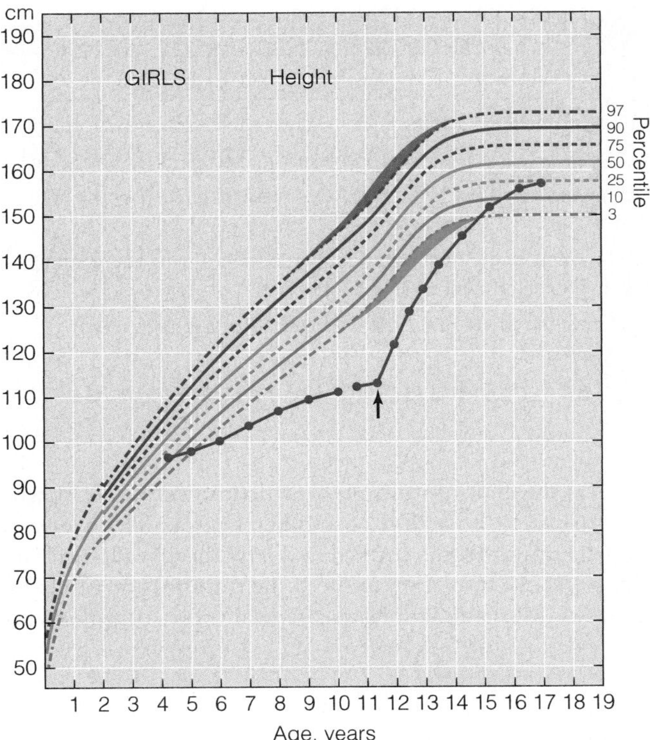

Figure 5.1 This shows the catch-up growth that has occurred in a girl following treatment at around age 11 for her celiac syndrome.

SOURCE: Cameron, N., (2002). Human growth curve, canalization, and catch-up growth. In N. Cameron (Ed.), *Human Growth and Development* (p. 19). NY: Academic Press. Copyright © 2002. Reprinted with permission of Elsevier.

docrine glands is the **pituitary gland,** the so-called master gland located at the base of the brain. Directly controlled by the hypothalamus of the brain, it triggers the release of hormones from all other endocrine glands by sending hormonal messages to those glands. Moreover, the pituitary produces **growth hormone,** which triggers the production of specialized hormones that directly regulate growth. Children who lack adequate growth hormone are unlikely to exceed 4 feet (or 130 cm) in height as adults but can now be treated successfully with synthetic growth hormone (Vance, Mauras, & Wood, 1999). By contrast, administering human growth hormone to children who are simply short and do not have an endocrine problem is likely to do no good and can even backfire. Hormone treatment tends to induce an early and short puberty, and treated children are either early in attaining the height they would have reached anyway or end up smaller than they would otherwise have been (Rosenfeld, 1997).

The thyroid gland also plays a key role in physical growth and development and in the development of the nervous system. Babies born to mothers who had a thyroid deficiency during pregnancy have lower IQ scores as children (Haddow et al., 1999). Thyroid deficiency during infancy can also lead to mental retardation and slow growth if unnoticed and untreated (Robertson, 1993). Children who develop a thyroid deficiency later in life will not suffer brain damage, because most of their brain growth has already occurred, but their physical growth will slow drastically.

In Chapter 4, you learned about another critical role of the endocrine system. A male fetus will not develop male reproductive organs unless (1) a gene on his Y chromosome triggers the development of the testes (which are endocrine glands), and (2) the testes secrete the most important of the male hormones, testosterone. Male sex hormones become highly important again during adolescence. When people speak of adolescence as a time of "raging hormones," they are quite right. The testes of a male secrete large quantities of testosterone and other male hormones (called **androgens**). These hormones stimulate the production of growth hormone, which in turn triggers the adolescent growth spurt. Androgens are also responsible for the development of the male sex organs and contribute to sexual motivation during adulthood.

Meanwhile, in adolescent girls, the ovaries (also endocrine glands) produce larger quantities of the primary female hormone, **estrogen,** and of progesterone. Estrogen increases dramatically at puberty, stimulating the production of growth hormone and the adolescent growth spurt, much as testosterone does in males. It is also responsible for the development of the breasts, pubic hair, and female sex organs and for the control of menstrual cycles throughout a woman's reproductive years. Finally, the adrenal glands secrete androgen-like hormones that contribute to the maturation of the bones and muscles in both sexes. There is also evidence that the maturation of the adrenal glands during middle childhood results in sexual attraction well before puberty in both boys and girls (McClintock & Herdt, 1996) and relates to sexual orientation in adulthood (Arlt et al., 1999). The roles of different endocrine glands in physical growth and development are summarized in Table 5.1.

In adulthood, endocrine glands continue to secrete hormones, under the direction of the hypothalamus and the pituitary, to regulate bodily processes. For example, thyroid hormones help the body's cells metabolize (break down) foods into usable nutrients, and the adrenal glands help the body cope with stress. Throughout the life span, then, the endocrine system works with the nervous system to keep the body on an even keel. Yet changes occur; for example, declines in levels of sex hormones are associated with menopause. And, as you will see in Chapter 17, some theorists believe that changes in the functioning of the endocrine glands late in life bring about aging and death.

In short, the endocrine system, in collaboration with the nervous system, is centrally involved in growth during childhood, physical and sexual maturation during adolescence, functioning over the life span, and aging later in life.

The Nervous System

None of the physical or mental achievements that we regard as human would be possible without a functioning nervous system. Briefly, the nervous system consists of the brain and spinal cord (central nervous system) and the neural tissue that extends into all parts of the body (peripheral nervous system). Its basic unit is a **neuron** (see Figure 5.2). Although neurons come in many shapes and sizes, they have some common fea-

Table 5.1 Hormonal Influences on Growth and Development

Endocrine Gland	Hormones Produced	Effects on Growth and Development
Pituitary	Growth hormone	Regulates growth from birth through adolescence; triggers adolescent growth spurt
	Activating hormones	Signal other endocrine glands (such as ovaries and testes) to secrete their hormones
Thyroid	Thyroxine	Affects growth and development of the brain and helps regulate growth of the body during childhood
Testes	Testosterone	Is responsible for development of the male reproductive system during the prenatal period; directs male sexual development during adolescence
Ovaries	Estrogen and progesterone	Is responsible for regulating the menstrual cycle; estrogen directs female sexual development during adolescence
Adrenal glands	Adrenal androgens	Play a supportive role in the development of muscle and bones; contribute to sexual motivation

tures. Branching, bushy dendrites receive signals from other neurons, and the long axon of a neuron transmits signals to other neurons or, in some cases, directly to a muscle cell. The axon of one neuron makes a connection with another neuron at a tiny gap called a **synapse.** By releasing neurotransmitters stored at the ends of its axons, one neuron can either stimulate or inhibit the action of another neuron. The axons of many neurons become covered by a fatty sheath called *myelin,* which acts like insulation to speed the transmission of neural impulses. Myelination begins prenatally but continues for

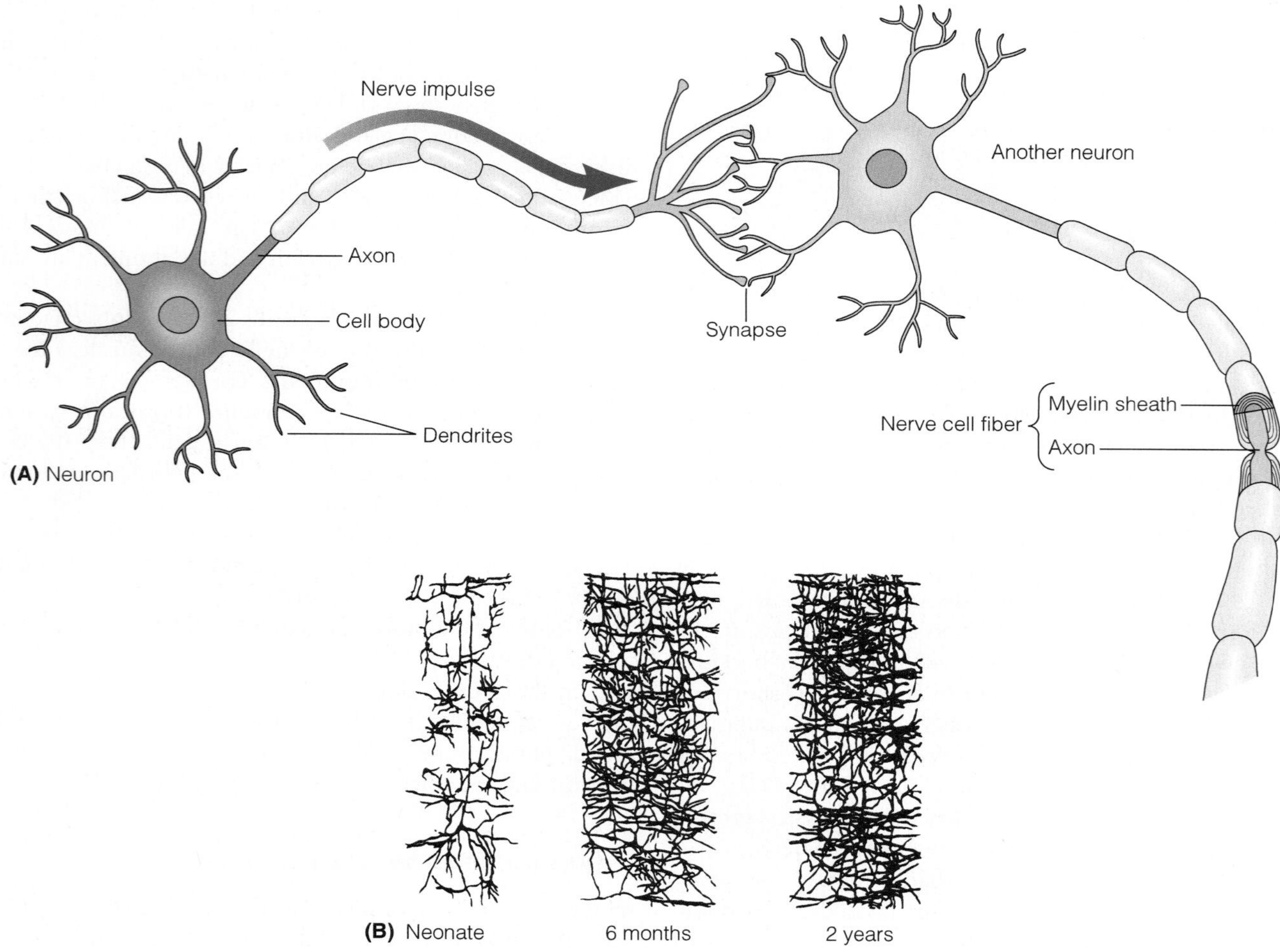

Figure 5.2 Parts of a neuron. (A) Although neurons differ in size and function, they all contain three main parts: the dendrites, which receive messages from adjacent neurons; the cell body; and the axon, which sends messages across the synapse to other neurons. (B) The formation of dendrites leading to new connections among existing neurons, as well as the myelination of neural pathways, accounts for much of the increase in brain weight during a baby's first 2 years.

many years after birth, proceeding from the spinal cord to the hindbrain, midbrain, and forebrain.

Now imagine a brain with as many as 100 billion neurons and each neuron communicating through synapses to thousands of others. How does this brain develop to make adults more physically and mentally capable than infants? Is it that adults have more neurons than infants do? Do they have more synapses connecting neurons or a more organized pattern of connections? And what happens to the brain in later life?

Brain Development

In Chapter 4, we traced the amazing evolution of the brain during the prenatal period. Here, we pick up the story by looking at what goes on in the brain from birth onward. Although the brain is proportionately the largest and most developed part of the body at birth, much development takes place after birth. At birth, the brain weighs about 25% of its adult weight; by age 2, it reaches 75% of its adult weight; and by age 5, the brain has achieved 90% of its adult weight. The myelination of neurons continues throughout childhood and into adolescence, and the different areas of the brain become more specialized.

The development of the brain early in life is not entirely caused by the unfolding of a maturational program; it is the product of a genetic program and early experience. Assuming that the infant has normal opportunities to explore and experience the world, the result will be a normal brain and normal development. However, the lack of normal experiences can interfere with normal brain development. Classic studies conducted by David Hubel and Torsten Wiesel showed that depriving newborn kittens of normal visual experience by suturing one eye closed for 8 weeks resulted in a lack of normal connections between that eye and the visual cortex—and blindness even after the eye had been reopened (Hubel & Wiesel, 1970). Even as little as 1 week of deprivation during the critical period of the first 8 weeks after birth can lead to permanent vision loss in the kitten (Kandel & Jessell, 1991). By contrast, depriving an adult cat's eye of light does no permanent damage. In humans, the critical period for the visual cortex appears to extend 6 years; children who have cataracts or for some other reason are unable to see during their first 6 years suffer permanent damage to their vision (Thompson, 2000). Similarly, children with strabismus (short, jerky movements of the two eyeballs resulting in an inability to integrate the images from both eyes into a single image) initially have good visual acuity in both eyes. But if the condition is not corrected early, children typically lose vision in the eye that they "tune out" to focus on a single image from the other eye (Kandel & Jessell, 1991).

This research shows that the immature brain has great **plasticity;** that is, it is responsive to the individual's experiences and can develop in a variety of ways (Kolb & Whishaw, 2003). On the negative side, the developing brain is highly vulnerable to damage if it is exposed to drugs or diseases (recall the description of teratogens in Chapter 4) or if it is deprived of sensory and motor experiences. On the positive side, this highly adaptable brain can often recover successfully from injuries. Neurons that are not yet fully committed to their specialized functions can often take over the functions of damaged neurons. Moreover, the immature brain is especially able to benefit from stimulating experiences. Rats that grow up in enriched environments with plenty of sensory stimulation develop larger, better-functioning brains with more synapses than rats that grow up in barren cages (Greenough, Black, & Wallace, 1987; Nilsson et al., 1999). Brain plasticity is greatest early in development. However, the organization of synapses within the nervous system continues to change in response to experience throughout the life span. Animals put through their paces in mazes grow bushier dendrites, but their brains lose some of their complexity if the animals are then moved to less-stimulating quarters (Thompson, 2000).

In short, the critical period for brain development—the time when it proceeds most rapidly—is during the late prenatal period and early infancy. The developing brain is characterized by a good deal of plasticity: normal genes may provide rough guidelines about how the brain should be configured, but early experience determines the architecture of the brain.

One important feature of the developing organization of the brain is the **lateralization,** or asymmetry, of the two hemispheres of the cerebral cortex. Instead of developing identically, the functions controlled by the two hemispheres diverge (Springer & Deutsch, 1997). In most people, the left cerebral hemisphere controls the right side of the body and is adept at the *sequential processing* needed for analytic reasoning and language processing. The right hemisphere generally controls the left side of the body and is skilled at the *simultaneous processing* of information needed for understanding spatial information and processing visual–motor information. Although it is an oversimplification, the left hemisphere is often called the *thinking* side of the brain, whereas the right hemisphere is called the *emotional* brain.

But having two hemispheres of the brain is not the same as having two brains. The hemispheres "communicate" and work together through the corpus callosum, "the superhighway of neurons connecting the halves of the brain" (Gazzaniga, 1998, p. 50). Even though one hemisphere might be more active than the other during certain tasks, they both play a role in all activities. For example, the left hemisphere is considered the seat of language because it controls word content, grammar, and syntax, but the right hemisphere processes melody, pitch, sound intensity, and the affective content of language (Gazzaniga, 2000; Hellige, 1993).

If one hemisphere is damaged, it may be possible for the other hemisphere to "take over" the functions lost. For example, in a small sample of children who had their left hemispheres removed to try to reduce or eliminate severe seizures, all regained normal use of language (Vining et al., 1997; de Bode & Curtiss, 2000). The sample included two children who were 12 and 13 years old at the time of surgery—fairly old in terms of brain development. Thus, although the left hemisphere processes language in most people (perhaps 92%), the right hemisphere may also be able to fill this function (Knecht et al., 2000; Gazzaniga, 1998).

When does the brain become lateralized? Signs of brain lateralization are clearly evident at birth. Newborns are more likely to turn their heads to the right than to the left (Thompson & Smart, 1993), and one-quarter clearly prefer the right hand in their grasp reflex (Tan & Tan, 1999). Left hemispheric specialization is evident among 5- to 12-month-old babies who engaged in babbling, thought by many to be a precursor of language (Holowka & Petitto, 2002). This evidence suggests that young brains are already organized in a lateralized fashion. Still, preference for one side of the body over the other becomes more stable and systematic throughout childhood.

Signs of lateralization so early in life suggest that it has a genetic basis. Further support for the role of genes comes from family studies of handedness. Overall, about 9 in 10 people rely on their right hands (or left hemispheres) to write and perform other motor activities. In families where both parents are right-handed, the odds of having a left-handed child are only 2 in 100. These odds increase to 17 in 100 when one parent is left-handed and to 46 in 100 when both parents are left-handed (Springer & Deutsch, 1997). This suggests a genetic basis to handedness, although it could also indicate that children become left-handed because of experiences provided by left-handed parents. However, experience would not account for head-turning preferences in young infants or for the differential activation of the left and right hemispheres observed in newborns when listening to speech sounds. Thus, nature seems to account better than nurture for much of the lateralization of the brain.

Overall, then, the brain appears to be structured very early so that the two hemispheres of the cortex will be capable of specialized functioning. As we develop, most of us come to rely more on the left hemisphere to carry out language activities and more on the right hemisphere to do such things as perceive spatial relationships. We also come to rely more consistently on one hemisphere, usually the left, to control many of our physical activities.

When does the brain complete its development? In the past, the answer to this question might have been adolescence, childhood, or even infancy. Today, however, the answer is that brain development is never truly complete; the brain changes across the life span. Nonetheless, there are periods when the brain experiences growth spurts (Thompson et al., 2000). These growth spurts seem to occur at the times in infancy, childhood, and adolescence when Jean Piaget and others believe major cognitive breakthroughs occur (see, for example, Epstein, 2001; Kwon & Lawson, 2000; Somsen et al., 1997). For example, teenagers are more likely than children to ask hypothetical "what if" questions and to reason about weighty abstractions such as truth and justice. Reorganization of the brain may be responsible for such breakthroughs in adolescent thinking. For example, maturation of the prefrontal lobes during adolescence enables students to focus on task-relevant material and block task-irrelevant information (Casey, Giedd & Thomas, 2000; Kwon & Lawson, 2000).

Other changes in the brain also take place between ages 12 and 20. By about age 16, the brain reaches its full adult weight (Tanner, 1990). Myelination of certain pathways, including those that allow people to concentrate for lengthy periods, continues during adolescence, which may help explain why infants, toddlers, school-age children, and even young adolescents have shorter attention spans than do older adolescents and adults (Tanner, 1990). New evidence indicates that myelination continues well into adulthood, which may explain why adults are better able than teenagers to integrate thoughts and emotions (Benes, 1998). The speed at which the nervous system processes information also continues to increase during adolescence (Kail, 1991).

Finally, although 12-year-olds, even those who are intellectually gifted, are often "clever," they are rarely what people would call "wise." They can solve many problems correctly, but they are not as skilled as older adolescents or adults at showing foresight or adopting broad perspectives on problems (Segalowitz, Unsal, & Dywan, 1992). Although changes in the brain during adolescence are less dramatic than those earlier in life, it is likely that some of the cognitive growth researchers observe during the teenage years becomes possible only because of further brain development. For instance, when coupled with appropriate physical and social experiences, maturation of the brain contributes to the development of scientific reasoning ability. Changes in the brain during adolescence may also account for some of the risky behaviors associated with this period (see the Explorations box on page 117).

The Aging Brain

Many people fear that aging means losing brain cells and ultimately becoming "senile." As you will see in Chapter 16, Alzheimer's disease (and other conditions that cause serious brain damage and dementia) is not part of normal aging; it does not affect most older people. Normal aging is associated with gradual and relatively mild degeneration within the nervous system—some loss of neurons, diminished functioning of many remaining neurons, and potentially harmful changes in the tissues surrounding and supporting the neurons, such as the protective myelin covering (Hof & Mobbs, 2001; Peters, 2002). Just as brain weight and volume increase over the childhood years, they decrease over the adult years, especially after age 50 (Courchesne et al., 2000; Resnick, 2000). As people age, more of their neurons atrophy or shrivel, transmit signals less effectively, and ultimately die (Hof & Mobbs, 2001). Elderly adults may end up with 5 to 30% fewer neurons, depending on the brain site studied, than they had in young adulthood. Neuron loss is greater in the areas of the brain that control sensory and motor activities than in either the association areas of the cortex (involved in thought) or the brain stem and lower brain (involved in basic life functions such as breathing) (Whitbourne, 2004).

Other signs of brain degeneration besides neuron loss include declines in the levels of important neurotransmitters; the formation of "senile plaques," hard areas in the tissue surrounding neurons that may interfere with neuronal function-

Explorations

Can Brain Development Explain Why Adolescents Take More Risks Than Adults?

Adolescents are notorious for taking chances that most adults would not take. They often display poor judgment and decision making when it comes to alcohol, drug, and cigarette use and to their sexual activities and driving. In a 1-year period, for example, 10 Kansas City adolescents were killed in a series of automobile accidents that resulted from "hill hopping"—getting a car airborne as it crests the top of a hill (Williams, 2000). According to the National Center for Health Statistics (2000b), other risky behaviors during adolescence include the following:

- Smoking frequently (reported by 17% of adolescents)
- Drinking alcohol (about 50%)
- Drinking and driving (13%)
- Riding with a driver who has been drinking (33%)
- Using marijuana (27%)
- Carrying weapons (17%)
- Having unprotected sex (42%)

© Jim Cummins/CORBIS

Various explanations have been offered for adolescents' risk taking, including the need to separate from parents and the influence of the peer group (for example, Arnett, 2002). Several researchers are beginning to find connections between brain development and risky behavior during adolescence. Linda Spear (2000b) found that the prefrontal cortex—that part of the brain involved in control of emotions and decision making—decreases in size and undergoes a reorganization of neuronal connections during adolescence (see also Casey, Giedd, & Thomas, 2000). The prefrontal cortex appears to be particularly important in planning and thinking through the consequences of decisions. In other research, teenagers had less activity in a part of the brain that has been associated with a desire for reward (Bjork et al., 2004). This underactivity may mean that teens need more stimulation to achieve the same level of reward that others achieve with less stimulation, leading them to engage in more risky behaviors.

Thus, a growing body of research suggests some connection between brain activity and risk-taking behavior during the teen years. Neurotransmitters (brain chemicals) may help explain this link. Animal research reveals that one chemical, dopamine, reaches peak levels during adolescence in the prefrontal cortex and limbic system before dropping and then leveling off (Lewis et al., 1998). This chemical is involved in novelty seeking and in determining the motivational value of activities (Spear, 2000a). If this holds true for human adolescents, then their risky behaviors may reflect a combination of seeking new experiences and changing incentive value of stimuli—both influenced by changes in brain chemistry and incomplete development of the prefrontal cortex during adolescence. So far, the research with humans seems to support this brain–behavior connection. The adolescent brain, then, is still a work in progress, and some risk taking by teenagers may be par for the course until further brain developments, such as maturation of the prefrontal cortex, refine their good judgment and decision making.

ing and are seen in abundance in people with Alzheimer's disease; and reduced blood flow to the brain, which may starve neurons of the oxygen and nutrients they need to function (Hof & Mobbs, 2001). One of the main implications of such degeneration, as you will see later, is that older brains typically process information more slowly than younger brains do.

On the positive side, research shows that the brain can change in response to experience and develop new capabilities

Mental "exercise" later in life is likely to contribute to neural growth in the aging brain and compensate for neural degeneration.

throughout the life span (see Nelson & Luciana, 2001). Neurons can form new synapses and extend their dendrites (Kolb & Whishaw, 2003), thus filling in gaps left by dying neurons. This self-repair demonstrates at least some degree of plasticity in the aging brain, just as in the young brain.

What does it mean for older adults that both degeneration and plasticity—both losses and gains—characterize the aging brain? In some people, degeneration may win and declines in intellectual performance will occur. In other people, plasticity may prevail; their brains may form new and adaptive neural connections faster than they are lost so that performance on some tasks may actually improve with age (at least until very old age). As you will see in Chapters 7, 8, and 9, older adults vary widely in how effectively they learn, remember, and think and in how well their intellectual abilities hold up as they age. On average, however, plasticity and growth may make up for degeneration until people are in their 70s and 80s. One key to maintaining or even improving performance in old age is to avoid the many diseases that can interfere with nervous system functioning. Another key is to remain intellectually active—to create an "enriched environment" for the brain. You can reject the view that aging involves nothing but a slow death of neural tissue. Old brains *can* learn new tricks.

Principles of Growth

To complete this explanation of the building blocks of growth and physical development, we will look at three principles that underlie growth. Knowledge of these principles allows researchers to make general predictions about growth patterns. It is easiest to see these principles in action during infancy when growth is fast. For instance, you have probably noticed that young infants seem to be all head compared with older children and adults. That is because growth follows the **cephalocaudal principle** according to which growth occurs in a head-to-tail direction. This pattern is clear in Figure 5.3: The head is far ahead of the rest of the body during the prenatal period and accounts for about 25% of the newborn's length and 13% of total body weight. But the head accounts for only 12% of an adult's height and 2% of adult weight (Zemel, 2002). During the first year after birth, the trunk grows the fastest; in the second year, the legs are the fastest growing part of the body.

When infants are growing from the head downward, they are also growing and developing muscles from the center outward to the extremities. This **proximodistal principle** of

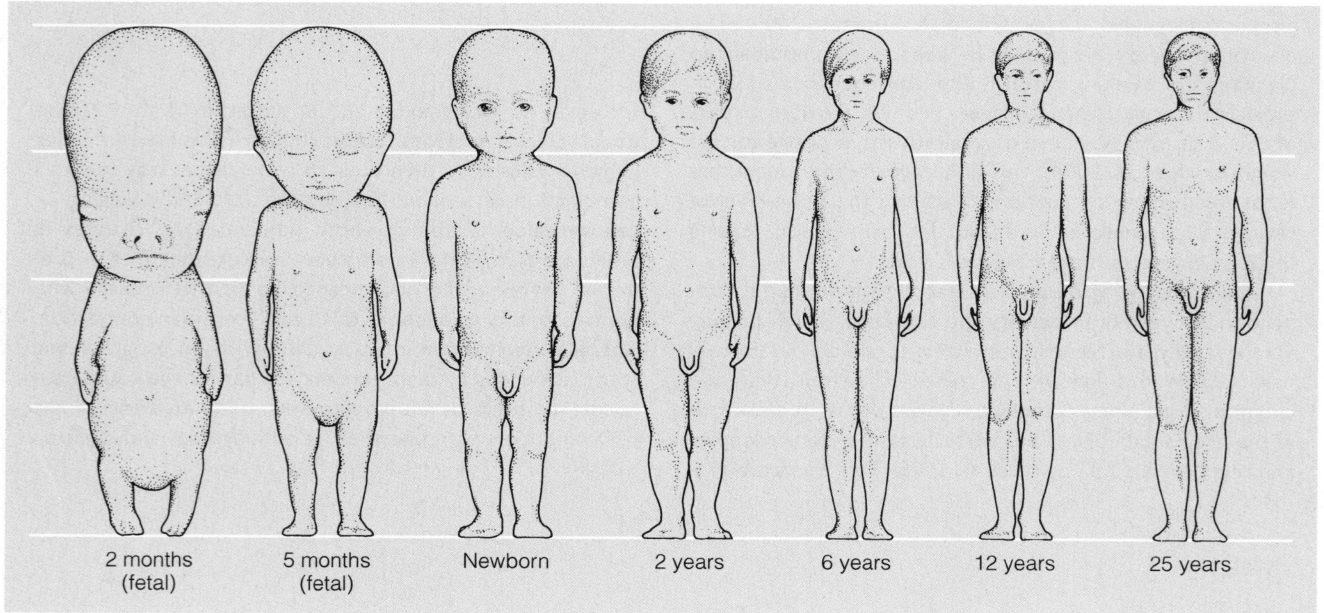

Figure 5.3 Changes in the proportions of the human body from fetal period through adulthood. The head represents 50% of body length at 2 months after conception but only 12 to 13% of adult height. By contrast, the legs constitute only about 12 to 13% of the length of a 2-month-old fetus but 50% of an adult's height.

growth can be seen during the prenatal period, when the chest and internal organs form before the arms, hands, and fingers. During the first year after birth, the trunk is rapidly filling out but the arms remain short and stubby until they undergo their own period of rapid development.

A third important principle of growth and development is the **orthogenetic principle.** This means that development starts globally and undifferentiated and moves toward increasing differentiation and hierarchical integration (Werner, 1957). Consider a human who starts as a single, undifferentiated cell at conception. As growth proceeds, that single cell becomes billions of highly specialized cells (neurons, blood cells, liver cells, and so on). These differentiated cells become organized, or integrated, into functioning systems such as the brain or the digestive system.

Having looked at the building blocks of growth and development, you are ready to examine the development and aging of the physical self. We concentrate on the body (its size, composition, and functioning) and the use of body and brain in physical activities such as locomotion and finely controlled movements.

Summing Up

It is clear that genetic and environmental factors are closely intertwined in the development of the physical self. The plasticity of the infant brain allows it to select certain neural connections over others in response to normal early experiences and to benefit from enriching stimulation. During childhood, neural transmission speeds up and lateralization of various brain functions, although present at birth, becomes more evident in behavior. During adolescence, the brain, especially the prefrontal cortex, continues to develop, permitting sustained attention and strategic planning. The aging brain exhibits both degeneration and plasticity. Neurons atrophy and die, and blood flow to the brain decreases; but the aging brain forms new synapses to compensate for neural loss and reorganizes itself in response to learning experiences. Physical growth proceeds according to the cephalocaudal (head-to-tail), proximodistal (center outward), and orthogenetic (global and undifferentiated to integrated and differentiated) principles. ■

The Infant

Infancy is characterized by rapid growth, continued brain development, emergence of locomotor skills, and impressive sensory and reflexive capabilities. Understanding the newborn's capacities and limitations brings a fuller appreciation of the dramatic changes that take place between birth and adulthood.

Rapid Growth

Newborns are typically about 20 inches long and weigh 7 to 7½ pounds. However, weight and length at birth can mislead about eventual weight and height because the growth of some fetuses is stunted by a poor prenatal environment (Lejarraga, 2002). Size during the first few months after birth is related more to prenatal experiences (environment) than to size of parent (genes). This is easy to see with the birth of twins and other multiples, whose prenatal growth is significantly restricted by siblings competing for the limited space in the mother's womb.

In the first few months after birth, infants grow rapidly, gaining nearly an ounce of weight a day and an inch in length each month. By age 2, they have already attained about half of their eventual adult height and weigh 27 to 30 pounds. Although we usually think of growth as a slow and steady process, daily measurements of infant length show that babies grow in fits and starts (Lampl, 2002). They may grow a couple of centimeters a day then not grow for a few weeks before experiencing another little growth spurt. In the end, 90 to 95% of an infant's days are growth free, yet their occasional bursts of physical growth add up to substantial increases in size.

Bones and muscles are also developing quickly during infancy. At birth, most bones are soft, pliable, and difficult to break. They are too small and flexible to allow newborns to sit up or balance themselves when pulled to a standing position. The soft cartilage-like tissues of the young infant gradually ossify (harden) into bony material as calcium and other minerals are deposited into them. In addition, more bones develop, and they become more closely interconnected. As for muscles, young infants are relative weaklings. They have all the muscle cells they will ever have, but their strength will increase as their muscles grow.

Newborn Capabilities

Newborns used to be viewed as helpless little organisms ill prepared to cope with the world outside the womb. We now know that they are equipped to begin life. Just what can a newborn do? Among the most important capabilities are reflexes, functioning senses, a capacity to learn, and organized, individualized patterns of waking and sleeping.

Reflexes

One of the newborn's greatest strengths is a full set of useful reflexes. A **reflex** is an unlearned and involuntary response to a stimulus, such as when the eye automatically blinks in response to a puff of air. Reflexes can be contrasted with the newborn's spontaneous arm waving, leg kicking, and thrashing—movements that have no obvious stimulus. Table 5.2 lists some reflexes that can be readily observed in all normal newborns. These seemingly simple reactions are quite varied and complex patterns of behavior.

Some reflexes are called *survival reflexes* because they have clear adaptive value. Examples include the breathing reflex (useful for obvious reasons), the eye-blink reflex (which protects against bright lights or foreign particles), and the sucking reflex (needed to obtain food). Those called *primitive reflexes* are not clearly useful; many are believed to be remnants of evolutionary history that have outlived their purpose (but see Schott & Rossor, 2003, for another perspective). Babinski reflex is a good example. Why would it be adaptive

Table 5.2 Major Reflexes of Full-Term Newborns

Reflexes	Developmental Course	Significance
SURVIVAL REFLEXES		
Breathing reflex	Permanent	Provides oxygen; expels carbon dioxide
Eye-blink reflex	Permanent	Protects eyes from bright light or foreign objects
Pupillary reflex: Constriction of pupils to bright light; dilation to dark or dimly lit surroundings	Permanent	Protects against bright light; adapts visual system to low illumination
Rooting reflex: Turning a cheek toward a tactile (touch) stimulus	Weakens by 2 months; disappears by 5 months	Orients child to breast or bottle
Sucking reflex: Sucking on objects placed (or taken) into mouth	Is gradually modified by experience over the first few months after birth; disappears by 7 months	Allows child to take in nutrients
Swallowing reflex	Is permanent but modified by experience	Allows child to take in nutrients; protects against choking
PRIMITIVE REFLEXES		
Babinski reflex: Fanning then curling toes when bottom of foot is stroked	Disappears 12–18 months after birth	Presence at birth and disappearance in first year indicate normal neurological development
Grasping reflex: Curling fingers around objects (such as a finger) that touch the baby's palm	Disappears in first 3–4 months; is replaced by a voluntary grasp	Presence at birth and later disappearance indicate normal neurological development
Moro reflex: Loud noise or sudden change in position of baby's head will cause baby to throw arms outward, arch back, then bring arms toward each other	Disappears by 4 months; however, child continues to react to unexpected noises or a loss of bodily support by showing startle reflex (which does not disappear)	Presence at birth and later disappearance (or evolution into startle reflex) indicate normal neurological development
Swimming reflex: Infant immersed in water will display active movements of arms and legs and will involuntarily hold breath (thus staying afloat for some time)	Disappears in first 4–6 months	Presence at birth and later disappearance indicate normal neurological development
Stepping reflex: Infants held upright so that their feet touch a flat surface will step as if to walk	Disappears in first 8 weeks unless infant has regular opportunities to practice it	Presence at birth and later disappearance indicate normal neurological development

Preterm infants may show little to no evidence of primitive reflexes at birth, and their survival reflexes are likely to be irregular or immature. However, the missing reflexes will typically appear soon after birth and will disappear a little later than they do among full-term infants.

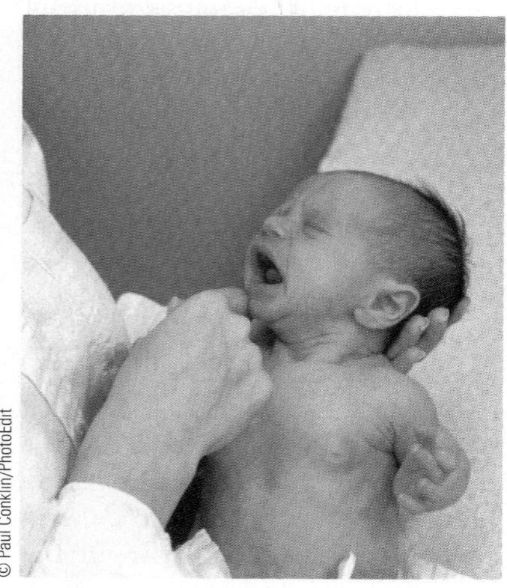

Rooting reflex

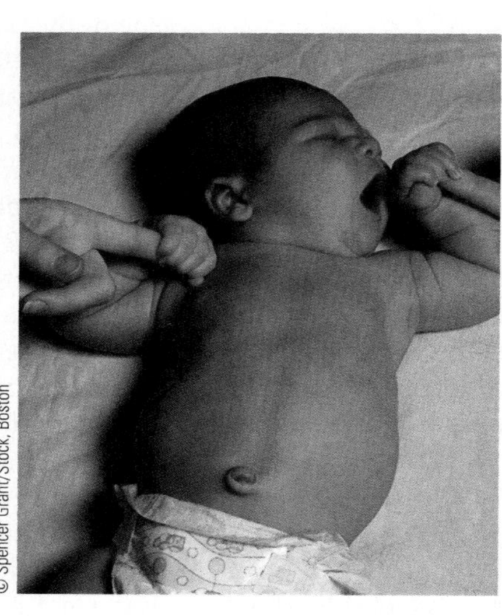

Grasping reflex

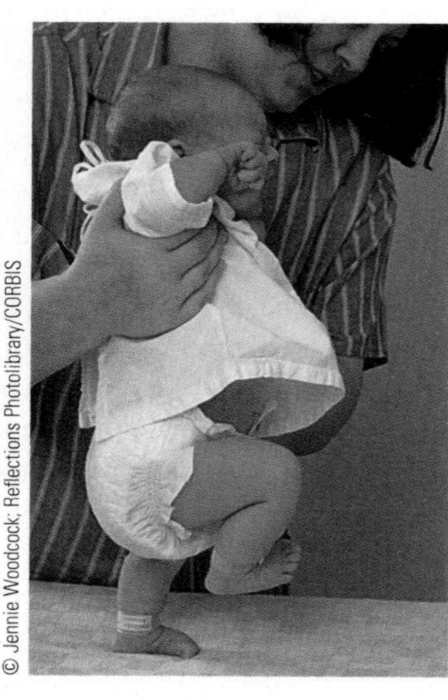

Stepping reflex

for infants to fan their toes when the bottoms of their feet are stroked? We do not know. Other primitive reflexes may have some adaptive value, at least in some cultures. For example, the grasping reflex may help infants carried in slings or on their mothers' hips to hang on. Finally, some primitive reflexes—for example, the stepping reflex—are forerunners of useful voluntary behaviors that develop later in infancy. The expression of primitive reflexes at age 6 weeks, however, is not related to the expression of later motor behaviors (Bartlett, 1997). Thus, infants who demonstrate a strong primitive grasping reflex at 6 weeks are not necessarily the infants who demonstrate a strong voluntary grasp later in infancy.

Primitive reflexes typically disappear during the early months of infancy. For instance, the grasping reflex becomes weak by 4 months. These primitive reflexes are controlled by the lower, subcortical areas of the brain and are lost as the higher centers of the cerebral cortex develop and make voluntary motor behaviors possible. Even though many primitive reflexes are not very useful to infants, they have proven to be extremely useful in diagnosing infants' neurological problems. If such reflexes are not present at birth—or if they last too long in infancy—physicians know that something is wrong with a baby's nervous system. The existence of reflexes at birth tells them that infants come to life ready to respond to stimulation in adaptive ways. The disappearance of certain reflexes tells them that the nervous system is developing normally and that experience is affecting both brain and behavior.

Behavioral States

Another sign that newborns are equipped for life is their ability to establish organized and individualized patterns of daily activity. Settling into an organized sleep–wake pattern is an indication that the baby is integrating biological, physiological, and psychosocial information (Sadeh, Raviv, & Gruber, 2000). Infants must move from short sleep–wake cycles distributed throughout the day and night to a pattern that includes longer sleep periods at night with longer wake periods during the day. Much to their tired parents' dismay, newborns have no clear sense of night or day and may wake every 1 to 4 hours. By 3 months, infants begin to establish a predictable sleep–wake cycle; by 6 months three-quarters have settled into a fairly consistent pattern (Minard, Freudigman, & Thoman, 1999). They spend more time asleep at night and awake during the day, and many sleep through the night. Newborns spend half of their sleeping hours in active sleep, also called **REM sleep** (for the rapid eye movements that occur during it). Infants older than 6 months spend only 25 to 30% of their total sleep in REM sleep, which more closely resembles the 20% that adults spend in REM sleep.

Why do young infants sleep so much and spend so much more time in REM sleep than adults? Daphne and Charles Maurer (1988) suggest that infants use sleep to regulate sensory stimulation. Being bombarded by too much stimulation can "overload" the immature nervous system. To reduce the stimulation, infants tend to become less active, grow quieter, and shift into sleep. This may explain why infants are notoriously fussy at the end of a busy day—often at dinnertime when parents are tired and hoping for some peace. The infant's nervous system can be overstimulated by the flood of stimulation received during the day. Somehow, the arousal needs to be reduced—perhaps by crying and then sleeping. Adults sometimes marvel at how infants can sleep through the loudest noises and the brightest lights, but being able to do so may serve a valuable function. As the Explorations box on page 122 shows, sleep is important across the life span and inadequate sleep can take its toll in a variety of ways.

Research on infant states also makes it clear that newborns have a good deal of individuality (Thoman & Whitney, 1990). In one study a newborn was observed to be in an alert waking state only 4% of the time, whereas another was alert 37% of the time (Brown, 1964). Similarly, one newborn cried only 17% of the time, but another spent 39% of its time crying. Premature babies spend more time in transitions from one state to another, and the time they spend in any particular state is shorter than it is for full-term infants (Wyly, 1997). Such variations among infants have obvious implications for parents. It is likely to be far more pleasant to be with a baby who is often alert and rarely cries than it is to interact with a baby who is rarely attentive and frequently fussy. As you saw in Chapter 3, both genetic endowment and environment contribute to these kinds of differences in infant temperament.

Life becomes easier for parents (in some ways) as infants age. As Table 5.3 shows, infants gradually spend more time awake and less time eating, fussing, and crying. Although their sleep times do not change much, their sleep patterns do: they sleep for longer periods at night and take fairly predictable naps during the day.

Sensing and Learning

As you saw in Chapter 4, the sensory systems are developing before birth, and all of the senses are functioning reasonably well at birth. Newborns see and hear, and they respond to tastes, smells, and touches in predictable ways. For instance, newborns can visually track slow-moving objects, they can turn in the direction of sounds, they can turn from unpleasant odors; they are responsive to touch, and they show preferences for sweet tastes (Wyly, 1997). We will explore these sensory capabilities further in Chapter 6.

Table 5.3 Percentage of Day (24-Hour Period) Spent in Various Behavioral States at 2, 6, 12, and 40 Weeks

Behavior	2 Weeks	6 Weeks	12 Weeks	40 Weeks
Sleeping	59%	56%	57%	55%
Awake	14	19	25	34
Feeding	17	15	11	8
Fussing	5	6	5	3
Crying	4	3	2	<1

Note especially the increase in time awake. Because of rounding, the columns do not total 100%.

SOURCE: Adapted from St. James-Roberts & Plewis, 1996, Table 2.

Are Today's Children (and Adults) Sleep Deprived?

"Impaired by sleep loss, individuals start a task feeling fine. Minutes later, however, heads begin to nod, and the rate of deterioration accelerates. Instead of being able to sustain attention for a 45-minute lecture in a classroom, for example, a student might be able to manage only 3 to 5 minutes" (National Academy of Sciences, 2000, p. 15).

How much sleep do people need, and what happens when they do not get enough? As the figure in this Explorations box illustrates, sleep needs change across age, with infants needing the most and adults the least number of hours per night. Experts recommend that 2- to 5-year-olds should get at least 12 hours of sleep every night, school-age children should get at least 10 hours, and teens should get about 9 hours of sleep (see, for example, W. Cole, 2003).

Among preschoolers, lack of a good night's sleep is associated with behavioral problems such as acting out and not complying with requests (Lavigne et al., 1999). Teachers report that at least 10% of their elementary school-age students have trouble staying awake in the classroom (Owens et al., 2000). School-age children who get a poor night's sleep, as measured by how restless they were during the night, perform poorly on a variety of memory tasks (Steenari et al., 2003).

Getting a good night's sleep only seems to get more difficult as children move into middle school. Katia Fredriksen and her colleagues (2004) found that sixth graders who got little sleep had lower self-esteem, poorer grades, and more depression symptoms than their well-rested peers. Furthermore, hours of sleep obtained declined during middle school; girls were more likely than boys to cut their sleep short by getting up earlier in the morning. By extending their sleep just 40 to 60 minutes, 9- to 12-year-olds can increase their performance significantly (Sadeh, Gruber, & Raviv, 2003).

Teenagers are especially likely to be at risk for daytime sleepiness and the consequences associated with fatigue. Changes in the sleep–wake cycle, melatonin production, and circadian rhythms during adolescence mean that the "natural" time for falling asleep shifts later to at least 11:00 p.m. Teens report later bedtimes from age 10 to age 17 (Wolfson &

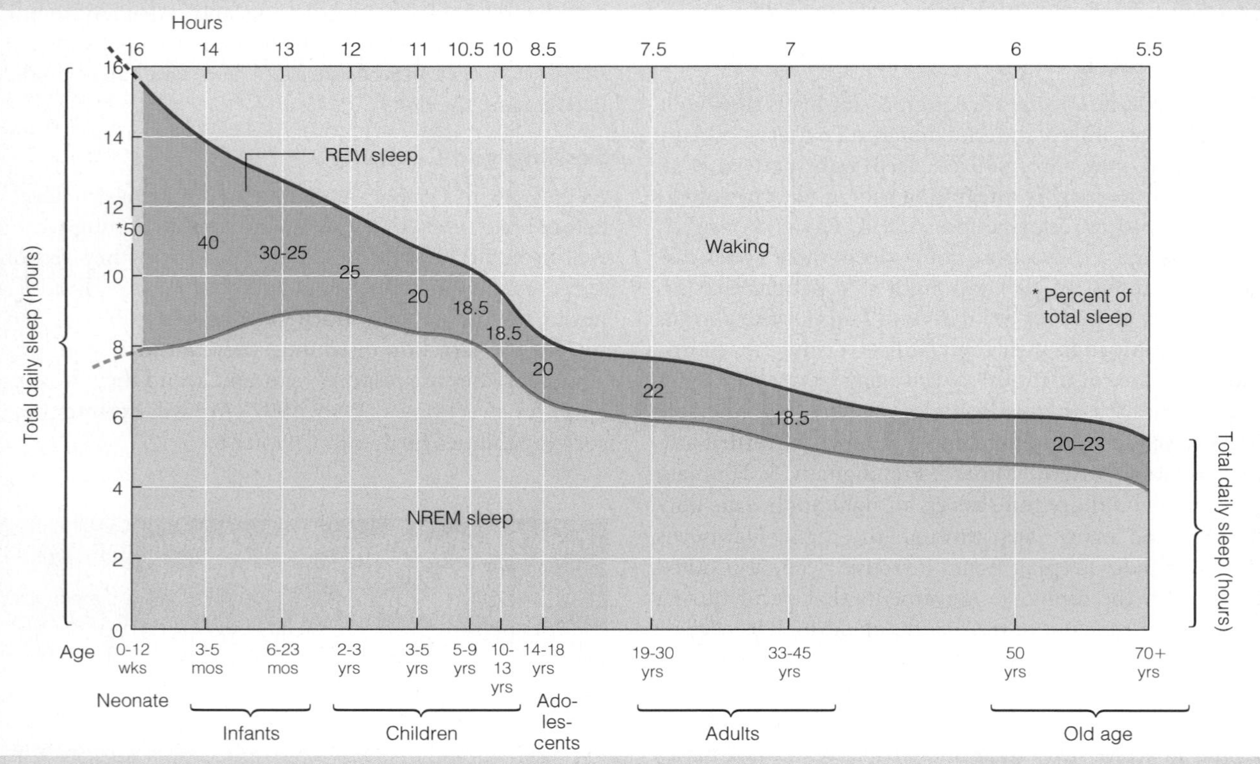

Figure 5.1 Graph showing changes with age in the total amount of daily sleep and the percentage of REM sleep. There is a sharp drop in the amount of REM sleep after the early years, falling from 8 hours at birth to less than 1 hour in old age. The change in the amount of non-REM (NREM) sleep is much less marked, falling from 8 hours to about 5 hours over the life span.

SOURCE: http://www.sleephomepages.org/sleepsyllabus/fr-c.html

Carskadon, 1998). Although psychosocial factors may contribute to later bedtimes than in childhood (for example, talking late into the night with friends), biological factors—puberty in particular—seem primarily responsible (National Sleep Foundation, 2004). Teens who go to bed at 11:00 p.m. should not wake up until around 8:00 a.m. if they are to get the recommended amount of sleep. However, most teens (84%) find themselves getting out of bed before 7:00 a.m., and 25% get up by 6:00 a.m., to get to school on time. High schools typically start earlier than middle or elementary schools, often by 7:30 a.m. and usually to accommodate bus schedules. Thus, just when their biological clocks are pushing back sleep times at night, schools are getting teens up earlier in the morning.

What are the consequences for teens who do not get enough sleep? Teens report greater sleepiness during the day and are quicker to fall asleep than younger children who get the same amount of sleep. Sleepiness is associated with decreased motivation or trouble initiating and maintaining activity, especially on "boring" tasks (Dahl, 1999). Tired teens may be able to successfully navigate a favorite class or read a particularly good book, but these same teens may have trouble completing an assignment in their least favorite subject or studying for an exam. Teens who have had their sleep restricted display increased sleepiness in proportion to the number of nights that their sleep is reduced. But surprisingly—at least to many adults—these same teens "perk up" in the evenings and show high levels of energy that discourage them from going to bed early (National Academy of Sciences, 2000).

Teens who sleep less at night or who stay up later on the weekends than their peers report higher levels of depression, irritability, and lack of tolerance for frustration (Dahl, 1999; Wolfson & Carskadon, 1998). They may also have difficulty controlling their emotional responses, which leads to greater expression of aggression or anger (Dahl, 1999). Like younger children, teens who do not get enough sleep have trouble concentrating in school, experience short-term memory problems, and may doze off in class (National Sleep Foundation, 2004).

In addition to causing lapses of attention, sleep deprivation also slows reaction times. Together, these increase the likelihood of accidents, which may help explain why adolescents have higher rates of car accidents than any other age group. Becoming drowsy or falling asleep behind the wheel of a car contributes to more than 100,000 accidents every year, and more than half of these accidents involve young drivers (National Sleep Foundation, 2004). Another 1 million car crashes every year are caused by driver inattention, a correlate of sleepiness.

Finally, what about adults and older adults? Young adults sleep 7 to 8 hours per night; this decreases to 6½ to 7½ hours during middle age and drops even further during old age. When they are raising children, which corresponds to the time career demands are likely to be high, many adults (about two-thirds) report that they do not get enough sleep (National Sleep Foundation, 2004). And one out of every five parents reports that daily functioning is impaired at least several days a week because that person feels so tired. The implications of this for worker productivity and safety are tremendous.

© Yellow Dog Productions/Getty Images

Older adults, although they sleep less at night, often compensate by taking a nap during the day. They are also more likely to report sleep problems such as difficulty staying asleep and repeated awakenings during the night. Changes in physiology, such as decreased production of melatonin and growth hormone, both of which help regulate sleep, contribute to the sleep problems experienced by older adults. In addition, older adults are more likely to experience health problems such as arthritis and congestive heart failure that disrupt sleep and to take medications that decrease sleep (National Sleep Foundation, 2004).

For all ages, learning more about sleep needs and the effects of sleep deprivation can lead to healthy lifestyle changes. Adhering to a regular bedtime and wake time on the weekends and on school and work days can help maintain healthy sleep habits. Unfortunately, "sleeping in" on the weekends alters the sleep–wake cycle and makes it more difficult to get up early for work or school Monday morning. So, next time you find yourself dozing off in class or at work, do not jump to the conclusion that the work you are doing is boring. It may be that your sleep–wake cycle is out of sync with the schedule imposed on you by school or work.

Another strength of newborns is their ability to learn from their experiences. They can, for example, learn to suck faster if sucking produces pleasant-tasting sugary liquid rather than plain water (Lipsitt, 1990). In other words, they can change their behavior according to its consequences. This is an example of the process of operant conditioning introduced in Chapter 2.

Newborn infants are competent and ready for life. They have a range of reflexes, functioning senses, a capacity to learn, and an organized and unique pattern of waking and sleeping. But when you think about newborns in comparison with adults, it is also clear that newborns are limited beings. Their brains are not nearly as developed as they will be by the end of infancy. Their capacity to move voluntarily and intentionally is limited, and although their senses are working, they cannot interpret stimuli as well as an older individual can. They can learn, but they are slow learners compared with older children, often requiring many learning trials before they form an association between stimulus and response. And they clearly lack important social and communication skills. In short, newborns have strengths and limitations—strengths that can serve as building blocks for later development and limitations that show much remains to be accomplished.

Table 5.4 Age Norms for Important Motor Milestones During the First Year

Age (in months)	Milestone
2	Lifts head up when lying on stomach
3	Rolls over from stomach to back; holds head steady when being carried
4	Grasps a cube or other small object
5	Sits without support toward end of month
6	Stands holding on to something
7	Rolls over from back to stomach and may begin to crawl or creep; shows thumb opposition
8	Pulls self up to standing position
9	Walks holding on to furniture; bangs two objects together
10	Plays clapping games (e.g., pat-a-cake)
11	Stands alone
12	Walks well alone; drinks from a cup

Based on Anglo American, Hispanic, and African American children in the United States. Indicates the age at which 50% of infants have demonstrated the skill. Keep in mind that there are large individual differences in when infants display various developmental milestones.
SOURCES: Bayley, 1993; Frankenburg et al., 1992.

Physical Behavior

The motor behaviors of newborns are far more organized and sophisticated than they appear at first glance, but newborns are not ready to dance or thread needles. By age 2, however, immobile infants have become toddlers, walking up and down stairs by themselves and using their hands to accomplish simple self-care tasks and to operate toys. How do the motor skills involved in walking and manipulating objects develop?

Locomotor Development

Table 5.4 shows the age at which half of U.S. infants master particular motor milestones. This average age of mastery is called the **developmental norm** for a skill. Developmental norms such as these must be interpreted carefully. They depend on the group studied (children walk earlier today than they used to and walk earlier in some cultures than in others), and they hide a good deal of variation among children, even in the sequence in which skills are mastered (von Hofsten, 1993). Finally, most children who master a skill earlier or later than the developmental norm are still within the normal range of development. Parents should not be alarmed if their child is 1 or 2 months "behind" the norm; only significantly delayed achievement of new skills is cause for concern.

Can you recognize the workings of the cephalocaudal and proximodistal principles of development in the milestones in Table 5.4? Early motor development follows the cephalocaudal principle because the neurons between the brain and the muscles acquire a myelin sheath in a head-to-tail manner. Thus, infants can lift their heads before they can control their trunks enough to sit, and they can sit before they can control their legs to walk. The proximodistal principle of development is also evident in early motor development. Activities involving the trunk are mastered before activities involving the arms and legs, and activities involving the arms and legs are mastered before activities involving the hands and fingers or feet and toes. Therefore, infants can roll over before they can walk or bring their arms together to grasp a bottle, and children generally master **gross motor skills** (skills such as kicking the legs or drawing large circles that involve large muscles and whole body or limb movements) before mastering **fine motor skills** (skills such as picking Cheerios off the breakfast table or writing letters of the alphabet that involve precise movements of the hands and fingers or feet and toes). As the nerves and muscles mature downward and outward, infants gradually gain control over the lower and the peripheral parts of their bodies.

The orthogenetic principle is also evident in early motor development. A young infant is likely to hurl his body as a unit at a bottle of milk held close by (a global response). An older infant gains the ability to move specific parts of her body separately (a differentiated response); she may be able to extend one arm toward the bottle without extending the other arm, move the hand but not the arm to grasp it, and so on, making distinct, differentiated movements. Finally, the still older infant is able to coordinate separate movements in a functional sequence—reaching for, grasping, and pulling in the bottle while opening his mouth to receive it and closing his mouth when the prize is captured (an integrated response).

Crawling. Life changes dramatically for infants and their parents when the infants first begin to crawl or creep, normally around 7 months. Different infants find different ways to navigate at first; one may slither on her belly in a kind of combat crawl, another may use only his forearms to pull ahead, another may chug backward. However, most infants around 10 months old end up crawling on their hands and knees, and they all seem to figure out that the best way to keep their balance is to move the diagonal arm and leg at the same time (Freedland & Bertenthal, 1994).

With their new mobility, infants are better able to explore the objects around them and to interact with other people. Experience moving through the spatial world contributes to cognitive, social, and emotional development (Bertenthal, Campos, & Kermoian, 1994). For example, crawlers, and non-crawlers mobile with the aid of special walkers, are better able to search for and find hidden objects than are infants of the same age who are not mobile. Crawling also contributes to more frequent social interactions with parents and to the emergence of a healthy fear of heights.

Walking. Although parents must be on their toes when their infants first begin walking, they take great delight in witnessing this new milestone in motor development, which occurs around infants' first birthday. According to Esther Thelen (1984, 1995), the basic motor patterns required for walking are present at birth. They are evident in the newborn's stepping reflex and in the spontaneous kicking of infants lying down. Indeed, Thelen noticed that the stepping reflex and early kicking motions were identical. She began to question the traditional understanding that early reflexes, controlled by subcortical areas of the brain, are inhibited once the cortex takes control of movements. Thelen showed that it simply requires more strength to make the walking motion standing up (as in the stepping reflex) than to make it lying down (as in kicking). She demonstrated that babies who no longer showed the stepping motion when placed on a table did show it when suspended in water because less muscle power was needed to move their chunky legs. The upshot? Infants need more than a more mature nervous system to walk; they must also develop more muscle and become less top-heavy. Even when they begin to walk, they lack good balance partly because of their big heads and short legs. Steps are short; legs are wide apart; and hips, knees, and ankles are flexed. There is much teetering and falling, and a smooth gait and good balance will not be achieved for some time. Thelen's point is that adults would walk funny, too, if they, like infants, were "fat, weak, and unstable" (Thelen, 1984, p. 246).

☾ Young toddlers have difficulty maintaining their balance because of their large, heavy heads and torsos and their weak muscles.

How do infant "walkers" affect the emergence of walking? Do they enhance walking, perhaps by allowing infants to exercise their legs without having to support the full weight of their bodies? To answer these questions, Andrea Siegel and Roger Burton (1999) studied three groups of infants: One group used no walkers; a second group used older-model walkers that had large leg openings and allowed the infants to see their legs and feet; and a third group used newer-model walkers designed to be safer than the older model with small leg openings and large opaque trays. These newer walkers helped prevent infants from slipping out of the seat, but they blocked the infants' view of their legs and feet. Infants who did not use either type of walker sat up, crawled, and walked earlier than infants with the old-style walkers, and they in turn walked earlier than infants with newer walkers. Why? Infants in the newer walkers with the opaque trays did not receive sensory feedback about their movements; they could not see how their movements altered the positions of their legs relative to other body parts and to the stationary environment. And infants who did not use walkers enjoyed unrestricted movement and sensory feedback about the effects of their movement. As you will see later in this section, infants need feedback to learn how to coordinate their body movements with the demands of their environment.

Walker use also affected scores on the Bayley scales, a measure of motor and mental development. As Figure 5.4 shows, infants in the newer walkers scored significantly lower on motor development than the other two groups and scored significantly lower on mental development than infants in the no-walker group. The newer walkers restrict visual–motor experiences when infants are seeking new levels of interaction with their environment. Emerging skills of crawling, reaching, and grasping are restricted, which limits what infants can learn about their environment. These infants likely catch up in mental development to their no-walker peers once they stop using walkers, usually around 10 months when they are capable of climbing out of these contraptions.

Manipulating Objects

If you look at what infants can do with their hands, you will find another progression from reflexive activity to more voluntary, coordinated behavior. As you have seen, newborns come equipped with a grasping reflex. It weakens from age 2 to 4 months, and for a time infants cannot aim their grasps well. They take swipes at objects and even make contact more than you would expect by chance, but they often miss. And rather than opening their hands to grasp what they are reaching for, they make a fist (Wallace & Whishaw, 2003).

By the middle of the first year, infants can once again grasp objects well, although they use a rather clumsy, clamp-

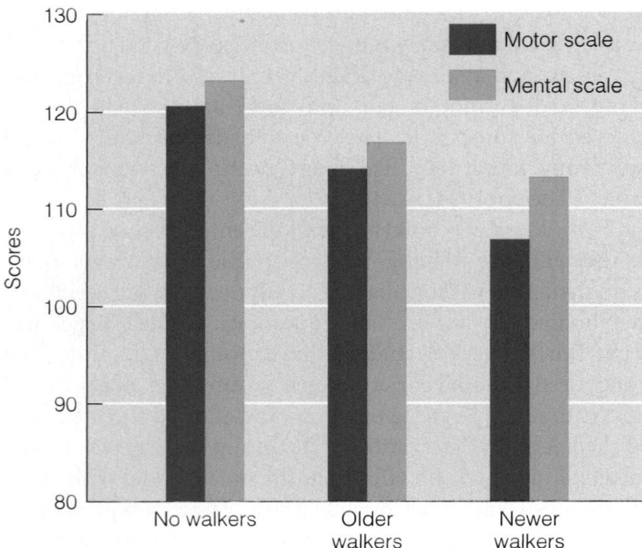

Figure 5.4 Scores on the Bayley Scales of Mental and Psychomotor Development for infants who use no walkers, older (can see their feet) walkers, or newer (feet are not visible) walkers.

SOURCE: Adapted with permission from Siegel, A. C., & Burton, R. V. (1999). Effects of baby walkers on motor and mental development in human infants. *Journal of Development and Behavioral Pediatrics, 20*, 355–361.

like grasp in which they press the palm and outer fingers together. As they gain postural control of their trunks and heads and visual control of their eyes, they become increasingly skillful at reaching for and manipulating objects with their hands (Bertenthal & von Hofsten, 1998). The workings of the proximodistal principle of development can be seen when infants who could control their arms and then their hands finally become able to control the individual fingers enough to use a **pincer grasp.** Involving only the thumb and the forefinger (or another finger), the pincer grasp appears as early as 5 months (Wallace & Whishaw, 2003).

By 16 months, infants can scribble with a crayon, and by the end of the second year they can copy a simple horizontal or vertical line and even build towers of five or more blocks. They are rapidly gaining control of specific, *differentiated* movements, then *integrating* those movements into whole, coordinated actions. They use their new locomotor and manipulation skills to learn about and adapt to the world around them. By cornering bugs and stacking Cheerios, they develop their minds.

Emergence of Motor Skills

How do motor skills emerge? Thelen (1996) observed infants throughout their first year and discovered that they spent a great deal of time engaged in **rhythmic stereotypies.** The infants moved their bodies in repetitive ways—rocking, swaying, bouncing, mouthing objects, and banging their arms up and down. Thelen found that infants performed these rhythmic stereotypies shortly before a new skill emerged but not after the skill had become established. Thus, infants might rock back and forth while on their hands and knees, but once they were crawling, they no longer rocked.

Esther Thelen and Linda Smith (1994) propose a **dynamic systems approach** to explain such motor developments. According to this view, developments take place over time through a "self-organizing" process in which children use the sensory feedback they receive when they try different movements to modify their motor behavior in adaptive ways (Smith & Thelen, 1993). In this view, motor milestones such as crawling and walking are the learned outcomes of a process of interaction with the environment in which infants do the best they can with what they have to achieve their goals (Thelen, 1995). Neural maturation, physical growth, muscle strength, balance, and other characteristics of the child interact with gravity, floor surfaces, and characteristics of the specific task to influence what children can and cannot learn to do with their bodies. Recall the infants who could not see their legs or feet in the newer walkers: it took them longer to achieve certain motor milestones than infants who could see their legs and learn how their movements affected their relationship to their environment.

Consistent with the dynamic systems approach, Karen Adolph and Anthony Avolio (2000) found that young toddlers could adjust their walking to changes in both body dimensions and slope of a walkway. The researchers had infants walk on slopes of different degrees while wearing a vest with removable "saddlebags" that could be weighted to simulate changes in their body dimensions (see Figure 5.5). The weights added mass and shifted the infants' center of gravity, akin to what happens when infants grow. Would infants be able to compensate for the changes in their body and their environment? Yes—they adjusted their motor skills to adapt to rapid "growth" of their bodies and to changes in their environment (Adolph, 1997). Like adults carrying a heavy load on their shoulders, infants bent their knees and kept their

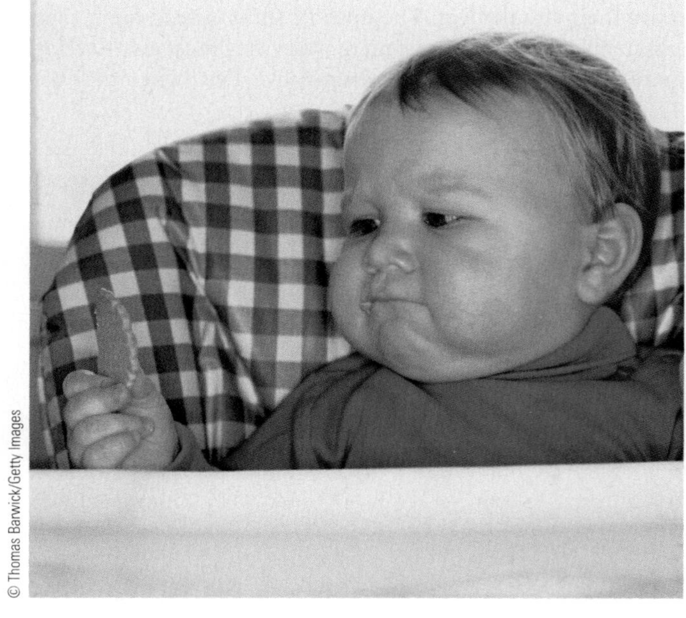

Once infants have mastered the pincer grasp, they can pick up all sorts of objects.

Figure 5.5 Adolph and Avolio's walkway with adjustable slope. Infants are outfitted with weighted saddlebags to alter their body mass and center of gravity. While an experimenter stays beside infants to ensure safety, parents stand at the end of the walkway and encourage their child to walk toward them.
SOURCE: Adolph & Avolio (2000)

upper bodies stiffly upright to maintain their balance with heavier loads. Infants also seemed to recognize when the walkway was too steep to travel safely—they either avoided it or scooted down on their bottoms or on their hands and knees.

How does this dynamic systems perspective fit the nature–nurture theme of development? According to Thelen (1995), toddlers walk not because their genetic code programs them to do so but because they learn that walking works well given their biomechanical properties and the characteristics of the environments they must navigate. In the dynamic systems approach, nature (maturation) and nurture (sensory and motor experience) are both essential and largely inseparable. Feedback from the senses and from motor actions is integrated with the ever-changing abilities of the infant. Having learned how to adjust one motor skill (such as crawling) to successfully navigate environmental conditions, however, does not mean that infants will generalize this knowledge to other motor skills (such as walking; see Adolph & Avolio, 2000). Different motor skills present different challenges. Crawling infants, for instance, must learn to avoid such dangers as bumping their head on table legs. Walking infants face other challenges, such as not toppling over when turning around. To master these challenges, infants need opportunities to gather feedback from each motor activity.

Finally, an important contribution of the dynamic systems approach to motor development is its integration of action with thought. The motor behaviors we have been describing are not separate and distinct from the child's knowledge. Children have to think about how to organize their movements to optimize what they are able to get from their ever-changing environment. Thus, there is far more to motor development than implied by norms indicating when we might expect infants to sit up, stand alone, or walk independently. The emergence of motor skills is complex and is closely connected to perceptual–cognitive developments (Bushnell & Boudreau, 1993).

Summing Up

The physical changes that occur during the short period of infancy are awe-inspiring. Infants gain significant height and weight, their bones harden, and their muscles become stronger. Reflexes and sensory capabilities allow infants to gather information from their surroundings and interact in increasingly meaningful ways with their environments. They proceed from not even being able to sit up by themselves to crawling, walking, and picking up everything in sight. According to the dynamic systems perspective, children engage in a self-regulating process by using sensory feedback they receive from their movements to modify their motor behavior in adaptive ways. During no other postnatal period are there such dramatic changes. Still, 2-year-olds have a long way to go before their physical selves reach maturity. ■

The Child

Development of the body and of motor behavior during childhood is slower than it was during infancy, but it is steady. You need only compare the bodies and the physical feats of the 2-year-old and the 10-year-old to be impressed by how much change occurs over childhood.

Steady Growth

From age 2 until puberty, children gain about 2 to 3 inches in height and 5 to 6 pounds in weight every year (National Center for Health Statistics, 2000a). During middle childhood (ages 6–11), children may seem to grow little, probably because the gains are small in proportion to the child's size (4–4½ feet and 60–80 pounds) and therefore harder to detect. The cephalocaudal and proximodistal principles of growth continue to operate. As the lower parts of the body and the extremities fill out, the child takes on more adultlike body proportions. The bones continue to grow and harden, and the muscles strengthen.

Physical Behavior

Infants and toddlers are capable of controlling their movements in relation to a *stationary* world, but children master the ability to move capably in a *changing* environment (Sayre & Gallagher, 2001). They must learn to modify their movements to adapt to changes in environment. This allows them to bring their hands together at just the right time to catch a ball and to avoid bumping into moving people when walking through a crowded mall. They also refine many motor skills. For example, young children throw a ball only with the arm, but older children learn to step forward as they throw. Thus, older children can throw a ball farther than younger ones can, not just because they are bigger and stronger but also because they can integrate multiple body movements—raising their arm, turning their body, stepping forward with one foot, and pushing their body forward with the other foot (Sayre & Gallagher, 2001).

The toddler in motion appears awkward compared with the older child, who takes steps in more fluid and rhythmic strides and is better able to avoid obstacles. And children quickly become able to do more than just walk. By age 3, they can walk or run in a straight line, although they cannot easily turn or stop while running. Kindergarten children can integrate two motor skills—hopping on one foot with walking or running—into mature skipping (Loovis & Butterfield,

Applications

Promoting Lifelong Health with Physical Activity

It is clear that physical activity has beneficial effects on physical functioning across the life span. For instance, children who participate in a systematic exercise program are more physically fit than children who lead a more sedentary lifestyle (see Tuckman, 1999, for a review). Similarly, exercise by older adults can improve cardiovascular and respiratory functioning, slow bone loss, and strengthen muscles. In one study, older athletes (average age 69 years) were compared with older nonathletes on several physiological measures following exercise. The athletes showed better oxygen uptake capacity and greater cardiovascular stamina than the nonathletes (Jungblut et al., 2000). In another study, elderly adults who did low-intensity exercise and weight lifting for 1 year became stronger and more flexible and experienced less pain as a result (Sharpe et al., 1997). Exercise also reduces the number of sick days, doctor visits, and hospitalizations of older adults (German et al., 1995). Overall, it is estimated that regular exercise by older adults can delay the onset of physical disabilities by up to 7 years (Vita et al., 1998).

The benefits of exercise go beyond physical fitness; physical activity may enhance cognitive and psychological functioning. In a review of studies on children's participation in physical activity and their academic performance, Roy Shepard (1997) concluded that increased physical activity was associated with improved academic skills. But these data are largely correlational, and many factors may explain the connection between physical activity and academic performance. For instance, Mark Tremblay and colleagues (Tremblay, Inman, & Willms, 2000) found that regular participation in physical activity did *not* strongly influence 12-year-olds' academic performance, but it did positively affect their self-esteem. Students who are healthier and feel better about themselves may perform better in the classroom.

Older adults also reap multiple benefits from participating in exercise programs. Exercise can make aging adults feel less stressed and happier, and it can enhance their cognitive functioning (Barnes et al., 2003; Rowe & Kahn, 1998; Yaffe et al., 2001). Physical activity is also associated with a lower incidence of depression among older adults (Lampinen, Heikkinen, & Ruoppila, 2000).

© Bob Daemmrich/Stock, Boston

2000). With each passing year, school-age children can run a little faster, jump a little higher, and throw a ball a little farther. Their motor skills are also responsive to practice. In one study, children improved their arm movements 25 to 30% with practice—an impressive accomplishment compared with the 10% improvement shown by adults who practiced (Thomas, Yan, & Stelmach, 2000). There are some gender differences in motor skills, with boys slightly ahead in throwing and kicking and girls somewhat ahead in hopping and the side gallop (van Beurden et al., 2002). These differences seem to arise primarily from practice and different expectations for males and females rather than from inherent differences between males and females. The Applications box beginning on page 128 explores some of the benefits of physical activity for children and for adults.

From age 3 to 5, eye–hand coordination and control of the small muscles are improving rapidly, giving children more sophisticated use of their hands. At age 3, children find it difficult to button their shirts, tie their shoes, or copy simple designs. By age 5, children can accomplish all of these feats and can cut a straight line with scissors or copy letters and numbers with a crayon. By age 8 or age 9, they can use household tools such as screwdrivers and have become skilled performers at games that require eye–hand coordination. Handwriting quality and speed also improve steadily from age 6 to age 15 (van Galen, 1993).

Unfortunately, we live in an era that inadvertently promotes physical inactivity. The average child watches 3 hours of television every day (Huston et al., 1999), and schools have reduced recess time and physical education requirements (Tremblay, Pella, & Taylor, 1996). Time riding in cars and sitting at the computer has increased, and walking and physical activity time has decreased. As a result, as many as 30% of American children are estimated to be overweight (Wolfe et al., 1994), and being an overweight child or adolescent usually means becoming an overweight adult (Boodman, 1995). Children who watch more than 5 hours of television a day are about 5 times more likely to be overweight than children who watch 0 to 2 hours a day, perhaps because they get little exercise and eat the junk foods they see advertised on TV (Gortmaker et al., 1996). Weight-loss programs are likely to be more successful with child "couch potatoes" than with adult ones, however; self-control may not be as necessary if parents can control their children's eating habits for them (Wilson, 1994).

Teenagers face increased risks of obesity because their metabolism rates slow as they mature physically. Individuals who are overweight as adolescents—even those who slim down as adults—run a greater-than-average risk of coronary heart disease and a host of other health problems some 55 years later (Must et al., 1992). Middle-aged adults also run a special risk of gaining weight, especially if they become less physically active but keep eating as much as they did as younger adults (Haber, 1994).

Obesity—being 20% or more above the "ideal" weight for your height, age, and sex—is clearly a threat to health. Rates of obesity have been increasing in U.S. society at all ages levels, even among children (Dwyer & Stone, 2000). Obese people do not live as long as their normal-weight peers, and they are at greater risk for such problems as heart and kidney disease, high blood pressure, diabetes, liver problems, and even arthritis. Obesity is usually the product of both nature and nurture: heredity is perhaps the most important factor (Grilo & Pogue-Geile, 1991), but poor eating habits, inactivity, and even parenting beliefs contribute (Gable & Lutz, 2000). One intriguing finding comes from a study comparing obese and nonobese children on several factors, including eating habits and activities (Gable & Lutz, 2000). Surprisingly, the two groups did not differ in their consumption of high-fat, high-sugar junk foods. They did differ in their activities: obese children watched more television, participated in fewer extracurricular activities, and engaged in less active play. So perhaps parents should worry less about the junk food their children consume—as long as it is not excessive or a substitute for healthy foods—and focus more on getting their children involved in physical activities.

Exercise is clearly beneficial to physical and mental health over the life span. What exercise cannot do is halt the inevitable aging process. Even frequent joggers gain weight and add inches to their waists as they enter middle age (Williams, 1997). True, people who exercise generally weigh less and have slimmer waists than those who do not, but a 30-year-old man who runs 20 to 30 miles a week until he is 50 would add almost 2 inches to his waist anyway; he would have to run farther each year to avoid it. To try to beat aging, then, it is not enough to remain active; he must become *more* active over the years (Williams, 1997).

As this section shows, physical and psychological development are intimately intertwined throughout the life span. Changes in the body require psychological adjustments and bring psychological change. Newly mobile infants benefit cognitively and emotionally from access to a larger physical and social world; adolescents alter their body images in response to physical and sexual maturation; and aging adults change in response to disease and disability. Psychological and social factors influence reactions to these physical changes.

© Dennis MacDonald/PhotoEdit

Children are not as coordinated in preschool as they will be a few years later.

Finally, older children have quicker reactions than young children do. When dogs suddenly run in front of their bikes, they can do something about it. In studies of **reaction time,** a stimulus, such as a light, suddenly appears and the subject's task is to respond to it as quickly as possible—for example, by pushing a button. These studies reveal that reaction time improves steadily throughout childhood (Eaton & Ritchot, 1995; Yan et al., 2000). As children age, they can carry out any number of cognitive processes more quickly (Kail, 1991; van Galen, 1993). This speeding up of neural responses with age contributes in important ways to steady improvements in memory and other cognitive skills from infancy to adolescence (see Chapter 8).

Summing Up

In short, no matter what aspect of physical growth and motor behavior you consider, you can see steady and impressive improvement over the childhood years. Although these changes are not as dramatic as those witnessed during infancy or those that will occur during the adolescent years, they bring the child closer to becoming a full-fledged adult. ■

The Adolescent

Adolescents are intensely focused on their physical self, and rightly so—dramatic physical changes are taking place during this period. Consider your own transformation from child to adult. You rapidly grew taller and took on the body size and proportions of an adult during a growth spurt. Moreover, you experienced **puberty**—the processes of biological change that result in an individual's attaining sexual maturity and becoming capable of producing a child. We look at both of these processes.

© Laura Dwight/CORBIS

These 3-year-olds may think they are playing, but stringing beads also exercises their eye–hand coordination and fine motor skills.

The Growth Spurt

As noted earlier in the chapter, the **adolescent growth spurt** is triggered by an increase in the level of growth hormones circulating through the body during adolescence. Boys and girls grow at different rates, as do different body parts. Girls' peak rate of growth for height is just under 12 years; for boys it is 13.4 years (Geithner et al., 1999). The peak rate of growth for weight is 12.5 years for girls and 13.9 years for boys. Thus, boys lag behind girls by 1 to 2 years. Both sexes return to a slower rate of growth after the peak of their growth spurts. Like infants, adolescents may grow in spurts rather than continuously (Lampl, 2002). Girls achieve their adult height by around 16 years; boys are still growing at 18, 19, or even 20 years (National Center for Health Statistics, 2000a).

Muscles also develop rapidly in both sexes, with boys normally gaining a greater proportion of muscle mass than girls do. Total body weight increases in both sexes, but it is distributed differently: girls gain extra fat, primarily in the breasts, hips, and buttocks; boys develop broader shoulders.

Sexual Maturation

Long before the physical signs of puberty are evident, the body is changing to prepare for sexual maturity. The adrenal glands increase production of adrenal androgens as early as age 6 to age 8, which contributes partly to such secondary sex characteristics as pubic and axillary (underarm) hair (Spear, 2000a). But the more obvious signs of sexual maturity emerge with increased production of gonadal hormones (those produced by the testes or ovaries): androgens in males and estrogen and progesterone in females. The gonadal hormones are primarily responsible for the development of secondary sexual characteristics and sexual maturity.

© David Young-Wolff/PhotoEdit, Inc.

Although there are large individual differences, girls typically mature earlier than boys, which sometimes leads to girls' towering over the boys in their classes.

For girls, the most dramatic event in the sexual maturation process is **menarche**—the first menstruation—normally between age 11 and age 14 with an average of $12^1/_2$ years for non-Hispanic white girls and 12 years for non-Hispanic black girls (Anderson, Dallal, & Must, 2003; Chumlea et al., 2003). Menstruation is the process of shedding the lining of a uterus prepared to support a fertilized egg. However, young girls often begin to menstruate before they have begun to ovulate, so they may not be capable of reproducing until several years after menarche (Spear, 2000a).

After decreasing during the first half of the 20th century, the average age of menarche has not changed much in recent decades, at least in industrialized nations (Chumlea et al., 2003; Viner, 2002). However, there is a great deal of variability in when secondary sex characteristics appear. Sexual maturation also proceeds at different rates in different ethnic groups. Several studies have found that African American and Mexican American girls begin to experience pubertal changes earlier than European American girls (Chumlea et al., 2003; Wu, Mendola, & Buck, 2002). At age 9, for example, 49% of African American girls have begun to develop breasts compared with only 16% of European American girls and 25% of Mexican American girls (Wu, Mendola, & Buck, 2002). A few girls (1% of European Americans and 3% of African Americans) show signs of breast or pubic hair development at age 3, and a few have not begun to mature even at age 12 (Herman-Giddens et al., 1997).

For the average boy, the sexual maturation process begins around age 11 to age $11^1/_2$ with an initial enlargement of the testes and scrotum (the saclike structure that encloses the testes). Unpigmented, straight pubic hair appears soon thereafter, and about 6 months later, the penis grows rapidly about the same time that the adolescent growth spurt begins (see Figure 5.6). The marker of sexual maturation most like menarche in girls is **semenarche,** or a boy's first ejaculation—the emission of seminal fluid in a "wet dream" or while masturbating. It typically occurs around age 13. Just as girls often do not ovulate until some time after menarche, boys often do not produce viable sperm until some time after their first ejaculation.

Somewhat later, boys begin to sprout facial hair, first at the corners of the upper lip and finally on the chin and jawline. As the voice lowers, many boys have the embarrassing experience of hearing their voices "crack" uncontrollably up and down between a squeaky soprano and a deep baritone, sometimes within a single sentence. Boys may not see the first signs of a hairy chest until their late teens or early 20s, if at all.

What determines an adolescent's rate of development? Genes are part of the answer: identical twins typically experience changes at similar times, and early or late maturation tends to run in families (Tanner, 1990). In both sexes, the changes involved in physical and sexual maturation are triggered when the hypothalamus of the brain stimulates activity in the endocrine system (see the description at the beginning of this chapter).

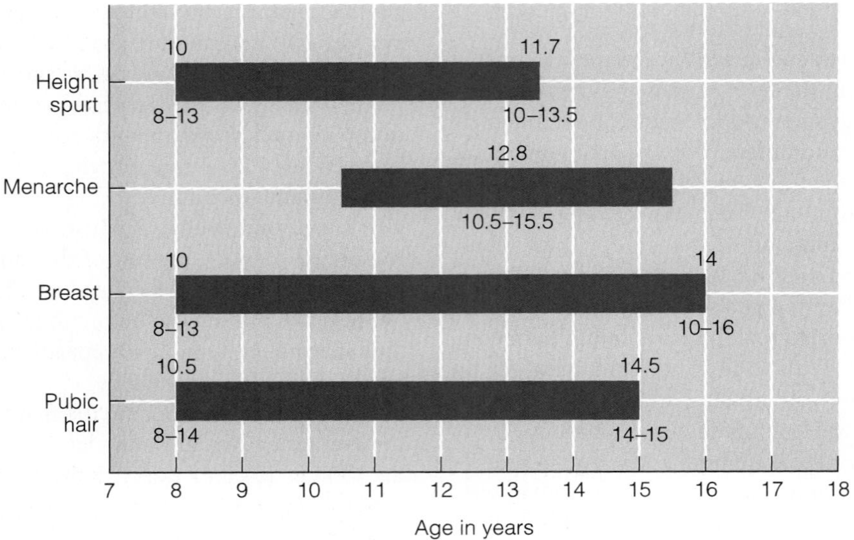

(A) Females

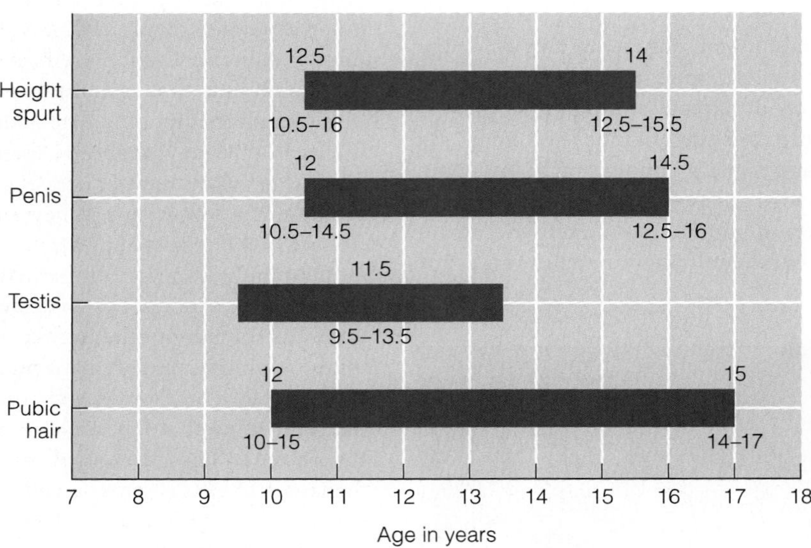

(B) Males

Figure 5.6 Sequence of events in the sexual maturation of females (A) and males (B). The numbers represent the variation among individuals in the ages at which each aspect of maturation begins or ends. For example, growth of the penis may begin as early as age $10\frac{1}{2}$ or as late as age $14\frac{1}{2}$.

Boys and girls have similar levels of both male and female sex hormones during childhood. By the time sexual maturation is complete, however, males have larger quantities of male hormones (androgens, including testosterone) circulating in their blood than females do, whereas females have larger quantities of female hormones (estrogen, progesterone, and others).

Physical and sexual maturation, then, are processes set in motion by the genes and executed by hormones. But environment also plays its part in the timing of maturation. This is dramatically illustrated by the **secular trend**—the historical trend in industrialized societies toward earlier maturation and greater body size. In 1840, for example, the average age of menarche was $16^1/_2$ years, a full 4 years later than it is today (Rees, 1993). Today, researchers can still find cultures in which sexual maturity is reached much later than it is in Western nations. For example, in one region of Saudi Arabia the average age of menarche is 15, and in one part of New Guinea the average girl does not reach menarche until age 18 (Dosoky & Amoudi, 1997; Tanner, 1990).

What explains the secular trend? Better nutrition and advances in medical care seem to be the major factors (Johnston, 2002). Worldwide, the age of menarche is earlier in countries with good nutrition, long life expectancies, and high literacy rates, reflecting the effect of both biological and environmental factors (Thomas et al., 2001). In industrialized nations, today's children are more likely than their parents or grandparents to reach their genetic potential for maturation and growth because they are better fed and less likely to experience growth-retarding illnesses. Even within the relatively affluent U.S. society, poorly nourished adolescents—both boys and girls—mature later than well-nourished ones do. Girls who are taller and heavier as children tend to mature earlier than other girls (St. George, Williams, & Silva, 1994). By contrast, girls who engage regularly in strenuous physical activity and girls who suffer from anorexia nervosa (the life-threatening eating disorder that involves dieting to the point of starvation) may begin menstruating late or stop menstruating after they have begun. These variations seem to be tied not to overall weight but to skeletal development, particularly maturation of the pelvic bones necessary for delivering a baby (Ellison, 2002).

Research by Bruce Ellis and Judy Garber (2000) shows that family and marital stress also affects the timing of puberty in girls. Girls whose mothers were depressed were likely to experience early puberty, as were girls who had a stepfather or mother's boyfriend present in the home. In particular, girls who were relatively young when an unrelated male moved into the house and whose mothers and stepfathers or boyfriends had a more conflicted, stressful relationship were likely to experience early sexual maturity. In other research, however, Croatian girls living under the stressful conditions of war showed delayed sexual maturation (Prebeg & Bralic, 2000). And girls from lower socioeconomic backgrounds lag several months behind their higher socioeconomic counterparts, possibly because of less adequate nutrition and health care (Dosoky & Amoudi, 1997). Truly, then, physical and sexual maturation are the products of an interaction between heredity and environment, with some environments delaying maturation and others hastening it.

Psychological Implications

As noted previously, there are large individual differences in the timing of physical and sexual maturation. An early-maturing girl may develop breast buds at age 8 and reach menarche at age 10, whereas a late-developing boy may not begin to experience a growth of his penis until age 14½ or a height spurt until age 16. Within a middle school, then, there is a wide assortment of bodies, ranging from entirely childlike to fully adultlike. No wonder adolescents are self-conscious about their appearance.

What psychological effects do the many changes associated with puberty have on adolescents? In many cultures, girls approaching or experiencing puberty tend to become concerned about their appearance and worry about how others will respond to them. One adolescent girl may think she is too tall, another that she is too short. One may try to pad her breasts; another may hunch her shoulders to hide hers. Not surprisingly, research confirms that individual reactions to menarche vary widely, with many girls reporting a mixture of positive and negative feelings and some confusion about the process (Koff & Rierdan, 1995; Moore, 1995). Unfortunately, cultural views about menstruation are often negative, and girls internalize these negative myths about what to expect. Many also develop poor body images because they are bothered by the weight gains that typically accompany menarche (Seiffge-Krenke, 1998).

What about boys? Their body images are more positive than those of girls, and they are more likely to welcome their weight gain and voice changes (Benjat & Hernández-Guzmán, 2002; Martin, 1996). But they hope to be tall, hairy, and handsome, and they may become preoccupied with their physical and athletic prowess. Whereas menarche is a memorable event for girls, boys are often unaware of some of the physical changes they are experiencing. They notice their first ejaculation, but they rarely tell anyone about it and often were not prepared for it (Stein & Reiser, 1994). Although males express a mix of positive and negative reactions to becoming sexually mature, they generally react more positively to semenarche than girls do to menarche; 62% of boys regard semenarche positively, whereas only 23% of girls view menarche positively (Seiffge-Krenke, 1998).

Pubertal changes may prompt changes in family relations. Adolescents physically distance themselves from their parents by engaging in less body contact, especially with fathers, and they go to great lengths to avoid being seen naked by their parents (Schulz, 1991, in Seiffge-Krenke, 1998). Likewise, parents seem to restructure the parent–child relationship, placing greater distance between themselves and their children. Perhaps as a result of the barriers erected between adolescents and their parents, teens become more independent and less close to their parents (Steinberg, 1989). They are also more likely to experience conflicts with their parents, especially with their mothers—more often about minor issues such as unmade beds, late hours, and loud music than about core values. Hormone changes in early adolescence may contribute to this increased conflict with parents and to moodiness, bouts of depression, lower or more variable energy levels, and restlessness (Buchanan, Eccles, & Becker, 1992). However, cultural beliefs about family relations and about the significance of becoming an adult also influence parent–child interactions during adolescence. For example, many Mexican American boys and their parents appear to become closer rather than more distant during the peak of pubertal changes (Molina & Chassin, 1996).

Even when parent–child relationships are disrupted during early adolescence, they become warmer once the pubertal transition is completed. Parents—mothers and fathers alike—can help adolescents adjust successfully to puberty by maintaining close relationships and helping adolescents accept themselves (Swarr & Richards, 1996). Overall, you should not imagine that the physical and hormonal changes of puberty cause direct and straightforward psychological changes in the individual. Instead, biological changes interact with psychological characteristics of the person and with changes in the social environment to influence how adolescence is experienced (Magnusson, 1995; Paikoff & Brooks-Gunn, 1991).

Early versus Late Development

If "timely" maturation has psychological implications, what is it like to be "off time"—to be an especially early or late developer? The answer depends on whether we are talking about males or females and also on whether we examine their adjustment during adolescence or later on.

Consider the short-term effect of being an early- or late-developing boy. Early-developing boys are judged to be socially competent, attractive, and self-assured, and they enjoy greater social acceptance by their peers (Bulcroft, 1991). The only negative aspect of being an early-maturing boy is earlier involvement in substance use and other problem behaviors such as bullying (Kaltiala-Heino et al., 2003). By comparison, late maturation in boys has several disadvantages. Late-maturing boys tend to be more anxious and less sure of themselves, and they experience more behavior and adjustment problems (Dorn, Susman, & Ponirakis, 2003). As a group, they even score lower than other students do, at least in early adolescence, on school achievement tests (Dubas, Graber, & Petersen, 1991).

Now consider early- and late-maturing girls. Traditionally, physical prowess has not been as important in girls' peer groups as in boys', so an early-developing girl may not gain much status from being larger and more muscled. In addition, because girls develop about 2 years earlier than boys do, a girl may be subjected to ridicule for a time—the only one in her grade who is developed and thus the target of some teasing. Perhaps for some of these reasons, early maturation appears to be more of a disadvantage than an advantage for girls. Many studies report an association between early maturation and lower self-esteem among girls (see, for example, Forys & Rider, 2000; Williams & Currie, 2000). The early-maturing girl tends to be less popular than her prepubertal classmates, and she is more likely to report symptoms of depression and anxiety, especially if she had psychological problems as a child (Graber et al., 1997; Hayward et al., 1997). In addition, early-maturing girls often end up socializing with an older peer group; consequently, they are likely to become involved in dating, drinking, having sex, and engaging in minor troublemaking at an early age (Dick et al., 2000; Lanza & Collins, 2002).

Late-maturing girls (like late-maturing boys) may experience some anxiety as they wait to mature, but they are not nearly as disadvantaged as late-maturing boys. Indeed, whereas later-developing boys tend to perform poorly on school achievement tests, later-developing girls outperform other students (Dubas, Graber, & Petersen, 1991). Perhaps late-developing girls focus on academic skills when other girls have shifted some of their focus to extracurricular activities.

Do differences between early and late developers persist into later adolescence and adulthood? Typically, they fade with time. By late high school, for example, differences in academic performance between early and late maturers have already disappeared (Dubas, Graber, & Petersen, 1991), and early-maturing girls are no longer less popular than other girls (Hayward et al., 1997). However, there may be lasting effects of some of the risky behaviors engaged in by early-maturing girls (such as sex and drinking). And some research shows that early-maturing girls have a greater likelihood than all other groups of experiencing lifetime adjustment problems, including both anxiety and depression (Graber et al., 1997). Some of the advantages of being an early-maturing boy may carry over into adulthood, but early-maturing boys also seem to be more rigid and conforming than late-maturing ones, who may learn some lessons about coping in creative ways from their struggles as adolescents (Jones, 1965).

Overall, then, late-maturing boys and early-maturing girls are especially likely to find the adolescent period disruptive. However, psychological differences between early- and late-maturing adolescents become smaller and more mixed in quality by adulthood. It is also important to note that differences between early and late maturers are relatively small and that many factors besides the timing of maturation influence whether this period goes smoothly or not. For example, girls who make the transition from elementary to middle school when they experience puberty exhibit greater adjustment problems than girls who do not experience a school transition and pubertal changes at the same time (Simmons & Blyth, 1987).

Finally, and perhaps most important, the effects of the timing of puberty depend on the adolescent's perception of whether pubertal events are experienced early, on time, or late (Seiffge-Krenke, 1998). Thus, one girl may believe she is a "late bloomer" when she does not menstruate until age 14. But another girl who exercises strenuously may believe that menarche at age 14 is normal because delayed menarche is typical of serious athletes. Peer and family-member reactions to an adolescent's pubertal changes are also instrumental in determining the adolescent's adjustment. This may help explain the difference in adjustment between early-maturing boys and early-maturing girls. Parents may be more concerned and negative about their daughter's emerging sexuality than they are about their son's. These attitudes may be inadvertently conveyed to teens, affecting their experience of puberty and their self-concept.

Physical Behavior

The dramatic physical growth that occurs during adolescence makes teenagers more physically competent than children. Rapid muscle development over the adolescent years makes both boys and girls noticeably stronger than they were as children (Seger & Thorstensson, 2000). Their performance of large-muscle activities continues to improve: An adolescent can throw a ball farther, cover more ground in the standing long jump, and run much faster than a child can (Keough & Sugden, 1985). However, as the adolescent years progress, the physical performance of boys continues to improve, whereas that of girls often levels off or even declines (Seger & Thorstensson, 2000).

Clearly, larger muscles enable boys to outperform girls in activities that require strength. But biological differences cannot entirely explain sex differences in physical performance (Smoll & Schutz, 1990). Gender-role socialization may be partly responsible. As girls mature sexually and physically, they are often encouraged to be less "tomboyish" and to become more interested in traditionally "feminine" (often more sedentary) activities. Studies of world records in track, swimming, and cycling suggest that as gender roles have changed in the past few decades, women have been improving their performances, and the male–female gap in physical performance has narrowed dramatically (Sparling, O'Donnell, & Snow, 1998; Whipp & Ward, 1992). A small gender gap remains in some areas of physical activity, largely related to biological differences—greater muscle mass in males, greater body fat in females, and differences in oxygen transport capacity (Sparling, O'Donnell, & Snow, 1998). But as today's girls participate more often in sports and other strenuous physical activities, their performance on tests of large-muscle activity is likely to remain stable or improve during adolescence, rather than declining as it did in previous generations. Then both young women and young men will be likely to enter adulthood in peak physical condition.

Summing Up

The adolescent period, then, is marked by physical growth and attainment of sexual maturity. These changes are significant and have psychological implications. Most adolescents, but especially girls, react to the maturation process with mixed feelings and worry about their physical appearance and capabilities. Early maturation tends to give boys an advantage over their peers but appears to be disadvantageous for girls. For girls, the best course would be to mature "on time," that is, when peers are experiencing the same changes. ■

The Adult

The body of the mature adolescent or young adult is at its prime in many ways. It is strong and fit; its organs are functioning efficiently. But it is aging, as it has been all along. Physical aging occurs slowly and steadily over the life span.

Physical Changes

Physical changes begin to have noticeable effects on appearance and functioning in middle age and have an even more significant effect by the time old age is reached, although more in some people than in others. We will now examine the physical aging process.

Appearance and Structure

Only minor changes in physical appearance occur in the 20s and 30s, but many people notice signs that they are aging as they reach their 40s. Skin becomes wrinkled, dry, and loose, especially among people who have spent more time in the sun. Hair thins and often turns gray from loss of pigment-producing cells. And to most people's dismay, they put on extra weight throughout much of adulthood as their metabolism declines but their eating and exercise habits do not adjust accordingly (Kart, Metress, & Metress, 1992). Among middle-aged adults, more than half are overweight, whereas only 2% are underweight (Centers for Disease Control, 2002). Indeed, more middle-aged people are overweight than in the normal weight range.

The body shows additional effects of aging in old age. After gaining weight throughout early and middle adulthood, people typically begin to lose weight starting in their 60s (Haber, 1994). Loss of weight in old age is usually coupled with loss of muscle over the span of adulthood. However, it is not age per se that reduces muscle mass but rather the sedentary lifestyle adopted by many older adults (Harper, 1999). When Abby King and colleagues (2000) surveyed nearly 3000 women in middle and later adulthood, they found that only 9% met the criteria for being regularly active. And as age increased, level of activity decreased. Age is not the only culprit, however, in making adults less active; low level of education, poor neighborhood characteristics, and personal factors (such as caregiving responsibilities and lack of energy) also influence whether or not adults exercise (King et al., 2000).

Aging is also associated with decreased bone density which, with reduced muscle mass and joint changes, can lead to shortened stature, stooped posture, fractures, and pain. Most older adults are not bothered by the slight decrease in height they experience (about half an inch for men and an inch for women by age 70), but they are troubled by joint pain and fractures because these changes can impair mobility and detract from the quality of life.

Extreme bone loss in later life results from **osteoporosis,** a disease in which a serious loss of minerals leaves the bones fragile and easily fractured. It involves pain and can result in death if the victim falls and fractures a hip. As many as one-third of elderly adults who fracture a hip die within 1 year (Rose & Maffulli, 1999). Osteoporosis is a special problem for older women, who never had as much bone mass as men and whose bones tend to thin rapidly after menopause (Henderson & Goltzman, 2000). European and Asian women with light frames, those who smoke, and those with a family history of osteoporosis are especially at risk. Women with osteoporosis may eventually develop the so-called dowager's hump, a noticeably rounded upper back. One long-term victim lost almost 6 inches in height by age 70 (far more than the average loss of 1 inch) and ended up with her ribcage sitting on her hipbones (Franklin, 1995).

What can be done to prevent osteoporosis? For starters, dietary habits can influence a person's risk for osteoporosis. Many individuals do not get enough calcium to develop strong bones when they are young or to maintain bone health as they age (Kart, Metress, & Metress, 1992). Weight-bearing exercises such as walking or jogging can help prevent osteoporosis, as can the hormone replacement therapy (HRT) that some women take following menopause (but see page 138 for concerns about HRT). It is increasingly evident that good bone health starts in childhood and adolescence (Krucoff, 2000). Girls and young women who are physically active and eat a healthy diet develop higher bone density that protects them from bone loss in later life.

The joints also age over the adult years. The cushioning between bones wears out, and the joints stiffen. Many older adults experience pain or discomfort from arthritis, or joint inflammation. The most common joint problem among older adults is **osteoarthritis,** which results from gradual deterioration of the cartilage that cushions the bones from rubbing against one another. For some older adults, joint disease is deforming and painful and limits their activities. The older person who can no longer fasten buttons, stoop to pick up dropped items, or even get into and out of the bathtub may easily feel incompetent and dependent (Whitbourne, 2001).

Functioning and Health

Aging also involves a gradual decline in the efficiency of most bodily systems from the 20s on (Christofalo, 1988; Whitbourne, 2001). Most systems increase to a peak sometime between childhood and early adulthood and decline slowly thereafter. No matter what physical function you look at—the capacity of the heart or lungs to meet the demands of exercise, the ability of the body to control its temperature, the ability of the immune system to fight disease, or strength—the gradual effects of aging are evident. For example, Monique Samson and her colleagues (2000) assessed handgrip strength in healthy men and women between age 20 and age 80. Women showed only small decreases in muscle strength before age 55 but much larger decreases after age 55. Men showed steady loss of muscle strength across all ages studied.

It should be noted, however, that individual differences in physiological functioning increase with age (Harris et al., 1992). That is, aerobic capacity and other physiological measurements vary more widely among 70-year-olds than among 20-year-olds. Even though the average old person is less physiologically fit than the average young person, not all older people have poor physiological functioning. Older adults who remain physically active retain greater strength (Amara et al., 2003).

Another fact of physical aging is a decline in the **reserve capacity** of many organ systems—that is, their ability to respond to demands for extraordinary output, such as in emergencies (Goldberg & Hagberg, 1990). For example, old and young people do not differ much in resting heart rates, but

© Bob Daemmrich/Stock, Boston

Some older adults have a good deal of reserve capacity and can perform strenuous activities even in their 80s and 90s.

Table 5.5 Physical Skills of Adults 70 and Older

Skill	Men	Women
Walk one-quarter mile	88%	82%
Climb 10 stairs without resting	92	88
Stoop, crouch, or kneel	90	84
Reach over head	97	86

SOURCE: Federal Interagency Forum on Aging-Related Statistics, 2000, Table 18b.

older adults, unless they are disease-free, will have lower maximal heart rates (Lakatta, 1990). This means that older adults who do not feel very old as they go about their normal routines may feel very old if they try to run up mountains.

By the time people are 65 or older, it is hard to find many who do not have something wrong with their bodies. Acute illnesses such as colds and infections become less frequent from childhood on, but chronic diseases and disorders become more common. National health surveys indicate that many of the 70-and-older age group have at least one chronic impairment—whether a sensory loss, arthritis, hypertension, or a degenerative disease (Federal Interagency Forum, 2000). Arthritis alone affects 50% of elderly men and 64% of elderly women; in addition, about 45% have hypertension (high blood pressure), and about 22% have heart disease (Federal Interagency Forum, 2000). Among older adults who live in poverty, many of whom are members of a minority group, health problems and difficulties in day-to-day functioning are even more common and more severe (Clark & Maddox, 1992; Hobbs, 1996). Still, as Table 5.5 shows, most adults maintain the physical capabilities that allow them to function successfully.

Psychological Implications

Some people, influenced by societal stereotypes to equate "old" with "unattractive," find the physical changes in their appearance and functioning that occur with age difficult to accept. American society values youth and devalues old age and the physical changes that often accompany it. What are the psychological implications of growing older under these conditions? Negative stereotypes about older adults abound—they are sickly, frail, forgetful, unattractive, dependent, or otherwise incompetent. Such stereotypes can lead to **ageism,** or prejudice against elderly people. Most elderly adults have internalized these negative views but believe they apply to other older adults and not to themselves.

Laura Hurd (1999) interviewed women between age 50 and age 90 who attended programs at a "senior center." She found that the women actively worked to distance themselves from the "old" category and to remain in the "not old" category. These categories were defined not by age but by what individuals can and cannot do. Generally, the women believed that they were not old because they had the physical and mental abilities to avoid nursing home care. In particular, they believed that remaining active—both physically and socially—was the key to avoiding becoming old. Women who considered themselves "not old" believed that men and women who were old had given in to the stereotypes of aging by being inactive and solitary.

As you have seen, many older adults, even those who consider themselves "not old," have chronic diseases and impairments. Still, 72% of people 65 and older say they are in excellent, very good, or good health (Federal Interagency Forum, 2000). Moreover, relatively few say they need assistance with daily activities, although the figure climbs with age—from 9% of those age 65 to age 69 to 50% of those age 85 and older (Hobbs, 1996). Although having a chronic disease or disability tends to lower an older person's sense of well-being, many people with arthritis, diabetes, and other difficulties are no less content with their lives than anyone else (Kempen, Ormel, & Relyveld, 1997). Clearly, most older people are able to retain their sense of well-being and their ability to function independently despite an increased likelihood of impairments.

The Reproductive System

During most of adulthood, the sex hormones that start to be secreted during adolescence help ensure interest in sexual behavior and the ability to have children, but they also have psychological implications and affect the experience of aging. In men, testosterone levels fluctuate annually, with the highest levels detected in June and July (Andersson et al., 2003), and daily (Harman & Talbert, 1985). Men with high levels of testosterone tend to be more sexually active and aggressive than other men (Schiavi et al., 1991; Archer, 1991), Otherwise, it is not clear that changes in men's hormone levels are tied to changes in their moods and behavior.

By contrast, hormone levels in women shift drastically each month as they progress through their menstrual cycles. These shifts have psychological implications for some women. Estrogen and progesterone levels rise to a peak at midcycle, when a woman is ovulating, and decline as she approaches her menstrual period. The cyclic changes in hormones may lead to such symptoms as bloating, moodiness, breast tenderness, and headaches during the days just before the menstrual flow, symptoms collectively referred to as **premenstrual syndrome (PMS)**. Among women age 21 to age 64, 41% report that they experience PMS and another 17% report at least some symptoms before menstruation (Singh et al., 1998). Many adolescent women (88%) report moderate or severe symptoms (Cleckner-Smith, Doughty, & Grossman, 1998).

However, there is some debate about the validity of PMS. In research where women are simply asked to complete mood surveys every day and do not know that their menstrual cycles are being studied, most report little premenstrual mood change (Englander-Golden et al., 1986). This suggests that expectations and not hormones play a role in many cases of PMS. Only a few women—probably fewer than 5%—experience significant PMS. Changes in estrogen and progesterone levels may be responsible for the severe PMS these women experience (Schmidt et al., 1998). Women with severe PMS may find relief when treated with antidepressant drugs such as Prozac (Dimmock et al., 2000). For women with milder forms of PMS, treatment with calcium and vitamin D may alleviate symptoms because low estrogen levels can interfere with the absorption of these substances by the body (Thys-Jacobs, 2000). Clearly, individuals vary in how they experience menstrual cycles.

You now know that genetic endowment influences the extent to which a woman experiences both premenstrual and menstrual distress (Condon, 1993; Kendler et al., 1992). Social factors also play a role. Learned societal stereotypes of what women "should" experience at different phases of the menstrual cycle appear to influence what women experience and report (Ainscough, 1990; Englander-Golden et al., 1986). Most likely, then, biological, psychological, social, and cultural factors all contribute to a woman's experience of the menstrual cycle during her adult life (McFarlane & Williams, 1990).

Female Menopause

Like other systems of the body, the reproductive system ages. The ending of a woman's menstrual periods in midlife is called **menopause.** The average woman experiences menopause at age 51, and the usual age range is from 45 to 54 (National Institutes of Health, 2002). The process takes place gradually over 5 to 10 years as periods become either more or less frequent and less regular. Levels of estrogen and other female hormones decline so that the woman who has been through menopause has a hormone mix that is less "feminine" and more "masculine" than that of the premenopausal woman. When menopause is completed, a woman is no longer ovulating, no longer menstruating, and no longer capable of conceiving a child.

The age at which a woman reaches menopause is somewhat related to both the age at which she reached menarche and the age at which her mother reached menopause (Varea et al., 2000). Although life expectancy has increased and the age of menarche has decreased over history as part of the secular trend, the age of menopause does not appear to have changed much and is similar from culture to culture (Brody et al., 2000). What has changed is that women are now living long enough to experience a considerable period of postmenopausal life.

Society holds rather stereotypic views of menopausal women. They are regarded as irritable, emotional, depressed, and unstable. How much truth is there to this stereotype? Not much. About two-thirds of women in U.S. society experience **hot flashes**—sudden experiences of warmth and sweating, usually centered around the face and upper body, that occur at unpredictable times, last for a few seconds or minutes, and are often followed by a cold shiver (Robinson, 1996). Many also experience vaginal dryness and irritation or pain during intercourse. Still other women experience no symptoms.

What about the psychological symptoms—irritability and depression? Again, researchers have discovered wide variation among menopausal women—and not much truth to the negative stereotypes. In a particularly well-designed study, Karen Matthews and her associates (Matthews, 1992; Matthews et al., 1990) studied 541 initially premenopausal women over a 3-year period, comparing those who subsequently experienced menopause with women of similar ages who did not become menopausal. The typical woman entering menopause initially experienced some physical symptoms such as hot flashes. Some women also reported mild depression and temporary emotional distress, probably in reaction to their physical symptoms, but only about 10% could be said to have become seriously depressed in response to menopause. Typically, menopause had no effect on the women's levels of anxiety, anger, perceived stress, or job dissatisfaction. When women do experience severe psychological problems during the menopausal transition, they often had those problems well before the age of menopause (Greene, 1984).

Women who have been through menopause generally say it had little effect on them or that it even improved their lives; they are usually more positive about it than women who have not been through it yet (Gannon & Ekstrom, 1993; Wilbur, Miller, & Montgomery, 1995). For most women, menopause brings no changes in sexual interest and activity, although sexual activity gradually declines in both women and men over the adult years (Laumann, Paik, & Rosen, 1999). In short, despite all the negative stereotypes, menopause seems to be "no big deal" for most women.

Why do some women experience more severe menopausal symptoms than others do? Again, part of the answer may lie with biology. Women who have a history of menstrual problems (such as PMS) report more menopausal symptoms, both physical and psychological (Morse et al., 1998). Thus, some women may experience greater biological changes. But psychological and social factors of the sort that influence women's reactions to sexual maturation and to their menstrual cycles also influence the severity of menopausal symptoms. For example, women who expect menopause to be a negative experience are likely to get what they expect (Matthews, 1992). There is also a good deal of variation across cultures in how menopause is experienced (see the Explorations box on this page). It appears that the effect of menopause is colored by the meaning it has for the woman, as influenced by her society's prevailing views of menopause and by her own personal characteristics.

For years, **hormone replacement therapy,** or **HRT** (taking estrogen and progestin to compensate for hormone loss at menopause), was considered an effective cure for the symptoms that many women experience with menopause. This hormone treatment relieves physical symptoms of menopause, such as hot flashes and vaginal dryness, and prevents or slows osteoporosis (National Institutes of Health, 2002). Unfortunately, researchers have learned that this relief comes with a price. HRT increases women's chances of developing breast cancer and experiencing heart attacks and strokes (Women's Health Initiative, 2004). For most women, these risks outweigh the benefits of HRT, particularly if the hormones estrogen and progestin are taken over a long period. For women with severe menopausal symptoms associated with decreasing production of hormones, short-term HRT (for example, up to 2 years) may be warranted.

Explorations

Cultural Differences in the Experience of Menopause

The physical changes involved in menopause are universal, but the psychological experience of it is not. Consider hot flashes, the most frequent complaint of menopausal women. Nearly three-quarters of American and Canadian women report experiencing at least one hot flash during the menopausal period, but only one in five Japanese women recall having had any (Lock, 1993; Shaw, 1997). Even within the United States, Japanese and Chinese women report fewer menopausal symptoms than African American, European American, and Hispanic women (Gold et al., 2000). In Zimbabwe, women experience the same symptoms as reported by women in Western cultures, but they view these as part of a normal and healthy stage of life and not as an unhealthy sign of loss (McMaster, Pitts, & Poyah, 1997). Thus, they tend not to seek treatment or complain about their "symptoms."

Marcha Flint (1982) surveyed women of a high and socially advantaged caste in India and found that women who had not reached menopause looked forward to it and that women who had reached it were pleased that they had. Why? According to Flint, menopause brought social rewards to these Indian women. They were freed from the taboos associated with menstruation that had kept them veiled and segregated from male society as younger women. They could now mingle with men other than their husbands and fathers and even drink the local brew with the fellows. Moreover, they still had meaningful work roles and were seen as wise by virtue of their years. In North American society, by comparison, aging often means a loss of status for older women, and menopause is regarded as a medical condition of aging to be treated with hormones.

Not all women share this negative and medical view of menopause, even when the broader culture around them embraces this view. Some American women, for instance, report that menopause is insignificant relative to other things going on in their lives (Winterich & Umberson, 1999). Others regard menopause as a normal life transition, even an opportunity to embark on new life options (Adler et al., 2000). So again, biological, psychological, and social factors all play parts in how a seemingly common event is interpreted differently by different individuals.

Increasingly, women are considering alternative treatments such as soy, but the benefits and pitfalls of these alternatives have not been documented. Lifestyle changes such as exercising and getting adequate sleep may be the best options for menopausal women because they alleviate some complaints and are safe.

Male Andropause

Obviously, men cannot experience menopause because they do not menstruate. They also do not experience the sharp drop in hormones that accompanies menopause in women (Gould, Petty, & Jacobs, 2000). But over the past several years, some research has pointed to the possibility that men experience andropause as they age. **Andropause,** slower and not as dramatic as menopause in women, is characterized by decreasing levels of testosterone and a variety of symptoms including low libido, fatigue and lack of energy, erection problems, memory problems, and loss of pubic hair (Tan & Pu, 2004; Vermeulen, 2000; Wu, Yu, & Chen, 2000). By age 80, men have between 20 and 50% of the testosterone that they had at age 20. The sperm produced by older men may not be as active as those produced by younger men. Still, men can have children long after women are capable of bearing children. Men in their 90s have been known to father children.

Some research reports that, among men over age 50 with symptoms of andropause, testosterone levels are markedly lower than levels in men without symptoms (Wu, Yu, & Chen, 2000). But other research does not show a clear connection between andropause symptoms and testosterone levels (see, for example, Vermeulen, 2000). In one study, for example, half of 50- to 70-year-old men complained of erectile dysfunction despite having sufficient levels of testosterone; most of these cases of erectile dysfunction are caused by medical conditions such as diabetes and not by lower hormone production (Gould, Petty, & Jacobs, 2000).

In sum, the changes associated with andropause in men are more gradual, more variable, and less complete than those associated with menopause in women. As a result, men experience fewer psychological effects. Frequency of sexual activity does decline as men age. However, this trend cannot be blamed entirely on decreased hormone levels, because sexual activity often declines even when testosterone levels remain high (Gould, Petty, & Jacobs, 2000; see also Chapter 12 on sexuality).

Physical Behavior

How well can older adults carry out the physical activities of daily life? Obviously, those who have severe arthritis may have difficulty merely walking or dressing themselves without pain, but here we focus on two more typical changes in physical behavior over the adult years: a slowing of behavior and a decreased ability to engage in strenuous activities.

Slowing Down

You may have noticed, as you breeze by them on the sidewalk, that older adults often walk more slowly than young people do. Indeed, research suggests that the amount of time stoplights provide for pedestrians to cross the street is not enough for the 99% of people age 72 or older who walk at a pace slower than 4 feet per second (Langlois et al., 1997). Some older adults also walk as if they were treading on a slippery surface—with short, shuffling steps and not much arm movement (Murray, Kory, & Clarkson, 1969). Why is this?

Difficulty with balance is one likely culprit. The sensory systems involved in balance do not function as well in old age as they did in earlier years (Ochs et al., 1985). Indeed, balance is often used as an indicator of older adults' functional mobility—their ability to stand, sit, walk, and turn (Shumway-Cook, Brauer, & Woollacott, 2000). Individuals with poor balance may compensate by walking more slowly. More generally, older adults who have fallen or fear they will fall make many adaptive changes in their walk to protect themselves (Newstead et al., 2000).

An older person's slow pace of walking may also be caused by loss of strength and reduced cardiovascular functioning (Buchner, 1997). The pace at which adults of any age choose to walk and the fastest pace at which they can walk are associated with their cardiovascular capacity and their muscle mass (Cunningham et al., 1982). Older people with strong hearts and muscles may walk briskly, but those who have cardiovascular limitations may be slow.

On average, older adults perform many motor actions more slowly and with less coordination than younger adults do (Morgan et al., 1994; Stelmach & Nahom, 1992). The underlying reason is a slowing of the brain. Gerontologist James Birren has argued that *the* central change that comes about as people age is a slowing of the nervous system (Birren & Fisher, 1995). It affects not only motor behavior but also mental functioning, and it affects most elderly people to at least some degree. You have already seen that young children have slow reaction times. Speed on a variety of perceptual–motor tasks then improves and peaks among young adults, only to gradually decrease among middle-aged and older adults (Earles & Salthouse, 1995; Yan, Thomas, & Stelmach, 1998). In a study comparing younger adults (18–24 years) with older adults (62–72 years) on five motor tasks, the older adults performed more slowly on all five (Francis & Spirduso, 2000). The older adults were especially slow on fine motor tasks requiring object manipulation, such as inserting pegs in holes. They also have more trouble when tasks are novel and when they are complex—for example, when any one of several stimuli might appear on a screen and each requires a different response (Sliwinski et al., 1994; Spirduso & MacRae, 1990). On average, older adults take $1\frac{1}{2}$ to 2 times longer than young adults to respond on a range of cognitive tasks that require speedy answers (Lima, Hale, & Myerson, 1991).

You should not expect all old people to be slow in all situations, however. The reaction times of older adults vary greatly (Yan, Thomas, & Stelmach, 1998; Yan et al., 2000). Physically fit older people and those free from cardiovascular diseases have quicker reactions than peers who lead sedentary lives or have diseases, although they are still likely to be slower than they were when they were younger (Earles & Salthouse,

1995; Spirduso & MacRae, 1990). Aerobic exercise or experience playing video games can also speed the reactions of older adults (Dustman et al., 1989, 1992). In addition, experience can help elderly people compensate for a slower nervous system so that they can continue to perform well on familiar motor tasks (Salthouse, 1984).

The slowing of the nervous system and of motor performance is one important fact of aging. Another is that many people become out of shape. Typically, adults decrease their involvement in vigorous physical activity as they get older—females earlier than males (Ruchlin & Lachs, 1999). By late adulthood, they may find that they get tired just climbing stairs or carrying groceries; running a marathon is out of the question. Because of declines in reserve capacity, aging bodies are at a greater disadvantage when they must perform tasks requiring maximal strength, speed, or endurance than when they are asked to perform normal daily activities (Goldberg & Hagberg, 1990). The average older person tires more quickly and needs more time to recover after vigorous activity than the average younger person.

Yet again, diversity is greater among older adults than among younger ones. Some older people can perform vigorous physical activities with distinction. For instance, at age 84, James Dooley is still an active downhill skill racer (Tyre, 2004). Mary Jansen, a grandmother, started training for her first marathon when she was 54 years old (Tyre, 2004). At 62, she has competed in a variety of races, and although she has not yet won a race, she always finishes. And Michael Stones and Albert Kozma (1985) cite the example of a 98-year-old man who could run a marathon (26.2 miles) in 7½ hours!

Disease, Disuse, and Abuse

As you have seen, many aspects of physical functioning decline over the adult years in many individuals. But an important question arises: when researchers look at the performance of older people, are they seeing the effects of aging alone or the effects of something else? The "something else" could be disease, disuse of the body, abuse of the body—or all three.

Most older people have at least some chronic *disease* or impairment, such as arthritis or heart disease. How would an elderly person function if she could manage to stay disease-free? Birren and his colleagues (1963) addressed this question in a classic study of men age 65 to 91. Extensive medical examinations were conducted to identify two groups of elderly men: (1) those who were almost perfectly healthy and had no signs of disease and (2) those who had slight traces of some disease in the making but no clinically diagnosable diseases. Several aspects of physical and intellectual functioning were assessed in these men, and the participants were compared with young men.

The most remarkable finding was that the healthier group of older men hardly differed from the younger men. They were equal in their capacity for physical exercise, and they beat the younger men on measures of intelligence requiring general information or knowledge of vocabulary words. Their main limitations were the slower brain activity and reaction times that seem to be so basic to the aging process. Overall, aging in the absence of disease had little effect on physical and psychological functioning. However, the men with slight traces of impending disease were deficient on several measures. Diseases that have progressed to the point of symptoms have even more serious consequences for performance.

So it is possible that disease, rather than aging, accounts for many declines in functioning in later life (Houx, Vreeling, & Jolles, 1991). We must note, however, that Birren and his colleagues had a tough time finding the perfectly healthy older people they studied. Most older people experience both aging and disease, and it is difficult to separate the effects of the two. Although aging and disease are distinct, increased vulnerability to disease is one part—and an important part—of normal aging.

Disuse of the body also contributes to steeper declines in physical functioning in some adults than in others (Wagner et al., 1992). John Masters and Virginia Johnson (1966) proposed a "use it or lose it" maxim to describe how sexual functioning deteriorates if a person engages in little or no sexual activity. The same maxim can be applied to other systems of the body. Muscles atrophy if they are not used, and the heart functions less well if a person leads a sedentary life. Changes such as these in some aging adults are much like the changes observed in people of any age confined to bed for a long time (Goldberg & Hagberg, 1990). The brain also needs "mental exercise" to display plasticity and to continue to function effectively in old age (Black, Isaacs, & Greenough, 1991). In short, most systems of the body seem to thrive on use, but too many people become inactive as they age (Ruchlin & Lachs, 1999).

Finally, *abuse* of the body contributes to declines in functioning in some people. Excessive alcohol consumption, a high-fat diet, and smoking are all clear examples (Haber, 1994). In addition, although elderly adults are rarely recreational drug abusers, many take several prescribed medications. Drugs typically affect older adults more powerfully than they do younger adults; they can also interact with one another and with the aging body's chemistry to impair functioning (Cherry & Morton, 1989; Lamy, 1986).

Overall, then, poor functioning in old age may represent any combination of the effects of aging, disease, disuse, and abuse. We may not be able to do much to change basic aging processes, but we can change our lifestyles to optimize the odds of a long and healthy old age.

Summing Up

Declines in physical systems and capabilities begin in early adulthood, with steeper declines evident among older adults. Most older adults successfully adjust to these changes, although there may be psychological consequences just as there are during adolescence. Disease, disuse, and abuse all influence the physical behavior of adults. For both sexes, changes in the reproductive system are a normal part of aging. Neither women nor men seem to suffer much as their ability to have children wanes or disappears. Sexual activity becomes less frequent, but it remains an important part of life for most older adults. ■

Summary Points

1. Each of the many systems of the human body develops and ages at its own rate, guided by a genetic program set into action by the brain and the hormones released by the endocrine system. Endocrine glands such as the pituitary, thyroid, testes, and ovaries regulate behavior by secreting hormones directly into the bloodstream.

2. The nervous system consists of the brain and the spinal cord. The amazingly complex processes of the endocrine and nervous systems normally work like a well-oiled machine, but their operation can be hindered or enhanced by environmental forces. Brain development is most rapid during the late prenatal period and early infancy. There is a good deal of plasticity of brain functions during this early developmental period, although even older brains retain some plasticity.

3. The procession of physical growth is orderly, obeying the cephalocaudal, proximodistal, and orthogenetic principles.

4. Newborns have a range of reflexes (both survival and primitive), working senses, a capacity to learn, and organized sleeping and waking states. During infancy, significant growth takes place. In addition, bones harden and muscles strengthen. According to the dynamic systems approach, early motor development is influenced by maturation and by normal opportunities to interact with environment.

5. During childhood, the body steadily grows, and large-muscle and small-muscle control and reaction time improve. Children learn to coordinate their movements within a changing environment.

6. The adolescent growth spurt and pubertal changes make adolescence a time of dramatic physical change. Girls reach menarche (first menstruation) at an average age of $12^1/_2$; boys experience semenarche (first ejaculation) a bit later. Rates of maturation vary widely, partly because of genetic makeup and partly because of nutrition and health status.

7. Most adolescent girls and boys react to the maturation process with mixed feelings, worry about their physical appearance and capabilities, and experience heightened conflict with parents in early adolescence. Early maturation tends to give boys an advantage over their peers but appears to be disadvantageous for girls. Physical capabilities of boys improve, but those of many girls level off or even decline during adolescence, perhaps because of gender stereotypes.

8. Most systems of the body reach a peak of functioning between childhood and early adulthood and decline gradually thereafter; decreases in reserve capacity are especially noticeable. However, individual differences in physiological functioning become greater with age. Older adults lose bone density, which may lead to fractures or osteoporosis. Good bone health starts in childhood with adequate calcium and is maintained with regular physical activity.

9. During the reproductive years of adulthood, some women experience mood swings during the menstrual cycle, but few women are incapacitated by PMS. Men's hormone levels also fluctuate, although not in monthly cycles. Women reach menopause and lose their reproductive capacity around age 50; most experience hot flashes and vaginal dryness, but few experience severe psychological symptoms. The reproductive systems of men age more gradually and less completely during the male andropause.

10. As people age, their nervous systems, reaction times, and motor behavior slow; their capacity for vigorous activity is also reduced. Aging, disease, disuse, and abuse of the body all affect performance in later life. Healthy older people function much like younger people except for their slower reactions, but the development of chronic diseases is a fact of aging for most people.

Critical Thinking

1. You now know that the architecture of the brain is created in response to early experience rather than laid down by the genes. In what ways might a brain "fine-tuned" by experience be superior to a brain whose structure is entirely determined at birth?

2. Recall a time when you learned a new motor skill—for example, how to rollerblade or hit a golf ball. Can you apply the dynamic systems approach to understand how your skill developed over time and what influenced its development?

3. Many (indeed, most) stereotypes of the physical aging process are negative and depressing. What in this chapter gives you reason to be more optimistic about aging, and why? Cite specific concepts and research findings.

4. Suppose you set as your goal reaching age 100 in superb physical condition. Describe and justify a plan for achieving your goal, then indicate why you might not make it despite your best efforts.

Key Terms

catch-up growth, 112
endocrine gland, 112
pituitary gland, 113
growth hormone, 113
androgens, 113
estrogen, 113
neuron, 113
synapse, 114
plasticity, 115
lateralization, 115
cephalocaudal principle, 118
proximodistal principle, 118
orthogenetic principle, 119
reflex, 119
REM sleep, 121
developmental norm, 124
gross motor skills, 124
fine motor skills, 124
pincer grasp, 126
rhythmic stereotypies, 126
dynamic systems approach, 126
reaction time, 130
puberty, 130
adolescent growth spurt, 131
menarche, 131
semenarche, 131
secular trend, 132
osteoporosis, 135
osteoarthritis, 136
reserve capacity, 136
ageism, 136
premenstrual syndrome (PMS), 137
menopause, 137
hot flashes, 137
hormone replacement therapy (HRT), 138
andropause, 139

Media Resources

Websites to Explore

Visit Our Website

For a chapter tutorial quiz and other useful features, visit the book's companion website at *http://psychology.wadsworth.com/sigelman_rider5e*. You can also connect directly to the following sites:

Health

Medline Plus provides extensive information on health issues and includes recent scholarly research on each covered topic. Discovery Health is sponsored by the group that produces the Discovery Channel for television.

Sleep
The Sleep Foundation maintains a website with scholarly information on sleep needs, habits, and problems.

Early Brain Development
The Zero to Three website examines brain development from the prenatal period through the first 3 postnatal years. Topics covered include critical periods, environmental influences, and risk factors.

Developmental Psychology
The Psi Café is a website maintained by an instructor at Portland State University. It contains links to myriad psychology resources and has a page devoted to developmental psychology.

The Secret Life of the Brain
In 2002, PBS premiered a five-part series on the brain. Its companion website summarizes each of the five episodes and offers web-exclusive features such as a three-dimensional exploration of the brain.

Understanding the Data: Exercises on the Web

For additional insight on the data presented in this chapter, try the exercises for these figures at *http://psychology.wadsworth.com/sigelman_rider5e:*

Figure 5.1 Catch-up growth in a girl following treatment for celiac syndrome at around age 11

Table 5.3 Percentage of day (24-hour period) spent in various behavioral states at 2, 6, 12, and 40 weeks

Figure 5.6 Sequence of events in the sexual maturation of females and males

Life-Span CD-ROM

Go to the Wadsworth Life-Span CD-ROM for further study of the concepts in this chapter. The CD-ROM includes narrated concept overviews, video clips, a multimedia glossary, and additional activities to expand your learning experience. For this chapter, check out the following clips, and others, in the video library:

VIDEO Newborn Reflexes

VIDEO Infancy and Toddlerhood: Fine Motor Development

VIDEO Physical Changes with Aging

DEVELOPMENTAL
PsychologyNow™

Developmental PsychologyNow is a web-based, intelligent study system that provides a complete package of diagnostic quizzes, a personalized study plan, integrated multimedia elements, and learning modules. Check it out at *http://psychology.wadsworth.com/sigelman_rider5e/now.*

CHAPTER six

Perception

EQUIPPED WITH AN IMMATURE NERVOUS SYSTEM, a baby arrives into a clamorous world of stimuli that come both from within and without her growing body. In the early months of life, a normally developing child begins the task of making order out of the sensations that stream unbidden and unchanneled through her maturing senses. First she must attain control over her body's motions and internal sensations and over her own attention . . . these abilities to process sights, sounds, and other sensations and to organize responses in a calm, focused manner support mastery of further basic skills of development (Greenspan, 1997, p. 45).

Psychologists have long distinguished between sensation and perception. **Sensation** is the process by which sensory receptor neurons detect information and transmit it to the brain. From birth, infants sense their environment. They detect light, sound, odor-bearing molecules in the air, and other stimuli. But do they make "sense" of it? **Perception** is the interpretation of sensory input: recognizing what you see, understanding what is said to you, knowing that the odor you have detected is a sizzling steak, and so on. It is affected by the individual's history of learning experiences. Does a newborn perceive the world, then, or merely sense it? And what happens to sensory and perceptual capacities as the person ages? Perhaps we should start with a more basic question: Why should you care about the development of sensation and perception?

In what ways are the perceptual experiences of infants and adults similar, and in what ways are they different because of the adult's greater experience with the world?

Sensation and perception are at the heart of human functioning. Everything you do depends on your ability to perceive the world around you. You would have a tough time as a student if you could neither read printed words nor understand speech. Indeed, you would not be able to walk to class without the aid of the body senses that control movement. Possibly one reason that sensation and perception may not seem important is that they occur so effortlessly for most people. And as long as the sensory–perceptual systems are in good working order, we tend to take them for granted. But as soon as there is a "glitch" in the system, we become painfully aware of the limitations imposed when, for example, we lose our vision or sense of smell.

There is another reason to be interested in sensation and perception. They have been at the center of a debate among philosophers and, more recently, developmental scientists about how we gain knowledge of reality.

Issues of Nature and Nurture

Does the ability to perceive the world around us depend solely on innate biological factors, or is this ability acquired through experience and learning? Philosophers were raising this nature–nurture issue about perception long before anyone had conducted research on the perceptual capabilities of young infants. **Empiricists** such as the 17th-century British philosopher John Locke (1690/1939) took the nurture side of the nature–nurture issue; they believed that the infant enters the world as a tabula rasa (blank slate) that knows nothing except what is learned through the senses. Empiricists think infants perceive the world differently than adults do; only by accumulating perceptual experience do they learn how to interpret sensory stimuli in meaningful ways.

Nativists take the nature side of the nature–nurture issue and argue that we come into the world equipped with knowledge that allows us to perceive a meaningful world. For example, Rene Descartes (1638/1965) and Immanuel Kant (1781/1958) believed that we are born with an understanding of the spatial world. Presumably, infants do not need to learn that receding objects will appear smaller or that approaching objects will seem larger; perceptual understandings such as these are innate or at least mature rapidly. According to nativists, these abilities have been built into the human nervous system through the course of evolution, making the infant perceiver similar to the adult perceiver.

Many of today's developmental theorists take less extreme stands on the nature–nurture issue. They understand that humans' innate biological endowment, maturational processes, and experience all contribute to perceptual development. Yet they grapple with nature–nurture issues, and some still take a strong stand on either the nature or the nurture side of the debate. Some have concluded that infants are equipped almost from birth to interpret sensory experience much as adults do (Spelke, 1994), whereas others argue that perceptual areas of the brain and perceptual skills evolve gradually as infants respond to sights, sounds, and other stimuli (Smith & Katz, 1996). Researchers who study perceptual development attempt to determine which perceptual capacities are evident so early in life that they seem innate and which take longer to emerge and appear to be learned. They also attempt to identify the kinds of experiences required for normal perceptual development, sometimes by studying children deprived of certain experiences. Their work is some of the most exciting in developmental psychology.

Nature–nurture issues also arise in the study of declines in sensory and perceptual abilities in later life. Are these declines universal, suggesting that they are the product of fundamental aging processes? Or do they differ greatly from person to person and result from factors other than aging, such as disease, exposure to ultraviolet rays, loud noise, or other environmental influences known to damage the senses? Just as researchers must pin down the contributions of nature and nurture to early perceptual development, they must clarify their roles in perceptual aging.

In the next section, we look closely at sensation and perception in infancy because this is when most fundamental perceptual capacities emerge. Later, you will see how much more "intelligent" the senses become during childhood and adolescence and will question the image of old age as a time of little more than sensory decline.

Summing Up

Empiricists argue that, as a newborn, a person is a "blank slate" and must acquire an understanding of the world through experience with sensory inputs. In contrast, the nativists believe that each person is born with some innate understanding of how to interpret sensory information. ■

The Infant

The pioneering American psychologist William James (1890) claimed that sights, sounds, and other sensory inputs formed a "blooming, buzzing confusion" to the young infant. James was actually noting that impressions from the several senses are fused rather than separable, but his statement has since been quoted to represent the view that the world of the young infant is hopelessly confusing.

Today, the accepted view is that young infants have far greater perceptual abilities than anyone suspected. Their senses are functioning even before birth, and in the early months after birth they show many signs that they are perceiving a coherent rather than a chaotic world. Why the change in views? It is not that babies have become smarter. It is that researchers have become smarter. They have developed more sophisticated methods of studying what infants can and cannot do. Infants, after all, cannot tell researchers directly what they perceive, so the trick has been to develop ways to let their behavior speak for them.

Assessing Perceptual Abilities

As researchers have devised more ingenious ways of testing the perceptual capacities of young infants, they have uncovered more sophisticated capacities at younger ages. The main methods used to study infant perception are the habituation, preferential looking, evoked potentials, and operant conditioning techniques (Gibson & Pick, 2000; Kellman & Banks, 1998).

Habituation

Humans of all ages lose interest in a stimulus if it is presented repeatedly. This process of learning to be bored is called **habituation.** Researchers can use this process to uncover what is going on inside the infant's mind. Suppose researchers repeatedly present the same visual stimulus (such as a blue circle) to an infant; eventually the infant becomes bored and looks away—the infant habituates. If this infant regains interest when a different stimulus (such as a red circle) is substituted, researchers know that the infant has discriminated between the two stimuli (Gibson & Pick, 2000). This procedure can be used to test for discrimination of stimuli by all the senses—vision, audition, touch, and even taste and smell.

Preferential Looking

Alternatively, researchers can present an infant with two stimuli at the same time and measure the length of time the infant spends looking at each. A preference for one over the other, like responding to a novel stimulus in the habituation paradigm, indicates that the infant discriminates the two stimuli (see Figure 6.1). What if the infant looks equally long at the two stimuli? Then it is unclear what researchers can conclude; the infant may discriminate the stimuli but may simply not like one better than the other. It is also possible that infants have a preference but do not display it with preferential looking (Rovee-Collier, 2001). They may reveal this preference when tested with an alternative method, such as an opportunity to interact with the preferred object.

Evoked Potentials

Researchers can get an idea of how the brain responds to stimulation by measuring its electrical activity with small metal disks (electrodes) attached to the skin's surface. The infant simply sits in a comfortable seat and watches or listens to various stimuli. The electrodes and computer record the brain's response to these stimuli so that researchers can "see" what is going on inside the brain.

Operant Conditioning

As you learned in Chapter 2, humans will repeat a response that has a pleasant consequence; that is, they are capable of learning through operant conditioning. Young infants are not

Figure 6.1 Researchers must devise special ways to assess infants' perceptual abilities. Here, an experimenter and camera record how much time the infant looks at each stimulus. The visual preference test was pioneered by Robert Fantz in the early 1960s.

SOURCE: Adapted with permission from Schiffman, H.R. (2000). *Sensation and perception* (5th ed.) New York: Wiley, p. 295, Fig. 11.4. Copyright © 2000 by John Wiley & Sons, Inc.

easily conditioned, but they can learn to suck faster or slower or to turn the head to the side when a certain stimulus is presented if they are reinforced for that response. Suppose that you want to determine whether infants can distinguish two speech sounds. First, an infant might be conditioned over several trials to turn his head every time he hears a sound—perhaps by being shown an interesting toy or being given a taste of milk. Then, a second sound would be presented; if the infant turns his head, it suggests that the two sounds are perceived as equivalent; if the infant does *not* turn his head, you can conclude that the two sounds have been discriminated.

Methods for studying infant perception have their limitations. For example, infants can fail to respond to some difference between stimuli for reasons unrelated to an inability to discriminate between them (Rosser, 1994). Still, these techniques, with others, have revealed a good deal about what infants perceive and what they do not, as you will now see.

Vision

Most of us tend to think of vision as our most indispensable sense. Because vision is indeed important, we examine its early development in some detail before turning to the other major senses.

Basic Capacities

The eye functions by taking in stimulation in the form of light and converting it to electrochemical signals to the brain. How well does the newborn's visual system work? Fairly well, despite being the one sense that receives no experience before birth (Slater, 2004). From the first minutes after birth, the infant can detect changes in brightness and can visually track a slow-moving picture or object, although not as sensitively as an adult (Slater, 2004). The ability to discriminate degrees of brightness develops rapidly. By only 2 months after birth, infants can distinguish a white bar that differs only 5% in luminance from a solid white background (Peeples & Teller, 1975). In other words, a 2-month-old would be able to distinguish shades of white paint, a task that challenges many adults trying to select just the right shade of white from many paint samples.

Very young infants also see the world in color, not in black and white as some early observers thought (Adams, Maurer, & Davis, 1986). How do researchers know this? Suppose they accustom an infant to a blue disk using the habituation technique. What will happen if they then present either a blue disk of a different shade or a green disk? Infants 4 months old will show little interest in a disk of a different blue but will be attentive to a green disk—even when the light reflected from these two stimuli differs in wavelength from the original blue stimulus by the same amount (Schiffman, 2000). Thus, 4-month-olds appear to discriminate colors and categorize portions of the continuum of wavelengths of light into the same basic color categories (red, blue, green, and yellow) that adults do. Color vision is present at birth, but newborns often cannot discriminate color differences because their receptors are not yet mature. By 2 to 3 months, however, color vision is mature (Schiffman, 2000).

Are objects clear or blurry to young infants? This is a matter of **visual acuity**, or the ability to perceive detail. By adult standards, the newborn's visual acuity is poor, but it improves rapidly during the first 6 months (Schiffman, 2000). You have undoubtedly heard of 20/20 vision, as measured by the familiar Snellen eye chart with the big *E* at the top. Infants cannot be asked to read eye charts. However, they do prefer to look at a patterned stimulus rather than a blank one—unless it is so fine-grained that it looks no different from a blank. By presenting increasingly fine-grained striped disks paired with blank disks to infants using the preferential looking technique, researchers can find the point at which their perception of the stripes is lost and translate this into an estimate of visual acuity.

Estimates of newborns' acuity range from 20/600 to as poor as 20/1200 (Schiffman, 2000). At best, this means that an adult with normal vision can see at 600 feet what the infant sees clearly at only 20 feet. Objects are blurry to the young infant unless they are about 8 inches from the face or are bold patterns with sharp light–dark contrasts—the face of a parent, for example. The young infant's world is also blurred because of limitations in **visual accommodation**—the ability of the lens of the eye to change shape to bring objects at different distances into focus. It is likely to take 6 months to 1 year before the infant can see as well as an adult (Schiffman, 2000; Slater, 2004).

In short, the eyes of the young infant are not working at peak levels, but they are working. As one researcher summarizes it: Infants are able to see what they need to see (Hainline,

1998). Even newborns can perceive light and dark, focus on nearby objects, distinguish colors, and see simple patterns. But does all this visual stimulation make any sense?

Pattern Perception

Over years of testing, researchers have found that even young infants prefer to look at certain patterns more than others. What are the properties of patterns that "turn infants on?" For one thing, young infants are attracted to patterns that have a large amount of light–dark transition, or **contour;** they are responsive to sharp boundaries between light and dark areas (Banks & Shannon, 1993). This is perhaps why it was once mistakenly thought that infants could only see in black and white. They can detect color, but often the pastel colors presented to young infants do not have enough contrast to be interesting. Black and white objects, however, offer this contrast.

Second, young infants are attracted to *movement*, especially the onset of motion (Abrams & Christ, 2003). Newborns can and do track a moving target with their eyes, although their tracking at first is imprecise and likely to falter unless the target is moving slowly (Easterbrook et al., 1999; Slater, 2004). Attractive and interesting targets, such as faces, elicit more visual tracking than other targets (Gamé, Carchon, & Vital-Durand, 2003). Infants also look longer at moving objects and perceive their forms better than those of stationary ones (Johnson & Aslin, 1995; Slater 2004).

Finally, young infants seem to be attracted to *moderately complex* patterns. They prefer a clear pattern (for example, a bold checkerboard pattern) to either a blank stimulus or an elaborate one such as a page from the *New York Times* (Fantz & Fagan, 1975). As infants mature, they prefer more complex stimuli.

One special pattern that has garnered much attention from researchers is the human face. Early research showing that young infants preferred to look at schematic drawings of faces rather than other patterned stimuli seemed to suggest an inborn tendency to orient to faces (see, for example, Johnson & de Haan, 2001). But as you have just learned, infants prefer contour, movement, and moderate complexity. Human faces have all of these physical properties. In addition, recent research shows that newborns have a bias toward viewing patterns that have more information in their upper visual field, that is, patterns that are "top-heavy" (Cassia, Turati, & Simion, 2004; Turati, 2004). Again, faces are top-heavy. When presented with a normal face and a face that is scrambled but still top-heavy (see Figure 6.2), newborns do not prefer one over the other, but they prefer a normal (upright) face to one that is upside down or one that is scrambled and not top-heavy (Cassia, Turati, & Simion, 2004).

To recap what has been covered up to this point, researchers know that infants younger than 2 months have visual preferences, and they also know something about the physical properties of stimuli that attract infants' attention. Martin Banks and his colleagues have offered a simple explanation for these early visual preferences: Young infants prefer to look at whatever they can see well (Banks & Ginsburg, 1985). Based on a complex mathematical model, Banks has been able to predict how different patterns might look to a young infant. Figure 6.3 gives an example. Because the young infant's eye is small and its neural receptors are immature, it has poor visual acuity and sees a highly complex checkerboard as a big, dark blob. The pattern in a moderately complex checkerboard can be seen. Less-than-perfect vision would therefore explain why young infants prefer moderate complexity to high complexity. Indeed, limited vision can account for several of the infant's visual preferences. Young infants seem to actively seek the visual input they can see well—input that will stimulate the development of the visual centers of their brains (Banks & Shannon, 1993; Hainline, 1998).

At 2 months, Jordan is attracted to the mobile's well-defined contours (or light–dark contrasts) and bold patterns (which are neither too simple nor too complex).

Finding that young infants discriminate patterns and prefer some over others raises another question. Can infants really perceive forms or patterns? For example, do they just see an angle or two when they view a triangle, or do they see a whole triangular form that stands out from its background as a distinct shape? Some research suggests that even newborns and 1-month-olds are sensitive to information about whole shapes or forms (Slater, 2004). But most studies point to an important breakthrough in the perception of forms starting around 2 or 3 months. Part of the story is told in Figure 6.4.

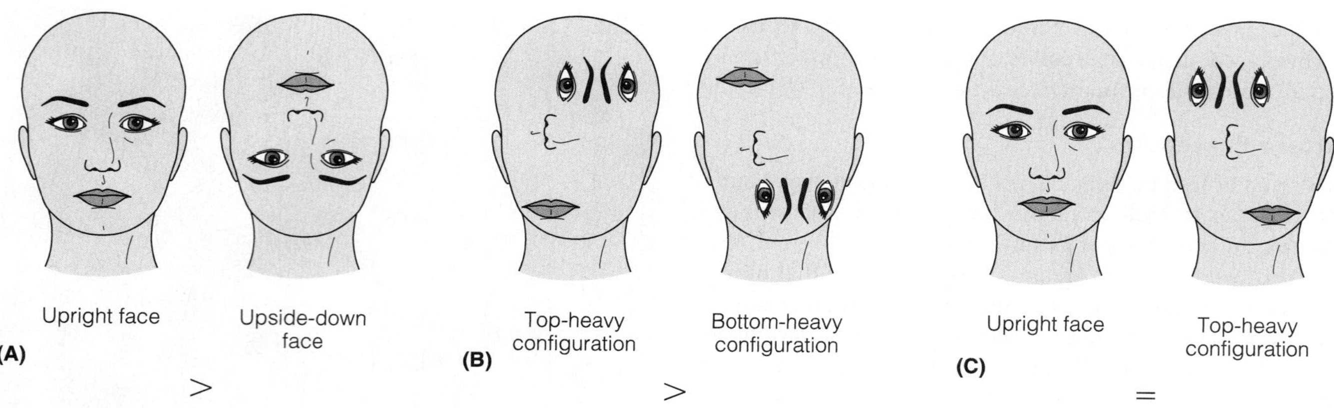

Figure 6.2 In a series of studies, Cassia, Turati, and Simion (2004) showed that newborns prefer an upright face over an upside-down one (A) and prefer a top-heavy configuration over a bottom-heavy one (B), but do not show a preference for an upright face when paired with a top-heavy configuration (C).

SOURCE: Cassia, Turati, & Simion (2004, p. 381).

One-month-olds focus on the outer contours of forms such as faces (Johnson, 1997). Even babies a few days old can recognize their mothers' faces—but only when they can see the shape of the mother's head, not when they have only her facial features to work with (Pascalis et al., 1995). Starting around 2 months, infants no longer focus on some external boundary or contour; instead, they explore the interiors of figures thoroughly (for example, looking at a person's facial features rather than just at the chin, hairline, and top of the head). It is as though they are no longer content to locate where an object starts and where it ends, as 1-month-olds tend to do; they seem to want to know what it is. During this time, infants also become better at shifting their gaze from one object to another (Butcher, Kalverboer, & Geuze, 2000). Initially, their gaze seems to become "stuck" on the fixated object, and they have difficulty shifting it to another object. As you might imagine, this difficulty with shifting gaze limits what young infants can take in from their environment.

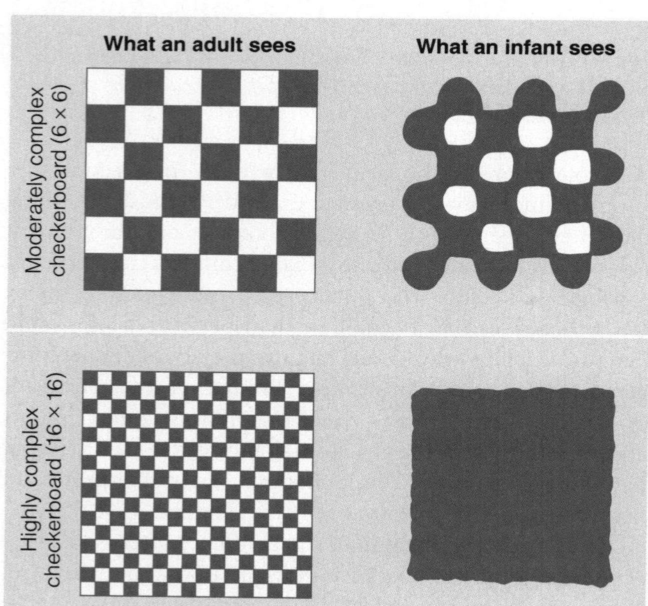

Figure 6.3 What the young eye sees. By the time these two checkerboards are processed by eyes with undeveloped vision, only the checkerboard at top left may have a pattern remaining. Blurry vision in early infancy helps explain a preference for moderately complex rather than highly complex stimuli.

SOURCE: From Mussen, P. H. (1983). *Handbook of child psychology: Vol. 2. Infancy and developmental psychology* (4th ed.). New York: Wiley. Copyright © 1983 by John Wiley & Sons, Inc. Adapted with permission.

Much remains to be learned about early perception of faces. An intense nature–nurture debate still rages about whether infants have an innate ability to perceive face forms or can do so only after they have had some experience looking at faces (Johnson & de Haan, 2001; Slater, 2004). Still, we can conclude that infants truly perceive a meaningful face form, not merely an appealing pattern, by 2 to 3 months of age. Infants smile when they see faces as though they recognize them as familiar and appreciate their significance. So it goes with pattern perception more generally: As infants gain experience with different objects, their attention is drawn to certain objects not only because they have certain physical properties, but also because their forms are recognized as familiar.

Depth Perception

Another important aspect of visual perception involves perceiving depth and knowing when objects are near or far. Although it can take years to learn to judge the size of objects in the distance, very young infants have some intriguing abilities to interpret spatial cues involving nearby objects. For example, they react defensively when objects move toward their faces; blinking in response to looming objects first appears around 1 month and becomes more consistent over the next few months (Nanez & Yonas, 1994). Moreover, even newborns seem to operate by the principle of **size constancy:** They recognize that an object is the same size despite changes in its distance from the eyes. In one study, newborns who were habituated to a particular cube presented at different distances

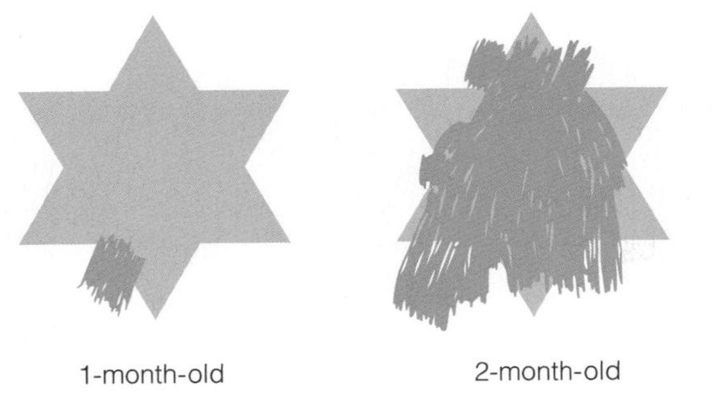

Visual scanning of a geometric figure by 1- and 2-month-old infants

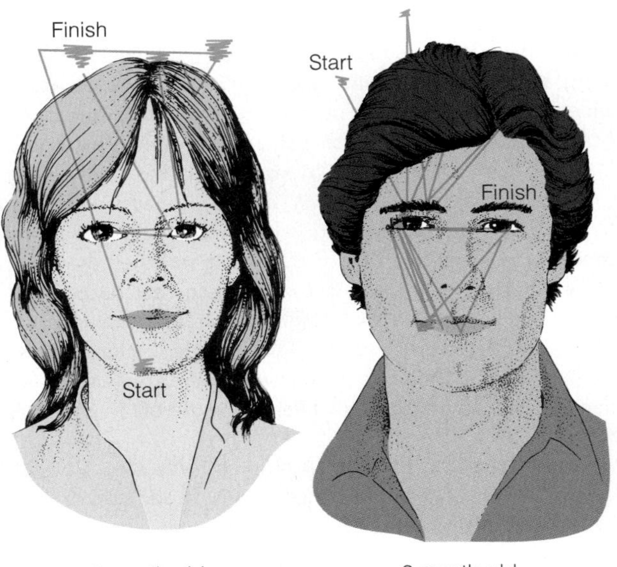

Visual scanning of the human face by 1- and 2-month-old infants

Figure 6.4 Visual scanning in early infancy. The 1-month-old seems to be trying to locate where an object begins and ends, whereas the 2-month-old seems to be on the way to figuring out what an object is by exploring it inside and out.

SOURCE: Adapted from Salapatek, P. (1975). Pattern perception in early infancy. In L. B. Cohen & P. Salapatek (Eds.), *Infant perception: From sensation to cognition* (Vol. 1). New York: Academic Press. Copyright © 1975 by Academic Press, Inc. Reprinted by permission.

preferred to look at a different-sized cube when given a choice (Slater, Mattock, & Brown, 1990). This was the case even when the new cube filled the same amount of the visual field as the original cube. This indicates that infants recognize the size of an object even when the object is presented at different distances and thus produces different images on the retina.

Does this evidence of early spatial perception mean that infants who have begun to crawl know enough about space to avoid crawling off the edges of beds or staircases? The first attempt to examine depth perception in infants was carried out in classic research by Eleanor Gibson and Richard Walk (1960) using an apparatus called the **visual cliff.** This cliff (see the photo on this page) consists of an elevated glass platform divided into two sections by a center board. On the "shallow" side a checkerboard pattern is placed directly under the glass. On the "deep" side the pattern is several feet below the glass, creating the illusion of a drop-off or "cliff." Infants are placed on the center board and coaxed by their mothers to cross both the shallow and the deep sides. Testing infants 6½ months of age and older, Gibson and Walk found that 27 of 36 infants would cross the shallow side to reach Mom, but only 3 of 36 would cross the deep side. Most infants of crawling age (typically 7 months or older) clearly perceive depth and are afraid of drop-offs.

But the testing procedure used by Gibson and Walk depended on the ability of infants to crawl. Would younger infants who cannot yet crawl be able to perceive a drop-off? Joseph Campos and his colleagues (Campos, Langer, & Krowitz, 1970) found that when they slowly lowered babies over the shallow and deep sides of the visual cliff, babies as young as 2 months had a slower heart rate on the deep side than on the shallow side. Why slower? When we are afraid, our hearts beat faster, not slower. A slow heart rate is a sign of interest. So, 2-month-old infants *perceive a difference* between the deep and the shallow sides of the visual cliff, but they have not yet learned to *fear* drop-offs.

Fear of drop-offs appears to be learned through crawling—and perhaps falling now and then, or at least coming close to it (Campos, Bertenthal, & Kermoian, 1992). Some beginning crawlers will shuffle right off the ends of beds or the tops of stairwells if they are not watched carefully. However, fear of drop-offs is stronger in infants who have logged a few weeks of crawling than in infants of the same age who do not yet crawl; also, providing infants who do not crawl with walkers that allow them to move about hastens the development of a healthy fear of heights (Campos, Bertenthal, & Kermoian, 1992). Both maturation and normal experiences moving about contribute to the perception and interpretation of depth, it seems.

Organizing a World of Objects

Another challenge in perceptual development is to separate the visual field into distinct objects, even when parts of objects are hidden behind other objects. From an early age, infants show remarkable abilities to organize and impose order on visual scenes in much the same way that adults do. For example,

© Mark Richards/PhotoEdit

An infant on the edge of a visual cliff, being lured to cross the "deep" side.

Can Babies Count?

Although you may think it ridiculous to ask whether babies can count, some developmentalists have discovered that very young infants have some impressive understandings of the abstract quality we call *number*. Karen Wynn (1992) sought to determine whether 5-month-old infants could add and subtract numbers by seeing how long infants looked at different addition and subtraction "problems." Her test procedure, summarized in the figure here, involved showing the infant a display area with a single Mickey Mouse doll in it, raising a screen to hide the doll, and having the infant watch as a hand placed a second doll in the display area and came out empty. The infant was then observed to see how long she looked at each of two outcomes when the screen was dropped again: a correct outcome in which two dolls were in the display area when the screen was removed (1 + 1 = 2) or an incorrect outcome in which only one doll was present (1 + 1 = 1).

Which of these two events attracted more attention? Infants looked longer at the incorrect outcome, as though surprised by the mathematical error it represented. They also looked longer at a 1 + 1 = 3 scenario than at the correct 1 + 1 = 2 outcome. These 5-month-olds also seemed able to subtract: They were surprised when one doll removed from a pair of dolls resulted in two dolls rather than one. Babies can count sounds, too: Research using auditory sequences shows that 6-month-old infants can distinguish 16 from 8 sounds and that 9-month-old infants can tell the difference between 12 and 8 sounds, although they cannot distinguish 10 from 8 sounds (Lipton & Spelke, 2003). Like the research with visual stimuli, this research suggests a general, but increasingly precise, understanding of numbers during the first year.

But do such findings really show that babies can count and understand numerical functions? In Wynn's research, that infants look more at incorrect mathematical outcomes than at correct ones is difficult to interpret (Canfield & Smith, 1996): What competencies are babies actually showing? Some research has replicated Wynn's findings (see, for example, Simon, Hespos, & Rochat, 1995), lending support to the idea that infants have an innate sensitivity to numerical knowledge. The picture becomes muddled, however, when we look at other research. Tony Simon (1997, 1999) suggests that these findings show babies come equipped with—or quickly develop—an ability to distinguish "same" from "different" but do not yet understand numbers or precise addition and subtraction. According to this view, at steps 3 and 4 in Wynn's experiment (see the figure in this Explorations box), babies develop some sort of mental representation of two objects. When the screen drops and two objects are revealed (the correct outcome), the image in front of the infant matches the mental representation he formed. But in the incorrect outcome, the screen drops to reveal one object, which does not match the infant's mental representation. Thus, longer looking times in the incorrect conditions may reveal only a general understanding of same versus different, not of mathematical processes.

Ann Wakeley and her colleagues (Wakeley, Rivera, & Langer, 2000), who found no evidence of addition and subtraction by infants using Wynn's procedures, suggest another explanation for the mixed findings. It may be that at 5 or 6 months, infants' numerical knowledge is "variable and fragile" (p. 1531). Overall, then, numerical competence is not so clearly innate. Early competence may be evident in some infants under some task conditions, but much remains to be learned later in life. Clearly, babies still have a lot to learn before they will be ready to study calculus.

Katherine Van Giffen and Marshall Haith (1984) reported that 3-month-olds, but not 1-month-olds, will focus their attention on a small irregularity in an otherwise well-formed circle or square pattern, as if they appreciated that it is a deviation from an otherwise well-formed and symmetrical pattern.

Infants must also determine where one object ends and another begins. Elizabeth Spelke and her colleagues (Kellman & Spelke, 1983; Spelke, 1990) have concluded that young infants are sensitive to several cues about the wholeness of objects, especially cues available when an object moves. For example, 4-month-olds seem to expect all parts of an object to move in the same direction at the same time, and they therefore use common motion as an important cue in determining what is or is not part of the same object (Kellman & Spelke, 1983). It takes infants longer, until about 6 months of age, to determine the stationary boundaries of objects (Gibson & Pick, 2000). Amy Needham (1999) has found that 4-month-old babies, like adults, use object shape to figure out that two objects side by side are separate. They also use *good form* (for example, logical continuation of a line) to perceive an object's unity or wholeness (Johnson et al., 2000). Thus, babies appear to have an unlearned ability to organize a visual scene into distinct objects, and they are better able to make sense of a world in motion—a world like the one they live in—than to make sense of a stationary world.

The Infant as an Intuitive Theorist

That is not all. Researchers have been exploring infants' understandings of the physical laws that govern objects. For example, Spelke and her colleagues have been testing infants to determine what they know of Newtonian physics and the basic laws of object motion (Spelke & Hermer, 1996). Do babies

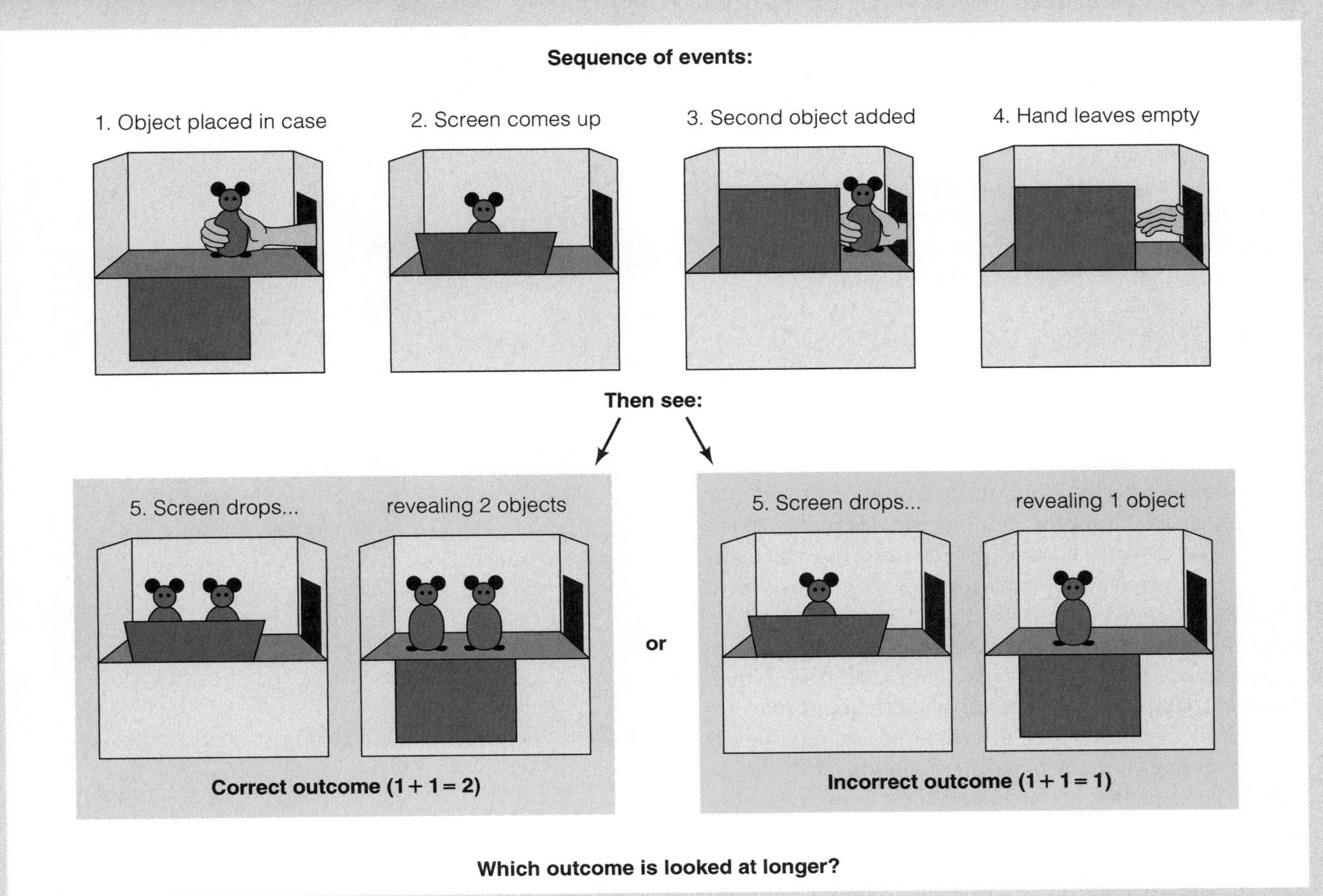

SOURCE: Reprinted with permission from Wynn, K. (1992). Addition and subtraction by human infants. *Nature, 358,* 749–750. Copyright © 1992 by MacMillian Magazines Limited.

know that a falling object will move downward along a continuous path until it encounters an obstruction? Spelke's studies suggest that infants only 4 months of age seem surprised when a ball dropped behind a screen is later revealed below a shelf rather than resting on it. They look longer at this "impossible" event than at the comparison event in which the ball's motion stops when it reaches a barrier. By 6 months, infants seem surprised when a ball drops behind a screen and then, when the screen is lifted, appears to be suspended in midair rather than lying at the bottom of the display unit (Kim & Spelke, 1992; Spelke et al., 1992). This hints that they know something about the laws of gravity.

Findings such as these have led some developmentalists to conclude that young infants do more than just sense the world—that they come equipped with organized systems of knowledge, called **intuitive theories,** that allow them to make sense of the world (Wellman & Gelman, 1992; Gelman, 1996). From an early age, children distinguish between the domains of knowledge adults know as physics, biology, and psychology. They organize their knowledge in each domain around causal principles and seem to understand that different causal forces operate in different domains (for example, that desires influence the behavior of humans but not of rocks). According to this intuitive theories perspective, young infants have innate knowledge of the world, and they perceive and even reason about it much as adults do. Coming to know the physical world is then a matter of fleshing out understandings they have had all along rather than constructing entirely new ones as they age (Spelke, 1994).

As you will see in the Explorations box beginning on page 150, some researchers also believe that babies understand number concepts long before they ever step into a math class.

All in all, it is becoming clearer that young infants know a good deal more about the world around them than anyone imagined, although they learn more as they get older.

Hearing

Hearing is at least as important to us as vision, especially because we depend on it to communicate with others through spoken language. As Anne Fernald (2004) notes, "while vision may be primary in enabling infants to learn about the physical world, audition plays a powerful role in initiating infants into a social world" (p. 37).

The process of hearing begins when moving air molecules enter the ear and vibrate the eardrum. These vibrations are transmitted to the cochlea in the inner ear and are converted to signals that the brain interprets as sounds.

Basic Capacities

Newborns can hear well—better than they can see. They can also localize sounds: They are startled by loud noises and will turn from them, but they will turn toward softer sounds (Field et al., 1980; Morrongiello et al., 1994). Even unborn infants can hear some of what is going on in the world outside the womb as much as 3 months before birth (Fernald, 2004). Researchers have detected changes in fetal heart rates that correspond to changes in sounds from the mother's environment (Fifer, Monk, & Grose-Fifer, 2004)

Although the auditory sense is working before birth, infants appear to be a little less sensitive to very soft sounds than adults are (Fernald, 2004). As a result, a soft whisper may not be heard. Still, newborns can discriminate among sounds within their range of hearing that differ in loudness, duration, direction, and frequency or pitch, and these basic capacities improve rapidly during the first months after birth (Fernald, 2004). In general, the sounds that penetrate the womb before birth are the ones that are the easiest for the infant to hear after birth (Eliot, 1999).

From birth, infants will look in the direction of an interesting sound. This ability to localize sound improves and becomes more voluntary by 4 months.

Speech Perception

Young infants seem to be well equipped to respond to human speech; they can discriminate basic speech sounds—called **phonemes**—very early in life. Peter Eimas (1975b, 1985) pioneered research in this area by demonstrating that infants 2 to 3 months old could distinguish similar consonant sounds (for example, *ba* and *pa*). Indeed, infants seem to detect the difference between the vowels *a* and *i* from the second day after birth (Clarkson & Berg, 1983). They can even distinguish between standard sounds (those that occur regularly in a language) and deviant sounds (those that occur rarely) in the first few days after birth (Ruusuvirta et al., 2003). By 3 months, they have developed a sound category system that allows them to recognize a phoneme as the same phoneme even when it is spoken by different people (Marean, Werner, & Kuhl, 1992; Winkler et al., 2003). These are impressive accomplishments.

Infants can actually make some speech sound discriminations better than adults (Werker & Desjardins, 1995). They begin life biologically prepared to learn any language humans anywhere speak. As they mature, they become especially sensitive to the sound differences significant in their own language and less sensitive to sound differences irrelevant to that language. For example, young infants can easily discriminate the consonants *r* and *l* (Eimas, 1975a). So can adults who speak English, French, Spanish, or German. However, the Chinese and Japanese languages make no distinction between *r* and *l*, and adult native speakers of those languages cannot make this particular auditory discrimination as well as young infants can (Miyawaki et al., 1975). Similarly, infants raised in English-speaking homes can make discriminations important in Hindi but nonexistent in English, but English-speaking adults have trouble doing so (Werker et al., 1981).

By 1 year of age, when infants are just beginning to utter their first words, they have already become insensitive to contrasts of sounds that are not made in their native language (Werker & Desjardins, 1995). Their early auditory experiences have shaped the formation of neural connections, or synapses, in the auditory areas of their brains so that they are optimally sensitive to the sound contrasts that they have been listening to and that are important in the language they are acquiring.

Newborns are especially attentive to female voices (Ecklund-Flores & Turkewitz, 1996), but can they recognize their mother's voice? Indeed they can. Unborn fetuses can distinguish their mother's voice from a stranger's voice. How do we know this? Canadian researchers measured fetal heart rate in response to a tape recording (played over the mother's stomach) of either their mother's voice or a stranger's voice (Kisilevsky et al., 2003). Heart rates increased in response to their mother's voice and decreased in response to the stranger's voice, indicating that they detected a difference between the two. Following birth, newborns will learn to suck faster on a special pacifier when it activates a recording of the mother's voice (DeCasper & Fifer, 1980).

Does this early recognition extend to fathers' voices? Apparently not. Even by 4 months, infants show no preference for their father's voice over the voice of a strange man (Ward & Cooper, 1999). They can detect the difference between various male voices, however, indicating that the lack of preference for the father's voice cannot be because of a failure to distinguish it.

Why would infants prefer their mother's but not their father's voice? You must look at what is happening before birth to answer this. Anthony DeCasper and Melanie Spence (1986) had mothers recite a passage (for example, portions of Dr. Seuss's *The Cat in the Hat*) many times during the last 6 weeks of their pregnancies. At birth, the infants were tested to see if they would suck more to hear the story they had heard before birth or to hear a different story. Remarkably, they preferred the familiar story. Somehow these infants were able to recognize the distinctive sound pattern of the story they had heard in the womb. Auditory learning before birth could also explain why newborns prefer to hear their mother's voice to those of unfamiliar women but do not show a preference for their father's voice. They are literally bombarded with their mother's voice for months before birth, giving them ample opportunity to learn its auditory qualities.

You have now learned that hearing is more developed than vision at birth. Infants can distinguish between speech sounds and recognize familiar sound patterns such as their mother's voice soon after birth. Within the first year, they lose sensitivity to sound contrasts insignificant in the language they are starting to learn, and they further refine their auditory perception skills. Unfortunately, some infants experience hearing problems, placing them at risk for language and communication problems. The Applications box on page 154 examines the importance of early identification and treatment of hearing problems.

Taste and Smell

Can newborns detect different tastes and smells? Both of these senses rely on the detection of chemical molecules. The sensory receptors for taste—taste buds—are located mainly on

☾ From birth, infants respond to tastes. In response to a sugar solution, newborns part their lips, lick their upper lips, make sucking movements, and sometimes smile. In response to bitter tastes, they purse their lips or open their mouths with the corners down and drool.

Applications

Aiding Infants and Children with Hearing Impairments

Although sensory impairments can change the course of normal life-span development, much can be done to help even individuals born totally deaf or blind develop in positive directions and function effectively in everyday life. Let's briefly examine interventions for infants and children who have hearing impairments. Why tackle hearing impairments and not another sensory system? Because several estimates suggest that hearing impairments take a heavy toll on the individual and on society. Researchers at Johns Hopkins University, for example, estimate that more than $1 million will be spent over the lifetime of each infant or child who becomes deaf before acquiring language (Mohr et al., 2000).

For the 1 to 3 in 1000 infants born deaf or hearing impaired, early identification and treatment are essential if they are to master spoken language. Unfortunately, the average hearing-impaired child is not identified until age 2, usually when it becomes clear that his language skills have not developed normally (National Institutes of Health, 1993). Because children who receive no special intervention before age 3 usually have lasting difficulties with speech and language, the Joint Committee on Infant Hearing (2000) recommended that all newborns in the United States be given hearing tests soon after birth. As a result, many states require a hearing test before babies leave the hospital (Hosaka, 1999). How do you test the hearing of newborns? By using the auditory evoked potentials described at the beginning of the chapter and determining whether sounds trigger normal activity in the brain. Infants' behaviors also give physicians clues about their hearing. Does she turn her head when spoken to? Does he react to loud noises? Is she soothed by your voice? If the answers to these questions are no, a more thorough examination is warranted.

Once hearing-impaired infants are identified, interventions can be planned. Many programs attempt to capitalize on whatever residual hearing these children have by equipping them with hearing aids. Today, even profoundly deaf children can be helped to hear through an advanced amplification device called the **cochlear implant** (see the illustration in this Applications box). The device is implanted in the inner ear

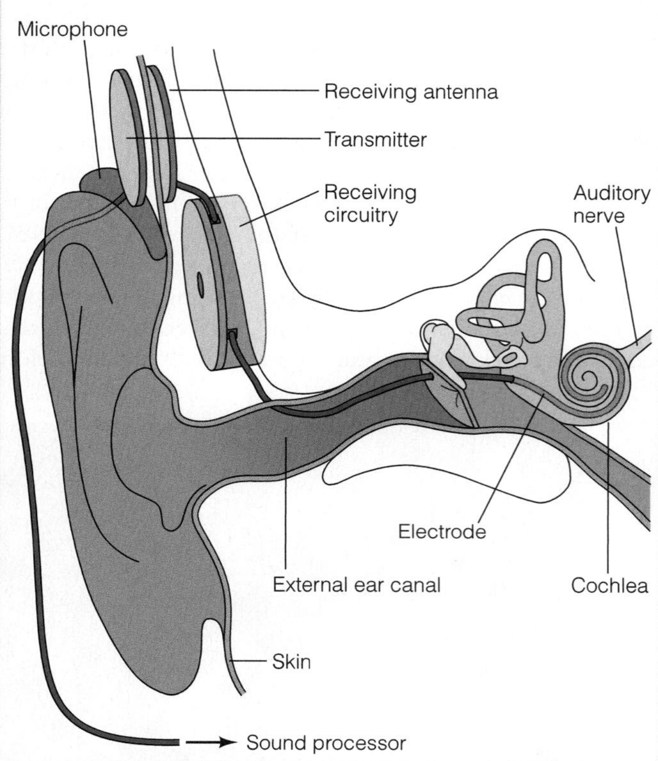

the tongue. In ways not fully understood, taste buds respond to chemical molecules and produce perceptions of sweet, salty, bitter, or sour tastes. At birth, babies can clearly distinguish sweet, bitter, and sour tastes and show a preference for sweets. Indeed, sugar water—but not plain water—seems to have a marvelous ability to calm even premature babies and can help them cope with painful events such as needle pricks (Barr et al., 1999; Smith & Blass, 1996).

Different taste sensations also produce distinct facial expressions in the newborn. Jacob Steiner and his colleagues (Ganchrow, Steiner, & Daher, 1983; Steiner, 1979) have found that newborns lick their lips and sometimes smile when they are tasting a sugar solution but purse their lips and even drool to get rid of the foul taste when they are given bitter quinine. Their facial expressions become increasingly pronounced as a solution becomes sweeter or more bitter, suggesting that newborns can discriminate different concentrations of a substance. Even before birth, babies show a preference for sweets when they swallow more amniotic fluid that contains higher concentrations of sugars than amniotic fluid with lower concentrations of sugar (Fifer, Monk, & Grose-Fifer, 2004).

Recent research by Julie Mennella and her colleagues (2004) suggests that food preferences may be influenced by early tastes that we are exposed to during infancy. Starting at 2 weeks of age, Mennella fed infants one of two formulas for 7 months. One formula was bland, and the other was bitter and tasted sour, at least to most adults. After this period, the babies who had been fed the sour formula continued to consume it, but the other infants refused when it was offered to through surgery and connected to a microphone worn outside the ear. It works by bypassing damaged hair cells and directly stimulating the auditory nerve with electrical impulses. By 2000, more than 8000 infants and children had received cochlear implants; the number implanted increases every year (Schery & Peters, 2003).

Deaf children provided with cochlear implants around age 4 recognize more spoken words and speak more intelligibly than do children who receive them later in childhood, though even children given implants later in life can benefit (O'Donoghue, Nikolopoulos, & Archbold, 2000). Indeed, research shows that the rate of language development among children with cochlear implants is similar to that of children with normal hearing (Schery & Peters, 2003). In addition, speech production and speech perception are improved in children who have cochlear implants compared with children who have traditional hearing aids (Schery & Peters, 2003). Performance is especially enhanced with earlier implantation and more auditory training following the implant.

Why, then, are not all hearing-impaired children provided with cochlear implants? First, they require surgery and are expensive—although the expense of cochlear implants may be offset by educational savings down the road (Cheng et al., 2000). Also, despite their benefits, cochlear implants do not have the full support of the deaf community (Tucker, 1998). Deaf children who use them, some say, will be given the message that they should be ashamed of being deaf. They will be deprived of participation in the unique culture that has developed in communities of deaf people who share a common language and identity. Because their hearing will still be far from normal, they may feel they do not belong to either the deaf or the hearing world (Arana-Ward, 1997; Fryauf-Bertschy et al., 1997).

Another important element in early intervention programs for hearing-impaired children is parent involvement (Maxon & Brackett, 1992). In one program for hearing-impaired children, infants are fitted with hearing aids and teachers then go into the home to show parents how to make their children more aware of the world of sound (Bess & McConnell, 1981). For instance, on hearing the screech of a car's brakes outside, parents might put their hands to their ears, rush their child to the window, and talk about the noise. Similarly, parents are urged to slam doors, deliberately rattle pots and pans, and create other such opportunities for the child to become alert to sounds. All the while, parents are using words to describe everyday objects, people, and events.

This combination of the right amplification device and auditory training in the home has proven effective in improving the ability of hearing-impaired infants and preschoolers to hear speech and learn to speak. Yet for other deaf and severely hearing-impaired children, the most important thing may be early exposure to sign language. Early intervention programs for parents of deaf infants can teach them strategies for getting their infants' attention and involving them in conversations using sign (Chen, 1996). The earlier in life deaf children acquire some language system, whether spoken or signed, the better their command of language is likely to be later in life (Mayberry & Eichen, 1991). Deaf children whose parents are deaf and use sign language with them, as well as deaf children of hearing parents who participate in early intervention programs, generally show normal patterns of development, whereas children who are not exposed to any language system early in life suffer for it (Marschark, 1993).

them. By 4 to 5 years, children fed the unpleasant-tasting formula were more likely to consume other sour-tasting foods (for example, a sour-flavored apple juice) than children exposed to only bland-tasting formula (Mennella & Beauchamp, 2002). This research may be key to helping researchers understand why some people are picky eaters, whereas others are open to a wide variety of tastes. Greater exposure to a variety of flavors during infancy—what a breast-fed baby with a mother who eats many different foods might experience—may lead to a more adventuresome eater later on. These early experiences with different flavors may also extend to the prenatal period and exposure to different chemicals in the amniotic fluid (Fifer, Monk, & Grose-Fifer, 2004).

The sensory receptors for smell, or **olfaction,** are located in the nasal passage. Like taste, the sense of smell is working well at birth. Newborns react vigorously to unpleasant smells such as vinegar or ammonia and turn their heads away (Rieser, Yonas, & Wilkner, 1976). Even babies born at 28 weeks of gestation are capable of detecting various odors. Newborns also reliably prefer the scent of their own amniotic fluid over that of other amniotic fluid, suggesting that olfactory cues are detectable prenatally (Schaal, Barlier, & Soussignan, 1998). Exposure to familiar amniotic fluid can also calm newborns, resulting in less crying when their mothers are absent (Varendi et al., 1998). Furthermore, babies who are breast-fed can recognize their mothers solely by the smell of their breasts or underarms within 1 or 2 weeks of birth (Cernoch & Porter, 1985; Porter et al., 1992). Babies who are bottle-fed cannot, probably because they have less contact with their mothers' skin. On the flip side, mothers can identify their newborns by smell (Porter,

1999). Thus, the sense of smell we often take for granted may help babies and their parents get to know each other.

Touch, Temperature, and Pain

Receptors in the skin detect touch or pressure, heat or cold, and painful stimuli. The sense of touch seems to be operating nicely before birth and, with the body senses that detect motion, may be among the first senses to develop (Eliot, 1999; Field, 1990). You saw in Chapter 5 that newborns respond with reflexes if they are touched in appropriate areas. For example, when touched on the check, a newborn will turn its head and open its mouth. Even in their sleep, newborns will habituate to strokes of the same spot on the skin but respond again if the tactile stimulation is shifted to a new spot—from the ear to the lips, for example (Kisilevsky & Muir, 1984). And like the motor responses described in Chapter 5, sensitivity to tactile stimulation develops in a cephalocaudal direction, so the face and mouth are more sensitive than lower parts of the body. No wonder babies like to put everything in their mouths—the tactile sensors in and around the mouth allow babies to collect a great deal of information about the world. Most parents quickly recognize the power of touch for soothing a fussy baby. Touch has even greater benefits. Premature babies who are systematically stroked over their entire body gain weight and settle into a regular sleep–wake pattern faster than premature babies who are not massaged (Field, 1995b; Scafidi, Field, & Schanberg, 1993).

Newborns are also sensitive to warmth and cold; they can tell the difference between something cold and something warm placed on their cheeks (Eliot, 1999). Finally, young babies clearly respond to painful stimuli such as needle pricks (Guinsburg et al., 2000). For obvious ethical reasons, researchers have not exposed infants to severely painful stimuli. However, analyses of babies' cries and facial movements as they receive injections and have blood drawn leave no doubt that these procedures are painful (Delevati & Bergamasco, 1999). For example, researchers have compared infants born to diabetic mothers, who have their heels pricked every few hours after birth to test their blood sugar levels, with infants born to nondiabetic mothers (Taddio, 2002). Both groups of infants have blood drawn from the back of their hands before they leave the hospital so several routine tests can be conducted. The infants who have already had their heels pricked show a larger response to having blood drawn than the infants who have never experienced the presumably painful needle pricks in their feet. Indeed, some infants who had already experienced the heel pricks began to grimace when the nurse was preparing their skin for the needle prick, indicating that they had learned from their prior experiences that a painful moment was coming.

Such research challenges the medical wisdom of giving babies who must undergo major surgery little or no anesthesia. It turns out that infants are more likely to survive heart surgery if they receive deep anesthesia that keeps them unconscious during the operation and for a day afterward than if they receive light anesthesia that does not entirely protect them from the stressful experience of pain (Anand & Hickey, 1992). And the American Academy of Pediatrics (2000) recommends that local anesthesia be given to newborn males undergoing circumcision.

You have now seen that each of the major senses is operating in some form at birth and that perceptual abilities improve dramatically during infancy. Let us ask one final question about infant perception: Can infants meaningfully integrate information from the different senses?

Integrating Sensory Information

It would obviously be useful for an infant attempting to understand the world to be able to put together information gained from viewing, fingering, sniffing, and otherwise exploring objects. It now seems clear that the senses function in an integrated way at birth. For instance, newborns will look in the direction of a sound they hear, suggesting that vision and hearing are linked. Moreover, infants 8 to 31 days old expect to feel objects that they can see and are frustrated by a visual illusion that looks like a graspable object but proves to be nothing but air when they reach for it (Bower, Broughton, & Moore, 1970). Thus, vision and touch, as well as vision and hearing, seem to be interrelated early in life. This integration of the senses helps babies perceive and respond appropriately to the objects and people they encounter (Hainline & Abramov, 1992; Walker-Andrews, 1997).

A more difficult task is to recognize through one sense an object familiar through another; this is called **cross-modal perception.** This capacity is required in children's games that involve feeling objects hidden in a bag and identifying what they are by touch alone. Some researchers (for example, Streri, 2003; Streri & Gentez, 2004) report that newborns can recognize an object by sight that they had previously touched with their hand. But other researchers have had trouble demonstrating cross-modal perception in such young infants (for example, Maurer, Stager, & Mondloch, 1999). Apparently, early cross-modal perception is a fragile ability dependent on various task variables such as which hand is used to manipulate the object (Streri & Gentez, 2004). Consistent oral-to-visual cross-modal transfer is shown by 3 months of age, and other forms of cross-modal perception are reliably displayed at 4 to 7 months (Streri & Pecheux, 1986; Walker-Andrews, 1997). By that age, for example, infants integrate vision and hearing to judge distance; they prefer to look at an approaching train that gets louder and a departing one that gets quieter rather than at videos in which sound and sight are mismatched (Pickens, 1994). Nevertheless, performance on more complex cross-modal perception tasks that require matching patterns of sounds with patterns of visual stimuli continues to improve throughout childhood and even adolescence (Bushnell & Baxt, 1999).

Researchers now conclude that impressions from the different senses are "fused" early in life, much as William James believed, but they do not create the "blooming, buzzing confusion" he described. Rather, this early sensory integration may make it easier for babies to perceive and use information

© Mary Kate Denny/PhotoEdit

☾ Intersensory perception. The ability to recognize through one sense (here, touch) what has been learned through another (vision) increases with age during infancy and childhood. Here, the birthday girl must identify prizes in the bag by touch alone.

that comes to them through multiple channels simultaneously (Walker-Andrews, 1997). Then, as the separate senses continue to develop and each becomes a more effective means of exploring objects, babies become more skilled at cross-modal perception and are able to coordinate information gained through one sense with information gained through another.

Influences on Early Perceptual Development

The perceptual competencies of even very young infants are remarkable, as is the progress made within the first few months after birth. All major senses begin working before birth and are clearly functioning at birth; parents would be making a huge mistake to assume that their newborn is not taking in the sensory world. Many perceptual abilities—for example, the ability to perceive depth or to distinguish melodies—emerge within just a few months of birth. Gradually, basic perceptual capacities are fine-tuned, and infants become more able to interpret their sensory experiences—to recognize a pattern of light as a face, for example. By the time infancy ends, the most important aspects of perceptual development are complete (Bornstein, 1992). The senses and the mind are working to create a meaningful world of recognized objects, sounds, tastes, smells, and bodily sensations.

The fact that perceptual development takes place so quickly can be viewed as support for the "nature" side of the nature–nurture debate. Many basic perceptual capacities appear to be innate or to develop rapidly in all normal infants. What, then, is the role of early sensory experience in perceptual development?

Early Experience and the Brain

As you saw in Chapter 5, sensory experience is critically important in determining the organization of the developing brain. To expand a bit on this theme, imagine what visual perception would be like in an infant who was blind at birth but later had surgery to permit vision. This is the scenario for perhaps 3 of every 5000 infants with congenital **cataracts,** a clouding of the lens that leaves these infants nearly blind from birth if it is not corrected (Lambert & Drack, 1996). In the past, surgery to remove cataracts was often delayed until infants were older. But such delays meant that infants had weeks, months, or even years with little or no visual input. Consequently, some never developed normal vision even after the lens was removed.

It turns out that the visual system requires stimulation early in life, including patterned stimulation, to develop normally. Although the visual system has some plasticity throughout childhood, the first 3 to 4 months after birth are considered critical (Lambert & Drack, 1996). During this time, the brain must receive clear visual information from both eyes. Unfortunately, not all infants with cataracts are identified early enough to benefit from surgery. In the United Kingdom, for example, only 57% of infants with cataracts are diagnosed by 3 months (Rahi & Dezateux, 1999). Even after surgery restores their sight, these infants have difficulty, at least initially, perceiving their visual world clearly (Maurer et al., 1999). Acuity after surgery is what you might find in a newborn without cataracts—in other words, rather poor. But it improves significantly during the month following surgery (Maurer et al., 1999).

Years after corrective surgery, individuals who missed out on early visual experience because of congenital cataracts show normal visual abilities to see details of faces (for example, different facial expressions) but struggle to identify different orientations of the same face (Geldart et al., 2002). What might account for this pattern? Sybil Geldart and her colleagues (2002) speculate that learning about things such as the general orientation of faces (for example, a forward-facing versus a profile shot) occurs very early when normal infants' visual acuity is still poor and when infants with cataracts receive limited or no visual experience. Finer distinctions (for example, differences in facial expressions) are learned later when acuity is sharper for normal infants and for infants with cataracts once vision has been restored. Clearly, these findings suggest that early visual experiences influence later visual perception.

The same message about the importance of early experience applies to the sense of hearing: Exposure to auditory stimulation early in life affects the architecture of the developing brain, which in turn influences auditory perception skills (Finitzo, Gunnarson, & Clark, 1990). Children with hearing impairments who undergo cochlear implant, which bypasses damaged nerve cells in their inner ear, may struggle for months to understand the meaning of signals reaching their brain through the implant before they derive benefits (Allum et al., 2000; see also the Applications box on page 154). Although the brain is being fed information, it must learn how to interpret these signals. Otherwise, the signals are a crashing jumble of nonsense that can be worse than not hearing (Colburn, 2000). The conclusion is clear: Maturation alone is not enough; normal perceptual development also requires normal perceptual experience. The practical implication is also clear: Visual and hearing problems in children should be detected and corrected as early in life as possible (Joint Committee on Infant Hearing, 2000).

The Infant's Active Role

Parents need not worry about arranging the right sensory environment for their children because young humans actively seek the stimulation they need to develop properly. Infants are active explorers and stimulus seekers; they orchestrate their own perceptual, motor, and cognitive development by exploring their environment and learning what it will allow them to do (Gibson, 1988; Gibson & Pick, 2000).

According to Eleanor Gibson (1988), infants proceed through three phases of exploratory behavior:

1. From birth to 4 months they explore their immediate surroundings, especially their caregivers, by looking and listening, and they learn a bit about objects by mouthing them and watching them move.

2. From 5 to 7 months, once the ability to voluntarily grasp objects has developed, babies pay far closer attention to objects, exploring objects with their eyes as well as with their hands.

3. By 8 or 9 months, after they have begun to crawl, infants extend their explorations into the larger environment and carefully examine the objects they encounter on their journeys, learning all about their properties. Whereas a young infant may merely mouth a new toy and look at it now and then, a 12-month-old will give it a thorough examination—turning it, fingering it, poking it, and watching it intently (Ruff et al., 1992).

By combining perception and action in their exploratory behavior, infants actively create sensory environments that meet their needs and contribute to their own development (Eppler, 1995). As children become more able to attend selectively to the world around them, they become even more able to choose the forms and levels of stimulation that suit them best.

Cultural Variation

Do infants who grow up in different cultural environments encounter different sensory stimulation and perceive the world in different ways? Perceptual preferences obviously differ from culture to culture. In some cultures, people think hefty women are more beautiful than slim ones or relish eating sheep's eyeballs or chicken heads. Are more basic perceptual competencies also affected by socialization?

People from different cultures differ little in basic sensory capacities, such as the ability to discriminate degrees of brightness or loudness (Berry et al., 1992). However, their perceptions and interpretations of sensory input can vary considerably. For example, you have already seen that children become insensitive, starting at the end of the first year after birth, to speech sound contrasts that they do not hear because they are not important in their primary language. Michael Lynch and his associates (1990) have shown that the same is true for perceptions of music. Infants from the United States, they found, noticed equally notes that violated either Western musical scales or the Javanese pelog scale. This suggests that humans are born with the potential to perceive music from a variety of cultures. However, American adults were less sensitive to bad notes in the unfamiliar Javanese musical system than to mistuned notes in their native Western scale, suggesting that their years of experience with Western music had shaped their perceptual skills.

Another example of cultural influence concerns the ability to translate perceptions of the human form into a drawing. In Papua New Guinea, where there is no cultural tradition of drawing and painting, children ages 10 to 15 who have had no schooling do not have much luck drawing the human body; they draw scribbles or tadpolelike forms far more often than children in the same society who have attended school and have been exposed many times to drawings of people (Martlew & Connolly, 1996; see Figure 6.5). We all have the capacity to create two-dimensional representations, but we apparently develop that capacity more rapidly if our culture provides us with relevant experiences. Many other examples

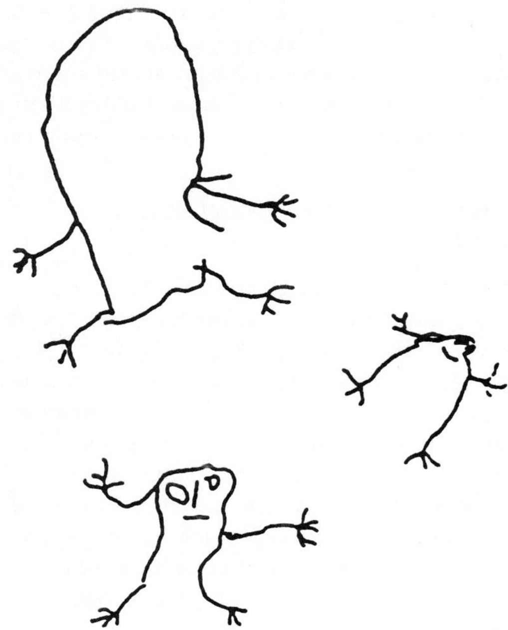

Figure 6.5 Children ages 10 to 15 in Papua New Guinea, unless they have attended school, lack experience with drawings of the human form and produce drawings much like those done by far younger children (such as 4-year-olds) in U.S. society. Cultural experience influences the ability to translate visual perceptions into representations on the page.

of the effects of cultural learning experiences on visual and auditory perception can be cited (Berry et al., 1992).

Summing Up

The visual system is fairly well developed at birth. Infants under 2 months of age discriminate brightness and colors and are attracted to contour, moderate complexity, and movement. Starting at 2 or 3 months, they more clearly perceive whole patterns such as faces and seem to understand a good deal about objects and their properties, guided by intuitive theories of the physical world. Spatial perception also develops rapidly, and by about 7 months infants not only perceive drop-offs but also fear them.

Young infants can recognize their mother's voice and distinguish speech sounds that adults cannot discriminate. The senses of taste and smell are also well developed at birth. In addition, newborns are sensitive to touch, temperature, and pain. The senses are interrelated at birth, but as infants develop, performance on cross-modal perception tasks improves. ■

The Child

If most sensory and perceptual development is complete by the end of infancy, what is left to accomplish during childhood? Mostly, it is a matter of learning to use the senses more intelligently. For example, children rapidly build knowledge of the world so that they can recognize and label what they sense, giving it greater meaning. As a result, it becomes even harder to separate perceptual development from cognitive development.

The Development of Attention

Much of perceptual development in childhood is really the development of **attention**—the focusing of perception and cognition on something in particular. Youngsters become better able to use their senses deliberately and strategically to gather the information most relevant to a task at hand.

Infants actively use their senses to explore their environment, and they prefer some sensory stimuli to others. Still, there is some truth to the idea that the attention of the infant or very young child is "captured by" something and that of the older child is "directed toward" something. Selective as they are, 1-month-old infants do not deliberately choose to attend to faces and other engaging stimuli. Instead, a novel stimulus attracts their attention and, once their attention is "caught," they sometimes seem unable to turn away (Butcher, Kalverboer, & Geuze, 2000; Ruff & Rothbart, 1996). As children get older, three things change: their attention spans become longer, they become more selective in what they attend to, and they are better able to plan and carry out systematic strategies for using their senses to achieve goals.

Longer Attention Span

Young children have short attention spans. Researchers know that they should limit their experimental sessions with young children to a few minutes, and nursery-school teachers often switch classroom activities every 15 to 20 minutes. Even when they are doing things they like, such as watching a television program or playing with a toy, 2- and 3-year-olds spend far less time concentrating on the program or the toy than older children do (Ruff & Capozzoli, 2003; Ruff & Lawson, 1990). In one study of sustained attention, children were asked to put strips of colored paper in appropriately colored boxes (Yendovitskaya, 1971). Children ages 2 to 3 worked for an average of 18 minutes and were easily distracted; children ages 5 to 6 often persisted for 1 hour or more. Further improvements in attention span occur later in childhood as those parts of the brain involved with attention become further myelinated (see Chapter 5).

More Selective Attention

Although infants clearly deploy their senses in a selective manner, they are not good at controlling their attention—deliberately concentrating on one thing while ignoring something else, what is known as **selective attention.** With age, attention becomes more discriminating, starting in infancy. As infants approach 2 years, they become able to form plans of action, which then guide what they focus on and what they ignore (Ruff & Rothbart, 1996). Between approximately 2 years and 3½ years, there is a significant increase in focused attention; further increases in attention occur throughout childhood (Ruff & Capozzoli, 2003). These findings should suggest to teachers of young children that performance will be better if distractions in task materials and in the room are kept to a minimum.

More Systematic Attention

Finally, as they age, children become more able to plan and carry out systematic perceptual searches. You have already seen that older infants are more likely than younger ones to thoroughly explore a pattern. Research with children in the former Soviet Union reveals that visual scanning becomes considerably more detailed or exhaustive over the first 6 years after birth (Zaporozhets, 1965). But the most revealing findings come from studies of how children go about a visual search. Elaine Vurpillot (1968) recorded the eye movements of 4- to 10-year-olds trying to decide whether two houses, each with several windows containing various objects, were identical or different. As Figure 6.6 illustrates, children ages 4 and 5 were not systematic. They often looked at only a few windows and, as a result, came to wrong conclusions. In contrast, most children older than 6 were very systematic; they typically checked each window in one house with the corresponding window in the other house, pair by pair. Improvements in visual search continue to be made throughout childhood and into early adulthood (Burack et al., 2000).

Summing Up

Learning to control attention is an important part of perceptual development during childhood. Infants and young children are selectively attentive to the world around

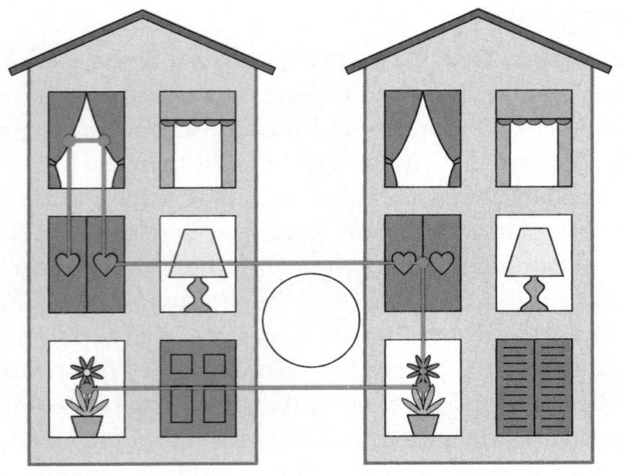
5-year-old: "The same"

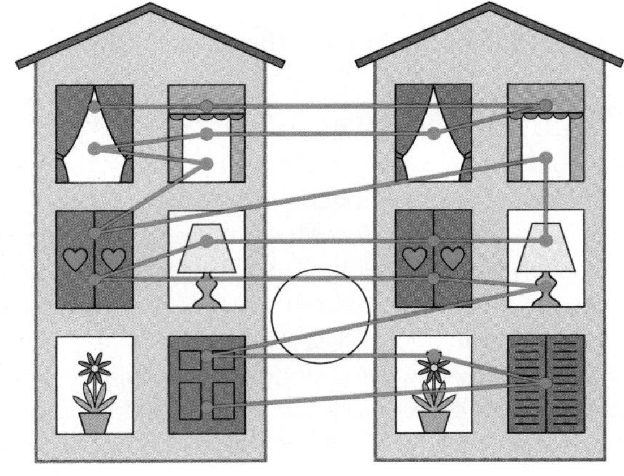
8-year-old: "Not the same"

Figure 6.6 Are the houses in each pair identical or different? As indicated by the lines, 8-year-olds are more likely than 5-year-olds to answer correctly because they systematically scan the visual features of the two pictures.

SOURCE: Adapted from Vurpillot (1968).

them, but they have not fully taken charge of their attentional processes. With age, children become more able to concentrate on a task for a long period, to focus on relevant information and ignore distractions, and to use their senses in purposeful and systematic ways to achieve goals. As you might expect, infants and children who can control and sustain their attention are more successful at problem solving (Choudhury & Gorman, 2000). ■

The Adolescent

There is little to report about perception during adolescence, except that some developments of childhood are not completed until then. For example, portions of the brain that help regulate attention are not fully myelinated until adolescence (Tanner, 1990). Perhaps this helps explain why adolescents and young adults have incredibly long attention spans on occasion, as when they spend hours cramming for tests or typing term papers into the wee hours of the morning. The ability to sustain attention improves considerably between childhood and adulthood (McKay et al., 1994).

In addition, adolescents become still more efficient at ignoring irrelevant information so that they can concentrate on the task at hand. Not only do they learn more than children do about material they are supposed to master, but they also learn less about distracting information that could potentially interfere with their performance (Miller & Weiss, 1981). Similarly, adolescents can divide their attention more systematically between two tasks. For instance, Andrew Schiff and Irwin Knopf (1985) watched the eye movements of 9-year-olds and 13-year-olds during a two-part visual search task. Children were to push a response key when particular symbols appeared at the center of a screen and to remember letters flashed at the corners of the screen. The adolescents developed efficient strategies for switching their eyes from the center to the corners and back at the right times. The 9-year-olds had an unfortunate tendency to look at blank areas of the screen or to focus too much attention on the letters in the corners of the screen, thereby failing to detect the symbols in the center.

☾ Adolescents are skilled at dividing their attention among several tasks.

Summing Up

Basic perceptual and attentional skills are perfected during adolescence. Adolescents are better than children at sustaining their attention and using it selectively and strategically to solve the problem at hand. ■

The Adult

What becomes of sensory and perceptual capacities during adulthood? There is good news and bad news, and we might as well dispense with the bad news first: Sensory and perceptual capacities decline gradually with age in the normal person. Whispers become harder to hear, seeing in the dark becomes difficult, food may not taste as good, and so on. Often these declines begin in early adulthood and become noticeable in the 40s, sometimes giving middle-aged people a feeling that they are getting old. Further declines take place in later life, to the point that you would have a hard time finding a person age 65 or older who does not have at least a mild sensory or perceptual impairment. The good news is that these changes are gradual and usually minor. As a result, we can usually compensate for them, making small adjustments such as turning up the volume on the TV set or adding a little extra seasoning to food. Because the losses are usually not severe, and because of the process of compensation, only a minority of old people develop serious problems such as blindness and deafness.

The losses we are describing take two general forms. First, sensation is affected, as indicated by raised **sensory thresholds.** The threshold for a sense is the point at which low levels of stimulation can be detected—a dim light can be seen, a faint tone can be heard, a slight odor can be detected, and so on. Stimulation below the threshold cannot be detected, so the rise of the threshold with age means that sensitivity to very low levels of stimulation is lost. (You saw that the very young infant is also insensitive to some very low levels of stimulation.)

Second, perceptual abilities decline in some aging adults. Even when stimulation is intense enough to be well above the detection threshold, older people sometimes have difficulty processing or interpreting sensory information. As you will see, they may have trouble searching a visual scene, understanding rapid speech in a noisy room, or recognizing the foods they are tasting.

So, sensory and perceptual declines are typical during adulthood, although they are far steeper in some individuals than in others and can often be compensated for. These declines involve both a rise of thresholds for detecting stimulation and a loss of some perceptual abilities.

Vision

We begin with a question that concerns many people as they get older: Will I lose my eyesight? For most people, the answer is no. Fewer than 2% of adults older than 70 are blind in both eyes, and only 4.4% are blind in one eye (Campbell et al., 1999). Still, that does not mean that you will go through old age with no vision problems. As Table 6.1 shows, 9 in 10 people will wear corrective lenses; 1 in 4 will have **cataracts,** or cloudiness of the normally clear lens; and some will need to use a magnifying glass to help them see. Why do these changes in the visual system occur, and is there anything you can do to prevent losses? Before we answer these questions, briefly review the basic workings of the visual system.

As Figure 6.7 shows, light enters the eye through the cornea and passes through the pupil and lens before being projected (upside down) on the retina. From here, images are relayed to the brain by the optic nerve at the back of each eye. The pupil of the eye automatically becomes larger or smaller depending on the lighting conditions, and the lens changes shape, or accommodates, to keep images focused on the retina. In adolescents and young adults, the visual system is normally at peak performance. Aging brings changes to all components of the visual system.

Table 6.1 Percentage of Adults 70 Years and Older Who Experience Vision Problems

Vision Condition	Percentage of Adults 70 and Older
Blind in one eye	4.4
Blind in both eyes	1.7
Other trouble seeing	14.4
Glaucoma	7.9
Cataract(s)	24.5
Use a magnifier	17.0
Wear glasses	91.5

SOURCE: Adapted from Campbell et al., 1999.

Changes in the Pupil

As we age, our pupils become somewhat smaller and do not change as much when lighting conditions change. As a result, older adults experience greater difficulty when lighting is dim, when it is bright, and when it suddenly changes. Approximately one-third of adults older than 85 exhibit a tenfold loss of the ability to read low-contrast words in dim lighting (Brabyn, 2000). Put another way, an 82-year-old can see with 20/30 acuity (20/20 is considered optimal) when lighting and contrast are good, but her acuity drops to 20/120 when lighting and contrast are poor (Enoch et al., 1999). Such an adult often has difficulty reading menus in restaurants with "mood" lighting. To compensate, she might use a small flashlight. And restaurants could help by providing menus printed with sharp contrast (black print on a pure white background).

When walking into the sunlight after watching a movie in a darkened theater, older adults' pupils are slower than younger adults' to change from large to small, a process that helps reduce the glare of bright lights. In one study, adults older than 85 years took more than 2 minutes to recover from glare, whereas adults younger than 65 needed less than 15 seconds (Brabyn, 2000).

Similarly, **dark adaptation**—the process in which the eyes adapt to darkness and become more sensitive to the low level of light available—occurs more slowly in older individuals than in younger ones (Fozard & Gordon-Salant, 2001) As a result, the older person driving at night may have special problems when turning onto a dark road from a lighted highway.

Changes in the Lens

The lens of the eye also undergoes change with age. It has been gaining new cells since childhood, making it denser and less flexible later in life. It cannot change shape, or accommodate, as well to bring objects at different distances into focus. The lens is also yellowing, and both it and the gelatinous liquid behind it are becoming less transparent. The thickening of the

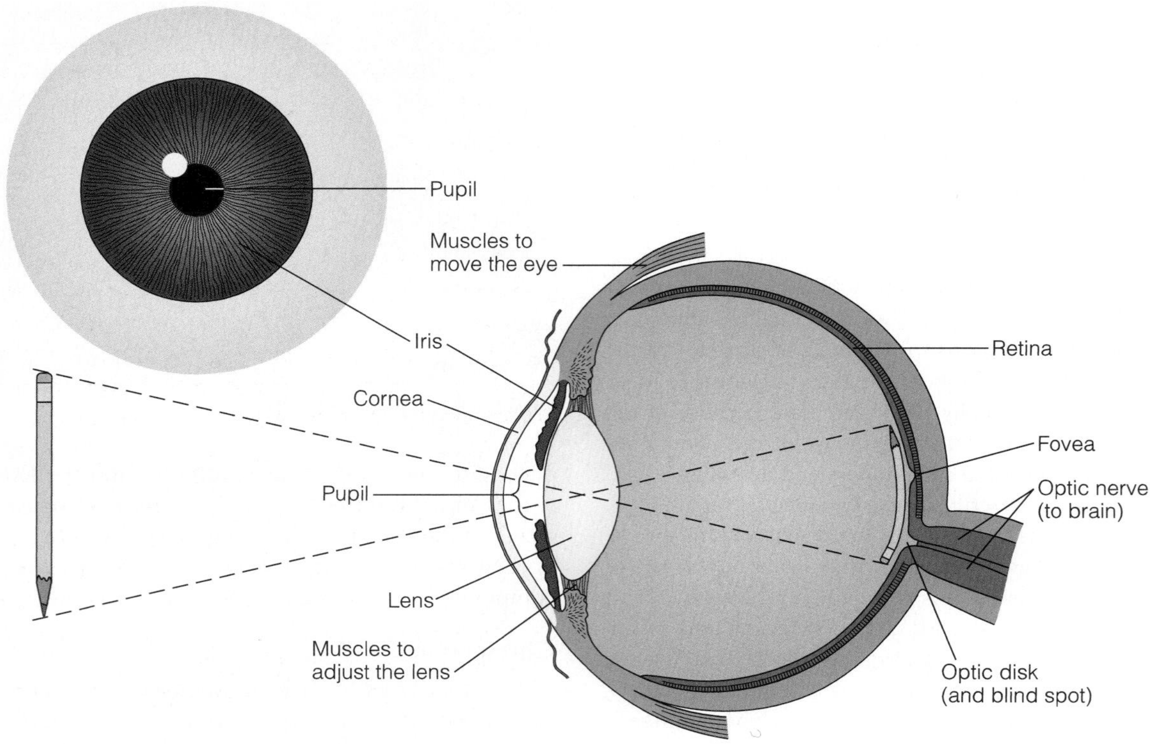

Figure 6.7 The human eye and retina. Light passes through the cornea, pupil, and lens and falls on the light-sensitive surface of the retina, where images of objects are projected upside down. The information is relayed to the brain by the optic nerve.

lens with age leads to **presbyopia,** or the decreased ability of the lens to accommodate objects close to the eye (Fozard & Gordon-Salant, 2001). Over the years, an adult may, without even being aware of it, gradually move newspapers and books farther from the eye to make them clearer—a form of compensation for decline. Eventually, however, the arms may simply be too short to do the trick any longer. Middle-aged adults cope with problems of near vision by getting reading glasses (or, if they also have problems with distance vision, bifocals); reading fine print may still be a problem, however.

☾ As adults age, they typically find they are more bothered by glare and need corrective lenses.

As for distance vision, visual acuity as measured by standard eye charts increases in childhood, peaks in the 20s, remains steady through middle age, and steadily declines in old age (Evans et al., 2002; Klein et al., 2001). The implications for the average adult are fairly minor. For example, in one major study, 76% of older adults (75 years and older) had good corrected vision (Evans et al., 2002). At worst, most of them could see at 20 feet what a person with standard acuity can see at 25 feet—not a big problem. Among adults in their 90s, 37% are visually impaired, but only 7% are blind. Several studies show that women experience greater declines in visual acuity than men (see, for example, van der Pols et al., 2000). Older women with declining vision are more susceptible to falling and fracturing a bone, which is a serious threat to their independence (Coleman et al., 2004). Fracturing a hip often triggers a shift from independent to assisted living and can even be fatal. And poor vision that is not correctable can seriously decrease older adults' quality of life. According to one estimate, older adults with poor visual acuity (20/40 or worse) were as impaired as those with a major medical problem such as stroke (Chia et al., 2004).

Thus, even though most of us will not be blind, we will need to wear corrective lenses and regularly monitor our vision. The minority of elderly people who experience serious declines in visual acuity typically suffer from pathological conditions of the eye. These conditions become more prevalent in old age but are not part of aging itself. For example, cataracts are the leading cause of visual impairment in old age. Most older adults have some degree of lens clouding, and significant clouding is present in roughly half of adults older than 75 years, often from lifelong heavy exposure to sunlight and its damaging ultraviolet rays (Fozard & Gordon-Salant, 2001). Fortunately, cataracts can be removed through surgery, improving vision and preventing blindness.

Retinal Changes

Researchers also know that the web of sensory receptor cells in the retina may die or not function in later life as efficiently as they once did. The serious retinal problem **age-related macular degeneration** results from damage to cells in the retina responsible for central vision. Thus, vision becomes blurry; it also begins to fade first from the center of the visual field, making reading and many other activities impossible. With the success of corrective surgery for cataracts, age-related macular degeneration is now a leading cause of blindness in older adults (Congdon et al., 2004). The causes of macular degeneration are largely unknown, but some research points to a genetic role; other research shows a connection with cigarette smoking (Evans, 2001). Currently, there is no treatment for macular degeneration, but several researchers are working to develop retinal implants that would stimulate the remaining cells of the retina and restore some useful vision (Boston Retinal Implant Project, 2004).

Changes in the retina also lead to decreased visual field, or a loss of peripheral (side) vision (Fozard & Gordon-Salant, 2001). Looking straight ahead, an older adult may see only half of what a young adult sees to the left and the right of center. Can you think of activities that might be hindered by a decreased visual field? Driving a car comes to mind. For example, when approaching an intersection, you need to be able to see what is coming toward you as well as what is coming from the side roads. The Explorations box on page 164 describes some other sensory changes that might make driving more hazardous for older people.

Significant loss of peripheral vision can lead to tunnel vision, a condition often caused by retinitis pigmentosa or by glaucoma. **Retinitis pigmentosa (RP)** is a group of hereditary disorders that all involve gradual deterioration of the light-sensitive cells of the retina. Symptoms of RP can appear as early as childhood, but it is more likely to be diagnosed in adulthood, when the symptoms have become more apparent. Individuals with RP often have a history of visual problems at night and a gradual loss of peripheral vision. There is no cure for retinal deterioration, but some promising research suggests that treatment with vitamin A can slow (not eliminate) the progress of the disease (Berson, 2000; Sibulesky et al., 1999).

In **glaucoma,** increased fluid pressure in the eye can damage the optic nerve and can cause a progressive loss of peripheral vision and, ultimately, blindness. It becomes more common over age 50. The key is to prevent the damage before it occurs, using eyedrops or surgery to lower eye fluid pressure. In many cases, however, the damage is done before people experience visual problems; only regular eye tests can reveal the buildup of eye pressure that spells trouble (Fozard & Gordon-Salant, 2001).

To recap, you can expect some changes in vision as you age. Sensory thresholds increase with age so that you need higher levels of stimulation than when you were young. Acuity, or sharpness of vision, decreases, and it takes longer for eyes to adapt to changes. Fortunately, it is possible to correct or compensate for most of these "normal" changes. Some older adults will experience more serious visual problems, such as those caused by changes in the retina, but early detection and treatment can preserve vision in most adults.

Attention and Visual Search

As you learned earlier in this chapter, perception is more than just seeing. It is using the senses intelligently and allocating attention efficiently. Young children have more difficulty performing complex visual search tasks and ignoring irrelevant information than older children do. Do older adults also have more difficulty than younger adults?

Older adults do worse than younger ones on several tests that require dividing attention between two tasks (divided attention) or selectively attending to certain stimuli while ignoring others (selective attention; see Juola et al., 2000; Madden & Langley, 2003). The more distracters a task involves, the more the performance of elderly adults falls short of the performance of young adults. In everyday life, this may translate into difficulty carrying on a conversation while driving or problems locating the asparagus amid all the frozen vegetables at the supermarket.

In one test of visual search skills, Charles Scialfa and his colleagues (Scialfa, Esau, & Joffe, 1998) asked young adults and elderly adults to locate a target (for example, a blue horizontal line) in a display where the distracter items were clearly different (for example, red vertical lines) or in a more difficult task where the distracters shared a common feature with the target (for example, blue vertical and red horizontal lines). Older adults were slower and less accurate on the more challenging search task. They were also more distracted by irrelevant information; they were especially slow compared with young adults when the number of distracter items in the display was high. In some situations, elderly people appear to have difficulty inhibiting responses to irrelevant stimuli so that they can focus their attention more squarely on relevant stimuli (Erber, 2005). Older adults can improve their visual search performance with practice, and they are more successful when they strategically use a feature of the display (for example, color) to help guide their search (Madden, Gottlob, & Allen, 1999).

In short, older adults have their greatest difficulties in processing visual information when the situation is *novel* (when they are not sure exactly what to look for or where to look) and when it is *complex* (when there is a great deal of distracting information to search through or when two tasks must be performed at once). By contrast, they have fewer problems when

Explorations

Aging Drivers

Older drivers are perceived by many as more accident prone and slower than other drivers. Perhaps you have had the experience of zipping down the interstate when a slow-moving car driven by an elderly adult pulls into your path, forcing you to brake quickly. Is this experience representative, and is the stereotype of older drivers accurate? This is an important question, because 20% of all drivers will be older than 65 years by 2030 (Braver & Trempel, 2004; Lyman et al., 2002).

It is true that older adults (70 years and older) are involved in more automobile fatalities than middle-aged adults (see the figure in this Explorations box). But the most accident-prone group is young drivers between 16 and 24 years (U.S. Department of Transportation, 1997). When you take into account that young people drive more than elderly people do, it turns out that both elderly drivers and young drivers have more accidents *per mile driven* than middle-aged drivers have (Williams & Carsten, 1989).

Why is driving hazardous for elderly adults? Clearly, vision is essential to driving; vision accounts for approximately 90% of the information necessary to operate and navigate a car (Messinger-Rapport, 2003). Visual acuity or clarity is one component of problematic driving, but as noted in the main text, poor acuity is fairly easy to correct. Therefore, although older adults cite concerns about eyesight as one reason to limit or avoid driving, it cannot account for all the problems older drivers have (Ragland, Satariano, & MacLeod, 2004).

Diminished peripheral vision also makes driving hazardous (Owsley et al., 1998). Good drivers must be able to see vehicles and pedestrians approaching from the side. Half of the fatal automobile accidents involving older drivers occur at intersections, and older drivers are more than twice as likely as young drivers to have problems making left-hand turns (Uchida, Fujita, & Katayama, 1999). Not only must drivers see obstacles moving toward them, they must evaluate the speed and trajectory of these objects and integrate this information with their own speed and trajectory to determine a course of action. For example, is the car approaching from the left going to hit my car, or will I be through the intersection before it reaches me? Unfortunately, perceiving moving objects is a problem for older adults, even those who have good visual acuity (Erber, 2005). And simultaneously processing multiple pieces of information is also difficult for older adults. Thus,

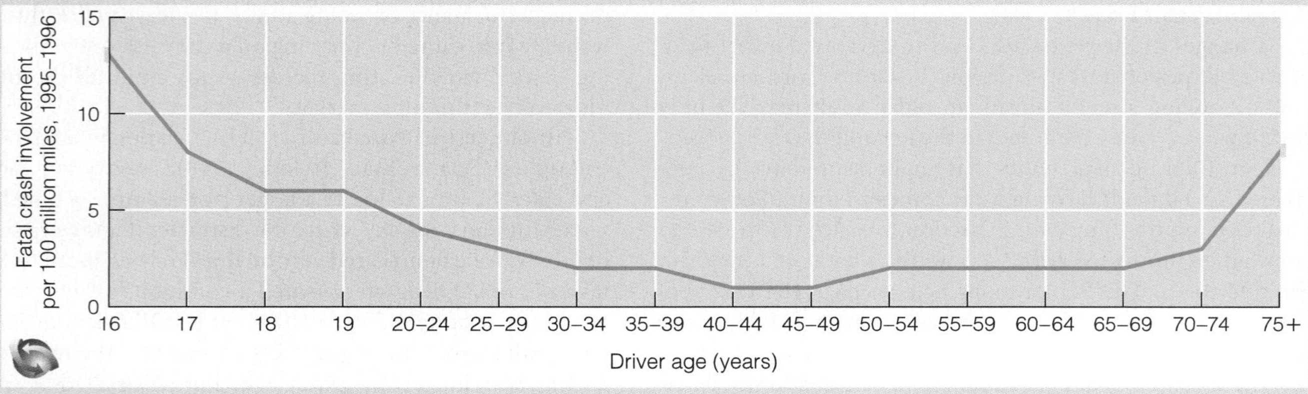

they have clear expectations about what they are to do and when the task is not overly complex. Thus, an older factory worker who has inspected radios for years may be just as speedy and accurate as a younger worker at this well-practiced, familiar task, but he might perform relatively poorly if suddenly asked to inspect pocket calculators and look for a much larger number of possible defects—a novel and complex task.

Hearing

There is some truth to the stereotype of the hard-of-hearing older person. The older the age group, the greater the percentage of people who have at least mild hearing loss: as many as 90% of individuals older than 65 have impaired hearing (Fozard & Gordon-Salant, 2001). Most older people experience mild to moderate hearing impairments, some experience severe hearing loss, and only a few are deaf (Dalton et al., 2004).

Basic Capacities

Sources of hearing problems range from excess wax buildup in the ears to infections to a sluggish nervous system. Most age-related hearing problems seem to originate in the inner ear, however (Fozard & Gordon-Salant, 2001). The cochlear hair cells that serve as auditory receptors, their surrounding structures, and the neurons leading from them to the brain older drivers have trouble reading street signs while driving (Dewar, Kline, & Swanson, 1995), and they are less able than younger adults to quickly change their focus from the dashboard to the rearview mirror to the road ahead.

After understanding the dynamics of a potentially dangerous situation, the driver must be able to react quickly to threats (for example, a child chasing a ball into the street). As you learned in Chapter 5, older adults typically have slower response times than younger adults; thus, they need more time to react to the same stimulus. Finally, older adults are slower to recover from glare and to adapt to the dark, which makes night driving problematic.

But the driving records of older adults are not as bad as might be expected, because many of them compensate for visual and other perceptual difficulties and slower reactions by driving less frequently, especially in conditions believed to be more hazardous—at night, during rush hour, and when the weather is poor (Messinger-Rapport, 2003). Older adults with visual problems such as cataracts and those with cognitive problems are more likely to limit their driving than older adults without these problems (Messinger-Rapport, 2003). Some states have responded to concerns about elderly drivers with mandatory road retesting for license renewal (Cobb & Coughlin, 1998). But most states have no distinct policies about license renewal for older adults. It is not that states do not care; rather, they face strong opposition from groups such as the American Association of Retired Persons and individual older adults (Cobb & Coughlin, 1998). To give up driving is to give up a big chunk of independence, something anyone would be loathe to do. Most people want to find ways to drive safely as long as possible. By understanding the strengths and limitations of their sensory–perceptual abilities, older adults will be in a good position to keep driving safely. Remember that the next time you are stuck behind a slow driver.

© David Young-Wolff/PhotoEdit

An older adult is likely to find the ice cream as efficiently as a younger adult in a familiar supermarket but may have difficulty with this visual search task if the supermarket is unfamiliar.

degenerate gradually over the adult years. The most noticeable result is a loss of sensitivity to high-frequency or high-pitched sounds, the most common form of **presbycusis,** or problems of the aging ear. Thus an older person may have difficulty hearing a child's high voice, the flutes in an orchestra, and high-frequency consonant sounds such as *s, z,* and *ch* (Whitbourne, 2001) but may have less trouble with deep voices, tubas, and sounds such as *b.* After age 50, lower-frequency sounds also become increasingly difficult to hear (Kline & Scialfa, 1996). Thus, to be heard by the average older adult, a sound—especially a high-pitched sound but ultimately any sound—must be louder than it needs to be to exceed the auditory threshold of a younger adult.

Is this loss of hearing with age the inevitable result of basic aging processes, or is it caused by other factors? Researchers know that the loss is more noticeable among men than among women, that men are more likely to work in noisy industrial jobs, and that those who hold such jobs experience more hearing loss than other men (Martin & Clark, 2002; Reuben et al., 1998). But even when adults who have held relatively quiet jobs are studied, men show detectable hearing losses earlier in life (in their 30s) and lose hearing sensitivity at a faster rate than women do (Pearson et al., 1995). It seems, then, that most people, men more than women, will experience some loss of sensitivity to high-frequency sounds as part of the basic aging process, but that certain people will experience more severe losses because of their experiences. As Table 6.2 shows, loud sounds—those above 75 decibels—may leave the listener with a loss of hearing. Fans of loud music, beware: The noise at rock concerts and night clubs is often in the 120- to 130-decibel range; this is loud enough to cause a temporary rise in hearing thresholds) and possibly even permanent hearing loss in individuals regularly exposed to it (Hetu & Fortin, 1995). And if you can hear the music coming from the headset of your friend's MP3 player, your friend may be damaging her hearing (Schiffman, 2000).

Speech Perception

Perhaps the most important thing we do with our ears in everyday life is listening to other people during conversations. The ability to hear is one requisite for understanding speech, but this complex auditory perception task also depends on cognitive processes such as attention and memory. How well do aging adults do?

Older adults typically have more difficulty understanding speech than younger adults do, even under ideal listening conditions. However, this age difference becomes small when dif-

Noise	Number of Decibels
Whisper	30
Quiet room	40
Normal speech	60
City traffic	80
Lawnmower	90
Rock music	110
Jet plane takeoff	120
Jackhammer	130
Firearm discharge	140

Table 6.2 Noise Levels

The healthy ear can detect sounds starting at 0 decibels. Damage to hearing can start between 75 and 80 decibels and is more likely with long-term exposure to loud sounds.

ferences in hearing are controlled (Schneider, Daneman, et al., 2000). Thus, older adults' difficulties with speech perception under good listening conditions are largely because of hearing problems rather than cognitive declines. However, under poor listening conditions—for example, loud background noise—differences between older and young adults are larger even when individual differences in hearing are accounted for (Schneider, Daneman, et al., 2000). Thus, older adults may recall fewer details of a conversation that takes place in a crowded, noisy restaurant.

In addition, auditory perception tasks, like visual perception tasks, are more difficult for older people when they are novel and complex. In familiar, everyday situations, older adults are able to use contextual cues to interpret what they hear (Fozard & Gordon-Salant, 2001). In one study, for example, elderly adults were about as able as young adults to recall meaningful sentences they had just heard (Wingfield et al., 1985). However, they had serious difficulty repeating back

Applications

Aiding Adults with Hearing Impairments

In the Applications box on page 154, we examined ways to help infants and children who have hearing impairments, often from birth. Here, we consider the other end of the life span. What can be done to assist hearing-impaired adults, most of whom were born with normal hearing? Many are reluctant to admit that they have a hearing problem, so few older adults with hearing loss use hearing aids (Popelka et al., 1998). Those who do not have their hearing corrected may suffer depression, decreased independence, and strained relationships (Appollonio et al., 1996). Imagine how hard social interaction can become if you cannot understand what is being said, misinterpret what is said, or have to keep asking people to repeat what they said. One 89-year-old woman became extremely depressed and isolated: "There is an *awfulness* about silence . . . I am days without speaking a word. It is affecting my voice. I fear for my mind. I cannot hear the alarm clock, telephone ring, door bell, radio, television—or the human voice" (Meadows-Orlans & Orlans, 1990, pp. 424–425). We tend to think of vision as our most important sense, but hearing impairments may be more disruptive than visual impairments to cognitive and social functioning. Still, many individuals cope well with their hearing impairments and maintain active, satisfying lifestyles.

Hearing aids, although beneficial, cannot restore normal hearing; they tend to distort sounds and to magnify background noise as well as what the wearer is trying to hear. In addition, many older people are ill served by hearing aids that are of poor quality or that are poorly matched to their specific hearing problems. Because cochlear implants work best for individuals exposed to spoken language before they lost their hearing, elderly people are ideal candidates for them. They tolerate the surgical procedure required for implantation well, and their hearing test scores increase significantly (Kelsall, Shallop, & Burnelli, 1995). In addition, adults who receive cochlear implants report that their quality of life has improved significantly (Faber & Grontved, 2000). Cochlear implants, however, cannot work overnight miracles; it can take months, even years, to learn how to interpret the messages relayed by the implant to the brain (Colburn, 2000).

Finally, the physical and social environment can be modified to help people of all ages with hearing losses (National Institute on Aging & National Institute on Deafness, 1996). For example, furniture can be arranged to permit face-to-face contact; lights can be turned on to permit use of visual cues such as gestures and lip movements. Then there are the simple guidelines we can follow to make ourselves understood by hearing-impaired people. One of the most important is to avoid shouting. Shouting not only distorts speech but also raises the pitch of the voice (therefore making it more difficult for elderly people to hear); it also makes it harder for the individual to read lips. It is best to speak at a normal rate, clearly but without overarticulating, with your face fully visible at a distance of about 3 to 6 feet.

With modern technology, appropriate education, effective coping strategies, and help from those who hear, hearing-impaired and deaf individuals of all ages can thrive.

grammatical sentences that made no sense or random strings of words, especially when these meaningless stimuli were spoken rapidly. So, an older person may be able to follow an ordinary conversation but not a technical presentation on an unfamiliar topic—especially if the speaker makes the task harder by talking too fast.

Overall, then, most older adults have only mild hearing losses, especially for high-frequency sounds, and only minor problems understanding everyday speech; in addition, they can compensate for their difficulties successfully—for example, by reading lips and relying on contextual cues. Novel and complex speech heard under poor listening conditions is likely to cause more trouble. Fortunately, there is much they can do to improve hearing or compensate for its loss, as the Applications box on page 166 describes.

Taste and Smell

Does the aging of sensory systems also mean that older people become less able to appreciate tastes and aromas? Studies designed to measure taste thresholds suggest that with increasing age, some of us have more difficulty detecting weak taste stimulation—for example, a small amount of salt on food or a few drops of lemon juice in a glass of water (Mattes, 2002; Schiffman, 1997). Thus, older adults may report that food tastes bland and use larger amounts of salt and seasonings than used when they were younger. In addition, both middle-aged and older adults sometimes have difficulty discriminating among tastes that differ in intensity (Nordin et al., 2003). In one study, for example, adults over 70 were less able than young adults to reliably judge one solution to be saltier, more bitter, or more acidic than another (Weiffenbach, Cowart, & Baum, 1986). Interestingly, older adults did not have difficulty distinguishing degrees of sweetness; people do not seem to lose the sweet tooth they are born with.

The ability to perceive odors also typically declines with age. Sensitivity to odors increases from childhood to early adulthood then declines during adulthood, more so with increasing age (Finkelstein & Schiffman, 1999; Ship et al., 1996). Age takes a greater toll on the sense of smell than on the sense of taste (Rolls, 1999). However, differences among age groups are usually small, and many older people retain their sensitivity to odors. Women are more likely than men to maintain their ability to label odors in scratch-and-sniff tests (Ship & Weiffenbach, 1993), partly because they are less likely than men to have worked in factories and been exposed to chemicals (Corwin, Loury, & Gilbert, 1995). Also, healthy adults of both sexes retain their sense of smell better than do those who have diseases and take medications (Ship & Weiffenbach, 1993). Again, then, perceptual losses in later life are part of the basic aging process but vary from person to person depending on environmental factors.

How do declines in the senses of taste and smell affect the older person's enjoyment of food? Susan Schiffman (1977) blindfolded young adults and elderly adults and asked them to identify blended foods by taste and smell alone. As Table 6.3 reveals, the older people were correct less often than the college students were. But was this because of a loss of taste sensitivity or smell sensitivity? Or was it a cognitive problem—difficulty coming up with the name of a food that was sensed?

Claire Murphy (1985) attempted to shed light on these questions by presenting young and elderly adults with 12 of the blended foods used by Schiffman. She observed that older people often came up with the wrong specific label but the right idea (identifying sugar as fruit or salt as peanuts, for example). Thus, at least some of their difficulty may have been cognitive. Murphy also tested women whose nostrils were blocked and found that both young and elderly women did miserably when they could not smell and had to rely on taste alone. This finding suggests that a reduced ability to identify foods in old age is less because of losses in the sense of taste

Table 6.3 Age Differences in Recognition of Foods

	Percentage Recognizing Food	
Pureed Food Substance	**College Students (ages 18–22)**	**Elderly People (ages 67–93)**
Fruits		
Apple	93	79
Banana	93	59
Pear	93	86
Pineapple	93	86
Strawberry	100	79
Tomato	93	93
Vegetables		
Broccoli	81	62
Cabbage	74	69
Carrot	79	55
Celery	89	55
Corn	96	76
Cucumber	44	28
Green bean	85	62
Green pepper	78	59
Potato	52	59
Meat/Fish		
Beef	100	79
Fish	89	90
Pork	93	72
Other		
Rice	81	55
Walnut	33	28

Elderly adults have more difficulty than young college students in identifying most blended foods by taste and smell alone. Percentages of those recognizing food include reasonable guesses such as "orange" in response to "apple." Notice that some foods (for example, cucumber) are difficult for people of any age to identify by taste and smell alone. Appearance and texture are important to the recognition of such foods.

SOURCE: Schiffman, S. (1977). Food recognition by the elderly. *Journal of Gerontology, 32.* Reprinted by permission.

than because of losses in the sense of smell and declines in the cognitive skills required to remember and name what has been tasted (Murphy, Nordin, & Acosta, 1997).

If foods do not have much taste, an older person may lose interest in eating and may not get proper nourishment (Rolls, 1999). Alternatively, an older person may overuse seasonings such as salt or may eat spoiled food, which can threaten health in other ways. Yet these problems can be remedied. For example, when flavor enhancers were added to the food in one nursing home, elders ate more, gained muscle strength, and had healthier immune system functioning than they did when they ate the usual institutional fare (Schiffman & Warwick, 1993).

Conclusions about changes in taste and smell must be considered in perspective. These sensory and perceptual abilities are highly variable across the life span, not just older adulthood. Many older adults will not experience deficits: They can continue to smell the roses and enjoy their food.

Touch, Temperature, and Pain

By now, you have seen numerous indications that older adults are often less able than younger adults to detect weak sensory stimulation. This holds true for the sense of touch. The detection threshold for touch increases and sensitivity is gradually lost from middle childhood on (Erber, 2005). It is not clear that minor losses in touch sensitivity have many implications for daily life, however.

Similarly, older people may be less sensitive to changes in temperature than younger adults are (Frank et al., 2000). Some keep their homes too cool because they are unaware of being cold; others may fail to notice that it is too hot. Because older bodies are also less able than younger ones to maintain an even temperature, elderly people face an increased risk of death in heat waves or cold snaps (Worfolk, 2000).

It seems only fair that older people should also be less sensitive to painful stimulation, but are they? They are indeed less likely than younger adults to report *weak* levels of stimulation as painful, although the age differences in pain thresholds are not large or consistent (Verrillo & Verrillo, 1985). Yet older people seem to be no less sensitive to stronger pain stimuli. Unfortunately, older adults are more likely to experience chronic pain than younger adults but are less likely to obtain adequate pain relief (Gloth, 2000). Adults with arthritis, osteoporosis, cancer, and other diseases who also experience depression and anxiety are especially likely to perceive pain. Treating these secondary conditions and administering effective pain relief can improve the daily functioning and psychological well-being of older adults.

The Adult in Perspective

Of all the changes in sensation and perception during adulthood that we have considered, those involving vision and hearing appear to be the most important and the most universal. Not only are these senses less keen, but they also are used less effectively in such complex perceptual tasks as searching a cluttered room for a missing book or following rapid conversation in a noisy room. Declines in the other senses are less serious and do not affect as many people.

Although people compensate for many sensory declines, their effects cannot be entirely eliminated. At some point, aging adults find that changes in sensory abilities affect their activities. As Table 6.4 shows, older adults with one or two sensory impairments are more likely to experience difficulty with basic tasks of living—walking, getting outside, getting in or out of bed or a chair, taking medicines, or preparing meals. Notice, however, that even older adults without sensory impairments report some difficulty with these tasks. People who are limited by sensory impairments usually have physical or intellectual impairments as well, most likely because of general declines in neural functioning that affect both perception and cognition (Baltes & Lindenberger, 1997; Salthouse et al., 1996). Most older adults, even those with sensory impairments, are engaged in a range of activities and are living full lives. Thus, although most adults will experience some declines in sensory abilities with age, these changes do not need to detract from their quality of life.

Summing Up

During adulthood, sensory and perceptual capacities gradually decline in most individuals, although many changes are minor and can be compensated for. Changes in the lens, pupil, cornea, and retina of the eye contribute to decreased vision as we age. Hearing difficulty associated with aging most commonly involves loss of sensitiv-

Table 6.4 Percentage of Older Adults with Various Impairments Who Report Limits on Activities

Activity	With Visual Impairments	With Hearing Impairments	With Both Visual and Hearing Impairments	Without Visual or Hearing Impairments
Difficulty walking	43.3%	30.7%	48.3%	22.2%
Difficulty getting outside	28.6	17.3	32.8	11.9
Difficulty getting in or out of a bed or chair	22.1	15.1	25.0	10.4
Difficulty taking medicines	11.8	7.7	13.4	5.0
Difficulty preparing meals	18.7	11.6	20.7	7.8

SOURCE: Adapted from Campbell et al. (1999).

ity to high-frequency (high-pitched) sounds. Hearing aids can significantly improve older adults' abilities to detect sounds. Even elderly people without significant hearing losses may experience difficulty understanding novel and complex speech spoken rapidly under poor listening conditions. Many older people have difficulty recognizing or enjoying foods, largely because of declines in the sense of smell and memory; touch, temperature, and pain sensitivity also decrease slightly, but intense pain stimuli still hurt. ■

Summary Points

1. Sensation is the detection of sensory stimulation; perception is the interpretation of what is sensed. Developmentalists and philosophers differ about whether basic knowledge of the world is innate (the nativist position) or must be acquired through the senses (the empiricist position).

2. Methods of studying infant perception include habituation, evoked potentials, preferential looking, and operant conditioning techniques.

3. From birth, the visual system is working reasonably well. The auditory sense is well developed at birth. Very young infants can recognize their mother's voice and can make distinctions among speech sounds that adults may no longer be able to make. The other senses are also well developed at birth.

4. During childhood we learn to sustain attention for longer periods, to direct it more selectively (filtering out distracting information), and to plan and carry out more systematic perceptual searches.

5. During adolescence, the ability to sustain and control attention improves further, and sensation and perception are at their peaks.

6. Throughout adulthood, sensory abilities gradually decline. However, these changes can often be compensated for with, for example, corrective lenses for the eyes, amplification devices for the ears, and more spices for the taste buds. Moderate to severe declines that are not corrected can lead to declines in activities and quality of life among older adults.

Critical Thinking

1. Drawing on your knowledge of the sensory and perceptual capacities of newborns, put yourself in the place of a newborn just emerging from the womb and describe your perceptual experiences.

2. You have been hired to teach a cooking course to elderly adults. First, analyze the perceptual strengths and weaknesses of your students: What perceptual tasks might be easy for them, and what tasks might be difficult? Second, considering at least three senses, think of 10 strategies you can use to help your students compensate for the declines in perceptual capacities that some of them may be experiencing.

3. You are the coordinator for social and educational activities at your community center, which means you work with people of all ages, ranging from the youngest infants to the oldest adults. In planning activities, what is important to know about capturing and holding the attention of different age groups?

4. You have an unlimited budget for redesigning a local child care center that serves children 6 weeks to 6 years old. Given what you know about sensory and perceptual capabilities of infants and young children, what equipment and toys will you purchase, and how will you remodel and redecorate the rooms?

Key Terms

sensation, 144
perception, 144
empiricist, 144
nativist, 144
habituation, 145
visual acuity, 146
visual accommodation, 146
contour, 147
size constancy, 148
visual cliff, 149
intuitive theories, 151
phoneme, 152
cochlear implant, 154
olfaction, 155
cross-modal perception, 156
attention, 159
selective attention, 159
sensory threshold, 161
cataracts, 161
dark adaptation, 161
presbyopia, 162
age-related macular degeneration, 163
retinitis pigmentosa (RP), 163
glaucoma, 163
presbycusis, 165

Media Resources

Websites to Explore

Visit Our Website

For a chapter tutorial quiz and other useful features, visit the book's companion website at *http://psychology.wadsworth.com/sigelman_rider5e.* You can also connect directly to the following sites:

Senses Data
From the Howard Hughes Medical Institute, the web page titled "Seeing, Hearing, and Smelling the World" provides a great deal of scholarly, yet easy to understand, material on the senses.

Hearing Impairments
The Center for Assessment and Demographic Studies at Gallaudet University provides a scholarly paper on the demographics of hearing impairments in the United States.

Understanding the Data: Exercises on the Web

For additional insight on the data presented in this chapter, try the exercises for these figures at *http://psychology.wadsworth.com/sigelman_rider5e:*

Unnumbered figure in Explorations box titled "Aging Drivers"

Table 6.4 Percentage of Older Adults with Various Impairments Who Report Their Activities Are Limited

Life-Span CD-ROM

Go to the Wadsworth Life-Span CD-ROM for further study of the concepts in this chapter. The CD-ROM includes narrated concept overviews, video clips, a multimedia glossary, and additional activities to expand your learning experience.

Developmental PsychologyNow is a web-based, intelligent study system that provides a complete package of diagnostic quizzes, a personalized study plan, integrated multimedia elements, and learning modules. Check it out at *http://psychology.wadsworth.com/sigelman_rider5e/now.*

CHAPTER seven

Cognition

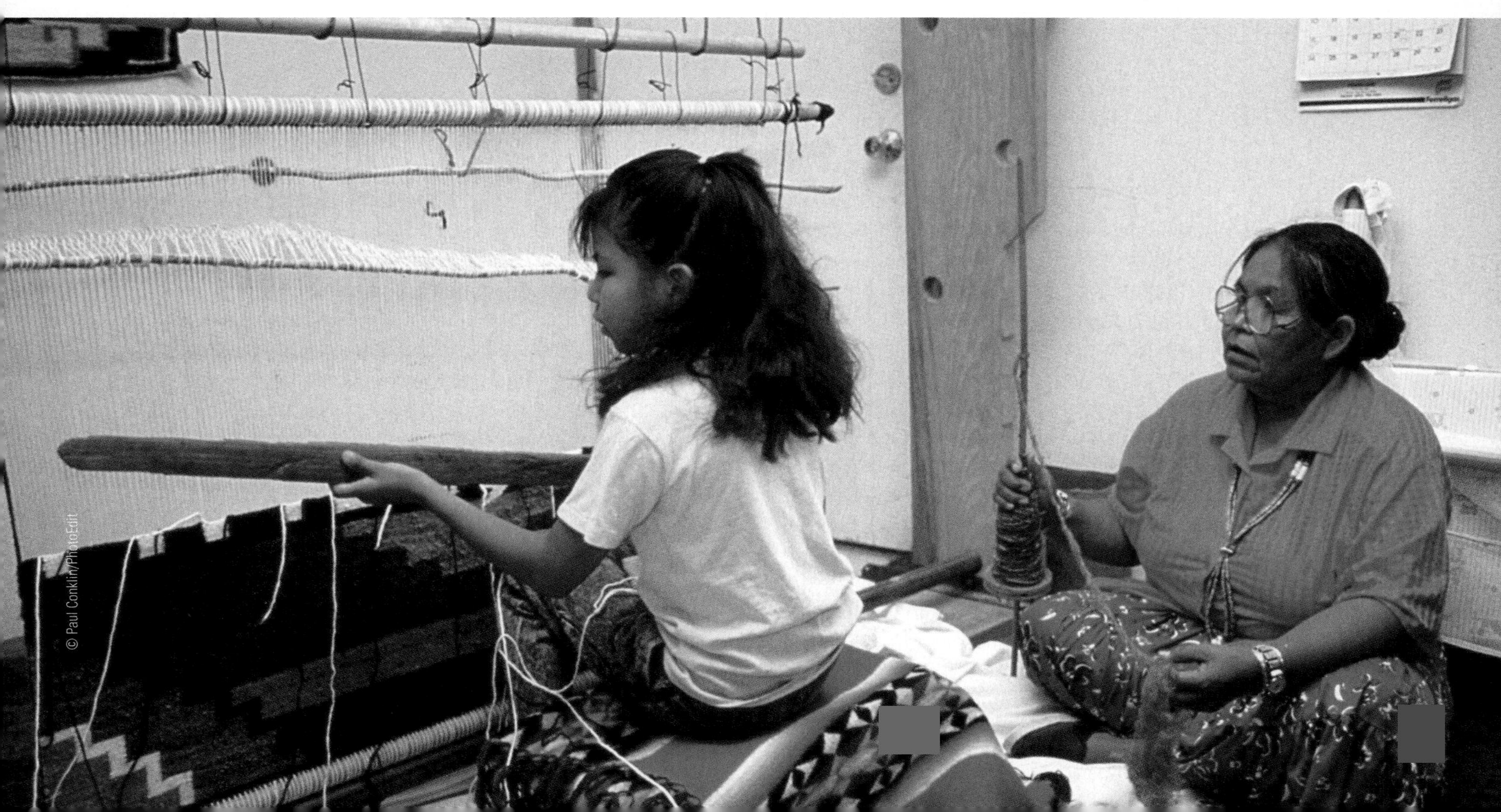

LAURA (3 YEARS OLD), removing an opened can of soda from the refrigerator, to her mother: "Whose is this? It's not yours 'cause it doesn't have lipstick."

Matt (11 years old) wanted to go to a hobby store on Memorial Day. His mother, doubting it was open, told him to call. Matt went to the phone, returned, and said, "Let's go." They arrived to find the store closed. The frustrated mother: "I thought you called." Matt: "I did, but they didn't answer, so I figured they were too busy to come to the phone" (DeLoache, Miller, & Pierroutsakos, 1998, p. 801).

From an early age, humans think and reason about the world around them—sometimes coming to logical conclusions. At age 3, Laura shows remarkable logic when she concludes that a soda cannot be her mother's because it does not have lipstick on it. By contrast, Matt, age 11, does not use the rational powers we assume 11-year-olds possess, perhaps because his wishes get in the way.

In this chapter, we begin to examine the development of **cognition**—the activity of knowing and the processes through which knowledge is acquired and problems are solved. Humans are cognitive beings throughout the life span, but as the preceding examples suggest, their minds change in important ways. We concentrate on the influential theory of cognitive development proposed by Jean Piaget, who traced growth in cognitive capacities during infancy, childhood, and adolescence, and then ask what becomes of these capacities during adulthood. We also consider an alternative view: Lev Vygotsky's sociocultural perspective on cognitive development. Both theorists have changed how we think about cognitive functioning and education. We explore Piaget and Vygotsky's ideas for improving cognitive skills at the end of this chapter; we will revisit these ideas in Chapter 10 when we cover language and education.

Piaget's Constructivist Approach

Piaget was an exceptional person. As you learned in Chapter 2, Piaget became intrigued by children's mistakes because he noticed that children of the same age often made similar kinds of mental mistakes—errors typically different from those made by younger or older children. Could these age-related differences in error patterns reflect developmental steps, or stages, in intellectual growth? Piaget thought so, and he devoted his life to studying *how* children think, not just *what* they know (Flavell, 1963). Although many of Piaget's ideas were initially formulated in the 1920s, there was little knowledge of his work in North America until the 1960s, when John Flavell's (1963) summary of Piaget's theory appeared in English.

Interested in basic questions of philosophy, Piaget defined his field of interest as **genetic epistemology**—the study of how humans come to know reality and basic dimensions of it such as space, time, and causality. Epistemology is the branch of philosophy that studies knowledge of reality, and *genetic* can be translated as *emergence* or *development.* In other words, Piaget sought to shed new light on the nature of human knowledge by studying how children come to know the world.

His studies began with close observation of his own three children as infants: how they explored new toys, solved simple problems that he arranged for them, and generally came to understand themselves and their world. Later, Piaget studied larger samples of children through what has become known as his **clinical method,** a flexible question-and-answer technique used to discover how children think about problems. Consider the following exchange between Piaget and 6-year-old Van (Piaget, 1926, p. 293):

> Piaget: Why is it dark at night?
> Van: Because we sleep better, and so that it shall be dark in the rooms.
> Piaget: Where does the darkness come from?
> Van: Because the sky becomes grey.
> Piaget: What makes the sky become grey?
> Van: The clouds become dark.
> Piaget: How is that?
> Van: God makes the clouds become dark.

Many contemporary researchers consider the method imprecise because it does not involve asking standardized questions of all children tested, but Piaget (1926) believed that the investigator should have the flexibility to pursue an individual child's line of reasoning to fully understand that child's mind. Using his naturalistic observations of his own children and the clinical method to explore how children understand everything from the rules of games to the concepts of space and time, Piaget formulated his view of the development of intelligence.

What Is Intelligence?

Piaget's definition of intelligence reflects his background in biology: *intelligence is a basic life function that helps an organism adapt to its environment.* You can see adaptation when you watch a toddler figuring out how to work a jack-in-the-box, a school-age child figuring out how to divide treats among friends, or an adult figuring out how to operate a new digital camera. The newborn enters an unfamiliar world with few means of adapting to it other than working senses and reflexes. But Piaget viewed infants as active agents in their own development, learning about the world of people and things by observing, investigating, and experimenting.

Knowledge gained through active exploration takes the form of a scheme (sometimes called *schema* in the singular and *schemata* in the plural). **Schemes** are cognitive structures—organized patterns of action or thought that people construct to interpret their experiences (Piaget, 1952, 1977). For example, the infant's grasping actions and sucking responses are early behavioral schemes, patterns of action used to adapt to different objects. During their second year, children develop symbolic schemes, or concepts. They use internal mental symbols such as images and words to represent or stand for aspects of experience, such as when a young child sees a funny dance and carries away a mental model of how it was done. Older children become able to manipulate symbols in their heads to help them solve problems.

As children develop more sophisticated schemes, or cognitive structures, they become increasingly able to adapt to their environments. Because they gain new schemes as they develop, children of different ages will respond to the same stimuli differently. The infant may get to know a shoe mainly as something to chew, the preschooler may decide to let the shoe symbolize or represent a telephone and put it to her ear, and the school-age child may mentally count its shoelace eyelets.

The grasping scheme. Infants have a range of behavioral schemes that allow them to explore new objects. Each scheme is a general pattern of behavior that can be adjusted to fit specific objects.

How Does Intelligence Develop?

Piaget took an interactionist position on the nature–nurture issue: Children are neither born with innate ideas nor programmed with knowledge by adults. Instead, Piaget viewed humans as active creators of their own intellectual development. As we noted in Chapter 2, Piaget took a position called *constructivism,* maintaining that children "construct reality," or actively create knowledge of the world, from their experiences (Siegler & Ellis, 1996). Their knowledge of the world takes the form of cognitive structures or schemes, which change as children organize and reorganize their existing knowledge and adapt to new experiences.

Piaget believed that all schemes—all forms of understanding—are created through the operation of two inborn intellectual functions, which he called organization and adaptation. These processes operate throughout the life span. Through **organization,** children systematically combine existing schemes into new and more complex ones. Thus, their minds are not cluttered with an endless number of independent facts; they contain instead logically ordered and interrelated actions and ideas. For example, the infant who gazes, reaches, and grasps will organize these simple schemes into the complex structure of visually directed reaching. Complex cognitive structures in older children grow out of reorganizations of more primitive structures.

Adaptation is the process of adjusting to the demands of environment. It occurs through two complementary processes, assimilation and accommodation. Imagine that you are a 2-year-old, that the world is still new, and that you see your first horse. What will you make of it? You likely will try to relate it to something familiar. **Assimilation** is the process by which we interpret new experiences in terms of existing schemes or cognitive structures. Thus, if you already have a scheme that mentally represents your knowledge of dogs, you may label this new beast "doggie." Through assimilation, we deal with our environment in our own terms, sometimes bending the world to squeeze it into our existing categories. Throughout the life span, we rely on our existing cognitive structures to understand new events.

But if you notice that this "doggie" is bigger than most dogs and that it has a mane and an awfully strange "bark," you may be prompted to change your understanding of the world of four-legged animals. **Accommodation** is the process of modifying existing schemes to better fit new experiences. Perhaps you will need to invent a new name for this animal or ask what it is and revise your concept of four-legged animals accordingly.

If we always assimilated new experiences, our understandings would never advance. Piaget believed that all new experiences are greeted with a mix of assimilation and accommodation. Once we have schemes, we apply them to make sense of the world, but we also encounter puzzles that force us to modify our understandings through accommodation. According to Piaget, when new events seriously challenge old schemes, or prove our existing understandings to be inadequate, we experience cognitive conflict. This cognitive disequilibrium then stimulates cognitive growth and the formation of more adequate understandings (Piaget, 1985; see Figure 7.1).

Intelligence, then, develops through the interaction of the individual with the environment. Nature provides the complementary processes of assimilation and accommodation that make adaptation to environments possible. As a result of the interaction of biological maturation and experience, humans progress through four distinct stages of cognitive development:

1. The sensorimotor stage (birth to roughly 2 years)
2. The preoperational stage (roughly 2 to 7 years)
3. The concrete operations stage (roughly 7 to 11 years)
4. The formal operations stage (roughly 11 years and beyond)

These stages represent qualitatively different ways of thinking and occur in an invariant sequence—that is, in the same order in all children. However, depending on their experiences, children may progress through the stages at different rates, with some moving more rapidly or more slowly than

Equilibrium

Current understanding of the world (internal data) is consistent with external data.

Small furry animals with fluffy tails are called cats. They meow and smell nice.

Disequilibrium

Along comes a new piece of information that does not fit with current understanding of the world, leading to disequilibrium—an uncomfortable state of mind that the child seeks to resolve.

That's strange—this small furry creature has a fluffy tail but it doesn't meow and it certainly doesn't smell nice!

Assimilation and Accommodation

This unbalanced (confused) state can be resolved through the processes of organization and adaptation (assimilation and accommodation).

This can't be a cat. Mommy called it a skunk, which must be a different kind of animal.

Equilibrium

These lead to a new way of understanding the world—a new state of equilibrium.

I'll have to remember that skunks and cats are different types of animals.

Figure 7.1 Process of change in Jean Piaget's theory.

others. Thus, the age ranges associated with the stages are only averages. A child's stage of development is determined by his reasoning processes, not his age.

Summing Up

According to Piaget, children progress through four stages of cognitive development, creating more complex schemes for understanding their world. Along with maturation and experience, two innate processes, organization and adaptation, drive children's new understandings. Adaptation involves the complementary processes of assimilating new experiences into existing understandings and accommodating existing understandings to new experiences. ■

The Infant

Piaget's sensorimotor stage, spanning the 2 years of infancy, involves coming to know the world through senses and actions. The dominant cognitive structures are behavioral schemes—patterns of action that evolve as infants begin to coordinate sensory input (seeing and mouthing an object) and motor responses (grasping it). Because infants solve problems through their actions rather than with their minds, their mode of thought is qualitatively different from that of older children.

Substages of the Sensorimotor Stage

The six substages of the sensorimotor stage are outlined in Table 7.1. At the start of the sensorimotor period, infants may not seem highly intelligent, but they are already active explorers of the world around them. Researchers see increasing signs of intelligent behavior as infants pass through the substages, because they are gradually learning about the world and about cause and effect by observing the effects of their actions. They are transformed from reflexive creatures who adapt to their environment using their innate reflexes to reflective ones who can solve simple problems in their heads.

The advances in problem-solving ability captured in the six substages of the sensorimotor period bring many important changes. Consider changes in the quality of infants' play activities. During the first month, young infants react reflex-

Table 7.1 The Substages and Intellectual Accomplishments of the Sensorimotor Period

Substage	Description
1. Reflex activity (birth to 1 month)	Active exercise and refinement of inborn reflexes (e.g., accommodate sucking to fit the shapes of different objects)
2. Primary circular reactions (1–4 months)	Repetition of interesting acts centered on the child's own body (e.g., repeatedly suck a thumb, kick legs, or blow bubbles)
3. Secondary circular reactions (4–8 months)	Repetition of interesting acts on objects (e.g., repeatedly shake a rattle to make an interesting noise or bat a mobile to make it wiggle)
4. Coordination of secondary schemes (8–12 months)	Combination of actions to solve simple problems (e.g., bat aside a barrier to grasp an object, using the scheme as a means to an end); first evidence of intentionality
5. Tertiary circular reactions (12–18 months)	Experimentation to find new ways to solve problems or produce interesting outcomes (e.g., explore bath water by gently patting it then hitting it vigorously and watching the results or stroke, pinch, squeeze, and pat a cat to see how it responds to varied actions)
6. Beginning of thought (18-24 months)	First evidence of insight; solve problems mentally, using symbols to stand for objects and actions, visualize how a stick could be used (e.g., move an out-of-reach toy closer); no longer limited to thinking by doing

ively to internal and external stimulation. In the primary circular reactions substage (1–4 months), they are more interested in their own bodies than in manipulating toys. By the third substage of secondary circular reactions (4–8 months), they derive pleasure from repeatedly performing an action, such as sucking or banging a toy. In the fourth substage (8-12 months), they can combine actions to achieve simple goals. Later, when they reach the substage of tertiary circular reactions (12–18 months), they experiment in varied ways with toys, exploring them thoroughly and learning all about their properties. With the final substage, the beginning of thought (about 18 months), comes the possibility of letting one object represent another so that a cooking pot becomes a hat or a shoe becomes a telephone—a simple form of pretend play made possible by the capacity for symbolic thought. It is also in this stage, according to Piaget, that infants can imitate models no longer present, because they can now create and later recall mental representations of what they have seen.

The Development of Object Permanence

Another important change during the sensorimotor period concerns the infant's understanding of the existence of objects. According to Piaget, newborns lack an understanding of **object permanence** (also called *object concept*). This is the fundamental understanding that objects continue to exist—they are permanent—when they are no longer visible or otherwise detectable to the senses. It probably does not occur to you to wonder whether your coat is still in the closet after you shut the closet door (unless perhaps you have taken a philosophy course). But very young infants, because they rely so heavily on their senses, seem to operate as though objects exist only when they are perceived or acted on. According to Piaget, infants must construct the notion that reality exists apart from their experience of it.

Piaget believed that the concept of object permanence develops gradually over the sensorimotor period. Up through roughly 4 to 8 months, it is out of sight, out of mind; infants will not search for a toy if it is covered with a cloth or screen. By substage 4 (8–12 months), they master that trick but still rely on their perceptions and actions to "know" an object (Piaget, 1954). After his 10-month-old daughter, Jacqueline, had repeatedly retrieved a toy parrot from one hiding place, Piaget put it in a new spot while she watched him. Amazingly, she looked in the original hiding place. She seemed to assume that her behavior determined where the object would appear;

At 5 months, almost everything ends up in Eleanor's mouth. According to Jean Piaget, infants in the sensorimotor stage of development learn a great deal about their world by investigating it with their senses and acting motorically on this information.

© Amy Etra/PhotoEdit

Until an infant masters the concept of object permanence, objects that are outside of his visual sight are "out of mind."

she did not treat the object as if it existed apart from her actions or from its initial location. The surprising tendency of 8- to 12-month-olds to search for an object in the place where they last found it (A) rather than in its new hiding place (B) is called the **A-not-B error.** The likelihood of infants making the A-not-B error increases with lengthier delays between hiding and searching and with the number of trials in which the object is found in spot A (Marcovitch & Zelazo, 1999).

In substage 5, the 1-year-old overcomes the A-not-B error but continues to have trouble with invisible displacements—as when you hide a toy in your hand, move your hand under a pillow, and then remove your hand leaving the toy under the pillow. The infant will search where the object was last seen, seeming confused when it is not in your hand and failing to look under the pillow, where it was deposited. Finally, by 18 months or so, the infant is capable of mentally representing such invisible moves and conceiving of the object in its final location. According to Piaget, the concept of object permanence is fully mastered at this point.

Does research support Piaget? Recent studies suggest that infants may develop at least some understanding of object permanence far earlier than Piaget claimed (Baillargeon, 2002; Luo et al., 2003). For example, Renee Baillargeon and her colleagues have used a method of testing for object concept that does not require reaching for a hidden object, only looking toward where it should be. In one study, infants as young as $2^1/_2$ months seemed surprised (as demonstrated by looking longer) when a toy that had disappeared behind one screen (left side of Figure 7.2) reappeared from behind a second screen (right side of Figure 7.2) *without* appearing in the open space between the two screens (Aguiar & Baillargeon, 1999).

At this young age, however, understanding of occluded objects is still limited. Consider the scenario shown in Figure 7.3. In the high-window condition, a toy is hidden as it moves along a track behind a block that has a window located at its top. There is nothing odd about this condition. In the low-window condition, a toy *should* be visible as it moves along a track behind a block that has a window located at its bottom, but it is not. To someone who understands the properties of object permanence, this should strike them as odd. At $2^1/_2$ months, infants do not show signs that they detect a difference between an object moving along a track under the high- and low-window conditions. But, just 2 weeks later, 3-month-olds look longer at the low-window event compared with the high-window event (Aguiar & Baillargeon, 2002). Thus, by 3 months, infants have gained an understanding that objects have qualities that should permit them to be visible when nothing is obstructing them.

In an unusual study of toddlers' advanced understanding of object permanence, researchers compared healthy 2-year-olds with 2-year-olds with spinal muscular atrophy (SMA), which is characterized by normal IQ but severe muscle problems limiting children's movement (Riviere & Lecuyer, 2003). Based on Piaget's original reaching task, infants watch as a hand picks up a toy and then "visits" three separate cloths, depositing the toy under the second location before moving to the last cloth. Healthy toddlers incorrectly searched under the third cloth for the toy, whereas the SMA toddlers correctly searched under the second cloth. In a second study, researchers made healthy toddlers wait before they were allowed to search, and with this delay, they too responded correctly by searching under the second cloth. What explains this? Healthy toddlers may quickly and impulsively search at the location where an object is likely to be hidden (where the hand was last seen), but when given more time to think about it, they can go beyond their first impulsive response to search successfully. SMA toddlers have this extra time "built in." Because of their muscle problems, SMA toddlers are slower at searching and have less experience with manual searches than other children. They are less likely to make an impulsive reach in the wrong direction because of the time and effort required to reach. This research suggests that success at object permanence tasks may depend on more than a cognitive awareness of the properties of objects: success also could be influenced

Figure 7.2 Test stimuli used by Aguiar and Baillargeon (1999, 2002). The doll moves behind the screen on the left and reappears on the right side of the second screen without appearing in the space between the screens.

SOURCE: Aguiar & Baillargeon (2002). Developments of young infant's reasoning about occluded objects. *Cognitive Psychology, 45,* 267–336. © 2002. Reprinted with permission from Elsevier.

Figure 7.3 There is nothing to be surprised about in the high-window event, but in the low-window event, the doll should (but does not) appear in the middle space as it moves along the track.

SOURCE: Aguiar & Baillargeon (2002). Developments of young infant's reasoning about occluded objects. *Cognitive Psychology, 45,* 267–336. © 2002. Reprinted with permission from Elsevier.

by task conditions such as the time interval between seeing something hidden and being able to search for it.

In general, then, it seems that babies sometimes know a good deal more about object permanence than they reveal through their actions when they are given the kinds of search tasks originally devised by Piaget (Baillargeon, 2002). Such findings, however, are not necessarily inconsistent with Piaget's findings (Haith & Benson, 1998). Indeed, Piaget contended that looking behaviors were developmental precursors to the reaching behaviors that he assessed. He did not believe, however, that looking represented complete understanding of object permanence (Fischer & Bidell, 1991; Haith & Benson, 1998). An analysis of infants' looking behaviors by Carolyn Rovee-Collier (2001) suggests that Piaget was wise to distinguish between infants' looking and reaching. In some situations, looking may developmentally precede reaching for an object, as Piaget suggested. In other situations, however, infants' actions may reveal a more sophisticated understanding of the world than looking would indicate. Regardless of the specific measure researchers use, infants gradually become more skilled at acting on their knowledge by searching in the right spot. They improve their looking and reaching skills between 8 and 12 months, and by the end of the sensorimotor period, they are masters of even very complex hide-and-seek games (Moore & Meltzoff, 1999; Newman, Atkinson, & Braddick, 2001).

The Emergence of Symbols

The crowning achievement of the sensorimotor stage is internalizing behavioral schemes to construct mental symbols that can guide future behavior. Now the toddler can experiment mentally and can therefore show a kind of insight into how to solve a problem. This new **symbolic capacity**—the ability to use images, words, or gestures to represent or stand for objects and experiences—enables more sophisticated problem solving. To illustrate, consider young Lucienne's actions after she watches her father—Piaget—place an interesting chain inside a matchbox (Piaget, 1952, pp. 337–338):

> [To open the box], she only possesses two preceding schemes: turning the box over in order to empty it of its contents, and sliding her fingers into the slit to make the chain come out. It is of course this last procedure that she tries first: she puts her finger inside and gropes to reach the chain, but fails completely. A pause follows during which Lucienne manifests a very curious reaction. . . . She looks at the slit with great attention; then several times in succession, she opens and shuts her mouth, at first slightly, then wider and wider! [Then] . . . Lucienne unhesitatingly puts her finger in the slit, and instead of trying as before to reach the chain, she pulls so as to enlarge the opening. She succeeds and grasps the chain.

Lucienne uses the symbol of opening and closing her mouth to "think" through the problem. In addition to permitting mental problem solving, the symbolic capacity will appear in the language explosion and pretend play so evident in the preschool years.

In all, children's intellectual achievements during the six substages of the sensorimotor period are remarkable. By its end, they have become deliberate thinkers with a symbolic capacity that allows them to solve some problems in their heads, and they have a grasp of object permanence and many other concepts.

Summing Up

According to Piaget, infants progress through six substages of the sensorimotor period by perceiving and acting on the world; they progress from using their reflexes to adapt to their environment to using symbolic or representational thought to solve problems in their heads.

Their symbolic capacity permits full mastery of object permanence, or the understanding that objects continue to exist even when not perceived by the child. ■

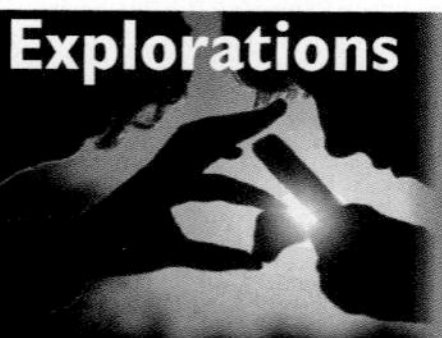

The Child

No one has done more to make us aware of the surprising turns that children's minds can take than Piaget, who described how children enter the preoperational stage of cognitive development in their preschool years and progress to the stage of concrete operations as they enter their elementary school years.

The Preoperational Stage

The preoperational stage of cognitive development extends from roughly 2 to 7 years of age. The symbolic capacity that emerged at the end of the sensorimotor stage runs wild in the preschool years and is the greatest cognitive strength of the preschooler. Imagine the possibilities: The child can now use words to refer to things, people, and events that are not physically present. Instead of being trapped in the immediate present, the child can refer to past and future. Pretend or fantasy play flourishes at this age: blocks can stand for telephones, cardboard boxes for trains. Some children—especially firstborns and only children who do not have ready access to play companions—even invent **imaginary companions** (Bouldin

Explorations

Can There Really Be a Santa Claus?

Many young children around the world believe in Santa Claus, St. Nicholas, the Tooth Fairy, or a similar magical being. At what point, and why, do their beliefs in these figures begin to waiver? According to Piaget's theory, children would begin to seriously question the existence of Santa Claus when they acquire concrete-operational thought. With their ability to reason logically, they may begin to ask questions such as, "How can Santa Claus get around to all those houses in one night?" "How can one sleigh hold all those gifts?" "Why haven't I ever seen a reindeer fly?" and "How does Santa get into houses without chimneys?"

What made sense to the preoperational child no longer adds up to the logical, concrete-operational thinker. With their focus on static endpoints, preschool-age children may not have a problem imagining presents for all the children in the world (or at least, those on the "nice" list) sitting at the North Pole waiting to be delivered and then sitting under decorated trees Christmas morning. But once children understand transformations, they are confronted with the problem of how all those presents get from the North Pole to the individual houses in record time. The logical thinker notes that the gifts under the tree are wrapped in the same paper that Mom has in her closet. Some children question why gifts sport certain brand labels if Santa and his elves spent the year making gifts in their workshop.

© Creasource/PictureQuest

As adults, we can resolve some of these inconsistencies for children to help maintain children's beliefs in Santa Claus. We can, for example, point out that Santa has many helpers and that reindeer native to the North Pole are unlike those ever seen in the wild or in a zoo. Some parents get tough and simply tell their children that nonbelievers will not get any presents. So the level of cognitive development and the surrounding culture play roles in whether or not children believe in Santa Claus and for how long.

& Pratt, 1999; Gleason, Sebanc, & Hartup, 2000). Some are humans, and some are animals; they come with names like Ariel, Nutsy, Little Chop, and Bazooie (Taylor, Cartwright, & Carlson, 1993). Their inventors know their companions are not real. Although parents may worry about such flights of fancy, they are normal. In fact, imaginative uses of the symbolic capacity are associated with advanced cognitive and social development (Singer & Singer, 1990; Taylor, 1999).

Yet the young child's mind is limited compared with that of an older child, and it was the limitations of preoperational thinking that Piaget explored most thoroughly. Although less so than infants, preschoolers are highly influenced by their immediate perceptions. They often respond as if they have been captured by, or cannot go beyond, the most perceptually salient aspects of a situation. This focus on **perceptual salience,** or the most obvious features of an object or situation, means that preschoolers can be fooled by appearances. They have difficulty with tasks that require them to use logic to arrive at the right answer. We can best illustrate this reliance on perceptions and lack of logical thought by considering Piaget's classic tests of conservation (also see the Explorations box on page 178).

Lack of Conservation

One of the many lessons about the physical world that children must master is the concept of **conservation**—the idea that certain properties of an object or substance do not change when its appearance is altered in some superficial way (see Figure 7.4). So, find a 4- or 5-year-old and try Piaget's conservation-of-liquid-quantity task. Pour equal amounts of water into two identical glasses, and get the child to agree that they have the same amount of water. Then, as the child watches, pour the water from one glass into a shorter, wider glass. Now ask whether the two containers—the tall, narrow glass or the shorter, broader one—have the same amount of water to drink or whether one has more water. Children younger than 6 or 7 will usually say that the taller glass has more water than the shorter one. They lack the understanding that the volume of liquid is conserved despite the change in the shape it takes in different containers.

How can young children be so easily fooled by their perceptions? According to Piaget, the preschooler is unable to engage in **decentration**—the ability to focus on two or more dimensions of a problem at once. Consider the conservation task: the child must focus on height and width simultaneously and recognize that the increased width of the short, broad container compensates for its lesser height. Preoperational thinkers engage in **centration**—the tendency to center attention on a single aspect of the problem. They focus on height alone and conclude that the taller glass has more liquid; or, alternatively, they focus on width and conclude that the short, wide glass has more. In this and other ways, preschoolers seem to have one-track minds.

A second contributor to success on conservation tasks is **reversibility**—the process of mentally undoing or reversing an action. Older children often display mastery of reversibility by suggesting that the water be poured back into its original container to prove that it is still the same amount. The young child shows irreversibility of thinking and may insist that the water would overflow the glass if it were poured back. Indeed, one young child tested by a college student shrieked, "Do it again!" as though pouring the water back without causing the glass to overflow were some unparalleled feat of magic.

Finally, preoperational thinkers fail to demonstrate conservation because of limitations in **transformational thought**—the ability to conceptualize transformations, or processes of change from one state to another, as when water is poured from one glass to another (see Figure 7.4). Preoperational thinkers engage in **static thought,** or thought that is fixed on end states rather than the changes that transform one state into another.

Preoperational children do not understand the concept of conservation, then, because they engage in centration, irreversible thought, and static thought. The older child, in the

In this conservation-of-area-task, Rachel first determines that the yellow boards have the same amount of space covered by blocks. But after the blocks are rearranged on one of the boards, she fails to conserve area, indicating that one board now has more open space.

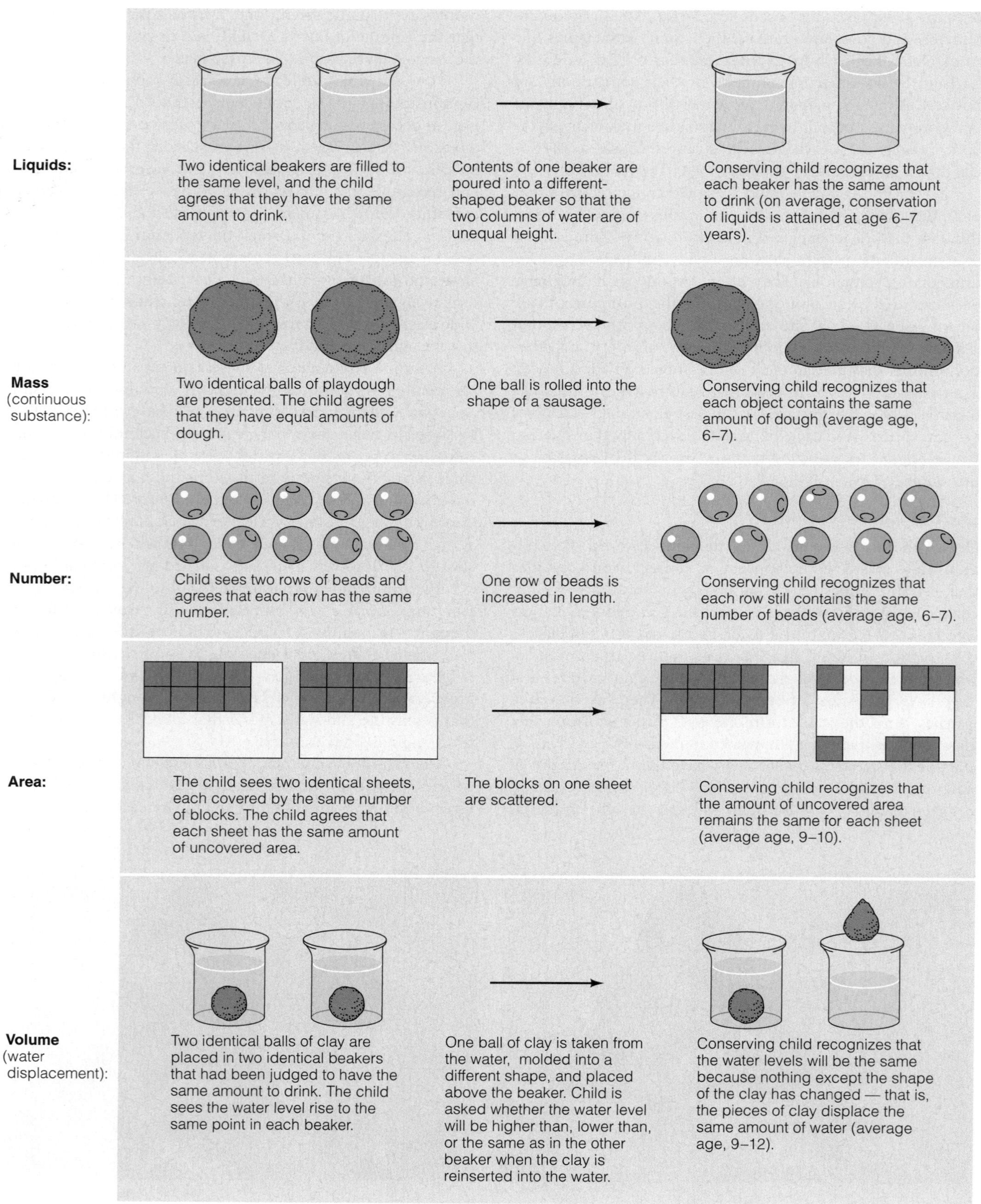

Figure 7.4 Some common tests of the child's ability to conserve.

stage of concrete operations, has mastered decentration, reversibility, and transformational thought. The correct answer to the conservation task is a matter of logic to the older child; there is no longer a need to rely on perception as a guide. Indeed, a 9-year-old tested by another of our students grasped the logic so well and thought the question of which glass had more water so stupid that she asked, "Is this what you do in college?"

Egocentrism

Piaget believed that preoperational thought also involves **egocentrism**—a tendency to view the world solely from one's own perspective and to have difficulty recognizing other points of view. For example, he asked children to choose the drawing that shows what a display of three mountains would look like from a particular vantage point. Young children often chose the view that corresponded to their own position (Piaget & Inhelder, 1956). Similarly, young children often assume that if they know something, other people do, too (Ruffman & Olson, 1989). The same holds for desires: the 4-year-old who wants to go to McDonald's for dinner may say that Mom and Dad want to go to McDonald's, too, even if Mom does not like burgers or chicken nuggets and Dad would rather order Chinese take-out.

Difficulty with Classification

The limitations of relying on perceptions and intuitions are also apparent when preoperational children are asked to classify objects and think about classification systems. When 2- or 3-year-old children are asked to sort objects on the basis of similarities, they make interesting designs or change their sorting criteria from moment to moment. Older preoperational children can group objects systematically on the basis of shape, color, function, or some other dimension of similarity (Inhelder & Piaget, 1964). However, even children ages 4 to 7 have trouble thinking about relations between classes and subclasses or between wholes and parts. Given a set of wooden beads, most of which are brown but a few of which are white, preoperational children do fine when they are asked whether all the beads are wooden and whether there are more brown beads than white beads. That is, they can conceive of the whole class (wooden beads) or of the two subclasses (brown and white beads). However, when the question is, "Which would make the longer necklace, the brown beads or the wooden beads?" they usually say, "The brown beads." They cannot simultaneously relate the whole class to its parts; they lack what Piaget termed the concept of **class inclusion**—the logical understanding that the parts are included within the whole. Notice that the child centers on the most striking perceptual feature of the problem—brown beads are more numerous than white ones—and is again fooled by appearances.

Did Piaget Underestimate the Preschool Child?

Are preschool children really as bound to perceptions and as egocentric as Piaget believed? Many developmentalists believe that Piaget underestimated the competencies of preschool children by giving them very complex tasks to perform (Bjorklund, 1995). Consider a few examples of the strengths uncovered by researchers using simpler tasks.

Rochel Gelman (1972) simplified Piaget's conservation-of-number task (shown in Figure 7.4) and discovered that children as young as 3 have some grasp of the concept that number remains the same even when items are rearranged spatially. She first got children to focus their attention on number by playing a game in which two plates, one holding two toy mice and one with three toy mice, were presented; and the plate with the larger number was always declared the winner. Then Gelman started introducing changes, sometimes adding or subtracting mice but sometimes just bunching up or spreading out the mice. Young children were not fooled by spatial rearrangements; they seemed to understand that number remained the same. However, they showed their limitations when given larger sets of numbers they could not count.

Similarly, by reducing tasks to the bare essentials, several researchers have demonstrated that preschool children are not as egocentric as Piaget claimed. In one study, 3-year-olds were shown a card with a dog on one side and a cat on the other (Flavell et al., 1981). The card was held vertically between the child (who could see the dog) and the experimenter (who could see the cat). When children were asked what the experimenter could see, these 3-year-olds performed flawlessly.

Finally, preschool children seem to have a good deal more understanding of classification systems than Piaget believed. Sandra Waxman and Thomas Hatch (1992) asked 3- and 4-year-olds to teach a puppet all the different names they could think of for certain animals, plants, articles of clothing, and pieces of furniture. The goal was to see whether children knew terms associated with familiar classification hierarchies—for example, if they knew that a rose is a type of flower and is a member of the larger category of plants. Children performed well, largely because a clever method of prompting responses was used. Depending on which term or terms the children forgot to mention (rose, flower, or plant), they were asked about the rose: "Is this a dandelion?" "Is this a tree?" "Is this an animal?" Often, children came up with the correct terms in response (for example, "No, silly, [it's not an animal] it's a plant!"). Even though young children typically fail the tests of class inclusion that Piaget devised, then, they appear to have a fairly good grasp of familiar classification hierarchies.

Studies such as these have raised important questions about the adequacy of Piaget's theory and have led to a more careful consideration of the demands placed on children by cognitive assessment tasks. Simplified tasks that focus youngsters' attention on relevant aspects of the task and do not place heavy demands on their memories or verbal skills tend to reveal that young children develop sound understandings of the physical world earlier than Piaget thought. Yet Piaget was right in arguing that preschool children, although they have several sound intuitions about the world, are more perception-bound and egocentric thinkers than elementary school children are. Preschool children still depend on their perceptions to guide their thinking, and they fail to grasp the logic behind concepts such as conservation. They also have difficulty applying their emerging understanding to complex tasks that involve coordinating two or more dimensions.

The Concrete Operations Stage

About the time children start elementary school, their minds undergo another transformation. Piaget's third stage of cognitive development extends from roughly 7 to 11 years of age. The concrete operations stage involves mastering the logical operations missing in the preoperational stage—becoming able to perform mental actions on objects, such as adding and subtracting Halloween candies, classifying dinosaurs, or arranging objects from largest to smallest. This allows school-age children to think effectively about the objects and events they experience in everyday life. For every limitation of the preoperational child, there is a corresponding strength of the concrete-operational child. These contrasts are summarized in Table 7.2.

Conservation

Given the conservation-of-liquid task (Figure 7.4), the preoperational child centers on either the height or the width of the glasses, ignoring the other dimension. The concrete-operational child can decenter and juggle two dimensions at once. Reversibility allows the child to mentally reverse the pouring process and imagine the water in its original container. Transformational thought allows the child to better understand the process of change involved in pouring the water. Overall, armed with logical operations, the child now knows that there must be the same amount of water after it is poured into a different container; the child has logic, not just appearance, as a guide.

Looking back at the conservation tasks in Figure 7.4, you will notice that some forms of conservation (for example, mass and number) are understood years earlier than others (area or volume). Piaget maintained that operational abilities evolve in a predictable order as simple skills that appear early are reorganized into increasingly complex skills. He used the term **horizontal décalage** for the idea that different cognitive skills related to the same stage of cognitive development emerge at different times.

Seriation and Transitivity

To appreciate the nature and power of logical operations, consider the child's ability to think about relative size. A preoperational child given a set of sticks of different lengths and asked to arrange them from biggest to smallest is likely to struggle, awkwardly comparing one pair of sticks at a time. Concrete-operational children are capable of the logical operation of **seriation,** which enables them to arrange items mentally along a quantifiable dimension such as length or weight. Thus they perform this seriating task quickly and correctly.

Concrete-operational thinkers also master the related concept of **transitivity,** which describes the necessary relations among elements in a series. If, for example, John is taller than Mark, and Mark is taller than Sam, who is taller—John or Sam? It follows logically that John must be taller than Sam, and the concrete operator grasps the transitivity of these size relationships. Lacking the concept of transitivity, the preoperational child will need to rely on perceptions to answer the question; she may insist that John and Sam stand next to each other to determine who is taller. Preoperational children probably have a better understanding of such transitive relations than Piaget gave them credit for (Gelman, 1978; Trabasso, 1975), but they still have difficulty grasping the logical necessity of transitivity (Chapman & Lindenberger, 1988).

Table 7.2 Comparison of Preoperational and Concrete-Operational Thinking

Preoperational Thinkers	Concrete-Operational Thinkers
Fail conservation tasks because they have: • *Irreversible thought*—Cannot mentally undo an action • *Centration*—Center on a single aspect of a problem rather than two or more dimensions at once • *Static thought*—Fail to understand transformations or processes of change from one state to another	Solve conservation tasks because they have: • *Reversibility of thought*—Can mentally reverse or undo an action • *Decentration*—Can focus on two or more dimensions of a problem at once • *Transformational thought*—Can understand the process of change from one state to another
Perceptual salience. Understanding is driven by how things look rather than derived from logical reasoning.	*Logical reasoning.* Children acquire a set of internal operations that can be applied to a variety of problems.
Transductive reasoning. Children combine unrelated facts, often leading them to draw faulty cause–effect conclusions simply because two events occur close together in time or space.	*Deductive reasoning.* Children draw cause–effect conclusions logically, based on factual information presented to them.
Egocentrism. Children have difficulty seeing things from other perspectives and assume that what is in their mind is also what others are thinking.	*Less egocentrism.* Children understand that other people may have thoughts different from their own.
Single classification. Children classify objects by a single dimension at one time.	*Multiple classification.* Children can classify objects by multiple dimensions and can grasp class inclusion.

Other Advances

The school-age child overcomes much of the egocentrism of the preoperational period, becoming increasingly better at recognizing other people's perspectives. Classification abilities improve as the child comes to grasp the concept of class inclusion and can bear in mind that subclasses (brown beads and white beads) are included in a whole class (wooden beads). Mastery of mathematical operations improves the child's ability to solve arithmetic problems and results in an interest in measuring and counting things precisely (and sometimes in fury if companions do not keep accurate score in games). Overall, school-age children appear more logical than preschoolers because they possess a powerful arsenal of "actions in the head."

But surely, if Piaget proposed a fourth stage of cognitive development, there must be some limitations to concrete operations. Indeed, there are. This mode of thought is applied to objects, situations, and events that are real or readily imaginable (thus the term *concrete operations*). As you will see in the next section, concrete operators have difficulty thinking about abstract ideas and unrealistic hypothetical propositions.

Summing Up

In Piaget's preoperational stage (ages 2–7), children make many uses of their symbolic capacity but are limited by their dependence on appearances, lack of logical mental operations, and egocentrism. They fail to grasp the concept of conservation because they engage in centration, irreversible thinking, and static thought, although recent research suggests that preschool children's capacities are greater than Piaget supposed. School-age children enter the stage of concrete operations (ages 7–11) and begin to master conservation tasks through decentration, reversibility, and transformational thought. They can think about relations, grasping seriation and transitivity, and they understand the concept of class inclusion. ■

The Adolescent

Although tremendous advances in cognition occur from infancy to the end of childhood, other transformations of the mind are in store for the adolescent. If teenagers become introspective, question their parents' authority, dream of perfect worlds, and contemplate their futures, cognitive development may help explain why.

The Formal Operations Stage

Piaget set the beginning of the formal operations stage of cognitive development around age 11 or 12 and possibly later. If concrete operations are mental actions on objects (tangible things and events), formal operations are mental actions on ideas. Thus the adolescent who acquires formal operations can mentally juggle and think logically about ideas, which cannot be seen, heard, tasted, smelled, or touched. In other words, formal-operational thought is more hypothetical and abstract than concrete-operational thought; it also involves adopting a more systematic and scientific approach to problem solving (Inhelder & Piaget, 1964).

Hypothetical and Abstract Thinking

If you could have a third eye and put it anywhere on your body, where would you put it, and why? That question was posed to 9-year-old fourth-graders (concrete operators) and to 11- to 12-year-old sixth-graders (the age when the first signs of formal operations often appear). In their drawings, all the 9-year-olds placed the third eye on their foreheads between their existing eyes; many thought the exercise was stupid. The 11- and 12-year-olds were not as bound by the realities of eye location. They could invent ideas contrary to fact (for example, the idea of an eye in a palm) and think logically about the implications of such ideas (see Figure 7.5). Thus, concrete operators deal with realities, whereas formal operators can deal with possibilities, including those that contradict known reality. This may be one reason adolescents come to appreciate absurd humor, as shown in the Explorations box on page 185.

Formal-operational thought is also more abstract than concrete-operational thought. The school-age child may define the justice system in terms of police and judges; the adolescent may define it more abstractly as a branch of government concerned with balancing the rights of different interests in society. Also, the school-age child may be able to think logically about concrete and factually true statements, as in this syllogism: If you drink poison, you will die. Fred drank poison. Therefore, Fred will die. The adolescent can engage in such if–then thinking about contrary-to-fact statements ("If you drink milk, you will die") or symbols (If P, then Q. P, therefore, Q).

Problem Solving

Formal operations also permit systematic and scientific thinking about problems. One of Piaget's famous tests for formal-operational thinking is the pendulum task (see Figure 7.6). The child is given several weights that can be tied to a string to make a pendulum and is told that he may vary the length of the string, the amount of weight attached to it, and the height from which the weight is released to find out which of these factors, alone or in combination, determines how quickly the pendulum makes its arc. How would you go about solving this problem?

The concrete operator is likely to jump right in without much advanced planning, using a trial-and-error approach. That is, the child may try a variety of things but fail to test different hypotheses systematically—for example, the hypothesis that the shorter the string is, the faster the pendulum swings, all other factors remaining constant. Concrete operators are therefore unlikely to solve the problem. They can draw proper conclusions from their observations—for example, from watching as someone else demonstrates what happens if a pendulum with a short string is compared with a pendulum with a long string.

Figure 7.5 Where would you put a third eye? Tanya (age 9) did not show much inventiveness in drawing her "third eye." But Ken (age 11) said of his eye on top of a tuft of hair, "I could revolve the eye to look in all directions." John (also 11) wanted a third eye in his palm: "I could see around corners and see what kind of cookie I'd get out of the cookie jar." Ken and John show early signs of formal-operational thoughts.

What will the formal-operational individual do? In all likelihood, the child will first sit and think, planning an overall strategy for solving the problem. All the possible hypotheses should be generated; after all, the one overlooked may be the right one. Then it must be determined how each hypothesis can be tested. This is a matter of **hypothetical-deductive reasoning,** or reasoning from general ideas to their specific implications. In the pendulum problem, it means starting with a hypothesis and tracing the specific implications of this idea in an if–then fashion: "If the length of the string matters, then I should see a difference when I compare a long string with a short string while holding other factors constant." The trick in hypothesis testing is to vary each factor (for example, the length of the string) while holding all others constant (the weight, the height from which the weight is dropped, and so on). (It is, by the way, the length of the string that matters; the shorter the string, the faster the swing.)

In sum, formal-operational thought involves being able to think systematically about hypothetical ideas and abstract concepts. It also involves mastering the hypothetical-deductive approach that scientists use—forming many hypotheses and systematically testing them through an experimental method.

Progress toward Mastery

Are 11- and 12-year-olds really capable of all these sophisticated mental activities? Anyone who has had dealings with this age group will know that the answer to this question is usually not. Piaget (1970) described the transition from concrete operations to formal operations as taking place gradually

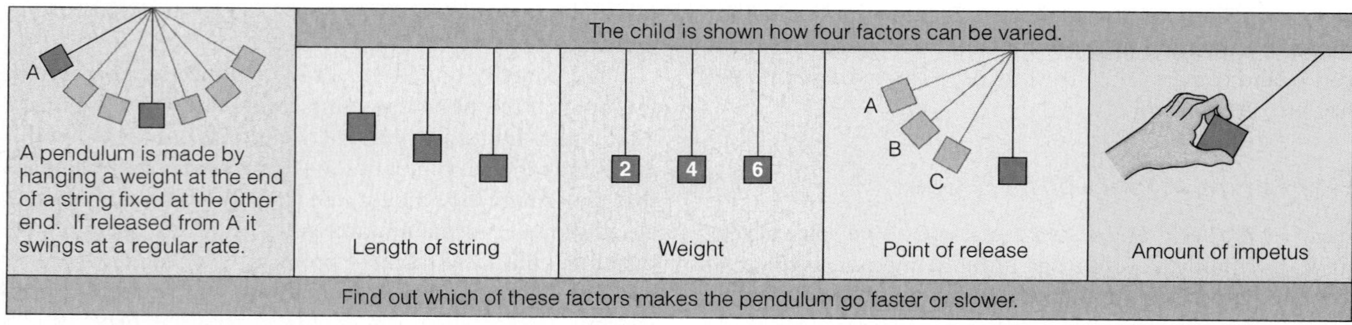

Figure 7.6 The pendulum problem.

Source: Labinowicz (1980).

Explorations

Children's Humor and Cognitive Development

At age 4, John repeatedly tells his mother the following joke: Why did the football coach go to the bank? Answer: To get his quarter back. When his mom asks him why this is funny, he replies that the coach lost his quarter and needed to get it back. He misses the whole idea that the humor of the joke depends on the double meaning of "quarter back." He repeats it only because of the chuckles it elicits from his listeners, who are amused not by the joke but because he is so earnest in his attempt to tell a joke. What really tickles John's funny bone is anything that looks or sounds silly—calling a "shoe" a "floo" or a "poo," for example. Once children realize that everything has a correct name, playing with language by mislabeling things and using taboo words such as "poo-poo" becomes wonderfully amusing (Frankel, 2003; McGhee, 1979).

With the onset of concrete-operational thought and advances in awareness of the nature of language, children come to appreciate jokes and riddles that involve linguistic ambiguities. The "quarter back" joke boils down to a classification task. School-age children who have mastered the concept of class inclusion can keep the class and subclasses in mind at once and move mentally between the two meanings of "quarter back." Appreciation of such puns is high among second-graders (7- to 8-year-olds) and continues to grow until fourth or fifth grade (Frankel, 2003; McGhee & Chapman, 1980). And the better children are at solving riddles, the better they tend to be at reading and other language tasks (Ely, 1997).

As their command of language strengthens, children also become more able to understand sarcasm, irony, and other discrepancies between what is said and what is meant, such as when a teacher says to a noisy 8-year-old, "My, but you're quiet today" (Capelli, Nakagawa, & Madden, 1990; Creusere, 1999). The more they understand ironic statements, the more they appreciate the humor in them (Dews et al., 1996). Irony not only conveys humor, but it may also allow speakers to convey serious points with less offense to their listeners (Creusere, 1999). You are more likely to hear an adolescent than a younger child "soften" a criticism with an ironic comment ("Well, aren't you in a pleasant mood today" to a grumpy sibling).

Children's tastes in humor change again when they enter the stage of formal operations around age 11 or 12. Simple riddles and puns are no longer cognitively challenging enough, it seems, and are likely to elicit loud groans (McGhee, 1979). Adolescents appreciate jokes that involve an absurd or contrary-to-fact premise and a punch line that is logical if the absurd premise is accepted. The humor in "How do you fit six elephants into a Volkswagen?" depends on appreciating that "three in the front and three in the back" is a perfectly logical answer only if you accept the hypothetical premise that multiple elephants could fit into a small car. Reality-oriented school-age children may simply consider this joke stupid; after all, elephants cannot fit into cars. Clearly, then, children cannot appreciate certain forms of humor until they have the required cognitive abilities. Research on children's humor suggests that children and adolescents are most attracted to jokes that challenge them intellectually by requiring them to use the cognitive skills they are just beginning to master (McGhee, 1979).

over years. Many researchers have found it useful to distinguish between early and late formal operations. For example, 11- to 13-year-olds just entering the formal operations stage are able to consider simple hypothetical propositions such as the three-eye problem. But most are not yet able to devise an overall game plan for solving a problem or to systematically generate and test hypotheses. These achievements are more likely later in adolescence.

Consider the findings of Suzanne Martorano (1977), who gave 80 girls in grades 6, 8, 10, and 12 a battery of 10 Piagetian tasks. Among them were the pendulum problem; a task requiring students to identify all the possible combinations of chemicals that could produce a particular chemical reaction; and analyzing how the behavior of a balance beam is affected by the heaviness of weights on the beam and their distances from the fulcrum, or center. The 6th- and 8th-graders (ages

© Charles Gupton/CORBIS

Adolescents are more likely than children to benefit from some types of science instruction because formal-operational thought opens the door for reasoning about abstract and hypothetical material.

11–12 and 13–14) accomplished only 2 or 3 of the 10 tasks on the average; the 10th- and 12th-graders (ages 15–16 and 17–18) accomplished an average of 5 or 6. Similarly, 10th- and 11th-graders (ages 16–17) demonstrate more advanced scientific reasoning than 7th- and 8th-graders (ages 13–14) when asked to consider evidence and evaluate theories regarding religion and social class (Klaczynski, 2000). Still, the responses of older adolescents contain biases similar to those shown by younger adolescents. Both age groups more readily accept evidence consistent with their preexisting beliefs than evidence inconsistent with these beliefs (Kuhn, 1993; Klaczynski & Gordon, 1996a, 1996b). Thus, although reasoning skills improve over the adolescent years, adolescents do not consistently show formal operations and logical scientific reasoning skills on all tasks (Klaczynski & Narasimham, 1998).

Contrary to Piaget's claim that intuitive reasoning is replaced by scientific reasoning as children age, the two forms of reasoning—intuitive and scientific—seem to coexist in older thinkers (Klaczynski, 2000, 2001). Being able to shift between intuitive and scientific reasoning provides flexibility in problem-solving situations as long as the thinker can effectively select the appropriate strategy. However, like children (and adults), adolescents often seem to adopt an intuitive strategy, leading them to conclusions inconsistent with scientific judgment (Klaczynski, 2001). With age, however, adolescents are increasingly able to **decontextualize,** or separate prior knowledge and beliefs from the demands of the task at hand (Klaczynski, 2000; Stanovich & West, 1997). For example, someone who believes that males are better at math than females may find it difficult to accept new evidence that girls attain higher classroom math grades than boys if their prior beliefs (their intuitions) do not allow them to scientifically process the new information. Decontextualizing increases the likelihood of using reasoning to analyze a problem logically rather than relying on intuition or faulty existing knowledge.

There is some evidence that today's teens (ages 13–15) are better able than earlier cohorts to solve formal-operational tasks. For example, 66% of teens tested in 1996 showed formal-operational thought on a probability test, whereas 49% of teens tested in 1967 showed such skills (Flieller, 1999). Why might formal-operational skills improve over time? Changes in school curricula are the likely explanation. The achievement of formal-operational thinking depends on specific experiences, such as exposure to math and science education (Laurendeau-Bendavid, 1977). Research with Western and African populations shows that both age and education level influence performance on formal-operational tasks; college and university students outperform adults with no advanced education, who in turn outperform adolescents (Mwamwenda & Mwamwenda, 1989; Mwamwenda, 1999).

Progress toward the mastery of formal operations is slow, at least as measured by Piaget's scientific tasks. These findings have major implications for secondary-school teachers, who are often trying to teach abstract material to students with a range of thinking patterns. Teachers may need to give concrete thinkers extra assistance by using specific examples and demonstrations to help clarify general principles.

Implications of Formal Thought

Formal-operational thought contributes to other changes in adolescence—some good, some not so good. First, the good news: As you will see in upcoming chapters, formal-operational thought may prepare the individual to gain a sense of identity, think in more complex ways about moral issues, and understand other people. Advances in cognitive development help lay the groundwork for advances in many other areas of development.

Now, the bad news: Formal operations may also be related to some of the more painful aspects of the adolescent experience. Children tend to accept the world as it is and to heed the words of authority figures. The adolescent armed with formal operations can think more independently, imagine alternatives to present realities, and raise questions about everything from why parents set certain rules to why there is injustice in the world. Questioning can lead to confusion and sometimes to rebellion against ideas that do not seem logical enough. Some adolescents become idealists, inventing perfect worlds and envisioning logical solutions to problems they detect in the imperfect world around them, sometimes losing sight of practical considerations and real barriers to social change. Just as infants flaunt the new schemes they develop, adolescents may go overboard with their new cognitive skills, irritate their parents, and become frustrated when the world does not respond to their flawless logic.

Some years ago, David Elkind (1967) proposed that formal-operational thought also leads to **adolescent egocentrism**—difficulty differentiating one's own thoughts and feelings from those of other people. The young child's egocentrism is rooted in ignorance that different people have different perspectives, but the adolescent's reflects an enhanced ability to reflect about one's own and others' thoughts. Elkind identified two types of adolescent egocentrism: the imaginary audience and the personal fable.

The **imaginary audience** phenomenon involves confusing your own thoughts with those of a hypothesized audience for your behavior. Thus, the teenage girl who ends up with pizza sauce on the front of her shirt at a party may feel extremely self-conscious: "They're all thinking what a slob I am! I wish I could crawl into a hole." She assumes that everyone in the room is as preoccupied with the blunder as she is. Or a teenage boy may spend hours in front of the mirror getting ready for a date then may be so concerned with how he imagines his date is reacting to him that he hardly notices her: "Why did I say that? She looks bored. Did she notice my pimple?" (She, of course, is equally preoccupied with how she is playing to her audience. No wonder teenagers are often awkward and painfully aware of their every slip on first dates.)

The second form of adolescent egocentrism is the **personal fable**—a tendency to think that you and your thoughts and feelings are unique (Elkind, 1967). If the imaginary audience is a product of the inability to differentiate between self and other, the personal fable is a product of differentiating too much. Thus, the adolescent in love for the first time imagines that no one in the history of the human race has ever felt such heights of emotion. When the relationship breaks up, no one—least of all a parent—could possibly understand the crushing agony. The personal fable may also lead adolescents to feel that rules that apply to others do not apply to them. Thus, they will not be hurt if they speed down the highway without wearing a seat belt or drive under the influence of alcohol. And they will not become pregnant if they engage in sex without contraception, so they do not need to bother with contraception. As it turns out, high scores on measures of adolescent egocentrism are associated with behaving in risky ways (Greene et al., 1996; Holmbeck et al., 1994).

☾ A teenage girl may feel that everyone is as preoccupied with her appearance as she is, a form of adolescent egocentrism known as the imaginary audience phenomenon.

Elkind hypothesized that the imaginary audience and personal fable phenomena should increase when formal operations are first being acquired and then decrease as adolescents get older, gain fuller control of formal operations, and assume adult roles that require fuller consideration of others' perspectives. Indeed, both the self-consciousness associated with the imaginary audience and the sense of specialness associated with the personal fable are most evident in early adolescence and decline by late high school (Elkind & Bowen, 1979; Enright, Lapsley, & Shukla, 1979). Adolescent egocentrism may persist, however, when adolescents have insecure relationships with their parents that may make them self-conscious and may make them appear to lack self-confidence even as older adolescents (Ryan & Kuczkowski, 1994).

Contrary to what Piaget and Elkind hypothesized, however, researchers have been unable to link the onset of the formal operations stage to the rise of adolescent egocentrism (Gray & Hudson, 1984; O'Connor & Nikolic, 1990). It seems that adolescent egocentrism may arise when adolescents acquire advanced social perspective-taking abilities and contemplate how other people might perceive them and react to their behavior (Lapsley et al., 1986; Vartanian & Powlishta, 1996).

Furthermore, recent research by Joanna Bell and Rachel Bromnick (2003) suggests that adolescents are preoccupied with how they present themselves in public not because of an imaginary audience but because of a real audience. That is, research indicates that adolescents are aware that there are real consequences to how they present themselves. Their popularity and peer approval, as well as their self-confidence and self-esteem, are often influenced by how others (the real audience) perceive them. Adults, too, are aware that their actions and appearance are often judged by others, but although these adult concerns are usually assumed to be realistic, similar concerns by adolescents are sometimes viewed, perhaps unfairly, as trivial (Bell & Bromnick, 2003).

Summing Up

Adolescents often show the first signs of formal operations at 11 or 12 and gradually master the hypothetical-deductive reasoning skills required to solve scientific problems. Cognitive changes result in other developmental advances and may contribute to confusion, rebellion, idealism, and adolescent egocentrism (the imaginary audience and the personal fable). ■

The Adult

Do adults think differently than adolescents do? Does cognition change over the adult years? Until fairly recently, developmentalists have not asked such questions. Piaget indicated that the highest stage of cognitive development, formal operations, was fully mastered by most people between age 15 and age 18. Why bother studying cognitive development in adulthood? As it turns out, it has been worth the effort. Research has revealed limitations in adult performance that must be explained, and it suggests that at least some adults progress beyond formal operations to more advanced forms of thought (Jacobs & Klaczynski, 2002).

Limitations in Adult Cognitive Performance

If many high school students are shaky in their command of formal operations, do most of them gain fuller mastery after the high school years? Gains are indeed made between adolescence and adulthood (Blackburn & Papalia, 1992). However, only about half of all college students show firm and consistent mastery of formal operations on Piaget's scientific reasoning tasks (Neimark, 1975). Similarly, sizable percentages of American adults do not solve scientific problems at the formal level, and there are some societies in which no adults solve formal-operational problems (Neimark, 1975).

Why do more adults not do well on Piagetian tasks? An average level of performance on standardized intelligence tests seems to be necessary for a person to achieve formal-operational thought (Inhelder, 1966). What seems more important than basic intelligence, however, is formal education (Neimark, 1979). In cultures in which virtually no one solves Piaget's problems, people do not receive advanced schooling. If achieving formal-operational thought requires education, Piaget's theory may be culturally biased, and his stages may not be as universal as he believed.

But neither lack of intelligence nor lack of formal education is a problem for most college students. Instead, they have difficulty with tests of formal operations when they lack expertise in a domain of knowledge. Piaget (1972) suggested that adults are likely to use formal operations in a field of expertise but to use concrete operations in less familiar areas. This is precisely what seems to happen. For example, Richard De Lisi and Joanne Staudt (1980) gave three kinds of formal-operational tasks—the pendulum problem, a political problem, and a literary criticism problem—to college students majoring in physics, political science, and English. As Figure 7.7 illustrates, each group of students did well on the problem relevant to that group's field of expertise. On problems outside their fields, however, about half the students failed. Possibly, then, many adolescents and adults fail to use formal reasoning on Piaget's scientific problems simply because these problems are unfamiliar to them and they lack expertise.

As Kurt Fischer (1980; Fischer, Kenny, & Pipp, 1990) maintains, each person may have an optimal level of cognitive performance that will show itself in familiar and well-trained content domains. However, performance is likely to be highly inconsistent across content areas unless the person has had a chance to build knowledge and skills in all these domains. More often, adults may use and strengthen formal modes of thinking only in their areas of expertise. By adopting a contextual perspective on cognitive development, you can appreciate that the individual's experience and the nature of the tasks she is asked to perform influence cognitive performance across the life span (Salthouse, 1990).

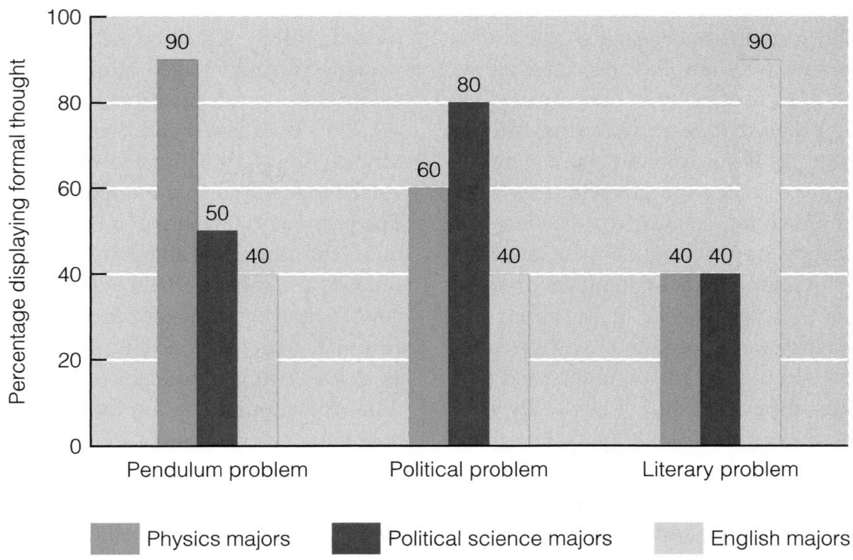

Figure 7.7 Expertise and formal operations. College students show the greatest command of formal-operational thought in the subject area most related to their major.

SOURCE: Data from De Lisi & Staudt (1980).

Growth beyond Formal Operations?

Some researchers have been asking why adults sometimes perform so poorly on cognitive tasks; others have been asking why they sometimes perform so well. Take Piaget. Was his ability to generate a complex theory of development no more than the application of formal-operational thought? Or are there advances in cognitive development during adulthood that would better explain the remarkable cognitive achievements of some adults?

Several intriguing ideas have been proposed about stages of cognitive development that may lie beyond formal operations—that is, about **postformal thought** (Commons, Richards, & Armon, 1984; Labouvie-Vief, 1992; Sinnott, 1996; Yan & Arlin, 1995). As noted earlier, adolescents who have attained formal operations sometimes get carried away with their new powers of logical thinking. They insist that there is a logically correct answer for every question—that if you simply apply logic, you will arrive at the right answer, at some absolute truth. Perhaps formal-operational adolescents need a more complex way of thinking to adapt to the kinds of problems adults face every day—problems in which there are many ways to look at an issue, no one right answer, and yet a need to make a decision (Sinnott, 1996).

How might thought be qualitatively different in adulthood than it is in adolescence? What might a truly adult stage of cognitive development be like? Several researchers have suggested that adults are more likely than adolescents to see knowledge as relative rather than absolute (Kitchener et al., 1989; Labouvie-Vief, 1992). **Relativistic thinking,** in this sense, means understanding that knowledge depends on the subjective perspective of the knower. An absolutist assumes that truth lies in the nature of reality and that there is only one truth; a relativist assumes that his starting assumptions influence the "truth" discovered and that a problem can be viewed in multiple ways.

Consider this logic problem: "A grows 1 cm per month. B grows 2 cm per month. Who is taller?" (Yan & Arlin, 1995, p. 230). The absolutist might say, "B," based on the information given, but the relativist would be more likely to say, "It depends." It depends on how tall A and B were to begin with and on how much time passes before their heights are measured. The relativistic thinker will recognize that the problem is ill defined and that further information is needed, and he will be able to think flexibly about what the answer would be if he made certain assumptions rather than others.

Or consider this problem, given to preadolescents, adolescents, and adults by Gisela Labouvie-Vief and her colleagues (1983, p. 5):

> John is known to be a heavy drinker, especially when he goes to parties. Mary, John's wife, warns him that if he gets drunk one more time she will leave him and take the children. Tonight John is out late at an office party. John comes home drunk.

Does Mary leave John? Most preadolescents and many adolescents quickly and confidently said, "Yes." They did not question the assumption that Mary would stand by her word; they simply applied logic to the information they were given. Adults were more likely to realize that different starting assumptions were possible and that the answer depended on which assumptions were chosen. One woman, for example, noted that if Mary had stayed with John for years, she would be unlikely to leave him now. This same woman said, "There was no right or wrong answer. You could get logically to both answers" (p. 12). Postformal thinkers seem able to devise more than one logical solution to a problem (Sinnott, 1996).

In a fascinating study of cognitive growth over the college years, William Perry (1970) found that beginning college students often assumed that there were absolute, objective truths to be found by consulting their textbooks or their professors. They looked to what they believed were authoritative sources for *the* answer to a question, as if all problems have a single, correct answer. As their college careers progressed, they often became frustrated in their search for absolute truths. They saw that many questions seemed to have several answers, depending on the perspective of the respondent. Taking the extremely relativistic view that any opinion was as good as any other, several of these students said they were not sure how they could ever decide what to believe. Eventually, many understood that some opinions can be better supported than others; they were then able to commit themselves to specific positions, fully aware that they were choosing among relative perspectives.

Between adolescence and adulthood, then, many people start as absolutists, become relativists, and finally make commitments to positions despite their more sophisticated awareness of the nature and limits of knowledge (Sinnott, 1996). Not surprisingly, students at the absolute level of thinking use fewer thinking styles, sticking mainly with traditional modes of thinking (Zhang, 2002). Students who are relativistic thinkers use a greater variety of thinking styles, including ones that promote creativity and greater cognitive complexity.

It has also been suggested that advanced thinkers thrive on detecting paradoxes and inconsistencies among ideas and trying to reconcile them—only to repeatedly challenge and change their understandings (Basseches, 1984; Riegel, 1973). Advanced thinkers also seem to be able to think systematically and logically about abstract systems of knowledge (Fischer, Kenny, & Pipp, 1990; Richards & Commons, 1990). Where the concrete-operational thinker performs mental actions (such as addition) on concrete objects and the formal-operational thinker performs mental actions on ideas, the postformal thinker seems able to manipulate systems of ideas—for example, by comparing and contrasting psychological theories or analyzing abstract similarities and differences between mathematical operations such as addition and division.

It is not yet clear whether relativistic thinking or other forms of advanced thinking might qualify as a new, postformal stage of cognitive development. It is clear, however, that these types of thinking are shown by only a minority of adults, particularly those who have received advanced education, who are open to rethinking issues, and who live in a culture that nourishes their efforts to entertain new ideas (Irwin, 1991; Sinnott, 1996). It is also clear that cognitive growth does not end in adolescence. Yet age does not tell us much about how adults think; life circumstances and the demands placed on people to think at work, in the home, and in the community often tell us more.

Aging and Cognitive Skills

What becomes of cognitive capacities in later adulthood? Some mental abilities decline as the average person ages, and it appears that older adults often have trouble solving Piagetian tests of formal-operational thinking (Blackburn & Papalia, 1992). Indeed, elderly adults sometimes perform poorly relative to young and middle-aged adults even on concrete-operational tasks assessing conservation and classification skills.

This does not mean that elderly adults regress to immature modes of thought. For one thing, these studies have involved cross-sectional comparisons of different age groups. The poorer performance of older groups does not necessarily mean that cognitive abilities are lost as people age. It could be caused by a cohort effect, because the average older adult today has had less formal schooling than the average younger adult has had. Older adults attending college tend to perform as well as younger college students on tests of formal operations (Blackburn, 1984; Hooper, Hooper, & Colbert, 1985). Moreover, brief training can quickly improve the performance of older adults long out of school, which suggests that the necessary cognitive abilities are there but merely need to be reactivated (Blackburn & Papalia, 1992).

Questions have also been raised about the relevance of the skills assessed in Piagetian tasks to the lives of older adults (Labouvie-Vief, 1985). Not only are these problems unfamiliar to many older adults, but they also resemble the intellectual challenges that children confront in school, not those that

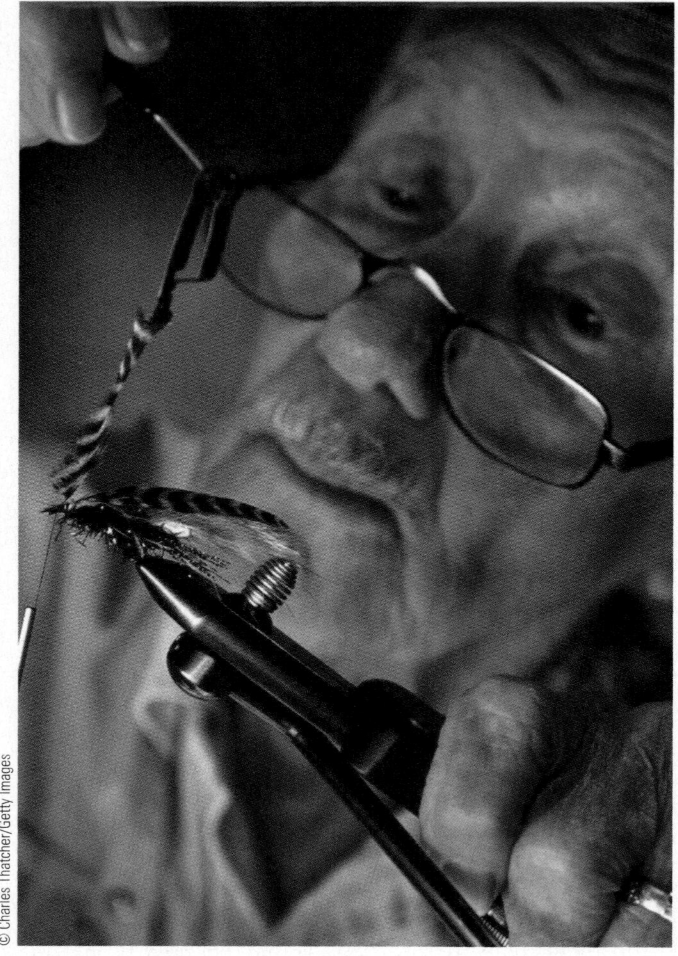

Adults think efficiently once they gain expertise on the job.

most adults encounter in everyday contexts. Thus, older people may not be motivated to solve them. Also, older adults may rely on modes of cognition that have proved useful to them in daily life but that make them look cognitively deficient in the laboratory (Salthouse, 1990).

Consider this example: Kathy Pearce and Nancy Denney (1984) found that elderly adults, like young children but unlike other age groups, often group two objects on the basis of some functional relationship between them (for example, putting a pipe and matches together because matches are used to light pipes) rather than on the basis of similarity (for example, putting a pipe and a cigar together because they are both ways of smoking tobacco). In school and in some job situations, Pearce and Denney suggest, people are asked to group objects on the basis of similarity, but in everyday life it may make more sense to associate objects commonly used together.

Such findings suggest that what appear to be deficits in older people may merely be differences in style. Similar stylistic differences in classification skills have been observed cross-culturally and can, if researchers are not careful, lead to the incorrect conclusion that uneducated adults from non-Western cultures lack basic cognitive skills. A case in point: Kpelle adults in Africa, when asked to sort foods, clothing, tools, and cooking utensils into groups, sorted them into pairs based on functional relationships. "When an exasperated experimenter finally asked, 'How would a fool do it?' he was given sorts of the type that were initially expected—four neat piles with foods in one, tools in another, and so on" (Glick, 1975, p. 636).

So, today's older adults appear not to perform concrete and formal-operational tasks as well as their younger contemporaries do. Planners of adult education for senior citizens might bear in mind that some (although by no means all) of their students may benefit from more concrete forms of instruction. However, these differences may be related to factors other than age, such as education and motivation; an age-related decline in operational abilities has not been firmly established. Most importantly, older adults who perform poorly on unfamiliar problems in laboratory situations often perform far more capably on the sorts of problems that they encounter in everyday contexts (Cornelius & Caspi, 1987; Salthouse, 1990).

Summing Up

Adults are most likely to display formal-operational skills in their areas of expertise. Some adults, especially well-educated ones, may advance to postformal modes of thought such as relativistic thinking. Although aging adults often perform less well than younger adults on Piagetian tasks, factors other than biological aging may explain this. ■

Piaget in Perspective

Now that you have examined Piaget's theory of cognitive development, it is time to evaluate it. We start by giving credit where credit is due, then we consider challenges to Piaget's version of things.

Piaget's Contributions

Piaget is a giant in the field of human development. As one scholar quoted by Harry Beilin (1992) put it, "assessing the impact of Piaget on developmental psychology is like assessing the impact of Shakespeare on English literature or Aristotle on philosophy—impossible" (p. 191). It is hard to imagine that researchers would know even a fraction of what they know about intellectual development without his groundbreaking work.

One sign of a good theory is that it stimulates research. Piaget asked fundamentally important questions about how humans come to know the world and showed that we can answer them "by paying attention to the small details of the daily lives of our children" (Gopnik, 1996, p. 225). His cognitive developmental perspective has been applied to almost every aspect of human development, and the important questions he raised continue to guide the study of cognitive development.

We can credit Piaget with some lasting insights (Flavell, 1996). He showed us that infants are active in their own development—that from the start they seek to master problems and to understand the incomprehensible by using the processes of assimilation and accommodation to deal with cognitive disequilibrium. He taught us that young people think differently than older people do—and often in ways we never would have suspected. The reasoning of preschoolers, for example, often defies adult logic, but it makes sense in light of Piaget's insights about their egocentrism and reliance on the perceptual salience of situations. School-age children have the logical thought processes that allow them to excel at many tasks, but they draw a blank when presented with hypothetical or abstract problems. And adolescents are impressive with their scientific reasoning skills and their ability to wrestle with abstract problems, but they may think so much about events that they get tangled with new forms of egocentrism.

Finally, Piaget was largely right in his basic description of cognitive development. The sequence he proposed—sensorimotor to preoperational to concrete operations to formal operations—seems to describe the course and content of intellectual development for children and adolescents from the hundreds of cultures and subcultures that have been studied (Flavell, Miller, & Miller, 1993). Although cultural factors influence the rate of cognitive growth, the direction of development is always from sensorimotor thinking to preoperational thinking to concrete operations to, for many, formal operations (or even postformal operations).

Challenges to Piaget

Partly because Piaget's theory has been so enormously influential, it has had more than its share of criticism (Lourenco & Machado, 1996). We focus on five major criticisms:

1. *Underestimating young minds.* Piaget seems to have underestimated the cognitive abilities of infants and young children, although he emphasized that he was more interested in understanding the sequences of changes than the specific ages at which they occur (Lourenco & Machado, 1996). When researchers use more familiar problems than Piaget's and reduce

tasks to their essentials, hidden competencies of infants and young children are sometimes revealed.

2. *Failing to distinguish between competence and performance.* Piaget sought to identify underlying cognitive competencies that guide performance on cognitive tasks. But there is an important difference between understanding a concept and passing a test designed to measure it. The age ranges Piaget proposed for some stages may have been off target partly because he tended to ignore the many factors besides competence that can influence task performance—everything from the individual's motivation, verbal abilities, and memory capacity to the nature, complexity, and familiarity of the task used to assess mastery. Piaget may have been too quick to assume that children who failed one of his tests lacked competence; they may only have failed to demonstrate their competence in a particular situation.

Perhaps more importantly, Piaget may have overemphasized the idea that knowledge is an all-or-nothing concept (Schwitzgebel, 1999). Instead of having or not having a particular competence, children probably gain competence gradually and experience long periods between understanding and not understanding. Many of the seemingly contradictory results of studies using Piagetian tasks can be accounted for with this idea of gradual change in understanding. For instance, Piaget argued that infants do not show understanding of object permanence until 9 months, but other research indicates that at least some understanding of object permanence is present at 4 months (Schwitzgebel, 1999). If researchers accept that conceptual change is gradual, then they can stop debating whether competence is present or not present at a particular age.

3. *Wrongly claiming that broad stages of development exist.* According to Piaget, each new stage of cognitive development is a coherent mode of thinking applied across a range of problems. Yet individuals are often inconsistent in their performance on different tasks that presumably measure the abilities defining a given stage. Researchers increasingly are arguing that cognitive development is domain specific—that is, it is a matter of building skills in particular content areas—and that growth in one domain may proceed much faster than growth in another (Fischer, Kenny, & Pipp, 1990).

4. *Failing to adequately explain development.* Several critics suggest that Piaget did a better job of describing development than of explaining how it comes about (Bruner, 1997). To be sure, Piaget wrote extensively about his interactionist position on the nature–nurture issue and did as much as any developmental theorist to tackle the question of how development comes about. Presumably, humans are always assimilating new experiences in ways that their level of maturation allows, accommodating their thinking to those experiences, and reorganizing their cognitive structures into increasingly complex modes of thought. Yet this explanation is vague. Researchers need to know far more about how specific maturational changes in the brain and specific kinds of experiences contribute to important cognitive advances.

5. *Giving limited attention to social influences on cognitive development.* Some critics say Piaget paid too little attention to how children's minds develop through their social interactions with more competent individuals and how they develop differently in different cultures. Piaget's child often resembles an isolated scientist exploring the world alone, but children develop their minds through interactions with parents, teachers, peers, and siblings. True, Piaget had interesting ideas about the role of peers in helping children overcome their egocentrism and adopt other perspectives (see Chapter 13 on moral development). And some scholars believe that this criticism is an unfair simplification of Piaget's position on the social nature of development (Matusov & Hayes, 2000). Still, as you will see shortly, the significance of social interaction and culture for cognitive development is the basis of the perspective on cognitive development offered by one of Piaget's early critics, Lev Vygotsky.

Summing Up

Piaget's theory of cognitive development might have been stronger if he had designed tasks that could better reveal the competencies of infants and young children, if he had explored the many factors besides underlying competence that influence performance, if he had been able to provide more convincing evidence that his stages are coherent, if he had been more specific about why development proceeds as it does, and if he had more fully considered social and cultural influences on the development of thought. It may be unfair, however, to demand of an innovator who accomplished so much that he achieve everything. ■

Vygotsky's Sociocultural Perspective

You can gain additional insight into Piaget's view of cognitive development by considering the quite different sociocultural perspective of Lev Vygotsky (1962, 1978; see also Rowe & Wertsch, 2004). This Russian psychologist was born in 1896, the same year as Piaget, and was an active scholar in the 1920s and 1930s when Piaget was formulating his theory. For many years, Vygotsky's work was banned for political reasons in the Soviet Union, and North American scholars lacked English translations of his work, which limited consideration of Vygotsky's ideas until recent decades. In addition, Vygotsky died of tuberculosis at age 38 before his theory was fully developed. However, his main theme is clear: cognitive growth occurs in a sociocultural context and evolves out of the child's social interactions.

Culture and Thought

Culture and society play a pivotal role in Vygotsky's theory. Indeed, intelligence in the Vygotskian model is held by the group, not the individual, and is closely tied to the language system and tools the group has developed over time (Case, 1998). Culture and social experiences affect how we think, not just what we think.

© Sidney Bahrt/Photo Researchers, Inc.

According to Lev Vygotsky's theory, cognitive development is shaped by the culture in which children live and the kinds of problem-solving strategies that adults and other knowledgeable guides pass on to them.

Consider some research by Vygotsky's colleague, Alexander Luria, who tested groups of 9- to 12-year-old children growing up in different social environments. Children were given target words and asked to name the first thing that came to mind when they heard each word. Luria found that children growing up in a remote rural village with limited social experiences gave remarkably similar responses, whereas children growing up in a large city gave more distinctly individual answers. Vygotsky and Luria believed that this difference reflected the city children's broader exposure to various aspects of culture. On their own, the rural children were unable to develop certain types of knowledge. Knowledge, then, depends on social experiences.

Vygotsky would not be surprised to learn that formal-operational thought is rarely used in some cultures; he expected cognitive development to vary from society to society depending on the mental tools the culture values and makes available. How do children acquire their society's mental tools? They acquire them by interacting with parents and other more experienced members of the culture and by adopting their language and knowledge (Frawley, 1997).

Social Interaction and Thought

Consider this scenario: Annie, a 4-year-old, receives a jigsaw puzzle, her first, for her birthday. She attempts to work the puzzle but gets nowhere until her father sits down beside her and gives her some tips. He suggests that it would be a good idea to put the corners together first. He points to the pink area at the edge of one corner piece and says, "Let's look for another pink piece." When Annie seems frustrated, he places two interlocking pieces near each other so that she will notice them. And when she succeeds, he offers words of encouragement. As Annie gets the hang of it, he steps back and lets her work more independently. This kind of social interaction, said Vygotsky, fosters cognitive growth.

How? First, Annie and her father are operating in what Vygotsky called the **zone of proximal development**—the gap between what a learner can accomplish independently and what she can accomplish with the guidance and encouragement of a more skilled partner. Skills within the zone are ripe for development and are the skills at which instruction should be aimed. Skills outside the zone are either well mastered already or still too difficult. In this example, Annie obviously becomes a more competent puzzle-solver with her father's help than without it. More importantly, she will internalize the problem-solving techniques that she discovered in collaboration with her father, working together in her zone of proximal development, and will use them on her own, rising to a new level of independent mastery. What began as a social process involving two people becomes a cognitive process within one.

An important implication of the zone of proximal development is that knowledge is not a fixed state and no single test or score can adequately reflect the range of a person's knowledge. The mind has potential for unlimited growth. Development consists of moving toward the upper range of the zone using the tools of society. The upper limit continues to move upward in response to cultural changes (Smagorinsky, 1995). Support for Vygotsky's idea of the zone of proximal development comes from various sources, including research showing that children's performance on assisted learning tasks is a good predictor of their future achievement (Meijer & Elshout, 2001). And research on pairing less-skilled readers with more-skilled ones shows that reading fluency increases substantially when the less-skilled readers are provided with a model of good reading and encouragement (Nes, 2003).

In many cultures, children do not go to school with other children to learn, nor do their parents explicitly teach them

© Laura Dwight/CORBIS

By working with a more knowledgeable partner, this child is able to accomplish more than would be possible on his own. According to Lev Vygotsky, the difference between what a child can accomplish alone and with a partner is the zone of proximal development.

Applications

Improving Cognitive Functioning

What do the theories of Piaget and Vygotsky have to contribute to the goal of optimizing mental functioning? As Piaget's views first became popular in the United States and Canada, psychologists and educators designed studies to determine whether they could speed cognitive development and help children and adults solve problems more effectively. Some researchers had a different motive: to challenge Piaget's view that concepts such as conservation cannot be mastered until the child is intellectually ready.

What has been learned from these training studies? Generally, they suggest that many Piagetian concepts can be taught to children who are slightly younger than the age at which the concepts would naturally emerge. Training is sometimes difficult, and it does not always generalize well to new problems, but progress can be achieved. Dorothy Field (1981), for example, demonstrated that 4-year-olds could be trained to recognize the identity of a substance such as a ball of clay before and after its appearance is altered—that is, to understand that although the clay looks different, it is still the same clay and has to be the same amount of clay. Field found that nearly 75% of the children given this identity training could solve at least three of five conservation problems 2 to 5 months after training.

Similar training studies have demonstrated that children who function at the late concrete operations stage can be taught formal operations (Adey & Shayer, 1992). Researchers have had even more luck improving the cognitive performance of older adults, sometimes with simple interventions (Blackburn & Papalia, 1992). Such studies suggest that many elderly individuals who perform poorly on Piagetian problem-solving tasks simply need a quick refresher course to demonstrate their underlying competence. Make no mistake: No one has demonstrated that 2-year-olds can be taught formal operations. But at least these studies establish that specific training experiences can somewhat speed a child's progress through Piaget's stages or bring out more-advanced capacities in an adult performing at a less-advanced level.

Piaget disapproved of attempts by Americans to speed children's progress through his stages (Piaget, 1970). He believed that parents should simply provide young children with opportunities to explore their world and that teachers should use a discovery approach in the classroom that allows children to learn by doing. Given their natural curiosity and normal opportunities to try their hand at solving problems, children would construct ever more-complex understandings on their own. Many educators began building Piaget's ideas about discovery-based education into school curricula, especially in science classes (Gallagher & Easley, 1978). Teachers have also taken seriously Piaget's notion that children understand material best if they can assimilate it into their existing understandings. So, for example, they have designed curricula to guide severely mentally retarded adults through the substages of the sensorimotor period (Williams, 1996). Finding out what the learner already knows or can do and providing instruction

tasks such as weaving and hunting. Instead, they learn through **guided participation**—by actively participating in culturally relevant activities with the aid and support of their parents and other knowledgeable guides (Rogoff, 1998). Jerome Bruner (1983) had a similar concept in mind when he wrote of the many ways in which parents provide "scaffolding" for their children's development, structuring learning situations so that learning becomes easier. By calling attention to guided participation processes in the zone of proximal development, Vygotsky was rejecting Piaget's view of children as independent explorers in favor of the view that they learn more sophisticated cognitive strategies through their interactions with more mature thinkers. To Piaget, the child's level of cognitive development determines what he can learn; to Vygotsky, learning in collaboration with more knowledgeable companions drives cognitive development.

The Tools of Thought

In Vygotsky's view, adults use a variety of tools to pass culturally valued modes of thinking and problem solving to their children. Spoken language is clearly the most important tool, but writing, using numbers, and applying problem-solving and memory strategies also convey information and enable thinking (Bodrova & Leong, 1996; Crain, 2000; Vygotsky, 1978). The type of tool used to perform a task influences performance on the task. Consider a study by Dorothy Faulkner and her colleagues (2000) with 9- and 10-year-old children. Children worked in pairs on a science project (Inhelder and Piaget's chemical combination task), using either a computer simulation of the task or the actual physical materials. The children who worked with the computerized version talked more, tested more possible chemical combinations, and completed the task more quickly than children who worked with the physical materials. The computer, then, was a tool that changed the nature of the problem-solving activity and influenced performance, as Vygotsky would have predicted.

Look more closely at Vygotsky's notion of how tools—especially language—influence thought. Whereas Piaget maintained that cognitive development influences language development, Vygotsky argued that language shapes thought matched to the child's level of development are in the spirit of Piaget.

What would Vygotsky recommend to teachers who want to stimulate cognitive growth? As you might guess, Vygotsky's theoretical orientation leads to a different approach to education than Piaget's does—a more social one. Whereas students in Piaget's classroom would most likely be engaged in independent exploration, students in Vygotsky's classroom would be involved in guided participation, "co-constructing" knowledge during interactions with teachers and more knowledgeable peers. The roles of teachers and other more skillful collaborators would be to organize the learning activity, break it into steps, provide hints and suggestions carefully tailored to the student's abilities, and gradually turn over more of the mental work to the student. According to Vygotsky's sociocultural perspective, the guidance provided by a skilled partner will then be internalized by the learner, first as private speech and eventually as silent inner speech. Education ends up being a matter of providing children with tools of the mind important in their culture, whether hunting strategies or computer skills (Bodrova & Leong, 1996; Berk & Winsler, 1995).

Is there evidence that Vygotsky's guided participation approach might be superior to Piaget's discovery approach? Consider what Lisa Freund (1990) found when she had 3- to 5-year-old children help a puppet with a sorting task: deciding which furnishings (sofas, beds, bathtubs, stoves, and so on) should be placed in each of six rooms of a dollhouse that the puppet was moving into. First, the children were tested to determine what they already knew about proper furniture placement. Then, each child worked at a similar task, either alone (as might be the case in Piaget's discovery-based education, although here children were provided with corrective feedback by the experimenter) or with his or her mother (Vygotsky's guided learning). Finally, to assess what they had learned, Freund asked the children to perform a final, rather complex, furniture-sorting task. The results were clear: Children who had sorted furniture with help from their mothers showed dramatic improvements in sorting ability, whereas those who had practiced on their own showed little improvement. Moreover, the children who gained the most from guided participation with their mothers were those whose mothers talked the most about how to tackle the task. Collaborating with a competent peer can also produce cognitive gains that a child might not achieve working alone (Azmitia, 1992; Gauvain & Rogoff, 1989).

So, children do not always learn the most when they function as solitary scientists, seeking discoveries on their own; often, conceptual growth springs more readily from children's interactions with other people—particularly with competent people who provide an optimal amount of guidance. Yet it would seem that many children might benefit most from the best of both worlds: opportunities to explore on their own and supportive companions to offer help when needed.

in important ways and that thought changes fundamentally once we begin to think in words (Bodrova & Leong, 1996). Piaget and Vygotsky both noticed that preschool children often talk to themselves as they go about their daily activities, almost as if they were play-by-play sports announcers. ("I'm putting the big piece in the corner. I need a pink one. Not that one—this one.") Two preschool children playing next to each other sometimes carry on separate monologues rather than conversing. Piaget (1926) regarded such speech as egocentric—further evidence that preoperational thinkers cannot yet take the perspectives of other people (in this case, their conversation partners) and therefore have not mastered the art of social speech. He did not believe that egocentric speech played a useful role in cognitive development.

In contrast, Vygotsky called children's recitations **private speech**—speech to oneself that guides one's thought and behavior. Rather than viewing it as a sign of cognitive immaturity, he saw it as a critical step in the development of mature thought and as the forerunner of the silent thinking-in-words that adults engage in every day. Adults guide children's behavior with speech, a tool that children appropriate and initially use externally, just as adults did with them. Gradually, this regulatory speech is internalized.

Studies conducted by Vygotsky and other researchers support his claim (Berk, 1992). For example, in one set of studies, Vygotsky (1962) measured children's private speech first as they worked unimpeded on a task, then as they worked to overcome an obstacle placed in their path. Their use of private speech increased dramatically when they confronted an interruption of their work—a problem to solve. Thus, young children rely most heavily on private speech when they are struggling to solve difficult problems (Berk, 1992). Even adults sometimes revert to thinking aloud when they are stumped by a problem (John-Steiner, 1992).

The incidence of private speech varies with age and task demands. Both 3- and 4-year-olds use private speech, but 4-year-olds are more likely to use it systematically when engaged in a sustained activity. Four-year-olds are presumably more goal oriented than 3-year-olds and use private speech to regulate their behavior and achieve their goals (Winsler, Carlton, & Barry, 2000). As the task becomes familiar and children gain competence, the use of private speech decreases (Duncan &

Table 7.3 A Comparison of Vygotsky and Piaget

Vygotsky's Sociocultural View	Piaget's Cognitive Developmental View
Cognitive development is different in different social and historical contexts.	Cognitive development is mostly the same universally.
Appropriate unit of analysis is the social, cultural, and historical context in which the individual develops.	Appropriate unit of analysis is the individual.
Cognitive growth results from social interactions (guided participation in the zone of proximal development).	Cognitive growth results from the child's independent explorations of the world.
Children and their partners "co-construct" knowledge.	Each child constructs knowledge on his or her own.
Social processes become individual psychological ones (e.g., social speech becomes inner speech).	Individual, egocentric processes become more social (e.g., egocentric speech becomes social speech).
Adults are especially important (because they know the culture's tools of thinking).	Peers are especially important (because children must learn to take peers' perspectives into account).
Learning precedes development (tools learned with adult help become internalized).	Development precedes learning (children cannot master certain things until they have the requisite cognitive structures).

Pratt, 1997). Private speech is also more frequent during open-ended activities (such as pretend play) that have several possible outcomes than during closed-ended tasks that have a single outcome (Krafft & Berk, 1998). Open-ended activities tend to be directed more by the child than by an adult; they allow children to alter the difficulty level of the task so that it is appropriately challenging. In contrast, adult-directed activities provide fewer opportunities for children to regulate their own behavior.

Intellectually capable children rely more heavily on private speech in the preschool years and make the transition to inner speech earlier in the elementary school years than their less academically capable peers do (Berk & Landau, 1993; Kohlberg, Yaeger, & Hjertholm, 1968). This suggests that the preschool child's self-talk is indeed a sign of cognitive maturity, as Vygotsky claimed, rather than a sign of immature egocentrism, as Piaget claimed.

In addition, heavy use of private speech contributes to effective problem-solving performance—if not immediately, then when children encounter similar problems in the future (Behrend, Rosengren, & Perlmutter, 1989; Bivens & Berk, 1990). The amount of private speech and the nature of what the child says are both related to performance (Chiu & Alexander, 2000). In particular, children who use metacognitive private speech ("No, I need to change this. Try it over here. Yes, that's good.") show greater motivation toward mastery; that is, they are more likely to persist on a task without adult intervention (Chiu & Alexander, 2000). Thus, private speech not only helps children think their way through challenging problems but also allows them to incorporate into their own thinking the problem-solving strategies they learned during their collaborations with adults. Notice that, as in guided participation, what is at first a social process becomes an individual psychological process. In other words, social speech (for example, the conversation between Annie and her father as they jointly worked a puzzle) gives rise to private speech (Annie talking aloud, much as her father talked to her, as she then tries to work the puzzle on her own), which in turn goes "underground" to become first mutterings and lip movements and then inner speech (Annie's silent verbal thought).

Evaluation of Vygotsky

Although many scholars find Vygotsky's ideas a refreshing addition to Piaget's, some concerns should be noted. Piaget has been criticized for placing too much emphasis on the individual and not enough on the social environment; Vygotsky has been criticized for placing too much emphasis on social interaction (Feldman & Fowler, 1997). Vygotsky seemed to assume that all knowledge and understanding of the world is transmitted through social interaction. But at least some understanding is individually constructed, as Piaget proposed. Vygotsky and Piaget are often presented as opposites on a continuum representing the extent to which cognitive development derives from social experience. However, a careful reading of the two theorists reveals that they are not as dissimilar as they are often presented to be (DeVries, 2000; Matusov & Hayes, 2000). Both Piaget and Vygotsky acknowledge the importance of the social context of development. Still, there are differences in their emphasis. Table 7.3 summarizes some of the differences between Vygotsky's sociocultural perspective and Piaget's cognitive developmental view. The Applications box on page 194 explains their views on improving cognitive functioning.

Pause for a moment and consider the remarkable developmental accomplishments we described in this chapter. The capacity of the human mind for thought is awesome. Because the human mind is so complex, you should not be surprised that it is not yet understood. Piaget attacked only part of the puzzle, and he only partially succeeded. Vygotsky alerted us to sociocultural influences on cognitive development but died before he could formalize his theory. As you will see in Chapters 8 and 9, other ways to think about mental development are needed.

Summing Up

Vygotsky's sociocultural perspective stresses social influences on cognitive development that Piaget largely ignored. Children's minds develop (1) in response to cultural influences; (2) in collaborative interactions with skilled partners, or guided participation, on tasks within their zone of proximal development; and (3) as they incorporate what skilled partners say to them into what they say to themselves. As social speech is transformed into private speech and then into inner speech, the culture's preferred tools of problem solving work their way from the language of competent guides into the thinking of the individual.

Summary Points

1. Jean Piaget, through his clinical method, formulated four stages of cognitive development in which children construct increasingly complex schemes through an interaction of maturation and experience.

2. Children adapt to the world through the processes of organization and adaptation (assimilating new experiences to existing understandings and accommodating existing understandings to new experiences).

3. Piaget proposed four stages of cognitive development, each representing a qualitatively different level of thought. In the sensorimotor stage, infants construct simple schemes by taking in information through their senses and acting motorically on it. In the preoperational stage, preschool-age children do not yet reason logically; instead they rely on perceptually salient features of a task or object. Concrete-operational thinkers can reason logically about concrete information, and formal-operational thinkers can apply their logical reasoning to hypothetical problems.

4. Piaget has made huge contributions to the field of human development but has been criticized for underestimating the capacities of infants and young children, not considering factors besides competence that influence performance, failing to demonstrate that his stages have coherence, offering vague explanations of development, and underestimating the role of language and social interaction in cognitive development.

5. Lev Vygotsky's sociocultural perspective emphasizes cultural and social influences on cognitive development more than Piaget's theory does. Through guided participation in culturally important activities, children learn problem-solving techniques from knowledgeable partners sensitive to their zone of proximal development.

6. Language is the most important tool that adults use to pass culturally valued thinking and problem solving to their children. Language shapes their thought and moves from social speech to private speech and later to inner speech.

Critical Thinking

1. Considering the differences between preoperational thought, concrete-operational thought, and formal-operational thought, what should parents keep in mind as they interact with their 4-year-old, 8-year-old, and 17-year-old children?

2. Create descriptions of a Piagetian preschool and a Vygotskian preschool. What are the main differences in how children will be assessed, what they will be taught, and how they will be taught?

3. How might Piaget's theory be updated to accommodate the research findings that have emerged since he constructed his theory?

4. Piaget and Vygotsky differed in their views of the importance of the individual versus society. Compare their positions on individual versus society in terms of cognitive development.

5. How important is it to achieve formal operational thought? What limitations would you experience at work and school if you operated at a concrete operational level all the time and never progressed to formal operational thought?

Key Terms

cognition, 172
genetic epistemology, 172
clinical method, 172
scheme (schema), 172
organization, 173
adaptation, 173
assimilation, 173
accommodation, 173
object permanence, 175
A-not-B error, 176
symbolic capacity, 177
imaginary companions, 178
perceptual salience, 179
conservation, 179
decentration, 179
centration, 179
reversibility, 179
transformational thought, 179
static thought, 179
egocentrism, 181
class inclusion, 181
transductive reasoning, 182
horizontal décalage, 182
seriation, 182
transitivity, 182
hypothetical-deductive reasoning, 184
decontextualize, 186
adolescent egocentrism, 187
imaginary audience, 187
personal fable, 187
postformal thought, 189
relativistic thinking, 189
zone of proximal development, 193
guided participation, 194
private speech, 195

Media Resources

Websites to Explore

Visit Our Website

For a chapter tutorial quiz and other useful features, visit the book's companion website at *http://psychology.wadsworth.com/sigelman_rider5e*. You can also connect directly to the following sites:

Piaget

The Jean Piaget Society provides biographical information, links to other Piaget resources on the web, and lists of suggested readings for those who would like to learn more about Piaget's research and writings.

Review of Vygotsky
Maintained by an instructor at the University of Colorado at Denver, the web page titled "Celebrities in Cognitive Science" contains links to profiles, interviews, papers, and other articles on cognitive scientists living and dead, including Lev Vygotsky.

Understanding the Data: Exercises on the Web

For additional insight on the data presented in this chapter, try the exercises for the following figure at *http://psychology.wadsworth.com/sigelman_rider5e:*

Figure 7.7 Expertise and formal operations

Life-Span CD-ROM

Go to the Wadsworth Life-Span CD-ROM for further study of the concepts in this chapter. The CD-ROM includes narrated concept overviews, video clips, a multimedia glossary, and additional activities to expand your learning experience. For this chapter, check out the following clips, and others, in the video library:

VIDEO Jean Piaget's Sensorimotor Stage

VIDEO Preoperational Thinking: Piaget's Conservation Experiments

DEVELOPMENTAL
PsychologyNow™

Developmental PsychologyNow is a web-based, intelligent study system that provides a complete package of diagnostic quizzes, a personalized study plan, integrated multimedia elements, and learning modules. Check it out at *http://psychology.wadsworth.com/sigelman_rider5e/now.*

CHAPTER e i g h t

Memory and Information Processing

IN HIS BOOK *The Mind of a Mnemonist,* Aleksandr Luria (1987) describes the case of "S," a newspaper reporter who never took notes at news briefings yet would later demonstrate verbatim recall of all that was said. S thought it rather strange that other reporters had to carry notebooks and were always writing copious notes in them. S could look at a chart with 50 digits for 2 to 3 minutes then reproduce it perfectly in any order, even in reverse or diagonally. Imagine how you might perform on tests if you had S's memory. Obviously, S's memory ability is highly unusual. Most of us have more ordinary skills with a host of strengths and weaknesses. Even so, our memory is a vital aspect of who we are and what we do, allowing us to function in the present, act on the past, and plan for the future.

In this chapter, we consider how memory develops and changes over the life span. We also continue examining cognitive development by looking at a view different from Jean Piaget's and Lev Vygotsky's approaches, described in the last chapter. Cognitive psychologists, influenced by the rise of computer technology, began to think of the brain as a computer that processes input and converts it to output (correct answers on tests, for example). This information-processing perspective has revealed much about how the capacities to acquire, remember, and use information change over the life span.

The Information-Processing Approach

According to Howard Gardner (1985), the "cognitive revolution" in psychology that generated the information-processing approach could not have occurred without a demonstration of the inadequacies of the behaviorist approach and the rise of computer technology.

Showing deficiencies in the behaviorist approach was easiest in relation to complex learning and memory tasks. Consider learning from this textbook. Obviously, some complex processes occur between when you register the pattern of print on this page and when you write an essay about it. To account for these processes, behaviorists such as John B. Watson and B. F. Skinner (see Chapter 2) would have to describe chains of mental stimuli and responses between an external stimulus (for instance, the printed page) and an overt response. This approach proved cumbersome at best, as more cognitively oriented learning theorists, such as Albert Bandura, recognized.

Then came computers with their capacity for systematically converting input to output. The computer seemed to provide a good analogy to the human mind, and efforts to program computers to play chess and solve other problems as well as human experts do have revealed a great deal about the strengths and limitations of human cognition (Newell & Simon, 1961; Simon, 1995).

Any computer has a limited capacity, associated with its hardware and software, for processing information. The computer's hardware is the machine itself—its keyboard (or input system), its storage capacity, and so on. The mind's "hardware" is the nervous system, including the brain, the sensory receptors, and their neural connections. The computer's software consists of the programs used to manipulate stored and received information: word processing, statistics programs, and the like. The mind, too, has its "software"—rules, strategies, and other mental "programs" that specify how information is to be registered, interpreted, stored, retrieved, and analyzed.

The computer, then, was the model for the **information-processing approach** to human cognition, which emphasizes the basic mental processes involved in attention, perception, memory, and decision making. When the information-processing approach began to guide studies of development, the challenge became one of determining how the hardware and software of the mind change over the life span. Just as today's more highly developed computers have greater capacity than those of the past, maturation of the nervous system plus experience presumably enables adults to remember more than young children can and to perform more complex cognitive feats with greater accuracy (Kail & Bisanz, 1992).

Memory Systems

Figure 8.1 presents an early and influential conception of the human information-processing system offered by Richard Atkinson and Richard Shiffrin (1968). If your history professor says that the U.S. Constitution was ratified in 1789, this statement is an environmental stimulus. Assuming that you are not lost in a daydream, your **sensory register** will log it, holding it for a fraction of a second as a kind of afterimage (or, in this example, a kind of echo). Much that strikes the sensory register quickly disappears without further processing. Attentional processes (see Chapter 6) have a good deal to do with which sensory stimuli enter the sensory register and which are processed further. If you think you may need to remember 1789, it will be moved into **short-term memory,** which can hold a limited amount of information (perhaps only about seven items or chunks of information) for several seconds. For example, short-term memory can hold onto a telephone number while you dial it. Today, cognitive researchers distinguish between passive and active forms of short-term memory and use the term **working memory** to refer to a mental "scratch pad" that temporarily stores information while actively operating on it (Baddeley, 1986, 1992). It is what is "on one's mind," or in one's consciousness, at any moment. As you know, people can juggle only so much information at once without having some of it slip away.

To illustrate working memory, look at the following seven numbers. Then look away and add the numbers in your head while trying to remember them:

7 2 5 6 1 4 7

Most likely, having to actively manipulate the numbers in working memory to add them disrupted your ability to re-

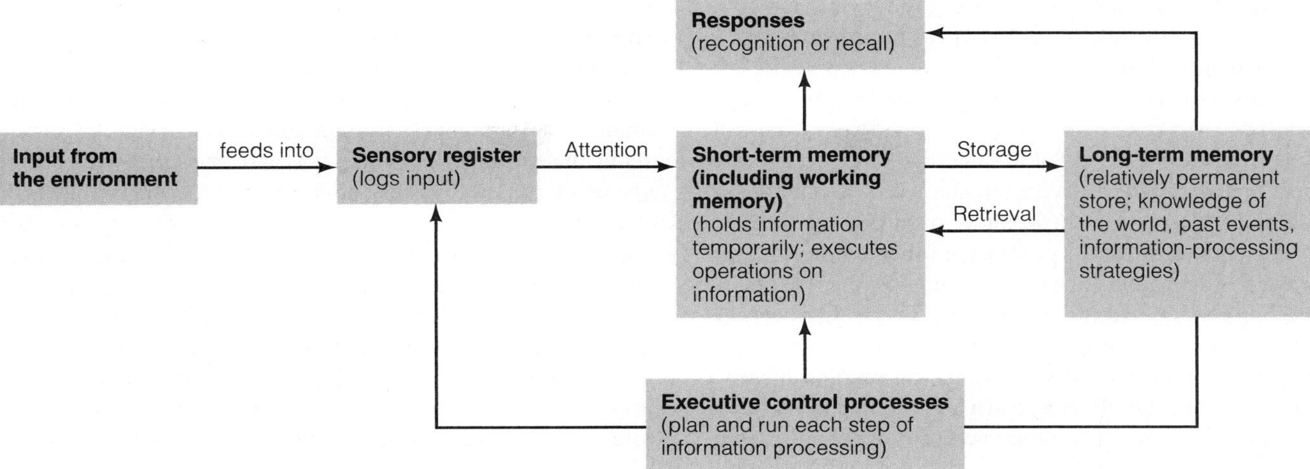

Figure 8.1 A model of information processing.

SOURCE: Adapted from Atkinson, R. C., & Shiffrin, R. M. (1968). Human memory: A proposed system and its control processes. In K. W. Spence & J. T. Spence (Eds.), *The psychology of learning and motivation: Advances in research and theory* (Vol 2). New York: Academic Press. Copyright © 1968 by Academic Press. Reprinted by permission.

hearse them to remember them. People who are fast at adding numbers would have better luck than most people, because they would have more working memory space left for remembering the items (Byrnes, 1996).

To be remembered for any length of time, information must be moved from short-term memory into **long-term memory,** a relatively permanent store of information that represents what most people mean by memory. More than likely, you will hold the professor's statement in short-term memory just long enough to record it in your notes. Later, as you study your notes, you will rehearse the information in working memory to move it into long-term memory so that you can retrieve it the next day or week when you are taking the test.

This simplified model shows what you must do to learn and remember something. The first step is **encoding** the information: getting it into the system, learning it, and moving it from the sensory register to short-term memory then to long-term memory while organizing it in a form suitable for storage. If it never gets in, it cannot be remembered. Then there is **storage**—holding information in the long-term memory store. Memories fade over time unless they are appropriately stored in long-term memory. Finally, there is **retrieval**—the process of getting information out when it is needed. People say they have successfully remembered something when they can retrieve it from long-term memory.

Retrieval can be accomplished in several ways. If you are asked a multiple-choice question about when the Constitution was ratified, you need not actively retrieve the correct date; you merely need to recognize it among the options. This is an example of **recognition memory.** If, instead, you are asked, "When was the Constitution ratified?" this is a test of **recall memory;** it requires active retrieval without the aid of cues. Between recognition and recall memory is **cued recall memory,** in which you would be given a hint or cue to facilitate retrieval (for example, "When was the Constitution ratified? It is the year the French Revolution began and rhymes with *wine.*"). Most people find questions requiring recognition memory easier to answer than those requiring cued recall and those requiring cued recall easier than those requiring pure recall. This holds true across the life span, which suggests that many things people have apparently encoded or learned are "in there someplace" even though they may be difficult to retrieve without cues. Breakdowns in remembering may involve difficulties in initial encoding, storage, or retrieval.

Implicit and Explicit Memory

Memory researchers have concluded that the long-term memory store responds differently depending on the nature of the task. They distinguish between **implicit memory,** which occurs unintentionally, automatically, and without awareness, and **explicit memory,** which involves deliberate, effortful recollection of events. Explicit memory is tested through traditional recognition and recall tests. When implicit memory is tested, learners do not even know their memory is being assessed. For example, individuals might be exposed to a list of words (*orange, tablet, forest,* and so on) to be rated for likeability, not to be memorized. In a second task, they are given word stems such as *tab*_____ and asked to complete them with the first word that comes to mind. People who are exposed to the word *tablet* in the initial task are more likely than people who are not exposed to the word to come up with *tablet* rather than *table* or *tabby* to complete the word stem, demonstrating that they learned something from their earlier exposure to the words even though they were not trying to learn. Adults with amnesia do poorly on tests of explicit memory in which they study words and then are asked to finish word stems such as *tab*_____ with a word they studied earlier. Amazingly, however, if they are merely exposed to a list of words and then given an implicit memory test that asks them to write the first word that comes to mind, they do fine (Graf, Squire, & Mandler, 1984). Many forms of amnesia destroy explicit memory but leave implicit memory intact

(Schacter, 1996). In other words, these are two distinct components of long-term memory that operate independently.

Some scholars believe that implicit memory develops earlier in infancy than explicit memory (Schneider, 2004). Others believe that both forms of memory are evident early in infancy (Rovee-Collier, 1997). All agree that the two types of memory follow different developmental paths. Explicit memory capacity increases from infancy to adulthood then declines in later adulthood. By contrast, implicit memory capacity changes little; young children often do no worse than older children and elderly adults often do no worse than younger adults on tests of implicit memory (Schneider, 2004; Schneider & Bjorklund, 1998). Research on implicit memory shows that young and old alike learn and retain a tremendous amount of information from their everyday experiences without any effort.

Problem Solving

Now imagine that you are asked how many years passed between the signing of the Declaration of Independence (1776, remember?) and the ratification of the Constitution. This is a simple example of **problem solving,** or use of the information-processing system to achieve a goal or arrive at a decision (in this case, to answer the question). Here, too, the information-processing model describes what happens between stimulus and response. The question will move through the memory system. You will need to draw on your long-term memory to understand the question, then you will have to search long-term memory for the two relevant dates. Moreover, you will need to locate your stored knowledge of the mathematical operation of subtraction. You will then transfer this stored information to working memory so that you can use your subtraction "program" (1789 minus 1776) to derive the correct answer.

Notice that processing information successfully requires both knowing what you are doing and making decisions. This is why the information-processing model (see Figure 8.1) includes **executive control processes** involved in planning and monitoring what is done. These control processes run the show, guiding the selection, organization, manipulation, and interpretation of information throughout. Stored knowledge about the world and about information processing guides what is done with new information.

Cognitive psychologists now recognize that information processing is more complex than this model or similar models suggest (Bjorklund, 1997). For example, they appreciate that people, like computers, engage in "parallel processing," carrying out many cognitive activities simultaneously rather than performing operations in a sequence. They also appreciate that different processing approaches are used in different domains of knowledge. Still, the information-processing approach to cognition has the advantage of focusing attention on how people remember things or solve problems, not just on what they recall or what answer they give. A young child's performance on a problem could break down in any number of ways: The child might not be paying attention to the relevant aspects of the problem, might be unable to hold all the relevant pieces of information in working memory long enough to do anything with them, might lack the strategies for transferring new information into long-term memory or retrieving information from long-term memory as needed, might simply not have enough stored knowledge to understand the problem, or might not have the executive control processes needed to manage the steps for solving problems. If researchers can identify how information processes in the younger individual differ from those in the older person, they will gain much insight into cognitive development.

Many processes involved in memory and problem solving improve between infancy and adulthood then decline somewhat in old age, although this pattern is not uniform for all processes or all people. Our task in this chapter is to describe these age trends and, of greater interest, to try to determine why they occur.

Summing Up

The information-processing approach uses a computer analogy to illustrate how the mind processes information. The human "computer" takes in information through the sensory registers. If the person pays attention to the information, it is further processed in the short-term and working memory and may eventually be stored in long-term memory. Encoding and retrieval strategies influence memory performance. Explicit memory is deliberate and effortful and changes over the life span, whereas implicit memory is automatic and relatively stable over the life span. Finally, stored memories are instrumental to success at solving problems. ■

The Infant

You have already seen that infants explore the world thoroughly through their senses. But are they remembering anything of their experiences? First, look at what research on information processing has helped developmentalists or researchers learn about early memory; then, consider whether infants demonstrate problem-solving skills.

Memory

Assessing infant memory requires some ingenuity because infants cannot just tell researchers what they recall (Bauer, 2004; Rovee-Collier & Barr, 2004). Several methods have been used to uncover infants' memory capabilities. Here we consider imitation, habituation, and operant conditioning techniques before examining infants' abilities to recall previously presented information.

Imitation

Researchers may be able to learn something about memory by noting whether or not infants can imitate an action performed by a model. Some studies suggest that young infants, even newborns, can imitate certain actions, such as sticking

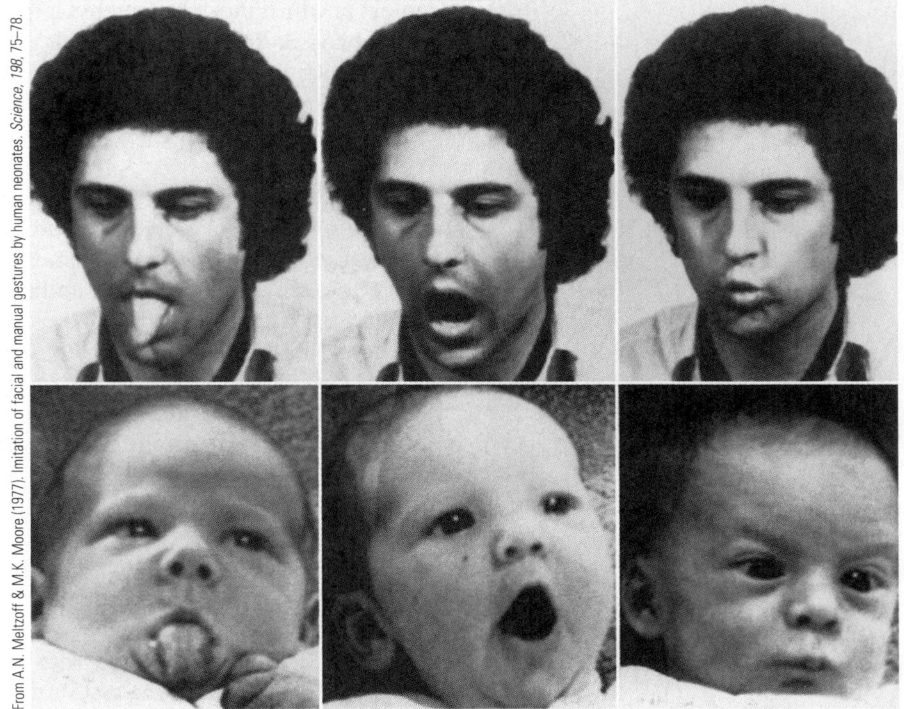
From A.N. Meltzoff & M.K. Moore (1977). Imitation of facial and manual gestures by human neonates. *Science, 198*, 75–78.

Andrew Meltzoff is one researcher who has demonstrated imitation of facial expressions in newborns. These sample photographs are from videotaped recordings of 2- to 3-week-old infants imitating tongue protrusion, mouth opening, and lip protrusion. Of the three responses shown here, tongue protrusion is the most reliably observed.

out the tongue or opening the mouth (see Meltzoff, 2004, for a review; see also the photo on this page). These findings are exciting because they challenge Piaget's claim that infants cannot imitate actions until about 1 year, when they have some ability to represent mentally what they have seen.

At first, such findings were viewed with skepticism by some, who believed that early tongue protrusions did not demonstrate true imitation but instead reflected reflexive responses to specific stimuli or attempts to "explore" interesting sights (for example, Bjorklund, 1995; Jones, 1996). However, observations of infants sticking out their tongues and moving their mouths in ways consistent with a model have now been replicated with different populations (Meltzoff & Moore, 1997). In addition, 6-month-olds display **deferred imitation,** the ability to imitate a novel act after a delay, which clearly requires memory ability (Barr, Dowden, & Hayne, 1996; Bauer, 2004).

Habituation

Another method to assess memory uses habituation, a simple and often overlooked form of learning introduced in Chapter 6. Habituation—learning *not* to respond to a repeated stimulus—might be thought of as learning to be bored by the familiar (for example, the continual ticking of a clock) and is evidence that a stimulus is recognized as familiar. From birth, humans habituate to repeatedly presented lights, sounds, and smells; such stimuli are recognized as "old hat" (Bauer, 2004; Rovee-Collier & Barr, 2004). In other words, newborns are capable of recognition memory and prefer a new sight to something they have seen many times. As they age, infants need less "study time" before a stimulus becomes old hat, and they can retain what they have learned for days or even weeks (Bahrick & Pickens, 1995).

Operant Conditioning

To test long-term memory of young infants, Carolyn Rovee-Collier and her colleague devised a clever task that relies on the operant conditioning techniques introduced in Chapter 2 (Rovee-Collier & Barr, 2004). When a ribbon is tied to a baby's ankle and connected to an attractive mobile (see the photo on page 204), the infant will shake a leg now and then and learn in minutes that leg kicking brings about a positively reinforcing consequence: the jiggling of the mobile.

To test infant memory, the mobile is presented later to see whether the infant will kick again. To succeed at this task, the infant must not only recognize the mobile but also recall that the thing to do is to kick. When given two 9-minute training sessions, 2-month-olds remember how to make the mobile move for up to 2 days, 3-month-olds for about 1 week, and 6-month-olds for about 2 weeks (Rovee-Collier & Boller, 1995). By 18 months, infants can remember for at least 3 months (Rovee-Collier & Barr, 2004). The researchers could enhance young infants' memory by giving them three 6-minute learning sessions rather than two 9-minute sessions (Rovee-Collier, 1999). Although the total training time is the same in the two conditions, the distributed training is more effective. As it

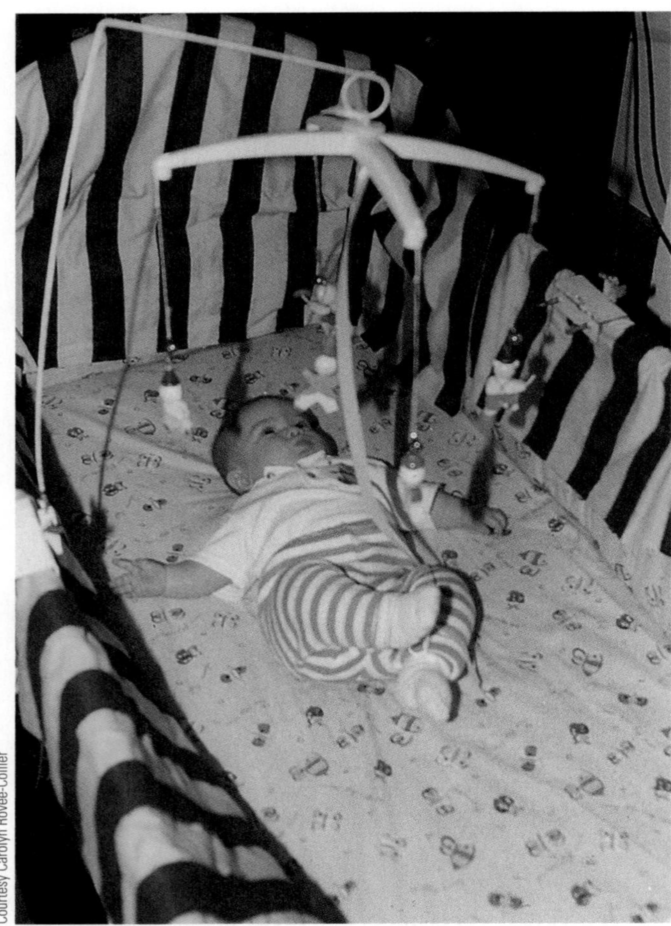

☾ When ribbons are tied to their ankles, young infants soon learn to make a mobile move by kicking their legs. Carolyn Rovee-Collier has made use of this operant conditioning paradigm to find out how long infants will remember the trick for making the mobile move.

turns out, distributed practice is beneficial across the life span (Son, 2004).

What if stronger cues to aid recall are provided? Rovee-Collier and her colleague (2004) found that 2 to 4 weeks after their original learning experience infants who were reminded of their previous learning by seeing the mobile move kicked up a storm as soon as the ribbon was attached to their ankles, whereas infants who were not reminded showed no sign of remembering to kick. It seems, then, that cued recall (in this case, memory cued by the presence of the mobile or, better yet, its rotation by the experimenter) emerges during the first couple of months after birth and that infants remember best when they are reminded of what they have learned. Other research shows that verbal reminders are also effective with 15-month-olds, helping them remember an event after a month as well as they did after a week (Bauer, Hertsgaard, & Wewerka, 1995; Bauer et al., 2000).

However, this research also suggests that young infants have difficulty recalling what they have learned if cues are insufficient. They have trouble remembering whether the mobile (for example, the specific animals hanging from it) or the context in which they encountered it (for example, the design on the playpen liner) is even slightly different from the context in which they learned. In short, early memories are *cue-dependent* and *context-specific.*

Recall

When are infants capable of pure recall—of actively retrieving information from memory when no cues are available? As noted earlier, infants as young as 6 months, given repeated exposure to a model's actions, can imitate novel behaviors (for example, pushing a button on a box to produce a beep) after a 24-hour delay (Barr, Dowden, & Hayne, 1996; Meltzoff, 1988). As infants age, they demonstrate recall or deferred imitation over longer periods. For instance, 14- to 16-month-olds show deferred imitation after delays of 4 months (Meltzoff, 1995). By 24 months of age, recall is more flexible—less bound by the specific cues present at the time of learning (Herbert & Hayne, 2000; Klein & Meltzoff, 1999).

Patricia Bauer (1996, 2000) and her colleagues have shown sequences of actions to infants of different ages then asked them to imitate what they saw—for example, putting a teddy bear in bed, covering him with a blanket, and reading him a story. Infants as young as 13 months can reconstruct a sequence of actions for as long as 3 months afterward. Older infants (16 and 20 months) can store and retrieve events for 12 months after exposure (Bauer et al., 2000). Much like children and adults, they remember best when they have repeated exposures to what they are to remember, when they are given plenty of cues to help them remember, and when the events they must remember occur in a meaningful or logical order.

By age 2, infants have become verbal and can use words to reconstruct events that happened months earlier. In one study, for example, researchers interviewed young children about emergency room visits for accidents the children had between about 1 and 3 years (Peterson & Rideout, 1998). Interviews were conducted soon after the ER visits and 6, 12, 18, or 24 months later. Children who were 18 months or younger at the time of their ER visit were unable to verbally recall aspects of their visits after a 6-month delay, but children 20 months or older were able to do so. Children who were at least 26 months old at the time of their ER visit could retain and answer verbal questions about their experiences for at least 2 years following the event.

Problem Solving

Infants, like children and adults, face problem-solving tasks every day. For example, they may want to obtain an object beyond their reach or make a toy repeat the interesting sound it produced earlier. Can infants overcome obstacles to achieve desired goals? It appears they can. In one study, infants were presented with an object out of their reach; however, by pulling on a cloth, they could drag the object to within reach (Willats, 1990). Although 6-month-olds did not retrieve the object, 9-month-olds solved this problem. Even the younger infants were successful when given hints about how they might retrieve the object (Kolstad & Aguiar, 1995). Simple

Infants begin to learn problem-solving strategies around 6 months of age.

problem-solving behaviors such as this improve considerably over the first 2 years after birth, then, as you will see shortly, flourish during childhood.

Summing Up

Using imitation, habituation, and operant conditioning techniques, researchers have gone from believing that infants have no memory beyond a few seconds to appreciating that even young 1-year-olds can recall experiences for weeks and even months under certain conditions. Infants clearly show recognition memory for familiar stimuli at birth and cued recall memory by about 2 months. As they age, they can retain information longer. More explicit memory, which requires actively retrieving an image of an object or event no longer present, appears to emerge toward the end of the first year. By age 2, it is even clearer that infants can consciously and deliberately recall events that happened long ago, for they, like adults, use language to represent and describe what happened. Simple problem solving improves throughout infancy. ■

The Child

The 2-year-old is already a highly capable information processor, as evidenced by the rapid language learning that takes place at this age. But dramatic improvements in learning, memory, and problem solving occur throughout the childhood years as children learn everything from how to flush toilets to how to work advanced math problems.

Explaining Memory Development

In countless situations, older children learn faster and remember more than younger children do. For example, 2-year-olds can repeat back about two digits immediately after hearing them, 5-year-olds about four digits, and 10-year-olds about six digits. And second-graders not only are faster learners than kindergartners but also retain information longer (Howe, 2000). Why is this? Here are four major hypotheses about why learning and memory improve, patterned after those formulated by John Flavell and Henry Wellman (1977):

1. *Changes in basic capacities.* Older children have higher-powered "hardware" than younger children do; their brains have more working memory space for manipulating information and can process information faster.

2. *Changes in memory strategies.* Older children have better "software"; they have learned and consistently use effective methods for putting information into long-term memory and retrieving it when they need it.

3. *Increased knowledge about memory.* Older children know more about memory (for example, how long they must study to learn things thoroughly, which kinds of memory tasks take more effort, and which strategies best fit each task).

4. *Increased knowledge about the world.* Older children know more than younger children about the world in general. This knowledge, or expertise, makes material to be learned more familiar, and familiar material is easier to learn and remember than unfamiliar material.

Do Basic Capacities Change?

Because the nervous system continues to develop in the early years after birth, it seems plausible that older children remember more than younger children do because they have a better "computer"—a larger or more efficient information-processing system. However, we can quickly rule out the idea that the storage capacity of long-term memory enlarges. There is no consistent evidence that it changes after the first month of life (Perlmutter, 1986). In fact, young and old alike have more room for storage than they could ever use. Nor does the capacity of the sensory register to take in stimuli seem to change much (Schneider & Bjorklund, 1998). It does seem, however, that the speed of mental processes improves with age and that this allows older children and adults to perform more mental operations at once in working memory than young children can (Halford, 2004; Kail & Salthouse, 1994).

This idea has been featured in revisions of Piaget's theory of cognitive development proposed by neo-Piagetian theorists such as Robbie Case (1985; Marini & Case, 1994). Case seeks to build on Piaget's insights into cognitive development but has also been strongly influenced by the information-processing approach. He proposes that more advanced stages of cognitive development are made possible because children make better use of the available space in their working memory. For example, Piaget stressed the preschooler's tendency to *center* on one aspect of a problem and lose sight of another (for example, to attend to the height of a glass but ignore its width, or vice versa). Perhaps, say the neo-Piagetians, this is not a matter of lacking certain cognitive structures; perhaps young children simply do not have enough working memory capacity to keep both pieces of information in mind at once and to coordinate them. Similarly, young children may do poorly on memory tasks because they cannot keep the first items on a list in mind while processing later ones. And they may fail to solve mathematical problems correctly because they cannot keep the facts of the problem in mind while they are performing the calculations.

To test the capacity of short-term memory, researchers quickly present a list of items (such as numbers) then count the number of items that a person can recall in order. Measured this way, short-term memory capacity seems to improve from age 2 to adulthood from just over two items to close to seven items (Rose et al., 1997). In addition, older children are able to manipulate more information at once in working memory (Case, 1985; Kail, 1990). Partly, this is because they have become faster and more efficient at executing basic mental processes, such as identifying numbers or words to be learned (Kail, 1991); these processes become automatic so that they can be done with little mental effort. This, in turn, frees space in working memory for other purposes, such as storing the information needed to solve a problem.

Some research suggests that the degree of improvement in short-term memory capacity evident as children age depends on what is being tested. That is, short-term memory capacity is domain-specific—it varies with background knowledge (Schneider, 2004). Greater knowledge in a domain or area of study increases the speed with which new, related information can be processed. In other words, the more you know about a subject, the faster you can process information related to this subject. Other research, however, indicates that developmental changes in capacity are general, not domain-specific (Schneider, 2004; Swanson, 1999). So which is it?

Improvements with age in operating speed and working memory efficiency could be because of maturational changes in the brain; the older child's greater familiarity with numbers, letters, and other stimuli; or both (Bjorklund, 1995). There is agreement, however, that speed of processing affects short-term memory capacity; older children process information faster than younger children can, and this is one reason memory improves over childhood (Gathercole, 1998).

Do Memory Strategies Change?

If shown the 12 items in Figure 8.2, 4-year-olds might recall only 2 to 4 of them, 8-year-olds would recall 7 to 9 items, and adults might recall 10 to 11 of the items after a delay of several minutes. Are there specific memory strategies that evolve during childhood to permit this dramatic improvement in performance?

Children as young as 2 years can deliberately remember to do "important" things, such as reminding Mom to buy candy at the grocery store (Somerville, Wellman, & Cultice, 1983). They are more likely to use external memory aids (for example, pointing at or holding a toy pig when asked to remember where it was hidden) if they are instructed to remember than if they are not (Fletcher & Bray, 1996). Yet preschoolers have not mastered many effective strategies for moving information into long-term memory. For example, when instructed to remember toys they have been shown, 3- and 4-year-olds will look carefully at the objects and will often label them once, but they only rarely use the memory strategy called **rehearsal**—the repeating of items they are trying to learn and remember (Baker-Ward, Ornstein, & Holden, 1984). To rehearse the objects in Figure 8.2, you might simply say, "apple, truck, grapes . . ." repeatedly. John Flavell and his associates found that only 10% of 5-year-olds repeated the names of pictures they were asked to recall, but more than half of 7-year-olds and 85% of 10-year-olds used this strategy (Flavell, Beach, & Chinsky, 1966).

Figure 8.2 A memory task. Imagine that you have 120 seconds to learn the 12 objects pictured here. What tricks or strategies might you devise to make your task easier?

Another important memory strategy is **organization,** or classifying items into meaningful groups. You might lump the apple, the grapes, and the hamburger in Figure 8.2 into a category of foods and form other categories for animals, vehicles, and baseball equipment. You would then rehearse each category and recall it as a cluster. Another organizational strategy, chunking, is used to break a long number (6065551843) into manageable subunits (606-555-1843, a phone number). Organization is mastered later in childhood than rehearsal. Until about age 9 or 10, children are not much better at recalling lists of items that lend themselves readily to grouping than they are at recalling lists of unrelated words (Flavell & Wellman, 1977).

Finally, the strategy of **elaboration** involves actively creating meaningful links between items to be remembered. Elaboration is achieved by adding something to the items, in the form of either words or images. Creating and using a sentence such as "the apple fell on the horse's nose" could help you remember two of the items in Figure 8.2. Elaboration is especially helpful in learning foreign languages. For example, you might link the Spanish word *pato* (pronounced pot-o) to the English equivalent *duck* by imagining a duck in a pot of boiling water.

Memory or encoding strategies develop in a fairly predictable order, with rehearsal emerging first, followed by organization, and then by elaboration. Children do not suddenly start using strategies, however. According to Patricia Miller (1990, 1994; Miller & Seier, 1994), they typically progress through four phases on their way to successful strategy use. Initially, children have a **mediation deficiency,** which means they cannot spontaneously use or benefit from strategies, even if they are taught how to use them. This gives way to a different kind of problem, a **production deficiency,** in which children can use strategies they are taught but do not produce them on their own. The third phase is a **utilization deficiency,** in which children spontaneously produce a strategy but their task performance does not yet benefit from using the strategy. Finally, children exhibit effective strategy use by both producing and benefiting from a memory strategy.

There is ample evidence of utilization deficiencies across various age groups and for different types of strategies (see, for example, Coyle & Bjorklund, 1996; Miller & Seier, 1994; also see Schneider, 2004, for a review). Why would children who use a strategy fail to benefit from it? One possibility is that using a new strategy is mentally taxing and leaves no free cognitive resources for other aspects of the task (Bjorklund et al., 1997). Once using the strategy becomes routine, then other components of the task can be addressed simultaneously. Whatever the reason for utilization deficiencies, they reflect a child–task interaction; that is, they depend on how difficult a task is for a particular child rather than on task difficulty per se (Bjorklund et al., 1997).

Using effective storage strategies to learn material is only half the battle; retrieval strategies can also influence how much is recalled. Indeed, retrieving something from memory can often be a complex adventure when solving problems, such as when you try to remember when you went on a trip by searching for cues that might trigger your memory ("Well, I still had long hair then, but it was after Muffy's wedding, and . . ."). Strange as it may seem, even when young schoolchildren are shown how to use the memory strategy of elaboration, they may not do as well as older children on memory tests because it does not occur to them to use the images they worked so hard to create to help them retrieve what they have learned (Pressley & Levin, 1980). In general, young children rely more on external cues for both encoding and retrieving information than do older children (Schneider & Pressley, 1997). Thus, young children may need to put their toothbrushes next to their pajamas so that they have a physical reminder to brush their teeth before they go to bed. Older children are less likely to need such external cues but may continue to use them throughout elementary school (Eskritt & Lee, 2002). In many ways, then, command of memory strategies increases over the childhood years, but the path to effective strategy use is characterized more by ups and downs than by steady increases (Schneider, 2004).

Does Knowledge about Memory Change?

The term **metamemory** refers to knowledge of memory and to monitoring and regulating memory processes (Schneider, 2004). It is knowing, for example, what your memory limits are, which memory strategies are more or less effective, and which memory tasks are more or less difficult (Flavell, Miller, & Miller, 1993). It is also noting that your efforts to remember something are not working and that you need to try something different (Schneider, 2004). Metamemory is one aspect of **metacognition,** or knowledge of the human mind and of the range of cognitive processes. Your store of metacognitive knowledge might include an understanding that you are better at learning language than at learning algebra, that it is harder to pay attention to a task when there is distracting noise in the background than when it is quiet, and that it is wise to check a proposed solution to a problem before concluding that it is correct.

When do children first show evidence of metacognition? If instructed to remember where the *Sesame Street* character Big Bird has been hidden so that they can later wake him up, even 2- and 3-year-olds will go stand near the hiding spot, or at least look or point at that spot; they do not do these things as often if Big Bird is visible and they do not need to remember where he is (DeLoache, Cassidy, & Brown, 1985). By age 2, then, children understand that to remember something, you have to work at it. Researchers have found that 3-year-olds understand the difference between thinking about an object and perceiving it and that 4-year-olds realize behavior is guided by beliefs (Flavell, 1999). These findings indicate that metacognitive awareness is present at least in a rudimentary form at a young age (Kuhn, 2000).

In another study (Ghetti & Alexander, 2004), children and adults were asked to rate the salience and memorability of past events. Even 5-year-olds detected differences in the salience of events and expected that more salient events would be easier to remember. These findings contrast with earlier ones in which children were asked to predict how many items they would be able to remember (for example, Yussen & Levy, 1975). Under these conditions, preschoolers' estimates were highly unrealistic—as if they believed they could perform any memory feat imaginable—and they were unfazed by information about how another child had done on the task. But if researchers gave children more time before asking them to estimate how much they would be able to recall of what they had just studied, accuracy was good among children as young as age 6 (Schneider, Roth, & Ennemoser, 2000). When asked immediately after the learning task, children (and adults) overestimated their future ability to remember, presumably based on what was still in their short-term memory. After a few minutes, this information is typically lost from short-term memory, and children base their estimates on what has made it into long-term memory.

Are increases in metamemory a major contributor to improved memory performance over the childhood years? Children with greater metamemory awareness demonstrate better memory ability, but several factors influence the strength of this relationship (Bjork & Bjork, 1998; Schneider, 2004). Researchers are most likely to see a connection between metamemory and memory performance among older children and among children who have been in situations in which they must remember something (DeMarie & Ferron, 2003; Schneider & Bjorklund, 1998). Not only is task experience important, but the nature of the task is also relevant. Awareness of memory processes benefits even young children on tasks that are simple and familiar and where connections between metamemory knowledge and memory performance are fairly obvious (Schneider & Sodian, 1988). Yet children who know what to do may not always do it, so good metamemory is no guarantee of good recall (Schneider & Pressley, 1997). It seems that children not only must know that a strategy is useful but also must know why it is useful to be motivated to use it and to benefit from its use (Justice et al., 1997). The links between metamemory and memory performance, although not perfect, are strong enough to suggest the merits of teaching children more about how memory works and how they can make it work more effectively for them.

Does Knowledge of the World Change?

Ten-year-olds know considerably more about the world in general than 2-year-olds do. The individual's knowledge of a content area to be learned, or **knowledge base,** as it has come to be called, clearly affects learning and memory performance. Think about the difference between reading about a topic that you already know well and reading about a new topic. In the first case, you can read quickly because you are able to link the information to the knowledge you have already stored. All you really need to do is check for any new information or information that contradicts what you already know. Learning about a highly unfamiliar topic is more difficult ("It's Greek to me").

Perhaps the most dramatic illustration of the powerful influence of knowledge base on memory was provided by Michelene Chi (1978). She demonstrated that even though adults typically outperform children on tests of memory, this age difference could be reversed if children have more expertise than adults. Chi recruited children who were expert chess players and compared their memory skills with those of adults who were familiar with the game but lacked expertise. On a test of memory for sequences of digits, the children recalled fewer than the adults did, demonstrating their usual deficiencies. But on a test of memory for the locations of chess pieces, the children clearly beat the adults (see Figure 8.3). Because they were experts, these children were able to form more and larger mental chunks, or meaningful groups of chess pieces, which allowed them to remember more. When child experts were compared with adult experts, there were no differences in performance (Schneider et al., 1993).

Pause to consider the implications: On most tasks, young children are the novices and older children or adults are the experts. Perhaps older children and adults recall longer strings of digits because they are more familiar with numbers than young children are, not because they have better basic learning capacities. Perhaps they recall more words in word lists simply because they have more familiarity with language. Perhaps memory improves over childhood simply because older children know more about all kinds of things than younger children do (Bjorklund, 1995).

In their areas of expertise—whether baseball, dinosaurs, Yu-Gi-Oh cards, or *Lord of the Rings*—children appear to develop highly specialized and effective strategies of information processing, just as the young chess players studied by Chi apparently had (see Schneider & Bjorklund, 1998, for review). Indeed, children with low general intellectual ability but high expertise sometimes understand and remember more about stories in their area of expertise than do children with higher intellectual ability but less expertise (Schneider, Bjorklund, & Maier-Bruckner, 1996). It seems that the more you know, the more you *can* know. It also seems that how well a child does on a memory task depends not only on age but also on familiarity with the specific task.

Revisiting the Explanations

We can now draw four conclusions about the development of learning and memory:

1. Older children have a greater information-processing *capacity* than younger children do, particularly in the sense that they are faster information processors and can juggle more information in working memory.

2. Older children use more effective *memory strategies* in encoding and retrieving information.

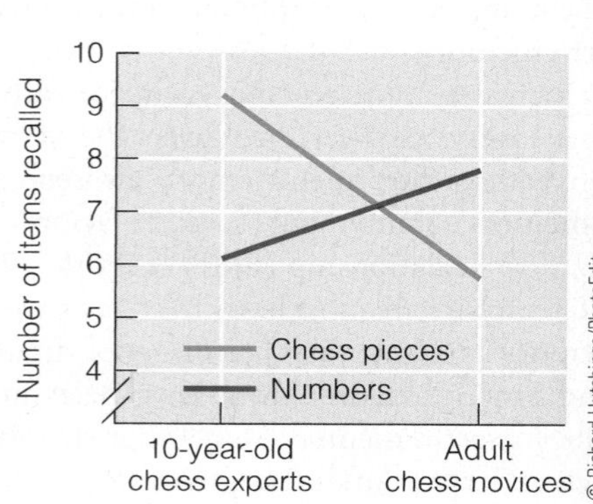

Figure 8.3 Effects of expertise on memory. Michelene Chi found that child chess experts outperformed adult chess novices on a test of recall for the location of chess pieces (although, in keeping with the usual developmental trend, these children could not recall strings of numbers as well as adults could).

SOURCE: Adapted from Chi, M. T. H. (1978). Knowledge structures and memory development. In R. Siegler (Ed.), *Children's thinking: What develops?* Hillsdale, NJ: Erlbaum. Copyright © 1978 by Lawrence Erlbaum Associates, Inc. Reprinted by permission.

3. Older children know more about memory, and good *metamemory* may help children choose more appropriate strategies and control and monitor their learning more effectively.

4. Older children know more in general, and their larger *knowledge base* improves their ability to learn and remember.

Is there a best hypothesis? Darlene DeMarie and John Ferron (2003) tested whether a model that includes three of these factors—basic capacities, strategies, and metamemory—could explain recall memory better than a single factor. For both younger (5–8 years) and older (8–11 years) children, the three-factor model predicted memory performance better than a single-factor model. Use of memory strategies was an especially strong direct predictor of recall. Importantly, there were also correlations among factors. Having good basic capacities, for example, was related to advanced metamemory and to command of strategies and had both direct and indirect influences on recall. So all these phenomena may contribute something to the dramatic improvements in learning and memory that occur over the childhood years. We return to these four hypotheses when we consider changes in learning and memory in adulthood.

Autobiographical Memory

Much of what children remember and talk about consists of everyday events that have happened to them. Children effortlessly remember all sorts of things: a birthday party last week, where they left their favorite toy, what to do when they go to a fast-food restaurant. Such **autobiographical memories** are essential ingredients of present and future experiences. Look at how autobiographical memories are stored and organized and at factors that influence their accuracy.

When Do Autobiographical Memories Begin?

You learned earlier in this chapter that infants and toddlers are able to store memories. You also know that children and adults have many specific autobiographical events stored in long-term memory. Yet research shows that older children and adults exhibit **childhood** (or infantile) **amnesia;** that is, they have few autobiographical memories of events that occurred before about age 2 or age 3 (Hayne, 2004; Neisser, 2004).

To determine how old we have to be when we experience significant life events to remember them, JoNell Usher and Ulric Neisser (1993) asked college students who had experienced the birth of a younger sibling, a hospitalization, the death of a family member, or a family move early in life to answer questions about those experiences (for example, who told them their mothers were going to the hospital to give birth, what they were doing when she left, and where they were when they first saw the new baby). As Figure 8.4 shows, the proportion of memory questions students were able to answer increased dramatically as age at the time of the experience increased. Overall, children had to be at least age 2 to recall the birth of a sibling or hospitalization and age 3 to recall the death of a family member or a move.

Why do we remember little about our early years? As you have seen, infants and toddlers are certainly capable of encoding their experiences (Fivush, 2002; Howe, 2000; Rovee-

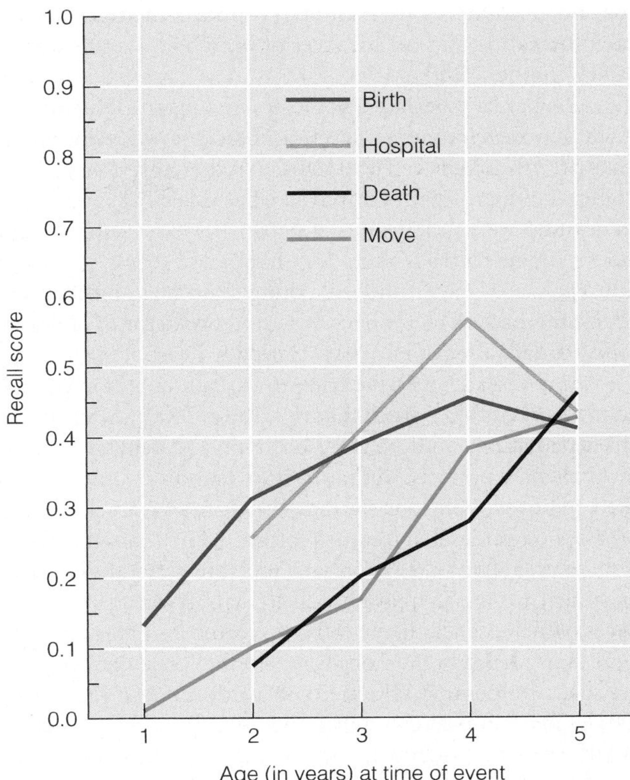

Figure 8.4 College students' recall of early life events increases as a function of how old they were at the time of the event.

SOURCE: From Usher, J. A., & Neisser, U. (1993). Childhood amnesia and the beginnings of memory for four early life events. *Journal of Experimental Psychology: General, 122,* 155–165. Copyright © 1993 by the American Psychological Association. Reprinted by permission.

Collier, 1997). Also, young preschool children seem able to remember a good deal about events that occurred when they were infants even though older children and adults cannot (Bauer, 1996; Fivush, Gray, & Fromhoff, 1987). One explanation of childhood amnesia is that infants and toddlers may not have enough space in working memory to hold the multiple pieces of information about actor, action, and setting needed to encode a coherent memory of an event (White & Pillemer, 1979). As you learned earlier in this chapter, functional working memory capacity increases with age.

Also, infants do not use language, and adults do. Because autobiographical memory relies heavily on language skills, we would expect such memories to increase with increased language skills (Marian & Neisser, 2000). Gabrielle Simcock and Harlene Hayne (2002) assessed the verbal skills of young children (27, 33, and 39 months old) who participated in a unique event. After a 6- or 12-month delay, children were tested for both verbal and nonverbal recall of the unique event. Their nonverbal recall improved across the age groups but was good for all the children. Verbal recall was poor and relied entirely on the simpler verbal skills present at the time of encoding rather than the more developed verbal skills present at the time of recall. In other words, "children's verbal reports of the event were frozen in time" (p. 229). So a relative lack of verbal skills during our first few years may limit what we are able to recall from this period. However, this language explanation does not account for why children cannot remember nonverbal information such as the faces of preschool classmates (Lie & Newcombe, 1999).

Alternatively, perhaps memories no longer useful once we reach new developmental levels and face new developmental tasks are no longer retrieved and are therefore lost (Rovee-Collier & Boller, 1995). Or maybe what is lacking is a sense of self around which memories of personally experienced events can be organized as "events that happened to *me*" (Howe & Courage, 1993, 1997). Indeed, young children's ability to recognize themselves in a mirror is a good predictor of children's ability to talk about their past (Harley & Reese, 1999).

Some researchers have tried to explain childhood amnesia in terms of **fuzzy-trace theory** (Howe, 2000). According to this explanation, children store verbatim and general accounts of an event separately. Verbatim information is unstable and likely to be lost over long periods (Leichtman & Ceci, 1993); it is easier to remember the gist of an event than the details (Brainerd & Reyna, 1993; Koriat, Goldsmith, & Pansky, 2000). With age, we are increasingly likely to rely on gist memory traces, which are less likely to be forgotten and are more efficient than verbatim memory traces in the sense that they take less space in memory (Brainerd & Gordon, 1994; Klaczynski, 2001). Children pass through a transition period from storing largely verbatim memories to storing more gist memories, and the earlier verbatim memories are unlikely to be retained over time (Howe, 2000).

Finally, there is evidence that although children may lose explicit recall of early experiences, they retain some implicit memories, at least for nonverbal information (such as classmates' faces; see Lie & Newcombe, 1999). As you can see, there are plenty of ideas about the causes of childhood amnesia but still no firm explanation of why a period of life that is highly important to later development is a blank for most of us.

Scripts

As children engage in routine daily activities such as getting ready for bed or eating at a fast-food restaurant, they construct **scripts** of these activities (Nelson, 1986). Scripts represent the typical sequence of actions related to an event and guide future behaviors in similar settings (Schank & Abelson, 1977). For instance, children who have been to a fast-food restaurant might have a script like this: Wait in line, tell the person behind the counter what you want, pay for the food, carry the tray of food to a table, open the packages and eat the food, gather the trash, and throw it away before leaving. With this script in mind, children can act effectively in similar settings. Children as young as 3 years use scripts when reporting familiar events (Nelson, 1997). When asked about their visit to a fast-food restaurant the day before, children report generally what happens when they go to the restaurant rather than what specifically happened during yesterday's visit (Kuebli & Fivush, 1994). As children age, their scripts become more detailed. Perhaps more important than age, however, is experience: Children with greater experience of an event develop richer scripts than children with less experience (DeMarie, Norman, & Abshier, 2000).

Eyewitness Memory

Children's scripts affect their memory. For example, when presented with information inconsistent with their scripts, preschoolers may misremember the information so that it

☾ Children develop scripts in memory for routine activities that guide their behavior in these situations.

better fits their script (Nelson & Hudson, 1988). This indicates that memory is a reconstruction, not an exact replication (Koriat, Goldsmith, & Pansky, 2000). This, in turn, has significant implications for **eyewitness memory** (or testimony), or people reporting events that they witnessed or experienced—for example, you reporting that you saw your little brother snitch some candy before dinner. Children are increasingly asked to report events that have happened in the context of abuse cases or custody hearings (Bruck & Ceci, 1999; Ceci & Bruck, 1998). To what extent can you "trust" a child's memory in these situations? What factors influence the accuracy of children's eyewitness memory?

When asked generally about events ("Tell me what happened at Uncle Joe's house"), preschoolers recall less information than older children, but the recall of both groups is accurate (Fivush & Hammond, 1989; Howe, Courage, & Peterson, 1994). Specific questions ("Was Uncle Joe wearing a red shirt?") elicit more information, but accuracy of recall begins to slip (Hilgard & Loftus, 1979). This is especially true as the questions become more directed or leading ("Uncle Joe touched you here, didn't he?"). Preschool-age children, more so than older children and adults, are suggestible; they can be influenced by information implied in direct questioning and by relevant information introduced after the event (Bjorklund, Brown, & Bjorklund, 2002).

Perhaps it is unfortunate, then, that preschoolers, because they initially offer less information in response to open-ended questions, are asked a larger number of directed questions (Baker-Ward et al., 1993; Price & Goodman, 1990). They are also frequently subjected to repeated questioning, which increases errors in reporting among children (Bjorklund, Brown, & Bjorklund, 2002). Although repeated questioning with general, open-ended questions can increase accuracy, repeated questioning with directed or closed questions can decrease it (Memon & Vartoukian, 1996). For example, in a study with 5- and 6-year-olds, researchers "cross-examined" children about events that occurred on a field trip to a police station during which the children saw a jail cell and police car and were fingerprinted and photographed (Zajac & Hayne, 2003). After a delay of 8 months, children's memories were probed using irrelevant, leading, and ambiguous questions like those you might hear in a courtroom. Many children "cracked" under the pressure as evidenced by backing down and changing their answers in response to the questioning. Fully one out of three children changed *all* their answers, and most changed at least one answer. So although children can demonstrate accurate recall when asked clear and unbiased questions, this study shows that young children's memory for past events can quickly become muddied when the questioning becomes tough.

Problem Solving

Memories are vital to problem-solving skills. To solve any problem, a person must process information about the task, as well as use stored information, to achieve a goal. How do problem-solving capacities change during childhood? Piaget provided one answer to this question by proposing that children progress through broad stages of cognitive growth, but information-processing theorists were not satisfied with this explanation. They sought to pinpoint more specific reasons why problem-solving prowess improves so dramatically as children age.

Consider the problem of predicting what will happen to the balance beam in Figure 8.5 when weights are put on each side of the fulcrum, or balancing point. The goal is to decide which way the balance beam will tip when it is released. To judge correctly, you must take into account both the number of weights and their distances from the fulcrum. Piaget believed that concrete operational thinkers can appreciate the significance of either the amount of weight or its distance from the center but will not grasp the inverse relationship between the two factors. Only when they reach the stage of formal operations will new cognitive structures allow them to understand that balance can be maintained by decreasing a weight *and* moving it farther from the fulcrum or by increasing a weight *and* moving it closer to the fulcrum (Piaget & Inhelder, 1969).

Robert Siegler (1981, 2000) proposed that the information-processing perspective could provide a fuller analysis. His **rule assessment approach** determines what information about a problem children take in and what rules they then formulate to account for this information. This approach assumes that children's problem-solving attempts are not hit or miss but are governed by rules and that children fail to solve problems because they fail to encode all the critical aspects of the problem and are guided by faulty rules.

Siegler (1981) administered balance beam problems to individuals ages 3 to 20. He detected clear age differences in the extent to which both weight and distance from the fulcrum were taken into account in the rules that guided decisions about which end of the balance beam would drop. Few 3-year-olds used a rule; they guessed. By contrast, 4- and 5-year-olds were governed by rules. More than 80% of these children used a simple rule that said the side of the balance beam with greater weight would drop; they ignored distance from the fulcrum. By age 8, most children had begun to consider distance from the fulcrum and weight under some conditions: when the weight on the two sides was equal, they appreciated that the side of the balance beam with the weights farthest from the fulcrum would drop. By age 12, most children considered both weight and distance on a range of problems, although they still became confused on complex problems in which one side had more weights but the other had its weights farther from the fulcrum. Finally, 30% of 20-year-olds

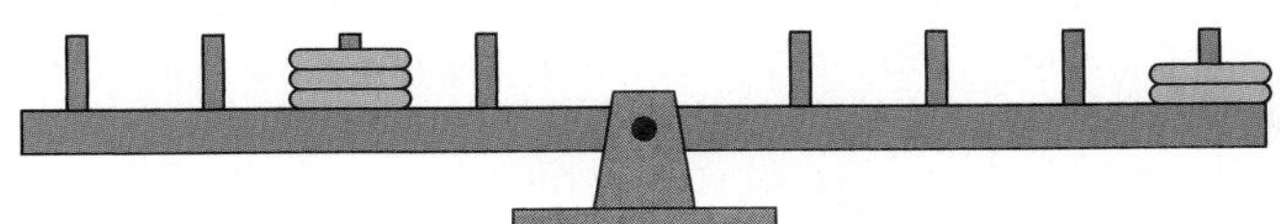

Figure 8.5 The balance beam apparatus used by Robert Siegler to study children's problem-solving abilities. Which way will the balance beam tip?

discovered the correct rule—that the pull on each arm is a function of weight times distance. For example, if there are three weights on the second peg to the left and two weights on the fourth peg to the right, the left torque is $3 \times 2 = 6$ and the right torque is $2 \times 4 = 8$, so the right arm will drop.

The increased accuracy of young adults comes with a price—increased time to solve the problem (van der Maas & Jansen, 2003). Although, in general, information processing time gets faster with age, the complex rules needed to successfully solve all the variations of the balance beam problem demands more time. So on some problems, adults are slower than children because they are using a more sophisticated strategy.

In most important areas of problem solving, Siegler (1996) concluded, children do not simply progress from one way of thinking to another as they age, as his balance beam research suggested. Instead, in working problems in arithmetic, spelling, science, and other school subjects, most children in any age group use multiple rules or problem-solving strategies rather than just one. In working a subtraction problem such as $12 - 3 = 9$, for example, children sometimes count down from 12 until they have counted off 3 and arrive at 9 but other times count from 3 until they reach 12. In one study of second- and fourth-graders, more than 90% of the children used three or more strategies in working subtraction problems (Siegler, 1989).

Similarly, Michael Cohen (1996) found that most preschoolers used all possible strategies when attempting to solve a practical mathematical problem in the context of playing store. He also found that children's selection and use of strategies became more efficient over multiple task trials; that is, they increasingly selected strategies that would allow them to solve the task in fewer steps.

Such results suggest that cognitive development works much as evolution does, through a process of natural selection in which many ways of thinking are available and the most adaptive survive (Siegler, 1996, 2000; DeLoache, Miller, & Pierroutsakos, 1998). Rather than picturing development as a series of stages resembling stairsteps, Siegler argues, we should picture it as overlapping waves, as shown in Figure 8.6. At each age, children have multiple problem-solving strategies available to them; it is not "one child (or age), one rule." As children gain more experience, which typically occurs as they age, they use less-adaptive strategies less and more-adaptive strategies more; occasionally, new strategies may appear. Strategies evolve from their initial acquisition in a particular context to their generalization to other contexts, which helps strengthen the fledgling strategies (Chen & Siegler, 2000). Gradually, children not only learn to choose the most useful strategy for a problem but also become increasingly effective at executing new strategies. Familiarity with a task and with strategies frees processing space, allowing children to engage in more metacognitive analysis of the strategies at their disposal (Whitebread, 1999).

Notice the difference between this information-processing explanation and Piaget's explanation of cognitive change. Piaget argued that change is qualitative, with new, more effective

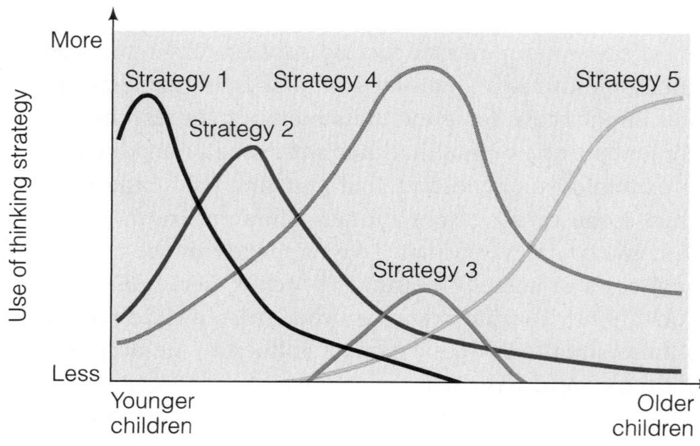

Figure 8.6 Cognitive development may resemble overlapping waves more than a staircase leading from one stage to another. Children of a particular age typically use multiple thinking strategies rather than just one.

SOURCE: Siegler (1996).

strategies replacing older, less effective strategies all at once as children move from one stage to another. Siegler argues that strategies emerge gradually and become more effective over time, with multiple strategies available any time.

Imagine how effective teachers might be if they, like Siegler, could accurately diagnose the information-processing strategies of their learners to know what each child is noticing (or failing to notice) about a problem and what rules or strategies each child is using. Like a good car mechanic, the teacher would be able to pinpoint the problem and encourage less use of faulty strategies and rules and more use of adaptive ones. Much remains to be learned about how problem-solving strategies evolve as children age, and why. However, the rule assessment approach and overlapping waves model give a fairly specific idea of what children are doing (or doing wrong) as they attack problems and illustrate how the information-processing approach to cognitive development provides a different view of development than Piaget's account does.

Summing Up

Memory improves during childhood with increased efficiency of basic information-processing capacities, greater use of memory strategies, improvement in metamemory, and growth of general knowledge base. Much of what we remember is autobiographical. Even though infants and toddlers show evidence of memory, older children and adults often experience childhood amnesia, or lack of memory for events that happened during infancy and early childhood. Such childhood amnesia may occur because of space limitations in working memory or because early events are stored in ways that make later retrieval difficult or because children store more verbatim information and less gist. By age 3, children store routine daily events as scripts that they can draw on in similar situations. Our scripts influence what we remember about an event, which is also influenced by information related to but coming after the event. Even young children can use systematic rules to solve problems, but their problem-solving skills improve as they replace faulty rules with ones that incorporate all the relevant aspects of the problem. ■

The Adolescent

Although parents in the midst of reminding their adolescent sons and daughters to do household chores or homework may wonder whether teenagers process any information, learning, memory, and problem solving continue to improve considerably during the adolescent years. How does this improvement occur?

First, new learning and memory strategies emerge. It is during adolescence that the memory strategy of elaboration is mastered (Schneider & Pressley, 1997). Adolescents also develop and refine advanced learning and memory strategies highly relevant to school learning—for example, note-taking and underlining skills. Ann Brown and Sandra Smiley (1978) asked students from 5th to 12th grade (approximately 11–18 years) to read and recall a story. Some learners were asked to recall the story immediately; others were given an additional 5 minutes to study it before they were tested. Amazingly, fifth-graders gained almost nothing from the extra study period except for those few who used the time to underline or take notes. The older junior high school students benefited to an extent, but only senior high school students used underlining and note-taking methods effectively to improve their recall. When some groups of students were told specifically that they could underline or take notes if they wished, fifth-graders still did not improve, largely because they tended to underline everything rather than to highlight the most important points.

Second, adolescents make more deliberate use of strategies that younger children use unconsciously (Bjorklund, 1985). For example, they may deliberately organize a list of words instead of simply using the organization or grouping that happens to be there already. And they use existing strategies more selectively. For example, they are adept at using their strategies to memorize the material on which they know they will be tested and at deliberately forgetting anything else (Bray, Hersh, & Turner, 1985; Lorsbach & Reimer, 1997). To illustrate, Patricia Miller and Michael Weiss (1981) asked children to remember the locations of animals that had been hidden behind small doors, ignoring the household objects hidden behind other doors. As Figure 8.7 shows, 13-year-olds recalled more than 7- and 10-year-olds about where the animals had been hidden, but they remembered less about task-irrelevant information (the locations of the household objects). Apparently, they are better able to push irrelevant information out of working memory so that it does not interfere with task performance (Lorsbach & Reimer, 1997). So, during elementary school, children get better at distinguishing between what is relevant and what is irrelevant, but during adolescence they advance further by selectively using their memory strategies only on the relevant material. If it is not going to be on the test, forget it!

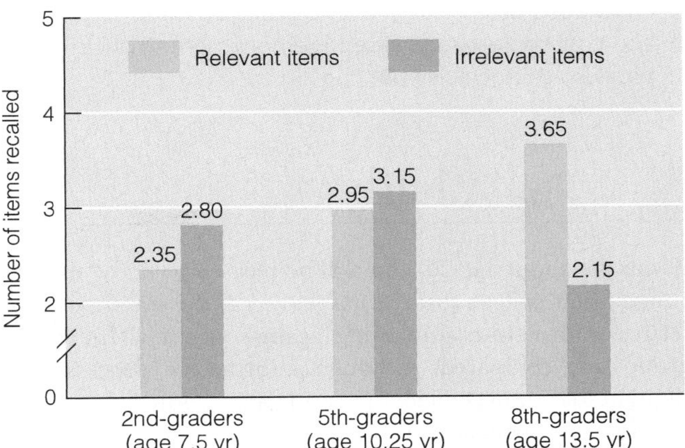

Figure 8.7 Adolescents are better able than children to concentrate on learning relevant material and to ignore irrelevant material.

SOURCE: Miller & Weiss (1981).

Adolescents make other strides besides these changes in memory strategies. Basic capacities continue to increase; for example, adolescents perform any number of cognitive operations more speedily than children do (Kail, 1991). Adolescents continue to expand their knowledge base, so they may do better than children on some tasks simply because they know more about the topic. Metamemory and metacognition also improve. For example, adolescents become better able to tailor their reading strategies to different purposes (studying versus skimming) and better able to realize when they do not understand something (Baker & Brown, 1984). They can monitor their strategy choice, selecting elaboration over rote repetition when they realize that the former is more effective (Pressley, Levin, & Ghatala, 1984). They are also fairly accurate at monitoring whether or not they have allocated adequate study time to learn new material (Kelemen, 2000). Teens typically allocate more study time to information judged to be difficult, indicating that they understand this material needs additional processing to be retained (Thiede & Dunlosky, 1999). Interestingly, when pressed for time, college students devote more study time to easy items (Son & Metcalfe, 2000). Apparently, they decide it is futile to work on the difficult material when they do not have adequate time, so they spend their time on what seems most likely to pay off. Hopefully, you can see the implication of this for your own studying: Set aside enough time to study all the material; otherwise, you may end up in a time crunch reviewing only the easy material.

Growth in strategies, basic capacities, knowledge base, and metacognition probably also helps explain the growth in everyday problem-solving ability that occurs during the adolescent years. Teenagers perfect several information-processing skills and become able to apply them deliberately and spontaneously across a variety of tasks.

Summing Up

Adolescents are able to use more sophisticated memory strategies, although they often rely on the strategy of rehearsal that served them well during childhood. Their knowledge bases and metamemory skills also improve and contribute to increased memory performance and problem-solving ability. ■

The Adult

If you are about age 20, you will be pleased to know that the young adult college student has served as the standard of effective information processing against which all other age groups are compared. Although information processes are thought to be most efficient in young adults, improvements in cognitive performance continue during the adult years before aging begins to take its toll on some memory and problem-solving capacities.

Developing Expertise

Comparing people new to their chosen fields of study with those more experienced tells researchers that experience pays off in more effective memory and problem-solving skills. In Chapter 7, you saw that people in Piaget's highest stage of cognitive development, formal operations, often perform better in their areas of specialization than in unfamiliar areas. Similarly, information-processing research shows that adults often function best cognitively in domains in which they have achieved expertise (Byrnes, 1996; Ericsson, 1996; Glaser & Chi, 1988). It seems to take about 10 years of training and experience to become a true expert in a field and to build a rich and well-organized knowledge base (Ericsson, 1996). But once this base is achieved, the expert not only knows and remembers more but thinks also more effectively than individuals who lack expertise.

Consider first the effects of knowledge base on memory. How might adults who are baseball experts and adults who care little for baseball perceive and remember the same game? George Spilich and his associates (1979) had baseball experts and novices listen to a tape of a half inning of play. Experts recalled more of the information central to the game—the important plays and the fate of each batter, in proper order—whereas novices were caught by facts such as the threatening weather conditions and the number of people attending the game. Experts also recalled more details—for example, noting that a double was a line drive down the left-field line rather than just a double. At any age, experts in a field are likely to remember new information in that content domain more fully than novices do (Morrow et al., 1994).

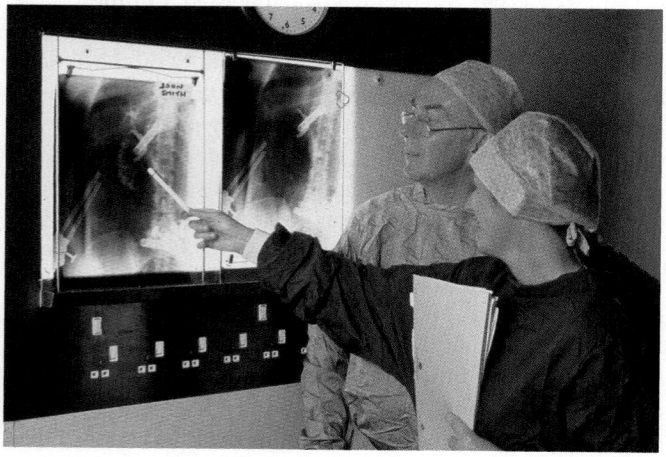

In addition, experts are able to use their elaborately organized and complete knowledge bases to solve problems effectively and efficiently (Proffitt, Coley, & Medin, 2000). They are able to size up a situation quickly, see what the problem really is, and recognize how the new problem is similar to and different from problems encountered in the past (Glaser & Chi, 1988). They can quickly, surely, and almost automatically call up the right information from their extensive knowledge base to devise effective solutions to problems and to carry them out efficiently.

Are the benefits of expertise content-specific, or does gaining expertise in one domain carry over into other domains and make a person a more generally effective learner or problem solver? This is an interesting and important question. One research team (Ericsson, Chase, & Faloon, 1980) put an average college student to work improving the number of digits he could recall. He practiced for about 1 hour a day, 3 to 5 days a week, for more than $1^1/_2$ years—more than 200 hours in all. His improvement? He went from a memory span of 7 digits to one of 79 digits. His method involved forming meaningful associations between strings of digits and running times—for example, seeing 3492 as "3 minutes and 49 point 2 seconds, near world-record mile time" (p. 1181). It also involved chunking numbers into groups of three or four then organizing the chunks into large units.

Did all this work pay off in a better memory for information other than numbers? Not really. When he was given letters of the alphabet to recall, this young man's memory span was unexceptional (about six letters). Clearly the memory ability he developed was based on strategies of use only in the subject matter he was trying to remember. Similarly, Rajan Mahadevan, a man with an exceptional memory for arrays of numbers, turns out to possess no special ability for remembering the positions and orientations of objects (Biederman et al., 1992), and Shakuntala Devi, a woman who can solve complex mathematical problems in her head at amazing speeds, is apparently average at performing other cognitive operations (Jensen, 1990). Each expert apparently relies on domain-specific knowledge and domain-specific information-processing strategies to achieve cognitive feats (Ericsson & Kintsch, 1995; Schunn & Anderson, 1999).

Sometimes, domain expertise can be a hindrance. Tax experts typically outperform tax novices on hypothetical tax cases that do not fit a general tax principle (Marchant et al., 1991). But when primed to think about a general tax princi-

☾ Adults who have gained proficiency in their chosen fields can draw from their well-organized knowledge bases to find just the right information to fit the problem at hand. Solving problems is automatic and effortless for experts.

ple, experts had more trouble than novices on a tax case that violated this principle, presumably because they had trouble "overriding" the rich source of information activated in their memory (Lewandowsky & Kirsner, 2000). And although older adults know more about the world than younger adults, they do not always perform better when given an explicit memory task (Foos & Sarno, 1998). In one study, for example, older adults first demonstrated that they had greater knowledge of U.S. presidents than younger adults. Both groups were then given a set of 20 presidents' names to study for as long as they wanted before being tested for recall and recognition of the list (Foos & Sarno, 1998). The younger adults outperformed the older ones. The older adults spent less time studying the list than the younger adults, possibly because they were confident that they already knew the familiar material.

It is evident that experts know more than novices do, their knowledge base is more organized, and they are able to use their knowledge and the specialized strategies they have devised to learn, remember, and solve problems efficiently in their areas of expertise—but not in other domains. In effect, experts do not need to think much; they are like experienced drivers who can put themselves on "autopilot" and carry out well-learned routines quickly and accurately. By gaining expertise over the years, adults can often compensate for losses in information-processing capacities, the next topic.

Autobiographical Memory

Earlier in this chapter, we examined the emergence of autobiographical memories and you learned that most adults do not remember much about their early years. What, then, do adults remember about their pasts? To begin to understand the nature of autobiographical memories, Christopher Burt and his colleagues (2003) had some adults record their daily experiences in diaries and others take photographs, creating a visual diary of their experiences. Both groups were then tested for recall of their experiences after an interval of 4 or 5 months. From this, Burt and his colleagues learned that autobiographical memories of an event often include what was initially recorded as several episodes rather than a single episode. Thus, memories for events in a person's past are complex integrations of multiple episodes occurring over time.

Other research indicates that memories of our former selves are often negative compared with our current perceptions (Berntsen & Rubin, 2002; Ross & Wilson, 2003). Thus, a woman might recall that she used to be awkward in social situations compared with how comfortable and sophisticated she is now. Or a couple may recall how intolerant they were as young parents compared with how tolerant they are now. At the time these people were supposedly so awkward or intolerant, they did not perceive themselves that way; only in hindsight do people have this perspective. The extent to which people recall their past selves as worse than their current selves depends on whether they feel that their past selves are distant enough from their current selves, regardless of how much time has passed (Ross & Wilson, 2003).

Finally, research on autobiographical memory has revealed that people recall more information from their late teens and early 20s than from any other time frame except for the near present (Fitzgerald, 1999; Rubin, 2002; Rybash, 1999). Figure 8.8 shows the number of memories recalled by 70-year-old adults. Not surprisingly, they recalled a lot from their recent past (for example, age 65). But the number of memories recalled from about ages 15 to 25 was higher than the number recalled from other points of the life span. Why? Possibly, this period of life is more memorable because it is instrumental in shaping who people are as adults and is often full of significant life changes (Fitzgerald, 1999). David Rubin (2002) suggests that the *bump*, as he calls it, occurs because memories from adolescence and early adulthood are more easily accessible than memories from other periods of the life span. They are more accessible because of their distinctiveness and the effort applied to understanding the meaning of the events recalled (Rubin, Rahhal, & Poon, 1998).

Memory and Aging

No less an expert on learning than B. F. Skinner complained about memory problems: "One of the more disheartening experiences of old age is discovering that a point you have just made—so significant, so beautifully expressed—was made by you in something you published a long time ago" (Skinner, 1983, p. 242). Most elderly adults report that they have at least minor difficulties remembering things (Smith et al., 1996). They are especially likely to have trouble remembering names

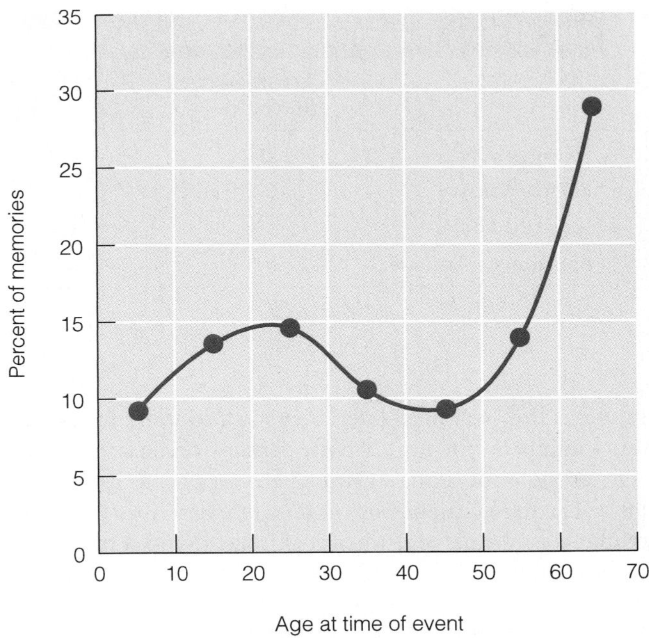

Figure 8.8 The distribution of autobiographical memories over the life span of older adults (70 years).

SOURCE: Rubin, Wetzler, & Nebes (1986, pp. 202–221). Reprinted by permission of Cambridge University Press.

Forgetting: What Is Normal and What Is Not?

As we age, or watch parents and grandparents age, how can we distinguish between normal forgetfulness and abnormal memory changes? Many older adults worry that forgetting an appointment or where they put their reading glasses is a precursor to the pathological memory loss associated with Alzheimer's disease (see Chapter 16). Fortunately, most of us will not develop Alzheimer's disease (AD) and the atypical memory changes that accompany it. Most will, however, exhibit some changes in memory and information-processing skills. So how can we discriminate between normal memory changes and those associated with disease?

Giovanni Carlesimo and his colleagues (1998) compared the memory performance of healthy younger, elderly, and very old adults with that of adults with Alzheimer's disease. The table in this Explorations box shows how the four groups compared on a digit-span test assessing how many pieces of information can be held in short-term memory and on immediate and delayed recall of semantically related items. The digit span of Alzheimer's disease patients was worse than that of their healthy age-mates, although it was not markedly different from that of very old adults. However, recall was clearly deficient in Alzheimer's disease patients compared not only with their age-mates but also with very old healthy adults. Even more striking was the difference in the extent to which the groups took advantage of the semantic relatedness of items to help their memory. The last column shows that the three healthy groups of adults performed at above-chance levels in categorizing items, whereas the Alzheimer's disease patients were below chance and sharply different from all the healthy groups. Clearly, normal aging does not take nearly the toll on memory skills that Alzheimer's disease does.

How, then, can family members and professionals recognize the difference between normal and unhealthy memory deficits? Cynthia Green (2001) suggests three criteria that can be used to alert us to atypical memory problems:

- Has memory gotten noticeably worse over the past 6 months?
- Do memory problems interfere with everyday activities at home or work?
- Are family and friends concerned about an individual's memory problems?

Answering "yes" to these questions may indicate unusual memory loss that should be evaluated by a professional.

In practical terms, it is normal to forget where you put something but abnormal to forget how to use it (Cherry & Smith, 1998). Thus, do not worry when Grandpa cannot find his car keys, but be alert if he cannot remember how to use them when they are in his hand. Similarly, it is normal to forget a new phone number you recently looked up in the phone book but abnormal to forget phone numbers you have known and used for years.

Age, Memory Performance, and Clustering Scores of Healthy Adults and Adults with Alzheimer's Disease

	Average Age (in years)	Digit Span	Immediate Recall	Delayed Recall	Clustering Index
Young Adults	29	6.4	51	12	+0.25
Elderly Adults	67	5.5	39	9	+0.24
Very Old Adults	83	4.6	34	7	+0.30
Alzheimer's Patients	67	4.3	18	2	−0.13

and items they will need later; they are also more upset than young adults by memory lapses, perhaps because they view them as signs of aging (Cavanaugh, Grady, & Perlmutter, 1983). The Explorations box on this page describes when forgetfulness is normal and when it is indicative of a more serious problem.

Areas of Strength and Weakness

Much research indicates that, on average, older adults learn new material more slowly and sometimes learn it less well than young and middle-aged adults do and that they remember what they have learned less well. However, the following qualifications are important:

- Most of the research is based on cross-sectional studies that compare age groups, which suggests that the age differences detected could be related to factors other than age.
- Declines, when observed, typically do not become noticeable until the late 60s and 70s. Indeed, the memory of "young-old" adults (60–70 years) is more similar to that of young adults (18–34 years) than to that of older adults (71–82 years; Cregger & Rogers, 1998).

Researchers who study memory now believe there is a third type of memory loss between normal loss with age and pathological loss from disease (Petersen et al., 1997, 2001). Some individuals may develop **mild cognitive impairment.** They experience significant memory problems—forgetting important appointments, trouble learning new names, and repeating themselves to the same person—but otherwise do not appear to be suffering from dementia. At least not yet. Some research suggests that as many as 80% of those with mild cognitive impairment will eventually develop Alzheimer's disease (Morris et al., 2001).

The good news is that age-related memory loss may be preventable, and some losses may be reversible. Reducing stress, for example, is one way to improve memory performance (Bremner & Narayan, 1998). Chronic stress elevates levels of cortisol in the brain, which impedes memory. A study by the MacArthur Foundation found that three things predicted good memory over time: physical fitness and activity, mental activity, and a sense of control over life events (Rowe & Kahn, 1998). Mental activity—working crossword puzzles, reading, playing musical instruments—increases connections among neurons. Physical activity seems to release chemicals that protect neurons involved in cognitive function. Thus, remaining physically and mentally active can help protect against memory loss associated with aging. Having a sense of control over memory can boost both confidence and memory performance.

In sum, significant memory loss is not likely among healthy older adults. It is true that, relative to young adults, older adults exhibit poorer memory performance in some situations. But these changes are minor and can often be avoided by remaining physically and mentally active. Families and professionals should be on the lookout for older adults who show marked declines in their memory performance. They may be experiencing mild cognitive impairment and may eventually develop Alzheimer's disease and impaired memory.

• Difficulties in remembering affect elderly people more noticeably as they continue to age and are most severe among the oldest elderly people.

• Not all older people experience these difficulties.

• Not all kinds of memory tasks cause older people difficulty.

Studies of memory skills in adulthood suggest that the aspects of learning and memory in which older adults look most deficient in comparison with young and middle-aged adults are some of the same areas in which young children compare unfavorably with older children (for reviews, see Guttentag, 1985; Smith & Earles, 1996). The following sections describe some of the major weaknesses—and, by implication, strengths—of the older adult.

Timed Tasks. On average, older adults are slower than younger adults are to learn and retrieve information; they may need to go through the material more times to learn it equally well and may need more time to respond when their memory is tested. Thus, they are hurt by time limits (Finkel et al., 2003b).

Unfamiliar Content. Older adults fare especially poorly compared with younger adults when the material to be learned is unfamiliar or meaningless—when they cannot tie it to their existing knowledge. In a convincing demonstration of how familiarity influences memory, researchers had young and elderly adults examine words likely to be more familiar to the young adults at the time of the testing (for example, *dude, disco,* and *bummer*) and words from the past likely to be more familiar to the older adults (for example, *pompadour, gramophone,* and *vamp*). Young adults outperformed older adults on the "new" words, but older adults outperformed young adults on the "old" words (Barrett & Wright, 1981). Many memory tasks involve learning unfamiliar material and thus do not allow older adults to use their knowledge base.

Artificial Tasks. Memory is often assessed in the artificial context of the laboratory, which may be more detrimental to older adults than to young ones. In a recent meta-analysis of prospective memory, or memory for future events (for example, remembering that you must take your medicine at bedtime), Julie Henry and her colleagues (2004) reported that older adults performed significantly worse in laboratory contexts. In naturalistic contexts, however, the older adults outperformed the younger adults. So when the task is meaningful, older adults may be able to draw on their greater experience or knowledge bases to enhance their memory performance.

Unexercised Skills. Older adults are also likely to be at a disadvantage when they are required to use learning and memory skills that they rarely use in daily life; they hold their own when they can rely on well-practiced skills that have become effortless and automatic with practice. For example, Lynne Reder, Cynthia Wible, and John Martin (1986) found that elderly adults were just as good as young adults at judging whether sentences presented to them were plausible based on a story they had read. Judging whether something makes sense in the context of what has been read is a well-exercised ability. However, older adults were deficient when it came to judging whether specific sentences had or had not appeared in the story—a skill seldom used outside school. It seems that older adults read to get the gist or significance of a story and do not bother with the details, a strategy that may be adaptive if they have no need to memorize details and if their ability to do so has fallen off with age (Adams, 1991; Stine-Morrow, Loveless, & Soederberg, 1996). In other ways, age differences are smaller when well-practiced skills are assessed than when less-practiced skills are assessed (Denney, 1982).

Recall versus Recognition. Older adults are likely to be more deficient on tasks requiring recall memory than on tasks requiring only recognition of what was learned (Charles, Mather, & Carstensen, 2003). In one study of memory for high school classmates (Bahrick, Bahrick, & Wittlinger, 1975), even adults who were almost 35 years past graduation could recognize which of five names matched a picture in their yearbook about 90% of the time. However, the ability to actively recall names of classmates when given only their photos as cues dropped considerably as the age of the rememberer increased. A large gap between recognition and recall shows that older people have encoded and stored the information but cannot retrieve it without the help of cues. Sometimes older adults fail to retrieve information because they never thoroughly encoded or learned it, but at other times they simply cannot retrieve information that is "in there."

Explicit Memory Tasks. Finally, older adults seem to have more trouble with explicit memory tasks that require mental effort than with implicit memory tasks that involve more automatic mental processes (Light & LaVoie, 1993; Mitchell & Bruss, 2003). Some researchers report a small decline with age even in implicit memory, but the larger loss is in explicit memory (Maki, Zonderman, & Weingartner, 1999).

Overall, these findings suggest that older adults, like young children, have difficulty with tasks that are cognitively demanding—that require speed, the learning of unfamiliar material, the use of unexercised abilities, recall rather than recognition, or explicit and effortful rather than implicit and automatic memory. Yet older adults and young children have difficulty for different reasons, as you will now see.

Explaining Declines in Old Age

In asking why some older adults struggle with some learning and memory tasks, first return to the hypotheses used to explain childhood improvements in performance: knowledge base, metamemory, strategy use, and basic processing capacities. Then consider some additional possibilities.

Knowledge Base. Start with the hypothesis that differences in knowledge base explain differences between older and younger adults. You immediately encounter a problem: Young children may lack knowledge, but elderly adults do not. Indeed, older adults are generally at least as knowledgeable as young adults (Camp, 1989; Hess & Pullen, 1996). They often equal or surpass younger adults on measures of vocabulary and knowledge of word meanings (Light, 1991; West, Crook, & Barron, 1992). Moreover, they know a lot about the world. For example, they know more than younger adults about real-world categories of information such as U.S. presidents, countries, international cities, and bodies of water (Foos & Sarno, 1998). They also still know a surprising amount of information they learned in high school Spanish, algebra, and geometry courses taken as many as 50 years earlier (Bahrick, 1984; Bahrick & Hall, 1991). So, deficiencies in knowledge base are probably not the source of most memory problems that many older adults display. On the contrary, gains in knowledge probably help older adults compensate for losses in information-processing efficiency (Salthouse, 1993). Thus, older pilots are as adept as younger pilots and better than nonpilots at repeating back flight commands, but they show the usual effects of aging if they are given tasks less relevant to their work (Morrow et al., 1994). Older adults perform better than younger adults on memory tasks in which they can spontaneously use analogies, another indication that a rich knowledge base can aid memory (Caplan & Schooler, 2001). Knowledge enhances learning (Kaplan & Murphy, 2000). Indeed, as Paul Baltes has put it, "Knowledge is power!" (Baltes, Smith, & Staudinger, 1992, p. 143).

Metamemory. Could elderly adults, like young children, be deficient in the specific knowledge called metamemory? Is their knowledge of some of the strategies that prove useful in school learning—and in laboratory memory tasks—rusty? This theory sounds plausible, but research shows that older adults seem to know as much as younger adults about such things as which memory strategies are best and which memory tasks are hardest (Light, 1991). Yet there is a difference between knowing about memory and believing that you can remember things. Older adults do express more negative beliefs about their memory skills than younger adults do

☾ Many adults continue to expand their knowledge bases well into old age.

(Cavanaugh, 1996). Although memory loss may contribute to a drop in confidence in memory skills, negative beliefs about memory skills also appear to hurt memory performance (Cavanaugh, 1996; McDonald-Miszczak, Hertzog, & Hultsch, 1995).

Becca Levy and Ellen Langer (1994) suggest that part of the problem lies in U.S. society's negative stereotypes of aging—specifically, the stereotype of elderly people as forgetful. These researchers tested the memory of young and elderly adults (ages 59–91) in three groups: hearing Americans, deaf Americans, and hearing Chinese. In both the American deaf and Chinese cultures, elders are respected and negative stereotypes of intellectual aging are not as prevalent as they are among hearing Americans. As Figure 8.9 shows, young adults in the three groups performed about equally well on a set of recall tasks, but Chinese elders clearly outperformed both deaf American elders (who were second best) and hearing American elders. Elderly Chinese adults scored only a little lower than young Chinese adults despite having less education. In addition, those older people in the study who believed that aging brings about memory loss performed more poorly than those who did not hold this belief. Levy (1996) has also shown that activating negative stereotypes in the minds of elderly adults (through rapid, subliminal presentation of words such as *Alzheimer's* and *senile* on a computer screen) causes them to perform worse on memory tests and to express less confidence in their memory skills than when positive stereotypes of old age are planted in their minds (through words such as *wise* and *sage*). Findings such as these clearly call into question the idea of a universal decline in memory skills in later life and point to the influence of culture and its views of aging on performance.

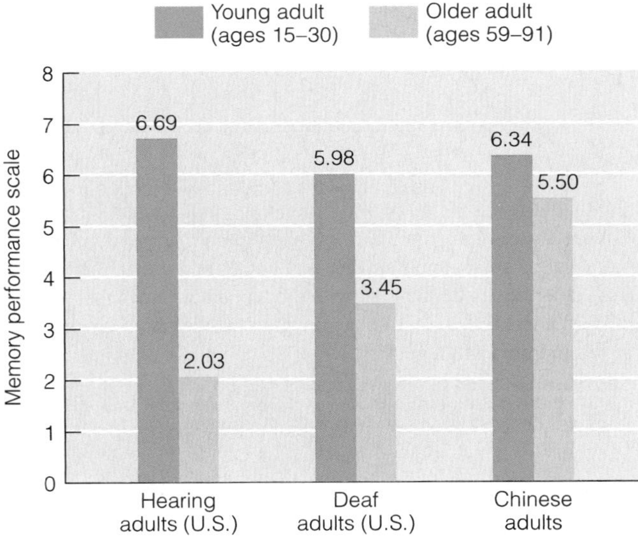

Figure 8.9 Declines in memory skills in old age are not universal. In Chinese culture, elderly people are not stereotyped as forgetful or senile. Perhaps as a result, Chinese elders perform almost as well as young Chinese adults on memory tasks, whereas in the United States, elders, especially in the hearing population, perform poorly.

SOURCE: From Levy, B., & Langer, E. (1994). Aging free from negative stereotypes: Successful memory in China and among the American deaf. *Journal of Personality and Social Psychology, 66*, 989–997. Copyright © 1994 by the American Psychological Association. Reprinted by permission.

Memory Strategies. What about the hypothesis that failure to use effective memory strategies accounts for deficits in old age? Many older adults do not spontaneously use strategies such as organization and elaboration even though they know them and are capable of using them (Light, 1991; Smith & Earles, 1996). This may be an important part of the problem when older adults are asked to deliberately memorize something. But why do many older adults fail to use effective strategies?

Basic Processing Capacities. The answer may lie in the fourth hypothesis—the notion that basic processing capacities change with age. Which capacities? Much attention has focused on declines in the capacity to use working memory to operate actively on a lot of information simultaneously. Working memory capacity increases during childhood and adolescence, peaks around age 45, then begins to decline (Swanson, 1999). Moreover, an adult's working memory capacity predicts how well he will perform on a range of cognitive tasks (Engle et al., 1999; Salthouse, 1992).

Both young children and older adults, it seems, need to devote more space in working memory than older children or young adults do to carrying out basic mental operations such as recognizing stimuli (Guttentag, 1985; Kail & Salthouse, 1994). This leaves less space for other purposes, such as thinking about or rehearsing material. You have seen that both young children and older adults do relatively well when learning and remembering can take place automatically—when mental effort is not required—but they struggle when they must exert a great deal of mental effort or carry out several activities at once. For example, research shows that trying to memorize a list of words while walking is more problematic for older adults than for middle-aged or younger adults (Li et al., 2001; Lindenberger, Marsiske, & Baltes, 2000).

Limitations in working memory capacity are most likely rooted in slower functioning of the nervous system both early and late in life (Earles & Kersten, 1999; Salthouse, 1992; also see Chapter 5). Much research shows that speed of processing increases during childhood and adolescence, peaks in early adulthood, then declines slowly over the adult years (Frieske & Park, 1999; Kail & Salthouse, 1994). Much research also shows that age differences in performance on cognitive tasks often shrink when age differences in speed of information processing are taken into account and controlled. Experience in a domain of learning can certainly enhance performance, but if children and older adults generally have sluggish "computers," they simply may not be able to keep up with the processing demands of complex learning and memory tasks (Kail & Salthouse, 1994). Slow neural transmission, then, may be behind limitations in working memory in both childhood and old age. Limitations in working memory, in turn, may contribute not only to limitations in long-term memory but also to difficulties performing a range of cognitive tasks, including problem-solving tasks and tests of intelligence, even those that

Applications

Improving Memory and Study Skills

Have you noticed that the material in this chapter has great potential value to teachers? The information-processing perspective has yielded better methods for diagnosing learning problems and improving instruction. Here we focus on interventions aimed at boosting the memory skills of young children and older adults. Just how much can be achieved through training?

Garrett Lange and Sarah Pierce (1992) took on the challenge of teaching the memory strategy of organization (grouping) to 4- and 5-year-olds. Using pictures of objects and animals as the stimuli, they taught these preschoolers a "group-and-name trick" that involved sorting items to be learned into groups based on similarity, naming the group, naming the items within the group, and, at recall, naming the group before calling out the items within that group. Because such memory-training programs have not always been successful, these researchers attempted to increase motivation through encouragement and praise. They even included training in metamemory: They made sure children understood the rationale for the sorting strategy, knew when it could be used, and could see firsthand that it could improve their performance.

How successful was the training? These children did virtually no sorting of items to be learned before they were trained, but they did a good deal of it after training, even 7 days later. They clearly learned to use the organization strategy they were taught. They also outperformed untrained control children on measures of recall. However, the gains in recall were fairly small compared with the much larger gains in strategy use. These young children demonstrated utilization deficiencies: They could not derive full benefit from the memory strategy they were taught, possibly because they did not have the working memory capacity to carry out the strategy. Other programs that teach memory strategies and metacognitive skills to elementary school children often work much better, especially with children who are underachievers and who may be capable of executing strategies but fail to do so on their own (Hattie, Biggs, & Purdie, 1996). Still, the benefits of training are often domain-specific; they do not generalize to learning tasks different from those that were the focus of training. Perhaps this makes sense if you realize that the strategies that work best in learning math skills may be different from the strategies that work best in learning historical facts or basketball skills.

How well do older adults respond to attempts to teach them more effective memory strategies? To answer this, consider the interesting work of Paul Baltes and his colleagues. In one study (Kliegl, Smith, & Baltes, 1990), these researchers trained young adults (ages 19–29) and old adults (ages 60–80) in a mnemonic technique called the **method of loci.** It involves devising a mental map of a route through a familiar place (such as the person's home) and then creating images that link items to be learned to landmarks along the route. For example, the German adults in the study were taught to associate words on word lists with well-known landmarks in Berlin; they continued to practice for many sessions so that their maximal level of performance could be assessed.

The accomplishments of these adults were remarkable, as the figure in this Applications box shows. Older adults improved from recalling fewer than 3 words in correct order

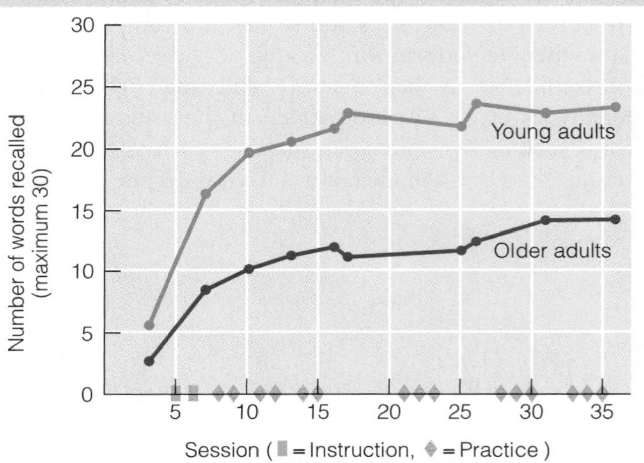

Trained to use the method of loci then given many practice sessions, young adults improve their ability to recall word lists more than older adults do, suggesting that aging places limits on maximal performance. Still, elderly adults benefit considerably from training in this memory strategy.

SOURCE: Adapted from Baltes, P. B., & Kliegl, R. (1992). Further testing of limits of cognitive plasticity: Negative age differences in a mnemonic skill are robust. *Developmental Psychology, 28,* 121–125. Copyright © 1992 by the American Psychological Association. Reprinted by permission.

have no time limits (Fry & Hale, 1996; Kail & Salthouse, 1994).

To this point, then, you might conclude that many older adults, although they have a vast knowledge base and a good deal of knowledge about learning and memory, experience declines in basic processing capacity that make it difficult for them to carry out memory strategies that will drain their limited working-memory capacity. But the basic processing capacity hypothesis cannot explain everything about age differences in memory (Light, 1991). You must consider some additional hypotheses, including sensory changes and a variety of contextual factors.

Sensory Changes. As you learned in Chapter 6, older adults experience declines in sensory abilities. Might these affect memory performance? Yes indeed. Research shows after hearing a 30-word list only once to recalling 13 words, and young adults upped their performance even more, from 6 to more than 20 words. In another study, even older adults (ages 75–101) were similarly trained to use the method of loci then tested to see whether training influenced memory performance (Singer, Lindenberger, & Baltes, 2003). Again, it did, although not as much as with the "younger" old adults. Very old adults improved from about 3 to 7 words after training.

These findings show that there is a great deal of cognitive plasticity and potential throughout the life span. As Baltes and his colleagues put it, older adults have considerable "reserve capacity" that can be tapped through intensive training. Despite limitations in basic processing capacity, older adults can master powerful memory techniques that enable them to outperform young adults who have not learned and practiced these techniques. Memory training programs can also improve aspects of metamemory, including elders' negative beliefs about their memory capacities and their memory monitoring skills (Dunlosky, Kubat-Silman, & Hertzog, 2003; Floyd & Scogin, 1997).

This study and others also show that older adults, especially those who have experienced steep cognitive declines, profit less from memory training than young adults do (Verhaeghen & Marcoen, 1996). Both children and elderly adults coached to use memory strategies often fail to use them in new learning situations, perhaps because these strategies simply require too much mental effort (Singer et al., 2003).

What, then, is the solution? If some memory strategies are too mentally taxing for many young children and elderly adults, it may make more sense to capitalize on their memory strengths. Knowing that implicit memory holds up better than explicit memory, for example, Cameron Camp and his colleagues (Camp et al., 1996; Camp & McKitrick, 1992) have tried to help patients with dementia caused by Alzheimer's disease use the implicit memory capacities that they, like people with amnesia, retain even though they have serious deficits in explicit memory. For example, they have taught patients with Alzheimer's disease to remember the names of staff members by having the patients name photos of staff members repeatedly and at ever-longer intervals between trials. People who could not retain names for more than a minute were able to recall the names weeks later after training. The technique appears to work because it uses implicit memory processes; adults learn effortlessly when they repeatedly encounter the material to be learned.

Finally, it sometimes makes more sense to change the learning environment than to change the learner (Pressley, 1983). If, for example, young children and some older adults do not spontaneously organize the material they are learning to make it more meaningful, it can be organized for them. Giving children practice at learning highly organized material can help them master the grouping strategy on their own (Best, 1993). Similarly, if the material to be learned is unfamiliar, you can use examples or analogies that will help learners relate it to something that is familiar (for example, teaching a senior citizens' group about the federal budget by likening it to their personal budgets). If young children and older adults need more time, let them set their own pace.

To use a real-world example, older adults have more trouble understanding and remembering information about their drug prescriptions than young adults do (Morrell, Park, & Poon, 1989). Yet by writing clear, organized instructions and spending time explaining to older patients what they are to do, health care professionals can simplify the learning task (Morrell, Park, & Poon, 1989). Alternatively, older adults can be given external memory aids. Denise Park and her colleagues (1992) explored the benefits of two such aids: an organization chart (a poster or pocket-sized table giving an hour-by-hour account of when drugs should be taken) and a medication organizer (a dispenser with columns for different days of the week and pill compartments for times of the day). Adults over 70 more often took their pills correctly when they were given both the chart and the organizer than when they were given one or neither. Because researchers know that poor health is one contributor to poor memory functioning, it makes especially good sense to reduce the cognitive demands on old and ailing patients by letting external memory aids do the mental work for them. Surely the best of all possible worlds for the learner would be one in which materials and teaching techniques are tailored to the learner's information-processing capacities and in which training is offered in how to stretch those capacities.

that visual and auditory skills are often better predictors than processing speed of cognitive performance among older adults (Anstey, Hofer, & Luszcz, 2003; Lindenberger & Baltes, 1994). As noted in Chapter 6, many older adults experience some hearing loss. When young adults are tested under moderately noisy conditions, a situation that mimics the hearing loss experienced by many older adults, their short-term memory performance decreases (Murphy et al., 2000). Sensory loss at any age may tax available processing resources, leading to memory deficits.

Contextual Contributors. Many researchers have adopted a contextual perspective on learning and memory, which combines biological and genetic factors with environmental and situational factors (Blanchard-Fields, Chen, & Norris, 1997; Dixon, 1992). They emphasize that performance on learning and memory tasks is the product of an interaction among (1) characteristics of the learner, such as goals, motivations, abilities, and health; (2) characteristics of the task or situation; and (3) characteristics of the broader environment, including the cultural context, in which a task is performed. They are not convinced that there is a universal biological decline in basic learning and memory capacities because older individuals often perform capably in certain contexts.

First, cohort differences in education and IQ can explain age differences in some learning and memory skills. Elderly people today are less educated, on average, than younger adults are, and they are further removed from their school days. When education level is controlled for, age differences nearly disappear (Nilsson et al., 2002). Moreover, education can compensate for aging. Older adults who are highly educated or who have high levels of intellectual ability often perform as well as younger adults (Cherry & LeCompte, 1999; Haught et al., 2000).

Similarly, health and lifestyle differences between cohorts may contribute to age differences in learning and memory. Older adults are more likely than younger adults to have chronic or degenerative diseases, and even mild diseases can impair memory performance (Houx, Vreeling, & Jolles, 1991; Hultsch, Hammer, & Small, 1993). Older adults also lead less active lifestyles and perform fewer cognitively demanding activities than younger adults do, on average. These age group differences in lifestyle also contribute to age differences in cognitive performance (Finkel & McGue, 1998; Luszcz, Bryan, & Kent, 1997). Older college professors, perhaps because they remain mentally active, outperform other older adults and perform similarly to young professors on some tests of recall (Shimamura et al., 1995).

The implications of such research are clear: Declines in information-processing skills are not inevitable or universal. Nature may place some boundaries on the information-processing system, but nurture plays a significant role in sustaining memory and problem-solving skills. Older adults may be able to maintain their memory skills if they are relatively well-educated, stay healthy, and exercise their minds. Simply reviewing material after its presentation can help them improve their memory performance (Koutstaal et al., 1998; see the Applications box on page 220 for more ways to improve memory across the life span). At the same time, factors such as education and health cannot account completely for age differences in cognitive performance (Smith & Earles, 1996).

Perhaps the truth lies somewhere between the basic processing capacity view, which emphasizes nature by pointing to a universal decline in cognitive resources such as speed and working memory that affect performance on many cognitive tasks, and the contextual view, which emphasizes nurture. Contextual theorists stress variability from person to person and situation to situation based on cohort differences, motivational factors, and task demands. Most adults, at least if they live to an advanced old age, may experience some loss of basic processing resources. However, they may also have developed specialized knowledge and strategies that allow them to compensate for these losses as they carry out the everyday cognitive activities most important to them (Baltes, Smith, & Staudinger, 1992).

Problem Solving and Aging

You know that problem-solving skills improve steadily from early childhood through adolescence, but what becomes of them in adulthood? On the one hand, you might expect to see a decline in problem-solving prowess paralleling declines in learning and memory performance. On the other hand, if adults increase their knowledge bases and develop expertise as they age, might not older adults outwit younger novices on many problem-solving tasks?

When given traditional problem-solving tasks to perform in the laboratory, young adults typically perform better than middle-aged adults, who in turn outperform older adults (Denney, 1989). However, consider research using the Twenty Questions task. Subjects are given an array of items and asked to find out, using as few questions as possible, which item the experimenter has in mind (see Figure 8.10). The soundest problem-solving strategy is to ask **constraint-seeking questions**—ones that rule out more than one item (for example, "Is it an animal?"). Young children and older adults tend to pursue specific hypotheses instead ("Is it a pig?" "Is it a pencil?"). Consequently, they must ask more questions to identify the right object. However, older adults do far better if the task is altered to make it more familiar; they then draw on their knowledge base to solve the problem. For example, when Nancy Denney (1980) used an array of playing cards, older adults asked plenty of

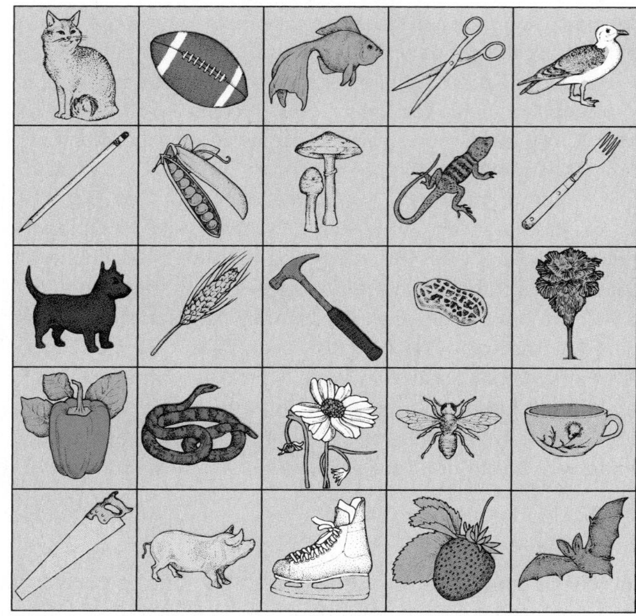

Figure 8.10 A Twenty Questions game. You can try it on a young child or a friend by thinking of one item in the group and asking your testee to find out which it is by asking you yes–no questions. Look for the constraint-seeking questions (for example, "Is it animate?"), and note the total number of questions required to identify the correct item.

constraint-seeking questions ("Is it a heart?" "Is it a face card?"). Thus, older adults are capable of using effective problem-solving strategies but do not use them in some contexts, especially when given unfamiliar tasks in a laboratory.

What if adults are asked to deal with real-life problems such as grease fires in the kitchen, warm refrigerators, or family squabbles? Nancy Denney and Kathy Pearce (1989) asked elderly adults to help them devise everyday problems that would be meaningful and familiar to older individuals. One problem was to generate ideas about how a 65-year-old recently widowed woman could improve her social life; another was to advise an elderly couple living on Social Security what to do when they were unable to pay their heating bill one winter. On these everyday problems, performance increased from early adulthood to middle age and declined in old age.

Other findings echo this one: When given everyday problems to which they can apply the expertise they have gained through experience, middle-aged adults often outperform young adults. Elderly adults sometimes equal and sometimes do worse than young and middle-aged adults; either way, they show smaller deficits than they do on unfamiliar problems in the laboratory (Berg & Klaczynski, 1996; Marsiske & Willis, 1995). Ultimately, declines in basic capacities may limit the problem-solving skills of many elderly adults, not only in the laboratory but also in real life (Denney, 1989; Kasworm & Medina, 1990). You should bear in mind, however, that cognitive competence among older adults varies widely because of differences in health, education, experience, and so on.

Finally, some cognitive researchers believe that what appear to be cognitive deficits in old age may be signs of cognitive adaptation and growth (Dixon, 1992; Perlmutter, 1986). Older adults may let little-needed cognitive skills grow rusty to maintain and strengthen those skills most useful to them in everyday life. They may use their expertise in important domains to compensate for losses in basic processing capacities (Baltes, Smith, & Staudinger, 1992). Children improve their ability to do all kinds of things; older adults may improve their ability to perform critical learning, memory, and problem-solving tasks and may forget the rest.

Summing Up

Adults increasingly develop larger and more organized knowledge bases that aid memory and problem solving. Some older adults, however, may begin to experience problems on tasks that require speed or working with unfamiliar material or unexercised skills. Contextual factors such as motivation, cohort, and the nature of the task also influence memory. The message about problem-solving skills is similar to that about memory capacities. Although performance on unfamiliar, meaningless laboratory tasks often appears to decline after early adulthood, the ability to perform more familiar, everyday information-processing tasks often improves through middle age and is maintained until late in life. ■

Summary Points

1. The information-processing approach uses a computer analogy to illustrate how the mind processes information. The human "computer" puts information into a sensory register, into short-term and working memory, then into long-term memory during encoding; stores it; retrieves it (demonstrating recognition, cued recall, or recall memory); and uses it to solve problems.

2. Infants are capable of remembering from the start. They show recognition memory at birth, simple recall in the presence of cues at 2 or 3 months, recall in the absence of cues toward the end of the first year, and deliberate, conscious attempts to retrieve memories by age 2.

3. Learning and memory continue to improve during childhood: (a) Basic information-processing capacity increases as the brain matures and fundamental processes are automated to free working-memory space; (b) memory strategies such as rehearsal, organization, and elaboration improve; (c) metamemory improves; and (d) the general knowledge base grows, improving the processing of new information in areas of expertise.

4. According to Robert Siegler, even young children use systematic rules to solve problems, but their problem-solving skills improve as they replace faulty rules with ones that incorporate all the relevant aspects of the problem. Multiple strategies are used at any age so that development proceeds through a natural selection process and resembles overlapping waves more than a set of stairsteps leading from one way of thinking to the next.

5. Adolescents master advanced learning strategies such as elaboration, note taking, and underlining; use their strategies more deliberately and selectively; and use their increased metacognitive abilities to guide learning and remembering.

6. As adults gain expertise in a domain, they develop large and organized knowledge bases and highly effective, specialized, and automated ways of retrieving and using their knowledge. Many older adults perform less well than young adults on memory tasks that require speed, the learning of unfamiliar or meaningless material, the use of unexercised abilities, recall rather than recognition memory, and explicit rather than implicit memory. Contextual factors such as cohort differences and the irrelevance of many laboratory tasks to everyday life also contribute to age differences in memory.

7. On average, older adults also perform less well than younger adults on laboratory problem-solving tasks, but everyday problem-solving skills are likely to improve from early adulthood to middle adulthood and to be maintained in old age.

Critical Thinking

1. You are a first-grade teacher, and one of the first things you notice is that some of your students remember a good deal more

than others about the stories you read to them. Based on what you have read in this chapter, what are your main hypotheses about why some children have better memories than other children the same age?

2. As a teacher in an Elderhostel program, you want to base your teaching methods on knowledge of the information-processing capacities of elderly adults. What practical recommendations would you derive from (a) the view that there is a universal decline with age in basic processing capacities and (b) the contextual perspective on cognitive aging?

3. Using the information processing model presented in the chapter (see Figure 8.1), explain why Dan, a 7-year-old, does not perform as well as Dave, a 17-year-old, when asked to recall a TV program on the Civil War both watched last week.

4. Revisit Figure 8.8 showing the distribution of autobiographical memories over the life span. What factors might account for the rise and fall of autobiographical memories at different phases of the life span?

Key Terms

information-processing approach, 200
sensory register, 200
short-term memory, 200
working memory, 200
long-term memory, 201
encoding, 201
storage, 201
retrieval, 201
recognition memory, 201
recall memory, 201
cued recall memory, 201
implicit memory, 201
explicit memory, 201
problem solving, 202
executive control processes, 202
deferred imitation, 203
rehearsal, 206
organization (as memory strategy), 206
elaboration, 206
mediation deficiency, 206
production deficiency, 207
utilization deficiency, 207
metamemory, 207
metacognition, 207
knowledge base, 208
autobiographical memories, 209
childhood amnesia, 209
fuzzy-trace theory, 210
script, 210
eyewitness memory, 211
rule assessment approach, 211
mild cognitive impairment , 217
method of loci, 220
constraint-seeking questions, 220

Media Resources

Websites to Explore

Visit Our Website

For a chapter tutorial quiz and other useful features, visit the book's companion website at *http://psychology.wadsworth.com/sigelman_rider5e.* You can also connect directly to the following sites:

Memory and Aging

The website of the Memory and Aging Research Center at University of California at Los Angeles contains links to scholarly information.

Implicit and Explicit Memory

For those seeking greater depth, read an article by researchers at the University of Sheffield that outlines a new theoretical framework for explicit and implicit memory.

Memory Loss and the Brain

The newsletter of the Memory Disorders Project at Rutgers–Newark provides information about many of the issues covered in the chapter, including mild cognitive impairment. There are also links to memory games that let you test your memory.

AmoebaWeb

Honored in October 2001 by the American Psychological Association as the website of the month, AmoebaWeb catalogs websites and Internet pages relevant to multiple areas of psychology, including memory. Psychologist Douglas Degelman at Vanguard University of Southern California maintains it.

Understanding the Data: Exercises on the Web

For additional insight on the data presented in this chapter, try the exercises for these figures at *http://psychology.wadsworth.com/sigelman_rider5e:*

Figure 8.3 Effects of expertise on memory

Figure 8.7 Adolescents are better able than children to concentrate on learning relevant material and to ignore irrelevant material

Life-Span CD-ROM

Go to the Wadsworth Life-Span CD-ROM for further study of the concepts in this chapter. The CD-ROM includes narrated concept overviews, video clips, a multimedia glossary, and additional activities to expand your learning experience.

Developmental PsychologyNow is a web-based, intelligent study system that provides a complete package of diagnostic quizzes, a personalized study plan, integrated multimedia elements, and learning modules. Check it out at *http://psychology.wadsworth.com/sigelman_rider5e/now.*

CHAPTER nine

Intelligence and Creativity

GREG SMITH WAS MEMORIZING BOOKS at 14 months of age and adding numbers at 18 months (Lenhart, 1999). He sped from second to eighth grade in 1 year and completed high school in less than 2 years. He started college full-time when he was 10 years old and hopes to eventually earn three doctoral degrees.

At age 35, Michael lives in an institution for the mentally retarded. He has been labeled profoundly retarded and has an IQ score of 17, as nearly as it can be estimated. Michael responds to people with grins and is able to walk haltingly, but he cannot feed or dress himself and does not use language.

As these examples indicate, the range of human cognitive abilities is immense. So far, much of the material on cognitive development in this book has focused on what human minds have in common, not on how they differ. Piaget, after all, was interested in identifying universal stages of cognitive development. And the information-processing approach has been used mainly to understand the basic cognitive processes all people rely on to learn, remember, and solve problems.

This chapter continues the exploration of how the human mind normally changes over the life span. Here we introduce still another approach to the study of the mind: the psychometric, or testing, approach to intelligence, which led to the creation of intelligence tests. Many people find it hard to say anything nice about IQ tests. These measures have their limitations and they have been misused. Yet they have also provided researchers with a good deal of information about intellectual development and about variations in intellectual performance. This chapter examines how performance on intelligence tests typically changes and stays the same over the life span, what IQ tests reveal about a person, and why people's IQ scores differ. It also looks at both gifted and mentally retarded individuals from a life-span perspective. Finally, it considers creativity, a type of intellectual ability not measured by traditional intelligence tests. Before going further, take the quiz in Table 9.1 to see if you may have some misconceptions about intelligence and intelligence tests; this chapter will clarify why the correct answers are correct.

© AP/Wide World Photos

Some gifted children thrive as college students. Some minds develop faster and farther than others.

What Is Intelligence?

There is no clear consensus on the definition of intelligence. As noted in Chapter 7, Piaget defined intelligence as thinking or behavior that is adaptive. Other experts have offered different definitions, many of them centering on the ability to think abstractly or to solve problems effectively (Sternberg, 2000). Early definitions of intelligence tended to reflect the assumption that intelligence reflects innate ability, genetically determined and thus fixed at conception. But it has become clear that intelligence is not fixed, that it is changeable and subject to environmental influence (Perkins, 1996). As a result, an in-

Table 9.1 What Do You Know about Intelligence and Creativity?

Answer each question true or false:

1. On the leading tests of intelligence, a score of 100 is average.
2. Most scholars now conclude that there is no such thing as general intelligence; there are only separate mental abilities.
3. Individuals who are intellectually gifted are typically gifted in all mental abilities.
4. Intellectually gifted children do well in school but are more likely than most children to have social and emotional problems.
5. IQ predicts both a person's occupational status and his success compared with others in the same occupation.
6. On average, performance on IQ tests declines for people in their 70s and 80s.
7. Qualities associated with wisdom are as common among young and middle-aged adults as among elderly adults.
8. It has been established that children's IQs are far more influenced by their environments than by their genes.
9. How well a child does on a test of creativity cannot be predicted well from her IQ score.
10. Creative achievers (great musicians, mathematicians, writers, and so on) typically do all their great works before about age 40 or 45 and produce only lesser works from then on.

Answers: 1-T, 2-F, 3-F, 4-F, 5-T, 6-T, 7-T, 8-F, 9-T, 10-F

dividual's intelligence test scores sometimes vary considerably over a lifetime. Bear in mind that understanding of this complex human quality has changed since the first intelligence tests were created at the turn of the century—and that there is still no single, universally accepted definition of intelligence.

The Psychometric Approach

The research tradition that spawned the development of standardized tests of intelligence is the **psychometric approach.** According to psychometric theorists, intelligence is a trait or a set of traits that characterizes some people to a greater extent than others. The goals, then, are to identify these traits precisely and to measure them so that differences among individuals can be described. But from the start, experts could not agree on whether intelligence is one general cognitive ability or many specific abilities.

Early on, Charles Spearman (1927) proposed a two-factor theory of intelligence consisting of a general mental ability (called *g*) that contributes to performance on many different kinds of tasks. This *g* factor is what accounts for Spearman's observation that people were often consistent across a range of tasks. However, he also noticed that a student who excelled at most tasks might score low on a particular measure (for example, memory for words). So he proposed a second aspect of intelligence: *s,* or special abilities, each of which is specific to a particular kind of task.

Later, Louis Thurstone (1938; Thurstone & Thurstone, 1941) analyzed test scores obtained by eighth-graders and college students and identified seven fairly distinct factors that he called *primary mental abilities:* spatial ability, perceptual speed (the quick noting of visual detail), numerical reasoning (arithmetic skills), verbal meaning (the defining of words), word fluency (speed in recognizing words), memory, and inductive reasoning (the formation of a rule to describe a set of observations). Thus, Thurstone concluded that Spearman's general ability factor should be broken into several distinct mental abilities.

Raymond Cattell and John Horn have greatly influenced current thinking concerning intelligence by focusing attention on two broad dimensions of intellect: fluid intelligence and crystallized intelligence (Cattell, 1963; Horn & Cattell, 1967; Horn & Noll, 1997). **Fluid intelligence** is the ability to use your mind actively to solve novel problems—for example, to solve verbal analogies, remember unrelated pairs of words, or recognize relationships among geometric figures. The skills involved—reasoning, seeing relationships among stimuli, and drawing inferences—are usually not taught and are believed to be relatively free of cultural influences (see Figure 9.1). **Crystallized intelligence,** in contrast, is the use of knowledge acquired through schooling and other life experiences. Tests of general information (At what temperature does water boil?), word comprehension (What is the meaning of *duplicate*?), and numerical abilities are all measures of crystallized intelligence. Thus, fluid intelligence involves using your mind in new and flexible ways, whereas crystallized intelligence involves using what you have already learned through experience.

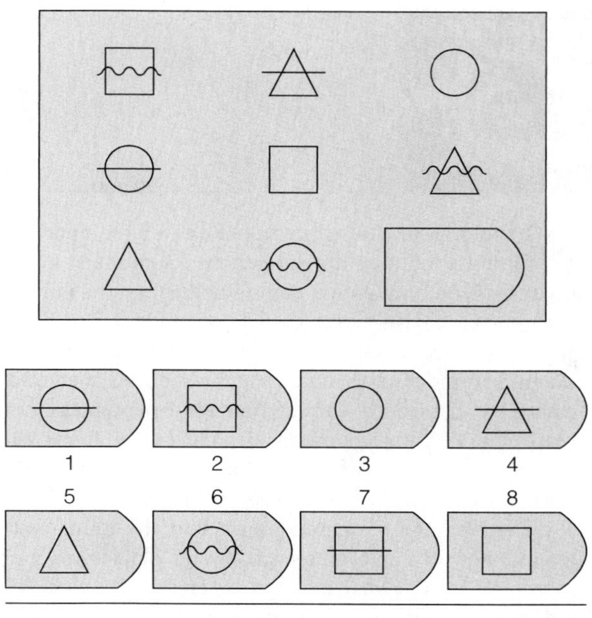

Figure 9.1 An item assessing fluid intelligence (similar to those in a test called the Raven Progressive Matrices Test). Which of the numbered pieces completes the design?

Obviously, there is no single answer to the question, what is intelligence? Nonetheless, some consensus is emerging. Intelligence is most often viewed as a hierarchy that includes (1) a general ability factor at the top that influences how well people do on a range of cognitive tasks; (2) a few broad dimensions of ability that are distinguishable in factor analyses (for example, fluid intelligence, crystallized intelligence, memory capacity, perceptual skills, and processing speed); and (3) at the bottom, many specific abilities such as numerical reasoning, spatial discrimination, and word comprehension that also influence how well a person performs cognitive tasks that tap these specific abilities (Carroll, 1993; Horn & Noll, 1997).

In the end, the intelligence tests guided by psychometric theories have emphasized general intellectual ability by summarizing performance in a single IQ score, and they have assessed only some of the specialized abilities humans possess. Critics believe traditional psychometric tests have not fully described what it means to be an intelligent person and some have offered alternative ways of thinking about intelligence that represent challenges to the traditional view. Reading about these approaches in the following sections will help you capture the nature of intelligence and appreciate the limitations of the tests used to measure it. In addition, the Explorations box on page 228 examines two traditional psychometric tests and two modern alternatives.

Gardner's Theory of Multiple Intelligences

Howard Gardner (1993, 1999/2000; Chen & Gardner, 1997) rejects the idea that a single IQ score is a meaningful measure of human intelligence. He argues that there are many intelli-

Explorations

Measuring Intelligence

At the turn of the last century, Alfred Binet and Theodore Simon produced the forerunner of modern intelligence tests. In 1904, they were commissioned by the French government to devise a test that would identify "dull" children who might need special instruction. Binet and Simon devised a large battery of tasks measuring the skills believed to be necessary for classroom learning: attention, perception, memory, reasoning, verbal comprehension, and so on. Items that discriminated between normal children and those described by their teachers as slow were kept in the final test.

The test was soon revised so that the items were age-graded. For example, a set of "6-year-old" items could be passed by most 6-year-olds but by few 5-year-olds; "12-year-old" items could be handled by most 12-year-olds but not by younger children. This approach permitted the testers to describe a child's **mental age**—the level of age-graded problems that the child is able to solve. Thus, a child who passes all items at the 5-year-old level but does poorly on more advanced items—regardless of the child's actual age—is said to have a mental age of 5.

Binet's test became known as the Stanford-Binet Intelligence Scale after Lewis Terman of Stanford University translated and published a revised version of the test for use with American children. Terman developed a procedure for comparing a child's mental age (MA) with their chronological age (CA) by calculating an **intelligence quotient (IQ),** which consisted of MA divided by CA and then multiplied by 100 ($IQ = MA/CA \times 100$). An IQ score of 100 indicates average intelligence, regardless of a child's age: The normal child passes just the items that age-mates typically pass; mental age increases each year, but so does chronological age. The child of 8 with a mental age of 10 has experienced rapid intellectual growth and has a high IQ (specifically, 125); if she still has a mental age of 10 when she is 15 years old, then she has an IQ of only 67 and is clearly below average compared with children of the same age.

The Stanford-Binet, now in its fifth edition, is still in use (Roid, 2003). Its **test norms**—standards of normal performance expressed as average scores and the range of scores around the average—are based on the performance of a large, representative sample of people (2-year-olds through adults) from many socioeconomic and racial backgrounds. The concept of mental age is no longer used to calculate IQ; instead, individuals receive scores that reflect how well or how poorly they do compared with others of the same age. An IQ of 100 is still average, and the higher the IQ score an individual attains, the better the performance is in comparison with that of age-mates.

David Wechsler constructed a set of intelligence tests also in wide use. The Wechsler Preschool and Primary Scale of Intelligence is for children between ages 3 and 8 (Wechsler, 2002). The Wechsler Intelligence Scale for Children (WISC-III) is appropriate for schoolchildren ages 6 to 16 (Wechsler, 1991), and the Wechsler Adult Intelligence Scale is used with adults (Wechsler, 1997). The Wechsler tests yield a verbal IQ score based on items measuring vocabulary, general knowledge, arithmetic reasoning, and the like and a performance IQ based on such nonverbal skills as the ability to assemble puzzles, solve mazes, reproduce geometric designs with colored blocks, and rearrange pictures to tell a meaningful story. As with the Stanford-Binet, a score of 100 is defined as average performance for the person's age. A person's full-scale IQ is a combination of the verbal and performance scores.

Scores on both the Stanford-Binet and Wechsler Scales form a **normal distribution,** or a symmetrical, bell-shaped spread around the average score of 100 (see the Figure in this Box). Scores around the average are common; very high and very low scores are rare. About two-thirds of people taking one of these IQ tests have scores between 85 and 115. Fewer

gences, most of which have been ignored by the developers of standardized intelligence tests. Instead of asking, "How smart are you?" researchers should be asking, "How are you smart?" and identifying people's strengths and weaknesses across the full range of human mental faculties (Chen & Gardner, 1997). Gardner (1993, 2000) argues that there are at least eight distinct intellectual abilities:

1. *Linguistic intelligence.* Language skills, such as those seen in the poet's facility with words.
2. *Logical–mathematical intelligence.* The abstract thinking and problem solving shown by mathematicians and computer scientists and emphasized by Piaget.
3. *Musical intelligence.* Based on an acute sensitivity to sound patterns.
4. *Spatial intelligence.* Most obvious in great artists who can perceive things accurately and transform what they see.
5. *Bodily-kinesthetic intelligence.* The skillful use of the body to create crafts, perform, or fix things; shown, for example, by dancers, athletes, and surgeons.
6. *Interpersonal intelligence.* Social intelligence, social skill, exceptional sensitivity to other people's motivations and moods; demonstrated by salespeople and psychologists.
7. *Intrapersonal intelligence.* Understanding of one's own feelings and inner life.
8. *Naturalist intelligence.* Expertise in the natural world of plants and animals.

Traditional IQ tests emphasize linguistic and logical–mathematical intelligence and to some extent test spatial in-

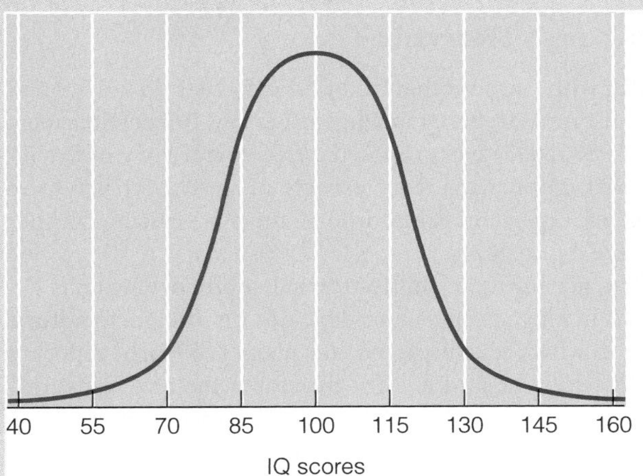

The approximate distribution of IQ scores.

than 3% have scores of 130 or above, a score often used as one criterion of giftedness. Similarly, fewer than 3% have IQs below 70, a cutoff commonly used to define mental retardation.

Several alternatives to these traditional tests have been proposed. Alan Kaufman and Nadeen Kaufman, for example, designed the Kaufman Assessment Battery for Children (K-ABC-II; Kaufman & Kaufman, 2003). This test, based on information-processing theory, focuses on how children solve problems rather than on what problems they solve (Kaufman, 2001; Sparrow & Davis, 2000). The K-ABC-II, which is appropriate for children ages 3 through 18, has two subscales. One measures a child's ability to process information sequentially; the other measures the ability to integrate several pieces of information. The test also has a separate section of questions to assess children's achievement or acquired knowledge.

Another promising approach, called **dynamic assessment,** attempts to evaluate how well children learn new material when an examiner provides them with competent instruction (Haywood & Tzuriel, 2002; Lidz, 1997; Lidz & Elliott, 2001). Reuven Feuerstein and his colleagues, for example, have argued that, even though intelligence is often defined as the potential to learn from experience, IQ tests typically assess what has been learned, not what can be learned (Feuerstein, Feuerstein, & Gross, 1997). This approach may be biased against children from culturally different or disadvantaged backgrounds who lack opportunities to learn what the tests measure.

Feuerstein developed the Learning Potential Assessment Device to assess children's ability to learn new things with the guidance of an adult who provides increasingly helpful cues. This test interprets intelligence as the ability to learn quickly with minimal guidance. Feuerstein believes that learners first need a "mediator," a guide who structures and interprets the environment for them; then, they are able to learn more from their experiences on their own. This approach should remind you of Lev Vygotsky's theory, described in Chapter 7, that children acquire new ways of thinking through their social interactions with more experienced problem solvers; it is based partly on Vygotsky's work. The dynamic assessment of learning capacity provides information beyond what traditional IQ tests provide about a child's intellectual competence and likely achievement (Haywood & Tzuriel, 2002; Lidz, 1997).

Trying to boil a person's intelligence down to a single score is a formidable task. A single score derived from a test that assesses only some of the many intelligences that humans can display does not do justice to the complexity of human mental functioning. Moreover, it is a measure of the individual's performance at one point—an estimate that is not always a good indicator of the person's underlying intellectual competence.

telligence, perhaps because those are the forms of intelligence Western societies value most highly and work the hardest to nurture in school. But IQ tests can be faulted for ignoring most of the other forms of intelligence. Although Gardner does not claim that his is the definitive list of intelligences, he presents evidence suggesting that each of these eight abilities is distinct. For example, it is clear that a person can be exceptional in one ability but poor in others—witness **savant syndrome,** the phenomenon in which extraordinary talent in a particular area is displayed by a person otherwise mentally retarded (Treffert, 2000). Leslie Lemke, one such individual, is blind, has cerebral palsy, is mentally retarded, and could not talk until he was an adult (Treffert, 2000). Yet he can hear a musical piece once and play it flawlessly on the piano or imitate songs in perfect German or Italian even though his own speech is still primitive. He apparently has a high level of musical intelligence. Other savants, despite IQs below 70, can draw well enough to gain admittance to art school or calculate on the spot what day of the week it was January 16, 1909 (Hermelin & Rutter, 2001). Some scholars think that the skills shown by savants are so specific and depend so much on memory that they do not qualify as separate "intelligences" (Nettelbeck & Young, 1996). However, Gardner insists that savant syndrome simply cannot be explained by theories that emphasize a general intelligence factor, *g*.

Gardner also marshals evidence to show that each intelligence has its own distinctive developmental course. Many great musical composers and athletes, for example, revealed

© Pam Driscol Gallery, CO

Alonzo Clemons has trouble with some of the basic tasks of living, but he can quickly sculpt incredibly detailed and accurate replicas of animals that he has seen only briefly.

their genius in childhood, whereas exceptional logical–mathematical intelligence typically shows up later, after the individual has gained the capacity for abstract thought and has mastered an area of science. Finally, Gardner links his distinct intelligences to distinct structures in the brain, arguing that the eight intelligences are neurologically distinct.

Sternberg's Triarchic Theory

Agreeing with Gardner that traditional IQ tests do not capture all that it means to be an intelligent person, Robert Sternberg (1985, 1988, 2003) has proposed a **triarchic theory of intelligence** that emphasizes three aspects of intelligent behavior: contextual, experiential, and information-processing components (see Figure 9.2).

First, according to the **contextual subtheory,** what is defined as intelligent behavior depends on the sociocultural context in which it is displayed. Sternberg (1999a, b) reports a study in which he and a colleague tested the analogical reasoning skills of second-graders in a school where instruction was conducted in English in the morning and in Hebrew in the afternoon. Some children got all of the problems wrong, suggesting they were not bright. However, the children had been tested with English problems in the afternoon when they normally would have received problems in Hebrew; consequently, the children read the problems from right to left. In their normal classroom context, this would have been a smart thing to do. Thus, Sternberg argues that what is defined as intelligent behavior depends on the sociocultural context in

Experiential subtheory

How experiences affect intelligence and how intelligence affects a person's experiences. Includes:
1. Ability to deal with novelty
2. Ability to automatize processing

Intelligence

Contextual subtheory

Behaviors considered intelligent in a particular culture. Includes:
1. Adaptation
2. Selection
3. Shaping

Componential (information-processing) subtheory

Cognitive processes that underlie intelligent behavior. Includes:
1. Metacomponents (e.g., strategy construction, strategy selection, and solution monitoring)
2. Performance components (e.g., encoding and comparing)
3. Knowledge acquisition components (e.g., selective encoding, selective combination, and selective comparison)

Figure 9.2 Robert Sternberg's triarchic theory of intelligence.

which it is displayed. Intelligent people adapt to the environment they are in (for example, a job setting), shape that environment to make it suit them better, or find a better environment. Such people have "street smarts." Psychologists, according to Sternberg, must begin to understand intelligence as behavior in the real world, not as behavior in taking tests (Sternberg et al., 1995).

This perspective views intelligent behavior as varying from one culture or subculture to another, from one period in history to another, and from one period of the life span to another. Each culture or subculture defines the ingredients of intelligent behavior in its own way (Sternberg, 2003). The challenge, then, is to devise ways of measuring intelligence that are appropriate across cultures.

Just as intelligent behavior varies from one culture to another, it changes over time. Numerical abilities may not play as important a role in intelligent behavior now that calculators and computers are widely used, for example, whereas analytical skills may be more important than ever in a complex, urban world. And certainly the infant learning how to master new toys shows a different kind of intelligence than the adult mastering a college curriculum. Thus, the definition of the intelligent infant must differ from the definition of the intelligent adult.

The second aspect of the triarchic theory focuses on the role of experience in intelligence. According to this **experiential subtheory,** what is intelligent when a person first encounters a new task is not the same as what is intelligent after extensive experience with that task. The first kind of intelligence, response to novelty, requires active and conscious information processing. Sternberg believes that relatively novel tasks provide the best measures of intelligence because they tap the individual's ability to come up with good ideas or fresh insights.

In daily life, however, people also perform more or less intelligently on repetitive tasks (reading the newspaper, for example). This second kind of intelligence reflects **automatization,** or an increased efficiency of information processing with practice. It is intelligent to develop little "programs in the mind" for performing common, everyday activities efficiently and unthinkingly. Thus, according to Sternberg, it is crucial to know how familiar a task is to a person before assessing that person's behavior. For example, giving people of two different cultural groups an intelligence test whose items are familiar to one group and novel to the other introduces culture bias into the testing process, making it difficult to obtain a fair assessment of the groups' relative abilities.

The third aspect of the triarchic theory, the **componential subtheory,** focuses on information-processing components. As an information-processing theorist, Sternberg believes that the theories of intelligence underlying the development of IQ tests ignore how people produce intelligent answers. He argues that the components of intelligent behavior range from identifying the problem to carrying out strategies to solve it; a full picture of intelligence includes not only the number of answers people get right but also the processes they use to arrive at their answers and the efficiency with which they use those processes.

So, to fully assess how intelligent people are, researchers must consider the *context* in which they perform (their age, culture, and historical period), their previous *experience* with a task (whether their behavior reflects response to novelty or automatized processes), and their *information-processing* strategies. Individuals who are intelligent, according to this triarchic model, are able to carry out logical thought processes efficiently and effectively to solve both novel and familiar problems and to adapt to their environment.

Sternberg (1999, 2003) recently expanded his triarchic theory of intelligence to what he calls the theory of **successful intelligence.** According to this view, people are intelligent "to the extent that they have the abilities needed to succeed in life, according to their own definition of success within their sociocultural context" (2003, p. xvi). Thus, intelligence is not just the ability to do well in school, something measured by traditional intelligence tests, but also the ability to do well in life (Sternberg, 2004). Smart people find ways to optimize their strengths and minimize their weaknesses so that they can succeed. They select environments (including occupations) that suit their profile of abilities, or, to the extent it is possible, they modify their abilities or environments. Unfortunately, today's widely used tests of intelligence do not reflect this sophisticated view of intelligence.

☾ How would you define an intelligent child? Mexican American parents, like Cambodian, Filipino, and Vietnamese parents, say that intelligent children are motivated, socially skilled, and able to manage their own behavior. European American parents place less emphasis on these noncognitive aspects of intelligence (Okagaki & Sternberg, 1993). Each cultural group defines intelligence in its own way.

Summing Up

The psychometric or testing approach to cognition defines intelligence as a set of traits that allows some people to think and solve problems more effectively than others. It can be viewed as a hierarchy consisting of a general factor *g*, broad abilities such as fluid and crystallized intelligence, and many specific abilities. Gardner's theory of multiple intelligences, with its focus on eight distinct forms of intelligence, offers an alternative view.

Sternberg's triarchic theory of intelligence, with its contextual, experiential, and information-processing components, offers another. ■

The Infant

As you saw in Chapters 7 and 8, the mind develops rapidly in infancy. But how can an infant's intellectual growth be measured? Is it possible to identify infants who are more or less intelligent than their age-mates? And how well does high (or low) intelligence in infancy predict high (or low) intelligence in childhood and adulthood?

Developmental Quotients

None of the standard intelligence tests can be used with children much younger than 3, because the test items require verbal skills and attention spans that infants do not have. Some developmentalists have tried to measure infant intelligence by assessing the rate at which infants achieve important developmental milestones. Perhaps the best known and most widely used of the infant tests is the Bayley Scales of Infant Development (Bayley, 1993). This test, designed for infants ages 1 to 42 months, has the following three parts:

1. The *motor scale,* which measures the infant's ability to do such things as grasp a cube and throw a ball

2. The *mental scale,* which includes adaptive behaviors such as reaching for a desirable object, searching for a hidden toy, and following directions

3. The *behavior rating scale,* a rating of the child's behavior on dimensions such as goal-directedness, emotional regulation, and social responsivity

On the basis of the first two scores, the infant is given a **developmental quotient (DQ)** rather than an IQ. The DQ summarizes how well or how poorly the infant performs in comparison with a large norm group of infants the same age.

Infant Intelligence and Later Intelligence

As they age, infants progress through many developmental milestones of the kind assessed by the Bayley scales, so such scales are useful in charting infants' developmental progress. They are also useful in diagnosing neurological problems and mental retardation—even when these conditions are mild and difficult to detect through standard pediatric or neurological examinations (Escalona, 1968; Honzik, 1983). But developmentalists have also been interested in the larger issue of continuity versus discontinuity in intellectual development: Is it possible to predict which infants are likely to be gifted, average, or mentally retarded during the school years?

Not from their DQ Scores. Correlations between infant DQ and child IQ are low, sometimes close to zero. The infant who does well on the Bayley scales or other infant tests may or may not obtain a high IQ score later in life (Honzik, 1983; Rose et al., 1989). True, the infant who scores low on an infant test often turns out to be mentally retarded, but otherwise there seems to be a good deal of discontinuity between early and later scores—at least until a child is 4 or older.

What might explain the poor connection between scores on infant development scales and children's later IQs? Perhaps the main reason is that infant tests and IQ tests tap qualitatively different kinds of abilities (Columbo, 1993). Piaget would undoubtedly approve of this argument. Infant scales focus heavily on the sensory and motor skills that Piaget believed are so important in infancy; IQ tests such as the Stanford-Binet and WISC-III emphasize more abstract abilities, such as verbal reasoning, concept formation, and problem solving.

Robert McCall (1981, 1983) offers a second explanation, arguing that the growth of intelligence during infancy is highly influenced by powerful and universal maturational processes. Maturational forces pull infants back on course if environmental influences cause them to stray. For this reason, higher or lower infant test scores are likely to be nothing more than temporary deviations from a universal developmental path. As the child nears age 2, McCall argues, maturational forces become less strong, so individual differences become larger and more stable over time. Consistent differences related to both individual genetic makeup and environment begin to emerge.

Should researchers give up on trying to predict later IQ on the basis of development in infancy? Perhaps not yet. The information-processing approach has given new life to the idea that there is continuity in intelligence from infancy to childhood. Several researchers have found that certain measures of infant attention predict later IQ better than infant intelligence tests do. For example, speed of habituation (the speed with which an infant loses interest in a repeatedly presented stimulus) and preference for novelty (the infant's tendency to prefer a novel stimulus to a familiar one), assessed in the first year of life, have an average correlation of about +0.45 with IQ in childhood, particularly with verbal IQ and memory skills (McCall & Carriger, 1993; Rose & Feldman, 1997; Rose, Feldman, & Jankowski, 2003). Fast reaction time in infancy (time taken to look in the direction of a visual stimulus as soon as it appears) predicts later IQ about as well (Dougherty & Haith, 1997).

Perhaps, then, researchers can characterize the "smart" infant as the speedy information processor—the infant who quickly becomes bored by the same old thing, seeks novel experiences, and soaks up information rapidly. There seems to be some continuity between infant intelligence and childhood intelligence after all. Such Bayley scale accomplishments as throwing a ball are unlikely to carry over into vocabulary-learning or problem-solving skills in childhood. However, the extent to which the young infant processes information quickly can predict the extent to which he will learn quickly and solve problems efficiently later in childhood.

Summing Up

The Bayley scales include motor, mental, and behavior ratings to assess infant development. Although traditionally used as a measure of infant intelligence, they do not correlate well with later IQ scores. Instead, infant measures that capture speed of information processing and preference for novelty are better at predicting later intelligence. ■

The Child

Over the childhood years, children generally become able to answer more questions, and more difficult questions, on IQ tests. That is, their mental ages increase. But what happens to the IQ scores of individual children, which reflect how they compare with peers?

How Stable Are IQ Scores during Childhood?

It was once assumed that a person's IQ reflected her genetically determined intellectual capacity and therefore would remain stable over time. In other words, a child with an IQ of 120 at age 5 was expected to obtain a similar IQ at age 10, 15, or 20. Is this idea supported by research? As you have seen, infant DQs do not predict later IQs well. However, starting around age 4 there is a fairly strong relationship between early and later IQ, and the relationship grows even stronger by middle childhood. Table 9.2 summarizes the results of a longitudinal study of 220 children from ages 4 to 12 (Weinert & Schneider 1999; Weinert & Hany, 2003). The shorter the interval between two testings, the higher the correlation between children's IQ scores on the two occasions. Even when several years have passed, however, IQ seems to be a stable attribute: the scores that children obtain at age 7 are clearly related to those they obtain 5 years later, at age 12.

These correlations do not reveal everything, however. They are based on a large group of children, and they do not necessarily mean that the IQs of individual children will remain stable over the years. As it turns out, many children show sizable ups and downs in their IQ scores over the course of childhood. Patterns of change differ considerably from child to child, as though each were on a private developmental trajectory (Gottfried et al., 1994). One team of researchers looked at the IQ scores of 140 children who had taken intelligence tests at regular intervals from age 2 to age 17 (McCall, Applebaum, & Hogarty, 1973). The average difference between a child's highest and lowest scores was a whopping 28.5 points. About one-third showed changes of more than 30 points, and one child changed by 74 IQ points.

How do researchers reconcile the conclusion that IQ is relatively stable with this clear evidence of instability? They can still conclude that, within a group, children's standings (high or low) in comparison with peers stay stable from one point to another during the childhood years (Sternberg, Grigorenko, & Bundy, 2001). But many individual children experience drops or gains in IQ scores over the years. Remember, however, that this relates to performance on IQ tests rather than underlying intellectual competence. IQ scores are influenced not only by people's intelligence but also by their motivation, testing procedures and conditions, and many other factors. As a result, IQ may be more changeable over the years than intellectual ability.

Table 9.2 Correlations of IQs Measured at Various Ages

Age of Child	Correlation with IQ at Age 9	Correlation with IQ at Age 12
4	0.46	0.42
5	0.47	0.49
7	0.81	0.69
9	—	0.80

SOURCE: Adapted from Weinert & Hany, 2003, p. 171, Table 10.1.

Causes of Gain and Loss

Some wandering of IQ scores upward or downward over time is just random fluctuation—a good day at one testing, a bad day at the next. Yet there are patterns. Children whose scores fluctuate the most tend to live in unstable home environments; their life experiences have fluctuated between periods of happiness and turmoil.

In addition, some children gain IQ points over childhood and others lose them. Who are the gainers, and who are the losers? Gainers seem to have parents who foster achievement and who are neither too strict nor too lax in child rearing (McCall, Applebaum, & Hogarty, 1973). Noticeable drops in IQ with age often occur among children who live in poverty. Otto Klineberg (1963) proposed a **cumulative-deficit hypothesis** to explain this: impoverished environments inhibit intellectual growth, and these negative effects accumulate over time. There is some support for the cumulative-deficit hypothesis, especially when a child's parents are not only poor but also low in intellectual functioning themselves (Jensen, 1977; Ramey & Ramey, 1992). The Explorations box on page 234 examines the success of early intervention programs designed to raise the IQ scores and academic success of children living in poverty.

Summing Up

During childhood, IQ scores become more stable so that scores at one point in time are generally consistent with scores obtained at a second point. Despite group stability, the scores of individuals can fluctuate over time. Greater changes are evident when children grow up in unstable environments. Overall, there is both continuity and change in IQ scores during childhood; IQ scores remain stable for many children, and mental ages rise. ■

Explorations

Early Intervention for Preschool Children

During the 1960s, several programs were launched to enrich the early learning experiences of disadvantaged preschoolers. Project Head Start is perhaps the best known of these interventions. The idea was to provide a variety of social and intellectual experiences that might better prepare these children for school. At first, Head Start and similar programs seemed to be a smashing success; children in the programs were posting average gains of about 10 points on IQ tests. But then discouragement set in: By the time children reached the middle years of grade school, their IQs were no

© Michael Newman/PhotoEdit, Inc.

High-quality Head Start programs provide the nutrition, health care, parent training, and intellectual stimulation that can get disadvantaged children off to a good start.

The Adolescent

Intellectual growth is rapid during infancy and childhood. What happens during adolescence, and how well does IQ predict school performance?

Continuity between Childhood and Adulthood

Intellectual growth continues its rapid pace in early adolescence then slows and levels off in later adolescence (Thorndike, 1997). A spurt in brain development, some studies suggest, occurs around age 11 or age 12, when children are believed to enter Piaget's formal operational stage (Case, 1992; Andrich & Styles, 1994). Brain development may give children the information-processing speed and working memory capacity they need to perform at adultlike levels on IQ tests (Kail & Salthouse, 1994). Thus, basic changes in the brain in early adolescence may underlie a variety of cognitive advances—the achievement of formal operations, improved memory and information-processing skills, and better performance on tests of intelligence.

Although adolescence is a time of impressive mental growth, it is also a time of increased stability of individual differences in intellectual performance. During the teen years, IQ scores become even more stable than they were in childhood and predict IQ in middle age well (Eichorn, Hunt, & Honzik, 1981). Even while adolescents as a group are experiencing cognitive growth, then, each adolescent is establishing a characteristic level of intellectual performance that will most likely higher than those of control-group children (Gray, Ramsey, & Klaus, 1982). Such findings led Arthur Jensen (1969, p. 2) to conclude that "compensatory education has been tried and it apparently has failed."

But that was not the end of the story. Children in some of these programs have been followed into their teens and even 20s. Irving Lazar and Richard Darlington (1982) reported on the long-term effects of 11 early intervention programs in several areas of the United States. Other follow-up studies of Head Start and similar early education programs for disadvantaged children have been conducted since then (Campbell & Ramey, 1995; Guralnick, 1997). These long-term studies indicate the following:

- Children who participate in early intervention programs show immediate gains on IQ and school achievement tests, whereas nonparticipants do not. However, the gains rarely last more than 3 or 4 years after the program has ended. Effects on measures other than IQ are more encouraging.
- Compensatory education improves both children's and mothers' attitudes about achievement. When asked to describe something that has made them feel proud of themselves, program participants are more likely than nonparticipants to mention scholastic achievements or (in the case of 15- to 18-year-olds) job-related successes. Mothers of program participants tend to be more satisfied with their children's school performance and to hold higher occupational aspirations for their children.
- Program participants are more likely to meet their school's basic requirements than nonparticipants are. They are less likely to be assigned to special education classes, to be retained in a grade, or to drop out of high school.
- There is even some evidence (although not in all studies) that teenagers who have participated in early compensatory education are less likely than nonparticipants to become pregnant, to require welfare assistance, and to be involved in delinquent behavior.

In sum, longitudinal evaluations suggest that compensatory education has been tried and it works. Programs seem most effective if they start early, last long, and involve several components. For example, Craig Ramey and his colleagues (Campbell et al., 2001; Campbell & Ramey, 1995) have reported outstanding success with the Abecedarian Project, an early intervention for extremely disadvantaged, primarily African American, children that involved an intellectually stimulating day care program, home visits and efforts to involve parents in their children's development, and medical and nutritional care from early infancy to kindergarten entry. Program participants outperformed nonparticipants throughout childhood and into adolescence. By age 15, the impressive IQ advantage they had shown as young children had narrowed to less than 5 points, but they continued to perform better on math and reading achievement tests, were less likely to have been held back a grade, and were less in need of special education services. Some children in the study were randomly assigned to a group whose intervention did not begin until school age, when a teacher worked with their regular teachers and their parents over a 3-year period. These children did not show as many gains as those who received the preschool intervention, suggesting that it is best to intervene early in children's lives (Campbell & Ramey, 1995).

be carried into adult life unless the individual's environment changes dramatically.

IQ and School Achievement

The original purpose of IQ tests was to estimate how well children would do in school and they do this fairly well. The correlation between children's and adolescents' IQ scores and their grades is about +0.50, making general intellectual ability one of the best predictors of school achievement available (Neisser et al., 1996). Adolescents with high IQs are also less likely to drop out of high school and more likely to go on to college than their peers with lower IQs; the correlation between IQ and years of education obtained averages +0.55 (Neisser et al., 1996). However, IQ scores do not predict college grades as well as they predict high school grades (Brody & Brody, 1976). Most college students probably have at least the average intellectual ability needed to succeed in college; success is therefore more influenced by personal qualities such as motivation. Overall, an IQ score is a good predictor of academic achievement, but it does not reveal everything about a student. Factors such as work habits, interests, and motivation to succeed also affect academic achievement.

Summing Up

IQ scores continue to stabilize as intellectual performance reaches near-adult level. IQ scores have proved useful at predicting academic achievement of adolescents. ■

The Adult

Do IQ scores predict achievement and success after people have left school? Does performance on IQ tests change during the adult years? And do IQ scores decline in old age, as performance on Piagetian cognitive tasks and some memory tasks does?

IQ and Occupational Success

There is a relationship between IQ and occupational status. Professional and technical workers perform higher on IQ tests than white-collar workers, who in turn score higher than blue-collar, or manual, workers (Schmidt & Hunter, 2004). As shown in Figure 9.3, the average IQ score of workers increases as the prestige of the occupation increases (Nyborg & Jensen, 2001). This is true for both African American and European American workers, although the relationship is stronger among African American samples. The reason for this relationship is clear: It undoubtedly takes more intellectual ability to complete law school and become a lawyer (a high-status occupation) than it does to be a farmhand (a low-status occupation). However, the prestige or status of the occupation is not as important as the complexity of the work (Gottfredson, 1997; Kuncel, Hezlett, & Ones, 2004). Greater intelligence is required to handle more complex or cognitively challenging work. Still, IQs vary considerably in every occupational group, so many people in low-status jobs have high IQs.

Now a second question: Are bright lawyers, electricians, or farmhands more successful or productive than their less intelligent colleagues? The answer here is also yes. The correlation between scores on tests of intellectual ability and such measures of job performance as supervisor ratings averages +0.30 to +0.50 (Neisser et al., 1996). General intellectual ability seems to predict job performance in a range of occupations better than any other indicator, and it predicts likelihood of success as accurately for members of racial and ethnic minority groups as for whites (Gottfredson, 2002; Schmidt & Hunter, 1998, 2004). More intellectually capable adults are better able to learn what they need to know about their occupations and to solve the problems that arise. This literally pays off, as shown in Figure 9.4: Individuals with greater cognitive ability earn more money that those with lower cognitive ability (Ceci & Williams, 1997).

IQ and Health

People who score higher on measures of intelligence tend to be healthier and live longer than those who score lower (Gottfredson, 2004). Research in Scotland has investigated the relationship between intelligence and health. Nearly everyone in the country born in 1921 completed an intelligence test in 1932 when they were 11 years old. Following up on health and death records decades later, researchers found that individuals who scored one standard deviation (15 points) below other individuals were less likely to be alive at age 76 and more likely to have experienced stomach or lung cancers and cardiovascular or coronary heart disease (Deary, Whalley, & Starr, 2003; Whalley & Deary, 2001).

A common explanation for this connection between IQ and health is socioeconomic status: Smart people may have better jobs, giving them the resources to obtain better health care. But when living conditions are statistically controlled (that is, held constant), there is still a connection between intelligence and health (Gottfredson & Deary, 2004). Similarly,

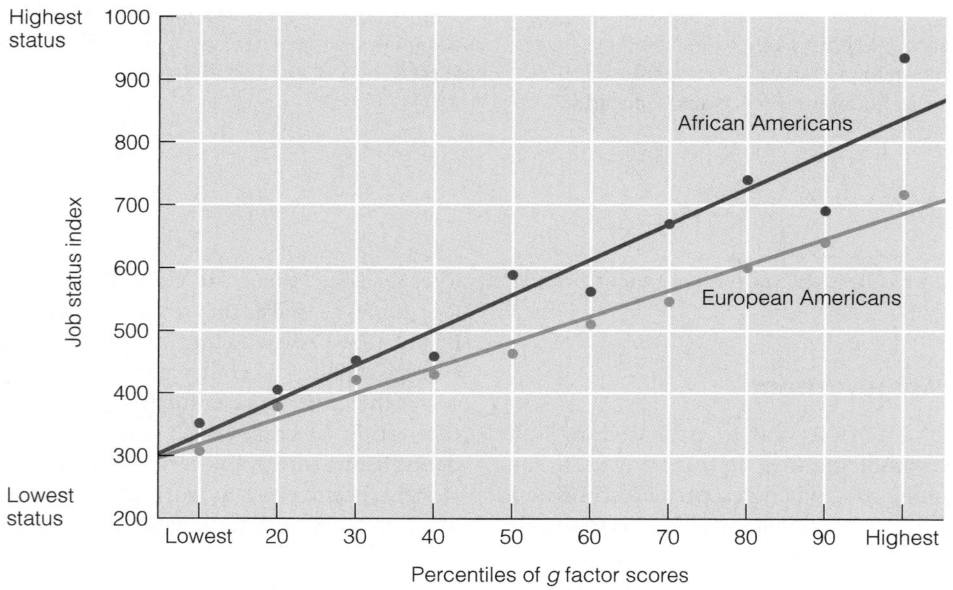

Figure 9.3 Job status in relation to intelligence test performance for African Americans and European Americans.

SOURCE: Reprinted from Nyborg, H., & Jensen, A. R. (2001). *Intelligence, 29*, Fig. 1, p. 15. Copyright © 2001 with permission from Elsevier Science.

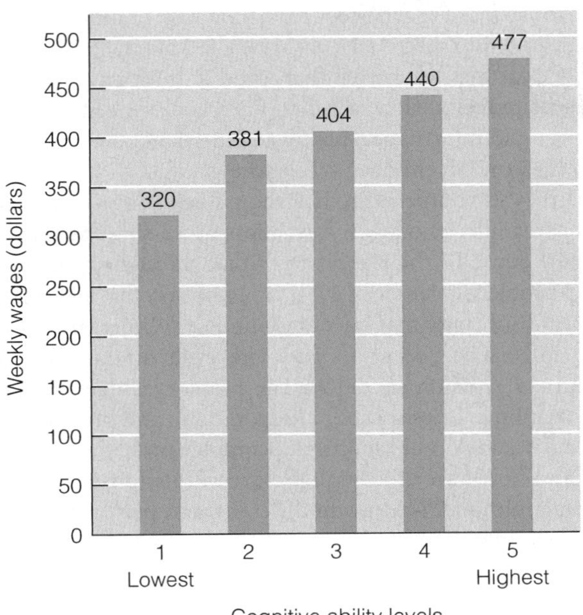

Figure 9.4 Weekly wages by level of cognitive ability.

Source: From Ceci, S. J. & Williams, W. M. (1997). Schooling, intelligence, and income. *American Psychologist, 53,* 1056. Copyright © 1997 by the American Psychological Association. Reprinted by permission.

providing equal access to health care reduces but does not eliminate the social class differences in health (Steenland, Henley, & Thun, 2002).

So what else could be going on? Linda Gottfredson (2004) argues that good health takes more than access to material resources. It requires some of the abilities measured by intelligence tests, such as efficient learning and problem solving. In other words, successfully monitoring health and properly applying treatment protocols requires a certain amount of intelligence. Consider the chronic illness diabetes. Successful management requires acquiring knowledge of the disease symptoms and course, identifying signs of inappropriate blood sugar levels, and making judgments about how to respond to blood sugar fluctuations. A patient's IQ predicts how much knowledge of diabetes he or she acquires during the year following diagnosis (Taylor et al., 2003). Other research shows that many people with diabetes who have limited literacy, which correlates with intelligence, do not know the signs of high or low blood sugar and do not know how to correct unhealthy levels (Williams et al., 1998).

Research on relationships between IQ and health is relatively new and ongoing. But it suggests that IQ influences socioeconomic status, which in turn influences health, and also influences health directly. Smarter people are able to apply their intellectual skills to understanding and managing their health.

Changes in IQ with Age

Perhaps no question about adult development has been studied as thoroughly as that of how intellectual abilities change with age. Alan Kaufman (2001) examined cross sections of adults ranging in age from 16 to 89 who were tested with the Wechsler Adult Intelligence Scale. As Figure 9.5 shows, IQs rise slightly until age 44 then decline, with the steepest declines starting around age 80. But recall the description of cross-sectional designs in Chapter 1. Cross-sectional studies compare people of different cohorts who have had different levels of education and life experiences because they were born at different times. Could the apparent declines in IQ with age reflect cohort differences?

Kaufman (2001) also studied the longitudinal performance of seven cohorts of adults over a 17-year period. The results of this longitudinal study were similar to those obtained cross-sectionally. There was a loss of about 5 IQ points from age 40 to age 57; losses of 7 to 8 points from age 50 to age 67 and from age 60 to age 77; and losses of about 10 points from age 67 to age 84 and from age 72 to age 89. Do intellectual abilities decline with age, as these data suggest? It depends on which abilities are examined. In both the cross-sectional and longitudinal studies, verbal IQ was essentially unchanged with age, at least until the person's 80s. In contrast, performance IQ peaked by ages 20 to 24 then steadily declined.

There is also data on changes in IQ with age from a comprehensive sequential study directed by K. Warner Schaie (1983, 1996). Schaie's study began in 1956 with a sample of

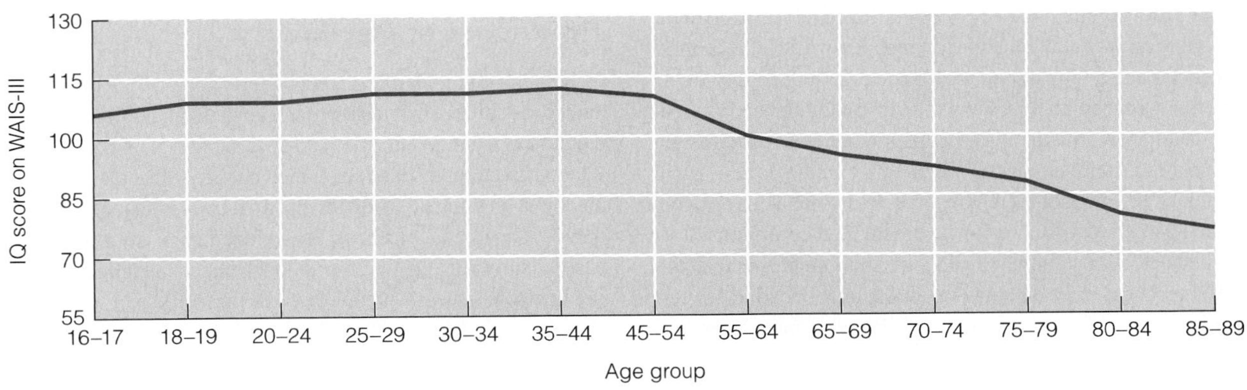

Figure 9.5 IQ scores by age.

Source: Based on data from Kaufman (2001).

members of a health maintenance organization ranging in age from 22 to 70. They were given a revised test of primary mental abilities that yielded scores for five separate mental abilities: verbal meaning, spatial ability, reasoning, numerical ability, and word fluency. Seven years later, as many of them as could be found were retested. In addition, a new sample of adults ranging from their 20s to their 70s was tested. This design made it possible to determine how the performance of the same individuals changed over 7 years and to compare the performance of people who were 20 years old in 1956 with that of people who were 20 years old in 1963. This same strategy was repeated in 1970, 1977, and 1984, giving the researchers a wealth of information about different cohorts including longitudinal data on some people over a 28-year period.

Several findings have emerged from this important study. First, it seems that *when a person was born* has at least as much influence on intellectual functioning as age does. In other words, cohort or generational effects on performance exist. This evidence confirms the suspicion that cross-sectional comparisons of different age groups yield too grim a picture of declines in intellectual abilities during adulthood. Specifically, recently born cohorts (the youngest people in the study were born in 1959) tended to outperform earlier generations (the oldest were born in 1889) on most tests. Yet on the test of numerical ability, people born between 1903 and 1924 performed better than both earlier and later generations. So different generations may have a special edge in different areas of intellectual performance. Overall, though, judging from Schaie's findings, young and middle-aged adults today can look forward to better intellectual functioning in old age than their grandparents experienced.

Another important message of Schaie's study, and of other research, is that patterns of aging differ for different abilities. Fluid intelligence (those abilities requiring active thinking and reasoning applied to novel problems, as measured by tests such as the primary mental abilities tests of reasoning and space) usually declines earlier and more steeply than crystallized intelligence (those abilities involving the use of knowledge acquired through experience, such as in answering the verbal meaning test used by Schaie). Consistently, adults lose some of their ability to grapple with new problems starting in middle age, but their crystallized general knowledge and vocabulary stay steady throughout middle and older adulthood (Rabbitt, Chetwynd, & McInnes, 2003; Singer et al., 2003). Some research even shows that knowledge, such as vocabulary, is higher among older adults than among younger adults (Field & Gueldner, 2001; Verhaeghen, 2003).

Why is this? Tests of performance and fluid IQ are often timed, and, as noted in Chapter 8, performance on timed or speeded tests declines more in old age than performance on unspeeded tests does. Performance, fluid, and speeded IQ test items may be less familiar to older adults who have been out of school for years than to younger adults; in this sense, the tests may be subtly biased against older adults (Berg, 2000). Declines in these fluid aspects of intelligence have also been linked to the slowing of central nervous system functioning that most people experience as they age (Salthouse, 1996; Sliwinski & Buschke, 1999; Zimprich & Martin, 2002).

A clear message here is that speed of information processing is related to intellectual functioning across the life span. Not only is rapid information processing in infancy associated with high IQ scores in childhood, but young adults with quick reaction times also outperform their more sluggish age-mates on IQ tests and adults who lose information-processing speed in later life lose some of their ability to think through complex and novel problems (Jensen, 1993). It is not just that older adults cannot finish tests that have time limits; declines in performance intelligence occur in later life even on untimed tests (Kaufman & Kaufman, 1997). The problem is that the slower information processor cannot keep in mind and process simultaneously all relevant aspects of a complex problem.

You now have an overall picture of intellectual functioning in adulthood. Age group differences in performance suggest that older adults today are at a disadvantage on many tests compared with younger adults, partly because of deficiencies in the amount and quality of education they received early in life. But actual declines in intellectual abilities associated with aging are generally minor until people reach their late 60s or 70s. Even in old age, declines in fluid intelligence, performance intelligence, and performance on speeded tests are more apparent than declines in crystallized intelligence, verbal intelligence, and performance on untimed tests. As you will soon see, declines in fluid intelligence can be reduced when adults remain cognitively stimulated through work or other activities (Weinert & Hany, 2003).

One last message of this research is worth special emphasis: Declines in intellectual abilities are not universal. Even among the 81-year-olds in Schaie's study, only about 30 to 40% had experienced a significant decline in intellectual ability in the previous 7 years (Schaie, 1990). Moreover, although few 81-year-olds maintained all five mental abilities, almost all retained at least one ability from testing to testing and about half retained four out of five (Schaie, 1989). The range of differences in intellectual functioning in a group of older adults is extremely large (Dixon, 2003). Anyone who stereotypes all elderly adults as intellectually limited is likely to be wrong most of the time.

Predictors of Decline

What is most likely to affect whether or not a person experiences declines in intellectual performance in old age? *Poor health,* not surprisingly, is one risk factor. People who have cardiovascular diseases or other chronic illnesses show steeper declines in mental abilities than their healthier peers (Schaie, 1996). Diseases (and most likely the drugs used to treat them) also contribute to a rapid decline in intellectual abilities within a few years of death (Johansson, Zarit, & Berg, 1992; Singer et al., 2003). This phenomenon has been given the depressing label **terminal drop.** Perhaps there is something, then, to the saying "Sound body, sound mind."

A second factor in decline is an *unstimulating lifestyle.* Schaie and his colleagues found that the biggest intellectual declines were shown by elderly widows who had low social status, engaged in few activities, and were dissatisfied with their lives (Schaie, 1996). These women lived alone and seemed disengaged from life. Individuals who maintain their performance or even show gains tend to have above-average socioeconomic status, advanced education, intact marriages, intellectually capable spouses, and physically and mentally active lifestyles. Interestingly, married adults are affected by the intellectual environment they provide for each other. Their IQ test scores become more similar over the years, largely because the lower-functioning partner's scores rise closer to those of the higher-functioning partner (Gruber-Baldini, Schaie, & Willis, 1995; Weinert & Hany, 2003).

The moral is "Use it or lose it." This rule, applicable to muscular strength and sexual functioning, also pertains to intellectual functioning in later life. The plasticity of the nervous system throughout the life span enables elderly individuals to benefit from intellectual stimulation and training, to maintain the intellectual skills most relevant to their activities, and to compensate for the loss of less-exercised abilities (Dixon, 2003; Weinert & Hany, 2003; see also the Applications box on this page). There is still much to learn about how health, lifestyle, and other factors shape the individual's intellectual growth and decline. What is certain is that most people can look forward to many years of optimal intellectual functioning before some of them experience losses of some mental abilities in later life.

Potential for Wisdom

Many people believe, incorrectly, as you have seen, that intellectual decline is an inevitable part of aging—yet many people also believe that old people are wise. Indeed, this belief has been expressed in many cultures throughout history. It is also featured in Erik Erikson's influential theory of life-span development. Erikson says that older adults often gain wisdom as they face the prospect of death and attempt to find meaning in their lives (see Chapter 11). Notice, too, that the word *wise* is rarely used to describe children, adolescents, or even young adults (unless perhaps it is to call one of them a *wise guy*). Is the association between wisdom and old age just a stereotype, or is there some truth to it?

But first, what is wisdom, and how can researchers assess it? There is no consensus on these questions, and, until recently, little research (Sternberg, 2003). Researchers do know that wisdom is not the same as high intelligence: There are many highly intelligent people who are not wise. Paul Baltes and his colleagues offer this definition of **wisdom:** "expert knowledge in the fundamental pragmatics of life that permits exceptional insight, judgment, and advice about complex and uncertain matters" (Pasupathi, Staudinger, & Baltes, 2001, p. 351). Similarly, Robert Sternberg (2003) defines a wise person as someone who can combine successful intelligence with creativity to solve problems that require balancing multiple interests or perspectives. In addition, the wise person has the

Applications

IQ Training for Aging Adults

Can you teach old dogs new tricks? And can you reteach old dogs who have suffered declines in mental abilities the old tricks they have lost? K. Warner Schaie and Sherry Willis (1986) sought to find out by training elderly adults in spatial ability and reasoning, two of the fluid mental abilities most likely to decline in old age. Within a group of older people ranging in age from 64 to 95 who participated in Schaie's longitudinal study of intelligence, they first identified individuals whose scores on one of the two abilities had declined over a 14-year period and individuals who had remained stable over the same period. The goal with the decliners would be to restore lost ability; the goal with those who had maintained their ability would be to improve it. Participants took pretests measuring both abilities, received 5 hours of training in either spatial ability or reasoning, and then were given posttests on both abilities. The spatial training involved learning how to rotate objects in space, at first physically and then mentally. Training in reasoning involved learning how to detect a recurring pattern in a series of stimuli (for example, musical notes) and to identify what the next stimulus in the sequence should be.

The training worked. Both those who had suffered ability declines and those who had maintained their abilities before the study improved, although decliners showed significantly more improvement in spatial ability than nondecliners did. Schaie and Willis estimated that 40% of the decliners gained enough through training to bring them back to the level of performance they had achieved 14 years earlier, before decline set in. What is more, effects of the training among those who had experienced declines in performance were still evident 7 years later (Schaie, 1996).

The larger messages? You can teach old dogs new tricks—and reteach them old tricks—in a short amount of time. This research does not mean that cognitive abilities can be restored in elderly people who have Alzheimer's disease or other brain disorders and have experienced significant neural loss. Instead, it suggests that many intellectual skills decline in later life because they are not used—and that these skills can be revived with a little coaching and practice. This research, combined with research on children, provides convincing evidence of the plasticity of cognitive abilities over the entire life span.

☾ People tend to believe that age brings wisdom. It can—but wisdom is rare even in later life.

following five qualities (Baltes & Staudinger, 2000; Pasupathi, Staudinger, & Baltes, 2001):

- Rich factual knowledge about life (a knowledge base regarding such areas as human nature, interpersonal relations, and critical events in life)
- Rich procedural knowledge (such as strategies for giving advice and handling conflicts)
- A life-span contextual perspective (consideration of the contexts of life—family, education, work, and others)
- Relativism of values and life priorities (acknowledgment and tolerance of different values)
- Recognition and management of uncertainty (understanding that knowledge of the world is limited and the future is unknown)

Does wisdom typically increase with age, or are life experiences more important than age in determining whether or not a person is wise? Ursula Staudinger, Jacqui Smith, and Paul Baltes (1992) attempted to find out by interviewing young (ages 25–35) and elderly (ages 65–82) women who were clinical psychologists or similarly well-educated professionals in other fields. The goal was to assess the relative contributions of age and specialized experience to wisdom, based on the assumption that clinical psychologists gain special sensitivity to human problems from their professional training and practice.

These women were interviewed about a person named Martha, who had chosen to have a family but no career and who met an old friend who had chosen to have a career but no family. The women were asked to talk about how Martha might review and evaluate her life after this encounter. Answers were scored for the five preceding qualities judged to be indicators of wisdom.

What was found? First, wisdom proved to be rare; it seems that only about 5% of the answers given by adults to problems such as these qualify as wise (Smith & Baltes, 1990). Second, expertise proved to be more relevant than age to the development of wisdom. That is, clinical psychologists, whether young or old, displayed more signs of wisdom than other women did. Older women were generally no wiser—or less wise—than younger women.

Age, then, does not predict wisdom, at least among adults (there is some evidence that age is related to wisdom-related performance among adolescents; see Pasupathi, Staudinger, & Baltes, 2001). Yet the knowledge base that contributes to wisdom, like other crystallized intellectual abilities, holds up well later in life (Baltes et al., 1995). Older adults, like younger adults, are more likely to display wisdom if they have life experiences (such as work as a clinical psychologist) that sharpen their insights into the human condition. The immediate social context also influences the degree to which wisdom is expressed; wiser solutions to problems are generated when adults have an opportunity to discuss problems with someone whose judgment they value and when they are encouraged to reflect after such discussions (Staudinger & Baltes, 1996). Thus, consulting with your fellow students and work colleagues and thinking about their advice may be the beginning of wisdom.

Finally, wisdom seems to reflect a particular combination of intelligence, personality, and cognitive style (Baltes & Staudinger, 2000). For example, individuals who have a cognitive style of comparing and evaluating relevant issues and who show tolerance of ambiguity are more likely to demonstrate wisdom than individuals without these characteristics. In addition, external factors influence the development of wisdom. Monika Ardelt (2000) found that a supportive social environment during early adulthood was positively associated with wisdom 40 years later.

At this early stage in the study of wisdom, there is much disagreement about what it is, how it develops, and how it is related to other mental abilities. However, research on wisdom provides further evidence that different mental faculties develop and age differently over the adult years.

Summing Up

IQ is related to the status or prestige of an adult's occupation and to her success within that occupation. Intelligence also affects health and longevity. Both cross-sectional studies and longitudinal studies tend to show age-related decreases in IQ. Schaie's sequential study suggests that (1) date of birth (cohort) influences test performance, (2) no major declines in mental abilities occur until the late 60s or 70s, (3) some abilities (especially fluid ones) decline more than others (especially crystallized ones), and (4) not all people's abilities decline. Decline is most likely in those who have poor health and unstimulating lifestyles. A few adults display wisdom, which requires a rich knowledge base along with particular personality traits and cognitive styles that foster wisdom. ■

Factors That Influence IQ Scores

Now that we have surveyed changes in intellectual functioning over the life span, we will address a different question: Why do children or adults who are the same age differ in IQ? Part of the answer is that they differ in the kinds of motivational and situational factors that can affect performance on a given day. Yet there are real differences in underlying intellectual ability that need to be explained. As usual, the best explanation is that genetic and environmental factors interact to make us what we are.

Genes

The pioneers of the IQ testing movement believed that individual differences in IQ exist simply because some people inherit better genes at conception than others do. Even though IQ scores are now known not to be determined entirely by genes, heredity helps explain individual differences in intellectual performance. As you saw in Chapter 3, identical twins obtain more similar IQ scores than fraternal twins do even when they have been raised apart (you might want to look again at Table 3.3). Moreover, the IQs of adopted children, once they reach adolescence, are more strongly correlated with those of their biological parents than with those of their adoptive parents. Overall, most researchers find that about half of the variation in IQ scores within a group of individuals is associated with genetic differences among them (Plomin & Spinath, 2004). Some researchers report that genetic influence on IQ differences is somewhat greater than environmental influences (Rowe, Vesterdal, & Rodgers, 1999). In either case, as much as half of the variation in scores is attributable to differences in the environments in which people develop. Children growing up in the same home show family resemblance in IQ scores (an effect of shared environment) when they are young children but not by the time they reach adolescence and adulthood (Bartels et al., 2002; Loehlin, Horn, & Willerman, 1997; McGue et al., 1993). Most effects of environment on IQ are unique to the individual and are not shared by siblings (Maccoby, 2000).

Although differences in IQ are linked to differences in genetic makeup, this says nothing about the extent to which IQ can be increased. Height, for example, is even more strongly associated with genetic endowment than IQ. Yet it can clearly be decreased by poor nutrition or increased by good nutrition, and it has increased over several generations as nutrition has improved (Sternberg, 1997). So look further at aspects of the environment in infancy and early childhood that can stimulate or inhibit intellectual growth. Then you will see how far this information can go in explaining differences in IQ scores associated with socioeconomic status and race or ethnicity.

Home Environment

Research by Arnold Sameroff and his colleagues (1993) provides a broad overview of some of the environmental factors that put children at risk for having low IQ scores—and, by implication, some of the factors associated with higher IQs. These researchers assessed the 10 risk factors shown in Table 9.3 at age 4 and again at age 13. Every factor was related to IQ at age 4, and most predicted IQ at age 13. In addition, the greater the number of these risk factors affecting a child, the

Table 9.3 How 10 Environmental Risk Factors Associated with Low IQ Affect Children

	Mean IQ at Age 4	
Risk Factor	**Child Experienced Risk Factor**	**Child Did Not Experience Risk Factor**
Child is member of minority group	90	110
Head of household is unemployed or low-skilled worker	90	108
Mother did not complete high school	92	109
Family has four or more children	94	105
Father is absent from family	95	106
Family experienced many stressful life events	97	105
Parents have rigid child-rearing values	92	107
Mother is highly anxious or distressed	97	105
Mother has poor mental health or diagnosed disorder	99	107
Mother shows little positive affect toward child	88	107

SOURCE: Based on Sameroff et al. (1993).

lower his IQ. Which risk factors the child experienced was less important than how many he experienced. Clearly, it is not good for intellectual development to grow up in a disadvantaged home with an adult unable to provide much intellectual nurturance.

In what ways do parents and the home influence children's intellectual development? A widely used assessment of the intellectual stimulation of the home environment is the **Home Observation for Measurement of the Environment (HOME) inventory** (Bradley et al., 2001). Sample items from the preschool version of a HOME inventory are shown in Table 9.4 (Caldwell & Bradley, 1984). Bradley and his colleagues (1989) have found that scores on the HOME can predict the IQs of African American and European American children at age 3, with correlations of about 0.50 (see also Cleveland et al., 2000). HOME scores continue to predict IQ scores between ages 3 and 6 (Espy, Molfese, & DiLalla, 2001). Gains in IQ from age 1 to age 3 are likely to occur among children from stimulating homes, whereas children from families with low HOME scores often experience drops in IQ over the same period. The early IQ scores of Mexican American children are not closely related to their families' HOME scores, however, so researchers know less about how the home environments provided by Hispanic parents influence their children's intellectual development.

What aspects of the home environment best predict high IQs? Studies using the HOME inventory indicate that the most important factors are parental involvement with the child and opportunities for stimulation (Gottfried et al., 1994). However, the amount of stimulation parents provide to their young children may not be as important as whether that stimulation is responsive to the child's behavior (a smile in return for a smile) and matched to the child's competencies so that it is neither too simple nor too challenging (Miller, 1986; Smith, Landry, & Swank, 2000). In short, an intellectually stimulating home is one in which parents are eager to be involved with their children and are responsive to their developmental needs and behavior. This may help explain why some research finds a connection between family size and birth, which is examined in the Explorations box on page 243.

Do differences in stimulation in the home create individual differences in IQ? More intelligent parents are more likely than less intelligent parents to provide intellectually stimulating home environments for their children and to pass on to their children genes that contribute to high intelligence; that is, there is evidence of the gene–environment correlations described in Chapter 3. Maternal IQ, for example, is correlated with a child's IQ at 3 years and with family income and quality of home environment (Bacharach & Baumeister, 1998). So, are bright children bright because of the genes they inherited or because of the home environment their bright parents provided? Keith Yeates and his colleagues (1983) evaluated these alternative hypotheses in a longitudinal study of 112 mothers and their children, ages 2 to 4. They measured the mothers'

Table 9.4 Subscales and Sample Items from the HOME Inventory

Subscale 1: Emotional and Verbal Responsivity of Parent (11 items)	
SAMPLE ITEMS:	Parent responds verbally to child's vocalization or verbalizations. Parent's speech is distinct, clear, and audible. Parent caresses or kisses child at least once.
Subscale 2: Avoidance of Restriction and Punishment (8 items)	
SAMPLE ITEMS:	Parent neither slaps nor spanks child during visit. Parent does not scold or criticize child during visit. Parent does not interfere with or restrict child more than three times during visit.
Subscale 3: Organization of Physical and Temporal Environment (6 items)	
SAMPLE ITEMS:	Child gets out of house at least four times a week. Child's play environment is safe.
Subscale 4: Provision of Appropriate Play Materials (9 items)	
SAMPLE ITEMS:	Child has a push or pull toy. Parent provides learning facilitators appropriate to age—mobile, table and chairs, highchair, playpen, and so on. Parent provides toys for child to play with during visit.
Subscale 5: Parental Involvement with Child (6 items)	
SAMPLE ITEMS:	Parent talks to child while doing household work. Parent structures child's play periods.
Subscale 6: Opportunities for Variety in Daily Stimulation (5 items)	
SAMPLE ITEMS:	Father provides some care daily. Child has three or more books of his or her own.

SOURCE: Adapted from Caldwell & Bradley (1984).

Explorations

Family Size and Birth Order

Years ago, the case was made that birth order influenced intellectual and academic performance, with firstborn children scoring the highest on intellectual tests and later-born children scoring progressively worse (Zajonc, 1976). After being dismissed for a time, this possible link between birth order and intelligence has recently been reexamined (Downey, 2001; Rodgers, 2001; Zajonc, 2001a, b). How might birth order affect intelligence? According to Zajonc (2001a, b), firstborn children benefit from having their parents' undivided attention and are exposed primarily to adult language. Subsequent children are exposed to their parents' attention and language, but they are also exposed to their older sibling's language and they must share their parents' attention. According to the resource dilution model, parents have only so many resources (time, energy, money, and so on); once these resources are used up, there are no more to go around (Downey, 2001). For a time, firstborns get all the resources; later-borns get fewer resources because the finite resources must be shared among more children. Firstborns are further advantaged because they are in a position to teach their younger siblings, and teaching others seems to promote intellectual development. Later-born children may not have opportunities to teach younger siblings.

Not all the research shows a clear connection between birth order and intelligence (Armor, 2001; Zajonc, 2001), and in those studies that do, the difference in test scores between firstborns and later-borns is only a few points. Thus, a firstborn might score 118 on an intelligence test and a younger sibling 115; this 3-point difference is unlikely to have practical significance for what the two siblings are able to accomplish in life (Armor, 2001).

Finally, birth order is connected to family size. When researchers compare fifth-born children, for example, with firstborns, some of the firstborns may have four or more siblings (as would be the case for the fifth-born child), but many have only one or two siblings. Thus, the children come from families of different sizes. Research suggests that, in general, children from larger families have lower IQ scores than children from smaller families. What this research does not tell is whether growing up in a large family leads to lower IQs or whether lower-IQ parents tend to have more children and pass their lower-IQ genes on to them (Rodgers et al., 2000).

IQs, the children's IQs from age 2 to age 4, and the families' HOME environments. The best predictor of a child's IQ at age 2 was the mother's IQ, just as a genetic hypothesis would suggest; home environment had little effect. But the picture changed by the time children were 4 years old, when the mother's IQ and the quality of the home environment were about equally important predictors of a child's IQ. Moreover, the researchers established statistically that differences in the quality of the home environment influenced children's IQs beyond the effects of their mothers' IQs, and that much of the effect of a mother's IQ could be attributed to high-IQ mothers providing more stimulating home environments than low-IQ mothers (Bacharach & Baumeister, 1998). In addition, adopted children's IQ scores rise considerably when they are moved from less stimulating to more stimulating homes (Turkheimer, 1991), and the quality of day care children receive predicts their verbal IQ scores (Broberg et al., 1997).

Thus, the argument that genetic influences can fully explain the apparent effects of home environment on IQ does not hold up. Yet researchers cannot ignore genetic influences; gifted children are more likely than their less gifted peers to seek intellectual stimulation (Gottfried et al., 1994). Overall, intellectual development seems to go best when a motivated, intellectually capable child begging for intellectual nourishment is fortunate enough to get it from involved and responsive parents.

Social Class

Children from lower-class homes average some 10 to 20 points below their middle-class age-mates on IQ tests. This is true in all racial and ethnic groups (Helms, 1997). Socioeconomic status affects IQ scores as well as children's rate of intellectual growth (Espy, Molfese, & DiLalla, 2001). What if socioeconomic conditions were to improve?

Over the 20th century, average IQ scores have increased in all countries studied, a phenomenon called the **Flynn effect** after its discoverer, James Flynn (1987, 1998, 1999). In the United States, the increase has amounted to 3 to 4 IQ points per decade. Most researchers argue that increases of this size cannot be caused by genetic evolution and therefore must have environmental causes (but see Mingroni, 2004). Interestingly, the Flynn effect is clearer for measures of fluid intelligence than for measures of crystallized intelligence, even though you might expect crystallized intelligence to benefit more from improved educational opportunities. Flynn believes that a good portion of the trend reflects increases not in true intellectual capacity but in performance on IQ tests, because today's test takers are probably more test-wise than test takers of the past. Flynn also suggests that improved nutrition, education, and living conditions over the course of the 20th century have contributed to real improvements in intellectual functioning. Increases in children's IQs over a 20-year period are apparently not caused by speedier processing of information, however, so the search for explanations continues (Nettelbeck & Wilson, 2004).

Similarly, improving the economic conditions of children's homes can improve their IQs. For example, Sandra Scarr and Richard Weinberg have charted the intellectual growth of African American and European American children adopted before their first birthday (Scarr & Weinberg, 1983; Weinberg, Scarr, & Waldman, 1992). Many of these children came from disadvantaged family backgrounds and had biological parents who were poorly educated and somewhat below average in IQ. They were placed in middle-class homes with adoptive parents who were highly educated and above average in intelligence. Throughout childhood and adolescence, these adoptees have posted average or above average scores on standardized IQ tests—higher scores than they would have obtained if they had stayed in the disadvantaged environments offered by their natural parents. Research with French children who were adopted later—around age 5—indicates that increases in IQ are much larger among children adopted into affluent homes with highly educated parents than among those adopted into disadvantaged homes (Duyme, Dumaret, & Tomkiewicz, 1999).

Could social class differences in IQ be caused by differences in the quality of the home environment that parents of different socioeconomic levels provide? Yes, at least partially. Scores on the HOME inventory are higher in middle-class homes than in lower-class homes, indicating that middle-class homes are more intellectually stimulating on average (Bradley et al., 1989; Gottfried, 1984). Poor nutrition, drug abuse, disruptive family experiences, and other factors associated with poverty may also contribute to the social-class gap in IQ (Gottfried & Gottfried, 1984).

Race and Ethnicity

Most studies find racial and ethnic differences in IQ scores and this has sparked much controversy. In the United States, for example, Asian American and European American children tend to score higher, on average, on IQ tests than African American, Native American, and Hispanic American children (Neisser et al., 1996). Different subcultural groups sometimes show distinctive profiles of mental abilities; for example, black children often do particularly well on verbal tasks, whereas Hispanic children, perhaps because of language differences, tend to excel on nonverbal items (Neisser et al., 1996; Taylor & Richards, 1991). It is essential to keep in mind that we are talking about *group averages.* Like the IQ scores of white children, those of minority children run the range from the mentally retarded to the gifted. Researchers certainly cannot predict an individual's IQ merely on the basis of racial or ethnic identity. Having said that, why do these average group differences exist? Consider the following hypotheses: bias in the tests, motivational factors, genetic differences among groups, and environmental differences among groups.

© Scholastic Studio 10/Index Stock Imagery

Differences in intellectual functioning within any racial or ethnic group are far greater than differences among groups.

Culture Bias

There may be **culture bias** in testing; that is, IQ tests may be more appropriate for children from white middle-class backgrounds than for those from other subcultural groups (Helms, 1992; Lopez, 1997). Low-income African American children who speak a dialect of English different from that spoken by middle-class Anglo children, as well as Hispanic children who hear Spanish rather than English at home, may not understand some test instructions or items. What is more, their experiences may not allow them to become familiar with some of the information called for on the tests (for example, What is a 747? Who wrote *Hamlet*?).

Minority-group children often do not have as much exposure to the culture reflected in the tests as nonminority children do. If IQ tests assess "proficiency in European American culture," minority children are bound to look deficient (Helms, 1992). Using IQ tests designed to be fair to all ethnic groups and introducing procedures to help minority children feel more comfortable and motivated can cut the usual IQ gap between African American and European American children in half (Kaufman, Kamphaus, & Kaufman, 1985). But, even though standardized IQ test items sometimes have a white middle-class flavor, group differences in IQ probably cannot be traced solely to test bias. Culture-fair IQ tests include items that should be equally unfamiliar (or familiar) to people from all ethnic groups and social classes—for example, items that require completing a geometric design with a piece that matches the rest of the design. Still, racial and ethnic differences emerge on such tests (Jensen, 1980). In addition, IQ tests predict future school achievement as well for African Americans and other minorities as they do for European Americans (Neisser et al., 1996).

Motivational Factors

Another possibility is that minority individuals are not motivated to do their best in testing situations because they are anxious or resist being judged by whites (Moore, 1986; Ogbu, 1994; Steele, 1997). They may be wary of strange examiners, may see little point in trying to do well, and may shake their heads before the question is completed as if to say they do not know the answer. Disadvantaged children score some 7 to 10 points better when they are given time to get to know a friendly examiner or are given a mix of easy and hard items so that they do not become discouraged by a long string of difficult items (Zigler et al., 1982). Even though most children do better with a friendly examiner, it seems that African American children, even those from middle-class homes, are often less comfortable in testing situations than white middle-class children are (Moore, 1986).

Claude Steele and his colleagues have argued that the performance of African Americans is especially likely to suffer whenever negative stereotypes of their group come into play (Steele, 1997, 1999; Steele & Aronson, 1995; see also Sackett, Hardison, & Cullen, 2004). In one study, female students at Stanford University were given difficult test items. Some students were told that they were taking a test of verbal abilities and would get feedback about their strengths and weaknesses; others were told that they were going to do some verbal problems but that their ability would not be evaluated. As Figure 9.6 shows, African American students performed poorly when they were led to believe that the test would reveal their level of intellectual ability, but performed more like European American students when they did not think their ability would be judged. Even being asked to identify their race in a personal information section at the start of a test of intellectual ability can undermine the performance of African American college students (Steele & Aronson, 1995).

Why? Steele concluded that African Americans perform poorly on IQ tests partly because of **stereotype threat**—fear that they will be judged to have the qualities associated with negative stereotypes of African Americans (see also Aronson et al., 1999). It is not that African Americans have internalized stereotypes and believe they are intellectually inferior, according to Steele. Instead, they become anxious and unable to perform well in testing situations that arouse concerns about being negatively stereotyped.

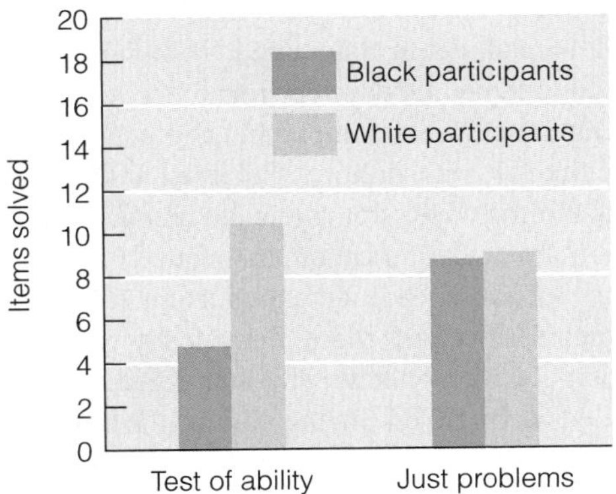

Figure 9.6 African American students perform poorly on tests of mental abilities when they think they are taking a test that may result in their being stereotyped as unintelligent.

SOURCE: From Steele, C. M., & Aronson, J. (1995). Stereotype threat and the intellectual test performance of African Americans. *Journal of Personality and Social Psychology, 69.* Copyright © 1995 by the American Psychological Association. Reprinted by permission.

Other research has demonstrated that positive stereotypes about a group can increase the performance of members of that group. Margaret Shih and her colleagues (Shih, Pittinsky, & Ambady, 1999) gave Asian American women a math test under one of three conditions. In one, their identity as women was made salient; in another, their Asian American identity was made salient; and in a third condition, no identity was emphasized. Consistent with stereotypes, these women performed worse when their gender was emphasized and better when their ethnic background was emphasized, relative to the group that was not primed to think about either identity. So, stereotypes can either hinder or enhance performance, depending on whether a person identifies with a group that is viewed negatively or positively.

The effects of stereotype threat can be reduced by providing students with a mentor. Catherine Good and her colleagues (2003) had college students serve as mentors to seventh-graders likely to experience stereotype threat as a result of being female, impoverished, and a member of a minority group. The mentors encouraged students to interpret their academic troubles as a result of the transition to a new school for seventh grade. In addition, they talked about intelligence being flexible and responsive to new learning. Following such mentoring, the students performed better on standardized tests than students who did not receive mentoring. These findings provide a practical means for eliminating or reducing the negative influence of stereotype threat.

Genetic Influences

Perhaps no idea in psychology has sparked more heated debate than the suggestion that racial and ethnic differences in IQ scores could be caused by group differences in genetic makeup. Differences in genetic makeup contribute, with differences in environment, to IQ differences within either the European American or the African American population. Scholars such as Arthur Jensen (1969) and Herrnstein and Murray (1994) have gone a step further to suggest that IQ differences between European Americans and African Americans may be because of genetic differences between the races.

However, most psychologists do not think the evidence that heredity contributes to within-group differences says much about the reasons for between-group differences. Richard Lewontin (1976) makes this point with an analogy. Suppose that corn seeds with different genetic makeups are randomly drawn from a bag and planted in two fields—one that is barren and one that has fertile soil. Because all the plants within each field were grown in the same soil, their differences in height would have to be because of differences in genetic makeup. A genetic explanation of differences would fit. But, if the plants in the fertile field are generally taller than those in the barren field, this between-field variation must be entirely because of environment. Similarly, even though genes partially explain individual differences in IQ within African American and European American groups, the average difference between the racial groups may still reflect nothing more than differences in the environments they typically experience. There is no direct evidence that differences in genetic makeup between the races account for average group differences in IQ (Neisser et al., 1996).

Environmental Influences

It is time to return to an environmental hypothesis about racial and ethnic differences in IQ. Many of the intellectual and academic differences attributed to race or ethnicity probably reflect racial and ethnic differences in socioeconomic status instead (Patterson, Kupersmidt, & Vaden, 1990). Research on adopted children is relevant here. Placement in more advantaged homes has allowed lower-income African American children to equal or exceed the average IQ in the general population and to exceed the IQs of comparable African American children raised in more disadvantaged environments by 20 points (Moore, 1986; Scarr & Weinberg, 1983; Weinberg, Scarr, & Waldman, 1992). This could not have happened if African American children were genetically deficient.

The major message of this research is that children, whatever their racial background, perform better on IQ tests when they grow up in intellectually stimulating environments with involved, responsive parents and are exposed to the "culture of the tests and the schools" (Scarr & Weinberg, 1983, p. 261). How much of the racial gap in IQ can be explained by racial differences in neighborhood and family socioeconomic conditions, mother's education, and qualities of the home environment? Jeanne Brooks-Gunn, Pamela Klebanov, and Greg Duncan (1996) used statistical procedures to correct for these environmental differences between African American and European American children so that they could estimate what the IQ difference would be if the two racial groups had been raised in similar environments. Without any controls for environmental differences, there was an IQ gap of 18 points. The gap narrowed to 8 points when family and neighborhood income levels were controlled and was reduced to 3 points, a trivial difference, when racial differences in the provision of a stimulating home environment (HOME scores) were also controlled. In short, that more African American than European American children live in poverty and have limited learning opportunities at home has a lot to do with the racial difference in average IQ scores.

Summing Up

Individual differences in IQ scores are related to both genetic and home environmental factors. The lower average IQ scores of some minority groups may be better explained by culture bias in testing, low motivation (including anxiety caused by negative group stereotypes), and low socioeconomic status than by genetic differences. Minority children perform better when they grow up in intellectually stimulating homes. ■

The Extremes of Intelligence

Although we have identified some of the factors that contribute to individual differences in intellectual performance, you cannot fully appreciate the magnitude of these differences without considering people at the extremes of the IQ continuum. Just how different are mentally retarded and gifted individuals? And how different are their lives?

Mental Retardation

Mental retardation is currently defined by the American Association on Mental Retardation (AAMR, 2002) as significantly below-average intellectual functioning with limitations in areas of adaptive behavior such as self-care and social skills and originating before age 18. To be diagnosed as mentally retarded, an individual must obtain an IQ score of 70 or lower and have difficulties meeting age-appropriate expectations in important areas of everyday functioning. According to this definition, mental retardation is not merely a deficiency within the person; rather, it is the product of the interaction between person and environment, strongly influenced by the type and level of supportive help the individual receives (Reiss, 1994).

Individuals with mental retardation differ greatly in their levels of functioning (see Table 9.5). An adult with an IQ in the range of about 55 to 70 is likely to have a mental age comparable to that of an 8- to 12-year-old child. Individuals with mild mental retardation can learn both academic and practical skills in school, and they can potentially work and live independently or with occasional help as adults. Many of these individuals are integrated into regular classrooms, where they excel academically and socially relative to comparable individuals who are segregated into special classrooms (Freeman, 2000). At the other end of the continuum, individuals with IQs below 20 to 25 and mental ages below 3 years ("profoundly retarded") show major delays in all areas of development and require basic care, sometimes in institutional settings. However, they, too, can benefit considerably from training.

Mental retardation has many causes. Severely and profoundly retarded people are often affected by **organic retardation,** meaning that their retardation is because of some identifiable biological cause associated with hereditary factors, diseases, or injuries. Down syndrome, the condition associated with an extra 21st chromosome, and PKU are familiar examples of organic retardation associated with genetic factors (Simonoff, Bolton, & Rutter, 1996; see also Chapter 3). Other forms of organic retardation are associated with prenatal risk factors—an alcoholic mother, exposure to rubella, and so on (see Chapter 4). Because many organically retarded children are seriously delayed or have physical defects, they can often be identified at birth or during infancy. However, the most common form of mental retardation, **cultural–familial retardation,** is typically milder and appears to be caused by a combination of a low genetic potential and a poor, unstimulating environment (Simonoff, Bolton, & Rutter, 1996). Whereas children with organic retardation come from all socioeconomic levels, children with cultural–familial retardation often come from poverty areas and have a parent or sibling who is also retarded (Zigler, 1995). From one-half to three-quarters

Table 9.5 Levels and Characteristics of Mental Retardation

	Level			
	Mild	**Moderate**	**Severe**	**Profound**
APPROXIMATE RANGE OF IQ SCORES	52 to 70	35 to 51	20 to 34	Below 19
DEGREE OF INDEPENDENCE	Usually independent	Some independence; needs some supervision	May be semi-independent with close supervision	Dependent; needs constant supervision
EDUCATIONAL ACHIEVEMENT	Can do some academic work—usually to sixth-grade level; focus is on career	Focus is on daily living skills rather than academics; some career training	Focus is on self-care (toileting, dressing, eating) and communication skills	Focus is on self-care, mobility, and basic communication education

SOURCE: Based on Barack, Hodapp, & Zigler (1998).

of mental retardation is of the cultural–familial type: exact cause unknown (Zigler & Hodapp, 1991).

Historically, about 3% of school-age children have been classified as mentally retarded, although this rate is decreasing because fewer children are diagnosed as mildly retarded today (Patton, 2000). What becomes of these children as they grow up? Generally, they proceed along the same paths and through the same sequences of developmental milestones as other children do (Zigler & Hodapp, 1991). Their IQs remain low because they do not achieve the same level of growth that others do. They, like nonretarded people, show signs of intellectual aging in later life, especially on tests that require speed (Devenny et al., 1996). Individuals with Down syndrome may experience even greater intellectual deterioration later in life because they are at risk for premature Alzheimer's disease (Day & Jancar, 1994).

As for their outcomes in life, consider a follow-up study of individuals with mild and borderline mental retardation who had been placed in segregated special education classes during the 1920s and 1930s (Ross et al., 1985). The individuals studied had a mean IQ of 67. They were compared with their siblings and with nonretarded peers about 35 years later. Generally, these mentally retarded adults had poor life outcomes in middle age in comparison with nonretarded groups (see also Schalock et al., 1992). About 80% of the men with retardation were employed, but they usually held semiskilled or unskilled jobs that required little education or intellectual ability. Women often married and became homemakers. Compared with nonretarded peers, men and women with retardation also fared worse on other counts. For example, they had lower incomes, less adequate housing, poorer adjustment in social relationships, and greater dependency on others.

Yet the authors of the study found grounds for optimism. These individuals had done much better during adulthood than stereotyped expectations of people with mental retardation would predict. Most of them worked and had married, and about 80% reported having had no need for public assistance in the 10 years before they were interviewed. This study, like others before it, suggests that many children labeled mentally retarded by the schools—and who have difficulty with the tasks demanded of them in school—"vanish" into the general population after they leave school. Apparently they can adapt to the demands of adult life. As the authors put it, "It does not take as many IQ points as most people believe to be productive, to get along with others, and to be self-fulfilled" (Ross et al., 1985, p. 149).

Giftedness

The gifted child used to be identified solely by an IQ score—one that was at least 130. Programs for gifted children still focus mainly on those with very high IQs, but there is increased recognition that some children are gifted because they have special abilities rather than because they have high general intelligence. Even high-IQ children are usually not equally talented in all areas; contrary to myth, they cannot just become anything they choose (Winner, 1996). More often, high-IQ children have exceptional talent in an area or two and otherwise are good, but not exceptional, performers (Achter, Benbow, & Lubinski, 1997). So, today's definitions emphasize

Gifted children have either high IQ scores or special abilities. This young girl is performing with the Pacific Symphony of Orange County, California.

that **giftedness** involves having a high IQ or showing special abilities in areas valued in society, such as mathematics, the performing and visual arts, or even leadership.

Joseph Renzulli (1998) has long argued that giftedness emerges from a combination of above-average ability, creativity, and task commitment. According to this view, someone might have a high IQ and even creative ability, but Renzulli questions whether they are truly gifted if they are not motivated to use this intelligence. Here we focus on individuals with exceptional IQs.

How early can intellectually gifted children be identified? By toddlerhood, according to a longitudinal study by Allen Gottfried and his colleagues (1994). They tracked a large sample of children from age 1 to age 8, determined which children had IQs of 130 or above at age 8, and then looked for differences between these gifted children and other children earlier in life. The gifted children turned out to be identifiable as early as 18 months, primarily by their advanced language skills. They were also highly curious and motivated to learn; they even enjoyed the challenge of taking IQ tests more than most children. Linda Silverman and her colleagues at the Gifted Development Center have used the Characteristics of Giftedness Scale to identify gifted children (Rogers, 1986; Silverman, Chitwood, & Waters, 1986). They have found that gifted children can be distinguished from average children in terms of: rapid learning, extensive vocabulary, good memory, long attention span, perfectionism, preference for older companions, excellent sense of humor, early interest in reading, strong ability with puzzles and mazes, maturity, and perseverance

The rest of the story of the development of high-IQ children is told by a major longitudinal study launched in 1921 by Lewis Terman, developer of the Stanford-Binet test (Holahan & Sears, 1995; Terman, 1954; Oden, 1968). The participants were more than 1500 California schoolchildren nominated by their teachers as gifted and who had IQs of 140 or higher. It soon became apparent that these high-IQ children (who came to be called *Termites*) were exceptional in many other ways. For example, they had weighed more at birth and had learned to walk and talk sooner than most toddlers. They reached puberty somewhat earlier than average and had better-than-average health. Their teachers rated them as better adjusted and more morally mature than their less intelligent peers. And, although they were no more popular than their classmates, they were quick to take on leadership responsibilities. Taken together, these findings destroy the stereotype that most gifted children are frail, sickly youngsters who are socially inadequate and emotionally immature.

Another demonstration of the personal and social maturity of most gifted children comes from a study of high-IQ children who skipped high school and entered the University of Washington as part of a special program to accelerate their education (Robinson & Janos, 1986). Contrary to the common wisdom that gifted children will suffer socially and emotionally if they skip grades and are forced to fit in with much older students, these youngsters showed no signs of maladjustment (see also Kulik & Kulik, 1992). On several measures of psychological and social maturity and adjustment, they equaled their much older college classmates and similarly gifted students who attended high school. Many of them thrived in college, for the first time finding friends like themselves—friends who were like-minded rather than like-aged (Boothe, Sethna, & Stanley, 2000).

Most of Terman's gifted children remained as remarkable in adulthood as they had been in childhood. Fewer than 5% were rated as seriously maladjusted. Their rates of such problems as ill health, mental illness, alcoholism, and delinquent behavior were but a fraction of those observed in the general population (Terman, 1954), although they were no less likely to divorce (Holahan & Sears, 1995).

The occupational achievements of the men in the sample were impressive. In middle age, 88% were employed in professional or high-level business jobs, compared with 20% of men in the general population (Oden, 1968). As a group, they had taken out more than 200 patents and written some 2000 scientific reports, 100 books, 375 plays or short stories, and more than 300 essays, sketches, magazine articles, and critiques. And gifted women? Because of the influence of gender-role expectations during the period covered by the study, gifted women achieved less than gifted men vocationally, often interrupting their careers or sacrificing their career goals to raise families. Still, they were more likely to have careers, and distinguished ones, than most women of their generation.

Finally, the Termites aged well. In their 60s and 70s, most of the men and women in the Terman study were highly active, involved, healthy, and happy people (Holahan & Sears, 1995). The men kept working longer than most men do and stayed involved in work even after they retired. The women too led exceptionally active lives. Contrary to the stereotype that gifted individuals burn out early, the Termites continued to burn bright throughout their lives.

Yet, just as it is wrong to view intellectually gifted children as emotionally disturbed misfits, it is inaccurate to conclude that intellectually gifted children are models of good adjustment, perfect in every way. Some research suggests that children with IQs closer to 180 than 130 are often unhappy and socially isolated, perhaps because they are so out of step with their peers, and sometimes even have serious problems (Winner, 1996). In *Terman's Kids,* Joel Shurkin (1992) describes several less-than-happy life stories of some of Terman's Termites. A woman who graduated from Stanford at age 17 and was headed for success as a writer became a landlady; an emotionally disturbed boy took cyanide at age 18 after being rejected in love.

These are exceptions, however. Overall, most of Terman's gifted children moved through adulthood as healthy, happy, and highly productive individuals. Yet some fared better than others. Even within this elite group, for example, the quality of the individual's home environment was important. The most well-adjusted and successful adults had highly educated parents who offered them both love and intellectual stimulation (Tomlinson-Keasey & Little, 1990).

Summing Up

The extremes of intelligence are represented by mental retardation at one end of the continuum and giftedness at the other end. Mental retardation is defined by deficits in adaptive behavior with low IQ scores. Functioning varies by level of retardation, but is often better than expected during adulthood. Giftedness has most often been defined by high IQ scores, although more recent definitions recognize special talents not measured by traditional IQ tests. Life outcomes are generally above average. ■

What Is Creativity?

Despite their many positive outcomes in life, not one of Terman's high-IQ gifted children became truly eminent. Recall that Terman had teachers nominate bright children for inclusion in the study. Is it possible that teachers overlooked some children who would be considered gifted by today's criteria because of their special talents rather than their high IQs? Might they have missed children capable of outstanding work in a particular area such as music, art, or writing? The word *creativity* comes to mind. Perhaps creativity is more important than IQ in allowing a Michelangelo or a Mozart to break new ground. But what is creativity, and what is known about its development?

Creativity is most often defined as the ability to produce novel responses appropriate in context and valued by others—products both original and meaningful (Csikszentmihalyi, 1996; Simonton, 1999; Sternberg, 2003). J. P. Guilford (1967, 1988) proposed that creativity involves divergent rather than convergent thinking. **Divergent thinking** requires coming up with a variety of ideas or solutions to a problem when there is no one right answer. **Convergent thinking** involves "converging" on the best answer to a problem and is precisely what IQ tests measure. The most common measure of creativity, at least in children, is called **ideational fluency,** or the sheer number of different (including novel) ideas that a person can generate. Quick—list all the uses you can think of for a pencil. An uncreative person might say you could write letters, notes, postcards, and so forth; by contrast, one creative person envisioned a pencil as "a backscratcher, a potting stake, kindling for a fire, a rolling pin for baking, a toy for a woodpecker, or a small boat for a cricket" (Richards, 1996, p. 73).

Creativity and divergent thinking are distinct from general intelligence and convergent thinking. Indeed, correlations between scores on creativity measures and scores on IQ tests are low to moderate, depending on the area of creativity measured (Sternberg, 2003). Creativity and general intelligence are related in the sense that highly creative people rarely have below-average IQs. Thus, a minimum of intelligence is probably required for creativity (Runco, 1992; Simonton, 1999). However, among people who have average or above-average IQs, an individual's IQ score is essentially unrelated to her level of creativity. In all likelihood, then, the IQs posted by you and your classmates will not necessarily predict which of you will give the most creative answers to the problems in Figure 9.7.

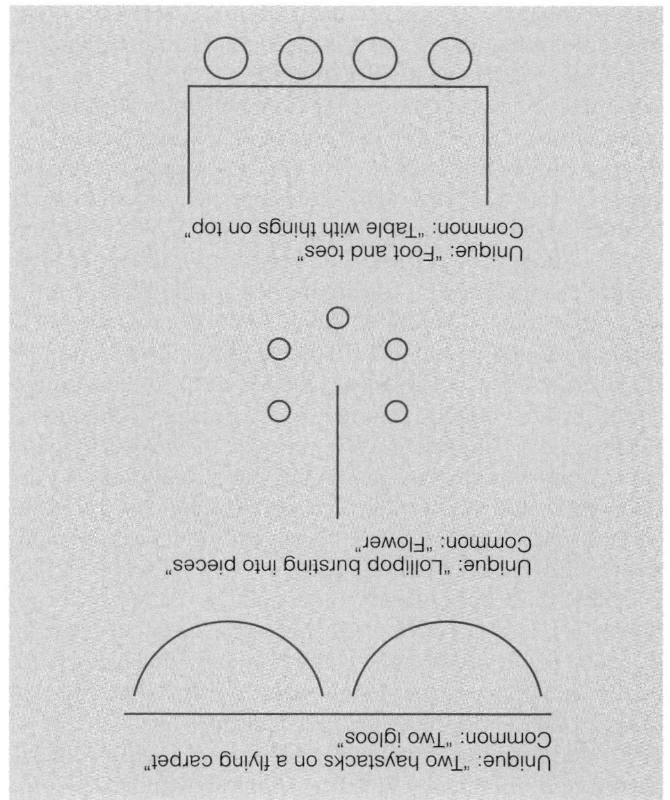

Figure 9.7 Are you creative? Indicate what you see in each of the three drawings. Below each drawing you will find examples of unique and common responses, drawn from a study of creativity in children.
SOURCE: Wallach & Kogan (1965).

Creativity in Childhood and Adolescence

What is the child who scores high on tests of creativity like? To answer this, one group of researchers compared children who had high creativity scores but normal-range IQ scores with children who scored high in IQ but not in creativity (Getzels and Jackson, 1962). Personality measures suggested that the creative children showed more freedom, originality, humor, violence, and playfulness than the high-IQ children. Perhaps as a result, the high-IQ children were more success-oriented and received more approval from teachers. Compared with their less creative peers, creative children also engaged in more fantasy or pretend play, often inventing new uses for familiar objects and new roles for themselves (Kogan, 1983). Finally, these children are more open to new experiences and ideas (Simonton, 1999).

Although average IQ scores differ across racial and socioeconomic groups, scores on creativity tests often do not (Kogan, 1983). Moreover, genetic influences (a source of individual differences in IQ) have little to do with performance on tests of creativity; twins are similar in the degree of creativity they display, but identical twins are no more similar than fraternal twins (Plomin, 1990; Reznikoff et al., 1973). This suggests that certain qualities of the home environment tend to make brothers and sisters alike in their degree of creativity. What qualities? Although there is little research to go on, parents of creative children and adolescents tend to value nonconformity and independence, accept their children as they are, encourage their curiosity and playfulness, and grant them a good deal of freedom to explore new possibilities on their own (Harrington, Block, & Block, 1987; Runco, 1992). In some cases, the parent–child relationship is even distant; a surprising number of eminent creators seem to have experienced rather lonely, insecure, and unhappy childhoods (Ochse, 1990; Simonton, 1999). Out of their adversity may have come an active imagination and a strong desire to develop their talents. Overall, then, creative abilities are influenced by factors distinct from those that influence the cognitive abilities measured on IQ tests.

How does the capacity to be creative change with age? Researchers are not sure. Performance on tests of creativity generally improves over the childhood and adolescent years, but there appear to be certain ages at which it drops off (Kogan, 1983). Howard Gardner (Gardner, Phelps, & Wolf, 1990) suggests that preschool children are highly original, playful, and uninhibited but that school-age children become restricted in their creative expression as they attempt to master their culture's rules for art, music, dance, and other creative endeavors so that they can do things the "right" way. During adolescence, Gardner believes, some individuals give up the desire to express themselves creatively but others regain the innovativeness and freedom of expression they had as preschoolers and put it to use, with the technical skills they gained as children, to produce highly creative works. The ages at which creativity flourishes or is stifled seem to vary from culture to culture depending on when children are pressured to conform (Torrance, 1975). Overall, the developmental course of creativity is not so predictable or steady as the increase in mental age seen on measures of IQ. Instead, creativity seems to wax and wane with age in response to developmental needs and cultural demands.

How well does performance on tests of creativity predict creative accomplishments, such as original artwork or outstanding science projects? Some researchers have found that scores on creativity tests administered in either elementary or secondary school predict creative achievements, such as inventions and novels, in adulthood (Howieson, 1981; Runco, 1992; Torrance, 1988). However, just as it is a mistake to expect IQ to predict accomplishments, it may also be a mistake to expect tests of creativity to do so with any great accuracy (Albert, 1996). Why? First, creativity is expressed in different ways at different points in the life span; engaging in imaginative play as a child is correlated with high scores on tests of creativity (Russ, 1996) but may have little to do with being a creative scientist or musician as an adult. Also, creativity tests, like IQ tests, attempt to measure general cognitive abilities when many specific talents exist, and each (artistic, mathematical, musical, and so on) requires distinct skills and experiences, as suggested by Gardner's theory of multiple intelligences.

Researchers are now looking at individuals who show exceptional talent in a particular field and are trying to identify the factors that contribute to their accomplishments (Sternberg & Lubart, 1996). David Feldman (1982, 1986), for example, has studied children who are prodigies in such areas as chess, music, and mathematics. These individuals were generally similar to other children in areas outside their fields of expertise. What contributed to their special achievements? On the nature side, they had *talent* as well as a powerful *motivation* to develop their special talents—a real passion for what they were doing. Olympic gymnast Olga Korbut put it well: "If gymnastics did not exist, I would have invented it" (Feldman, 1982, p. 35). On the nurture side, these achievers were blessed with *environments* that recognized, valued, and nurtured their talent and motivation (see also Winner, 1996). They were strongly encouraged and supported by their families and intensively tutored or coached by experts. According to Feldman, the child with creative potential in a specific field must become intimately familiar with the state of the field if he is to advance or transform it, as the groundbreaking artist or musician does. But parents and trainers must not be too pushy. For example, David Helfgott, the Australian pianist who was the subject of the movie *Shine,* was nearly destroyed by an abusive father who pushed him unmercifully to master difficult pieces (Page, 1996). Cellist Yo-Yo Ma, a prodigy himself, says this about nurturing young musicians:

> If you lead them toward music, teach them that it is beautiful, and help them learn—say, "Oh, you love music, well, let's work on this piece together, and I'll show you something . . ." That's a *creative* nurturing. But if you just push them to be stars, and tell them they'll become rich and famous—or, worse, if you try to live through them—that is damaging (Page, 1996, p. G10).

K. Anders Ericsson and Neil Charness (1994) go even farther than Feldman in emphasizing the importance of environment in the development of creative talent. Indeed, they maintain that it is practice rather than innate talent that makes great creators great—that nature is overrated and nurture is underrated when it comes to creative achievement. Their research shows that prolonged training in a set of skills can alter cognitive and physiological processes and permit levels of performance that would have been unimaginable without training. Motivation also enters in, however, because only some individuals are willing to do what Ericsson and Charness believe is necessary to become outstanding in a field—work hard every day over a period of more than 10 years.

Creative Achievement in Adulthood

Studies of creativity during the adult years have focused on a small number of so-called eminent creators in such fields as art, music, science, and philosophy. The big question has been this: When in adulthood are such individuals most productive and most likely to create their best works? Is it early in adulthood, when they can benefit from youth's enthusiasm and freshness of approach? Or is it later in adulthood, when they have fully mastered their field and have the experience and knowledge necessary to make a breakthrough in it? And what becomes of the careers of eminent creators in old age?

Early studies by Harvey Lehman (1953) and Wayne Dennis (1966) provided a fairly clear picture of how creative careers unfold (see also Simonton, 1990). In most fields, creative production increases steeply from the 20s to the late 30s and early 40s then gradually declines thereafter, although not to the same low levels that characterized early adulthood. Peak times of creative achievement also vary from field to field. As Figure 9.8 shows, the productivity of scholars in the humanities (for example, historians and philosophers) continues well into old age and peaks in the 60s, possibly because creative work in these fields often involves integrating knowledge that has crystallized over years. By contrast, productivity in the arts (for example, music or drama) peaks in the 30s and 40s and declines steeply thereafter, perhaps because artistic creativity depends on a more fluid or innovative kind of thinking. Scientists seem to be intermediate, peaking in their 40s and declining only in their 70s. Even within the same general field, differences in peak times have been noted. For example, poets reach their peak before novelists do, and mathematicians peak before other scientists do (Dennis, 1966; Lehman, 1953).

Still, in many fields (including psychology), creative production rises to a peak in the late 30s or early 40s, and both the total number of works and the number of high-quality works decline thereafter (Simonton, 1990). This same pattern can be detected across different cultures and historical periods. Even so, the percentage of a creator's works that are major, significant ones changes little over the years (Simonton, 1990). This means that many creators are still producing outstanding works in old age—sometimes their greatest works—not just rehashes of earlier triumphs. Michelangelo, for instance, was in his 70s and 80s when he worked on St. Peter's Cathedral, and Goethe was polishing *Faust* at 83. Indeed, the most eminent among the eminent seem to start early and finish late (Simonton, 1990).

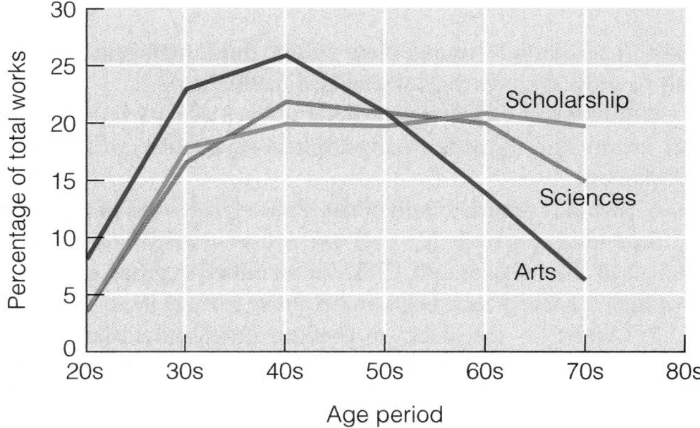

Figure 9.8 Percentage of total works produced in each decade of the lives of eminent creators. The "scholarship" group includes historians and philosophers; the "sciences" category includes natural and physical scientists, inventors, and mathematicians; the "arts" creators include architects, musicians, dramatists, poets, and the like.

SOURCE: Based on data from Dennis (1966).

How can researchers account for changes in creative production over the adult years? One explanation, proposed long ago (Beard, 1874, in Simonton, 1984), is that creative achievement requires both enthusiasm and experience. In early adulthood, the enthusiasm is there, but the experience is not; in later adulthood, the experience is there, but the enthusiasm or vigor has fallen off. People in their 30s and 40s have it all.

Dean Simonton (1984, 1990, 1991) has offered another theory: Each creator may have a certain potential to create that is realized over the adult years; as the potential is realized, less is left to express. According to Simonton, creative activity involves two processes: ideation (generating creative ideas) and elaboration (executing ideas to produce poems, paintings, or scientific publications). After a career is launched, some time elapses before any ideas are generated or any works are completed. This would explain the rise in creative achievement between the 20s and 30s. Also, some kinds of work take longer to formulate or complete than others, which helps explain why a poet (who can generate and carry out ideas quickly) might reach a creative peak earlier in life than, say, a historian (who may need to devote years to the research and writing necessary to complete a book once the idea for it is hatched).

Why does creative production begin to taper off? Simonton (1990, 1991) suggests that older creators may simply have used up much of their stock of potential ideas. They never exhaust their creative potential, but they have less of it left to realize. Simonton argues, then, that changes in creative production over the adult years have more to do with the nature of the creative process than with a loss of mental ability in later life. Creators who start their careers late are likely to experience the same rise and fall of creative output that others do, only later in life. And those lucky creators with immense creative potential to realize will not burn out; they will keep producing great works until they die.

What about mere mortals? Here, researchers have fallen back on tests designed to measure creativity. In one study, scores on a test of divergent thinking abilities decreased at least modestly after about age 40 and decreased more steeply starting around 70 (McCrae, Arenberg, & Costa, 1987). It seems that elderly adults do not differ much from younger adults in the originality of their ideas; the main difference is that they generate fewer of them (Jaquish & Ripple, 1981). Generally, then, these studies agree with the studies of eminent achievers: Creative behavior becomes less frequent in later life, but it remains possible throughout the adult years.

Summing Up

Creativity is the ability to produce novel and socially valuable work. It requires divergent thinking rather than the convergent thinking captured by traditional IQ tests. Creativity increases throughout childhood and adoles-

Table 9.6 Comparison of Approaches to Intelligence

	Piagetian Theory	Vygotskian Theory	Information-Processing Approach	Psychometric Approach
WHAT IS INTELLIGENCE?	Cognitive structures that help people adapt	Tools of culture	Attention, memory, and other mental processes	Mental abilities and scores on IQ tests
WHAT CHANGES WITH AGE?	Stage of cognitive development	Ability to solve problems without assistance of others and use of inner speech	Hardware (speed) and software (strategies) of the mind	Mental age (difficulty of problems solved)
WHAT IS OF MOST INTEREST?	Universal changes	Culturally influenced changes and processes	Universal processes	Individual differences

cence. Eminent creators are typically more productive during their 30s and 40s than before or after but continue to produce great works in later life.

Our account of cognitive development over the life span is now complete. We hope you appreciate that each of the four major approaches to the mind that we have considered—the Piagetian cognitive-developmental approach and Vygotsky's theory described in Chapter 7, the information-processing approach explained in Chapter 8, and the psychometric or testing approach covered here—offers something of value. Table 9.6 lists how these four approaches compare with their views of intelligence. Perhaps we can summarize it this way: Piaget has shown that comparing the thought of a preschooler with the thought of an adult is like comparing a tadpole with a frog. Modes of thought change qualitatively with age. Vygotsky has highlighted the importance of culturally transmitted modes of thinking and interactions with others. The information-processing approach has helped researchers understand thinking processes and explain why the young child cannot remember as much information or solve problems as effectively as the adult can. Finally, the psychometric approach has told researchers that, if they look at the range of tasks to which the mind can be applied, they can recognize distinct mental abilities that each person consistently displays in greater or lesser amounts. You need not choose one approach and reject the others. Your understanding of the mind is likely to be richer if all three approaches continue to thrive. There are truly many intelligences, and it is foolish to think that a single IQ score can describe the complexities of human cognitive development. ■

Summary Points

1. Most modern intelligence tests are based on the psychometric approach, which assumes that intelligence consists of a set of traits that can be measured. The Stanford-Binet and Wechsler scales are the most common intelligence tests and compare an individual's performance on a variety of cognitive tasks with the average performance of age-mates.

2. In infancy, mental growth is rapid and is measured by DQs derived from tests such as the Bayley scales. However, infant scores do not predict later IQ as well as measures of speed of information processing such as rapid habituation and preference for novelty do.

3. During childhood, mental growth continues, and IQs at one age can predict IQs at later ages. However, many individuals show wide variations in their IQ scores over time. Those who gain IQ points often have favorable home environments, whereas disadvantaged children often show a cumulative deficit.

4. IQ is relatively stable throughout adolescence and adulthood. IQ scores predict school achievement and years of education obtained. IQ scores are also correlated with occupational status and health in adulthood. Among older adults, fluid intelligence is more likely to show declines than crystallized intelligence.

5. Individual differences in IQ at a given age are linked to genetic factors and to intellectually stimulating qualities of the home environment.

6. Mentally retarded individuals show varied levels of functioning, depending on their IQs and the causes (organic or cultural–familial) of their retardation. Children identified as gifted on the basis of high IQ scores have been found above average in all ways.

7. Creativity—the ability to produce novel and socially valued works—is a distinct mental ability that demands divergent rather than convergent thinking; it is largely independent of IQ (above a certain minimum level), increases with age during childhood, and is fostered in homes where independence is valued. Performance on creativity tests declines in later life, but creative capacities clearly survive into old age.

Critical Thinking

1. How does intelligence change across the life span? Outline the pattern you would expect to find from infancy to older adulthood

and indicate what tests you would use to assess intelligence at different ages.

2. Imagine that you are chosen to head a presidential commission on intelligence testing whose task it is to devise a better IQ test for use in the schools than any that currently exists. Drawing on material in this chapter, sketch out the features of your model IQ test. What would be included and excluded from your definition of intelligence? How would you measure intelligence? In what ways would your test improve upon the tests that are currently used?

3. Putting together material from Chapters 7, 8, and 9, how would you describe the cognitive functioning of a typical 70-year-old person? What are the greatest cognitive strengths of older adults, what are their greatest limitations, and how much can an individual do to optimize her functioning?

4. The Maori are a socioeconomically disadvantaged group in New Zealand, a country colonized by the British long ago. Maori children typically score lower on IQ tests than children of British background. Knowing what you know about minorities in the United States, what are your top two hypotheses about why Maori children perform relatively poorly, and how might you test these hypotheses?

Key Terms

psychometric approach, 227
fluid intelligence, 227
crystallized intelligence, 227
mental age, 228
intelligence quotient (IQ), 228
test norms, 228
normal distribution, 228
dynamic assessment, 229
savant syndrome, 229
triarchic theory of intelligence, 230
contextual subtheory, 231
experiential subtheory, 231
automatization, 231
componential subtheory, 231
successful intelligence, 231
developmental quotient (DQ), 232
cumulative-deficit hypothesis, 233
terminal drop, 238
wisdom, 239
Home Observation for Measurement of the Environment (HOME) inventory, 242
Flynn effect, 243
culture bias, 244
stereotype threat, 245
mental retardation, 246
organic retardation, 246
cultural–familial retardation, 246
giftedness, 248
creativity, 249
divergent thinking, 249
convergent thinking, 249
ideational fluency, 249

Media Resources

Websites to Explore

Visit Our Website

For a chapter tutorial quiz and other useful features, visit the book's companion website at *http://psychology.wadsworth.com/sigelman_rider5e.* You can also connect directly to the following sites:

The Role of Intelligence in Modern Society
An article by Earl Hunt, published in 1995 in *The American Scientist,* addresses the controversy raised by Richard Herrnstein and Charles Murray's book, *The Bell Curve.*

Gardner's Multiple Intelligences
Follow up on the material in the chapter regarding Howard Gardner's eight intelligences by pursuing one of the links provided by the Psi Café website.

Mental Retardation
The website for the Association for Retarded Citizens offers a wealth of resources on mental retardation.

Understanding the Data: Exercises on the Web

For additional insight on the data presented in this chapter, try the exercises for these figures at *http://psychology.wadsworth.com/sigelman_rider5e:*

Unnumbered figure in Explorations box titled Measuring Intelligence

Figure 9.4 Weekly wages by level of cognitive ability

Figure 9.6 African American students perform poorly on tests of mental abilities when they think they are taking a test that may result in their being stereotyped as unintelligent

Figure 9.8 Percentage of total works produced in each decade of the lives of eminent creators

Life-Span CD-ROM

Go to the Wadsworth Life-Span CD-ROM for further study of the concepts in this chapter. The CD-ROM includes narrated concept overviews, video clips, a multimedia glossary, and additional activities to expand your learning experience. For this chapter, check out the following clip, and others, in the video library:

VIDEO Culture and Intelligence

Developmental PsychologyNow is a web-based, intelligent study system that provides a complete package of diagnostic quizzes, a personalized study plan, integrated multimedia elements, and learning modules. Check it out at *http://psychology.wadsworth.com/sigelman_rider5e/now.*

CHAPTER ten

Language and Education

© Robin Sachs/PhotoEdit, Inc.

AS THE COOL STREAM GUSHED over one hand, she [Annie] spelled into the other the word water, first slowly, then rapidly. I stood still, my whole attention fixed upon the motions of her fingers. Suddenly I felt a misty consciousness as of something forgotten—a thrill of returning thought; and somehow the mystery of language was revealed to me. I knew then that W-A-T-E-R meant the wonderful cool something that was flowing over my hand. . . . I left the well-house eager to learn. Everything had a name, and each name gave birth to a new thought. As we returned to the house every object which I touched seemed to quiver with life (Keller, 1954).

There is possibly no more important skill than mastering some type of language system. Consider how the world changed for Helen Keller, deaf and blind from a young age, when she finally realized that every object, every person, every concept could be represented with a symbol. From this point on, she was able to communicate with the people around her and participate in the world in ways that were not available without a tool such as sign or spoken language. As you learned in Chapter 7, psychologist Lev Vygotsky argued that language is the primary vehicle through which adults pass culturally valued modes of thinking and problem solving to their children. He also believed that language is our most important tool of thinking.

In this chapter, we begin by examining how and when language is acquired. Basic language skills become established largely through an informal education system consisting of parents, other grown-ups, peers, and even the media. We then consider formal education, which uses basic language skills to cultivate the reading, writing, thinking, and problem-solving skills that allow individuals to become fully functioning members of society. Getting the most out of education requires more than acquiring language and literacy skills, however. As Terrel Bell, former secretary of education asserted, "there are three things to remember about education. The first one is motivation. The second one is motivation. The third one is motivation" (quoted in Maehr & Meyer, 1997, p. 372). Thus, we also examine achievement motivation and its relationship to education and educational outcomes.

Mastering Language

Although language is one of the most intricate forms of knowledge we will ever acquire, all normal children master a language early in life. Indeed, many infants are talking before they can walk. Can language be complex, then? It certainly can be. Linguists (scholars who study language) have yet to fully describe the rules of English (or of any other language), and so far computers cannot understand speech as well as most 5-year-olds can. What is the task young language learners face?

What Must Be Mastered

Linguists define **language** as a communication system in which a limited number of signals—sounds or letters (or gestures, in the case of the sign language used by deaf people)—can be combined according to agreed-upon rules to produce an infinite number of messages. To master a spoken language such as English, a child must learn basic sounds, how sounds are combined to form words, how words are combined to form meaningful statements, what words and sentences mean, and how to use language effectively in social interactions. That is, the child must master five aspects of language: phonology, morphology, syntax, semantics, and pragmatics.

Phonology is the sound system of a language, and the basic units of sound in any given language are its phonemes. A child in an English-speaking country must learn the 45 phonemes used in English (which correspond roughly to the familiar vowel and consonant sounds) and which ones can be combined in English and which ones cannot (for example, *st*- but not *sb*-). Other languages have other basic sounds (or, in a sign language, basic hand shapes and motions). Children must learn to hear and to pronounce the phonemes of their language to make sense of the speech they hear and to be understood when they speak.

Rules of **morphology** are rules for forming words from sounds. Rules of morphology in English include the rule for forming past tenses of verbs by adding *-ed*, the rule for forming plurals by adding *-s*, and rules for using other prefixes and suffixes. Exceptions to these rules also must be learned.

Rules of **syntax** are rules for forming sentences from words. Consider these three sentences: (1) Fang Fred bit. (2) Fang bit Fred. (3) Fred bit Fang. The first, as even young children recognize, violates the rules of English sentence structure or syntax, although this word order would be acceptable in German. The second and third are both grammatical English sentences, but their different word orders convey different meanings. Children must master rules of syntax to understand or use language, from simple declarative sentences such as these to complex sentences with many clauses and phrases.

Semantics is the aspect of language that concerns meanings. Words stand for things, and the child must map the relationships between words and things. Knowledge of semantics is also required to interpret sentences, speeches, or paragraphs. Grasping semantics depends on understanding the world and thus on cognitive development.

Finally, language learners must master **pragmatics**—rules specifying how language is used appropriately in different social contexts. That is, children have to learn when to say what to whom. They must learn to communicate effectively by taking into account who the listener is, what the listener already knows, and what the listener needs or wants to hear. "Give me that cookie" may be grammatical English, but the child is far more likely to win Grandma's heart (not to mention a cookie) with a polite "May I please try one of your yummy cookies, Grandma?"

In short, mastering language is an incredible challenge that requires learning phonology, semantics, morphology, syntax, and pragmatics. What is more, human communication involves not only language but also forms of nonverbal communication (facial expressions, tone of voice, gestures, and so on). For example, **intonation**—the variations in pitch, loudness, and timing used when saying words or sentences—can be important. Using intonation, speakers emphasize grammatically important words, signal that they are asking questions rather than making statements, and so on. Children must also learn these nonverbal signals, which often clarify the meaning of a verbal message and are important means of communicating. We now look at the course of language development then ask how nature and nurture contribute to the child's remarkable accomplishment.

© Laura Dwight/CORBIS

A mother draws her 3-month-old infant into a "conversation."

The Course of Language Development

For the first 10 to 13 months of life, infants are not yet capable of speaking meaningful words, but they are building up to that achievement.

Before the First Words

As you learned in Chapter 6, newborns seem to tune in to human speech immediately. Very young infants can distinguish between phonemes such as *b* and *p* or *d* and *t* (Eimas, 1975a). Before they ever speak a word, infants are also becoming sensitive to pauses in speech that fall between clauses, phrases, and words rather than in the middle of these important language units (Fisher & Tokura, 1996; Myers et al., 1996). Infants as young as $7\frac{1}{2}$ months can segment speech into meaningful words, a skill that improves over the next several months (Houston et al., 2000; Jusczyk, 1999; Jusczyk, Houston, & Newsome, 1999). This shows sensitivity to phonology and may help infants learn the rules of grammar.

What about producing sounds? From birth, infants produce sounds—cries, burps, grunts, and sneezes. These sounds help exercise the vocal cords and give infants an opportunity to learn how airflow and different mouth and tongue positions affect sounds. Furthermore, parents typically respond to these prelinguistic sounds as if they were genuine efforts to communicate (McCune et al., 1996). For instance, in response to her 3-month-old's hiccup sound, a mother replies, "My goodness! What's going on in there? Huh? Tell Mommy." The mother draws her infant into a sort of dialogue. Such prelinguistic sounds, and the feedback infants receive, will eventually be incorporated into meaningful speech sounds (Hoff, 2004). Perhaps most impressive about this early verbal and nonverbal "dance" between infants and their caregivers is that it relates positively to later attachment between them and to the cognitive development of the infant (Jaffe et al., 2001).

The next milestone in vocalization, around 6 to 8 weeks of age, is **cooing**—repeating vowel-like sounds such as "oooooh" and "aaaaah." Babies coo when they are content and often in response to being spoken to in a happy voice. Do infants this age understand the words spoken to them? Not likely—they primarily respond to the "melody" of speech. Parents can say some rather nasty things to their young infants ("You're driving me nuts today!") as long as they say them with a happy voice (Hirsh-Pasek, Golinkoff, & Hollich, 1999).

Around 3 to 4 months, infants expand their vocal range considerably as they begin to produce consonant sounds. They enter a period of **babbling** between about 4 and 6 months, repeating consonant–vowel combinations such as "baba" or "dadadada," which is what Jean Piaget would call a primary circular reaction—the repeating of an interesting noise for the pleasure of making it.

Up to about 6 months, infants all over the world, even deaf ones, sound pretty much alike, but the effects of experience soon become apparent. Without auditory feedback, deaf infants fall behind hearing infants in their ability to produce well-formed syllables (Koopmans-van Beinum, Clement, & van den Dikkenberg-Pot, 2001). By the time infants are about 8 months old, they babble with something of an accent; adults can often tell which language infants have been listening to from the sound of their babbling (Poulin-Dubois & Goodz, 2001). These advanced babblers increasingly restrict their sounds to phonemes in the language they are hearing, and they pick up the intonation patterns of that language (Hoff, 2004). Once these intonation patterns are added to an infant's babbles, the utterances sound much like real speech until, as Erika Hoff (2004) puts it, "you listen closely and realize that the infant is producing the melody of language without the words" (p. 103).

As they attempt to master the semantics of language, infants come to understand many words before they can produce them. That is, comprehension (or reception) is ahead of production (or expression) in language development. Before they understand the specific words in a command (such as "Get the ball"), they will obey it in familiar contexts, probably by interpreting tone of voice and context cues (Hoff, 2004). Shortly before speaking their first true words, however, as they approach 1 year, they really seem to understand familiar words. How do they figure out what words mean? When Mom points to a small, four-legged furry animal and says "Furrball," how do infants learn that this refers to the cat and not to its movement or to its tail or to the animal next door? Several researchers note the importance of **joint attention** in early word learning (Carpenter, Nagell, & Tomasello, 1998; Woodward & Markman, 1998). Infants listen to parents repeatedly labeling and pointing at objects, directing their gaze, and otherwise making salient the connection between words and their referents (Hollich, Hirsh-Pasek, & Golinkoff, 2000). If Mom says "cat" when both she and her child are looking at the furry animal, then this likely is the referent for the label. Infants also tend to assume that a word refers to a whole object rather than to some part of the object (Pan, 2005; Woodward & Markman, 1998). Thus, infants realize that Furrball refers to the family's whole cat and not to individual properties of the cat.

The First Words

An infant's first meaningful word, spoken around 1 year, is a special event for parents. First words have been called **holophrases** because a single word sometimes conveys an entire sentence's worth of meaning. These single-word "sentences" can serve different communication functions depending on the way they are said and the context in which they are said (Barrett, 1995). For example, 17-month-old Shelley used the word *ghetti (spaghetti)* in three different ways over a 5-minute period. First, she pointed to the pan on the stove and seemed to be asking, "Is that spaghetti?" Later, the function of her holophrase was to name the spaghetti when shown the contents of the pan, as in "It's spaghetti." Finally, there was little question that she was requesting spaghetti when she tugged at her companion's sleeve as he was eating and used the word in a whining tone.

Although there are limits to the meaning that can be packed into a single word and its accompanying tone of voice and gestures, 1-year-olds in the holophrastic stage of language development seem to have mastered such basic language functions as naming, questioning, requesting, and demanding. When they begin to use words as symbols, they also begin to use nonverbal symbols—gestures such as pointing, raising their arms to signal "up," or panting heavily to say "dog" (Acredolo & Goodwyn, 1988; Camaioni, 2004; Lock, 2004).

What do 1-year-olds talk about? They talk mainly about familiar objects and actions (Nelson, Hampson, & Shaw, 1993; Pan, 2005; and see Table 10.1). Katherine Nelson (1973) studied 18 infants as they learned their first 50 English words and found that nearly two-thirds of these early words were common nouns representing objects and people that the children interacted with daily *(mommy, kitty)*. These objects were nearly all things that the children could manipulate *(bottles, shoes)* or that were capable of moving on their own *(animals, trucks)*. Children also acquire words that facilitate social interactions *(hello, bye-bye, no)*.

Initial language acquisition proceeds literally one word at a time. Three or four months may pass before the child has a vocabulary of 10 words (Nelson, 1973). Then, in what is called the **vocabulary spurt,** around 18 months when the child has mastered about 30 to 50 words, the pace of word learning quickens dramatically (Bloom, 1998; Goldfield & Reznick, 1996). At 20 months, children are producing an average of 150 words, and just 4 months later, this has doubled to 300 words (Camaioni, 2004). What changes? During the vocabulary spurt, toddlers seem to arrive at the critical realization, as Helen Keller did, that everything has a name; they then want to learn all the names (Reznick & Goldfield, 1992).

Table 10.1 Examples of Words Used by Children Younger than 20 Months

Category	Words
Sound effects	*baa baa, meow, moo, ouch, uh-oh, woof, yum-yum*
Food and drink	*apple, banana, cookie, cheese, cracker, juice, milk, water*
Animals	*bear, bird, bunny, dog, cat, cow, duck, fish, kitty, horse, pig, puppy*
Body parts and clothing	*diaper, ear, eye, foot, hair, hand, hat, mouth, nose, toe, tooth, shoe*
House and outdoors	*blanket, chair, cup, door, flower, keys, outside, spoon, tree, TV*
People	*baby, daddy, gramma, grampa, mommy, [child's own name]*
Toys and vehicles	*ball, balloon, bike, boat, book, bubbles, plane, truck, toy*
Actions	*down, eat, go, sit, up*
Games and routines	*bath, bye, hi, night-night, no, peek-a-boo, please, shhh, thank you, yes*
Adjectives and descriptors	*all gone, cold, dirty, hot*

SOURCE: Pan, 2005.

With such a rapidly increasing vocabulary, it should come as no surprise that children sometimes make mistakes. Although they rarely get the meaning entirely wrong, they often use a word too broadly or too narrowly (Pan, 2005). One error is **overextension,** or using a word to refer to too wide a range of objects or events, as when a 2-year-old calls all furry, four-legged animals "doggie." The second, and opposite, error is **underextension,** as when a child initially uses the word *doggie* to refer only to basset hounds like the family pet. Notice that both overextension and underextension are examples of Piaget's concept of assimilation, using existing concepts to interpret new experiences. Getting semantics right seems to be mainly a matter of discriminating similarities and differences—for example, categorizing animals on the basis of size, shape, the sounds they make, and other perceptual features (Clark & Clark, 1977).

But might children know more about the world than their semantic errors suggest? Yes, 2-year-olds who say "doggie" when they see a cow will point to the cow rather than the dog when asked to find the cow (Thompson & Chapman, 1977). Children who overextend the word *doggie* in their speech are no less able than children who do not to look toward the cow rather than the dog when asked, "Where's the cow?" (Naigles & Gelman, 1995). Children may overextend the meaning of certain words such as *doggie* not because they misunderstand word meanings but because they want to communicate, have only a small vocabulary with which to do so, and have not yet learned to call something a "whatchamacall-it" when they cannot come up with the word for it (Naigles & Gelman, 1995).

You must be careful about applying these generalizations about early language acquisition to all children because they mask large individual differences in speaking style (Camaioni, 2004; Goldfield & Snow, 2005). As Figure 10.1 shows, one 24-month-old may have a vocabulary of approximately 50 words, and another may be able to produce more than 500 words (Fenson et al., 1994). Some children use a referential style—lots of nouns referring to objects. Others seem to treat language as a social tool; they use an expressive style of speaking with more personal pronouns and memorized social routines such as "bye-bye" and "I want it" (Bates et al., 1994; Nelson, 1973). Culture exerts some influence: Infants learning English use many nouns and few verbs in their early speech, whereas infants learning Korean use more verbs (Gopnik & Choi, 1995). More important, differences in the daily language experiences of children contribute to the differences in their speech. Both quantity of speech (how many words the child hears in the home) and quality of speech (how sophisticated the speech is) affect young children's vocabularies (Hoff, 2004; Weizman & Snow, 2001). So, individual differences in language acquisition are the norm rather than the exception.

Telegraphic Speech

The next step in language development, normally taken about 18 to 24 months of age, is combining two words into a simple sentence. Toddlers all over the world use two-word sentences to express the same basic ideas (see Table 10.2). Early combinations of two, three, or more words are sometimes called **telegraphic speech** because, like telegrams, these sentences contain critical content words and omit frills such as articles, prepositions, and auxiliary verbs.

It is ungrammatical in adult English to say "No want" or "Where ball." However, these two-word sentences are not just random word combinations or mistakes; they reflect children's systematic rules for forming sentences. Psycholinguists such as Lois Bloom (1998) believe it is appropriate to describe children's early sentences in terms of a **functional grammar**—one that emphasizes the semantic relationships among words, the meanings being expressed, and the functions served by sentences (such as naming, questioning, or commanding). For example, young children often use the same word order to convey different meanings. "Mommy nose" might mean "That's Mommy's nose" in one context, but for one 22-month-old girl one afternoon it meant "Mommy, I've just wiped my runny nose the length of the living room couch." Word order sometimes does matter: "Billy hit" and "Hit Billy" may mean different things. Body language and tone of voice also communicate meanings, such as when a child points and whines to request ice cream, not merely to note its existence.

Between age 2 and age 5, children learn to speak sentences that are remarkably complex and adultlike. Table 10.3 gives an inkling of how fast things move in the particularly important period from age 2 to age 3. From the two-word stage of language acquisition, children progress to three-word telegraphic sentences then to longer sentences, beginning to add the little function words such as articles and prepositions that were often missing in their early telegraphic sentences (Hoff, 2004). They increasingly infer the rules of adult language.

How do people know when children are mastering new rules? Oddly enough, their progress sometimes reveals itself in new "mistakes." Consider the task of learning rules of morphology for forming plurals and past tenses. Typically this

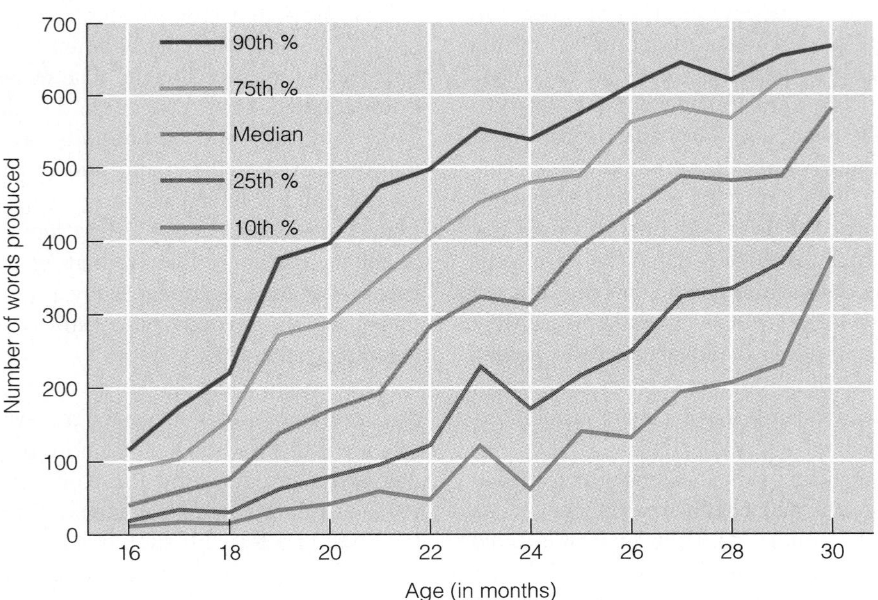

Figure 10.1 The range of individual differences in vocabulary size from 16 to 30 months.

SOURCE: Fenson et al. (1994).

Table 10.2 Two-Word Sentences Serve Similar Functions in Different Languages

Function of Sentence	Language	
	English	German
To locate or name	*There book*	*Buch da (book there)*
To demand	*More milk*	*Mehr milch (more milk)*
To negate	*No wet*	*Nicht blasen (not blow)*
To indicate possession	*My shoe*	*Mein ball (my ball)*
To modify or qualify	*Pretty dress*	*Armer wauwau (poor doggie)*
To question	*Where ball*	*Wo ball (where ball)*

SOURCE: Adapted from Slobin, 1979. Reprinted by permission of Addison-Wesley Longman, Inc.

happens sometime during the third year (Hoff, 2004). A child who has been saying "feet" and "went" may suddenly start to say "foots" and "goed." Does this represent a step backward? Not at all. The child was probably using the correct irregular forms at first by imitating adult speech without understanding the meaning of plurality or verb tense. The use of "foots" and "goed" is a breakthrough: The child has inferred the morphological rules of adding *-s* to pluralize nouns and adding *-ed* to signal past tense. At first, however, the youngster engages in **overregularization,** overapplying the rules to cases in which the proper form is irregular. When the child masters exceptions to the rules, she will say "feet" and "went" once more.

Children must also master rules for creating variations of the basic declarative sentence; that is, they must learn the rules for converting a basic idea such as "I am eating pizza" into such forms as questions ("Am I eating pizza?"), negative sentences ("I am not eating pizza"), and imperatives ("Eat the pizza!"). The prominent linguist Noam Chomsky (1968, 1975) drew attention to the child's learning of these rules by proposing that language be described in terms of a **transformational grammar,** or rules of syntax for transforming basic underlying thoughts into a variety of sentence forms.

How do young children learn to phrase the questions that they so frequently ask to fuel their cognitive growth? The earliest questions often consist of nothing more than two- or three-word sentences with rising intonation ("See kitty?"). Sometimes *wh-* words such as *what* or *where* appear ("Where kitty?"). During the second stage of question asking, children begin to use auxiliary, or helping, verbs, but their questions are of this form: "What Daddy is eating?" "Where the kitty is going?" Their understanding of transformation rules is still incomplete (Tager-Flusberg, 2005). Finally, they learn the transformation rule that calls for moving the auxiliary verb ahead of the subject (as in the adultlike sentence "What is Daddy eating?").

By the end of the preschool period (ages 5–6), children's sentences are much like those of adults even though they have never had a formal lesson in grammar. It is an amazing accomplishment. Yet there is more growth that needs to occur.

Table 10.3 Samples of Kyle's Speech at 24 Months and 35 Months

At 24 Months (his second birthday party)	At 35 Months (playing with a potato bug)
Want cake now. Boons! Boons! [pointing to balloons] They mine! [referring to colors] I wan' see. See sky now. Ow-ee [pointing to knee].	*Mother:* Kyle, why don't you take the bug back to his friends? *Kyle:* After I hold him, then I'll take the bug back to his friends. Mommy, where did the bug go? Mommy, I didn't know where the bug go. Find it. Maybe Winston's on it [the family dog]. Winston, get off the bug! [Kyle spots the bug and picks it up.] *Mother:* Kyle, *please* let the bug go back to his friends. *Kyle:* He does not want to go to his friends. [He drops the bug and squashes it, much to his mother's horror.] I stepped on it and it will not go to his friends.

At 24 months, Kyle speaks in telegraphic sentences no more than three words long; by 35 months, his sentences are much longer and more grammatically complex, although not free of errors, and he is better able to participate in the give-and-take of conversation (despite not heeding his mother and respecting the dignity of potato bugs).

Later Language Development

School-age children improve their pronunciation skills, produce longer and more complex sentences, and continue to expand their vocabularies. The average first-grader starts school with a vocabulary of about 10,000 words and adds somewhere between 5 and 13 new words a day throughout the school years (Anglin, 1993; Bloom, 1998). During adolescence, with the help of formal operational thought, teens become better able to understand and define abstract terms (McGhee-Bidlack, 1991). They also become better able to infer meanings that are not explicitly stated (Beal, 1990).

School-age children also begin to think about and manipulate language in ways previously impossible (Ely, 2005; Klein, 1996). They can, for example, interpret passive sentences such as "Goofy was liked by Donald" and conditional sentences such as "If Goofy had come, Donald would have been delighted" (Boloh & Champaud, 1993; Sudhalter & Braine, 1985). Command of grammar continues to improve through adolescence; teenagers' spoken and written sentences become increasingly long and complex (Christie, 2002).

Children are also mastering the pragmatics of language, becoming increasingly able to communicate effectively in different situations (Oliver, 1995). They increasingly use **decontextualized language** as they move from talking about the immediate conversational context ("I see a dog over there") to talking about past or remote events ("I saw a dog while on vacation last week"; Ely, 2005). They can tell stories about events that happened in the past or are not part of the current context. By adolescence, these narratives are often detailed and lengthy.

Throughout childhood and adolescence, advances in cognitive development are accompanied by advances in language and communication skills. For example, as children become less cognitively egocentric, they are more able to take the perspective of their listeners (Hoff, 2004). Middle childhood and adolescence also bring increased **metalinguistic awareness,** or knowledge of language as a system (Ely, 2005). Children with metalinguistic awareness understand the concept of words and can define words (semantics). Adolescents are increasingly able to define abstract words (such as *courage* or *pride*) but are still outperformed by adults on difficult words (such as *idleness* or *goodness;* Nippold et al., 1999). Development of metalinguistic awareness also means that children and adolescents can distinguish between grammatically correct and grammatically incorrect sentences (syntax) and can understand how language can be altered to fit the needs of the specific social context in which it is used (pragmatics).

What happens to language skills during adulthood? Adults simply hold onto the knowledge of the phonology they gained as children, although elders can have difficulty distinguishing speech sounds if they have hearing impairments or deficits in the cognitive abilities required to make out what they hear (Sommers, 1997). They also retain their knowledge of grammar or syntax. Older adults tend to use less complex sentences than younger adults do, however. Also, those with memory difficulties may have trouble understanding sentences that are highly complex syntactically (for example, "The children warned about road hazards refused to fix the bicycle of the boy who crashed"); they may not be able to remember the beginning of the sentence by the time they get to the end (Kemtes & Kemper, 1997; Stine, Soederberg, & Morrow, 1996).

Meanwhile, knowledge of the semantics of language, of word meanings, often expands during adulthood, at least until people are in their 70s or 80s (Obler, 2005; Schaie, 1996). After all, adults gain experience with the world from year to year, so it is not surprising that their vocabularies continue to grow and that they enrich their understandings of the meanings of words. However, older adults more often have the "tip-of-the-tongue" experience of not being able to come up with the name of an object (or especially a person's name) when they need it (Au et al., 1995; Kemper & Mitzner, 2001). This problem is a matter of not being able to retrieve information stored in memory rather than a matter of no longer knowing the words.

Adults also refine their pragmatic use of language—adjusting it to different social and professional contexts (Obler, 2005). Physicians, for example, must develop a communication style that is effective with their patients. Partners who have been together for years often develop a unique way of communicating with one another that is distinctly different from how they communicate with others. Overall, command of language holds up well in later life unless the individual experiences major declines in cognitive functioning (Kemper & Mitzner, 2001; Stine et al., 1996).

How Language Develops

We cannot help but be awed by the pace at which children master the fundamentals of language during their first 5 years of life, but we must also appreciate the continued growth that occurs in childhood and adolescence and the maintenance of language skills throughout the life span. How are these remarkable skills acquired? Theorists attempting to explain language acquisition have differed considerably in their positions on the nature–nurture issue, as illustrated by the learning, nativist, and interactionist perspectives on language development (Bohannon & Bonvillian, 2005).

The Learning Perspective

How do children learn language? To answer this, you have another opportunity to examine the role of nature and nurture. Intuitively, many people believe that language learning is a matter of nurture: Children imitate what they hear, receiving praise when they get it right and being corrected when they get it wrong. Different learning theorists emphasize different aspects of this broad process. Social learning theorist Albert Bandura (1971) and others emphasize observational learning—learning by listening to then imitating older companions. Behaviorist B. F. Skinner (1957) and others have emphasized the role of reinforcement. As children achieve better approximations of adult language, parents and other adults praise meaningful speech and correct errors. Children are also reinforced by getting what they want when they speak correctly. In general, learning theorists consider the child's social environment to be critical to what and how much she learns.

How well does the learning perspective account for language development? It is no accident that children learn the language their parents speak, down to the regional accent. Children learn the words they hear spoken by others—even when the words are not spoken directly to them (Akhtar, Jipson, & Callanan, 2001). For example, 2-year-olds can learn object labels and verbs by "eavesdropping" on a conversation between two adults (so be careful about what you say within earshot of toddlers). In addition, young children are more likely to start using new words if they are reinforced for doing so than if they are not (Whitehurst & Valdez-Menchaca, 1988). Finally, children whose caregivers frequently encourage them to converse by asking questions, making requests, and the like are more advanced in early language development than those whose parents are less conversational (Bohannon & Bonvillian, 2005; Pine, 1994).

However, learning theorists have had an easier time explaining the development of phonology and semantics than accounting for how syntactical rules are acquired. For example, after analyzing conversations between mothers and young children, Roger Brown, Courtney Cazden, and Ursula Bellugi (1969) discovered that a mother's approval or disapproval depended on the truth value or semantics of what was said, not on the grammatical correctness of the statement. Thus, when a child looking at a cow says, "Her cow" (accurate but grammatically incorrect), Mom is likely to provide reinforcement ("That's right, darling"), whereas if the child were to say,

A is for *apple*. The learning perspective helps explain how young children learn the meaning of words.

"There's a dog, Mommy" (grammatically correct but untruthful), Mom would probably correct the child ("No, silly—that's a cow"). Similarly, parents seem just as likely to reward a grammatically primitive request ("Want milk") as a well-formed version of the same idea (Brown & Hanlon, 1970). Such evidence casts doubt on the idea that the major mechanism behind syntactic development is reinforcement.

Could imitation of adults account for the acquisition of syntax? You have already seen that young children produce many sentences they are unlikely to have heard adults using ("All gone cookie," overregularizations such as "It swimmed," and so on). These kinds of sentences are not imitations. Also, an adult is likely to get nowhere in teaching syntax by saying "Repeat after me" unless the child already has at least some knowledge of the grammatical form to be learned (Baron, 1992; McNeill, 1970). Young children frequently imitate other people's speech, and this may help them get to the point of producing new structures. But it is hard to see how imitation and reinforcement alone can account for the learning of grammatical rules.

The Nativist Perspective

In contrast to the learning theorists who adopt a nurture perspective, nativists minimize the role of the language environment and maximize the role of the child's biologically programmed capacities in explaining language development (see, for example, Chomsky, 1995; Pinker, 2002; see also Maratsos, 1998). Chomsky (1968, 1975, 1995) proposed that humans have an inborn mechanism for mastering language called the **language acquisition device (LAD).** The LAD was conceived as an area in the brain equipped to identify certain universal features of language and to figure out the specific rules of any particular language. To learn to speak, children need only to hear other humans speak; using the LAD, they quickly grasp the rules of whatever language they hear (see Figure 10.2).

What evidence supports a nativist perspective on language development? First, there are areas of the brain that specialize in language functions; Broca's area in the frontal lobe controls speaking, for example, whereas Wernicke's area controls speech recognition (Bear, Connors, & Paradiso, 2001). Second, children acquire an incredibly complex communication system rapidly. For example, 7-month-olds are able to extract grammatical rules of language and generalize these rules to novel items (Marcus & Vijayan, 1999). Researchers have also demonstrated that 18-month-olds show an understanding of syntax that they could not have acquired solely from information provided by the researchers (Lidz, Waxman, & Freedman, 2003). Third, children all progress through the same sequences at roughly similar ages, and they even make the same kinds of errors, which suggests that language development is guided by a species-wide maturational plan. Fourth, these universal aspects of early language development occur despite cultural differences in the styles of speech that adults use in talking to young children. In some cultures, for example, parents believe that babies are incapable of understanding speech and do not even talk directly to them (Crago, Allen, & Hough-Eyamir, 1997).

Finally, there is evidence that the capacity for acquiring language has a genetic basis. Some of our linguistic competencies, including the ability to combine symbols to form short sentences, are shared with chimpanzees and other primates, suggesting that they arose during the course of evolution and are part of our genetic endowment as humans (Greenfield & Savage-Rumbaugh, 1993; Pinker, 2000). Identical twins score more similarly than fraternal twins on measures of verbal skills, and certain speech, language, and reading disorders run in families, indicating that individual heredity influences the course of language development (Lewis & Thompson, 1992; Plomin, 1990).

Although nativists are correct to emphasize the importance of biologically based capacities in language acquisition, the nativist perspective has two major limitations. First, attributing language development to a built-in LAD does not really explain it. Explanations would require knowing how

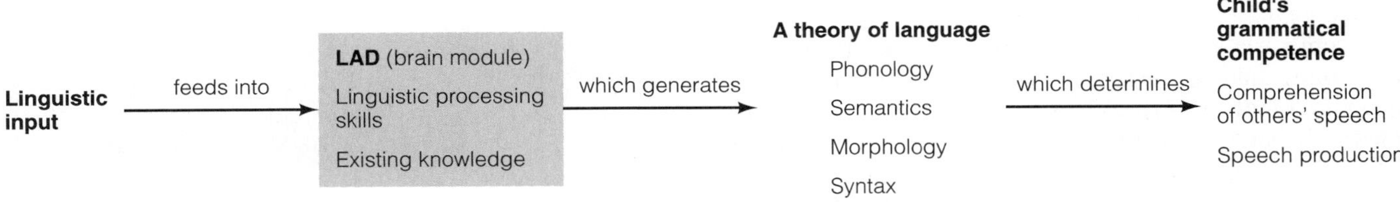

Figure 10.2 The language acquisition device (LAD).

such an inborn language processor sifts through language input and infers the rules of language (Moerk, 1989). Second, nativists, in focusing on the defects of learning theories of language development, tend to underestimate the contributions of children's language environment. The nativists base much of their argument on three assumptions: (1) that the only thing children need to develop language is exposure to speech, (2) that the speech children hear is so incredibly complex that only a highly powerful brain could detect regularities in it, and (3) that adults give children little useful feedback about whether their sentences are grammatically correct. These assumptions now seem to be largely inaccurate, and most researchers currently believe that language development depends on both nature and nurture.

The Interactionist Perspective

Interactionists believe that both learning theorists (nurture) and nativists (nature) are correct: Children's biologically based competencies and their language environment interact to shape the course of language development (Bohannon & Bonvillian, 2005; Bloom, 1998). They emphasize that acquisition of language skills depends on and is related to the acquisition of many other capacities: perceptual, cognitive, motor, social, and emotional. They point out that the capacity for acquiring language is not unique (as nativists who speak of the LAD claim); milestones in language development often occur at the same time as milestones in other aspects of cognitive development and involve the same underlying mental processes (Bates, O'Connell, & Shore, 1987). For example, young children first begin to use words as meaningful symbols when they begin to display nonlinguistic symbolic capacities, such as the ability to use gestures (waving bye-bye), and begin to engage in pretend play (treating a bowl as if it were a hat).

The interactionists' position is not unlike that taken by Piaget (1970). He believed that milestones in cognitive development pave the way for progress in language development and that maturation and environment interact to guide both cognitive development and language development. Like Piaget (but unlike learning theorists), many interactionists argue that language development depends on the maturation of cognitive abilities such as the capacity for symbolic thought. However, the interactionist position also emphasizes—as Vygotsky did but Piaget did not—ways in which social interactions with adults contribute to cognitive and linguistic development. Language is primarily a means of communicating—one that develops in the context of social interactions as children and their companions strive to get their messages across (Tomasello, 1999).

Long before infants use words, Jerome Bruner (1983) says, their caregivers show them how to take turns in conversations—even if the most these young infants can contribute when their turn comes is a laugh or a bit of babbling. As adults converse with young children, they create a supportive learning environment—a scaffold in Bruner's terms, a zone of proximal development in Vygotsky's—that helps the children grasp the regularities of language (Bruner, 1983; Harris, 1992). For example, parents may go through their children's favorite picture books at bedtime and ask "What's this?" and "What's that?" This gives their children repeated opportunities to learn that conversing involves taking turns, that things have names, and that there are proper ways to pose questions and give answers. Soon the children are asking "What's this?" and "What's that?"

As children gain new language skills, adults adjust their styles of communication accordingly. Language researchers use the term **child-directed speech** to describe the speech adults use with young children: short, simple sentences spoken slowly, in a high-pitched voice, often with much repetition, and with exaggerated emphasis on key words (usually words for objects and activities). For example, the mother trying to get her son to eat his peas might say, "Eat your *peas* now. Not the cracker. See those *peas?* Yes, eat the *peas.* Oh, such a good boy for eating your *peas.*" Mothers also convey more exaggerated emotions (positive and negative) when speaking to their infants than when speaking to other adults (Kitamura & Burnham, 2003). Child-directed speech seems to be used by adults speaking to young children in most language communities that have been studied (Fernald et al., 1989). And infants, from the earliest days of life, seem to pay more attention to the high-pitched sounds and varied intonational patterns of child-directed speech than to the speech adults use when communicating with one another (Cooper et al., 1997; Pegg, Werker, & McLeod, 1992).

Would children learn language just as well if adults talked to them in an adultlike style? Perhaps not. The nativists seem

Adults are not the only ones who use child-directed speech. Children also adjust their speech to their listener.

to have underestimated the contributions of environment to language development. Mere exposure to speech is not enough; children must be actively involved in using language (Locke, 1997). Catherine Snow and her associates, for example, found that a group of Dutch-speaking children, although they watched a great deal of German television, did not acquire German words or grammar (Snow et al., 1976). True, there are cultural groups (the Kaluli of New Guinea, the natives of American Samoa, and the Trackton people of the Piedmont Carolinas) in which child-directed speech does not seem to be used. Children in these societies still seem to acquire language without noticeable delays (Gordon, 1990; Ochs, 1982; Schieffelin, 1986). Yet even these children overhear speech and participate in social interactions in which language is used, and that is what seems to be required to master a human language (Lieven, 1994). Those parents who use child-directed speech further simplify the child's task of figuring out the rules of language (Harris, 1992; Kemler Nelson et al., 1989). They converse with children daily in attention-getting and understandable ways about the objects and events that have captured the youngsters' attention.

Adults speaking to young children also use certain communication strategies that foster language development. For example, if a child says, "Kitty goed," an adult may respond with an **expansion**—a more grammatically complete expression of the same thought ("Yes, the cat went in the car"). Adults use conversational techniques such as expansions mainly to improve communication, not to teach grammar (Penner, 1987). However, these techniques also serve as a subtle form of correction after children produce grammatically incorrect sentences and show children more grammatical ways to express the same ideas (Bohannon & Stanowicz, 1988; Saxton, 1997). It is not quite true, then, that adults provide no corrective feedback concerning children's grammatical errors, as nativists claim. True, they rarely say, "No, that's wrong; say it this way." Nevertheless, they provide subtle corrective feedback through their responses to children, and this feedback helps children grow linguistically (Bohannon & Bonvillian, 2005).

How can adults best facilitate young children's language learning? What cognitive capacities enable children to learn how language works? Much remains to be learned about language development, but it does seem to require the interaction of a biologically prepared child with at least one conversational partner, ideally one who tailors her own speech to the child's level of understanding.

A Critical Period for Language?

Young children are so adept at learning languages that some scholars have wondered whether a critical (or at least sensitive) period for language acquisition may exist. Some years ago, Eric Lenneberg (1967) said that there is such a critical period and that it lasts until puberty, when the development of lateralization of language functions in the left hemisphere of the brain is completed. Although researchers now know that lateralization of the brain occurs more rapidly than Lenneberg thought (Locke, 1997; and see Chapter 5), they continue to be interested in determining whether young children are uniquely capable of language learning.

What evidence supports the critical period hypothesis of language acquisition? Some comes from studies of deaf children, some of whom (especially those with hearing parents) do not have an opportunity to learn any language, oral or signed, in their early years. Rachel Mayberry (1994) studied language mastery in deaf college students exposed to American Sign Language (ASL) at different ages and found that the rule "the earlier, the better" applies (see also Mayberry, Lock, & Kazmi, 2002). Mastery of the morphology, syntax, and semantics of sign language was greatest among students exposed to it in infancy or early childhood. Those who learned sign later in their development (ages 9–16) mastered it better if they had had some exposure to English early in life than if they had not been exposed to any language system before they encountered sign language. The Explorations box on page 264 provides more details on how the language development of deaf children compares with that of hearing children.

Elissa Newport and her colleagues (Newport, 1991) uncovered similar evidence of a critical period for second language learning. In one study (Johnson & Newport, 1989), native speakers of Korean or Chinese who had come to the United States between age 3 and age 39 were tested for mastery of English grammar. Among those who began learning English before puberty, those who learned it earliest knew it best. Among those who arrived in the United States after puberty, performance was generally poor regardless of age of arrival or number of years using English. Such findings have been used to argue that there is a critical period for language acquisition that ends around puberty. But other research shows that, even beyond puberty, age of arrival in the United States is related to proficiency in English as a second language (Birdsong, 1999). Thus, adults relocating at age 25 develop greater proficiency than adults relocating at age 30, an advantage related more to age than to length of residence in the United States (Stevens, 1999). And although adults are generally less likely than children to ever attain nativelike proficiency in a second language—suggesting a critical period—some adults achieve such proficiency (Birdsong, 1999).

Young children may have advantages over adults when learning a second language. This does not necessarily mean that there is a critical period for language acquisition. Children are generally immersed in their second language through school and peer-group activities. This greater exposure may facilitate second language acquisition partly by making the new language dominant in their lives. Adults, by contrast, may be more likely to continue using their native language as their dominant mode of communication, making second language acquisition more difficult (Jia & Aaronson, 1999).

It is possible that the language processing areas of the brain are shaped for a lifetime by early experience with language in ways that limit later learning of other languages. But it seems unlikely that there is a hard-and-fast critical period for language acquisition. It might be more accurate to say there is a "sensitive" period during which languages are most easily and flawlessly acquired. Perhaps the main message is

Explorations

Language Acquisition among Deaf Children

Many deaf children gain their first exposure to language by learning ASL. This is a true language. For example, signs are arbitrary symbols, not attempts to mimic objects and events, and they are used according to a system of grammatical rules that determines their ordering. You ought to be able to learn some interesting lessons about language acquisition in general, then, by studying language acquisition among deaf children.

On average, deaf children acquire sign language in much the same sequence and at much the same rate as hearing children acquire spoken language, and they make many of the same kinds of errors along the way (Bellugi, 1988; Masataka, 2000). Interestingly, deaf infants whose parents are deaf "babble" in sign language. They experiment with gestures in much the same way that hearing infants experiment with sounds in preparation for their first meaningful communications (Petitto & Marentette, 1991). They then sign their first meaningful single words around 12 months, use their first syntax (combinations of two signs) between 18 and 24 months, and master many rules of morphology, such as past tense formation, between 2 and 3 years (Meier, 1991). Just as hearing children have difficulty with the pronunciation of certain words and overgeneralize certain rules, deaf children make predictable errors in their signing (Meier, 1991). Moreover, for both deaf and hearing children, advances in language development are linked closely to advances in cognitive development; for example, putting signs or words together in sentences happens

© Stephen McBrady/PhotoEdit, Inc.

that young children are supremely capable of learning languages and advancing their cognitive development in the process. Meanwhile, college students learning a foreign language for the first time must appreciate that they may never speak it as well as someone who learned it as a young child.

Developing language competence may be our earliest and greatest learning challenge, but it is only the beginning. There is much more to be mastered during the school years and beyond. Language lays the foundation for acquiring reading, writing, and countless other skills required for productive citizenship. But unlike language, which seems to develop effortlessly in the absence of formal education, these other skills typically require directed education. In the following sections, we look at education across the life span, examining changes in motivation for learning and changes in educational environments as learners get older.

Summing Up

To acquire language, children must master phonology (sound), semantics (meaning), morphology (word struc-

around the same age that children put sequences of actions together in their play (Spencer, 1996).

The language environment experienced by deaf infants is also far more similar to that of hearing infants than you would imagine. For example, deaf mothers sign in child-directed speech; they present signs at a slower pace, repeat signs more, and exaggerate their signing motions more when they talk to their infants than when they talk to their deaf friends (Masataka, 1996). Moreover, just as hearing babies prefer the exaggerated intonations of child-directed speech, deaf infants pay more attention and give more emotional response when they are shown videos of infant-directed signing than tapes of adult-directed signing.

Finally, it turns out that language areas of the brain develop much the same in deaf children exposed to sign as in hearing children exposed to speech. For example, Helen Neville and her colleagues (1997) examined brain activity during the processing of sentences by deaf and hearing ASL users, hearing individuals (interpreters) who acquired sign late in life, and hearing individuals who did not know ASL. Mostly, reliance on areas of the left hemisphere of the cortex to process sentences was as evident among those who acquired ASL early in life as among hearing individuals who acquired English early in life. Reliance on the left hemisphere to process syntax was not as clear among individuals who acquired a language later in life. Early learners of ASL used their right hemispheres more in responding to sentences, perhaps because spatial skills based in the right hemisphere come into play in interpreting the gestures of someone who is signing.

As you have seen, language development is sometimes delayed among deaf children of hearing parents if they cannot hear well enough to understand spoken language but are not exposed to sign language (Mayberry, 1994). Overall, then, studies of language acquisition among deaf children suggest that young humans are biologically prepared to master language and will do so if given the opportunity, whether that language is signed or spoken and whether it involves visual–spatial skills or auditory ones (Meier, 1991).

ture), and syntax (sentence structure). They must also learn how to use language appropriately (pragmatics) and how to understand nonverbal communication. Infants are able to discriminate speech sounds and progress from crying, cooing, and babbling to one-word holophrases (at 12 months) and then to telegraphic speech (at 18 months). During the preschool years, language abilities improve dramatically, as illustrated by overregularizations and new transformation rules. School-age children and adolescents refine their language skills and become less egocentric communicators. Theories of language development include learning theories, nativist theories, and interactionist theories that emphasize the child's biologically based capacities and experience conversing with adults who use child-directed speech and strategies such as expansion that simplify the language-learning task. ■

The Infant

Before children begin their formal education, they are learning a great deal from the informal curriculum of their lives. Above all, they are learning to master their environments.

Mastery Motivation

Infants seem to be intrinsically motivated to master their environment (Morgan, MacTurk, & Hrncir, 1995). This **mastery motivation** can be seen clearly when infants struggle to open kitchen cabinets, take their first steps, or figure out how new toys work—and derive great pleasure from their efforts (Jennings & Dietz, 2003; Masten & Reed, 2002).

Much evidence supports the claim that infants are curious, active explorers constantly striving to understand and to exert control over the world around them. This, you should recall, was one of Piaget's major themes. A striving for mastery or

Every day, infants and young children display their innate mastery motive.

competence appears to be inborn and universal and will display itself in the behavior of all normal infants without prompting from parents. Even so, some infants appear to be more mastery oriented than others. Given a new push toy, one baby may simply look at it, but another may mouth it, bang it, and push it across the floor (Jennings & Dietz, 2003). Why might some infants have a stronger mastery motive than others?

Mastery motivation seems higher when parents frequently provide sensory stimulation designed to arouse and amuse their babies—tickling them, bouncing them, playing games of pat-a-cake, giving them stimulating toys, and so on (Busch-Rossnagel, 1997). Mastery motivation also flourishes when infants grow up in a responsive environment that provides plenty of opportunities to see for themselves that they can control their environments and experience successes (Maddux, 2002; Masten & Reed, 2002). Consider the toddler who, faced with the challenge of retrieving a cookie from the kitchen counter, struggles to maneuver a chair across the room and to climb up without tipping the chair or falling off. When Mom offers to help him, he shrieks, "Me do it!" And when he does it, he feels a sense of accomplishment that will increase the likelihood he will tackle future challenges. Parents who return smiles and coos or respond promptly to cries show infants they can affect people around them. By contrast, the children of parents who are depressed show less interest in and persistence on challenging tasks, perhaps because their parents are not responsive to them (Redding, Harmon, & Morgan, 1990).

An infant's level of mastery motivation affects her later achievement behavior. Babies who actively attempt to master challenges at 6 and 12 months score higher on tests of mental development at 2 and 3 years than their less mastery-oriented peers (Jennings & Dietz, 2003; Messer et al., 1986). In short, infants are intrinsically motivated to master challenges, but parents may help strengthen this inborn motive by stimulating their infants appropriately and responding to their actions. What about infants and toddlers who spend considerable amounts of time away from their parents? Is their motivation influenced by time spent in preschool?

Early Education

As you have seen in previous chapters, babies learn a great deal in the first few years of life. But do infants and toddlers need specific educational experiences? Manufacturers of products such as "Baby Einstein" videos and "Baby Mozart" compact discs hope that parents will buy into the idea that early stimulation is critical to infants' intellectual development (McCormick, 1998). Formal programs such as Bookstart, which promotes literacy early by providing 6- to 9-month-old infants and their parents with books and literacy information, have even been developed (Hall, 2001; Wade & Moore, 1998).

Despite its popular appeal, most experts dispute the idea that children need special educational experiences during their first 3 years (Bruer, 1999; Kagan, 1998). And some, such as David Elkind (1987), author of *Miseducation: Preschoolers at Risk,* fear that the push for earlier education may be going too far and that young children today are not given enough time simply to be children—to play and socialize as they choose. Elkind even worries that children may lose their self-initiative and intrinsic motivation to learn when their lives are orchestrated by parents who pressure them to achieve at early ages. Is there anything to these concerns?

Some research seems to confirm Elkind's fears. In one study (Hyson, Hirsch-Pasek, & Rescorla, 1989), 4-year-olds in preschools with strong academic thrusts gained an initial advantage in basic academic skills such as knowledge of letters and numbers but lost it by the end of kindergarten. What is more, they proved to be less creative, more anxious in testing situations, and more negative toward school than children who attended preschool programs with a social rather than academic emphasis. Similarly, Deborah Stipek and her colleagues (1995) have found that highly academic preschool programs raise children's academic achievement test scores but decrease their expectancies of success and pride in accomplishment. So, it may be possible to undermine achievement motivation by overemphasizing academics in the preschool years (Garner, 1999).

However, preschool programs that offer a healthy mix of play and academic skill-building activities can be beneficial to young children, especially disadvantaged ones (Barnett, 2002; Gorey, 2001). Although many children who attend preschool programs are no more or less intellectually advanced than those who remain at home, disadvantaged children who attend programs specially designed to prepare them for school experience more cognitive growth and achieve more success in school than disadvantaged children who do not attend such programs (Barnett, 2002). Consider again the Abecedarian Project, a full-time educational program from infancy (starting around 4–5 months) to age 5 for children from low-income families (Campbell et al., 2001; and see Chapter 9). Compared with children who did not participate, Abecedarian children showed impressive cognitive gains during and immediately after the program (see Figure 10.3). Although their performance level compared with test norms decreased over the subsequent years, these children continued to show an advantage over children who did not receive this intensive early educational experience (Nelson, Westhues, & MacLeod, 2003).

Thus, early education can provide disadvantaged children with a boost that has lasting consequences, lending support to the basic idea of Head Start. Positive effects on later school achievement are especially likely if the preschool experience not only stimulates children's cognitive growth but also gets parents more involved with their children's education and includes follow-up during elementary school (Nelson et al., 2003). More generally, preschool programs that build school readiness skills but also allow plenty of time for play and social interaction can help all children make a smooth transition to kindergarten and elementary school (Parker et al., 1999).

Summing Up

Mastery motivation, the forerunner of achievement motivation, is an urge for mastery evident in infancy and is

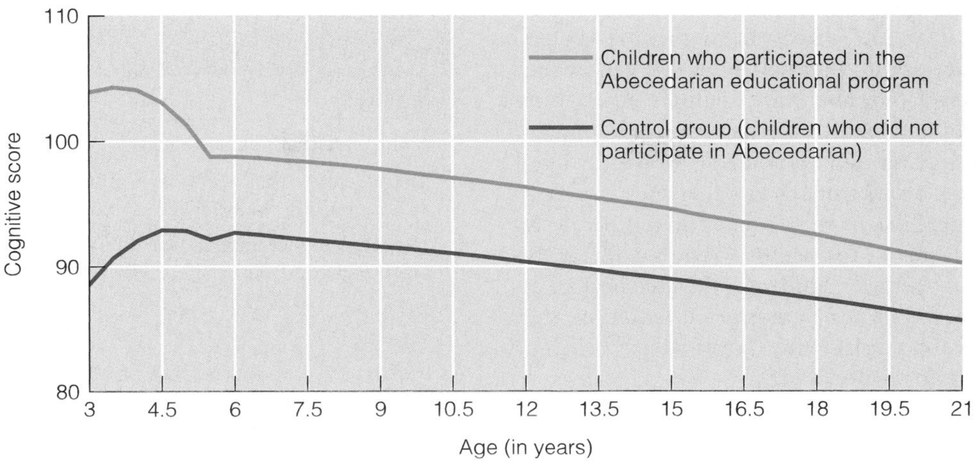

Figure 10.3 Cognitive growth curves as a function of preschool treatment.

SOURCE: Campbell et al. (2001). Copyright © 2001 American Psychological Association. Reprinted by permission.

nurtured by sensory stimulation and a responsive environment at home. Early education can help prepare disadvantaged children for formal schooling, but an overemphasis on academics at the expense of other activities may hinder young children's development. ■

The Child

With infancy behind them, children begin to show true achievement motivation. Even by age 2, they seem capable of appraising their performances as successes or failures and look to others for approval when they succeed and for disapproval when they fail (Stipek, Recchia, & McClintic, 1992). By age 3, children have clearly internalized standards of performance and experience true pride or shame, depending on how successfully they meet those standards (Stipek et al., 1992). Some children are clearly more achievement oriented and high achieving than others, however, and it is these differences we now seek to explain.

Achievement Motivation

All children occasionally experience failure in their efforts to master challenges and meet achievement standards. What are the differences between children who persist and triumph in

© Reflections Photolibrary/CORBIS

Preschools that offer a healthy combination of preacademic and social activities can help children prepare for school.

the face of failure and those who give up? Carol Dweck (2002; Heyman, Dweck, & Cain, 1992) finds that high achievers tend to attribute their successes to internal and stable causes such as high ability. However, they blame their failures either on external factors beyond their control ("That test was impossibly hard," "That professor's grading is biased") or—and this is even more adaptive—on internal causes that they can overcome (particularly insufficient effort). They do not blame the internal but stable factor of low ability ("I'm terrible at this and will never do any better"). Students with this healthy attributional style are said to have a **mastery orientation;** they thrive on challenges and persist in the face of failure, believing that their increased effort will pay off.

By contrast, children who tend to be low achievers often attribute their successes either to the internal cause of hard work or to external causes such as luck or the easiness of the task. Thus, they do not experience the pride and self-esteem that come from viewing themselves as highly capable. Yet they often attribute their failures to an internal and stable cause—namely, lack of ability. As a result, they have low expectancies of success and tend to give up. Dweck describes children with this attributional style as having a **learned helplessness orientation**—a tendency to avoid challenges and to cease trying when they experience failure, based on the belief that they can do little to improve.

Age Differences

Are children capable of analyzing the causes of success and failure in this way? Perhaps not when they are young. Before age 7 or so, children tend to be unrealistic optimists who think they can succeed on almost any task (Stipek & Mac Iver, 1989). With age, children's perceptions of their academic abilities become more accurate (Wigfield et al., 1997). Even after repeated poor performances, young children often continue to think they have high ability and will do well, whereas older children tend to become helpless (Miller, 1985; Ruble, Eisenberg, & Higgins, 1994). Young children can be made to feel helpless if their failures are clear-cut and they conclude they have been bad (Burhans & Dweck, 1995), but they are clearly less susceptible than older children to learned helplessness.

Why is this? Young children are protected from damaging self-perceptions partly because they do not yet fully understand the concept of ability as a stable capacity (Nicholls & Miller, 1984; Pomerantz & Ruble, 1997). They believe that ability is a changeable quality and that they can become smarter if they work hard. This view of ability encourages them to adopt **learning goals** in achievement situations, aiming to learn new things so that they can improve their abilities (Covington, 2000; Dweck & Leggett, 1988).

As children age, they begin to see ability as a fixed trait that does not change much with effort. As a result, more of them adopt **performance goals** in school; they aim to *prove* their ability rather than to *improve* it and seek to be judged smart rather than dumb (Dweck & Leggett, 1988; Erdley et al., 1997; and see Table 10.4). These changes in the understanding of ability are probably caused both by cognitive development—especially an increased ability to analyze the causes of successes and failures and to infer enduring traits from behavior—and by an accumulation of feedback in school (Stipek, 1984).

Table 10.4 Comparison of Learning and Performance Goals

Learning Goals
• Ability as a changeable trait
• Ability to focus on increasing competence or knowledge ("I understand this material better than I did before")
• Self-regulated learning; ability to monitor understanding of material and adjust behavior (for example, effort) accordingly
• Deep-level processing of material (for example, learning to understand)
• Feelings of pride and satisfaction associated with success, with failures indicating a need for more effort or different learning strategies
Performance Goals
• Ability as a fixed trait
• Ability to focus on increasing status relative to others ("I did better on this than the other students did")
• Other-regulated learning; ability to monitor performance relative to peers and increase effort (approach) to outperform them or decrease effort (avoidance) to save face (to say that failures are because of a lack of effort, not incompetence)
• Superficial-level processing of material (for example, memorizing for a test)
• Feelings of anxiety and shame associated with failure; boastful feelings associated with success

SOURCES: Based on Covington, 2000; Elliot & Church, 1997.

Importantly, children who continue to focus on learning goals tend to do better in school than those who switch to performance goals (Butler, 1999; Stipek & Gralinski, 1996; Covington, 2000). As Table 10.4 illustrates, when students believe that ability is a fixed entity that they either have or do not have and conclude that they lack it, they set performance goals rather than learning goals; figuring that hard work will not pay off, they run the risk of becoming helpless in the classroom (Dweck & Leggett, 1988). Even gifted students can fall into this trap (Ablard & Mills, 1996). What can parents and schools do to foster healthy patterns of achievement motivation?

Parent Contributions

As you saw earlier, parents can foster mastery motivation in infancy by providing their babies with appropriate sensory stimulation, being responsive, and (as you will see in Chapter 14) building a secure attachment relationship. Parents can then strengthen their children's achievement motivation by stressing and reinforcing independence and self-reliance at an early age, encouraging children to do things on their own (Peterson & Steen, 2002). They can also emphasize the importance of doing things well, or meeting high standards of performance (Deci & Ryan, 1992). As children begin formal schooling, parents can help foster high levels of achievement motivation by getting involved with their child's education (Stevenson & Stigler, 1994).

Finally, parents can provide a cognitively stimulating home environment (Gottfried, Fleming, & Gottfried, 1998). This includes having reading material in the home, engaging in intellectual discussions, attending lectures or cultural events, visiting museums, and holding high expectations for children's education. By doing these things, parents stimulate intellectual curiosity and a desire to learn. Children who are encouraged and supported in a positive manner are likely to enjoy new challenges and feel confident about mastering them. They are also unlikely to make the kinds of counterproductive attributions ("I'm dumb") that can cause them to lose interest in schoolwork (Glasgow et al., 1997). Children typically feel competent when their parents are satisfied with their performance (McGrath & Repetti, 2000). By contrast, parents can undermine a child's school performance and intrinsic motivation to learn if they are uninvolved and offer little guidance or if they are highly controlling, nag continually about homework, offer bribes for good grades, and criticize bad grades (Ginsburg & Bronstein, 1993). Thus, parents need to strike a healthy balance between being supportive and being controlling.

School Contributions

How do schools affect achievement? Nearly every school asserts that the major goal of classroom instruction is improvement of children's learning. Many of these same schools, however, are structured in ways that focus on the external rewards that students can earn (such as grades or stickers). As a result, they may encourage children to set performance goals rather than learning goals (Covington, 2000). Many classrooms are competitive places where students try to outdo each other to earn the best grades and gain teacher recognition. Schools may serve their students better by de-emphasizing grades as endpoints and focusing on the process of learning. In many classes, students receive a grade (good or bad), indicating their performance on a test or project, and that is the end of it. If they did not fully learn the material, they are given no opportunity to do so: They learn that the grade, not learning, is the goal.

Martin Covington (2000, 1998) believes that schools can foster children's academic motivation by downplaying the competitive race for the best grades in class. How might this work? Consider some research by Elaine Elliott and Carol Dweck (1988). They asked fifth-graders to perform a novel task. The students were led to believe that they had either low or high ability and were warned that they would soon be performing similar tasks that would prove difficult. Half the children worked under a performance goal (not unlike the goals emphasized in many classrooms): They were told that their performance would be compared with that of other children and evaluated by an expert. The remaining children were induced to adopt a learning goal: Although they would make some mistakes, they were told, working at the tasks would "sharpen the mind" and help them at school.

As expected, the only children who displayed the telltale signs of helplessness (that is, deteriorating performance and attribution of failure to low ability) were those who believed they had low ability and were pursuing a performance goal. For them, continuing to work on the difficult task meant demonstrating again that they were stupid. By contrast, even "low ability" students who pursued a learning goal persisted despite their failures and showed remarkably little frustration, probably because they believed they could grow from their experience. Perhaps, then, teachers undermine achievement motivation by distributing gold stars and grades and frequently calling attention to how students compare with one another (Deci, Koestner, & Ryan, 1999). Children might be better off if teachers nurtured their intrinsic motivation to master challenges (Boggiano & Katz, 1991; Butler, 1990). Then, slow learners could view their mistakes as a sign that they should change strategies to improve their competencies rather than as further proof that they lack ability.

Finally, the school climate can influence achievement. Academic achievement is greater when schools encourage family involvement and regular parent–teacher communication and when they develop a system that makes family involvement possible (Rimm-Kaufman & Pianta, 1999). Schools can also try to capture students' enthusiasm for learning from the start of schooling. Students who start out liking school are typically the ones who like school later; they also participate more in the classroom, which leads to higher levels of achievement (Ladd, Buhs, & Seid, 2000).

To recap what you have learned so far, children approach achievement tasks with either a mastery orientation or a learned helplessness orientation, based on how they view their academic triumphs and disasters. As they age, children understand the concept of ability as a stable trait and shift from focusing on learning goals to focusing on performance goals. These changes, brought about by both cognitive development and feedback in school, give them a more realistic picture of their own strengths and weaknesses but also make them more vulnerable to learned helplessness. Yet some children remain far more motivated to succeed in school than others, and parents and schools have a lot to do with that.

Learning to Read

Perhaps the most important achievement in school is acquiring the ability to read. Mastery of reading paves the way for mastering other academic skills. Skilled readers consume more printed material than unskilled readers or nonreaders, giving them an advantage in other academic areas that increasingly rely on reading skills over the school years (Stanovich, 1986). Unlike language acquisition, a natural learning task that typically requires no formal education, reading acquisition is an "unnatural" task (Stanovich & Stanovich, 1999). Learning to read almost always requires direct instruction. How do children master this complex and important skill?

Mastering the Alphabetic Principle

Before children can read, they must understand the **alphabetic principle**—the idea that the letters in printed words represent the sounds in spoken words in a systematic way (Byrne, 1998; Treiman, 2000). According to Linnea Ehri (1999), this is a four-step process. First, children in the prealphabetic phase memorize selected visual cues to remember words. They can "read" text that they have memorized during previous readings. For instance, seeing a picture of a dinosaur on a page in a favorite book cues a child to recall the words she has often heard her mother read when they turned to this page. Or, a child in the prealphabetic phase might recognize a word by its shape (physically, the printed word *bed* looks different than the word *egg*).

In the partial alphabetic phase, children learn the shapes and sounds of letters. For example, they recognize the curved shape of the letter *C* and begin to associate this with a particular sound. These children begin to connect at least one letter in a word—usually the first—to its corresponding sound. Not surprisingly, children typically recognize the initial letter of their first name before other letters (Treiman & Broderick, 1998).

Complete connections between written letters and their corresponding sounds are acquired during the full alphabetic phase. In this phase, children acquire full **phonological awareness**—the sensitivity to the sound system of language that enables them to segment spoken words into sounds or phonemes (Carroll et al., 2003). Children who have phonological awareness can recognize that *cat* and *trouble* both have the phoneme /t/ in them, can tell you how many distinct sounds there are in the word *bark*, and can tell you what will be left if you take the /f/ sound out of *fat*. Children can decode words never before seen by applying their knowledge of phonetics. They can decipher the new word *mat* from their previous understanding of the word *cat* and the letter *m*.

In addition to decoding unfamiliar words, children in the full alphabetic phase use sight reading for familiar words. Sight reading is fast and works well for words that are hard to decode (such as those with unusual spellings) or frequently encountered. If you regularly run across the word *alligator* in your readings, you may initially read this by decoding it, or "unpacking" each sound then putting the sounds together. But after many encounters with this word, you can sight-read it, or recall it from memory, without having to decode every sound.

Finally, in the consolidated alphabetic phase, letters that regularly occur together are grouped as a unit. For instance, the letter sequence *ing,* which frequently appears at the end of verbs, is perceived as a single unit rather than as three separate letters. This grouping speeds the processing of the multisyllabic words that older children are increasingly exposed to in their books.

Thus, the basic components of literacy include mastering a language system, understanding connections between sounds and their printed symbols (the alphabetic principle), and discriminating phonemes that make up words (phonological awareness). How does the child pull all this together into reading?

Emergent Literacy

Several activities help promote **emergent literacy**—the developmental precursors of reading skills in young children (Whitehurst & Lonigan, 1998). Emergent literacy includes knowledge, skills, and attitudes that will facilitate the acquisition of reading ability. For instance, reading storybooks to preschoolers positively influences their later literacy (Roskos, Christie, & Richgels, 2003). Repetitious storybook reading enhances children's vocabulary and allows them to see the connection between printed and spoken words (Whitehurst & Lonigan, 1998). With each successive reading, parents ask increasingly complex questions about the text, moving the child from a superficial to a deeper understanding (van Kleeck et al., 1997). Even older children benefit from reading the same book on multiple occasions (Faust & Glenzer, 2000) and from shared reading with a parent (Clarke-Stewart, 1998). Parents, with their greater mastery of reading, can help their fledgling readers develop an understanding of printed words. If you think of this in Vygotsky's framework, it is an example of parent and child operating in the zone of proximal development.

Repeatedly reading the same story fosters vocabulary and deepens children's understanding of the story content.

Rhyming stories and games can help foster phonological awareness. For this reason, listening to books with a rhyming structure (for example, Dr. Seuss's *The Cat in the Hat*) can benefit children. Young children's sensitivity to rhyme (for example, *cat–sat*) helps predict their later reading success (Bryant, 1998; Goswami, 1999).

By assessing preschool children's emergent literacy skills, parents can develop a fairly accurate idea of what their later reading skills will be (Lonigan, Burgess, & Anthony, 2000). In particular, differences among children in knowledge of letters (for example, knowing the alphabet) and phonological awareness predict later differences in their reading ability (Carroll et al., 2003). In addition, semantic knowledge, reflected in children's ability to retrieve words and provide word definitions, can predict later reading ability (Roth, Speece, & Cooper, 2002). This suggests that parents can help children get a head start on reading by encouraging activities such as rhyming, repeating the ABCs, and defining words.

Skilled and Unskilled Readers

After children have received reading instruction, why are some children quick, advanced readers but others struggle to master the most basic reading material? For starters, skilled readers have a solid understanding of the alphabetic principle—the notion that letters must be associated with phonemes. Thus, when they see the letter *b,* they know the sound that it represents. A large body of research also confirms that reading ability is influenced by a child's level of phonological awareness (Adams, Treiman, & Pressley, 1998; Bus & van Ijzendoorn, 1999). Children with higher levels of phonological awareness usually become better readers than children with lower levels of phonological awareness (Schneider, Roth, & Ennemoser, 2000).

But there is more to being a skilled reader than connecting letters with sounds. Analyses of eye movement patterns show that unskilled readers skip words or parts of words, whereas skilled readers' eyes hit all the words (Perfetti, 1999). Skilled readers do not use context to help them identify words, although they may use context to help with comprehension. As noted previously, they rely on phonology to identify words, something most unskilled readers have trouble with.

Some children have serious difficulties learning to read, even though they have normal intellectual ability and no sensory impairments or emotional difficulties that could account for their problems. These children have **dyslexia,** or a reading disability. A minority have the kind of visual perception problem that used to be seen as the heart of dyslexia; they cannot distinguish between letters with similar appearances, or they read words backward (*top* might become *pot*). However, it is now clear that the difficulties of most dyslexic children involve auditory perception more than visual perception (see, for example, Temple et al., 2000).

Specifically, children who become dyslexic readers often show deficiencies in phonological awareness well before they enter school (Bruck, 1992; Vellutino et al., 1996). There is even evidence that the brains of dyslexic children respond differently to speech sounds soon after birth (Molfese, 2000). This suggests that a perceptual deficit may develop during the prenatal period of brain development. Because dyslexic children have difficulty analyzing the sounds in speech, they also have trouble detecting sound–letter correspondences, which in turn impairs their ability to recognize printed words automatically and effortlessly (Bruck, 1990; Vellutino, 1991). They must then devote so much effort to decoding the words on the page that they have little attention to spare for interpreting and remembering what they have read. Dyslexic children continue to perform poorly on tests of phonological awareness and tests of word recognition as adolescents and adults, even if they have become decent readers (Bruck, 1990, 1992; Shaywitz et al., 1999). It is now clear that dyslexia is a lifelong disability, not just a developmental delay that is eventually overcome (Shaywitz et al., 1999).

How Should Reading Be Taught?

What does all this suggest about teaching children to read? For years a debate has raged over the merits of two broad approaches to reading instruction: the phonics approach and the whole-language approach (see, for example, Chall, 1967; Lemann, 1997). The phonics (or code-oriented) approach teaches children to analyze words into their component sounds; that is, it systematically teaches them letter–sound correspondence rules (Vellutino, 1991). By contrast, the whole-language (or look–say) approach emphasizes reading for meaning and teaches children to recognize specific words by sight or to figure out what they mean using clues in the surrounding context. It assumes that the parts of printed words (the letters) are not as meaningful as the whole words and that by focusing on whole words children can learn to read as effortlessly and naturally as they learn to understand speech.

Research strongly supports the phonics approach. To read well, children must somehow learn that spoken words are made up of sounds and that the letters of the alphabet correspond to these sounds (Foorman, 1995). Teaching phonological awareness skills can pay off in better reading skills (National Reading Panel, 1999). Table 10.5 shows what happened when a third-grade boy with poor phonological awareness tried to read by the look–say method. He ended up with an incorrect interpretation and lost the intended meaning of the sentence. Better decoding skills (phonics) might have enabled him to read the sentence accurately.

With this in mind, several programs have been developed for at-risk and dyslexic children who have special difficulty discriminating speech sounds that are made rapidly, such as *b, d,* and *t.* By playing an entertaining computer game, children are able to practice discriminating pairs of these hard-to-distinguish sounds, which are altered so that they are stretched in time and thereby made easier to perceive (Merzenich et al., 1996; Tallal et al., 1996). After only a month

Table 10.5 One Boy's Misreading of the Sentence "A Boy Said, 'Run, Little Girl.'"

Words in Target Sentence	Strategies Employed by Reader	Words "Read"
A	Sight word known to reader	A
boy	Unknown; uses beginning *b* to guess *baby*	baby
said, "Run	*Said* unknown; jumps to the next word *(run),* which he recognizes, then uses the *s* in *said* and his knowledge of syntax to generate *is running*	is running
little	Sight word known to reader	little
girl."	Unknown; uses beginning *g* to guess *go*	go

SOURCE: Adapted from Ely, 2001.

of such game playing, children's ability to recognize fast sequences of speech sounds and to understand language improves dramatically. These gains eventually pay off in improved reading performance as children become more able to sound out words on the page (Foorman et al., 1998). Despite the importance of phonological awareness, however, children must also make sense of what they are reading—they must be able to read for meaning. Thus, reading programs should use both phonics and whole-language instruction, teaching letter–sound correspondences but also helping children find meaning and enjoyment in what they read (Adams, 1990).

The debate over reading instruction and its effectiveness raises a broader question about just how well schools are doing at educating children. Look at what factors contribute—or do not contribute—to effective schools.

Effective Schools

Some schools are clearly better than others at accomplishing their objectives. You can regularly read news reports of schools above or below the national average in the percentage of students they graduate or the achievement scores of their students—two common measures of school effectiveness. As you read the next sections, you may be surprised by some factors that do and do not have a bearing on how effective a school is (Molnar, 2002; Reynolds, 1992; Rutter & Maughan, 2002).

Less Important Factors

Many people assume that pouring financial resources into schools will automatically increase school effectiveness. But the relationship between funding and student outcome is complex. Some research shows that as long as schools have reasonable resources, the precise amount of money spent per pupil plays only a minor role in determining student outcomes (Hanushek, 1997; Rutter, 1983). Other research suggests that increased resources, if applied directly to classroom instruction, can increase student achievement in the earlier grades (Wenglinsky, 1998). Thus, simply adding money to school budgets is unlikely to improve school effectiveness unless schools invest this money wisely.

Another factor that has relatively little to do with a school's effectiveness is average class size (Ehrenberg et al., 2001; Rutter & Maughan, 2002). Within a range of 18 to 40 students per class, reducing class sizes (from, say, 36 to 24 students) is unlikely to increase student achievement (Hanushek, 1997, 1998). Instead, tutoring students in the early grades (kindergarten through third), especially disadvantaged and low-ability ones, one-on-one or in small groups makes a big difference in their learning of reading and mathematics (Blatchford et al., 2002; Finn, 2002). However, more modest reductions in the student–teacher ratio do not seem to be worth the large amount of money they cost.

What about the amount of time spent in school? Most children go to school for 6 hours on about 180 days of each school year. Many people assume that schools could improve student outcomes if they lengthened the school day or year. But research shows that the modest increases in time that some schools have implemented have only minimal effects on achievement (Glass, 2002c). Thus, adding 30 minutes to each school day or lengthening the school year by 15, 20, or even 25 days has negligible effects on student outcomes. Similarly, redistributing school days so that they are evenly spread across the year rather than bunched between September and May does not improve student achievement.

Finally, it matters little whether or not a school uses **ability grouping,** in which students are grouped according to ability then taught in classes or work groups with others of similar academic or intellectual standing. Grouping by ability has no clear advantage over mixed-ability grouping for most students (Glass, 2002a). It *can* be beneficial, especially to higher-ability students, if it results in a curriculum more appropriate to students' learning needs (Glass, 2002a; Kulik & Kulik, 1992). However, low-ability students are unlikely to benefit and may suffer if they are denied access to the most effective teachers, taught less material than other children, and stigmatized as "dummies" (Mac Iver, Reuman, & Main, 1995; Mehan et al., 1996). Too often, this is what happens. As Hugh Mehan and his colleagues (1996) put it, "It is not that dumb kids are placed in slow groups or low tracks; it is that kids are made dumb by being placed in slow groups or low tracks" (p. 230). The Explorations box on page 274 takes a closer look at mixing students with different abilities and backgrounds.

These, then, are examples of school characteristics that do not seem to contribute a great deal to effective education. A school that has limited financial support (assuming it exceeds a basic minimum), places most students (except perhaps beginning readers) in relatively large classes, and combines students in mixed-ability learning groups or classes is often just as effective as a school that has ample financial resources, small classes, and ability grouping.

Factors That Matter

So what does influence how well children perform? To understand why some schools are more effective than others, you must consider characteristics of the students, characteristics of the teachers, characteristics of the learning environment, and the interaction between student and environment.

First, a school's effectiveness is a function of what it has to work with—the students it takes in and the teachers who provide the instruction (Wang, Haertel, & Walberg, 1993). With respect to the children, genetic differences among children contribute to differences in aptitude among them (Rutter & Maughan, 2002). As you learned in Chapters 3 and 9, IQ scores have a genetic component, and children with higher IQs attain higher grades throughout their 12 years of school (Gutman, Sameroff, & Cole, 2003). Schools cannot eliminate these genetic differences among children but they can influence (that is, raise) overall levels of academic achievement (Rutter & Maughan, 2002). In addition, academic achievement, on average, tends to be higher in schools with a preponderance of economically advantaged students; children are better able to make academic progress in school when they come from homes that are stocked with computers, books, and intellectually stimulating toys (Brookover et al., 1979; Portes & MacLeod, 1996). However, this does not mean that schools are only as good as the students they serve. Many schools that serve disadvantaged populations are highly effective at motivating students and preparing them for jobs or further education (Reynolds, 1992).

Finally, studies of the effects of schools provide another illustration of the interaction of nature and nurture. High-achieving parents pass their genes to their children, providing genetic potential for high achievement to their children (Rutter & Maughan, 2002). These same high-achieving parents are likely to select schools that have strong academic reputations, often by choosing to live in a neighborhood served by a "good" school district (Rutter & Maughan, 2002). This is an example of a passive gene–environment correlation, described in Chapter 3, in which children are influenced by their parent's genes directly through genetic transmission and indirectly through the environments their parents create for them.

As for the effects of teachers on school achievement, Andrew Wayne and Peter Youngs (2003) reviewed research on the relationship between teacher characteristics and student achievement. They found that student achievement scores rose with increases in the quality of their teachers' undergraduate institutions and their teachers' licensure examination scores. There was also a connection between teachers' coursework and student achievement, but only in high school mathematics. Thus, high school math teachers are more effective, as measured by student achievement gains, when they have completed more math courses as part of their teacher training. Similarly, in a review of teacher characteristics, Gene Glass (2002b) concluded that student achievement is enhanced when students are taught by regularly licensed teachers who have more experience.

Third, the learning environment of some schools allows them to nurture achievement. Basically, the effective school environment is a comfortable but businesslike setting in which teachers are involved with students, students are motivated to learn, and serious teaching takes place (Mac Iver et al., 1995; Phillips, 1997; Rutter, 1983). More specifically, in effective schools and classrooms, teachers:

- Strongly emphasize academics. They demand a lot from their students, expect them to succeed, regularly assign homework, and work hard to achieve their objectives in the classroom.
- Create a task-oriented but comfortable atmosphere. For example, they waste little time starting activities or dealing with distracting discipline problems, provide clear instructions and feedback, and encourage and reward good work.
- Manage discipline problems effectively. For example, they enforce the rules on the spot rather than sending offenders to the principal's office, and they avoid the use of physical punishment.

Effective schools also have supportive parents and supportive communities behind them (Comer, 1997). Students achieve more when their parents are interested in and value school and school achievement; participate in parent–teacher conferences, PTA meetings, and other school events; and participate in homework and other school-related activities at home (Hill & Craft, 2003; Hill & Taylor, 2004). Parents' involvement in school is also associated with better social skills and fewer behavioral problems among their children (Kohl et al., 2000; Marcon, 1999). Parents with less education are typically less involved in their children's education than highly educated parents are, yet they can have a greater effect on their children's grades if they become involved (Bogenschneider, 1997; Downey, 2002).

In a comfortable and task-oriented classroom, children are motivated to learn.

Finally, characteristics of the student and characteristics of the school environment often interact to affect student outcome. This is an example of the concept of **goodness of fit**—an appropriate match between the student's characteristics and her environment. Much educational research has been based on the assumption that one teaching method, organizational system, or philosophy of education will prove superior for all students, regardless of their ability levels, learning styles, personalities, and cultural backgrounds. This assumption is often wrong. Instead, many educational practices are highly effective with some kinds of students but ineffective with other students. The secret is to find an appropriate match between the learner and the teaching method.

To illustrate goodness of fit between learners and environments, highly achievement-oriented students adapt well to unstructured classrooms in which they have a good deal of choice, whereas less achievement-oriented students often do better with more structure (Peterson, 1977). Sometimes an alternative teaching method works as well as a traditional one for highly capable students but only one of these methods suits less capable students. In one study, for example, highly distractible students got more from computer-assisted instruction than from a teacher's presentation of the same material, whereas more attentive students benefited equally from both methods (Orth & Martin, 1994). Finally, students tend to have more positive outcomes when they and their teacher share similar backgrounds (Goldwater & Nutt, 1999). Evidence of the importance of the fit between student and classroom environment implies that educational programs are likely to be most effective when they are highly individualized—tailored to suit each student's developmental competencies and needs.

Explorations

Making Integration and Inclusion Work

For many minority students of the past, especially African Americans, additional barriers to school success were created by school segregation. Black children in many states were forced to attend "black schools" that were clearly inferior to "white schools." In its landmark decision in the case of *Brown v. Board of Education of Topeka* in 1954, the Supreme Court ruled that segregated schools were "inherently unequal" and declared that they must be desegregated. More than 50 years have passed since this ruling (Pickren, 2004). What has been learned about desegregation during this time?

In general, the effects of school integration on children's racial attitudes, self-esteem, and school achievement have been mixed (Gray-Little & Carels, 1997; Stephan, 1978). Some studies suggest that both African American and European American children tend to have higher self-esteem and higher achievement when they attend racially mixed schools, but the effects are often small (Gray-Little & Carels, 1997). White prejudice toward black students often does not decrease much. The self-esteem of black children in integrated schools is only sometimes higher than that of black children in segregated schools (Gray-Little & Carels, 1997). And although minority students sometimes achieve more in integrated schools, especially if they begin to attend them early in their academic careers, school integration often has little effect on achievement (Rossell, Armor, & Walberg, 2002).

Children with developmental disabilities (mental retardation, learning disabilities, physical and sensory handicaps, and other special learning needs) have had a similar history. They used to be placed in separate schools or classrooms—or, in some cases, rejected as unteachable by the public schools. But the Individuals with Disabilities Education Act (an extension of the 1975 Education for All Handicapped Children Act) requires schools to provide such children with a free and appropriate education that occurs "to the maximum extent appropriate . . . with children who are not disabled."

What has been achieved? Studies of developmentally disabled children integrated into regular classrooms through a practice called **inclusion** (formerly called *mainstreaming*)—to

Summing Up

During childhood, some children develop higher levels of achievement motivation than others; they tend to have mastery-oriented rather than helpless attribution styles, and they set learning rather than performance goals in the classroom. To read, children must master the alphabetic principle and develop phonological awareness so that they can grasp letter–sound correspondence rules. Emergent literacy activities such as listening to storybooks facilitate later reading. Compared with unskilled readers, skilled readers have better understanding of the alphabetic principle and greater phonological awareness. A school's effectiveness is not influenced much by financial support, class size, time spent in school, or use of ability grouping. Instead, students perform best when (1) they are intellectually capable and motivated; (2) their teachers create an effective learning environment; and (3) there is a good fit between children's characteristics and the kind of instruction they receive. ■

The Adolescent

Adolescents make critical decisions about such matters as how much time to devote to studying, whether to work part-time after school, whether to go to college, and what to be when they grow up. They become more capable of making these educational and vocational choices as their cognitive and social skills expand; in turn, the choices they make shape their de-emphasize the philosophy that children with special learning needs should spend the entire school day rather than only parts of it in a regular classroom and truly be included in the normal educational process—have yielded mixed results. Compared with similar students who attend segregated special education classes, these mainstreamed youngsters sometimes fare better in terms of academic performance, self-esteem, and social adjustment but sometimes do not (Buysse & Bailey, 1993; Hunt & Goetz, 1997; Manset & Semmel, 1997). The outcome depends partly on the severity of the child's disability. The performance of higher-functioning disabled children often benefits from inclusion in the regular classroom, whereas the performance of lower-functioning children is similar in integrated and segregated classrooms (Holahan & Costenbader, 2000). In terms of peer acceptance, children with severe disabilities are better accepted by their normally developing peers than are children with mild disabilities in homogeneous regular classrooms, where those with more severe disabilities presumably stand out as different, prompting other students to adjust their expectations (Cook & Semmel, 1999). Children with mild disabilities do not markedly stand out in homogeneous classrooms and therefore do not achieve "special" status; these children are better accepted in heterogeneous classrooms (Cook & Semmel, 1999).

What researchers seem to be learning about both racial integration and inclusion is that simply putting diverse students into the same schools and classrooms accomplishes little. Instead, something special must be done to ensure that students of different ethnic backgrounds and ability levels interact in positive ways and learn what they are supposed to be learning.

One promising model uses **cooperative learning,** in which diverse students are assigned to work teams and are reinforced for performing well as a team (Salend, 1999; Slavin, 1986; Stevens & Slavin, 1995). Consider research conducted by Uri Treisman at the University of California at Berkeley in the 1970s (Fullilove & Treisman, 1990). Treisman studied African Americans and Asian Americans enrolled in first-year calculus. The Asian Americans did well in the class, whereas the African Americans performed poorly. But this was not the only difference between the two groups of students. The African American students worked independently on work related to the class; the Asian Americans worked in small study groups and often combined studying with socializing, something the African American students rarely did. Treisman decided to see whether working together and receiving support from peers could boost the African American students' performance—it did (see also Duncan & Dick, 2000).

In cooperative learning classrooms, children of different races and ability levels interact in a context where the efforts of even the least capable team members are important to the group's success. Elementary-school students like school better and learn more when they participate in cooperative learning groups than when they receive traditional instruction (Johnson, Johnson, & Maruyama, 1983; O'Donnell & O'Kelly, 1994; Stevens & Slavin, 1995). Moreover, team members gain self-esteem from their successes, and minority students and students with developmental disabilities are more fully accepted by their peers. In short, racial integration and inclusion can succeed if educators deliberately design learning experiences that encourage students from different backgrounds to pool their efforts to achieve common goals. Interventions such as this are important if children are to be ready for the challenges of secondary school.

velopment. But many of them lose interest in school when they leave elementary school.

Declining Levels of Achievement

You might think that adolescents would become more dedicated to academic success once they begin to realize that they need a good education to succeed in life. But consider what Deborah Stipek (1984, p. 153) concluded after reviewing studies on the development of achievement motivation from early childhood to adolescence:

> On the average, children value academic achievement more as they progress through school, but their expectations for success and self-perceptions of competence decline, and their affect toward school becomes more negative. Children also become increasingly concerned about achievement outcomes and reinforcement (e.g., high grades) associated with positive outcomes and less concerned about intrinsic satisfaction in achieving greater competence.

Many of the negative trends Stipek describes become especially apparent as young adolescents make the transition from elementary school to middle school (typically grades 6 to 8) or junior high school (grades 7 to 9). At this critical juncture, achievement motivation, self-esteem, and grades may all decline. Figure 10.4 shows the academic trajectories for four groups of students studied by Leslie Gutman and his colleagues: those with high and low IQ scores who had either many or few risk factors (Gutman, Sameroff, & Cole, 2003). Risk factors included minority group status, mothers' educational level and mental health, stressful life events, family size,

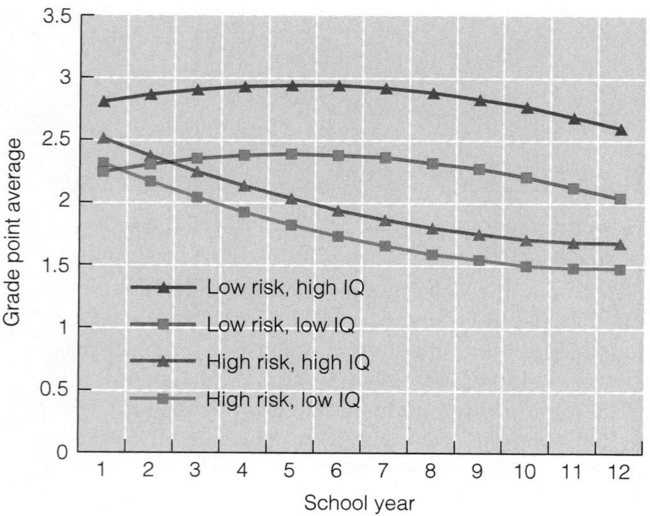

Figure 10.4 Grade point average from 1st grade to 12th grade for students with high and low risk and IQ.
SOURCE: Gutman, Sameroff, & Cole (2003), p. 785, Figure 1.

and father absence. Students with more risk factors showed a steady decline in academic achievement throughout their schooling, regardless of whether they had high or low IQ scores to begin with. Students with few risk factors showed a slight increase in achievement until around grade 6 or 7, at which time achievement began to drop slowly.

What might explain these discouraging trends? Consider six contributors: family characteristics, cognitive growth, negative feedback, peer pressures, pubertal changes, and poor fit between the adolescents and the schools they attend.

Family Characteristics

Several family characteristics are associated with lower achievement and greater absences from school. Being a member of a minority group, growing up in a single-parent family, and having a mother with less education or with mental health problems are potential academic risk factors (Gutman, Sameroff, & Eccles, 2002; Gutman et al., 2003). In contrast, living in a small, caring family with a stable parent who uses consistent discipline can bolster school performance (Gutman et al., 2002).

Cognitive Growth

As you saw earlier, children become increasingly capable of analyzing the causes of events, interpreting feedback from teachers, and inferring enduring traits such as high or low ability from their behavior (Stipek & Mac Iver, 1989). The result is that they view their strengths and weaknesses more realistically—and lose some of their high academic self-esteem and high expectancies of success (Stipek & Mac Iver, 1989; Wigfield et al., 1997).

Negative Feedback

Declines in achievement motivation may also be caused by changes in the kinds of feedback students receive as they age (Eccles, Lord, & Midgley, 1991; Stipek & Mac Iver, 1989). Preschool teachers often praise their young charges merely for trying and do not hand out much criticism. As Stipek notes (1984), it would be unthinkable for an adult to say to a 5-year-old exhibiting a drawing, "What an ugly picture. You sure can't draw very well" (p. 156). The positive feedback young children receive for their efforts may contribute to their tendency to set learning rather than performance goals and to sense that hard work can overcome any barrier (Rosenholtz & Simpson, 1984). By contrast, elementary- and secondary-school teachers increasingly reserve praise, high grades, and other forms of approval for students who turn in high-quality products. Effort alone is not enough. As they progress through school, then, children receive more feedback telling them precisely what capabilities they have and what capabilities they lack.

Peer Pressures

The adolescent's environment also changes in the sense that peers become increasingly important and sometimes can undermine parents' and teachers' efforts to encourage school achievement. Many years ago, when James Coleman (1961) asked high school students how they would like to be remembered, only 31% of the boys and 28% of the girls wanted to be remembered as bright students. They were more concerned with having the athletic and social skills that lead to popularity. Not much has changed (see Suitor & Reavis, 1995).

Peer pressures that undermine achievement motivation tend to be especially strong for many lower-income minority students. In particular, African American and Hispanic peer cultures in many low-income areas actively discourage academic achievement, whereas European American and especially Asian American peer groups tend to value and encourage it (Steinberg, Dornbusch, & Brown, 1992). High-achieving African American students in some inner-city schools risk being rejected by their African American peers if their academic accomplishments cause them to be perceived as "acting white" (Fordham & Ogbu, 1986). They may feel that they have to abandon their cultural group and racial identity to succeed in school, and this takes a psychological toll (Arroyo & Zigler, 1995; Ogbu, 2003). Alternatively, they may disengage from academics to preserve their cultural identity with a group that does not value academics (Ogbu, 2003). Although African American parents are as likely as European American parents to value education and to provide the kind of authoritative parenting that encourages school achievement, their positive influences are sometimes canceled out by negative peer influences (Steinberg et al., 1992).

For those African American teens who belong to a supportive peer group, academic achievement is strengthened (Gutman et al., 2002). In addition, African American teens who strongly value their ethnic group membership and have positive beliefs about how society views African Americans tend to have more positive beliefs about education (Chavous et al., 2003).

Pubertal Changes

It has also been suggested that the transition to middle school or junior high school is difficult because young adolescents are often experiencing major physical and psychological changes when they are switching schools. Roberta Simmons and Dale Blyth (1987) found that girls who were reaching puberty when they were moving from sixth grade in an elementary school to seventh grade in a junior high school were more likely to experience drops in self-esteem and other negative changes than girls who remained in a K–8 school during this vulnerable period.

Could it be that more adolescents would remain interested in school if they did not have to change schools when they are experiencing pubertal changes? This idea became an important part of the rationale for middle schools (grades 6 to 8), which were developed to make the transition from elementary school to high school easier for early adolescents (Braddock & McPartland, 1993). Yet Jacquelynne Eccles and her colleagues (Eccles, Lord, & Midgley, 1991; Eccles, Midgley, et al., 1993) have shown that students do not necessarily find the transition to middle school any easier than the transition to junior high school. These researchers suspect that when adolescents make a school change is less important than what their new school is like.

By adolescence, some students have little motivation to achieve in the classroom.

Poor Person–Environment Fit

Eccles and her colleagues offer a goodness-of-fit explanation for declining achievement motivation in adolescence, arguing that the transition to a new school is likely to be especially difficult when the new school, whether a junior high or a middle school, is ill matched to the developmental needs of early adolescents. These researchers have found that the transition to middle school or junior high school often involves going from a small school with close student–teacher relationships, a good deal of choice regarding learning activities, and reasonable discipline to a larger, more bureaucratized environment in which student–teacher relationships are impersonal, good grades are more emphasized but harder to come by, opportunities for choice are limited, assignments are not as intellectually stimulating, and discipline is rigid—all when adolescents are seeking more rather than less autonomy and are becoming more rather than less intellectually capable. Students who had what Carol Dweck calls learning goals in elementary school perceive an increased emphasis on performance goals when they move to middle school (Anderman & Midgley, 1997).

Eccles and her colleagues have demonstrated that the fit between developmental needs and school environment is an important influence on adolescent adjustment to school. In one study (Mac Iver & Reuman, 1988), the transition to junior high school brought about a decline in intrinsic motivation to learn mainly among students who wanted more involvement in classroom decisions but ended up with fewer such opportunities than they had in elementary school. In another study (Midgley, Feldlaufer, & Eccles, 1989), students experienced negative changes in their attitudes toward mathematics only when their move from elementary school to junior high resulted in less personal and supportive relationships with math teachers. For those few students whose junior high school teachers were more supportive than those they had in elementary school, interest in academics increased.

The message? Declines in academic motivation and performance are not inevitable during early adolescence. Students may indeed form more realistic expectancies of success as their growing cognitive abilities allow them to use the increasingly informative feedback they receive from teachers. Experiencing pubertal changes at the same time as other stressful changes and needing to downplay academics to gain popularity may also hurt school achievement. However, educators can help keep adolescents engaged in school by creating school environments that provide a better fit to the developmental needs and interests of adolescents. Whether they are called middle schools or junior high schools, such schools should provide warm, supportive relationships with teachers, intellectual challenges, and increased opportunities for self-direction (Eccles, Midgley, et al., 1993). Specially designed school transition programs can help students adjust to high school and reduce the risk that they will drop out (Smith, 1997).

Science and Mathematics Education

Elementary schools necessarily spend much time on reading and writing skills. But secondary-school teachers take these skills largely for granted and focus energy on other academic areas. More advanced skills of concrete then formal operational thought enable children to tackle more challenging academic tasks. Much attention has been focused on mathematics and science, skills important for success in many industrialized nations. How well do secondary-school students perform in science and math? And how might achievement in these areas be optimized?

Table 10.6 shows average mathematics and science achievement test scores of eighth-grade students in various countries. Students in the United States score above the international average but significantly below achievement levels in nations such as Singapore, Japan, and Korea. When researchers looked at the best students—those in the top 10% of all eighth-graders surveyed in the 38 nations—only 9% of U.S. students met the criteria in math and only 15% met it in science. In comparison, the nation with the largest percentage of students in the top 10% was Singapore, with 46% in math and 32% in science. What might account for these international differences in math and science achievement? Are students in some nations simply more intelligent than students in other nations?

Cross-cultural research conducted by Harold Stevenson and his colleagues (Chen & Stevenson, 1995; Stevenson & Lee, 1990; Stevenson, Chen, & Lee, 1993) shows that American schoolchildren perform about as well on IQ tests as their Asian counterparts when they enter school (Stevenson et al., 1985). They score at least as well as Japanese and Chinese students on tests of general information not typically covered in school (Stevenson et al., 1993). Instead, the achievement gap between American and Asian students seems to be rooted in cultural differences in attitudes concerning education and educational practices. Here is what some of this cross-cultural research on education and achievement shows:

• Asian students spend more time being educated. Elementary-school teachers in Asian countries devote more class time to academics. The classroom is a businesslike place

Table 10.6 Average Mathematics and Science Achievement of Eighth-Grade Students in Various Nations (1999 scores)

Mathematics		Science	
Singapore	604	Chinese Taipei	569
Republic of Korea	587	Singapore	568
Chinese Taipei	585	Hungary	552
Hong Kong SAR	582	Japan	550
Japan	582	Republic of Korea	549
Netherlands	540	Netherlands	545
Hungary	532	Australia	540
Canada	531	Czech Republic	539
Slovenia	530	England	538
Russian Federation	526	Slovenia	533
Australia	525	Canada	533
Czech Republic	520	Hong Kong SAR	530
Malaysia	519	Russian Federation	529
United States	502	United States	515
England	496	New Zealand	510
New Zealand	491	Italy	493
INTERNATIONAL AVERAGE	487	Malaysia	492
Italy	479	INTERNATIONAL AVERAGE	488
Cyprus	476	Thailand	482
Romania	472	Romania	472
Thailand	467	Cyprus	460
Turkey	429	Iran	448
Iran	422	Turkey	433
Chile	392	Chile	420
Philippines	345	Philippines	345
Morocco	337	Morocco	323
South Africa	275	South Africa	243

☐ Average is significantly higher than the U.S. average
☐ Average does not differ significantly from the U.S. average
☐ Average is significantly lower than the U.S. average

SOURCE: Martin et al., 2000.

where little time is wasted; Asian students spend about 95% of their time "on task" (in activities such as listening to the teacher and completing assignments), whereas American students spend only about 80% of their time "on task" (Stigler, Lee, & Stevenson, 1987). Asian students also attend school for more hours per day and more days per year (Stevenson, Lee, & Stigler, 1986).

• Asian students, especially Japanese students, are assigned and complete considerably more homework than American students (Larson & Verma, 1999; Stevenson & Lee, 1990). When American students are working or socializing with friends, Asian students are hitting the books (Fuligni & Stevenson, 1995). Researchers from the Brookings Institution report that American students spend, on average, only 20 minutes a day on homework (Mathews, 2003).

• Asian parents are strongly committed to the educational process. About 40% think their children should have 3 hours or more of homework each day (Ebbeck, 1996). Asian parents are rarely satisfied with how their children are doing in school or with the quality of education their children are receiving; American parents seem to settle for less (Mathews, 2003). Asian parents also receive frequent communications from their children's teachers in notebooks children carry to and from school each day. They find out how their children are progressing and follow teachers' suggestions for encouraging and assisting their children at home (Stevenson & Lee, 1990).

• Asian peers also value school achievement and have high standards; time spent with peers often involves doing homework rather than engaging in activities that interfere with homework (Chen & Stevenson, 1995).

• Asian parents, teachers, and students all share a strong belief that hard work or effort will pay off in better academic performance (that is, they set what Dweck calls learning goals), whereas Americans tend to put more emphasis on ability as a cause of good or poor performance. The result may be that Americans give up too quickly on a child who appears to have low intellectual ability. In doing so, they may help create a case of learned helplessness.

This cross-cultural research carries an important message: The secret of effective education is to get teachers, students, and parents working together to make education the top priority for youth, to set high achievement goals, and to invest the day-by-day effort required to attain those goals. Many states and local school districts have begun to respond to evidence that American schools are being outclassed by schools in other countries by strengthening curricula, tightening standards for teacher certification, and raising standards for graduation and promotion from grade to grade.

Integrating Work and School

Unlike teens in many other industrialized nations, a sizable number (between one-third and one-half) of teens in the United States and Canada work part-time during their high school careers (Bachman et al., 2003; Thomas, 1998). How do these early work experiences affect their development and, in particular, their school achievement?

Laurence Steinberg and his associates have compared working and nonworking high school students in terms of such outcomes as autonomy from parents, self-reliance, self-esteem, sense of investment in school, academic performance, delinquency, and drug and alcohol use (Greenberger & Steinberg, 1986; Steinberg & Dornbusch, 1991; Steinberg, Fegley, & Dornbusch, 1993). Overall, this research offers more bad news than good. The good news is that working students seem to gain knowledge about work, consumer issues, and financial management and sometimes about greater self-reliance. However, high school students who worked 20 or more hours a week had lower grade-point averages than those of students who did not work or who worked only 10 or fewer hours per week (Steinberg & Dornbusch, 1991). Working students were also more likely than nonworkers to be disengaged from school—bored and uninvolved in class and prone to cut class and spend little time on homework.

In addition, the more adolescents worked, the more independent they were of parental control, the more likely they were to be experiencing psychological distress (anxiety, depression, and physical symptoms such as headaches), and the more frequently they used alcohol and drugs and engaged in delinquent acts. These negative effects of work generally increased as the number of hours a student worked increased.

Jerald Bachman and his colleagues (2003) have found that not-yet-employed students who want to work long hours tend to be disenchanted with school, have low grades, and are more likely to use alcohol and cigarettes. Once they start working, the disenchantment and problem behaviors are exacerbated (Bachman et al., 2003; Steinberg et al., 1993). Similarly, longitudinal research on adolescents and work confirms that academically struggling students are the ones likely to work more hours (Warren, LePore, & Mare, 2000). Kusum Singh and Mehmet Ozturk (2000) reached a similar conclusion from their research on employment during high school and performance in mathematics and science courses. They found that students with low achievement in science and math were more likely to work part-time than students with high achievement in these courses. Working reduced the number of math and science courses that students enrolled in. Ultimately, students who work during high school may limit their future educational and vocational prospects by limiting their exposure to potentially important coursework.

Not all research findings are this discouraging. Jeylen Mortimer and his colleagues (1996) also conducted a longitudinal study of high school students but controlled for differences between working and nonworking students on factors such as family background and prior academic performance. In their study, working 20 hours or more a week did not hurt academic achievement, self-esteem, or psychological adjustment once other factors were controlled. Students who worked 1 to 20 hours a week actually earned better grades than either nonworkers or students who worked more than 20 hours a week. As in Steinberg's study, however, students who worked more than 20 hours used alcohol more frequently than students who were not employed.

When all the research is examined as a package, the findings suggest that working while attending high school is often more damaging than beneficial. Much depends on the nature of the work adolescents do. Many teenagers work in food service jobs (pouring soft drinks behind the counter at fast food restaurants, scooping ice cream, and the like) or perform manual labor (especially cleaning or janitorial work). These routine and repetitive jobs offer few opportunities for self-direction or decision making and only rarely call on academic skills such as reading and mathematics (Greenberger & Steinberg, 1986). They are not the kinds of jobs that build character or teach new skills. Adolescents experience increases in mastery motivation and become less depressed over time when the work they do provides opportunities for advancement and teaches useful skills, but they lose mastery motivation and become more depressed when they hold menial jobs that interfere with their schooling (Shanahan et al., 1991; Call, Mortimer, & Shanahan, 1995). And working long hours has negative effects on adolescents when their jobs are menial but not when their jobs are high quality (Barling, Rogers, & Kelloway, 1995).

Judging from this research, many adolescents who are flipping hamburgers might be better off postponing work or working only a limited number of hours so that they can concentrate on obtaining a solid education and exploring their career options (Greenberger & Steinberg, 1986). However, those adolescents lucky enough to land intellectually challenging jobs, especially jobs that tie in with their emerging vocational interests and teach them useful skills, can benefit from their work experiences.

Pathways to Adulthood

The educational paths and attainments of adolescents are partially set long before they enter adolescence. Because many individuals' IQ test scores remain stable from childhood on, some children enter adolescence with more aptitude for schoolwork than others do (see Chapter 9). Moreover, some students have more achievement motivation than others. Clearly, a bright and achievement-oriented student is more likely to obtain good grades and go on to college and is less likely to drop out of school than a student with less ability and less need to achieve. By early elementary school, and sometimes even before they enter school, future dropouts are often identifiable by such warning signs as low IQ and achievement test scores, poor grades, aggressive behavior, low socioeconomic status, and troubled homes (Ensminger & Slusarcick, 1992; Gamoran et al., 1997).

This does not mean that adolescents' fates are sealed in childhood, however; experiences during adolescence clearly make a difference. Some teenagers make the most of their intellectual abilities, whereas others who have the ability to do well in school drop out or get poor grades. The quality of an adolescent's school, the extent to which her parents are authoritative and encourage school achievement, and the extent to which her peers value school can make a big difference (Brown et al., 1993; Rutter et al., 1979; Steinberg et al., 1992).

The stakes are high. Students who achieve good grades are more likely to complete high school; recently, 91% of European American students, 84% of African American students, and an alarmingly low 63% of Hispanic students achieved this milestone (National Center for Education Statistics, 2001). They then stand a chance of being among the 34% of whites, 18% of blacks, and 10% of Hispanics who complete 4 years of college or more (Hoffman, Llagas, & Snyder, 2003). These youth, in turn, are likely to have higher career aspirations and to end up in higher-status occupations than their peers who do not attend college or do not even finish high school (McCaul et al., 1992). If their grades are good, they are likely to perform well in those jobs and advance far in their careers (Roth et al., 1996). In a real sense, then, individuals are steered along "high success" or "low success" routes starting in childhood. Depending on their own decisions and family, peer, and school influences, adolescents are more distinctly "sorted" in ways that will affect their adult lifestyles, income levels, and adjustment. Meanwhile, high school dropouts not only have less successful careers but also miss out on the beneficial effects that every year of schooling has on intellectual functioning (Ceci & Williams, 1997). In addition, they experience more psychological problems than those who stay in school (Kaplan, Damphousse, & Kaplan, 1994).

© Black Star Publishing/PictureQuest

☾ Working in fast-food restaurants is not the kind of intellectually challenging work that can contribute positively to adolescent development.

Summing Up

Achievement motivation tends to decline as children move into middle school and high school. Various factors may account for this, including family characteristics, cognitive development, more negative teacher feedback, peer pressures, puberty, and poor person–environment fit. Middle school and high school include a greater focus on science and mathematics education. U.S. students score close to the international average but below several other countries in math and science. Cross-cultural research suggests that the success of Asian schools is rooted in more class time spent on academics, more homework, more parent involvement, more peer support, and a strong belief that hard work pays off. ■

The Adult

The lives of adults are dominated by work—paid or unpaid, outside the home or within the home. What becomes of achievement motivation and literacy during the adult years? What educational options are available to adults, and what are the benefits of lifelong education?

Achievement Motivation

The level of achievement motivation that we acquire in childhood and adolescence carries into adulthood to influence our decisions and life outcomes (Wlodkowski, 1998). For instance, women who have a strong need to achieve are more likely than less achievement-oriented women to work outside the home (Krogh, 1985). Adults with strong achievement needs are also likely to be more competent workers than adults who have little concern with mastering challenges (Helmreich, Sawin, & Carsrud, 1986; Spence, 1985).

What happens to achievement motivation in later life? Is there any support for the common belief that older adults lose some of their drive to excel? Joseph Veroff, David Reuman, and Sheila Feld (1984) explored this question by analyzing motivational themes in stories that American adults told in response to pictures. Older men displayed only slightly lower levels of achievement motivation than young or middle-aged men did. Here, then, there is no support for the stereotyped idea that older adults are "unmotivated" or have ceased to pursue goals (Filipp, 1996; McAdams, de St. Aubin, & Logan, 1993).

Veroff and his associates (1984) did find that achievement motivation declined fairly steeply from age group to age group among women (see also Mellinger & Erdwins, 1985). However, this age trend pertained mainly to career-related motivation and an interest in striving for success in competitive situations. Women's motivation in other areas remains high. Many women set aside career-achievement goals after they have children and make nurturing those children their priority (Krogh, 1985). However, highly educated women often regain a strong motive to achieve outside the home once their children are older and they could invest more energy in outside work. Apparently, then, women are especially likely to be motivated to achieve career success when they have the educational background that would allow them to pursue attractive career goals and when they are not pursuing family-related goals.

Overall, adults' achievement-related motives are far more affected by changes in work and family contexts than by the aging process (Filipp, 1996). Adults of different ages are often more alike than they are different, and different people tend to retain their characteristic levels of achievement motivation over the years, much as they retain many personality traits (Stevens & Truss, 1985). There is little evidence that elderly adults inevitably lose their motivation to pursue important goals. Moreover, those elders who have a strong sense of purpose and direction and feel they are achieving their goals en-

© Gabe Palmer/CORBIS

Many older adults remain motivated to learn and seek challenging experiences.

joy greater physical and psychological well-being than those who do not (Hooker & Siegler, 1993; Rapkin & Fischer, 1992; Reker, Peacock, & Wong, 1987). Throughout the life span, then, setting and achieving goals are important.

Literacy

Literacy is the ability to use printed information to function in society, achieve goals, and develop one's potential (Kirsch et al., 1993). Few adults are completely illiterate, but many adults do not have functional literacy skills despite years of formal education. The National Adult Literacy Survey, which uses a 5-point scale to estimate literacy, finds that about 22% of adults in the United States demonstrate the lowest level of literacy skills (Kirsch et al., 1993). This is roughly equivalent to a third-grade or lower reading ability; such an adult could probably find an expiration date on a driver's license or locate a specific word or phrase in a short body of text but would have trouble filling out an application or reading a simple book to a child. Although one-quarter of this group consists of immigrants learning English as a second language, most individuals in this group are U.S.-born citizens. Nearly two-thirds did not finish high school. When the U.S. literacy rate is compared with rates in other countries, researchers find that the United States has one of the largest pockets of illiterate adults but also has some of the most highly literate adults (U.S. Department of Education, 1997). Thus, literacy in the United States is unevenly distributed.

Literacy contributes to economic security through occupational advancement. Nearly half of the adults with the lowest literacy scores live in poverty, whereas few adults with the highest literacy scores do (Bowen, 1999). Improving the literacy skills of impoverished adults, however, does not automatically raise them out of poverty. For many low-income and functionally illiterate adults, other obstacles must be overcome, including addiction, discrimination, and disabilities (Bowen, 1999).

Programs to raise the literacy level of adults are rarely successful. Several factors limit the success of such programs. For one thing, despite having limited literacy skills, many of these adults (75%) reported that they could read or write "well" or "very well"—attitudes that must make it difficult to motivate them to improve their literacy skills. Second, adults do not stay in literacy programs long enough to make improvements (Amstutz & Sheared, 2000). The dropout rate is as high as 70 to 80%, and many leave in the first weeks of the program (Quigley & Uhland, 2000). Adults who do not persist report that the programs are boring and do not meet their needs (Imel, 1996; Kerka, 1995; Quigley, 1997). Materials, for example, are often geared toward children, not adults who often have families, jobs, and different interests than children do.

Continuing Education

Increasingly, adults are seeking education beyond basic literacy skills. Nearly 40% of college students are 25 years or older, representing 15 million adults enrolled in college (National Center for Education Statistics, 1998). The number of "older" adults attending college is expected to increase as the overall population ages. Whether we call them adult learners, nontraditionals, returning students, mature students, or lifelong learners, these adults represent a diverse group. They bring different work and life experiences to the classroom, and they report a variety of reasons for enrolling in postsecondary education (Kopka & Peng, 1993).

Many "traditional" students (17- to 24-year-olds) are motivated to attend college by external expectations, but older students are often motivated by internal factors (Dinmore, 1997). Women are more likely to return to the classroom for personal enrichment or interest, whereas men are more likely to take classes required or recommended for their work (Sargant et al., 1997). The internal motivation of adult students often leads to deeper levels of processing information (Harper & Kember, 1986). In other words, returning students may put forth greater effort to truly understand material because they want to learn and want (or need) to use the material. Traditional students who do not have the benefit of experience may learn the material necessary to do well on an examination but may not process the material in ways that will lead to long-term retention.

Continued or lifelong education has its drawbacks. Mainly, it is often difficult for adults already busy with jobs and family to find the time to take classes. Successful continuing education programs must devise ways to schedule classes at convenient times and must be responsive to the lifestyles of their adult learners (Parnham, 2001). Yet the benefits of lifelong education typically outweigh drawbacks. For instance, continued education allows adults to remain knowledgeable and competitive in fields that change rapidly. Adults who return to school for bachelor's or master's degrees can also advance their careers, particularly if their education and work are closely related (Senter & Senter, 1997). Finally, higher education is associated with maintaining or improving physical and mental health (Fischer, Blazey, & Lipman, 1992).

Summing Up

Adults of different ages are similar in their levels of achievement motivation, although women who turn their attention to child rearing may lose some of their career-oriented achievement motivation. Some adults, despite years of education, have not acquired the skills of functional literacy. Literacy programs have had minimal success in improving literacy rates. Adults increasingly are seeking continued educational opportunities for both personal and work-related reasons.

In this and previous chapters, you have examined a great deal of material on thinking and learning across the life span. How can principles of cognitive development be used to improve education for all ages? Before closing this chapter, we summarize, in the Applications box on page 283, what theorists Piaget and Vygotsky contribute to education and what research on information processing, intelligence, and perception suggests about optimal learning environments. ■

Applications

What Can Theory and Research Contribute to Education?

To help you appreciate the practical implications for school reform and school achievement of the material in Chapters 6 through 9, we provide the following recommendations.

Piaget

- Provide opportunities for independent, hands-on interaction with the physical environment, especially for younger children. Children need to "see" for themselves how things work and from this construct their own understanding of the world.
- Be aware of children's cognitive strengths and limitations (their stage of development). For example, teachers and parents should recognize that a preoperational child is cognitively unable to master multidimensional or abstract tasks.
- With the child's current level of understanding in mind, create some disequilibrium by presenting new information slightly above the child's current level. Children who experience disequilibrium—cognitive discomfort with their understanding (or lack of understanding)—will work to resolve it, achieving a higher level of mastery of the material.
- Encourage interaction with peers, which will expose children to other perspectives and give them an opportunity to reevaluate and revise their own view.
- Connect abstract ideas to concrete information as much as possible.

Vygotsky

- Provide opportunities for children to interact with others who have greater mastery of the material—an older peer, teacher, or parent. These more advanced thinkers can help "pull" children to a level of understanding they would be unable to achieve on their own.
- Encourage students, especially young ones, to talk to themselves as they work on difficult tasks. Such private speech can guide behavior and facilitate thought.
- Present challenging tasks, but do not expect students to complete such tasks successfully without guidance. With support, students can accomplish more difficult tasks than those they would be able to achieve independently.
- Help children master the cognitive tools of their culture—writing, computers, and so on—so that they can function successfully in the culture.

Research on Information Processing

- Provide opportunities for rehearsal and other memory strategies to move information into long-term memory. Realize that young children do not spontaneously use memory strategies but can use them when prompted.
- Structure assignments so that retrieval cues are consistent with cues present at acquisition to facilitate retrieval of information from long-term memory.
- Enable learners to develop some knowledge base and expertise in domains of study. This means presenting "facts and figures" through readings, lectures, observations, and other appropriate methods. When beginning a new lesson, start with and build on what students already know.
- Assess the knowledge and strategies required to solve assigned problems; then determine which aspects of a task pose difficulties for learners and target these for further instruction.
- Be aware that well-learned and frequently repeated tasks become automatized over time, freeing information-processing capacity for other tasks. For example, reading is labor intensive for those new to the task, but with practice, the process of reading becomes "invisible" and learners focus their processing resources on other aspects of the task.

Research on Intelligence

- Realize that individual differences in intelligence have implications for the classroom. Students at both ends of the continuum may need special educational services to optimize their learning.
- Recognize that although IQ scores do a reasonably good job of predicting achievement in the classroom, such tests have weaknesses that limit their usefulness, especially in assessing members of minority groups.

Research on Sensory and Perceptual Abilities

- Test all children early and regularly for sensory and perceptual problems that might limit their ability to benefit from regular classroom instruction.
- Be aware of developmental differences in attention span. Clearly, a young child will not be able to attend to a task for as long as a teenager. Determine what "captures" students' attention at different ages.
- Minimize distractions in the learning environment. Younger students have trouble "tuning out" background noise and focusing on the task at hand.

Summary Points

1. The complex process of language acquisition appears to occur effortlessly through an interaction of inborn readiness and a language environment. Over the first few years of life, children master many elements of language, including phonology, semantics, morphology, syntax, and pragmatics. Language skills are refined throughout childhood and adolescence. Most language abilities remain strong throughout adulthood.

2. Precursors of achievement motivation can be seen among infants who strive to master their environments. Opportunities to succeed are important for children of all ages. Without such opportunities, children are at risk for developing a learned helplessness orientation.

3. Learning to read is typically an effortful process that relies on understanding the alphabetic principle and acquiring phonological awareness. There is a great deal of variability in reading ability among children and among adults.

4. Effective schools are characterized by a focus on academics and a good fit between the learners and the instruction they receive. Student achievement is not strongly influenced by spending, class size, ability grouping, or length of the school day or year.

5. Some students (for example, those from advantaged homes) typically outperform others, and some learning environments (especially those in which teachers create a motivating, comfortable, and task-oriented setting and involve parents in their children's schooling) are generally more conducive to learning than others. Still, what works best for one kind of student may not work as well for another kind of student.

6. Achievement motivation and grades tend to drop during adolescence for a variety of reasons. Students from Asian cultures often outperform U.S. adolescents in mathematics and science, partly because they spend many more hours a week on homework and have parents who highly value academics.

7. Level of achievement carries over from adolescence into adulthood. There may be some decline in achievement motivation among women who set aside career goals to raise children, but career goals reemerge as their children age, especially among women with higher levels of education. Some adults struggle with literacy, and some return to school.

Critical Thinking

1. Research shows that achievement motivation and grades often drop as students move through middle school and high school. Develop a program to combat this trend, keeping in mind that students of different backgrounds may lose motivation for different reasons.

2. Based on what you have learned about memory, thinking, problem solving, and language skills, how would you teach students of different ages? What would you need to do differently for the different ages?

3. Using the material on effective schools, evaluate your local school district and indicate ways it could improve to become a highly effective school.

4. What are the advantages and disadvantages of grouping children by ability versus grouping them by age in the classroom?

Key Terms

language, 255
phonology, 255
morphology, 255
syntax, 255
semantics, 255
pragmatics, 255
intonation, 256
cooing, 256
babbling, 256
joint attention, 256
holophrase, 257
vocabulary spurt, 257
overextension, 257
underextension, 257
telegraphic speech, 258
functional grammar, 258
overregularization, 259
transformational grammar, 259
decontextualized language, 259
metalinguistic awareness, 260
language acquisition device (LAD), 261
child-directed speech, 262
expansion, 263
mastery motivation, 265
mastery orientation, 268
learned helplessness orientation, 268
learning goal, 268
performance goal, 268
alphabetic principle, 269
phonological awareness, 270
emergent literacy, 270
dyslexia, 271
inclusion, 272
cooperative learning, 273
ability grouping, 274
goodness of fit, 275
literacy, 282

Media Resources

Websites to Explore

Visit Our Website

For a chapter tutorial quiz and other useful features, visit the book's companion website at *http://psychology.wadsworth.com/sigelman_rider5e*. You can also connect directly to the following sites:

Reading Instruction
From the Center for Academic and Reading Skills, Barbara Foorman and her colleagues describe their "Scientific Approach to Reading Instruction."

National Network for Child Care
This website provides information about all aspects of child development. Look for the links that relate to language development, reading, and education.

Baby Babble
The late psychologist Peter Jusczyk of Johns Hopkins University wrote a book about how children acquire language. The *Johns Hopkins Magazine* published an interesting article titled "The Origins of Babble" about Jusczyk's research.

Psychology of Language
Psychology professor Roger Kreuz at the University of Memphis maintains a web page listing psychology of language resources such as current researchers, organizations, journals, and databases.

The American Speech–Language–Hearing Association
The website of the American Speech–Language–Hearing Association posts information pages geared toward the general public. One of these pages features speech and language development.

Understanding the Data: Exercises on the Web

For additional insight on the data presented in this chapter, try the exercises for these figures at *http://psychology.wadsworth.com/sigelman_rider5e:*

Figure 10.1 The range of individual differences in vocabulary size from 16 to 30 months

Figure 10.4 Grade point average from 1st grade to 12th grade for students with high and low risk and IQ

Life-Span CD-ROM

Go to the Wadsworth Life-Span CD-ROM for further study of the concepts in this chapter. The CD-ROM includes narrated concept overviews, video clips, a multimedia glossary, and additional activities to expand your learning experience. For this chapter, check out the following clips, and others, in the video library:

VIDEO Early and Middle Childhood: Language Development

VIDEO Learning Deaf Language

DEVELOPMENTAL PsychologyNow™

Developmental PsychologyNow is a web-based, intelligent study system that provides a complete package of diagnostic quizzes, a personalized study plan, integrated multimedia elements, and learning modules. Check it out at *http://psychology.wadsworth.com/sigelman_rider5e/now.*

CHAPTER e l e v e n

Self and Personality

UNTIL RECENTLY, I TRIED to establish my identity by acquiring the interests of the people I dated. I enjoyed heavy metal music when I was dating a headbanger. If I dated someone who smoked, I also smoked. Eventually I became more secure with my identity. I no longer feel the need to acquire someone else's interests in order to stabilize or prolong a relationship.

The college student who wrote this is describing how she changed in the process of finding her identity. In what ways have you changed as a person over the years? In what ways have you remained the same? If you have changed considerably, why do you think that is? If you feel like "the same old person," what might account for that? Finally, project ahead: What do you think you will be like as a person when you are 70, and why?

Do humans remain "the same people" in most significant respects, or do they undergo dramatic transformations in personality from infancy to old age? The issue of continuity (stability) and discontinuity (change) in the individual is central in the study of human development (see Chapter 2). This chapter is about the ways in which personalities, and perceptions of those personalities, change—and remain the same—over the life span; it is also about the implications of personality for adjustment. We begin by clarifying some terms and laying out key theoretical perspectives on personality. Then you will see how self-perceptions and aspects of temperament and personality change from infancy to old age.

Conceptualizing the Self

Personality is often defined as an organized combination of attributes, motives, values, and behaviors unique to each individual. Most people describe personalities in terms of personality traits—dispositions such as sociability, independence, dominance, and so on. Traits are assumed to be relatively consistent across different situations and over time; if you peg a classmate as insecure, you expect this person to behave insecurely at school and at work, now and next year.

When you describe yourself, you may not be describing your personality so much as revealing your **self-concept**—your perceptions, positive or negative, of your unique attributes and traits. We all know people who seem to have unrealistic self-conceptions—the fellow who thinks he is "God's gift to women" (who do not agree) or the woman who believes she is a dull plodder (but is actually brilliant). A closely related aspect of self-perception is **self-esteem**—your overall evaluation of your worth as a person, high or low, based on all the positive and negative self-perceptions that make up your self-concept. Self-concept is about "what I am," whereas self-esteem concerns "how good I am" (Harter, 1999). This chapter examines how self-concept and self-esteem change and remain the same over the life span. It also takes up the question of how adolescents pull together their various self-perceptions to form an **identity**—an overall sense of who they are, where they are heading, and where they fit into society.

Summing Up

Personality is an organized combination of attributes unique to the individual. Self-concept is an individual's perception of those attributes, whereas self-esteem is his overall evaluation of his worth, and identity is a sense of who he is, where he is going, and how he fits in society. ■

Perspectives on Personality Development

To get a feel for current debates about the nature of personality development, look at the striking differences among three major theoretical perspectives on the nature of personality and personality development: psychoanalytic theory, trait theory, and social learning theory.

Psychoanalytic Theory

Psychoanalytic theorists generally use in-depth interviews, dream analysis, and similar techniques to get below the surface of the person and her behavior and to understand the inner dynamics of personality. As you should recall from Chapter 2, Sigmund Freud believed that biological urges residing within the id push all children through universal stages of psychosexual development, starting with the oral stage of infancy and ending with the genital stage of adolescence. Freud did not see psychosexual growth continuing during adulthood. He believed that the personality was formed during the first 5 years of life and showed considerable continuity thereafter. Anxieties arising from harsh parenting, overindulgence, or other unfavorable early experiences, he said, would leave a permanent mark on the personality and reveal themselves in adult personality traits.

The psychosocial theory of personality development formulated by neo-Freudian Erik Erikson was also introduced in Chapter 2 and will be highlighted in this chapter. Like Freud, Erikson concerned himself with the inner dynamics of personality and proposed that the personality evolves through systematic stages that confront people with different challenges (Erikson 1963, 1968, 1982). Compared with Freud, however, Erikson placed more emphasis on social influences such as peers, teachers, and cultures; the rational ego and its adaptive powers; possibilities for overcoming the effects of harmful early experiences; and the potential for growth during the adult years. Later in this chapter, you will encounter the work of Daniel Levinson and colleagues (1978), a psychoanalytic theorist best known for saying that adults experience a midlife crisis.

Erikson and Levinson clearly did not agree with Freud that the personality is largely formed by the end of early childhood; they appreciated possibilities for personality change

© Jose Luis Pelaez, Inc./CORBIS

Do you share Sigmund Freud's belief that the personality is formed during the first 5 years of life?

and development throughout the life span. Yet Freud, Erikson, and other psychoanalytic theorists agreed on this: people everywhere progress through the same stages of personality development, undergoing similar personality changes at similar ages.

Trait Theory

The approach to personality that has most strongly influenced efforts to study it is trait theory, based on the psychometric approach that guided the development of intelligence tests (see Chapter 9). According to this approach, personality is a set of trait dimensions along which people can differ (for example, sociable–unsociable, responsible–irresponsible). (You may want to complete the brief personality scale in the Explorations box on page 289 before reading further.) To identify distinct trait dimensions, researchers construct personality scales and use the statistical technique of factor analysis to identify groupings of personality scale items that are correlated with each other but not with other groupings of items. Trait theorists assume that personality traits are relatively enduring; like psychoanalytic theorists, they expect to see carryover in personality over the years. Unlike psychoanalytic theorists, however, they do not believe that the personality unfolds in a series of stages.

How many personality trait dimensions are there? Just as scholars have disagreed about how many distinct mental abilities exist, they have disagreed about how many personality dimensions exist. However, a consensus is forming around the idea that human personalities can be described in terms of five major dimensions, called the **Big Five** (Digman, 1990; McCrae & Costa, 2003). These five personality dimensions—openness to experience, conscientiousness, extraversion, agreeableness, and neuroticism—have emerged from factor analyses of personality scales and are described in Table 11.1. If you score the personality scale in the Explorations box on page 289, you will get a rough sense of where you fall on the Big Five trait dimensions.

There is evidence that all five of the Big Five trait dimensions are genetically influenced and that they are at least roughly related to dimensions of temperament evident in infancy (McCrae & Costa, 2003). The Big Five also seem to be universal; they capture personality differences in cultures with different parenting styles, value systems, and languages (McCrae, 2004; McCrae et al., 2000). This is true even though levels of Big Five traits differ from culture to culture (for example, Europeans appear to be more extroverted on average

Table 11.1 The Big Five Personality Dimensions

Dimension	Basic Definition	Key Characteristics
Openness to experience	Curiosity and interest in variety vs. preference for sameness	Openness to fantasy, esthetics, feelings, actions, ideas, values
Conscientiousness	Discipline and organization vs. lack of seriousness	Competence, order, dutifulness, striving for achievement, self-discipline, deliberation
Extraversion	Sociability and outgoingness vs. introversion	Warmth, gregariousness, assertiveness, activity, seeking excitement, positive emotions
Agreeableness	Compliance and cooperativeness vs. suspiciousness	Trust, straightforwardness, altruism, compliance, modesty, tender-mindedness
Neuroticism	Emotional instability vs. stability	Anxiety, hostility, depression, self-consciousness, impulsiveness, vulnerability

As a mnemonic device, notice that the first letters of the dimensions spell *ocean.*

Explorations

A Brief Personality Scale

Here are several personality traits that may or may not apply to you. Write a number next to each statement to indicate the extent to which you agree or disagree with that statement. You should rate the extent to which the pair of traits applies to you, even if one characteristic applies more strongly than the other.

1 = Disagree strongly
2 = Disagree moderately
3 = Disagree a little
4 = Neither agree nor disagree
5 = Agree a little
6 = Agree moderately
7 = Agree strongly

I see myself as:

1. ______ Extraverted, enthusiastic
2. ______ Critical, quarrelsome
3. ______ Dependable, self-disciplined
4. ______ Anxious, easily upset
5. ______ Open to new experiences, complex
6. ______ Reserved, quiet
7. ______ Sympathetic, warm
8. ______ Disorganized, careless
9. ______ Calm, emotionally stable
10. ______ Conventional, uncreative

To score yourself, reverse the scoring of items marked here with *R* so that a score of 1 becomes 7, 2 becomes 6, 3 becomes 5, 4 stays 4, 5 becomes 3, 6 becomes 2, and 7 becomes 1. Then add the pair of scores listed here for each of the Big Five personality dimensions:

Extraversion = Item 1 + item 6R = ______

Agreeableness = Item 2R + item 7 = ______

Conscientiousness = Item 3 + item 8R = ______

Low neuroticism (high emotional stability) = Item 4R + item 9 = ______

Openness to experience = Item 5 + item 10R = ______

To help you see where you stand, mean scores for a sample of 1813 individuals tested by Samuel Gosling and colleagues (2003) were 4.44 for extraversion, 5.23 for agreeableness, 5.40 for conscientiousness, 4.83 for low neuroticism (high emotional stability), and 5.38 for openness to experience.

SOURCE: Gosling, Rentfrow, & Swann, 2003, p. 525.

than Asians or Africans) and even though traits may be expressed differently in different cultures. You will soon see what happens to these trait dimensions as we age.

Social Learning Theory

Finally, social learning (or social cognitive) theorists such as Albert Bandura (1986) and Walter Mischel (1973; Mischel & Shoda, 1995; Shoda & Mischel, 2000) not only reject the notion of universal stages of personality development but also have questioned the existence of enduring personality traits that show themselves in a variety of situations and over long stretches of the life span. Instead, they emphasize that people change if their environments change. An aggressive boy can become a warm and caring man if his aggression is no longer reinforced; a woman who has been socially withdrawn can become more outgoing if she begins to socialize with friends who serve as models of outgoing, sociable behavior. From this perspective, personality is a set of behavioral tendencies shaped by interactions with other people in specific social situations.

Social learning theorists believe strongly in situational influences on behavior (Shoda & Mischel, 2000). They argue that consistency over time in personality is most likely if the social environment remains the same. Thus, if Rick the rancher continues to run the same ranch in the same small town for a lifetime, he might stay the "same old Rick." However, most of us experience changes in our social environments as we become older. Just as we behave differently when we are in a library than when we are at a party, we become "different people" as we take on new roles, develop new relationships, or move to new locations.

An excellent example of this principle comes from research on the relationship between birth order and personality. How would you characterize firstborns? Second-borns? Last-borns? Many of us have strong beliefs about the differences; we think of firstborns as bossy and dominant, for example, and last-borns as rebellious and spoiled. Yet most research reveals few consistent differences between the personalities of firstborns and those of later-borns (Harris, 2000b). Why might we be misled into thinking such differences exist? Judith Rich Harris (2000b) notes that we see members of our families in a family context and observe real differences in personality in that context. Firstborns often are bossy when they baby-sit younger siblings, for example. However, the differences are created by the family context and do not necessarily carry over into other situations. Thus, for example, the same firstborn may not be bossy in interactions with peers who are similar in age and competence and cannot be pushed around as easily as younger brothers and sisters. Different context, different personality.

To the social learning theorist, then, personality development is an individual process whose direction depends on each person's social experiences and social environments. Theorists who adopt a contextual–systems perspective on development (see Chapter 2) make similar assumptions. Contextual theorists are likely to say that personality traits, considered apart from the social contexts that shape and give meaning to a person's actions, are meaningless abstractions.

This chapter explores continuity and discontinuity in self-conceptions and personality traits across the life span. When do infants become aware of themselves as unique individuals, and when do they begin to display unique personalities? What influences how children perceive and evaluate themselves, and to what extent can we detect in them the personalities they will have as adults? How do adolescents go about finding their identities as individuals? Finally, do people's personalities and self-perceptions change systematically over the adult years, or do they remain essentially the same, and what does it all mean for their adjustment?

Summing Up

Psychoanalytic theorists, trait theorists, and social learning theorists do not see eye to eye about what personality is and how it develops. Psychoanalytic theorists explore the inner dynamics of personality and propose universal, age-related personality changes. Freud believed that the personality emerges in the first 5 years and remains largely stable thereafter, whereas Erikson and Levinson saw more discontinuity and believed that stagelike personality changes occur throughout the life span. Trait theorists, based on factor analyses of responses to personality scales, emphasize the continuity of major dimensions of personality such as the Big Five (openness to experience, conscientiousness, extraversion, agreeableness, and neuroticism). Social learning and contextual theorists question the existence of traits and call attention to the potential for discontinuity in personality across situations and over time. ■

The Infant

When do infants display an awareness that they exist and a sense of themselves as distinct individuals? We will explore this issue and then see whether there is evidence that infants have unique "personalities."

The Emerging Self

Psychoanalytic theorist Margaret Mahler (Mahler, Pine, & Bergman, 1975) likened the newborn to a "chick in an egg" that had no reason to differentiate itself from its surrounding environment. Development, to Mahler, was about "hatching," differentiating self from other, especially mother, and dealing with tensions between being separate from and one with other people. Finding a sense of self, she believed, happened in the context of the parent–child relationship.

As it turns out, infants may be born without a sense of self, but they quickly develop an implicit, if not conscious, sense of self through their perceptions of their bodies and actions (Rochat & Striano, 2000). The capacity to differentiate self from world becomes even more apparent in the first 2 or 3 months of life as infants discover that they can cause things to happen. For example, 2-month-old infants whose arms are connected by strings to audiovisual equipment delight in producing the sight of a smiling infant's face and the theme from *Sesame Street* by pulling the strings (Lewis, Alessandri, & Sullivan, 1990). When the strings are disconnected and they can no longer produce such effects, they pull harder and become frustrated and angry. Over the first 6 months of life, then, infants discover properties of their physical selves, distinguish between the self and the rest of the world, and appreciate that they can act upon other people and objects (Thompson, 1998).

In the second half of their first year, infants realize that they and their companions are separate beings with different perspectives, ones that can be shared (Thompson, 1998). This is illustrated by the phenomenon of *joint attention,* in which infants about 9 months or older and their caregivers share perceptual experiences by looking at the same object at the same time (Mitchell, 1997). When an infant points at an object and looks toward her companions in an effort to focus their attention on the object, she shows awareness that self and other do not always share the same perceptions.

Around 18 months, infants recognize themselves visually as distinct individuals. To establish this, Michael Lewis and Jeanne Brooks-Gunn (1979) used an ingenious technique first used with chimpanzees to study **self-recognition**—the ability to recognize oneself in a mirror or photograph. Mother daubs a spot of rouge on an infant's nose and then places the infant in front of a mirror. If the infant has some mental image of his own face and recognizes his mirror image as himself, he should soon notice the red spot and reach for or wipe his own nose rather than the nose of the mirror image. When infants 9 to 24 months old were given this rouge test, the youngest infants showed no self-recognition: they seemed to treat the image in the mirror as if it were "some other kid." Some 15-month-olds recognized themselves, but only among 18- to 24-month-olds did most infants show clear evidence of self-recognition. They touched their noses rather than the mirror, apparently realizing that they had a strange mark on their faces that warranted investigation. They knew exactly who that kid in the mirror was. At the time they first pass the "rouge test" of self-recognition, infants also take more interest

© Joseph Pobereskin/Getty Images

☾ Does this boy know that he is the fascinating tot in the mirror? Probably not if he is younger than 18 months, which is about when self-recognition is mastered by most toddlers.

in watching a video of themselves than in watching a video of another infant, whereas younger infants often seem to be more interested in other babies than in themselves (Nielsen, Dissanayake, & Kashima, 2003).

As babies learn to recognize themselves, they also form a **categorical self**; that is, they classify themselves into social categories based on age, sex, and other visible characteristics, figuring out what is "like me" and what is "not like me." Before they are 18 months old, toddlers can tell themselves apart from toddlers of the other sex or from older individuals but are less able to distinguish between photos of themselves and photos of other infants of the same sex. As they approach age 2, they also master this task (Brooks-Gunn & Lewis, 1981; Lewis & Brooks-Gunn, 1979). By 18 to 24 months, then, most infants have an awareness of who they are—at least as a physical self with a unique appearance and as a categorical self belonging to specific age and gender categories. They even begin to use their emerging language skills to talk about themselves and to construct stories about events in their lives, past and present (Thompson, 1998).

What does it take to become self-aware? First, the ability to recognize the self depends on *cognitive development* (Bertenthal & Fischer, 1978). Mentally retarded children are slow to recognize themselves in a mirror but can do so once they have attained a mental age of at least 18 months (Hill & Tomlin, 1981). Second, self-awareness depends on *social experiences*. Chimpanzees who have been raised without contact with other chimps fail to recognize themselves in a mirror as normal chimps do (Gallup, 1979). Moreover, human toddlers who have formed secure attachments to their parents are better able to recognize themselves in a mirror and know more about their names and genders than do toddlers whose relationships are less secure (Pipp, Easterbrooks, & Harmon, 1992).

The critical role of social interaction in the development of the self was appreciated long ago by Charles Cooley (1902) and George Herbert Mead (1934). Cooley used the term **looking-glass self** to emphasize that our understanding of self is a reflection of how other people respond to us; that is, our self-concepts are the images cast by a social mirror. Through their actions and words, parents and other companions communicate to infants that they are babies and are either girls or boys. Later, social feedback helps children determine what they are like and what they can and cannot do well. Throughout life, we forge new self-concepts from the social feedback we receive, good or bad (Harter, 1999). Thus the development of the self is closely related to both cognitive development and social interaction, beginning in infancy.

Awareness of the self paves the way for many important emotional and social developments. Toddlers who recognize themselves in the mirror are more able than those who do not to talk about themselves and to assert their wills (DesRosiers et al., 1999). They are more likely to experience self-conscious emotions such as embarrassment—for example, if asked to show off by dancing in front of strangers (Lewis et al., 1989). Toddlers who have gained self-awareness are also more able to coordinate their own perspectives with those of other individuals—for example, to communicate with their playmates by imitating their actions (Asendorpf, Warkentin, & Baudonnière, 1996) or to cooperate with peers to achieve common goals such as retrieving toys from containers (Brownell & Carriger, 1990).

Temperament

Even though it takes infants some time to become aware of themselves as individuals, they are individuals with distinctive personalities from the first weeks of life. The study of infant personality has centered on dimensions of temperament—early, genetically based tendencies to respond in predictable ways to events that serve as the building blocks of personality. Learning theorists have tended to view babies as "blank slates" who can be shaped in any number of directions by their experiences. However, it is now clear that babies differ from the start in characteristics such as how they react to stimuli (for example, whether they smile or fuss and how strongly) and how they regulate these reactions (for example, whether they attend to arousing stimuli or avoid them; Rothbart, Ahadi, & Evans, 2000). Temperament has been defined and measured in several ways, as you will now see.

Emotionality, Activity, and Sociability

Arnold Buss and Robert Plomin (1984) have called attention to three dimensions of temperament: **emotionality, activity,** and **sociability.** Some babies are more emotionally reactive, or easily and intensely irritated by events, than others are. Some are highly active; others are relatively sluggish. Some are very sociable, or interested in and responsive to people; others are more standoffish. Behavioral genetics research on twins and adopted children shows that these three aspects of temperament are partly influenced by genetic endowment. Identical twins have similar temperaments, whereas fraternal twins hardly resemble each other (Buss & Plomin, 1984; Rowe, 1994). Growing up in the same home does little to make adoptive brothers and sisters alike in these aspects of temperament, but the individual's unique experiences have an effect (Schmitz et al., 1996).

Behavioral Inhibition

Jerome Kagan and his colleagues identified another aspect of early temperament that they believe is highly significant—**behavioral inhibition,** or the tendency to be extremely shy, restrained, and distressed in response to unfamiliar people and situations (Kagan, 1994, 2003; Reznick et al., 1986). In the language of Buss and Plomin, inhibited children could be considered extremely high in emotionality and low in sociability. Kagan (1989) estimates that about 15% of toddlers have this inhibited temperament, whereas 10% are extremely uninhibited, eager to jump into new situations.

At 4 months, infants who will turn into inhibited toddlers wriggle and fuss and fret more than most infants in response to new sights and sounds such as a moving mobile (Fox et al., 2001). At 21 months, they take a long time to warm up to a strange examiner, retreat from unfamiliar objects such as a large robot, and fret and cling to their mothers, whereas uninhibited toddlers readily and enthusiastically interact with strangers, robots, and all manner of new experiences (Kagan, 1994). In follow-up tests at $5\frac{1}{2}$ and $7\frac{1}{2}$ years of age, children who were highly inhibited as toddlers proved more likely than those who had been uninhibited to be shy in a group of strange peers and to be afraid to try a balance beam. Overall, of the children who had maintained the same temperament from age 2 to age 7, about half still had the same temperament by adolescence, suggesting a fair amount of continuity in this dimension of temperament (Kagan, 1994).

Kagan and his colleagues have concluded that behavioral inhibition is biologically rooted. They have found that youngsters with an inhibited temperament show distinctive physiological reactions to novel events; for example, they become highly aroused (as indicated by high heart rates) in situations that barely faze other children (Kagan, 1994). Even as adults, individuals who were inhibited toddlers show stronger responses to novel faces in the part of the brain called the amygdala than do adults who were uninhibited early in life, whereas they respond no differently to familiar faces (Schwartz et al., 2003). Finally, behavioral inhibition is genetically influenced. In one study (DiLalla, Kagan, & Reznick, 1994), the correlation between the inhibition scores of identical twins was +0.82, and that for fraternal twins +0.47. Possibly, genes affect temperament by influencing the development of the nervous system and the way it responds to stimuli.

Yet genes and environment interact. Kagan and his colleagues also found that if the parents of inhibited children overprotect their sensitive children from stress, or if they become angry and impatient with their timid children's behavior, these children do not learn to control their inhibition as they develop and they remain inhibited. By contrast, when parents prepare inhibited youngsters for potentially upsetting experiences, then make reasonable but firm demands that they cope, early inhibition may be overcome (Kagan, 1994).

© A. Ramey/PhotoEdit

Children with an inhibited temperament are not sure they want to try new experiences.

Easiness and Difficultness

Finally, researchers have learned much about infant temperament from the classic work of Alexander Thomas, Stella Chess, and their colleagues (Chess & Thomas, 1999; Thomas & Chess, 1986). These researchers gathered information about nine dimensions of infant behavior, including typical mood, regularity or predictability of biological functions such as feeding and sleeping habits, tendency to approach or withdraw from new stimuli, intensity of emotional reactions, and adaptability to new experiences and changes in routine. Based on the overall patterning of these temperamental qualities, most infants could be placed into one of three categories (Table 11.2):

- **Easy temperament.** Easy infants are even tempered, typically content or happy, and open and adaptable to new experiences such as the approach of a stranger or their first taste of strained plums. They have regular feeding and sleeping habits, and they tolerate frustrations and discomforts.
- **Difficult temperament.** Difficult infants are active, irritable, and irregular in their habits. They often react negatively (and vigorously) to changes in routine and are slow to adapt to new people or situations. They cry frequently and loudly and often have tantrums when they are frustrated by such events as being restrained or having to live with a dirty diaper.

Table 11.2 Summary of Temperament Categories

Researchers	Dimension
Buss and Plomin	Emotionality Activity Sociability
Kagan	Behaviorally inhibited temperament Uninhibited temperament
Thomas and Chess	Easy temperament Difficult temperament Slow-to-warm-up temperament

- **Slow-to-warm-up temperament.** Slow-to-warm-up infants are relatively inactive, somewhat moody, and only moderately regular in their daily schedules. Like difficult infants, they are slow to adapt to new people and situations, but they typically respond in mildly, rather than intensely, negative ways. For example, they may resist cuddling by looking away from the cuddler rather than by kicking or screaming. They eventually adjust, showing a quiet interest in new foods, people, or places.

Of the infants in Thomas and Chess's longitudinal study of temperament, 40% were easy infants, 10% were difficult infants, and 15% were slow-to-warm-up infants, The remaining third could not be clearly placed in one category because they shared qualities of two or more categories. Thomas and Chess went on to study the extent of continuity and discontinuity in temperament from infancy to early adulthood (Chess & Thomas, 1984; Thomas & Chess, 1986). Difficult infants who had fussed when they could not have more milk often became children who fell apart if they could not work mathematics problems correctly. By adulthood, however, an individual's adjustment had little to do with her temperament during infancy, suggesting a good deal of discontinuity over this long time span. Apparently, many easy infants turn into maladjusted adults, and many difficult infants outgrow their behavioral problems. Both continuity and discontinuity in temperament are evident (Guerin et al., 2003).

Goodness of Fit

Differences in temperament appear to be rooted in genetically based differences in levels of certain neurotransmitters and in the functioning of the brain (Ebstein, Benjamin, & Belmaker, 2003). But what determines whether temperamental qualities persist? Much may depend on what Thomas and Chess call the **goodness of fit** between child and environment—the extent to which the child's temperament is compatible with the demands and expectations of the social world to which he must adapt. A good example comes from observations of the Masai of East Africa (DeVries, 1984). In most settings, an easy temperament is likely to be more adaptive than a difficult one, but among the Masai during famine, babies with difficult temperaments outlived easy babies. Why? Perhaps because Masai parents believe that difficult babies are future warriors or perhaps because babies who cry loud and long get noticed and fed. As this example suggests, a particular temperament may be a good fit to the demands of one environment but maladaptive under other circumstances. The goodness-of-fit concept is an excellent example of the theme that individual predispositions and the environment interact to influence developmental outcomes.

Explorations

Goodness of Fit and the Case of Carl

The case of Carl illustrates the significance for later personality development of the match between a child's temperament and his social environment. Early in life, Carl was one of the most difficult children Stella Chess and Alexander Thomas had ever encountered: "Whether it was the first bath or the first solid foods in infancy, the beginning of nursery and elementary school, or the first birthday parties or shopping trips, each experience evoked stormy responses, with loud crying and struggling to get away" (1984, p. 188). Carl's mother became convinced that she was a bad parent, but his father accepted and even delighted in Carl's "lusty" behavior. He patiently and supportively waited for Carl to adapt to new situations. As a result, Carl did not develop serious behavioral problems as a child.

Carl's difficult temperament came out in force when he entered college and had to adapt to a new environment. He became extremely frustrated and thought about dropping out but eventually reduced his course load and got through this difficult period successfully. By age 23, he was no longer considered by the researchers to have a difficult temperament. How different his later personality and adjustment might have been had the fit between his difficult temperament and his parents' demands and expectations been poor. When children have difficult temperaments and grow up with parents who cannot control their behavior effectively, they are likely to have serious behavioral problems as children and adolescents (Guerin et al., 2003; Maziade et al., 1990). Clearly, then, healthy personality development depends on the goodness of fit between child and home environment. The moral for parents is clear: get to know your baby as an individual, and allow for his personality quirks.

The difficult children studied by Chess and Thomas (1999), like Kagan's inhibited toddlers, often continued to display difficult temperaments later in life if the person–environment fit was bad—for example, if their parents were impatient and overly demanding with them. However, difficult infants whose parents adapted to their temperaments and gave them more time to adjust to new experiences enjoyed a good fit to the environment and became able to master new situations effectively and energetically (see the Explorations box on page 293).

Parents' personalities and perceptions help determine whether an infant's home environment is a good or poor fit to her personality. Mothers who are low in empathy tend to use threats and physical force with infants who show a lot of negative emotion, perhaps because they cannot understand why these babies are so irritable (Clark, Kochanska, & Ready, 2000). By contrast, mothers who are high in empathy are able to refrain from strong-arm tactics even when they are faced with an irritable child. They are therefore able to provide care that is a better fit to the child's difficult temperament. Similarly, whereas parents who perceive their infants to be high in negative emotionality may strengthen their infants' tendencies to be irritable, parents who perceive their babies' temperaments more positively may contribute to a more sunny disposition over time (Pauli-Pott et al., 2003). Infants' temperaments and their parents' parenting behaviors reciprocally influence and interact over time to steer the direction of later personality development (Sanson, Hemphill, & Smart, 2004). Teaching parents of irritable babies how to interpret their infants' cues and respond sensitively and appropriately to them can produce calmer infants who cry less and become less irritable preschoolers than temperamentally similar children whose mothers do not receive training (van den Boom, 1995; Crockenberg & Leerkes, 2003).

Summing Up

In sum, 2- to 3-month-olds discover they are physically distinct from the world around them and can act upon it. By 18 to 24 months, toddlers show self-awareness by recognizing themselves in a mirror, and they form a categorical self. Cognitive development and experiences with the social looking glass make this new self-awareness possible. Moreover, each toddler has distinct temperamental qualities sketched in the genetic code and expressed from the first days of life—qualities such as emotionality, activity, and sociability; behavioral inhibition; and an easy, difficult, or slow-to-warm-up temperament (see Table 11.2). However, the personality is by no means set in infancy; there is both continuity and discontinuity in development. Early temperamental qualities may or may not be elaborated into later personality traits, depending on the goodness of fit between the individual's predispositions and his social environment and on the kinds of transactions that take place between child and significant others. ■

The Child

Children's personalities continue to form, and children acquire much richer understandings of themselves as individuals, as they continue to experience cognitive growth and interact with other people. Ask children of different ages to tell you about themselves. You will find their responses amusing, and you will learn something about how children come to know themselves as individuals.

Elaborating on a Sense of Self

Once toddlers begin to talk, they can and do tell us about their emerging self-concepts. By age 2, some toddlers are already using the personal pronouns *I, me, my,* and *mine* (or their names) when referring to the self and *you* when addressing a companion (Lewis & Brooks-Gunn, 1979; Stipek, Gralinski, & Kopp, 1990). Toddlers also show their emerging categorical selves when they describe themselves in terms of age and sex ("Katie big girl").

The preschool child's self-concept is concrete and physical (Damon & Hart, 1988). Asked to describe themselves, preschoolers dwell on their physical characteristics ("I look like a kid. I have skin. I have clothes."), their possessions ("I have a bike."), their physical activities and accomplishments ("I can jump."), and their preferences ("I like cake."). One exuberant 3-year-old said the following (Harter, 1999, p. 37):

> I'm 3 years old and I live in a big house with my mother and father and my brother, Jason, and my sister, Lisa. I have blue eyes and a kitty that is orange and a television in my own room. I know all of my ABC's, listen: A, B, C, D, E, F, G, H, J, L, K,O, M, P, Q, X, Z. I can run real fast. I like pizza and I have a nice teacher at preschool. I can count up to 100, want to hear me? I love my dog Skipper.

Few young children mention their psychological traits or inner qualities. At most, young children use global terms such

© Ariel Skelley/CORBIS

Preschool children emphasize the "active self" in their self-descriptions, noting things they can do but saying little about their psychological traits.

as *nice* or *mean* and *good* or *bad,* to describe themselves and others (Livesley & Bromley, 1973). However, their descriptions of their characteristic behavioral patterns and preferences ("I like to play by myself at school") may provide the foundation for their later personality trait descriptions ("I'm shy"; Eder, 1989).

Self-conceptions become more sophisticated around age 8, partly because of cognitive development (Harter, 2003). First, children begin to form social identities, defining themselves as part of social units ("I'm a Kimball, a second-grader at Brookside School, a Brownie Scout"; Damon & Hart, 1988). Second, they begin to describe their enduring inner qualities using personality trait terms such as *funny* and *smart* (Harter, 1999; Livesley & Bromley, 1973). Third, they are now capable of **social comparison**—of using information about how they compare with other individuals to characterize and evaluate themselves (Pomerantz et al., 1995). The preschooler who said she could hit a baseball becomes the elementary-school child who says she is a better batter than her teammates.

Young children often seem oblivious to information about how they compare with others and seem to have difficulty interpreting and acting on such information when they receive it (Butler, 1990; Ruble, 1983). They tend to believe that they are the greatest, even in the face of compelling evidence that they have been outclassed. By contrast, first-grade children glance at each other's papers, ask "How many did you miss?," say things like "I got more right than you did," and, in the process, learn about their strengths and weaknesses (Frey & Ruble, 1985; Pomerantz et al., 1995).

The looking-glass self takes shape as children receive social feedback from the people around them.

Although social comparison generally becomes more common with age, the extent to which children engage in social comparison is greatly influenced by the sociocultural context. Social comparison is common in the United States because parents, teachers, and others place heavy emphasis on individual achievement. However, Israeli children living in communal kibbutzim do less of it than children raised in Israeli cities, perhaps because cooperation and teamwork are so strongly emphasized in the kibbutzim (Butler & Ruzany, 1993).

Self-Esteem

As children amass a range of perceptions of themselves and engage in social comparisons, they begin to evaluate their worth. Susan Harter (1999, 2003) has developed self-perception scales for use across the life span and has found that preschool children distinguish two broad aspects of self-esteem: their competence (both physical and cognitive) and their personal and social adequacy (for example, their social acceptance). By mid–elementary school, children differentiate among five aspects of self-worth, all measured by Harter's self-perception scale: scholastic competence (feeling smart or doing well in school); social acceptance (being popular or feeling liked); behavioral conduct (staying out of trouble); athletic competence (being good at sports); and physical appearance (feeling good-looking). When Harter's scale was given to third- through ninth-graders, even third-graders showed that they had well-defined positive or negative feelings about themselves. Moreover, children made clear distinctions between their competency in one area and their competency in another. They did not just have generally high or generally low self-esteem.

This suggests that self-esteem is multidimensional rather than unidimensional. As children organize their perceptions of themselves over the elementary-school years, they differentiate more sharply among distinct aspects of the self-concept. Self-esteem is also hierarchical in nature; children integrate self-perceptions in distinct domains to form an overall, abstract sense of self-worth (Harter, 1999; Marsh & Ayotte, 2003). Figure 11.1 shows the kind of self-esteem hierarchy that results, with global self-worth at the top and specific dimensions of self-concept below it.

The accuracy of children's self-evaluations increases steadily over the elementary-school years (Marsh, Craven, & Debus, 1999; Harter, 1999). Children as young as 5 already have some sense of whether they are worthy and lovable (Verschueren, Buyck, & Marcoen, 2001). However, the self-esteem scores of young children (4- to 7-year-olds) sometimes reflect their desires to be liked or to be good at various activities as much as they reveal their competencies. Overall, they

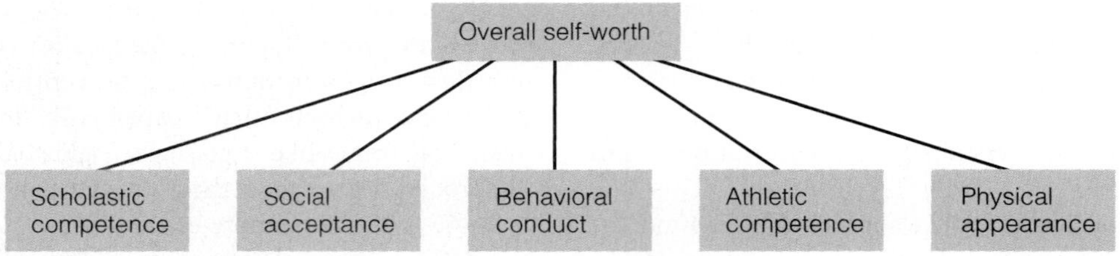

Figure 11.1 The multidimensional and hierarchical nature of self-esteem.
SOURCE: Harter (1996).

tend to have unrealistically positive views of themselves (Eccles, Wigfield, et al., 1993; Harter & Pike, 1984).

Starting about age 8, partly because of cognitive development, children's self-evaluations become more accurate. For example, those with high scholastic self-esteem are more likely than those with low scholastic self-esteem to be rated as intellectually competent by their teachers, and those with high athletic self-esteem are frequently chosen by peers in sporting events (Harter, 1999). At the same time, children are increasingly realizing what they "should" be like and are forming an ever-grander **ideal self.** As a result, the gap between the real self and the ideal self increases with age, and older children run a greater risk than younger children do of thinking that they fall short of what they could or should be (Glick & Zigler, 1985; Oosterwegel & Oppenheimer, 1993).

Influences on Self-Esteem

Why do some children have higher self-esteem than others? It is simple: Some children are more competent than others, and, apart from their competence, some children receive more positive social feedback than others (Harter, 1999). Children who are more capable and socially attractive than other children experience more success in areas important to them and come out better in social comparisons (Luster & McAdoo, 1995). For example, achievement in school has a positive effect on academic self-concept; a positive academic self-concept, in turn, contributes to future academic achievement (Guay, Marsh, & Boivin, 2003).

Apart from competence, social feedback from parents, teachers, and peers plays a critical role in shaping self-perceptions. Most notably, children with high self-esteem tend to be securely attached to parents who are warm and democratic (Arbona & Power, 2003; Coopersmith, 1967). Parents who are loving, form secure attachments with their children, and frequently communicate approval and acceptance help their children think positively about themselves (Doyle, Markiewicz, et al., 2000). Saying, through words, looks, or actions, "You're not important" or "Why can't you be more like your older brother?" is likely to have the opposite effect. This is the concept of the looking-glass self in action: children will form self-concepts that reflect the evaluations of significant people in their lives.

Parents whose children have high self-esteem also enforce clearly stated rules of behavior and allow their children to express their opinions and participate in decision making. This democratic parenting style most likely gives children a firm basis for evaluating their behavior and sends them the message that their opinions are respected. The relationship between high self-esteem and a warm, democratic parenting style has been observed in most ethnic groups in the United States and in other countries (Scott, Scott, & McCabe, 1991; Steinberg, Dornbusch, & Brown, 1992). Interestingly, children with high self-esteem may also contribute to their own high self-esteem by actively seeking positive feedback; children with low self-esteem do not seem as hungry for pats on the back and therefore may not get as many (Cassidy et al., 2003).

The judgments of other people, with all the information that children collect by observing their own behavior and comparing it with that of their peers, shape children's overall self-evaluations. Once a child's level of self-esteem has been established, it tends to remain stable over the elementary-school years. Moreover, high self-esteem is positively correlated with a variety of measures of good adjustment (Coopersmith, 1967; Harter, 1999).

Forming Personality

The biologically based response tendencies called temperament are shaped, with the help of the individual's social experiences, into a full-blown personality during childhood. Although links between temperament in early childhood and later personality are often weak, such links have been identified (Halverson et al., 2003; Sanson, Hemphill, & Smart, 2004). For example, in a longitudinal study of 1000 children in New Zealand, Avshalom Caspi and his colleagues (Caspi, 2000; Caspi, Harrington, et al., 2003) found that inhibited 3-year-olds who are shy and fearful tend to become teenagers who are cautious and unassertive and young adults who have little social support, tend to be depressed, and are barely engaged in life. By contrast, 3-year-olds who are difficult to control, irritable, and highly emotional tend to be difficult to manage later in childhood and end up as impulsive adolescents and adults who do not get along well with other people at home and on the job, are easily upset, get into scrapes with the law, and abuse alcohol. Finally, well-adjusted ("easy") 3-year-olds tend to remain well adjusted. Interestingly, the assessments of personality at age 3 that proved predictive of later personality and adjustment were made on the basis of only 90 minutes of observation by an adult examiner who did not know the child (see Pesonen et al., 2003).

Yet relationships between early temperament and later personality are not well understood. Temperament researchers and personality researchers have tended to go their separate ways, developing distinct conceptual schemes and methods of assessing individual differences. Efforts are only recently being made to map various dimensions of temperament onto Big Five personality trait dimensions and to study Big Five trait dimensions in childhood. For example, high activity, high sociability, and low shyness or inhibition in the preschool period have been found to correlate with extraversion in middle childhood, and high negative emotionality is related to later neuroticism (Hagekull & Bohlin, 1998). The ability of infants to regulate themselves, or to exert effortful control over their attention and arousal (for example, to calm themselves) may also be linked to later conscientiousness, and an uninhibited temperament that embraces novelty may relate to openness to experience (Rothbart, Ahadi, & Evans, 2000; Sanson, Hemphill, & Smart, 2004). Charles Halverson and his colleagues (2003) report that parents in all seven countries they studied describe children as young as age 3 in Big Five terms, suggesting that these adult personality dimensions begin to show themselves in early childhood and need to be studied more thoroughly during childhood.

Yet we cannot accept Freud's view that the personality is mostly formed by age 5. The correlations between early childhood traits and adult traits are small. Some dimensions of personality do not seem to "gel" until the elementary-school years, when they begin to predict adult personality and adjustment much better (Hartup & van Lieshout, 1995; Shiner, Masten, & Roberts, 2003). Other aspects of personality do not seem to stabilize until adolescence or even early adulthood (Caspi & Roberts, 2001; McCrae & Costa, 2003). The older the child, the more accurately personality traits predict later personality and adjustment.

Certain behavioral patterns are probably reinforced and strengthened as years pass because they set in motion certain kinds of social interactions and evoke certain reactions from other people (Caspi, Elder, & Bem, 1987, 1988). For example, a child who has an explosive personality and is irritable and prone to temper tantrums may lose friends and alienate teachers as a child, lose jobs or experience marital problems as an adult, and therefore experience a snowballing of the negative consequences of his early personality. He may also evoke hostile reactions from other people that reinforce his tendency to be ill tempered.

Summing Up

In sum, major changes in self-conceptions occur about age 8 as children shift from describing their physical and active selves to talking about their psychological and social qualities. Other changes include increased social comparison, formation of a multidimensional and hierarchically organized self-concept with an overall sense of self-worth at the top, more accurate self-evaluation, and widening of the ideal self–real self gap. Competence, with positive social feedback from warm, democratic parents and others, contributes to high self-esteem. Some aspects of temperament may translate into Big Five personality traits and carry over into adulthood, but other aspects of personality do not gel until middle childhood and still others do not stabilize until adolescence or early adulthood. ■

The Adolescent

Perhaps no period of the life span is more important to the development of the self than adolescence. Adolescence is truly a time for "finding oneself," as research on adolescent self-conceptions, self-esteem, identity formation, and vocational choice illustrates.

Self-Conceptions

Raymond Montemayor and Marvin Eisen (1977) learned a great deal about the self-concepts of children and adolescents from grades 4 to 12 by asking students to write 20 different answers to the question "Who am I?" What age differences can you detect in these answers given by a 9-year-old, an $11\frac{1}{2}$-year-old, and a 17-year-old (pp. 317–318)?

> **9-year-old:** My name is Bruce C. I have brown eyes. I have brown hair. I love! sports. I have seven people in my family. I have great! eye sight. I have lots! of friends. I live at. . . . I have an uncle who is almost 7 feet tall. My teacher is Mrs. V. I play hockey! I'm almost the smartest boy in the class. I love! food . . .. I love! school.
>
> **$11\frac{1}{2}$-year-old:** My name is A. I'm a human being . . . a girl . . . a truthful person. I'm not pretty. I do so-so in my studies. I'm a very good cellist. I'm a little tall for my age. I like several boys. . . . I'm old fashioned. I am a very good swimmer. . . . I try to be helpful. . . . Mostly I'm good, but I lose my temper. I'm not well liked by some girls and boys. I don't know if boys like me. . . .
>
> **17-year-old:** I am a human being . . . a girl . . . an individual. . . . I am a Pisces. I am a moody person . . . an indecisive person . . . an ambitious person. I am a big curious person. . . . I am lonely. I am an American (God help me). I am a Democrat. I am a liberal person. I am a radical. I am conservative. I am a pseudoliberal. I am an Atheist. I am not a classifiable person (i.e., I don't want to be).

There are several notable differences between the self-descriptions of children and adolescents (Damon & Hart, 1988; Harter, 1999, 2003). First, self-descriptions become *less physical and more psychological* as children age. Second, self-portraits become *less concrete and more abstract.* Recall Piaget's theory that children begin to shift from concrete operational to formal operational thinking at about age 11 or 12. Children entering adolescence (11- to 12-year-olds) go beyond describing their traits in largely concrete terms ("I love! food") and more often generalize about their broader personality traits ("I am a truthful person"). High school students' self-descriptions are even more abstract, focusing not only on personality traits but also on important values and ideologies or beliefs ("I am a pseudoliberal").

Third, adolescents reflect more about what they are like; they are *more self-aware* than children are (Selman, 1980). Indeed, their new ability to think about their own and other people's thoughts and feelings can make them painfully self-conscious. Fourth, adolescents have a *more differentiated* self-concept than children. For example, the child's "social self," which reflects perceived acceptance by peers, splits into distinct aspects such as acceptance by the larger peer group, acceptance by close friends, and acceptance by romantic partners (Harter, 1999). Finally, older adolescents gain the ability to combine their differentiated self-perceptions into a *more integrated, coherent self-portrait.* Instead of merely listing traits, they organize their self-perceptions, including those that seem contradictory, into a coherent picture—a theory of what makes them tick.

To illustrate the phases through which adolescents pass in coming to know and accept themselves, consider an interesting study by Susan Harter and Ann Monsour (1992). Adolescents 13, 15, and 17 years old were asked to describe themselves when they are with their parents, with friends, in romantic relationships, and in the classroom. The adolescents were then asked to sort through their self-descriptions, identify any opposites or inconsistencies, and indicate which opposites confused or upset them.

The 13-year-olds were unaware of inconsistencies within themselves—and when they did detect any, they were not especially bothered by them. By age 15, students identified many more inconsistencies and were clearly confused by them (see Figure 11.2). One ninth-grade girl, for example, recognizing her tendency to be happy with friends but depressed at home, said, "I really think of myself as a happy person, and I want to be that way with everyone because I think that's my true self, but I get depressed with my family and it bugs me because that's not what I want to be like" (Harter & Monsour, 1992, p. 253). These 15-year-olds, especially the girls, seemed painfully aware that they had several different selves and were concerned about figuring out which was the "real me."

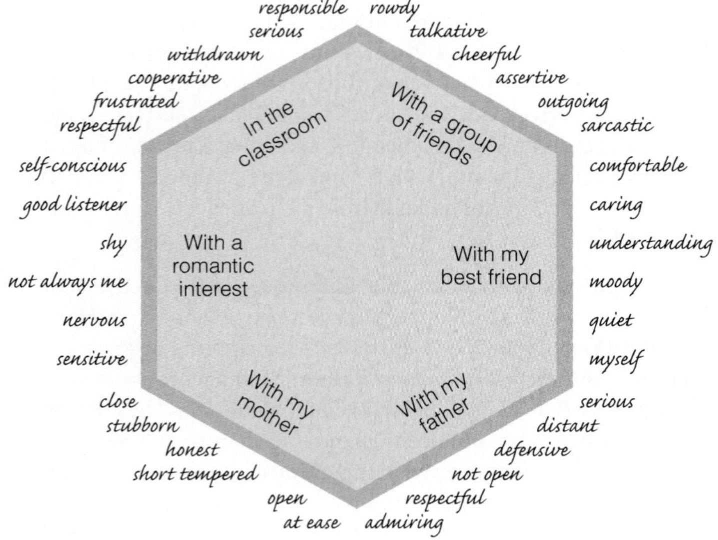

Figure 11.2 The multiple selves experienced by a 15-year-old girl. Can you identify any inconsistencies in her self-perceptions?
SOURCE: Harter (1999).

The oldest adolescents studied by Harter and Monsour, the 17-year-olds, overcame many of the uncomfortable feelings the 15-year-olds had. They were able to integrate their conflicting self-perceptions into a more coherent view of themselves. Thus a 17-year-old boy might conclude that it is understandable to be relaxed and confident in most situations but nervous on dates if he has not had much dating experience. He might realize that the concept of moodiness can explain being cheerful on some occasions but irritable on others. Harter and Monsour believe that cognitive development—specifically the ability to compare abstract trait concepts and integrate them through higher-order concepts such as moodiness—is behind this change in self-perceptions.

In sum, self-understandings become more psychological, abstract, differentiated, and integrated and self-awareness increases from childhood to adolescence and over the course of adolescence. At first oblivious to contradictions within the self, teenagers become painfully aware of them and, eventually, can better integrate their various selves. Many adolescents even become sophisticated personality theorists who reflect upon the workings of their own personalities and those of their companions.

Self-Esteem

Overall, self-esteem tends to decrease from childhood to early adolescence, partly because adolescents are more knowledgeable and realistic than children about their strengths and weaknesses (Jacobs et al., 2002; Robins et al., 2002) and because they move from elementary school to middle school or junior high school and may become temporarily unsure of themselves (Cole et al., 2001). This dip in self-esteem affects some teens more than others. It tends to be greatest among white females, especially those facing multiple stressors—for example, making the transition from elementary school to middle school, coping with pubertal changes, beginning to date, and perhaps dealing with a family move all at the same time (Gray-Little & Hafdahl, 2000; Simmons et al., 1987). A drop in self-esteem also tends to be especially likely among adolescents who base their self-worth on the approval of others and then experience losses of approval (Harter & Whitesell, 2003). In addition, self-esteem is affected by how competent an adolescent's classmates are, as shown in the Explorations box on page 299.

Overall, adolescence is not as hazardous to the self as most people believe. Although some adolescents experience significant drops in self-esteem in early adolescence, most emerge from this developmental period with higher self-esteem than they had at the onset (Robins et al., 2002). Apparently, they revise their self-concepts in fairly minor ways as they experience the physical, cognitive, and social changes

Explorations

Big Fish in a Little Pond

If the goal is high self-esteem, is it better to be a big fish in a small pond or a small fish in a big pond? Herbert Marsh and Kit-Tai Hau (2003) conducted an ambitious study involving more than 100,000 15-year-olds in 26 countries to better understand the **big-fish–little-pond effect,** in which, holding factors such as academic competence equal, a student's academic self-concept is likely to be more positive in an academically unselective school than in a highly selective one with many high-achieving students. Marsh and Hau found that individual achievement is positively related to academic self-concept, as they expected. However, they also found that *schoolwide average achievement* is negatively related to academic self-concept. That is, a student's academic self-concept tends to be less positive when the average academic achievement of her classmates is high (when she is a small fish in a big pond) than when school average academic achievement is low (when she is a big fish in a small pond).

The big-fish–little-pond effect suggests that making the transition from regular classes to classes for gifted students, or from an unselective high school to a selective college or university, could threaten an adolescent's self-esteem. Indeed, gifted children moved from regular classes into gifted programs sometimes suffer drops in academic self-concept (Marsh et al., 1995). The big-fish–little-pond effect may also explain why special education students tend to have higher academic self-esteem when they are placed in homogeneous special education classes than when they are placed in regular classes with higher-achieving classmates (Marsh & Hau, 2003). This is just what you would expect if students who have high-achieving classmates fare poorly in social comparisons with students whose classmates are not so high achieving. Unfortunately, this means that otherwise desirable educational decisions such as including students with learning disabilities and mental retardation in the mainstream of education may have unintended side effects, undermining self-esteem and possibly future academic achievement.

☾ A little fish in a big pond is likely to have lower academic self-esteem than a big fish in a little pond.

of adolescence. Assuming that they have opportunities to feel competent in areas important to them and have the approval and support of parents, peers, and other important people in their lives, they are likely to feel good about themselves (Harter, 1999).

Forging a Sense of Identity

Erikson (1968) characterized adolescence as a critical period in the lifelong process of forming an identity as a person and proposed that adolescents experience the psychosocial conflict of **identity versus role confusion.** The concept of identity, explained at the start of the chapter, refers to a firm and coherent definition of who you are, where you are going, and where you fit into society. To achieve a sense of identity, the adolescent must somehow integrate the many separate perceptions that are part of the self-concept into a coherent sense of self and must feel that she is, deep down, the same person yesterday, today, and tomorrow—at home, at school, or at work (van Hoof, 1999). The search for identity involves grappling with many important questions: What kind of career do I want? What religious, moral, and political values can I really call my own? Who am I as a man or woman and as a sexual being? Where do I fit into the world? What do I really want out of my life?

If you have struggled with such issues, you can appreciate the uncomfortable feelings that adolescents may experience when they cannot seem to work out a clear sense of who they are. Erikson believed that many young people in complex societies such as that of the United States experience a full-blown and painful "identity crisis"; indeed, he coined the term. There are many reasons they might do so. First, their bodies change; therefore, they must revise their body images (a part of their self-concepts) and adjust to being sexual beings. Second, cognitive growth allows adolescents to think systematically about hypothetical possibilities, including possible future selves. Third, social demands are placed on them to "grow up"—to decide what they want to do in life and to get on with it. According to Erikson (1968), our society supports youths by allowing them a **moratorium period**—a time in high school and college when they are relatively free of responsibilities and can experiment with different roles to find themselves (see Arnett, 2000). But our society also makes establishing an identity harder than it may be in many other cultures by giving youths a huge number of options and encouraging them to believe they can be anything they want to be.

(Adolescents sometimes experiment with a variety of looks in their search for a sense of identity.

Developmental Trends

James Marcia (1966) expanded on Erikson's theory and stimulated much research on identity formation by developing an interview that allows investigators to assess where an adolescent is in the process of identity formation. Adolescents are classified into one of four identity statuses based on their progress toward an identity in each of several domains (for example, occupational, religious, and political–ideological). The key questions are whether an individual has experienced a *crisis* (or has seriously grappled with identity issues and explored alternatives) and whether he has achieved a *commitment* (that is, resolution of the questions raised). On the basis of crisis and commitment, the individual is classified into one of the four identity statuses shown in Table 11.3.

How long does it take to achieve a sense of identity? Philip Meilman's (1979) study of college-bound boys between 12 and 18, 21-year-old college males, and 24-year-old young men provides an answer (see Figure 11.3). Most of the 12- and 15-year-olds were in either the identity diffusion or the foreclosure status. At these ages, many adolescents simply have not yet thought about who they are—either they have no idea or they know that any ideas they do have are likely to change (the **diffusion status,** with no crisis and no commitment). Other adolescents may say things like "I'm going to be a doctor like my dad" and appear to have their acts together. However, it becomes apparent that they have never thought through on their own what suits them best and have simply accepted identities suggested to them by their parents or other people (the **foreclosure status,** involving a commitment without a crisis).

As Figure 11.3 indicates, progress toward identity achievement becomes more evident starting at age 18. Notice that diffusion drops off steeply and more individuals begin to

Table 11.3 The Four Identity Statuses as They Apply to Religious Identity

	No Commitment Made	Commitment Made
No Crisis Experienced	**Diffusion Status**	**Foreclosure Status**
	The individual has not yet thought about or resolved identity issues and has failed to chart directions in life. Example: "I haven't really thought much about religion, and I guess I don't know what I believe exactly."	The individual seems to know who she is but has latched onto an identity prematurely with little thought (e.g., by uncritically becoming what parents or other authority figures suggest she should). Example: "My parents are Baptists, and I'm a Baptist; it's just the way I grew up."
Crisis Experienced	**Moratorium Status**	**Identity Achievement Status**
	The individual is experiencing an identity crisis, actively raising questions, and seeking answers. Example: "I'm in the middle of evaluating my beliefs and hope that I'll be able to figure out what's right for me. I like many of the answers provided by my Catholic upbringing, but I've also become skeptical about some teachings and have been looking into Unitarianism to see if it might help me answer my questions."	The individual has resolved her identity crisis and made commitments to particular goals, beliefs, and values. Example: "I really did some soul-searching about my religion and other religions, too, and finally know what I believe and what I don't."

fall into the **moratorium status,** in which they are currently experiencing a crisis or actively exploring identity issues. Presumably, entering the moratorium status is a good sign; if the individual can find answers to the questions raised, he will move to the identity achievement status. About 20% of the 18-year-olds, 40% of the college students, and slightly more than half of the 24-year-olds in Meilman's study had achieved a firm identity based on a careful weighing of alternatives (the **identity achievement status**).

Is the identity formation process different for females than it is for males? In most respects, no (Meeus et al., 1999; Kroger, 1997). Females progress toward achieving a clear sense

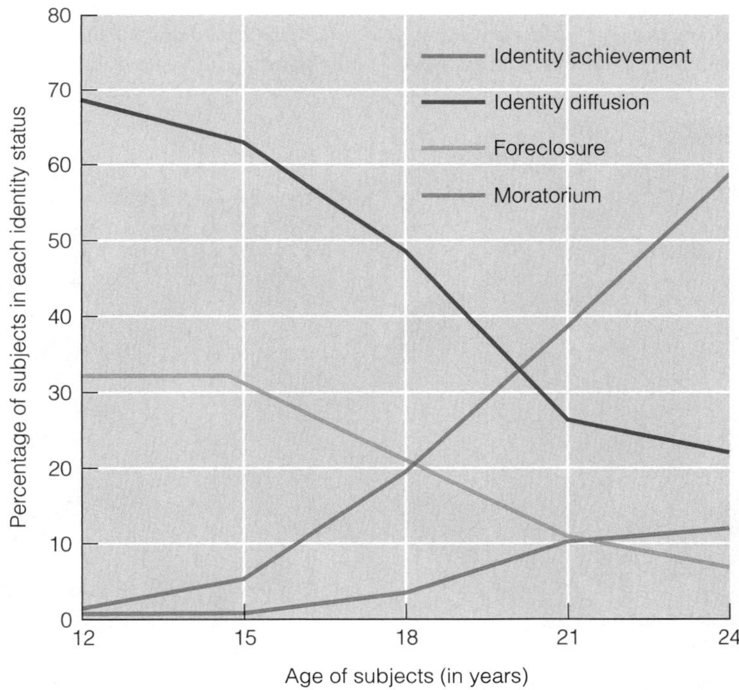

Figure 11.3 Percentage of subjects in each of James Marcia's four identity statuses as a function of age. Note that only 4% of the 15-year-olds and 20% of the 18-year-olds had achieved a stable identity.

SOURCE: Based on Meilman (1979).

Forging a Positive Ethnic Identity

The process of identity development includes forging an **ethnic identity**—a sense of personal identification with an ethnic group and its values and cultural traditions (Phinney, 1996). Everyone has an ethnic and racial background, but members of minority groups tend to put more emphasis than white adolescents on defining who they are ethnically or racially, probably because majority group members do not think of themselves as having an ethnicity (Laursen & Williams, 2002; Bracey, Bamaca, & Umana-Taylor, 2004).

The process begins during the preschool years, when children learn that different racial and ethnic categories exist and gradually become able to classify themselves correctly (Spencer & Markstrom-Adams, 1990). For example, Mexican American preschool children learn behaviors associated with their culture, such as how to give a Chicano handshake, but they often do not know until about age 8 what ethnic labels apply to them, what they mean, or that they will last a lifetime (Bernal & Knight, 1997).

The formation of a positive ethnic identity during adolescence seems to proceed through the same identity statuses as the formation of a vocational or religious identity (Phinney, 1993). School-age children and young adolescents say either that they identify with their racial or ethnic group because their parents and others in their ethnic group influenced them to do so (foreclosure status) or that they have not given the issue much thought (diffusion status). Between age 16 and age 19, many minority youths move into the moratorium and achievement statuses with respect to ethnic identity. One Mexican American female described her moratorium period this way: "I want to know what we do and how our culture is different from others. Going to festivals and cultural events helps me to learn more about my own culture and about myself" (Phinney, 1993, p. 70).

A positive ethnic identity is most likely to be achieved when parents teach their children about their group's cultural traditions, try to prepare them to live in a culturally diverse society and deal with prejudice, and provide the warm and democratic parenting that seems to foster self-esteem and healthy identity development (Bernal & Knight, 1997; Marshall, 1995). Minority youth may have difficulty feeling good about themselves if they encounter prejudice—if, for example, they are called racist names or treated by teachers as if they were incompetent (Nyborg & Curry, 2003).

Once formed, a positive ethnic identity can protect adolescents' self-concepts from the damaging effects of racial discrimination (Wong, Eccles, & Sameroff, 2003), breed high self-esteem (Bracey et al., 2004), and promote academic achievement and good adjustment (Laursen & Williams, 2002). Most minority adolescents cope well with the special challenges they face in identity formation. They settle questions of ethnic identity and resolve other identity issues around the same ages that European American youth do (Markstrom-Adams & Adams, 1995), and they wind up feeling good about themselves (Gray-Little & Hafdahl, 2000).

of identity at about the same rate that males do. However, one reliable sex difference has been observed: Although today's college women are just as concerned about establishing a career identity as men are, they attach greater importance to and think more about the aspects of identity that center on sexuality, interpersonal relations, and balancing career and family goals (S. L. Archer, 1992; Kroger, 1997; Meeus et al., 1999). These concerns probably reflect the continuing influence of traditional gender roles.

Judging from such research, identity formation *takes a long time.* Many young men and women move from the diffusion or the foreclosure status to the moratorium status then achieve a sense of identity in their late teens or early 20s (Waterman, 1982). But this is by no means the end of the identity formation process. Some adults continue in a moratorium status for years; others reopen the question of who they are after thinking they had all the answers earlier in life (Kroger, 1996). Even in their 60s, some adults are reworking and strengthening their sense of identity (Zucker, Ostrove, & Stewart, 2002).

Not only does identity formation take a long time but it also *occurs at different rates in different domains of identity* (Kroger, 1996). For example, Sally Archer (1982) assessed the identity statuses of 6th- to 12th-graders in four domains: occupational choice, gender-role attitudes, religious beliefs, and political ideologies. Only 5% of the adolescents were in the same identity status in all four areas, and more than 90% were in two or three statuses across the four areas. It is common for some aspects of identity to take shape earlier than others. The process of identity formation may be even more complex for members of racial and ethnic minority groups. As the Explorations box on page 302 shows, they face the challenge of forming a positive ethnic identity.

Finally, the patterns of identity development discovered in longitudinal studies *are not always consistent with theory* (Meeus et al., 1999; van Hoof, 1999). For example, some youth may settle on an identity early and only later reflect on their choice rather than experiencing a moratorium phase on their way to achieving an identity (Meeus et al., 1999). In addition, not all changes in identity status reflect forward progress toward maturity; adolescents sometimes slide backward before they move forward again (Reis & Youniss, 2004). In short, identity development is complex. It takes a long time, occurs at different rates in different domains, and does not always unfold in the theoretically expected way from diffusion or foreclosure to moratorium to identity achievement.

Influences on Identity Formation

The adolescent's progress toward achieving identity is a product of at least four factors: (1) cognitive growth, (2) relationships with parents, (3) experiences outside the home, and (4) the broader cultural context. *Cognitive development* enables adolescents to imagine and contemplate possible future identities. Adolescents who have achieved solid mastery of formal operational thought, who think in complex and abstract ways, and who are self-directed and actively seek relevant information when they face decisions are more likely to raise and resolve identity issues than other adolescents (Berzonsky & Kuk, 2000; Waterman, 1992).

Second, adolescents' *relationships with parents* affect their progress in forging an identity (Markstrom-Adams, 1992; Waterman, 1982). Youths in the diffusion status of identity formation are more likely than those in the other categories to be neglected or rejected by their parents and to be distant from them. It can be difficult to forge an identity without first having the opportunity to identify with respected parental figures and to take on some of their desirable qualities. At the other extreme, adolescents in the foreclosure status appear to be extremely close—sometimes too close—to parents who are loving but overly protective and controlling. Because foreclosed adolescents love their parents and have little opportunity to make decisions on their own, they may never question parental authority or feel a need to forge a separate identity. Perhaps that is why achievement of identity is more likely when adolescents move out of the house to attend college than when they stay at home during college (Jordyn & Byrd, 2003).

By comparison, students classified in the moratorium and identity achievement statuses appear to have a solid base of affection at home combined with freedom to be individuals. Adolescents who make good progress in identity formation tend to be securely attached to their parents, especially if they are females and are close to their mothers (Samuolis, Layburn, & Schiaffino, 2001). In addition, their parents set rules and monitor their activities (Sartor & Youniss, 2002). In family discussions, these adolescents experience a sense of closeness and mutual respect but also feel free to disagree with their parents (Grotevant & Cooper, 1986). Notice that this is the same warm and democratic parenting style that seems to help younger children gain a strong sense of self-esteem.

Experiences outside the home are a third influence on identity formation. For example, adolescents who attend college are exposed to diverse ideas and encouraged to think through issues independently. Although college students may be more confused for a time about their identities than peers who begin working after high school (Munro & Adams, 1977), going to college provides the kind of moratorium period Erikson felt was essential to identity formation. By contrast, conflicts with peers may impede identity formation or cause reversion to the diffusion or foreclosure status (Reis & Youniss, 2004).

Finally, identity formation is influenced by *the broader cultural context* in which it occurs—a point Erikson emphasized. The notion that adolescents should forge a personal identity after carefully exploring many options may well be peculiar to modern industrialized Western societies (Cote & Levine, 1988; Flum & Blustein, 2000). As was true of adolescents in earlier eras, adolescents in many traditional societies today simply adopt the adult roles they are expected to adopt in their culture, without much soul-searching or experimentation. Among the Navajo, for example, a coming-of-age ceremony for pubertal young women called Kinaaldá efficiently transforms a girl into an ideal Navajo woman around age 12 or 13 and connects her to her community (Markstrom & Iborra, 2003). For many adolescents in traditional societies, what Marcia calls identity foreclosure may be the most adaptive route to adulthood (Cote & Levine, 1988).

In Western industrialized societies, however, the adolescent who is able to raise serious questions about the self and answer them—that is, the individual who achieves identity—is likely to be better off for it. Identity achievement is associated with psychological well-being and high self-esteem, complex thinking about moral issues and other matters, a willingness to accept and cooperate with other people, and a variety of other psychological strengths (Waterman, 1992). Erikson recognized that identity issues can and do crop up later in life, even for people who form a positive sense of identity during adolescence. Nonetheless, he quite rightly marked the adolescent period as a key time in life for defining who we are.

Vocational Identity and Choice

Vocational identity is a central aspect of identity with major implications for adult development. How do adolescents choose careers that express their sense of self as they prepare for adulthood? According to an early theory of vocational choice proposed by Eli Ginzberg (1972, 1984), vocational choice unfolds in three stages: (1) the fantasy stage, (2) the tentative stage, and (3) the realistic stage. In the *fantasy stage* of vocational development, children up to about age 10 years base their choices primarily on wishes and whims, wanting to be zookeepers, professional basketball players, firefighters, rock stars, or whatever else strikes them as glamorous and exciting. As Linda Gottfredson (1996) emphasizes, however, children are already beginning to narrow their ideas about future careers to those consistent with their emerging self-concepts—as humans rather than as bunnies or ninja turtles, as males rather than as females, and so on. As early as kindergarten, for instance, almost all boys choose traditionally masculine occupations, and most girls name traditionally female occupations such as nurse or teacher (Etaugh & Liss, 1992; Phipps, 1995). Still, most children make pretty unrealistic choices of careers, and most have few clues about what it takes to achieve their dream careers (Phipps, 1995). It may be different in societies in which children begin to participate in adult work at age 3 or 4 and have real responsibilities for child care, farming, and household tasks at age 5 to age 7 (Rogoff et al., 2003).

During Ginzberg's second stage of vocational choice, the *tentative stage,* adolescents age 11 to age 18 begin to weigh factors other than their wishes and to make preliminary decisions. After considering their interests ("Would I enjoy counseling people?"), they take into account their capacities ("Am I skilled at relating to people, or am I too shy and insecure for this kind of work?"), then think about their values ("Is it really important to me to help people, or do I value power or money more?").

As adolescents leave this tentative stage, they begin to take into account the realities of the job market and the physical and intellectual requirements for different occupations (Ginzberg, 1972, 1984). During Ginzberg's third stage of vocational choice, the *realistic stage,* from about age 18 to age 22, they narrow things to specific choices based not only on their interests, capacities, and values but also on their accumulating knowledge of available career opportunities and their requirements, and they begin serious preparation for their chosen occupations (Walls, 2000). By late adolescence, they are in a good position to consider the availability of job openings in a field such as school counseling, the years of education required, the work conditions, and other relevant factors.

The main developmental trend evident in Ginzberg's stages is increasing realism about vocational options. As adolescents narrow career choices in terms of both personal factors (their own interests, capacities, and values) and environmental factors (the opportunities available and the realities of the job market), they seek the vocation that best suits them. According to vocational theorists such as John Holland (1985), vocational choice is just this: an effort to find an optimal fit between one's self-concept and personality and an occupation (see also Super, Savickas, & Super, 1996).

As they age, adolescents from lower-income families, especially minority group members living in poverty and facing limited opportunities, stigmatization, and stress, may have difficulty forming a positive vocational identity (Phillips & Pittman, 2003). They may lower their career aspirations and

To make realistic vocational choices, adolescents must become familiar with the requirements of different jobs—for example, through internships.

aim toward the jobs they think they are likely to get rather than the jobs they most want (Armstrong & Crombie, 2000; Rojewski & Yang, 1997). Similarly, the vocational choices of females have been and continue to be constrained by traditional gender norms. Young women who have adopted traditional gender-role attitudes and expect to marry and start families early in adulthood are likely to set their educational and vocational sights low, figuring that they cannot "have it all" (Mahaffy & Ward, 2002). Although more young women aspire toward high-status jobs now, many others, influenced by gender norms, do not seriously consider traditionally male-dominated jobs, doubt their ability to attain such jobs, and aim instead toward feminine-stereotyped, and often lower-status and lower-paying, occupations (Armstrong & Crombie, 2000; Morinaga, Frieze, & Ferligoj, 1993).

Many other teenagers simply do not do as Erikson and vocational theorists would advise—explore a range of possible occupations, then make a choice. Those who do consider a range of options are more likely than those who do not to choose careers that fit their personalities (Grotevant & Cooper, 1986). A good fit between person and vocation, in turn, is associated with greater job satisfaction and success (Spokane, Meir, & Catalano, 2000; Verquer, Beehr, & Wagner, 2003). The saving grace is that those who do not explore thoroughly as adolescents have plenty of opportunities to change their minds as adults.

Summing Up

During adolescence, self-awareness increases and self-concepts become more psychological, abstract, and integrated. Self-esteem may dip temporarily in early adolescence, especially among adolescents facing a school transition and multiple stressors. Resolving Erikson's crisis of identity versus role confusion means progressing from the diffusion and foreclosure statuses to the moratorium and identity achievement statuses, a process that extends into late adolescence and early adulthood and is facilitated by cognitive development, warm and democratic parenting, and opportunities to explore. In establishing vocational identities, adolescents progress through Ginzberg's fantasy, tentative, and realistic stages and seek a good fit between self and occupation, but the choices of low-income youth and females are often constrained. ■

The Adult

We enter adulthood having gained a great deal of understanding of what we are like as individuals—but we are not done developing. How do self-conceptions change and stay the same over the adult years, and to what extent are they shaped by the culture in which the individual develops? How do personality traits change, and how are both self-concepts and personalities related to the psychological changes adults experience as their careers unfold?

Self-Conceptions

It is clear that adults differ from one another in their self-perceptions; both age and cultural context will help you understand that variation.

Age Differences

In Western society, it is commonly believed that adults gain self-esteem as they cope successfully with the challenges of adult life but then lose it as aging, disease, and losses of roles and relationships take their toll in later life. Is there truth to this view? A large survey over the Internet of more than 300,000 people ages 9 to 90 conducted by Richard Robins and his colleagues (2002) suggests there is. Self-esteem tends to be high in childhood, to drop in adolescence, to rise gradually through the adult years until the mid-60s, then to drop in late old age, as shown in Figure 11.4. The same analysis showed that males generally have higher self-esteem than females except in childhood and very old age.

So there is some support for the idea that self-esteem increases during the adult years and drops in late adulthood, although only in the 70s and 80s. Yet other work suggests that elderly adults are more like young- and middle-aged adults than different in both levels of self-esteem and in the ways in which they describe themselves (Helgeson & Mickelson, 2000; Ruth & Coleman, 1996). Moreover, correlations between self-esteem at one age and self-esteem at a subsequent age are generally large, in the 0.50 to 0.70 range (Trzesniewski, Donnellan, & Robins, 2003). There is little truth, then, to the stereotyped view that most older adults suffer from a poor self-image, even if self-esteem drops for some adults in very old age. How, then, do most elderly people manage to maintain positive self-images for so long, even as they experience some of the disabilities and losses that come with aging?

First, *older people adjust their ideal selves to be more in line with their real selves.* Carol Ryff (1991) asked young, middle-aged, and elderly adults to assess their ideal, likely future, present, and past selves with respect to various dimensions of well-being, including self-acceptance. Figure 11.5 shows the average scores on the self-acceptance scale. Ratings of the present self changed little across the adult years. However, older adults scaled down their visions of what they could ideally be and what they likely will be. They also judged more positively what they had been. As a result, their ideal, future, present, and past selves converged. Notice, then, that the gap between the ideal self and the real self that widens during childhood and adolescence, and that gives us a sense of falling short, apparently closes again in later life, helping us maintain self-esteem.

Second, *people's goals and standards change with age* so that what seem like losses or failures to a younger person may not be perceived as such by the older adult (Helgeson & Mickelson, 2000; Carstensen & Freund, 1994). A 45-year-old may be devastated at being passed over for a promotion, whereas a 60-year-old nearing retirement may not be any more bothered by this slight than 45-year-olds are bothered by "not being able to jump on their beds and draw pictures

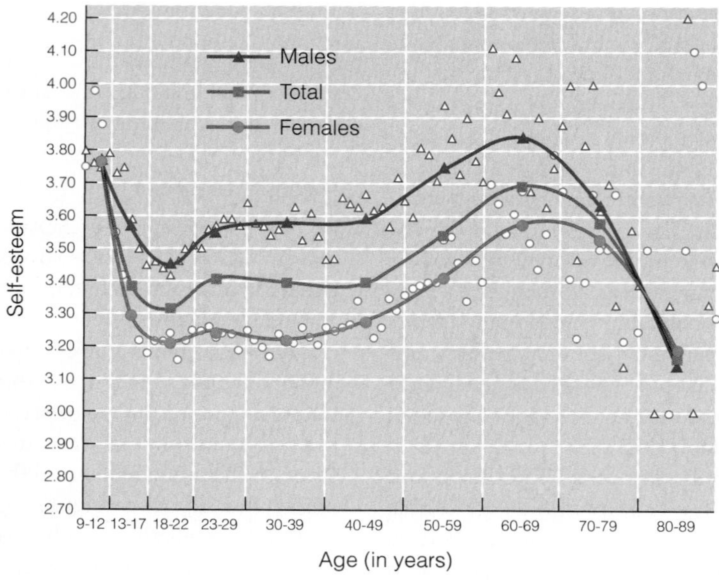

Figure 11.4 Self-esteem dips in early adolescence and rises during the adult years until it declines in very old age. Males have higher scores than females except in childhood and late old age.
SOURCE: Robins et al. (2002).

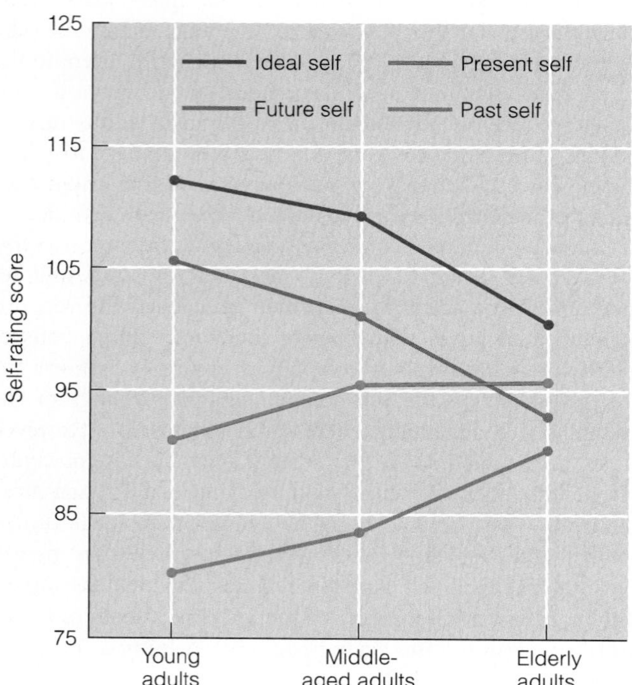

Figure 11.5 Favorability of ratings of their ideal, likely future, present (real), and past selves by young, middle-aged, and elderly adults. The gap between the ideal and the real self that widens during childhood and adolescence shrinks during adulthood, as indicated by the converging lines in the graph. As they age, adults become more comfortable with the idea of remaining as they are and as they have been.
SOURCE: Adapted from Ryff (1991).

with crayons" (Carstensen & Freund, 1994, p. 87). For the older adult with a disability, walking a mile may be as much a triumph as running a mile might have been earlier in life (Rothermund & Brandtstädter, 2003b). As our goals and standards change over the life span, we apply different measuring sticks in evaluating ourselves and do not mind failing to achieve goals no longer important.

Third, older adults maintain self-esteem because *the people with whom they compare themselves are also old* (Helgeson & Mickelson, 2000; Brandtstädter & Greve, 1994). Older adults do not compare themselves with young adults but with people who have the same kinds of chronic diseases and impairments they have—or worse ones. If they want to feel good about themselves, they may even strategically select worse-off elders for social comparison (Frieswijk et al., 2004; Rothermund & Brandtstädter, 2003a), as in, "I'm getting around much better than Bessy is." Indeed, some observers argue that stereotypes of aging in our society are so bleak that older adults can feel better about their own aging simply by conjuring up an image of the typical "old person" (Brandtstädter & Greve, 1994). On balance, however, negative stereotypes of old age probably have more damaging than beneficial effects on the self-perceptions of elderly people, as shown in the Applications box on page 308.

Overall, then, adults of different ages generally describe themselves in similar ways, but self-esteem appears to rise in early and middle adulthood and to drop off in late old age. Many older adults are able to maintain self-esteem by perceiving a smaller gap than younger adults do between their real and ideal selves, evaluating their self-worth by different standards, and making social comparisons with other older people. Overall, powerful mechanisms are at work to protect self-esteem in the face of some of the challenges of aging and negative stereotypes of aging (Wahl & Kruse, 2003).

Cultural Differences

By adulthood, self-conceptions show the imprint not only of individual experiences such as positive or negative feedback from parents but also of broader cultural influences. In an **individualistic culture,** individuals define themselves as individuals and put their own goals ahead of their social group's goals, whereas in a **collectivist culture,** people define themselves in terms of group memberships and give group goals higher priority than personal goals (Triandis, 1989, 1995). Individualistic cultures emphasize socializing children to be independent and self-reliant, whereas collectivist ones emphasize interdependence with others, social harmony, and subordination of self-interest to the interests of the group. North American and Western European societies typically have an individualistic orientation, whereas many societies in Latin America, Africa, and Asia are collectivist. All cultures include a mix of individualism and collectivism, however; the cultural differences we are describing are matters of degree (Oyserman, Coon, & Kemmelmeier, 2002).

How do self-conceptions differ in individualistic and collectivist cultures? Hazel Markus and her colleagues have been studying cultural differences in the meaning of self in the United States and Japan (Cross, 2000; Markus, 2004; Markus, Mullally, & Kitayama, 1997). They have found that being a person in the United States (an individualistic culture) means being your own person—independent, unique, and differentiated from the rest of the social world, whereas being a person in Japan (a collectivist culture) means being interdependent, connected to others in social groups, and embedded in society. Thus, when asked to describe themselves, American adults talk about their unique personal qualities but Japanese adults more often refer to their social roles and identities and mention other people (for example, "I try to make my parents happy").

In addition, Americans describe their generalizable personality traits—traits they believe they display in most situations and relationships. By contrast, Japanese adults describe their behavior in specific contexts such as home, school, or work and may describe themselves differently depending on the social situation or context they are talking about. Indeed, the Japanese language has no word to refer to *I* apart from social context (Cross, 2000). In short, Americans think like trait theorists, whereas Japanese people seem to adopt a social learning theory or contextual perspective on personality, expecting people to react differently in different situations. The result is that Westerners are more likely than Easterners to feel that they have an inner self consistent across situations and over time (Tafarodi et al., 2004).

Finally, Americans are obsessed with maintaining high self-esteem; most believe that they are above average in most respects. Japanese adults are more modest and self-critical (Cross, 2000). They readily note their inadequacies and seem reluctant to "stand out from the crowd" by calling attention to their positive qualities. In Japan, making a point of your strengths would mean slighting the importance of your group (Shweder et al., 1998, p. 907; also see Table 11.4 for a summary of these differences).

Interestingly, some of these cultural differences in self-descriptions can be detected as early as age 3 or 4 when children are asked to talk about themselves and their experiences (Wang, 2004). American children talk about their roles, preferences, characteristics, and feelings, whereas Chinese children describe themselves in terms of social roles and social routines such as family dinners. They are a good deal more modest, too, saying things like "I sometimes forget my manners." Parents may contribute to these cultural differences through everyday conversations with their children; for example, American mothers tell stories in which their children are the stars, whereas Chinese mothers talk about the experiences of the family as a group (Wang, 2004).

Cross-cultural studies of individualistic and collectivist cultures challenge the Western assumption that a person cannot develop normally without individuating himself from others and coming to know his identity as an individual. They also suggest that our methods for studying the self—asking people who they are, having them respond to personality scale items about how they generally behave across social contexts—may be culturally biased. Many of the world's people seem to get on quite nicely by being part of a collective and not thinking much about how they differ from other group members. It is wise to bear in mind, then, that self-conceptions are culturally defined.

Continuity and Discontinuity in Personality

To address questions of continuity and change in adult personality, we must ask two questions: Do *individual* adults retain their rankings on trait dimensions compared with others in a group over the years? Do *average* scores on personality trait measures increase, decrease, or remain the same as age increases?

Table 11.4 Views of the Self in Individualistic and Collectivist Cultures

Individualistic (e.g., United States)	Collectivist (e.g., Japan)
Separate	Connected
Independent	Interdependent
Traitlike, personal qualities transcend specific situations and relationships	Flexible, different in different social contexts
Need for self-esteem results in seeing self as above average	Self-critical, aware of inadequacies
Emphasis on uniqueness	Emphasis on group memberships and similarities to others

SOURCE: Based on Markus, Mullally, & Kitayama, 1997.

Stereotypes of Aging and Self-Perceptions in Old Age

Are the self-perceptions of elderly adults affected by the negative stereotypes of aging rampant in our society? Becca Levy (2003) argues that stereotypes of old people learned in childhood often become self-stereotypes when people reach old age. She cites studies indicating that children learn early to take a dim view of elderly people, to stereotype them as sick, weak, forgetful, and incompetent. These negative stereotypes are reinforced over the years and are available to be applied to the self once a person begins to think of himself as an "old person." Aging adults often go to great lengths to deny that they are old—a sign in itself that old age is negatively perceived in our society—but eventually they can deny no longer, apply the "old" label, and run the risk of negatively stereotyping themselves.

To demonstrate that aging self-stereotypes can negatively affect the behavior of elderly adults, Levy and her associates (Hausdorff, Levy, & Wei, 1999) used a priming technique. Words reflecting either negative stereotypes of aging or positive stereotypes of aging were flashed rapidly on a computer screen to elderly participants in the study so that the words were perceived but were below the level of awareness. After the priming experience, these adults were asked to walk down a hall wearing measuring devices on their feet that registered how rapidly they walked and how lightly they stepped (how long their feet were off the ground). Most people assume that a slow, shuffling gait in old age is caused by either biological aging or illness. This study demonstrated that social stereotypes are also relevant. Older adults primed with positive stereotypes of aging clocked faster speeds and more foot-off-the-floor time than older adults exposed to negative stereotypes. As Chapter 8 revealed, Levy (1996) has also found that priming older adults with words such as *senile* results in poorer memory performance than priming them with words such as *wise*.

Levy and her colleagues (2002) have even found that middle-aged adults who have positive perceptions of their own aging (for example, who disagree with statements such as "Things keep getting worse as I get older") end up not only in better health in old age but live more than 7 years longer than adults who have less positive self-perceptions of aging. This was the case even when age, health, socioeconomic status, and other relevant variables were controlled. Bear in mind that this is a correlational study and that unmeasured health or mental health problems may have negatively affected people's self-perceptions of aging.

Klaus Rothermund and Jochen Brandtstädter (2003a) conducted an interesting study that tested Levy's view against competing hypotheses about the relationship between aging stereotypes and self-perceptions in later life. They asked the following:

- Do aging stereotypes contaminate self-perceptions, as Levy (2003) argues?
- Alternatively, do aging stereotypes offer such a dismal view of old age that they give the self-concepts of aging adults a boost by allowing them to compare themselves with worse-off others?
- Instead, might aging stereotypes reflect self-perceptions rather than shape them so that adults experiencing the negative effects of aging begin to take a dim view of old people in general?

Do People Retain Their Rankings?

Paul Costa, Robert McCrae, and their colleagues have closely studied personality change and continuity by giving adults from their 20s to their 90s personality tests and administering these tests repeatedly over the years (McCrae & Costa, 2003). Focusing on the Big Five dimensions of personality listed in Table 11.1, they have found a good deal of *stability in rankings within a group,* as indicated by high correlations between scores on the same trait dimensions at different ages. In other words, the person who tends to be extraverted as a young adult is likely to be extraverted as an elderly adult, and the introvert is likely to remain introverted over the years. Similarly, the adult who shows high or low levels of neuroticism, conscientiousness, agreeableness, or openness to new experiences is likely to retain that ranking compared with that of peers years later. Correlations between personality trait scores on two occasions 20 to 30 years apart average about 0.60 across the five personality dimensions. Correlations of this size suggest consistency in personality over time but also room for change in response to life events (McCrae & Costa, 2003; Morizot & Le Blanc, 2003).

The tendency to be consistent increases with age. In a meta-analysis of 152 studies in which personality was assessed on two or more occasions, Brent Roberts and Wendy DelVecchio (2000) found that the average correlation between scores at two testings 6 to 7 years apart was 0.31 in infancy and early childhood, 0.54 in the college years, 0.64 at age 30, and 0.74 from age 50 on. Because they are still forming, personalities are unsettled in childhood and even in a person's teens and 20s. McCrae and Costa (2003) conclude that rankings on the Big Five are stable by the time adults are in their 30s, but Roberts and DelVecchio (2000) conclude that personalities stabilize even more by age 50 or 60.

These researchers asked German adults ages 54 to 77 at the start of the study to rate a "typical old person" and to rate themselves on the same scale. The sample was then studied over 8 years so that relationships between earlier and later stereotyped beliefs and self-perceptions could be assessed. The adults in this study clearly had a more positive view of themselves than they had of the typical old person, although they became more charitable in their evaluations of old people as they aged. Overall, the results supported Levy's view that aging stereotypes damage self-perceptions. Holding negative aging stereotypes at the outset of the study led to negative self-perceptions later, whereas early self-perceptions did not affect later aging stereotypes. The link between negative stereotypes of old age and negative self views was especially strong among the oldest adults in the study, perhaps helping explain the tendency for self-esteem to drop in late old age.

This research points to the value of combating ageist stereotypes and calling attention to positive aspects of old age and aging. Intervention might best begin in childhood. For example, intergenerational programs in which elderly adults work with children in the schools not only help children learn but also can improve their attitudes toward old people (Cummings, Williams, & Ellis, 2003). Interventions to combat ageism also need to be aimed at elderly people. For example, Levy's (2003) work suggests that activating positive stereotypes of aging before elderly people perform cognitive tasks may boost their performance, at least temporarily.

Some years ago, Judith Rodin and Ellen Langer (1980) set out to boost the self-esteem of elderly nursing home residents after discovering that 80% blamed physical aging for many of their difficulties in functioning and did not consider that the nursing home environment could be a source of their problems. In an experiment, Rodin and Langer exposed one group of nursing home residents to a new theory highlighting environmental causes of their limitations in functioning: That they had difficulty walking, for example, was attributed to the nursing home floors, which were tiled and therefore slippery for people of any age. Compared with an untreated control group and a group that received medical information that physical aging was not the major source of their difficulties, the group that learned to attribute everyday problems in functioning to the nursing home environment rather than to old age became more active, more sociable, and even more healthy.

Ultimately, societal-level change may be needed. Some countries (China, for example) clearly have more positive views of old age than America does (Levy & Langer, 1994). It may be possible for our ageist society, by instituting new social policies and programs, to reduce ageism and promote more positive views of aging across the life span (Braithwaite, 2002). Meanwhile, it seems that elderly people who can avoid taking negative stereotypes of old people to heart and who can avoid blaming the difficulties they encounter on the ravages of old age—that is, older adults who can avoid thinking like ageists—stand a good chance of feeling good about themselves.

Do Mean Personality Scores Change?

Do most people change systematically in common directions over the years? You may be consistently more extraverted than your best friend over the years, and yet both of you, with your peers, could become less extraverted at age 70 than you were at age 20. A second major meaning of continuity in personality, *stability in the average level of a trait,* is relevant in assessing the truth of stereotypes of older adults—for example, that they are more rigid, grumpy, depressed, and passive than younger adults.

Early cross-sectional studies suggested that younger and older adults have different personalities on average. However, some age-group differences have turned out to be generational, or cohort, differences rather than true maturational changes. That is, people's personalities are affected by when they were born and by the experiences they had in their formative years (Schaie & Parham, 1976). For example, Jean Twenge (2000) has shown that recent cohorts of children and adults have scored higher on measures of anxiety and neuroticism than earlier generations did. Indeed, the average child living in the United States in the 1980s reported levels of anxiety higher than those reported by children receiving psychiatric treatment in the 1950s. Possibly high crime and divorce rates and other social problems are making it harder for us to feel connected to others and safe today (Twenge, 2000).

When age-group differences appear consistently in different cultures undergoing different social changes at different times, they are not likely to be because of cohort effects. McCrae, Costa, and their colleagues (2000) have examined age-group differences in scores on the Big Five personality dimensions in countries as diverse as Turkey, the Czech Republic, and Japan. They find that neuroticism, extraversion (especially excitement-seeking tendencies), and openness to experience all decline modestly from adolescence to middle

© Royalty-Free/CORBIS

☾ Middle-aged adults tend to be less neurotic, extraverted, and open to experiences but more agreeable and conscientious than adolescents.

age, whereas agreeableness and conscientiousness increase modestly over this same age range. That is, during the years from adolescence to middle adulthood, we become less anxious and emotionally unstable, less outgoing, less open to new experiences, more cooperative and easy to get along with, and more disciplined and responsible.

Longitudinal studies confirm some of these patterns of change in the Big Five (McCrae & Costa, 2003). Generally, longitudinal studies point to personality growth from adolescence to middle adulthood—for example, to increased achievement orientation and self confidence (Haan, 1981; Jones & Meredith, 1996), and to increased dominance and independence (Helson, Jones, & Kwan, 2002). The studies are not all consistent, however, and the age changes in personality are not always large (McCrae & Costa, 2003).

What personality changes can people expect from middle age to old age? There are only a few signs that most people change in similar ways during this period. Activity level—the tendency to be energetic and action oriented, an aspect of extraversion—begins to decline in people's 50s and continue declining through the 80s and 90s (McCrae & Costa, 2003). People may also become more introverted and introspective in later life (Field & Millsap, 1991; Leon et al., 1979). Still, most of us will not undergo similar personality changes as part of the aging experience. Either we will remain much the same or we will change in response to life experiences in our own ways and at our own times (Helson, Jones, & Kwan, 2002).

Evidence of similar age differences in personality in different cultures, coupled with evidence that the Big Five personality trait dimensions are genetically influenced, has led McCrae and Costa (2003) to conclude that the Big Five:

- Are biologically based temperaments
- Are relatively resistant to environmental influences
- Undergo a universal process of maturational change

McCrae and Costa go on to theorize that evolution is behind maturational changes in personality. For our ancestors, they argue, a good deal of extraversion and openness to new experiences during adolescence might have proved useful in exploring the environment and, in the process, finding mates and other valued resources. For adults raising children, a keen sense of responsibility (conscientiousness) and helpfulness (agreeableness) may have proved more adaptive. This may explain why extraversion, openness to experience, and neuroticism appear to decrease from adolescence to middle age and why conscientiousness and agreeableness increase.

Although they are convinced that developmental trends in Big Five personality dimensions are universal, McCrae and Costa acknowledge that cultural and social influences shape the specific ways in which people adapt to their environments and learn habits and attitudes. Still, these leading experts on adult personality conclude that personality changes lives more than lives change personality: "Ask not how life's experiences change personality; ask instead how personality shapes lives and gives order, continuity, and predictability to the life course." (p. 235).

Not everyone agrees with the McCrae–Costa position that personality is largely biologically based and firmly in place by around age 30. For example, Ravenna Helson and her colleagues (2002) find that mean personality scores continue to change after age 30 and that societal changes such as an increased emphasis on individualism affect adults' personalities. Even McCrae and Costa (2003) allow that some aspects of personality are more changeable and more subject to environmental influence than the Big Five personality dimensions are—for example, attitudes and values, social roles, relationships, and self-concept.

What should you conclude, then? Most evidence points to (1) a good deal of cross-age consistency in people's rankings compared with other people on Big Five personality trait dimensions such as extraversion and neuroticism but also changes in rankings; (2) cohort effects suggesting that the historical context in which people grow up affects their personality development; (3) personality growth from adolescence to middle adulthood, or a strengthening of qualities such as achievement orientation and changes in the Big Five suggesting less neuroticism, extraversion, and openness to experience but more conscientiousness and agreeableness; and (4) little personality change from middle adulthood to later adulthood except for modest decreases in activity level and increases in introversion. In short, there is both continuity and discontinuity in personality during adulthood, and although some aspects of personality may be largely biologically based, others are more environmentally influenced.

Why Do People Change or Remain the Same?

Having figured out that personality exhibits both stability and change over the life span, developmentalists naturally want to know why people stay the same and why they change. What makes a personality stable? First, *heredity* is at work. As we have explained, genes contribute to individual differences in adult personality, including all five of the Big Five personality factors (Borkenau et al., 2001; Loehlin et al., 1998). Second, *lasting effects of childhood experiences* may contribute; you have seen, for example, that parents can either help a child overcome a difficult temperament or contribute to it becoming an enduring pattern of response. Third, traits may remain stable because people's *environments remain stable.* Fourth, *gene–environment correlations* may promote continuity. That is, genetic endowment may influence the kinds of experiences we have, and those experiences, in turn, may strengthen our genetically based predispositions (Roberts & Caspi, 2003; also see Chapter 3). Thus, an extravert's early sociability will elicit friendly responses from others, and she will seek and create environments to her liking—places where she can socialize and where her initial tendency to be extraverted will be strengthened. The individual genetically predisposed to be an introvert, by contrast, may avoid crowds, keep to herself, and therefore remain an introverted individual, comfortable with herself and her lifestyle. In a kind of snowball effect, the consequences of having one early temperament rather than another will cumulate over the years (Caspi, 1998).

What, then, might cause the significant changes in personality that some adults experience? *Biological factors* such as disease could contribute. The nervous system deterioration associated with Huntington's disease or Alzheimer's disease, for example, can cause victims to become moody, irritable, and irresponsible (McCrae & Costa, 2003). Adults also change in response to *changes in the social environment,* including major life events (Caspi, 1998; Maiden et al., 2003). For example, young adults who land good jobs after college tend to gain confidence, whereas those who face job insecurity and unemployment in their early careers lose it (Mortimer, Finch, & Kumka, 1982). In this way, life events help determine whether traits evident in early adulthood will persist or change, much as social learning theorists claim.

Finally, change is more likely when there is *a poor fit between person and environment* (Roberts & Robins, 2004). For example, Florine Livson (1976) discovered that independent women who did not have traditionally feminine traits experienced more personality change during midlife than traditional women who fit the stereotypically feminine roles of wife and mother better. Bothered by the mismatch between their personalities and their traditionally feminine roles, the nontraditional women redirected their lives in their 40s, expressed their masculine sides, and experienced improvements in psychological health by their 50s. Similarly, men who fit the traditional male role changed less over the years than nontraditional men who felt cramped by this role and who, after a crisis in their 40s, began to express their more feminine, emotional sides (Livson, 1981). For both men and women, then, a mismatch between personality and environment (or lifestyle) prompted personality change. This message about the importance of person–environment fit is the one that has emerged from research on children with different temperaments.

Thus, genes, lasting effects of early childhood experiences, stable environments, and gene–environment correlations (in which people seek and experience environments that match and reinforce earlier predispositions) all contribute to the considerable continuity seen in adult personality. Change in personality becomes more likely if people's biologies or environments change considerably or if there is a poor fit between their personalities and their lifestyles. To the extent that there is continuity in personality, people can predict what they and other people will be like in the future or how they will respond to life events. For example, individuals who score high on measures of neuroticism and low on measures of extraversion are likely to experience more negative and fewer positive life events than other people (Magnus et al., 1993) and to have more difficulty coping with negative life events when they occur (Hoffman, Levy-Shiff, & Malinski, 1996), whereas older adults who are extraverted and open to experience adapt well to potential stressors such as moving, gaining rather than losing self-esteem (Kling et al., 2003).

Eriksonian Psychosocial Growth

Researchers who conclude that adults hardly change over the years typically study personality by administering standardized personality scales. These tests were designed to assess enduring traits and probably reveal the most stable aspects of personality. Researchers who interview people in depth about their lives or look at aspects of personality such as perceived social acceptance and loneliness often detect considerably more change and growth (Asendorpf & van Aken, 2003; McCrae & Costa, 2003).

This is clear in research on Erikson's theory of psychosocial development through the life span. Erikson's eight stages of psychosocial development, listed in Table 11.5, will be reviewed briefly here, with emphasis on their implications for development during adulthood. Both maturational forces and social demands, Erikson believed, push humans everywhere through these eight psychosocial crises. Later conflicts may prove difficult to resolve if early conflicts were not resolved successfully. For development to proceed optimally, a healthy balance between the terms of the conflict must be struck.

The Path to Adulthood

During Erikson's first psychosocial conflict, **trust versus mistrust,** infants learn to trust other people if their caregivers are responsive to their needs; otherwise, the balance of trust versus mistrust will tip in the direction of mistrust. Erikson believed that infants, in resolving the psychosocial conflict of basic trust versus mistrust, begin to recognize that they are separate from the caregivers who respond to their needs. Indeed, as you saw earlier in this chapter, infants begin to dis-

Table 11.5 The Eight Stages of Erikson's Psychosocial Theory

Stage	Age Range	Central Issue
1. Trust vs. mistrust	Birth to 1 year	Can I trust others?
2. Autonomy vs. shame and doubt	1 to 3 years	Can I act on my own?
3. Initiative vs. guilt	3 to 6 years	Can I carry out my plans successfully?
4. Industry vs. inferiority	6 to 12 years	Am I competent compared with others?
5. Identity vs. role confusion	12 to 20 years	Who am I?
6. Intimacy vs. isolation	20 to 40 years	Am I ready for a relationship?
7. Generativity vs. stagnation	40 to 65 years	Have I left my mark?
8. Integrity vs. despair	65 years and older	Has my life been meaningful?

tinguish self from other (typically the mother) during the first 2 or 3 months of life.

Toddlers acquire an even clearer sense of themselves as individuals as they struggle with the psychosocial conflict of **autonomy versus shame and doubt.** According to Erikson, they develop a sense of themselves and assert that they have wills of their own. Consistent with this view, toddlers recognize themselves in a mirror and lace their speech with "me" and "no" around 18 months of age. Four- and 5-year-olds who have achieved a sense of autonomy then enter Erikson's stage of **initiative versus guilt.** They develop a sense of purpose by devising bold plans and taking great pride in accomplishing the goals they set. As you have seen, preschoolers define themselves primarily in terms of their physical activities and accomplishments.

A sense of initiative, Erikson believed, paves the way for success when elementary-school children face the conflict of **industry versus inferiority** and focus on mastering important cognitive and social skills. As you have seen, elementary-school children seem intent on evaluating their competencies; they engage in more social comparison than younger children and are likely to acquire a sense of industry rather than one of inferiority if those comparisons turn out favorably.

According to Erikson, children who successfully master each of these childhood psychosocial conflicts gain new ego strengths. Moreover, they learn a good deal about themselves and position themselves to resolve the adolescent crisis of *identity versus role confusion,* Erikson's fifth stage and a concept introduced earlier in this chapter. As you have seen in some detail, adolescence is a time for raising and answering identity questions. But what happens to adolescents with newfound identities during the adult years? Erikson thought that stagelike changes in personality continue during adulthood.

Early Adult Intimacy

As Erikson saw it, early adulthood is a time for dealing with the psychosocial conflict of **intimacy versus isolation.** He theorized that a person must achieve a sense of individual identity before becoming able to commit himself to a shared identity with another person—that is, you must know yourself before you can love someone else. The young adult who has no clear sense of self may be threatened by the idea of entering a committed, long-term relationship and being "tied down," or he may become overdependent on a romantic partner (or possibly a close friend) as a source of identity.

Does identity indeed pave the way for genuine intimacy? To find out, Susan Whitbourne and Stephanie Tesch (1985) measured identity status and intimacy status among college seniors and 24- to 27-year-old alumni from the same university. The researchers interviewed people about their closest re-

Early adulthood is the time, according to Erik Erikson, for deciding whether to commit to a shared identity with another person.

lationships and placed each person in one of six intimacy statuses. These included being a social isolate with no close relationships, being in a shallow relationship with little communication or involvement, being in a deep relationship but not yet being ready to make a long-term commitment to a partner, and being in a genuinely intimate relationship that has it all—involvement, open communication, and a long-term commitment. College graduates had progressed farther than college seniors in resolving intimacy issues; more of them were in long-term, committed relationships. In addition, the college graduates who had well-formed identities were more likely than those who did not to be capable of genuine and lasting intimacy.

As Erikson theorized, then, we must know ourselves before we can truly love another person. Yet Erikson believed that women resolve identity questions when they choose a mate and fashion an identity around their roles as wife and mother-to-be. Is this rather sexist view correct? Not quite. Influenced by traditional sex-role expectations, some women resolve intimacy issues before identity issues: they marry, raise children, and only after the children are more self-sufficient ask who they are as individuals (Hodgson & Fischer, 1979). Other women with feminine gender-role orientations tackle identity and intimacy issues simultaneously, perhaps forging a personal identity that centers on caring for other people or defining themselves in the context of a love relationship (Dyk & Adams, 1990).

However, still other women with more masculine gender-role orientations tend to follow the identity-before-intimacy route that characterizes men, settling on a career then thinking about a serious relationship (Dyk & Adams, 1990). Overall, then, Erikson's theory seems to fit men better than it fits women because fewer women follow the hypothesized identity-then-intimacy path. Sex differences in routes to identity and intimacy are likely to diminish, however, as more women postpone marriage to pursue careers.

Midlife Generativity

Does psychosocial growth continue in middle age? George Vaillant (1977), a psychoanalytic theorist, conducted an in-depth longitudinal study of mentally healthy Harvard men from college to middle age and a longitudinal study of blue-collar workers (Vaillant, 1983; Vaillant & Milofsky, 1980). Vaillant found support for Erikson's view that the 20s are a time for intimacy issues. He found that in their 30s, men shifted their energies to advancing their careers and were seldom reflective or concerned about others. Finally, in their 40s, many men became concerned with Erikson's issue of **generativity versus stagnation,** which involves gaining the capacity to generate or produce something that outlives you and to care about the welfare of future generations through such activities as parenting, teaching, mentoring, and leading (de St. Aubin, McAdams, & Kim, 2004; Slater, 2003). Vaillant's 40-something men expressed more interest in passing on something of value, either to their own children or to younger people at work. They reflected on their lives and experienced the kind of intellectual vitality that adolescents sometimes experience as they struggle with identity issues. Few experienced a full-blown and turbulent midlife crisis, just as few had experienced a severe identity crisis as college students. Nonetheless, they were growing as individuals, often becoming more caring and self-aware as they entered their 50s. One of these men expressed the developmental progression Vaillant detected perfectly: "At 20 to 30, I think I learned how to get along with my wife. From 30 to 40, I learned how to be a success in my job. And at 40 to 50, I worried less about myself and more about the children" (1977, p. 195).

Dan McAdams and others have been studying midlife generativity in more depth (de St. Aubin, McAdams, & Kim, 2004). Their studies show that middle-aged men and women are more likely than young adults to have achieved a sense of generativity (McAdams, Hart, & Maruna, 1998; Timmer, Bode, & Dittmann-Kohli, 2003). Moreover, those adults who have achieved a sense of identity and intimacy are more likely than other adults to achieve generativity, as Erikson predicted (Christiansen & Palkovitz, 1998). Adults who score high on measures of generativity are caring people, committed parents, productive workers and mentors, and community leaders. Influenced by gender roles, women often express generativity through caring for their families; men typically express it through their careers and leadership roles in the community (McAdams & Logan, 2004). In Big Five terms, generative adults tend to be agreeable, open to new experiences, and low in neuroticism (McAdams et al., 1998), and they are more satisfied with their lives (McAdams & Logan, 2004). Overall, research on generativity supports Erikson's view that both women and men are capable of impressive psychosocial growth during middle adulthood.

Old Age Integrity

Elderly adults, according to Erikson, confront the psychosocial issue of **integrity versus despair.** They try to find a sense of meaning in their lives that will help them face the inevitability of death. Most older adults, when asked what they would do differently if they had their lives to live over, say there is little, if anything, they would change (Erikson, Erikson, & Kivnick, 1986). This suggests that most older adults attain a sense of integrity. But how?

Some years ago, gerontologist Robert Butler (1963) proposed that elderly adults engage in a process called **life review,** in which they reflect on unresolved conflicts of the past to come to terms with themselves, find new meaning and coherence in their lives, and prepare for death (see Webster & Haight, 2002). Do older adults engage in life review, and does it help them achieve a healthy sense of integrity? Contrary to stereotypes, elderly people do not spend more time dwelling in the past than younger people do (Webster & McCall, 1999). However, whereas younger adults often reminisce to relieve boredom or to work on identity issues, older adults use their reminiscences to evaluate and integrate the pieces of their lives and to prepare for death—exactly what life review is all about (Molinari & Reichlin, 1984–1985; Webster & McCall, 1999). Elderly adults are also more likely than younger adults to focus on positive experiences and to emphasize the positive

© Royalty-Free/CORBIS

Reminiscence and life review can help older adults achieve a sense of integrity.

emotions associated with them when they reminisce, which may help them accept their lives and feel good about themselves (Pasupathi & Carstensen, 2003).

As it turns out, elders who use the life review process to confront and come to terms with their lives display a stronger sense of ego integrity and better overall adjustment than those who do not reminisce and those who mainly stew about how poorly life has treated them (Taft & Nehrke, 1990; Wong & Watt, 1991). Believing that life review can be beneficial in later life, Butler and others have used it as a form of therapy, asking elderly adults to reconstruct and reflect on their lives with the help of photo albums and other memorabilia. Participation in life review therapy can indeed benefit elderly adults (Molinari, 1999; Webster & Haight, 2002).

On balance, Erikson's view that humans experience psychosocial growth throughout the life span has gained support from research. Although few studies have directly tested Erikson's ideas about psychosocial development during childhood, his theorizing about the adolescent stage of identity versus role confusion has been tested extensively and is well supported. In addition, achieving a sense of identity in adolescence paves the way for forming a truly intimate relationship with another person as a young adult, many middle-aged adults go on to attain a sense of generativity, and many older adults work toward a sense of integrity through the process of life review.

Midlife Crisis?

Where in all this evidence of stability in personality traits such as extraversion and neuroticism and of Eriksonian psychosocial growth is the midlife crisis that many people believe is a standard feature of personality development in middle age? Although Erikson saw few signs of a midlife crisis, another psychoanalytic theorist, Daniel Levinson (1986, 1996; Levinson et al., 1978), did. He proposed an influential stage theory of adult development based on intensive interviews with men and later reported that it fit women as well (Levinson, 1996).

Levinson's stages describe the unfolding of what he calls an individual's **life structure**—an overall pattern of life that reflects the person's priorities and relationships with other people and the larger society. Levinson proposes that adults go through a repeated process of first building a life structure and then questioning and altering it. Structure-building periods, during which the person pursues career, family, and personal goals, alternate with transitional periods, when the person questions her life decisions. Levinson believed that his stages, outlined in Table 11.6, are both maturational in nature and universal. Environmental factors will influence the specifics of

Table 11.6 Levinson's Stages of Adult Development

Stage	Age	Characteristics
Early adult transition	17–21	Young people make the transition from adolescence to early adulthood, try to establish independence from parents, and explore possibilities for an adult identity. They form the dream, a vision of their life goals.
Entering the adult world	22–28	Adults build their first life structure, often by making and testing a career choice and by getting married. They work to succeed; find a supportive spouse, mentor, or both if possible; and do not question their lives much.
Age 30 transition	28–33	In this period of questioning, adults ask whether their career choices and marriages are what they want. If uncomfortable feelings arise from their questioning, they ignore them and plug away, make small adjustments in their life structure, or plan major life changes (e.g., a job change, a divorce, or a decision to return to school).
Settling down	33–40	This is a time for building and living a new, and often different, life structure and for "making it," or realizing one's dream. An adult may outgrow his need for a mentor and become his own person. As in the structure-building period of entering the adult world, adults tend to be ambitious, task oriented, and unreflective.
Midlife transition	40–45	In this major period of questioning, Levinson believes successful adults ask whether the dreams they formulated as young adults were worth achieving. If they have not achieved their dreams, they face that they may never achieve them. They may make major changes in their life structures.

an adult's life, but the basic pattern of building, questioning, and rebuilding will still be evident under the surface.

According to Levinson, the transition period from age 40 to age 45 is an especially significant time developmentally, a time of **midlife crisis**—of a person questioning his entire life structure and raising unsettling issues about where he has been and where he is heading. Most middle-aged men Levinson studied did not seek divorces, quit their jobs, buy red sports cars, or behave like lovesick adolescents, as popular images of the midlife crisis would have it. However, Levinson characterized 80% of the men in his study as having experienced a bona fide crisis—a period of intense inner struggles and disturbing realizations—in their early 40s. And, in his in-depth study of 45 women between age 35 and age 45, Levinson (1996) concluded that women experience significant crises during both the age 30 transition (28 to 33) and the midlife transition (40 to 45) often centered on the balancing of career and family.

Many researchers agree that middle age is a time when many important issues arise and when some men and women perceive themselves to be engaged in a painful self-evaluation process (Hermans & Oles, 1999; Rosenberg, Rosenberg, & Farrell, 1999). Still, there is not much support for Levinson's claim that most adults experience a genuine "crisis" in their early 40s. Although many middle-aged adults evaluate their lives, only a minority experience a painful upheaval that could be called a crisis (Hedlund & Ebersole, 1983; Vaillant, 1977). What is more, people question their lives at a variety of ages rather than only in their early 40s and often do so in response to specific life events such as a heart attack or a divorce.

If a stage of midlife crisis in the early 40s was widespread, researchers might expect men and women to experience significant personality changes at midlife or to show signs of emotional disturbance, decreasing well-being, or dissatisfaction with their job. This does not seem to be the case (Charles, Reynolds, & Gatz, 2001; McCrae & Costa, 2003; Warr, 1992). In sum, Levinson may have overestimated the extent to which midlife crisis occurs. It would seem more appropriate to call the phenomenon midlife *questioning,* to recognize that it can occur in response to life events at a variety of ages, and to appreciate that it is usually not a true psychological crisis.

Vocational Development and Adjustment

Although Levinson's concept of midlife crisis is not well supported, he was right to emphasize that adults revise important life decisions as they develop. To illustrate, consider vocational development during adulthood, a reflection of personality and self-concept (Judge & Bono, 2001). After much experimenting in early adulthood, people settle into chosen occupations, ideally ones that suit their self-concepts and personalities, in their 30s and strive for success. Ultimately, they prepare for the end of their careers, make the transition into retirement, and attempt to establish a satisfying lifestyle during their "golden years."

Establishing a Career

Much as Levinson discovered, early adulthood is a time for exploring vocational possibilities, launching careers, making tentative commitments, revising them if necessary, seeking advancement, and establishing yourself firmly in what you hope is a suitable occupation. Using data from a longitudinal study of males tracked from adolescence to age 36 (see Super, Savickas, & Super, 1996), Susan Phillips (1982) examined whether men's decisions about jobs at different ages were tentative and exploratory (for example, "to see if I really liked that kind of work") or more final (for example, "to get started in a field I wanted [to enter]"). The proportions of decisions that were predominantly exploratory were 80% at age 21, 50% at age 25, and 37% at age 36. From age 21 to age 36, then, young adults progressed from wide-open exploration of different career possibilities to tentative or trial commitments to a stabilization of their choices. Even in their mid-30s, however, about a third of adults were still exploring what they wanted to be when they grew up. The average man held *seven* full-time jobs or training positions between age 18 and age 36 (Phillips, 1982). The picture for women is similar (Jenkins, 1989).

After their relatively unsettled 20s and decision-making 30s, adults often reach the peaks of their careers in their 40s (Simonton, 1990). They often have major responsibilities and define themselves in terms of their work. Personality is an important influence on how it goes. For example, aggressive boys tend to become poorly adjusted adolescents and then men with unstable careers and long stretches of unemployment (Margit et al., 2003; Roenkae & Pulkkinen, 1995). By contrast, adults who score high in conscientiousness and extraversion and low in neuroticism tend to achieve more vocational success and are more satisfied with their jobs than other workers (Bajor & Baltes, 2003; Seibert & Kraimer, 2001). Person–environment fit can be critical, too: people tend to become dissatisfied and open to changing jobs when the fit between their personality and aptitudes and the demands of their job is poor (Bretz & Judge, 1994).

Gender is another significant influence on vocational development. Although women are entering a much wider range of fields today than they were a few decades ago, most secretaries, teachers, and nurses are still women. Partly because they are clustered in traditionally feminine-stereotyped occupations, U.S. women earn about 80 cents for every dollar men earn (Associated Press, 2003). Why the gap? It is probably caused by a combination of the influence of gender-role norms on the choices women make in their careers and of discrimination in the workplace.

Gender-role norms have prompted many women to subordinate career goals to family goals. Women often interrupt their careers, drop down to part-time work, or take less-demanding jobs so that they can bear and raise children (Moen, 1992). In the process, they hurt their chances of rising to high-paid, more responsible positions. Meanwhile, the women who make it to the top of the career ladder, especially in male-dominated fields, sometimes achieve this success by remaining single, divorcing, or limiting their childbearing (Jenkins, 1989). Overall, women without children achieve more in their careers than women with children (Carr et al., 1998; Wilson, 2003). Each additional child reduces a woman's earnings further (Avellar & Smock, 2003).

☾ Gender roles and career choices illustrated in *Doonesbury.*

The second factor limiting women's vocational development, discrimination, is evidenced by the following:

• Traditionally "female" jobs pay less than "male" jobs even when the intellectual demands of the work are similar (England, Reid, & Kilbourne, 1996).

• Women who enter jobs with the same management degrees and salaries as men, and receive equal performance ratings, still do not rise as far in the organization or earn as much as men (Cox & Harquail, 1991).

• Women earn about 20% less than men even when researchers control for women typically working less, stepping out of the work force more, and entering lower-paying occupations more often than men do (Associated Press, 2003).

Thus, although we make preliminary vocational choices as adolescents, we remain open to making new choices as young adults and take some time to settle on careers that fit our personalities and gender roles. Vocational experiences affect personality development and adjustment. For example, people whose work is complex and intellectually challenging grow as a result of the intellectual stimulation they receive on the job, becoming more able to handle intellectual problems adeptly, more self-confident, and even more tolerant of other people (Kohn & Schooler, 1982; Schooler, Mulatu, & Oates, 1999).

The Aging Worker

Many people believe that adults become less able or less motivated to perform well on the job as they approach retirement. As it turns out, the job performance of workers in their 50s and 60s is similar overall to that of younger workers (Avolio & Sosik, 1999; Hansson et al., 1997). Not only are older workers generally as competent as younger workers, but they tend to be more satisfied with their jobs, more involved in their work, and less interested in finding new jobs than younger workers are (Rhodes, 1983).

Why is the performance of older workers not hurt by some of the age-related physical and cognitive declines described in this book? First, these declines typically do not become significant until people are in their 70s and 80s, long after they have retired. Second, many older workers have accumulated a good deal of on-the-job expertise that helps them continue to perform well (Hansson et al., 1997). Finally, the answer may lie in the strategies that aging adults use to cope with aging. Gerontologists Paul and Margaret Baltes (1990) have theorized that older people can best cope with aging through a strategy they call **selective optimization with compensation** (Baltes & Baltes, 1990; Baltes & Freund, 2003). Three processes are involved: *selection* (focus on the skills the person most needs and wants to keep sharp), *optimization* (practice of those skills to keep them sharp), and *compensation* (development of ways to get around the need for other skills). Using selective optimization with compensation, an overworked 60-year-old lawyer might, for example, avoid spreading herself too thin by delegating lower-priority tasks to younger workers (selection), putting a lot of time into staying up-to-date in her main area of specialization (optimization), and making up for her failing memory by taking more notes at meetings (compensation).

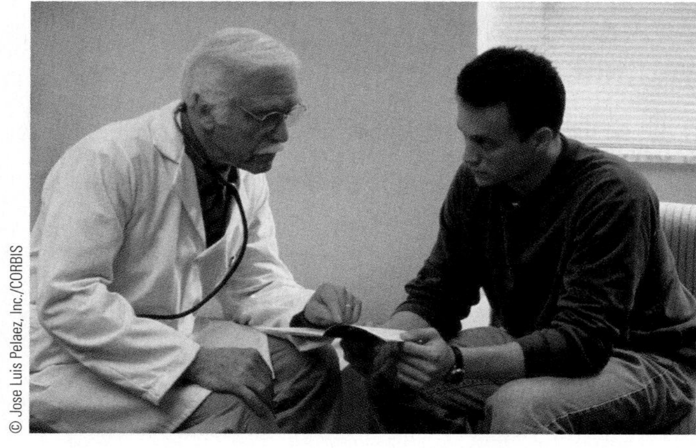

☾ Older workers generally perform as well as younger ones, possibly because they use selective optimization with compensation to cope with aging.

In a study of this coping strategy (Abraham & Hansson, 1995), workers age 40 to age 69 completed scales measuring their reliance on selection, optimization, and compensation strategies. Among older adults in the sample, especially those with highly stressful jobs, heavy reliance on selective optimization with compensation helped workers maintain a high level of performance and achieve their goals at work. The federal government seems to have recognized that older workers are typically effective workers. It has raised or eliminated mandatory retirement ages, increased the age of eligibility for receiving Social Security, and, through the Age Discrimination in Employment Act, protected older workers from age discrimination in hiring and retention (Hansson et al., 1997).

Retirement

A century ago, most adults continued working as long as they were able. As late as 1930, more than half of all men age 65 or older were still working (Palmore et al., 1985). The introduction of Social Security in 1934, affluence, and increased availability of private pension plans has changed that, making it financially possible for more men and women to retire and to do so earlier. In 1960, for example, 78% of men age 60 to age 64 were still in the labor force; by 2000, only 55% were (Samuelson, 2002).

How do people adjust to the final chapter of the work life cycle? Robert Atchley (1976) proposed that adults progress through a series of phases as they make the transition from worker to retiree. The process of adjustment begins with a *preretirement phase* in which workers nearing retirement gather information, talk about retirement, and plan for the future (Ekerdt, Kosloski, & DeViney, 2000). Deciding when to retire is an important part of the process. Some workers are forced to retire early because of poor health or because they are pushed out of their jobs, but others choose to retire early because they have enough money to do so, do not feel attached to their jobs, or simply like the idea (Beehr et al., 2000; Hansson et al., 1997).

Just after they retire, workers often experience a *honeymoon phase* in which they relish their newfound freedom—perhaps they head for the beach, golf course, or camping grounds and do all the projects they never had time to do while they worked. Then, according to Atchley, many enter a *disenchantment phase* as the novelty wears off; they feel aimless and sometimes unhappy. Finally, they move to a *reorientation phase* in which they begin to put together a realistic and satisfying lifestyle. Research supports this view. For example, David Ekerdt and his colleagues (Ekerdt, Bossé, & Levkoff, 1985) found that (1) men who had been retired only a few months were in a honeymoon period in which they were highly satisfied with life and optimistic about the future, (2) men who had been retired 13 to 18 months were rather disenchanted, and (3) men who had been retired for longer periods were relatively satisfied (see also Gall, Evans, & Howard, 1997).

Clearly retirement takes some getting used to. After retirees have adjusted, however, are they worse off than they were before they retired? Negative images of the retired person abound in our society; the retiree supposedly ends up feeling useless, old, bored, sickly, and dissatisfied with life. Yet research shows that retirement has few effects on adults (Gall et al., 1997; Hansson et al., 1997; Palmore et al., 1985). Retirement's most consistent effect is to reduce the individual's income—on average, to about three-fourths of what it was before retirement (Palmore et al., 1985). Retired people generally do not experience a decline in health simply because they retire. Poor health more often causes retirement than retirement causes poor health. Retirees' activity patterns and social lives do not change much either (Palmore et al., 1985). Retirement typically has no noticeable effect on the size of people's social networks, the frequency of their social contacts, or their satisfaction with the social support they receive. Finally, retirement does not seem to disrupt marriages or reduce life satisfaction or mental health.

Overall, then, retirees are likely to experience an adjustment process involving preretirement then honeymoon, disenchantment, and reorientation phases. They end up adapting successfully to retirement and to the drop in income that it typically involves. Yet there are huge individual differences in adjustment. What makes for a favorable adjustment? Adults who retire voluntarily rather than involuntarily, enjoy good health, have the financial resources to live comfortably, and are married or otherwise have strong social support typically fare better than those forced to retire because of poor health or those who find themselves with inadequate incomes and few social ties (Gall et al., 1997; Palmore et al., 1985; Szinovacz & Ekerdt, 1995).

Personality and Successful Aging

What makes not only for a successful transition to retirement but also, more generally, for a happy and fulfilling old age? Theories of successful aging have been offered to answer that question. **Activity theory** holds that aging adults will find their lives satisfying to the extent that they can maintain their previous lifestyles and activity levels, either by continuing old activities or by finding substitutes—for example, by replacing work with hobbies, volunteer work, or other stimulating pursuits (Havighurst, Neugarten, & Tobin, 1968; Fry, 1992). According to this theory, psychological needs do not really change as people enter old age: most aging individuals continue to want an active lifestyle.

By contrast, **disengagement theory** says that successful aging involves a withdrawal of the aging individual from society that is satisfying to both (Cumming & Henry, 1961; Achenbaum & Bengtson, 1994). The aging individual is said to have needs different from those he once had and to seek to leave old roles behind and reduce activity. Meanwhile, society both encourages and benefits from the older person's disengagement.

Which is it? Throughout this text, you have seen evidence that individuals who remain active in old age benefit from their activity. Those who are physically active maintain their health longer (see Chapter 5), those who are intellectually active maintain their cognitive functions longer (see Chapter 9),

© Chuck Savage/CORBIS

Many older adults subscribe to the activity theory of aging, attempting to find substitutes for lost roles and activities. Others find happiness through disengagement and prefer to sit and watch.

and those who remain involved in meaningful social relationships are likely to be more satisfied with their lives (see Chapter 14). In other words, there is more support for activity theory than for disengagement theory.

But before you conclude that activity theory explains all you need to know about successful aging, add three qualifications. First, the relationship between level of activity and life satisfaction or well-being is surprisingly weak (Fry, 1992). Apparently, many inactive individuals are nonetheless satisfied with their lives, and many busy individuals are nonetheless miserable. This suggests that quality of activity is probably more important than its quantity (Pinquart & Sorensen, 2000).

Second, some messages of disengagement theory have merit (Achenbaum & Bengtson, 1994). As you saw earlier in this chapter, for example, older adults sometimes become more introspective than they were earlier in life. This sort of psychological withdrawal could be viewed as a form of disengagement. Moreover, most older people today withdraw voluntarily from certain roles and activities. Most retire, for example, and society generally supports the concept of their doing so.

But third, neither activity theory nor disengagement theory adequately allows that the personality traits people carry with them from childhood influence their well-being in old age. Generally, for example, people who are highly extraverted and conscientious and score low in neuroticism have a greater sense of well-being than other adults (Siegler & Brummett, 2000). Even more important, a good fit between the individual's lifestyle and the individual's needs, preferences, and personality may be the real secret to successful aging (Fry, 1992; Seleen, 1982). Activity theorists assume that most people will benefit from maintaining an active lifestyle; disengagement theorists assume that most people will be best off if they disengage. In fact, an energetic and outgoing person may want to maintain her active lifestyle in old age, whereas a person who always found work to be a hassle may like nothing better than to sit in a rocking chair and might be miserable if forced to continue working or to participate in a retirement community's sing-alongs, dances, and skits.

Still other older adults may find satisfaction in maintaining a few highly important roles, relationships, and personally meaningful projects but selectively withdrawing from others (Turk-Charles & Carstensen, 1999; Lawton et al., 2002). That is, selective optimization with compensation, which as you saw helps aging workers maintain good job performance, may also work as a strategy for maintaining a sense of well-being in old age (Freund & Baltes, 1998; Baltes & Carstensen, 2003). By selecting a few priority areas, optimizing competencies in those areas, and compensating for performance declines in other areas, older adults can continue to feel good about themselves and their lives. In short, you cannot assume, as both activity theory and disengagement theory do, that what suits one suits all. Rather, you should again adopt an interactional model of development that emphasizes the goodness of fit between person and environment. In the next chapter, we explore some fascinating interactions between biology and environment that contribute to differences between males and females.

Summing Up

People of different ages describe themselves in largely similar ways, and older adults are generally able to maintain self-esteem by closing the gap between the ideal and the real self, altering goals and standards, and comparing themselves with other aging people until self-esteem drops for some in late old age. There is both continuity and discontinuity in personality; individual rankings on Big Five dimensions stay stable after 30, but mean scores shift toward less neuroticism, extraversion, and openness to experience—and more agreeableness and conscientiousness—from adolescence to middle age. Few systematic changes occur from middle age to old age except for a decrease in activity level and an increase in introversion. Stability may be caused by genes, early experience, stable environments, and gene–environment correlations; change may be caused by biological or environmental changes and a poor person–environment fit.

Erikson's theory of psychosocial development is supported by evidence that resolution of conflicts centering on trust, autonomy, initiative, and industry pave the way for identity achievement in adolescence and for intimacy, generativity, and integrity in adulthood. Levinson's stage theory of adult development, featuring a midlife crisis in the person's 40s, is only partly supported, although adults do evaluate their lives and make changes at various times. In support of Levinson, adults engage in much career exploration before they settle down in their 30s and achieve peak vocational success in their 40s. Personality and gender play a role in vocational development, and older workers remain productive and satisfied, perhaps partly through the use of the coping device of selective optimization with compensation.

Retiring workers experience preretirement, honeymoon, disenchantment, and reorientation phases and typically experience a drop in income but little change in health or psychological well-being. More generally, neither activity theory nor disengagement theory explains successful aging because a good fit between lifestyle and personality is important. ■

Summary Points

1. Personality is an organized combination of attributes unique to the individual; self-concept is a person's perceptions of his attributes; and self-esteem is his overall evaluations of his worth.

2. Psychoanalytic theorists maintain that we all experience stagelike personality changes at similar ages and that early personality affects later personality, but Erik Erikson and Daniel Levinson saw more potential for growth during adulthood than Sigmund Freud did. Trait theorists believe that aspects of personality such as the Big Five trait dimensions are enduring and do not propose stages of personality development. By contrast, social learning theorists and contextual theorists maintain that people can change in any number of directions at any time in life if their social environments change.

3. Early in their first year, infants sense that they are separate from the world around them; by 18 to 24 months, they display self-recognition and form a categorical self based on age and sex.

4. Infants differ in temperament: emotionality, activity, and sociability; behavioral inhibition; and easy, difficult, and slow-to-warm-up temperaments. Temperament is partially influenced by genetic endowment, shaped by the goodness of fit between child and environment, and only moderately related to later personality.

5. Whereas the self-concepts of preschool children are largely focused on physical characteristics and activities, 8-year-olds describe their inner psychological traits and evaluate their competencies through social comparison. Children are most likely to develop high self-esteem when they are competent, fare well in social comparisons (like big fish in small ponds), and have warm, democratic parents. During middle childhood, personality traits become more consistent and enduring.

6. During adolescence, self-concepts become more psychological, abstract, and integrated, and self-awareness increases. Most adolescents experience only temporary disturbances in self-esteem at the onset of adolescence and gain self-esteem thereafter.

7. In resolving Erikson's conflict of identity versus role confusion, many college-age youths progress from diffusion or foreclosure status to moratorium status to identity achievement status. Identity formation is uneven across domains of identity, often continues into adulthood, and is influenced by cognitive development and social experiences such as interactions with loving parents who encourage individuality.

8. According to Eli Ginzberg, adolescents' vocational choices become increasingly realistic as they progress through the fantasy, tentative, and realistic stages. Social factors sometimes constrain the choices made by females and by low-income youth of both sexes.

9. Older adults maintain self-esteem by converging their ideal selves and their real selves, changing their goals and standards of self-evaluation, and comparing themselves with other aging adults, but sometimes they lose self-esteem in late old age. Self-conceptions differ in individualistic cultures (where generalizable traits are emphasized) and collectivist cultures (where personality is more situational).

10. Individuals' rankings on Big Five dimensions of personality become more stable with age, but there is both continuity and discontinuity in personality during adulthood. From adolescence to middle adulthood, people gain personal strengths, and Big Five profiles shift from neuroticism, extraversion, and openness to experience toward agreeableness and conscientiousness. From middle age to old age, a decrease in activity level and an increase in introversion may occur.

11. Stability of personality may be caused by genetic makeup, lasting effects of early experience, stable environments, and gene–environment correlations. Personality change may be associated with biological or environmental changes or a poor fit between person and environment.

12. Erikson's theory of psychosocial development is supported by evidence that resolution of conflicts centering on trust, autonomy, initiative, and industry paves the way for achieving a sense of identity in adolescence and that identity then lays a foundation for

achieving intimacy in early adulthood, generativity in middle age, and a sense of integrity through life review in old age.

13. Levinson's theory that adults experience a recurring process of building and questioning life structures—highlighted by a midlife crisis—is only partly supported. Midlife crisis in a person's early 40s does not seem to be universal, although adults do reevaluate their lives.

14. Young adults engage in much career exploration and questioning before they settle down in their 30s and achieve peak success in their 40s. Personality and gender influence vocational success, and work activities influence personality. Older workers are as productive as and more satisfied than younger workers, possibly because they use selective optimization with compensation to cope with aging.

15. Retiring workers experience an adjustment process with preretirement, honeymoon, disenchantment, and reorientation phases; they typically experience a drop in income but little change in health or psychological well-being. In attempting to identify paths to successful adjustment in old age, neither activity theory nor disengagement theory places enough emphasis on person–environment fit and selective optimization with compensation.

Critical Thinking

1. Write three brief descriptions of yourself to show how you might have answered the question "Who am I?" at age 4, age 9, and age 18. What developmental changes in self-conceptions do your self-descriptions illustrate?

2. Gracie the toddler tends to become stressed when her routines are changed, a stranger comes to the door, or she is asked to try something she has never tried before. Help her parents understand her temperament and what it may mean for her personality as a 21-year-old.

3. Zhenyu is having a terrible time achieving a sense of identity during adolescence; he has been drifting aimlessly for years. Drawing on the material in this chapter, explain why this may be the case.

4. Aunt Rosalia is about to retire and wants to establish a satisfying lifestyle for her old age. What would an activity theorist, a disengagement theorist, and a theorist who supports selective optimization with compensation recommend that she do?

Key Terms

personality, 287
self-concept, 287
self-esteem, 287
identity, 287
Big Five, 288
self-recognition, 290
categorical self, 291
looking-glass self, 291
emotionality 291
activity, 291
sociability, 292
behavioral inhibition, 292
easy temperament, 292
difficult temperament, 292
slow-to-warm-up temperament, 293
goodness of fit, 293
social comparison, 295
ideal self, 296
big-fish–little-pond effect, 299
identity versus role confusion, 300
moratorium period, 300
diffusion status, 300
foreclosure status, 300
moratorium status, 301
identity achievement status, 301
ethnic identity, 302
individualistic culture, 307
collectivist culture, 307
trust versus mistrust, 311
autonomy versus shame and doubt, 312
initiative versus guilt, 312
industry versus inferiority, 312
intimacy versus isolation, 312
generativity versus stagnation, 313
integrity versus despair, 313
life review, 313
life structure, 314
midlife crisis, 315
selective optimization with compensation, 316
activity theory, 317
disengagement theory, 317

Media Resources

Websites to Explore

Visit Our Website

For a chapter tutorial quiz and other useful features, visit the book's companion website at *http://psychology.wadsworth.com/sigelman_rider5e.* You can also connect directly to the following sites:

The Big Five Personality Dimensions
Get acquainted with the Big Five and the specific traits that belong under each of the five major dimensions. You will find background information, a comparison of this model of personality with others, and information about tests available for assessing the Big Five dimensions.

Personality Theorists from Freud to Piaget
C. George Boeree, a psychology professor at Shippensburg University, has written and compiled an e-text on different personality theories, including that of Erik Erikson. For each theorist, he offers a brief biography, a summary of the theory, a discussion, and additional readings for further exploration.

Midlife
This site, intended to be "inspirational," is dedicated to middle age and its characteristics and challenges.

Eldercare
ElderWeb is an online sourcebook with links directly to articles about Eldercare topics, sites where you can search for services by location and state-specific benefits information. It also has a page devoted to financial planning.

Retirement
A public education program of the nonpartisan Employee Benefit Research Institute, Choose to Save® maintains a website that promotes planning for a secure financial future. It includes tools such as worksheets and online calculators that help consumers of all ages plan their retirement.

Understanding the Data: Exercises on the Web

For additional insight on the data presented in this chapter, try the exercises for these figures at *http://psychology.wadsworth.com/sigelman_rider5e:*

Figure 11.3 Percentage of subjects in each of James Marcia's four identity statuses as a function of age

Figure 11.5 Favorability of ratings of their ideal, likely future, present (real), and past selves by young, middle-aged, and elderly adults

Life-Span CD-ROM

Go to the Wadsworth Life-Span CD-ROM for further study of the concepts in this chapter. The CD-ROM includes narrated concept overviews, video clips, a multimedia glossary, and additional activities to expand your learning experience. For this chapter, check out the following clips, and others, in the video library:

VIDEO Infancy and Toddlerhood: Temperament

VIDEO Early and Middle Childhood: Play

DEVELOPMENTAL Psychology Now™

Developmental PsychologyNow is a web-based, intelligent study system that provides a complete package of diagnostic quizzes, a personalized study plan, integrated multimedia elements, and learning modules. Check it out at *http://psychology.wadsworth.com/sigelman_rider5e/now.*

CHAPTER twelve

Gender Roles and Sexuality

DEVELOPMENTAL PSYCHOLOGIST CAROLE BEAL (1994) learned an interesting lesson about the significance of being a girl or a boy when she was interviewing 9-year-olds:

> I had just finished one interview and was making some quick notes when the next child came into the office. I looked up, and an odd thing happened: I could not tell whether the child was a boy or a girl. The usual cues were not there: The child's hair was trimmed in a sort of pudding-bowl style, not really long but not definitively short either. The child was dressed in a gender-neutral outfit of jeans, sneakers, and a loose T-shirt, like most of the children at the school. The name on the interview permission slip was "Cory," which did not clarify matters much as it could be either a boy's or a girl's name. Still puzzled, I began the interview and found myself becoming increasingly frustrated at not knowing Cory's sex. I quickly realized how many unconscious assumptions I usually made about boys and girls; for example, that a girl would probably like a particular story about a horse and be willing to answer a few extra questions about it, or that a boy would probably start to get restless after a certain point and I would have to work a bit harder to keep his attention. (p. 3)

Unlike Cory, most children are readily identified as girls or boys and treated accordingly. How much does it matter, in terms of development, whether a child is perceived and treated as a girl or as a boy? How much does it matter whether a child is a girl or a boy biologically? These are the kinds of questions we tackle in this chapter.

Gender matters. When proud new parents telephone to announce a birth, the first question friends and family tend to ask is "Is it a boy or a girl?" Before long, girls discover that they are girls, and many acquire a taste for frilly dresses and dolls, and boys discover that they are boys and often wrestle each other on the lawn. As an adult, you are probably keenly aware of being either a man or a woman and may define yourself partly in terms of your "feminine" or "masculine" qualities. In short, being female or male is a highly important aspect of the self throughout the life span. Before you read any further, try the quiz in Table 12.1 to see if you know which of the many ideas about male–female differences have some truth to them.

Table 12.1 Which of These Sex Differences Is Real?

Which of the following do you think are consistent sex differences that have been demonstrated in studies comparing males and females? Mark each statement T (true) or F (false). Answers are printed upside down; they will be clarified in the discussion that follows.

____ 1. Males are more aggressive than females.

____ 2. Males are more active than females.

____ 3. Females are more social than males.

____ 4. Females have stronger verbal abilities than males.

____ 5. Males have greater achievement motivation than females.

____ 6. Males are more analytical than females.

____ 7. Females are more suggestible and prone to conform than males.

____ 8. Females are more emotionally unstable than males.

____ 9. Males are more rational and logical than females.

____ 10. Males have greater spatial and mathematical abilities than females.

Answers: 1-T, 2-T, 3-F, 4-T, 5-F, 6-F, 7-F, 8-F, 9-F, 10-T.

Male and Female

What difference does it make whether a person is a male or a female? It matters in terms of physical differences, psychological differences, and differences in roles played in society. The physical differences are undeniable. A zygote that receives an X chromosome from each parent is a genetic (XX) female, whereas a zygote that receives a Y chromosome from the father is a genetic (XY) male. In rare cases of gender chromosome abnormalities (see Chapter 3), this is not the case; a girl may have only one X chromosome or a boy may have three chromosomes (XYY or XXY). Chromosomal differences result in different prenatal hormone balances in males and females, and hormone balances before and after birth are responsible for the facts that the genitals of males and females differ and that only females can bear children. Moreover, males typically grow to be taller, heavier, and more muscular than females, although females may be the hardier sex in that they live longer and are less susceptible to many physical disorders (Giampaoli, 2000). As you will see later in the chapter, some theorists argue that biological differences between males and females are responsible for psychological and social differences.

However, there is much more to being male or female than biology. Virtually all societies expect the two sexes to adopt different **gender roles**—the patterns of behavior that females and males should adopt in a particular society (for example, the roles of wife, mother, and woman or of husband, father, and man). Characteristics and behaviors viewed as desirable for males or females are specified in **gender-role norms**—society's expectations or standards concerning what males and females *should be* like. Each society's norms generate **gender-role stereotypes,** overgeneralized and largely inaccurate beliefs about what males and females *are* like.

Through the process of **gender typing,** children not only become aware that they are biological males or females but also acquire the motives, values, and patterns of behavior that their culture considers appropriate for members of their biological sex. Through the gender-typing process, for example, Susie may learn a gender-role norm stating that women should strive to be good mothers and gender-role stereotypes indicating that women are more skilled at nurturing children than men are. As an adult, Susan may then adopt the traditional feminine role by switching from full- to part-time work when her first child is born and devoting herself to the task of mothering.

It would be a mistake, then, to attribute any differences that we observe between girls and boys (or women and men) solely to biological causes. They could just as easily be caused by differences in the ways males and females are perceived and raised. But before we try to explain sex differences, perhaps we should describe what these differences are believed to be and what they actually are.

Gender Norms and Stereotypes

Which sex is more likely to express emotions? To be neat and organized? To be competitive? To use harsh language? If you are like most people, you undoubtedly have ideas about how men and women differ psychologically and can offer some answers to these questions.

The female's role as childbearer has shaped the gender-role norms that prevail in many societies, including our own. At the heart of the feminine gender role is **communality,** an orientation that emphasizes connectedness to others and includes traits of emotionality and sensitivity to others (Best & Williams, 1993; Conway & Vartanian, 2000). Simon Baron-Cohen (2003) goes so far as to argue that the female brain is "hard-wired for empathy," which is a significant component of communality (p. 1). Girls who adopt communal traits will presumably be prepared to play the roles of wife and mother—to keep the family functioning and to raise children successfully. By contrast, the central aspect of the masculine gender role is **agency,** an orientation toward individual action and achievement that emphasizes traits of dominance, independence, assertiveness, and competitiveness. Boys have been encouraged to adopt agentic traits to fulfill the traditionally defined roles of husband and father, which involve providing for the family and protecting it from harm. Taking this one step further, Baron-Cohen (2003) claims that men's focus on work, achievement, and independence stems from the male brain's tendency to **systemize,** or analyze and explore how things work.

Norms in many cultures mandate that females play a communal role and males play an agentic role, which leads us to form stereotypes saying that females possess communal traits and males possess agentic traits (Williams & Best, 1990). Unfortunately, feminine traits are stereotyped as more childlike and less adultlike than masculine traits, placing adults perceived as having feminine traits at a disadvantage (Powlishta, 2000). If you are thinking that these stereotypes have disappeared as attention to women's rights has increased and as more women have entered the labor force, think again. Although some change has occurred, adolescents and young adults still endorse many traditional stereotypes about men and women (Botkin, Weeks, & Morris, 2000; Lueptow, Garovich-Szabo, & Lueptow, 2001).

Moreover, males and females continue to describe themselves differently. When Jean Twenge (1997) analyzed studies conducted from 1970 to 1995 in which standard scales assessing gender-relevant traits had been administered, she found that men and women in the mid-1990s described themselves more similarly than men and women did 20 years previously, largely because modern women saw themselves as having more masculine traits. However, male and female personality profiles continued to differ in ways consistent with gender stereotypes. Might beliefs about sex differences, then, have a basis in fact?

Are There Gender Differences?

Much research has attempted to answer the question of whether there are sex or gender differences in behavior. Although differences in some areas have been identified, other areas show no gender differences. As you review the areas in which there are some differences, keep in mind that these are often small, group differences. That is, even when research shows that women score higher (or lower) than men on average, there will be individual women who score lower (or higher) than individual men. With this in mind, here is what the research shows:

- *Females sometimes display greater verbal abilities than males, but the difference is small.* According to Eleanor Maccoby and Carol Jacklin's (1974) classic review of more than 1500 studies, girls tend to develop verbal skills at an earlier age than boys and show a small but consistent advantage on tests of vocabulary, reading comprehension, and speech fluency. Sex differences in verbal ability have all but disappeared in more recent studies, but girls continue to achieve higher classroom grades in English (Feingold, 1988; Hyde & Linn, 1988; Nowell & Hedges, 1998; Wentzell, 1988).
- *Males outperform females on tests of spatial ability* (for example, arranging blocks in patterns or identifying the same figure from different angles; see Figure 12.1). Although Maccoby and Jacklin concluded in their 1974 review that these differences emerge only in adolescence, differences on some tests—especially mental rotations—can be detected in childhood and persist across the life span (Choi & Silverman, 2003; Nordvik & Amponsah, 1998; Voyer, Voyer, & Bryden, 1995).
- Most, but not all, research finds that males outperform females, on average, on tests of mathematical ability. In particular, Janet Hyde and her associates (Hyde, Fennema, & Lamon, 1990) conclude that *girls have a slight edge in calculation skills; the sexes do not differ in their understanding of math concepts; and males outperform females on mathematical word problems, starting in adolescence.* The male advantage in mathematical problem-solving skills is especially clear in samples of high math performers; that is, more males than females are mathematically talented (Stumpf & Stanley, 1996). Some research shows that this male advantage is evident in the earliest grades (Nowell & Hedges, 1998; Robinson et al., 1996). As it turns out, more males than females are also low math achievers; on several cognitive ability tests, more males than females show up at both the top and the bottom of the scale (Feingold, 1992).
- *Males engage in more physical and verbal aggression than females, starting as early as age 2* (Buss & Perry, 1992; Eagly &

Figure 12.1 A spatial ability task. Are the two figures in each pair alike or different? The task assesses the ability to mentally rotate visual information and is a task on which average differences between males and females are large.
SOURCE: Shepard & Metzler (1971).

Steffen, 1986). Males commit more serious crimes (Barash, 2002), but sex differences are clearer for physical aggression than for other forms of aggression. For example, females tend to specialize in subtle, indirect, and relational forms of aggression such as gossiping about and excluding others (Bjorkqvist, 1994; Crick & Bigbee, 1998).

• Even before birth and throughout childhood, *boys are more physically active* than girls (Almli, Ball, & Wheeler, 2001); they fidget and squirm more as infants and run around more as children.

• *Boys are more developmentally vulnerable,* not only to prenatal and perinatal stress (for example, they die more often before birth) but also to several diseases and to disorders such as reading disabilities, speech defects, hyperactivity, emotional problems, and mental retardation (Henker & Whalen, 1989; Jacklin, 1989; Raz et al., 1994).

• *Girls are more compliant with requests from adults,* although they are no more likely than boys to give in to peers (Maccoby, 1998).

• *Girls are more tactful and cooperative,* as opposed to forceful and demanding, when attempting to persuade others to comply with them (Baron-Cohen, 2003; Maccoby, 1998).

• *Both males and females report that females are more nurturant and empathic; sex differences in behaviors, however, are small but show females empathizing more than males* (Baron-Cohen, 2003; Deutsch, 1999; Feingold, 1994b). Females take more interest in and are more responsive to infants (Reid & Trotter, 1993).

• *Females are somewhat more anxious, cautious, and fearful,* although not in social situations (Feingold, 1994b). They are also more prone to develop anxiety disorders and phobias (Pigott, 2002).

• *Males show a small edge over females in self-esteem* (Kling et al., 1999; Robins et al., 2002). Overall, the largest gender difference in self-esteem is found during late adolescence, but the difference is evident throughout adulthood.

• *Males are more likely to engage in risky behaviors,* although this varies with age and has decreased somewhat over the years (Byrnes, Miller, & Schafer, 1999; Pinker, 2002).

Despite such evidence of gender differences from some researchers, others take the contrasting view that even the largest of the "real" psychological differences between the sexes are trivial. For example, if you imagine all the differences in aggressiveness among individuals, from the most aggressive to the least aggressive person in a group, it turns out that only 5% of that variation can be traced directly to whether a person is male or female (Hyde, 1984); apparently, the remaining 95% of the variation is caused by other differences among people. It is worth reiterating the point we made at the beginning of this section: *Average* levels of a behavior such as aggression may be noticeably different for males and females, but within each sex there are both extremely aggressive and extremely nonaggressive individuals. Thus, it is impossible to predict accurately how aggressive a person is simply by knowing his or her gender. Sex differences in most other abilities and personality traits are similarly small. Moreover, some sex differences are smaller today than they used to be (Hyde et al., 1990; Stumpf & Stanley, 1996).

As it turns out, many of our stereotypes of males and females are just that—overgeneralizations unsupported by fact. Despite some differences, females and males are more psychologically similar than different.

Why do unfounded stereotypes persist? Partly because we, as the holders of male–female stereotypes, are biased in our perceptions. We are more likely to notice and remember behaviors that confirm our beliefs than to notice and remember exceptions, such as independent behavior in a woman or emotional sensitivity in a man (Martin & Halverson, 1981). Alice Eagly's (1987) **social-role hypothesis** suggests that differences in the roles that women and men play in society do a lot to create and maintain gender-role stereotypes (see also Eagly & Steffen, 2000). For example, men have traditionally occupied powerful roles in business and industry that require them to be dominant and forceful. Women have more often filled the role of homemaker and therefore have been called upon to be nurturant and sensitive to their children's needs. As a result, we begin to see men as dominant or agentic by nature and women as nurturant or communal by nature. We lose sight that it is differences in the social roles they play that

According to Alice Eagly's social-role hypothesis, this man would be perceived as nurturant, warm, and caring because he has assumed the role of caregiver.

cause men and women to behave differently. It could be that sex differences in behavior might be reversed if women ran companies and men raised children.

As Eagly's social-role hypothesis suggests, we must adopt a contextual perspective on psychological differences between males and females. Sex differences evident in one culture or social context often are not evident in another (Deaux & Major, 1990; Feingold, 1994a). For example, women do better on tests of mathematical ability—and sometimes outperform men—in countries such as Israel, where women have excellent occupational opportunities in technical fields (Baker & Jones, 1992). This suggests that sex differences in abilities are not biologically inevitable. From a contextual perspective, it is silly to speak about the "nature of women" or the "nature of men." Differences between males and females can be large or small depending on the social contexts in which they find themselves.

Although psychological sex differences are often small, however, it makes a difference in society whether a person is male or female. First, gender norms and stereotypes, even when they are unfounded, affect how we perceive ourselves and other people. As long as people expect females to be less competent in math than males, for example, females may lack confidence in their abilities and perform less competently (Eccles, Jacobs, & Harold, 1990). That many stereotypes are unfounded does not make them less potent.

In addition, even though males and females are similar psychologically, they are steered toward different roles in society. In childhood, girls and boys conform to their gender roles by segregating themselves by sex and developing different interests and play activities (Maccoby, 1998). As adolescents and adults, males and females pursue different vocations and lifestyles. Although more women are entering male-dominated fields today than in the past, they are underrepresented in many traditionally male-dominated fields, and men rarely enter female-dominated fields (U.S. Department of Labor, 2001). If you go to a college graduation ceremony today, you will still see relatively few women among the engineers and few men among the nursing graduates. More men are sharing child-rearing and household responsibilities with their partners, but most couples still divide the labor along traditional lines, so that the woman is primarily responsible for child care and housework and the man is primarily responsible for income and money management (Bianchi et al., 2000; Perkins & DeMeis, 1996). When we think about who asks whom out on a date, who stays home from work when a child has the chicken pox, or who sews the buttons back on shirts, we must conclude that, despite significant social change, traditional gender roles are alive and well.

Summing Up

In short, we continue to live in a society where, for better or worse, being male or female matters. The psychological differences between the sexes may be few and small, but the physical differences are always visible, and the roles that most men and women play in society continue to differ. Now, trace how girls and boys master their "gender-role curriculum" and how they apply what they learn throughout their lives. ■

The Infant

At birth there are few differences, other than the obvious anatomical ones, between males and females, and even these few differences tend to be small and inconsistent. Nonetheless, it does not take long after newborns are labeled as girls or boys for gender stereotypes to affect how they are perceived and treated—and for infants to notice that males and females are different.

Differential Treatment

When the baby is still in the hospital delivery room or nursery, parents tend to use masculine terms when talking to or about their infant son (such as "big guy" or "tiger") and to comment on the strength of his cries, kicks, and grasps. Girl infants are more likely to be labeled "sugar" or "sweetie" and to be described as soft, cuddly, and adorable (Maccoby, 1980). Even when objective examinations reveal no such differences between boys and girls at birth, adults perceive boys as strong, large featured, and coordinated and view girls as weaker, finer featured, and more awkward (Rubin, Provenzano, & Luria, 1974; see also Karraker, Vogel, & Lake, 1995). Soon boys and girls are decked out in either blue or pink and provided with "sex-appropriate" hairstyles, toys, and room furnishings (Pomerleau et al., 1990).

In one study (Condry & Condry, 1976), college students watched a videotape of a 9-month-old infant who was introduced as either a girl ("Dana") or a boy ("David"). Students who saw "David" interpreted his strong reaction to a jack-in-the-box as anger, whereas students who watched "Dana" concluded that the same behavior was fear. Although stereotyping of boys and girls from birth could be partly the effect of differences between the sexes (Beneson, Philippoussis, & Leeb, 1999), it may also be a cause of such differences.

Early Learning

Yet infants are not merely the passive targets of other people's reactions to them; they are actively trying to get to know the social world around them and to get to know themselves. By the end of the first year, babies can already distinguish women from men in photographs (women are the long-haired ones), and they look longer when male or female voices match properly with male or female faces than when a male voice is paired with a female face or vice versa (Fagot & Leinbach, 1993; Poulin-Dubois et al., 1994). As they begin to categorize other people as males and females, they also figure out which of these two significant social categories they belong to. By 18 months, most toddlers seem to have an emerging understanding that they are either like other males or like other females, even if they cannot verbalize it (Lewis & Weinraub, 1979). Almost all children give verbal proof that they have acquired a basic sense of **gender identity,** or an awareness that they are either a boy or a girl, by age 2½ to age 3 (Levy, 1999; Warin, 2000).

As they acquire their gender identities, boys and girls are also beginning to behave differently. By the end of their second year, boys usually prefer trucks and cars to other playthings, whereas girls of this age would rather play with dolls and soft toys (Smith & Daglish, 1977; Wood, Desmarais, & Gugala, 2002). Many 18- to 24-month-old toddlers will refuse to play with toys regarded as appropriate for the other sex—even when there are no other toys to play with (Caldera, Huston, & O'Brien, 1989). As they approach age 2, then, infants are already beginning to behave in ways considered gender appropriate in our society.

Summing Up

In sum, the 2 years of infancy lay the groundwork for later gender-role development. Because their sex is important to those around them, and because they see that males and females differ, infants begin to form categories of "male" and "female," establish a basic gender identity, and pursue "gender-appropriate" pastimes. ■

The Child

Much of the action in gender-role development takes place during the toddler and preschool years. Having already come to understand their basic gender identity, young children rapidly acquire gender stereotypes, or ideas about what males and females are supposedly like, and gender-typed behavioral patterns, or tendencies to favor "gender-appropriate" activities and behaviors over those typically associated with the other sex.

Acquiring Gender Stereotypes

Remarkably, young children begin to learn society's gender stereotypes around the time they become aware of their basic gender identities. Judith Blakemore (2003) showed pictures of toys to 3- to 11-year-olds and asked them whether boys or girls would usually play with each toy. Toys included masculine-stereotyped ones (for example, GI Joe dolls) and feminine-stereotyped ones (for example, Barbie dolls). Even the youngest children (3 years) knew that girls, but not boys, play with Barbie dolls and vice versa for GI Joes. They also recognized that boys and girls differ in clothes and hairstyles.

In other research, girls as young as 24 months understood which activities were masculine and which ones were feminine (Poulin-Dubois et al., 2002; see also Serbin, Poulin-Dubois, & Eichstedt, 2002). Boys, however, did not show the same understanding until at least 6 months later. Even by 18 months of age, girls can match photos of gender-stereotypic toys with faces of boys or girls (Serbin et al., 2001). So children, at least girls, are aware of gender stereotypes at an early age.

Over the next several years, children acquire considerably more "knowledge" about the toys and activities considered appropriate for girls or boys (Blakemore, 2003; Serbin, Powlishta, & Gulko, 1993). For instance, Gary Levy and his associates (2000) asked 4- and 6-year-olds whether men or women would be better in two masculine-stereotyped occupations (car mechanic and airplane pilot) and two feminine-stereotyped occupations (clothes designer and secretary). Children believed that men would be more competent than women as mechanics and pilots whereas women would make better designers and secretaries. Boys and girls also expressed positive emotions at the thought of growing up and holding gender-stereotypic occupations. They reacted negatively, however, when asked to consider holding gender-counterstereotypic occupations.

How seriously do children take the gender-role norms and stereotypes that they are rapidly learning? It depends on how old they are. Robin Banerjee and Vicki Lintern (2000) tested the rigidity of 4- to 9-year-olds' gender-stereotypic beliefs with four brief stories in which characters had either gender-stereotypic interests (for example, a boy named Tom who was best friends with another boy and liked playing with airplanes) or gender-counterstereotypic interests (for example, a boy named John who was best friends with a girl and liked playing with doll carriages). Children were then asked whether the target child would like to play with dolls, play football, skip, or play with toy guns. Younger children (4- and 6-year-olds) were considerably more rigid in their beliefs than older children; they did not believe that boys would want to play with dolls or skip (stereotypic girl activities) or that girls would want to play with footballs or toy guns (stereotypic boy activities). Consistent with earlier research (Damon, 1977), rigidity about gender stereotypes increased from 4 to 6 years of age then decreased significantly from age 6 to age 8 or 9. Why? Between ages 4 and 6, most children acquire a clear understanding that their sex will remain constant, making them intolerant of anyone who violates traditional gender-role standards. These norms now have the force of absolute moral laws and must be obeyed: boys must not play with dolls.

Eleanor Maccoby (1998) suggests that young children may exaggerate gender roles to cognitively clarify these roles. Once their gender identities are more firmly established, children can afford to be more flexible in their thinking about what is "for boys" and what is "for girls." They still know the stereotypes, but they no longer believe as many of them (Signorella, Bigler, & Liben, 1993). Other research suggests that children's rigidity about gender-role violations depends on how essential or valued a behavior is to children's understanding of gender identity (Blakemore, 2003). Thus, children believe it would be bad for boys to wear dresses because dresses are strongly associated with the feminine gender role. But if boys wanted to play with a toy kitchen, this would not be too bad because, although the toy kitchen may be associated with the feminine gender role, it is not considered an essential aspect of the feminine gender role (Blakemore, 2003).

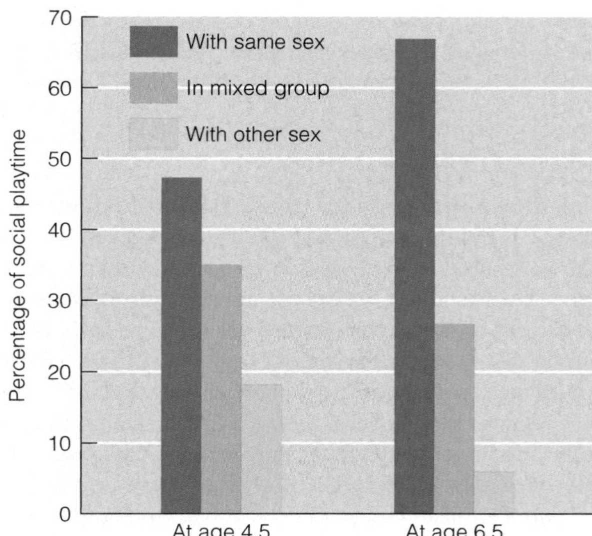

Figure 12.2 Do children prefer playmates of their own sex? Apparently so. Both boys and girls spend more time playing with same-sex peers, especially at age 6.

SOURCE: Maccoby & Jacklin (1987).

Gender-Typed Behavior

Finally, children rapidly come to behave in "gender-appropriate" ways. As you have seen, preferences for gender-appropriate toys are detectable in infancy. Apparently, babies establish preferences for "boys' toys" or "girls' toys" even before they have established clear identities as males or females or can correctly label toys as "boy things" or "girl things" (Blakemore, LaRue, & Olejnik, 1979; Fagot, Leinbach, & Hagan, 1986). In childhood, preference for same-sex toys is still evident, although occasionally both boys and girls would like to play with "boys' toys" more than "girls' toys" (Klinger, Hamilton, & Cantrell, 2001). Moreover, children quickly come to favor same-sex playmates. Several studies show that by 30 to 36 months of age, children form new friendships primarily with same-sex partners (see, for example, Howes, 1988; Martin & Fabes, 2001).

© Joe Gemignani/CORBIS

© Richard Hutchings/PhotoEdit

☾ Do boys and girls segregate themselves into same-sex play groups because they have different play styles?

During the elementary-school years, boys and girls develop even stronger preferences for peers of their own sex and show increased **gender segregation,** separating themselves into boys' and girls' peer groups and interacting far more often with their own sex than with the other sex (Maccoby, 1998). Gender segregation occurs in a variety of cultures, from Kenya to India to the Philippines, and it increases with age (Leaper, 1994; Whiting & Edwards, 1988). At age $4^1/_2$, children in the United States spend 3 times more time with same-sex peers than with peers of the other sex; by age $6^1/_2$, they spend 11 times more time (see Figure 12.2; Maccoby & Jacklin, 1987). This is partly because of incompatibilities between boys' and girls' play styles. Boys are too rowdy, domineering, and unresponsive to suit the tastes of many girls, so girls gravitate toward other girls and develop a style of interacting among themselves different from the rather timid style they adopt in the company of boys (Maccoby, 1998; Moller & Serbin, 1996).

As it turns out, children who insist most strongly on clear boundaries between the sexes and avoid consorting with "the enemy" tend to be socially competent and popular, whereas children who violate gender segregation rules tend to be less well adjusted and run the risk of being rejected by their peers (Kovacs, Parker, & Hoffman, 1996; Sroufe et al., 1993). Boys face stronger pressures to adhere to gender-role expectations than girls do. This may be why they develop stronger gender-typed preferences at earlier ages (Banerjee & Lintern, 2000; O'Brien et al., 2000). Just ask your female classmates if they were tomboys when they were young; you are likely to find that about half were (Bailey, Bechtold, & Berebaum, 2002). But we challenge you to find many male classmates who willingly admit they were sissies in their youth. The masculine role is clearly defined in our society, and boys are ridiculed and rejected if they do not conform to it (Martin, 1990).

Summing Up

Gender-role development proceeds with remarkable speed. By the time they enter school, children have long been aware of their basic gender identities, have acquired many stereotypes about how the sexes differ, and have come to prefer gender-appropriate activities and same-sex playmates. During middle childhood, their knowledge continues to expand as they learn more about gender-stereotyped psychological traits, but they also become more flexible in their thinking about gender roles. Their behavior, especially if they are boys, becomes even more gender typed, and they segregate themselves even more from the other sex. ■

The Adolescent

After going their separate ways in childhood, boys and girls come together in the most intimate ways during adolescence. How do they prepare for the masculine or feminine gender roles they will be asked to play in adulthood?

Adhering to Gender Roles

As you have just seen, young elementary-school children are highly rigid in their thinking about gender roles, whereas older children think more flexibly, recognizing that gender norms are not absolute, inviolable laws. Curiously, children again seem to become highly intolerant of certain role violations and to become stereotyped in their thinking about the proper roles of males and females in adolescence. They are more likely than somewhat younger children to make negative judgments about peers who violate expectations by engaging in cross-sex behavior or expressing cross-sex interests (Alfieri, Ruble, & Higgins, 1996; Sigelman, Carr, & Begley, 1986).

Consider what Trish Stoddart and Elliot Turiel (1985) found when they asked children ages 5 to 13 questions about boys who wear a barrette in their hair or put on nail polish and about girls who sport a crew haircut or wear a boy's suit. Both the kindergartners and the adolescents judged these behaviors to be wrong, whereas third- and fifth-graders viewed them far more tolerantly. Like the elementary-school children, eighth-graders clearly understood that gender-role expectations are just social conventions that can easily be changed and do not necessarily apply in all societies. However, these adolescents had also begun to conceptualize gender-role violations as a sign of psychological abnormality and could not tolerate them.

Increased intolerance of deviance from gender-role expectations is tied to a larger process of **gender intensification,** in which sex differences may be magnified by hormonal changes associated with puberty and increased pressure to conform to gender roles (Boldizar, 1991; Galambos, Almeida, & Petersen, 1990). Boys begin to see themselves as more masculine; girls emphasize their feminine side. Girls often become more involved with their mothers, and boys spend more time with their fathers (Crouter, Manke, & McHale, 1995). Why might this gender intensification occur? Hormonal influences may be at work, or adolescents may emphasize gender more once they mature physically and begin to look like either a man or a woman. Parents may also contribute: as children enter adolescence, mothers do more with their daughters and fathers do more with their sons (Crouter et al., 1995).

Peers may be even more important. Adolescents increasingly find that they must conform to traditional gender norms to appeal to the other sex. A girl who was a tomboy and thought nothing of it may find, around age 12 or 13, that she must dress and behave in more "feminine" ways to attract boys and must give up her tomboyish ways (Burn, O'Neil, & Nederend, 1996). A boy may find that he is more popular if he projects a more sharply "masculine" image. Social pressures on adolescents to conform to traditional roles may even help explain why sex differences in cognitive abilities sometimes become more noticeable as children enter adolescence (Hill & Lynch, 1983; Roberts et al., 1990). Later in adolescence, teenagers again become more comfortable with their identities as men and women and more flexible in their thinking.

We have now surveyed some major milestones in gender-role development from infancy to adolescence—the development of basic gender identity in toddlerhood, gender segregation in childhood, and a return to rigid thinking about gender as part of gender intensification during adolescence. Now comes the most intriguing question about gender-role development in childhood and adolescence: How can it be explained?

Explaining Gender-Role Development

"Once there was a baby named Chris... [who] went to live on a beautiful island . . . [where] there were only boys and men; Chris was the only girl. Chris lived a very happy life on this island, but she never saw another girl or woman" (Taylor, 1996, p. 1559). Do you think Chris developed traditionally masculine or traditionally feminine characteristics? When Marianne Taylor (1996) asked children about Chris's toy preferences, occupational aspirations, and personality traits, she found that 4- to 8-year-olds took the nature side of the nature–nurture controversy: They expected Chris's biological status as a girl to determine her development. The 9- and 10-year-olds in the

study emphasized the role of nurture in Chris's development, expecting her to be influenced by the masculinizing environment in which she was raised. Where do you come down in this debate, and why?

Several theories about the development of gender roles have been proposed. Some theories emphasize the role of biological differences between the sexes, whereas others emphasize social influences on children. Some emphasize what society does to children; others focus on what children do to themselves as they try to understand gender and all its implications. Briefly examine a biologically oriented theory then consider the more "social" approaches offered by psychoanalytic theory, social learning theory, cognitive developmental theory, and gender schema theory.

Biosocial Theory

The biosocial theory of gender-role development proposed by John Money and Anke Ehrhardt (1972) calls attention to the ways in which biological events influence the development of boys and girls. But it also focuses on ways in which early biological developments influence how people react to a child and suggests that these social reactions have much to do with children's assuming gender roles.

Chromosomes, Hormones, and Social Labeling. Money and Ehrhardt stress that the male (XY) or female (XX) chromosomes most of us receive at conception are merely a starting point in biological differentiation of the sexes. Several critical events affect a person's eventual preference for the masculine or feminine role (see also Breedlove, 1994):

1. If certain genes on the Y chromosome are present, a previously undifferentiated tissue develops into testes as the embryo develops; otherwise, it develops into ovaries.

2. The testes of a male embryo normally secrete more of the male hormone testosterone, which stimulates the development of a male internal reproductive system, and another hormone that inhibits the development of female organs. Without these hormones, the internal reproductive system of a female will develop from the same tissues.

3. Three to four months after conception, secretion of additional testosterone by the testes normally leads to the growth of a penis and scrotum. If testosterone is absent (as in normal females), or if a male fetus's cells are insensitive to the male sex hormones he produces, female external genitalia (labia and clitoris) will form.

4. The relative amount of testosterone alters the development of the brain and nervous system. For example, it signals the male brain to stop secreting hormones in a cyclical pattern so that males do not experience menstrual cycles at puberty.

Thus, fertilized eggs have the potential to acquire the anatomical and physiological features of either sex. Events at each critical step in the sexual differentiation process determine the outcome.

Once a biological male or female is born, social labeling and differential treatment of girls and boys interact with biological factors to steer development. Parents and other people label and begin to react to children on the basis of the appearance of their genitalia. If children's genitals are abnormal and they are mislabeled as members of the other sex, this incorrect label will affect their future development. For example, if a biological male were consistently labeled and treated as a girl, he would, by about age 3, acquire the gender identity of a girl. Finally, biological factors reenter the scene at puberty when large quantities of hormones are released, stimulating the growth of the reproductive system and the appearance of secondary sex characteristics. These events, with a person's earlier self-concept as a male or female, provide the basis for adult gender identity and role behavior. The complex series of critical points in biological maturation and social reactions to biological changes that Money and Ehrhardt (1972) propose is diagrammed in Figure 12.3. But how much is nature, and how much is nurture?

Evidence of Biological Influences. Much evidence suggests that biological factors influence the development of males and females in many species of animals (Breedlove, 1994). Evolutionary psychologists notice that most societies socialize males to have agentic traits and females to have communal ones; they conclude that traditional gender roles may be a reflection of species heredity (Archer, 1996; Buss, 1995). In addition, individual differences in masculinity and femininity may be partly genetic. Twin studies suggest that individual heredity accounts for 20 to 50% of the variation in the extent to which people describe themselves as having masculine and feminine

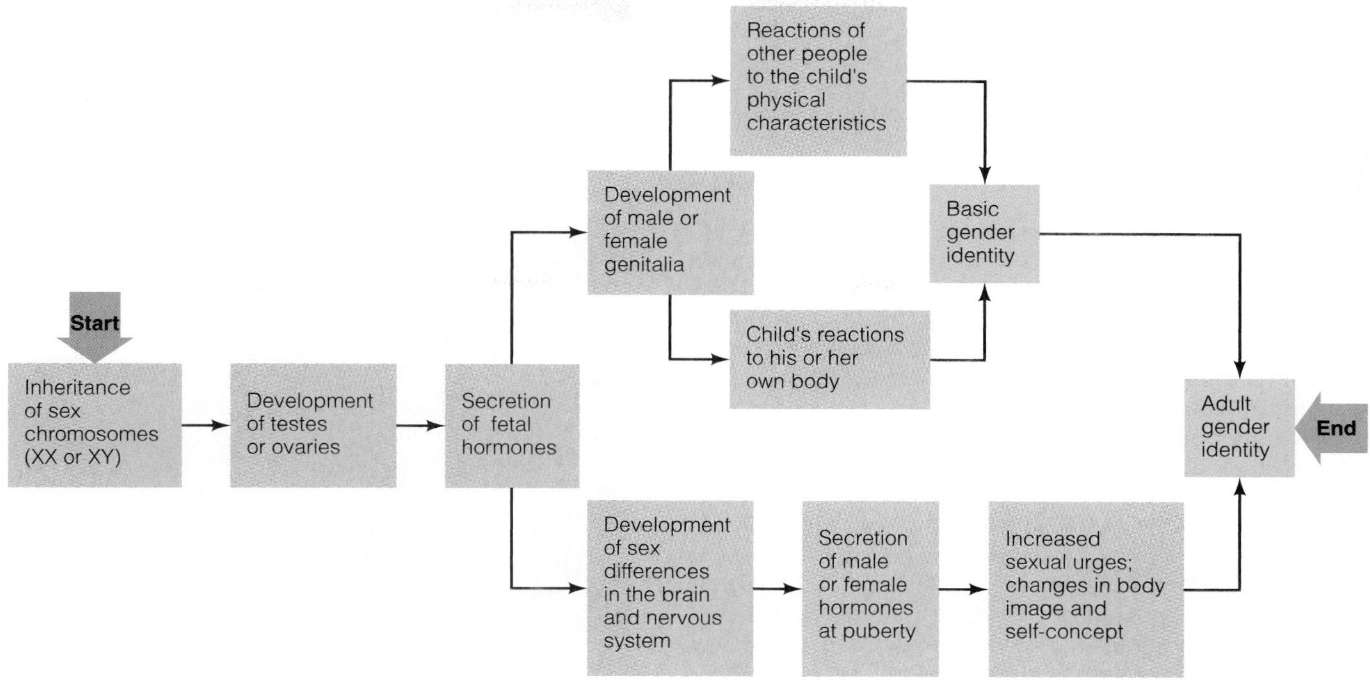

Figure 12.3 Critical events in John Money and Anke Ehrhardt's biosocial theory of gender typing.

SOURCE: Money & Ehrhardt (1972).

psychological traits (Loehlin, 1992; Mitchell, Baker, & Jacklin, 1989). In other words, experience does not explain everything.

Biological influences on development are also evident in studies of children exposed to the "wrong" hormones prenatally (Ehrhardt & Baker, 1974; Money & Ehrhardt, 1972; see also Gandelman, 1992). Before the consequences were known, some mothers who previously had problems carrying pregnancies to term were given drugs containing progestins, which are converted by the body into the male hormone testosterone. These drugs had the effect of masculinizing female fetuses so that, despite their XX genetic endowment and female internal organs, they were born with external organs that resembled those of a boy (for example, a large clitoris that looked like a penis and fused labia that resembled a scrotum). Several of these **androgenized females** (girls exposed to excess androgens) were recognized as genetic females, underwent surgery to alter their genitals, and were then raised as girls. When Money and Ehrhardt compared them with their sisters and other girls, it became apparent that many more androgenized girls were tomboys and preferred boys' toys and vigorous activities to traditionally feminine pursuits (see also Meyer-Bahlburg et al., 2004). As adolescents, they began dating somewhat later than other girls and felt that marriage should be delayed until they had established their careers. A high proportion (37%) described themselves as homosexual or bisexual (Money, 1985; see also Dittman, Kappes, & Kappes, 1992). Androgenized females also perform better than most other females on tests of spatial ability, further evidence that early exposure to male hormones has "masculinizing" effects on a female fetus (Kimura, 1992; Resnick et al., 1986).

In addition, male exposure to testosterone and other male hormones may be part of the reason males are more likely than females to commit violent acts (Rubinow & Schmidt, 1996). Evidence from experiments conducted with animals is quite convincing. For example, female rhesus monkeys exposed prenatally to the male hormone testosterone often threaten other monkeys, engage in rough-and-tumble play, and try to "mount" a partner as males do at the beginning of a sexual encounter (Young, Goy, & Phoenix, 1964; Wallen, 1996). Men with high testosterone levels tend to have high rates of delinquency, drug abuse, abusiveness, and violence, although nature interacts with nurture so that these links between testosterone and antisocial behavior are not nearly as evident among men high in socioeconomic status as among men low in socioeconomic status (Dabbs & Morris, 1990).

Because testosterone levels rise as a result of aggressive and competitive activities, it has been difficult to establish unambiguously that high concentrations of male hormones cause aggressive behavior in humans (Archer, 1991). Still, animal studies show that early experiences can alter the developing nervous systems of males and females and, in turn, their behavior (Breedlove, 1994). Much evidence suggests that prenatal exposure to male or female hormones has lasting effects on the organization of the brain and, in turn, on sexual behavior, aggression, cognitive abilities, and other aspects of development (Rubinow & Schmidt, 1996). Yet biology does not dictate gender-role development. Instead, gender-role development evolves from the complex interaction of biology, social experience, and the individual's behavior.

Explorations

Is the Social Label Everything, or Is Biology Destiny?

When biological sex and social labeling conflict, which wins out? Consider the unfortunate case of a male identical twin whose penis was damaged beyond repair during a botched circumcision (Money & Tucker, 1975). On the advice of Dr. John Money, the parents agreed to a surgical procedure that removed what was left of the damaged penis and altered their 21-month-old boy's external genitals to appear feminine. From then on, they treated him like a girl. By age 5, this boy-turned-girl was reportedly different from her genetically identical brother. According to Money and the team in charge of her treatment, she clearly knew she was a girl; had developed strong preferences for feminine toys, activities, and apparel; and was far neater and daintier than her brother. This, then, is a vivid demonstration that the most decisive influence on gender-role development is how a child is labeled and treated during the critical period for such development. Or is it?

Milton Diamond and H. Keith Sigmundson (1997) followed up on this "John" turned "Joan" and found that the story had a twist ending (see also Colapinto, 1997; 2000). Joan was never comfortable with doll play and other traditionally feminine pursuits; she preferred to dress up in men's clothing, play with her twin brother's toys, and take things apart to see how they worked. She used the jumping rope she was given to whip people and tie them up; she was miserable when she was forced to become a Girl Scout rather than a Boy Scout and make daisy chains (Colapinto, 1997). Somewhere around age 10, she had the distinct feeling that she was not a girl: "I began to see how different I felt and was . . . I thought I was a freak or something . . . but I didn't want to admit it. I figured I didn't want to wind up opening a can of worms" (Colapinto, 2000, pp. 299–300). Being rejected by other children because of her masculine looks and feminine dress and being called "cave-woman" and "gorilla" also took their toll, as did continued pressure from psychiatrists to behave in a more feminine manner. Finally, at age 14 and after years of inner turmoil and suicidal thinking, Joan had had it and simply refused to take the female hormones prescribed for her and pretend to be a girl any longer. When finally told that she was a chromosomal male, Joan was relieved: "Suddenly it all made sense why I felt the way I did. I *wasn't* some sort of weirdo" (Colapinto, 1997, p. 92). She then received male hormone shots, a double mastectomy, and surgery to construct a penis and emerged as a nice young man who eventually dated girls, married at age 25, and appears to be comfortable with his hard-won identity as John. He now speaks out against the sex reassignment treatment that has long been applied to infants with injured or am-

John–Joan–John

Evidence of Social-Labeling Influences. We must also take seriously the social aspect of Money and Ehrhardt's biosocial theory. How a child is labeled and treated can considerably affect gender development. For instance, some androgenized females were labeled as boys at birth and raised as such until their abnormalities were detected. Money and Ehrhardt (1972) report that the discovery and correction of this condition (by surgery and relabeling as a girl) caused few adjustment problems if the sex change took place before 18 months. After age 3, sexual reassignment was exceedingly difficult because these genetic females had experienced prolonged masculine gender typing and had already labeled themselves as boys. These findings led Money and Ehrhardt to conclude that there is a critical period (between 18 months and 3 years) for the establishment of gender identity when the label society attaches to the child is likely to stick. Yet some studies in which infants are presented to some people as boys but to others as girls indicate that labeling has little effect on how people perceive and treat these infants (Stern & Karraker, 1989). And, as the Explorations box on this page shows, biological males who are labeled as girls during the so-called critical period sometimes adopt a male gender identity later in life despite their biguous genitals (Colapinto, 1997). This case study shows that we should back off from the conclusion that social learning is all that matters. Apparently, biology matters, too.

A second source of evidence that biology matters is a study of 18 biological males in the Dominican Republic who had a genetic condition that made their cells insensitive to the effects of male hormones (Imperato-McGinley et al., 1979; see also Herdt & Davidson, 1988). They had begun life with ambiguous genitals, were mistaken for girls, and so were labeled and raised as girls. However, under the influence of male hormones produced at puberty, they sprouted beards and became entirely masculine in appearance. How, in light of Money and Ehrhardt's critical-period hypothesis, could a person possibly adjust to becoming a man after leading an entire childhood as a girl?

Amazingly, 16 of these 18 individuals seemed able to accept their late conversion from female to male and to adopt masculine lifestyles, including the establishment of heterosexual relationships. One retained a female identity and gender role, and the remaining individual switched to a male gender identity but still dressed as a female. This study also casts doubt on the notion that socialization during the first 3 years is critical to later gender-role development. Instead, it suggests that hormonal influences may be more important than social influences. It is possible, however, that Dominican adults, knowing that this genetic disorder was common in their society, treated these girls-turned-boys differently from other girls when they were young or that these youngsters recognized on their own that their genitals were not normal (Ehrhardt, 1985). As a result, these "girls" may never have fully committed themselves to being girls.

What studies such as these of individuals with genital abnormalities appear to teach us is this: We are predisposed by our biology to develop as males or females; the first 3 years of life are a sensitive period perhaps, but not a critical period, for gender-role development; and both biology and social labeling contribute to gender-role development.

early labeling and socialization, suggesting that we should refer to a sensitive rather than a critical period. Once again, then, we see both nature and nurture at work in development.

Psychoanalytic Theory

As is true of thinking about most areas of development, thinking about gender-role development was shaped early on by Sigmund Freud's psychosexual theory. The 3- to 6-year-old child in Freud's phallic stage is said to harbor a strong, biologically based love for the parent of the other sex, experience internal conflict and anxiety as a result of this incestuous desire, and resolve the conflict through a process of **identification** with the same-sex parent. According to Freud, a boy experiencing his **Oedipus complex** loves his mother, fears that his father will retaliate by castrating him, and is forced to identify with his father, thereby emulating his father and adopting his father's attitudes and behaviors. Freud believed that a boy would show weak masculinity later in life if his father was inadequate as a masculine model, was often absent from the home, or was not dominant or threatening enough to foster a strong identification based on fear.

Meanwhile, a preschool-age girl is said to experience an **Electra complex** involving a desire for her father (and envy of him for the penis she lacks) and a rivalry with her mother. To resolve her unconscious conflict, she identifies with her mother. Her father also contributes to gender-role development by reinforcing her for "feminine" behavior resembling that of her mother. Thus, Freud emphasized the role of emotions (love, fear, and so on) in motivating gender-role development and argued that children adopt their roles by patterning themselves after their same-sex parents.

We can applaud Freud for identifying the preschool years as a critical time for gender-role development. In addition, his view that boys, because of fear of castration, have a more powerful motivation than girls to adopt their gender role is consistent with the finding that boys seem to learn gender stereotypes and gender-typed behaviors faster and more completely than girls do. It is also true that boys whose fathers are absent from the home tend to be less traditionally sex-typed than other boys (Stevenson & Black, 1988). Finally, Freud's notion that fathers play an important role in the gender typing of their daughters and of their sons has been confirmed (Parke, 1996).

On other counts, however, psychoanalytic theory has not fared well. Many preschool children are so ignorant of male and female anatomy that it is hard to see how most boys could fear castration or most girls could experience penis envy (Bem, 1989). Moreover, Freud assumed that a boy's identification with his father is based on fear, but most researchers find that boys identify most strongly with fathers who are warm and nurturant rather than overly punitive and threatening (Hetherington & Frankie, 1967; Mussen & Rutherford, 1963). Finally, children are not especially similar psychologically to their same-sex parents (Maccoby & Jacklin, 1974). Apparently, other individuals besides parents influence a child's gender-related characteristics. It seems we must look elsewhere for more complete explanations of gender-role development.

Social Learning Theory

According to social learning theorists, children learn masculine or feminine identities, preferences, and behaviors in two ways. First, through *differential reinforcement,* children are rewarded for sex-appropriate behaviors and are punished for behaviors considered more appropriate for members of the other sex. Second, through *observational learning,* children adopt the attitudes and behaviors of same-sex models. In this

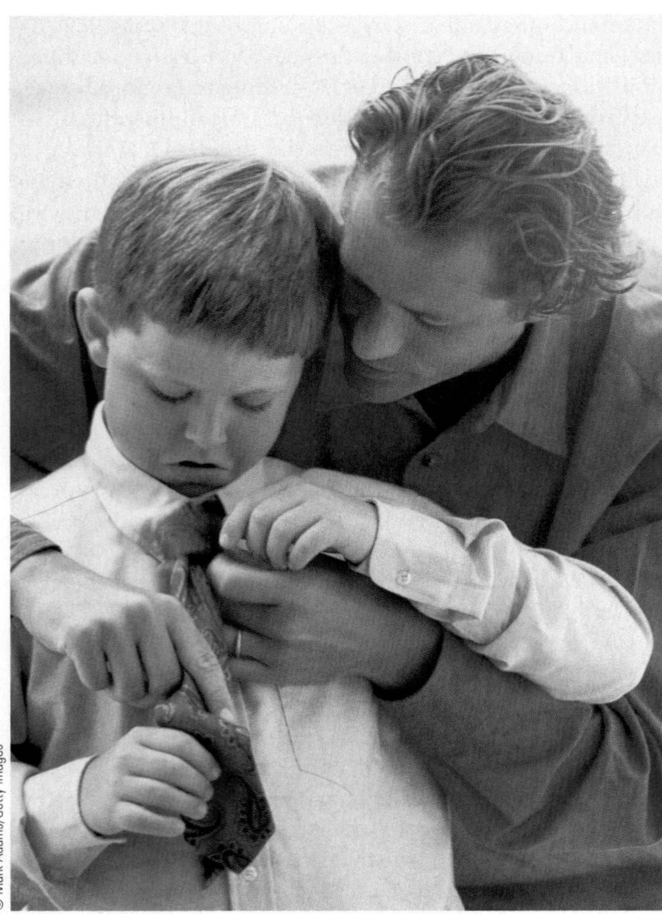
© Mark Adams/Getty Images

According to psychoanalytic theory, children become appropriately "masculine" or "feminine" through identification with the same-sex parent. Social learning theorists call this process observational learning.

view, children's gender-role development depends on which of their behaviors people reinforce or punish and on what sorts of social models are available. Change the social environment, and you change the course of gender-role development.

Differential Reinforcement. Parents use differential reinforcement to teach boys how to be boys and girls how to be girls (Lytton & Romney, 1991). By the second year of life, parents are already encouraging sex-appropriate play and discouraging cross-sex play, before children have acquired their basic gender identities or display clear preferences for male or female activities (Fagot & Leinbach, 1989). By 20 to 24 months, daughters are reinforced for dancing, dressing up (as women), following their parents around, asking for help, and playing with dolls; they are discouraged from manipulating objects, running, jumping, and climbing. By contrast, sons are often reprimanded for such "feminine" behavior as playing with dolls or seeking help and are often actively encouraged to play with "masculine" toys such as blocks, trucks, and push-and-pull toys (Fagot, 1978). Mothers and fathers may also discipline their sons and daughters differently, with fathers more likely to use physical forms of discipline (such as spanking) than mothers and mothers more likely to use reasoning to explain rules and consequences (Conrade & Ho, 2001; Russell et al., 1998). In addition, boys end up on the receiving end of a spanking more often than girls do (Day & Peterson, 1998).

In recent research by Barbara Morrongiello and Kerri Hogg (2004), mothers were asked to imagine how they would react if their 6- to 10-year-old son or daughter misbehaved in some way that might be dangerous (for example, bicycling fast down a hill they had been told to avoid). Mothers reported that they would be angry with their sons but disappointed and concerned with their daughters for misbehaving and putting themselves in harm's way. Boys will be boys, they reasoned, but girls should know better. To prevent future risky behaviors, mothers said they would be more rule-bound with their daughters but would not do anything different with their sons. After all, there is no point in trying to prevent these risky behaviors in boys because it is "in their nature." Girls' behavior, on the other hand, can be influenced, so it is worth enforcing an existing rule or instituting a new one.

Does this "gender curriculum" in the home influence children? It certainly does. Parents who show the clearest patterns of differential reinforcement have children who are relatively quick to label themselves as girls or boys and to develop strongly sex-typed toy and activity preferences (Fagot & Leinbach, 1989; Fagot, Leinbach, & O'Boyle, 1992). Fathers play a central role in gender socialization; they are more likely than mothers to reward children's gender-appropriate behavior and to discourage behavior considered more appropriate for the other sex (Leve & Fagot, 1997; Lytton & Romney, 1991). Women who choose nontraditional professions are more likely than women in traditionally female fields to have had fathers who encouraged them to be assertive and competitive (Coats & Overman, 1992). Fathers, then, seem to be an especially important influence on the gender-role development of both sons and daughters.

Could differential treatment of boys and girls by parents also contribute to sex differences in ability? Possibly so. Jacquelynne Eccles and her colleagues (1990) have conducted several studies to determine why girls tend to shy from math and science courses and are underrepresented in occupations that involve math and science (see also Benbow & Arjmand, 1990). They suggest that parental expectations about sex differences in mathematical ability become self-fulfilling prophecies. The plot is something like this:

1. Parents, influenced by societal stereotypes about sex differences in ability, expect their sons to outperform their daughters in math and expect their sons will be more interested in math and science than their daughters (Tenenbaum & Leaper, 2003).

2. Parents attribute their sons' successes in math to ability but credit their daughters' successes to hard work. Perhaps as a result of this, fathers talk differently to their sons and daughters when discussing science with them (Tenenbaum & Leaper, 2003). With their sons, they use more scientific terms, provide more detailed explanations, and ask more abstract questions than with their daughters. These differences rein-

force the belief that girls lack mathematical talent and turn in respectable performances only through plodding effort.

3. Children begin to internalize their parents' views, so girls come to believe that they are "no good" in math. Girls report that they are less competent and more anxious about their performance than boys (Pomerantz, Altermatt, & Saxon, 2002).

4. Thinking they lack ability, girls become less interested in math, less likely to take math courses, and less likely to pursue career possibilities that involve math after high school.

In short, parents who expect their daughters to have trouble with numbers get what they expect. The negative effects of low parental expectancies on girls' self-perceptions are evident regardless of their performance. Indeed, girls feel less competent than do boys about math and science even when they outperform the boys (Pomerantz et al., 2002). Girls whose parents are nontraditional in their gender-role attitudes and behaviors do not show the declines in math and science achievement in early adolescence that girls from more traditional families display, so apparently the chain of events Eccles describes can be broken (Updegraff, McHale, & Crouter, 1996).

Peers, like parents, reinforce boys and girls differentially. As Beverly Fagot (1985) discovered, boys only 21 to 25 months of age belittle and disrupt each other for playing with "feminine" toys or with girls, and girls express their disapproval of other girls who choose to play with boys. Some scholars believe peers contribute at least as much to gender typing as parents do (Beal, 1994). And, as shown in the Explorations box on this page, teachers may contribute by paying more attention to boys than to girls.

Observational Learning. Social learning theorists call attention to differential treatment of girls and boys by parents, peers, and teachers; they also emphasize that observational learning contributes in important ways to gender typing. Children see which toys and activities are "for girls" and which are "for boys" and imitate individuals of their own sex. Around age 6 or 7, children begin to pay much closer attention to same-sex models than to other-sex models; for exam-

Explorations

Are Single-Sex Schools Good for Girls?

To what extent do teachers treat girls and boys differently in the classroom? We can probably all think of instances in which teachers subtly communicate that boys and girls are different—for example, when teachers ask the boys in the room to help move furniture for the class party but the girls to pour punch. Some scholars feel that sexist treatment in the classroom undermines the confidence and achievement of girls (Beal, 1994). What does research reveal?

Several studies suggest that teachers pay more attention to boys than to girls (Jussim & Eccles, 1992; Sadker & Sadker, 1994). Teachers call on boys more often and give them more feedback. It is not that boys are praised more than girls; instead, they tend to receive both more positive and more negative feedback (Brody, 1985; Hamilton et al., 1991). A good part of the attention they receive is occasioned by their troublemaking, but attention, positive or negative, may signal to girls that boys matter more than they do.

Concerned that girls are being held back academically by this differential treatment, some scholars and educators argue forcefully that girls would be better off in all-girl schools or classrooms than in coed ones, and some school systems are experimenting with same-sex education (Sadker & Sadker, 1994). What does the evidence show? Some early studies suggested that all-girl schooling was advantageous to girls (Lee & Bryk, 1986). However, these studies often did not control properly for differences between the students and the educational programs in same-sex and coed schools. More recent and more carefully designed studies of students attending Catholic schools find few differences in school-related attitudes and levels of achievement (LePore & Warren, 1997; Marsh, 1989; Signorella, Frieze, & Hershey, 1996). In a 1997 study of all-girl, all-boy, and coed Catholic high schools, for example, students in single-sex schools generally did no better than students in coed schools. The few differences observed suggested that boys benefit more academically from same-sex schooling than girls do (LePore & Warren, 1997). It seems, then, that all-girl schooling is not as beneficial as some educators believe; perhaps the reason is that sexist treatment of girls (and boys) can occur in any type of school (Lee, Marks, & Byrd, 1994).

ple, they will choose toys that members of their own sex prefer even if it means passing up more attractive toys (Frey & Ruble, 1992). Children who see their mothers perform so-called masculine tasks and their fathers perform household and child care tasks tend to be less aware of gender stereotypes and less gender typed than children exposed to traditional gender-role models at home (Sabattini & Leaper, 2004; Turner & Gervai, 1995). Similarly, boys with sisters and girls with brothers have less gender-typed activity preferences than children who grow up with same-sex siblings (Colley et al., 1996; Rust et al., 2000).

Not only do children learn by watching the children and adults with whom they interact, but they also learn from the media—radio, television, movies, magazines—and even from their picture books and elementary-school readers. Although sexism in children's books has decreased over the past 50 years, male characters are still more likely than female characters to engage in active, independent activities such as climbing, riding bikes, and making things, whereas female characters are more often depicted as passive, dependent, and helpless, spending their time picking flowers, playing quietly indoors, and "creating problems that require masculine solutions" (Diekman & Murnen, 2004; Kortenhaus & Demarest, 1993). And college textbooks used by students in teacher education programs still portray males in more stereotypically masculine activities and assign more negative masculine traits such as aggression to males than to females (Yanowitz & Weathers, 2004). Teachers may have trouble bucking gender stereotypes with the students in their classrooms when their own teaching training included gender-stereotypic portrayals.

It is similar in the world of television: Male characters dominate in children's programs, prime-time programs, and advertisements (Barner, 1999; Glascock, 2001). Even on shows with an equal number of male and female characters, the male characters assume more prominent roles (Ogletree et al., 2004). Typically, men are influential individuals who work at a profession, whereas many women—especially those portrayed as married—are passive, emotional creatures who manage a home or work at "feminine" occupations such as nursing (Signorielli & Kahlenberg, 2001). Women portrayed as single are often cast in traditionally male occupations. The message children receive is that men work regardless of their marital status and they do important business, but women only work at important jobs if they are single (Signorielli & Kahlenberg, 2001). Children who watch a large amount of television are more likely to choose gender-appropriate toys and to hold stereotyped views of males and females than their classmates who watch little television (Signorielli & Lears, 1992). As more women play detectives and more men raise families on television, children's notions of female and male roles are likely to change. Indeed, watching nonsexist programs is associated with holding less stereotyped views of the sexes (Rosenwasser, Lingenfelter, & Harrington, 1989; Signorielli, 1990).

To recap, there is much evidence that both differential reinforcement and observational learning contribute to gender-role development. However, social learning theorists often portray children as the passive recipients of external influences: parents, peers, television characters, and others show them what to do and reinforce them for doing it. Perhaps this perspective does not put enough emphasis on what children contribute to their own gender socialization. Youngsters do not receive gender-stereotyped birthday presents simply because their parents foist those toys upon them. Instead, parents tend to select gender-neutral and often educational toys for their children, but their boys beg for trucks and their girls demand tea sets (Robinson & Morris, 1986).

Cognitive Theories

Some theorists have emphasized cognitive aspects of gender-role development, noting that as children acquire understanding of gender, they actively teach themselves to be girls or boys. Lawrence Kohlberg based his cognitive theory on Jean Piaget's cognitive developmental theory, whereas Carol Martin and Charles Halverson Jr. based their theory on an information-processing approach to cognitive development.

Cognitive Developmental Theory. Kohlberg (1966a) proposed a cognitive theory of gender typing that is different from the other theories you have considered and that helps explain why boys and girls adopt traditional gender roles even when their parents do not want them to do so. Among Kohlberg's major themes are the following:

- Gender-role development depends on stagelike changes in cognitive development; children must acquire certain understandings about gender before they will be influenced by their social experiences.
- Children engage in self-socialization; instead of being the passive targets of social influence, they actively socialize themselves.

According to both psychoanalytic theory and social learning theory, children are influenced by their companions to adopt male or female roles before they view themselves as girls or boys and identify with (or habitually imitate) same-sex models. Kohlberg suggests that children first understand that they are girls or boys and then actively seek same-sex models and a range of information about how to act like a girl or a boy. To Kohlberg, it is not "I'm treated like a boy; therefore, I must be a boy." It is more like "I'm a boy, so now I'll do everything I can to find out how to behave like one."

What understandings are necessary before children will teach themselves to behave like boys or girls? Kohlberg believes that children everywhere progress through the following three stages as they acquire an understanding of what it means to be a female or a male:

1. Basic gender identity is established by age 2 or 3, when children can recognize and label themselves as males or females (Campbell, Shirley, & Caygill, 2002).
2. Somewhat later, usually by age 4, children acquire **gender stability**—that is, they come to understand that gender identity is stable over time. Boys invariably become men, and girls grow up to be women.
3. The gender concept is complete, somewhere between age 5 and age 7, when children achieve **gender consistency** and

realize that their sex is also stable across situations. Now, children know that their sex cannot be altered by superficial changes such as dressing up as a member of the other sex or engaging in cross-sex activities.

Children 3 to 5 years of age often do lack the concepts of gender stability and gender consistency; they often say that a boy could become a mommy if he really wanted to or that a girl could become a boy if she cut her hair and wore a hockey uniform (Warin, 2000). This changes over kindergarten and early grade-school years (Szkrybalo & Ruble, 1999). As children enter Piaget's concrete operational stage of cognitive development and come to grasp concepts such as conservation of liquids, they also realize that gender is conserved despite changes in appearance. In support of Kohlberg's theory, Jo Warin (2000) found that children who have achieved the third level of understanding display more gender-stereotypic play preferences than children who have not yet grasped gender consistency.

Criticisms? Sandra Bem (1989) has shown that children need not reach the concrete operations stage to understand gender stability and consistency if they have sufficient knowledge of male and female anatomy to realize that people's genitals make them male or female. The most controversial aspect of Kohlberg's cognitive developmental theory, however, has been his claim that only when children fully grasp that their biological sex is unchangeable, around age 5 to age 7, do they actively seek same-sex models and attempt to acquire values, interests, and behaviors consistent with their cognitive judgments about themselves. Although some evidence supports Kohlberg, this chapter shows that children learn many gender-role stereotypes and develop clear preferences for same-sex activities and playmates long before they master the concepts of gender stability and gender consistency and then, according to Kohlberg, attend more selectively to same-sex models (Ruble & Martin, 1998). It seems that only a rudimentary understanding of gender is required before children learn gender stereotypes and preferences.

Gender Schema Theory. Martin and Halverson (1981, 1987) have proposed a somewhat different cognitive theory, an information-processing one, that overcomes the key weakness of Kohlberg's theory. Like Kohlberg, they believe that children are intrinsically motivated to acquire values, interests, and behaviors consistent with their cognitive judgments about the self. However, Martin and Halverson argue that self-socialization begins as soon as children acquire a basic gender identity, around age 2 or 3. According to their schematic-processing model, children acquire **gender schemata**—organized sets of beliefs and expectations about males and females that influence the kinds of information they will attend to and remember.

First, children acquire a simple in-group–out-group schema that allows them to classify some objects, behaviors, and roles as appropriate for males and others as appropriate for females (cars are for boys, girls can cry but boys should not, and so on). Then, they seek more elaborate information about the role of their own sex, constructing an own-sex schema. Thus, a young girl who knows her basic gender identity might first learn that sewing is for girls and building model airplanes is for boys. Then, because she is a girl and wants to act consistently with her own self-concept, she gathers a great deal of information about sewing to add to her own-sex schema, largely ignoring any information that comes her way about how to build model airplanes (see Figure 12.4).

Consistent with this schematic-processing theory, children appear to be especially interested in learning about objects or activities that fit their own-sex schemata. In one study,

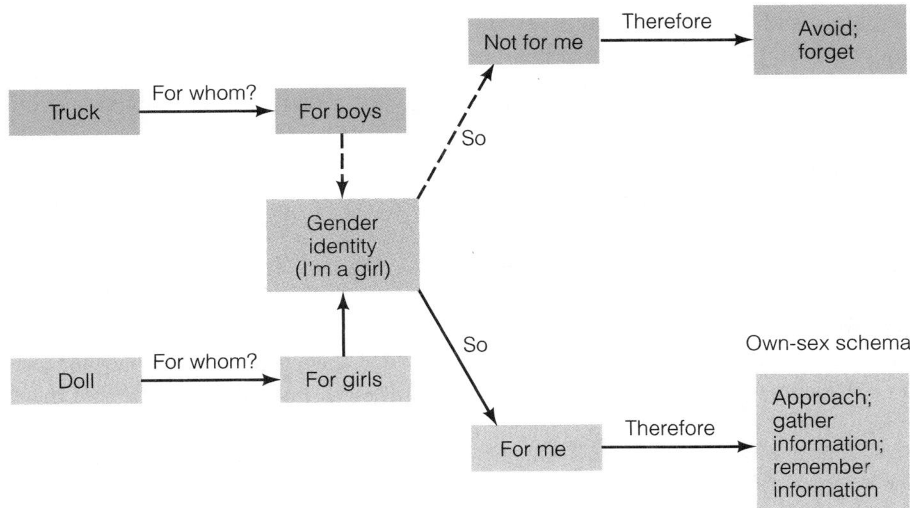

Figure 12.4 Gender schema theory in action. A young girl classifies new information according to an in-group–out-group schema as either "for boys" or "for girls." Information about boys' toys and activities is ignored, but information about toys and activities for girls is relevant to the self and is added to an ever-larger own-sex schema.

Source: Adapted from Martin & Halverson (1987).

4- to 9-year-olds were given boxes of gender-neutral objects (hole punches, burglar alarms, and so on) and were told that some objects were "girl" items and some were "boy" items (Bradbard et al., 1986). Boys explored boy items more than girls did, and girls explored girl items more than boys did. A week later, the children easily recalled which items were for boys and which were for girls; they had apparently sorted the objects according to their in-group–out-group schemata. In addition, boys recalled more in-depth information about boy items than did girls, whereas girls recalled more than boys about these same objects if they had been labeled girl items. If children's information-gathering efforts are guided by their own-sex schemata in this way, you can easily see how boys and girls might acquire different stores of knowledge as they develop.

Once gender schemata are in place, children will distort new information in memory so that it is consistent with their schemata (Liben & Signorella, 1993; Martin & Halverson, 1983). For example, Martin and Halverson (1983) showed 5- and 6-year-olds pictures of children performing gender-consistent activities (for example, a boy playing with a truck) and pictures of children performing gender-inconsistent activities (for example, a girl sawing wood). A week later, the children easily recalled the sex of the actor performing gender-consistent activities; when an actor expressed gender-inconsistent behavior, however, children often distorted the scene to reveal gender-consistent behavior (for example, by saying that it was a boy, not a girl, who had sawed wood). This research gives some insight into why inaccurate gender stereotypes persist. The child who believes that women cannot be doctors may be introduced to a female doctor but is likely to remember meeting a nurse and may insist that women cannot be doctors.

An Attempt at Integration

The biosocial, social learning, and cognitive perspectives all contribute to our understanding of sex differences and gender-role development. The biosocial model offered by Money and Ehrhardt notes the importance of biological developments that influence how people label and treat a child. Yet socialization agents—not only parents, as noted by Freud, but also siblings, peers, and teachers, as noted by social learning theorists—are teaching children how to be girls or boys well before they understand that they are girls or boys. Differences in social learning experiences may also help explain why, even though virtually all children form gender concepts and schemata, some children are far more gender typed than others in their preferences and activities (Serbin, Powlishta, & Gulko, 1993).

Kohlberg's cognitive developmental theory and Martin and Halverson's gender schema approach convince us that cognitive growth and self-socialization processes also contribute to gender-role development. Once children acquire a basic gender identity as a boy or a girl and form gender schemata, they become highly motivated to learn their appropriate roles. When they finally grasp, from age 5 to age 7, that their sex will never change, they become even more determined to learn their gender roles and pay special attention to same-sex models. Parents who want to avoid socializing their children into traditional gender roles are often amazed to see their children turn into traditional girls and boys on their own.

In short, children have a male or female biological endowment that helps guide their development, are influenced by other people from birth on to become "real boys" or "real girls," and actively socialize themselves to behave in ways that seem consistent with their understandings that they are either boys or girls (see Table 12.2). Most developmentalists today would agree that what children learn regarding how to be male or female depends on an interaction between biological factors and social influences. Thus, we must respect the role of genes and hormones in gender-role development but also view this process from a contextual perspective and appreciate that the patterns of male and female development that we observe in society today are not inevitable. In another era, in another culture, the process of gender-role socialization could produce different kinds of boys and girls.

Summing Up

Theories of gender-role development include the biosocial theory proposed by Money and Ehrhardt, which emphasizes prenatal biological developments and stresses the importance of how a child is labeled and treated during a critical period for gender identity information. From Freud's psychoanalytic perspective, gender-role development results from the child's identification with the same-sex parent. Social learning theorists focus on differential reinforcement and observational learning. Cognitive perspectives emphasize understanding of gender and active self-socialization: Kohlberg's cognitive developmental theory emphasizes that children master gender roles once they master the concepts of gender identity, gender stability, and gender consistency. Gender schema theory holds that children socialize themselves as soon as they have a basic gender identity and can construct gender schemata. Each theory has some support, but none is completely right. ■

The Adult

You might think that once children and adolescents have learned their gender roles, they simply play them out during adulthood. Instead, as people face the challenges of adult life and enter new social contexts, their gender roles and their concepts of themselves as men and women change.

Changes in Gender Roles

Although males and females fill their masculine or feminine roles throughout their lives, the specific content of those roles changes considerably over the life span. The young boy may act out his masculine role by playing with trucks or wrestling

Table 12.2 An Integrative Overview of the Gender-Typing Process

Developmental Period	Events and Outcomes	Pertinent Theory or Theories
Prenatal period	The fetus develops male or female genitalia, which others will react to once the child is born.	Biosocial
Birth to 3 years	Parents and other companions label the child as a boy or a girl; they begin to encourage gender-consistent behavior and discourage cross-sex activities. As a result of these social experiences and the development of basic classification skills, the young child acquires some gender-typed behavioral preferences and the knowledge that he or she is a boy or a girl (basic gender identity).	Social learning
3 to 6 years	Once children acquire a basic gender identity, they begin to seek information about sex differences, form gender schemata, and actively try to behave in ways viewed as appropriate for their own sex.	Gender schema
7 to puberty	Children finally acquire the concepts of gender stability and consistency, recognizing that they will be males or females all their lives and in all situations. They begin to look closely at the behavior of same-sex models to acquire attributes consistent with their firm self-categorization as male or female.	Cognitive developmental
Puberty and beyond	The biological changes of adolescence, with social pressures, intensify gender differences and stimulate formation of an adult gender identity.	Biosocial Social learning Gender schema Cognitive developmental

with his buddies; the grown man may play his role by holding down a job. Moreover, the degree of difference between male and female roles also changes. Children and adolescents adopt behaviors consistent with their "boy" or "girl" roles, but the two sexes otherwise adopt similar roles in society—namely, those of children and students. Even as they enter adulthood, males' and females' roles differ little because members of both sexes are often single and in school or working.

However, the roles of men and women become more distinct when they marry and, especially, when they have children. In most couples, for example, the wife typically does more housework than her husband, whether or not she is employed—about 17 to 18 hours per week for her compared with 10 hours for him (Bianchi et al., 2000). If this does not seem like a large discrepancy on a weekly basis, consider that over 1 year, wives contribute more than 400 hours to housework beyond the amount their husbands contribute. By their silver wedding anniversary, wives will have logged about 10,000 more hours than husbands have. Furthermore, specific tasks tend to be parceled out along traditional lines—she does the cooking, he takes out the garbage (Bianchi et al., 2000). The birth of a child tends to make even egalitarian couples divide their labors in more traditional ways than they did before the birth (Cowan & Cowan, 2000). She becomes primarily responsible for child care and household tasks; he tends to emphasize his role as breadwinner and center his energies on providing for the family. Even as men increase their participation in child care and housework, they tend to play a helper role and spend only two-thirds as much time with their children as women do (Bianchi, 2000).

What happens after the children are grown? The roles played by men and women become more similar again starting in middle age, when the nest empties and child care responsibilities end. The similarity between gender roles continues to increase as adults enter old age; as retirees and grandparents, men and women lead similar lives. It would seem, then, that the roles of men and women are fairly similar before marriage, maximally different during the child-rearing years, and similar again later (Gutmann, 1997).

Masculinity, Femininity, and Androgyny

Do the shifts in the roles played by men and women during adulthood affect them psychologically? For years, psychologists assumed that masculinity and femininity were at opposite ends of a continuum. If a person possessed highly masculine traits, then that person must be very unfeminine; being highly feminine implied being unmasculine. Bem (1974) challenged this assumption by arguing that individuals of either sex can be characterized by psychological **androgyny**—that is, by a balancing or blending of both masculine-stereotyped traits (for example, being assertive, analytical, and independent) and feminine-stereotyped traits (for example, being affectionate, compassionate, and understanding). In Bem's model, then, masculinity and femininity are two separate dimensions of personality. A male or female who has many masculine-stereotyped traits and few feminine ones is defined as a masculine sex-typed person. One who has many feminine- and few masculine-stereotyped traits is said to be a feminine sex-typed

© Tom Stewart/CORBIS

☾ After the androgyny shift, women may feel freer to express their "masculine" side, and men may express "feminine" qualities that they suppressed during the parenting years.

person. The androgynous person possesses both masculine and feminine traits, whereas the undifferentiated individual lacks both kinds of attributes (see Figure 12.5).

How many of us are androgynous? Research with college students using self-perception inventories that contain both a masculinity (or instrumentality) scale and a femininity (or expressivity) scale found that roughly 33% of the test takers were "masculine" men or "feminine" women; about 30% were androgynous, and the remaining individuals were either undifferentiated (low on both scales) or sex reversed (masculine sex-typed females or feminine sex-typed males) (Spence & Helmreich, 1978). Around 30% of children can also be classified as androgynous (Boldizar, 1991; Hall & Halberstadt, 1980). Although constructed in the 1970s, these inventories remain valid measures of gender roles today (Holt & Ellis, 1998). Androgynous individuals exist, and in sizable numbers. But do perceived masculinity, femininity, and androgyny change over the adult years?

Masculinity	Femininity: High	Femininity: Low
High	Androgynous	Masculine sex-typed
Low	Feminine sex-typed	Undifferentiated

Figure 12.5 Categories of gender-role orientation based on viewing masculinity and femininity as separate dimensions of personality.

Changes with Age

David Gutmann (1987, 1997) has offered the intriguing hypothesis that gender roles and gender-related traits in adulthood are shaped by what he calls the **parental imperative**—the requirement that mothers and fathers adopt different roles to raise children successfully. Drawing on his own cross-cultural research and that of others, he suggests that in many cultures, young and middle-aged men must emphasize their "masculine" qualities to feed and protect their families, whereas young and middle-aged women must express their "feminine" qualities to nurture the young and meet the emotional needs of their families.

According to Gutmann, this changes dramatically starting in midlife, when men and women are freed from the demands of the parental imperative. Men become less active and more passive, take less interest in community affairs, and focus more on religious contemplation and family relationships. They also become more sensitive and emotionally expressive. Women, meanwhile, are changing in the opposite direction. After being passive, submissive, and nurturing in their younger years, they become more active, domineering, and assertive in later life. In many cultures, they take charge of the household after being the underlings of their mothers-in-law and become stronger forces in their communities. In short,

Gutmann's parental imperative hypothesis states that, over the course of adulthood, psychologically "masculine" men become "feminine" men and "feminine" women become "masculine" women—that the psychological traits of the two sexes flip-flop.

A similar hypothesis is that adults experience a midlife **androgyny shift.** Instead of giving up traits they had as young adults, men and women retain their gender-typed qualities but add qualities traditionally associated with the other sex; that is, they become more androgynous. Ideas along this line were proposed by the psychoanalytic theorist Carl Jung (1933), who believed that we have masculine and feminine sides all along but learn to integrate them and express both facets of our human nature only in middle age. Now look at how these ideas have fared.

What age-related differences do researchers find when they administer masculinity and femininity scales to men and women of different cohorts? In one study, Shirley Feldman and her associates (Feldman, Biringen, & Nash, 1981) gave Bem's androgyny inventory to individuals at eight different stages of the family life cycle. Consistent with Gutmann's notion of a parental imperative, taking on the role of parent seemed to lead men to perceive themselves as more masculine in personality and women to perceive themselves as having predominantly feminine strengths. Among adults beyond their parenting years, especially among grandparents, sex differences in self-perceptions were smaller. Contrary to Gutmann's hypothesis, however, grandfathers did not replace their masculine traits with feminine traits, and grandmothers did not become less feminine and more masculine. Instead, both sexes appeared to experience an androgyny shift: Grandfathers retained their masculine traits and gained feminine attributes; grandmothers retained their feminine traits and took on masculine attributes (see also Wink & Helson, 1993). This finding is particularly interesting because today's older people should, if anything, be more traditionally gender typed than younger adults who have grown up in an era of more flexible gender norms.

Is Androgyny Advantageous?

If a person can be both assertive and sensitive, both independent and understanding, being androgynous sounds psychologically healthy. Is it? College students—both males and females—believe that the ideal person is androgynous (Slavkin & Stright, 2000). Bem (1975, 1978) demonstrated that androgynous men and women behave more flexibly than more sex-typed individuals. For example, androgynous people, like masculine sex-typed people, can display the "masculine" agentic trait of independence by resisting social pressure to conform to undesirable group activities. Yet they are as likely as feminine sex-typed individuals to display the "feminine" communal trait of nurturance by interacting positively with a baby. Androgynous people seem to be highly adaptable, able to adjust their behavior to the demands of the situation at hand (Shaffer, Pegalis, & Cornell, 1992). Perhaps this is why androgynous parents are viewed as warmer and more supportive than nonandrogynous parents (Witt, 1997). In addition, androgynous individuals appear to enjoy higher self-esteem and are perceived as better adjusted than their traditionally sex-typed peers, although this is largely because of the masculine qualities they possess (Boldizar, 1991; Spence & Hall, 1996).

Before you jump to the conclusion that androgyny is a thoroughly desirable attribute, can you imagine any disadvantages of androgyny? During childhood, expressing too many of the traits considered more appropriate in the other sex can result in rejection by peers and low self-esteem (Lobel, Slone, & Winch, 1997). In addition, you may need to distinguish between the androgynous individual who possesses *positive* masculine and feminine traits and the one who possesses *negative* masculine and feminine traits (Woodhill & Samuels, 2003, 2004). People with positive androgyny score higher on measures of mental health and well-being than those with negative androgyny (Woodhill & Samuels, 2003). It may be premature, then, to conclude that it is better in all respects to be androgynous rather than either masculine or feminine in orientation. Still, you can at least conclude that it is unlikely to be damaging for men to become a little more feminine or for women to become a little more masculine than they have traditionally been. The Applications box on page 342 looks at whether researchers have had any success in changing gender-role attitudes and behavior.

Summing Up

Adults are influenced by the changing demands of gender roles. Marriage and parenthood appear to cause men and women to adopt more traditionally sex-typed roles. Freed from the parental imperative, middle-aged and elderly adults tend to experience a shift toward androgyny, blending desirable masculine-stereotyped and feminine-stereotyped qualities (although not switching personalities). Androgyny tends to be associated with good adjustment and adaptability. ■

Sexuality over the Life Span

A central part of the process of becoming a woman or a man is the process of becoming a sexual being, so it is appropriate that we examine sexual development here. It is a lifelong process that starts in infancy.

Are Infants Sexual Beings?

Sigmund Freud made the seemingly outrageous claim that humans are sexual beings from birth onward. We are born, he said, with a reserve of sexual energy redirected toward different parts of the body as we develop. Freud may have been wrong about some things, but he was right that infants are sexual beings.

Babies are biologically equipped at birth with male or female chromosomes, hormones, and genitals. Moreover, young infants in Freud's oral stage of development appear to derive

Applications

Changing Gender-Role Attitudes and Behavior

Some people believe that the world would be a better place if boys and girls were no longer socialized to adopt traditional masculine or feminine roles, interests, and behaviors. Children of both sexes would then have the freedom to be androgynous; women would no longer suffer from a lack of assertiveness in the world of work, and men would no longer be forced to suppress their emotions. Just how successful are efforts to encourage more flexible gender roles?

In several projects designed to change gender-role behavior, children have been exposed to nonsexist films, encouraged to imitate models of cross-sex behavior, reinforced by teachers for trying cross-sex activities, and provided with nonsexist educational materials (Katz, 1986; Katz & Walsh, 1991). For example, Rebecca Bigler and Lynn Liben (1990) reasoned that if they could alter children's gender stereotypes, they could head off the biased information processing that stereotypes promote. They exposed 6- to 11-year-olds to a series of problem-solving discussions emphasizing that (1) the most important considerations in deciding who could perform well in such traditionally masculine or feminine occupations as construction worker and beautician are the person's interests and willingness to learn and (2) the person's gender is irrelevant. Compared with children who received no such training, program participants showed a clear decline in occupational stereotyping, especially if they had entered the study with firm ideas about which jobs are for women and which are for men. Moreover, this reduction in stereotyping brought about the predicted decrease in biased information processing: Participants were more likely than nonparticipants to remember counterstereotypic information presented to them in stories (for example, recalling that the garbage man in a story was a woman).

Yet many efforts at change that work in the short run fail to have lasting effects. Children encouraged to interact in mixed-sex groups revert to their preference for same-sex friends as soon as the program ends (Lockheed, 1986; Serbin, Tonick, & Sternglanz, 1977). Why is it so difficult to change children's thinking? Perhaps because children are groomed for their traditional gender roles from birth and are bombarded with traditional gender-role messages every day. A short-term intervention project may have little chance of succeeding in this larger context.

Other research shows that it is often difficult to change the gender schemata we have constructed. Farah Hughes and Catherine Seta (2003) gave fifth-graders descriptions of men and women behaving in ways inconsistent with traditional gender stereotypes. The children were then asked to rate the likelihood that another man or woman would behave in gender-inconsistent ways. Despite being exposed to a model of inconsistent gender-stereotypic behavior, children believed that the other man (although not the other woman) would behave in a gender-consistent manner. The authors interpret this in terms of gender schema theory and children's desire to maintain their stereotypic gender schemata by countering an inconsistent piece of information with a highly consistent one. It also illustrates that simply exposing children to models of inconsistent gender roles is not going to miraculously lead to changes in the way they think about gender-stereotypic behavior: Men should still behave in masculine ways. Consistent with other research presented in this chapter, Hughes and Seta found that women were given more flexibility in terms of gender roles.

pleasure from sucking, mouthing, biting, and other oral activities. But the clincher is this: Both male babies and female babies have been observed to touch and manipulate their genital areas, to experience physical arousal, and to undergo what appear to be orgasms (Hyde & DeLamater, 2003; Leung & Robson, 1993). Parents in some cultures, well aware of the pleasure infants derive from their genitals, occasionally use genital stimulation as a means of soothing fussy babies (Ford & Beach, 1951).

What should you make of this infant sexuality? Infants feel bodily sensations, but they are hardly aware that their behavior is "sexual" (Crooks & Baur, 2005). Infants are sexual beings primarily in the sense that their genitals are sensitive and their nervous systems allow sexual responses. They are also as curious about their bodies as they are about the rest of the world. They enjoy touching all parts of their body, especially those that produce pleasurable sensations, and are likely to continue touching themselves unless reprimands from parents or other grown-ups discourage this behavior (at least in front of adults). From these early experiences, children begin to learn what human sexuality is about and how the members of their society regard it.

Childhood Sexuality

Although boys and girls spend much of their time in gender-segregated groups, they are nonetheless preparing for the day they will participate in sexual relationships with the other sex. They learn a great deal about sexuality and reproduction, continue to be curious about their bodies, and begin to interact with the other sex in ways that will prepare them for dating in adolescence.

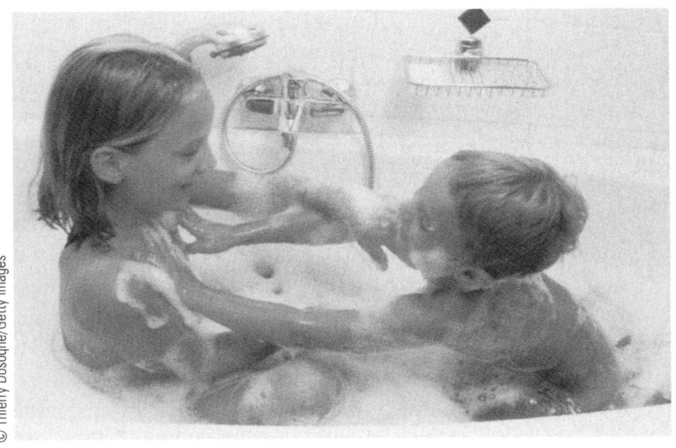

Preschoolers are naturally curious about the human body.

Knowledge of Sex and Reproduction

With age, children learn that sexual anatomy is the key differentiator between males and females, and they acquire a more correct and explicit vocabulary for discussing sexual organs (Brilleslijper & Baartman, 2000; Gordon, Schroeder, & Abrams, 1990). As Anne Bernstein and Philip Cowan (1975) have shown, children's understandings of where babies come from also change as they develop cognitively. Young children often seem to assume either that babies are just there all along or that they are somehow manufactured, much as toys might be. According to Jane, age 3½, "You find [the baby] at a store that makes it. . . . Well, they get it and then they put it in the tummy and then it goes quickly out" (p. 81). Another preschooler, interpreting what he could of an explanation about reproduction from his mom, created this scenario (author's files):

> The woman has a seed in her tummy that is fertilized by something in the man's penis. *(How does this happen?)* The fertilizer has to travel down through the man's body into the ground. Then it goes underground to get to the woman's body. It's like in our garden. *(Does the fertilizer come out of his penis?)* Oh no. Only pee-pee comes out of the penis. It's not big enough for fertilizer.

As these examples illustrate, young children construct their own understandings of reproduction well before they are told the "facts of life." Consistent with Piaget's theory of cognitive development, children construct their understanding of sex by assimilating and accommodating information into their existing cognitive structures. Children as young as age 7 know that sexual intercourse plays a role in the making of babies, but their understanding of just how this works is limited (Cipriani, 2002; Hyde & DeLamater, 2003). By age 12, most children have integrated information about sexual intercourse with information about the biological union of egg and sperm and can provide an accurate description of intercourse and its possible outcomes. Thus, as children mature cognitively and as they gain access to information, they are able to construct ever more accurate understandings of sexuality and reproduction.

Sexual Behavior

According to Freudian theory, preschoolers in the phallic stage of psychosexual development are actively interested in their genitals and seek bodily pleasure through masturbation, but school-age children enter a latency period during which they repress their sexuality and turn their attention instead to schoolwork and friendships with same-sex peers. It turns out that Freud was half right and half wrong.

Freud was correct that preschoolers are highly curious about their bodies, masturbate, and engage in both same-sex and cross-sex sexual play. He was wrong to believe that such activities occur infrequently among school-age children. By age 6, about half of children have engaged in sexual play (playing doctor or house), and sexual exploration (such as looking at and touching genitals) is increasingly common in elementary school (Larsson & Svedin, 2002; Okami, Olmstead, & Abramson, 1997; Simon & Gagnon, 1998). Elementary-school aged children in Freud's latency period may be more discreet about their sexual experimentation than preschoolers, but they have by no means lost their sexual curiosity. Surveys show, for example, that about two-thirds of boys and one-half of girls have masturbated by age 13 (Janus & Janus, 1993; Larsson & Svedin, 2002).

Gilbert Herdt and Martha McClintock (2000) have gathered evidence that age 10 is an important point in sexual development, a time when many boys and girls experience their first sexual attraction (often for a member of the other sex if they later become heterosexual or for a member of their own sex if they later become gay or lesbian). This milestone in development appears to be influenced by the maturation of the adrenal glands (which produce male androgens). It comes well before the maturation of the sex organs during puberty and therefore challenges the view of Freud (and many of the rest of us) that puberty is the critical time in sexual development. As Herdt and McClintock note, our society does little to encourage fourth-graders to have sexual thoughts, especially about members of their own sex, so perhaps a hormonal explanation of early sexual attraction makes more sense than an environmental one. Indeed, the adrenal glands mature around age 6 to age 8 and produce low, but increasing, amounts of androgens (McClintock & Herdt, 1996).

Yet sexual development is also shaped by the sociocultural context in which children develop. Eric Widmer and his colleagues (Widmer, Treas, & Newcomb, 1998) compared attitudes toward sex in 24 countries and found wide variations in sexual beliefs. Still, the researchers were able to discern four sets of beliefs that characterized most of the countries. The "teen permissive" countries, which included Germany, Austria, and Sweden, reported the highest levels of acceptance of both early teenage sex and premarital sex. The United States, Ireland, Northern Ireland, and Poland were categorized as sexual conservatives. People in these countries were most disapproving of all types of nonmarital sex. For example, they were more likely than people in other countries to report that teenage sex, extramarital sex, and homosexual sex were "always wrong." Several countries—the Netherlands, Norway, the Czech Republic, Canada, and Spain—were classified as homosexual permissives because of their relatively high acceptance of homosexual sex. Otherwise, these countries were similar in attitudes to the sexual conservatives. Most of the remaining countries were classified as moderate and were rather heterogeneous in their sexual attitudes.

In the United States, children learn from their peers how to relate to the other sex. As Barrie Thorne's (1993) observations in elementary schools demonstrate, boys and girls may be segregated by gender, but they are hardly oblivious to each other. They talk constantly about who likes whom and who is cute; they play kiss-and-chase games in which girls attempt to catch boys and infect them with "cooties"; and they have steady boyfriends and girlfriends (if only for a few days). At times, boys and girls seem like mortal enemies. But by loving and hating each other, kissing and running away, they are grooming themselves for more explicitly sexual—but still often ambivalent—heterosexual relationships later in life (Thorne, 1993).

Childhood Sexual Abuse

Every day in this country, children, adolescents, and even infants are sexually abused by the adults closest to them. A typical scenario would be this: A girl age 12 or 13—although it happens to boys, too—is abused repeatedly by her father, stepfather, or another male relative or family friend (Putnam, 2003; Trickett & Putnam, 1993). Estimates of the percentages of girls and boys who are sexually abused vary wildly, perhaps because so many cases go unreported and because definitions vary substantially. In one representative sample of U.S. adults, 27% of the women and 16% of the men reported having experienced some form of childhood sexual abuse, ranging from being touched in ways they considered abusive to being raped (Finkelhor et al., 1989). Controlling for differences in definitions and samples, Kevin Gorey and Donald Leslie (1997) report that 17% of women and 8% of men have experienced childhood sexual abuse. In any case, childhood sexual abuse is a serious and widespread social problem. Unfortunately, only one out of every four abused children tells someone about the abuse within the first 24 hours and one in four remains silent, never telling anyone about his or her painful experience (Kogan, 2004).

What is the effect of sexual abuse on the victim? Kathleen Kendall-Tackett, Linda Williams, and David Finkelhor (1993) offer a useful account, based on their review of 45 studies. No single distinctive "syndrome" of psychological problems characterizes abuse victims. Instead, they may experience any number of problems commonly seen in emotionally disturbed individuals, including anxiety, depression, low self-esteem, aggression, acting out, withdrawal, and school learning problems. Roughly 20 to 30% experience each of these problems, and boys seem to experience the same types and degrees of disturbance as girls do.

Many of these aftereffects boil down to lack of self-worth and difficulty trusting others (Cole & Putnam, 1992). A college student who had been abused repeatedly by her father and other relatives wrote this about her experience (author's files):

> It was very painful, emotionally, physically, and psychologically. I wanted to die to escape it. I wanted to escape from my body. . . . I developed a "good" self and a "bad" self. This was the only way I could cope with the experiences. . . . I discovered people I trusted caused me harm. . . . It is difficult for me to accept the fact that people can care for me and expect nothing in return. . . . I dislike closeness and despise people touching me.

Two problems seem to be especially linked to being sexually abused. First, about a third of victims engage in sexualized behavior, acting out sexually by putting objects in vaginas, masturbating in public, behaving seductively, or if they are older, behaving promiscuously (Kendall-Tackett et al., 1993). One theory is that this sexualized behavior helps victims master or control the traumatic events they experienced (Tharinger, 1990). Second, about a third of victims display the symptoms of **posttraumatic stress disorder.** This clinical disorder, involving nightmares, flashbacks to the traumatizing events, and feelings of helplessness and anxiety in the face of danger, affects some soldiers in combat and other victims of extreme trauma (Kendall-Tackett et al., 1993).

In a few children, sexual abuse may contribute to severe psychological disorders including multiple-personality disorder, the splitting of the psyche into distinct personalities (Cole & Putnam, 1992; Ross et al., 1991). Yet about a third of children seem to experience no psychological symptoms (Kendall-Tackett et al., 1993). Some of these symptomless children may experience problems in later years. Nevertheless, some children are less severely damaged and more able to cope than others are.

Which children have the most difficulty? The effects of abuse are likely to be most severe when the abuse involved penetration and force and occurred frequently over a long period, when the perpetrator was a close relative such as the father, and when the child's mother did not serve as a reliable source of emotional support (Beitchman et al., 1991; Kendall-Tackett et al., 1993; Trickett & Putnam, 1993). Children are likely to recover better if their mothers believe their stories and can offer them a stable and loving home environment (Kendall-Tackett et al., 1993). Psychotherapy aimed at treating the anxiety and depression many victims experience and teaching them coping and problem-solving skills so that they will not be revictimized can also contribute to the healing process (Finkelhor & Berliner, 1995). Recovery takes time, but it does take place.

Adolescent Sexuality

Although infants and children are sexual beings, sexuality assumes far greater importance once sexual maturity is achieved. Adolescents must incorporate into their identities as males or females concepts of themselves as sexual males or females. Moreover, they must figure out how to express their sexuality in relationships. As part of their search for identity, teenagers raise questions about their sexual attractiveness, their sexual values, and their goals in close relationships. They also experiment with sexual behavior—sometimes with good outcomes, sometimes with bad ones.

Sexual Orientation

Part of establishing a sexual identity, part of an individual's larger task of resolving Erikson's conflict of identity versus role confusion, is becoming aware of one's **sexual orientation**—that is, one's preference for sexual partners of the same or other sex. Sexual orientation exists on a continuum; not all cultures categorize sexual preferences as ours does (Paul, 1993), but we commonly describe people as having primarily heterosexual, homosexual, or bisexual orientations. Most adolescents establish a heterosexual sexual orientation without much soul-searching. For youths attracted to members of their own sex, however, the process of accepting that they have a homosexual orientation and establishing a positive identity in the face of negative societal attitudes can be a long and torturous one. Many have an initial awareness of their sexual preference before reaching puberty but do not accept being gay or lesbian, or gather the courage to "come out," until their mid-20s (Savin-Williams, 1995). Among 17- to 25-year-olds with same-sex attractions, fewer than half have told both their parents and about one-third have not told either parent about their sexual orientation (Savin-Williams & Ream, 2003). Those who had disclosed to one or both parents did so around age 19. By this age, most are out of high school and have achieved some independence from their parents, which may give them the confidence to share this information.

Experimentation with homosexual activity is fairly common during adolescence, but few adolescents become part of the estimated 5 to 6% of adults who establish an enduring homosexual or bisexual sexual orientation (Smith, 1991). Contrary to societal stereotypes of gay men as effeminate and lesbian women as masculine, gay and lesbian individuals have the same range of psychological and social attributes that heterosexual adults do. Knowing that someone prefers same-sex romantic partners reveals no more about his personality than knowing that someone is heterosexual.

What influences the development of sexual orientation? Part of the answer lies in the genetic code. Twin studies have established that identical twins are more alike in sexual orientation than fraternal twins (Bailey & Pillard, 1991; Bailey et al., 1993). As Table 12.3 reveals, however, in about half the identical twin pairs, one twin is homosexual or bisexual but the other is heterosexual. This means that environment contributes at least as much as genes to the development of sexual orientation (Bailey, Dunne, & Martin, 2000).

Research also shows that many gay men and lesbian women expressed strong cross-sex interests when they were young, despite being subjected to the usual pressures to adopt a traditional gender role (Bailey et al., 2000; LeVay, 1996). Richard Green (1987), for example, studied a group of highly feminine boys who did not just engage in cross-sex play now and then but who strongly and consistently preferred female roles, toys, and friends. He found that 75% of these boys (compared with 2% of a control group of gender-typical boys) were exclusively homosexual or bisexual 15 years later. Yet the genetic research by J. Michael Bailey and Richard Pillard suggests that sexual orientation is every bit as heritable among gay men who were typically masculine boys and lesbian women who were typically feminine girls as among those who showed early cross-sex interests (Bailey & Pillard, 1991; Bailey et al., 1993). All that is clear, then, is that many gay and lesbian adults know from an early age that traditional gender-role expectations do not suit them.

Table 12.3 Percentage of Twins Who are Concordant for Homosexual or Bisexual Sexual Orientation.

	Identical Twins	Fraternal Twins
Both male twins are gay or bisexual if one is	52%	22%
Both female twins are lesbian or bisexual if one is	48%	16%

SOURCES: Male figures from Bailey & Pillard, 1991; female figures from Bailey et al., 1993.

Note: Higher rates of concordance (similarity) for identical twin pairs than for fraternal twin pairs provide evidence of genetic influence on homosexuality. Less-than-perfect concordance points to the additional operation of environmental influences.

What environmental factors may help determine whether a genetic predisposition toward homosexuality is actualized? We do not know yet. The old psychoanalytic view that male homosexuality stems from having a domineering mother and a weak father has received little support (LeVay, 1996). Growing up with a gay or lesbian parent also seems to have little effect on later sexual orientation (Patterson, 2004). Nor is there support for the idea that homosexuals were seduced into a homosexual lifestyle by older individuals.

A more promising hypothesis is that hormonal influences during the prenatal period influence sexual orientation (Ellis et al., 1988; Meyer-Bahlburg et al., 1995). For example, androgenized females are more likely than most other women to adopt a lesbian or bisexual orientation, suggesting that high prenatal doses of male hormones may predispose at least some females to homosexuality (Dittman et al., 1992; Money, 1988). Another possibility is that nature and nurture interact. Biological factors may predispose an individual to have certain psychological traits, which in turn influence the kinds of social experiences the person has, which in turn shape her sexual orientation (Byne, 1994). However, no one yet knows which factors in the prenatal or postnatal environment contribute, with genes, to a homosexual orientation (Byne, 1994; LeVay, 1996).

Sexual Morality

Whatever their sexual orientation, adolescents establish attitudes regarding what is and is not appropriate sexual behavior. The sexual attitudes of adolescents changed dramatically during the 20th century, especially during the 1960s and 1970s, yet many of the old values have endured (Caron & Moskey, 2002). Three generalizations emerge from the research on sexual attitudes.

First, most adolescents have come to believe that sex with affection is acceptable. They no longer buy the traditional view that premarital intercourse is always morally wrong.

They do not go so far as to view casual sex as acceptable, although males have more permissive attitudes about this than females. Most adolescents insist that the partners be in a romantic relationship or feel a close emotional involvement with each other (Caron & Moskey, 2002).

A second finding is that the **double standard** has declined over the years. According to the double standard, sexual behavior that is viewed as appropriate for males is considered inappropriate for females; there is one standard for males, another for females. In the "old days," a young man was expected to sow some wild oats and gain some sexual experience, whereas a young woman was expected to remain a virgin until she married. Although the double standard has declined, it has by no means disappeared (Crawford & Popp, 2003). Fathers still look more favorably on the sexual exploits of their sons than on those of their daughters (Brooks-Gunn & Furstenberg, 1989), and college students still tend to believe that a woman who has many sexual partners is more immoral than an equally promiscuous man (Crawford & Popp, 2003; Blumberg, 2003). Adolescent girls generally hold less permissive attitudes about sex than adolescent boys do (Milhausen & Herold, 1999). However, Western societies have been moving toward a single standard of sexual behavior used to judge both males and females.

A third generalization that emerges from research on sexual attitudes is that adolescents are confused about sexual norms. Adolescents continually receive mixed messages about sexuality (Ponton, 2001). They are encouraged to be popular and attractive to the other sex, and they watch countless television programs and movies that glamorize sexual behavior. Yet they are told to value virginity and to fear and avoid pregnancy, bad reputations, and AIDS and other STDs. Adults often tell teens that they are too young to engage in sexual activity with a peer, yet they make teens feel ashamed about masturbating (Halpern et al., 2000; Ponton, 2001). The standards for males and females are now more similar, and adolescents tend to agree that sexual intercourse in the context of emotional involvement is acceptable; but teenagers still must forge their own codes of behavior, and they differ widely in what they decide.

☾ Many of today's adolescents become involved in sexual activity early and give little thought to the long-term consequences of their behavior.

Sexual Behavior

If attitudes about sexual behavior have changed over the years, has sexual behavior itself changed? Yes, it has. Today's teenagers are involved in more intimate forms of sexual behavior at earlier ages than adolescents of the past were. Several themes emerge from the research on teens' sexual behavior:

- Rates of sexual activity climbed in the 1960s and continued to climb through the 1980s before leveling off and even declining in the 1990s (Althaus, 2001).
- The percentages of both males and females who have had intercourse increased steadily throughout the 20th century.
- Perhaps reflecting the decline of the double standard, the sexual behavior of females has changed much more than that of males, and the difference between the sexes has narrowed (Althaus, 2001).

The percentage of adolescents with sexual experience increases steadily over the adolescent years. About 20% of white teens report having sexual intercourse by age 15, and 50% have had intercourse sometime between age 15 and age 19 (Althaus, 2001). The rate is somewhat higher among black teens, with 30% of 14-year-olds reporting they have engaged in sex (DiIorio et al., 2001). By age 21 to age 24, 85% reported having had sexual intercourse (Meschke et al., 2000). Of course, rates of sexual activity depend greatly on how sexual activity is defined. What constitutes "having sex"? Virtually all college students—both male and female—agree that penile–vaginal intercourse is having sex, but only 38% believe that oral sex constitutes having sex (Pitts & Rahman, 2001). Perhaps this is why there are higher rates of oral sex than intercourse among today's high school students (Prinstein, Meade, & Cohen, 2003). Their cognitive schema of having sex does not include oral sex (or anal sex for some teens), so they can engage in oral sex without feeling as though they are really having sex.

Early sexual involvement is most likely among adolescents whose mothers were teenage parents; indeed, twin studies indicate that age of first intercourse is genetically influenced (Dunne et al., 1997). In addition, adolescents who become sexually active early have little invested in school; instead, they are involved in problem behaviors such as substance abuse and delinquency (Crockett et al., 1996). The factors that predict timing of first intercourse differ for males and females (Meschke et al., 2000). First intercourse is later for girls who do not date alone often and whose parents have always been married. Boys with higher levels of achievement orientation and less focus on popularity tend to delay first intercourse. Interestingly, teen couples in which the young woman is highly feminine and the young man is highly masculine are more likely to have had sex and to have had early sex than other combinations of couples (Udry & Chantala, 2004). Furthermore, in these couples, the girl's previous sexual experience, not the boy's, determined how early the couple started having sex (Udry & Chantala, 2004).

Males and females feel differently about their sexual encounters. Teenage boys often report that their first sexual intercourse was pleasurable, whereas teenage girls respond more negatively, with some feelings of disappointment (Hyde & DeLamater, 2003). Among girls who have been sexually active, many wish they waited longer to start having sex (National Campaign to Prevent Teenage Pregnancy, 2002). Females are more insistent than males that sex and love—physical intimacy and emotional intimacy—go together. In one survey, 61% of college women, but only 29% of college men, agreed with the idea of "no intercourse without love" (Darling, Davidson, & Passarello, 1992; see also de Gaston, Weed, & Jensen, 1996). Females are also more likely than males to have been in a steady relationship with their first sexual partner (Darling et al., 1992). This continuing gap between the sexes can sometimes create misunderstandings and hurt feelings, and it may partly explain why females are more likely than males to wish they had waited to have sex (de Gaston, Jensen, & Weed, 1995).

It is clear that sexual involvement is part of the average adolescent's experience. This is true of all major ethnic groups, rich and poor. The differences in sexual activity among social groups have been shrinking (Forrest & Singh, 1990). Although most adolescents seem to adjust successfully to becoming sexually active, there have also been some casualties among those who are psychologically unready for sex or who end up with an unintended pregnancy or an STD.

Sexually active adolescent couples often fail to use contraception, partly because they are cognitively immature and do not take seriously the possibility that their behavior could have unfortunate long-term consequences (Loewenstein & Furstenberg, 1991; Morrison, 1985). Although condom use has increased over the past decade, it is still low (Kaplan et al., 2001). In one study, for example, only 45% of adolescent males said they always used a condom during intercourse (Kaplan et al., 2001). Adolescent females report less frequent condom use than males, possibly because their sexual partners are often several years older and because condom use among males declines from mid- to late adolescence (Kaplan et al., 2001; Sneed et al., 2001). This may reflect that adolescent couples who are in long-term, monogamous relationships stop using condoms because they no longer fear transmission of HIV or STDs.

For the adolescent who gives birth, the consequences of teenage sexuality are likely to include an interrupted education, a low income, and a difficult start for both her and her child (Furstenberg, Brooks-Gunn, & Chase-Lansdale, 1989). This young mother's life situation and her child's developmental status are likely to improve later, especially if she goes back to school and limits her family size, but she is likely to remain economically disadvantaged compared with her peers who postpone parenthood until their 20s (Furstenberg, Brooks-Gunn, & Morgan, 1987).

What effect has the threat of AIDS had on adolescent sexual behavior? Most studies find change, but perhaps not enough. As noted, teens are more likely to use condoms (at least some of the time) than they used to be, and rates of teenage pregnancy have begun to decline recently as a result (Vobejda & Havemann, 1997). However, few adolescents are doing what they would need to do to protect themselves from HIV infection: abstaining from sex or using a condom (latex with a spermicide) *every* time. No wonder many educators are calling for stronger programs of sex education and distribution of free condoms at school. There is little chance of preventing the unwanted consequences of teenage sexuality unless more adolescents either postpone sex or practice safer sex. One encouraging finding is that warmth and connectedness between mothers and their children can delay the age of first intercourse (Sieving, McNeely, & Blum, 2000), as can parent–child communication about sexuality (Blake et al., 2001).

Adult Sexuality

Adults' sexual lifestyles are as varied as their personalities and intellects. Some adults remain single—some of them actively seeking a range of partners, others having one partner at a time, and still others leading celibate lives. More than 9 of 10 Americans marry, and most adults are married at any given time. Men have more sexual partners than women during their adult lives, but most members of both sexes have just one sexual partner at a time (Laumann et al., 1994).

Among married couples, there is a small decline in quality of sex over the course of marriage (Liu, 2003). And married women report somewhat less satisfaction with their sex lives than do married men (Liu, 2003). On average, married middle-aged couples have sex about once a week and report that they would have sex more often if they were not so busy and tired from their jobs and raising kids (Deveny, 2003).

What becomes of people's sex lives as they age? Many young people can barely conceive of their parents or—heaven forbid—their grandparents as sexual beings. We tend to stereotype older adults as sexless or asexual. But we are wrong: people continue to be sexual beings throughout the life span. Perhaps the most amazing discoveries about sex in late adulthood are those of Bernard Starr and Marcella Weiner (1981), who surveyed 800 elderly volunteers ages 60 to 91. In this group, more than 90% said they like sex, almost 80% were still sexually active, and 75% said that their sex lives were the same as or were better than when they were younger. One 70-year-old widow, asked how often she would like to have sex, was not bashful at all about replying, "Morning, noon, and night" (p. 47).

Obviously, people can remain highly interested in sex and sexually active in old age. Yet Starr and Weiner's findings are likely to be exaggerated because only the most sexually active people may have agreed to complete such a survey. More reliable findings are reported by Tom Smith (1991) based on a survey of a representative sample of American adults that asked about many things, including sexual behavior. As Figure 12.6 shows, the percentage of adults who reported at least some sexual contact in the past year declined steadily from age group to age group, although almost a third of adults in their 70s and older were still sexually active. Men were more likely

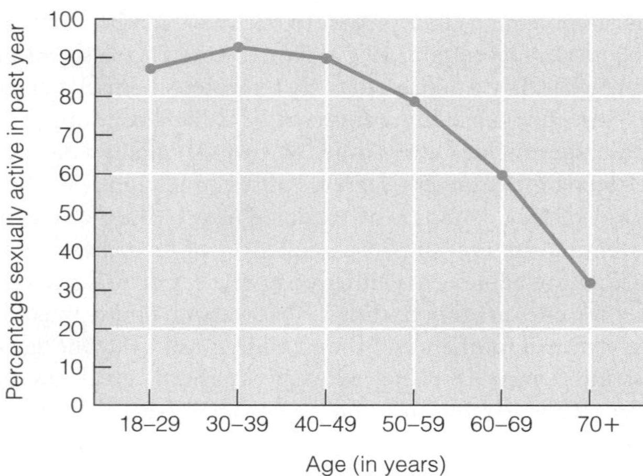

Figure 12.6 Percentage of U.S. adults of different ages who reported having at least one sexual partner in the past year. Cross-sectional data such as these can be misleading about the degree to which sexual activity declines with age, but longitudinal studies also point to decreased involvement.

SOURCE: Adapted from Smith (1991).

to be sexually active than women, and, as you might expect, adults were more likely to be sexually active if they were married (91%) than if they were separated or divorced (74–80%) or widowed (only 14%) (see also Gott & Hinchliff, 2003).

How can we explain declines with age in sexual interest and activity? Consider first the physiological changes in sexual capacity that occur with age, as revealed by the pioneering research of William Masters and Virginia Johnson (1966, 1970). Males are at their peak of sexual responsiveness in their late teens and early 20s and gradually become less responsive thereafter. A young man is easily and quickly aroused; his orgasm is intense; and he may have a refractory, or recovery, period of only minutes before he is capable of sexual activity again. The older man is likely to be slower—slower to arouse, slower to ejaculate after being aroused, and slower to recover afterward. In addition, levels of male sex hormones decline gradually with age in many men. This may contribute to diminished sexual functioning among older men (Schiavi et al., 1991), although most researchers do not believe that hormonal factors fully explain the changes in sexual behavior that most men experience (Kaye, 1993).

Physiological changes in women are far less dramatic. Females reach their peak of sexual responsiveness later than men do, often not until their late 30s. Women are capable of more orgasms in a given time span than men are because they have little or no refractory period after orgasm, and this capacity is retained into old age. As noted in Chapter 5, menopause does not seem to reduce sexual activity or interest for most women. However, like older men, older women typically are slower to become sexually excited. Moreover, some experience discomfort associated with decreased lubrication.

The physiological changes that men and women experience do not explain why many of them become less sexually active in middle and old age. Masters and Johnson concluded that both men and women are physiologically capable of sexual behavior well into old age. Women retain this physiological capacity even longer than men, yet they are less sexually active in old age.

Apparently, we must turn to factors other than biological aging to explain changes in sexual behavior. In summarizing these factors, Pauline Robinson (1983) quotes Alex Comfort (1974): "In our experience, old folks stop having sex for the same reason they stop riding a bicycle—general infirmity, thinking it looks ridiculous, and no bicycle" (p. 440).

Under the category of infirmity, diseases and disabilities, as well as the drugs prescribed for them, can limit sexual functioning (Marsiglio & Donnelly, 1991). This is a particular problem for men, who may become impotent if they have high blood pressure, coronary disease, diabetes, or other health problems. Mental health problems are also important: Many cases of impotence among middle-aged and elderly men are attributable to psychological causes such as stress at work and depression rather than to physiological causes (Persson & Svanborg, 1992).

The second source of problems is social attitudes that view sexual activity in old age as ridiculous, or at least inap-

Most older adults continue to be sexual beings who seek love and affection.

propriate. Old people are stereotyped as sexually unappealing and sexless (or as "dirty old men") and are discouraged from expressing sexual interests. These negative attitudes may be internalized by elderly people, causing them to suppress their sexual desires (Kaye, 1993; Purifoy, Grodsky, & Giambra, 1992). Older females may be even further inhibited by the double standard of aging, which regards aging in women more negatively than aging in men (Arber & Ginn, 1991).

Third, there is the "no bicycle" part of Comfort's analogy—the lack of a partner, or at least of a willing and desirable partner. Most older women are widowed, divorced, or single and face the reality that there just are not enough older men to go around. Moreover, most of these men are married, and those who are single are often looking for a younger partner (Robinson, 1983). Lack of a partner, then, is the major problem for elderly women, many of whom continue to be interested in sex, physiologically capable of sexual behavior, and desirous of love and affection.

Perhaps we should add one more element to Comfort's bicycle analogy: lack of cycling experience. Masters and Johnson (1966, 1970) proposed a "use it or lose it" principle of sexual behavior to reflect two findings. First, an individual's level of sexual activity early in adulthood predicts his level of sexual activity in later life. The relationship is not necessarily causal, by the way; it could simply be that some people are more sexually motivated than others throughout adulthood. A second aspect of the use it or lose it rule may be causal, however: Middle-aged and elderly adults who experience a long period of sexual abstinence often have difficulty regaining their sexual capacity.

Summing Up

We are sexual beings from infancy onward. School-age children engage in sex play and appear to experience their first sexual attractions around age 10. In adolescence, forming a positive sexual identity is an important task, one that can be difficult for those with a gay or lesbian sexual orientation. During the past century, we have witnessed increased endorsement of the view that sex with affection is acceptable, a weakening of the double standard, and increased confusion about sexual norms.

Many older adults continue having sexual intercourse, and many of those who cease having it or have it less frequently continue to be sexually motivated. Elderly people can continue to enjoy an active sex life if they retain their physical and mental health, do not allow negative attitudes surrounding sexuality in later life to stand in their way, and have a willing and able partner. ■

Summary Points

1. Differences between males and females can be detected in the physical, psychological, and social realms; gender differences arise from an interaction of biological influences and socialization into gender roles (including the learning of gender-role norms and stereotypes).

2. Research comparing males and females indicates that the two sexes are far more similar than different psychologically. The average male is more aggressive and better at spatial and mathematical problem-solving tasks, but less adept at verbal tasks, than the average female. Males also tend to be more active, assertive, and developmentally vulnerable than females, who tend to be more compliant with adults' requests, tactful, nurturant, and anxious. Most sex differences are small, however, and some are becoming smaller.

3. During infancy, boys and girls are similar but adults treat them differently. By age 2, infants have often gained knowledge of their basic gender identity and display "gender-appropriate" play preferences.

4. Gender typing progresses most rapidly during the toddler and preschool years, with 2- and 3-year-olds already learning gender stereotypes; school-age children are at first rigid and then more flexible in their thinking about gender norms, and they segregate themselves by sex.

5. Adolescents become intolerant in their thinking about gender-role deviations and, through gender intensification, show increased concern with conforming to gender norms.

6. Theories of gender-role development include John Money and Anke Ehrhardt's biosocial theory, Sigmund Freud's psychoanalytic perspective, social learning theory, and the cognitive theories including Lawrence Kohlberg's cognitive developmental theory and the gender schema theory. Each theory has some support, but none is completely right.

7. Sexuality is an important component of our development throughout the life span. Infants and children are curious about their bodies and begin experimenting with sexual behaviors. A significant increase in sexual behavior occurs during adolescence. Most adults marry and engage in regular sexual activity, with declines evident as they age. Declines in the physiological capacity for sex cannot fully explain declines in sexual activity; poor physical or mental health, lack of a partner, negative societal attitudes, and periods of sexual abstinence also contribute.

Critical Thinking

1. Jen and Ben are fraternal twins whose parents are determined that they should grow up to be androgynous. Nonetheless, when the twins are only 4, Jen wants frilly dresses and loves to play with her Barbie doll, and Ben wants a machine gun and loves to pretend he's a football player and tackle people. Each seems headed for a traditional gender role. Which of the theories in this chapter do you think explains this best, which has the most difficulty explaining it, and why did you reach these conclusions?

2. Fewer women than men become architects. Drawing on the material in this chapter, explain the extent to which nature and nurture may be responsible for this, citing evidence.

3. The extent to which males and females differ changes from infancy to old age. When are gender differences in psychological characteristics and roles played in society greatest, and when are they least evident? How would you account for this pattern?

4. What factors are likely to influence the age at which young people today become sexually active? If you wanted to delay the age of first intercourse, what would be some ways to do this?

Key Terms

gender role, 323
gender role norms, 323
gender-role stereotypes, 323
gender typing, 323
communality, 324
agency, 324
systemize, 324
social-role hypothesis, 325
gender identity, 327
gender segregation, 328
gender intensification, 329
androgenized female, 331
identification, 333
Oedipus complex, 333
Electra complex, 333
gender stability, 336
gender consistency, 336
gender schema (*plural:* schemata), 337
androgyny, 339
parental imperative, 340
androgyny shift, 341
posttraumatic stress disorder, 344
sexual orientation, 345
double standard, 346

Media Resources

Websites to Explore

Visit Our Website

For a chapter tutorial quiz and other useful features, visit the book's companion website at *http://psychology.wadsworth.com/sigelman_rider5e.* You can also connect directly to the following sites:

Gender, Diversities, and Technology Institute
Billing itself as "an incubator for new ideas and approaches, a generator of new policy," the Gender, Diversities, and Technology Institute focuses on gender equity in education, technology, and the workplace. The Publications page on its website contains several articles available for downloading.

Sexual Health
The site of the Planned Parenthood Federation has a wealth of information about sexual and reproductive health, birth control, STDs, and sex education.

Another resource on sexual health is the Sexuality Information and Education Council of the United States. This nonprofit organization aims to promote and advocate comprehensive sexual health education through media outreach, public policy, information dissemination, and educational programs, including two geared toward youth development and school health education. If you click the Publications tab, you will find a myriad of fact sheets on issues related to sexuality education and lesbian, gay, bisexual, and transgender youth.

Teen Intimacy and Sexuality
The Teen Intimacy and Sexuality subcategory on the Developmental Psychology page at the Psi Café features links related to a range of topics, including the development of intimacy and sexual orientation.

Sex: Unknown
This PBS program explores the complicated terrain of gender identity. You can watch it in its entirety on the companion website. The site also contains information about intersex conditions and the embryonic development of gender within the womb. In addition, you can read various stories from people who have struggled with gender identity, including an essay by Max Beck, a man raised as a woman.

Understanding the Data: Exercises on the Web

For additional insight on the data presented in this chapter, try the exercises for the following figure and table at *http://psychology.wadsworth.com/sigelman_rider5e:*

Figure 12.2 Do children prefer playmates of their own sex?

Table 12.3 Percentage of Twins Who Are Concordant for Homosexual or Bisexual Sexual Orientation

Life-Span CD-ROM

Go to the Wadsworth Life-Span CD-ROM for further study of the concepts in this chapter. The CD-ROM includes narrated concept overviews, video clips, a multimedia glossary, and additional activities to expand your learning experience. For this chapter, check out the following clips, and others, in the video library:

VIDEO Early and Middle Childhood: Gender Issues

VIDEO Influences on Teen Sexuality

VIDEO Sex over 45

Developmental PsychologyNow is a web-based, intelligent study system that provides a complete package of diagnostic quizzes, a personalized study plan, integrated multimedia elements, and learning modules. Check it out at *http://psychology.wadsworth.com/sigelman_rider5e/now.*

CHAPTER thirteen

Social Cognition and Moral Development

ON MARCH 5, 2001, Charles "Andy" Williams, age 15, took a .22-caliber revolver from his father's locked gun collection and went on a shooting spree at Santana High School in suburban San Diego (Fletcher & Waxman, 2001). Another in a long line of youthful murderers, the most notorious of which were the Columbine High School duo of Eric Harris and Dylan Klebold, Williams injured 13 and killed 2. And a nation wondered why.

Williams was always talking big, his friends said, so they just ignored him when he bragged that he was going to steal a car or, shortly before the shooting, that he was going to take a gun to school and shoot the place up. A short, skinny loner who had long been the target of name-calling and bullying, he had moved to California with his father within a year of the incident and immediately became the target of even worse taunting, to the point that he talked of killing himself. Not able to fit in with the high school crowd, he hung out with skateboarders who experimented with drugs. He was a latchkey child who spent a lot of time at friends' houses. He showed no remorse when interviewed by the police. His friends had the sense that he was mad at something (Booth & Snyder, 2001). Yet they also could not believe that he did what he did: "He didn't seem like that kind of person" (Fletcher & Waxman, 2001, p. A4). When asked about her son, his mother, who had been divorced from Williams's father for a decade, could only say tearfully, "He's lost" (Booth & Snyder, 2001).

What might have been going through Williams's head as he played out his drama? Did he think about the consequences of his act, for himself and others? Did he have empathy for his victims? Did he know that what he was doing was wrong? Should this 15-year-old have been tried as an adult? Did he have the same capacity to judge right and wrong that an adult has? Apparently the court thought so: He was sentenced to 50 years to life and will be eligible for parole at age 65 (Moran, 2002, http://signonsandiego.com/news/metro/santana/index.html).

In this chapter, we continue our examination of the development of the self by exploring how we come to understand the world of people and think through social issues, especially issues of right and wrong, and how our thinking about self and others is related to our behavior. We begin with the broad topic of **social cognition**—thinking about the perceptions, thoughts, emotions, motives, and behaviors of self, other people, groups, and even whole social systems (Flavell, 1985). We then look closely at thinking about moral issues and ask how children acquire a set of moral standards, how they decide what is right and wrong, how their thoughts and emotions influence what they do, and how their moral decision making changes over the life span. In the process, you stand to gain some insights into why Andy Williams shot his classmates.

Charles "Andy" Williams, age 15, in court, accused of murder in a school shooting in Santee, California. The obvious question: Why?

Social Cognition

Infants come to know parents, siblings, and other companions by appearance and form expectations about how these companions will behave. However, young infants cannot analyze the personalities of other people or recognize that their companions have their own distinct motives, feelings, and thoughts. These skills are examples of social cognition. We have already touched on some important aspects of social cognitive development in this book, for example, that older children think differently than younger children about what they are like as individuals and about how males and females differ. Here we focus on developmental changes in the ability to understand human psychology, describe other people, and adopt other people's perspectives.

Developing a Theory of Mind

Imagine that you are a young child, are brought to the laboratory, and are led through the research scenario portrayed in Figure 13.1. A girl named Sally puts her marble in her basket and leaves the room. While she is gone, Anne moves the marble to her box. Sally returns to the room. Now you are asked the critical question: Where will Sally look for her marble?

This task, called a **false belief task,** assesses the understanding that people can hold incorrect beliefs and that these beliefs, even though incorrect, can influence their behavior. The task was used in a pioneering study by Simon Baron-Cohen, Alan Leslie, and Uta Frith (1985) to determine whether young children, children with Down syndrome, and children with autism (see Chapter 16) have a theory of mind. A **theory of mind** is the understanding that people have mental states such as desires, beliefs, and intentions and that these mental states guide (or cause, if you like) their behavior. We all rely on a theory of mind, also called mind-reading skills, to predict and explain human behavior. We refer to mental states every day, saying, for example, that people did what they did

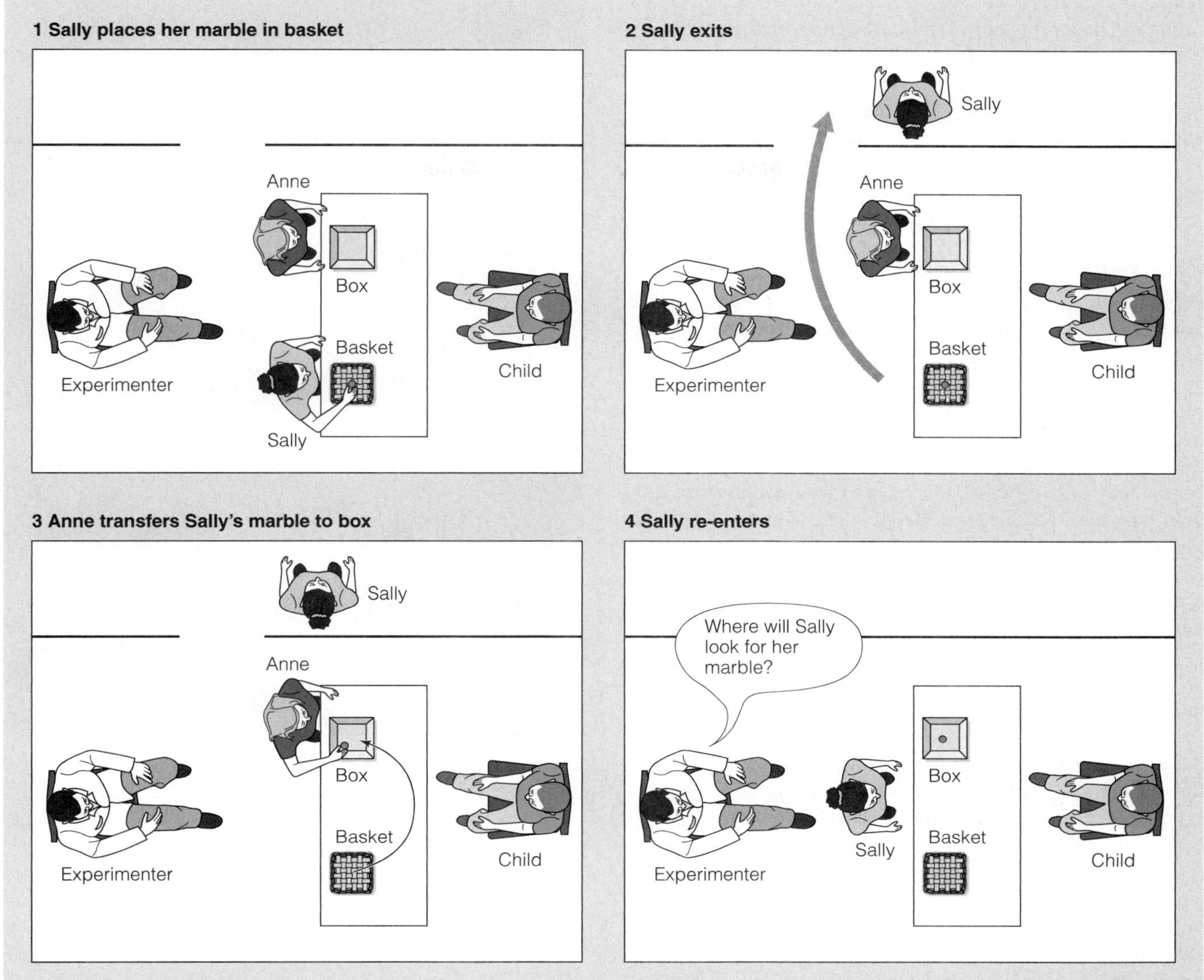

Figure 13.1 The experimental arrangement in the false belief task involving Sally and Anne. Because Sally does not know that Anne transferred Sally's marble from Sally's basket to Anne's box, she falsely believes it is in her basket. The child who has a theory of mind should say that she will look for it there.

SOURCE: Adapted from Baron-Cohen et al. (1985).

because they wanted to, intended to, or believed that doing so would have a desired effect.

Children who pass the false belief task in Figure 13.1, and therefore show evidence of having a theory of mind to explain human behavior, say that Sally will look for her marble in the basket (where she falsely believes it to be) rather than in the box (where it is). Children who have a theory of mind believe that Sally's behavior will be guided by her false belief about the marble's location; they are able to set aside their own knowledge of where the marble ended up after Anne moved it. In the study by Baron-Cohen and his colleagues, about 85% of 4-year-olds of normal intelligence and older children with Down syndrome passed the false belief task. Yet despite mental ages greater than those of the children with Down syndrome, 80% of the autistic children failed. They incorrectly said Sally would look where they knew the marble to be (in the box) rather than where Sally had every reason to believe it was (in the basket).

This study served as the basis for hypothesizing that autistic children display severe social deficits because they lack a theory of mind and suffer from a kind of mind blindness (Baron-Cohen, 1995; and see Chapter 16 on autism). Imagine trying to understand and interact with people if you were unable to appreciate such fundamentals of human psychology as people look for things where they believe they are, choose things that they want, reject things that they hate, and sometimes attempt to plant false beliefs in others (that is, lie).

Temple Grandin, a woman with autism who is intelligent enough to be a professor of animal sciences, describes having to compensate for lack of a theory of mind: she must create a memory bank of how people behave and what emotions they express in various situations and then "compute" how people might be expected to behave in similar situations (Sacks, 1993). Just as we cannot understand falling objects without employing the concept of gravity, we cannot hope to understand humans without invoking the concept of mental states.

First Steps

Research on theory of mind has not only stimulated much thought about the nature and causes of autism but also prompted many researchers to ask when and how normal children develop the components of a theory of mind. Although children normally do not pass false belief tasks until age 4 or at the earliest age 3, researchers have detected forerunners of a theory of mind as early as the end of the first year of life and believe that a theory of mind begins to form long before children pass false belief tasks (Flavell, 1999; Gopnik, Capps, & Meltzoff, 2000). Four abilities are considered precursors or early signs of a theory of mind: joint attention, pretend play, imitation, and emotional understanding (Charman, 2000). All four, as it turns out, are deficient in autistic children.

Starting around 9 months, infants and their caregivers begin to engage in much *joint attention,* both looking at the same object at the same time. At this age, infants sometimes point to toys then look toward their companions, encouraging others to look at what they are looking at. By doing so, infants show awareness that other people have different perceptual experiences than they do—and that two people can share a perceptual experience.

© IFA Bilderteam/eStock Photography/PictureQuest

☾ Even 1-year-olds show awareness that other people can have mental states (perceptions) different from their own when they point at objects so that their companions and they can jointly attend to the same object.

Similarly, when infants engage in their first simple pretend play, between 1 and 2 years, they show at least a primitive understanding of the difference between pretense (a kind of false belief) and reality (see Chapter 14). They know the difference between a pretend tea party and a real one, for example. Yet if you pretend to spill pretend tea on the table and hand a 2-year-old a paper towel, he will quickly wipe it up, no questions asked (Harris, 1989).

In addition, imitation of other people in the first year of life reveals an ability to mentally represent their actions and possibly the goals or intentions behind them. Finally, emotional understanding, as evidenced by comforting a playmate who is crying (see a later section) or teasing a sibling in the second year of life, reflect an understanding that other people have emotions and that these emotions can be influenced (Flavell, 1999).

We have even more solid evidence that children are developing theories of mind when they begin to refer to mental states in their speech starting around age 2 (Bretherton & Beeghly, 1982). For example, Ross (at 2 years, 7 months) was asked why he keeps asking why and replied, "I want to say 'why,'" explaining his behavior in terms of his desire; Adam (at 3 years, 3 months) commented about a bus, "I thought it was a taxi," showing awareness that he held a false belief about the bus (Wellman & Bartsch, 1994, p. 345).

Finally, some research suggests that children as young as $2\frac{1}{2}$ years old will attempt to deceive an adult about which of several containers holds a bag of gold coins and jewels (Chandler, Fritz, & Hala, 1989). They seem capable of trying to plant a false belief in another person if they are shown how to erase telltale footprints leading toward the hiding place and to lay new footprints heading in the wrong direction. Other studies suggest that 3-year-olds may be too young to deceive other people deliberately; they sometimes lay false tracks even when they are supposed to help someone find a prize rather than keep someone from finding it (Sodian, 1994). Interestingly, 77% of the mothers polled in one study said 4-year-olds are capable of deliberately lying, but only 29% thought 3-year-olds have this capacity to plant false beliefs (Stouthamer-Loeber, 1991). Overall, children clearly understand perceptions, desires, pretense, and hide-and-seek deception games before they pass false belief tasks. A theory of mind forms gradually, starting in infancy (Charman, 2000; Wellman, Phillips, & Rodriguez, 2000).

Desire and Belief–Desire Psychologies

Henry Wellman (1990) has theorized that children's theories of mind first take shape about age 2 as a **desire psychology.**

Toddlers talk about what they want and even explain their own behavior and that of others in terms of wants or desires. This early desire psychology could be seen even among 18-month-olds in a clever study by Betty Repacholi and Alison Gopnik (1997). An experimenter tried two foods—Goldfish crackers and broccoli florets—and expressed happiness in response to one but disgust in response to the other. Because the toddlers almost universally preferred the crackers to the broccoli, the acid test was a scenario in which toddlers saw the experimenter express her liking for broccoli but her disgust at the crackers ("Eww! Crackers! I tasted crackers! Eww!"). When confronted with the two bowls of food and asked to give the experimenter some, would these toddlers give her broccoli or crackers? The 14-month-olds in the study either did not comply with the request or gave the experimenter crackers, despite her distaste for them. However, the 18-month-olds gave her broccoli (undoubtedly against their better judgment), showing that they were able to infer her desire from her previous emotional reactions to the two foods.

By age 4, children normally progress to a **belief–desire psychology.** Not only do they understand that people's desires guide their behavior, but they also understand that two people can have different beliefs and they begin to pass false belief tasks like the one about Sally and her marble, demonstrating an understanding that beliefs are not always an accurate reflection of reality (Wellman & Liu, 2004). They appreciate that people do what they do because they *desire* certain things and they *believe* that certain actions will help them fulfill their desires. Based on a meta-analysis of 178 studies of theory of mind, Henry Wellman, David Cross, and Julanne Watson (2001) concluded that research strongly supports this shift from a desire psychology at age 2 to a belief–desire psychology at age 4, sometimes earlier if the tasks are simplified.

However, it is better to think of theory of mind as a set of understandings that children begin to develop well before age 4, and continue to refine and learn to use long afterward, than to view it as something children "have" at 4 years (Mitchell, 1997; Wellman & Liu, 2004). In late elementary school, children are still mastering the complexities of thinking about other people's beliefs (Bosacki, 2000; Keenan, 2003)—for example, making sense of statements such as, "Mary thinks that Jeff thinks that she hates him." Moreover, it is not until then that children grasp that different human minds construct different views of reality and that their interpretations of events are influenced by these views (Flavell, 1999).

Nature and Nurture

What roles do nature and nurture play in the development of theory of mind? On the nature side, evolutionary theorists argue that having a theory of mind proved adaptive to our ancestors and became part of our biological endowment as a species (Bjorklund & Pellegrini, 2002; Mitchell, 1997). You can easily imagine that theory-of-mind skills would help humans function as members of a social group, gain resources, and therefore survive. Social behaviors such as bargaining, conflict resolution, cooperation, and competition depend on understanding other people and predicting their behavior accurately. As it turns out, chimpanzees, gorillas, and other great apes share with humans basic, although not advanced, theory-of-mind skills, including a capacity to deceive others to get what they want and to grasp what competitors have seen or have not seen about where food has been hidden (Hare, Call, & Tomasello, 2001; Tomasello, Call, & Hare, 2003).

Developing a theory of mind also requires a certain level of biological maturation, especially neurological and cognitive development. This may be why children everywhere develop a theory of mind and progress from a desire psychology to a belief–desire psychology in the same manner (Tardif & Wellman, 2000). Abnormal brain development in children with autism is suspected to be behind their great difficulty passing theory-of-mind tasks. One view is that evolution may have equipped the normal human brain with a specialized module or modules devoted to understanding mental states (Leslie, 1994; Scholl & Leslie, 2001). Using neuroimaging techniques, researchers are beginning to identify areas of the brain in the prefrontal cortex and temporal lobes that are activated during theory-of-mind tasks and seem to be uniquely involved in thinking about people's beliefs (Gallagher & Frith, 2003; Saxe, Carey, & Kanwisher, 2004). The "brain module" view is not firmly supported, however. Other researchers argue that theory-of-mind skills are the outgrowth of broader maturational changes in the brain and in cognitive functioning (Gopnik et al., 2000). For example, children seem to need to attain a certain level of language development before they can master false belief tasks (Ruffman et al., 2003). This may be because both language development and theory of mind require representational or symbolic thinking skills or because language provides the vehicle through which humans can think about and share information about their mental states.

On the nurture side of the nature–nurture debate is evidence that acquiring a theory of mind, much like acquiring language, requires not only a normal human brain but also experience interacting with other humans and participating in a "community of minds" (Nelson et al., 2003). Children with siblings seem to grasp the elements of a theory of mind earlier than children without siblings (Jenkins & Astington, 1996). Engaging in pretend play with siblings may be especially helpful, because this provides good practice in understanding that belief and reality are not necessarily the same (Taylor & Carlson, 1997; Youngblade & Dunn, 1995). In multichild families, there may also be more talk about mental states ("She thought you were done with your ice cream," "He didn't mean to step on your head"). This kind of mind talk seems to contribute to early mastery of a theory of mind (Dunn et al., 1991).

Parents are important, too. They can contribute positively to the development of theory-of-mind skills by forming secure attachments with their children, being sensitive to their needs and perspectives, and talking about their own emotions and beliefs (Symons & Clark, 2000). Mothers who talk in elaborated ways about mental states and use them to explain everyday behavior tend to have children with advanced theory-of-mind skills (Peterson & Slaughter, 2003). So do mothers who encourage their children, after they have misbehaved, to imagine what others may have thought or felt (Pears & Moses, 2003). As children discuss everyday experiences with their parents, they begin to appreciate that they and other people do not always have the same perspectives, thoughts, or feelings. Children who are physically abused, especially as toddlers, are slow to master theory-of-mind tasks, possibly because they are deprived of such parent–child conversations about mental states (Cicchetti et al., 2003).

Children in certain cultures are also deprived of opportunities to "talk psychology" every day, and the effects are evident. Among the Junin Quechua people of Peru, adults rarely talk about beliefs and thoughts and have few words in their language for them. The result is that children as old as 8 years have trouble understanding that beliefs can be false (Vinden & Astington, 2000). Similarly, children as old as age 15 in a region of Papua New Guinea could not answer questions about other people's thoughts that 5-year-olds in our society handle easily (Vinden & Astington, 2000). So, although children everywhere develop theories of mind, there are cultural differences in the extent to which people focus on overt behavior versus mental states in talking about and explaining other people's behavior and in the number of terms they have for mental states. These cultural differences may help explain differences in the rate at which children master theory-of-mind tasks (Lillard, 1998; Vinden & Astington, 2000). Alternatively, our tasks may underestimate children in some non-Western cultures. Children who fail Western theory-of-mind tasks sometimes show keen sensitivity to the mental states of others in culturally important, everyday situations such as teaching younger siblings how to do chores (Greenfield et al., 2003; Maynard, 2002).

Finally, sensory impairments can delay the development of theory-of-mind understandings. Although they eventually catch up to their seeing peers, blind children are slow to master false belief tasks, probably because they do not get as much social input as other children (Peterson, Peterson, & Webb, 2000). Deaf children of hearing parents also take longer than usual to master false belief tasks. Deaf children of deaf parents develop theory-of-mind skills on schedule, however, probably because they are able to communicate easily and frequently with their companions in sign language (Peterson & Siegal, 1999; Woolfe, Want, & Siegal, 2002). That deaf children with limited language experience show deficits in theory-of-mind performance rivaling those of autistic children casts doubt on the brain module view of theory of mind, because there is no evidence that deaf children's brains function improperly (Wellman & Lagattuta, 2000). Instead, from a nurture perspective, it may be that autistic children simply lack the social input they need to learn to read minds.

In sum, acquiring a theory of mind—the foundation for all later social cognitive development—begins with first steps such as joint attention, pretend play, imitation, and emotional understanding and advances from a desire psychology to a belief–desire psychology universally. It is the product of both nature and nurture; that is, it requires normal neurological and cognitive growth and social and language experiences that involve talking about mental states with parents, siblings, and other companions. Forming a theory of mind has many important consequences for development. Children who have mastered theory-of-mind tasks generally tend to have more advanced social skills and better social adjustment than those who have not (Keenan, 2003; Repacholi et al., 2003), and as

☾ Deaf children who can communicate with their companions through sign language develop theory-of-mind skills on schedule.

you will see later, they think more maturely about moral issues. However, mind-reading skills can be used for evil and good ends; bullies and manipulative children often prove as adept as socially competent children at mind reading (Repacholi et al., 2003).

Describing Other People

Although research on theory of mind shows that even preschool children are budding psychologists, they still have a way to go to understand other people in terms of their enduring personality traits and to use their knowledge of other people's personalities to predict how they will react and what they will do. In studies of person perception, children are sometimes asked to describe people they know—parents, friends, disliked classmates, and so on. The descriptions offered by young children and older children are very different.

As you discovered in Chapter 11, children younger than 7 or 8 describe themselves primarily in physical rather than psychological terms. They describe other people that way, too (Livesley & Bromley, 1973; Yuill, 1993). Thus, 4-year-old Evan says of his father, "He has one nose, one Mom, two eyes, brown hair." And 5-year-old Keisha says, "My daddy is big. He has hairy legs and eats mustard. Yuck! My daddy likes dogs—do you?" Not much of a personality profile there.

Young children perceive others in terms of their physical appearance, possessions, and activities. When they use psychological terms, the terms are often global, evaluative ones such as "nice" or "mean," "good" or "bad," rather than specific personality-trait labels (Livesley & Bromley, 1973; Ruble & Dweck, 1995). Moreover, they do not yet view traits as enduring qualities that can predict how a person will behave in the future or explain why a person behaves as he does. The 5-year-old who describes a friend as "dumb" may be using this trait label only to describe that friend's recent "dumb" behavior; he may expect "smart" behavior tomorrow. Indeed, young children tend to be optimists, believing that negative traits today are likely to change into positive ones tomorrow (Lockhart, Chang, & Story, 2002). Young children sometimes use information about classmates' previous behavior, good or bad, to predict their future behavior if the task is simple enough (Droege & Stipek, 1993). Yet they appear to do so based on their evaluations of how "good" or "bad" the person is rather than based on inferring specific personality traits and expecting them to be expressed consistently (Alvarez, Ruble, & Bolger, 2001). So, when the traits portrayed in stories about characters can be categorized cleanly as either good or bad (for example, generous versus selfish), 5- and 6-year-olds can predict future behavior that is either generous or selfish based on concluding that the character is either good or bad. However, when traits cannot be so clearly labeled as good or bad (for example, tough versus sensitive), children can infer the character's trait but do not seem to use that information to predict future behavior.

Around age 7 or 8, children become more able to "get below the surface" of humans and infer their enduring psychological traits. Thus, 10-year-old Kim describes her friend Tonya: "She's funny and friendly to everyone, and she's in the gifted program because she's smart, but sometimes she's too bossy." Over the elementary-school years, children increasingly believe that traits such as being smart or getting along with others characterize other children across situations and over time, and yet they also begin to appreciate that people can change their traits if they work at it (Pomerantz & Saxon, 2001). As children reach age 11 or 12, they make more use of psychological traits to explain why people behave as they do, saying, for instance, that Mike pulled the dog's tail because Mike is cruel (Gnepp & Chilamkurti, 1988). Clearly, then, children become more psychologically minded as their emerging social cognitive abilities permit them to make inferences about enduring inner qualities from the concrete behavior they observe in the people around them.

When asked to describe people they know, adolescents offer personality profiles that are even more psychological than those provided by children (Livesley & Bromley, 1973). They see people as unique individuals with distinctive personality traits, interests, values, and feelings. Moreover, they are able to create more integrated, or organized, person descriptions, analyzing how an individual's diverse and often inconsistent traits fit together and make sense as a whole personality. Dan, for example, may notice that Noriko brags about her abilities at times but seems unsure of herself at other times, and he may integrate these seemingly discrepant impressions by concluding that Noriko is basically insecure and boasts only to hide her insecurity. Some adolescents spend hours psychoanalyzing their friends and acquaintances, trying to figure out what makes them tick.

As was the case for self-descriptions, then, you can detect a progression in person perception from (1) physical descriptions and global evaluations of other people as good or bad during the preschool years to (2) more differentiated descriptions that refer to specific personality traits starting at age 7 or 8 and finally to (3) more integrated personality profiles that show how even seemingly inconsistent traits fit together during adolescence.

Role-Taking Skills

Another important aspect of social cognitive development involves outgrowing the egocentrism that Jean Piaget believed characterizes young children and developing **role-taking skills**—the ability to adopt another person's perspective and understand her thoughts and feelings in relation to your own. Role-taking skills are really theory of mind in action (Blair, 2003). They are essential in thinking about moral issues from different points of view, predicting the consequences of a person's actions for others, and empathizing with others (Gibbs, 2003). Robert Selman (1976, 1980; Yeates & Selman, 1989) contributed greatly to our understanding of role-taking abilities by asking children questions about interpersonal dilemmas (Selman, 1976, p. 302):

> Holly is an 8-year-old girl who likes to climb trees. She is the best tree climber in the neighborhood. One day while

climbing down from a tall tree, she falls... but does not hurt herself. Her father sees her fall. He is upset and asks her to promise not to climb trees anymore. Holly promises.

Later that day, Holly and her friends meet Shawn. Shawn's kitten is caught in a tree and can't get down. Something has to be done right away or the kitten may fall. Holly is the only one who climbs trees well enough to reach the kitten and get it down but she remembers her promise to her father.

To assess how well a child understands the perspectives of Holly, her father, and Shawn, Selman asks: "Does Holly know how Shawn feels about the kitten? How will Holly's father feel if he finds out she climbed the tree? What does Holly think her father will do if he finds out she climbed the tree? What would you do in this situation?" Children's responses to these questions led Selman (1976) to conclude that role-taking abilities develop in a stagelike manner:

- Children 3 to 6 years old are largely egocentric, assuming that others share their point of view. If young children like kittens, for example, they assume that Holly's father does, too, and therefore will be delighted if Holly saves the kitten.
- By age 8 to 10, as concrete operational cognitive abilities solidify, children appreciate that two people can have different points of view even if they have access to the same information. Children are able to think about their own thoughts and about the thoughts of another person, and they realize that their companions can do the same. Thus, they can appreciate that Holly may think about her father's concern for her safety but conclude that he will understand her reasons for climbing the tree.
- Adolescents who have reached the formal operational stage of cognitive development, at roughly age 12, become capable of mentally juggling multiple perspectives, including the perspective of the "generalized other," or the broader social group. The adolescent might consider how fathers in general react when children disobey them and consider whether Holly's father is similar to or different from the typical father (Selman, 1980; Yeates & Selman, 1989). Adolescents thus become mental jugglers, keeping in the air their own perspective, that of another person, and that of an abstract "generalized other" representing a larger social group.

© Michael Newman/PhotoEdit

☾ Adolescents who have advanced role-taking, or social perspective-taking, skills are better able than those who do not to resolve conflicts with their parents (Selman et al., 1986). They are better able to adopt the perspectives of their parents (and parents in general) and to identify a mutually beneficial agreement.

These advances in social cognition have important implications for children's and adolescents' relationships. Experience interacting with peers seems to sharpen role-taking skills; sophisticated role-taking skills, in turn, help make the child a more sensitive and desirable companion. Children whose role-taking skills are advanced are more likely than agemates who perform poorly on tests of role taking to be sociable and popular and to have established close peer relationships (Kurdek & Krile, 1982; LeMare & Rubin, 1987). What is more, coaching in perspective taking can help improve the social behavior of disruptive children (Grizenko et al., 2000).

Social Cognition in Adulthood

As you saw in earlier chapters, nonsocial cognitive abilities, such as those used in remembering text and testing scientific hypotheses, often improve during early and middle adulthood and decline in later life, at least in many older adults. Do important social cognitive skills, such as the ability to think through theory-of-mind problems or adopt other people's perspectives, also increase early in adulthood but decline in later life?

Social cognitive development during adulthood appears to involve both gains and losses (Blanchard-Fields, 1996; Hess, 1999). For example, Fredda Blanchard-Fields (1986) presented adolescents, young adults, and middle-aged adults with three dilemmas that required them to engage in role taking and to integrate discrepant perspectives: two conflicting historical accounts, a conflict between a teenage boy and his parents over whether he must visit his grandparents with the family, and a disagreement between a man and a woman about an unintended pregnancy. Adults, especially middle-aged ones, were better able than adolescents to see both sides of the issues and to integrate the perspectives of both parties into a workable solution. Here, then, is evidence that the social cognitive skills of adults may continue to improve after adolescence. Through a combination of social experience and cognitive growth, middle-aged adults have the potential to become sophisticated students of human psychology. As you saw in Chapter 9, a few even gain a kind of wisdom that gives them exceptional insight into the complexities of human existence.

Do elderly people continue to display the sophisticated social cognitive skills that middle-aged adults display? The evidence is mixed. They perform as well as young and middle-aged adults on some social cognitive tasks (Hess, 1994; Pratt & Norris, 1999). Yet other studies suggest that, on average, older adults are not always as adept as middle-aged adults at taking others' point of view, integrating different perspectives, and thinking in complex ways about the causes of people's behavior (Blanchard-Fields, 1996; Pratt et al., 1996).

Consider what happens when adults are given theory-of-mind tasks suitable for adults. Susan Sullivan and Ted Ruffman (2004) used one in which a burglar leaving a crime scene is stopped by a policeman who saw the burglar drop his glove. The burglar turns himself in, and the key question is what the burglar was thinking about the policeman's thoughts. In a previous study, elderly adults performed as well as college students on theory-of-mind tasks (Happé, Winner, & Brownell, 1998). However, Sullivan and Ruffman found that adults who averaged age 73 performed more poorly than adults who averaged 30 and that age differences in fluid intelligence largely accounted for this variation (see also Maylor et al., 2002). This suggests that the declines in working memory and processing speed that limit the performance of older adults on nonsocial cognitive tasks also take some toll on their ability to take in and manipulate social information (Hess, 1999). Still, social cognitive abilities appear to hold up better than nonsocial cognitive abilities, possibly because the areas of the cortex that support social cognition and emotional understanding age more slowly than the areas that support nonsocial cognition (MacPherson, Phillips, & Della Sala, 2002).

The most important message about adult social cognition, however, is that some older adults maintain their social cognitive abilities extremely well and others do not. Whether they do or do not depends far more on the extent and nature of their social experiences than on their age. Those elderly adults who have the sharpest social cognitive skills tend to be socially active and involved in meaningful social roles such as spouse, grandparent, church member, and worker (Dolen & Bearison, 1982). They have opportunities to talk to other people about problems they are experiencing, they tend to be well-educated, and they are in good health (Pratt et al., 1996). It is mainly when elderly people become socially isolated or inactive that their reasoning about personal and interpersonal issues becomes less complex.

© Walter Hodges/CORBIS

Social cognitive skills hold up well when older adults are socially active.

Having examined some important and dramatic changes in social cognition over the life span, focus on an important area of development in which social cognitive skills play a crucial role: moral development.

Summing Up

Social cognition, thinking about self and others, takes shape in infancy through joint attention, pretend play, imitation, and emotional understanding—precursors of a theory of mind, or an understanding of mental states and their role in guiding behavior. Children progress from a desire psychology at 2 years to a belief–desire psychology at 4 years, when they are able to pass false belief tasks. Developing a theory of mind depends on both nature (normal neurological and cognitive maturation) and nurture (social and language experience that may be missed by autistic children, deaf children with hearing parents, and children in cultures in which people talk little about mental states).

Children's descriptions of other people reveal that preschool children focus on physical features and activities, whereas 7- and 8-year-olds begin to describe inner psychological traits and use trait inferences to predict future behavior. Adolescents are better able to integrate trait descriptions. With age, children also gain role-taking skills. Social cognitive skills often improve in early and middle adulthood but sometimes decline in old age because of declines in working memory and processing speed, especially in socially isolated adults. ■

Perspectives on Moral Development

Although we could debate endlessly what **morality** is (see Gibbs, 2003), most of us might agree that it involves the ability to distinguish right from wrong, to act on this distinction, and to experience pride when we do the right things and guilt or shame when we do not. Accordingly, three basic components of morality have been of interest to developmental scientists:

1. The *affective,* or emotional, component consists of the feelings (guilt, concern for others' feelings, and so on) that surround right or wrong actions and that motivate moral thoughts and actions.

© Mary Kate Denny/PhotoEdit

Learning to resist the temptation to break moral rules (here, one about taking turns) is an important part of moral development.

2. The *cognitive* component centers on how we conceptualize right and wrong and make decisions about how to behave, drawing on social cognitive skills such as role taking.

3. The *behavioral* component reflects how we behave when, for example, we experience the temptation to cheat or are called upon to help a needy person.

Each of the three major theoretical perspectives on moral development focuses on a different component of morality. So, we will look at what psychoanalytic theory, and more modern perspectives rooted in it, says about moral affect; what cognitive developmental theory says about moral cognition or reasoning; and what social learning (or social cognitive) theory reveals about moral behavior.

Moral Affect: Psychoanalytic Theory and Beyond

What kind of **moral affect,** or emotion related to matters of right and wrong, do you feel if you contemplate cheating or lying? Chances are you experience such negative feelings as shame, guilt, anxiety, and fear of being detected—feelings that keep you from doing things you know are wrong. **Empathy**—the vicarious experiencing of another person's feelings (for example, smiling at the good fortune of another or experiencing another person's distress)—is another important moral affect (Hoffman, 2000). Empathizing with individuals who are suffering can motivate **prosocial behavior**—positive social acts, such as helping or sharing, that reflect a concern for the welfare of others. Positive emotions, such as pride and self-satisfaction when you have done the right thing, are also an important part of morality. To experience any of these emotions, you need to be capable of evaluating whether you have exceeded or fallen short of standards of behavior (Tangney, 2003). We are generally motivated to avoid negative moral emotions and to experience positive ones by acting in moral ways.

Assuming that young infants are unlikely to feel these sorts of moral emotions, when do they arise? Sigmund Freud's (1960) psychoanalytic theory offered an early answer (see Chapter 2). As you will recall, Freud believed that the mature personality has three components: the selfish and irrational id, the rational ego, and the moralistic superego. The superego, or conscience, has the important task of ensuring that any plans formed by the ego to gratify the id's urges are morally acceptable. Infants and toddlers, Freud said, lack a superego and are essentially "all id." They will therefore act on their selfish motives unless their parents control them.

The superego is formed during the phallic stage (ages 3–6), when children are presumed to experience an emotional conflict over their love for the other-sex parent. To resolve his Oedipus complex, Freud said, a boy identifies with and patterns himself after his father, particularly if the father is a threatening figure who arouses fear. Not only does he learn his masculine role in this manner, but through the process of identification, he also takes on his father's moral standards as his own. Similarly, a girl resolves her Electra complex by identifying with her mother and internalizing her mother's moral standards. However, Freud believed that, because they do not experience the intense fear of castration that boys experience, females develop weaker superegos than males do.

Having a superego, then, is like having a parent inside your head—there, even when your parent is not, to tell you what is right or wrong and to arouse emotions such as shame and guilt if you so much as think about doing wrong. We can applaud Freud for pointing out that emotion is an important part of morality, that early relationships with parents contribute in important ways to moral development, and that children must somehow internalize moral standards if we want them to behave morally even when no authority figure is present to detect and punish them.

However, the specifics of Freud's theory are largely unsupported:

1. Cold, threatening, and punitive parents who make their children anxious about losing their parents' love do not raise morally mature youngsters; instead, as modern psychoanalytic thinkers appreciate, children form strong consciences when they are securely attached to warm and responsive parents (Hoffman, 2000).

2. Males do not appear to have stronger superegos than females; if anything, females are more able to resist temptation (Silverman, 2003).

3. Moral development begins well before the phallic stage, as you will see shortly.

4. Children who are 6 or 7 years old, and who have presumably achieved moral maturity by resolving their Oedipal conflicts, are far from completing their moral growth.

Although the particulars of Freud's theory of moral development lack support, the themes that emotions play a critical role in motivating morality and that early relationships with caregivers steer moral development are taken seriously today (Eisenberg, 2000; Kochanska, 2002). As you will see shortly, Martin Hoffman (2000) has developed a perspective that features our evolved ability to feel empathy for other people as the foundation of the motivation to behave morally, other researchers have called attention on the importance of guilt as a motivator of moral behavior (Tangney, 2003), and still others have shown that a secure and warm parent–child attachment early in life fosters moral development.

Moral Reasoning: Cognitive Developmental Theory

Cognitive developmental theorists study morality by looking at the development of **moral reasoning**—the thinking process that occurs when we decide whether an act is right or wrong. These theorists assume that moral development depends on social cognitive development, particularly role-taking or perspective-taking skills that allow us to picture how our victims might react to our misdeeds or how people in distress must feel. These skills also allow us to get beyond our egocentric perspective to construct a concept of reciprocity, or mutual give and take, in human relationships (Gibbs, 2003). Moral reasoning is said to progress through an invariant sequence—a fixed and universal order of stages, each of which represents a consistent way of thinking about moral issues that is different from the stage preceding or following it. To cognitive developmental theorists, what is of interest is how we decide what to do, not what we decide or what we actually do. A young child and an adult may both decide not to steal a pen, but the reasons they give for their decision may be entirely different. Jean Piaget paved the way for the influential theory of moral development put forth by Lawrence Kohlberg.

Piaget's View

Piaget (1965) studied children's concepts of rules by asking Swiss children about their games of marbles and explored children's concepts of justice by presenting them with moral dilemmas to ponder. For example, he told children about two boys, John, who accidentally knocked over a tray of 15 cups when coming to dinner as requested, and Henry, who broke only one cup when sneaking jam from the cupboard. The key question he posed was which child was naughtier, and why.

Based on children's responses to such questions, Piaget formulated a theory of moral development that included a premoral period and two moral stages:

• **Premoral period.** During the preschool years, children show little awareness or understanding of rules and cannot be considered moral beings.

• **Heteronomous morality.** Children 6 to 10 years old take rules seriously, believing that they are handed down by parents and other authority figures and are sacred and unalterable (the term **heteronomous** means under the rule of another). They also judge rule violations as wrong based on the extent of damage done, not taking into account whether the violator had good or bad intentions.

• **Autonomous morality.** At age 10 or 11, most children enter a final stage of moral development in which they begin to appreciate that rules are agreements between individuals—agreements that can be changed through a consensus of those individuals. In judging actions, they pay more attention to whether an actor's intentions were good or bad than to the consequences of his act; thus, they see Henry, the misbehaving boy who broke one cup, as naughtier than John, the well-intentioned boy who broke 15.

According to Piaget, progress through these stages depends on both cognitive maturation and social experiences, not so much with parents as with peers. Because peers are equals, they must learn to take one another's perspectives and to resolve disagreements among themselves through negotiation, which sharpens their role-taking skills and helps them discover principles of fairness. By contrast, parents can impose their rules on children through brute force. According to Piaget, then, moral growth requires developing, through interactions with peers, an ability to recognize and coordinate multiple perspectives on moral issues (Gibbs, 2003).

Kohlberg's View

Inspired by Piaget's pioneering work, Kohlberg (1963, 1981, 1984; Colby & Kohlberg, 1987) formulated a highly influential cognitive developmental theory of moral development. Born in 1927, Kohlberg put his moral principles into action as a youth by helping transport Jewish refugees from Europe to Israel after World War II, spent most of his career at Harvard University, and died in 1987 when, suffering from a painful physical condition, he committed suicide by walking into the Atlantic Ocean (Walsh, 2000).

Kohlberg began his work by asking 10-, 13-, and 16-year-old boys questions about various moral dilemmas to assess how they thought about these issues. Careful analysis of the responses led Kohlberg to conclude that moral growth progresses through a universal and invariant sequence of three broad moral levels, each of which is composed of two distinct stages. Each stage grows out of the preceding stage and represents a more complex way of thinking about moral issues. According to Kohlberg, a person cannot skip stages, and a person who has reached a higher stage will not regress to earlier stages.

Think about how you would respond to the following moral dilemma posed by Kohlberg and his colleagues (Colby et al., 1983, p. 79):

> There was a woman who had very bad cancer, and there was no treatment known to medicine that would save her. Her doctor, Dr. Jefferson, knew that she had only about 6 months to live. She was in terrible pain, but she was so weak that a good dose of a pain killer like ether or morphine would make her die sooner. She was delirious and

almost crazy with pain, and in her calm periods she would ask Dr. Jefferson to give her enough ether to kill her. She said she couldn't stand the pain and she was going to die in a few months anyway. Although he knows that mercy killing is against the law, the doctor thinks about granting her request.

Should Dr. Jefferson give her the drug that would make her die? Why or why not? Should the woman have the right to make the final decision? Why or why not? These are among the questions that people are asked after hearing the dilemma. Remember, Kohlberg's goal is to understand how an individual thinks, not whether she is for or against providing the woman with the drug. Individuals at each stage of moral reasoning might endorse either of the alternative courses of action, but for different reasons. Following are Kohlberg's three levels of moral reasoning, and the two stages within each level.

Level 1: Preconventional Morality At the level of **preconventional morality**, rules are external to the self rather than internalized. The child conforms to rules imposed by authority figures to avoid punishment or to obtain personal rewards. The perspective of the self dominates: What is right is what one can get away with or what is personally satisfying.

- *Stage 1: Punishment-and-Obedience Orientation.* The goodness or badness of an act depends on its consequences. The child will obey authorities to avoid punishment but may not consider an act wrong if it will not be punished. The greater the harm done or the more severe the punishment, the more "bad" the act is.
- *Stage 2: Instrumental Hedonism.* A person at the second stage of moral development conforms to rules to gain rewards or satisfy personal needs. There is some concern for the perspectives of others, but it is motivated by the hope of benefit in return. "You scratch my back and I'll scratch yours" and "an eye for an eye" are the guiding philosophies.

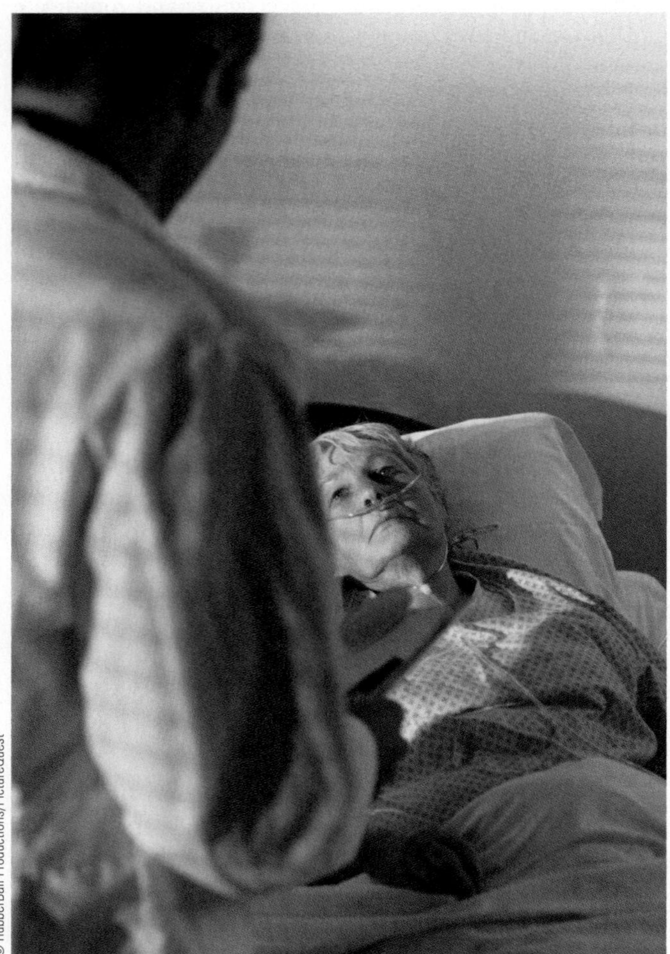

Moral dilemma: Should a doctor give a pain-ridden and terminal patient a drug that would hasten her death?

Level 2: Conventional Morality At the level of **conventional morality**, the individual has internalized many moral values. He strives to obey the rules set by others (parents, peers, the government) to win their approval or to maintain social order. The perspectives of other people are clearly recognized and given serious consideration. The child may now be able to take the perspective of a potential victim of a prank, for example, and realize that the victim might find the prank humiliating rather than amusing (Gibbs, 2003).

- *Stage 3: "Good Boy" or "Good Girl" Morality.* What is right is now what pleases, helps, or is approved by others. People are often judged by their intentions; "meaning well" is valued, being "nice" is important. Other people's feelings should be considered.
- *Stage 4: Authority and Social Order–Maintaining Morality.* Now what is right is what conforms to the rules of legitimate authorities. The reason for conforming is not so much a fear of punishment as a belief that rules and laws maintain a social order worth preserving. Doing one's duty and respecting law and order are valued.

Level 3: Postconventional Morality At the final level of moral reasoning, **postconventional morality**, the individual defines what is right in terms of broad principles of justice that have validity apart from the views of particular authority figures. The individual may distinguish between what is morally right and what is legal, recognizing that some laws—for example, the racial segregation laws that Dr. Martin Luther King Jr. challenged—violate basic moral principles. Thus, the person transcends the perspectives of particular social groups or authorities and begins to take the perspective of all individuals.

- *Stage 5: Morality of Contract, Individual Rights, and Democratically Accepted Law.* At this "social contract" stage, there is an increased understanding of the underlying purposes served by laws and a concern that rules should be arrived at through a democratic consensus so that they express the will of the majority and maximize social welfare. Whereas the person at stage 4 is unlikely to challenge an established law, the moral reasoner at stage 5 might call for democratic change in a law that compromises basic rights. The principles embodied in the U.S. Constitution illustrate stage 5 morality.

• *Stage 6: Morality of Individual Principles of Conscience.* At this "highest" stage of moral reasoning, the individual defines right and wrong on the basis of self-generated principles that are broad and universal in application. The stage 6 thinker does not just make up whatever principles she chooses. She discovers, through reflection, abstract principles of respect for all individuals and for their rights that all religions or moral authorities would view as moral. Kohlberg (1981) described stage 6 thinking as a kind of "moral musical chairs" in which the person facing a moral dilemma is able to take the "chair," or perspective, of each person or group that could potentially be affected by a decision and to arrive at a solution that would be regarded as just from every chair. Stage 6 is Kohlberg's vision of ideal moral reasoning, but it is so rarely observed that Kohlberg stopped attempting to measure its existence.

In the Explorations box on page 364, we present examples of how people at the preconventional, conventional, and postconventional levels might reason about the mercy-killing dilemma. Progress through Kohlberg's stages of moral reasoning depends partly on the development of perspective-taking abilities (Selman, 1980). Specifically, as individuals become more able to consider perspectives other than their own, moral reasoning progresses from an egocentric focus on personal welfare at the preconventional level, to a concern with the perspectives of other people (parents, friends, and other members of society) at the conventional level, and to an ability to coordinate multiple perspectives and determine what is right from the perspective of all people at the postconventional level (Carpendale, 2000).

Moral Behavior: Social Learning Theory

Social learning theorists such as Albert Bandura (1991, 2002; Bandura et al., 2001), whose social cognitive theory was introduced in Chapter 2, have been primarily interested in the behavioral component of morality—in what we do when faced with temptation or with an opportunity to behave prosocially. These theorists say that moral behavior is learned in the same way that other social behaviors are learned: through observational learning and reinforcement and punishment principles. They also consider moral behavior to be strongly influenced by situational factors—for example, by whether a professor proctors an examination to reduce the chances of cheating.

Applying his social cognitive perspective, Bandura goes on to emphasize that moral thinking is linked to moral action through cognitive self-regulatory mechanisms that involve monitoring and evaluating our own actions (or anticipated actions), disapproving of ourselves when we contemplate doing wrong, and approving of ourselves when we behave responsibly or humanely. By applying consequences to ourselves in this way, we become able to exert self-control, inhibit urges to misbehave, and keep our behavior in line with internalized standards of behavior. Sometimes this system of moral self-regulation can triumph over strong situational influences pushing us to do wrong. However, we have also devised mechanisms of **moral disengagement** that allow us, even though we know the difference between right and wrong, to avoid condemning ourselves when we engage in immoral behavior. For example, we disengage morally by justifying doing harm as morally right (as in war), minimizing the extent of harm done, or blaming the victim or someone else for what we did (Bandura, 2002). Many of us learn the right moral standards, but some people hold themselves strictly to those standards and others find it easy to disengage morally.

To highlight the difference between Bandura's social cognitive theory and other perspectives, consider how different theorists might try to predict whether a teenager (we will call him Waldo) will cheat on his upcoming math test. Freud would want to know whether Waldo identified strongly with his father in early childhood. If he did, presumably he has developed a strong superego and will be less likely to cheat, lie, or steal than a child with a weak superego (unless his father had a weak superego).

Kohlberg would be more interested in Waldo's cognitive development and, specifically, in the stage at which he reasons about moral dilemmas. Although his level of moral reasoning does not necessarily predict the decision he will make, Kohlberg would expect Waldo's mode of decision making to be consistent across many situations. Moreover, because Kohlberg believes that each higher stage permits a more adequate way of making moral decisions, he might expect the child whose moral reasoning is advanced to be less likely to cheat than the child who still thinks at the preconventional level and is "looking out for number one." Notice that both the psychoanalytic perspective and the cognitive developmental perspective view morality as a kind of personality trait—a quality that each of us possesses and that consistently influences our judgments and actions.

© Barbara Stitzer/PhotoEdit

How many students in your class would admit to having cheated in high school? Fifty years ago, only about one in five college students admitted to it, but in recent surveys at least three in five, and often more, admit to having cheated in high school (Kleiner & Lord, 1999). Techniques have changed, too; use of preprogrammed calculators, cell phones to relay information about the test, hidden miniature cameras, and online term-paper mills suggest that cheating has gone "high-tech." Why do you think cheating is so rampant in schools today?

Explorations

Sample Responses to the Mercy-Killing Dilemma at Kohlberg's Three Levels of Moral Reasoning

Preconventional Morality

Give the Drug

Stage 1: The doctor should give the terminally ill woman a drug that will kill her because there is little chance that he will be found out and punished and because she would not have to live with her agony anymore.

Stage 2: He should give her the drug; he might benefit from the gratitude of her family if he does what she wants. He should think of it as the right thing to do if it serves his purposes.

Do Not Give the Drug

Stage 1: The doctor runs a big risk of losing his license and being thrown in prison if he gives her the drug.

Stage 2: He has little to gain by taking such a big chance. If the woman wants to kill herself, that is her business, but why should he help her if he stands to gain little in return?

Conventional Morality

Give the Drug

Stage 3: Most people would understand that the doctor was motivated by concern for the woman rather than by self-interest. They would be able to forgive him for what was essentially an act of kindness.

Stage 4: The doctor should give the woman the drug because of the Hippocratic oath, which spells out a doctor's duty to relieve suffering. This oath is binding and should be taken seriously by all doctors.

Do Not Give the Drug

Stage 3: Most people are likely to disapprove of mercy killing. The doctor would clearly lose the respect of his colleagues and friends if he administered the drug. A good person simply would not do this.

Stage 4: Mercy killing is against the laws that citizens are obligated to uphold. The Bible is another compelling authority, and it says, "Thou shalt not kill." The doctor simply cannot take the law into his own hands; rather, he has a duty to uphold the law.

Postconventional Morality

Give the Drug

Stage 5: Although most of our laws have a sound basis in moral principle, laws against mercy killing do not. The doctor's act is morally justified because it relieves the suffering of an agonized human without harming other people. Yet if he breaks the law in the service of a greater good, he should still be willing to be held legally accountable because society would be damaged if everyone simply ignored laws they do not agree with.

Stage 6: We must consider the effects of this act on everyone concerned—the doctor, the dying woman, other terminally ill people, and all people everywhere. Basic moral principle dictates that all people have a right to dignity and self-determination as long as others are not harmed by their decisions. Assuming that no one else will be hurt, then, the dying woman has a right to live and die as she chooses. The doctor is doing right by respecting her integrity as a person and saving her, her family, and all of society from needless suffering.

Do Not Give the Drug

Stage 5: The laws against mercy killing protect citizens from harm at the hands of unscrupulous doctors and selfish relatives and should be upheld because they prevent harm. If the laws were to be changed through the democratic process, that might be another thing. But right now the doctor can best serve society by adhering to them.

Stage 6: If we truly adhere to the principle that human life should be valued above all else and all lives should be valued equally, it is morally wrong to "play God" and decide that some lives are worth living and others are not. Before long, we would have a world in which no life has value.

By contrast, Bandura would be most interested in the moral habits Waldo has learned, the expectations he has formed about the probable consequences of his actions, his ability to self-regulate his behavior, and his ultimate behavior. If Waldo's parents have consistently reinforced him when he has behaved morally and punished him when he has misbehaved; if he has been exposed to models of morally acceptable behavior rather than brought up in the company of liars, cheaters, and thieves; and if he has well-developed self-regulatory mechanisms that cause him to take responsibility for his actions rather than to disengage morally, he is likely to behave in morally acceptable ways. Yet Bandura and other social learning theorists believe in the power of situational influences and predict that Waldo may still cheat on the math test if he sees his classmates cheating and getting away with it or if he is under pressure to get a B in math.

We are now ready to trace the development of morality from infancy to old age. Our coverage charts the development of the self as a moral being, examining moral affect, cognition, and behavior over the life span.

Summing Up

Morality has affective, cognitive, and behavioral components. Moral affect, including guilt, empathy, and pride, is the focus of Freudian psychoanalytic theory, with its emphasis on the formation of the superego and internalization of parental values during the preschool years. Moral reasoning was the focus of Piaget's pioneering work on premoral, heteronomous, and autonomous stages of moral development and the progression to an understanding of the need to consider intentions as well as consequences in judging actions and of rules as a consensus of equals rather than the dictates of authority. Kohlberg's preconventional, conventional, and postconventional levels of morality, each with two stages, capture a progression from selfish egocentrism to concern for others' perspectives to consideration of the reasons behind the rules and the perspectives of all. Finally, moral behavior is the focus of social learning theory approaches to morality; social cognitive theorist Bandura views morality as learned behavior influenced by both self-regulatory cognitive processes and situational influences. ■

The Infant

Do infants have a sense of right or wrong? If a baby takes a toy that belongs to another child, would you label the act stealing? If an infant bashes another child in the head with a toy, would you insist that the infant be put on trial for assault? Of course not. Adults in our society, including psychologists, view infants as **amoral**—that is, lacking any sense of morality. Because we do not believe that infants are capable of evaluating their behavior in relation to moral standards, we do not hold them morally responsible for wrongs they commit (although we attempt to prevent them from harming others). Nor do we expect them to be "good" when we are not around to watch them. Yet it is now clear that these initially amoral creatures begin to learn fundamental moral lessons during their first 2 years of life (Emde et al., 1991; Kochanska, 1993).

Early Moral Training

Moral socialization begins early. Roger Burton (1984) relates how his daughter Ursula, age 1½, was so taken by the candy that she and her sisters had gathered on Halloween that she snatched some from her sisters' bags. The sisters immediately said, "No, that's mine," and conveyed their outrage in the strongest terms. A week later, the sisters again found some of their candy in Ursula's bag and raised a fuss, and it was their mother's turn to explain the rules to Ursula. The problem continued until finally Burton came upon Ursula looking at some forbidden candy. Ursula looked up and said, "No, this is Maria's, not Ursula's" (p. 199).

It is through such social learning experiences, accumulated over years, that children come to understand and internalize moral rules and standards. Children must learn two lessons, really: to associate negative emotions with violating rules and to exert self-control, or inhibit their impulses, when they are tempted to violate rules (Kochanska, 1993, 2002). Ursula and other young children learn from being reprimanded to associate the act of stealing with negative emotional responses. As they near age 2, children are already beginning to show visible signs of distress when they break things or otherwise violate standards of behavior (Cole, Barrett, & Zahn-Waxler, 1992; Kagan, 1981). Made to think that they have caused a doll's head to fall off, some toddlers even show signs of guilt, as opposed to mere distress, and try frantically to make amends (Kochanska, Casey, & Fukumoto, 1995). This means 18- to 24-month-old children are beginning to internalize rules and to anticipate disapproval when they fail to comply with them.

In her research on early moral socialization, Grazyna Kochanska (1997b, 2002) has found that moral development goes best when a **mutually responsive orientation** exists between caregiver and child—when there is a close, affectively positive, and cooperative relationship in which child and caregiver are attached to each other and are sensitive to each other's needs. Such a relationship makes children want to comply with caregivers' rules and adopt their values and standards. These children then learn moral emotions such as guilt and empathy, develop the capacity for advanced moral reasoning, and become able to resist temptation because they have learned to regulate their behavior without external control.

It is also important for parents to discuss their toddlers' behavior in an open way, expressing their feelings and evaluating acts as good or bad (Laible & Thompson, 2000). This

Children learn early that some acts have distressing consequences.

kind of emotion-centered discussion contributes more to the development of conscience than does talk about the physical damage done by the child or about family rules of conduct. It is even beneficial for children to be involved in verbal squabbles with their parents if it means hearing how their parents evaluate behavior, justify their positions, and talk about emotions (Laible & Thompson, 2002). By establishing rules, reacting to children's rule-breaking behavior, and working during everyday conversations toward mutual understandings of what is acceptable and what is not, parents give children a clear rule system to internalize and teach them to associate guilt with wrongdoing (Emde et al., 1991; Gralinski & Kopp, 1993).

Prosocial Behavior

Not only are infants capable of internalizing rules of behavior, but they also are not so selfish, egocentric, and unconcerned about other people as Freud, Piaget, Kohlberg, and many other theorists have assumed. Perhaps the strongest evidence of this comes from studies of empathy and prosocial behavior. Even newborns display a primitive form of empathy: They become distressed by the cries of other newborns, suggesting that empathy may be part of our evolutionary heritage (Hoffman, 2000; Martin & Clark, 1982). It is unlikely that young infants distinguish between another infant's distress and their own, however.

From age 1 to age 2, infants become capable of a truer form of empathy that is likely a key motivator of moral behavior, according to Martin Hoffman (2000), and that becomes more sophisticated with age as role-taking skills develop. They understand that someone else's distress is different from their own, and they try to comfort the person in distress. Carolyn Zahn-Waxler and her colleagues (1992) report that more than half of the 13- to 15-month-old infants they observed engaged in at least one act of prosocial behavior—helping, sharing, expressing concern, comforting, and so on. These behaviors became increasingly common from age 1 to age 2, when all but one child in the study acted prosocially.

Consider some concrete examples of early empathy described by Hoffman (2000). One 10-month-old, watching a peer cry, looked sad and buried her head in her mother's lap, as she often did when she was distressed. A 2-year-old brought his own teddy bear to comfort a distressed friend; when it failed to do the trick, he offered the friend's teddy instead, beginning to show an ability to take the perspective of the friend. Finally, consider the reaction of 21-month-old John to his distressed playmate, Jerry (Zahn-Waxler, Radke-Yarrow, & King, 1979, pp. 321–322):

> Today Jerry was kind of cranky; he just started... bawling and he wouldn't stop. John kept coming over and handing Jerry toys, trying to cheer him up. . . . He'd say things like "Here, Jerry," and I said to John, "Jerry's sad; he doesn't feel good; he had a shot today." John would look at me with his eyebrows wrinkled together like he really understood that Jerry was crying because he was unhappy.

Summing Up

Infants are amoral in some senses, particularly when it comes to making judgments of right and wrong; yet their "moral socialization" has begun. A secure attachment and a mutually responsive orientation between parent and child contribute to the development of a conscience. By age 2, children have internalized rules of conduct, and they become distressed when they violate the rules. They also show the rudiments of empathy when others are distressed, an important motivator of moral behavior that may be part of our species heredity. ■

The Child

From age 2 to age 12, children's standards of morality and their motivation to live up to these standards grow out of their social experiences in their family, peer group, and society. Research on moral development during childhood has explored how children of different ages think about moral issues and how they behave when their moral values are tested. As you will see, Piaget and Kohlberg probably underestimated children. Other researchers have looked more closely at the moral reasoning of children and find that they engage in some fairly sophisticated thinking about right and wrong from an early age.

Weighing Intentions

Consider Piaget's claim that young children (heteronomous thinkers) judge acts as right or wrong on the basis of their consequences, whereas older children (autonomous thinkers) judge on the basis of the intentions that guided the act. His moral-decision story about the two boys and the cups—asking whether a child who causes a small amount of damage in the service of bad intentions is naughtier than a child who causes a large amount of damage despite good intentions—was flawed in that it confounded the two issues, goodness of intentions and amount of damage done.

Sharon Nelson (1980) overcame this flaw in an interesting experiment. In the study, 3-year-olds listened to stories in which a character threw a ball to a playmate. The actor's motive was described as *good* (his friend had nothing to play with) or *bad* (the actor was mad at his friend), and the consequences of his act were either *positive* (the friend caught the ball and was happy to play with it) or *negative* (the ball hit his friend in the head and made him cry). To make the task simpler, Nelson showed children drawings of what happened (see Figure 13.2 for an example).

Not surprisingly, the 3-year-olds in the study judged acts that had positive consequences more favorably than acts that caused harm. However, they also judged the well-intentioned child who had wanted to play more favorably than the child who intended to hurt his friend, regardless of the consequences of his actions. Apparently, then, even young children can base their moral judgments on both an actor's intentions and the consequences of his act.

Figure 13.2 Examples of drawings used by Sharon Nelson to convey an actor's intentions to preschool children. Here you see negative intent and a negative consequence.
SOURCE: Nelson (1980).

Overall, Piaget was correct to conclude that young children assign more weight to consequences and less weight to intentions than older children do, but he was wrong to conclude that young children are incapable of considering both intentions and consequences when they evaluate others' conduct.

Understanding Rules

Piaget also said that 6- to 10-year-old heteronomous children view rules as sacred prescriptions laid down by respected authority figures. These moral absolutes cannot be questioned or changed. However, Elliot Turiel (1978, 1983) has observed that children distinguish between two kinds of rules in daily life: **moral rules,** or standards that focus on the welfare and basic rights of individuals, and **social-conventional rules,** standards determined by social consensus that tell us what is appropriate in particular social settings. Moral rules include rules against hitting, stealing, lying, and otherwise harming others or violating their rights. Social-conventional rules are more like rules of social etiquette; they include the rules of games and school rules that forbid eating snacks in class or using the restroom without permission.

Even preschool children in our society understand that moral and social-conventional rules are different and that moral rules are more compelling and unalterable (Nucci & Nucci, 1982; Smetana, Schlagman, & Adams, 1993). Judith Smetana (1981), for example, discovered that children as young as age 2 regard moral transgressions such as hitting, stealing, or refusing to share as more serious and deserving of punishment than social-conventional violations such as not staying in their seats in nursery school or not saying grace before eating. Remarkably, these youngsters indicated that it was always wrong to hit people or commit other moral transgressions, rule or no rule, whereas they felt that it would be OK for children to get out of their seats at nursery school or violate other social conventions if there were not rules against it.

Piaget also thought that 6- to 10-year-old children view any law laid down by adults as sacred. Instead, they appear to be capable of questioning adult authority (Tisak & Tisak, 1990). These children say it is fine for parents to enforce rules against stealing and other moral violations, but they believe that it can be inappropriate and unjustifiable for parents to arbitrarily restrict their children's friendships. And they maintain that not even God can proclaim that stealing is morally right and make it so (Nucci & Turiel, 1993). In other words, school-age children will not blindly accept any dictate offered by an authority figure as legitimate.

Applying Theory of Mind

Theory-of-mind research has also given us insights into the moral sensibilities of young children. Because they understand that intentions matter, 4-year-old children who have a theory of mind and pass false belief tasks may cry, "I didn't mean it! I didn't mean it!" when they stand to be punished. Moreover, their understandings of an actor's beliefs at the time he committed a harmful act ("Donnie didn't know Marie was in the box when he pushed it down the stairs!") influence their judgments about whether the act was intentional and therefore how bad it was (Chandler, Sokol, & Wainryb, 2000). Preschool children who pass theory-of-mind tasks are also more able than those who fail them to distinguish between lying (deliberately promoting false beliefs) and simply having facts wrong (Peterson & Siegal, 2002).

Having a theory of mind also helps young children understand people's emotional reactions to others' actions, an important consideration in judging right and wrong. At only 3 years, for example, children can use their emerging theory-of-mind skills to figure out that Lewis, who likes tarantulas but fears puppies, will be upset if his friend gives him a puppy—and that it is therefore bad to give Lewis a puppy, even though it may be nice to give almost any other child a puppy (Helwig, Zelazo, & Wilson, 2001). Preschool children who have mastered theory-of-mind tasks are also especially attuned to other people's feelings and welfare when they think through the morality of such acts as snatching a friend's toy or calling the friend a bad name (Dunn, Cutting, & Demetriou, 2000). In short, research on the development of theory of mind gives us additional reasons to appreciate that much moral growth occurs during early childhood.

Thinking through Kohlberg's Dilemmas

Many of the early emerging moral sensitivities that we have been describing were missed by Kohlberg. The hypothetical moral dilemmas that he devised to assess stages of moral reasoning (for example, the mercy-killing dilemma presented earlier) were intended for adolescents and adults and are too complex to be used to assess moral thinking during the preschool years. The youngest children Kohlberg studied were age 10. As a result, Kohlberg did not have much to say about young children except that they are preconventional moral reasoners, as are most school-age children. By his yardstick, children generally take an egocentric perspective on morality, defining as right those acts that are rewarded and as wrong those acts that are punished (Colby et al., 1983). At best, older school-age children are beginning to make the transition to conventional moral reasoning by displaying a stage 3 concern with being a good boy or a good girl who takes others' perspectives and is concerned with others' approval.

Overall, then, both Piaget and Kohlberg failed to appreciate how much moral growth takes place during childhood (Nucci, 2001). We now know that even preschool children are capable of judging acts as right or wrong according to whether the actor's intentions were good or bad; do not view all rules as absolute, sacred, and unchangeable; challenge adult authority when they believe it is illegitimate; and use their theories of mind to analyze people's motives and the emotional consequences of their acts.

Behaving Morally

To many people, the goal of moral socialization is to produce an individual who not only has internalized moral rules but also will abide by them. Can children be trusted to do so? Consider a classic study of moral behavior reported by Hugh Hartshorne and Mark May (1928–1930). Their purpose was to investigate the moral character of 10,000 children (ages 8–16) by tempting them to lie, cheat, or steal in a variety of situations. It readily became apparent that almost all children espoused "sound" moral values, saying that honesty was good, that cheating and stealing were wrong, and so on. Yet most children cheated or otherwise broke one of their moral rules in at least one of the situations the researchers created to test their moral behavior. In other words, Hartshorne and May had a tough time finding children who not only espoused the right values but consistently acted according to those values. Most children's moral behavior was inconsistent from situation to situation.

Reanalyses of these data and new studies suggest that children are somewhat more consistent in their behavior than Hartshorne and May concluded (Burton, 1963; Hoffman, 2000). And, across a set of situations, some children are more honest, more likely to resist temptation, or more helpful than other children. Still, moral thought, affect, and behavior are not as closely interrelated in childhood as they will be by adolescence or adulthood (Blasi, 1980).

Why are children relatively inconsistent in their moral behavior? One explanation may be that they are reasoning at Kohlberg's preconventional level. When punishment and reward are the primary considerations in defining acts as right or wrong, perhaps it is not surprising that a child may see nothing much wrong with cheating when the chances of detection and punishment are slim. In addition, as social learning theorists would emphasize, moral inconsistency results from situational influences on behavior—such factors as the importance of the goal that can be achieved by transgressing and the amount of encouragement provided by peers (Burton, 1976).

Nurturing Morality

How, then, can parents best raise a child who can be counted on to behave morally in most situations? You have already seen that a mutually responsive orientation between parent and child helps (Kochanska, 2002). Social learning theorists would also advise parents to reinforce moral behavior, punish immoral behavior, and serve as models of moral behavior. Reinforcers such as praise can strengthen prosocial behaviors such as sharing (Fischer, 1963; Perry & Parke, 1975). Punishment of misdeeds can also contribute to moral growth if it is not overly harsh, if it teaches children to associate negative emotions with their wrongdoing, if it is accompanied by an explanation of why the forbidden act is wrong and should be avoided, and if it is supplemented by efforts to encourage and reinforce more acceptable behavior (Gershoff, 2002; Perry & Parke, 1975). The problem with punishment, especially severe physical punishment, is that it may have undesirable side effects (such as making children resentful or overly anxious or teaching them that aggression is an appropriate means of solving problems). Finally, parents can serve as models of moral behavior and will be especially effective if they state the rule they are following and a rationale for not committing a prohibited act (Grusec et al., 1979).

The important work of Martin Hoffman (2000) has provided additional insights into how to foster not only moral behavior but also moral thought and affect. As you saw earlier, Hoffman (2000) believes that empathy is a key motivator of moral behavior and that the key task in socialization, therefore, is to foster empathy for others. Many years ago, Hoffman (1970) reviewed the child-rearing literature to determine which approaches to discipline were associated with high levels of moral development. Three major approaches were compared:

1. **Love withdrawal.** Withholding attention, affection, or approval after a child misbehaves—in other words, creating anxiety by threatening a loss of reinforcement from parents
2. **Power assertion.** Using power to administer spankings, take away privileges, and so on—in other words, using punishment
3. **Induction.** Explaining to a child why the behavior is wrong and should be changed by emphasizing how it affects other people

Suppose that little Angel has just put the beloved family cat through a cycle in the clothes dryer. Using love withdrawal, a parent might say, "How could you do something like that? I can't even bear to look at you!" Using power assertion, a parent might say, "Get to your room this minute; you're going to get it." Using induction, a parent might say, "Angel, look how scared Fluffball is. You could have killed her, and you know how sad we'd be if she died." Induction, then, is a matter of providing rationales or explanations that focus special attention on the consequences of wrongdoing for other people (or cats).

Which approach best fosters moral development? Induction is more often positively associated with children's moral maturity than either love withdrawal or power assertion (Brody & Shaffer, 1982). In Hoffman's (2000) view, induction works well because it breeds empathy. Anticipating empathic distress if we contemplate harming someone keeps us from doing harm; empathy for individuals in distress motivates us to help them (Hoffman, 2000).

Love withdrawal has been found to have positive effects in some studies but negative effects in others. The use of power assertion is more often associated with moral immaturity than with moral maturity. When parents are physically abusive, children feel less guilt than other children and engage in more immoral behaviors such as stealing (Koenig, Cicchetti, & Rogosch, 2004). The use of power tactics such as restraining and commanding to keep young children from engaging in prohibited acts is associated with less rather than more moral behavior in other contexts (Kochanska, Aksan, & Nichols, 2003). It is a vicious cycle: parental power tactics lead to noncompliant children, and noncompliant children prompt increasingly controlling parental behavior (Smith et al., 2004).

Despite evidence that power assertion interferes with the internalization of moral rules and undermines the child's capacity to exert self-control, Hoffman (2000) concludes that power assertion can be useful occasionally, as long as it does not arouse too much fear, because it can motivate a child to pay close attention to inductions. Like other techniques, it works best in the context of a loving and mutually responsive parent–child relationship.

© Image Source/Picture Quest

Most youngsters can be tempted to steal if the situational factors are right. Children's moral conduct is fairly inconsistent from situation to situation.

Hoffman's work provides a fairly clear picture of how parents can best contribute to the moral growth of their children. As he puts it, the winning formula is "a blend of frequent inductions, occasional power assertions, and a lot of affection" (Hoffman, 2000, p. 23). Yet we must also appreciate that a particular moral socialization technique can have different effects depending on the particular misdeed, child, parent, and context. More important than the particular socialization strategies a parent uses may be the quality of the parent–child relationship and the parent's understanding of the particular child and of the situation at hand (Grusec, Goodnow, & Kuczynski, 2000). To illustrate, the history of the parent–child relationship can influence the effectiveness of a parent's efforts to control a child's behavior. For example, abused children tend to be most compliant with requests to clean a playroom if their mothers do not show much negative emotion, whereas nonabused children are more compliant if their mothers do show negative emotion (Koenig, Cicchetti, & Rogosch, 2000).

A child's temperament also helps determine how morally trainable she is and what approach to moral training is used. Grazyna Kochanska has found that children are likely to be easy to socialize (1) if they are by temperament fearful or inhibited (see Chapter 11), and therefore are more likely than fearless or uninhibited children to become appropriately anxious and distressed when they are disciplined, and (2) if they are capable of effortful control, and therefore are able to inhibit their urges to engage in wrongdoing or to stop themselves from doing something once they have begun (Kochanska, Murray, & Coy, 1997; Kochanska & Knaack, 2003). Children high in both fearfulness and effortful control can be socialized easily using positive disciplinary techniques such as induction; as a result, their parents are likely to use induction frequently and may rarely need to resort to power assertion (Keller & Bell, 1979). However, children who are not easily led to associate guilt and other negative emotions with their wrongdoings or who have difficulty controlling their impulses may drive their parents to use more power-assertive (and ineffective) discipline, which is likely to impede moral development (Anderson, Lytton, & Romney, 1986; Lytton, 1990).

Finally, a child's biologically based temperament may interact with his parents' socialization approach to influence moral development. Kochanska (1995, 1997a) finds that fearful, inhibited children, who are hesitant to try activities such as jumping on a trampoline or putting on an ape mask and who become highly anxious when reprimanded, can be effectively socialized to refuse to touch certain toys and to comply cheerfully with requests through a gentle approach to discipline that capitalizes on their anxiety but does not terrorize them so much that they miss the lesson they are to learn (Fowles & Kochanska, 2000). Toddlers who are fearless or uninhibited do not respond to the gentle reprimands that work with inhibited children, but they do not respond to being treated harshly, either. Fearless children are most likely to learn to comply with rules and requests when the parent–child relationship is characterized by a mutually responsive orientation and the child therefore wants to cooperate (Fowles & Kochanska, 2000). Here, then, is another example of the importance of the goodness of fit between a child's temperament and her social environment. What works for one child may not work for another. Given appropriate socialization, most children will internalize rules of conduct, experience moral emotions, and learn to regulate their own behavior.

Summing Up

Both Piaget and Kohlberg failed to appreciate how much moral growth takes place in early childhood. We now know that even young children are capable of judging acts as right or wrong according to whether the actor's intentions were good or bad, do not view all rules as sacred (for example, they distinguish between social-conventional and moral rules), challenge adult authority when they believe it is illegitimate, and use their theories of mind to analyze people's motives and the emotional consequences of their acts. Young children have by no means completed their moral growth, but they appear to be on their way to becoming moral beings long before late childhood and early adolescence, when Piaget's autonomous stage and Kohlberg's stage 3 (conventional level) of moral reasoning are likely to be reached. When it comes to moral behavior, situational influences contribute to much moral inconsistency during childhood. Reinforcement, modeling, and the disciplinary approach of induction (as opposed to power assertion and love withdrawal) can foster moral growth, but a child's socialization history and temperament also influence his response to moral training. ■

The Adolescent

As adolescents gain the capacity to think about abstract and hypothetical ideas, and as they begin to chart their future identities, many of them reflect on their values and moral standards. Indeed, some come to view being a moral person (being caring, fair, honest, and so on) as an important part of who they are. Their moral identity then motivates moral action, and they end up being more capable of advanced moral reasoning and more likely to engage in moral behavior than adolescents who do not incorporate morality in their sense of identity (Aquino & Reed, 2002; Gibbs, 2003). At the other extreme are the adolescents who end up engaging in serious antisocial behavior.

Changes in Moral Reasoning

Although most teenagers break the law occasionally, adolescence is a period of considerable growth in moral reasoning and a time when many individuals become increasingly motivated to behave morally. Consider first the results of a 20-year longitudinal study that involved repeatedly asking the 10-, 13-, and 16-year-old boys originally studied by Kohlberg to respond to moral dilemmas (Colby et al., 1983). Figure 13.3 shows the percentage of judgments offered at each age that reflected each of Kohlberg's six stages.

Several interesting developmental trends can be seen here. Notice that the preconventional reasoning (stage 1 and 2 thinking) that dominates among 10-year-olds decreases considerably during the teen years. During adolescence, conventional reasoning (stages 3 and 4) becomes the dominant mode of moral thinking. So, among 13- to 14-year-olds, most moral judgments reflect either a stage 2 (instrumental hedonism) approach—"You scratch my back and I'll scratch yours"—or a stage 3 (good boy or good girl) concern with being nice and earning approval. More than half of the judgments offered by 16- to 18-year-olds embody stage 3 reasoning, and about a fifth were scored as stage 4 (authority and social order–maintaining morality) arguments. These older adolescents were beginning to take a broad societal perspective on justice and were concerned about acting in ways that would help maintain the social system.

In short, the main developmental trend in moral reasoning during adolescence is a shift from preconventional to conventional reasoning. During this period, most individuals seem to rise above a concern with external rewards and punishments. They begin to express a genuine concern with living up to the moral standards that parents and other authorities have taught them and ensuring that laws designed to make human relations just and fair are taken seriously and maintained. Many teens also begin to view morality as an important part of their identity and want to be able to think of themselves as honest, fair, and caring individuals (Damon &

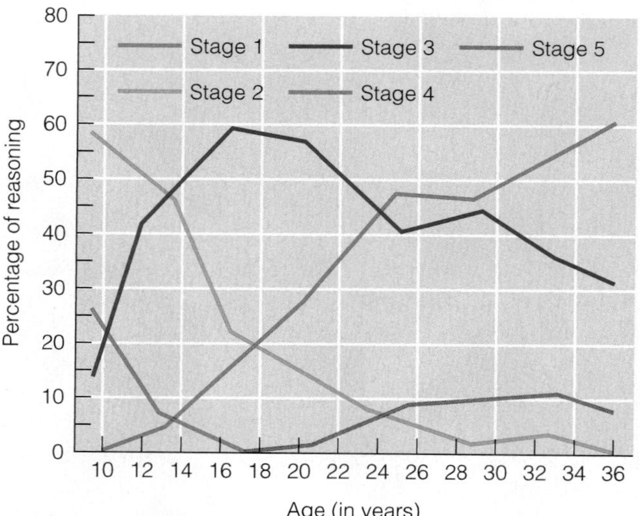

Figure 13.3 Average percentage of moral reasoning at each of Lawrence Kohlberg's stages for males from age 10 to age 36.

SOURCE: Colby et al. (1983).

Hart, 1992). Postconventional reasoning does not emerge until adulthood if at all.

Antisocial Behavior

Although most adolescents internalize society's moral standards, a few youths, such as Andy Williams described at the beginning of the chapter, are involved in serious antisocial conduct—muggings, rapes, armed robberies, knifings, or drive-by shootings. Indeed, crime rates peak during adolescence in most societies, especially for "hell-raising" crimes such as vandalism (Agnew, 2003). Most severely antisocial adults started their antisocial careers in childhood and continued them in adolescence. The consequences of their early misbehavior cumulate, they become juvenile delinquents, and they find themselves leaving school early, participating in troubled relationships, having difficulty keeping jobs, and engaging in criminal behavior as adults (Loeber & Farringon, 2000; Maughan & Rutter, 2001). Nevertheless, most children and adolescents who engage in aggressive behavior and other antisocial acts do not grow up to be antisocial adults (Maughan & Rutter, 2001). There seem to be at least two subgroups of antisocial youths: one group that is persistently antisocial across the life span and a larger group that behaves antisocially mainly during adolescence, perhaps in response to peer pressures, and outgrows this behavior in adulthood (Moffitt & Caspi, 2001; Quinsey et al., 2004). Our focus here is on the chronically and seriously aggressive adolescents.

What causes some youths to become menaces to society? Might adolescents who engage repeatedly in aggressive, antisocial acts be cases of arrested moral development who have not internalized conventional values? Juvenile delinquents are more likely than nondelinquents to rely on preconventional, egocentric moral reasoning (Gregg, Gibbs, & Basinger, 1994; Trevethan & Walker, 1989). Aggressive youths are less likely to show empathy or concern for others in distress (Blair, 2003; Hastings et al., 2000). Some offenders clearly lack a sense of right and wrong and feel little remorse about their criminal acts.

© Alan Danaher/Getty Images

☾ Use of power assertion by adults is linked to moral immaturity rather than moral maturity.

Yet the relationship between moral reasoning and antisocial behavior is weak. Many delinquents are capable of conventional moral reasoning but commit illegal acts anyway (Blasi, 1980). This suggests that to understand the origins of antisocial conduct, we must consider a wider range of factors (see Gibbs, 2003; Quinsey et al., 2004).

Dodge's Social Information-Processing Model

Kenneth Dodge and his colleagues have advanced our understanding by offering a social information-processing model of behavior that has been used to analyze contributors to aggressive behavior (Crick & Dodge, 1994; Dodge, 1986; Dodge & Pettit, 2003). Imagine that you are walking down the aisle in a classroom and trip over a classmate's leg. As you fall to the floor, you are not sure what happened. Dodge and other social information-processing theorists believe that the individual's reactions to frustration, anger, or provocation depend not so much on the social cues in the situation as on the ways in which she processes and interprets this information.

An individual who is provoked (as by being tripped) progresses through six steps in information processing, according to Dodge:

1. *Encoding of cues:* Taking in information
2. *Interpretation of cues:* Making sense of this information and deciding what caused the other person's behavior
3. *Clarification of goals:* Deciding what to achieve in the situation
4. *Response search:* Thinking of possible actions to achieve the goal
5. *Response decision:* Weighing the pros and cons of these alternative actions
6. *Behavioral enactment:* Doing something

People do not necessarily go through these steps in precise order; we can cycle among them or work on two or more simultaneously (Crick & Dodge, 1994). And at any step, we may draw not only on information available in the immediate situation but also on a stored database that includes memories of previous social experiences and information about the social world.

As you might imagine, the skills involved in carrying out these six steps in social information processing improve with age (Dodge & Price, 1994; Mayeux & Cillessen, 2003). Older children are more able than younger ones to do such things as encode all the relevant cues in a situation, accurately interpret cues to determine why another person behaved as he did, generate a range of responses, and carry off intended behaviors skillfully. Why, then, are some children of a given age more aggressive than others?

Highly aggressive youths, including adolescents incarcerated for violent crimes, show deficient or biased information processing at every step (Dodge, 1993; Slaby & Guerra, 1988). For example, a highly aggressive adolescent who is tripped by a classmate is likely to (1) process relatively few of the available cues in the situation and show a bias toward information suggesting that the tripping was deliberate rather than accidental (for example, noticing a fleeting smirk on the class-

Table 13.1 The Six Steps in Dodge's Social Information-Processing Model and Sample Responses of Aggressive Youth.

Step	Behavior	Likely Response of Aggressive Youth
1. Encoding of cues	Search for, attend to, and register cues in the situation	Focus on cues suggesting hostile intent; ignore other relevant information
2. Interpretation of cues	Interpret situation; infer other's motive	Infer that provoker had hostile intent
3. Clarification of goals	Formulate goal in situation	Make goal to retaliate
4. Response search	Generate possible responses	Generate few options, most of them aggressive
5. Response decision	Assess likely consequences of responses generated; choose the best	See advantages in responding aggressively rather than nonaggressively (or fail to evaluate consequences)
6. Behavioral enactment	Produce chosen response; act	Behave aggressively

Social information processors use a database of information about past social experiences, social rules, and social behavior at each step of the process and skip from step to step. See Crick & Dodge (1994) for further details and relevant research.

mate's face); (2) make an attribution of hostile intent inferring, based on the information gathered, that the classmate meant to cause harm; (3) set a goal of getting even (rather than a goal of smoothing relations); (4) think of only a few possible ways to react, mostly aggressive ones; (5) conclude, after evaluating alternative actions, that an aggressive response will have favorable outcomes (or perhaps not think through the possible negative consequences of an aggressive response); and (6) carry out the particular aggressive response selected (see Table 13.1).

Many aggressive youths also skip steps of the model and act impulsively, "without thinking"; they respond automatically based on their database of past experiences. These youths tend to see the world as a hostile place and are easily angered. If a situation is ambiguous (as a tripping or bumping incident is likely to be), they are more likely than nonaggressive youths to quickly attribute hostile intent to whoever harms them (Crick & Dodge, 1994; Orobio de Castro et al., 2002). Interestingly, 4- to 6-year-olds who are rejected by peers because of aggressive and otherwise irritating behavior do as well as their more popular peers on theory-of-mind tasks but appear to have developed what Happé and Frith (1996b) have dubbed a "theory of 'nasty minds,'" attributing hostile intentions and motives to other people even at this early age (Badenes, Estevan, & Garcia Bacete, 2000). Severely violent youths such as Andy Williams have often experienced abandonment, neglect, abuse, and other traumas that may have given them cause to view the world as a hostile place and to feel morally justified in going after anyone who threatens or wrongs them (Gibbs, 2003; Margolin & Gordis, 2000).

Aggressive youths also tend to evaluate the consequences of aggression far more positively than other adolescents do. They expect their aggressive acts to achieve the desired results, view being "tough" and controlling others as important to their self-esteem, and feel morally justified in acting because they believe they are only retaliating against individuals who are "out to get them" (Coie et al., 1991; Smithmyer, Hubbard, & Simons, 2000). They often belong to peer groups whose members value toughness and reinforce one another for bullying classmates or otherwise misbehaving (Poulin & Boivin, 2000).

Dodge's social information-processing model is helpful in understanding why children and adolescents might behave aggressively in particular situations. However, it leaves somewhat unclear the extent to which the underlying problem is *how one thinks* (how skilled the person is at processing social information), *what one thinks* (for example, whether the individual believes that other people are hostile or that aggression pays), or *whether one thinks* (how impulsive the person is). The role of emotions also needs more attention. Children who are by temperament high in emotionality but have difficulty regulating and controlling their emotions are especially likely to show deficiencies in social information processing and to engage in problem behavior, perhaps because their strong emotions cloud their thinking (Eisenberg et al., 1996; Lemerise & Arsenio, 2000). Finally, we need more research, like the work we will describe next, to tell us why only some children develop the social information-processing styles associated with aggressive behavior.

Patterson's Coercive Family Environments

Family influences on aggression may provide part of the answer. Gerald Patterson and his colleagues have found that highly antisocial children and adolescents often experience **coercive family environments** in which family members are locked in power struggles, each trying to control the others through coercive tactics such as threatening, yelling, and hitting (Patterson, DeBaryshe & Ramsey, 1989; Kiesner, Dishion, & Poulin, 2001). In some cases, parents use harsh discipline or are even abusive (Margolin & Gordis, 2000). Coercive family processes were first identified in families with boys who were out of control, but they also surface in the families of girls with conduct problems (Compton et al., 2003; Eddy, Leve, & Fagot, 2001). Parents learn (through negative reinforcement) that they can stop their children's misbehavior, temporarily at least, by threatening, yelling, and hitting. Meanwhile, children learn (also through negative reinforcement) that they can get their parents to lay off them by ignoring requests, whining, throwing full-blown temper tantrums, and otherwise being as difficult as possible. As both parents and children learn to rely on coercive tactics, parents increasingly lose control over their children's behavior until even the loudest lectures and hardest spankings have little effect and the child's conduct problems spiral out of control. It is easy to see how a child who has grown up in a coercive family environment might attribute hostile intent to other people and rely on aggressive tactics to resolve disputes.

Growing up in a coercive family environment sets in motion the next steps in the making of an antisocial adolescent (see Figure 13.4): The child, already aggressive and unpleasant to be around, ends up performing poorly in school and being rejected by other children. Having no better options, she becomes involved in a peer group made up of other low-achieving, antisocial, and unpopular youths and is then steered even further in the direction of a delinquent career by these colleagues in crime, who positively reinforce one another's talk about rule breaking and delinquent acts (Dishion, Andrews, & Crosby, 1995; Kiesner et al., 2001). Rejection by peers may further reinforce a tendency to attribute hostile intent to others and in the process strengthen aggressive tendencies (Dodge et al., 2003).

Overall, there is much support for the view that ineffective parenting in childhood contributes to behavioral problems, peer rejection, involvement with antisocial peers, and, in turn, antisocial behavior in adolescence. The pattern even seems to repeat itself across generations; aggressive youths who experienced coercive parenting become coercive parents and raise aggressive children (Conger et al., 2003; Thornberry et al., 2003).

Nature and Nurture

Severe antisocial behavior is the product of a complex interplay between genetic predisposition and social learning experiences (Quinsey et al., 2004; Dodge & Pettit, 2003). We can start by putting aggression in an evolutionary context. For example, males are more aggressive overall than females and engage in three or four times as much crime; the male edge in violence is evident in many cultures and in many species (Barash, 2002). It has been argued that aggression evolved in males because it serves adaptive functions in mate selection (Hilton, Harris, & Rice, 2000; Pellegrini & Long, 2003). Becoming dominant in the male peer group enables adolescent males to compete with other males for mates, bearing many offspring and therefore succeeding in passing their genes to future generations. Adolescent females can bear only so many children and therefore may not need to be as competitive (Barash, 2002). However, even they may boost their chances of finding mates by engaging in subtle and indirect forms of aggression such as spreading rumors about and "trashing" other females (Pellegrini & Long, 2003).

In addition, we now know that some individuals are more genetically predisposed than others to have difficult, irritable temperaments and other personality traits that incline them to show aggressive, delinquent, and criminal behavior (Cleveland, 2003; Rhee, & Waldman, 2002; Simonoff, 2001). Some aggressive individuals may be predisposed to violence by neurological deficits that affect their impulse control and verbal skills (Quinsey et al., 2004; Teichner & Golden, 2000). Behavioral genetic research suggests that genetic differences account for about 40% of the variation among individuals in antisocial behavior; nonshared environmental influences account for another 45% of the variation, and shared environmental influences common to siblings in the same family context account for about 15% (Rhee & Waldman, 2002).

Through the mechanism of gene–environment correlation, children who inherit a genetic predisposition to become aggressive may evoke the coercive parenting that Patterson and his colleagues find breeds aggression, even when they grow up with adoptive parents rather than with their biological parents. Coercive parenting, in turn, contributes to strengthening their aggressive tendencies (Lytton, 2000; O'Connor et al., 1998). When identical twin pairs are studied—therefore, only environmental influences can explain differences between the twins—the twin who receives the most negative treatment and the least warmth from his mother tends to become the more aggressive of the two twins (Caspi et al., 2004). When both genes predisposing a child to aggression and coercive parenting are at work, the child quickly becomes out of control and the parents become so frustrated that they may monitor their child's behavior less to avoid the unpleasant battles of will that result when they attempt to clamp down (Dodge & Pettit, 2003).

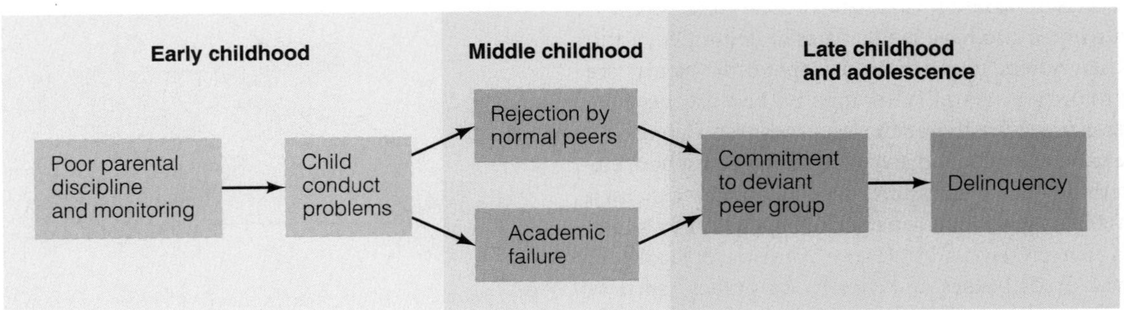

Figure 13.4 Gerald Patterson's model of the development of antisocial behavior starts with poor discipline and coercive cycles of family influence.

Source: Adapted from Patterson et al. (1989).

Many other risk and protective factors in the environment can help determine whether a child genetically predisposed to be aggressive ends up on a healthy or unhealthy developmental trajectory. The prenatal environment—for example, exposure to alcohol, opiate drugs, and lead poisoning—has been linked to conduct problems (Dodge & Pettit, 2003). Complications during delivery may also contribute, especially if the child later grows up in a deprived family environment (Arseneault et al., 2002).

Some cultural contexts are more likely to breed aggression than others. In Japan, a collectivist culture in which children are taught early to value social harmony, children are less angered by interpersonal conflicts and less likely to react to them aggressively than American children are (Zahn-Waxler et al., 1996). Hispanic youths who have been brought up with traditional Hispanic cultural values such as the importance of family are less likely than those who are more acculturated into American society to engage in antisocial behavior (Cota-Robles, 2003; Soriano et al., 2004). Could this be partly because children in the United States are so heavily exposed to violence on television every day? Research shows that children exposed to a lot of media violence are not only more aggressive in the short run but also more likely to engage in assaults, spouse abuse, and other forms of violence as adults (Anderson et al., 2003; Huesmann et al., 2003). More generally, the United States is an especially violent country. The homicide rate is only 0.5 homicides per 1 million people in Iceland; it is closer to 10 per 1 million in Europe, and it is more than 100 per 1 million in the United States (Barash, 2002).

Subcultural and neighborhood factors can also contribute to youth violence. Rates of aggression and violent crime are two to three times higher in lower socioeconomic neighborhoods and communities, especially transient ones, than in middle-class ones (Elliott & Ageton, 1980; Maughan, 2001). Community norms that support the use of violence to resolve conflicts and social stressors that make it difficult for parents to monitor and manage their children may both contribute (Jagers, Bingham, & Hans, 1996). So may witnessing community violence (Guerra, Huesmann, & Spindler, 2003). Interestingly, parental behaviors that can help control aggression, such as monitoring adolescents' comings and goings, appear to make even more of a difference in disadvantaged, unstable, violence-prone neighborhoods than they do in adequate ones (Beyers, Bates, et al., 2003; Cleveland, 2003).

Certain schools also have higher rates of delinquency and aggression than others, even when socioeconomic factors are controlled (Maughan, 2001). This may be because negative peer influences prevail in these schools; exposure to aggressive peers is a clear risk factor (Dodge & Pettit, 2003). In school environments that breed aggression, peer influences can turn even an adolescent without a genetic predisposition to be aggressive into an aggressive youth (Rowe, Almeida, & Jacobson, 1999). Because both bullies and victims of bullies (such as Andy Williams) are more likely than other youths to commit violent acts later in life, many schools are taking active steps to combat bullying instead of writing it off as normal child behavior (Strauss, 2001).

Gangs in inner-city areas are only part of the larger problem of youth violence.

Kenneth Dodge and Gregory Pettit (2003) have attempted to integrate all these influences on aggression in a biopsychosocial model, illustrated in Figure 13.5. It is based primarily on their research tracing the development of aggression among 585 boys and girls who were studied from preschool age to early adulthood. In the model, biological factors such as genes associated with aggression and sociocultural factors such as living in a violent area put certain children at risk from birth. Then, experiences with harsh and coercive parents, antisocial peers, and dysfunctional social institutions such as violence-ridden schools translate risk into reality. Interactions between person and environment over time determine whether the developmental path leads toward more or less antisocial behavior over the years. Cognitive and emotional processes also enter, as suggested by Dodge's social information-processing model; based on their life experiences, children build databanks of social knowledge about such things as norms for responding to aggression, aggressive tactics, and information-processing habits such as attributing hostile intent to others. The more risk factors at work, the greater the odds of an aggressive adult. Interactions among

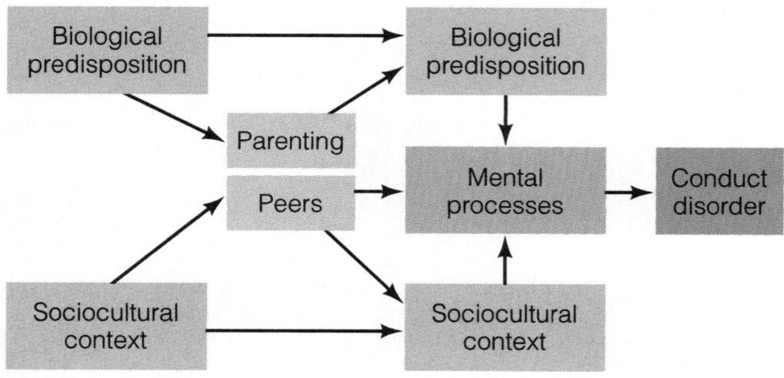

Figure 13.5 A biopsychosocial model of aggression highlights biological and sociocultural factors that predispose a child to aggression and combine with parent and peer influences to affect mental processes that directly cause a conduct disorder.

SOURCE: Dodge & Pettit (2003, p. 351, Figure 1).

factors can also be important; for example, only among children predisposed to aggression does rejection by peers increase the odds of a full-blown conduct disorder by adolescence (Dodge et al., 2003). In sum, many interacting factors, both biological and environmental, can put an individual on—or pull an individual off—a path to antisocial adulthood. Perhaps as a result, violence prevention and treatment programs can take many forms, as the Applications box on page 376 suggests.

Summing Up

In sum, adolescents normally shift from preconventional to conventional moral reasoning and incorporate moral values into their emerging sense of identity. The severe antisocial behavior that some adolescents display is more than a matter of immature moral reasoning, however, although many delinquent youths reason at Kohlberg's preconventional level. Antisocial behavior can also be traced to deficiencies in social information-processing skills that, according to Dodge and his colleagues, make youngsters quick to attribute hostile intentions to other people and convince them that aggression works. This information-processing style, in turn, may be rooted in genetically influenced temperamental traits that make for strong negative emotions and weak emotional control. Social learning experiences in the family (Patterson's coercive family environments), negative peer group influences and peer rejection, and wider school, neighborhood, and cultural influences also contribute, as suggested by the biopsychosocial model proposed by Dodge and Pettit. ■

The Adult

When adults assume responsibilities as parents, work supervisors, and community leaders, their moral decisions affect more people. How does moral thinking change during adulthood, and what else must we consider to gain a perspective on moral development across the life span?

Moral Development

As you have discovered (see Figure 13.3 on page 370), Kohlberg's postconventional moral reasoning appears to emerge only during the adult years (if it emerges). In Kohlberg's 20-year longitudinal study (Colby et al., 1983), most adults in their 30s still reasoned at the conventional level, although many of them had shifted from stage 3 to stage 4. A minority of individuals—one-sixth to one-eighth of the sample—had begun to use stage 5 postconventional reasoning, showing a deeper understanding of the basis for laws and distinguishing between just and unjust laws. Clearly, there is opportunity for moral growth in early adulthood.

Do these growth trends continue into later adulthood? Most studies find no major age differences in stage of moral reasoning, at least when relatively educated adults are studied and when the age groups compared have similar levels of education (Pratt & Norris, 1999). Older adults sometimes do worse than younger adults at gathering and coordinating information about the different perspectives that can be taken on a moral issue, perhaps because of declines in working memory or perhaps because they rely more on general rules in judging what is right and wrong and are not as interested in the details of different people's points of view (Pratt & Norris, 1999). However, even up to age 75, elderly adults seem to reason about moral issues as complexly as younger adults do, whether they are given Kohlberg's hypothetical dilemmas to ponder or asked to discuss real-life situations in which they were "unsure about the right thing to do" (Pratt et al., 1991, 1996).

In addition, older adults have a greater sense of having learned important lessons from moral dilemmas they have faced during their lives (Pratt & Norris, 1999). **Spirituality,** a search for ultimate meaning in life that may or may not be carried out in the context of religion, appears to increase from middle age to later adulthood (Wink & Dillon, 2002). Spirituality is especially evident among adults who are reflective seekers of knowledge and who experience adversity in their lives. Both postconventional moral reasoning (Pasupathi & Staudinger, 2001) and spirituality (Wink & Dillon, 2003) have been linked to the attainment of wisdom (see Chapter 9). It seems, then, that moral reasoning is an aspect of social cognitive development that holds up well in later life and that advanced moral reasoning may even be associated with increased spirituality and wisdom in adulthood.

Influences on Moral Development

Kohlberg argued (as did Piaget) that two factors are most important in moral development: cognitive growth and social experiences, particularly interactions with peers. As Kohlberg predicted, reaching the conventional level of moral reasoning and becoming concerned about living up to the moral standards of parents or society requires the ability to take other people's perspectives (Walker, 1980). Gaining the capacity for postconventional or "principled" moral reasoning requires still more cognitive growth—namely, a solid command of formal operational thinking, usually evident only in adulthood (Tomlinson-Keasey & Keasey, 1974; Walker, 1980). The person who bases moral judgments on abstract principles must be able to reason abstractly and take all possible perspectives on a moral issue. Milestones in moral development cannot be achieved without the requisite cognitive skills.

Kohlberg also stressed the need for social experiences that require the individuals to take the perspectives of others so that they can appreciate that they are part of a larger social order and that moral rules are a consensus of individuals in society. Interacting with people who hold views different from their own also creates cognitive disequilibrium—a conflict between existing cognitive structures and new ideas—which in turn stimulates new ways of thinking. Like Piaget, Kohlberg maintained that interactions with peers or equals, in which we experience and discuss differences be-

Applications

Combating Youth Violence

In recent years, U.S. society has been struggling with the problem of how to prevent youth violence and treat seriously aggressive children and adolescents such as Andy Williams, the troubled teenager described at the start of this chapter. Many believe that violence prevention needs to start in infancy or toddlerhood—perhaps even at conception—with a strong emphasis on positive parenting (Tremblay, 2000). Programs such as Fast Track, aimed at improving the social skills and self-control of young children at risk to become aggressive by using academic and social skills training at school, parent training, and home visits, have had some success in improving parenting and, in turn, reducing aggression (Conduct Problems Prevention Research Group, 1999). School-based prevention programs aimed at teaching social cognitive skills to either high-risk children or all children can also be effective (Aber, Brown, & Jones, 2003; Wilson, Lipsey, & Derzon, 2003). Here, we focus on how three perspectives described in this chapter—Lawrence Kohlberg's theory of moral reasoning, Kenneth Dodge's social information-processing model, and Gerald Patterson's coercive family environment model—have been applied to the challenge of treating youths who have already become antisocial.

Discussion of moral dilemmas may increase complexity of moral reasoning but does not necessarily reduce delinquency.

Improving Moral Reasoning

How can we foster stronger moral values and more advanced moral thinking among not-so-moral children and adolescents? If, as both Jean Piaget and Lawrence Kohlberg said, peers are more important than parents in stimulating moral growth, one sensible approach is to harness "peer power." This is what many psychologists and educators have tried to do, putting children or adolescents in pairs or small groups to discuss hypothetical moral dilemmas and creating school-based programs involving discussion of violations of both moral and social-conventional rules (see Nucci, 2001). The rationale is simple: Opportunities to take other people's perspectives and exposure to forms of moral reasoning more mature than their own will create cognitive disequilibrium, which will motivate children to devise more mature modes of thinking.

Does participation in group discussions of moral issues produce more mature moral reasoning? It appears so (Rest et al., 1999). Average changes that are the equivalent of about 4 to 5 years of natural development have been achieved in programs lasting only 3 to 12 weeks. Moreover, researchers have learned what kinds of discussion are most helpful. For example, it is important that students be exposed to reasoning that is more mature than their own (Lapsley, 1996). Also, moral growth is most likely when students actively transform, analyze, or otherwise act upon what their conversation partners have said—when they say things like "You're missing an important difference here" or "Here's something I think we can agree on" (Berkowitz & Gibbs, 1983; Nucci, 2001).

Participation in Kohlbergian moral discussion groups can even raise the level of moral thinking of institutionalized delinquents (Niles, 1986). However, unless it is combined with efforts to combat self-serving cognitions and teach social skills, efforts to foster mature moral judgment are unlikely to cause delinquents to cease being delinquent (Gibbs, 2003; Niles, 1986).

tween our own and others' perspectives, probably contribute more to moral growth than one-sided interactions with adult authority figures in which children are expected to defer to the adult's power. Were Piaget and Kohlberg right? As it turns out, peers are important, but so are parents, and not just by using inductive discipline and being warm, supportive parents.

Lawrence Walker and his colleagues (Walker, Hennig, & Krettenauer, 2000) directly compared parent and peer influences on moral development. Both 11- and 15-year-olds discussed moral dilemmas with a parent and then separately with a friend. Four years later, they were asked to respond to moral dilemmas. Interactions with both parents and friends influenced these individuals' moral development, but in somewhat different ways. Friends were more likely than parents to challenge and disagree with a child's or an adolescent's ideas, and they were most likely to contribute positively to moral growth when they confronted and challenged. Parents, because they functioned at more advanced stages of moral development than their children, en-

Building Social Information-Processing Skills

As you saw earlier, Dodge's social information-processing model identifies six steps at which a highly aggressive youth may display deficient or biased information processing. Nancy Guerra and Ronald Slaby (1990) coached small groups of incarcerated and violent juveniles of both sexes (1) to look for situational cues other than those suggesting hostile intentions, (2) to control their impulses so that they do not lash out without considering the consequences, and (3) to generate more nonaggressive solutions to conflicts. After a 12-week intervention, these adolescents showed dramatic improvements in social information-processing skills, believed less strongly in the value of aggression, and behaved less aggressively in their interactions with authority figures and other inmates.

Trained offenders were only somewhat less likely than untrained offenders (34% versus 46%) to violate their paroles after release, however, suggesting that they may have reverted to their antisocial ways once back in the environment in which their aggressive tendencies originated. Indeed, for young African American and Hispanic males in gang-dominated inner-city neighborhoods, being quick to detect others' hostile intentions and defend themselves against assault may be an important survival skill (Hudley & Graham, 1993).

Breaking Coercive Cycles

Patterson and his colleagues maintain that the secret to working with violent youths is to change the dynamics of interactions in their families so that aggressive tactics of controlling other family members are no longer reinforced and the cycle of coercive influence is broken. In one study, Patterson and his team (Bank et al., 1991) randomly assigned adolescent boys who were repeat offenders to either a special parent-training intervention or the service usually provided by the juvenile court. In the parent-training program, therapy sessions held with each family taught parents how to observe both prosocial and antisocial behaviors in their son, to communicate closely with their son's school, to gather teachers' reports on his performance and behavior at school, and, using methods derived from social learning theory, to establish behavioral contracts that detail what the youth can expect in the way of reinforcement for prosocial behavior and punishment for antisocial behavior.

Overall, the parent-training intervention was judged at least a partial success. It improved family processes, although it did not fully resolve the problems these dysfunctional families had. Rates of serious crime among this group dropped and remained lower even 3 years after the intervention ended. The usual juvenile services program also reduced crime rates but took longer to take effect.

Other research shows that peers can undermine the effectiveness of treatment programs. Programs that put antisocial adolescents together in treatment groups or facilities can increase problem behavior if they mainly provide antisocial youths with opportunities to reinforce one another's deviance (Dishion, McCord, & Poulin, 1999). A better strategy is to form groups with a mix of well-adjusted and aggressive youths (and hope that the well-adjusted ones prevail).

In sum, efforts to treat aggressive youths have included attempts to apply the work of Kohlberg (by discussing moral issues to raise levels of moral reasoning), Dodge (by teaching effective social information-processing skills), and Patterson (by replacing coercive cycles in the family environment with positive behavioral management techniques). Many interventions have achieved short-term gains in skills but have failed to reduce rates of antisocial behavior in the long run. The most promising approaches to preventing and treating aggressive youths appear to recognize that modifying patterns of antisocial behavior requires adopting a biopsychosocial perspective and seeking to change not only the individual but also his family, peers, and broader social environment (Dodge & Pettit, 2003; Elliott, Williams, & Hamburg, 1998).

gaged them in more intellectually stimulating discussions. Parents contributed most to development when they used a positive, supportive style in which they checked to make sure they understood what their children were trying to say and probed their thinking in a gentle, Socratic manner. They did more damage than good when they took an authoritarian approach and lectured about right and wrong (see also Walker & Taylor, 1991).

Other research suggests that children may think more actively and deeply about their own and their partners' moral ideas in discussions with peers than in talks with their mothers or other adults and that discussions with peers are more likely to stimulate moral growth (Kruger, 1992; Kruger & Tomasello, 1986). But although Piaget and Kohlberg were right to call attention to the role of peers in moral development, they failed to appreciate that parents also have much to contribute.

Another social experience that contributes to moral growth is advanced schooling. Adults who go on to college and receive years of education think more complexly about moral issues than do those who are less educated (Pratt et al., 1991). Advanced educational experiences not only contribute

© Najlah Feanny/CORBIS

Some school environments breed aggressive behavior.

to cognitive growth but also provide exposure to the diverse ideas and perspectives that produce cognitive conflict and soul-searching.

Finally, participating in a complex, diverse, and democratic society can stimulate moral development. Just as we learn the give and take of mutual perspective taking by discussing issues with our friends, we learn in a diverse democracy that the opinions of many groups must be weighed and that laws reflect a consensus of the citizens rather than the arbitrary rulings of a dictator. Indeed, cross-cultural studies suggest that postconventional moral reasoning emerges primarily in Western democracies (Snarey, 1985). Adults in homogeneous communities in traditional, non-Western societies may have less experience with the kinds of political conflicts and compromises that take place in more complex societies, so they may never have any need to question conventional moral standards.

In sum, advanced moral reasoning is most likely if the individual has acquired the necessary cognitive skills (particularly perspective-taking skills and, later, formal operational or abstract thinking). Moreover, an individual's moral development is highly influenced by social learning experiences, including interactions with parents, discussions with peers, exposure to higher education, and participation in democracy.

Kohlberg's Theory and Beyond

You have now seen that children think about hypothetical moral dilemmas primarily in a preconventional manner, that adolescents adopt a conventional mode of moral reasoning, and that a few adults progress to the postconventional level. Kohlberg appears to have discovered an important developmental progression in moral thought. He said that his stages form an invariant and universal sequence of moral growth, and longitudinal studies of moral growth in several countries support him (Colby & Kohlberg, 1987; Rest et al., 1999).

However, support for some parts of the stage progression is stronger than support for other parts. Questions have been raised about whether stages 1 and 2 adequately capture the moral thinking of children (Dawson & Gabrielian, 2003); as you saw earlier, young children are more sophisticated moral thinkers than either Piaget or Kohlberg recognized. Moreover, the idea that everyone progresses from preconventional to conventional reasoning is better supported than the idea that people continue to progress from conventional to postconventional reasoning (Boom, Brugman, & van der Heijden, 2001). Stage 3 or 4 seems to be the end of the developmental journey for most individuals worldwide (Snarey, 1985). Moreover, questions have been raised about whether the theory is biased against people from non-Western cultures, political conservatives, and women, as you shall now see.

Culture Bias?

Why does postconventional reasoning, as Kohlberg defines it, not seem to exist in traditional, non-Western societies? Critics charge that Kohlberg's highest stages reflect a Western ideal of justice centered on individual rights, making the stage theory biased against people who live in non-Western societies (Shweder, Mahapatra, & Miller, 1990). People in collectivist societies, which emphasize social harmony and place the good of the group ahead of the good of the individual, look like stage 3 conventional moral thinkers in Kohlberg's system but may have sophisticated concepts of justice that focus on the individual's responsibility for others' welfare (Snarey, 1985; Tietjen & Walker, 1985). Whereas American children learn to be relatively self-centered in their moral perspective, children in Asian collectivist cultures appear to learn earlier to consider others' perspectives and to care about the welfare of the family and other social groups (Fang et al., 2003). Cultural influences on moral development are explored further in the Explorations box on page 379.

Liberal Bias?

Critics charge that Kohlberg's theory is biased not only against non-Westerners but also against political conservatives. A person must hold liberal values—for example, opposing capital punishment or supporting civil disobedience in the name of human rights—to be classified as a postconventional moral reasoner, they say. In one study (de Vries & Walker, 1986), 100% of the college students who showed signs of postconventional thought opposed capital punishment, whereas none of the men and only a third of the women who were transitional between stage 2 and stage 3 moral reasoning opposed capital punishment. As Brian de Vries and Lawrence Walker (1986) note, it could be that opposition to capital punishment is a more valid moral position than support of capital punishment in that it involves valuing life highly. However, it could also be that the theory is unfair to law-and-order conservatives (Lapsley et al., 1984).

Gender Bias?

Criticisms of culture bias and liberal bias may have some merit, but no criticism of Kohlberg's theory has caused more stir than the charge that it is biased against women. Carol Gilligan (1977, 1982, 1993) was disturbed because Kohlberg's stages were developed based on interviews with males and that, in some studies, women seemed to reason at stage 3

Cultural Differences in Moral Thinking

Is each of the following acts wrong? If so, how serious is the violation?

1. A young married woman is beaten by her husband after going to a movie without his permission despite having been warned not to do so.
2. A brother and sister decide to marry and have children.
3. The day after his father died, the oldest son in a family gets a haircut and eats chicken.

These are 3 of 39 acts presented by Richard Shweder, Manamohan Mahapatra, and Joan Miller (1990, pp. 165–166) to children ages 5 to 13 and adults in India and the United States. You may be surprised to learn that Hindu children and adults rated the son's getting a haircut and eating chicken after his father's death among the most morally offensive of the 39 acts they rated. The husband's beating of his disobedient wife was not considered wrong. American children and adults, of course, viewed wife beating as far more serious than breaking seemingly arbitrary rules about appropriate mourning behavior. Although Indians and Americans agreed that a few acts, such as brother–sister incest, were serious moral violations, they did not agree on much else.

Moreover, Indian children and adults viewed the Hindu ban against behavior disrespectful of a dead father as a universal moral rule; they thought it would be best if everyone in the world followed it, and they strongly disagreed that it would be acceptable to change the rule if most people in their society wanted to change it. For similar reasons, they believed it is a serious moral offense for a widow to eat fish or for a woman to cook food for her family during her menstrual period. To orthodox Hindus, rules against such behaviors are required by natural law; they are not arbitrary social conventions. Similarly, Hindus regard it as morally necessary for a man to beat his disobedient wife to uphold his obligations as head of the family.

Shweder also observed different developmental trends in moral thinking in India and the United States, as the figure shows. With age, Indian children saw more issues as matters of universal moral principle, whereas American children saw fewer issues this way. Moreover, even the youngest children in both societies expressed moral outlooks similar to those expressed by adults in their own society and different from those expressed by either children or adults in the other society.

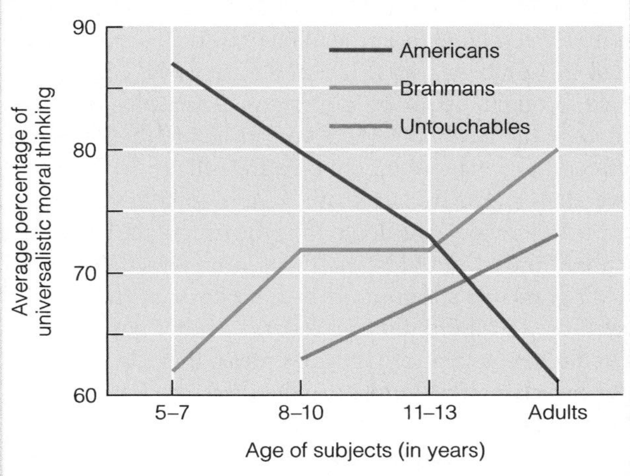

Based on such cross-cultural findings, Shweder calls into question Lawrence Kohlberg's claims that all children everywhere construct similar moral codes at similar ages and that certain universal moral principles exist. In addition, Shweder questions Elliot Turiel's claim that children everywhere distinguish from an early age between moral rules and more arbitrary social-conventional rules. Overall, then, these fascinating findings challenge the cognitive developmental position that important aspects of moral development are universal. Instead, they support a social learning or contextual perspective on moral development and suggest that children's moral judgments are shaped by the social context in which they develop.

How do we make sense of such conflicting findings? It seems likely that children all over the world think in more complex ways about moral issues as they age, as Kohlberg said, but that they also adopt different notions about what is right and what is wrong depending on what they are taught, as Shweder says. A study of Korean children (Baek, 2002) suggested just this: Like American children, Korean children appeared to progress through Kohlberg's general stages, but they drew on certain traditional Korean moral concepts in their answers that were not captured by Kohlberg's scoring system. In short, moral development appears to have both universal and culture-specific aspects.

when men usually reasoned at stage 4. She hypothesized that females develop a distinctly feminine orientation to moral issues, one that is no less mature than the orientation adopted by most men and incorporated into Kohlberg's theory.

Gilligan argues that boys, who traditionally are raised to be independent, assertive, and achievement oriented, come to view moral dilemmas as conflicts between the rights of two or more parties and to view laws and other social conventions as necessary for resolving these inevitable conflicts (a perspective reflected in Kohlberg's stage 4 reasoning). Girls, Gilligan argues, are brought up to be nurturant, empathic, and concerned with the needs of others and to define their sense of "goodness" in terms of their concern for other people (a perspective that approximates stage 3 in Kohlberg's scheme). What this difference boils down to is the difference between a "masculine" **morality of justice** (focused on laws defining individual rights) and a "feminine" **morality of care** (focused on a person's responsibility for the welfare of other people).

Despite the appeal of Gilligan's ideas, there is little support for her claim that Kohlberg's theory is systematically biased against females. In most studies, women reason just as complexly about moral issues as men do when their answers are scored by Kohlberg's criteria (Jaffee & Hyde, 2000). And females are, if anything, more likely than males to be able to resist the temptation to violate moral rules, although gender differences are often small (Silverman, 2003). Moreover, most studies do not support Gilligan's view that males and females think differently about moral dilemmas, and those that do find differences find only small ones indicating that females sometimes use more care reasoning than males and males sometimes use more justice reasoning than females (Jaffee & Hyde, 2000). Overall, it seems that both men and women use both types of reasoning—for example, care-based reasoning when they ponder dilemmas involving relationships and justice-based reasoning when issues of rights arise. The nature of the moral dilemma is far more important than the gender of the moral reasoner (Wark & Krebs, 1996). Finally, there is surprisingly little support for Gilligan's view that boys and girls are socialized differently in the area of morality (Lollis, Ross, & Leroux, 1996).

Although her hypothesis about sex differences in moral reasoning and their origin has not received much support, Gilligan's work has increased our awareness that both men and women often think about moral issues in terms of their responsibilities for the welfare of other people. Kohlberg emphasized only one way—a legalistic and abstract way—of thinking about right and wrong. Gilligan has called attention to the value of tracing the development of both a morality of justice and a morality of care in males and females (Brabeck, 1983; Moshman, 1999).

Supplementing Kohlberg

Kohlberg's theory focuses on moral reasoning or cognition. As a result, it has less to say about moral affect and behavior (Gibbs, 2003; Hoffman, 2000). It has been left to others to explore the emotional and behavioral components of morality more fully.

As Martin Hoffman (2000) emphasizes, empathy provides the motivation to take others' perspectives and needs seriously and to act to improve their welfare. Similarly, the anticipation of guilt motivates us to avoid doing wrong. Morality is more than cold cognition; "hot" emotions clearly play a role (Gibbs, 2003). Recognizing this, researchers today are looking more closely at what emotions children and adults

Adults in rural societies seem to have no need for postconventional moral reasoning because they share the same moral perspective.

© David Young-Wolff/PhotoEdit

Carol Gilligan maintains that girls are socialized into a morality of care rather than the morality of justice that interested Lawrence Kohlberg.

experience when they engage in immoral and moral behavior and at how they learn to regulate these emotions (Eisenberg, 2000). They are also looking at how morality becomes central to some people' identities and motivates them to live up to their values (Gibbs, 2003; Nucci, 2001).

In addition, researchers are looking more closely at the relationship between moral reasoning and moral behavior. Although a person may decide to uphold or to break a law at any of Kohlberg's stages of moral reasoning, Kohlberg argued that more advanced moral reasoners are more likely to behave morally than less advanced moral reasoners are. He would predict, for example, that the preconventional thinker might readily decide to cheat if the chances of being detected were small and the potential rewards were high. The postconventional thinker would be more likely to appreciate that cheating is wrong in principle, regardless of the chances of detection, because it infringes on the rights of others and undermines social order.

How well does a person's stage of moral reasoning predict his behavior? Individuals at higher stages of moral reasoning, especially when their empathy is aroused, are more likely than individuals at lower stages to behave prosocially (Gibbs, 2003). For instance, Elizabeth Midlarsky and her colleagues (1999) gave elderly adults moral dilemmas focused on prosocial behavior (for example, about whether to donate blood to a sick person at considerable cost to the donor). Adults whose responses to these moral dilemmas were based on abstract moral principles were more helpful in everyday life than those who reasoned at less advanced levels. Advanced moral reasoners are also less likely to cheat or to engage in delinquent and criminal activity (Judy & Nelson, 2000; Rest et al., 1999). For instance, Kohlberg (1975) found that only 15% of students who reasoned at the postconventional level cheated when given an opportunity to do so, compared with 55% of students at the conventional level reasoning and 70% of those at the preconventional level.

Still, relationships between stage of moral reasoning and moral behavior are typically weak, and researchers have struggled to explain why there is often a gap between thought and action (Bruggeman & Hart, 1996; Walker, 2004). As Albert Bandura (2002) emphasizes, we not only develop self-regulatory mechanisms that help us adhere to our internalized moral standards but also devise tactics of moral disengagement that let us distort reality, slither out from under responsibility for our actions, and commit acts that violate our moral values. Emotions also affect moral cognition and behavior. We reason less maturely, for example, in real interpersonal conflicts with romantic partners, when our egos are threatened and our self-interests are at stake, than we do when pondering hypothetical moral dilemmas of the sort Kohlberg posed (Krebs et al., 2002). In the end, we do best recognizing that the moral reasoning of interest to Piaget and Kohlberg, the moral emotions of interest to Freud and Hoffman, and the self-regulatory and moral disengagement processes of interest to Bandura—together with many other personal and situational factors—all help predict whether a person will behave morally or immorally in daily life.

We have now completed our series of chapters on the development of the self, or the person as an individual, looking at the development of self-conceptions and distinctive personality traits (Chapter 11), identities as males or females (Chapter 12), and now social cognitive skills and morality. But individual development does not occur in a vacuum. Repeatedly, you have seen that an individual's development may take different paths depending on the social and cultural context in which it occurs. Our task in upcoming chapters will be to put the individual even more squarely into a social context. It should become clear that throughout our lives we are both independent and interdependent—separate from and connected to other developing persons.

Summing Up

In sum, a few adults progress from the conventional to the postconventional level of moral reasoning during the adult years; moral reasoning skills are maintained in old age and may be tied to spirituality and wisdom for some. Overall, Kohlberg's theory of moral development describes a universal sequence of changes in moral reasoning extending from childhood through adulthood. The evidence supports

Kohlberg's view that both cognitive growth and experiences taking others' perspectives contribute to moral growth. However, the theory, although rightly emphasizing peer contributions to moral development, may not have appreciated parent contributions enough, and it may not be entirely fair to people who live in non-Western societies, who hold values other than liberal and democratic ones, or who emphasize what Gilligan calls a morality of care as opposed to a morality of justice. Furthermore, because Kohlberg's theory focuses on moral reasoning, it needs to be supplemented by other perspectives to help us understand how moral affect and moral behavior develop and how thought, emotion, and behavior interact to make us the moral beings we become. ■

Summary Points

1. Social cognition (thinking about self and others) is involved in all social behavior, including moral behavior. Starting in infancy with milestones such as joint attention and pretend play, children develop a theory of mind—an understanding that mental states exist and guide behavior. At age 2, they show evidence of a desire psychology; by age 4, they master a belief–desire psychology and pass false belief tasks. Developing a theory of mind requires normal neurological and cognitive growth and appropriate social and communication experience.

2. In characterizing other people, preschool children focus on their physical features and activities, whereas children 8 years and older describe people's inner psychological traits and adolescents integrate trait descriptions into personality profiles. With age, children also become more adept at role taking. Social cognitive skills often improve during adulthood but may decline late in life if a person is socially isolated.

3. Morality has cognitive, affective, and behavioral components; it is the ability to distinguish between right and wrong, to act on that distinction, and to experience appropriate moral emotions.

4. Sigmund Freud's psychoanalytic theory describes moral development in terms of the superego and moral emotions such as guilt; some modern theorists also emphasize the role of emotions and early parent–child relationships in moral development. Cognitive developmental theorist Jean Piaget distinguished premoral, heteronomous, and autonomous stages of moral thinking, and Lawrence Kohlberg proposed three levels of moral reasoning—preconventional, conventional, and postconventional—each with two stages. Social cognitive theorist Albert Bandura focused on how moral behavior is influenced by past learning, situational forces, self-regulatory processes, and moral disengagement.

5. Although infants are amoral in some respects, they begin learning about right and wrong through their early disciplinary encounters, and they internalize rules and display empathy and prosocial behavior by age 2. Their moral growth is facilitated by what Grazyna Kochanska calls a mutually responsive orientation between parent and child.

6. Kohlberg and Piaget underestimated the moral sophistication of young children (for example, their ability to consider intentions in judging acts, to distinguish between moral and social-conventional rules, and to question adult authority); most children display preconventional moral reasoning. Situational influences contribute to moral inconsistency. Reinforcement, modeling, and the disciplinary approach of induction can foster moral growth, and a child's temperament interacts with the approach to moral training parents adopt to influence outcomes.

7. During adolescence, a shift from preconventional to conventional moral reasoning is evident, and many adolescents incorporate moral values into their sense of identity as an individual.

8. Antisocial behavior can be understood in terms of Kenneth Dodge's steps in social information processing, Gerald Patterson's coercive family environments and the negative peer group influences they set in motion, and, more generally, a biopsychosocial model involving the interaction of genetic predisposition with social–environmental influences. Attempts to prevent and reduce youth violence have applied the work of Kohlberg (through moral discussion groups), Dodge (by teaching effective social information-processing skills), and Patterson (by altering coercive family environments).

9. Some adults progress from the conventional to the postconventional level of moral reasoning; elderly adults typically do not regress in their moral thinking, and some display advanced moral reasoning, spirituality, and wisdom.

10. Kohlberg's stages of moral reasoning form an invariant sequence, with progress through them influenced by cognitive growth and social experiences that involve taking others' perspectives. It has been charged that Kohlberg's theory is biased against people from non-Western cultures, conservatives, and women and men who express Gilligan's morality of care rather than a morality of justice. Other researchers emphasize that a full understanding of moral development requires attention not only to moral reasoning but also to moral affect and behavior.

Critical Thinking

1. Listen closely to a conversation in which your friends talk about people, and write down any statements in which they refer to people's beliefs, desires, intentions, and the like in attempting to explain someone's behavior. Can you find evidence that your friends have and use a theory of mind?

2. A preconventional thinker, a conventional thinker, and a postconventional thinker all face a moral dilemma the night before the final examination: A friend has offered them a key to the examination. Should they take it and use it or not? Provide examples of the reasoning you might expect at each of the three main levels of moral development—one argument in favor of cheating and one against it at each level. Are any of these arguments especially difficult to make?

3. Look back at the chapter's opening description of Andy Williams, the youth who murdered two people in a shooting rampage at his school. Drawing on material in this chapter, why do you think he might have done what he did? Profile him in terms of (a) his likely temperament, (b) his stage of moral reasoning, (c) his social information-processing style, (d) the discipline approaches his par-

ents used, and (e) other factors you think may have been significant contributors to his actions.

Key Terms

social cognition, 352
false belief task, 352
theory of mind, 352
desire psychology, 354
belief–desire psychology, 355
role-taking skills, 357
morality, 359
moral affect, 360
empathy, 360
prosocial behavior, 360
moral reasoning, 361
premoral period, 361
heteronomous morality, 361
autonomous morality, 361
preconventional morality, 362
conventional morality, 362
postconventional morality, 362
moral disengagement, 363
amoral, 365
mutually responsive orientation, 365
moral rules, 367
social-conventional rules, 367
love withdrawal, 368
power assertion, 368
induction, 368
coercive family environment, 372
spirituality, 375
morality of justice, 380
morality of care, 380

Media Resources

Websites to Explore

Visit Our Website

For a chapter tutorial quiz and other useful features, visit the book's companion website at *http://psychology.wadsworth.com/sigelman_rider5e.* You can also connect directly to the following sites:

Kohlberg

The Mental Help Net website details Lawrence Kohlberg's stages of moral development (although it uses different names for them) and provides some interesting values clarification surveys that can help you think about your own moral development.

Moral Development and Education

The Office for Studies in Moral Development and Moral Education at the University of Illinois–Chicago has on its website an overview of moral development and moral education that includes information about the theories of Jean Piaget, Lawrence Kohlberg, and Carol Gilligan. The website also details the research projects of faculty from different departments who study children's morality and character formation, especially as it relates to education.

Ethics Update on Gender Differences

Housed in the Values Institute at the University of San Diego, Ethics Updates bills itself as a website "dedicated to promoting the thoughtful discussion of difficult moral issues." It contains a wealth of resources on ethics-related theories and applied ethics dilemmas such as dealing with poverty, welfare, and bioethics. In its theory section, you can more thoroughly explore the ethical theory related to gender differences, including Carol Gilligan's ideas.

Youth Violence

For a major analysis of youth violence and how to combat it, see the website for *Youth Violence: A Report of the Surgeon General.* It provides statistics, summarizes research findings, confronts myths, and outlines strategies for preventing this major social problem.

Another useful reference is *Best Practices of Youth Violence Prevention: A Sourcebook for Community Action,* available at the National Center for Injury Protection and Control (NCIPC) site. This book, available online, draws on intervention research in areas such as parenting and conflict resolution skills. The NCIPC site also contains fact sheets about youth violence.

Understanding the Data: Exercises on the Web

For additional insight on the data presented in this chapter, try the exercise for the following figure at *http://psychology.wadsworth.com/sigelman_rider5e:*

Figure 13.3 Average percentage of moral reasoning at each of Lawrence Kohlberg's stages for males from age 10 to age 36

Life-Span CD-ROM

Go to the Wadsworth Life-Span CD-ROM for further study of the concepts in this chapter. The CD-ROM includes narrated concept overviews, video clips, a multimedia glossary, and additional activities to expand your learning experience.

DEVELOPMENTAL
PsychologyNow™

Developmental PsychologyNow is a web-based, intelligent study system that provides a complete package of diagnostic quizzes, a personalized study plan, integrated multimedia elements, and learning modules. Check it out at *http://psychology.wadsworth.com/sigelman_rider5e/now.*

CHAPTER fourteen

Attachment and Social Relationships

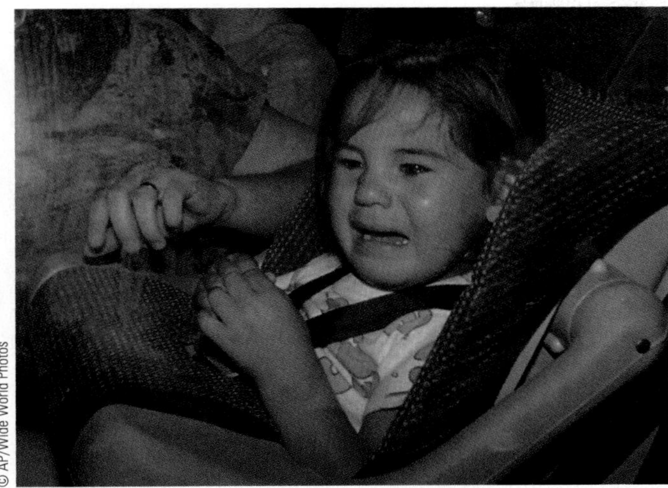
© AP/Wide World Photos

Baby Jessica leaves the only parents she knows.

THE LITTLE GIRL IN the photo is Baby Jessica, and she is about to be whisked away from the only parents she has ever known (Ingrassia & Springen, 1994). In August 1993, a nation watched in horror as this 2-year-old was taken from the DeBoers (the parents who thought they had adopted her, although the adoption was contested from the start and never finalized) and awarded by the court to the Schmidts (her biological parents).

How do you think this experience affected Jessica's development? Was she able to form close attachments to her biological parents? Was she scarred for life? You may be surprised to learn—as would some of the theorists described in this chapter—that by age 3 Jessica had been renamed Anna Jacqueline Schmidt and was reportedly a happy, well-adjusted preschooler (Ingrassia & Springen, 1994). According to her mother, Cara Schmidt, "Everyone guaranteed—*guaranteed*—that she would have short-term trauma, that she wouldn't eat, she wouldn't sleep, she'd cry. It didn't happen. She progressed, rapidly" (Ingrassia & Springen, 1994, p. 60). Jessica remembered the day of the van ride ("I got in the van and was crying and crying," p. 66), and she remembered her first parents, the DeBoers, but she did not pine for them.

The moral? We should not make too much of one case, but some would argue that Baby Jessica's story shows that children are resilient and that negative early experiences rarely ruin them for life. Yet Jessica had eight visits with her biological parents before being sent to live with them and therefore had an opportunity to begin to form an attachment to them (Ingrassia & Springen, 1994); maybe that explains why she was not traumatized. Or maybe she was scarred. We do not know whether her separation from the DeBoers had subtle effects on her development, perhaps making her fearful of abandonment by parents, friends, or, in her future, lovers.

Think about Jessica as you read this chapter. It concerns our closest relationships across the life span and their implications for development. Whatever you predict about Baby Jessica's future, you would probably agree that close interpersonal relationships play a critical role in our lives and in development. The poet John Donne wrote, "No man is an island, entire of itself"; it seems equally true that no human can become entire without the help of other humans.

This chapter addresses questions such as the following: What social relationships are especially important during different phases of the life span, and what is the character of these relationships? When and how do we develop the social competence it takes to interact smoothly with other people and to enter into intimate relationships with them? What are the developmental implications of being deprived of close relationships? We begin with some broad perspectives on social relationships.

Perspectives on Relationships

What is it that close social relationships contribute to our development? We can provide a reasonable answer by saying they provide learning experiences and social support. The learning experiences provided by social interactions affect virtually all aspects of development. We acquire language as young children, for example, because companions converse with us, serve as models of how to communicate, and reinforce our communication attempts. And other people teach us social skills and patterns of social behavior.

A second major function of close relationships is to provide **social support**—the emotional and practical help from others that bolsters us as individuals, protects us from stress, and enables us to cope. Many researchers use the term *social network* to describe the array of significant individuals who serve as sources of social support. Robert Kahn and Toni Antonucci (1980) prefer to describe these significant people as a **social convoy** to emphasize the idea of a social support system that changes in size and composition over the life span. An infant's social convoy may consist only of parents. The social convoy enlarges over the years as others (relatives, friends, supportive teachers, romantic partners, colleagues, and so on) join it, then it shrinks in old age (Levitt, Weber, & Guacci, 1993). As new members are added, some members drift away. Others remain in the convoy, but our relationships with them change, for example, when the infant son thoroughly dependent on his mother becomes the adolescent son clamoring for his independence—and later the middle-aged son who helps his mother manage her money and care for her house.

In sum, other people are important to us for an endless range of reasons, but their most critical roles in the developmental process are as sources of learning and social support. Yet developmental theorists have disagreed about which relationships are most critical to development. Many noted theorists have argued that no social relationship is more important than the first: the bond between parent and infant. Sigmund Freud (1930) left no doubt about his opinion: a stable mother–child relationship is essential for normal personality development. His follower Erik Erikson tended to agree, emphasizing the importance of responsive parenting to the development of trust in the parent–infant relationship. These theorists, in turn, influenced John Bowlby, the developer of attachment theory, to believe that the parent–infant relationship has lasting effects on later relationships and development. Yet, as you will see later, other theorists believe that peers are at least as significant as parents in the developmental process.

Attachment Theory

Attachment theory, today's most influential theory of parent–child and other close relationships, was formulated by Bowlby (1969, 1973, 1980, 1988), a British psychiatrist who died in 1990. It was elaborated on by his colleague Mary Ainsworth, an American developmental psychologist who died in 1999 (1989; Ainsworth et al., 1978). It was based on ethological theory, with its focus on the adaptive value of the evolved behavior of a species (see Chapter 2), and included concepts from psychoanalytic theory (Bowlby was a therapist trained in psychoanalytic thinking about mother–child relationships and their contribution to psychopathology) and cognitive theory (Bowlby believed that expectations about self and other are important, as you will see). Attachment theory replaced a learning theory perspective on early relationships, which held that caregivers become sources of reinforcement to infants through their association with food, comfort, and other primary reinforcers.

According to Bowlby (1969), an **attachment** is a strong affectional tie that binds a person to an intimate companion. It is also a behavioral system through which humans regulate their distress when under threat by seeking proximity to another person (see also Mikulincer & Shaver, 2003; Thompson & Raikes, 2003). For most of us, the first attachment we form, around 6 or 7 months of age, is to a parent. How do we know when baby Michael becomes attached to his mother? He will try to maintain proximity to her—crying, clinging, approaching, following, doing whatever it takes to maintain closeness. He will prefer her to other individuals, reserving his biggest smiles for her and seeking her when he is upset, discomforted, or afraid; she is irreplaceable in his eyes. He will also be confident about exploring his environment as long as he knows that his mother is there to provide the security he needs.

Notice that an infant attached to a parent is rather like an adult "in love." True, close emotional ties are expressed in different ways, and serve different functions, at different points in the life span. Adults, for example, do not usually feel compelled to follow their mates around the house, and they look to their loved ones for more than comforting hugs and smiles. Nonetheless, there are basic similarities among the infant attached to a caregiver, the child attached to a best friend, and the adolescent or adult attached to a mate or lover. Throughout the life span, the objects of our attachments are special, irreplaceable people with whom we are motivated to maintain proximity and from whom we derive a sense of security (Ainsworth, 1989).

Nature, Nurture, and Attachment

One of Bowlby's messages to his fellow psychiatrists was that it is normal rather than pathological to need other people throughout the life span. Using ethological theory and research, Bowlby argued that infants (and parents) are biologically predisposed to form attachments and to seek attachment figures to protect them. As you saw in Chapter 2, ethologists assume that all species, including humans, are born with innate behavioral tendencies that have contributed to the survival of the species over the course of evolution. It makes sense to think, for example, that young birds tended to survive if they stayed close to their mothers so that they could be fed and protected from predators—but that they starved and were gobbled up, and therefore failed to pass their genes to future generations, if they strayed. Thus, chicks, ducks, and goslings may have evolved so that they engage in **imprinting,** an innate form of learning in which the young will follow and become attached to a moving object (usually the mother) during a critical period early in life.

Groundbreaking ethologist Konrad Lorenz (1937) observed imprinting in young goslings and noted that it is automatic (young fowl do not have to be taught to follow), it occurs only within a critical period shortly after the bird has hatched, and it is irreversible—once the gosling begins to follow a particular object, whether its mother or Lorenz, it will remain attached to the object. The imprinting response is a prime example of a species-specific and largely innate behavior that has evolved because it has survival value.

What about human infants? Babies may not become imprinted to their mothers, but they certainly follow their love objects around. Bowlby argued that they come equipped with several other behaviors besides following, or proximity seeking, that help ensure adults will love them, stay with them, and meet their needs. Among these behaviors are sucking and clinging, signals such as smiling and vocalizing (crying, cooing, and babbling), and expressions of negative emotion (fretting and crying). Moreover, just as infants are programmed to

Ethologist Konrad Lorenz demonstrated that goslings would become imprinted to him rather than to their mother if he was the first moving object they encountered during their critical period for imprinting. Human attachment is more complex.

respond to the sight, sound, and touch of their caregivers, Bowlby argued that adults are biologically programmed to respond to an infant's signals. It is difficult for an adult to ignore a baby's cry or fail to warm to a baby's grin. In short, both human infants and human caregivers have evolved in ways that predispose them to form close attachments, and this ensures that infants will receive the care, protection, and stimulation they need to survive and thrive.

Just as the imprinting of goslings occurs during a critical period, human attachments form during what Bowlby viewed as a sensitive period for attachment, the first 3 years of life. But attachments do not form automatically. According to Bowlby, the development of a normal attachment requires human genes and a normal human environment—the environment in which attachment behaviors evolved. How secure a particular attachment relationship is depends on the ongoing interaction between infant and caregiver and on the ability of each partner to respond to the other's signals. The infant's preprogrammed signals to other people may eventually wane if the caregiver is unresponsive to them. And infants must learn to react sensitively to their caregiver's signals and adjust their own behavior accordingly. So, Bowlby believed that humans are biologically prepared to form attachments during a sensitive period early in life, but he also stressed that a normal human environment and mutual learning between caregiver and infant are critical to the unfolding of a secure relationship.

Implications of Attachment

Bowlby maintained that the quality of the early parent–infant attachment has important effects on later development, including the kinds of relationships people have with friends, romantic partners, and their children. He proposed that, based on their interactions with caregivers, infants construct **internal working models**—cognitive representations of themselves and other people that shape their expectations about relationships and their processing of social information (Bowlby, 1973; see also Bretherton, 1996). Securely attached infants who have received responsive care will form internal working models suggesting that they are lovable individuals and that other people can be trusted to care for them. By contrast, insecurely attached infants subjected to insensitive, neglectful, or abusive care may conclude that they are difficult to love, that other people are unreliable, or both. These insecure infants would be expected to have difficulties in later interpersonal relationships. They may, for example, be wary of entering close relationships or become jealous and overly dependent if they do.

In sum, attachment theory, as developed by Bowlby and elaborated by Ainsworth, claims that (1) the capacity to form attachments is part of our evolutionary heritage; (2) attachments unfold through an interaction of biological and environmental forces during a sensitive period early in life; (3) the first attachment relationship, the one between infant and caregiver, shapes later development and the quality of later relationships; and (4) internal working models of self and other serve as the mechanism through which early experience affects later development.

Peers and the Two Worlds of Childhood

A **peer** is a social equal, someone who functions at a similar level of behavioral complexity—often someone of similar age (Lewis & Rosenblum, 1975). Although the parent–infant relationship is important in development, some theorists argue that relationships with peers are at least as significant. In effect, they argue, there are "two social worlds of childhood"—one involving adult–child relationships and the other involving peer relationships and a wider peer culture—and these two worlds contribute differently to development (Harris, 1998; Youniss, 1980). Consider the views of three believers in peer influence: Jean Piaget, Harry Stack Sullivan, and Judith Rich Harris.

Piaget

Jean Piaget (1965) observed that relationships with peers are different from relationships with parents. Because parents have more power than children do, children are in a subordinate position and must defer to adult authority. By contrast, two children have equal power and influence and must learn to appreciate each other's perspectives, to negotiate and compromise, and to cooperate with each other if they hope to get along. For this reason, Piaget believed that peers can make a unique contribution to social development that adult authority figures cannot make. Specifically, as you saw in Chapter 13, peer relations help children understand that relationships are reciprocal and force them to hone their role-taking skills.

Sullivan

Another theorist who believed that peer relationships contribute significantly to development was neo-Freudian Harry Stack Sullivan (1953; see also Buhrmester & Furman, 1986). He believed that interpersonal needs change as we age and that different needs are gratified through different kinds of social relationships. The parent–child relationship is central until about age 6; infants need tender care and nurturance from their parents, and preschool children need their parents to serve as playmates and companions. From about age 6 on, however, peers become increasingly important. Young elementary-school children need acceptance by the peer group so that they will have opportunities to learn social skills within the group.

From around age 9 to 12, children begin to need intimacy in the form of a close friendship. Sullivan placed special emphasis on the developmental significance of **chumships,** or close friendships with peers of the same sex that emerge around age 9. It is with their close chums, he believed, that children become capable of truly caring about another person and learn the importance of trust, loyalty, and honesty in relationships. Sullivan believed that a close chumship could do much to make up for any insecurities caused by a poor parent–child relationship or by a rejection by the peer group. Moreover, the lessons about intimacy learned in the context of same-sex chumships would then carry over to the intimate romantic relationships formed during adolescence and adulthood.

© BananaStock/PictureQuest

☾ Harry Stack Sullivan viewed chumships as a training ground for intimate relationships.

Harris

More recently, Judith Rich Harris (1995, 1998, 2000b has written a controversial and influential book arguing that peers are far more important than parents in shaping development. In *The Nurture Assumption,* Harris (1998) made this strong claim: "Children would develop into the same sort of adults if we left their lives outside the home unchanged and left them in their schools and their neighborhoods—but switched all the parents around" (Harris, 1998, p. 359). She cites the example of immigrant children, who readily learn the local culture and language from peers even though their parents come from a different culture and speak a different language.

Harris argues that parent influence is overrated, reviewing behavioral genetics research of the sort we introduced in Chapter 3 to say that genes contribute to virtually all aspects of human development, that a child's genes influence the parenting she receives, and that, whatever parents do to children, it does little to make different children growing up in the same home more alike in the long run. Many studies that conclude that parenting matters, she charges, do not take into account genetic influences and therefore cannot separate the effects of parental genes from the effects of parental behavior. Moreover, she says that even when parenting behaviors can be shown to affect children, they do so mainly in the home environment; learning rarely generalizes outside the home and beyond childhood.

Harris argues that most important socialization for the world outside the home takes place in peer groups and makes children from different families alike. Children figure out which social category they belong to based on age, sex, and other characteristics and then want to be like members of their social group. They adopt the norms of behavior that prevail in their peer group, learn by observing other children, and take on their attitudes, speech, dress styles, and behavior. When children later gravitate toward peers who are similar to themselves, their genetically based tendencies are magnified; the budding delinquent becomes more delinquent, and the studious child becomes more studious.

Many developmental scientists have reacted strongly to Harris's message, charging that she overstates her case and offers too little evidence that peers are more important than parents (Collins et al., 2000; Vandell, 2000). Moreover, they say, she overlooks solid evidence that, even when genetic influences are taken into account, parenting does matter, although often by making children in the same family different from one another rather than similar, and that intervening to change how parents treat children can change the course of development (Begley, 1998; Vandell, 2000; and see, for example, research on coercive family environments in Chapter 13). Despite such criticisms, Harris deserves credit for stimulating greater attention to peer-group influences and for challenging developmentalists to demonstrate more convincingly, thorough research designs that take genes into account, that parents in fact influence their children's development. Moreover, some recent research inspired by her ideas supports her argument; for example, unrelated pairs of 11- and 12-year-olds who grow up in the same schools, neighborhoods, and communities tend to be similar in their religious practices and their smoking and drinking habits (Rose et al., 2003).

Summing Up

Social relationships provide learning opportunities and social support (through our changing social convoys). Debates about the relative significance of parents and peers for later development continue to rage. Following in Freud's footsteps, Bowlby, the developer with Ainsworth of attachment theory, draws on ethological theory and Lorenz's work on imprinting to argue that caregiver–infant attachment evolved to ensure survival, develops through an interaction of nature and nurture during a sensitive period early in life, and results in internal working models of self and other that shape later personality and social development. By contrast, Piaget (with his emphasis on peers as equals), Sullivan (with his emphasis on changing interpersonal needs and the significance of childhood chumships), and Harris (with her argument that children are socialized by neighborhood peers) have argued that relationships with peers are at least as significant. This chapter should convince you that close relationships with both caregivers and peers are essential to healthy development across the life span. ■

The Infant

Human infants are social beings from the start, but their social relationships change dramatically once they form close attachments to caregivers and develop the social skills that allow them to coordinate their own activities with those of other infants. Because attachments are emotional ties that have many implications for emotional development, we begin by setting

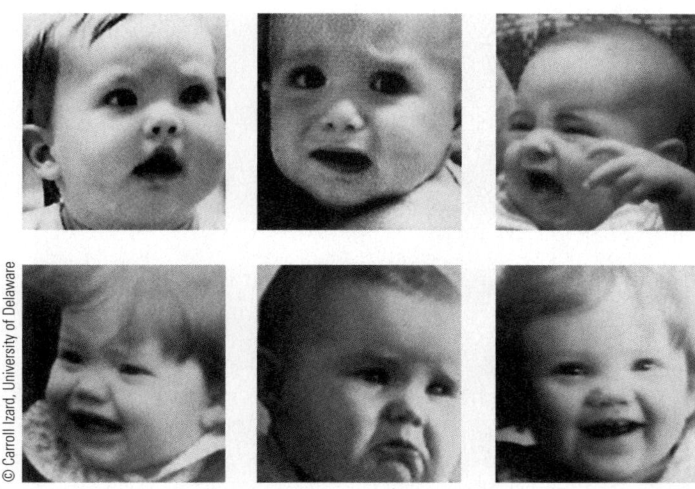

☾ Infants express a range of emotions.

the development of parent–infant attachment in the context of early emotional development.

Early Emotional Development

Carroll Izard (1982; Izard & Ackerman, 2000) and his colleagues maintain that basic emotions play critical roles in motivating and organizing behavior, and they have traced their early development. They have videotaped infants' responses to such events as grasping an ice cube, having a toy taken away, or seeing their mothers return after a separation. By analyzing specific facial movements (such as the raising of the brows and the wrinkling of the nose) and by asking raters to judge what emotion a baby's face reveals, Izard has established that very young infants express distinct emotions in response to different experiences and that adults can readily interpret which emotions they are expressing (see the photos on this page).

From Izard's work and that of others, we can piece together an account of the development of "primary" emotions (Lewis, 2000; also see Figure 14.1). At birth, babies show contentment, interest (by staring intently at objects), and distress (in response to pain or discomfort). Within the first 6 months, more specific emotions evolve from these three. By 3 months of age or so, contentment becomes joy, or excitement at the sight of something familiar such as Mom's face, and interest becomes surprise, such as when expectations are violated in games of peek-a-boo. Distress soon evolves into disgust (in response to foul-tasting foods) and sadness. Angry expressions appear as early as 4 months—about the time infants acquire enough control of their limbs to push unpleasant stimuli away. Fear makes its appearance as early as 5 months.

Next, as Figure 14.1 shows, come the so-called secondary or **self-conscious emotions.** These emotions, such as embarrassment, require an awareness of self and emerge around 18 months of age, when infants become able to recognize themselves in a mirror (see Chapter 11). At this age, they begin to show embarrassment when they are asked to perform for guests and empathy when a playmate breaks into tears (Lewis, 2000). Finally, when toddlers become able to judge their behavior against standards of performance, around age 2, they become capable of the self-conscious emotions of pride, shame, and guilt (Lewis, 2000).

Nature, Nurture, and Emotions

Primary emotions such as interest and fear seem to be biologically programmed. They emerge in all normal infants at roughly the same ages and are displayed and interpreted similarly in all cultures (Izard, 1982; Malatesta et al., 1989). The timing of their emergence is tied to cognitive maturation; for example, babies cannot fear strangers until they are able to represent mentally what familiar companions look like (Lewis, 2000). As Charles Darwin recognized long ago, basic emotions probably evolved in humans because they helped our ancestors appraise quickly and respond appropriately to novel stimuli and situations (Cole, Martin, & Dennis, 2004). Infants' emotional signals—whether expressions of joy or dis-

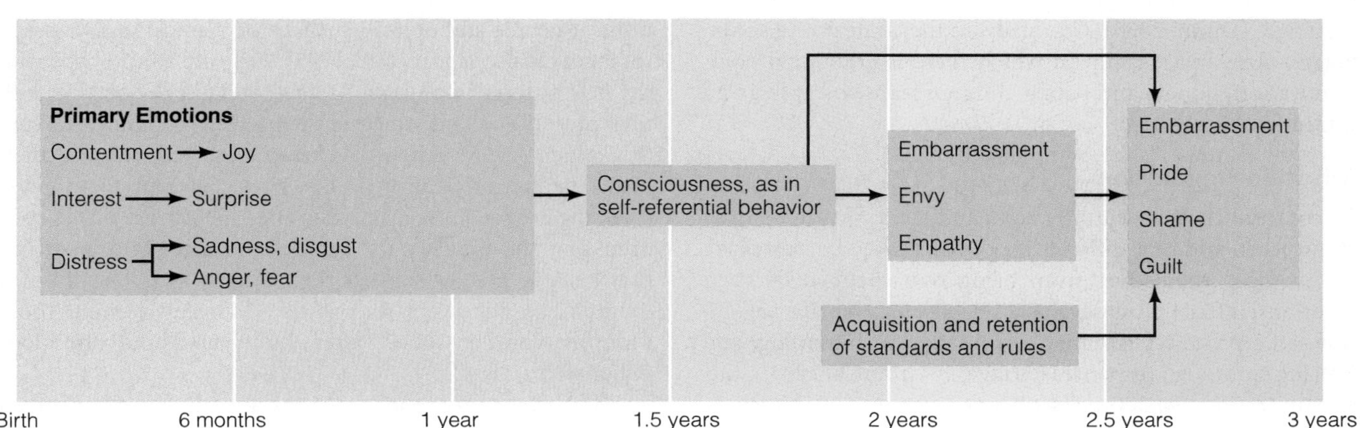

Figure 14.1 The emergence of different emotions. Primary emotions emerge in the first 6 months of life, secondary or self-conscious emotions emerge starting from about 18 months to 2 years.

SOURCE: Lewis (2000).

tress—help ensure that caregivers respond to them (Kopp & Neufield, 2003).

Whether an individual infant tends to be predominantly happy and eager to approach new stimuli, or he is irritable and easily distressed or angered, is influenced by his individual genetic makeup (Goldsmith, 2003). However, the studies that document genetic influence on temperamental qualities associated with emotional expression also reveal effects of the environment shared by siblings in the same family. This shows that nurture is also important in emotional development and that caregivers help shape an infant's predominant pattern of emotional expression.

Observational studies of face-to-face interactions between mothers and infants suggest that young infants display a range of positive and negative emotions, changing their expressions with lightning speed (once every 7 seconds) while their mothers do the same (Malatesta et al., 1986; Malatesta et al. 1989). Mothers mainly display interest, surprise, and joy, thus serving as models of positive emotions and eliciting positive emotions from their babies. What is more, mothers respond selectively to their babies' expressions; over the early months, they become increasingly responsive to their babies' expressions of happiness, interest, and surprise and less responsive to their negative emotions. Through basic learning processes, then, infants are trained to show a pleasant face more frequently and an unpleasant face less frequently—and they do just that over time. They are beginning to learn what emotional expressions mean in their sociocultural environment and which are socially acceptable (Sroufe, 1996; Saarni, 1999).

Toward the end of the first year, infants also begin to monitor their companions' emotional reactions in ambiguous situations and use this information to decide how they should feel and behave—a phenomenon called **social referencing** (Feinman, 1992). If their mothers are wary when a dog approaches, so are they; if their mothers pet a dog and smile, so may they. It is not just that 1-year-olds are imitating their parents' emotions; apparently they are able to understand what triggered these emotions and to regulate their behavior accordingly (Dunn, 2003). Gradually, in the context of a secure parent–child relationship in which there is emotional communication, infants and young children learn to express and understand emotions.

Emotion Regulation

To conform to their culture's rules and their caregiver's rules about when and how different emotions should be expressed, and to keep themselves from being overwhelmed by their emotions, infants must develop strategies for **emotion regulation**—the processes involved in initiating, maintaining, and altering emotional responses (Bridges & Grolnick, 1995; Cole, Martin, & Dennis, 2004; Eisenberg & Morris, 2002; Kopp & Neufield, 2003). Infants are active from the start in regulating their emotions, but at first they have only a few, simple emotion regulation strategies of their own and must rely heavily on caregivers to help them—for example, by stroking them gently or rocking them when they are distressed (Cole,

Parents help young infants develop emotion-regulation strategies

Michel, & Teti, 1994; Kopp, 1989). As infants age, and as they gain control of emotion regulation strategies first learned in the context of the parent–child relationship, they become increasingly capable of regulating their emotions on their own.

Very young infants are able to reduce their negative arousal by turning from unpleasant stimuli or by sucking vigorously on a pacifier (Mangelsdorf, Shapiro, & Marzolf, 1995). By the end of the first year, infants can also regulate their emotions by rocking themselves or, now that they are mobile, moving from upsetting events. They also actively seek attachment figures when they are upset because the presence of these individuals has a calming effect.

By 18 to 24 months, toddlers will try to control the actions of people and objects, such as mechanical toys, that upset them (Mangelsdorf et al., 1995). They are able to cope with the frustration of waiting for snacks and gifts by playing with toys and otherwise distracting themselves (Grolnick, Bridges, & Connell, 1996). They have been observed knitting their brows or compressing their lips in an attempt to suppress their anger or sadness (Malatesta et al., 1989). Finally, as children gain the capacity for symbolic thought and language, they become able to regulate their distress symbolically—for example, by repeating the words, "Mommy coming soon, Mommy coming soon," after Mom goes out the door (Thompson, 1994).

The development of emotions and the development of strategies for regulating emotions are closely intertwined with the development of attachment relationships (Bell & Calkins, 2000; Kopp & Neufield, 2003). Attachment figures play critical roles in helping infants regulate their emotions and in teaching them how to do so on their own. Attachment figures also arouse powerful emotions, positive and negative, that need to be controlled; infants can become uncomfortably overstimulated during joyful bouts of play with parents, and they can become highly distressed when their parents leave them. Finally, infants develop distinct styles of emotional expression designed to keep attachment figures close (Bridges & Grolnick, 1995). One infant may learn to suppress negative emotions such as fear and anger to avoid angering an irritable caregiver, whereas another may learn to scream loud and long to keep an unreliable caregiver close. Meanwhile, sensitive, responsive parenting is associated with low levels of fear, anger, and other negative emotions in infancy (Pauli-Pott, Mertesacker, & Beckmann, 2004). Clearly, emotions and emotion regulation develop in the context of attachment relationships and both affect and are affected by the quality of these and other relationships (Bell & Calkins, 2000).

An Attachment Forms

Like any relationship, the parent–infant attachment is reciprocal. Parents become attached to their infants, infants become attached to their parents, and the new relationship brings change.

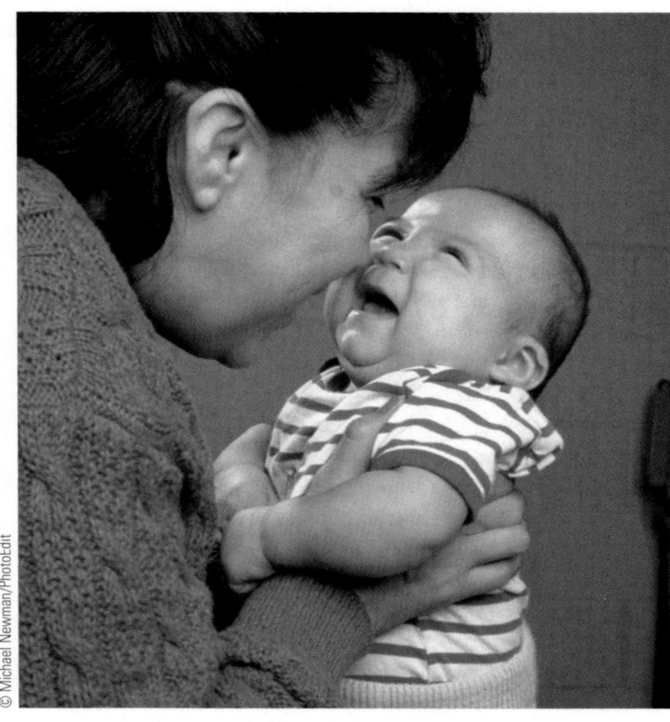

© Michael Newman/PhotoEdit

Smiling is one behavior that helps ensure adults will fall in love with babies.

The Caregiver's Attachment to the Infant

Parents often begin to form emotional attachments to their babies before birth. Mothers who have an opportunity for skin-to-skin contact with their babies during the first few hours after birth may feel a special bond forming (Klaus & Kennell, 1976). Studies of other primates suggest that the 2 or 3 weeks after birth is a sensitive period for bonding in which mothers are especially ready to respond to an infant; they will even adopt alien infants during this period, but not after it has passed, if they are separated from their own infants (Maestripieri, 2001). Moreover, premature human infants who have a daily session of skin-to-skin contact lying between their mothers' breasts while they are in the hospital nursery develop more rapidly neurologically, tolerate stress better, and later receive more sensitive parenting from their mothers and fathers than similar babies who do not receive this contact (Feldman & Eidelman, 2003; Feldman et al., 2003). Secure attachments can develop without such early contact, however, so it is neither crucial nor sufficient for the development of strong parent–infant attachments among humans.

What else helps an attachment form? Not only are babies cute, but their early reflexive behaviors such as sucking, rooting, and grasping help endear them to their parents (Bowlby, 1969). Smiling may be an especially important signal. Although it is initially a reflexive response to almost any stimulus, it is triggered by voices at 3 weeks of age and by faces at 5 or 6 weeks (Bowlby, 1969; Wolff, 1963). As soon as infants begin to coo and babble, their parents can enjoy "conversations" with them (Keller & Scholmerich, 1987; Stevenson et al., 1986).

Over the weeks and months, caregivers and infants develop **synchronized routines** much like dances, in which the partners take turns responding to each other's leads (Stern, 1977; Tronick, 1989). Note the synchrony as this mother plays peek-a-boo with her infant (Tronick, 1989, p. 112):

> The infant abruptly turns away from his mother as the game reaches its "peak" of intensity and begins to suck on his thumb and stare into space with a dull facial expression. The mother stops playing and sits back watching. . . . After a few seconds the infant turns back to her with an inviting expression. The mother moves closer, smiles, and says in a high-pitched, exaggerated voice, "Oh, now you're back!" He smiles in response and vocalizes. As they finish crowing together, the infant reinserts his thumb and looks away. The mother again waits. [Soon] the infant turns . . . to her and they greet each other with big smiles.

Smooth interactions like this are most likely to develop if caregivers limit their social stimulation to those periods when a baby is alert and receptive and avoid pushing things when the infant's message is "Cool it—I need a break from all this stimulation." Parents may have a difficult time establishing synchronized routines with irritable or unresponsive infants (Field, 1987). Moreover, some adults—for example, mothers suffering from depression—may have difficulty responding sensitively to their babies' signals (Hipwell et al., 2000; Stanley, Murray, & Stein, 2004). When synchrony in the vocalizations between parent and infant can be achieved, the likely outcome is a secure attachment relationship later in infancy (Jaffe et al., 2001).

In sum, infants play an active role in persuading adults to love them. Babies are physically appealing, have several reflexes that promote the formation of an attachment, and are highly responsive to people and capable of synchronizing their behavior with that of their "dance partners." As the caregiver and the infant perfect their interaction routines, the parent–infant attachment normally blossoms.

The Infant's Attachment to the Caregiver

Infants need time before they are developmentally ready to form attachments. They progress through the following phases (Ainsworth, 1973; Bowlby, 1969):

1. *Undiscriminating social responsiveness (birth to 2 or 3 months).* Very young infants are responsive to voices, faces, and other social stimuli, but any human interests them. They do not yet show a clear preference for one person over another.

2. *Discriminating social responsiveness (2 or 3 months to 6 or 7 months).* Infants begin to express preferences for familiar companions. They are likely to direct their biggest grins and most enthusiastic babbles toward those companions, although they are still friendly toward strangers.

3. *Active proximity seeking or true attachment (6 or 7 months to about 3 years).* Around 6 or 7 months, infants form their first clear attachments, most often to their mothers. Now able to crawl, an infant will follow her mother to stay close, protest when her mother leaves, and greet her mother warmly when she returns. Within weeks after forming their first attachments, most infants become attached to other people as well—fathers, siblings, grandparents, and regular baby-sitters (Schaffer & Emerson, 1964). By 18 months, few infants are attached to only one person, and some are attached to several.

4. *Goal-corrected partnership (3 years and older).* By about age 3, partly because they have more advanced social cognitive abilities, children can take a parent's goals and plans into consideration and adjust their behavior to achieve the all-important goal of maintaining optimal proximity to the attachment figure. Thus, a 1-year-old cries and tries to follow when Dad leaves the house to talk to a neighbor, whereas a 4-year-old probably understands where Dad is going and can control the need for his attention until he returns. The child capable of symbolic thinking can also maintain proximity symbolically—conjuring up a mental representation of the parent, possibly even imagining the reassuring things Mom might do or say to provide comfort. To participate in a goal-corrected partnership, children need to understand other people's needs and intentions, using their emerging theories of mind (see Chapter 13), and they need skills in communication and cooperation (Kobak & Esposito, 2004). This final, partnerlike phase of attachment lasts a lifetime.

Attachment-Related Fears

Infants no sooner experience the pleasures of love than they discover the agonies of fear. One form of fear, **separation anxiety,** is an important sign that an attachment has formed. Once attached to a parent, babies often become wary or fretful when separated from that parent and will follow the parent to try to avoid separation. Separation anxiety normally appears when infants are forming their first genuine attachments, peaks between 14 and 18 months, and gradually becomes less frequent and less intense throughout infancy and the preschool period (Weinraub & Lewis, 1977). Still, even children and adolescents may become homesick and distressed when separated from their parents for a long time (Thurber, 1995).

A second fearful response that often emerges shortly after an infant becomes attached to someone is **stranger anxiety**—a wary or fretful reaction to the approach of an unfamiliar person (Schaffer & Emerson, 1964). Anxious reactions to strangers—often mixed with signs of interest—become common between 8 and 10 months, continue through the first year, and gradually decline in intensity over the second year (Sroufe, 1996). The Explorations box on page 393 describes the circumstances under which stranger anxiety is most and least likely to occur and suggests how baby-sitters and health-care professionals can head off outbreaks of fear and trembling.

Exploratory Behavior

The formation of a strong attachment to a caregiver has another important consequence: It facilitates exploratory behavior. Ainsworth and her colleagues (1978) emphasized that an attachment figure serves as a **secure base** for exploration—a point of safety from which an infant can feel free to venture and to which she can return if frightened. Thus Wendy, a securely attached infant visiting a neighbor's home with Mom, may be comfortable cruising the living room as long as she can check occasionally to see that Mom is still on the couch but may freeze and fret if Mom disappears into the bathroom. Infants apparently need to rely on another person to feel confident about acting independently.

The Quality of the Attachment

Ainsworth made her most notable contribution to attachment theory by devising a way to assess differences in the quality of parent–infant attachments, thereby making Bowlby's psychoanalytic hypotheses testable (Thompson & Raikes, 2003; Weinfield et al., 1999). She and her associates created the **Strange Situation,** a now-famous procedure for measuring the quality of an attachment (Ainsworth et al., 1978). It consists of eight episodes that gradually escalate the amount of stress infants experience as they react to the approach of an adult stranger and the departure and return of their caregiver (see Table 14.1). On the basis of an infant's pattern of behavior across the episodes, the quality of his attachment to a parent can be characterized as one of four types: secure, resistant, avoidant, or disorganized–disoriented.

1. **Secure attachment.** About 60 to 65% of 1-year-olds in our society are securely attached to their mothers (Colin, 1996). The securely attached infant actively explores the room when alone with his mother because she serves as a secure base. The infant may be upset by separation but greets his mother warmly and is comforted by her presence when she returns. The securely attached child is outgoing with a stranger when his mother is present.

Explorations

Tips for Baby-Sitters Trying to Prevent Stranger Anxiety

It is not unusual for 1- or 2-year-olds meeting a new baby-sitter or being approached by a nurse or doctor at the doctor's office to break into tears and cling to their parents. Stranger-wary infants often stare at the stranger for a moment then turn away, whimper, and seek the comfort of their parents. Occasionally, infants become terrified and highly upset. Obviously, it is in the interests of baby-sitters and other "strangers" to be able to prevent such negative reactions. What might we suggest?

- *Keep familiar companions available.* Stranger anxiety is less likely to occur if an attachment figure is nearby to serve as a secure base. In one study, less than one-third of 6- to 12-month-olds were wary of an approaching stranger when they were seated on their mothers' laps (Morgan & Ricciuti, 1969). Yet about two-thirds of these infants frowned, turned away, whimpered, or cried if they were seated only 4 feet from their mothers. Baby-sitters would do well to insist that parents be present when they first meet the children they will tend. A security blanket or beloved stuffed animal can have much the same calming effect as a parent's presence for some infants (Passman, 1977).
- *Arrange for the infant's companions to respond positively to you.* As you have seen, infants about 9 months or older engage in social referencing, using other people's emotional reactions to guide their own responses to a situation. By implication, infants are likely to respond more favorably to a stranger's approach if their mothers or fathers greet the stranger warmly than if parents react neutrally or negatively toward the stranger.
- *Make the setting more "familiar."* Stranger anxiety is less likely to occur in familiar settings than in unfamiliar ones (Sroufe, Waters, & Matas, 1974). Stranger anxiety should be less severe if the baby-sitter comes to the child's home than if the child is taken to the baby-sitter's home or some other unfamiliar place. Yet an unfamiliar environment can become a familiar one if infants are given the time to get used to it, especially with their parents available as a secure base. L. Alan Sroufe and his colleagues (1974) found that more than 90% of 10-month-olds became upset if a stranger approached within 1 minute after they had been placed in an unfamiliar room. Only 50% did so when they were given 10 minutes to become accustomed to the room.
- *Be a sensitive, unobtrusive stranger.* Encounters with a stranger are likely to go best if the stranger initially keeps her distance and then approaches slowly while smiling, talking, and offering a familiar toy or suggesting a familiar activity (Bretherton, Stolberg, & Kreye, 1981; Sroufe, 1977). It also helps if the stranger, like any sensitive caregiver, takes her cues from the infant (Mangelsdorf, 1992). Babies prefer strangers they can control. Intrusive strangers who approach quickly and force themselves on infants (for example, by picking them up before they have time to adjust) probably get what they deserve.
- *Try not to look any stranger than you must.* Finally, infants are most likely to be afraid of people who violate their mental schemas or expectations (Kagan, 1972). Baby-sitters who have unusual physical features such as beards or Mohawks or who dress in unusual outfits elicit more wariness than those who resemble the people infants encounter every day. Baby-sitters who favor the latest faddish dress might try to make themselves more readily recognizable as members of the human race.

Table 14.1 The Episodes of the Strange Situation

Episode	Events	Attachment Behavior Observed
1	Experimenter leaves parent and baby to play	
2	Parent sits while baby plays	Use of parent as secure base
3	Stranger enters, talks to parent	Stranger anxiety
4	Parent leaves; stranger lets baby play, offers comfort if needed	Separation anxiety
5	Parent returns, greets baby, offers comfort if needed; stranger leaves	Reactions to reunion
6	Parent leaves	Separation anxiety
7	Stranger enters, offers comfort	Stranger anxiety; ability to be soothed by stranger
8	Parent returns, greets baby, offers comfort, lets baby return to play	Reactions to reunion

SOURCE: Based on Ainsworth et al., 1978.

2. Resistant attachment. About 10% of 1-year-olds show a resistant attachment, an insecure attachment characterized by anxious, ambivalent reactions. The resistant infant is anxious and often does not venture off to play even when his mother is present, which suggests that she does not serve as a secure base for exploration. Yet this infant becomes distressed when his mother departs, often showing more separation anxiety than the securely attached infant—perhaps because he is uncertain whether his mother will return. When his mother returns, the infant is ambivalent: He may try to remain near his mother but seems to resent her for having left, may resist if she tries to make physical contact, and may even hit and kick her in anger (Ainsworth et al., 1978). Resistant infants are also wary of strangers, even when their mothers are present. It seems, then, that resistant or ambivalent infants want affection and work hard to get the attention of their caregiver because they are never sure it will be forthcoming.

3. Avoidant attachment. Infants with avoidant attachments (about 15% of 1-year-olds) seem uninterested in exploring, show little distress when separated from their mothers, and avoid contact when their mothers return. These insecurely attached infants are not particularly wary of strangers but sometimes avoid or ignore them in much the same way that they avoid or ignore their mothers. Avoidant infants, then, seem to have distanced themselves from their parents, almost as if they were denying their need for affection or had learned not to express their emotional needs. Whereas the attachment system of the resistantly attached infant is hyperactivated, always alert to threats and ready to seek proximity to the attachment figure, the attachment system of the avoidantly attached infant is deactivated (Mikulincer & Shaver, 2003).

4. Disorganized–disoriented attachment. Ainsworth's work initially focused on secure, resistant, and avoidant attachment styles. Some infants do not develop any of these coherent ways of coping with their need for proximity to their caregiver when they are stressed. Up to 15% of infants—more in high-risk families—display what is now recognized as a fourth attachment classification, one that seems to be associated with later emotional problems (Atkinson & Goldberg, 2004; van IJzendoorn, Schuengel, & Bakermans-Kranenburg, 1999). Disorganized–disoriented attachment has features of both the resistant and the avoidant styles and reflects confusion about whether to approach or avoid the parent (Main & Solomon, 1990). Reunited with their mothers after a separation, these infants may act dazed and freeze or lie on the floor immobilized or they may seek contact but then abruptly move away as their mothers approach them, only to seek contact again. Unlike secure, resistant, or avoidant infants, infants with a disorganized–disoriented attachment have not been able to devise a coherent strategy for regulating negative emotions such as separation anxiety; they seem frightened of their parent and stuck between approaching and avoiding this frightening figure (Hesse & Main, 2000).

Table 14.2 summarizes the features of these four patterns of attachment, which have been the subject of considerable research. What determines which of these attachment patterns will characterize a parent–infant relationship? Early studies of the quality of attachments focused almost entirely on the qualities of caregivers that make infants form secure attachments to them, but we now know that infants also contribute to the attachment bond.

The Caregiver's Contributions

According to Freud, infants in the oral stage of psychosexual development become attached to the individual who provides them with oral pleasure, and the attachment bond will be most secure if a mother is relaxed and generous in her feeding practices. Early learning theorists put it differently but also believed that an infant learns positive emotional responses to her mother by associating her with food. In a classic study conducted by Harry Harlow and Robert Zimmerman (1959), the psychoanalytic and learning theory views dominant at the time were tested. Monkeys were reared with two surrogate mothers: a wire "mother" and a cloth "mother" wrapped in foam rubber and covered with terrycloth (see the photo on page 395). Half the infants were fed by the cloth mother, and the remaining infants were fed by the wire mother. To which mother did these infants become attached? There was no contest: Infants strongly preferred the cuddly cloth mother, regardless of which mother had fed them. Even if their food came from the wire mother, they spent more time clinging to the cloth mother, ran to her when they were upset or afraid, and showed every sign of being attached to her.

Table 14.2 Child Behaviors Associated with Attachment Styles in the Strange Situation Test and Related Parenting Styles

	Type of Attachment			
Child Behavior	**Secure**	**Resistant**	**Avoidant**	**Disorganized–Disoriented**
Explores when caregiver is present to provide a secure base for exploration?	Yes, actively	No, clings	Yes, but play is not as constructive as that of secure infant	No
Responds positively to stranger?	Yes, comfortable if caregiver is present	No, fearful even when caregiver is present	No, often indifferent, as with caregiver	No, confused responses
Protests when separated from caregiver?	Yes, at least mildly distressed	Yes, extremely upset	No, seemingly unfazed	Sometimes; unpredictable
Responds positively to caregiver at reunion?	Yes, happy to be reunited	Yes and no, seeks contact, but resents being left; ambivalent, sometimes angry	No, ignores or avoids caregiver	Confused; may approach or avoid caregiver or do both
Parenting Style	Sensitive, responsive	Inconsistent, often unresponsive (e.g., depressed)	Rejecting–unresponsive or intrusive–overly stimulating	Frightening (e.g., abusive) or frightened (e.g., overwhelmed)

Harlow's research demonstrated what he called **contact comfort,** or the pleasurable tactile sensations provided by a soft and cuddly "parent," is a more powerful contributor to attachment in monkeys than feeding or the reduction of hunger. Research with humans also contradicts Freud's view. Not only does contact comfort promote human attachments (Anisfeld et al., 1990), but many infants also become attached to someone other than the adult who feeds them, and variations in feeding schedules and the age at which infants are weaned have little effect on the quality of infants' attachments (Schaffer & Emerson, 1964).

We also know a great deal about the styles of parenting associated with each of the types of attachment characterized in Table 14.2. Infants who enjoy *secure* attachments to their parents have parents who are sensitive and responsive to their needs and emotional signals (Ainsworth et al., 1978; De Wolff & van IJzendoorn, 1997). These parents are good at reading and empathizing with their children's feelings (Oppenheim, Koren-Karie, & Sagi, 2001).

Babies who show a *resistant* pattern of attachment often have parents who are inconsistent in their caregiving; they react enthusiastically or indifferently, depending on their moods, and are frequently unresponsive (Isabella, 1993; Isabella & Belsky, 1991). Mothers who are depressed, for example, often have difficulty responding sensitively to their babies' signals and do not provide the comforting that helps babies regulate their negative emotions (Dawson & Ashman, 2000). The infant copes with unreliable caregiving by trying desperately—through clinging, crying, and other attachment behaviors—to obtain emotional support and comfort, and then becomes saddened and resentful when these efforts fail.

The parents of infants with an *avoidant* attachment tend to provide either too little or too much stimulation. Some are rejecting; they are impatient, unresponsive to the infant's signals, and resentful when the infant interferes with their plans (Ainsworth, 1979; Isabella, 1993). Other parents of infants with avoidant attachments have been called "intrusive"; they are overzealous and provide high levels of stimulation even when their babies become uncomfortably aroused and need a break so that they can regulate their emotions (Isabella &

The wire and cloth surrogate "mothers" used in Harry Harlow's research. This infant monkey has formed an attachment to the cloth mother that provides contact comfort even though it must stretch to the wire mother to feed.

Belsky, 1991; Swanson, Beckwith, & Howard, 2000). Infants with an avoidant attachment style may be responding adaptively by learning to avoid and make few emotional demands on adults who seem to dislike their company or who bombard them with stimulation they cannot handle.

Finally, a *disorganized–disoriented* style of attachment is evident in as many as 80% of infants who have been physically abused or maltreated (Carlson et al., 1989). It is also common among infants whose mothers are severely depressed or abuse alcohol and drugs and may, as a result, mistreat or neglect their babies (Beckwith, Rozga, & Sigman, 2002). The parents of infants with a disorganized attachment pattern have often suffered a loss or trauma and have unresolved feelings about it (Green & Goldwyn, 2002). They have been described as either frightening or frightened—as either hostile and intrusive individuals who provide a chaotic experience to their infants or fragile and fearful adults who are not up to the challenge of interacting with an infant (Lyons-Ruth et al., 2004; True, Pisani, & Ourmar, 2001). Infants with a disorganized attachment are understandably confused about whether to approach or avoid a parent who is loving one minute but angry and abusive or indifferent the next.

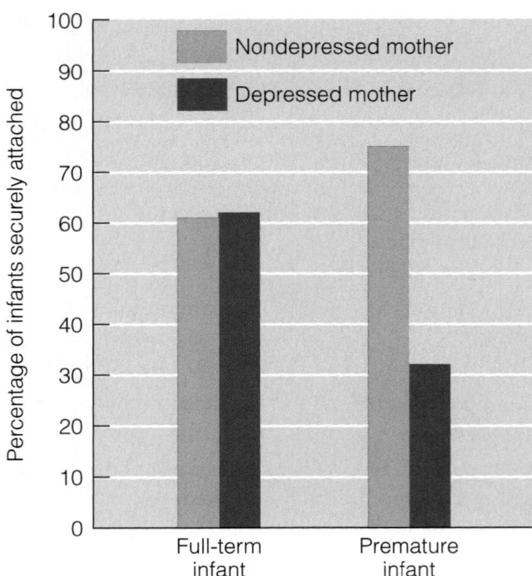

Figure 14.2 The combination of a depressed mother and a premature infant means low odds that a secure attachment will form.
SOURCE: Data from Poehlmann & Fiese (2001).

The Infant's Contributions

Clearly, the ways in which parents interact with their babies relate in predictable ways to the quality of the attachments that form. The infant's characteristics also have a bearing. Cognitive developmental theorists emphasize that the ability to form attachments depends partly on the infant's cognitive development. For example, the infant must recognize that close companions continue to exist even when they are absent to experience separation anxiety when a caregiver leaves the room (Kohlberg, 1969; Lester et al., 1974). That is, infants will not form attachments until they have acquired some concept of person permanence, a form of the object permanence concept studied by Jean Piaget and described in Chapter 7, which allows an infant to appreciate that an object still exists when it is removed from view. Person permanence, in turn, will not develop until infants undergo the brain growth that allows them to retrieve information from the recent past and compare it with the present (Kagan, 2003). An infant with neurological problems may therefore have difficulty forming a secure attachment (Cox, Hopkins, & Hans, 2000).

An infant's temperament also has an effect: An attachment is less likely to be secure if the infant is by temperament fearful, irritable, or unresponsive (Beckwith et al., 2002). Which has a stronger bearing on the quality of the attachment, then—the caregiver's style of parenting or the infant's temperament? Both are significant, and the two sometimes interact. To illustrate, Figure 14.2 shows the percentages of 12-month-olds who tested as securely attached as a function of whether they were difficult-to-read infants born prematurely and whether their mothers were depressed (Poehlmann & Fiese, 2001). Only when a depressed mother was coupled with a hard-to-read, premature infant did the odds of a secure attachment become low. Similarly, the combination of a mother with a low sense of self-efficacy as a parent and an infant with colic who cries endlessly makes for an insecure attachment (Stifter, 2003). Such findings point to the value of identifying and intervening to help parent–infant pairs in which both parent and child have characteristics associated with insecure attachments.

Overall, the caregiver's behavior has more to do with whether or not a secure attachment forms than do characteristics of the infant (Goldberg et al., 1986; Vaughn et al., 1989). If the infant's temperament were the main influence on security of attachment, we would not see so many infants securely attached to one parent but insecurely attached to the other (van IJzendoorn & De Wolff, 1997). Finally, even temperamentally difficult babies are likely to establish secure relationships with caregivers who are patient and adjust their caregiving to the baby's temperamental quirks (Mangelsdorf et al., 1990; van IJzendoorn et al., 1992). These findings are consistent with the goodness of fit model introduced in Chapter 11: Secure bonds evolve when parents can respond sensitively to whatever temperamental characteristics their babies display, whereas insecure bonds are more likely when there is a mismatch between caregiving style and infant temperament (Sroufe, 1985).

Contextual Contributors

In addition, the broader social context surrounding caregiver and infant can affect how they react to each other. For example, the stresses associated with living in poverty or experiencing marital difficulties may make it difficult for parents to be responsive to their babies and may therefore result in insecure attachments (Howes & Markman, 1989; Murray et al., 1996). The cultural context in which caregiver and baby interact also colors their relationship (Rogoff, 2003). For instance, German parents strongly encourage independence and discourage clingy behavior, which may explain why German infants are more likely than infants in many other societies to ignore or avoid their parents when they are reunited after a separation and why many of them are therefore classified as avoidantly attached when given the Strange Situation test (Grossmann et al., 1985). The Strange Situation may underestimate the number of securely attached infants in this culture. It may similarly underestimate the security of attachment of U.S. babies who regularly receive nonmaternal care and who therefore are rarely bothered by separations (Clarke-Stewart, Goossens, & Allhusen, 2001). By contrast, Japanese babies, who, like babies in many parts of the world, are rarely separated from their mothers early in life, become distressed by separations such as those they must endure in the Strange Situation. They are more likely than American babies to be classified as resistant as a result, but this does not suggest that they are maladjusted (Takahashi, 1990; van IJzendoorn & Sagi, 1999).

Could this mean that research on infant attachment is culturally biased? Fred Rothbaum and his colleagues (Rothbaum, Weisz et al., 2000) think so. They observe that in Western, *individualistic cultures,* optimal development means becoming an autonomous being, whereas in Eastern, *collectivist cultures,* such as Japan, the goal is to become integrated into the group. Instead of encouraging exploration, Japanese parents keep their infants in close contact and encourage them to be dependent. Understandably, these infants become upset when separated from their mothers in the Strange Situation. Most Japanese infants are probably securely attached when judged by their own culture's standards, Rothbaum argues. Some think he overstates the case and note that many predictions of attachment theory hold up in a variety of cultures (Posada & Jacobs, 2001). Still, characteristics of the caregiver, the baby, and the surrounding social environment all affect the quality of the emerging attachment, and what represents an adaptive attachment relationship in one culture may not be viewed as such in another.

Implications of Early Attachment

From Freud on, almost everyone has assumed that the parent–child relationship is critical in shaping human development. Just how important is it? Two lines of research offer some answers: studies of socially deprived infants and studies of the later development of securely and insecurely attached infants.

Japanese infants become anxious in the Strange Situation because they are rarely separated from their mothers.

Effects of Social Deprivation

What becomes of babies (like Baby Jessica described at the start of the chapter) who are separated from their caregivers as a result of illness, death, or other unforeseen circumstances? Worse yet, what happens to infants who never have an opportunity to form an attachment bond?

The daily separations from their parents that infants who attend day care facilities experience are unlikely to keep them from forming or maintaining close relationships with their parents. As the Explorations box on page 398 illustrates, day care can have positive or negative effects on child development, depending on several factors, and generally has a bit of both but normally does not damage development.

Infants who experience long-term separations from caregivers go through a grieving process but normally recover once they are reunited with their loved one, and infants who are permanently separated from a caregiver recover if they are able to maintain or form an attachment with someone else (Bowlby, 1960, 1980; Colin, 1996; and see Chapter 17). By contrast, infants who experience a series of such separations from caregivers or are moved from foster home to foster home may be permanently marred by their experiences of loving and losing. They sometimes even withdraw from human relationships (Bowlby, 1980; Colin, 1996).

It is better to have loved and lost, however, than never to have loved at all, say studies of infants who grow up in deprived institutional settings and never form attachments (Goldfarb, 1943, 1947; MacLean, 2003; Rutter & O'Connor, 2004). In the 1990s, children from deprived institutions in Romania were adopted into homes in the United States, the United Kingdom, and Canada after the fall of the Romanian government in 1990 (Gunnar, Bruce, & Grotevant, 2000). These adoptees reportedly spent their infancies in orphanages with 20 to 30 children in a room and only one caregiver for every 10 to 20 children; they spent most of their time rocking in their cribs with little human contact, much less hugs, bouts of play, and synchronous routines (L. Fisher et al., 1997). How have they turned out?

Infants who spent 8 months or more in deprived orphanages displayed eating problems and medical problems; many were withdrawn and seemed overwhelmed in interactions with their new siblings and peers (Fisher et al., 1997). For a substantial number, physical, cognitive, and social–emotional development were compromised (Gunnar et al., 2000; MacLean, 2003). Rapid recovery was evident once the children were adopted, however. In one study, 61% of the infants and young children were developmentally delayed in three or four areas tested when their adoptive parents first met them, but only 8% were still delayed in three or four areas 6 months later (Judge, 2003). Some formerly institutionalized children overcame their developmental problems entirely, and yet many of those institutionalized for more than 6 months never achieved

Explorations

Is Day Care Good for Infant Development?

© Owen Franken/CORBIS

With more than 60% of mothers in the United States working outside the home at least part-time, questions have naturally arisen about the effects of care outside the home on infant and child development. According to U.S. Department of Labor statistics, only about 30% of infants of working mothers are cared for by their parents; 30% are tended by a relative, 20% are in day care homes (typically run by a woman who takes a few children into her own home for payment), 10% are in large day care centers, and a small percentage are with nonrelatives in the child's home (Pungello & Kurtz-Costes, 1999).

Do infants who attend day care homes or centers suffer compared with infants who stay at home with a parent? Research suggests that they are not usually damaged by the experience but that the effects of day care depend on many factors (Clarke-Stewart, 1993; Scarr & Eisenberg, 1993). In a major longitudinal study conducted by teams of researchers in 10 cities in the United States, infants were assessed at 1, 6, 15, 24, 36, and 54 months of age (NICHD Early Child Care Research Network, 1997, 2003b). Efforts were made to control for child characteristics such as initial cognitive and language ability and social competence, as well as for family characteristics such as mother's education and quality of parenting, in assessing the effects of day care on development.

Infants receiving alternative forms of care were no less securely attached to their mothers overall than infants tended by their parents. A mother's sensitivity to her infant had a lot more to do with attachment security than whether or not an infant was in alternative care. Moreover, under some circumstances, high-quality day care made up for the negative effects of insensitive parenting.

Findings from the National Institute of Child Health and Human Development (NICHD) study are mixed regarding other aspects of development: Although children who spent a good deal of time in day care performed better than home-reared children on some measures of cognitive and language skills, spending many hours in day care also tended to be associated with higher levels of behavioral problems and conflicts with adults (NICHD Early Child Care Research Network, 2002a, 2003a). And although children who have more experience with peers in day care appear to interact adeptly with those peers in the day care setting, they are not more socially skilled than children who lack this experience in observed play with a friend, and their parents perceive them as behaving negatively in their interactions with playmates (NICHD Early Child Care Research Network, 2001a).

The most important message of research on day care is that some children do better in day care than others. Consider a few factors that influence how well infants adjust:

- *Quality of the day care.* Just as some parents are highly nurturant and others are neglecting or abusive, some day care experiences are more beneficial than at-home care and others are dreadful. An infant's development

normal levels of cognitive development, possibly because they lacked the intellectual stimulation necessary for normal brain development during infancy (Rutter & O'Connor, 2004). Generally, the longer children had experienced deprivation, the more likely they were to experience long-term difficulties.

Continuing problems in the area of interpersonal relationships were evident, too (Gunnar, et al., 2000; Rutter & O'Connor, 2004). These children have proved more likely than most infants to display abnormal patterns of attachment and social behavior, being emotionally withdrawn, indiscriminately friendly, or both (Smyke, Dumitrescu, & Zeanah, 2002; Zeanah, 2000). Thomas O'Connor and his colleagues (2003) compared attachment quality at age 4 among children who started their lives in deprived institutions in Romania and were adopted into British homes (either before 6 months or between 6 and 24 months of age) with British children adopted before 6 months of age. As Figure 14.3 shows, the longer the Romanian children had experienced early deprivation, the less likely they were to be securely attached and the more likely they were to show an abnormal pattern of insecure behavior that O'Connor and his associates called *disinhibited attachment.*

The children with a disinhibited attachment pattern were not very selective or discriminating in their responses to different adults. Many were indiscriminately friendly toward both a stranger and their parent in a Strange Situation test.

clearly will suffer if he ends up with an alcoholic baby-sitter or must compete for adult attention as one of many infants in a large, understaffed center. Good developmental outcomes are likely in high-quality day care that has a reasonable child-to-caregiver ratio (up to three infants, four toddlers, or eight preschoolers per adult); caregivers who have been educated for their roles and who are warm, emotionally expressive, and responsive to children; little staff turnover so that children can feel comfortable with and become attached to their caregivers; and planned, age-appropriate activities (Burchinal et al., 2000; Clarke-Stewart, 1993; Howes, Phillips, & Whitebrook, 1992). The NICHD study indicates that the extent to which his day care setting provides high-quality cognitive stimulation (for example, lots of language stimulation from caregivers, less time watching TV, and a stimulating physical environment) is linked to a child's cognitive functioning at age $4\frac{1}{2}$, even with characteristics of children and their parents controlled (NICHD Early Child Care Research Network, 2003b).

- *Characteristics of the child.* Some infants fare better in alternative care than others do. First, infants from disadvantaged homes experience faster intellectual growth if they attend a high-quality day care program specially designed to meet their needs than if they stay at home and receive little intellectual stimulation (Campbell & Ramey, 1994; Love et al., 2003). Second, girls tend to adapt better to day care than boys (Baydar & Brooks-Gunn, 1991; Belsky & Rovine, 1988). Third, infants and toddlers with easy temperaments are likely to adjust better than children who have difficult or slow-to-warm-up temperaments (Belsky & Rovine, 1988).
- *Parents' attitudes and behaviors.* The outcomes of day care placement are likely to be better if a mother has positive attitudes about working and about being a mother and if she has the personal qualities it takes to provide warm and sensitive care (Belsky & Rovine, 1988; Crockenberg & Litman, 1991). The quality of parenting that infants receive at home has far more to do with their development than the kind of alternative care they receive when they are not at home (NICHD Early Child Care Research Network, 2002b).

Most important of all may be interactions between some of these factors that suggest day care is good under some circumstances but not under others. In the NICHD (1997) study, for example, infants fared poorly if their mothers were not sensitive and responsive to them and if they were subjected to poor-quality day care; under these circumstances, about half of the infants were insecurely attached to their mothers. By contrast, infants who received high-quality care somewhere, either at home or at day care, were usually securely attached. Similarly, the combination of maternal insensitivity and many hours per week spent in day care is associated with insecure attachment (NICHD Early Child Care Research Network, 2001b).

In sum, you cannot draw simple conclusions about the effects of alternative care on infant development. Infants and young children who receive day care are, on average, not much different physically, cognitively, socially, or emotionally from infants and young children cared for at home. However, the effects of day care on specific children can range from growth-enhancing to harmful and are likely to be best when children interact with both responsive substitute caregivers and responsive parents.

They would eagerly approach the stranger in a coy or silly manner but then back off warily (rather than showing the normal pattern of wariness first and approach second). They were unable to regulate their emotions well enough to participate in a real, reciprocal social interaction. Interviews with their adoptive parents revealed that these children sometimes went off with a stranger in a new situation without ever checking back with the parent. Avoidant, resistant, and even disorganized attachments were rare among these previously institutionalized children. Although some of them had clearly formed secure attachments to their adoptive parents, the abnormal, disinhibited pattern of attachment was evident in half of the children deprived for more than 6 months.

Why does institutional deprivation have such damaging effects on development? Lack of proper nutrition, hygiene, and medical care; lack of stimulation; and lack of stable attachment relationships may all contribute (Gunnar et al., 2000). The deficits are probably not entirely caused by lack of sensory and intellectual stimulation; institutionalized children who are provided with such stimulation but lack a stable team of caregivers are still developmentally delayed and have emotional difficulties even as adolescents (Hodges & Tizard, 1989). Nor is the problem lack of a single "mother figure." In adequately staffed institutions in the People's Republic of China and Israel, infants cared for by a few responsive caregivers turn out quite normal (Kessen, 1975; Oppenheim, Sagi,

Infants do not develop normally if they lack continuing relationships with responsive caregivers—whether one or several.

& Lamb, 1988). We even know that institutionalized toddlers who receive care from a small number of caregivers are less likely to show abnormal attachment patterns than similar institutionalized toddlers who have many caregivers (Smyke et al., 2002). Apparently, then, normal development requires sustained interactions with responsive caregivers—whether one or a few.

On the one hand, then, studies of children from deprived institutions reveal that children have a good deal of resilience, provided that they are given reasonable opportunities to socialize and to find someone to love; on the other hand, they support Freud and Bowlby's view that early social experiences can have lasting effects on development.

Later Development of Securely and Insecurely Attached Infants

How much difference does having secure or insecure attachment to caregivers in infancy make later in life? According to Bowlby and Ainsworth's attachment theory, a secure attachment allows exploration from a secure base. This implies that securely attached children should be more cognitively competent (because they will be curious, explore the environment freely, and not shy from challenges) and more socially competent (because they will explore the world of people freely, expect positive reactions from others because of the positive internal working models they form, and have learned in the parent–child relationship how to interact smoothly with others). Does research support these predictions?

Indeed it does. In an early longitudinal study, Everett Waters and his associates (Waters, Wippman, & Sroufe, 1979) measured the quality of infants' attachments to their mothers at 15 months then observed these children in nursery school at 3 years. Children who had been securely attached as infants were more socially competent in the nursery-school setting than children who had been insecurely attached: They often initiated play activities, were sensitive to the needs and feelings of other children, and were popular with their peers (see also Clark & Ladd, 2000; Schneider, Atkinson, & Tardif, 2001). Securely attached infants also became children whom teachers described as curious, self-directed, and eager to learn, whereas insecurely attached children, lacking a secure base for exploration, were less independent.

Quality of attachment in infancy is also related to healthy emotional development. For example, Grazyna Kochanska (2001) assessed children at 9, 14, 22, and 33 months in laboratory situations designed to provoke fear (for example, the approach of an unpredictable toy dog), anger (confinement to a car seat), and joy (a hand puppet show). Infants with resistant attachments at 14 months were the most fearful and the least joyful of the children tested; they showed fear even in tests designed to provoke joy and displayed less positive emotion as they aged. Infants with avoidant attachments showed little emotional expression at first but became fearful by 33 months. Infants with disorganized attachments became angrier as they aged. Whereas these insecurely attached groups expressed more negative emotions with age, securely attached infants became less angry as they became older and were not overly fearful.

A secure attachment is also associated with a capacity to cope with stress and regulate emotions later in life. In experimental studies by Stephen Suomi (1997, 1999; Suomi & Levine, 1998), infant monkeys who experienced traumatic separations from their mothers were compared with monkeys

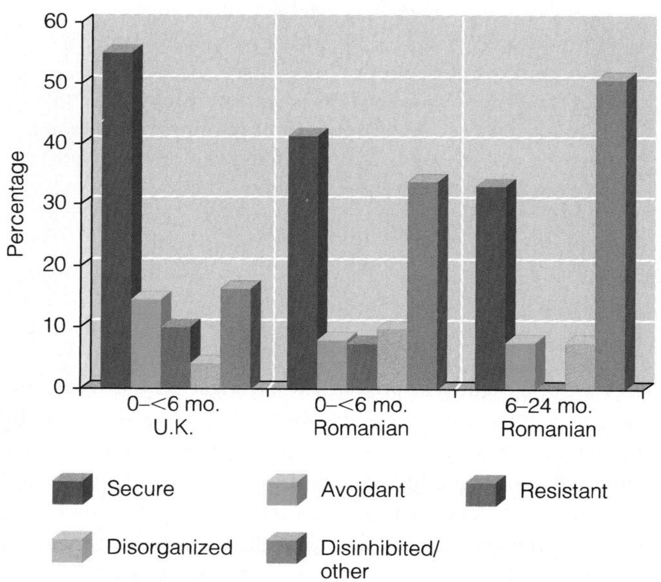

Figure 14.3 Percentages of secure, avoidant, resistant, disorganized, and disinhibited or other attachments among nondeprived British children adopted before 6 months of age, deprived Romanian children adopted in the United Kingdom before 6 months, and deprived Romanian children adopted between 6 and 24 months.
SOURCE: O'Connor et al. (2003).

who enjoyed secure attachment relationships with their mothers. Securely attached monkeys show more adaptive physiological responses to stress later in life and other positive outcomes, such as good parenting skills that result in their own infants' becoming securely attached (Suomi, 1997, 1999; Suomi & Levine, 1998). Research also demonstrates that young rhesus monkeys genetically prone to be highly emotionally reactive develop in healthy directions and are able to cope with stress if they are reared by calm mothers for the first 6 months of their lives (Suomi, 1997). These infants turn out to be socially incompetent if they are reared by emotionally reactive mothers. Similarly, human infants temperamentally prone to be anxious show less of a rise in cortisol (stress hormone) levels and are better able to cope physiologically with stressful experiences if they have enjoyed secure attachments than if they have not, indicating that nature and nurture interact to influence later coping capacities (Gunnar, 1998, 2000).

Do the effects of quality of attachment in infancy on social competence, curiosity, emotional development, and coping capacities last? In late childhood and adolescence, children who have enjoyed secure relationships with their parents continue to be well adjusted—intellectually, socially, and emotionally. They are self-confident and do well in school (Jacobsen & Hofmann, 1997), and they are accepted by the peer group and have close friends (Elicker, Englund, & Sroufe, 1992; Kerns, Klepac, & Cole, 1996). Infants who develop disorganized attachments are more likely than secure, resistant, or avoidant infants to develop psychological problems (Egeland & Carlson, 2004; van IJzendoorn et al., 1999). As you will see later, lasting effects of secure and insecure attachments can sometimes be detected even in adulthood.

How can researchers be sure that relationships between attachment security and later adjustment are not the product of genes shared by parent and child? Geert-Jan Stams and his colleagues (2002) reasoned that a study of adopted children might provide answers and followed a group of children placed in adoptive homes before 6 months until they were 7 years old. Children's temperaments, which are partly influenced by genes, predicted their social and cognitive development, personality, and tendency to display behavioral problems; children with an easy temperament were better adjusted than children with a difficult temperament. However, maternal sensitivity to the infant and the infant's attachment security also contributed to positive developmental outcomes, more than the contributions of temperament did, even though parent and child were not genetically related. Other qualities of the child besides temperament, as measured in this study, still might evoke certain responses from caregivers that then shape the child's development. In addition, researchers cannot always tell whether later adjustment is the product of early parenting and quality of attachment, later parenting and quality of attachment, or both. Still, evidence like this is consistent with the view that early parenting makes a difference in development.

In sum, children are unlikely to develop normally if their first relationships in life are repeatedly disrupted by separation or if they never have the opportunity to form an attachment. By contrast, a secure attachment during infancy has many positive implications for social, emotional, and intellectual development. Yet you must avoid concluding that infants who are insecurely attached to their mothers are doomed—or that infants who are securely attached to their mothers are forever blessed.

First, affectionate ties to fathers (or siblings or grandparents) can compensate for insecure mother–infant relationships (Main & Weston, 1981). Second, early attachments may have no long-term consequences if they change in quality later. Stressful life events such as divorce and illness often convert secure attachments into insecure ones, and lifestyle improvements can make insecure attachments more secure (Waters et al., 2000; Weinfield, Sroufe, & Egeland, 2000). In the end, infancy is not the only period of the life span that shapes development (Schaffer, 2000). As Arlene Skolnick (1986, p. 193) puts it, "Secure attachment to the mother does not make one invulnerable to later problems and socioemotional difficulties, and poor early relations with the mother do not doom a person to a life of loneliness, poor relationships, or psychopathology."

All things considered, the Bowlby–Ainsworth ethological attachment theory is well supported by research. Studies of the long-term consequences of early attachment support Bowlby's claim that "internal working models" of self and others formed early in life shape later relationships and development. Despite the significance of the infant–parent bond, however, many of us learn new social skills and different attitudes toward relationships in our later interactions not only with parents but also with peers, close friends, lovers, and spouses. It is time, then, to supplement this description of parent–child relations with a look at the "second world of childhood"—the world of peer relations.

First Peer Relations

Evolution seems to have equipped human infants not only with a capacity for forming attachments to caregivers but also with a capacity for entering social relationships with peers (Nash & Hay, 2003). Babies show an interest in other babies from an early age and begin to interact with them in earnest in about the middle of the first year. By then, infants will often smile or babble at their tiny companions, vocalize, offer toys, and gesture to one another, although many of the friendly gestures go unnoticed and unreciprocated (Hay, Nash, & Pedersen, 1983; Vandell, Wilson, & Buchanan, 1980). By around 6 months, infants even show evidence that they are biologically prepared for life in social groups, as illustrated by an ability to relate in meaningful ways to more than one peer at a time (Selby & Bradley, 2003; and see the photo on page 402).

By about 18 months, infants are able to engage in reciprocal, complementary play with peers (Mueller & Lucas, 1975; Mueller & Vandell, 1979). They turn rounds of imitation into social games (Eckerman & Stein, 1990; Howes & Matheson, 1992). They can also adopt and reverse roles in their play. Thus, the toddler who receives a toy may immediately offer a

© Laura Dwight/CORBIS

Even before 1 year of age, infants seem ready to engage in social interactions, not only in dyads but in groups.

toy in return, or the one who has been the chaser will become the chasee. Toward the end of the second year, infants have become proficient at this kind of turn-taking and reciprocal exchange, especially if they are securely attached to their parents (Fagot, 1997).

Surprising as it may seem, some infants also form special relationships with preferred playmates—friendships (Howes, 1996). On Israeli kibbutzim, where children are cared for in groups, Martha Zaslow (1980) discovered that many pairs of infants as young as 1 year became truly attached to each other. Hadara and Rivka, for instance, consistently sought each other as playmates, mourned each other's absence, and disturbed everyone with their loud babbling "conversations" when they were confined to their cribs. Clearly the caregiver–infant relationship is not the only important social relationship that develops during infancy; peer relations are well under way, too.

Summing Up

Biologically based primary emotions emerge in a universal sequence over the first months of life. Secondary, or self-conscious emotions, follow in the second and third years, and emotions increasingly become socialized through learning processes. As infants age, they rely less on caregivers and more on emotion regulation strategies to manage the emotions aroused by their social interactions.

Caregivers start to become attached to infants even before birth and find evolved behaviors such as smiling endearing. Although social from the start, as evidenced by their participation in synchronized routines, infants progress through phases of undiscriminating social responsiveness, discriminating social responsiveness, active proximity seeking, and goal-corrected partnership. The first attachment at 6 or 7 months brings with it both fearful emotions (separation and stranger anxiety) and confidence (using the attachment figure as a secure base for exploration). The experiences of caregivers and infants as they interact influence whether a secure, resistant, avoidant, or disorganized–disoriented attachment will be evident in Ainsworth's Strange Situation. The Freudian view that infants become attached to the one who feeds them was contradicted by Harlow's research on contact comfort in monkeys. Secure attachments are associated with sensitive, responsive parenting; resistant ones with inconsistent, unresponsive care; avoidant ones with either rejection or intrusiveness; and disorganized attachments with frightening or frightened parenting. Long-term consequences of the quality of early attachments are evident, but attachments often change, and early experience does not make or break later development, except perhaps for infants who experience repeated permanent separations or who spend months in severely deprived institutional settings and develop a disinhibited attachment style. ■

The Child

How do relationships with parents and peers change from infancy to childhood? And how important are children's social relationships to their development?

Parent–Child Attachments

The parent–child attachment changes qualitatively during childhood. According to John Bowlby (1969), it becomes a goal-corrected partnership in which parent and child accommodate to each other's needs; the child becomes a more sensitive partner and becomes more independent of the parent. Older preschoolers still seek attention and approval from their parents, and they rush to their parents for comfort when they are frightened or hurt. But they also become increasingly dependent on peers for social and emotional support (Furman & Buhrmester, 1992).

Peer Networks

From age 2 to age 12, children spend more time with peers and less time with adults. This trend emerged clearly in a study by Sharri Ellis and her colleagues (Ellis, Rogoff, & Cromer, 1981), who observed 436 children playing in their homes and around the neighborhood. Interestingly, this study revealed that youngsters of all ages spent less time with age-mates (defined as children whose ages were within 1 year of their own) than with children who were more than 1 year older or younger.

Another finding of this study is a familiar one: Even 1- to 2-year-olds played more often with same-sex companions than with other-sex companions, and this gender segregation became increasingly strong with age (see Chapter 12). Once in their sex-segregated worlds, boys and girls experience different kinds of social relationships. There is truth, for example, to the saying that boys travel in packs, whereas girls travel in pairs: boys spend more time than girls in groups, and girls spend more time than boys in dyads (Fabes, Martin, & Hanish, 2003). Overall, then, children spend an increasing amount of time with peers, typically same-sex children, roughly similar in age, who enjoy the same sex-typed activities.

Play

So important is play in the life of the child from age 2 to age 5 that these years are sometimes called *the play years.* This is when children hop about the room shrieking with delight, don capes and go off on dragon hunts, and whip up cakes and cookies made of clay, sand, or air. We can detect two major changes in play between infancy and age 5: it becomes more social, and it becomes more imaginative. After age 5 or so, the exuberant and fanciful play of the preschool years gives way to somewhat more serious play.

Play Becomes More Social

Years ago, Mildred Parten (1932) devised a useful method for classifying the types of play engaged in by nursery-school children of different ages. Her six categories of activity, arranged from least to most social, are as follows:

1. *Unoccupied play.* Children stand idly, look around, or engage in apparently aimless activities such as pacing.
2. *Solitary play.* Children play alone, typically with objects, and appear to be highly involved in what they are doing.
3. *Onlooker play.* Children watch others play, taking an active interest in and perhaps even talking to the players but not directly participating.
4. *Parallel play.* Children play next to one another, doing much the same thing, but they interact little (for example, two girls might sit near each other, both drawing pictures, without talking to each other to any extent).
5. *Associative play.* Children interact by swapping materials, conversing, or following each other's lead, but they are not united by the same goal (for example, the two girls may swap crayons and comment on each other's drawings as they draw).
6. *Cooperative play.* Children join forces to achieve a common goal; they act as a pair or group, dividing their labor and coordinating their activities in a meaningful way (for example, the two girls collaborate to draw a mural for their teacher).

The major message of Parten's study (and of others like it) is that play becomes increasingly social and socially skilled from age 2 to age 5 (Barnes, 1971; Smith, 1978; Howes & Matheson, 1992). Unoccupied and onlooker activities are rare at all ages. Solitary and parallel play become less frequent with age, although solitary play has its place throughout childhood.

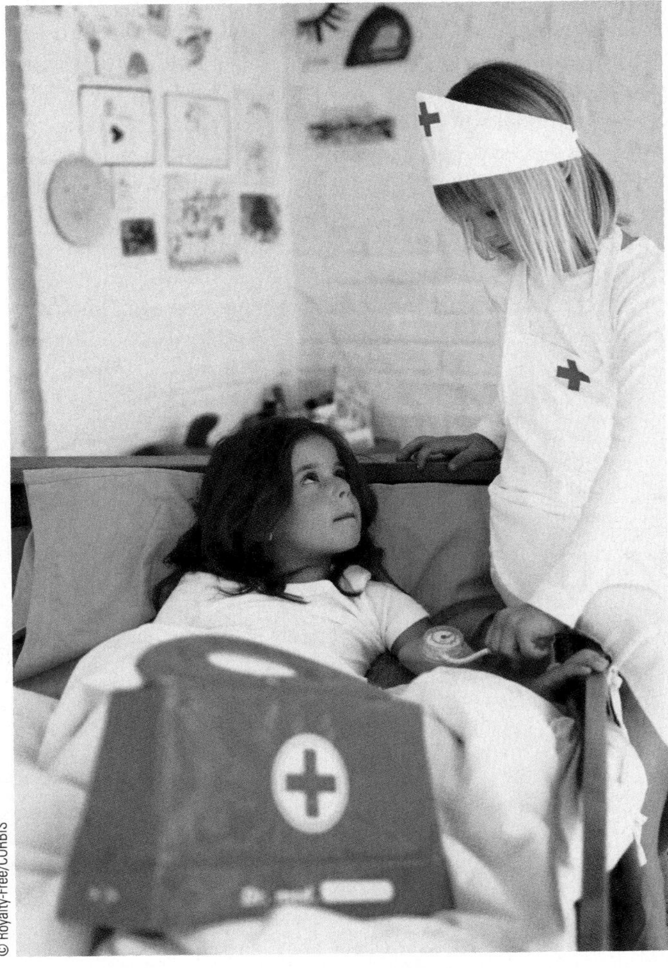

Social pretend play during the preschool years contributes to intellectual, social, and emotional development.

Meanwhile, associative and cooperative play, the most social and complex of the types of play, become more frequent with age and even more common during the school years (see Figure 14.4).

Play Becomes More Imaginative

The first **pretend play**—play in which one actor, object, or action symbolizes or stands for another—occurs around age 1, when an infant may raise an empty cup, or perhaps a forbidden treat, to her lips, smile, give a parent a knowing glance, and make loud lip-smacking sounds (Nicolich, 1977). The earliest pretend play is just like this: The infant performs actions that symbolize familiar activities such as eating, sleeping, and washing.

By age 2, toddlers readily join in pretense if you hand them a towel and suggest that they wipe up the imaginary tea you just spilled (Harris & Kavanaugh, 1993). Because there is no tea in sight, this willingness to clean it up is remarkable. It means that toddlers are capable of using their new symbolic capacity to construct a mental representation of a pretend event and of acting according to this representation. By age 3, most children even understand the difference between pretending to do something and trying but failing to do something (Rakoczy, Tomasello, & Striano, 2004). Shown a model pretending to write and behaving playfully then asked to take their turn, children pretend to write and do not seem bothered when the pen leaves no marks, understanding that when you pretend you do not want to "really" perform the action. Shown a model who tries to write but appears frustrated because the pen leaves no marks on the paper, children try to figure out how to make the pen work properly (accomplishable by removing the cap). Even 2-year-olds in the study grasped to some extent this distinction between intentionally acting-as-if (pretending) and doing or trying to do something.

Pretend play fully blossoms from age 2 to age 5, increasing in both frequency and sophistication (Howes & Matheson, 1992). As children age, they can depict heroes and heroines as different from themselves and can enact elaborate dramas using few or no props. Moreover, children combine their capacity for increasingly social play and their capacity for pretense into **social pretend play** (Howes & Matheson, 1992). Starting at age 2 or 3, children less often enact scenes on their own using dolls and other toys and more often cooperate with caregivers or playmates to enact dramas. These pretend play episodes can become elaborate and require a good deal of social competence. Consider the following example, in which a 5-year-old (M) wants her partner (E), playing the role of a mother, to leave her babies and come to M's house. The two girls negotiate what will happen next, managing to stay in role as they do so (Garvey, 1990, p. 137):

> *M:* You come here. The babies are sleeping now and . . . (interrupted).
> *E:* No, they'll cry when I leave 'cause they'll hear the car.
> *M:* Nooo. The car's broken. I have the car.
> *E:* All right, but one baby will have to take care of these little babies.

Although social pretend play is universal and becomes more frequent with age in all cultures, the quality of preschoolers' play is shaped by the culture in which they live (Haight et al., 1999). For example, U.S. children like to play superheroes and act out themes of danger and fantasy, whereas Korean children take on family roles and enact everyday activities (Farver & Lee-Shin, 1997). American children also talk a lot about their own actions, reject other children's ideas, and boss others around, whereas Korean children are more focused on their partners' activities and are more prone to make polite requests and agree with one another. Through their play, then, children in the United States (an individualistic culture) learn to assert their identities as individuals, whereas children in Korea (a collectivist culture) learn how to

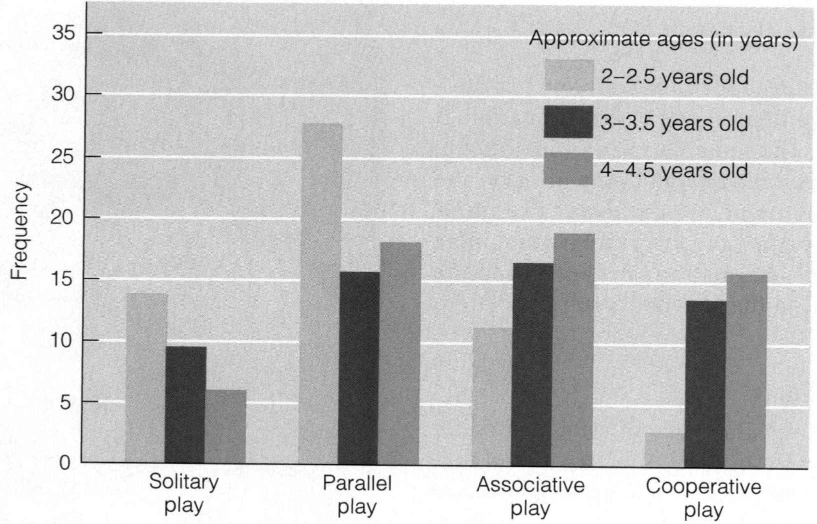

Figure 14.4 Frequency of activities engaged in by preschool children of different ages. With age, solitary and parallel play occur less frequently, whereas associative and cooperative play occur more frequently.

SOURCE: Adapted from Barnes (1971).

keep their egos and emotions under control to achieve group harmony.

Play Becomes More Rule-Governed

After they enter school, children engage less frequently in symbolic play. Now they spend more of their time playing organized games with rules—board games, games of tag or hide-and-seek, organized sports, and so on (Athey, 1984). They also develop individual hobbies, such as building model cars or making scrapbooks, that allow them to develop skills and gain knowledge.

According to Jean Piaget (1965), it is not until children enter the stage of concrete operations, around age 6 or 7, that they become capable of cooperating with other children to follow the rules of games. Older children—11- and 12-year-olds who are entering the stage of formal operations—gain a more flexible concept of rules, recognizing that rules are arbitrary agreements that can be changed as long as the players agree. Partly because of cognitive gains, then, the play of the school-age child is more organized and rule-governed—and less fanciful—than that of the preschool child.

What Good Is Play?

In 19th-century America, child's play was discouraged because it was viewed as a frivolous waste of time (Athey, 1984). Now we know better. Play contributes to virtually all areas of children's development. Indeed, that playful activity occurs among the young of so many species strongly suggests that play is an evolved behavior that helps the young adapt during childhood and prepares them for adult life (Bjorklund & Pellegrini, 2002). It is easy to imagine how girls playing house might be grooming themselves for traditional roles as mothers or how the rough-and-tumble play of boys, like the playful fights observed in young males of many species, might help them function in their peer groups and might prepare them to compete for mates as adolescents or to battle for survival as adults. In addition, play fosters cognitive, motor, and social skills and helps children cope with emotional problems.

Children who engage in a great deal of pretend play (or are trained to do so) perform better on tests of cognitive development, language skills, and creativity than children who rarely pretend (Fisher, 1992; Farver, Kim, & Lee-Shin, 2000). Engaging in social pretend play also allows children to hone their social skills and to construct their theories of mind; they learn, for example, that other children may have different mental states than they do and can act on the basis of false (pretend) beliefs (Lillard, 2001). Perhaps because of the social cognitive and social skills they gain, preschoolers who engage in a great deal of social pretend play tend to be more popular and socially skilled than children who do not (Connolly & Doyle, 1984; Farver et al., 2000).

Finally, play contributes to healthy emotional development by providing opportunities to express bothersome feelings, resolve emotional conflicts, and master challenges (Landreth & Homeyer, 1998). If Danny, for example, has recently been scolded by his mother for drawing on the wall, he may gain control of the situation by scolding his "child" for doing the same thing. And Jackie, an abused 5-year-old, apparently coped with his abuse by having an alligator puppet swallow a small child doll and then smashing the alligator with a mallet and burying it in the sandbox (Landreth & Homeyer, 1998).

Let it never be said, then, that play is useless; it is truly the child's work. Although children play because it is fun, not because it sharpens their skills, they contribute to their own development by doing so. Parents can help their children's development by becoming involved in the social give and take that play episodes require (Lindsey & Mize, 2000).

Peer Acceptance and Popularity

As children play and interact, they typically discover that they like some peers more than others. Researchers study peer-group acceptance through **sociometric techniques**—methods for determining who is liked and who is disliked in a group. In a sociometric survey, children in a classroom may be asked to nominate several classmates whom they like and several whom they dislike or to rate all of their classmates in terms of their desirability as companions (Cillessen & Bukowski, 2000; Hymel, McDougall, & Renshaw, 2002; Terry & Coie, 1991). It is important to find out who is liked and who is disliked; this allows children to be classified into the following, distinct categories of social status (Coie, Dodge, & Coppotelli, 1982):

1. *Popular.* Well liked by most and rarely disliked
2. *Rejected.* Rarely liked and often disliked
3. *Neglected.* Neither liked nor disliked; these isolated children seem to be invisible to their classmates
4. *Controversial.* Liked by many but also disliked by many; for example, the fun-loving child with leadership skills who also has a nasty habit of starting fights
5. *Average.* In the middle on both the liked and disliked scales

Why are some children more popular than others, and why are some children rejected by their peers? Popularity is affected by some personal characteristics that a child can do little about. For instance, physically attractive children are usually more popular than physically unattractive children, and children who are relatively intelligent tend to be more socially accepted than those who are not, probably because cognitive ability contributes to social competence (Bellanti, Bierman, & Conduct Problems Prevention Research Group, 2000). Social competence—the ability to apply social cognitive skills successfully in initiating social interactions, responding positively to peers, resolving interpersonal conflicts smoothly, and so on—clearly predicts popularity (Coie, Dodge, & Kupersmidt, 1990; Ladd, 1999). Children who are socially awkward, argumentative, and disruptive are unlikely to become popular.

"Rejected" children are usually highly aggressive, although some are socially isolated, submissive children who are overly sensitive to teasing and are seen by others as "easy to push around" (Parkhurst & Asher, 1992; Rabiner, Keane, & MacKinnon-Lewis, 1993). Rejected children are less aware than other children are of who likes them and who does not, one of many signs that they are not socially astute or socially

© Mary Kate Denny/PhotoEdit

☾ Children in the neglected category of sociometric status are shy and tend to hover on the fringes of a group without daring to enter it.

skilled (MacDonald & Cohen, 1995). Children who fall into the neglected category of sociometric status often have reasonably good social skills; they are usually nonaggressive and tend to be shy, withdrawn, and unassertive (Coie et al., 1990; Harrist et al., 1997). As a result, no one really notices them. Controversial children are interesting: They often show leadership qualities, like popular children, but they are also viewed as aggressive bullies, like many rejected children (DeRosier & Thomas, 2003; Miller-Johnson et al., 2003). Their social skills may allow them to con some classmates into liking them even though others dislike them.

To appreciate how social skills contribute to popularity, consider what happens when children try to enter and gain acceptance in play groups (Dodge et al., 1990; Putallaz & Wasserman, 1989). When children who ultimately become popular want to join a group's activity, they first hold back and assess what is going on, then smoothly blend into the group, commenting pleasantly about whatever the other children are discussing. By contrast, children who are eventually rejected by their peers tend to be pushy and disruptive. Jimmy, for example, may sit beside two boys who are playing a computer game and distract them by talking about a TV program he saw the night before. Even worse, he may criticize the way the boys are playing, start pecking computer keys, or threaten to turn off the computer if he is not allowed to play. By contrast, children who end up being neglected by their peers often hover around a group without taking positive steps to initiate contact, and they shy from peers who attempt to make contact with them.

In sum, popularity is affected by many factors. It helps to have an attractive face and cognitive skills, but it is probably more important to behave in socially competent ways. As you have seen, children who experienced secure attachments to their parents as infants tend to be popular because they have learned social skills and styles of interacting in the parent–child relationship that shape the quality of their relationships with peers. Influences on popularity vary from social context to social context, of course. For example, children who are shy are likely to be unpopular in Canada but popular in China, where being quiet and reserved is more socially desirable (Chen, Rubin, & Sun, 1992). The ingredients of popularity also change with age: establishing close relationships with members of the other sex may enhance popularity during adolescence, but consorting with "the enemy," and thereby violating norms of gender segregation, can detract from popularity during childhood (Sroufe et al., 1993).

Do the outcomes of these popularity polls matter? Yes—especially for the 10 to 15% of children who are rejected by their peers (Malik & Furman, 1993). Children who are neglected by peers often gain greater acceptance later, but those who are rejected, especially because of aggressive behavior, are likely to maintain their rejected status from grade to grade (Cillessen et al., 1992). More significantly, rejected children may end up with worse behavioral problems because they were rejected, perhaps because their social learning opportunities are limited or because they develop negative views of themselves and of their peers (Coie et al., 1992; Ladd & Troop-Gordon, 2003). Case in point: Peer rejection in sixth grade predicts poor adjustment in eighth grade, even with adjustment in sixth grade controlled (Wentzel, 2003).

Friendships

As Harry Stack Sullivan recognized, being accepted by the wider peer group and having close friends are distinct and serve different functions for children. Popular children are more likely than unpopular children to have friends, but many unpopular children enter at least one reciprocated friendship and many popular children do not. In one study of 7- and 8-year-olds, for example, 39% of children rejected by peers had at least one mutual friendship, whereas 31% of popular children lacked a friendship (Gest, Graham-Bermann, & Hartup, 2001).

Having friends increases the odds that a child will be happy and socially competent, especially if the friendships are with peers who are well adjusted and supportive (Vaughn et al., 2000; Hartup & Stevens, 1997), and reduces the odds that a child will be lonely and depressed (Nangle et al., 2003). Having friends not only teaches children how to participate in emotionally intimate relationships but also provides social support and comfort that can help children feel better about themselves, weather stressful events such as a divorce, and feel bolder when faced with challenges such as the first day of kindergarten (Hartup, 1996; Ladd, 1999). Moreover, as Sullivan theorized, a close chum can compensate for a poor relationship with parents, preventing maladjustment (Criss et al., 2002; Gauze et al., 1996).

Summing Up

Children participate in goal-corrected partnerships with their parents and spend increasing amounts of time with peers, with boys running in packs and girls interacting in pairs. Play becomes more social (as illustrated by associative and cooperative play) and imaginative (as illustrated by social pretend play) during the preschool years and more often involves organized games in elementary school. Physical attractiveness, cognitive ability, and especially social competence influence sociometric status, and peer rejection negatively affects development. Having friends, as distinct from gaining peer acceptance, also promotes development.

You can now appreciate that peers, and especially friends, may be as important as parents to child development. Parents may excel at caregiving and provide their children with a sense of emotional security that enables them to explore their environment and participate in social relationships. However, acceptance by and close relationships with peers may be critical in the learning of social skills and normal patterns of social behavior and can also provide a good deal of emotional support. ■

Going to college is a Strange Situation that activates attachment behaviors, such as hugging and e-mailing, designed to maintain contact with attachment figures.

The Adolescent

Although children are already highly involved in peer activities, adolescents spend even more time with peers and less time with parents. Although the quality of the individual's attachment to parents continues to be highly important throughout adolescence (Collins & Laursen, 2004), peers, including romantic partners, begin to rival or surpass parents as sources of intimacy and support (Furman & Buhrmester, 1992; Lempers & Clark-Lempers, 1992). Moreover, the quality of peer relations changes. Not only do adolescents begin to form boy–girl friendships and go on dates, but they also become more capable of forming deep and intimate attachments.

Attachments to Parents

Just as infants must have a secure base if they are to explore, adolescents seem to need the security, as well as the encouragement to explore, provided by supportive parents to become more independent and autonomous individuals (Kobak et al., 1993; Scharf, Mayseless, & Kivenson-Baron, 2004). Adolescents who enjoy secure attachment relationships with their parents generally have a stronger sense of identity, higher self-esteem, greater social competence, better emotional adjustment, and fewer behavioral problems than their less securely attached peers (Arbona & Power, 2003; Kenny & Rice, 1995). If adolescents have experienced separation from parents through divorce, death, or other reasons, their attachments to their parents are sometimes less secure and they may feel less equipped to cope with the challenges of adolescence (Woodward, Fergusson, & Belsky, 2000).

For many youths in our society, going off to college qualifies as a "naturally occurring strange situation"—a potentially stressful test of the youth's ability to cope with the unfamiliar (Kenny, 1987). Students who go home on weekends or call or e-mail home frequently during their first semester are engaging in attachment behavior just as surely as the infant who whimpers for his mommy. From an attachment theory perspective, experiencing separation anxiety in this situation is normal and adaptive. Preoccupation with parents typically decreases over the first semester and predicts adjustment problems only when it is extreme (Berman & Sperling, 1991).

College students who are securely attached to their parents display better psychological and social adjustment during the potentially difficult transition to college than students who are insecurely attached (Lapsley, Rice, & FitzGerald, 1990). In one study (Mayseless, Danieli, & Sharabany, 1996), securely attached students proved able to maintain close, caring relationships with their parents and form new relationships with romantic partners. Lacking a secure base for exploration, resistantly attached students had more difficulty forming romantic relationships and found even minor separations from their parents upsetting. And, true to form, avoidant youths claimed not to be bothered much by separation, as if denying that they could need their parents for anything. In another study (Scharf et al., 2004), having secure internal working models of relationships helped adolescents leave the nest and form close relationships not only with romantic partners but also with friends as they made the transition to adulthood.

Friendships

Friendships in early childhood are based on enjoying common activities; friendships in late childhood rest on mutual loyalty and caring (Aboud & Mendelson, 1996; Hartup & Stevens, 1997). Adolescent friendships increasingly hinge on intimacy and self-disclosure (Berndt & Perry, 1990; Buhrmester, 1996). Like children, teenagers form friendships with peers who are similar to themselves in observable ways. For example, most high school students, particularly African Americans, tend to choose friends of the same ethnic background (Hamm, 2000). However, adolescents increasingly choose friends whose psychological qualities—interests, attitudes, values, and personalities—match their own. Their friends are like-minded individuals who confide in each other.

Both nature and nurture contribute to the similarity of friends. Genes apparently influence friend selection because classmates' ratings indicate that the friends chosen by the members of an identical twin pair are more alike than the friends chosen by members of a fraternal twin pair (Rose, 2002). Once friends are friends, however, they become even more similar because of their mutual influence (Giordano, 2003).

Although same-sex friendships remain important throughout adolescence, teenagers increasingly form close cross-sex friendships. How do these other-sex friendships compare with same-sex friendships? Ruth Sharabany and her colleagues (Sharabany, Gershoni, & Hofman, 1981) asked 5th- to 11th-graders to assess their same- and cross-sex friendships in terms of such aspects of emotional intimacy as spontaneity, trust, loyalty, sensitivity to the other's feelings, and attachment. As you can see in Figure 14.5, same-sex friendships were highly intimate in most respects throughout this age range, but cross-sex friendships did not attain a high level of intimacy until 11th grade. These findings support Harry Stack Sullivan's view that children learn lessons about intimate attachments in their same-sex chumships that they only later apply in their heterosexual relationships.

In addition, girls tended to report higher degrees of intimacy in their friendships than boys did, and they achieve emotional intimacy in their cross-sex relationships at earlier ages. This may help explain why girls are later more likely than boys to describe their romantic relationships in terms of friendship-like qualities, such as disclosing feelings and providing emotional support (Feiring, 1999).

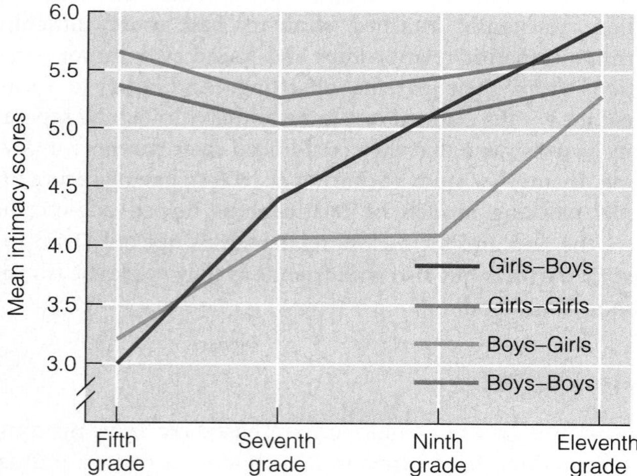

Figure 14.5 Changes during adolescence in the intimacy of same-sex and cross-sex friendships. The girls–boys scores reflect how girls rated the intimacy of their relationships with boys; the boys–girls scores reflect how boys rated their relationships with girls. Cross-sex friendships clearly become increasingly intimate during the adolescent years, achieving the levels of intimacy that characterize same-sex friendships throughout this developmental period.

SOURCE: Sharabany, Gershoni, & Hofman (1981).

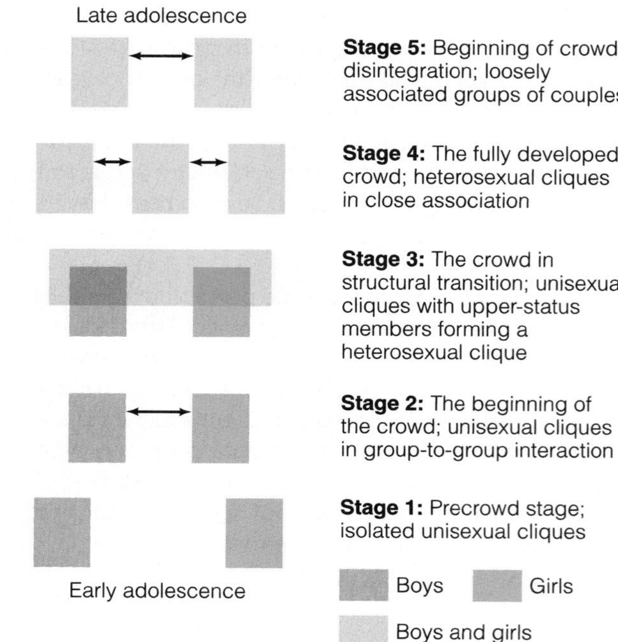

Figure 14.6 Stages in the evolution of the peer group during adolescence, from same-sex cliques (*bottom*) to dating couples (*top*).

SOURCE: Dunphy (1963).

Changing Social Networks

Elementary-school children take interest in members of the other sex, talk at length about who likes whom, develop crushes, and in the process prepare themselves for heterosexual relationships (Thorne, 1993). Still, we have to wonder how boys and girls who live in their own, gender-segregated worlds arrive at the point of dating "the enemy." Some time ago, Dexter Dunphy (1963) offered a plausible account of how peer-group structures change during adolescence to pave the way for dating relationships. His five stages, outlined in Figure 14.6, are still helpful today in understanding how peer relations lay the foundation for romantic attachments (see also Collins & Laursen, 2004; Connolly, Furman, & Konarski, 2000).

Cliques and Crowds

The process begins in late childhood, when boys and girls become members of same-sex **cliques,** or small friendship groups, and have little to do with the other sex. Then, members of boy cliques and girl cliques begin to interact more frequently. Just as parents provide a secure base for peer relationships, relationships with same-sex peers provide a secure base for romantic relationships. For an adolescent boy, talking to a girl at the mall with his friends and her friends there is far less threatening than doing so on his own. In the third stage, the most popular boys and girls form a heterosexual clique.

As less popular peers enter heterosexual cliques, a new peer-group structure, the **crowd,** completes its evolution. The crowd, a collection of several heterosexual cliques, is involved in arranging organized social activities—parties, outings to the lake or mall, and so on. Those adolescents who become members of a mixed-sex clique and a crowd (not all do) have many opportunities to get to know members of the other sex as both friends and romantic partners. Eventually, however, interacting with the other sex in group settings is not enough. Couples form and the crowd disintegrates in late high school after having served its purpose of bringing boys and girls together.

Not all high school crowds are alike. The names may vary, but every school has its crowds of, for example, "populars," "jocks," "druggies," and "losers," each consisting of adolescents who are similar to one another in some way (Brown, Mory, & Kinney, 1994). Everyone in high school seems to recognize these differences: "[The brains] all wear glasses and 'kiss up' to teachers and after school they all tromp uptown to the library" (Brown et al., 1994, p. 128), "The partiers goof off a lot more than the jocks do, but they don't come to school stoned like the burnouts do" (p. 133).

Which crowd or crowds an adolescent belongs to has important implications for her social identity and self-esteem; it is easier for her to feel good about herself if she is a "popular" or a "jock" than if she is a "dweeb," a "druggie," or a social isolate who does not belong to any crowd (Brown & Lohr, 1987). Indeed, self-perceived crowd membership in high school predicts later development; "brains" tend to graduate from college and have high self-esteem at age 24; "basket cases" are more likely than their peers to have seen a psychologist and attempted suicide; "jocks" achieve financial success but share with "criminals" a tendency to drink too much; and "criminals" prove to be the least well adjusted (Barber, Eccles, & Stone, 2001). Crowd membership may reflect personality traits, abilities, and values that existed before the adolescent ever got involved with a particular crowd; being the member of a particular crowd may then bring with it learning experiences that shape adjustment.

A common misconception is that peers are a negative influence on adolescent development. Overall, peers probably do more to foster and encourage positive behavior than to encourage antisocial behavior (Berndt & Murphy, 2002). Much depends on the crowd to which an adolescent belongs: "Druggies" encourage drug use, but "brains" discourage it. Adolescents are least likely to engage in delinquent behavior, become depressed, or feel lonely if they have friends and those friends do not engage in deviant behavior. Adolescents with deviant friends and adolescents without friends are more prone to delinquency and depression, although those with deviant friends are at least less lonely than those without friends (Brendgen, Vitaro, & Bukowski, 2000). Clearly the influences of peers and friends can be healthy or destructive, depending on which cliques and crowds an adolescent belongs to.

Dating

As Dunphy's model suggests, the transition to dating takes place in the context of the larger peer group (Collins & Laursen, 2004). These days, it involves heavy phone use, as illustrated by this snippet from the life of a seventh-grade boy, Chris, who was being pressured by his friends to have sex with Kim—and, of course, to report the details (Hersch, 1998, p. 130):

> The phone rings, and it is Kim, the first of what will be many long calls between them each day. Before long her friends start calling, too, and have long conversations with Chris about how the relationship is going. His friends call to see what's happening. The permutations seem endless. There are conference calls. Several people backed up on call waiting. Chris's bedroom phone is at the center of a huge communication network.

About 25% of 12-year-olds, 50% of 15-year-olds, and 70% of 18-year-olds say that they have been involved in a "special romantic relationship" in the past 18 months (Carver, Joyner, & Udry, 2003). Candice Feiring (1996) has provided a portrait of typical dating experiences in a sample of 15-year-olds. Almost 90% of these adolescents had dated by age 15, though only 21% were currently dating. Most couples did not go out alone on dates as much as they dated within the context of the peer group or crowd. When dating, couples saw each other or talked on the phone (for an average of 60 minutes per call) every day. These dating relationships were usually casual and short lived. Although partners were fascinated with one another, dating relationships were in most respects more like same-sex friendships than like adult romantic attachments; they were mainly sources of companionship rather than of love and security (Feiring, 1996). Perhaps this is why increased involvement in dating relationships often means less time spent with same-sex friends (Zimmer-Gembeck, 1999).

Dating relationships in early adolescence are more superficial and short lived than later dating relationships (Brown, Feiring, & Furman, 1999). It has been suggested that humans have an evolved tendency to compete with peers for mates and

Early dating is mainly about gaining confidence in the ability to date. No wonder there are awkward moments.

to engage in sexual experimentation with several partners before they narrow in on a steady mate (Weisfeld & Woodward, 2004). This is evident in B. Bradford Brown's (1999) view that adolescent romantic relationships evolve through the following four phases:

1. *Initiation phase.* In early adolescence, the focus is on the self—specifically, on coming to see oneself as a person capable of relating to members of the other sex in a romantic way.
2. *Status phase.* In midadolescence, having a romantic relationship, and having it with the "right kind" of partner, is important for the status it brings in the larger peer group.
3. *Affection phase.* In late adolescence, the focus is on the relationship rather than on the self or peer-group acceptance. Romantic relationships become more personal, caring relationships; they are set in the context of a small, mixed-sex clique rather than in the context of the larger crowd, with friends providing advice and emotional support.
4. *Bonding phase.* In the transition to young adulthood, the emotional intimacy achieved in the affection phase is coupled with a long-term commitment to create a lasting bond. We can speak of a true attachment bond.

Brown's phases were evident in an 8-year longitudinal study of German adolescents who were age 13 at the start of the study. The 13-year-olds who had romantic relationships tended to have relatively low quality and unstable, although emotionally intense, relationships that only lasted an average of about 3 months (Seiffge-Krenke, 2003). With age, relationships lasted longer (an average of 21 months by age 21) and became more emotionally intimate and supportive. Moreover, having a committed romantic relationship at age 21 was associated with having a positive self-concept at age 13, supportive peer relationships at age 15, and a supportive romantic relationship at age 17. Parents counted, too; supportive relationships with both mothers and fathers proved to be at least as important as supportive relationships with peers overall in predicting involvement in a love relationship in early adulthood (see also Miller & Hoicowitz, 2004). Other research suggests that adolescents who have secure attachment styles based on their early experiences in the parent–child relationship have more positive experiences dating than anxious or resistant ones, who fall in love and have sex a lot but are ever fearful of abandonment, and avoidant ones, who are reluctant to get emotionally involved (Tracy et al., 2003).

How does dating affect adolescent adjustment and development? Dating at an early age appears to have more negative than positive effects on social and emotional adjustment, either because troubled adolescents start dating early or because they get hurt or become involved in teenage problem behavior before their time (Collins, 2003; Compian, Gowen, & Hayward, 2004). However, both positive relationships in the family and positive relationships with same-gender peers can protect young adolescents from the negative effects of early dating (Brendgen et al., 2002; Doyle et al., 2003). Among older adolescents, dating typically has more positive than negative effects on development and can even compensate for a poor relationship with parents (Furman & Shaffer, 2003). Involvement in a steady relationship is good for self-esteem (although breakups hurt and can result in depression and even suicide), and adolescents who date tend to be better adjusted overall than those who do not (Collins, 2003; Furman & Shaffer, 2003).

Parent and Peer Influence

Should parents worry about losing influence over their children as adolescents become more involved in both same-sex and cross-sex relationships with peers? Studies of **conformity**—the tendency to yield to the opinions and wishes of others—show that conformity to parents' wishes tends to decrease gradually and steadily during adolescence. Conformity to peers, including peers who advocate lawbreaking, increases until about age 14 or 15 and then declines, although age differences are weak and depend on the issue at hand (Berndt, 1979; Berndt & Murphy, 2002). Thus, parents have some grounds for worrying that their adolescents may get into trouble by "going along with the crowd" to engage in delinquent acts, especially around age 14 or 15.

Increased dependence on peers in early adolescence may serve a positive function, however, representing a first step toward the development of autonomy (Steinberg & Silverberg, 1986). Although parents whose teenagers end up at the police station may not be comforted by this thought, teenagers may need the secure base that peer acceptance provides before they are ready to become autonomous in later adolescence. As adolescents progress in their quest for autonomy, they become less dependent on both parents and peers for guidance and more able to make their own choices, as evidenced by decreased conformity to peers in later adolescence.

Parents retain more influence over their adolescents than is commonly believed, however. Peers influence adolescents' social activities and tastes, but parents continue to be the major shapers of their educational and vocational plans and important values (Sebald, 1986; Wilks, 1986). More importantly, teenagers who have close attachments to warm and authoritative parents who establish and enforce clear standards of behavior are likely to be academically and socially competent and to associate with conventional rather than antisocial peer groups. As a result, they are less likely to be exposed to negative peer pressures—and are less susceptible to such pressures when they do encounter them—than are adolescents whose family relationships are poor (Brown et al., 1993; Fuligni & Eccles, 1993; Santor, Messervey, & Kusumakar, 2000).

Problems for youths who "get in with the wrong crowd" and engage in antisocial behavior usually begin at home with parents who are too strict and who fail to adjust to adolescents' needs for greater autonomy (Fuligni & Eccles, 1993) or with parents who fail to provide enough discipline and do not monitor their children's activities sufficiently (Brown et al., 1993; Dishion et al., 1991). When parents are warm and firm but not too controlling, a continual war of parents versus peers is unlikely. Instead, these two forces combine to guide development in positive directions. Adolescents are most

It is no accident that teenagers wear the same hairstyles and dress alike. Peers exert more influence than parents in these matters.

likely to be well adjusted when they have close attachments to both parents and peers (Laible, Carlo, & Raffaelli, 2000).

Summing Up

During adolescence, same-sex, and later cross-sex relationships, increasingly involve emotional intimacy and self-disclosure. According to Dunphy's model, the peer group is transformed from same-sex cliques to mixed-sex cliques and the crowd structure and finally to dating relationships, with the type of crowd an adolescent belongs to having implications for his self-esteem and development. According to Brown, dating relationships progress through initiation, status, affection, and bonding phases. Although conformity to parents declines during adolescence, and conformity to negative peer influences peaks around age 14 or 15, parents continue to be important forces in their children's lives, influencing life choices and values and, if their parenting is warm and firm, ensuring that their children are exposed to positive peer influences. ■

The Adult

Relationships with family and friends are no less important during adulthood than they are earlier in life, but they take on different qualities over the adult years. Examine how people's social networks change over the adult years, then look more closely at their romantic relationships and friendships.

Social Networks

With whom do adults of different ages interact, and how socially active are they? Young adults are busily forming romantic relationships and friendships, typically choosing to associate with people who are similar to themselves in important ways, just as children and adolescents do. The trend toward greater intimacy with the other sex that began in adolescence continues into early adulthood (Reis et al., 1993).

Young adults, especially single ones, seem to have more friends than middle-aged and older adults do. As adults marry, have children, take on increasing job responsibilities, and age, their social networks shrink (Fischer & Phillips, 1982; Fischer et al., 1989). The trend toward smaller social networks with age can be seen in many ethnic groups, but ethnic group differences are also evident. For example, from early adulthood on, African American adults' networks tend to be smaller, to be more dominated by kin, and to involve more frequent contact than those of European Americans (Ajrouch, Antonucci, & Janevic, 2001).

Laura Carstensen's (1992) **socioemotional selectivity theory** explains the shrinking social networks of aging adults as a choice they make to better meet their emotional needs (also see Lang & Carstensen, 2002; Turk-Charles & Carstensen, 1999). It is not, as many people believe, the result of increased loss and social isolation, Carstensen argues; it is an adaptive change that involves sacrificing the quantity of relationships to strengthen their quality and optimize emotional well-being. Less time left to live prompts older adults to put less emphasis on the goal of acquiring knowledge for future use and more emphasis on the goal of fulfilling their current emo-

Explorations

Emotional Experience in Adult Relationships

© Jim Richardson/CORBIS

Contrary to stereotype, elderly adults lead rich and generally positive emotional lives.

Laura Carstensen's socioemotional selectivity theory suggests that aging adults adopt the goal of optimizing their emotional experiences because they realize time is running out (Carstensen et al., 2003). Are they successful? To find out, Carstensen and her colleagues (2000) sampled the emotional experiences of African American and European American adults between age 18 and age 94 by paging them at random times over a 1-week period as they went about their lives. Contrary to ageist stereotypes, older adults did not have more dismal, depressing emotional lives than younger adults. Younger and older adults differed little in the frequency with which they experienced positive emotions, and negative emotions were less, not more, common among older adults. Older adults also experienced longer-lasting positive emotions and more fleeting negative moods, suggesting that they were better able than younger adults to regulate their emotions, savoring the happy experiences and cutting short the sad and angry ones. Finally, older adults appeared to have more complex emotional experiences, more often blending positive and negative emotions. Carstensen speculates that this may be because they "realize not only what they have but also that what they have cannot last forever" (p. 653).

Other research reinforces the conclusion that the emotional lives of elderly adults are rich and rewarding (Carstensen et al., 2003; Mroczek, 2004). Looking at close relationships with mothers, fathers, spouses, children, and friends in Japan and the United States, Hiroko Akiyama, Toni Antonucci, and their colleagues (2003) asked individuals ranging in age from 13 to 92 questions about how positive and negative in tone their interactions with significant others were. They then tried to understand what was behind age differences in the quality of each type of relationship.

As in the study by Carstensen and her colleagues (2000), there were no age differences in ratings of the positive tone of relationships, but older adults were less likely than younger adults to characterize their relationships as negatively toned by endorsing statements like, "My mother gets on my nerves." This decrease with age in negativity was evident in both Japan and the United States and for all relationships except relationships with spouses, which were perceived much the same across age groups. Also detected was a small increase in negativity in adults' relationships with their aging parents after a decrease in negativity in the parent–child relationship from early to middle adulthood.

What accounts for these age differences? Knowing people for a long time might be hypothesized to make a person more tolerant of their flaws, but it did not explain the decrease with age in negativity in relationships. Older adults, however, showed more social maturity (as indicated by their self-ratings of traits such as sensitivity and compassion) than younger adults, and they interacted less frequently with some members of their social convoy (a finding supportive of Carstensen's socioemotional selectivity theory). More social maturity was associated with less negativity in best-friend relationships. Less frequent contact proved to be even more important. It was correlated with low negativity in adults' interactions with both children and parents and did the most to explain the decrease with age in negative perceptions of relationships. Apparently we get along better with both our children and our parents when we no longer live with them. That spouses normally live together and interact frequently throughout their marriage may explain why the emotional quality of husband–wife relationships did not change much with age.

Carstensen would argue that the emotional experiences of older adults are less negative than those of younger adults because older adults have chosen to restrict their relationships to close ones and optimize their emotional experiences in those relationships. Akiyama and Antonucci offer other reasons, including that people simply get along better when they do not live together and interact frequently. Whatever the reasons, it appears that most of us can expect to lead rich emotional lives and to participate in rewarding relationships in later life.

tional needs. As a result, they actively choose to narrow their range of social partners to those who bring them emotional pleasure, usually family members and close friends, and let other social relationships fall by the wayside. Whereas younger adults need the social stimulation and new information that contacts with strangers and acquaintances often provide, and are even willing to sacrifice some emotional well-being to have many social contacts, older adults put their emotional well-being first.

Does the evidence support socioemotional selectivity theory? Middle-aged adults interact less frequently with acquaintances and friends than young adults do, but they interact often with their spouses and siblings and feel closer emotionally to the most significant people in their lives than younger adults do (Carstensen, 1992). Elderly adults drop even more friends and acquaintances from their networks, but they maintain a core of "very close" relationships. If they do not have living spouses or children, they strengthen relationships with other relatives or friends so that they can maintain this inner circle of intimates (Lang & Carstensen, 1994). Older adults end up just as satisfied, if not more satisfied, with their relationships than young adults and are less likely to want more friends (Lansford, Sherman, & Antonucci, 1998). The quality of their emotional experience seems to benefit from socioemotional selectivity, too, as the Explorations box on page 412 reveals.

Attachment Styles

Intrigued by parallels between an infant's attachment to a parent figure and a young adult's love for a romantic partner, researchers are studying adult romantic relationships from the perspective of attachment theory (Mikulincer & Shaver, 2003; Feeney & Noller, 1996). Obviously, parent–infant attachments and adult romantic attachments are not identical. Yet, like the infant who is attached to a parent, the adult who is in love experiences strong affection for her partner, wants to be close, takes comfort from the bond, and is upset by separations. And like the love of parent for infant, romantic love often involves deep attachment, commitment, and emotional intimacy (Hatfield & Rapson, 2000).

Like parent–child attachment, attachment between romantic partners is biologically adaptive and may be part of our evolutionary heritage; after all, it directly increases the odds of having children and the odds that these children will have two parents to help them survive (Diamond, 2003). Perhaps it is not surprising, then, that the concept of romantic love is not just a Western phenomenon, as many people believe. Instead, the phenomenon of romantic love has been documented in at least 88% of the world's cultures, including many in which marriages are arranged by family elders (Jankowiak & Fischer, 1992).

Table 14.3 shows a way of thinking about how the internal working models of self and other that we construct from our experiences in the parent–child relationship may affect our romantic relationships (Bartholomew & Horowitz, 1991; Crowell, Fraley, & Shaver, 1999). Adults with a *secure* working model feel good about both themselves and others; they are not afraid of entering intimate relationships or of being abandoned once they do. People with a *preoccupied* working model have a positive view of other people but feel unlovable. Like resistantly attached infants, they crave closeness to others as a means of validating their self-worth, are highly fearful of abandonment, and tend to become overly dependent on their partners.

Adults with a *dismissing* style of attachment have a positive view of self but do not trust other people. They dismiss the importance of close relationships, possibly because their care-

Table 14.3 Internal Working Models Associated with Views of Self and of Other People Based on Experiences in Relationships

		Model of Self	
		Positive	**Negative**
Model of Others	Positive	**SECURE** *Secure attachment history* Healthy balance of attachment and autonomy; freedom to explore	**PREOCCUPIED** *Resistant attachment history* Desperate for love to feel worthy as a person; worry about abandonment; express anxiety and anger openly
	Negative	**DISMISSING** *Avoidant attachment history* Shut out emotions; defend against hurt by avoiding intimacy, dismissing the importance of relationships, and being "compulsively self-reliant"	**FEARFUL** *Disorganized–disoriented attachment history* Need relationships but doubt own worth and fear intimacy; lack a coherent strategy for meeting attachment needs

Source: Adapted from Bartholomew & Horowitz, 1991.

It is also possible to look at these four types of attachment in terms of anxiety and avoidance dimensions (Gallo, Smith, & Ruiz, 2003; Mikulincer & Shaver, 2003): the secure type is low in both anxiety over relationships and avoidance of relationships; the preoccupied type is high in anxiety but low in avoidance; the dismissing type is low in anxiety but high in avoidance; and the fearful type is high in both anxiety and avoidance.

Internal Working Models of Attachment

Which of the internal working models of attachment in Table 14.3—secure, dismissing, preoccupied, or fearful—is expressed in each of the following statements (Bartholomew & Horowitz, 1991, p. 244, adapted from Hazan & Shaver, 1987)? And which internal working model best describes you?

1. "I want to be completely emotionally intimate with others, but I often find that others are reluctant to get as close as I would like. I am uncomfortable being without close relationships, but I sometimes worry that others don't value me as much as I value them."
2. "I am somewhat uncomfortable getting close to others. I want emotionally close relationships, but I find it difficult to trust others completely or to depend on them. I sometimes worry that I will be hurt if I allow myself to become too close to others."
3. "It is relatively easy for me to become emotionally close to others. I am comfortable depending on others and having others depend on me. I don't worry about being alone or having others not accept me."
4. "I am comfortable without close emotional relationships. It is very important to me to feel independent and self-sufficient, and I prefer not to depend on others or have others depend on me."

1. Preoccupied, 2. Fearful, 3. Secure, 4. Dismissing

givers were unreliable (Beckwith, Cohen, & Hamilton, 1999). Like avoidantly attached infants, they defend themselves against hurt by not expressing their need for love or their fear of abandonment. They deny that they need people or that relationships matter to them, find it hard to trust partners, feel that others want them to be more intimate than they wish to be, and keep partners at a distance. Bowlby (1973) described dismissing or avoidant individuals as "compulsively self-reliant." Finally, adults with a *fearful* working model resemble infants with a disorganized–disoriented attachment; they take a dim view of both themselves and other people and display a confusing mix of neediness and fear of closeness. You may wish to see if you can identify the internal working models expressed by the statements in the Explorations box on this page.

Mary Main and her colleagues have stimulated much research on adult attachment with their Adult Attachment Interview (AAI). It asks adults about their childhood experiences with attachment figures and about their current relationships with their parents and romantic partners, including their experiences with separation and rejection, then classifies respondents into categories similar to those in Table 14.3 based on their state of mind concerning attachment (Main, Kaplan, & Cassidy, 1985). Much is learned by seeing how freely and coherently adults talk about their early relationships and how objectively they view them. For example, dismissing adults prove unable to reflect on their early relationships with their parents; they may say all was great but provide no supporting evidence. Preoccupied adults have a lot to say, much of it emotionally charged, but they have difficulty integrating and gaining a perspective on their experiences. Secure (also called *autonomous*) adults are able to reflect on their family experience and make sense of it, even when they have had miserable childhoods.

Research using the AAI and similar instruments suggests that adults can be classified based on their predominant styles of attachment. In a pioneering study conceptualizing romantic love as attachment, Cindy Hazan and Phillip Shaver (1987) classified 56% of the adults they studied as having a secure attachment style, 19% as resistant, and 25% as avoidant. (They did not measure the fearful or disorganized–disoriented attachment style.) Adults' styles of attachment were related to the quality of their romantic relationships. For example, adults with a secure attachment style experience a good deal of trust and many positive emotions in their current love relationships, and their relationships tend to last longer than those of adults with insecure attachment styles. Avoidant lovers fear intimacy, whereas resistant individuals tend to be obsessed with their partners. Both avoidant and resistant adults report a lot of jealousy and emotional extremes of love and pain in their romantic relationships. They also feel unable to regulate their negative emotions or to manage conflicts with their partners (Creasey, Kershaw, & Boston, 1999).

Hazan and Shaver also discovered that adults with a secure attachment style recalled warm relationships with their parents during childhood. By contrast, adults with insecure attachment styles tended to remember their parents as unfair, critical, or cold. They also tend to have experienced abuse, neglect, and losses such as divorce or death in their early relationships or to have parents whose problems with substance abuse, depression, and so on made them unreliable caregivers (Mickelson, Kessler, & Shaver, 1997). Retrospective data such as these are not very convincing, however, because people may distort memories of the past to fit present realities. More convincing is a study by Rand Conger and his colleagues (2000) in which a warm parent–child relationship in seventh grade was linked in a longitudinal study to a high-

Romantic attachment shares qualities with parent-infant attachment.

quality romantic relationship in early adulthood. Moreover, in a study spanning the years from infancy to adulthood, adults who had experienced sensitive maternal care in infancy had positive mental representations of their romantic relationships (Grossmann et al., 2002b). The quality of an adult's romantic relationship was also related to the quality of the parent-child attachment, only weakly in infancy but more strongly at ages 6, 10, and 16.

These and other studies suggest that adults' styles of attachment are a reflection of their history of attachment relationships (Fraley, 2002). Here, then, is at least some support for Bowlby's (1973) hypothesis that internal working models of self and other formed on the basis of parent–child interactions affect the quality of later relationships. Receiving warm and supportive parenting as a child appears to be associated with engaging in warm, supportive behavior in romantic relationships as a young adult—and, as a result, enjoying a high-quality relationship (Conger et al., 2000).

As Bowlby theorized, internal working models of self and other also predict the capacity for exploration—the extent to which adults have the confidence and curiosity to explore their environments and to take on and master challenges (Mikulincer & Shaver, 2003). A secure attachment style in adulthood is associated with strong achievement motivation and a focus on mastering challenges as opposed to avoiding failure (Elliot & Reis, 2003). Securely attached adults also enjoy their work and are good at it, whereas preoccupied, or resistantly attached, adults want approval and grumble about not being valued enough by their bosses and coworkers. Dismissing, or avoidantly attached, adults bury themselves in their work and do little socializing (Hazan & Shaver, 1990).

The internal working models of self and other that grow out of early experiences in the family also affect an adult's capacity for caregiving—for empathizing with others, responding to their needs, and being a sensitive and responsive parent (Mikulincer & Shaver, 2003). Mothers and fathers who had secure relations with their parents tend to interact in more sensitive ways with their children and form more secure attachment relationships with them than parents whose early attachments were insecure (van IJzendoorn, 1995). Mothers whose AAIs reveal a dismissing attachment style experience little positive emotion, for example, whereas preoccupied mothers are anxious and behave angrily and intrusively with their infants (Adam, Gunnar, & Tanaka, 2004).

What is more, in a study of the intergenerational transmission of attachment styles, grandmothers who completed the AAI, mothers-to-be who completed the AAI when pregnant, and infants tested in the Strange Situation with their mothers all fell in the same attachment category in 64% of the cases (Benoit & Parker, 1994). Researchers are not yet sure how these family resemblances in attachment styles arise. They could be caused partly by genetic influences on temperament and behavior related to attachment. Intergenerational resemblances may also reflect a mother's current adjustment and orientation to relationships more than the lasting effects of her early experiences in the family; for example, a woman may recall her relationship with her mother positively if she enjoys a positive relationship with her infant and with her partner or negatively if she is depressed and unable to respond appropriately to her infant. However, it is also plausible that internal working models of relationships are passed from one generation to the next through observational learning.

Do attachment styles have bearing on adjustment in old age? Adults who recall loving relationships with their parents during childhood tend to have better physical and mental health than those who recall unsupportive relationships (Shaw et al., 2004). Interestingly, whereas most young and middle-aged adults appear to have secure adult attachment styles, Carol Magai and her colleagues (2001) have found that most European American and African American elderly adults fall in the dismissing–avoidant category based on their responses to attachment measures; they express some discomfort with closeness and tend to be compulsively self-reliant. Elderly people with either a secure or a dismissive (avoidant) attachment style tend to be happier than those whose styles are preoccupied or fearful, suggesting that the independent, dismissive style may be adaptive in old age, possibly helping adults who have lost spouses to adapt to life on their own (Webster, 1998).

Overall, internal working models of self and other, both those formed in childhood and those operating in adulthood, have implications for adult romantic relationships, exploration, work, relationships with children, and overall adjustment. But they are termed *working* models because they are subject to revision if later experiences in relationships suggest change is warranted. Although research on secure, preoccupied, dismissing, and fearful styles of attachment in adulthood is intriguing, remember that early attachment experiences may predict the future but do not determine it.

Adult Friendships

Friendships remain important across the life span, although they take on different characters at different ages (Blieszner & Roberto, 2004). Young adults typically have more friends than older adults do, but even adults age 85 and older usually have at least one close friend and are in frequent contact with their friends (Johnson & Troll, 1994). The friends of elderly adults are generally elderly; in one study, 68% of adults over age 75 had no one in their social network younger than 35, suggesting a good deal of age segregation (Uhlenberg & de Jong-Gierveld, 2004). Elderly adults seem fine with this, however: Almost three-fourths of the women Rebecca Adams (1985–1986) interviewed claimed that "old friends are the best friends," even though they continued to make new friends late in life.

What happens to friendships as older adults begin to develop significant health problems and disabilities? When one friend needs more aid than the other and is able to give less aid in return, this imbalance can strain the relationship (Silverstein & Waite, 1993). Social psychologists have long emphasized the importance of **equity,** or a balance of contributions and gains, to satisfaction with close relationships (Walster, Walster, & Berscheid, 1978). A person who receives more from a relationship than he gives is likely to feel guilty; a person who gives a great deal and receives little in return may feel angry or resentful.

Consistent with this equity view, involvement in relationships in which the balance of emotional support given and received is unequal is associated with lower emotional well-being and more symptoms of depression than involvement in more balanced relationships (Keyes, 2002; Ramos & Wilmoth, 2003). Interestingly, overbenefited, or dependent, friends in relationships often experience more distress than underbenefited, or support-giving, friends (Roberto & Scott, 1986). Being able to help other people, or at least to reciprocate help, tends to boost the self-esteem and reduce the depressive symptoms of elderly adults (Krause & Shaw, 2000; Ramos & Wilmoth, 2003). Perhaps because of gender-role norms, men who have a strong desire to be independent react especially negatively to receiving help (Nagumey, Reich, & Newsom, 2004). Perhaps because inequity threatens friendships, older adults usually call on family rather than friends when they need substantial help, unless they have no kin nearby (Felton & Berry, 1992; Kendig et al., 1988).

Close friendships that have lasted for years are particularly important to adults.

Adult Relationships and Adult Development

We have emphasized throughout this chapter that close attachments to other people are essential to normal cognitive, social, and emotional development. It should not surprise you to learn, then, that adults are better off in many ways if they enjoy meaningful social relationships. Research tells us this: The quality rather than the quantity of an individual's social relationships is most closely related to that person's sense of well-being or life satisfaction (O'Connor, 1995; Pinquart & Sorensen, 2000). Just as people can feel lonely despite being surrounded by other people, adults apparently can feel deprived of social support even though they receive a lot of it—or they can have restricted social networks yet be highly satisfied with their relationships.

The size of an adult's social network is not nearly as important as whether it includes at least one **confidant**—a spouse, relative, or friend to whom the individual feels especially attached and with whom thoughts and feelings can be shared (de Jong-Gierveld, 1986; Levitt, 1991). For most married adults in our society, spouses are the most important confidants, and the quality of an adult's marriage is one of the strongest influences on overall satisfaction with life (Fleeson, 2004). Men are particularly dependent on their spouses; women draw more on friends, siblings, and children for emotional support (Gurung, Taylor, & Seeman, 2003). For older adults whose spouses have died, children or friends often step in to fill these needs; for single adults, siblings sometimes become especially important (Connidis & Davies, 1992). Cultural factors enter, too: in Japan, for example, relationships with grown children appear to be more critical to the well-being of adults than relationships with husbands or wives (Sugisawa et al., 2002).

Applications

Building Stronger Social Relationships

How might some of the knowledge of social development captured in this chapter be applied to help humans develop more satisfying social relationships across the life span? As you have seen, parents who are likely to be insensitive to their infants, as well as infants who have difficult temperaments, are at risk for forming insecure attachments. In one study (van den Boom, 1995), low-income mothers in Holland with irritable babies were given a series of three 2-hour training sessions designed to make them more sensitive and responsive caregivers. Home visitors worked with the mothers during everyday interactions to help them recognize, interpret, and respond appropriately to their infants' positive and negative cues. Not only did the mothers who received training become more sensitive caregivers, but their infants also were more likely than those of mothers who received no training to be able to soothe themselves when upset, to be securely attached at age 1, and to remain securely attached at age 3. What is more, these children transferred positive skills they learned in the parent–infant relationship to their relationships with peers.

Other studies also suggest that parents who are responding insensitively to their infants can be trained in only a few sessions to be more sensitive caregivers and, as a result, to build more secure attachments with their infants (Bakermans-Kranenburg, van IJzendoorn, & Juffer, 2003). Also promising is toddler–parent psychotherapy based on attachment theory. In this approach, depressed parents are helped to understand how their internal working models of relationships (for example, their lingering anger at a mother who was not there for them in childhood) affect their interactions with their infants and how they can improve those interactions (Cicchetti, Toth, & Rogosch, 2004).

Children who are neglected or, worse, rejected by their peers are another group at risk. They can be helped through interventions designed to teach them the social and social cognitive skills they lack (Ladd, 1999; Malik & Furman, 1993). In social-skills coaching programs, an adult therapist models or displays social skills, explains why they are useful, allows children to practice them, then offers feedback to help children improve their skills. Sherrie Oden and Steven Asher (1977) coached third- and fourth-grade social isolates in four important social skills: how to participate in play activities, how to take turns and share, how to communicate effectively, and how to give attention and help to peers. Not only did the children who were coached become more outgoing and positive in their social behavior, but a follow-up assessment a year later also revealed that they had achieved gains in sociometric status within the classroom. Similar coaching programs have been found effective with lonely college students who have trouble relating to members of the other sex (Christopher, Nangle, & Hansen, 1993; Jones, Hobbs, & Hockenbury, 1982).

However, not all individuals who are lonely and isolated are socially incompetent. For some individuals, the real problem is a restricted social environment—a lack of opportunities to form close relationships (Rook, 1984, 1991). Such was the case for the socially isolated elderly people described by Marc Pilisuk and Meredith Minkler (1980). Living in inner-city hotels in San Francisco, these individuals were often prisoners in their rooms because of disability, poverty, and fear of crime. To change this situation, public health nurses began to offer free blood pressure checkups in the lobby of one hotel. As the nurses got to know the residents, they were able to draw them into conversations and to link individuals who had common interests. After about a year, the residents formed their own activities club; organized discussions, film showings, and parties; and were well on their way out of their social isolation. The trick was to change their social environment rather than their social skills. Programs in which home visitors befriend lonely elderly adults are also received well (Andrews et al., 2003).

Because development is influenced by both individual and environmental factors, it makes sense to think that children and adults who lack healthy social relationships can be helped most through efforts to improve their social skills and to change their social environments to increase opportunities for meaningful interaction. The goal might be to ensure that every person enjoys the many developmental benefits that come from a social convoy that includes a secure bond with at least one caregiver during infancy, one friend during childhood and adolescence, and an intimate romantic relationship or friendship in adulthood.

The amount of help key sources of social support provide is less important than whether interacting with them is rewarding or stressful. That is, quantity is less important than quality in relationships (Krause, 1995). Perhaps because of their personality traits, people who have positive (or negative) interactions in one relationship tend to have similar experiences in other relationships, creating a constellation of supportive (or stressful) relationships (Krause & Rook, 2003). Thus, an adult's interactions with grown children can undermine rather than increase well-being if the parent–child attachment is insecure (Barnas, Pollina, & Cummings, 1991), and negative exchanges with spouses, children, or other significant companions can have lasting negative effects on emotional well-being (Newsom et al., 2003).

So, a small number of close and harmonious relationships can make negative life events more bearable and improve the overall quality of an adult's life, and negative relationships can make life unpleasant. It is more than that, however: Social support, especially from family members, has positive effects on the cardiovascular, endocrine, and immune systems, keeps blood pressure in the normal range, improves the body's ability to cope with stress, and can contribute to better physical functioning and a longer life, especially in old age (Charles & Mavandadi, 2004; Uchino, Cacioppo, & Keicolt-Glaser, 1996). Close relationships can also help prevent declines in cognitive functioning (Zunzunegui et al., 2003). Susan Charles and Shahrzad Mavandadi (2004), noting that emotions and social relationships are closely linked starting in infancy, suggest that they may have evolved together. They go on to suggest that social relationships affect health and well-being through their effects, good or bad, on emotions and emotion regulation. Thus, separation from caregivers and social deprivation raise stress hormone levels in infants, whereas reunions with caregivers lower them (Gunnar, 2000). In addition, chronic emotional arousal because of poor emotion regulation in adulthood impairs the immune system and leaves people susceptible to disease, whereas close relationships help people keep their emotions under control (Charles & Mavandadi, 2004). Whatever the mechanisms, and whatever our ages, our well-being and developmental outcomes hinge considerably on the quality of our ties to our fellow humans—particularly on having a close bond with at least one person. It is fitting, then, that we conclude this chapter by illustrating, in the Applications box on page 417, approaches to improving social relationships across the life span.

Summing Up

Social networks shrink from early to later adulthood, although a core of close relationships is evident at all ages. According to Carstensen's socioemotional selectivity theory, this is because older adults, seeing less time ahead, focus on emotional fulfillment rather than acquisition of information for future use. As revealed by the AAI and other tools, adults have secure, preoccupied, dismissing, or fearful internal working models of self and other that are rooted in their early attachment experiences and that affect the quality of their romantic relationships, their ability to explore and to work productively, and their ability to form secure attachments with their own children. Adults continue to value friends, but disability and disease can introduce inequity into relationships, so older adults often turn first to family for help. Life satisfaction, as well as physical and cognitive functioning, tends to be maintained better in old age when people have at least one close confidant to help them regulate their emotions. ■

Summary Points

1. Social relationships contribute immensely to human development, primarily by providing critical learning opportunities and social support (through our changing social convoys). The developmental significance of early parent–child relationships was emphasized by Sigmund Freud and continues to be emphasized in the Bowlby–Ainsworth attachment theory, which draws on ethological, psychoanalytic, and cognitive theory to argue that attachments are built into the human species, develop through an interaction of nature and nurture during a sensitive period early in life, and affect later development by shaping internal working models of self and other.

2. The second world of childhood, the peer world, is believed to be especially important by Jean Piaget, who emphasized the reciprocal nature of peer relations; Harry Stack Sullivan, who held that childhood chumships can compensate for poor parent–child relationships or peer rejection and prepare children for romantic relationships; and more recently Judith Rich Harris, who argues that children are socialized more by peer groups than by parents.

3. Biologically based emotions such as anger and fear appear in the first year of life, and self-conscious emotions emerge in the second year; emotions are quickly socialized by caregivers. As infants age, they rely less on caregivers and more on their own emotion regulation strategies to manage their emotions in interactions with their attachment objects.

4. Because infants have endearing qualities, parents typically become attached to them before or shortly after birth. Parent and child establish synchronized routines, and infants progress through phases of undiscriminating social responsiveness, discriminating social responsiveness, active proximity seeking, and goal-corrected partnership. The formation of a first attachment around 6 or 7 months is accompanied by separation anxiety and stranger anxiety, as well as by exploration from a secure base.

5. Research using Mary Ainsworth's Strange Situation classifies the quality of parent–infant attachment as secure, resistant,

avoidant, or disorganized–disoriented. The Freudian view that infants become attached to those who feed them lacks support; Harry Harlow was correct to emphasize contact comfort. More generally, secure attachments are associated with sensitive, responsive parenting; resistant attachments with inconsistent, unresponsive care; avoidant attachments with either rejection or overstimulation; and disorganized–disoriented attachments with abuse. Infant characteristics (temperament and achievement of cognitive developmental milestones such as person permanence) also contribute.

6. Repeated long-term separations from attachment figures can result in withdrawal from relationships. Worse is social deprivation that makes it impossible for an infant to attach to anyone; recovery is evident, but so are disinhibited patterns of attachment and long-term developmental delays in children who spend much time in deprived institutions. By contrast, attending day care normally does not disrupt development or parent–child attachments, assuming that the quality of care at home and in the day care facility is reasonably good. Secure attachments contribute to later social competence and exploration, but attachment quality often changes over time; insecurely attached infants are not inevitably doomed to a lifetime of poor relationships.

7. Infants are interested in peers and become increasingly able to coordinate their own activity with that of their small companions. By 18 months, they participate in complementary interactive exchanges and form friendships.

8. From age 2 to age 12, children participate in goal-corrected partnerships with their parents and spend increasing amounts of time with peers, especially same-sex ones, engaging in increasingly social and imaginative play and later in organized games. Physical attractiveness, cognitive ability, and social competence contribute to popular—rather than rejected, neglected, or controversial—sociometric status. Children who are rejected by their peers or who have no friends are especially at risk for future problems.

9. During adolescence, same- and cross-sex friendships increasingly involve emotional intimacy and self-disclosure, and a transition is made from same-sex peer groups to mixed-sex cliques and larger crowds and finally to dating relationships, which at first meet self-esteem and status needs and later become more truly affectionate. Although susceptibility to negative peer pressure peaks around age 14 or 15, peers are more often a positive than a negative force in development, unless poor relationships with parents result in an adolescent's becoming involved with an antisocial crowd.

10. Most adults of all ages have high-quality relationships, but social networks shrink with age, possibly because of increased socioemotional selectivity. Adults have secure, preoccupied, dismissing, or fearful internal working models of self and others that appear to be rooted in their early attachment experiences and that affect their romantic relationships, approaches to work, and ability to form secure attachments with their own children.

11. Although adults are highly involved with their spouses or romantic partners, they continue to value friendships, especially long-lasting and equitable ones. Having at least one confidant has beneficial effects on life satisfaction and on physical and cognitive functioning.

Critical Thinking

1. Return to Baby Jessica, the little girl introduced at the start of the chapter who was taken at age 2 from the only parents she had ever known. Suppose she was observed at age 5 and found to have a resistant style of attachment to her mother. Now that you have read the chapter, hypothesize how she might have developed this attachment pattern and what kinds of relationships she will have as she grows up.

2. Ethological theory, psychoanalytic theory, and cognitive psychology all influenced John Bowlby as he formulated attachment theory. Which elements of attachment theory do you think most reflect each of these three theoretical perspectives, and why?

3. Billy, age 10, does not have a best friend and has never really had one. Why do you think this is, and what implications might lack of a friend have for Billy's later development?

4. Laura Carstensen's socioemotional selectivity theory suggests that adults narrow their social networks with age to better meet their emotional needs. Can you develop alternative hypotheses about why young adults might have larger social networks than elderly adults?

Key Terms

social support, 385
social convoy, 385
attachment theory, 386
attachment, 386
imprinting, 386
internal working model, 387
peer, 387
chumship, 387
self-conscious emotion, 389
social referencing, 390
emotion regulation, 390
synchronized routines, 391
separation anxiety, 392
stranger anxiety, 392
secure base, 392
Strange Situation, 392
secure attachment, 392
resistant attachment, 394
avoidant attachment, 394
disorganized–disoriented attachment, 394
contact comfort, 395
pretend play, 403
social pretend play, 404
sociometric techniques, 405
clique, 408
crowd, 408
conformity, 410
socioemotional selectivity theory, 411
equity, 416
confidant, 416

Media Resources

Websites to Explore

Visit Our Website

For a chapter tutorial quiz and other useful features, visit the book's companion website at *http://psychology.wadsworth.com/sigelman_rider5e*. You can also connect directly to the following sites:

Attachment

The website of developmental psychologist Everett Waters gives you an opportunity to read several papers on attachment theory and attachment research, including papers by attachment theorist Mary Ainsworth.

Pretend Play

This visually engaging and creative site focuses on pretend play, covering Jean Piaget's views on play, types of play, and more. A fun experience.

Day Care Quality

The site of the Child Welfare League of America offers guidance on judging the quality of day care centers.

Adult Attachment

This is the website of Phillip Shaver's Adult Attachment lab at the University of California at Davis. With papers on adult attachment and descriptions of measures of adult attachment styles, it offers a self-scoring Close Relationships Questionnaire that will allow you to see what your attachment style might be.

Understanding the Data: Exercises on the Web

For additional insight on the data presented in this chapter, try the exercises for these figures at *http://psychology.wadsworth.com/sigelman_rider5e:*

Figure 14.4 Frequency of activities engaged in by preschool children of different ages

Figure 14.5 Changes during adolescence in the intimacy of same-sex and cross-sex friendships

Life-Span CD-ROM

Go to the Wadsworth Life-Span CD-ROM for further study of the concepts in this chapter. The CD-ROM includes narrated concept overviews, video clips, a multimedia glossary, and additional activities to expand your learning experience. For this chapter, check out the following clips, and others, in the video library:

VIDEO Early and Middle Childhood: Play

VIDEO Attachment: Stranger Anxiety Secure Base Phenomenon

DEVELOPMENTAL PsychologyNow™

Developmental PsychologyNow is a web-based, intelligent study system that provides a complete package of diagnostic quizzes, a personalized study plan, integrated multimedia elements, and learning modules. Check it out at *http://psychology.wadsworth.com/sigelman_rider5e/now.*

CHAPTER fifteen

The Family

TWO COLLEGE STUDENTS, two takes on how divorce affects children's lives (Harvey & Fine, 2004, pp. 32–33 and 64):

> My brother, for instance, became very distant and cold toward my mother. He chose not to express any emotion. . . . I, on the other hand, became very sad. I didn't understand, because as I said, their marriage was perfect. I withdrew from my friends, couldn't sleep, and I cried all of the time.
>
> I look back at the divorce of my parents and I think it was a very important time in my life. It helped my [sic] to mature and to become more responsible. I have no regrets. I have lost a man who was intended to be my father, but gained a real dad.

For good or bad, we are all bound to our families. We are born into them, work our way toward adulthood in them, start our own as adults, and continue to lead linked lives in old age. We are part of our families, and they are part of us. James Garbarino (1992) has gone so far as to call the family the "basic unit of human experience" (p. 7).

This chapter examines the family and its central roles in human development throughout the life span. How has the family changed in recent years? How do infants, children, and adolescents experience family life, and how are they affected by their relationships with parents and siblings? How is adult development affected by such family transitions as marrying, becoming a parent, watching children leave the nest, and becoming a grandparent? Finally, what are the implications of the diversity that characterizes today's family lifestyles—and of such decisions as remaining childless or divorcing?

Understanding the Family

The family is a system, a system within other systems, a changing system, and a changing system in a changing world.

The Family as a System

Debate rages in the United States today about whether the marriage that forms the basis of a family must be between man and wife or can be between two men or two women. This illustrates that it may not be possible to define *family* in a way that applies across all cultures and eras; many forms of family life have worked and continue to work for humans (Coontz, 2000a; Leeder, 2004). However we define what a marriage is, proponents of **family systems theory** conceptualize a family as a system. This means that the family, like the human body, is truly a whole consisting of interrelated parts, each of which affects and is affected by every other part, and each of which contributes to the functioning of the whole (Fingerman & Bermann, 2000; Klein & White, 1996). In the past, developmentalists did not adopt this family systems perspective. They typically focused almost entirely on the mother–child relationship, assuming that the only process of interest within the family was the mother's influence on the child's development.

The **nuclear family** consists of husband–father, wife–mother, and at least one child. Even a simple man, woman, and infant "system" can be complex. An infant interacting with her mother is already involved in a process of reciprocal influence: The baby's smile is likely to be greeted by a smile from Mom, and Mom's smile is likely to be reciprocated by the infant's grin. However, the presence of both parents means that there is a family system involving husband–wife, mother–infant, and father–infant relationships (Belsky, 1981). Every individual and every relationship within the family affects every other individual and relationship through reciprocal influence. You can see why it was naive to think that the family could be understood by studying only the ways in which mothers mold their children.

Now think about how complex the family system becomes if we add another child (or two or six) to it. We must then understand the relationships between each parent and each of these children, the spousal relationship, and the relationships between siblings. The family becomes a system with parent–child, marital, and sibling subsystems (Parke, 2004). Or consider the complexity of an **extended family household,** in which parents and their children live with other kin—some combination of grandparents, siblings, aunts, uncles, nieces, and nephews. Extended family households are common in many cultures of the world (Ruggles, 1994). In U.S. society, African Americans, Hispanic Americans, and other ethnic minorities tend to place more emphasis on extended family bonds than European Americans do (Gadsden, 1999; Leyendecker & Lamb, 1999). Among African Americans, for example, economically disadvantaged single mothers can obtain needed help with child care and social support by living with their mothers (Burton, 1990; Taylor, 2000). Even when members of the extended family live in their own nuclear family households, they often share responsibility for raising children, to the benefit of the children.

© Rick Gomez/CORBIS

The family is a system in which reciprocal influence reigns.

The Family as a System within Other Systems

Whether a family is of the nuclear or the extended type, it does not exist in a vacuum. Adopting Urie Bronfenbrenner's bioecological model (see Chapter 1) will help you view the family as a system embedded in larger social systems such as a neighborhood, a community, a subculture, and a broader culture. The family experience in our culture is different from that in cultures where new brides become underlings in the households of their mothers-in-law or where men can have several wives. There is an almost infinite variety of family forms and family contexts in the world and a correspondingly wide range of developmental experiences within the family.

The Family as a Changing System

It would be difficult enough to study the family as a system if it kept the same members and continued to perform the same activities for as long as it existed. However, family membership changes as new children are born and as grown children leave the nest. Moreover, each family member is a developing individual, and the relationships between husband and wife, parent and child, and sibling and sibling develop in systematic ways over time. Because the family is truly a system, changes in family membership and changes in any individual or relationship within the family affect the dynamics of the whole.

The earliest theories of family development featured the concept of a **family life cycle**—a sequence of changes in family composition, roles, and relationships from the time people marry until they die (Hill & Rodgers, 1964). Family theorist Evelyn Duvall (1977) outlined eight stages of the family life cycle (see Table 15.1). In each stage, family members play distinctive roles and carry out distinctive developmental tasks—for example, establishing a satisfying relationship in the newlywed phase, adjusting to the demands of new parenthood in the childbearing phase, and adapting to the departure of children in the "launching" phase.

In this chapter, we look at the effect of these family transitions on adults, and we examine how the child's experience of the family changes as she develops. You will see, however, that an increasing number of people do not experience this traditional family life cycle. They remain single or childless, they marry multiple times, or they otherwise deviate from a scenario in which a man and woman form a nuclear family, raise children, and grow old together. As a result, many family researchers reject the simple concept of the family life cycle with its set stages (Dilworth-Anderson & Burton, 1996; Klein & White, 1996). However, they have embraced the concept that families, like the individuals in them, are developing organisms.

Table 15.1 Stages of the Family Life Cycle

Stage	Available Roles
1. Married couple without children	Wife Husband
2. Childbearing family (oldest child from birth to 30 months)	Wife–mother Husband–father Infant daughter or son
3. Family with preschool children (oldest child from 30 months to 6 years)	Wife–mother Husband–father Daughter–sister Son–brother
4. Family with school-age children (oldest child up to 12 years)	Wife–mother Husband–father Daughter–sister Son–brother
5. Family with teenagers (oldest child from 13 to 20 years)	Wife–mother Husband–father Daughter–sister Son–brother
6. Family launching young adults (First child gone to last child gone)	Wife–mother–grandmother Husband–father–grandfather Daughter–sister–aunt Son–brother–uncle
7. Family without children (empty nest to retirement)	Wife–mother–grandmother Husband–father–grandfather
8. Aging family (retirement to death)	Wife–mother–grandmother Husband–father–grandfather Widow or widower

SOURCE: Adapted from Duvall, 1977.

A Changing System in a Changing World

Not only is the family a system embedded within systems, and not only is it a developing system, but also the world in which it is embedded is ever changing. During the second half of the 20th century, several dramatic social changes altered the makeup of the typical family and the quality of family experience. Drawing on analyses of U.S. Census Bureau data and other surveys, we will highlight some of these trends, some of which are finally leveling off or even reversing (see Fox, 2001a; Teachman, 2000; U.S. Census Bureau, 2003; Whitehead & Popenoe, 2003):

1. *More single adults.* More adults are living as singles today than in the past, often living with a partner but unmarried. However, do not be deceived into thinking that marriage is out of style: more than 90% of adults can still be expected to marry at some time in their lives (Whitehead & Popenoe, 2003).

2. *Postponed marriage.* Many adults are not rejecting marriage but are simply delaying it and pursuing educational and career goals. The average age of first marriage decreased during the first half of the 20th century, but it has since risen again to about 25 for women and 27 for men (Whitehead & Popenoe, 2003) despite increased rates of teenage pregnancy.

3. *Fewer children.* Today's adults are also having fewer children and therefore spend fewer years of their lives raising

children. Increasing numbers of young women are also remaining childless; in 1998, 19% of women ages 40 to 44 were childless, compared with 10% in 1980 (Whitehead & Popenoe, 2003).

4. *More women working.* In 1950, 12% of married women with children younger than 6 years worked outside the home; now the figure is more than 60%, a truly dramatic social change (U.S. Census Bureau, 2003). Fewer children have a mother whose full-time job is that of homemaker.

5. *More divorce.* It is well known that the divorce rate has increased over the past several decades, although it leveled off around 1980. At least 4 in 10 newly married couples can expect to divorce (Vobejda, 1998).

6. *More single-parent families.* Partly because of a rising rate of out-of-wedlock births, but mostly because of the rise in divorce rates, more children live in single-parent families. In 1960, only 9% of children lived with one parent, usually a widowed one (Whitehead & Popenoe, 2003); in 2002, 23% of children younger than18 years lived with their mothers only and 5% lived with their fathers only (Fields, 2003).

7. *More children living in poverty.* The higher number of single-parent families has meant an increase in the proportion of children living in poverty. Almost 20% of children in the United States live in poverty today (U.S. Census Bureau, 2003). Fully 36% of African American children and almost 34% of Hispanic American children are poor, and more than one-third of children living in female-headed homes live in poverty.

8. *More remarriages.* As more married couples divorce, more adults are remarrying. Often they form new, **reconstituted families** that include at least a parent, a stepparent, and a child; sometimes they blend multiple children from two families into a new family. About 25% of American children will spend some time in a reconstituted, or blended, family (Hetherington & Jodl, 1994).

9. *More years without children.* Because modern couples are compressing their childbearing into a shorter time span, because some divorced individuals do not remarry, and mainly because people are living longer, adults today spend more of their later years as couples—or, especially if they are women, as single adults—without children in their homes (Johnson & Troll, 1996). Of adults age 65 and older, 24% live alone, 65% live with a spouse, and 11% live with someone else, such as a sibling or adult child (U.S. Census Bureau, 2003).

10. *More multigenerational families.* As a result of these same trends, more children today than in the past know their grandparents and even their great-grandparents, parent–child and grandparent–child relationships are lasting longer, and multigenerational bonds are becoming more important (Bengtson, 2001). As three- and even four-generation families have become more common, the result has been dubbed **the beanpole family,** characterized by more generations, but smaller ones, than in the past (Bengtson, Rosenthal, & Burton, 1990; Johnson & Troll, 1996).

11. *Fewer caregivers for aging adults.* Smaller families with fewer children, increases in the numbers of adults living alone, increased longevity, and the large Baby Boom generation poised to enter old age mean that we have more aging adults needing care from relatives and fewer relatives to provide it (E. Brody, 2004).

We will look at how some of these trends affect development later in this chapter. Some observers view these changes as evidence of a "decline of marriage and the family," noting the negative effects on human development of increased poverty, divorce, and single-parent families. They worry because most Americans now view marriage as an institution whose purpose is more to meet the emotional needs of adults than to raise children (Whitehead & Popenoe, 2003). Other scholars find good news with the bad in these trends (Teachman, 2000; L. White & Rogers, 2000). For example, postponing marriage improves its chances of success, men's and women's roles in the family are more equal than they used to be, more children have relationships with their grandparents and great-grandparents, and families are better off financially with two wage earners than with only one. Also, some of the trends suggesting the weakening of the family—for example, the rise in single-parent families and in numbers of children living in poverty—began to reverse in the 1990s. From this perspective, the family is not dying; it is just different. It may even be characterized as an "adaptable institution" in that it has survived despite many negative social changes (Amato et al., 2003).

Perhaps the most important message is this: the American family is more diverse than ever before (see Demo, Allen, & Fine, 2000). Our stereotyped image of the family—the traditional *Leave It to Beaver* nuclear family with a breadwinner–father, a full-time housewife–mother, and children—has become just that: a stereotype. By one estimate, about 45% of families in 1960, but only 12% of families in 1995, conformed to this pattern (Hernandez, 1997). Clearly we must broaden our image of the family to include the many dual-career, single-parent, reconstituted, childless, and other nontraditional families that exist today. We must also avoid assuming that families that do not fit the *Leave It to Beaver* model are deficient. Bear that in mind as we begin our excursion into family life.

Summing Up

In sum, family systems theorists view the family as a system in which all members affect all others; Bronfenbrenner and other ecological theorists see the family as a system embedded in other systems; and family development theorists insist that we understand the family life cycle. The world in which the family is embedded is constantly changing—in the last half century toward more single adults, postponed marriage, fewer children, more women working, more divorce, more single-parent families, more children in poverty, more reconstituted families, more years without children, more multigenerational families, and fewer caregivers for aging adults. Given the increased diversity of family forms, the *Leave It to Beaver* family is harder to find. ■

The Infant

We begin this look at family development by adopting a child's perspective and tracing a child's development in the family from infancy to adolescence. Later, we will adopt the perspective of this child's parents and see how the events of the family life cycle look to them.

Mother–Infant and Father–Infant Relationships

Once developmentalists took seriously the idea that the family is a system, they discovered the existence of fathers and began to look more carefully at how both mothers and fathers interact with their children and at what each parent contributes to a child's development. They have also asked how mothers' and fathers' roles have changed as more mothers have gone to work and as divorce rates have climbed.

Gender stereotypes would suggest that fathers are not cut out to care for infants and young children; however, the evidence suggests that they are (Lamb & Tamis-Lemonda, 2004; Parke, 1996; Phares, 1999). Researchers repeatedly find that fathers and mothers are more similar than different in the ways they interact with infants and young children. For example, when mothers and fathers are observed feeding their babies, fathers prove to be no less able than mothers to perform this caregiving task effectively and to ensure that the milk is consumed; nor are they less sensitive to the infant's cues during the feeding session (Parke & Sawin, 1976). Similarly, fathers, like mothers, become objects of their infants' love and serve as secure bases for their explorations (Cox et al., 1992). We have no basis for thinking that mothers are uniquely qualified to parent or that men are hopelessly inept around babies.

Fathers are just as capable as mothers of sensitive, responsive parenting.

However, that fathers are capable of sensitive parenting does not necessarily mean that they play the same roles as mothers in their children's lives. Fathers and mothers differ in both the quantity and the quality of the parenting they provide (Marsiglio et al., 2000; Lamb & Tamis-Lemonda, 2004), and we can ask how nature and nurture contribute to these differences. Consider first the matter of quantity. Mothers simply spend more time with children than fathers do (Bianchi, 2000). This gender difference is common across cultures, causing some to argue that it has been built into our genes during the course of evolution; it may even be related to the biological fact that mothers are more certain their children are theirs than fathers are (Bjorklund & Pellegrini, 2002).

True, fathers in our society are more involved with their children today than they were in the past (Marsiglio et al., 2000; Pleck & Masciadrelli, 2004). Some are sharing responsibility for child care equally with their spouses rather than just "helping" (Deutsch, 2001), especially if they hold egalitarian views about gender roles (Bulanda, 2004). Yet there is still a gap. In 1965, fathers spent about half as much time with their children as mothers did; in 1998, they spent about two-thirds as much time (Bianchi, 2000). Because mothers today spend less time on housework, because families are smaller, and because fathers are more involved, children in two-parent families may enjoy more time with their parents today than they used to (Bianchi, 2000). Yet increases in separation and divorce mean other children see little of their fathers.

Now consider the issue of quality. Mothers and fathers also differ in their typical styles of interacting with young children. When mothers interact with their babies, a large proportion of their time is devoted to caregiving: offering food, changing diapers, wiping noses, and so on. Fathers spend much of their time with children in playful interaction. They specialize in tickling, poking, bouncing, and surprising infants, whereas mothers hold, talk to, and play quietly with infants (Laflamme, Pomerleau, & Malcuit, 2002; Neville & Parke, 1997). Yet fathers are able to adopt a "motherlike" caregiver role if they have primary responsibility for their children, so their playful parenting may be more about being in the role of the "backup" parent than about being male rather than female (Phares, 1999). It seems then that both nature (evolution) and nurture (societal gender-role norms) contribute to mother–father differences in parental involvement and styles of interacting with young children.

In view of the roles that fathers play in their children's lives, what are their contributions to child development? Fathers contribute to healthy development by supporting their children financially, whether they live together or not (Marsiglio et al., 2000). They also contribute by being warm and effective parents, just as mothers do; in the end, that is more important than whether they serve as masculine role models (Lamb & Tamis-Lemonda, 2004). Babies are likely to be more socially competent if they are securely attached to both parents than if they are securely attached to just one (Main & Weston, 1981). In addition, children whose fathers are warm and involved with them tend to become high achievers in school (Cabrera et al., 2000). A father's tendency to challenge his young children during play, egging them on to take risks, may be particularly important, breeding a secure attachment style later in life and encouraging exploration (Grossmann et al., 2002). Finally, children generally have fewer psychological disorders and problems if their fathers are caring, involved, and effective parents than if they are not (Cabrera et al., 2000; Marsiglio et al., 2000).

Mothers, Fathers, and Infants: The System at Work

We now need to view the new family as a three-person system. The mother–child relationship cannot be understood without considering the father; nor can the father–child relationship be understood without taking the mother into account. This is because parents have **indirect effects** on their children through their ability to influence the behavior of their spouses. More generally, indirect effects within the family are instances in which the relationship between two individuals is modified by the behavior or attitudes of a third family member.

Fathers indirectly influence the mother–infant relationship in many ways. For example, mothers who have close, supportive relationships with their husbands tend to interact more patiently and sensitively with their babies than do mothers who are experiencing marital tension and who feel that they are raising their children largely without help (Cox et al., 1992; Lamb & Tamis-Lemonda, 2004). Meanwhile, mothers indirectly affect the father–infant relationship. For example, fathers are more likely to become involved in their children's education when their wives are involved (Flouri & Buchanan, 2003), and fathers who have just had arguments with their wives are less supportive and engaged when they interact with their sons than fathers who have just had pleasant conversations with their wives (Kitzmann, 2000). Parents can truly co-parent, working as a team, or they can undermine each other's effectiveness (Parke, 2004).

Summing Up

Mothers are tremendously important forces in human development, but fathers are, too. Although they spend less time than mothers with their children, and often adopt a playful rather than a caregiving role, they are capable of sensitive and responsive parenting and contribute in many positive ways to their children's development. Both mothers and fathers affect their children not only directly but also through indirect effects on their spouses. Overall, children are best off when the marital relationship is solid and couples provide mutual support and encouragement that allow both to be more sensitive and responsive parents. Socialization within the family is not a one-way street in which influence flows only from parent to child; it is more like the busy intersection of many avenues of influence. ■

The Child

As children reach age 2 or 3, parents continue to be caregivers and playmates, but they also become more concerned with teaching their offspring how (and how not) to behave, using some approach to child rearing and discipline to achieve this end. Siblings also serve as socialization agents and become an important part of the child's experience of the family.

Parenting Styles

How can I be a good parent? Certainly this question is uppermost in most parents' minds. You can go far in understanding which parenting styles are effective by considering just two dimensions of parenting: acceptance–responsiveness and demandingness–control (Darling & Steinberg, 1993; Maccoby & Martin, 1983; Schaefer, 1959).

Dimensions of Child Rearing

Parental **acceptance–responsiveness** refers to the extent to which parents are supportive, sensitive to their children's needs, and willing to provide affection and praise when their children meet their expectations. Accepting, responsive parents are affectionate and often smile at, praise, and encourage their children, although they also let children know when they misbehave. Less accepting and responsive parents are often quick to criticize, belittle, punish, or ignore their children and rarely communicate to children that they are loved and valued.

Demandingness–control (sometimes called *permissiveness–restrictiveness*) refers to how much control over decisions lies with the parent as opposed to with the child. Controlling and demanding parents set rules, expect their children to follow them, and monitor their children closely to ensure that the rules are followed. Less controlling and demanding parents (often called *permissive parents*) make fewer demands and allow their children a great deal of autonomy in exploring the environment, expressing their opinions and emotions, and making decisions about their activities.

By crossing these two dimensions, we have four basic patterns of child rearing to consider, as shown in Figure 15.1:

1. Authoritarian parenting. This is a restrictive parenting style combining high demandingness–control and low acceptance–responsiveness. Parents impose many rules, expect strict obedience, rarely explain why the child should comply with rules, and often rely on power tactics such as physical punishment to gain compliance.

2. Authoritative parenting. Authoritative parents are more flexible; they are demanding and exert control, but they are also accepting and responsive. They set clear rules and consistently enforce them, but they also explain the rationales for their rules and restrictions, are responsive to their children's needs and points of view, and involve their children in family decision making. They are reasonable and democratic in their approach; although it is clear that they are in charge, they communicate respect for their children.

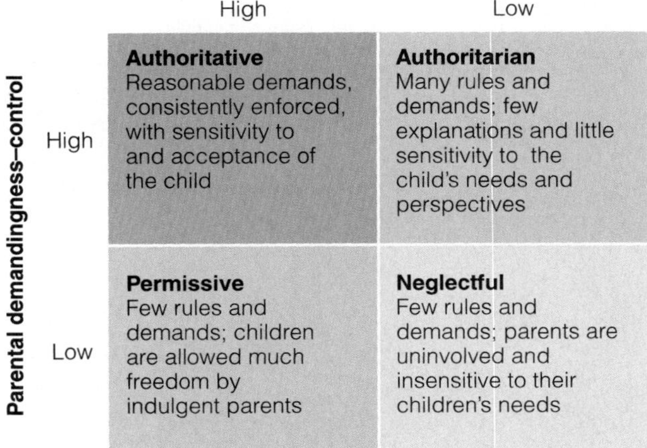

Figure 15.1 The acceptance–responsiveness and demandingness–control dimensions of parenting. Which combination best describes your parents' approach?

SOURCE: Based on Maccoby & Martin (1983).

3. Permissive parenting. This style is high in acceptance–responsiveness but low in demandingness–control. Permissive parents are indulgent; they have relatively few rules and make relatively few demands, encourage children to express their feelings and impulses, and rarely exert control over their behavior.

4. Neglectful parenting. Finally, parents who combine low demandingness–control and low acceptance–responsiveness are relatively uninvolved in their children's upbringing. They seem not to care much about their children and may even reject them—or else they are so overwhelmed by their own problems that they cannot devote sufficient energy to setting and enforcing rules (Maccoby & Martin, 1983).

We assume that you have no difficulty deciding that parental acceptance and responsiveness are preferable to parental rejection and insensitivity. As you have seen in this book, warm, responsive parenting is associated with secure attachments to parents, academic competence, high self-esteem, positive social skills, peer acceptance, a strong sense of morality, and many other virtues. By contrast, lack of parental acceptance and affection contributes to depression and other psychological problems (Ge et al., 1996).

The degree of demandingness and control is also important. The authoritarian, authoritative, and permissive parenting styles were originally identified and defined by Diana Baumrind (1967, 1977, 1991). In a pioneering longitudinal study, Baumrind found that children raised by authoritative parents were the best adjusted: They were cheerful, socially responsible, self-reliant, achievement oriented, and cooperative with adults and peers. Children of authoritarian parents tended to be moody and seemingly unhappy, easily annoyed, relatively aimless, and unpleasant to be around. Finally, children of permissive parents were often impulsive, aggressive, self-centered, rebellious, without self-control, aimless, and low in independence and achievement, although a warm, permissive style can be effective with an older, more independent child.

Subsequent research has shown that the worst developmental outcomes are associated with a neglectful, uninvolved style of parenting. Children of neglectful parents display behavioral problems such as aggression and frequent temper tantrums as early as age 3 (Miller et al., 1993). They tend to become hostile and antisocial adolescents who abuse alcohol and drugs and get in trouble (Lamborn et al., 1991; Weiss & Schwarz, 1996). Parents who provide little guidance and communicate that they do not care breed children who are resentful and prone to strike back at their uncaring parents and other authority figures.

In short, children develop best when they have love and limits. If they are indulged or neglected and given little guidance, they will not learn self-control, may become selfish and unruly, and may lack direction. If they receive too much guidance, as the children of authoritarian parents do, they will have few opportunities to learn self-reliance and may lack confidence in their own decision-making abilities. The link between authoritative parenting and positive developmental outcomes is evident in most ethnic groups and socioeconomic groups studied to date in the United States (Glasgow et al., 1997; Steinberg, 2001) and in a variety of other cultures (Scott, Scott, & McCabe, 1991; Vazonyi, Hibbert, & Snider, 2003).

Social Class, Economic Hardship, and Parenting

Parenting styles are not traitlike characteristics that parents display consistently regardless of the child, the child's age, or the context. Although parents differ in their broad approaches to parenting, they respond flexibly to the specific child-rearing situations that face them (Holden & Miller, 1999). With that as warning, we can note that middle-class and lower-class parents often pursue different goals, emphasize different values, and rely on different parenting styles in raising children. Compared with middle- and upper-class parents, lower- and working-class parents tend to stress obedience and respect for authority, be more restrictive and authoritarian, reason with their children less frequently, and show less warmth and affection (Maccoby, 1980; McLoyd, 1990). Although you will find a range of parenting styles in any social group, these average social-class differences in parenting have been observed in many cultures and across racial and ethnic groups in the United States.

Why might these social class differences exist? One explanation focuses on the skills needed by workers in white-collar and blue-collar jobs (Arnett, 1995; Kohn, 1969). Parents from lower socioeconomic groups may emphasize obedience to authority figures because that is what is required in blue-collar jobs like their own. Middle- and upper-class parents may reason with their children and stress individual initiative, curiosity, and creativity because these are the attributes that count for business executives, professionals, and other white-collar workers.

Most explanations, however, center on the stresses associated with low-income living and their effects on parenting

The stresses of economic hardship can make it hard to be an effective parent.

(McLoyd, 1990; Seccombe, 2000). Rand Conger and his associates (1992, 1995, 2002), for example, have shown that parents experiencing financial problems tend to become depressed, which increases conflict between them. Marital conflict, in turn, disrupts each partner's ability to be a supportive, involved, and effective parent—another example of indirect effects within the family. This breakdown in parenting then contributes to negative child outcomes such as low self-esteem, poor school performance, poor peer relations, and adjustment problems such as depression and aggression (see Figure 15.2).

Stresses are magnified for families living below the poverty line or moving in and out of poverty as a result of economic crises. Research shows that parents living in poverty tend to be restrictive, punitive, and inconsistent, sometimes to the point of being abusive and neglectful (Seccombe, 2000; Brooks-Gunn, Britto, & Brady, 1999). In high-crime poverty areas, parents may feel the need to be more authoritarian and controlling just to protect their children from danger (Taylor et al., 2000).

Although parenting practices do not account for all negative effects of poverty on child development, these effects are serious and far-reaching. Poverty tends to bring with it a physical environment characterized by pollution, noise, and crowded, unsafe living conditions and a social environment characterized by family instability, violence, harsh parenting, and limited cognitive stimulation (Evans, 2004). The effects on child development include health problems, emotional and behavioral problems, and school failure (Bradley & Corwyn, 2002; Evans, 2004). Federal and state welfare reform policies that require welfare mothers to work are not necessarily alleviating these problems. A single working mother

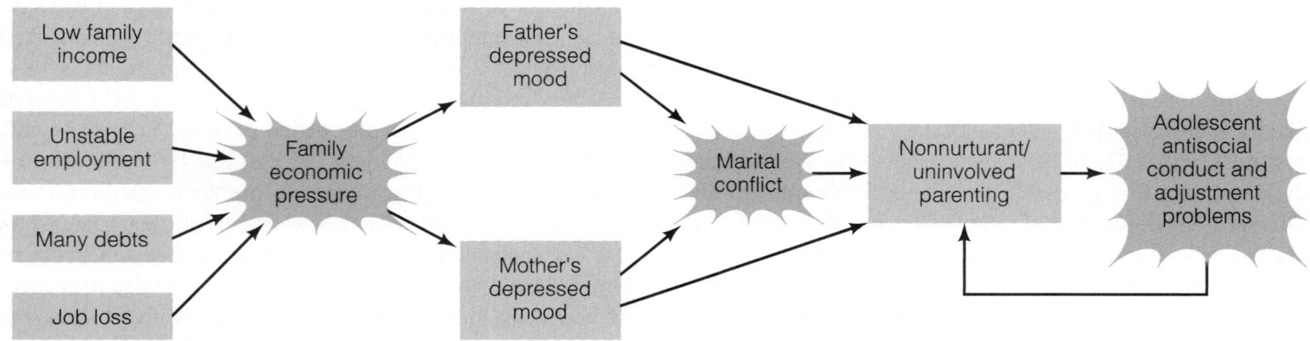

Figure 15.2 A model of the relationship among family economic stress, patterns of parenting, and adolescent adjustment.

SOURCE: Adapted from Conger et al. (1992).

with two children who earns a minimum wage is unlikely to earn enough to rise above the poverty line (Seccombe, 2000). She probably does not receive health coverage through her job, and she still has to worry about finding affordable child care and a myriad of other problems.

In sum, the more authoritarian parenting style used by many lower-income parents may reflect both an adaptive attempt to prepare children for jobs in which they will be expected to obey a boss and the effects of economic stress, particularly of living in poverty, on parenting.

Models of Influence in the Family

In thinking about influences within the family, we will bet that you, like most developmental scientists, think first about parents affecting children. But consider three different models of influence in the family: the parent effects, child effects, and transactional models.

Parent Effects Model

The study of human development has been guided through most of its history by a simple **parent effects model** of family influence. This model assumes that influences run one way, from parent (particularly mother) to child. You have just reviewed research demonstrating effects of parenting styles on child development. But what if you think a bit differently: Could it be that a child's behavior influences the style of parenting his parents adopt and that what appear to be parent effects are instead child effects?

Child Effects Model

A **child effects model** of family influence highlights instances in which children influence their parents rather than vice versa (Ambert, 1992; Crouter & Booth, 2003; Sanson, Hemphill, & Smart, 2004). One good example of a child effect is the influence of a child's age and competence on the style of parenting used with that child. For example, infants in their first year of life require and elicit sensitive care, whereas older infants who are asserting their wills and toddling here and there force parents to provide more instruction and discipline (Fagot & Kavanaugh, 1993). Normally, parents become less restrictive as their children mature and gradually, with parental guidance, become capable of making their own decisions (Steinberg, 2002).

Now consider the possibility that a child's personality influences the parenting she receives. Is it not possible that easygoing, manageable children cause their parents to be warm and authoritative? Could not difficult, stubborn, and aggressive children help mold parents who are rejecting and who either rule with an authoritarian iron hand or throw up their hands in defeat and become neglectful? Recall the description in Chapter 13 of the discipline techniques of induction, power assertion, and love withdrawal. In an early demonstration of child effects, Barbara Keller and Richard Bell (1979) set out to challenge the finding, reported in Chapter 13, that a parent's use of induction (explanations emphasizing the consequences of a child's behavior for other people) fosters moral maturity. Is it not possible instead, they reasoned, that children who are already "good" are more likely than less responsive children to elicit inductive explanations from adults? Keller and Bell had female college students attempt to convince 9-year-old girls to behave altruistically (for example, to spend more time sewing a pillow for a handicapped child than sewing a pillow for themselves). The girls had been coached to respond either attentively or inattentively.

As expected, students confronted with an attentive child used a great deal of induction, pointing out how other children might feel if the child behaved selfishly. By contrast, college students who interacted with an inattentive child relied on power-assertion techniques such as promising rewards for altruism and threatening penalties for selfishness. A study of the budding juvenile delinquents from age 14 to age 16 also revealed child effects on parents (Kerr & Stattin, 2003). In response to their delinquent child's difficult behavior at age 14, parents became less warm and emotionally supportive and less in control of their adolescents by the time the adolescents were 16. By contrast, these researchers could detect few links between parenting when adolescents were 14 and adolescent problem behavior at 16.

Transactional Model

Research now reveals that antisocial behavior probably results when a child genetically predisposed to be aggressive behaves in ways that elicit negative parenting and when this negative parenting, in turn, causes the child to become even more aggressive (Ge et al., 1996; O'Connor et al., 1998; and see Chapter 13). When such a destructive family process develops—the child elicits coercive and ineffective parenting from parents and parents contribute to the child's antisocial behavior—it becomes impossible to say who is more influential. This scenario is best described by a **transactional model** of family influence, in which parent and child are seen as influencing one another reciprocally (Sameroff, 1975; also see Cook, 2001). According to this model, child problems can develop if the relationship between parent and child goes bad as the two interact over time. Optimal child development is likely to result when parent–child transactions evolve in more positive directions.

Genes clearly have a role in family processes. The Explorations box on page 430 takes a closer look at how parents' genes and their cultural environments influence how they approach parenting. And, as Chapter 3 showed, a child's genetic endowment influences not only the child's behavior but also the parenting style and the home environment she experiences (Collins et al., 2000; Reiss et al., 2000). Through the process of gene–environment correlation (Scarr & McCartney, 1983; see Chapter 3), the genes children inherit (and share with their parents) influence how their parents and other people react to them and what experiences they seek. The child whose genes predispose him to antisocial behavior is likely to elicit a harsh, controlling style of parenting even from adoptive parents; the child's hostile behavior and the parent's ineffective parenting then feed on each other through a transactional process to aggravate the child's behavioral problems (Ge et al., 1996).

Genes, Culture, and Parenting

What determines the approach to parenting a mother or father adopts? Probably both nature and nurture. You have seen already that a child's genes may influence the kind of parenting he receives by evoking a certain kind of reaction from parents. Do a parent's genes also influence the kind of parenting she provides? Yes, say Jenae Neiderhiser and her colleagues (2004). They looked at genetic and environmental influences on mothers' parenting behavior in two samples. Using a sample consisting of sibling pairs of varying degrees of genetic relatedness from identical twin to unrelated siblings in stepfamilies, they could determine whether the genetic makeups of adolescents influenced the parenting they received. And in a sample of identical and fraternal twin mothers, they could see whether a mother's genes influenced her general parenting style, independent of a particular child's genetically influenced behavior. Data came from multiple sources—mothers, adolescents, and observers of parent–child interactions.

The team's complex analyses suggested that a mother's genes influence her positivity toward all her children. There were also signs that children's genes influence how positively their mothers treat them in particular. By contrast, a mother's negativity toward her adolescents, as well as her tendency to be controlling, seemed to be more influenced by a particular adolescent's genetically influenced characteristics than by a mother's genetic makeup. Thus, for example, a difficult child may evoke more negative reactions and more strong-armed control tactics from a parent than an easy child does.

Environmental influences, especially those unique to a particular child rather than shared with siblings, were also evident. But what environmental factors? The Neiderhiser study did not explore this question, but other research has pointed to a host of environmental influences on parenting. The type of parenting to which the parent was exposed as a child is one such influence, and it, in turn, is influenced by the cultural context in which the family lives. Parents of different cultures and ethnic backgrounds are socialized to hold different beliefs and values about child rearing that shape their parenting practices and, in turn, affect their children's development (MacPhee, Fritz, & Miller-Heyl, 1996; McLoyd et al., 2000). For example, Native American and Hispanic parents, probably because their cultures are collectivist and emphasize the goals of the group rather than of the individual, place more emphasis than European American parents on teaching children to be polite and respectful of authority figures (particularly their fathers) rather than to be independent and competitive (MacPhee et al., 1996). Some traditional Native American groups such as the Mayan and Navajo Indians also believe that the freedom and autonomy of young children must be respected. As a result, although parents may try to persuade children to do things, they feel it would be wrong to force them (Rogoff, 2003). Their children seem to do fine with this relatively permissive parenting style, learning at an early age to cooperate with their parents and with other people.

By contrast, African American parents and Asian or Asian American parents sometimes use a more authoritarian approach to parenting than most European American parents would use. They get good results with it because it is viewed as appropriate by parents and children alike in their sociocultural context. For example, physical, coercive discipline (short of abuse) is not as strongly linked to aggression and antisocial behavior among African American youths as it is among European Americans, possibly because it is viewed by African American children as a sign that their parents care (Deater-Deckard et al., 1996; Boykin-McElhaney & Allen, 2001). Authoritarian parenting also seems to mean something different to Chinese children than to American ones. Ruth Chao

Demonstrations of child effects and transactional effects within the family are important. Yet parent effects remain significant. By using more sophisticated research designs, researchers have gathered more solid evidence than ever that parents influence their children's development, even when genetic influences are controlled (Collins et al., 2000). For example, longitudinal studies demonstrate that parents who adopt an authoritative parenting style and who firmly demand that their children follow their rules have children who become more compliant and well-behaved over time than other children (Collins et al., 2000), whereas parents who respond angrily to children with behavioral problems can make those problems worse over time (P. M. Cole, 2003). Meanwhile, experimental studies show that parent training programs can positively affect child development by changing parenting practices (Forgatch & DeGarmo, 1999; Reynolds & Robertson, 2003). Still, we should not assume, as early child development researchers did, that parents are solely responsible for whether their children turn out "good" or "bad." We must remind ourselves repeatedly that the family is a system in which family members are influenced in reciprocal ways by both their genetic endowments and the environments they create for one another.

Sibling Relationships

A family system consisting of mother, father, and child is perturbed by the arrival of a new baby and becomes a new—and

© Charles Gupton/Stock, Boston

(1994, 2000) was puzzled because Chinese children do no better in school when their parents use an authoritative style of parenting than when their parents use an authoritarian style. She observed that Chinese parents offer their children clear and specific guidelines for behavior, believing that this is the best way to express their love and train their children properly. Although the style seems overly controlling to European Americans, Chinese children do not view it that way.

So, nature and nurture shape the parenting approach that parents use and its effectiveness. Parents' genes influence their general style of parenting, and their children's genes influence how each of them is treated. Cultural influences on parenting are also important. Although authoritative parenting is an effective parenting approach in most cultural contexts, other parenting styles can be effective if they are viewed as appropriate in a particular cultural context. As a result, you should be careful not to judge parenting in other cultures and subcultures as deficient just because it is not the style favored by middle-class European American parents (Ogbu, 1981).

considerably more complex—family system. How do children adapt to a new baby in the house, and how does the sibling relationship change as children age?

A New Baby Arrives

When Judy Dunn and Carol Kendrick (1982; see also Dunn, 1993) carefully studied young children's reactions to a new sibling, they found that mothers typically pay less attention to their firstborns after the new baby arrives than before. Partly for this reason, firstborns often find being "dethroned" a stressful experience. They become more difficult and demanding, or more dependent and clingy, and they often develop problems with their sleeping, eating, and toileting routines. Most of their battles are with their mothers, but a few firstborns are not above hitting, poking, and pinching their younger brothers or sisters. Security of attachment to their mothers decreases, especially if firstborns are 2 years old or older and can fully appreciate how much they have lost (Teti et al., 1996). Although positive effects such as an increased insistence on doing things independently are also common, it is clear that firstborns are not thrilled to have an attention-grabbing new baby in the house. They resent losing their parents' attention, and their own difficult behavior may alienate their parents further.

How can problems be minimized? Adjustment to a new sibling is easier if the marital relationship is good and if the firstborn had secure relationships with both parents before the younger sibling arrived—and continues to enjoy close re-

© Chris Lowe/Index Stock Imagery

☾ Firstborns do not always accept a newcomer in the family.

lationships afterward (Dunn & Kendrick, 1982; Teti et al., 1996). Parents are advised to guard against ignoring their firstborn, to continue providing love and attention, and to maintain the child's routines as much as possible. They can also encourage older children to become aware of the new baby's needs and feelings and to assist in her care (Dunn & Kendrick, 1982; Howe & Ross, 1990).

Ambivalence in Sibling Relationships

Fortunately, most older siblings adjust fairly quickly to having a new brother or sister (Dunn & Kendrick, 1982). Yet even in the best of sibling relationships, **sibling rivalry**—the spirit of competition, jealousy, and resentment between brothers and sisters—is normal. It may be rooted in an evolutionary fact: Although siblings share half their genes on average and are therefore more motivated to help one another than to help genetically unrelated individuals, siblings also compete with one another for their parents' time and resources to ensure their own survival and welfare (Bjorklund & Pellegrini, 2002).

The number of skirmishes between very young siblings can be as high as 56 per hour (Dunn, 1993). Jealousies, bouts of teasing, shouting matches, and occasional kicks and punches continue to be part of the sibling relationship throughout childhood; squabbles are most often about possessions (McGuire et al., 2000). Each combatant feels that he is blameless and has been terribly wronged by his sibling (Wilson et al., 2004). Levels of conflict decrease after early adolescence as teenagers spend more time away from the family (Furman & Buhrmester, 1992; Larson et al., 1996).

Some sibling relationships are consistently closer than others over the years (Dunn, Slomkowski, & Beardsall, 1994). Both the personalities of the siblings and the quality of parents' relationships with their children have a lot to do with how smooth or stormy the sibling relationship is (G. H. Brody & Stoneman, 1996). Sibling relationships are friendlier and less conflictual if mothers and fathers respond warmly and sensitively to all their children and do not unfairly favor one over another (Dunn, 1993; McHale et al., 2000). It is perceptions that matter most: Children are able to accept that differences in treatment can be fair, and therefore not objectionable, if they are based on differences in the ages, competencies, and personalities of the siblings (Kowal et al., 2002). Overall, the most important thing to know about sibling relationships is that they are ambivalent—they involve both closeness and conflict.

Contributions to Development

For most children, interactions with siblings are mostly positive, and siblings play mostly positive roles in one another's development. Even the battles may contribute positively to social development by teaching children how to assert themselves, manage conflict, and tolerate negative emotions (Bedford, Volling, & Avioli, 2000). Only when sibling relationships are extremely hateful and destructive and children experience harsh parenting should parents worry that siblings may contribute negatively to development (Garcia et al., 2000).

One of the important positive functions of siblings is to provide *emotional support.* Brothers and sisters confide in one another, often more than they confide in their parents (Howe et al., 2000). They protect and comfort one another in rough times. Even preschoolers jump in to comfort their infant siblings when their mothers leave them or when strangers approach (Stewart & Marvin, 1984).

© Penny Tweedie/Getty Images

☾ In many societies, older siblings are major caregivers for young children.

Second, older siblings often provide *caretaking* services for younger siblings; they baby-sit. Indeed, in a study of 186 societies, older children were the principal caregivers for infants and toddlers in 57% of the cultures studied (Weisner & Gallimore, 1977). In many societies, children as young as 5 years are involved in meaningful ways in the care of infants and toddlers (Rogoff, 2003).

Finally, older siblings serve as *teachers.* One 5-year-old was aware of how much her 2-year-old sister acquired from her through observational learning: "See. I said, 'Bye, I'm going on the slide,' and she said, 'Bye.' She says whatever I say." Older siblings may have more influence on their younger siblings' gender-role development than parents do (McHale et al., 2001). Older brothers and sisters are not always as skilled in teaching as parents are (Perez-Granados & Callanan, 1997), but they clearly feel a special responsibility to teach, and younger siblings actively seek their guidance.

Although having a large number of siblings has negative implications for cognitive development, most likely because each child receives less intellectual stimulation from adults, having at least one sibling has positive effects on a child's ability to relate to peers and to exert self-control, most likely because of the social skill learning that takes place in the sibling relationship (Downey & Condron, 2004). Moreover the quality of a child's sibling relationships predicts the quality of their later friendship relationships (Yeh & Lempers, 2004). Not all that is learned in the sibling relationship is good, of course. For example, having a troublemaking older sibling can be at least as important as having deviant peers in influencing adolescents to engage in troublemaking (Ardelt & Day, 2002).

One more note: An older sibling can affect a younger sibling not only directly but also through the indirect effects he has on parents. Gene Brody and his colleagues (2003, 2004) have discovered that, if an older sibling is competent, this contributes positively to his mother's psychological functioning (possibly because she feels good about herself as a parent), which makes her more likely to provide supportive parenting to a younger sibling, which in turn increases the odds that the younger sibling will also be competent. By contrast, an incompetent older sibling can set in motion a negative chain of events involving less supportive parenting and less positive outcomes for the younger sibling.

Summing Up

Parents who adopt an authoritative parenting style (as opposed to an authoritarian, permissive, or neglectful one) generally influence their children's development positively, whereas economic hardship undermines effective parenting. Children, meanwhile, as indicated by the child effects and transactional models, help influence where their parents fall on the acceptance and demandingness dimensions. When a couple has a second child, the family system changes profoundly. Involving both closeness and rivalry, sibling relationships offer emotional support, caretaking, and teaching and have both direct and indirect effects on development. ■

The Adolescent

When you picture the typical relationship between a teenager and her parents, do you envision a teenager who is out all the time with friends, resents every rule and restriction, and talks back at every opportunity? Do you imagine parents wringing their hands in despair and wondering if they will survive their children's adolescent years? Many people believe that the period of the family life cycle during which parents have adolescents in the house is a particularly stressful time, with close parent–child relationships deteriorating into bitter tugs of war. How much truth is there to these characterizations?

Ripples in the Parent–Child Relationship

Although many people believe that adolescents lose respect for their parents and feel less close to them than they did as children, these beliefs simply do not hold up. A temporary and modest increase in parent–child conflict is common at the onset of puberty (Steinberg, 2002), and family cohesion decreases modestly during the adolescent years (Baer, 2002). However, most adolescents still respect their parents and describe their family relationships in positive ways (Fuligni, 1998; Offer, Ostrov, & Howard, 1981). They also continue to respect the legitimacy of their parents' authority to set and enforce rules (Smetana, 2000). Mainly, adolescents and their parents squabble more about relatively minor matters such as disobedience, homework, household chores, and access to privileges such as use of the car.

They also seem less sure for a time about how to relate to each other. In an interesting study, problem-solving sessions between boys and their parents were observed every 2 years from age 9 to age 18. Isabela Granic and her colleagues (2003) then coded positive, neutral, negative, and hostile statements or acts on the part of child and parent. They found that the amount of changing from one type of behavior to another on the part of parent and child increased from age 9–10 to age 13–14 and then decreased by age 17 or age 18. This is illustrated in Figure 15.3, a sample chart showing that sequences of child and parent behavior in one family were more varied from age 13 to age 14 than before or after. It was as though parents and 13- and 14-year-olds were experimenting to figure out how to relate to each other now that the child had become a teenager. Conflict increased at this age, and adolescents became more active in initiating and controlling interactions. Before and after this period, each parent–child pair seemed to have a fairly stable style of interacting (for example, exchanging mostly positive behaviors or mostly negative behaviors rather than trying some of each).

Renegotiating the Relationship

Through experimentation and occasional arguments, the parent–child relationship changes during adolescence, not so much in its degree of closeness as in the balance of power between parents and adolescents. Most theorists agree that a key developmental task of adolescence is to achieve **autonomy**—

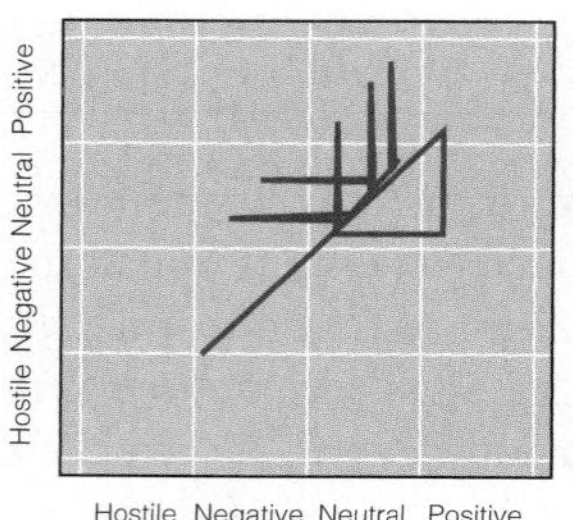

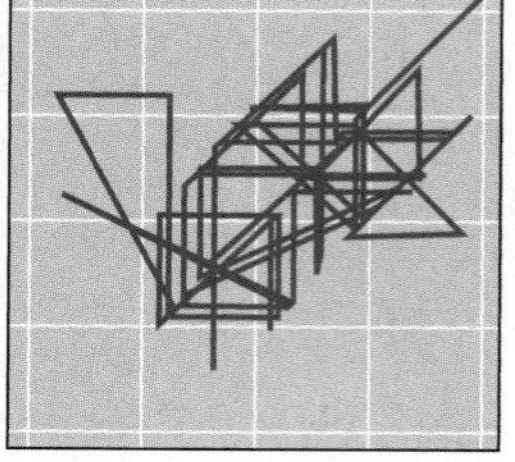

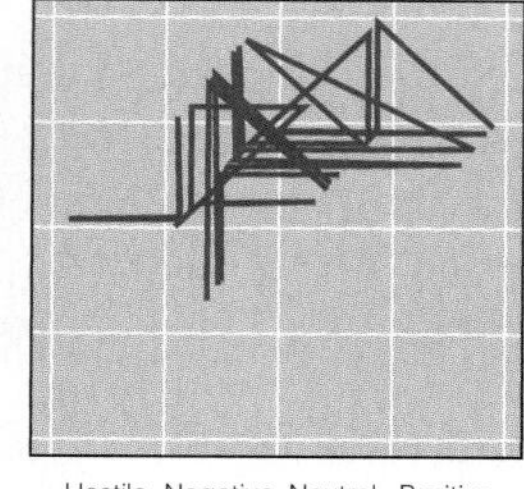

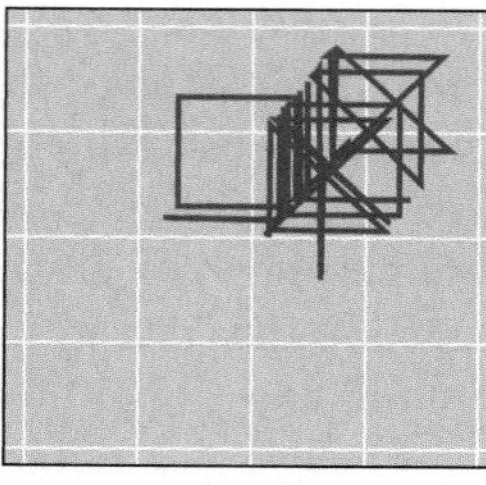

Figure 15.3 At age 13 or 14, sequences of behavior by parents and adolescents jump from positive to negative and negative to positive as though parents and children were trying to negotiate a new relationship.

SOURCE: © 2003 by the American Psychological Association. Reprinted by permission.

the capacity to make decisions independently and manage life tasks without being overly dependent on other people. If adolescents are to "make it" as adults, they cannot be rushing home for reassuring hugs after every little setback or depending on parents to get them to work on time or manage their checkbooks.

As children reach puberty and become more physically and cognitively mature and more capable of acting autonomously, they assert themselves more. As they do so, parents turn over more power to them, and the parent–child relationship changes from one in which parents are dominant to one in which parents and their sons and daughters are on a more equal footing (Steinberg, 2002). It is usually best for their development if adolescents maintain a close attachment with their families even as they are gaining autonomy and preparing to leave the nest (Kobak et al., 1993; Lamborn & Steinberg, 1993). Gaining some separation from parents is healthy; becoming detached from them is not (Beyers, et al., 2003). Some combination of autonomy and attachment, or independence and interdependence, is most desirable.

© Sean Justice/Getty Images

☾ Asian adolescents do not expect as much freedom as American adolescents do.

How much autonomy parents grant differs from culture to culture. Andrew Fuligni (1998) found that adolescents from different ethnic groups in the United States differ considerably in their beliefs about how much authority parents should have and how much autonomy adolescents should have. For example, Filipino and Mexican American adolescents are more likely than European American adolescents to believe that they should not disagree with their parents, and Chinese Americans are less likely to expect the freedom to go to parties and to date at a young age. Adolescents in Japan are even more strongly socialized to expect limited autonomy. They remain closer to their mothers and fathers than American adolescents throughout the adolescent years, do not feel as much need to distance themselves from their parents, and spend less time with peers (Rothbaum, Pott, et al., 2000). In collectivist Asian cultures, then, parents continue to impose many rules and the balance of power does not change as much, or at least as early, during adolescence as it does in the United States.

Across cultures, adolescents are most likely to become autonomous, achievement oriented, and well adjusted if their parents consistently enforce a reasonable set of rules, involve their teenagers in decision making, recognize their need for greater autonomy, monitor their comings and goings, gradually loosen the reins, and continue to be warm, supportive, and involved throughout adolescence (Beyers & Goossens, 1999; Lamborn et al., 1991). In other words, the winning approach is an authoritative style of parenting—the same style that fosters healthy child development. Although you should remind yourself that children also affect their parents, an authoritative parenting style gives adolescents opportunities to strengthen their independent decision-making skills and retain the benefit of their parents' guidance and advice. It creates a climate in which teenagers confide in their parents—and parents, therefore, do not have to spy to monitor where their children are and who they are with (Kerr & Stattin, 2003). When parents are rejecting and extremely strict, or rejecting and extremely lax, teenagers are most likely to be psychologically distressed and to get into trouble (Koestner, Zuroff, & Powers, 1991; Lamborn et al., 1991).

Summing Up

Most parents and their teenagers are able to work through some minor conflicts and maintain positive feelings for each other while renegotiating their relationship to allow the adolescent more freedom. With the help of an authoritative parenting style, most adolescents are able to achieve autonomy and shift toward a more mutual relationship with their parents. ■

The Adult

So far we have concentrated on the child's experience of family life. How do adults develop and change as they progress through the family life cycle?

Establishing the Marriage

In U.S. society, more than 90% of adults choose to marry at some point in their lives (Whitehead & Popenoe, 2003), and most choose to marry individuals they love. Marriages in many other cultures are not formed on the basis of love but are arranged by leaders of kin groups who are concerned with acquiring property, allies, and the rights to any children the marriage produces (Ingoldsby & Smith, 1995). As Corinne Nydegger (1986) put it, "These matters are too important to be left to youngsters" (p. 111). So, in reading what follows, remember that our way of establishing families is not the only way.

Marriage is a significant life transition for most adults: It involves taking on a new role (as husband or wife) and adjusting to life as a couple. We rejoice at weddings and view newlyweds as supremely happy beings. Indeed, they feel on top of the world, their self-esteem rises, and at least some of them adopt a more secure orientation toward attachment relationships as a result of marrying (Crowell, Treboux, & Waters, 2002; Giarrusso et al., 2000). Yet individuals who have just been struggling to achieve autonomy and assume adult roles soon find that they must compromise with their partners and adapt to each other's personalities and preferences.

Ted Huston and his colleagues have found that the honeymoon is short (Huston, McHale, & Crouter, 1986; Huston et al., 2001; also see Kurdek, 1999). In a longitudinal study of newlywed couples, these researchers discovered that perceptions of the marital relationship became less favorable during the first year after the wedding. For example, couples became less satisfied with their marriages and with their sex lives; they less frequently said "I love you," complimented each other, or disclosed their feelings to each other. Although they spent only somewhat less time together, more of that time was devoted to getting tasks done and less to having fun or just talking.

Although most couples are far more satisfied than dissatisfied with their relationships after the "honeymoon" is over, adapting to marriage clearly involves strains. Blissfully happy relationships evolve into still happy but more ambivalent ones as couples become somewhat disillusioned with each other and their relationship (Huston et al., 2001). Whether this

☾ The honeymoon is great, but it often ends quickly.

happens because couples begin to see "warts" that they did not notice before marriage, stop trying to be on their best behavior, have run-ins as an inevitable part of living together, or start to take each other for granted, it is normal.

Does the quality of a couple's relationship early in their marriage have any implications for their later marital adjustment? Apparently it does. Huston and his colleagues (2001) assessed couples 2 months, 1 year, and 2 years into their marriages and again 13 to 14 years after the wedding. It is commonly believed that marriages crumble when negative feelings build up and conflicts escalate, but Huston's findings provide little support for this escalating conflict view. Compared with couples who were happily married after 13 years, couples who remained married but were unhappy had had relatively poor relationships all along. Even as newlyweds, and probably even before they married, these couples were less blissfully in love and more negative toward each other than were couples who stayed married and remained happy in their marriages. Apparently, it is not the case that all marriages start out blissfully happy and then some turn sour: some start out sour. Even couples who divorced did not experience a buildup of conflict over time; often they lost their positive feelings for each other.

The establishment phase of the family life cycle involves a loss of enthusiasm for most couples. Some couples are already on the path to long-term marital satisfaction, whereas others are headed for divorce or for staying in a marriage that will continue to be less than optimal. Couples seem best off when they can maintain a high level of positive and supportive interactions to help them weather the conflicts that inevitably arise in any relationship (Fincham, 2003).

New Parenthood

How does the arrival of a new baby affect the wife, the husband, and the marital relationship? Some people believe that having children draws a couple closer together; others believe that children introduce additional strains into a relationship. Which is it?

On average, new parenthood is best described as a stressful life transition that involves both positive and negative changes (Cowan & Cowan, 2000; Nomaguchi & Milkie, 2003). On the positive side, parents claim that having a child brings them joy and fulfillment and contributes to their own growth as individuals (Emery & Tuer, 1993; Palkovitz, 2002). New parents are also more socially integrated than childless adults; they interact more with family and friends (Nomaguchi & Milkie, 2003).

But analyze the situation more closely. Couples have added new roles (as mothers and fathers) to their existing roles (as spouses, workers, and so on). New parents often find juggling work and family responsibilities stressful. They not only have an incredible amount of new work to do as caregivers, but they lose sleep, worry about their baby, find that they have less time to themselves, and often face financial difficulties. In addition, even egalitarian couples who previously shared household tasks begin to divide their labors along more traditional lines. She specializes in the "feminine" role by becoming the primary caregiver and housekeeper, often reducing her involvement in work outside the home, and he concentrates on his "masculine" role as provider (Cowan & Cowan, 2000; Sanchez & Thomson, 1997).

What are the effects of increased stress and of the tendency of husband and wife to establish more separate lifestyles? Marital satisfaction typically declines in the first year after a baby is born (Belsky, Lang, & Rovine, 1985; Gottman & Notarius, 2000). This decline is usually steeper for women than for men, primarily because the burden of child care responsibilities typically falls more heavily on mothers and they may resent what they regard as an unfair division of labor (Levy-Shiff, 1994). New mothers often feel trapped, isolated, and overwhelmed by their responsibility; new fathers worry about money (Fox, 2001b). Overall, women are more affected by parenthood in both positive and negative ways than men (Nomaguchi & Milkie, 2003).

However, individuals vary widely in their adjustment to new parenthood. Some new parents experience the transition as a bowl of cherries, others as the pits—as a full-blown crisis in their lives. Some get through the typical strains and conflicts of the first year and regain a high level of marital satisfaction; others do not (Cox et al., 1999). What might make this life event easier or harder to manage? We can answer that question by focusing on the nature of the event with which a parent must cope, the person who must cope with it, and the resources the individual has available.

The *event* is the baby. Clearly, infants who are difficult (for example, because of an illness that causes endless crying or an irritable temperament) create more stresses and anxieties for parents than infants who are quiet, sociable, responsive, and otherwise easy to love (Levy-Shiff, 1994; Meredith & Noller, 2003).

As for the *person,* some adults are better equipped than others to cope with stress; they have good problem-solving and communication skills and find adaptive ways to restructure and organize their lives to accommodate a new baby (Cox et al., 1999; Levy-Shiff, 1994). Similarly, parents who have realistic expectations about how parenthood will change their lives and about children tend to adjust more easily than those who expect the experience to be more positive than it turns out to be (Kalmuss, Davidson, & Cushman, 1992; Mylod, Whitman, & Borkowski, 1997). Mentally healthy parents also fare better than parents who are experiencing mental health problems such as depression going into new parenthood (Cox et al., 1999).

Attachment styles are also important. New parents who remember their own parents as warm and accepting are likely to experience a smoother transition to new parenthood than couples who recall their parents as cold or rejecting (Florsheim et al., 2003; van IJzendoorn, 1992). In an interesting study, Jeffry Simpson and his colleagues (2003) looked at adjustment during the transition to parenthood in relation to the styles of adult attachment described in Chapter 14. Viewing new parenthood as the kind of stressful transition likely to activate the attachment system, they administered scales to assess ambivalence and avoidance in romantic attachment relationships, husband's support for and anger toward his wife, and depression symptoms in a sample of 106 couples expecting their first child. As John Bowlby's attachment theory predicts, mothers who had a preoccupied (resistant) style of attachment—that is, emotionally needy and dependent women who expressed a lot of anxiety and ambivalence about romantic relationships—were likely to become increasingly depressed from before the birth to 6 months after birth if they perceived that their husbands gave them little support or were angry before the birth and if they then perceived that their husbands' support or anger worsened during the transition. Women with preoccupied (resistant) attachment styles who perceived low support from their husbands also experienced bigger declines in marital satisfaction than other mothers, and their husbands became less satisfied with the marriage (Rholes et al., 2001). Women with other attachment styles were not as vulnerable to depression and drops in marital satisfaction, even when they went into parenthood feeling that their partners were not supportive.

Finally, *resources* can make a great deal of difference to the new parent. Most important is spousal support: As suggested already, things go considerably better for a new mother when she has a good relationship with her husband, and when he shares the burden of child care and housework, than when she has no partner or an unsupportive one (Levy-Shiff, 1994; Demo & Cox, 2000). Social support from friends and relatives can also help new parents cope (Stemp, Turner, & Noh, 1986), as can interventions designed to help expecting parents prepare realistically for the challenges ahead and support one another as they deal with these challenges (Cowan & Cowan, 2000).

In sum, parents who have an easy baby to contend with; who possess positive personal qualities and coping skills, including a secure attachment style; and who receive reliable support from their partners and others are in the best position to cope adaptively with new parenthood, a transition normally both satisfying and stressful that can reduce marital satisfaction, especially for women.

The Child-Rearing Family

The child-rearing family is the family with children in it. What can parents look forward to as they have additional children and as their children age? A heavier workload! The stresses and strains of caring for a toddler are greater than those of caring for an infant, and the arrival of a second child means additional stress (O'Brien, 1996). Parents must not only devote time to the new baby but also deal with their firstborn child's normal anxieties about this change in lifestyle. They complain of the hassles of cleaning up food and toys, constantly keeping an eye on their children, and dealing with their perfectly normal but irritating demands for attention, failures to comply with requests, and bouts of whining (O'Brien, 1996). Because the workload increases, fathers often become more involved in child care after a second child is born (Phares, 1999). However, the mother who is raising children as a single parent or whose husband is not highly involved in family life may find herself without a moment's rest as she tries to keep up with two or more active, curious, mobile, and needy youngsters.

Additional challenges sometimes arise for parents when their children enter adolescence. As you saw earlier, parent–child conflicts become more frequent for a while as children enter adolescence. In addition, there is intriguing evidence that living with adolescents who are becoming physically and sexually mature and beginning to date may cause parents to engage in more than the usual amount of midlife questioning about what they have done with their lives and what they can expect next (Silverberg & Steinberg, 1990). Here, then, may be another example of child effects within the family system. Or is it? It is also possible that parents who are psychologically distressed and preoccupied with their own midlife problems cannot provide the emotional support their children need and cause them to seek it elsewhere, in the peer group. Parents who are insecure about attachment relationships sometimes have trouble letting go of their adolescents and serving as a secure base as their children seek to become more autonomous (Hock et al., 2001).

Children clearly complicate their parents' lives by demanding everything from fresh diapers and close monitoring to college tuition. By claiming time and energy that might otherwise go into nourishing the marital relationship and by adding stresses to their parents' lives, children seem to have a negative—although typically only slightly negative—effect on the marital relationship (Kurdek, 1999; Rollins & Feldman 1970). Yet when parents are interviewed about the costs and benefits of parenthood, they generally emphasize the positives and feel that parenthood has contributed a great deal to their personal development, making them more responsible and caring individuals (Palkovitz, 2002).

The Empty Nest

As children reach maturity, the family becomes a "launching pad" that fires adolescents and young adults into work and starting their own families. The term **empty nest** describes the family after the departure of the last child—a phase of the family life cycle that became common only in the 20th century (Fox, 2001a). Clearly, the emptying of the nest involves changes in roles and lifestyle for parents, particularly for

"Your attitude is sucking all the fulfillment out of motherhood."

mothers who have centered their lives on child rearing. There can be moments of deep sadness (Span, 2000, p. 15):

> Pamela automatically started to toss Doritos and yucky dip into her cart—and then remembered. "I almost burst into tears," she recalls. "I wanted to stop some complete stranger and say, 'My son's gone away to college.' I had such a sense of loss."

Overall, however, parents react positively to the emptying of the nest. Whereas the entry of children into the family causes modest decreases in marital satisfaction, the departure of the last child seems to be associated with either modest increases in marital satisfaction or at least a slowing of the decline in marital satisfaction that began early in the marriage (White & Edwards, 1990; Van Laningham, Johnson, & Amato, 2001). After the nest empties, women often feel that their marriages are more equitable and that their spouses are more accommodating to their needs (Mackey & O'Brien, 1995; Suitor, 1991). Only a few parents find this transition disturbing.

Why are parents generally not upset by the empty nest? Possibly it is because they have fewer roles and responsibilities and, therefore, experience less stress and strain. Empty nest couples also have more time to focus on their marital relationship and to enjoy activities together and more money to spend on themselves. Moreover, parents are likely to view the emptying of the nest as evidence that they have done their job of raising children well and have earned what Erik Erikson called a sense of generativity. One 44-year-old mother put it well: "I have five terrific daughters who didn't just happen. It took lots of time to mold, correct, love, and challenge them. It's nice to see such rewarding results." Finally, most parents continue to enjoy a good deal of contact with their children after the nest empties, so it is not as if they are really losing this important relationship (White & Edwards, 1990).

In recent years, an increasing number of adult children have been remaining in the nest or leaving then "refilling" it, often because of unemployment, limited finances, divorce, or other difficulties in getting their adult lives on track (Ward & Spitze, 1992; White & Rogers, 1997). Some parents find having adult children in the house distressing (Aquilino, 1991; Umberson, 1992). However, most empty nesters adapt, especially if their children are responsible young adults who are attending school or working rather than freeloading (White & Rogers, 1997). Having adult children in the house decreases the time couples spend alone together, but it does not seem to decrease marital happiness or increase marital conflict (Ward & Spitze, 2004). Young children in the house appear to affect marriages more than adult children do.

Grandparenthood

Although we tend to picture grandparents as white-haired, jovial elders who knit mittens and bake chocolate chip cookies, most adults become grandparents when they are middle-aged, not elderly, and when they are likely to be highly involved in work and community activities. The average age of first-time grandparenthood is 47 (Conner, 2000). Grandparenting styles are diverse, as illustrated by the results of a national survey of grandparents of teenagers conducted by Andrew Cherlin and Frank Furstenberg (1986). These researchers determined the prevalence of three major styles of grandparenting:

1. *Remote.* Remote grandparents (29% of the sample) were symbolic figures seen only occasionally by their grandchildren. Primarily because they were geographically distant, they were emotionally distant as well.

2. *Companionate.* This was the most common style of grandparenting (55% of the sample). Companionate grandparents saw their grandchildren frequently and enjoyed sharing activities with them. They only rarely played a parental role; they served as companions rather than as caregivers. Like most grandparents, they were reluctant to meddle in the way their adult children were raising their children and were happy not to have child care responsibilities. As one put it, "You can love them and then say, 'Here, take them now, go on home'" (Cherlin & Furstenberg, 1986, p. 55).

3. *Involved.* Finally, 16% of the grandparents assumed a parentlike role. Like companionate grandparents, they saw their grandchildren frequently and were playful with them, but unlike companionate grandparents, they often helped with child care, gave advice, and played other practical roles in their grandchildren's lives. Some involved grandparents were substitute parents who lived with and tended their grandchildren because their daughters were unmarried or recently divorced and worked outside the home.

You can see, then, that grandparenting takes many forms but that most grandparents see at least some of their grandchildren frequently and prefer a companionate role that is high in enjoyment and affection but low in responsibility. Most grandparents find the role gratifying, especially if they

Most grandparents prefer and adopt a companionate style of grandparenting.

see their grandchildren frequently and if they view the grandparent role as important and attach positive meanings to it (Reitzes & Mutran, 2004). Like grandparents, grandchildren often report a good deal of closeness in the grandparent–grandchild relationship and only wish they could see their grandparents more (Block, 2000).

Grandparents have been called "the family national guard" because they must be ever ready to come to the rescue when there is a crisis in the family and they never know when they will be called (Hagestad, 1985). When a teenage daughter becomes pregnant, grandmother and grandfather may find themselves serving as primary caregivers for the baby—sometimes in their 30s or even late 20s when they are not yet ready to become grandparents (Burton, 1996b). Similarly, grandparents may step in to help raise their grandchildren after a divorce; if their child does not obtain custody, however, their access to their grandchildren may be reduced or even cut off, causing them much anguish (Cooney & Smith, 1996).

Grandparents who do get "called to duty" sometimes make a real contribution to their grandchildren's development. For example, teenagers raised by single mothers tend to have low educational attainment and high rates of problem behavior, but they resemble children raised by two parents if they are raised by a single mother and at least one grandparent (DeLeire & Kalil, 2002). Involved grandparenting can take a toll, however: Grandmothers sometimes show symptoms of depression when grandchildren move in with them and they must become substitute parents (Szinovacz, DeViney, & Atkinson, 1999), and the risk of coronary heart disease is higher than average for grandmothers who care for grandchildren more than 8 hours a week (Lee et al., 2003). Grandparent care has been on the rise (Bryson & Casper, 1999). African Americans and other women of color are especially likely to be drawn into a highly involved caregiving role, especially when they live in the same household with their grandchildren and when their daughters work (Vandell et al., 2003). Although grandparents may benefit from the intellectual challenges and emotional rewards that parenting brings (Ehrle, 2001), their development and well-being can suffer if they become overwhelmed by their responsibilities.

Changing Family Relationships

Family relationships develop and change with time. See what becomes of relationships between spouses, siblings, and parents and their children during the adult years.

Marital Relationships

As you have seen, marital satisfaction, although generally high for most couples throughout their lives together, dips somewhat after the honeymoon period is over, dips still lower in the new-parenthood phase, continues to drop as new children are added to the family, and recovers only when the children leave the nest. Women, because they have traditionally been more involved than men in rearing children, tend to be more strongly affected by these family life transitions—for good or for bad—than men are. Although they are less happy with their marriages and more likely to have thoughts about divorce than men (Amato et al., 2003), their general happiness also depends more on how well their marriage is going (Kiecolt-Glaser & Newton, 2001).

The quality of marital relationships changes over the years. Although frequency of sexual intercourse decreases over the years, psychological intimacy often increases. The love relationship often changes from one that is passionate to one that is companionate, more like a best-friends relationship (Bierhoff & Schmohr, 2003). Elderly couples are even more affectionate than middle-aged couples when they interact, have fewer conflicts, and are able to resolve their conflicts without venting as many negative emotions (Carstensen, Levenson, & Gottman, 1995; Gagnon et al., 1999).

Overall, however, knowing what stage of the family life cycle an adult is in does not allow us to predict accurately how satisfied that person is with his marriage. Personality is probably more important. Happily married people have more pleasant personalities than unhappily married people; for example, they are more emotionally stable and vent negative feelings less often (Robins, Caspi, & Moffitt, 2000). Perhaps because it is influenced by personality, marital satisfaction tends to be stable over the years (Dickson, 1995; Huston et al., 2001). Moreover, the personalities of marriage partners are similar, and are likely to remain similar over the years, as each partner reinforces in the other the traits that brought them together (Caspi, Herbener, & Ozer, 1992). It is when "opposites attract" and find their personalities clashing day after day that marital problems tend to arise (Kurdek, 1991a; Russell & Wells, 1991).

The family life cycle ends with widowhood. Marriages face new challenges if one of the partners becomes seriously ill or impaired and needs care. Wives suffer more ill effects than daughters when they must care for a dying husband–father, but they generally cope reasonably well with their spouse's death, often feeling afterward that they have grown (Seltzer & Li, 2000; and see Chapter 17). By the time they reach age 65 or older, about 73% of men are still married and living with their wives, but about 59% of women are widowed or otherwise living alone (Spraggins, 2003).

Without question, the marital relationship is centrally important in the lives and development of most adults. Older adults who are divorced or widowed, especially if they have seen more than one relationship end, are lonelier than those who have partners (Peters & Liefbroer, 1997). Adults enjoy a boost in life satisfaction when they gain a spouse and a drop in life satisfaction when they lose one (Chipperfield & Havens, 2001). Overall, married adults are "happier, healthier, and better off financially" than other adults and are likely to remain so if they can weather bad times in their marriages (Waite & Gallagher, 2000).

Sibling Relationships

Relationships between brothers and sisters change once siblings no longer live together in the same home. Starting in adolescence, both closeness and conflict between siblings diminish as brothers and sisters forge their own lives. Sibling relationships also become more equal in adulthood (Buhrmester & Furman, 1990; Cicirelli, 1995). Victor Cicirelli (1982, 1995) finds that adult siblings typically see each other several times a year and communicate through phone calls or letters. Few discuss intimate problems or help one another, but siblings usually feel that they can count on each other in a crisis. And brothers and sisters are often there to support each other's life choices, help care for aging parents, and reminisce about their common past (Bedford & Volling, 2004).

The same ambivalence that characterizes sibling relationships during childhood seems to carry over into adulthood. Emotional closeness persists despite decreased contact; indeed, siblings often grow even closer in old age (Cicirelli, 1995). However, the potential for sibling rivalry persists, too. Conflict is far less frequent than during childhood, but old rivalries can and do flare up during adulthood (Cicirelli, 1995). Siblings who enjoyed a close relationship during childhood are likely to be drawn closer after significant life events such as a parent's illness or death, whereas siblings who had poor relationships during childhood are likely to clash in response to the same life events (Lerner et al., 1991; Ross & Milgram, 1982). Adult siblings also feel closer to each other when they feel that their parents treat them equally than when they feel that one of them is favored (Boll, Ferring, & Filipp, 2003).

In the end, the sibling relationship is typically the longest-lasting relationship we have, linking us to individuals who share many of our genes and experiences (Cicirelli, 1991). It is a relationship that can be close, conflictual, or, for most of us, some of both.

☾ Young adults and their parents often negotiate a more mutual, friendlike relationship.

Parent–Child Relationships

Parent and child generations in most families are in close contact and enjoy affectionate give-and-take relationships throughout the adult years. When aging parents eventually need support, children are there to help.

Forming More Mutual Relationships. As young adults leave the nest, they do not sever ties with their parents; instead, they and their parents jointly negotiate a relationship in which they move beyond playing out their roles as child and parent and become more like friends (Aquilino, 1997; Greene & Boxer, 1986). As a result, the parent–child relationship often becomes more positive between adolescence and early adulthood (Shulman & Ben-Artzi, 2003). This more mutual and warm relationship is especially likely to develop when children are married (but are still childless), are employed, and have moved out of their parents' house (Aquilino, 1997; Belsky et al., 2003). Relationships are also closer and less conflictual if parents were supportive, authoritative parents earlier in the child's life (Belsky et al., 2001). Children appreciate their more equal relationships with their parents (White, Speisman, & Costos, 1983, p. 73):

> I am understanding her now more than I ever did before. I have started to understand that I had to stop blaming her for everything in my life. I felt she had been a lousy parent. Now, I'm more understanding that my mother is a person and that she has her own problems and her own life. . . . I accepted her as a mother—but she actually is a human being.

What happens to the parent–child relationship when children become middle-aged and their parents become elderly? The two generations typically continue to care about, socialize with, and help each other throughout the adult years (Umberson & Slaten, 2000), and both generations gain self-esteem when the parent–child relationship is good (Giarrusso et al., 2000). Aging mothers enjoy closer relations and more contact with their children, especially their daughters, than aging fathers do (Umberson & Slaten, 2000). And African American, Hispanic American, and other minority elders often enjoy more supportive relationships with their families than European Americans do (Bengtson et al., 1996). These findings suggest that the predominant family form in the United States is neither the isolated nuclear family nor the extended family household but what has been called the **modified extended family**—an arrangement in which nuclear families live in separate households but have close ties and frequent communication and interaction with other kin (Litwak, 1960). Most elderly people in our society prefer this pattern. The last thing they want is to have to live with and burden their children when their health fails (E. Brody, 2004).

Relationships between the generations are not only close and affectionate, but they also are generally equitable: each generation gives something, and each generation gets something in return (Conner, 2000; Markides, Boldt, & Ray, 1986). If anything, aging parents give more (E. Brody, 2004). Contrary to myth, then, most aging families do not experience what has been called **role reversal**—a switching of roles late in life such that the parent becomes the needy, dependent one and the child becomes the caregiver (E. Brody, 2004). Only when parents reach advanced ages and begin to develop serious physical or mental problems does the parent–child relationship sometimes become lopsided.

Caring for Aging Parents. Elaine Brody (1985, 2004) uses the term **middle generation squeeze** (others call it the *sandwich generation* phenomenon) to describe the situation of middle-aged adults pressured by demands from both the younger and the older generations simultaneously. Put yourself in the shoes of Julia, a 52-year-old African American working woman (Burton, 1996b, p. 155):

> My girl and grand girl had babies young. Now, they keep on rushin' me, expectin' me to do this and that, tryin' to make me old 'fore my time. I ain't got no time for myself. I takes care of babies, grown children, and the old peoples. I work too. I get so tired. I don't know if I'll ever get to do somethin' for myself.

Julia's situation may not be typical, but it is certainly middle generation squeeze. Adults with children increasingly find themselves caring for their aging parents; indeed, middle-aged adults who have children are more likely than those who do not to be drawn into caring for parents and other aging relatives, possibly because they are more closely tied to kin networks (Gallagher & Gerstel, 2001). Spouses are the first in line to care for frail elders, assuming they are alive and up to the challenge, but most caregivers of ailing elders are daughters or daughters-in-law in their 40s and 50s. Daughters are about three times more likely than sons to assist aging parents (Dwyer & Coward, 1991). This imbalance exists partly because, according to traditional gender-role norms, women are the "kinkeepers" of the family and therefore feel obligated to provide care (E. Brody, 2004) and partly because women are less likely than men to have jobs that prevent them from helping (Sarkisian & Gerstel, 2004).

In many Asian societies, daughters-in-law are the first choice. Aging parents are often taken in by a son, usually the oldest, and cared for by his wife (Youn et al., 1999). In our society, where most aging parents do not want to have to live with their children, much elder care is provided from a distance (Bengtson et al., 1996). Either way, families are the major providers of care for the frail elderly today. We see little support here for the view that today's families have abandoned their elders or that adult children have failed to meet their **filial responsibility,** a child's obligation to his parents (E. Brody, 2004; Conner, 2000).

African American, Hispanic American, and Asian American families feel more strongly than European American ones that they have a responsibility to help ailing parents, and they do help more (Conner, 2000; Shuey & Hardy, 2003). Some ethnic groups have more potential helpers available, too; for example, compared with European American elders, African American ones can more often call on siblings and members of the extended family such as cousins and nieces and nephews for help if their children cannot help (Johnson, 2000). As a result, they are less likely to find themselves without family support when they reach advanced ages.

Middle-aged adults who must foster their children's (and possibly their grandchildren's) development while tending to their own development and caring for aging parents sometimes find their situation overwhelming. They may experience **caregiver burden**—psychological distress associated with the demands of providing care for someone with physical, cognitive, or both impairments. Although caring for an aging parent can be rewarding, many adult children providing such care experience emotional, physical, and financial strains (Aneshensel et al., 1995; Pinquart & Sorensen, 2003). A woman who is almost wholly responsible for a dependent elder may feel angry and resentful because she has no time for herself. She may experience role conflict between her caregiver role and her roles as wife, mother, and employee that undermines her sense of well-being (Stephens et al., 2001).

Not all caregivers feel that providing care is a burden or suffer negative mental health effects such as depression, however. The burden of care is likely to be perceived as especially weighty if the elderly parent engages in the disruptive and socially inappropriate behaviors often shown by people with dementia (Gaugler et al., 2000; Pinquart & Sorensen, 2003). The caregiver's personality also makes a difference; caregivers who lack a sense of mastery or control may have difficulty coping and may become more depressed over time (Li, Seltzer, & Greenberg, 1999). By contrast, those who have attained the sense of generativity that Erikson believes to be so important for middle-aged parents feel less caregiver burden than other women (Peterson, 2002).

© Tom Stewart/CORBIS

☾ Caring for an ailing parent can result in middle generation squeeze and caregiving burden.

The strain is also likely to be worse if a caregiving daughter is unmarried and, therefore, does not have a husband to lean on for practical and emotional support (E. Brody et al., 1992); if her marriage is an unsupportive one (Stephens & Franks, 1995); or if for other reasons she lacks social support (Clyburn et al., 2000). In the end, the caregiver–parent relationship and the marital relationship affect each other. A solid marriage can provide social support that lightens the burden of care; a troubled marriage can get in the way. Similarly, caring for an ailing parent can detract from the marital relationship, or it can improve it by making a daughter feel better about herself (Stephens & Franks, 1995).

Does it matter why adult children take on the burden of care? In an interesting attempt to find out, Cicirelli (1993) assessed whether daughters helped their aging mothers out of love ("I feel lonely when I don't see my mother often") or out of a sense of duty ("I feel that I should do my part in helping"). Both daughters who were highly motivated to help based on a strong attachment to their mothers and daughters who were motivated by a sense of obligation spent more time helping than women whose motivations to help were weaker. However, those who helped out of love experienced helping as far less stressful and burdensome than those who helped mainly out of a sense of duty (see also Lyonette & Yardley, 2003).

So, the caregivers most likely to experience psychological distress are those who must care for parents or spouses with behavioral problems, who lack social support, and whose assistance is not motivated by love. These individuals need support and relief from their burden. Interventions can help them sharpen their caregiving skills and learn to react less negatively to the difficult behavior often shown by elderly adults with dementia, reducing their sense of burden in the process (Ostwald et al., 1999; and see Schultz et al., 2003).

Summing Up

Marital satisfaction declines soon after the honeymoon period and again in response to new parenthood—a stressful transition especially if the baby is difficult, the parent is ill equipped to cope, and social support is lacking. The empty nest transition is generally smooth, and middle-aged adults enjoy playing a companionate grandparental role. Women are especially affected by family life cycle transitions, but marital satisfaction is more strongly influenced by personalities than by stage of family life.

Adult siblings continue to be both close and rivalrous. The parent–child relationship becomes more mutual in adulthood until some middle-aged adults, particularly daughters, experience the stress of caregiver burden. The child who is dependent on parents becomes the adult who can be interdependent with them—and sometimes becomes the person on whom aging parents depend. ■

Diversity in Family Life

Useful as it is, the concept of a family life cycle does not capture the diversity of adult lifestyles and family experiences. Many of today's adults do not progress in a neat and orderly way through the stages of the traditional family life cycle—marrying, having children, watching them leave the nest, and so on. A small number never marry; a larger number never have children. Some continue working when their children are young; others stop or cut back. And many adults move in and out of wedded life by marrying, divorcing, and remarrying. Examine some of these variations in family life.

Singles

It is nearly impossible to describe the "typical" single adult. This category includes not only young adults who have not yet married but also middle-aged and elderly people who experienced divorce or the death of a spouse or who never married. It is typical to start adulthood as a single person. Most adults in the 18 to 29 age range are not married (U.S. Census Bureau, 2003). Because adults have been postponing marriage, the number of young, single adults has been growing.

Cohabitation, living with a romantic partner without being married, is also on the rise (Amato et al., 2003). Some never-married people live together as a matter of convenience—because they are in a romantic relationship, need a place to live, and want to save money. They usually do not view cohabitation as a trial marriage, although they may later contemplate marriage if the relationship is working (Sassler, 2004). Other cohabiters have seen their marriages end and are looking for an alternative to marriage (Seltzer, 2000). Many have children; by one estimate, 4 out of 10 children will live in a family headed by a cohabiting couple sometime during childhood (Whitehead & Popenoe, 2003).

Single adults are diverse—not all are "swinging singles."

It makes sense to think that couples who live together before marrying would have more opportunity than those who do not to determine whether they are truly compatible. Yet couples who live together and then marry seem to be more dissatisfied with their marriages and more likely to divorce overall than couples who do not live together before marrying. These risks are not evident when a woman cohabits only with her future husband but are evident if she has more than one intimate premarital relationship (Teachman, 2003). It is unlikely that the experience of cohabitation itself is responsible (Booth & Johnson, 1988). Instead, it seems that the kinds of people who choose to cohabit with multiple partners may be more susceptible to marital problems and less committed to the institution of marriage than the kinds of people who do not. They tend, for example, to be less religious, less conventional in their family attitudes, less committed to the idea of marriage as a permanent arrangement, and more open to the idea of divorcing (Axinn & Barber, 1997; DeMaris & MacDonald, 1993). This may be why children who live with cohabiting biological parents have more emotional and behavioral problems and less engagement with school, on average, than children who live with married biological parents (Brown, 2004).

What of the 5% of adults who never marry? Stereotypes suggest that they are miserably lonely and maladjusted, but they often make up for their lack of spouse and children by forming close bonds with siblings, friends, or younger adults who become like sons or daughters to them (Rubinstein et al., 1991). As "old-old" people in their 80s and 90s, never-married people sometimes lack relatives who can assist or care for them (Johnson & Troll, 1996). Yet it is divorced rather than never-married single adults who tend to be the loneliest and least happy adults (Kurdek, 1991b; Peters & Liefbroer, 1997).

Childless Married Couples

Like single adults who never marry, married couples who remain childless do not experience all the phases of the traditional family life cycle. Many childless couples want children but cannot have them. However, a growing number of adults, especially highly educated adults with high-status occupations, voluntarily decide to delay having children or decide not to have them (Heaton, Jacobson, & Holland, 1999).

How are childless couples faring when their peers are having, raising, and launching children? Generally, they do well. Their marital satisfaction tends to be higher than that of couples with children during the child-rearing years (Kurdek, 1999). And middle-aged and elderly childless couples seem to be no less satisfied with their lives than parents whose children have left the nest (Allen, Blieszner, & Roberto, 2000; Rempel, 1985). However, elderly women who are childless and widowed may find themselves without anyone to help them if they develop health problems (Johnson & Troll, 1996). It seems, then, that childless couples derive satisfaction from their marriages and are happier than single adults but may suffer from a lack of social support late in life after their marriages end.

Dual-Career Families

As more mothers have gone to work outside the home, developmental scientists have naturally asked what effect maternal employment has on families. Some have focused on the concept of **spillover effects**—ways in which events at work affect home life and events at home carry over into the workplace. Most of their research has focused on negative spillover effects (Barnett et al., 1995; Perry-Jenkins, Repetti, & Crouter, 2000). However, positive spillover effects can also occur: A good marriage and rewarding interactions with children can protect a woman from the negative psychological effects of stresses at work and increase her job satisfaction (Barnett, 1994; Rogers & May, 2003), and a rewarding, stimulating job can have positive effects on her interactions within the family (Greenberger, O'Neil, & Nagel, 1994).

Overall, dual-career families are faring well. Women are giving up personal leisure time (not to mention sleep) and cutting back on housework to make time for their children; meanwhile, their husbands are slowly but steadily increasing their participation in household and child care activities (Cabrera et al., 2000; Coltrane, 2000). There is no indication that a mother's decision to work has damaging effects on child development; it can have positive or negative effects depending on the circumstances. It is likely to be best for children when it means an increase in family income, when mothers are satisfied with the choice they have made (that is, when they would rather be working than at home), when fathers become more involved, and when children are adequately supervised after school (Hoffman, 2000; Lerner & Noh, 2000). Girls may also benefit from the role model a working mother provides and tend to adopt less stereotyped views of men's and women's roles than children whose mothers do not work (Hoffman, 2000).

Having a working mother can be a negative experience, however (Goldberg, Greenberger, & Nagel, 1996). **Latchkey children** and adolescents can get into trouble when their parents do not monitor them and they lack adult supervision after school (Perry-Jenkins et al., 2000). They can also suffer if a working mother is unable to remain a warm and involved parent who shares "quality time" with them (Beyer, 1995). Martha Moorehouse (1991) found that 6-year-olds whose mothers began working full-time were more cognitively and socially competent (according to their teachers) than children whose mothers were homemakers if these youngsters frequently shared activities such as reading, telling stories, and talking with their mothers. However, they fared worse than children with stay-at-home mothers if they lost out on such opportunities.

Fortunately, most working mothers manage to spend almost as much time with their children as nonworking mothers do (Bryant & Zick, 1996; Nock & Kingston, 1988), and their husbands are more involved than ever in child care (Bianchi, 2000). As a result, most dual-career couples are able to enjoy the personal and financial benefits of working without compromising their children's development.

Gay and Lesbian Families

The family experiences of gay men and lesbian women are most notable for their diversity (Savin-Williams & Esterberg, 2000; Patterson, 2004). In the United States, several million gay men and lesbian women are parents, most through previous heterosexual marriages and others through adoption or artificial insemination (Flaks et al., 1995). Some no longer live with their children, but others raise them as single parents and still others raise them in families that have two mothers or two fathers. Other gay men and lesbian women remain single and childless or live as couples without children throughout their lives. The diverse families of gay and lesbian adults are poorly described by traditional family concepts such as the family life cycle, which were developed with heterosexual nuclear families in mind. Gay and lesbian families also face special challenges, as the recent national controversy over the legality of gay marriages suggests, because they are not fully recognized as families by society.

Those gay and lesbian adults who live as couples are likely to have more egalitarian relationships than heterosexual couples do. Rather than following traditional gender stereotypes, partners tend to work out a division of labor, through trial and error, based on who is especially talented at or who hates doing certain tasks (Huston & Schwartz, 1995). Otherwise, their relationships evolve through the same stages of development, are satisfying or dissatisfying for the same reasons, and are typically as rewarding as those of married or cohabiting heterosexuals (Kurdek, 1995).

© Ronnie Kaufman/CORBIS

☾ Children raised by lesbian couples develop much like other children do on average.

Is there reason to worry about the children? Not at all. Comparing lesbian mothers with heterosexual mothers in two-parent and single-parent homes, Susan Golombok and her colleagues (2003) found that lesbian mothers tend to hit children less and to engage in imaginative and domestic play more and that their lesbian partners are as involved in coparenting as fathers typically are. Overall, children who lived with two parents of the same sex were better off in terms of developmental outcomes than children living with a single mother and no different than children with two heterosexual parents. Overall, this study and others suggest that gay and lesbian adults who raise children are as likely as heterosexual parents to produce competent and well-adjusted children (Savin-Williams & Esterberg, 2000; Patterson, 2004). Moreover, contrary to what many people believe, their children are no more likely than the children of heterosexual parents to develop a homosexual or bisexual orientation (Patterson, 2004).

Divorcing Families

Orderly progress through the family life cycle is disrupted when a couple divorces. Divorce is not just one life event; rather, it is a series of stressful experiences for the entire family that begins with marital conflict before the divorce and includes a complex of life changes as the marriage unravels and its members reorganize their lives (Amato, 2000; Emery, 1999). Why do people divorce? What effects does divorce typically have on family members? And how can we explain, as illustrated by the two contrasting quotes at the start of this chapter, that some adults and children thrive after a divorce whereas others experience persisting problems?

Before the Divorce

Gay Kitson and her colleagues (Kitson, Babri, & Roach, 1985; Kitson, 1992) and Jay Teachman (2002) have pieced together a profile of the couples at highest risk for divorce. Generally, they are young adults, in their 20s and 30s, who have been married for an average of 7 years and often have young children. These days, only about 70% of marriages make it to the 10-year mark (Teachman, 2002). Couples are especially likely to divorce if they married as teenagers, had a short courtship, conceived a child before marrying, or are low in socioeconomic status—all factors that might suggest an unreadiness for marriage and unusually high financial and psychological stress accompanying new parenthood. Finally, their parents are likely to have divorced, and they are likely to be different from each other in demographic characteristics such as age and education (Teachman, 2002). Not surprisingly, divorcers also express low satisfaction with their marriages, think about breaking up, and express few positive emotions, many negative ones, or both when they interact (Gottman & Levenson, 2000).

Contrary to the notion that today's couples do not give their marriages a chance to work, research suggests that most divorcing couples experience a few years of marital distress and conflict and often try separations before they make the final decision to divorce (Kitson, 1992). Reasons for divorcing are no longer restricted to traditionally important precipitators such as nonsupport, alcoholism, or abuse (Gigy & Kelly, 1992). Instead, couples today typically divorce because they feel their marriages lack communication, emotional fulfillment, or compatibility. Wives tend to have longer lists of complaints than their husbands do and often have more to do with initiating the breakup (Thompson & Amato, 1999).

After the Divorce

Most families going through a divorce experience it as a genuine crisis—a period of considerable disruption that often lasts at least 1 to 2 years (Amato, 2000; Hetherington & Kelly, 2002). The wife, who usually obtains custody of any children, is likely to be angry, depressed, and otherwise distressed, although often she is relieved as well. The husband is also likely to be distressed, particularly if he did not want the divorce and feels shut off from his children. Both individuals must revise their identities (as single rather than married people) and revise their relationship. Both may feel isolated from former friends and unsure of themselves as they become involved in new romantic relationships. Divorced women with children are likely to face the added problem of getting by with considerably less money (Amato, 2000).

Because of all these stressors, divorced adults are at higher risk than married adults for depression and other forms of psychological distress, physical health problems, and even death (Amato, 2000; Lillard & Panis, 1996). Their adjustment is especially likely to be poor if they have little income, do not find a new relationship, take a dim view of divorce, and did not initiate the divorce (Wang & Amato, 2000). Some feel better about themselves and more in control of their lives after extracting themselves from a miserable marriage. Thus, divorce is at least temporarily stressful for most adults, but it can have negative or positive effects in the long run depending on the individual and the circumstances (Amato, 2000).

As you might suspect, psychologically distressed adults do not make the best parents. Moreover, children going through a divorce do not make the best children because they, too, are suffering. They are often angry, fearful, depressed, and guilty, especially if they fear that they were somehow responsible for what happened (Hetherington, 1981). They are also likely to be whiny, dependent, disobedient, and disrespectful. A vicious circle of the sort described by the transactional model of family in-

"Good" and "Bad" Divorces: Factors Influencing Adjustment

Some adults and children thrive after a divorce, whereas others suffer many negative and long-lasting effects. Why is this? Here are some factors that can make a big difference.

1. *Adequate financial support.* Families fare better after a divorce if the father pays child support and the family therefore has adequate finances (Amato & Sobolewski, 2004; Marsiglio et al., 2000). However, many noncustodial fathers do not pay child support or do not pay as much as they should, earning the label "deadbeat dads." Adjustment is likely to be more difficult for mother-headed families that fall into poverty and must struggle to survive.
2. *Good parenting by the custodial parent.* The custodial parent plays a critical role in what happens to the family. If she can continue to be warm, authoritative, and consistent, children are far less likely to experience problems (Hetherington & Kelly, 2002). It is difficult for parents to be effective when they are depressed and under stress, but parents who understand the stakes may be more able to give their children the love and guidance they need. Moreover, interventions can help them. Marion Forgatch and David DeGarmo (1999) randomly assigned divorced mothers of boys either to a parenting skills program designed to prevent them from becoming less positive and more coercive toward their children or to a control group. They found that training helped mothers rely less on coercive methods and remain positive toward their sons over a 12-month period. Better yet, these positive changes in their parenting behaviors were tied to improvements in their children's adjustment at school and at home (see also Wolchik et al., 2000).
3. *Good parenting by the noncustodial parent.* Children may suffer when they lose contact with their noncustodial parent. A quarter or more of children living with their mothers lose contact with their fathers, and many others see their fathers only rarely (Demo & Cox, 2000). More important than amount of contact, however, is quality of contact. Noncustodial fathers who are authoritative parents and who are emotionally close to their children can help children make a positive adjustment to life in a single-parent home (Amato & Sobolewski, 2004; Marsiglio et al., 2000).
4. *Minimal conflict between parents.* However their mothers and fathers parent, children should be protected from continuing marital conflict. If parents continue to squabble after the divorce and are hostile toward each other, both will likely be upset, their parenting is likely to suffer, and children will feel torn in their loyalties and experience behavioral problems (Amato, 1993). When parents can agree on joint custody, children's adjustment tends to be better than when custody is granted to one parent or the other (Bauserman, 2002). Working with a mediator to resolve issues, rather than

fluence results: children's behavioral problems and parents' ineffective parenting styles feed on each other.

Mavis Hetherington and her associates (Hetherington, Cox, & Cox, 1982; Hetherington & Kelly, 2002) have found that custodial mothers, preoccupied with their own problems, often become impatient and insensitive to their children's needs. In terms of the dimensions of child rearing we have described, they become less accepting and responsive, less authoritative, and less consistent in their discipline. They occasionally try to seize control of their children with a heavy-handed, authoritarian style of parenting, but more often they fail to carry through in enforcing rules and make few demands that their children behave maturely. Noncustodial fathers, meanwhile, are likely to be overly permissive, indulging their children during visitations (Amato & Sobolewski, 2004). This is not the formula for producing well-adjusted, competent children. The behavioral problems that children display undoubtedly make effective parenting difficult, but deterioration in parenting style aggravates those behavioral problems. When this breakdown in family functioning occurs, children are likely to display not only behavioral problems at home but also strained relations with peers, low self-esteem, academic problems, and adjustment difficulties at school (Amato, 2001; Hetherington & Kelly, 2002).

Families typically begin to pull themselves back together about 2 years after the divorce, and by the 6-year mark most differences between children of divorce and children of intact families have disappeared (Hetherington & Kelly, 2002). Yet even after the crisis phase has passed and most children and parents have adapted, divorce can leave a residue of negative effects on at least a few individuals that lasts years (Amato, 2000; Hetherington & Kelly, 2002). For example, as adolescents, children of divorce are less likely than other children to perceive their relationships with their parents, especially their fathers, as close and caring (Emery, 1999; Woodward, Fergusson, & Belsky, 2000), and many are still negative about what divorce has done to their lives and unhappy that it happened (Emery, 1999).

The negative aftereffects of the divorce experience even carry into adulthood. About 20 to 25% of Hetherington's chil-

having lawyers duke it out, helps keep noncustodial parents cooperating with their spouses and involved in their children's lives after the divorce. In an experiment by Robert Emery and his colleagues (2001) on mediation versus litigation, 30% of noncustodial parents randomly assigned to a mediator saw their children weekly or more, whereas only 9% of those assigned to the normal litigation approach did.

5. *Additional social support.* Divorcing adults are less depressed if they have close confidants (Menaghan & Lieberman, 1986). Children also benefit from having close friends to give them social support (Lustig, Wolchik, & Braver, 1992) and from participating in peer-support programs in which they and other children of divorce can share their feelings and learn positive coping skills (Grych & Fincham, 1992). Friends, relatives, school personnel, and other sources of social support outside the family can all help families adjust to divorce.
6. *Minimal other changes.* Generally, families respond most positively to divorce if additional changes are kept to a minimum—for example, if parents do not have to move, get new jobs, cope with the loss of their children, and so on (Buehler et al., 1985–1986). Obviously, it is easier to deal with a couple of stressors than a mountain of them. Although families cannot always control events, they can strive to keep their lives as simple as possible.

Mediation can help warring couples resolve their issues during a divorce.

Here, then, are the first steps on the path toward a positive divorce experience—as well as a better understanding of why divorce is more disruptive for some families than for others. As Paul Amato (1993) concludes, adjustment to divorce will depend on the "total configuration" of stressors the individual faces and on the resources he has available to aid in coping, including both personal strengths (such as good coping skills) and social supports.

dren of divorce still had emotional scars and psychological problems as young adults (Hetherington & Kelly, 2002). And a study of middle-aged adults revealed that 24% of those whose parents had divorced when they were younger had never married, compared with 14% of adults from intact families (Maier & Lachman, 2000). Adults whose parents divorced are also more likely than adults from intact families to experience marital conflict and divorce themselves (Amato, 1996).

Some researchers paint a particularly gloomy picture of the typical divorce, whereas others offer more encouraging messages. Judith Wallerstein and her colleagues (2000), in *The Unexpected Legacy of Divorce,* summarize years of interviews with children of divorce by concluding that most have struggled with relationships ever since. Many had not married, or if they married had divorced, and most did not want children for fear that their children would experience what they did. Wallerstein's findings might cause you to recommend that parents do all possible to hold a bad marriage together for the sake of the children. However, based on more careful sampling of divorced families and comparison families and more objective research methods, Mavis Hetherington, in her book *For Better or for Worse* (Hetherington & Kelly, 2002), concludes that most parents and children rebound from their crisis period and adapt well in the long run—and sometimes even undergo impressive growth as a result of their experience (Hetherington & Kelly, 2002; and see Harvey & Fine, 2004).

On the positive side, a conflict-ridden two-parent family is clearly more detrimental to a child's development than a cohesive single-parent family. Children from families experiencing marital conflict display more behavioral problems after a divorce than before, but they show even larger increases in behavioral problems if they remain with their warring parents (Morrison & Coiro, 1999)! Indeed, many of the behavioral problems that children display after a divorce are evident well before the divorce. They may be caused not by divorce but by long-standing family conflict or even by genes that predispose certain parents and their children to experience psychological problems (Cherlin et al., 1991; O'Connor et al., 2000). Moreover, whereas fathers who engage in low levels of antisocial behavior benefit their children by living with them, fathers who engage in high levels of antisocial behavior are likely to increase their children's conduct problems by spending more time living with them (Jaffee et al., 2003), suggesting that the presence of a second parent is not always a plus.

Perhaps the most important message of research on divorce is that the outcomes of divorce vary widely. As Alan Booth and Paul Amato (2001) conclude, "divorce may be beneficial or harmful to children, depending on whether it reduces or increases the amount of stress to which children are exposed" (p. 210). As you can see in the Explorations box on page 446, several factors can help facilitate a positive adjustment to divorce and prevent lasting damage—among them adequate finances, effective parenting by the custodial parent, effective parenting by the noncustodial parent, minimal conflict between parents, social support, and minimal additional changes and stressors.

Remarriage and Reconstituted Families

Within 3 to 5 years of a divorce, about 75% of single-parent families experience yet another major transition when a parent remarries and the children acquire a stepparent—and sometimes new siblings (Hetherington, 1989; Hetherington & Stanley-Hagan, 2000). Because about 60% of remarried couples divorce, some adults and children today find themselves in a recurring cycle of marriage, marital conflict, divorce, single status, and remarriage.

How do children fare when their custodial parent remarries? The first few years are a time of conflict and disruption as new family roles and relationships are ironed out (Hetherington & Stanley-Hagan, 2000). The difficulties are likely to be aggravated if both parents bring children to the family (Mekos, Hetherington, & Reiss, 1996). Girls are often so closely allied with their mothers that they may resent either a stepfather competing for their mother's attention or a stepmother attempting to play a substitute-mother role. Perhaps as a result, they tend to benefit less than boys do from remarriage, although most children adapt and fare well with time (Hetherington, Bridges, & Insabella, 1998). It seems that living in a reconstituted family as a child, like living in a single-parent family after a divorce, tends to increase the risk that individuals will enter marriages that are at risk to fail—for example, marriages in which the partners are young, have relatively little education, cohabit, and conceive a child before marriage (Teachman, 2004).

© IT Stock Free/PictureQuest

☾ Most children adjust to being part of a reconstituted family, but boys have an easier time than girls do.

Summing Up

Cohabitation tends to be associated with later marital problems. Childless married couples and gay and lesbian families generally fare well, and dual-career families can be good or bad for children depending on the quality of parenting children receive. Divorce creates a family crisis for 1 or 2 years and has long-term negative effects on some children, and becoming part of a reconstituted family is a more difficult transition for girls than for boys. Even this quick examination of diverse family experiences should convince you that it is difficult to generalize about the family. ■

The Problem of Family Violence

As this chapter makes clear, humans develop within a family context, and family relationships normally contribute positively to human development at every point in the life span. At the same time, families can be the cause of much anguish and of development gone astray. Nowhere is this more obvious than in cases of family violence (St. George, 2001, p. A20):

> From a young age, I have had to grow up fast. I see families that are loving and fathers who care for their children, and I find myself hating them. . . . I have nightmares pertaining to my father. I get angry and frustrated when family is around.

These sobering words were written by Sonyé Herrera, an abused adolescent who for years had been hit, threatened with guns, choked, and otherwise victimized—and had witnessed her mother abused—by an alcoholic father. The abuse continued even after the couple divorced. At age 15, unable to stand any more, Herrera had her father charged with assault, but he returned one afternoon when she was 15, hit her, and shot and killed both her and her mother before turning his gun on himself (St. George, 2001, p. A21).

Child abuse is perhaps the most visible form of family violence. Every day, infants, children, and adolescents are burned, bruised, beaten, starved, suffocated, sexually abused, or otherwise mistreated by their caretakers. About 3 million reports of child maltreatment are filed with social service agencies in the United States every year; in 2002, almost 900,000 of them were substantiated as true, a rate estimated to be 12 of every 1000 children (U.S. Department of Health and Human Services, 2004). Of the 900,000 children, 60% were neglected, 19% physically abused, 10% sexually abused, and

6% emotionally or psychologically abused; another 19% experienced still other types of maltreatment (and some children experienced more than one of the preceding types). Surveys reveal even higher rates, as much child abuse goes unreported. According to a national survey of U.S. families, for example, 11% of children had reportedly been kicked, bitten, hit, hit with an object, beaten, burned, or threatened or attacked with a knife or gun by a parent in the past year (Wolfner & Gelles, 1993).

Abuse of children by their caregivers is only one form of family violence. The potential for abuse exists in all possible relationships within the family. Children and adolescents batter, and in rare cases kill, their parents (Agnew & Huguley, 1989); siblings abuse one another in countless ways (Cicirelli, 1995). And spousal abuse, rampant in our society, appears to be the most common form of family violence worldwide. Globally, it is estimated that about one-third of women are beaten, coerced into sex, or emotionally abused by their partners (Murphy, 2003). An anthropological analysis of family violence in 90 nonindustrial societies by David Levinson (1989) revealed that wife beating occurred in 85% of them; in almost half of these societies, it occurred in most or all households, suggesting that it was an accepted part of family life.

Although spousal abuse is viewed as intolerable in most segments of U.S. society, Murray Straus and Richard Gelles (1986, 1990) nonetheless estimate, based on surveys they have conducted, that 16 of 100 married couples in the United States experience some form of marital violence in a year's time—often "only" a shove or a slap, but violence nonetheless—and that almost 6% experience at least one instance of severe violence (such as kicking or beating). Much "mild" spousal abuse is mutual; in more serious cases, one spouse, usually the woman, is repeatedly terrorized and injured by a partner whose goal is control (Johnson & Ferraro, 2000).

Elderly adults are also targets of family violence. Frail or impaired older people are physically or psychologically mistreated, neglected, financially exploited, and stripped of their rights—most often by adult children or spouses serving as their caregivers (Flannery, 2003; Wolf, 2000). No one knows how many cases of elder abuse there are, but all agree that many go unreported. Cognitive impairment is an important risk factor; in one sample of elderly adults with Alzheimer's disease, 5% had been physically abused by their caregivers in the year since they had been diagnosed (Paveza et al., 1992).

This is not a pretty picture. Here is a social problem of major dimensions that causes untold suffering and harms the development of family members of all ages. What can be done to prevent it, or to stop it once it occurs? To answer this question, you must first try to gain some insight into why family violence occurs.

Why Does Family Violence Occur?

The various forms of family violence have many similarities. Because child abuse has been studied the longest, we will look at what has been learned about the causes of child abuse.

The Abuser

Hard as it may be to believe, only about 1 child abuser in 10 appears to have a severe psychological disorder (Kempe & Kempe, 1978). Rather, the abusive parent is most often a young mother, most often acting alone (U.S. Department of Health and Human Services, 2004). She tends to have many children, to live in poverty, to be unemployed, and to have no partner to share her load (Wiehe, 1996; Wolfner & Gelles, 1993). Yet child abusers come from all races, ethnic groups, and social classes. Many of them appear to be fairly typical, loving parents—except for their tendency to become extremely irritated with their children and to do things they will later regret.

A few reliable differences between parents who abuse their children and those who do not have been identified. First, child abusers tend to have been *abused as children;* abusive parenting, like effective parenting, tends to be passed from generation to generation (van IJzendoorn, 1992; Conger et al., 2003). Although most maltreated children do not abuse their own children when they become parents, roughly 30% do (Kaufman & Zigler, 1989). They are also likely to become spousal abusers; about 60% of men who abuse their partners report that they either were abused or witnessed abuse as children, compared with about 20% of nonviolent men (Delsol & Margolin, 2004). Researchers do not know whether genes or environmental factors are primarily responsible for the intergenerational transmission of parenting. However, all forms of witnessing or being the target of violence in adults' families of origin predict all forms of perpetration and victimization later in life, suggesting that what children from violent homes learn is that violence is an integral part of human relationships (Kwong et al., 2003). The cycle of abuse is not inevitable, however; it can be broken if abused individuals receive emotional support from parent substitutes, therapists, or spouses and are spared from severe stress as adults (Egeland, Jacobvitz, & Sroufe, 1988; Vondra & Belsky, 1993).

Second, abusive mothers are often *battered by their partners* (Coohey & Braun, 1997; McCloskey, Figueredo, & Koss, 1995). Because adults are more likely to be in an abusive romantic relationship or marriage if they were abused or witnessed abuse as a child (Stith et al., 2000), abusive mothers may have learned through their experiences both as children and as wives that violence is the way to solve problems, or they may take out some of their frustrations about being abused on their children.

Third, abusers are often insecure individuals with *low self-esteem.* Their unhappy experiences in insecure attachment relationships with their parents, reinforced by their negative experiences in romantic relationships, may lead them to formulate negative internal working models of themselves and others (Pianta, Egeland, & Erickson, 1989; and see Chapter 14). These adults often feel like victims and feel powerless as parents (Bugental & Beaulieu, 2003). However, they have also learned to be victimizers (Pianta et al., 1989).

Fourth, abusive parents seem to have *unrealistic expectations* about what children can be expected to do at different ages and have difficulty tolerating the normal behavior of young children (Haskett, Johnson, & Miller, 1994). For example, Byron Egeland and his colleagues (Egeland, 1979; Egeland, Sroufe, & Erickson, 1983) found that when infants cry to communicate needs such as hunger, nonabusive mothers correctly interpret these cries as signs of discomfort, but abusive mothers often infer that the baby is somehow criticizing or rejecting them.

In short, abusive parents tend to have been exposed to harsh parenting and abusive relationships themselves, to have low self-esteem, and to find caregiving more stressful, unpleasant, and threatening to their egos than other parents do. Still, it has been difficult to identify a particular kind of person who is highly likely to turn into a child abuser. Could some children bring out the worst in parents?

The Abused

An abusive parent often singles out only one child in the family as a target; this offers a hint that child characteristics might matter (Gil, 1970). No one is suggesting that children are to blame for being abused, but some children appear to be more at risk than others. For example, children who have medical problems or who are difficult are more likely to be abused than quiet, healthy, and responsive infants who are easier to care for (Bugental & Beaulieu, 2003). Yet many difficult children are not mistreated, and many seemingly cheerful and easygoing children are.

Just as characteristics of the caregiver cannot fully explain why abuse occurs, then, neither can characteristics of children. There is now intriguing evidence that the combination of a high-risk parent and a high-risk child spells trouble. Specifically, the combination of a child who has a disability or illness or is otherwise difficult and a mother who feels powerless to deal with her child and overreacts emotionally when the child cannot be controlled increases the likelihood of abuse (Bugental, 2001). People who lack a sense of control as parents tend to feel threatened by children who are not responsive to them, become emotionally aroused, and may use force in a desperate attempt to establish that they have power. However, even the match between child and caregiver may not be enough to explain abuse. You should, as always, consider the ecological context surrounding the family system.

© Peggy & Ronald Barnett/CORBIS

Child abuse occurs in all ethnic and racial groups.

The Context

Consistently, abuse is most likely to occur when a parent is under great stress and has little social support (Cano & Vivian, 2003; Egeland et al., 1983). Life changes such as the loss of a job or a move to a new residence can disrupt family functioning and contribute to abuse or neglect (Wolfner & Gelles, 1993). Abuse rates are highest in deteriorating neighborhoods where families are poor, transient, socially isolated, and lacking in community services and informal social support. These high-risk neighborhoods are areas in which adults do not feel a sense of community and do not look after each other's children, neighborhoods in which the motto "It takes a village to raise a child" has little meaning (Korbin, 2001).

Finally, the larger macroenvironment is important. Ours is a violent society in which the use of physical punishment is common and the line between physical punishment and child abuse can be difficult to draw (Whipple & Richey, 1997). Parents who believe strongly in the value of physical punishment are more at risk than those who do not to become abusive if they are under stress (Crouch & Behl, 2001). Child abuse is less common in societies that discourage physical punishment and advocate nonviolent ways of resolving interpersonal conflicts (Gilbert, 1997; Levinson, 1989). Child abuse is particularly rare in Scandinavian countries, where steps have been taken to outlaw corporal (physical) punishment of children not only in schools but also at home (Finkelhor & Dziuba-Leatherman, 1994).

As you can see, child abuse is a complex phenomenon with a multitude of causes and contributing factors. It is not easy to predict who will become a child abuser and who will not, but abuse seems most likely when a vulnerable individual faces overwhelming stress with insufficient social support. Much the same is true of spousal abuse, elder abuse, and other forms of family violence.

What Are the Effects of Family Violence?

As you might imagine, child abuse is not good for human development. Physically abused and otherwise maltreated children tend to have many problems, ranging from physical injuries and cognitive and social deficits to behavioral problems and psychological disorders (Margolin & Gordis, 2000). Shaking and other physically abusive behaviors can cause brain damage in infants and young children, the stress of either being abused or witnessing abuse can interfere with normal brain development, and child neglect means receiving little of the intellectual stimulation from nurturing adults that contributes so much to intellectual growth (Eckenrode, Laird, & Doris, 1993).

Not surprisingly, then, intellectual deficits and academic difficulties are common among mistreated children (Malinosky-Rummell & Hansen, 1993; Shonk & Cicchetti, 2001). A particularly revealing study focused on 5-year-old identical and fraternal twins to rule out possible genetic influences on the association between exposure to domestic violence and intellectual development (Koenen et al., 2003). Children exposed to high levels of domestic violence had IQ scores 8 points lower, on average, than those of children who were not exposed to domestic violence, even taking genetic influences on IQ into account.

Behavioral problems are also common among physically abused children. Many tend to be explosively aggressive youngsters, rejected by their peers for that reason (Bolger & Patterson, 2001). They learn from their experience with an abusive parent to be supersensitive to angry emotions; as a result, they may perceive anger in peers where there is none and lash out to protect themselves (Reynolds, 2003). Even as adults, individuals who were abused as children not only tend to be violent, both inside and outside the family, but also tend to have higher-than-average rates of depression, anxiety, and other psychological problems (Margolin & Gordis, 2000).

The social skills of many abused children are also deficient (Darwish et al., 2001). One of the most disturbing consequences of physical abuse is a lack of normal empathy in response to the distress of others. When Mary Main and Carol George (1985) observed the responses of abused and nonabused toddlers to the fussing and crying of peers, they found that nonabused children typically attended carefully to the distressed child, showed concern, and even attempted to provide comfort. As shown in Figure 15.4, not one abused child showed appropriate concern in this situation. Instead, abused toddlers were likely to become angry and attack the crying child, reacting to the distress of peers much as their abusive parents react to their distress (Main & George, 1985, p. 410; see also Klimes-Dougan & Kistner, 1990):

> Martin (an abused boy of 32 months) tried to take the hand of the crying other child, and when she resisted, he slapped her on the arm with his open hand. He then turned away from her to look at the ground and began vocalizing very strongly, "Cut it out! CUT IT OUT!," each time saying it a little faster and louder. He patted her, but when she became disturbed by his patting, he retreated, hissing at her and baring his teeth. He then began patting her on the back again, his patting became beating, and he continued beating her despite her screams.

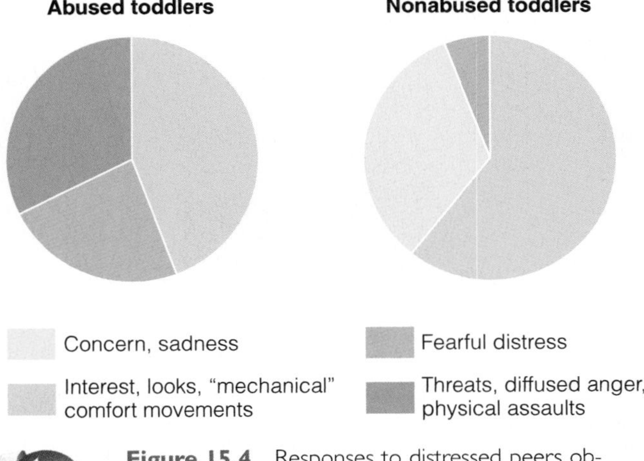

Figure 15.4 Responses to distressed peers observed in abused and nonabused toddlers in day care. Abused children distinguish themselves by a lack of concern and a tendency to become upset, angry, and aggressive when other children cry.

SOURCE: Adapted from Main & George (1985).

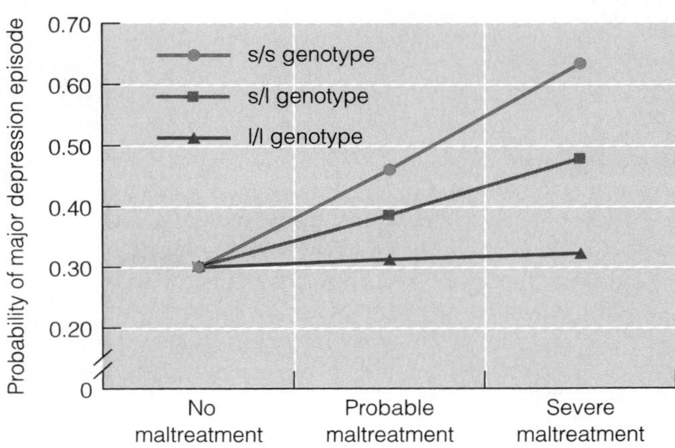

Figure 15.5 Genes interact to maltreatment as a child to influence the odds of depression as an adult. A short (s) variant of the gene studied increases risk, whereas a long (l) variant protects against depression.

SOURCE: Adapted from Caspi, Sugden et al. (2003, p. 388, Figure 2).

Remarkable as it may seem, many other neglected and abused children turn out fine. What distinguishes these children from the ones who have long-term problems? Part of the reason may be that they have genes that protect them from the negative psychological effects of abuse and possibly other stressful life events. As Figure 15.5 shows, Avshalom Caspi and his colleagues (Caspi et al., 2003) found that maltreatment during childhood increases the likelihood of clinical depression among individuals with a genetic makeup that predisposes them to depression but not among individuals with a genetic makeup known to protect against depression. Indeed, among individuals whose genes protect against depression, the rate of depression is no higher among adults who were maltreated as children than among adults who were not. Similarly, Caspi and his colleagues (2002) have studied maltreated children whose genes are associated with high levels of an enzyme, monoamine oxidase A, that clears neurotransmitters from the brain. These children are less likely to develop antisocial patterns of behavior as young adults than are maltreated children whose genes are associated with low levels of this enzyme. Low levels of the enzyme have been tied in previous studies to aggression. It seems, then, that genes and en-

Applications

Battling Family Violence

That family violence has many causes is discouraging. Where do we begin to intervene, and just how many problems must we correct before we can prevent or stop the violence and its damaging effects on development? Despite the complexity of the problem, progress is being made.

Consider first the task of preventing violence before it starts. This requires identifying high-risk families—a task greatly aided by the kinds of studies you have reviewed. For example, once we know that an infant is at risk for abuse because she is particularly irritable or unresponsive, it makes sense to help the child's parents appreciate the baby's positive qualities. Learning how to elicit smiles, reflexes, and other positive responses from premature infants makes parents more responsive to their babies, which in turn helps these at-risk babies develop more normally (Widmayer & Field, 1980).

Better yet, efforts to prevent abuse can be directed at the combination of a high-risk parent and a high-risk child. Daphne Bugental and her colleagues (Bugental & Beaulieu, 2003; Bugental et al., 2002) have focused on parents who feel powerless as parents and as a result often believe that their children are deliberately trying to annoy or get the best of them. Such parents are especially likely to become abusive if they face the challenge of raising a child who is unresponsive and difficult. In an intervention study, Bugental and her colleagues focused on high-risk mothers who had recently emigrated from Mexico to California and who scored high on a measure of family stress. Some had infants who were high risk (who were born prematurely or scored low on the Apgar examination at birth and were therefore at risk for future health problems), and others had infants who were low risk. The researchers designed a home visitation program aimed at empowering these mothers by teaching them to analyze the causes of caregiving problems without blaming either themselves or their children and to devise and try solutions to caregiving problems on their own. Families were randomly assigned to the empowerment program, another home visitation program without the empowerment training, or a control condition in which families were referred to regular community services.

After the intervention period, mothers in the empowerment training condition had more of a sense of power in the family than mothers in the other conditions did, and they reported fewer postpartum depression symptoms. The rate of physical abuse, including spanking and slapping, was only 4% in the empowerment group compared with 23% in the other home visitation group and 26% in the community referral group. Moreover, the children in the empowerment group were in better health and were better able to manage stress. Importantly, the benefits of the program were greatest for families with high-risk children. As the figure in this Applications box shows, after empowerment training, harsh parenting was unlikely whether the child was at medical risk or not, whereas in the control conditions, children at medical risk were treated far more harshly than low-risk children, suggesting that they were headed for trouble developmentally.

What about parents who are already abusive? Here the challenge is more difficult. Occasional visits from a social worker are unlikely to solve the problem. A more promising approach is Parents Anonymous, a self-help program based on Alcoholics Anonymous that helps caregivers understand their problems and gives them the emotional support they often lack. However, Robert Emery and Lisa Laumann-Billings (1998) argue that the social service system needs to distinguish more sharply between milder forms of abuse, for which supportive interventions such as Parents Anonymous are appropriate, and severe forms, where it may be necessary to prosecute the abuser and protect the children from injury and death by removing them from the home. Courts traditionally have been hesitant to break up families, but too often children who have been seriously abused are repeatedly abused.

A comprehensive approach is likely to be most effective. Abusive parents need emotional support and the opportunity to learn more effective parenting, problem-solving, and coping skills, and the victims of abuse need day care programs and developmental training to help them overcome cognitive, social, and emotional deficits caused by abuse (Malley-Morrison & Hines, 2004; Wiehe, 1996). The goal in combating child abuse and other forms of family violence must be to convert a pathological family system into a healthy one.

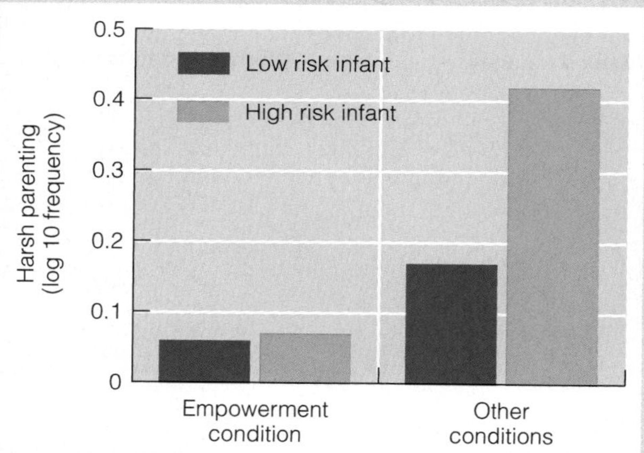

Empowerment training for low-income mothers under stress reduces harsh parenting practices, especially among mothers who are the most at risk of being abusive because their babies had medical problems or were born prematurely.

SOURCE: Bugental & Beaulieu, 2003, p. 352, Figure 1.

vironment interact to determine the life outcomes of abused and maltreated children. Maltreatment appears to do long-term damage to some children but to affect other children less, depending partly on whether their genes protect them from, or make them vulnerable to, the damaging effects of stress. Environmental factors can also make a big difference; for example, a close relationship with at least one nonabusive adult helps protect children against the destructive effects of abuse (Egeland et al., 1988).

Without question, child abuse has damaging long-term consequences for the cognitive, social, and emotional development of many victims. Moreover, witnessing marital violence has many of the same negative effects as being abused (Kitzmann et al., 2003). The important question then becomes this: Knowing what we know about the causes and effects of abuse, what can be done to prevent it, stop it, and undo the damage? What would you propose? The Applications box on page 452 offers some solutions.

Summing Up

Family violence occurs in all possible relationships within the family. A closer look at child abuse reveals that parent characteristics such as a history of abuse and low self-esteem, child characteristics such as medical problems and a difficult temperament, and contextual factors such as lack of social support and a culture that condones violence all contribute. Prevention efforts should therefore focus on empowering high-risk parents to deal with difficult and unresponsive children and treatment efforts on either strengthening social support for mild abusers or removing children from the reach of chronic, severe abusers. ■

Summary Points

1. The family, whether nuclear or extended, is best viewed as a changing social system embedded in larger social systems that are also changing.

2. Infants affect and are affected by their parents. Fathers are less involved in caregiving than mothers and specialize in challenging play. Developmental outcomes are likely to be positive when parents have positive indirect effects on development because of their positive influence on each other.

3. Child rearing can be described in terms of the dimensions of acceptance–responsiveness and demandingness–control; generally, children are more competent when their parents adopt an authoritative style of parenting, which is influenced by genes, socioeconomic status, and culture. Both genes and cultural context affect parenting styles. Research on the parent effects, child effects, and transactional models of family influence reminds us that children's problem behaviors are not always solely caused by ineffective parenting.

4. When a second child enters the family system, firstborns find the experience stressful. Sibling relationships are characterized by rivalry and affection and can have positive or negative effects on development. Parent–child relationships typically remain close in adolescence but involve some conflict and are renegotiated to become more equal.

5. Marital satisfaction declines somewhat as newlyweds adjust to each other and become parents, whereas the empty nest transition and grandparenthood are generally positive experiences. Marital satisfaction is also affected by earlier satisfaction, personality, and degree of similarity in personality.

6. In adulthood, siblings have less contact but normally continue to feel both emotionally close and rivalrous. Young adults often establish more mutual relationships with their parents. Middle-aged adults continue to experience mutually supportive relationships with their elderly parents but sometimes suffer from the stresses of middle generation squeeze and caregiver burden.

7. Among the adults whose lives are inadequately described by the traditional family life cycle concept are single adults (some of whom cohabitate), childless married couples, dual-career families, and gay and lesbian adults. Divorce creates a crisis in the family for 1 or 2 years; a few children experience long-lasting problems.

8. Parent characteristics, child characteristics, and contextual factors all contribute to child abuse and must be considered in formulating prevention and treatment programs.

Critical Thinking

1. Focusing on three key statistics about changes in the family, and drawing on other evidence in this chapter, make the case that the family in the United States is weaker today than it was 50 years ago. Now argue, using other statistics, that the family is stronger than it was 50 years ago.

2. A 16-year-old girl, drunk as a skunk, has plowed the family car into a tree and is being held at the police station for driving under the influence. Her father must pick her up. What would you expect an authoritarian, authoritative, permissive, and neglectful father to say and do in this situation, and what implications might their contrasting approaches have for this young women's development?

3. Martha, three months after her divorce, has become depressed and increasingly withdrawn. Her son Matt, age 7, has become a terror around the house and a discipline problem at school. From the perspective of (a) the parent effects model, (b) the child effects model, and (c) the transactional model of family influence, how would you explain what is going on in this single-parent family?

4. Martha has just married George and wonders how her experience of the family life cycle is likely to differ from his. Tell her.

Key Terms

family systems theory, 422
nuclear family, 422
extended family household, 422
family life cycle, 423
reconstituted family, 424
beanpole family, 424
indirect effect, 426
acceptance–responsiveness, 426
demandingness–control, 426
authoritarian parenting, 426
authoritative parenting, 426
permissive parenting, 427

neglectful parenting, 427
parent effects model, 429
child effects model, 429
transactional model, 429
sibling rivalry, 432
autonomy, 433
empty nest, 437
modified extended family, 440
role reversal, 441
middle generation squeeze, 441
filial responsibility, 441
caregiver burden, 441
cohabitation, 442
spillover effects, 443
latchkey children, 443

Media Resources

Websites to Explore

Visit Our Website

For a chapter tutorial quiz and other useful features, visit the book's companion website at *http://psychology.wadsworth.com/sigelman_rider5e*. You can also connect directly to the following sites:

Child Abuse and Neglect
The site of the National Clearinghouse on Child Abuse and Neglect Information is a rich source of information about the topic. It provides statistics, prevention approaches, and a searchable database.

Parents Anonymous
Parents Anonymous has chapters throughout the United States that offer support to parents in an effort to prevent child abuse and neglect. The national website has a network map that will help you find the Parents Anonymous organization in your state.

Grandparenthood
The website of the Foundation for Grandparenting is designed to help grandparents get the most out of grandparenthood. It includes ideas on the roles grandparents play and how they can relate to their grandchildren, research on grandparenthood, and updates on legislation affecting grandparents (for example, regarding visitation rights).

Family Studies
The World Wide Web Subject Catalog at the University of Kentucky has a page devoted to a multitude of Internet resources on family studies.

Understanding the Data: Exercises on the Web

For additional insight on the data presented in this chapter, try the exercises for these figures at *http://psychology.wadsworth.com/sigelman_rider5e:*

Figure 15.4 Responses to distressed peers observed in abused and nonabused toddlers in day care

Unnumbered Figure in Applications box "Battling Family Violence." Empowerment training for low-income mothers under stress reduces harsh parenting practices

Life-Span CD-ROM

Go to the Wadsworth Life-Span CD-ROM for further study of the concepts in this chapter. The CD-ROM includes narrated concept overviews, video clips, a multimedia glossary, and additional activities to expand your learning experience. For this chapter, check out the following clips, and others, in the video library:

VIDEO Deciding Whether to Have Children

VIDEO Adult Women Juggling Roles

Developmental PsychologyNow is a web-based, intelligent study system that provides a complete package of diagnostic quizzes, a personalized study plan, integrated multimedia elements, and learning modules. Check it out at *http://psychology.wadsworth.com/sigelman_rider5e/now.*

CHAPTER s i x t e e n

Developmental Psychopathology

PEGGY, A 17-YEAR-OLD FEMALE, was referred by her pediatrician to a child psychiatry clinic for evaluation of an eating disorder. She had lost 10 pounds in 2 months and her mother was concerned. . . . At the clinic she stated that she was not trying to lose weight, had begun to sleep poorly about 2 months ago unless she had several beers, and that she and friends "got trashed" on weekends. Her relationship with her parents was poor; she had attempted suicide a year previously with aspirin and was briefly hospitalized. The day before this evaluation she had taken a razor to school to try to cut her wrists, but it was taken away by a friend. She admitted being depressed and wanting to commit suicide and finally told of discovering that she was pregnant 4 months earlier. Her boyfriend wanted her to abort, she was ambivalent, and then she miscarried spontaneously about 2 months after her discovery. After that, "It didn't really matter how I felt about anything" (Committee on Adolescence, 1996, pp. 71–72).

We do not all have as many problems as Peggy, but it is the rare person who makes it through the life span without having at least some difficulty adapting to the challenges of living. Each phase of life has unique challenges, and some of us inevitably run into trouble mastering them. This chapter is about some of the ways in which human development can go awry. It is about how development influences psychopathology and how psychopathology influences development. By applying knowledge of life-span human development to the study of psychological disorders, you can understand them better. And by learning more about abnormal patterns of development, you can gain new perspectives on the forces that guide and channel—or block and distort—human development more generally.

What Makes Development Abnormal?

Clinical psychologists, psychiatrists, and other mental health professionals often apply three broad criteria in defining the line between normal and abnormal behavior and diagnosing psychological disorders:

1. *Statistical deviance.* Does the person's behavior fall outside the normal range of behavior? By this criterion, a mild case of the "blahs" or "blues" would not be diagnosed as clinical depression because it is so statistically common, but a more enduring, severe, and persistent case might be.

2. *Maladaptiveness.* Does the person's behavior interfere with personal and social adaptation or pose a danger to self or others? Psychological disorders disrupt functioning and create problems for the individual, other people, or both.

3. *Personal distress.* Does the behavior cause personal anguish or discomfort? Many psychological disorders involve personal suffering and are of concern for that reason alone.

Although these guidelines provide a start at defining abnormal behavior, they are vague. We must ask which forms of statistical deviation, which failures of adaptation, or which kinds of personal distress are significant.

DSM-IV Diagnostic Criteria

Professionals who diagnose and treat psychological disorders find more specific diagnostic criteria in the *Diagnostic and Statistical Manual of Mental Disorders,* published in 1994 by the American Psychiatric Association. The fourth edition of this manual, known as **DSM-IV,** spells out defining features and symptoms for the range of psychological disorders. Because we will be looking closely at depression in this chapter, we will use it here as an example of how DSM-IV defines disorders. Depression is a family of several affective or mood disorders, some relatively mild and some severe. One of the most important is **major depressive disorder,** defined in DSM-IV as at least one episode of feeling profoundly depressed, sad, and hopeless; of losing interest in the ability to derive pleasure from almost all activities; or both for at least 2 weeks (American Psychiatric Association, 1994). To qualify as having a major depressive episode, the individual must experience at least five of the following symptoms, including one of the first two, persistently during a 2-week period:

1. Depressed mood (or irritable mood in children and adolescents) nearly every day
2. Greatly decreased interest or pleasure in usual activities
3. Significant weight loss or weight gain (or in children, failure to make expected weight gains)
4. Insomnia or sleeping too much
5. Psychomotor agitation or sluggishness–slowing of behavior
6. Fatigue and loss of energy
7. Feelings of worthlessness or extreme guilt
8. Decreased ability to concentrate or indecisiveness
9. Recurring thoughts of death, suicidal ideas, or a suicide attempt

By these criteria, a man suffering from major depression might, for example, feel extremely discouraged; no longer seem to care about his job or even about sexual relations with his wife; lose weight or have difficulty sleeping; speak and move slowly as though lacking the energy to perform even the simplest actions; have trouble getting his work done; dwell on how guilty he feels about his many failings; and even begin to think he would be better off dead. Major depressive disorder would not be diagnosed if this man were merely a little "down," if his symptoms were directly caused by drug abuse or a medical condition, or if he were going through the normal grieving process after the death of a loved one. Many more people experience depressive symptoms than qualify as having a clinically defined depressive disorder.

Although some think DSM-IV does not say enough about cultural and developmental considerations (Christensen, Emde, & Fleming, 2004; Doucette, 2002), it notes that both should be taken into account in making a diagnosis of major depressive disorder. For example, DSM-IV indicates that Asians who are depressed tend to complain of bodily ailments such as tiredness rather than talking about psychological symptoms such as guilt (American Psychiatric Association, 1994). And although DSM-IV takes the position that depression in a child is fundamentally similar to depression in an adult, it points out that some depressed children express their depression by being irritable rather than sad.

Developmental Psychopathology

Psychologists and psychiatrists have long brought major theories of human development to bear in attempting to understand and treat psychological disorders. Freudian psychoanalytic theory once guided most thinking about psychopathology and clinical practice; behavioral theorists have applied learning principles to the understanding and treatment of behavioral problems; and cognitive psychologists have called attention to how individuals interpret their experiences and perceive themselves. More recently, evolutionary psychologists have begun asking interesting questions about adaptive functions of psychological disorders that may help individuals cope with abuse and other stressors (Fischer et al., 1997; Nesse, 2000).

In the past 2 decades, psychologists have become convinced of the need for a new field devoted to the study of abnormal behavior from a developmental perspective—**developmental psychopathology** (Cicchetti & Rogosch, 2002; Cummings, Davies, & Campbell, 2000; Rutter & Sroufe, 2000). As defined by L. Alan Sroufe and Michael Rutter (1984), developmental psychopathology is the study of the origins and course of maladaptive behavior. Developmental psychopathologists appreciate the need to evaluate abnormal development in relation to normal development and to study both. They seek to understand how disorders arise and how their expression changes as the individual develops, and they attempt to identify causal pathways and mechanisms involving the genes, the nervous system, the person, and the social environment that lead to normal or abnormal adjustment later in life (Pennington, 2002; Rutter & Sroufe, 2000). In short, they bring a life-span and contextual–systems perspective to the study of abnormal behavior.

Psychopathology as Development, Not as Disease

Some developmental psychopathologists fault DSM-IV and similar diagnostic systems for being rooted in a medical or disease model of psychopathology that views psychological problems as diseaselike entities that people either have or do not have. Sroufe (1997) argues that psychopathology is better seen as development than as disease; it is a pattern of adaptation that unfolds over time. From this perspective, a researcher cannot understand psychological disorder without understanding not only the person's characteristics, developmental status, and history of adaptation but also the transactions over time between person and social environment that either support or undermine healthy development (Cummings et al., 2000; Sameroff, 2000).

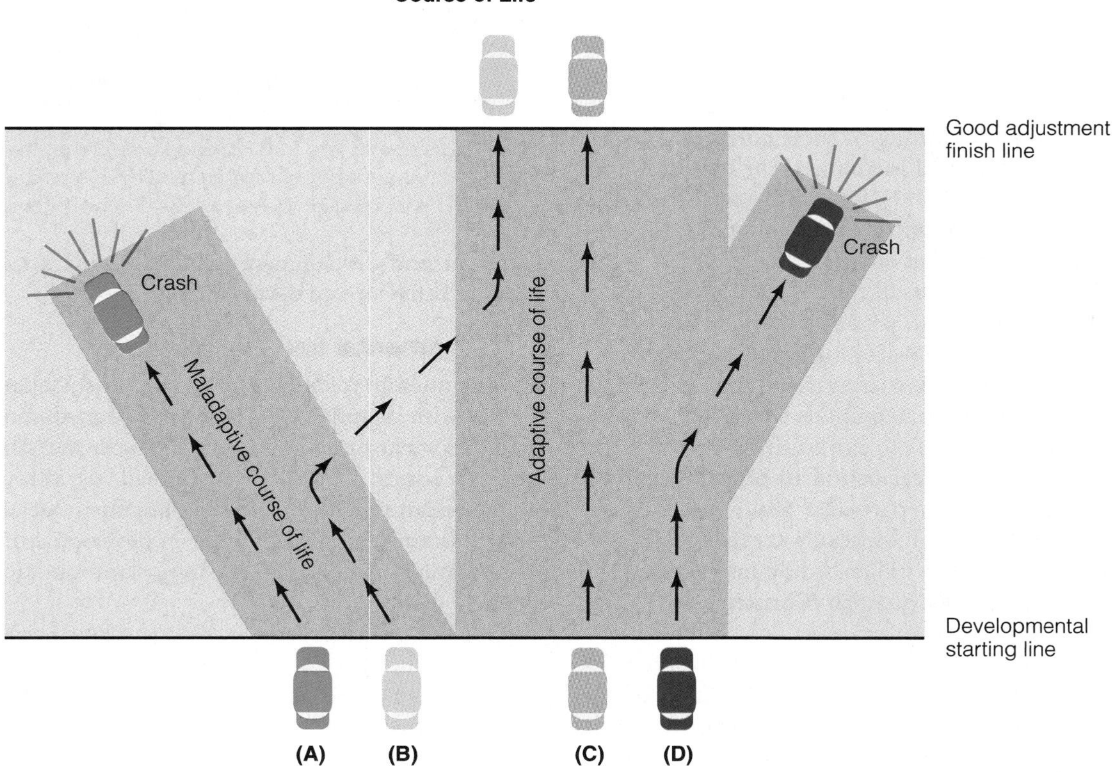

Figure 16.1 Developmental pathways leading to normal and abnormal outcomes. Some individuals start on a maladaptive course and deviate further from developmental norms as they age (route A); some start poorly but return to a more adaptive course later (route B); others stay on a route to competence and good adjustment all along (route C); and still others start off well but deviate later in life (route D).

SOURCE: Adapted from Sroufe (1997).

Figure 16.1 illustrates the concept of psychopathology as development. It portrays progressive branchings that lead development on either an optimal or a less-than-optimal course. Start with the assumption that normal human genes and normal human environments normally work to push development along a normal course and pull it back on course if it strays (Grossman et al., 2003). Some individuals—even some whose genes or experiences put them at risk to develop a disorder—manage to stay on a route to competence and good adjustment. Some start out poorly but get back on a more adaptive course later; others start off well but deviate later. Still others start on a maladaptive course and deviate further from developmental norms as they age because their early problems make it hard for them to master later developmental tasks and challenges. They may experience a developmental cascade in which genetic risk and early experiences such as a disturbed family environment lead to more negative experiences, lack of social support, and ultimately disorder (Kendler, Gardner, & Prescott, 2002). In the developmental pathways model, change is possible at many points, and the lines between normal and abnormal development are blurred. A model of this sort may seem complex, but it fits the facts of development.

Considering Social Norms and Age Norms

Developmental psychopathologists appreciate that behaviors are abnormal or normal only within particular social and developmental contexts (Cummings et al., 2000; Lopez & Guarnaccia, 2000). **Social norms** are expectations about how to behave in a particular social context—whether a culture, a subculture, or an everyday setting. What is normal in one social context may be abnormal in another. For example, John Weisz and his colleagues (1997) have discovered that Thai children are more likely than American children to have (or to be reported to have) symptoms of inner distress such as anxiety and depression and are less likely to engage in aggression and other forms of "acting out." One reason for the difference may be that the Thai culture places high value on emotional control and socializes children to internalize rather than vent their negative emotions. Both definitions and rates of abnormal behavior vary from culture to culture, from subculture to subculture, and from historical period to historical period. Abnormality is in the eye of a particular group of beholders. The cultural and social context (especially as expressed in parenting) also influences, and is influenced by, how psychological disorders play out over the life span (Christensen, Emde, & Fleming, 2004).

In addition, developmental psychopathologists recognize that abnormal behavior must be defined in relation to age norms—societal expectations about what behavior is appropriate or normal at various ages. This point is particularly important from a life-span perspective. The 4-year-old boy who frequently cries, acts impulsively, wets his bed, is afraid of the dark, and talks to his imaginary friend may be perceived as—and may be—normal. The 40-year-old who does the same things needs serious help. You simply cannot define abnormal behavior and development without having a solid grasp of normal behavior and development.

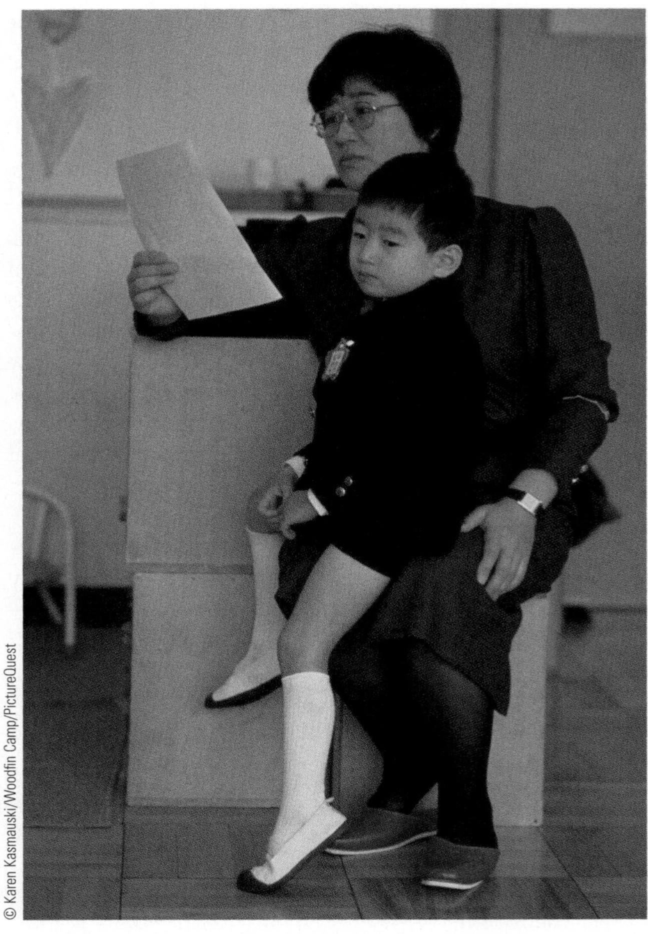

© Karen Kasmauski/Woodfin Camp/PictureQuest

As Japanese mothers have increased pressure on their children to succeed in school, cases of children refusing to attend school have become more prevalent (Kameguchi & Murphy-Shigematsu, 2001).

Developmental Issues

As they attempt to understand developmental pathways associated with adaptive or maladaptive functioning, developmental psychopathologists grapple with the same developmental issues that have concerned us throughout this book—most notably, the nature–nurture issue and the issue of continuity and discontinuity in development. Addressing these issues involves asking important questions such as these:

- How do biological, psychological, and social factors interact over time to give rise to psychological disorders?
- What are the important risk factors for psychological disorders, and what are the protective factors that keep some individuals who are at risk from developing disorders?
- Are most childhood problems passing phases that have no bearing on adjustment in adulthood, or does poor functioning in childhood predict poor functioning later in life?
- How do expressions of psychopathology change as the developmental status of the individual changes?

The Diathesis–Stress Model

In their efforts to understand how nature and nurture contribute to psychopathology, developmental psychopathologists have found a **diathesis–stress model** of psychopathology useful (Coyne & Whiffen, 1995; Ingram & Price, 2001). This model proposes that psychopathology results from the interaction over time of a predisposition or vulnerability to psychological disorder (a diathesis that can involve a particular genetic makeup, physiology, cognitions, personality, or a combination of these) and an experience of stressful events. This model helps to explain why "'bad' things have 'bad' effects among some—but not all—people, some—but not all—of the time" (Steinberg & Avenevoli, 2000).

Consider depression. We know that certain people are genetically predisposed to become depressed. Genetic factors account for about 40% of the variation in a group of people in symptoms of major depressive disorder; environmental factors unique to the individual rather than factors shared with siblings account for the rest (Glowinski et al., 2003). A genetic vulnerability to depression manifests itself as imbalances in several key neurotransmitters that affect mood and in such characteristics as high emotional reactivity to stress and self-defeating patterns of cognition in the face of negative events (Garber & Flynn, 2001).

According to the diathesis–stress model, however, individuals predisposed to become depressed are not likely to do so unless they experience significant losses or other stressful events, as illustrated in Figure 16.2. One stressful life event (such as the death of a loved one or a divorce) is usually not enough to trigger major depression, but when negative events pile up or become chronic, a vulnerable person may succumb. Meanwhile, individuals who do not have a diathesis—a vulnerability to depression—may be able to withstand high levels of stress without becoming depressed. For example, inheriting a particular variant of a gene involved in controlling levels of the neurotransmitter serotonin in the brain and experiencing multiple stressful events in early adulthood results in an especially high probability of major depression (Caspi, Sugden et al., 2003; and see Chapter 3). Among people with one or two of the high-risk genes, about 10% became depressed if they experienced no negative life events between ages 21 and 26, but 33% became depressed if they experienced four or more such events. By comparison, even when exposed to many stressful events, only 17% of individuals with two low-risk versions of the gene became depressed.

Depressive disorders (and many other psychological disorders) evolve from an interaction of diathesis and stress—or, to use developmental terminology, from the interplay of nature and nurture. It is messier than it appears at first glance. For example, it is clear that genes not only predispose some people to depression but also help shape their environment, including the extent to which they experience stressful life events (Rice, Harold, & Thapar, 2003). Moreover, the relationship between stress and disorder is reciprocal: Life stress aggravates disorder, and disorder makes lives more stressful (Grant et al., 2004). Finally, in a person genetically predisposed to depression, a depressive episode early in life in response to intense stress may bring about changes in gene activity and in the neurobiology of the stress response system (the hypothalamic–pituitary–adrenal axis); these changes may lower the threshold for a depressive episode (the diagonal line in Figure 16.2) so that later in life even mild stress can trigger depression (Grossman et al., 2003).

For some disorders we examine in this chapter, the diathesis for disorder is strong, probably more important than environmental influences in causing a disorder. Environment

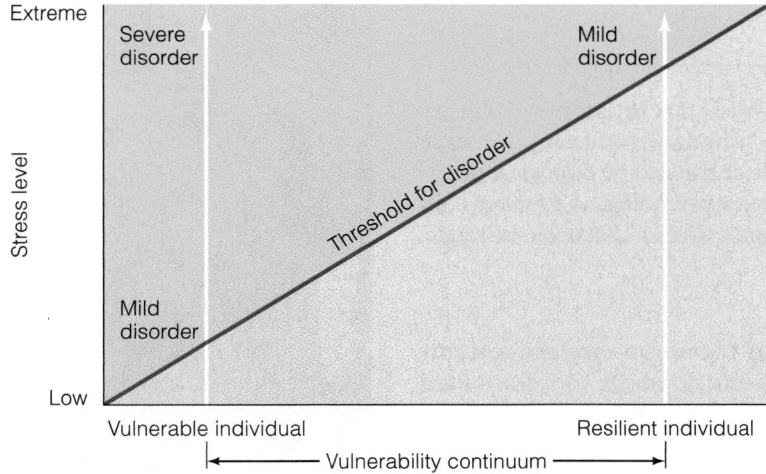

Figure 16.2 The diathesis–stress model. For a vulnerable individual, even mild stress can result in disorder. For an individual who is resilient and does not have a vulnerability or diathesis to disorder, it would take extremely high levels of stress to cause disorder; even then, the disorder might be only mild and temporary.

SOURCE: Adapted from Ingram & Price (2001).

may still play an important role, however, by shaping the course of the disorder and its effects on functioning and later development (Steinberg & Avenevoli, 2000). The depressed adolescent growing up in a hostile, disturbed family context, for example, is likely to fare worse than the depressed adolescent who receives a good deal of parental support and appropriate professional treatment.

This chapter highlights a sampling of developmental problems associated with each phase of the life span (for example, autism to illustrate disorders arising in infancy; attention deficit hyperactivity disorder, or ADHD, to illustrate childhood disorders; anorexia nervosa to illustrate disorders linked to adolescence; and Alzheimer's disease to illustrate disorders of old age). In addition, we look at depression in every developmental period to see whether and how its symptoms and significance change over the life span.

Summing Up

Diagnosing a psychological disorder such as major depressive disorder involves the consideration of the broad criteria of statistical deviance, maladaptiveness, and personal distress and the application of specific DSM-IV diagnostic criteria. Developmental psychopathology, the study of the origins and course of maladaptive behavior, offers a more developmental approach to psychological disorder, considering both social norms and age norms in diagnosis and charting developmental pathways leading to adaptive or maladaptive developmental outcomes. Questions about nature and nurture and about continuity and discontinuity must be answered, and diathesis–stress models must be developed, if researchers want to understand the development of psychological disorders. ■

The Infant

Adults worry about infants who do not eat properly, who cry endlessly, or who seem overly withdrawn and timid. Because infant development is strongly channeled by biological maturation, few infants develop severe psychological problems. Yet psychopathology exists in infancy, and its effects can be tragic.

Autism

> Jeremy, 3½ years old, has big brown eyes and a sturdy body. His mother carries him down the corridor toward the examiner, who greets them. Jeremy glances at the examiner's face but does not smile or say hello. They walk together into a playroom. Jeremy's mother puts him down, and he sits on the carpet in front of some toys. He picks up two blocks, bangs them together, and begins to stack the blocks, one on top of the other, not stopping until he has used the entire set. Jeremy does not look at the examiner or his mother while he works, nor when he finishes. And he does not make a sound. The examiner asks him to give her a red block. He does not respond. On their way out, Jeremy and his mother stop to look at a poster of a waterfall surrounded by redwood trees. "Yosemite Valley," Jeremy reads out—the name beneath the picture. His voice sounds automated, almost robotic (Sigman & Capps, 1997, p. 1).

Autism, first identified and described by Leo Kanner in 1943, is a disorder that begins in infancy and is characterized by deviant social development, deviant language and communication, and repetitive, stereotyped behavior. It is part of a larger group of related disorders called *pervasive developmental disorders*—disorders that appear early in life and are associated with gross abnormalities in several areas of development (American Psychiatric Association, 1994).

Picture the typical infant that we have described in this book: a social being who responds to others and forms close attachments starting at 6 or 7 months of age, a linguistic being who babbles and later uses one- and two-word sentences to converse, and a curious explorer who is fascinated by new objects and experiences. Now consider the three defining features of autism highlighted in DSM-IV (American Psychiatric Association, 1994; also see Frith, 2003; Klin et al., 2004; Volkmar et al., 2004):

1. *Deviant social development.* Autistic children have difficulty forming normal social relationships, responding appropriately to social cues, and sharing social experiences with other people. Like Jeremy, they seem to live in a world of their own, as though they find social contact aversive rather than pleasurable. They are far less likely than other infants to make eye contact, jointly attend to something with a social partner, seek other people for comfort, snuggle when held, and make friends. They also have difficulty reading other people's minds

© Jan Sonnenmair/Aurora

Many individuals with autism continue to function poorly as adolescents and adults, but some improve with age. One "improver," Jerry, described his childhood as a reign of "confusion and terror" in which "nothing seemed constant; everything was unpredictable and strange" (Bemporad, 1979, p.192).

and emotions or responding with empathy when others are distressed. Although they can form attachments to their parents, sometimes even secure ones, they often display what we referred to in Chapter 14 as a disorganized–disoriented pattern of attachment (Sigman & Capps, 1997).

2. *Deviant language and communicative skills.* Some autistic children are mute; others acquire language skills with some degree of success but still cannot communicate—that is, carry on a true conversation (Tager-Flusberg, 2000). As infants, autistic children often do not babble, gesture, or speak single words at the normal ages (Filipek et al., 2000). When they do speak, they may use a flat, robotlike tone; reverse pronouns (for example, use "you" to refer to the self); and engage in **echolalia** (a parroting of what someone else says).

3. *Repetitive, stereotyped behavior.* Autistic children seek sameness and repetition. They engage in stereotyped behaviors such as rocking, flapping their hands in front of their faces, or spinning toys; if they are more intellectually able, they carry out elaborate rituals such as a particular sequence of getting-dressed activities. They also become obsessed with particular objects and interests and can become highly distressed when their physical environment is altered (for example, when a chair in the living room is moved a few feet).

It is important to recognize that individuals with autism vary greatly in the degree and nature of their deficits. More mild cases of autism have been identified recently, and it is clear that there is a spectrum of autistic disorders that includes several syndromes (Brown, 2000c). Autism spectrum disorders include **Asperger syndrome,** in which the child has normal or above-average intelligence and good verbal skills, and clearly wants to establish social relationships, but has seriously deficient mind-reading and social skills. Affected children are sometimes called "little professors" because they talk rather stiffly and formally, and at mind-numbing length, about the particular subjects that obsess them. They have been largely invisible until recently, although people around them tend to view them as odd and socially aloof.

Rates of autism appear to have been rising, probably because of increased knowledge of the condition and increased diagnosis of higher-functioning individuals; autism in the narrow sense now affects about 10 of 10,000 children, and autism in the broader sense of a spectrum of disorders affects up to 40 children per 10,000 (Chakrabarti & Fombonne, 2001). At least 4 boys are affected for every girl (American Psychiatric Association, 1994), and among autistic individuals with normal IQs, there may be as many as 10 males for every female (Baron-Cohen, 2003).

Autistic children are autistic before age 3 and probably from birth. However, because at first they often seem to be normal and exceptionally good babies, or because physicians are slow to make the diagnosis even when parents express concerns about their child's development, many autistic children are not diagnosed until age 4 or later (Filipek et al., 2000; Klin et al., 2004). Efforts are being made to improve early screening and detection so that these children can receive early treatment. Autistic infants are given away by their lack of normal social responses—for example, by failure to display normal infant behaviors such as orientation to human voices, babbling, preference for human over nonhuman stimuli, eye contact and visual focus on faces in a scene (autistic babies tend to focus on objects in the background), joint attention, and reciprocity or taking turns, as in mutual smiling and peek-a-boo games (Klin et al., 2004).

Many people believe that autistic individuals are exceptionally intelligent. Some have average or above average IQs, but some are mentally retarded. With more higher-functioning children being diagnosed today, the percentage of children with autism who are also mentally retarded has dropped to under half but is still significant (Volkmar et al., 2004; Chakrabarti & Fombonne, 2001). Meanwhile, many autistic individuals, whether their IQs are high or low, show special talents such as the ability to quickly calculate days of the week corresponding to dates on the calendar or to memorize incredible amounts of information about train schedules (see Heaton & Wallace, 2004, and the description of savant syndrome in Chapter 9).

Autism used to be seen as a clear example of development that is qualitatively different from normal development. No more. The social impairment that defines autism is increasingly viewed as the extreme end of a genetically influenced continuum of social responsiveness, quantitatively rather than qualitatively different from normal social behavior (Constantino & Todd, 2003). In other words, many of us have some of the traits associated with autism to some degree, and the dividing line between normality and abnormality is arbitrary. Instead of apples and oranges—normal functioning versus autistic functioning—there are only degrees of appleness, a principle that appears to hold for most other psychological disorders.

Suspected Causes

Interest in solving the mysteries of autism is intense, and some fascinating hypotheses have been put forward in recent years to explain why individuals with autistic spectrum disorders show the symptoms they do. Many ideas have fallen by the wayside, such as the mistaken view that autism is caused by vaccination for measles, mumps, and rubella (Frith, 2003). We will outline three leading contenders, then introduce a new idea that has captured much attention. The main hypotheses are the theory-of-mind hypothesis, the executive function hypothesis, and the weak central coherence hypothesis (Frith, 2003).

• **Theory-of-mind hypothesis.** Individuals with autism regularly show limited understanding of mental states such as feelings, desires, beliefs, and intentions and of their role in human behavior—that is, they lack of what was characterized in Chapter 13 as a theory of mind (Baron-Cohen, 2000). As infants, they do not show some of the early precursors of theory of mind such as empathy for others, joint attention, pretend play, and imitation (Charman, 2000). As children, they have trouble understanding people's motives or appreciating that people can hold false beliefs. Indeed, they may not understand that people have beliefs, false or otherwise. Higher-functioning autistic individuals struggle to construct a theory of mind,

Explorations

Is Autism an Extreme Version of the Male Brain?

Many years ago, the discoverer of Asperger syndrome, Hans Asperger, suggested that the syndrome might reflect an extreme version of stereotypically masculine intelligence (Baron-Cohen, 2003). More recently, Simon Baron-Cohen (2003) has fleshed out Asperger's suggestion and proposed an **extreme male brain hypothesis** about autism. In his book *The Essential Difference,* Baron-Cohen lays out evidence that females tend to excel in empathizing, males in systematizing. Empathizing involves identifying people's thoughts and emotions and responding to them with appropriate emotions. Systematizing involves analyzing things to figure out how they work, extracting rules that determine what leads to what, and understanding systems. So, for example, little girls tend to be more interested than little boys in faces and in interacting with people, and women tend to be more able than men to read facial expressions of emotions and more likely to enter the helping professions. Meanwhile, little boys are more likely than little girls to enjoy playing with cars and trucks and building blocks and are more likely as adults to go into math, science, and engineering fields where they can work with predictable systems of objects rather than with ever-unpredictable people. Even when they are only a day old, girls prefer to look at a woman's face rather than a mechanical-looking mobile with some of the features of a face incorporated into it in a scrambled arrangement; by contrast, boys prefer the mechanical mobile (Connellan et al., 2000).

© Robert Maass/CORBIS

Baron-Cohen is quick to point out that not all women excel at empathizing and not all men excel at systematizing; there are simply average differences between the sexes, and they are likely caused by a combination of biological and environmental factors. Moreover, he notes that many people of both sexes have a balance of empathizing and systematizing skills, where both are strong or both are weak, rather than being strong in one and weak in the other. Of interest to us, however, are the individuals who are extremely weak in em-

but understanding people just does not come easily for them (Frith, 2003).

But is lack of a theory of mind the source of the social, emotional, and communicative problems autistic children display? Researchers are not sure. They note that autistic children are not so deficient on theory-of-mind tasks if they have good verbal ability (Yirmiya et al., 1996) and that theory-of-mind deficits help explain the social and communication problems of autistic individuals but do not explain other key features of autism, such as repetitive behavior (Joseph & Tager-Flusberg, 2004).

• **Executive dysfunction hypothesis.** Other researchers think that autism is rooted in a deficit in **executive functions,** the higher-level control functions associated with the prefrontal cortex of the brain that allow us to plan, change flexibly from one course of action to another, inhibit actions already begun, and the like (Hill, 2004; Ozonoff, 1997). Deficits in executive function would help explain why children with autism engage in repetitive, stereotyped behavior (they may not be able to switch to something else), cannot generate new ideas when asked to do so, have difficulty controlling their attention, and can be upset by change (Frith, 2003). But why are their planning and control deficits so much clearer for problems that concern people than for problems that concern objects, and how are their executive control deficits different from those of others with executive control problems, such as ADHD children?

• **Weak central coherence hypothesis.** A related idea is that autistic individuals focus on details and are unable to integrate their perceptions, see the "big picture," or form generalizations (Happé & Frith, 1996b). This would make a confusing, fragmented world; dealing with people in particular, given their unpredictability, would be challenging and possibly aversive. A focus on details rather than on the big picture also explains how autistic individuals are able to develop special talents and become trivia experts in specific areas. Yet autistic individuals often seem to get the big picture of what causes what when it comes to the world of objects (Baron-Cohen, 2003). Why does the world of people give them so much trouble?

Whether lack of a theory of mind, poor executive function, weak integrative abilities, or some other cognitive impairment pathizing and extremely strong in systematizing. They, Baron-Cohen argues, have the traits associated with autistic spectrum disorders. Clearly autistic individuals are weak at empathizing. Moreover, their repetitive actions (spinning plates or dropping sand through their fingers for hours) can be interpreted as attempts to systematize, to figure out the rules.

To assess group differences, John Lawson, Simon Baron-Cohen, and Sally Wheelwright (2004) gave males with Asperger syndrome, males without it, and females tasks to measure empathizing (understanding social outcomes when one person says something likely to upset another character in a story) and systematizing (predicting in mechanical diagrams how two levers or bobs will respond to the movement of another lever connected to them). On the empathizing tasks, females did better than males without Asperger syndrome; these males, in turn, outperformed males with Asperger syndrome. On the systematizing tasks, by contrast, both male groups outperformed the women.

Baron-Cohen also cites concrete cases of the extreme male brain at work. Richard, an award-winning mathematician, has Asperger syndrome. Despite his phenomenal ability to work math problems, he could not seem to master phones. Although he understood the mechanics of how they work, he did not know how to begin or end a conversation or what to say in between. He much preferred dealing with people one at a time rather than in groups, because people, unlike numbers, were too unpredictable for him. Noting that Isaac Newton and Albert Einstein had some similar traits, Baron-Cohen points out that Asperger syndrome tends to be common in families with many "male-brained" scientists and engineers. Exposure to a high dose of the male hormone testosterone during the prenatal period has been linked to strong spatial and mechanical abilities, so Baron-Cohen speculates that closer examination of the role of testosterone in brain development may yield a biological explanation for autism and tell us why it is so much more common among males than among females.

The extreme male brain hypothesis suggests that a disorder many thought to be a prime example of truly deviant human development may instead just represent one end of a continuum of intellectual functioning. Again, then, the boundaries between normality and abnormality are blurred, as developmental psychopathologists have emphasized. The extreme male brain hypothesis also calls attention to the strengths of individuals with autism and suggests that, if accommodations are made for their cognitive style, they can learn better and can be steered toward the kinds of mechanical and detail-oriented jobs that suit them. It is too soon, however, to say how valid the extreme male brain view of autism is. It does not fully explain why autistic individuals are so detail oriented and incapable of generalizing, for example; males without autism certainly can generalize. This hypothesis, like others actively being investigated today, requires further testing.

will prove to be at the heart of the problems autistic children display, this disorder clearly involves several cognitive impairments (Frith, 2003). It could be that the three hypotheses can be integrated; there is truth in each (Frith, 2003). Or it could be that there is no single core cognitive deficit or that what is at the root of autism is simply a lack of preference for social stimuli and social interaction (Volkmar et al., 2004). To make the mystery more intriguing, Simon Baron-Cohen (2003) has put forth an extreme male brain hypothesis regarding autistic spectrum disorders, described in the Explorations box on page 402.

What causes the impairments associated with autism? We are not yet sure. Early theorists suggested that rigid and cold parenting by "refrigerator moms" caused autism, but this harmful myth has long been put to rest (Achenbach, 1982). It is now understood that interacting with an autistic child can easily cause parents to be tense and frustrated and that the parents of autistic children are the source of genes that contribute to autism and therefore may have some autistic spectrum traits themselves. Bad parenting is not responsible for autism; rather, that autism is such a severe disorder present so early in life strongly suggests it has a biological basis.

Indeed, many autistic children display neurological abnormalities, and many of them have epilepsy (Volkmar et al., 2004). However, the neurological abnormalities are varied, and it is not clear which are most central to autism or how they arise. It has been observed, for example, that autistic children experience especially rapid and extensive brain growth during the first year of life, starting out with small heads at birth but ending up with big ones (Courchesne, Carper, & Akshoomoff, 2003). It is hypothesized that their neurons proliferate wildly during this sensitive period for brain development but do not become properly interconnected, perhaps accounting for the autistic child's special abilities and difficulties in integrating information (Volkmar et al., 2004).

Genes clearly contribute strongly to autism (Veenstra-Vanderweele & Cook, 2003). One research team found that if one identical twin was autistic, the other was autistic in 60% of the twin pairs studied; the concordance rate for fraternal twin pairs was 0% (Bailey et al., 1995). Moreover, when the broader spectrum of autism-related cognitive, linguistic, and social deficits was considered, 92% of the identical twins but only 10% of the fraternal twins were alike. Genes on several chromosomes have been implicated, and most likely individuals with autism inherit several genes that put them at risk (Pericak-Vance, 2003). That one identical twin can be autistic although the other is not suggests early environmental influences also contribute, although it is not clear how. One clear-cut biological defect that can explain all cases of autism will probably not be identified; autism is a complex spectrum of disorders with diverse neurological and behavioral characteristics and contributors.

Developmental Outcomes and Treatment

What becomes of autistic children as they age? The long-term outcome in the past has usually been poor, undoubtedly because autism is such a pervasive disorder, especially if it is accompanied by mental retardation. Many autistic individuals improve, but most are autistic for life, showing limited social skills even as adults (Howlin, Mawhood, & Rutter, 2000). Positive outcomes are most likely among those who have normal IQ scores and who can communicate through speech before they are 6 years old (Gillberg & Steffenburg, 1987).

Can treatment help autistic children overcome their problems? Researchers continue to search for drugs that will correct the suspected brain dysfunctions of these children, but they are a long way from discovering a "magic pill." Some autistic children are given drugs to control behavioral problems such as hyperactivity or obsessive–compulsive behavior, drugs that help them benefit from educational programs but do not cure autism (Volkmar, 2001).

The most effective approach to treating autism is intensive and highly structured behavioral and educational programming, beginning as early as possible, continuing throughout childhood, and involving the family (Connor, 1998; Koegel, Koegel, & McNerney, 2001). The goal is to make the most of the plasticity of the young brain during its sensitive period. O. Ivar Lovaas and his colleagues pioneered the application of reinforcement principles to shape social and language skills in autistic children. In one study, Lovaas (1987) compared two groups of autistic children treated at the University of California at Los Angeles. In the program, 19 children received intensive treatment—more than 40 hours a week of one-on-one treatment for 2 or more years during their preschool years. Trained student therapists worked with these children using reinforcement principles to reduce their aggressive and self-stimulatory behavior and to teach them developmentally appropriate skills such as how to imitate others, play with toys and with peers, use language, and master academic concepts. The training procedures involve many repetitions of simple learning tasks and the delivery of reinforcers such as bits of cereal for successful performance. Parents were taught to use the same behavioral techniques at home, and these children were mainstreamed into preschools that served normal children. The children who received this intensive treatment were compared with similarly disturbed children who, because of staff shortages or transportation problems, received a similar treatment program but were exposed to it for only 10 or fewer hours a week.

© Jan Sonnenmair/Aurora

Behavioral therapy starting early in life is effective with autistic children.

In the intensively trained group, all but 2 children scored in the mentally retarded range on tests of intellectual functioning at the start. Yet by age 6 or 7, their IQ scores averaged 83—about 30 points higher than the average in the control group. Moreover, 9 of the 19—47%—not only had average or above-average IQ scores at follow-up but also had been mainstreamed into regular first-grade classes and were adapting well. At age 13, 8 of the 19 treated students were still within the normal range of both IQ and school adjustment (Lovaas, Smith, & McEachin, 1989). In contrast, children in the comparison group displayed the usual intellectual deficits associated with autism, and most attended special classes for autistic and retarded children.

Some researchers have criticized this study's design (notice that it was not a true experiment with random assignment to treatment groups) and have concluded on the basis of later studies that early behavioral interventions usually do not convert autistic children into normally functioning ones (Gresham & MacMillan, 1998; Volkmar et al., 2004). However, research reinforces the conclusion that many autistic children, especially those who are young and are not severely retarded, have potential if they receive intensive cognitive and behavioral training and comprehensive family services starting early in life (Connor, 1998; Lovaas & Smith, 2003). It may be especially important to motivate autistic children to initiate social interactions so that they do not miss out on so many important social learning experiences (Koegel et al., 2001).

Depression

Does it seem possible that an infant could experience major depressive disorder as defined by DSM-IV? Infants are surely not capable of the negative cognitions common among depressed adults—the low self-esteem, guilt, worthlessness, hopelessness, and so on (Garber, 1984). After all, they have not yet acquired the capacity for symbolic thought that would allow them to reflect on their experience. Yet infants can exhibit some of the behavioral symptoms (such as loss of interest in

Explorations

Failure to Thrive

Infants diagnosed as having failure to thrive have, by definition, failed to grow normally. Outcomes associated with failure to thrive include illness, cognitive delays, and emotional maladjustment (Benoit & Coolbear, 2004). There are several possible causes underlying the basic failure to eat and grow normally (Chatoor & Ganiban, 2004; Lyons-Ruth, Zeanah, & Benoit, 2003). In some cases, an organic or biological cause, such as an illness, a heart defect, or deficiencies in the sensory and motor processes involved in feeding and swallowing, can be identified (Wright & Birks, 2000; Creskoff & Haas, 1999). Trauma to the gastrointestinal tract after choking or vomiting episodes can also be the root cause (Chatoor & Ganiban, 2004). In other cases, sometimes labeled nonorganic failure to thrive, the causes seem to be more emotional than physical. Indeed, it seems more correct to speak of a problem in the parent–child relationship than of a problem within the child (Benoit & Coolbear, 2004).

To illustrate, a normally developing boy whose mother was coping with marital problems and an unwanted pregnancy became the target of his mother's resentment when his father walked out on her. Soon this infant was a 13-month-old who was about the size of the average 7-month-old, whereas his fraternal twin sister grew at a normal rate (Gardner, 1972). Infants with nonorganic failure to thrive often have mothers who are stressed, depressed, and socially isolated and mothers whose own mothers were emotionally unresponsive or even abusive to them (Chatoor & Ganiban, 2004; Gorman, Leifer, & Grossman, 1993). These women tend to neglect their babies, interact insensitively with them, and express tension and anger rather than affection in their interactions (Lyons-Ruth et al, 2003). They often have unresolved losses and are insecure in their relationships; their babies are similarly insecure, often displaying a disorganized pattern of attachment in which they seem confused about how to relate to attachment figures (Ward, Lee, & Lipper, 2000). Some of these babies are fussy and unpredictable (Chatoor & Ganiban, 2004). Their difficultness may contribute to their parents' difficulties in responding to them and help produce an insecure attachment (Benoit & Coolbear, 2004).

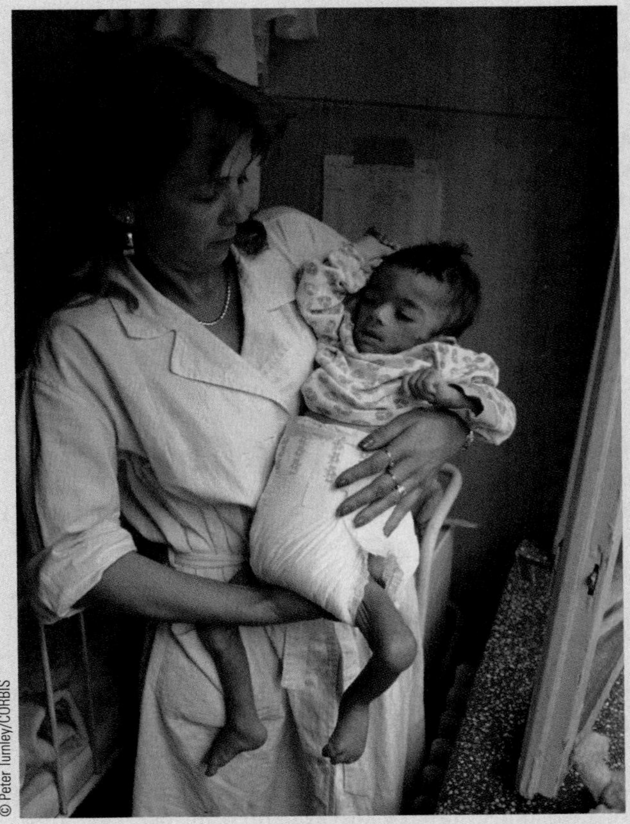

Babies with nonorganic failure to thrive gain weight and overcome their depression-like emotional symptoms quickly when they are removed from their homes (Bauchner, 1996). They tend to relapse if they are returned to parents who have not been helped to become more emotionally responsive. Their long-term development is likely to be especially poor if they have a history of both failure to thrive and maltreatment (Kerr, Black, & Krishnakumar, 2000), so intervening to change the family system is critical.

activities or psychomotor slowing) and **somatic symptoms** (bodily symptoms such as loss of appetite and disruption of normal sleep patterns) of depression. Researchers are still debating whether true depressive disorders can occur in infancy, but it is clear that babies can and do experience depression-like states and symptoms (Cytryn & McKnew, 1996).

Depressive symptoms are most likely to be observed in infants who lack a secure attachment relationship or who experience a disruption of an all-important emotional bond (Boris & Zeanah, 1999; Lyons-Ruth, Zeanah, & Benoit, 2003). It has long been observed that infants permanently separated from their mothers between 6 and 12 months of age tend to become sad, weepy, listless, unresponsive, and withdrawn and to show delays in virtually all aspects of their development (Spitz, 1946). Abused and neglected infants sometimes show similar symptoms (Zeanah, Boris, & Scheeringa, 1997). Infants who display a disorganized pattern of attachment, in which they do not seem to know whether to approach or avoid the attachment figure (see Chapter 14)—an attachment style common among abused children—are especially likely to show symptoms of depression (Lyons-Ruthet al., 2003; Egeland & Carlson, 2004).

Infants whose mothers are depressed are also at risk. They adopt an interaction style that resembles that of their depressed caregivers; they vocalize little and look sad, even when interacting with women other than their mothers, and they begin to show developmental delays by age 1 (Field, 1995a). They are at increased risk of becoming clinically depressed themselves later in life and of developing other psychological disorders. This may be because of a combination of genetic endowment and stressful experiences with their unpredictable mothers (that is, because of diathesis–stress). We know now that stress during the prenatal period or early in life can produce children with an overactive stress-response system who are easily distressed and unable to regulate their negative emotions effectively (Dawson & Ashman, 2000; Goodman, 2002). Moreover, these children are likely to interact negatively with their own children, increasing the chances that depression will be passed on to yet another generation (Whitbeck et al., 1992). Interventions can help depressed mothers understand and deal with their own attachment issues and appreciate and interact more sensitively with their babies (Cicchetti, Toth, & Rogosch, 2004).

Some infants who are neglected, abused, separated from attachment figures, or otherwise raised in a stressful or unaffectionate manner not only display depression-like symptoms but also may develop the life-threatening disorder called **failure to thrive.** These youngsters fail to grow normally, lose weight, and become seriously underweight for their age. They are the subject of the Explorations box on page 465.

Summing Up

Autism is characterized by deviant social development, deviant language and communication skills, and repetitive, stereotyped behavior. There are several autistic spectrum disorders, including Asperger syndrome, and genetics plays a strong role in them. Hypotheses about the brain dysfunctions and cognitive impairments at the root of this disorder include the theory-of-mind, executive dysfunction, weak central coherence, and extreme male brain hypotheses. Early behavioral intervention is the preferred treatment. Even babies can display many of the symptoms of depression, especially the behavioral and somatic ones, or a failure to thrive if they experience long-term or permanent separation from an attachment figure or are brought up by depressed, unresponsive, or rejecting caregivers. ■

The Child

Many children experience developmental problems—fears, recurring stomachaches, temper tantrums, and so on. A much smaller proportion are officially diagnosed as having one of the psychological disorders that typically begins in infancy, childhood, or adolescence—or as having one of the psychological disorders (such as major depressive disorder) that can occur at any age. Table 16.1 lists the major childhood disorders categorized in DSM-IV. In a study assessing children longitudinally through detailed interviews with parents and children administered from age 9 to age 16, more than one-third of children proved to have at least one diagnosable psychological disorder by age 16 (Costello et al., 2003). In addition, 1 in 5 young children and 1 in 10 older children qualified as having a diagnosable disorder in any given 3-month window (problems were at their lowest at age 12 before a rise in rates during adolescence).

Table 16.1 Some Psychological Disorders Usually First Diagnosed in Infancy, Childhood, or Adolescence

DSM-IV Category	Major Examples
Mental retardation	Subaverage general intellectual functioning
Learning disorders	Reading, math, and writing difficulties
Motor skill disorder	Developmental coordination disorder (extreme clumsiness, lack of coordination)
Communication disorders	Expressive language disorder; stuttering
Pervasive developmental disorders	Autism; similarly severe conditions
Attention deficit and disruptive behavioral disorders	Attention deficit hyperactivity disorder; conduct disorders (persistent antisocial behavior); oppositional defiant disorder
Feeding and eating disorders	Pica (eating nonnutritive substances such as paint or sand)
Tic disorders	Tourette's disorder (involuntary grimaces, grunts, foul language)
Elimination disorders	Enuresis (inappropriate urination); encopresis (inappropriate defecation)

SOURCE: Based on *DSM-IV*, American Psychiatric Association, 1994.

Many developmental problems of childhood can be placed in one of two broad categories that reflect whether the child's behavior is out of control or overly inhibited (Achenbach & Edelbrock, 1978). When children have **externalizing problems,** or undercontrolled disorders, they act out in ways that disturb other people and violate social expectations. They may be aggressive, disobedient, difficult to control, or disruptive (see the information in Chapter 13 on aggressive behavior). If their problems are severe, they may be diagnosed as having a conduct disorder or as hyperactive. **Internalizing problems,** or overcontrolled disorders, involve inner distress; they are more disruptive to the child than to other people and include anxiety disorders (such as persistent worrying about separation from loved ones), phobias, severe shyness and withdrawal, and depression. Externalizing behaviors mostly decrease from age 4 to age 18, whereas internalizing difficulties mostly increase (Bongers et al., 2003). Externalizing problems are more common among boys, whereas internalizing problems are more prevalent among girls—across cultures (Crijnen, Achenbach, & Verhulst, 1997). To give you a feel for these two categories of childhood disorder, we will look at one problem of externalization, hyperactivity, and one problem of internalization, depression.

Attention Deficit Hyperactivity Disorder

> The first year of proper school was a disaster for Greg. He spent most of the time being punished for getting out of his seat, for calling out, and for disrupting other children. The other children called him a "naughty Greg" and he became more and more discouraged and defiant. He did not seem to be learning anything at school at all. He was always in trouble. . . . At the end of the year the teacher told me that if she had to teach Greg for another year she would have resigned! (Selikowitz, 2004, p. 34)

When it was first identified, hyperactivity was defined principally as a problem of excess motor activity, and the term was used to describe children who could not seem to sit still and who were continually on the go. Now hyperactivity is viewed as a problem of attention. According to DSM-IV criteria, a child has **attention deficit hyperactivity disorder (ADHD)** if some combination of the following three symptoms is present (see also Selikowitz, 2004; Weyandt, 2001):

1. *Inattention.* The child does not seem to listen, is easily distracted, and does not stick to activities or finish tasks.
2. *Impulsivity.* The child acts before thinking and cannot inhibit an urge to blurt something out in class or have a turn in a group activity.
3. *Hyperactivity.* The child is perpetually fidgeting, finger tapping, chattering, and experiencing restlessness.

About 3 to 5% of school-age children, possibly more, are diagnosable as ADHD (American Psychiatric Association, 1994), at least two boys for every girl have the disorder (Pelham, Chacko, & Wymbs, 2004). Some critics believe that ADHD is overdiagnosed in the United States. It is more common here than in some countries, but it is reported throughout the world, and rates are consistently higher for boys than for girls (Luk, 1996).

Some children with ADHD, about as many of them girls as boys, are mainly inattentive but not hyperactive and impulsive; they are not disruptive but they often have difficulty in school (Weyandt, 2001). Those children with ADHD who are predominantly hyperactive and impulsive, as well as inattentive, often have conduct disorders or other externalizing problems. They are likely to irritate adults and become locked in coercive power struggles with their parents, interactions that only aggravate their problems (Barkley et al., 1991; Buhrmester et al., 1992). Because their behavior is so disruptive, they are also rejected by peers, which can have damaging effects on their adjustment and later development (Deater-Deckard, 2001; Whalen et al., 1989).

Not only do many children with ADHD have conduct disorders and behave aggressively, but many also have diagnosable learning disabilities, and some suffer from depression or anxiety disorders (Biederman et al., 1996). This co-occurrence of two or more conditions in the same individual is called **comorbidity** and is extremely common, especially during childhood. That is, many troubled individuals (like Peggy at the start of the chapter) have multiple psychiatric diagnoses rather than just one (Clark, Watson, & Reynolds, 1995). Comorbidity complicates the task of understanding the causes and consequences of any particular psychological disorder.

Developmental Course

ADHD expresses itself differently at different ages (Pelham et al., 2004). The condition often reveals itself in infancy. As infants, children with ADHD are often very active, have difficult temperaments, and show irregular feeding and sleeping patterns (Teeter, 1998). As preschool children, they are in perpetual motion, quickly moving from one activity to another. Because most young children are energetic and have short attention spans, behavior must be evaluated in terms of developmental norms; otherwise, we might mistake most average 3- and 4-year-olds for hyperactive children. Finally, by the grade-school years, overactive behavior is less of a problem, but children with ADHD are fidgety, restless, and inattentive to schoolwork (American Psychiatric Association, 1994).

What becomes of hyperactive children later in life? It used to be thought that they outgrew their problems, so parents sometimes delayed getting help, expecting their children's difficulties to go away by adolescence. Most children with ADHD do outgrow their overactive behavior (DuPaul & Stoner, 2003). This may have something to do with an opportunity for rewiring of the brain during a period in adolescence in which neurons proliferate and then are pruned back to complete the development of the frontal lobes (Selikowitz, 2004). But, despite improvements with development, most ADHD children continue to be less attentive and more impulsive than their peers (DuPaul & Stoner, 2003). An estimated 20% of ADHD children outgrow their problems, 20% continue to have severe problems as adults, and 60% continue to have at least mild problems throughout their lives (Selikowitz, 2004).

Adolescents with ADHD tend to be restless, to have difficulty concentrating on their academic work, and to behave impulsively; they often perform poorly in school or drop out, and they are prone to committing reckless delinquent acts without thinking about the consequences (Wallander & Hubert, 1985). The picture is more positive by early adulthood, yet many individuals with ADHD get in trouble because they have lapses of concentration, make impulsive decisions, and procrastinate (Wender, 1995). Especially if they had conduct disorders with ADHD as children, they are also likely to have more than their share of car accidents and law breaking, to abuse alcohol and drugs, and to have emotional problems as adults (Selikowitz, 2004; Weiss & Hechtman, 1993). The more severe the ADHD symptoms and any associated problems such as aggression in childhood, the more likely it is that later life outcomes will be poor (Pelham et al., 2004).

Suspected Causes

What causes this disorder? Researchers have long agreed that ADHD has a neurological basis, but they have had difficulty pinpointing it until recently. No consistent evidence of brain damage or of structural defects in the brain is found in most children with ADHD. Many cannot even be distinguished cleanly from non-ADHD children on the basis of neuropsychological tests because they do not all show clear deficits in neuropsychological functions or show them in the same areas (Doyle, Biederman et al., 2000). Still, it is widely agreed that the brains of children with ADHD work differently than the brains of other children do and that the cause is most likely differences in brain chemistry rather than physical brain damage.

Russell Barkley put forth the view that the frontal lobes of individuals with ADHD do not function properly, resulting in deficiencies in the executive functions that allow us to plan and control our behavior and to inhibit unwise responses (Barkley, 1997, 2000). This view has received much support. It now appears that the main problem is low levels of dopamine and related neurotransmitters that allow neurons in the frontal lobes to communicate with one another (Selikowitz, 2004). Abnormal functioning in an area of the brain specifically involved in regulating motor behavior has also been detected. Underactivity in this brain area seems to predict well the problems that children with ADHD have sitting still and paying attention (Teicher et al., 2000).

We also know that genes predispose some individuals to develop ADHD; one identical twin is highly likely to have it if the other does, and first-degree relatives of someone with ADHD (including parents) have four to five times the usual risk (Thapar, 2003). There is not one ADHD gene, however. Instead, researchers are identifying several specific gene variants that influence levels of dopamine and other relevant neurotransmitters in the brain and that are common in ADHD populations (Selikowitz, 2004; Thapar, 2003). Genes that tend to make humans restless and willing to take risks may have proved adaptive earlier in our evolutionary history, but inheriting too many of these genes today may not be adaptive (Selikowitz, 2004).

Environmental influences also enter, often not so much as the main cause of ADHD but as the forces that help determine whether a genetic potential turns into a reality and whether the individual adapts well or poorly as she develops. Low birth weight and prenatal exposure to nicotine, both associated with a shortage of oxygen prenatally, appear to contribute to some cases of ADHD, for example (Linnet et al., 2003). An intrusive, highly controlling parenting style may also contribute to, or at least aggravate, the problem in some cases; when parents are highly intrusive, infants and young children may not learn to regulate their own emotions and behavior effectively (Jacobvitz & Sroufe, 1987). Family risk factors such as marital conflict and socioeconomic disadvantage may also worsen the outcomes of children with ADHD (Biederman et al., 1995). By contrast, providing them with structured learning opportunities and appropriate reinforcement at home and at school can greatly improve their life outcomes (DuPaul & Stoner, 2003; Weyandt, 2001).

Are you one of the many people who believe that hyperactivity is caused by food additives such as red food coloring? High sugar intake? If so, your beliefs are largely incorrect. Although a few children with ADHD have allergic reactions to food additives, carefully controlled studies in which children and their families do not know whether they are getting a diet with food additives or a diet without them show that food additives have little effect on most children with ADHD (Bradley & Golden, 2001; Harley et al., 1978). Similarly, having hyperactive boys drink sugary drinks, rather than drinks containing the sugar substitute aspartame, has no effect on their behavior or learning performance (Milich & Pelham, 1986). All in all, ADHD is mainly caused by genetic influences on levels of dopamine and other neurotransmitters in the brain and environmental factors that improve or worsen ADHD symptoms and overall adjustment.

Treatment

Many children with ADHD are given stimulant drugs such as methylphenidate (Ritalin), and most are helped by these drugs. Although some observers are concerned that we do not yet know enough about the effects of stimulants on development, these drugs are now prescribed even for many preschool children with ADHD and have positive effects on how their behavior is judged by their parents and teachers (Short et al., 2004). Although it may seem odd to give overactive children stimulants, these drugs increase levels of dopamine and other relevant neurotransmitters in the frontal lobes of the brain to normal levels and, by doing so, allow these children to concentrate (Selikowitz, 2004). Listen to Greg's mother (she described his behavioral problems at the beginning of this section) on the topic: "The change in his behavior and mood was miraculous. One hour after the tablet I had my first proper conversation with Greg. For the first time in his life he was able to sit still and look at a book" (Selikowitz, 2004, p. 34).

Why, then, does controversy surround the use of stimulants with ADHD children? Some critics feel that these drugs are prescribed to too many children, including some who do not have ADHD. Although it is probably true that Ritalin and other stimulants are overprescribed in some communities, it is also true that many ADHD children who could benefit from drug treatment go untreated (Jensen, 2000). Other opponents of stimulant drug treatment are concerned that these drugs have undesirable side effects such as loss of appetite and headaches and do not correct the central problems that individuals with ADHD face or improve their academic and social functioning in the long run (Riddle, Kastelic, & Frosch, 2001). It is true that stimulants improve functioning only until their effects wear off at the end of the day (Schachar et al., 1997). And so far, there is not much evidence that individuals with ADHD who took stimulants as children are better off as adolescents or adults than those who did not (DuPaul & Stoner, 2003; Hart et al., 1995). Many experts have concluded that drugs alone cannot resolve all the difficulties faced by individuals with ADHD and their families.

What, then, is the best approach to treatment? The Multimodal Treatment of Attention Deficit Hyperactivity Disorder Study, a national study of 579 children with ADHD ranging in age from 7 to 9, is the best source of information about the pros and cons of medication and behavioral treatment for ADHD (Jensen et al., 2001). This study compared children who received optimally delivered medication, state-of-the-art behavioral treatment (a combination of parent training, child training through a summer program, and school intervention), a combination of the two approaches, or routine care in the community. The findings were clear: Medication alone was more effective than behavioral treatment alone or routine care in reducing ADHD symptoms. However, a combination of medication and behavioral treatment was superior to medication alone when the goal was defined as not only reducing ADHD symptoms but also improving academic performance, social adjustment, and parent–child relations.

So, medication is effective, especially if psychiatrists monitor doses closely and bear in mind that "children are not small adults" when it comes to drug dosages (Riddle et al., 2001). Medication can be even more effective, however, if supplemented by behavioral programs designed to teach children with ADHD to stay focused on tasks and to control their impulsiveness and by parent training designed to help parents understand and manage the behavior of these often-difficult youngsters (DuPaul & Stoner, 2003). The earlier children are diagnosed and treated, the better problems in family and peer relations that often flow from ADHD are prevented (Pelham et al., 2004).

Depression

As you saw earlier, the depression-like symptoms displayed by deprived or traumatized infants probably do not qualify as major depressive disorder. When, then, can children experience true clinical depression? For years many psychologists and psychiatrists, especially those influenced by psychoanalytic theory, argued that young children simply could not be depressed. Feelings of worthlessness, hopelessness, and self-blame were not believed to be possible until the child was older (Garber, 1984). Besides, childhood is supposedly a happy, carefree time, right? When it was finally appreciated that even very young children could become depressed, some researchers argued that childhood depression is qualitatively different from adult depression.

We now know that young children—as early as age 3—can meet the same criteria for major depressive disorder that are used in diagnosing adults (Garber & Flynn, 2001). Depression in children is rarer than depression in adolescents and adults, but an estimated 2% of children have diagnosable depressive disorders (Gotlib & Hammen, 1992). It used to be thought that depression in children was expressed in a masked manner as other problems. Many youngsters who show the key symptoms of depression have comorbid problems such as conduct disorder, ADHD, and anxiety disorder. These disorders are distinct problems, however, not just veiled symptoms of depression (Kaslow et al., 2000).

Developmentalists also appreciate that depression expresses itself somewhat differently in a young child than in an adult and believe it is premature to conclude that depression in children is the equivalent of depression in adults (Weiss & Garber, 2003). Like depressed infants, depressed preschool children are more likely to display the behavioral and somatic symptoms of depression (losing interest in activities, eating

Even young children can experience a major depressive episode.

Applications

Challenges in Treating Children and Adolescents

According to the Surgeon General of the United States, fewer than one in five U.S. children with psychological disorders receives treatment (Shute, 2001). Sometimes the child does not think she has a problem and resists. Other times, parents are dismissed by doctors or other professionals who say that that they are worrying too much or that their child is only going through "a phase" (Carter, Briggs-Gowan, & Davis, 2004). In addition, children are developing and their disorders are changing with them, making diagnosis tricky (Carter et al., 2004).

When children and adolescents do enter treatment, their therapists must recognize that they are not adults and cannot be treated as such (Holmbeck, Greenley, & Franks, 2003; Kazdin, 2003). First, children rarely seek treatment on their own; they are usually referred for treatment by parents who are disturbed by their behavior. This means that therapists must view the child and her parents as the "client."

Second, children's therapeutic outcomes often depend greatly on the cooperation of their parents (Bailey, 2000). Sometimes all members of the family must be treated for any enduring change in the child's behavior to occur—a principle derived from family systems theory. However, not all parents cooperate.

© SIU BioMed/Custom Medical Stock Photo

Play therapy can help young children who lack verbal skills express their feelings.

Third—a point familiar to students of human development—children function at different levels of cognitive and emotional development than adults do, and this must be taken into consideration in both diagnosing and treating their

poorly, and so on) than to display some of the cognitive symptoms (hopelessness) or to talk about being depressed (American Psychiatric Association, 1994; Kaslow et al., 2000). Yet even young children who are depressed sometimes express excessive guilt, claiming that they are bad (Weiss & Garber, 2003), and act out themes of death and suicide in their play (Luby, 2004). They can be recognized, through the application of developmentally sensitive modifications of DSM-IV criteria, because they are sad or irritable and show the same lack of interest in usually enjoyable activities that depressed adults do (Luby, 2004).

Children as young as age 2 or 3 are also capable of attempting suicide (Rosenthal & Rosenthal, 1984; Shaffer & Pfeffer, 2001). At age 3, Jeffrey repeatedly hurled himself down a flight of stairs and banged his head on the floor; upset by the arrival of a new brother, he was heard to say, "Jeff is bad, and bad boys have to die" (Cytryn & McKnew, 1996, p. 72). An 8-year-old, after writing her will, approached her father with a large rock and asked in all seriousness, "Daddy, would you crush my head, please?" (Cytryn & McKnew, 1996, pp. 69–70). Other children have jumped from high places, run into traffic, and stabbed themselves, often in response to abuse, rejection, or neglect. Moreover, children who attempt suicide once often try again (Shaffer & Pfeffer, 2001). The moral is clear: Parents and other adults need to appreciate that childhood is not always a happy, carefree time and that children can develop serious depressive disorders and suicidal tendencies. Children's claims that they want to die should be taken dead seriously.

Do depressed children tend to have recurring bouts of depression, becoming depressed adolescents and adults? Most children make it through mild episodes of sadness. However, 5- and 6-year-olds who report many depression symptoms are more likely than their peers to be depressed, to think suicidal thoughts, to struggle academically, and to be perceived as in need of mental health services when they are adolescents (Ialongo, Edelsohn, & Kellam, 2001). Moreover, it is estimated that half of children and adolescents diagnosed as having major depressive disorder have recurrences in adulthood (Kessler, Avenevoli, & Merikangas, 2001). Even if depressed children do not have further episodes, their depression can disrupt their intellectual development, school achievement, and social adjustment for years (Kovacs & Goldston, 1991).

Fortunately, most depressed children respond well to psychotherapy. Cognitive behavioral therapies that focus on changing distorted thinking have proved especially effective (Asarnow, Jaycox, & Tompson, 2001). But because children are problems (Kazdin, 2000). For example, young children cannot easily participate in therapies that require them to verbalize their problems and gain insight into the causes of their behavior. More developmentally appropriate techniques include play therapy, in which disturbed children are encouraged to act out concerns that they cannot easily express in words, and behavioral approaches that do not require insight and verbal skills.

Is psychotherapy for children and adolescents effective? John Weisz and Bahr Weiss (1993) pulled together research on two major categories of psychotherapy: behavioral therapies (those using reinforcement principles and modeling techniques to alter maladaptive behaviors and to teach more adaptive ones) and nonbehavioral therapies (primarily psychoanalytic therapies based on Freudian theory and other "talking cures" in which therapists help clients to express, understand, and solve their problems). These studies examined a range of problems (both externalizing and internalizing) and measured a range of outcomes (anxiety, cognitive skills and school achievement, personality and self-concept, social adjustment, and so on).

Judging from Weisz and Weiss's analysis, psychotherapy for children and adolescents works—at least as well as it works with adults—and the benefits are lasting (Kazdin, 2003). Moreover, externalizing problems such as hyperactivity and conduct disorder are just as responsive to treatment as internalizing problems such as phobias (Farmer et al., 2002). Behavioral therapies seemed to be more effective with children than nonbehavioral therapies, although such "talk therapies" have often proved equally effective in treating adults. However, more recent research suggests that cognitive behavioral therapy can be very effective with children, despite their cognitive limitations (Kazdin, 2003).

Today, psychiatrists are increasingly turning to medications to treat children—Ritalin for children with ADHD, Prozac and other antidepressants for depressed children as young as preschool age, and so on (Shute, Locy, & Pasternak, 2000). Both psychological and pharmacological treatments for children and adolescents with psychological disorders clearly achieve positive results (Asarnow et al., 2001). Yet they do not always work; for example, 40% or more of clinically depressed children and adolescents do not respond to psychotherapy, and about the same percentage do not respond to antidepressant medications (Asarnow et al., 2001). Apparently, then, we have much left to learn about the special challenges of treating children and adolescents with psychological problems.

not adults, treating children with depression and other psychological disorders poses several challenges for psychotherapists, as the Applications box on page 470 reveals. Many depressed children today are also being treated with antidepressant drugs such as Prozac (called *selective serotonin reuptake inhibitors*) that correct for low levels of the neurotransmitter serotonin in the brains of depressed individuals. Concerns have been raised, however, about their increasingly frequent use with children, about whether they are as effective with children as with adults, and about a recently discovered connection between their use by children and adolescents and an increased risk of suicide (Jensen et al., 1999; Vedantam, 2004).

Nature, Nurture, and Childhood Disorders

Most of us have a strong belief in the power of the social environment, particularly the family, to shape child development. This belief often leads us to blame parents—especially mothers—if their children are sad and withdrawn, uncontrollable and "bratty," or otherwise different from most children (see Chapter 15). Parents whose children develop problems often draw the same conclusion, feeling guilty because they assume they are at fault.

It is essential to view developmental disorders from a family systems perspective and to appreciate how emerging problems affect and are affected by family interactions. This perspective shows that the power of parents to influence their children's adjustment is not as great as many people believe. True, youngsters with depression and many other psychological disorders often come from problem-ridden families and have insecure attachments to their parents (Graham & Easterbrooks, 2000; van IJzendoorn & Bakermans-Kranenburg, 1996). They are also more likely than other children to have mothers, fathers, or both who have histories of psychological disorder (Connell & Goodman, 2002). Surely this means that children develop problems because they live in disturbed family environments with adults whose own psychological problems and marital conflicts make it difficult for them to parent effectively.

Or are there other interpretations? We cannot always be sure that unfavorable home environments cause childhood disorders. First, a child may have a genetic predisposition to disorder that would be expressed even if the child were adopted into another home early in life. In addition, "poor parenting" could be partly the effect of a child's disorder rather than its cause (Reiss et al., 2000). We cannot ignore the possibility that children's problem behaviors negatively affect their parents' moods, marital relationships, and parenting behaviors.

Unquestionably, family disruption and conflict and ineffective parenting contribute to and aggravate many childhood problems. Indeed, one study demonstrated that parents with psychological disorders often use less effective parenting approaches than parents without psychological disorders, but that their children were not likely to develop disorders unless the parenting they received was maladaptive (Johnson et al., 2001). Apparently, it was not sufficient to inherit a genetic predisposition to a disorder; as the diathesis–stress model suggests, a stressful environment was also necessary.

Overall, it is time to move beyond the simple view that parents are to blame for all their children's problems. It is also a mistake to view genes as the only important factor. Abnormal development, like normal development, is the product of both nature and nurture and of a history of complex transactions between person and environment in which each influences the other (Rutter, 2000).

Do Childhood Problems Persist?

The parents of children who develop psychological problems want to know this: Will my child outgrow these problems, or will they persist? Parents are understandably concerned with the issue of continuity versus discontinuity in development. You have already seen that autism, ADHD, and major depression tend to persist beyond childhood in many individuals. To answer the continuity–discontinuity question more fully, consider the spectrum of childhood problems.

Avshalom Caspi and his colleagues (1996) used data from a longitudinal study in New Zealand to determine whether children's behavioral styles, or temperamental characteristics, at age 3 predicted their susceptibility to psychological disorders at age 21—a span of 18 years. As Part A of Figure 16.3 shows, children who had externalizing problems as young children and were described as irritable, impulsive, and rough were more likely than either inhibited, overcontrolled children or well-adjusted children to be diagnosed as having antisocial personality disorder and to have records of criminal behavior as young adults.

Meanwhile, as Part B of Figure 16.3 shows, inhibited, internalizing children who were shy, anxious, and easily upset at age 3 were more likely than other children to be diagnosed as depressed later in life; contrary to prediction, they were not at significantly higher risk for anxiety disorders. This study and others point to *continuity* in susceptibility to problems over the years and suggest that early problems tend to have significance for later development (Costello et al., 2003; Mesman, Bongers, & Koot, 2001).

Relationships between early behavioral problems and later psychopathology in this study and others tend to be weak, however, so there is also *discontinuity* in development. Notice that most children with temperaments that put them at risk did not have diagnosable problems as adults. Similarly,

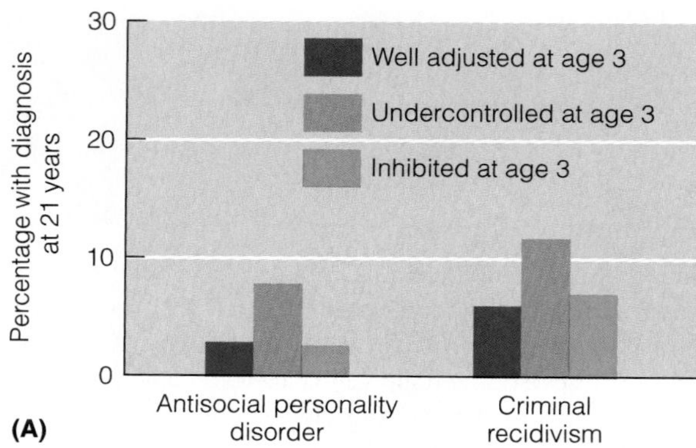

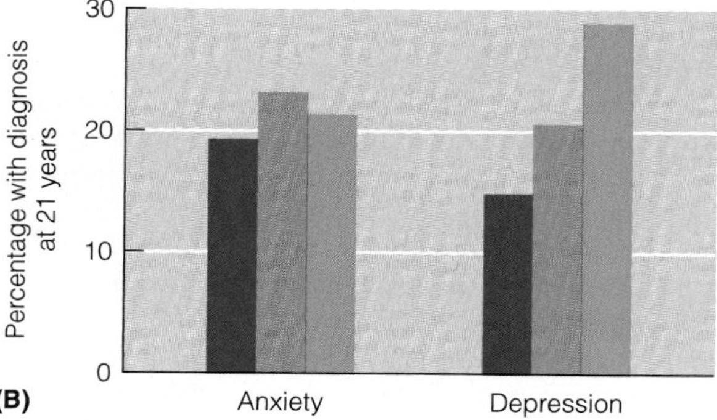

Figure 16.3 Relationships between behavior at age 3 and psychological disorders at age 21. Part A shows that children with uncontrolled, externalizing behavioral styles are more likely than other children to show antisocial behavior and repeated criminal behavior at age 21. Part B shows that inhibited, internalizing children are at high risk of depression, but not anxiety disorders, at 21.

SOURCE Adapted from Caspi et al. (1996).

in a 14-year follow-up of children and adolescents with behavioral and emotional problems, about 40% still had significant problems in adulthood, but most did not (Hofstra, Van der Ende, & Verhulst, 2000). In other words, having serious psychological problems as a child does not doom most individuals to a life of maladjustment.

Why might we see continuity of problem behavior in some children but discontinuity in others? If children have mild rather than severe psychological problems and receive help, their difficulties are likely to disappear. Some children also show remarkable resilience, functioning well despite exposure to risk factors for disorder or overcoming even severe early problems to become well adjusted (Garmezy, 1994; Small & Memmo, 2004). Such children appear to have protective factors working for them—processes that keep them from becoming maladjusted in the face of risk. These protective factors include their own competencies (especially intellectual ability and social skills) and strong social support (especially a stable family situation with at least one caring parent figure).

Summing Up

ADHD manifests itself from infancy into the adult years but is expressed differently at different ages. Genetically predisposed to ADHD, children with it are helped most by a combination of stimulant drugs that increase dopamine levels in their brains and behavioral therapy. Even young children can meet DSM-IV criteria for depression and become suicidal (although rarely). Nature and nurture conspire to produce such childhood disorders; they are not just the products of bad parenting. There is also both continuity and change in development: Some children remain maladapted, and others, especially those with mild problems and many protective factors, outgrow their difficulties. ■

The Adolescent

If any age group has a reputation for having problems and causing trouble, it is adolescents. This is supposedly the time when angelic children are transformed into emotionally unstable, unruly, problem-ridden delinquents. The view that adolescence is a time of emotional storm and stress was set forth by the founder of developmental psychology, G. Stanley Hall (1904). It has been with us ever since.

Storm and Stress?

Are adolescents really more likely than either children or adults to experience psychological problems? In truth, adolescents have a far worse reputation than they deserve. Most adolescents simply are not emotionally disturbed and do not develop serious problem behaviors such as drug abuse and chronic delinquency. Instead, significant mental health problems—real signs of storm and stress—characterize about 20% of adolescents (Kazdin, 2000; Offer & Schonert-Reichl, 1992). Moreover, many of these adolescents were maladjusted before they reached puberty and continue to be maladjusted during adulthood (Reinherz et al., 1999).

Yet adolescence is a period of heightened vulnerability to some forms of psychological disorder (Cicchetti & Rogosch, 2002). The 20% rate of diagnosable psychological disorder among adolescents is higher than an estimated rate of about 10% among children (Ford, Goodman, & Meltzer, 2003), although it is no higher than that for adults (Kazdin, 2000). Teenagers face greater stress than children; they must cope with physical maturation, changing brains and cognitive abilities, tribulations of dating, changes in family dynamics, moves to new and more complex school settings, societal demands to become more responsible and to assume adult roles, and more (Cicchetti & Rogosch, 2002; Hill, 1993). Mood swings, risk taking, and conflict with parents are all common (Arnett, 1999). Most adolescents cope with these challenges remarkably well, maintain the level of adjustment they had when they entered adolescence, and undergo impressive psychological growth, although it is not unusual for them to feel depressed, anxious, and irritable occasionally. For a minority, a buildup of stressors during adolescence can precipitate serious psychopathology. Their problems should not be dismissed as adolescent moodiness and irritability.

Many adolescents of both sexes get themselves into trouble by overusing alcohol and drugs, engaging in delinquent behavior, and displaying other so-called adolescent problem behaviors. These problem behaviors, although common, usually do not reach the level of seriousness to qualify as psychological disorders and typically wane as adolescents become adults (Jessor, 1998). Here we focus on two types of disorder that clearly become more prevalent in adolescence. Among females, diagnosable eating disorders such as anorexia nervosa can make the adolescent period treacherous. In addition, rates of depression increase dramatically from childhood to adolescence, especially among females, and suicide rates climb accordingly. These problems interfere with normal adolescent development; yet they become far more understandable when you view them in the context of this developmental period.

Anorexia Nervosa

Perhaps no psychological disorders are more associated with adolescence than the eating disorders that disproportionately strike adolescent girls, either during the transition from childhood to adolescence or during the transition from adolescence to adulthood (Keel & Fulkerson, 2001). Both anorexia nervosa and bulimia nervosa have become more common in recent years in several industrialized countries (Gordon, 2000; Milos et al., 2004). And both are serious—indeed, potentially fatal—conditions that are difficult to cure.

Anorexia nervosa, which literally means "nervous loss of appetite," has been defined as a refusal to maintain a weight that is at least 85% of the expected weight for the person's height and age (American Psychiatric Association, 1994). Anorexic individuals are also characterized by a strong fear of becoming overweight, a distorted body image (a tendency to view themselves as fat even when they are emaciated), and, if they are females, an absence of regular menstrual cycles. The typical individual with anorexia may begin dieting soon after reaching puberty and simply continue, insisting, even when she weighs only 60 or 70 pounds and resembles a cadaver, that she is well nourished and could stand to lose a few more pounds (Hsu, 1990). Praised at first for losing weight, she becomes increasingly obsessed with dieting and exercising and gains a sense of power by resisting the urging of parents and friends to eat more (Levenkron, 2000). Fewer than 3 in every 1000 adolescent girls suffer from this condition, and there are about 11 female victims for every 1 male victim (van Hoeken, Seidell, & Hoek, 2003).

Anorexia nervosa can be distinguished from **bulimia nervosa,** the so-called binge–purge syndrome, which involves recurrent episodes of consuming huge quantities of food followed by purging activities such as self-induced vomiting, use of laxatives, or rigid dieting and fasting (American Psychiatric

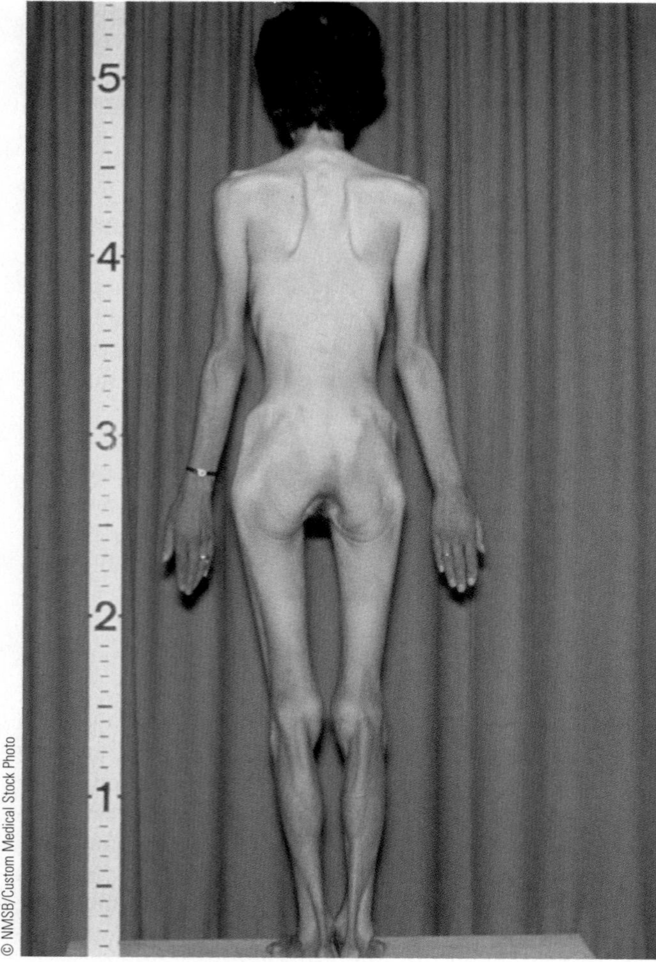

☾ Anorexia can be life threatening.

Association, 1994). Bulimia is especially prevalent in college populations, affecting few men but as many as 5% of college women (Hsu, 1990). A bulimic girl or woman typically binges on the foods that are taboo to dieters, eating entire half gallons of ice cream, multiple bags of cookies and potato chips, or whole pies and cakes—as much as *55,000 calories* in a single binge session (Johnson et al., 1982). Whereas individuals with anorexia are by definition underweight, individuals with bulimia can be found in all weight ranges (American Psychiatric Association, 1994). It is a myth that these eating disorders are restricted to European American females from upper middle-class backgrounds. They are evident at all socioeconomic levels (Gard & Freeman, 1996) and in all racial and ethnic groups, although African American females are less concerned with being thin and dieting than European American and Asian American females and have much lower rates of eating disorders (Wildes, Emery, & Simons, 2001).

Suspected Causes

Both nature and nurture contribute to eating disorders. On the nurture side, cultural factors are significant. We live in a society obsessed with thinness as the standard of physical attractiveness that makes it hard for young women to form positive identities (Gordon, 2000; Keel & Klump, 2003). As Western, and especially European American, values emphasizing the desirability of a slim figure have spread to other countries, rates of eating disorders in those countries have risen (Gordon, 2000). Interestingly, exposure to television on the island of Fiji converted girls raised to view plump bodies as a status symbol associated with the generous sharing of food into girls who feel too fat and try to control their weight (Becker et al., 2002).

Well before they reach puberty, large proportions of girls in our society associate being thin with being attractive, fear becoming fat, and wish they were thinner (Ricciardelli & McCabe, 2001). About a fourth of second-grade girls diet (Thelen et al., 1992). Being a 9-year-old in a school with girls as old as 13 rather than in a school with girls no older than 11 only heightens this cultural pressure to be thin and breeds the attitudes and dieting practices that lead to eating disorders (Wardle & Watters, 2004). As girls experience normal pubertal changes, they naturally gain fat and become, in their minds, less attractive. They have more reason than ever to be obsessed with controlling their weight (Murnen & Smolak, 1997). This may be why adolescence is a prime time for the emergence of eating disorders.

But why do relatively few adolescent females in our society become anorexic or bulimic, even though almost all of them experience social pressure to be thin? Most likely because genes serve as a diathesis, predisposing certain individuals more than others to develop eating disorders, at least if they live in a sociocultural context that encourages weight concern and if other environmental influences come into play (Bulik et al., 2000; Keel & Klump, 2003). Many biochemical abnormalities have been found in individuals with anorexia, although some may be consequences rather than causes of the condition (Wilson, Becker, & Hefferman, 2003). At least one gene involved in the control of appetite has been implicated (Vink et al., 2001), and even in early childhood adolescents and adults who later develop eating disorders experience conflicts over eating (Kotler et al., 2001). Genes may also contribute to the low levels of the neurotransmitter serotonin associated with both eating disorders and mood disorders (Keel & Fulkerson, 2001). And genes may put certain individuals at risk by influencing their personalities. Anorexic females tend to be introverted, anxious, and obsessive. They are perfectionists with low self-esteem and a high need for approval who desperately want to gain control of their lives and do so by dieting (Hsu, 1990; Wilson et al., 2003).

Yet an eating disorder may still not emerge unless a susceptible girl experiences disturbed family relationships and stressful events—unless heredity and environment interact in an unfavorable way (Keel & Fulkerson, 2001). Girls who are overly concerned about their weight tend to come from families preoccupied with weight (Gordon, 2000; Strober et al., 2000). They are often insecurely attached to their parents and have often constructed internal working models of self and other that lead them to think poorly of themselves and to expect others to think poorly of them (Sharpe et al.,

1998). Much emphasis has been placed on disturbed mother–daughter relationships, but poor father–daughter relationships may also contribute (Dominy, Johnson, & Koch, 2000). These young women seem unable to manage the adolescent task of gaining autonomy (Levenkron, 2000). So, family dynamics may contribute to anorexia, although it is not always clear whether disturbed family dynamics are contributors to, or only effects of, the condition (Gowers & Bryant-Waugh, 2004).

Ultimately, it may take a pileup of stressors to push a young woman over the edge. For example, vulnerable adolescents who are experiencing pubertal changes and weight gains, becoming involved in mixed-sex relationships, and changing schools may have more than they can handle and may then develop an eating disorder (Smolak & Levine, 1996). Emotional, sexual, or physical abuse sometimes precipitates the disorder (Kent & Waller, 2000). In anorexia nervosa, then, we have a prime example of the diathesis–stress model at work. A young woman who is at risk for it partly because of her genetic makeup may not develop anorexia unless she also grows up in a culture that overvalues thinness and in a family that makes it hard to forge an identity as an individual—and then faces an accumulation of stressful events.

Treatment

Individuals with bulimia respond better to treatment than those with anorexia, but both can be successfully treated (Wilson, Becker, & Hefferman, 2003). Effective therapies for individuals with eating disorders start with behavior modification programs designed to bring their eating behavior under control, help them gain weight if they are anorexic, and deal with any medical problems they may have, in a hospital or treatment facility if necessary (Patel, Pratt, & Greydarms, 2003). Then it is possible to move on to individual psychotherapy designed to help them understand and gain control over their problem, family therapy designed to help build healthier parent–child relationships, and medication for depression and related psychological problems. Cognitive behavioral therapy and antidepressant drugs appear to work well with bulimic patients (Gowers & Bryant-Waugh, 2004). Women with anorexia are more difficult to treat because they so strongly resist admitting that they have a problem and because the drugs tried to date do not seem to have reliable benefits. However, they can benefit from psychotherapy and family therapy (Gowers & Bryant-Waugh, 2004). Most overcome their eating disorders with time, although they may continue to have social and emotional difficulties and even diagnosable problems such as obsessive–compulsive disorder as adults (Wentz et al., 2001).

Depression and Suicidal Behavior

Children, especially girls, become more vulnerable to depression as they enter adolescence. Adults who suffer from bouts of depression often trace their first depressive episode to the adolescent period (Gotlib & Hammen, 2002). In one study of female adolescents, the rate of self-reported major depressive disorder at some time in the individual's life ranged from 1% among girls younger than age 12 to more than 17% among young women age 19 and older (Glowinski et al., 2003). Up to 35% of adolescents experience depressed moods at some time, and as many as 7% have diagnosable depressive disorders at any given time (Petersen et al., 1993). Symptoms are mostly like those displayed by depressed adults, although depressed adolescents sometimes act out and look more like delinquents than like victims of depression.

Why is adolescence a depressing period for some? For one thing, research suggests that genetic influences on symptoms of depression become stronger in adolescence than they were in childhood (Scourfield et al., 2003). Pubertal changes may be responsible or may at least provide another part of the answer. Xiaojia Ge and his colleagues (2003) studied African American adolescents at age 11 and again at age 13. For girls at both age 11 and age 13, being an early maturer was associated with high levels of major depression symptoms. Among boys, the early maturation effect was only temporary, evident at age 11 but not at age 13, as shown in Figure 16.4. This may be part of the reason that girls have higher depression rates than boys: the negative effects of early maturation last longer for them than for boys. However, boys who were on time or late at age 11 but who then underwent rapid pubertal growth became significantly more depressed from age 11 to age 13; this stressful pubertal change effect was not as evident among girls. Overall, then, pubertal changes and their timing contribute to increased depression rates in adolescence among both girls and boys but do so differently in the two sexes. To date, no clear and direct path from hormonal changes to depression has been identified (Kuehner, 2003).

Social factors also put adolescent females at risk for depression. They are more likely than males to experience a cumulation of stressful events in early adolescence (Ge et al.,

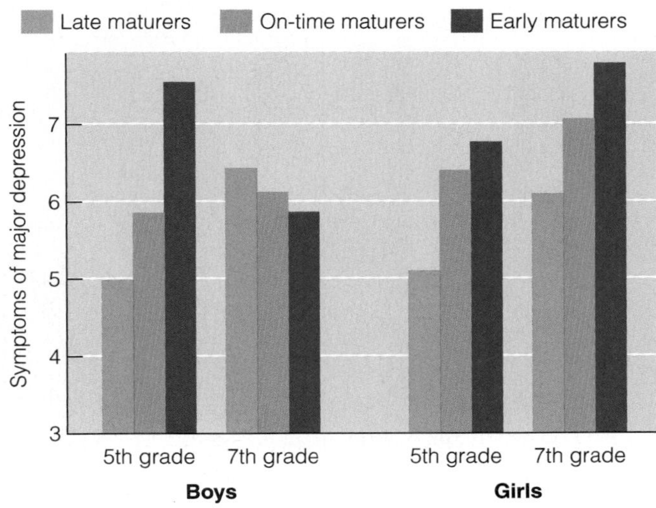

Figure 16.4 Early maturation is a risk factor for depression in adolescence—for boys, a temporary risk factor, but for girls a lasting one, evident in both fifth and seventh grades.

SOURCE: Ge et al. (2003, Figure 2, p. 435).

1994; Nolen-Hoeksema & Girgus, 1994). Stress in the mother–daughter relationship, heightened concern with body image, and early maturation can combine to put adolescent girls at risk (Seiffge-Krenke & Stemmler, 2002).

As depression becomes more common from childhood to adolescence, so do suicidal thoughts, suicide attempts, and actual suicides. Suicide is the third leading cause of death for this age group, far behind accidental injuries and just behind homicides; the yearly rate is now 10 per 100,000 15- to 24-year-olds, quite a bit higher than it was in 1950 (Freid et al., 2003). Nevertheless, probably because of increased use of antidepressants to treat depression, teenage suicide rates have been declining in the past 10 years (Gould et al., 2003; Olfson et al., 2003).

For every adolescent suicide, there are many unsuccessful attempts—as many as 50 to 200 by some estimates (Garland & Zigler, 1993). Also, suicidal thoughts that may not lead to action are even more common, to the point of being normal during this period (Shaffer & Pfeffer, 2001). In one survey of adolescents whose average age was 15, for instance, 56% reported at least one instance of suicidal thinking in their lives and 15% had attempted suicide (Windle & Windle, 1997).

Before you conclude that adolescence is the peak time for suicidal behavior, however, consider the suicide rates for different age groups, as shown in Figure 16.5. It is clear that adults are more likely to commit suicide than adolescents are. The suicide rate for females peaks in middle age, and the suicide rate for white males climbs throughout adulthood, making elderly white men the group most likely to commit suicide. As a result, increased attention is being focused on the problem of late-life suicide (Pearson, 2000).

Overall, males are more likely to commit suicide than females, by a ratio of at least three to one—a difference that holds up across most cultures studied (Girard, 1993; Shaffer & Pfeffer, 2001). When we look at suicide attempts, this ratio is reversed, with females leading males by a ratio of about three to one. Apparently, then, females attempt suicide more often than males do, but males more often commit suicide when they try, probably because they use more lethal techniques (especially guns).

If suicide rates are higher in adulthood than in adolescence, why do we hear so much about teenage suicide? Probably because adolescents attempt suicide more frequently than adults do. The typical adolescent suicide attempt has been characterized as a "cry for help"—a desperate effort to get others to notice and help resolve problems that have become unbearable (Berman & Jobes, 1991). The adolescent who attempts suicide often wants a better life rather than death (Lester, 1994). This by no means suggests that adolescent suicide attempts should be taken lightly. Their message is clear: "I've got serious problems; wake up and help me!"

Suicidal behavior in adolescence is most likely the product of diathesis–stress. Four key risk factors are youth psychological disorder, family pathology and psychopathology, stressful life events, and access to firearms (Gould et al., 2003; and see Beautrais, 2003). More than 90% of adolescent suicide victims, partly because of genetic predisposition, suffered from depression, substance use disorder, anxiety disorder, or another diagnosable psychological problem at the time of their death, so screening teenagers for depression and other psychological disorders makes great sense as an approach to prevention (Shaffer & Pfeffer, 2001). Many have histories of troubled family relationships, and often psychopathology and even suicide run in the family. In the period leading up to a suicide attempt, the adolescent has often experienced a buildup of stressful life events—deteriorating relationships

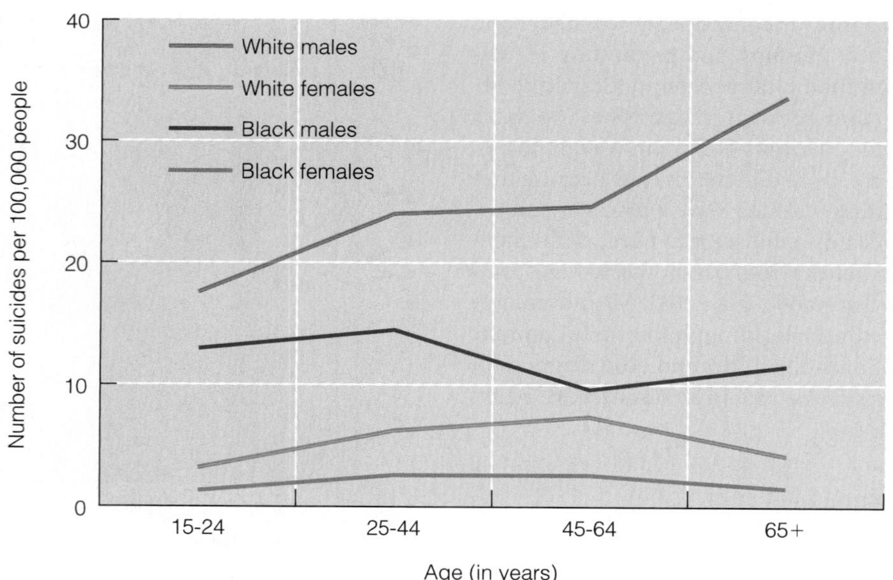

Figure 16.5 Number of suicides per 100,000 people by age and sex among European and African Americans in the United States.

SOURCE: Data from Freid et al. (2003).

with parents and peers, academic and social failures, run-ins with the law—and begun to feel incapable of coping (Berman & Jobes, 1991). The availability of firearms makes it easy to act on suicidal impulses. The adolescent who attempts suicide once may try again if he receives little help and continues to feel incapable of coping with problems. As a result, professional help is called for after an unsuccessful suicide attempt (Rotheram-Borus et al., 2000).

Summing Up

Although most adolescents do not experience storm and stress, rates of psychological disorder climb from about 10% in childhood to 20% in adolescence. Two problems that increase during adolescence, eating disorders and depression, strike females more than males, and both can be explained in terms of diathesis–stress. Females with anorexia nervosa are genetically predisposed to it but also tend to experience a culture obsessed with thinness, a disturbed family, and overwhelming stress. Depression and suicide are also associated with a genetically based vulnerability and a pileup of stressors. Still, most adolescents, even though they may diet or think a depressive or even suicidal thought now and then, emerge from this period as well-adjusted and competent young adults. ■

The Adult

Stressful experiences in childhood and adolescence increase a person's chances of psychological disorder later in life (Turner & Lloyd, 2004). Psychological problems then emerge when a vulnerable individual, perhaps one with a history of adversity, faces overwhelming stress. As it turns out, adults typically experience the greatest number of life strains in early adulthood (McLanahan & Sorensen, 1985; Pearlin, 1980). Life strains decrease from early to middle adulthood, perhaps as adults settle into more stable lifestyles. And, despite increased stress related to health problems, elderly adults report fewer hassles and strains overall than middle-aged adults do (Almeida & Horn, 2004; Martin, Grunendahl, & Martin, 2001). This may be because they have fewer roles and responsibilities to juggle or because they no longer perceive problems they have encountered before as stressful.

Age differences in stressful experiences may help explain age differences in rates of psychological disorder. In a major community mental health survey by the National Institute of Mental Health, adults age 18 or older were interviewed in their homes about the psychological symptoms they were experiencing, and estimates were then made of the percentages of respondents who met the criteria for several psychological disorders (Myers et al., 1984; Robins & Regier, 1991). Overall, a fairly large proportion of adults—15% to 22% of those surveyed in each city—were judged to have suffered from a diagnosable psychological disorder in the previous 6 months. Rates of affective disorders (major depression and related mood disorders), alcohol abuse and dependence, schizophrenia, anxiety disorders, and antisocial personality all decreased from early adulthood to late adulthood. (As you appreciate, this could be either a true age effect or a cohort effect suggesting that recent generations are more vulnerable than previous generations to psychological disorder.) The only type of impairment that increased with age was cognitive impairment, undoubtedly because some older adults were developing Alzheimer's disease and other forms of dementia (to be described shortly).

Mainly, it appears that young adults, because they experience more stress than older adults, are a group at high risk for mental health problems. With that as background, look more closely at one of the disorders to which young adults are especially susceptible, depression, and then turn to an examination of Alzheimer's disease and related cognitive impairments in later life.

Depression

Major depression and other affective disorders are among the most common psychological problems experienced by adults. Who gets depressed, and what does this reveal?

Age and Sex Differences

As just noted, and contrary to stereotypes of elderly people, older adults tend, if anything, to be less vulnerable to major depression and other severe affective disorders than young or middle-aged adults are (Blazer, 2003; Wolfe, Morrow, & Fredrickson, 1996). Unless older adults develop physical health problems that contribute to depression or experience increasing rather than decreasing levels of stress as they age, their mental health is likely to be good (Lynch & George, 2002; Wrosch, Schulz, & Heckhausen, 2004). Still, there are good reasons to be concerned about depression in old age. We know that depressed elders are more likely than depressed adolescents to take their own lives, and some studies show an increase in depression symptoms in late old age (Rothermund & Brandtstädter,

Although few elderly adults have diagnosed depression, a sizable minority experiences at least some symptoms of depression.

2003c). Also, although only about 1 to 3% of elderly adults have major depressive disorder, about 15% experience symptoms of depression (Mulsant & Ganguli, 1999). Might some of the individuals who report symptoms of depression have a more serious but undiagnosed depressive disorder?

Depression can be difficult to diagnose in later adulthood (Charney et al., 2003). Think about it: Symptoms of depression include fatigue, sleeping difficulties, cognitive deficits, and somatic complaints. What if a clinician notes these symptoms in an elderly person but interprets them as nothing more than normal aging, as the result of the chronic illnesses so common in old age, or as signs of dementia? A case of depression can easily be missed. Elderly adults who are depressed may also hide their depression, denying that they are sad and claiming instead that they have medical problems (Mulsant & Ganguli, 1999). This, too, can lead to underdiagnosis of depression in the elderly population. Yet overdiagnosis of depression in older adults can also occur if bodily complaints such as lack of energy caused by physical disease or disability are interpreted as symptoms of depression (Grayson et al., 2000).

Depression in elderly individuals is not so different from depression in young and middle-aged adults that different criteria must be developed to detect it. Still, clinicians working with elderly adults need to be sensitive to the differences between normal aging processes, disease, and psychopathology. Moreover, the fact that relatively few elderly people suffer from severe, diagnosable depression should not blind us to the fact that a much larger number feel depressed or demoralized and could benefit from treatment (Lynch & George, 2002). This is especially true of very old women who are physically ill, poor, socially isolated, or a combination of these (Blazer, 1993; Falcon & Tucker, 2000).

Starting in adolescence, and in a variety of cultures, females are more likely than males to be diagnosed as depressed—by a margin of about two to one (Kuehner, 2003). What accounts for this? It is not just because women are more likely than men to admit they are depressed or to seek help when they are depressed (Kessler, 2000). Nor is it clear that genetic factors contribute differently to depression in females than in males. Instead, higher rates of depression in females than in males have been linked to gender differences in a variety of factors (Kuehner, 2003; Nolen-Hoeksema, 2002): hormones and biological reactions to stress, levels of stress (including more experience of interpersonal stressors, especially sexual abuse, among women), ways of expressing distress (women being more likely to express classic depression symptoms, men being more likely to become angry or overindulge in alcohol and drugs), and styles of coping with distress (for example, women tend to ruminate about their problems, analyzing their despair, whereas men distract themselves from problems and may be better off for it). In short, there is no easy answer, but women are clearly more at risk than men for depression.

Treatment

One of the biggest challenges in treating adults with major depression and other psychological disorders is getting them to seek treatment. Elderly adults are especially likely to go undiagnosed and untreated, particularly if they are minority group members suspicious of the mental health system (Baldwin, 2000; Charney et al., 2003). Possibly this is because today's elderly generation grew up when it was considered shameful to have psychological problems. Older adults and members of their families may also believe, wrongly, that problems such as depression and anxiety are a normal part of getting older or becoming ill. Still another barrier to treatment may be negative attitudes among mental health professionals that cause them to prefer working with younger people, to perceive elderly individuals as untreatable, and to underdiagnose or misdiagnose their problems (Graham et al., 2003).

Despite these barriers, when depressed elderly adults seek psychotherapy, they benefit as much as younger adults (Karel & Hinrichsen, 2000; Powers et al., 2002). Moreover, those treated with antidepressant drugs, assuming they keep taking them, not only overcome their depression in most cases but also show improved cognitive functioning (Blazer, 2003; Butters et al., 2000). As with many psychological problems, the most effective approach is often a combination of drug treatment and psychotherapy (Hollon, Thase, & Markowitz, 2002). So, just as humans can fall prey to psychological problems at any point in the life span, they have an impressive capacity throughout the life span to overcome problems and to experience new psychological growth.

Aging and Dementia

Perhaps nothing scares us more about aging than the thought that we will become "senile." **Dementia,** the technical term for senility, is a progressive deterioration of neural functioning associated with memory impairment, declines in tested intellectual ability, poor judgment, difficulty thinking abstractly, and often personality changes. Becoming senile is not a nor-

Ronald Reagan brought attention to the tragedy of Alzheimer's disease.

mal part of the aging process. Yet rates of dementia increase steadily with age. Overall, dementia and other moderate and severe cognitive impairments affect about 5% of the 65-and-older population (Blazer, 1996; Regier et al., 1988).

Dementia is not a single disorder. Much damage can be done by labeling any older person with cognitive impairments as senile—or even as having Alzheimer's disease—and then assuming that she is a lost cause. Many different conditions can produce the symptoms we associate with senility, and some of them are curable or reversible. It is also a mistake to assume that any elderly person who becomes forgetful or absentminded—who occasionally misplaces keys or cannot remember someone's name—is becoming senile. As you saw in Chapter 8, small declines in memory capacities in later life are common and usually have little effect on daily functioning. If this were all it took to warrant a diagnosis of dementia, many young and middle-aged adults, not to mention textbook writers, would qualify. So look at some of the specific forms of dementia.

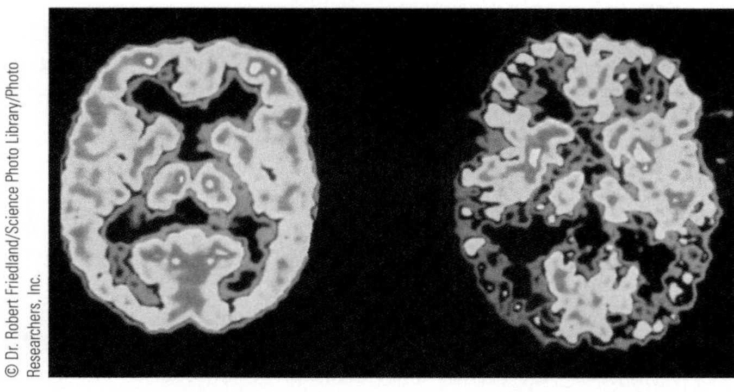

Positron emission tomography (PET scanning) shows metabolic activity in the brain and reveals areas of high brain activity (in red and yellow) and low brain activity (in blue or black). Here we see more activity in a normally functioning brain (left) than in the brain of a person with Alzheimer's disease (right).

Alzheimer's Disease

> With Alzheimer's disease, you just know you're going to forget things, and it's impossible to put things where you can't forget them because people like me can always find a place to lose things and we have to flurry all over the house to figure where in the heck I left whatever it was. . . . It's usually my glasses. . . . You've got to have a sense of humor in this kind of business, and I think it's interesting how many places I can find to lose things. . . . [People with Alzheimer's] want things like they used to be. And we just hate the fact that we cannot be what we used to be. It hurts like hell. (Cary Henderson, age 64, former history professor diagnosed with Alzheimer's disease at age 55; Rovner, 1994, pp. 12–13)

Alzheimer's disease, or *dementia of the Alzheimer's type* as it is termed in DSM-IV, is the most common cause of dementia, accounting for about 70% of all cases, including Ronald Reagan's (Tanzi & Parson, 2000). Dementia can strike in middle age but becomes increasingly likely with advancing age. Although the rate of Alzheimer's disease is about 5% for people older than age 65, it is more than 40% for people older than age 90 (Williams, 2003). Because more people are living into advanced old age, more will end up with the disease unless ways of preventing it or slowing its progress are found. It is estimated that about 4 million people in the United States have it now and that the number will more than triple by 2050 (Leifer, 2003).

Alzheimer's disease leaves two telltale signs in the brain (Selkoe, 1997; Williams, 1995): *senile plaques* (masses of dying neural material with a toxic protein called **beta-amyloid** at their core that injures neurons), and *neurofibrillary tangles* (twisted strands of neural fibers within the bodies of neural cells). Elderly adults without Alzheimer's disease have senile plaques and neurofibrillary tangles, too; it is not only the number but their type and location that mark the difference between Alzheimer's disease and normal aging (Snowdon, 1997). The results of Alzheimer's disease are progressive—and irreversible or incurable—deterioration of neurons, increasingly impaired mental functioning, and personality changes.

The first sign of Alzheimer's disease, detectable 2 to 3 years before dementia can be diagnosed, is usually difficulty learning and remembering verbal material (Howieson et al., 1997). As you saw in Chapter 8, mild cognitive impairment in some older adults is often an early warning that dementia will follow (Morris et al., 2001). In the early stages, free recall tasks are difficult but memory is good if cues to recall are provided; over time, individuals cannot recall even with the aid of cues and become increasingly frustrated (Grober & Kawas, 1997; Williams, 1995). As the disorder progresses, Alzheimer's patients have more trouble coming up with the words they want during conversations and may forget what to do next midway through making a sandwich or getting ready for bed. If tested, they may be unable to answer simple questions about where they are, what the date is, and who the president of the United States is. Eventually, they become incapable of caring for themselves, lose all verbal abilities, and die, some earlier and some later, but on average about 8 to 10 years after onset (National Institute on Aging, 2000; and see Figure 16.6). Not only do patients with Alzheimer's disease become increasingly unable to function, but they also often test the patience of caregivers by forgetting they have left something cooking on the stove, wandering away and getting lost, accusing people of stealing the items they have misplaced, seeing wild animals in their room, or taking off their clothes in public. Many become highly agitated and uncontrollable; large numbers suffer from depression; and some experience psychotic symptoms such as hallucinations (Gillick, 1998).

What causes Alzheimer's disease? Many cases appear to have a hereditary basis, but there is no single "Alzheimer's gene" (Tanzi & Parson, 2000). Alzheimer's disease strikes repeatedly and early in some families. By analyzing blood samples from families with many Alzheimer's victims, genetic researchers made a big breakthrough when they located a gene for the disease on the 21st pair of chromosomes. Anyone who

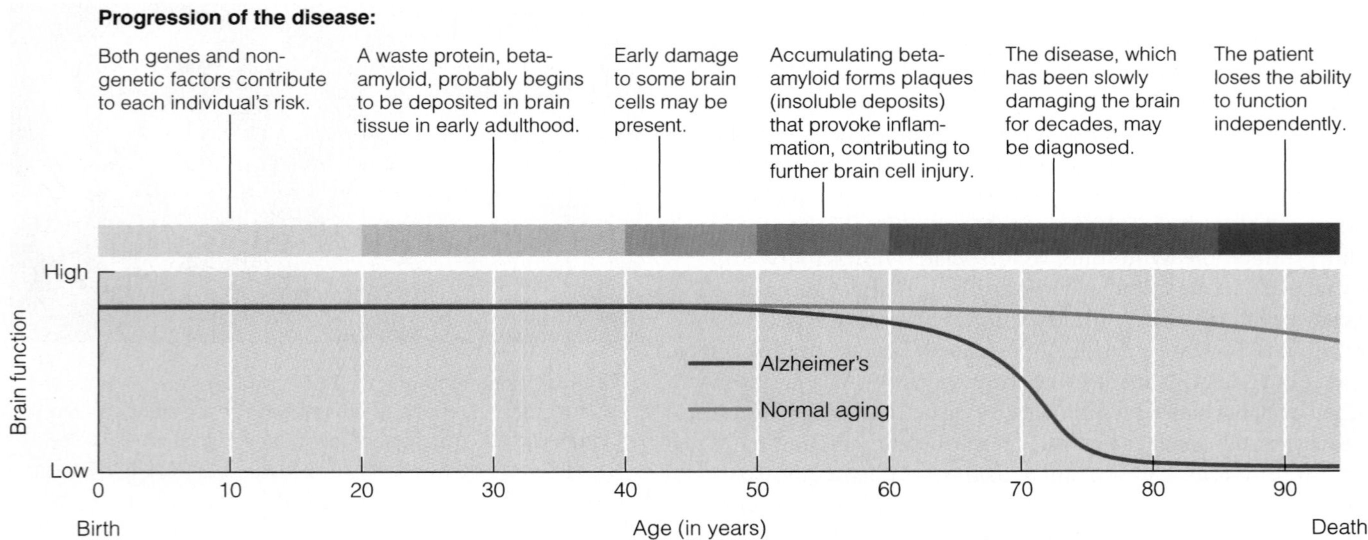

Figure 16.6 Alzheimer's disease emerges gradually over the adult years; brain cells are damaged long before noticeable cognitive impairment results in old age. Changes in brain functioning are significantly different from those associated with normal aging.

SOURCE: Adapted from Okie (2001).

inherits just one of these apparently dominant genes will eventually develop the disease. Genes on other chromosomes associated with early-onset Alzheimer's disease have since been discovered (Williams, 2003). However, only about 5% of cases of Alzheimer's disease begin before age 60; 95% are late-onset cases (Clark, 1999).

Genetic contributors to late-onset Alzheimer's disease are not as clear-cut or strong. Rather than making Alzheimer's disease inevitable, they only increase a person's risk (Tanzi & Parson, 2000; Williams, 2003). One variant of a gene on Chromosome 19 that is responsible for the production of ApoE, a protein involved in processing cholesterol, may be especially important. Having two of the risk-inducing ApoE4 genes means having up to eight times the normal risk of Alzheimer's disease; having one of the genes means two to four times the normal risk (Hendrie, 2001). Having another variant of the ApoE4 gene means having a good chance of maintaining cognitive functioning into very late adulthood (Riley et al., 2000). It is believed that the ApoE4 gene may increase the buildup of beta-amyloid—the damaging substance in senile plaques—and therefore speed the progression of Alzheimer's disease (National Institute on Aging, 2000). Yet not everyone with the ApoE4 gene, or even a pair of them, develops Alzheimer's disease, and many people with Alzheimer's disease lack the gene; therefore, other, as-yet unidentified genes, environmental factors, or both must also play a role.

What environmental factors? Head injuries in earlier adulthood increase the risk of Alzheimer's disease (Plassman et al., 2000), and a diet that increases the odds of high cholesterol and cardiovascular disease is recognized as another contributor (Hendrie, 2001; Nourhashemi et al., 2000). Moreover, people with little education are more at risk than people with lots of education, probably because they have less "cognitive reserve" or brain power to fall back on as aging and disease begin to take a toll on brain functioning (Gatz et al., 2001). Several pieces of evidence suggest that using their brains—and in the process forming new synapses or even brain cells—may help people hang on to their cognitive abilities (Verghese et al., 2003).

The search for causes, both genetic and environmental, continues. It increasingly appears that psychological disorders such as autism, ADHD, and Alzheimer's disease are not distinct abnormal entities. Rather, they sit at the extreme ends of dimensions of human difference, influenced by the same genetic and environmental factors that contribute to variation throughout the population (Plomin et al., 2003).

What is being done to prevent and treat Alzheimer's disease? Because victims have a deficit in the neurotransmitter acetylcholine, which is essential for normal learning and memory, researchers have developed drugs to correct this problem and related problems in neural functioning. No pill to prevent or reverse Alzheimer's disease has yet been discovered, but some drugs are regularly prescribed (Aricept, or donepezil, for example, and more recently Namenda, or memantine). They modestly improve cognitive functioning, reduce behavioral problems, and slow the progression of the disease in some patients (Grossberg & Desai, 2003). More such drugs are likely to follow, and researchers have hopes that a vaccine that would make the immune system mount an attack on beta-amyloid can be made to work, despite adverse reactions in the first trials with humans (Samuels & Davis, 2003).

Another promising approach attempts to combat the buildup of beta-amyloid in the brain. Antioxidants such as vitamins E and C may delay the onset and progression of Alzheimer's disease by inhibiting the damaging oxidating effects of beta-amyloid (National Institute on Aging, 2000). And lending support to the view that high cholesterol levels associated with the ApoE4 gene contribute to dementia, it has been found that statin drugs, widely prescribed for people with high cholesterol, improve cognitive functioning in people with dementia (Hajjar et al., 2002). It is beginning to look as though the same lifestyle factors that contribute to cardiovascular disease (eating too much and not getting enough exercise) increase the risk of dementia and that we can reduce our odds of Alzheimer's disease by living a healthy lifestyle from an early age (Pope, Shue, & Beck, 2003; Underwood, 2004).

Even if Alzheimer's disease cannot be prevented entirely, researchers are hopeful that its onset and progression can be slowed, especially if it is detected early. And, even though deterioration leading to death must be expected in today's Alzheimer's patients, a great deal can be done through the use of medications for behavioral problems, educational programs and psychological interventions for patients and their caregivers, and memory training to help people with the disease and their family members understand and cope with dementia and function better (Grossberg & Desai, 2003; Kasl-Godley & Gatz, 2000).

Other Causes of Cognitive Impairment

The second most common type of dementia, often occurring with Alzheimer's disease, is **vascular dementia** (Román, 2003). Also called multi-infarct dementia, it is caused by a series of minor strokes that cut off the blood supply to areas of the brain. Whereas Alzheimer's disease usually progresses slowly and steadily, vascular dementia often progresses in a steplike manner as each small stroke brings about a new deterioration in functioning (American Psychiatric Association, 1994). Whereas Alzheimer's disease impairs memory most, vascular dementia may do its greatest damage to executive functions (Román, 2003). And whereas Alzheimer's disease is more strongly influenced by genes, vascular dementia is more closely associated with environmental risk factors for cerebrovascular diseases that affect blood flow in the brain, such as smoking, eating a fatty diet, and being obese (Bergem, Engedal, & Kringlen, 1997; Kaplan & Sadock, 1998). Huntington's disease (a genetic disorder described in Chapter 3), Parkinson's disease, and even AIDS are among the other possible causes of irreversible dementia (Heston & White, 1991).

Some cases of dementia—perhaps 10 to 20%—are not related to any of these causes and, more important, are reversible or curable (Gurland, 1991; Lipton & Weiner, 2003). Such problems as alcoholism, toxic reactions to medication, infections, metabolic disorders, and malnutrition can cause symptoms of dementia. If these problems are corrected—for example, if the individual is taken off a recently prescribed medicine or is placed on a proper diet—a once "senile" person can be restored to normal mental functioning. By contrast, if that same person is written off as senile or as a victim of Alzheimer's disease, a potentially curable condition may become a progressively worse and irreversible one.

Similarly, some elderly adults are mistakenly diagnosed as suffering from irreversible dementia when they are experiencing **delirium.** This reversible condition emerges more rapidly than dementia, comes and goes over the course of the day, and is a disturbance of consciousness characterized by periods of disorientation, wandering attention, confusion, and hallucinations (American Psychiatric Association, 1994; Cole, 2004). Up to 50% of elderly hospital patients experience it in reaction to any number of stressors—for example, illness, surgery, drug overdoses, interactions of different drugs, or malnutrition (Cole, 2004). It is essential to watch for signs of delirium, identify possible causes such as an incorrect drug prescription, and intervene to change them quickly so that the individual can return to normal quickly (Flaherty & Morley, 2004). Death rates are high among elderly patients who experience delirium, are not identified, and are sent home from the hospital without treatment for it (Kakuma et al., 2003).

Finally, elderly adults who are depressed are all too frequently misdiagnosed as suffering from dementia because late-life depression brings with it cognitive impairments such as being forgetful and mentally slow (Butters et al., 2004). As you have seen, treatment with antidepressant drugs and psychotherapy can dramatically improve the functioning of such individuals. However, if their depression goes undetected and they are written off as senile, they, too, are likely to deteriorate further.

☾ Delirium is common among elderly hospital patients and can be treated.

The moral is clear: It is critical to distinguish among irreversible dementias (notably, dementia of the Alzheimer's type and vascular dementia), reversible dementias, delirium, depression, and other conditions that may be mistaken for irreversible dementias—including old age. This requires a thorough assessment, including a medical history, physical and neurological examinations, and assessments of cognitive functioning (Beck et al., 2000). Only after all other causes, especially potentially treatable ones, have been ruled out should a diagnosis of Alzheimer's disease be made. Unfortunately, many primary care physicians fail to notice symptoms of dementia or do not appreciate the importance of thorough testing to determine the underlying problem and whether it is treatable (Boise et al., 1999).

So ends our tour of psychopathology across the life span. It can be discouraging to read about the countless ways in which genes and environment can conspire to make human development go awry and about the high odds that most of us will experience a psychological disorder sometime during our lives. Yet research provides an increasingly solid basis for attempting to prevent developmental psychopathology through a two-pronged strategy of eliminating risk factors (such as abusive parenting) and strengthening protective factors (such as social support). If prevention proves impossible, most psychological disorders and developmental problems can be treated successfully, enabling the individual to move back onto a healthier developmental pathway.

Summing Up

Probably because young adults experience more life strains and stressors than older adults do, most psychological disorders besides those involving dementia or cognitive impairment are more common in early adulthood than in later adulthood. Depression tends to be most common among women; elderly adults may be underdiagnosed. The most common forms of dementia are Alzheimer's disease, in which a buildup of beta-amyloid within senile plaques damages neurons, and vascular dementia. These irreversible dementias must be carefully distinguished from correctible conditions such as reversible dementias, delirium, and depression. ■

Summary Points

1. To diagnose psychological disorders, clinicians consider statistical deviance, maladaptiveness, and personal distress and use DSM-IV. Developmental psychopathology is concerned with the origins and course of psychopathology; a diathesis–stress model has proved useful in understanding how nature and nurture contribute to psychological disorders.

2. Autism is characterized by deviant social responses, language and communication deficits, and repetitive behavior. It is genetically influenced, involves several key cognitive impairments, and responds to early behavioral training.

3. Infants who have been emotionally starved, maltreated, or separated from attachment figures, including infants whose parents are depressed and infants suffering from failure to thrive, display depression-like symptoms.

4. Children with ADHD, an externalizing disorder, display inattention, impulsivity, and hyperactivity. Stimulant drugs and behavioral training help, but many with ADHD do not entirely outgrow their problems.

5. Diagnosable depression, an internalizing disorder, can occur during childhood. It manifests itself somewhat differently at different ages, tends to recur, and can be treated successfully with antidepressant drugs and psychotherapy.

6. It is too simple to view "bad" parenting as the cause of all childhood problems; heredity also contributes. Despite some continuity, many childhood problems, especially mild ones, are only temporary.

7. Adolescents are more vulnerable than children but no more vulnerable than adults to psychological disorders. Anorexia nervosa arises when a genetically predisposed female who lives in a society that strongly encourages dieting experiences stressful events.

8. Risks of depression rise during adolescence, especially among females. Adolescents, in a cry for help, are more likely to attempt but less likely to commit suicide than adults.

9. Young adults experience both more life strains and more psychological disorders, including depression, than older adults.

10. Alzheimer's disease and vascular dementia, both irreversible dementias, must be carefully distinguished from correctible conditions such as reversible dementias, delirium, and depression.

Critical Thinking

1. Some say individuals with psychological disorders are qualitatively different from other people, whereas others say they just differ in degree, or quantitatively, from other people. Make both of these cases, using information in this chapter about two disorders.

2. Peggy, the young woman described at the beginning of the chapter, attempted suicide. Use the material on suicide in this chapter to explain why she might have done so, showing how both diathesis and stress may have contributed.

3. Lucille has struggled with major depressive disorder on and off for her entire life. Describe how she may have expressed her depression as an infant, preschool child, school-age child, adolescent, adult, and elderly adult.

4. Grandpa Fred is starting to display memory problems; sometimes he asks questions that he just asked, forgets where he left his car keys, and cannot come up with the names of visiting grandchildren. Fred's son Will is convinced that his father has Alzheimer's disease and is a lost cause. What possibilities would you like to rule out before accepting that conclusion—and why?

Key Terms

DSM-IV, 456
major depressive disorder, 456
developmental psychopathology, 457
social norm, 458
diathesis–stress model, 459
autism, 460
echolalia, 461
Asperger syndrome, 461
theory-of-mind hypothesis, 461
executive dysfunction hypothesis, 462
executive function, 462
weak central coherence hypothesis, 462
extreme male brain hypothesis, 462
somatic symptoms, 465
failure to thrive, 466
externalizing problem, 467
internalizing problem, 467
attention deficit hyperactivity disorder (ADHD), 467
comorbidity, 467
anorexia nervosa, 473
bulimia nervosa, 473
dementia, 478
Alzheimer's disease, 479
beta-amyloid, 479
vascular dementia, 481
delirium, 481

Media Resources

Websites to Explore

Visit Our Website

For a chapter tutorial quiz and other useful features, visit the book's companion website at *http://psychology.wadsworth.com/sigelman_rider5e.* You can also connect directly to the following sites:

General Resources on Psychological Disorders
The National Institute of Mental Health website provides general information and research updates on most of the disorders described in this chapter.

Another good reference, Mental Help Net, is a searchable site that includes pages on most disorders and on a variety of mental health topics, references to other websites, and help in finding therapists. For fun, take your problems to the computer therapist, Eliza Oracle.

Depression
Information about depression is available at the preceding general sites, but the Planet Rx website Depression.com has helpful information about research on and treatment of depression.

The TeenScreen program from Columbia University is a resource for school and mental health professionals and other leaders who want to begin a mental health and suicide risk screening effort in their own communities.

Dying to Be Thin
Watch this PBS program to learn more about the increasing prevalence of debilitating eating disorders. The companion website provides resources for seeking help and answers to frequently asked questions. You can also read testimonies from readers and viewers and learn more about the occurrence of eating disorders among men.

Autism
The Autism Society of America promotes research, education, advocacy, and awareness of issues related to this condition. Its website provides access to several informative articles.

Attention Deficit Hyperactivity Disorder
The organization Children and Adults with Attention Deficit Hyperactivity Disorder provides support and information to individuals with ADHD.
The Attention Deficit Disorder Association also has a useful site.

Alzheimer's Disease
The Alzheimer's Association website offers much useful information about the fundamentals of Alzheimer's disease; see especially the list of Ten Warning Signs that families can use to help them distinguish between normal cognitive decline and emerging Alzheimer's disease.

Another useful site is the Alzheimer's Disease Education and Referral Center by the National Institute on Aging, with a searchable database and a progress report on Alzheimer's research that was cited in this chapter.

Understanding the Data: Exercises on the Web

For additional insight on the data presented in this chapter, try the exercises for these figures at *http://psychology.wadsworth.com/sigelman_rider5e:*

Figure 16.3 Relationships between behavior at age 3 and psychological disorders at age 21

Figure 16.5 Elderly white males are most at risk for suicide

Life-Span CD-ROM

Go to the Wadsworth Life-Span CD-ROM for further study of the concepts in this chapter. The CD-ROM includes narrated concept overviews, video clips, a multimedia glossary, and additional activities to expand your learning experience. For this chapter, check out the following clip, and others, in the video library:

VIDEO Alzheimer's Disease: A Daughter's Experience

DEVELOPMENTAL PsychologyNow™

Developmental PsychologyNow is a web-based, intelligent study system that provides a complete package of diagnostic quizzes, a personalized study plan, integrated multimedia elements, and learning modules. Check it out at *http://psychology.wadsworth.com/sigelman_rider5e/now.*

CHAPTER seventeen

The Final Challenge: Death and Dying

KELLY COLASANTI'S HUSBAND CHRIS was one of the unlucky people working in the World Trade Center on September 11, 2001. The next morning, Kelly's 4-year-old daughter Cara stood outside her bedroom, and Kelly had to say something (Maraniss, Hull, & Schwartzman, 2001, p. A18):

> Cara had not wanted to accept her mother's word at first. "Maybe Daddy fainted," she said hours after she had been told. "If he did faint," Kelly answered, "he also stopped breathing and died." She could not believe her own words, but if nothing else, Cara had to know the truth.
>
> When the house emptied, Kelly gave Cara a bath, dressed her in pajamas and helped her into bed. She lay down in the adjoining trundle bed and started to tell a story that Chris loved to tell about his childhood—only she couldn't tell it so well. At the end of the story, the 4-year-old ordered her to leave and suggested that she go into the other room and read Harry Potter. Kelly was crushed; she wanted to sleep right there next to her daughter. She wandered across the hall and fell into bed, then got up and went to the closet for Chris's blue and green flannel bathrobe, the one he'd had forever. She took the robe to bed, burying her face in the cloth, again trying to smell him. Her chest went cold and her ribs ached and she opened her eyes, staring at the ceiling. My husband is dead, she said. I'm alone.

Death hurts. Whether we are 4, 34, or 84 when death strikes a loved one, it still hurts. By adulthood, most of us have experienced a significant loss, even if it was "only" the death of a beloved pet. Even when death is not striking so closely, it is there, lurking somewhere in the background as we go about the tasks of living—in the newspaper, on television, fleeting through our minds. Some psychologists argue that much of human behavior is an effort to defend against the terror of death (Pyszczynski, Solomon, & Greenberg, 2003). Yet sooner or later we all face the ultimate developmental task: the task of dying.

This chapter explores death and its place in life-span human development. What is death, and why do we die? How have theorists characterized the experiences of dying and bereaved people? How is death experienced in infancy, childhood, adolescence, and adulthood? Why do some individuals cope far more ably with death than others do? You will discover that death is part of the human experience throughout the life span, but that each person's experience of it depends on his level of development, personality, life circumstances, and sociocultural context. Finally, you will see what can be done to help dying and bereaved individuals.

Life and Death Issues

What is death? When are we most vulnerable to it, and what kills us? And why is it that all of us eventually die of "old age" if we do not die earlier? These "life and death" questions serve to introduce the topic of death and dying.

What Is Death?

There is a good deal of confusion in our society today about when life begins and when it ends. Proponents and opponents of legalized abortion argue vehemently about when life really begins. And we hear similarly heated debates about whether a person in an irreversible coma is truly alive and whether a terminally ill patient who is in agonizing pain should be kept alive with the help of life support machines or allowed to die naturally. Definitions of death as a biological phenomenon change; so do the social meanings attached to death.

Biological Definitions of Death

Biological death is hard to define because it is not a single event but a process (Medina, 1996). Different systems of the body die at different rates, and some individuals who have stopped breathing or who lack a heartbeat or pulse, and who would have been declared dead in earlier times, can now be revived before their brains cease to function. Moreover, basic bodily processes such as respiration and blood circulation can be maintained by life support machines in patients who have fallen into a coma and whose brains have ceased to function.

In 1968 an ad hoc committee of the Harvard Medical School offered a definition of biological death that has influenced modern legal definitions of death (Berger, 1993). The Harvard group defined biological death as **total brain death:** an irreversible loss of functioning in the entire brain, both the higher centers of the cerebral cortex that are involved in thought and the lower centers of the brain that control basic life processes such as breathing. Specifically, to be judged dead a person must meet the following criteria:

1. Be totally unresponsive to stimuli, including painful ones
2. Fail to move for 1 hour and fail to breathe for 3 minutes after being removed from a ventilator
3. Have no reflexes (for example, no eye blink and no constriction of the eye's pupil in response to light)
4. Register a flat electroencephalogram, indicating an absence of electrical activity in the cortex of the brain

As an added precaution, the testing procedure is repeated 24 hours later. Moreover, because a coma is sometimes reversible if the cause is either a drug overdose or an abnormally low body temperature, these conditions must be ruled out before a coma victim is pronounced dead.

Now consider some of the life and death issues that have revolved around this definition of biological death. In 1975, a now famous young woman named Karen Ann Quinlan lapsed into a coma at a party, probably because of the combination of alcohol and drugs she had consumed (Cantor, 2001; Urofsky, 1993). Quinlan was unconscious, but her bodily functioning was maintained with the aid of a ventilator and other life support systems. When a court finally granted her parents permission to turn off the respirator, on the grounds that patients are entitled to choose their own course of treatment (or to have their surrogates do so on their behalf), Quinlan continued to breathe without it, much to everyone's

Explorations

Should We Hasten Death?

Do you believe in euthanasia if a person is terminally ill and in constant pain? Before you answer, note that there are two very different forms of euthanasia. Active euthanasia, or "mercy killing," is deliberately and directly causing a person's death—for example, by administering a lethal dose of drugs to a pain-racked patient in the late stages of cancer or smothering a spouse who is in the late stages of Alzheimer's disease. Passive euthanasia, by contrast, means allowing a terminally ill person to die of natural causes—for example, by withholding extraordinary life-saving treatments, as happened when Karen Ann Quinlan was removed from her respirator. Between active euthanasia and passive euthanasia is **assisted suicide**—not killing someone, as in active euthanasia, but making available to a person who wishes to die the means by which she may do so. This includes physician-assisted suicide—for example, a doctor's writing a prescription for sleeping pills at the request of a terminally ill patient who has made known her desire to die, in full knowledge that she will probably take an overdose (Quill, 1993).

How do we as a society view these options? There is overwhelming support among medical personnel and members of the general public for passive euthanasia (Stillion & McDowell, 1996). And more than 68% of a Texas sample expressed support for assisted suicide, especially when the assistance is provided by a doctor rather than by a relative or friend (Worthen & Yeatts, 2000–2001). In addition, a surprising majority of Americans support active euthanasia in which a doctor ends a patient's life by some painless means if the patient and his family request it (Caddell & Newton, 1995). Minority group members seem less accepting of actions to hasten death than European Americans, however, possibly because they do not trust the medical establishment as much (Werth et al., 2002).

Although active euthanasia is still viewed as murder in the United States and most countries, it is now legal in most states to withhold extraordinary life-extending treatments from terminally ill patients and to "pull the plug" on life support equipment when that is the wish of the dying person or when the immediate family can show that the individual expressed, when she was able to do so, a desire to reject life support measures (Cantor, 2001). A **living will,** or an advance directive, allows people to state, when they are healthy and of sound mind, that they do not want any extraordinary medical procedures applied if they become hopelessly ill.

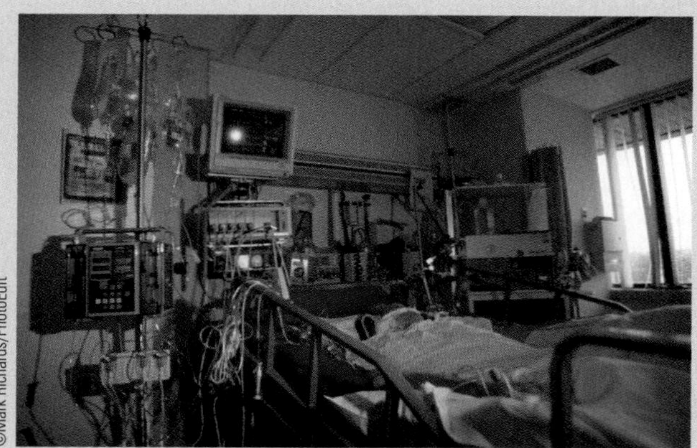
©Mark Richards/PhotoEdit

In 1997, Oregon became the first state to legalize physician-assisted suicide and allow terminally ill adults to request lethal medication. Although few people have used this option (Wineberg & Werth, 2003), other states have not followed Oregon's example. Indeed, several states have since passed laws against assisted suicide (Emanuel, 2001). This caution may be warranted, because terminal patients experience so many emotional ups and downs that it can be difficult to be certain that they truly want to end their lives (Chochinov et al., 1999). In addition, terminally ill patients are sometimes in no shape to make life-or-death decisions, and others speaking for them may not always have their best interests at heart (Cantor, 2001; Mishara, 1999).

On many life-or-death issues, right-to-die advocates, who maintain that people should have a say in how they die, fight right-to-life advocates, who say that everything possible should be done to maintain life and that nothing should be done to cut it short. It makes sense to think through these issues now in case you must someday decide whether you or a loved one should live or die.

surprise. She lived on in a vegetative state, lacking all consciousness and being fed through a tube, for 10 years.

This famous right-to-die case highlighted the different positions people can take on the issue of when a person is dead. The position laid out in the Harvard definition of total brain death (and in the laws of most states and nations) is quite conservative. By the Harvard criteria, Quinlan was not dead, even though she was in an irreversible coma, because the lower portion of her brain (the brain stem) was still functioning enough to support breathing and other basic bodily functions. Should not we keep such seemingly hopeless patients alive in case we discover ways to revive them? A more liberal position is that a person should be declared dead when the cerebral cortex is irreversibly dead, even if bodily functioning is still maintained by the more primitive portions of the brain. After all, is a person really a person if she lacks any awareness and if there is no hope that conscious mental activity will be restored?

Cases such as Quinlan's raise issues concerning **euthanasia**—a term meaning "happy" or "good" death that usually refers to hastening the death of someone suffering from an incurable illness or injury. The Explorations box on page 486 explores some of these issues. Clearly, we as a society continue to grapple with defining life and death and deciding whether euthanasia is morally and legally acceptable (Cantor, 2001; Emanuel, 2001).

Social Meanings of Death

Death is not only a biological process but also a psychological and social one. The social meanings attached to death vary widely from historical era to historical era and from culture to culture (Rosenblatt, 2001). Indeed, you have just discovered that society defines who is dead and who is alive. True, people everywhere die, and people everywhere grieve deaths. Moreover, all societies have evolved some manner of reacting to this universal experience—of interpreting its meaning, disposing of corpses, and expressing grief. Beyond these universals, however, the similarities end.

As Phillippe Ariès (1981) has shown, the social meanings of death have changed over the course of history. In Europe during the Middle Ages, people were expected to recognize that their deaths were approaching so that they could bid their farewells and die with dignity surrounded by loved ones. Since the late 19th century, Ariès argues, Western societies have engaged in a "denial of death." We have taken death out of the home and put it in the hospital and funeral parlor to be managed by physicians and funeral directors; as a result, we have less direct experience with it than our ancestors did (Röcke & Cherry, 2002; Taylor, 2003). We have made death a medical failure rather than a natural part of the life cycle. Right-to-die and death-with-dignity advocates have been arguing forcefully that we should return to the old ways, bringing death into the open, allowing it to occur more naturally, and making it again an experience to be shared within the family.

The experience of dying also differs from culture to culture today. A comparison of the experiences of terminal cancer patients in Scotland and Kenya is revealing (Murray et al., 2003). Scottish patients had far better medical care because their government provided free health care, social services, and financial aid, but they often felt that their emotional needs were not met and worried about burdening their families. In Kenya, patients lived in poverty and had no money with which to buy pain relievers, much less hospital care. Their main concern was fighting unbearable pain; yet they felt that their psychological, social, and spiritual needs were well met by their families, communities, and religious groups.

Finally, if we look at how people in other cultures grieve and mourn a death, we quickly realize that there are many alternatives to our Western ways and no single, biologically mandated grieving process (Klass, 2001; Rosenblatt, 2001).

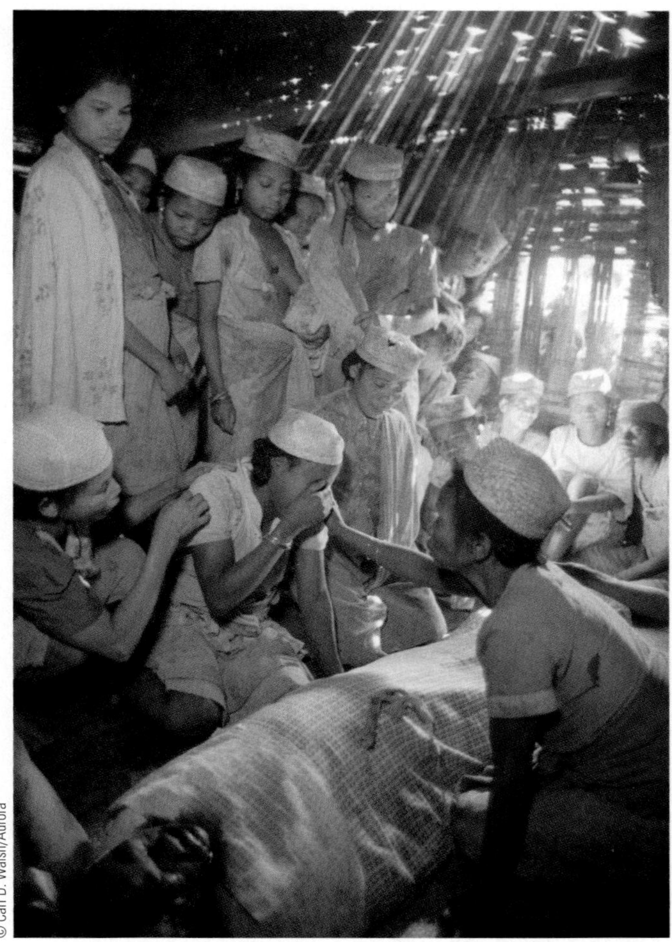

Mourning rituals differ considerably from culture to culture.

Depending on the society, "funerals are the occasion for avoiding people or holding parties, for fighting or having sexual orgies, for weeping or laughing, in a thousand different combinations" (Metcalf & Huntington, 1991, p. 24). Corpses are treated in a remarkable number of ways, too: They "are burned or buried, with or without animal or human sacrifice; they are preserved by smoking, embalming, or pickling; they are eaten—raw, cooked, or rotten; they are ritually exposed as carrion or simply abandoned; or they are dismembered and treated in a variety of these ways" (Metcalf & Huntington, 1991, p. 24). In most societies, there is some concept of spiritual immortality. Yet here, too, there is much variety, from concepts of heaven and hell to the idea of reincarnation to a belief in ancestral ghosts who can meddle in the lives of the living (Rosenblatt, 1993).

We need not look beyond North America to find considerable variation in the social meanings of death. Different ethnic and racial groups clearly have different rules for expressing grief. For example, it is customary among Puerto Ricans, especially women, to display intense, hysterical emotions after a death (Cook & Dworkin, 1992). Japanese Americans, by contrast, are likely to have been taught to restrain their grief—to smile so as not to burden others with their pain and to avoid the shame associated with losing self-control (Cook & Dworkin, 1992).

Different ethnic and racial groups also have different mourning practices. Irish Americans have traditionally believed that the dead deserve a good send-off, a wake with food, drink, and jokes—the kind of party the deceased might have enjoyed (McGoldrick et al., 1991). African Americans tend to regard the funeral not as a time for rowdy celebration but as a forum for expressing grief, in some congregations by wailing and singing spirituals (McGoldrick et al., 1991; Perry, 1993). Jewish families are even more restrained; they quietly withdraw from normal activities for a week of mourning, called *shivah,* then honor the dead again at the 1-month and 1-year marks (Cytron, 1993). The tradition among the Navajos is to try to forget the loved one rapidly and resume normal activities after only 3 or 4 days of mourning (Cook & Dworkin, 1992).

In short, the experiences of dying individuals and of their survivors are shaped by the historical and cultural context in which death occurs. Death may be universal, and the tendency to react negatively to the loss of the objects of our attachment may be universal (Parkes, 2000), but our specific experiences of death and dying are not. Death is truly what we make of it; there is no one "right" way to die or to grieve a death.

What Kills Us and When?

How long are we likely to live, and what is likely to kill us? In the United States the **life expectancy** at birth—the average number of years a newborn can be expected to live—is 76½ years (Freid et al., 2003). This average life expectancy disguises important differences between males and females, among racial and ethnic groups, and among social classes. The life expectancy for white males has risen to almost 75 years, whereas the life expectancy for white females is almost 80 years. Female hormones seem to protect women from high blood pressure and heart problems, and they are less vulnerable than men to violent deaths and accidents and to the effects of smoking, drinking, and similar health hazards (Kaplan & Erickson, 2000). No one is sure of all the reasons, but females live longer than men in most other countries as well. Meanwhile, life expectancies for African Americans, many of whom experience the health hazards associated with poverty, are a good deal lower than those for European Americans: 68 years for males, 75 years for females. Life expectancies are also lower—and have been rising less rapidly—in poor areas than in affluent areas (Malmstrom et al., 1999).

Life expectancies have increased steadily over the centuries, from 30 years in ancient Rome to around 80 years in modern affluent societies such as Japan and Sweden (Harman, 2001). Life expectancies in some countries lag far behind, however, as illustrated in Figure 17.1. In less-developed countries plagued by malaria, famine, AIDS, and other such killers—in Uganda, for example—the life expectancy barely exceeds 40 years (Kinsella & Gist, 1998; U.S. Agency for International Development, 2000).

Death rates change over the life span. Infants are relatively vulnerable; infant mortality in the United States has dropped considerably, however, and now stands at 7 out of 1000 live births (U.S. Bureau of the Census, 2003). Assuming that we survive infancy, we have a relatively small chance of dying during childhood, adolescence, or early adulthood. Death rates then climb steadily throughout middle age and old age.

What kills us? The leading causes of death change dramatically over the life span, as shown in Table 17.1 (Freid et al., 2003). Infant deaths are mainly associated with complications in the period surrounding birth and congenital abnormalities that infants bring with them to life. The leading cause of death among preschool and school-age children is accidents (especially car accidents but also poisonings, falls, fires, drownings, and so on). Adolescence and early adulthood are generally periods of good health. Accidents (especially car accidents), homicides, and suicides are the leading killers of adolescents; accidents and cancers kill young adults, but heart diseases also begin to take a toll.

Starting in the 45-to-64 age group, cancers and heart diseases begin to dominate the list of leading killers, probably because certain individuals' genetic endowments, unhealthy

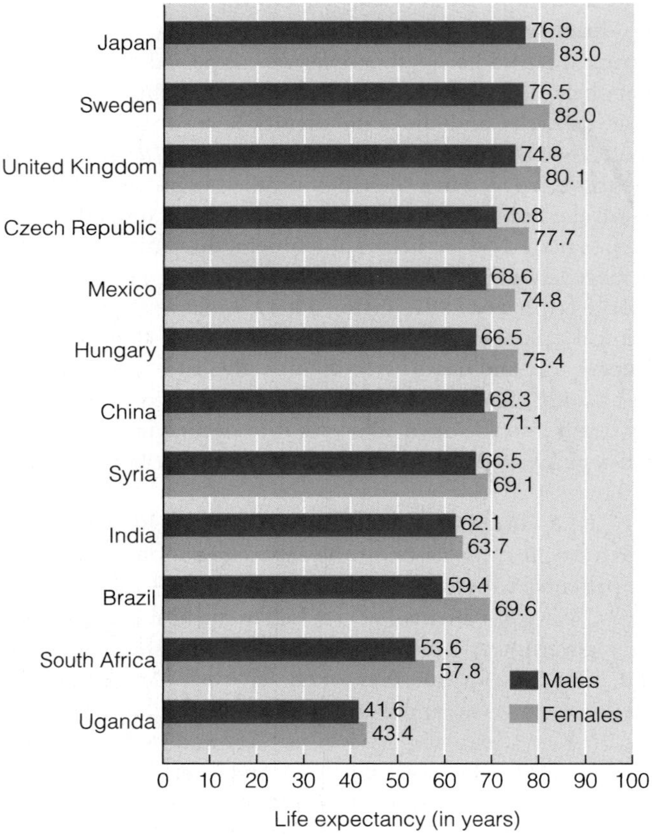

Figure 17.1 Male and female life expectancies at birth in selected countries. Life expectancies vary widely from country to country but are generally higher for females than for males.

SOURCE: Data from Kinsella & Gist (1998).

Table 17.1 Leading Causes of Death for Different Age Groups in the United States

Age Group	Total Deaths	No. 1 Cause	No. 2 Cause	No. 3 Cause
Under 1 year	27,568	Congenital anomalies	Short gestation, low birth weight	Sudden infant death syndrome
1 to 4 years	5,107	Accidents	Congenital anomalies	Cancers
5 to 14 years	7,095	Accidents	Cancers	Congenital anomalies
15 to 24 years	32,252	Accidents	Homicide	Suicide
25 to 44 years	133,357	Accidents	Cancers	Heart disease
45 to 64 years	412,204	Cancers	Heart disease	Accidents
65 years and older	1,798,420	Heart disease	Cancers	Cerebrovascular diseases

SOURCE: Based on data from Freid et al., 2003, Table 32, pp. 148–149.

lifestyles, or both put them at risk to develop these and other diseases prematurely (Horiuchi et al., 2003). The incidence of chronic diseases climbs steadily with age. Among adults 65 and older, heart disease leads the list by far, accounting for a third of all deaths, followed by cancers and cerebrovascular diseases (strokes). By this age, general aging processes that affect all of us are probably increasing the odds that one disease or another will strike (Horiuchi et al., 2003).

In sum, life expectancies are higher than ever. After we make it through the vulnerable period of infancy, we are at low risk of death through early adulthood and are most likely to die suddenly because of an accident if we do die. As we age, we become more vulnerable to death, especially because of chronic diseases. But now a more fundamental question: Why is it that all of us die? Why does no one live to be 200 or 600? To understand why death is an inevitable part of human development, you need the help of theories of aging.

Theories of Aging: Why Do We Age and Die?

There is no simple answer to the question of why we age and die. However, several theories have been proposed, and each of them says something important about the aging process. These theories can be divided into two main categories: **Programmed theories of aging** emphasize the systematic genetic control of aging processes; **damage theories of aging** call attention to more haphazard processes that cause errors in cells to accumulate and organ systems to deteriorate (Clark, 1999; Hayflick, 2004; Wickens, 1998). The question, really, is whether aging and death are the result of a biological master plan or of random insults to the body while we live.

Programmed Theories

Humans, like other species, have a characteristic **maximum life span**—a ceiling on the number of years that anyone lives. The longest documented and verified life so far is that of Jeanne Louise Calment, a French woman who died in 1997 at age 122 (Coles, 2004). Nearly blind and deaf and confined to a wheelchair, she maintained her sense of humor to the end, attributing her longevity to everything from having a stomach "like an ostrich's" to being forgotten by God (Trueheart, 1997). Calment and others who live almost as long are the basis for setting the maximum human life span around 120 years. There are probably only about 300 to 450 people documented to be age 110 and older alive today (Coles, 2004). Interestingly, the maximum life span has not increased much but the average life expectancy has been increasing dramatically (Wilmoth et al., 2000).

Humans are long-lived compared with most species. The maximum life span for the mouse is 3½ years, for the dog 20, for the chimpanzee 50, and for the long-lived Galapagos tortoise 150 (Walford, 1983). The fact that each species has its own characteristic maximum life span should convince us that specieswide genes influence how long people generally live.

Moreover, we know that the individual's genetic makeup, combined with environmental factors, influences how rapidly he ages and how long he lives compared with other humans. For example, genetic differences among us account for more than 50% of variation in the ability to stay free of major chronic diseases at age 70 or older (Reed & Dick, 2003). A fairly good way to estimate how long you will live is to average the longevity of your parents and grandparents (Medvedev, 1991). Recently, Terry Reed and his colleagues (2004) attempted to identify specific genes associated with long life in pairs of male fraternal twins who both made it to age 70 free of cardiovascular disease and prostate cancer. Several genes were located, including one on Chromosome 4 that had previously been found in families with many centenarians. Centenarians, it turns out, have exceptionally good cardiovascular health.

It is not clear yet exactly how genes influence aging and longevity. There are almost certainly several genes, rather than only one, involved in aging and death. And they are not just genes that increase or decrease susceptibility to the diseases that tend to kill people; they include genes that influence the human life span. Evolutionary theorists point to a puzzle: Genes that extend or shorten life will not be selected for in the course of evolution because they do not become relevant to adaptation until the reproductive years are over (Arking, 2004). However, genes that proved adaptive to our ancestors early in life but have negative effects later in life *could* have become common in our species over time (Olshansky & Carnes, 2004). For example, recent research suggests that a gene called p53, which protects against cancer early in life by affecting how cells respond to damage, can, if it is made overly active through genetic manipulation, contribute to cell aging (Dumble et al., 2004; Ferbeyre & Lowe, 2002). This suggests that cancer protection early in life may come at the price of aging later in life. If other such intriguing findings emerge, we might have to conclude that aging and death are the by-products of genes that served humans well during their reproductive years and therefore became more common in the species.

Biological researchers have also been exploring for some time the possibility that we are programmed with an "aging clock" in every cell of our bodies. Their work has built on that of Leonard Hayflick (1976, 1994), who grew cells in cultures, allowed them to divide or double, and measured the number of doublings that occurred. He discovered that cells from human embryos could double only a certain number of times—50 times, plus or minus 10—an estimate now referred to as the **Hayflick limit.** Hayflick also demonstrated that cells taken from human adults divide even fewer times, presumably because they have already used up some of their capacity for reproducing themselves. Moreover, the maximum life span of a species is related to the Hayflick limit for that species: The short-lived mouse's cells can go through only 14 to 28 doublings; the long-lived Galapagos tortoise's cells can manage 90 to 125.

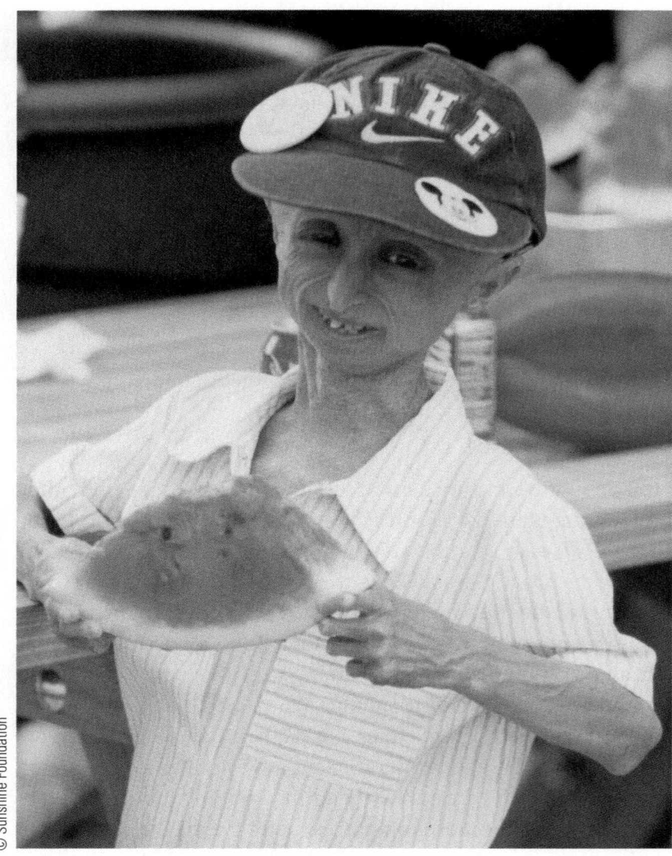

© Sunshine Foundation

Children with the genetic disorder progeria experience early graying, wrinkling, and hair loss, cardiovascular problems, Alzheimer's disease, and death. They provide clues to the genetic basis for aging.

Some believe that the cellular aging clock suggested by Hayflick's limit on cell division is timed by a shortening of **telomeres**—the stretches of DNA that form the tips of chromosomes (Bodnar et al., 1998; Klapper, Parwaresch, & Krupp, 2001). When a cell divides, each of its chromosomes replicates itself, but the chromosome's telomere does not. Instead, half of the telomere goes to one of the newly formed chromosomes and half goes to the other. The result is shorter telomeres as we age; eventually, the theory goes, this progressive shortening of telomeres makes cells unable to replicate and causes them to malfunction and die. It is not yet clear whether an eventual inability of cells to divide can explain the death of the whole organism (Masutomi et al., 2003; Wickens, 1998). Still, the idea that telomeres function as an aging clock within cells is a good example of a theory maintaining that aging and death are genetically programmed processes.

Using techniques of modern genetic analysis, researchers are identifying specific genes that become more or less active from middle age to old age and that therefore may be implicated in the basic aging process (Ly et al., 2000). Many of the genes that become less active with age in normal adults are also inactive in children who have **progeria,** a genetic disorder caused by a spontaneous (rather than inherited) gene mutation. The genetic mutation affects the membrane surrounding the nuclei of cells and makes victims age prematurely and die in their teens, often of heart disease (DeBusk, 1972; Eriksson et al., 2003). Many of the genes that normally become inactive with age also turn out to be involved in regulating cell division—for example, in stopping cells with genetic errors from dividing (Ly et al., 2000).

Other programmed theories of aging have centered on genetically guided, systematic changes in body systems, such as the neuroendocrine system and the immune system (Cristofalo, 1996; Knight, 2000). We know that the hypothalamus of the brain, guided by a genetic program, sets in motion the hormonal changes responsible for puberty and menopause (see Chapter 5). Possibly the hypothalamus also serves as an aging clock, systematically altering levels of hormones and brain chemicals in later life so that bodily functioning is no longer regulated properly and we die. Or perhaps aging is related to genetically governed changes in the immune system that decrease its ability to defend against potentially life-threatening foreign agents such as infections and cause it to mistake normal cells for invaders (Wickens, 1998). All of these programmed theories of aging hold that aging and dying are the inevitable products of our biological endowment as humans, and all have some support.

Damage Theories

In contrast to programmed theories of aging, damage theories generally propose that wear and tear—an accumulation of haphazard or random damage to cells and organs over the years—ultimately causes death. Like cars, we may have a limited warranty and simply give out after a certain number of years of use; as S. Jay Olshansky and Bruce Carnes (2004) put it, aging and death can be viewed as "the inadvertent but inevitable by-products of the degradation of biological structures and processes that evolved for growth, development, and reproduction rather than extended operation" (p. 154). Early in life, cells replicate themselves faithfully; later in life, this fidelity is lost and cells become increasingly damaged. Damage theorists believe that random damage, rather than genetically programmed change, is what biological aging is all about (Hayflick, 2004; Olshansky & Carnes, 2004).

According to the most promising damage theory, **free radical theory,** toxic by-products of the metabolism of oxygen damage cells and their functioning (Harman, 2001; Wickens, 1998). Free radicals are molecules that have an extra or "free" electron, are chemically unstable, and react with other molecules in the body to produce substances that damage normal cells, including their DNA. Over time, the genetic code contained in the DNA of more cells becomes scrambled, and the body's mechanisms for repairing such genetic damage simply cannot keep up with the chaos. More cells then function improperly or cease to function, and the organism eventually dies.

"Age spots" on the skin of older people are a visible sign of the damage free radicals and other products of oxidation can cause. Free radicals have also been implicated in some of the major diseases that become more common with age—most notably, cardiovascular diseases, cancer, and Alzheimer's disease (Harman, 2001). Moreover, they are implicated in the aging of the brain (Poon et al., 2004). However, the damage of most concern is damage to DNA because the result is more defective cells replicating themselves. Unfortunately, we cannot live and breathe without manufacturing free radicals because they are produced whenever oxygen is metabolized. No wonder many adults today are popping **antioxidants** such as vitamins E and C. At least when they are consumed in such foods as spinach and fruits rather than taken in pill form, antioxidants may increase longevity, although not for long, by inhibiting free radical activity and in turn helping prevent age-related diseases (Meydani, 2001). Caution is advised, though: Taking exceptionally high doses of vitamin E may shorten rather than prolong life (Stein, 2004).

Nature and Nurture Conspiring

The theories just described are some of the most promising explanations of why we age and die. Programmed theories of aging generally say that aging and dying are as much a part of nature's plan as sprouting teeth or uttering first words and may be the by-products of genes that contributed to early growth and development. The maximum life span, the role of individual genetic makeup in longevity, the telomere explanation of the Hayflick limit on cell replication, changes in the activity levels of certain genes as we age, and systematic changes in endocrine functioning and the immune system all suggest that aging and dying are genetically controlled. By contrast, damage theories of aging hold that we eventually succumb to haphazard destructive processes, most notably those caused by free radicals, that result in increasingly faulty DNA and abnormal cell functioning and ultimately a breakdown somewhere in the system.

Neither of these broad theories of aging has proved to be *the* explanation; instead, many interacting mechanisms involving both aging processes and disease processes are at work (Holliday, 2004; Knight, 2000). For example, genes influence the capacity of cells to repair environmentally caused damage, and the random damage caused by free radicals alters genetic material. John Medina (1996) put it this way: "Toxic waste products accumulate because genes shut off. Genes shut off because toxic waste products accumulate" (p. 291). In short, nature and nurture, biological and environmental factors, interact to bring about aging and dying—just as they interact to produce development.

The Applications box on page 492 explores efforts to apply research on theories of aging to the task of extending life, or finding the elusive fountain of youth. However, none of our efforts to delay death will keep us from dying. So turn to the question of how humans cope with death and dying.

Summing Up

In defining death as a biological process, the Harvard definition of total brain death has been influential; meanwhile, active euthanasia and assisted suicide are controversial. Our society tends to deny death, but the social meanings of death vary widely. The average life expectancy for a newborn in the United States is 76½ years and is higher for women than men; death rates decline after infancy and rise dramatically after early adulthood, when accidents give way to chronic diseases as primary causes of death. Programmed theories of aging claim that aging is governed largely by species heredity and individual genetic endowment and include the notion that the shortening of telomeres is behind the Hayflick limit on cell division. Damage theories of aging focus on random damage caused by destructive free radicals and other agents. In the end, genetic and environmental factors interact to bring about aging and death.

The Experience of Dying

People who die suddenly may be blessed, because those who develop life-threatening illnesses face the challenge of coping with the knowledge that they are seriously ill and are likely to die. Perhaps no one has done more to focus attention on the emotional needs of dying patients than psychiatrist Elisabeth Kübler-Ross (1969, 1974), whose "stages of dying" are widely known and whose 1969 book *On Death and Dying* revolutionized the care of dying people.

Applications

Can We Delay Death?

What does research on the basic causes of aging and death say about our prospects for finding the fountain of youth, or extending the life span? Aging Baby Boomers want to know, and in response a field of anti-aging medicine has sprung forth, bringing with it hucksters offering magic diets, cosmetic changes, and countless pills of no proven value (Binstock, 2004). Both genetic theories and damage theories of aging provide ideas about how to extend life.

It is not unthinkable that researchers might discover genetic mechanisms behind aging and dying and then devise ways of manipulating genes to increase longevity or even the maximum life span (Arking, 2004). Life spans of 200 to 600 years are probably not possible (and may not even be desirable), but some think researchers could raise the average age of death to around 112 years and allow 112-year-olds to function more like 78-year-olds (Miller, 2004). For example, researchers are looking for ways to keep telomeres from shortening and thus keep cells replicating longer. Others are trying to genetically engineer antioxidant enzymes that would slow the damage caused by free radicals or are trying to activate genes that improve the repair of damage caused by oxidation. Experiments with fruit flies have shown that the functioning of their DNA repair systems can be improved through genetic engineering, but the concept has not yet worked in mice (Arking, 2004).

Yet if aging is the result of random damage rather than a genetic program, or if many genetic and environmental factors contribute to it, the odds of long life through genetic engineering may be low because it will not be a simple matter of tinkering with a single "aging" gene. Moreover, what works for fruit flies or even mice does not always work for humans; gene therapy experiments with humans have been disappointing so far (Chapman, 2004). As students of human development know, ongoing interactions between genes and environmental factors are complex, and it is not always easy to predict the outcomes (Chapman, 2004).

At present, the only technique that has been demonstrated experimentally to extend the life span is **caloric restriction**—a highly nutritious but severely restricted diet representing a 30 to 40% or more cut in normal total caloric intake (Casadesus et al., 2004; Harman, 2001; Lane et al., 2001). Laboratory studies involving rats, and more recently primates, suggest that caloric restriction extends not only the average longevity but also the maximum life span of a species and that it delays or slows the progression of many age-related diseases (Bodkin et al., 2003; Lane et al., 2001). A 40% reduction in daily calories can result in a 40% decrease in body weight, a 40% increase in average longevity, and a 49% increase in the maximum life span of diet-restricted rats (Harman, 2001).

How does caloric restriction achieve these results? It clearly reduces the number of free radicals and other toxic products of metabolism (Wickens, 1998). By looking at the activity of genes in restricted-diet and normal-diet mice, researchers have also found that caloric restriction prevents an age-related decrease in the activity of genes involved in repairing the random damage caused by free radicals (Lee et al., 1999). In effect, eating little slows metabolism and changes cell functioning so that more emphasis is placed on damage repair (Arking, 2004).

However, we do not know whether caloric restriction works as well for humans as it apparently has for rats, what calorie counts and combinations of nutrients are optimal, or whether humans who have a choice would put up with being half-starved for most of their lives. We do know that centenarians are rarely obese (Arking, 2004). We also have some intriguing evidence from Biosphere II in Arizona. Four men and four women lived in this sealed ecological dome for 2 years. Crop shortages had them eating as little as about 1800 calories a day for the first 6 months and then about 2000 calories a day for the rest of their stay, mostly vegetables they grew themselves (Walford et al., 2002). They underwent a 15 to 20% weight loss.

Kübler-Ross's Stages of Dying

In interviews with terminally ill patients, Kübler-Ross (1969) detected a common set of emotional responses to the knowledge that the patient had a serious, and probably fatal, illness. She believed that similar reactions might occur in response to any major loss, so bear in mind that the family and friends of the dying person may experience some of these emotional reactions during the loved one's illness and after the death. Kübler-Ross's five "stages of dying" are as follows:

1. *Denial and isolation.* A common first response to dreadful news is to say, "No! It can't be!" **Denial** is a defense mechanism in which anxiety-provoking thoughts are kept out of, or "isolated" from, conscious awareness. A woman who has just been diagnosed as having lung cancer may insist that the diagnosis is wrong—or accept that she is ill but be convinced that she will beat the odds and recover. Denial can be a marvelous coping device: It can get us through a time of acute crisis until we are ready to cope more constructively. Even after dying patients face the facts and become ready to talk about

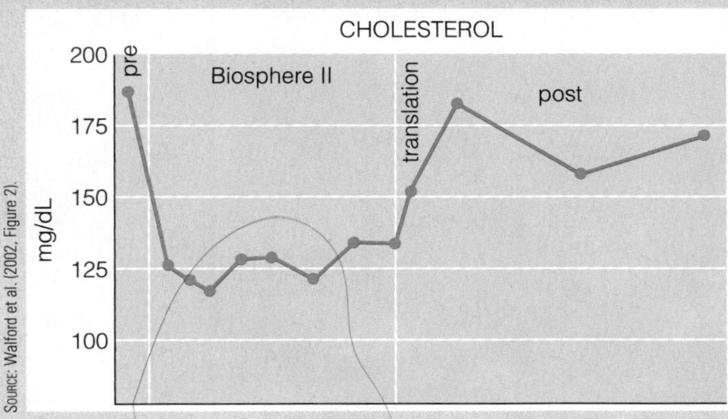

Cholesterol levels in 8 adults before, during, and after their 2-year residence in Biosphere II, when they were on a low-calorie but high-nutrition diet. Many other physiological measures show similarly dramatic changes.

Measurements such as the one for cholesterol shown in the graph in this Applications box indicated that these adults experienced significant improvements in several physiological indicators that have also been found to change in positive ways in calorie-restricted rats and monkeys. They had the energy to engage in an active lifestyle involving lots of physical labor during the 2-year period. (The physiological improvements in functioning also disappeared after they left Biosphere II and went back on normal diets.) We do not know whether they will live longer than they would have otherwise (Coles, 2004). We do know that starvation without good nutrition is bad for humans (and no fun), so experimenting with self-starvation before more evidence is in is not a good idea. While we wait for the breakthroughs that might extend the maximum life span of humans, we can at least reduce our chances of dying young. As suggested in Chapter 5, for example, we can stop smoking, drink only in moderation, eat nutritious food, exercise regularly, and take other steps to ward off the diseases that make us die prematurely.

Some think the search for the fountain of youth is misguided and will prove futile if humans, like cars, simply wear out at some point. As Leonard Hayflick (2004) notes, yesterday's searchers for immortality, who once "advocated sleeping with young virgins, encouraged monkey testicular grafting, or dined on yogurt have been replaced with today's practitioners of 'anti-aging medicine' who have put their faith in some equally unlikely modern equivalent" (p. 577). "If our society would learn to value old age to the same extent as we presently value youth," he adds, "then the drive to slow, stop, or reverse the aging process would be as unthinkable as intervening in the developmental processes of our youth" (p. 578).

dying, care providers and family members often engage in their own denial.

2. *Anger.* As the bad news begins to register, the dying person asks, "Why me?" Feelings of rage or resentment may be directed at anyone who is handy—doctors, nurses, or family members. Kübler-Ross advises those close to the dying person to be sensitive to this reaction so that they will not try to avoid this irritable person or become angry in return.

3. *Bargaining.* When the dying person bargains, he says, "Okay, me, but please. . . ." The bargainer begs for some concession from God, the medical staff, or someone else—if not for a cure, perhaps for a little more time, a little less pain, or provision for his children.

4. *Depression.* As the dying person becomes even more aware of the reality of the situation, depression, despair, and a sense of hopelessness become the predominant emotional responses. Grief focuses on the losses that have already occurred (for example, the loss of the ability to function as she once did) and the losses to come (separation from loved ones, the inability to achieve her dreams, and so on).

© Ken Ross

Psychiatrist Elisabeth Kübler-Ross called on physicians to emphasize caring rather than curing.

5. *Acceptance.* If the dying person is able to work through the emotional reactions of the preceding stages, he may accept the inevitability of death in a calm and peaceful manner. Kübler-Ross (1969) describes the acceptance stage this way: "It is almost void of feelings. It is as if the pain had gone, the struggle is over, and there comes a time for 'the final rest before the long journey,' as one patient phrased it" (p. 100).

In addition to these five stages of dying, Kübler-Ross emphasized a sixth response that runs throughout the stages: *hope.* She believed that it is essential for terminally ill patients to retain some sense of hope, even if it is only the hope that they can die with dignity.

Criticisms and Alternative Views

Kübler-Ross, who experienced a series of strokes and finally died peacefully and surrounded by family and friends at age 78 in 2004 (Holley, 2004), deserves immense credit for sensitizing our society to the emotional needs of dying people. She convinced medical professionals to emphasize caring rather than curing in working with such people. At the same time, there are flaws in her account of the dying person's experience (Kastenbaum, 2000). Among the most important points made by critics are these: dying is not stagelike; the course of an illness affects reactions to it; and individuals differ widely in their emotional responses to dying.

The major problem with Kübler-Ross's stages is that the dying process is simply not stagelike. Although dying patients often display symptoms of depression as death nears, the other emotional reactions Kübler-Ross describes seem to affect only minorities of dying people (Schulz & Aderman, 1974). Moreover, when these responses occur, they do not unfold in a set order. It might have been better if Kübler-Ross had, from the start, described her stages simply as common emotional reactions to dying. Unfortunately, some overzealous medical professionals have tried to push dying patients through the stages in order, believing incorrectly that their patients would never accept death unless they experienced the "right" emotions at the "right" times (Kastenbaum, 2000).

Edwin Shneidman (1973, 1980) offered an alternate view, arguing that dying patients experience a complex and ever-changing interplay of emotions, alternating between denial and acceptance of death. One day a patient may seem to understand that death is near; the next day she may talk of getting better and going home. Along the way many reactions—disbelief, hope, terror, bewilderment, rage, apathy, calm, anxiety, and others—come and go and are even experienced simultaneously. According to Shneidman, then, dying people experience many unpredictable emotional changes rather than distinct stages of dying. Research supports him and further suggests that anxiety and depression are common among dying patients and should be treated more often than they are to improve the quality of the person's last days (Chochinov & Schwartz, 2002). Many dying people also experience the confusion of delirium in their last weeks (Pessin, Rosenfeld, & Breitbart, 2002).

A second major problem in Kübler-Ross's theory is that it does not allow for differences in emotional responses to dying associated with the course or trajectory of an illness and the specific events that occur along the way (Glaser & Strauss,

1968). When a patient is slowly and gradually worsening over time, the patient, family members, and staff can all become accustomed to the death that lies ahead, whereas when the path toward death is more erratic, emotional ups or downs are likely each time the patient's condition takes a turn for better or worse. Kübler-Ross expects different patients to experience similar responses even when their diseases and pathways to death differ.

Finally, Kübler-Ross's approach overlooks the influences of each individual's personality on how she experiences dying. People cope with dying much as they have coped with life (Schulz & Schlarb, 1987–1988). For example, cancer patients who faced life's problems directly and effectively, were satisfied with their lives, and maintained good interpersonal relationships before they became ill displayed less anger and were less depressed and withdrawn during their illnesses than patients who were not so well adjusted before their illnesses (Hinton, 1975). Depending on their predominant personality traits, coping styles, and social competencies, some dying people may deny until the bitter end, some may "rage against the dying of the light," some may quickly be crushed by despair, and still others may display incredible strength. Most will display combinations of these responses, each in his own unique way. There is no right way to die.

Summing Up

Kübler-Ross stimulated much concern for dying patients by describing five stages of dying (denial and isolation, anger, bargaining, depression, and acceptance). The experiences of dying people are far more complex than Kübler-Ross's stages suggest, however. As Shneidman emphasizes, there is likely to be a complex interplay of many emotions and thoughts, with swings between acceptance and denial. Anxiety and depression are common. Moreover, experiences differ depending on the nature and course of the individual's condition and on the individual's personality and coping style. ■

The Experience of Bereavement

Most of us know more about the process of grieving a death than about the process of dying. To describe responses to the death of a loved one, we must distinguish among three terms: **Bereavement** is a state of loss, **grief** is an emotional response to loss, and **mourning** is a culturally prescribed way of displaying reactions to death. Thus, we can describe a bereaved person who grieves by experiencing such emotions as sadness, anger, and guilt and who mourns by attending the funeral and laying flowers on the grave each year.

Unless a death is sudden, relatives and friends, like the dying person, will experience many painful emotions before the death, from the initial diagnosis through the last breath (Grbich, Parker, & Maddocks, 2001). They, too, may alternate between acceptance and denial. They also may experience what has been termed **anticipatory grief**—grieving before death occurs for what is happening and for what lies ahead (Rando, 1986).

Yet no amount of preparation and anticipatory grief can eliminate the need to grieve after the death occurs. How, then, do we grieve?

The Parkes/Bowlby Attachment Model

Pioneering research on the grieving process was conducted by Colin Murray Parkes and his colleagues in Great Britain (Parkes, 1996, 1991; Parkes & Weiss, 1983). John Bowlby (1980), whose influential ethological theory of attachment was outlined in Chapter 14, and Parkes have conceptualized grieving in the context of attachment theory as a reaction to separation from a loved one. The grieving adult can be likened to the infant who experiences separation anxiety when her mother disappears from view and tries to retrieve her. As humans, we have evolved not only to form attachments but also to grieve their loss.

The **Parkes/Bowlby attachment model of bereavement** describes four predominant reactions. They overlap considerably and therefore should not be viewed as clear-cut stages even though the frequencies of different reactions change over time. These reactions are numbness, yearning, disorganization and despair, and reorganization (see also Jacobs et al., 1987–1988).

1. *Numbness.* In the first few hours or days after the death, the bereaved person is often in a daze—gripped by a sense of unreality and disbelief and almost empty of feelings. He may make plane reservations, call relatives, or order flowers—all as if in a dream. Underneath this state of numbness and shock is a sense of being on the verge of bursting, and occasionally painful emotions break through. The bereaved person is struggling to defend himself against the full weight of the loss; the bad news has not fully registered.

2. *Yearning.* As the numbing sense of shock and disbelief diminishes, the bereaved person experiences more agony. Grief comes in pangs or waves that typically are most severe from 5 to 14 days after the death. The grieving person has feelings of panic, bouts of uncontrollable weeping, and physical aches and pains. She is likely to be extremely restless, unable to concentrate or to sleep, and preoccupied with thoughts of the loved one and of the events leading to the death.

According to Parkes and Bowlby, the reaction that most clearly makes grieving different from other kinds of emotional distress is separation anxiety—the distress of being parted from the object of attachment. The bereaved person pines and yearns for the loved one and searches for the deceased. A widow may think she heard her husband's voice or saw him in a crowd; she may sense his presence in the house and draw comfort from it; she may be drawn to his favorite chair or wear his bathrobe. Ultimately, the quest to be reunited is doomed to fail.

Both anger and guilt are also common reactions during these early weeks and months of bereavement. Bereaved people often feel irritable and sometimes experience intense rage—at the loved one for dying, at the doctors for not doing a better job, at almost anyone. They seem to need to pin blame somewhere. Unfortunately, they often find reason to blame themselves—to feel guilty. A father may moan that he should have spent more time teaching his son gun safety; the friend of a young man who dies of AIDS may feel that he was not a good enough friend. One of the London widows studied by Parkes felt guilty because she never made her husband bread pudding.

3. *Disorganization and despair.* As time passes, pangs of intense grief and yearning become less frequent, although they still occur. As it sinks in that a reunion with the loved one is impossible, depression, despair, and apathy increasingly predominate. During most of the first year after the death, and longer in many cases, bereaved individuals often feel apathetic and may have difficulty managing and taking interest in their lives.

4. *Reorganization.* Eventually, bereaved people begin to pull themselves together again as their pangs of grief and periods of apathy become less frequent. They invest less emotional energy in their attachment to the deceased and more in their attachments to the living. If they have lost a spouse, they begin to make the transition from being a wife or husband to being a widow or widower, revising their identities. They may also revise their internal working models of attachment, thinking in new ways about their relationship with the person who died (Noppe, 2000). They begin to feel ready for new activities and possibly for new relationships or attachments.

Some Evidence

You will be looking soon at grief responses across the life span. For now, note that some researchers would disagree with the specifics of the Parkes/Bowlby view of bereavement. Like responses to dying, responses to loss tend to be messier and more individualized than the Parkes/Bowlby phases suggest (Röcke & Cherry, 2002). Most would agree on this: bereavement is a complex and multidimensional process that varies from person to person and often takes a long time. Many emotional reactions are involved, and their course and intensity differ from person to person. An analysis of research by George Bonanno and Stacey Kaltman (2000) suggests that modest disruptions in cognitive, emotional, physical, and interpersonal functioning are common, that they usually last for a year, and that less severe, recurring grief reactions may then continue for several years; see the "common grief" reaction in Figure 17.2. Although not captured in the Parkes/Bowlby model, positive thoughts about the deceased, expressions of love, and feelings of gaining from the loss are also part of the typical picture.

Yet different people grieve differently. A surprisingly high proportion of bereaved people, from 15 to 50% depending on the study, can be described as resilient. They experience minimal grief even in the early months after the death and minimal grief later on; they feel the loss but apparently cope effectively with it (Bonanno, 2004). About 15% can be characterized as chronic grievers: They continue to experience serious disruptions in functioning 1 to 2 or even more years after their loss, they often have diagnosable major depression or anxiety disorder, and they may therefore be candidates for treatment.

Meanwhile, we are sympathetic toward the bereaved immediately after a death—eager to help in any way we can—but we quickly grow weary of someone who is depressed, irritable, or preoccupied. We begin to think, sometimes after only a few days or weeks, that it is time for the bereaved person to cheer up and get on with life. We are wrong. To be of help to bereaved people, we must understand that their reactions of numbness and disbelief, yearning, and despair may linger a long time.

We have now presented some of the major theories of how people experience dying and bereavement. However,

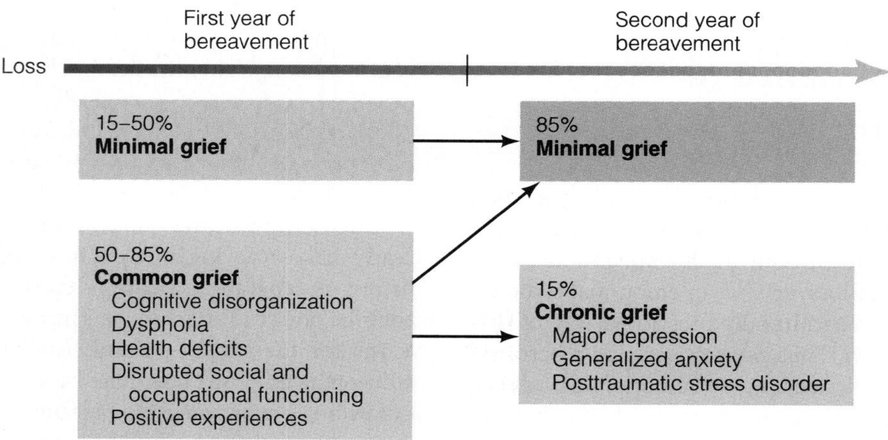

Figure 17.2 Patterns of grief differ greatly from person to person. Some people show little grief; many experience disrupted functioning for about a year and then minimal grief in the second year; and about 15% experience chronic and significant psychological problems.
SOURCE: Adapted from Bonanno & Kaltman (2000).

these theories have been based primarily on the responses of adults. How do infants, children, and adolescents respond to death? What does death even mean to infants and young children? A life-span perspective on death and dying is needed (Hayslip & Hansson, 2003).

Summing Up

Bereavement precipitates grief and mourning, which are expressed, according to the Parkes/Bowlby attachment model, in overlapping phases of numbness, yearning, disorganization and despair, and finally, after a year or more, reorganization. Research suggests that emotional reactions to bereavement may be more diverse and unpredictable than the model indicates, that a sizable number of individuals never experience significant grief, and that a minority experience chronic grief. ■

The Infant

Looking at bereavement from an attachment theory perspective makes us wonder how infants understand and cope with the death of an attachment figure. Infants surely do not comprehend death as the cessation of life, but they do gain an understanding of concepts that pave the way for an understanding of death. Infants may, for example, grasp the concepts of being and nonbeing, here and "all gone," from such experiences as watching objects and people appear and disappear, playing peek-a-boo, and even going to sleep and "coming alive" again in the morning (Maurer, 1961). Possibly, infants first form a global category of things that are "all gone" and later divide it into subcategories, one of which is "dead" (Kastenbaum, 2000).

The experience most directly relevant to an emerging concept of death is the disappearance of a loved one, and it is here that Bowlby's theory of attachment is helpful. After infants form their first attachments around 6 or 7 months, they begin to display signs of separation anxiety when their beloved caregivers leave them. They have begun to grasp the concept that people, like objects, have permanent existence, and they expect a loved one who has disappeared to reappear. According to Bowlby, they are biologically programmed to protest separations by crying, searching for their loved one, and attempting to follow, thereby increasing the chances that they will be reunited with the caregiver and protected from harm.

Bowlby (1980) observed that infants separated from their attachment figures display many of the same reactions that bereaved adults do. Infants first engage in vigorous *protest*—yearning and searching for the loved one and expressing outrage when they fail. One 17-month-old girl said only, "Mum, Mum, Mum" for 3 days after her mother died. She was willing to sit on a nurse's lap but would turn her back, as if she did not want to see that the nurse was not "Mum" (Freud & Burlingham cited in Bowlby, 1980).

Games of peek-a-boo help infants understand the concept of "all gone" and later the concept of death.

If, after a week or so, an infant has not succeeded in finding the loved one, he begins to *despair,* displaying depression-like symptoms. The baby loses hope, ends the search, and becomes apathetic and sad. Grief may be reflected in a poor appetite, a change in sleeping patterns, excessive clinginess, or regression to less mature behavior (Furman, 1984; and see the description in Chapter 16 of infant depression). Eventually, the bereaved infant enters a *detachment* phase, in which he takes renewed interest in toys and companions and may begin to seek new relationships. Infants will recover from the loss of an attachment figure most completely if they can rely on an existing attachment figure (for example, the surviving parent) or have the opportunity to attach themselves to someone new.

Summing Up

Infants who are at least 6 months of age and who have formed genuine attachment bonds are old enough to experience intense grief and depression-like symptoms when a parent or other loved one dies. Moreover, the responses they display—the protest and yearning, the despair or depression, and the detachment or reorganization—resemble adult grief responses. What is the difference? It is mainly that infants lack the concept of death as permanent separation or loss and the cognitive capacity to interpret what has happened. ■

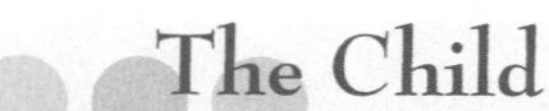

The Child

Much as parents would like to shelter their children from unpleasant life experiences, children encounter death in their early years, if only of bugs and birds. How do they come to understand and cope with their experiences of death?

Grasping the Concept of Death

Contrary to what many adults would like to believe, young children are highly curious about death, think about it with some frequency, and are willing to talk about it (Kastenbaum, 2000). Yet their beliefs about death often differ considerably from those of adults. In our society, a "mature" understanding of death has several components (Brent et al., 1996; Hoffman & Strauss, 1985; Kenyon, 2001; Slaughter, Jaakkola, & Carey, 1999). We see death as characterized by the following:

- *Finality.* It is the cessation of life and of all life processes, such as movement, sensation, and thought.
- *Irreversibility.* It cannot be undone.
- *Universality.* It is inevitable and happens to all living beings.
- *Biological causality.* It is the result of natural processes internal to the organism, even if external causes set off these internal changes.

Researchers have studied children's conceptions of death by asking them the sorts of questions contained in Table 17.2. Children between age 3 and age 5 have some understanding of death, especially of its universality (Brent et al., 1996). Rather than viewing death as a final cessation of life functions, however, many of them picture the dead as living under altered circumstances and retaining at least some of their capacities (Slaughter et al., 1999). According to these preschoolers, the dead may no longer possess all their biological and perceptual capacities, but they may have hunger pangs, wishes, and beliefs and may continue to love their Moms (Bering & Bjorklund, 2004).

Table 17.2 Western Children's Concepts of Death and Questions Pertaining to Them

Concept	Questions
Finality	Can a dead person move? Get hungry? Speak? Think? Dream? Do dead people know that they are dead?
Irreversibility	Can a dead person become a live person again? Is there anything that could make a dead animal come back to life?
Universality	Does everyone die at some time? Will your parents die someday? Your friends? Will you die?
Biological causality	What makes a person die? Why do animals die?

SOURCES: Based on Hoffman & Strauss, 1985; Florian & Kravetz, 1985; and other sources.

Some preschool-age children also view death as reversible rather than irreversible. They may liken it to sleep (from which a person can awaken) or to a trip (from which a person can return). With the right medical care, the right chicken soup, or a bit of magic, a dead person might be brought back to life (Speece & Brent, 1984). Finally, young children think death is caused by one external agent or another; they do not grasp the ultimate biological cause of death. One may say that people die because they eat aluminum foil; another may say the cause is eating a dirty bug or a Styrofoam cup (Koocher, 1974).

Children ages 5 to 7 make considerable progress in acquiring a mature concept of death. Most children this age understand that death is characterized by finality (cessation of life functions), irreversibility, and universality (Grollman, 1995; Speece & Brent, 1992). Recent research reveals that even preschool children can grasp these concepts if they understand that the function of the human body is to sustain life and that it needs food, air, and water to do so. They can then begin to infer that death is the opposite of life and that dead people no longer need to eat food or drink water (Slaughter & Lyons, 2003; Bering & Bjorklund, 2004). Understanding the biological causality of death is the hardest concept of death for children to master but is typically mastered by about age 10 (Kenyon, 2001). Paula, age 12, had clearly mastered the concept that all deaths ultimately involve a failure of internal biological processes: "When the heart stops, blood stops circulating, you stop breathing and that's it... there's lots of ways it can get started, but that's what really happens" (Koocher, 1974, pp. 407–408).

Children's level of understanding of death appears to be influenced by their level of cognitive development and their cultural and life experiences. Major breakthroughs in the understanding of death occur in the 5-to-7 age range—when Piaget would say children are making the transition from the preoperational stage of cognitive development to the concrete operational stage. Mature understanding of death is also correlated with IQ (Kenyon, 2001).

In addition, children's concepts of death are influenced by the cultural context in which they live and the specific cultural and religious beliefs to which they are exposed (Stambrook & Parker, 1987). For example, Jewish and Christian children in Israel, who are taught our Western concept of death, provide more "mature" answers to questions about death than Druze children, who are taught to believe in reincarnation (Florian & Kravetz, 1985). Understandably, a child who is taught that people are reincarnated after they die may not view death as an irreversible cessation of all life processes.

Within any society, children's unique life experiences will also affect their understanding of death. Children who have life-threatening illnesses or who have encountered violence and death in their own lives sometimes grasp death sooner than other children (O'Halloran & Altmaier, 1996). How parents and others communicate with children about death can also make a difference. How is a young child to overcome the

© Sesame Workshop

After the September 11 attack on the World Trade Center, the Sesame Workshop asked school-age children to draw pictures of their fears and worries. As one child wrote, "My worries is that terrist [sic] will harm my family, and I will be left with no family like the kids in New York" (Stepp, 2001, p. C4). Another child said: "I'm afraid we will be bombed again and it will be World War III. I hate technology" (Stepp, 2001, p. C1). Children's concepts of death are clearly affected by their sociocultural context and events like 9/11 and the Southeast Asian tsunami of 2004.

belief that death is temporary, for example, if parents and other adults claim that relatives who have died are "asleep"? And if a child is told that "Grandma has gone away," is it not logical to ask why she cannot hop a bus and return?

Experts on death insist that adults only make death more confusing and frightening to young children when they use such euphemisms. They point out that children often understand more than we think, as illustrated by the 3-year-old who, after her father explained that her long-ill and just deceased grandfather had "gone to live on a star in the sky," looked at him quizzically and said, "You mean he is dead?" (Silverman, 2000, pp. 2–3). Experts recommend that parents give children simple but honest answers to the many questions they naturally ask about death and capitalize on events such as the death of a pet to teach children about death and help them understand and express their emotions (Silverman, 2000). Appropriate programs can also help familiarize children with the concepts of life and death and accelerate the development of a mature understanding of death (Schonfeld & Kappelman, 1990; Slaughter & Lyons, 2003).

The Dying Child

Parents and doctors often assume that terminally ill children are unaware that they will die and are better off remaining so. Yet research shows that dying children are far more aware of what is happening to them than adults realize (Essa & Murray, 1994). Consider what Myra Bluebond-Langner (1977) found when she observed children ranging in age from 2 to 14 who had leukemia. Even preschool children arrived, over time, at an understanding that they were going to die and that death is irreversible. Despite the secretiveness of adults, these children noticed changes in their treatments and subtle changes in the way adults interacted with them, and they paid close attention to what happened to other children who had the same disease and were receiving the same treatments. Over time, many of these ill children stopped talking about the long-term future and wanted to celebrate holidays such as Christmas early. A doctor trying to get one boy to cooperate with a procedure said, "I thought you would understand, Sandy. You told me once you wanted to be a doctor." Sandy threw an empty syringe at the doctor and screamed, "I'm not going to be anything!" (p. 59).

How do terminally ill children cope with the knowledge that they are dying? They are not all the models of bravery that some people suppose them to be. Instead, they experience many of the emotions that dying adults experience (Waechter, 1984). Preschool children may not talk about dying, but they may reveal their fears by having temper tantrums or portraying violent acts in their pretend play. School-age children understand more about their situation and can talk about their feelings if given an opportunity to do so. They want to participate in normal activities so that they will not feel inadequate compared with their peers, and they want to maintain a sense of control or mastery, even if the best they can do is take charge of deciding which finger should be pricked for a blood sample.

So, children with terminal illnesses often become painfully aware that they are dying. They need the love and support of parents, siblings, and other significant individuals in their lives. In particular, they can benefit from a strong sense that their parents are there to care for them (Worchel, Copeland, & Barker, 1987) and from opportunities to talk about their feelings (Faulkner, 1997).

© Mark Sherman/Photo Network/PictureQuest

Children who are dying need to know that they are loved and to have opportunities to express their concerns and fears.

The Bereaved Child

Children's coping capacities are also tested when a parent, sibling, pet, or other loved one dies. Four major messages have emerged from studies of bereaved children: children grieve, they express their grief differently than adults do, they lack some of the coping resources that adults command, and they are vulnerable to long-term negative effects of bereavement (Osterweis, Solomon, & Green, 1984; Lieberman et al., 2003; Silverman, 2000).

Consider some of the reactions that have been observed in young children whose parents have died (Lewis & Lippman, 2004; Lieberman et al., 2003; Silverman, 2000). These children often misbehave or strike out in rage at their surviving parent; they can become unglued when routines such as playing airplane when eating oatmeal in the morning are not honored (Lieberman et al., 2003). They ask endless questions: Where is Daddy? When is he coming back? Will I get a new Daddy? Anxiety about attachment and separation are common; more than half of the bereaved children in one study reported being scared that other family members might die (Sanchez et al., 1994). At other times, bereaved children go about their activities as if nothing had happened, denying the loss or distracting themselves from it by immersing themselves in play. Alicia Lieberman and her colleagues (2003) characterize young children's responses as "cycles of intense distress, emotional withdrawal, anger, and emotional detachment" (p. 11). You can readily see how caregivers might be disturbed by some of these behaviors.

Because they lack some of the cognitive abilities and coping skills that older individuals command, it is natural that young children might have trouble grasping what has happened and attempt to deny and avoid emotions too overwhelming to face. Young children also have only concrete, behavioral coping strategies at their disposal. For example, 2-year-old Reed found comfort by taking out a picture of his mother and putting it on his pillow at night, then returning it carefully to the photo album in the morning (Lieberman et al., 2003). Older children are able to use cognitive coping strategies such as conjuring up mental representations of their lost parents (Compas et al., 2001).

What grief symptoms do children most commonly experience? Reactions differ greatly from child to child, but the preschooler's grief is likely to manifest itself in problems with sleeping, eating, toileting, and other daily routines (Osterweis et al., 1984; Oltjenbruns, 2001). Negative moods, dependency, and temper tantrums are also common. Older children express their sadness, anger, and fear more directly. However, somatic symptoms such as headaches and other physical ailments are also common (Worden & Silverman, 1996).

Well beyond the first year after the death, some bereaved children continue to display problems such as unhappiness, low self-esteem, social withdrawal, difficulty in school, and problem behavior (Worden & Silverman, 1996; Osterweis et al., 1984). In a longitudinal study of school-age children, one in five children who had lost a parent had serious adjustment problems 2 years after the death (Worden & Silverman, 1996; see also Downdney, 2000). Some even develop psychological problems that carry into adulthood—for example, depression and insecurity in later attachment relationships (Harris & Bifulco, 1991; Miralt, Bearor, & Thomas, 2001–2002).

However, most bereaved children—especially those who have effective coping skills and much social support—adjust quite well. They are especially likely to fare well if their surviving parent copes effectively with the loss (Kalter et al., 2002–2003). It is important for surviving parents and other adults who interact with bereaved children to recognize that children express their grief and cope with it in ways that reflect their level of development. It is also crucial to communicate to bereaved children that, although the lost parent cannot come back, the child will be loved and cared for (Lieberman et al., 2003). And, as this quote illustrates, it is good for children to be able to share their grief with others: "My father was a good man, a decent man, but he didn't know what to do. He was clueless. The message was not to talk about Mom. He thought he was protecting us from the pain by not reminding us of her" (Lewis & Lippman, 2004, p. xii).

Summing Up

Young children are naturally curious about death and form ideas about it from an early age. By age 5 to 7, and often earlier, they have mastered the concepts that death is final, irreversible, and universal and will later appreciate that death is ultimately caused by a failure of internal biological processes. Each child's grasp of death depends on her level of cognitive development, culture, and personal experiences of death. Terminally ill children often become painfully aware that they are dying. Bereaved children sometimes act out their grief and sometimes seem to deny the death because they lack coping skills. Some experience unhappiness, academic difficulties, and behavioral problems well beyond the first year mark, but most adjust with time. ■

The Adolescent

Adolescents typically understand death as the irreversible cessation of biological processes and are able to think in more abstract ways about it (Corr, 1995; Koocher, 1973). Adolescents do not necessarily face that they, too, will die; they take risks that they might not take if they truly believed that death is final, universal, and irreversible (Noppe & Noppe, 1996). However, they use their new cognitive capacities to ponder and discuss the meaning of death and such hypotheticals as an afterlife (Noppe & Noppe, 1997; Wass, 1991).

Indeed, a recent series of studies by Jesse Bering and David Bjorklund (2004) suggests that many adolescents and adults, although they clearly know that biological functions cease at death and although they believe more firmly than young children that all functions cease at death, share a belief with young children that psychological functions such as

Compared with children, adolescents often express abstract concepts of death influenced by their religious training. The 16-year-old girl who drew this picture explained: "The water represents the depth of death. The bubbles represent the releasing of the soul. The tree represents the memories we leave behind. The flame represents Hell and the halo represents Heaven."

knowing, believing, and feeling continue even after bodily functions have ceased. Belief in an afterlife is so common among humans, these researchers suggest, that it could be a product of evolution, although it could just as well be a learned belief because children are typically exposed to cultural beliefs about an afterlife from an early age.

Just as children's reactions to death and dying reflect their developmental capacities and needs, adolescents' reactions to becoming terminally ill are likely to reflect the themes of adolescence (Adams & Deveau, 1986; Stevens & Dunsmore, 1996). Concerned about their body images as they experience physical and sexual maturation, they may be acutely disturbed if their illness brings hair loss, weight gain, amputation, or other such physical changes. Wanting to be accepted by peers, they may feel like "freaks" or become upset when friends who do not know what to say or do abandon them. Eager to become more autonomous, they may be distressed by having to depend on parents and medical personnel and may struggle to assert their will and maintain a sense of control. Trying to establish their own identity and chart future goals, adolescents may be angry and bitter at having their dreams snatched from them.

Similarly, the reactions of adolescents to the deaths of family members and friends are likely to reflect the themes of the adolescent period (Balk & Corr, 2001; Tyson-Rawson, 1996). For example, even as teenagers become increasingly independent of their parents, they continue to depend heavily on their parents for emotional support and guidance. The adolescent whose parent dies may carry on an internal dialogue with the dead parent for years (Silverman & Worden, 1993). And, given the importance of peers in this developmental period, it is not surprising that adolescents are often devastated when a close friend dies in a car accident, commits suicide, or succumbs to a deadly disease. In one study, 32% of teenagers who lost a friend to suicide experienced clinical depression during the month after the suicide (Bridge et al., 2003). Yet grief over the loss of a friend is often not taken as seriously as grief over the loss of a family member (Ringler & Hayden, 2000).

Adolescents mostly grieve much as adults do. However, they are sometimes reluctant to express their grief for fear of seeming abnormal or losing control and may express their anguish instead through delinquent behavior and somatic ailments (Clark, Pynoos, & Goebel, 1994; Osterweis et al., 1984). The adolescent who yearns for a dead parent may feel that he is being sucked back into the dependency of childhood and may therefore bottle up these painful feelings (Raphael, 1983, p. 176):

> "When my mother died I thought my heart would break," recalled Geoffrey, age 14. "Yet I couldn't cry. It was locked inside. It was private and tender and sensitive like the way I loved her. They said to me, 'You're cool man, real cool, the way you've taken it,' but I wasn't cool at all. I was hot—hot and raging. All my anger, all my sadness was building up inside me. But I just didn't know any way to let it out."

Summing Up

By the time children reach adolescence, they have acquired a mature and more abstract concept of death, understanding it as a final cessation of life that is irreversible, universal, and biologically caused yet often believing in an afterlife. Whereas young children often express their grief indirectly through their behavior, older children and adolescents more directly express painful thoughts and emotions. In each period, children's reactions to bereavement or to the knowledge that they are dying reflect their developmental needs and the developmental tasks that they are facing. Thus, when a life-threatening illness strikes, the young child may most want reassurance of parental love and protection, the school-age child may most wish to keep up with peers in school, and the adolescent may most want to achieve a sense of identity and autonomy. ■

The Adult

For adults, dealing with the loss of a spouse or partner and accepting their own mortality can be considered normal developmental tasks (Röcke & Cherry, 2002). How, then, do adults cope with death and dying? We have already introduced models describing adults' experiences of dying and bereavement that partially answer that question. Here we will elaborate by examining bereavement from a family systems perspective then trying to define differences between normal and abnormal grief reactions.

Death in the Family Context

Given the importance of family attachments throughout the life span, it is not surprising that the deaths of family members are typically harder to bear than other deaths. You cannot fully understand bereavement unless you adopt a family systems approach and attempt to understand how a death alters relationships, roles, and patterns of interaction within the family, as well as interactions between the family and its environment (Shapiro, 2001; Silverman, 2000; Traylor et al., 2003). So examine some of the special challenges associated with three kinds of death in the family: the loss of a spouse, the loss of a child, and the loss of a parent.

The Loss of a Spouse

Most of what we know about bereavement is based on studies of widows and widowers. Experiencing the death of a spouse becomes increasingly likely as we age; it is something most women can expect to endure because women tend both to live longer than men and to marry men who are older than they are. The marital relationship is a central one for most adults, and the loss of a marriage partner or other romantic attachment figure can mean the loss of a great deal. Moreover, the death of a spouse often precipitates other changes—the need to move, enter the labor force or change jobs, assume responsibilities that the spouse formerly performed, parent single-handedly, and so on. Thus, widows or widowers must redefine their roles and even their identities in fundamental ways (Lopata, 1996; Parkes, 1996). If they are women, their wealth is also likely to decline substantially (Zick & Holden, 2000).

As noted earlier in this chapter, Colin Murray Parkes, in extensive research on widows and widowers younger than age 45, concluded that bereaved adults progress through overlapping phases of numbness, yearning, disorganization and despair, and reorganization. What toll does this grieving process take on the individual's physical, emotional, and cognitive functioning? Table 17.3 shows some of the symptoms that widows and widowers commonly report (Parkes, 1996; also see Bonanno & Kaltman, 2000). They are at risk for illness and physical symptoms such as loss of appetite and sleep disruption, and they tend to overindulge not only in alcohol but also in tranquilizers and cigarettes. Cognitive functions such as memory and decision making are often impaired, and emotional problems such as loneliness and anxiety are common. Most bereaved spouses do not become clinically depressed, but many display increased symptoms of depression in the year after the death (Wilcox et al., 2003).

Yet a recent study of bereaved elderly adults by George Bonanno and his colleagues reveals much diversity in patterns of response to loss. Members of a larger study sample who lost a spouse were studied longitudinally from an average of 3 years before the death of their spouse to 6 and 18 months afterward (Bonanno et al., 2002; Bonanno, Wortman, & Nesse, 2004). Gathering data both before and after the death of a spouse revealed patterns of adjustment over time that had not been evident in studies focused only on adjustment after a loss. Figure 17.3 graphs the average depression symptom scores displayed by the five subgroups of widows and widowers identified in the study:

- Common grief, with heightened then diminishing distress after the loss
- Chronic grief in which loss brings distress and the distress lingers
- Chronic depression in which individuals who were depressed before the loss remain so after it
- A depressed–improved pattern in which individuals who were depressed before the loss become less depressed after the death, perhaps because they were relieved of the stresses of coping with an unhappy marriage or an ill spouse
- A resilient pattern in which distress remains low

This study helps us understand that some bereaved people who display symptoms of depression were depressed even before the death, whereas others become depressed in response to their loss. The biggest surprise in the study, however, is that the resilient pattern involving low levels of distress turned out to be the most common pattern of response, char-

Table 17.3 Percentages of Bereaved and Nonbereaved Adults Reporting Various Symptoms within 14 Months of Loss

Symptoms	Bereaved	Nonbereaved
Admitted to hospital	12%	4%
Awakened during the night	27	8
Experienced changes in appetite	34	40
Increased alcohol consumption	19	2
Sought help for emotional problems	23	5
Wondered if anything is worthwhile	34	18
Worried by loneliness	44	17
Depressed or very unhappy (in past few weeks)	33	20
Felt restless	33	15
Believed memory was not all right	20	6
Found it hard to make up mind	36	22
Felt somewhat apart or remote even among friends	23	10

Responses were gathered in the Harvard Bereavement Study from men and women younger than age 45 who had lost their spouses 14 months before the interviews. Nonbereaved respondents were married adults matched to members of the bereaved sample so that they were similar in age, sex, family size, geographic area, nationality, and socioeconomic status.

SOURCE: Based on Parkes, 1996, Appendix Table 3.

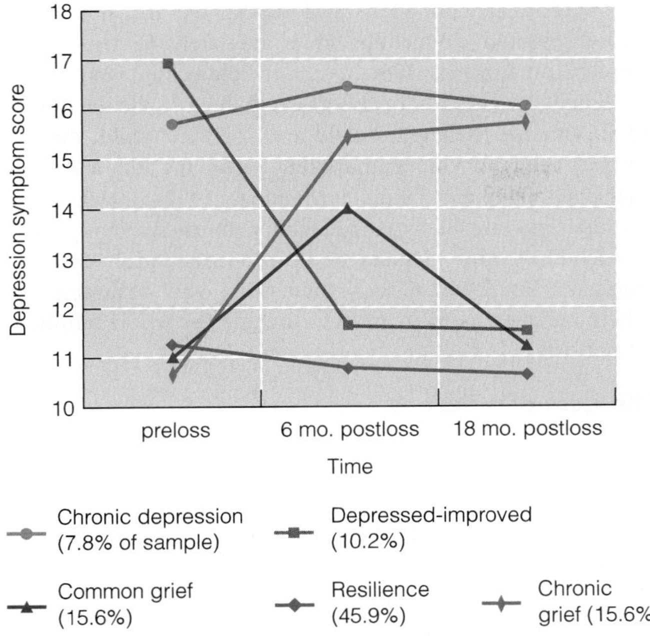

Figure 17.3 Depression symptom scores of five subgroups of elderly widows and widowers an average of 3 years before, 6 months after, and 18 months after the death of their spouse. In parentheses are the percentages of the sample showing each pattern. Notice that resilience—a low level of depression all along—is the most common response, contrary to our belief that all bereaved people must go through a period of significant distress.

acterizing almost half the sample. What is more, the resilient grievers were not just cold, unfeeling people who did not really love their partners. Rather, as indicated by the data collected before their spouses died, they seemed to be well adjusted and happily married people with good coping resources (Bonanno et al., 2002). Nor was there indication that they were defensively denying or avoiding painful feelings or that they needed counseling to help them express their grief (Bonanno, Wortman, & Nesse, 2004). Rather, although they experienced emotional pangs in the first months after the death, they were more comforted than most by positive thoughts of their spouses and simply seemed to cope effectively with their loss. Other research suggests that we should expect a greater proportion of young and middle-aged widows and widowers to display the common grief and chronic grief patterns of response, perhaps because the death of a spouse at these ages is off-time, unexpected, and more often violent (Kitson, 2000; Nolen-Hoeksema & Ahrens, 2002).

The individuals in Bonanno's study who were depressed before the death but recovered afterward are intriguing. They may have cared for spouses with dementia, cancer, and other terminal conditions for months or even years. Richard Schulz and his colleagues (Schulz et al., 2003) find that it is common among those who care for family members with dementia to experience more depression before the death than after. Indeed, more than 70% admit that the death came as a relief to both themselves and their loved one. As you saw in Chapter 15, caregiver burden can trigger depression (Schulz & Beach, 1999). Yet bereavement can also take a toll. For both reasons perhaps, widows and widowers as a group have higher-than-average rates not only of depression and illness but also of death (Stroebe, 2001b).

Many widows and widowers who experience significant grief begin to show signs of recovery in the second year after the death. Yet for some, grieving and symptoms of distress may continue for many, many years (Parkes & Weiss, 1983; Wortman & Silver, 2001). Darrin Lehman, Camille Wortman, and Allan Williams (1987) compared adults whose spouses had died in car accidents 4 to 7 years previously with similar nonbereaved adults. Even this long after their tragedies, bereaved adults showed more depression, hostility, and anxiety; had more worries; and felt less of a sense of psychological well-being than nonbereaved adults. Perhaps because these deaths were sudden and violent, 62% still had recurring thoughts that the death was unfair or that they had been cheated, and 68% said that they had been unable to find any meaning in the death.

In sum, the loss of a spouse can be a painful and damaging experience. During the first weeks and months after the death, the psychological pain is typically most acute, and the risks of developing serious physical or mental health problems or even dying are at a peak. Some widows and widowers experience emotional aftereffects for years, yet up to half of elderly widows and widowers show resilience and manage to cope without becoming highly distressed.

The Loss of a Child

> My child has died! My heart is torn to shreds. My body is screaming. My mind is crazed. The question is always present on my mind. Why? How could this possibly have happened? The anger is ever so deep, so strong, so frightening. (Bertman, 1991, p. 323, citing a mother's reflections on how she reacted to her 16-year-old daughter's death in a car accident after the initial numbness wore off)

No loss is more difficult for an adult than the death of a child (Cleiren, 1993; Rubin & Malkinson, 2001; Stroebe & Schut, 2001). Even when there is forewarning, the loss of a child is experienced as unexpected, untimely, and unjust (Sprang & McNeil, 1995). Compared with adults who have lost a spouse or a parent, parents who have lost a child are exceptionally angry, guilty, and depressed, and they have a greater number of physical complaints (Sanders, 1979–1980; Sprang & McNeil, 1995). Understandably, they experience a raging anger and often feel that they failed in their role as parent and protector (Rando, 1991). Their beliefs that the world is a good place, that life is meaningful, and that they are worthy people can all be shaken (Matthews & Marwit, 2003–2004). In one study, only 12% of parents whose adolescent or young adult child died of an accident, suicide, or homicide had found meaning in the death 1 year later, and only 57% had found it 5 years later (Murphy, Johnson, &

© Oleg Popov/Reuters/CORBIS

The death of a child can be devastating for parents.

Lohan, 2003b). The age of the child who dies has little effect on the severity of the grief: parents can experience severe grief reactions even after a miscarriage (Broen et al., 2004). Moreover, the death of an adult child is usually no less difficult to bear than the death of a younger child (Lesher & Bergey, 1988; Rubin & Malkinson, 2001).

The death of a child alters the family system, affecting the marital relationship, parenting, and the well-being of surviving siblings and grandparents. The marital relationship is likely to be strained because each partner grieves in a unique way and is not always able to provide emotional support for the other (Bohannon, 1990–1991). Strains are likely to be especially severe if the marriage was shaky before the death. The odds of marital problems and divorce tend to increase after the death of a child, although most couples stay together and some feel closer than ever (Dijkstra & Stroebe, 1998; Najman et al., 1993).

Grieving parents may also have difficulty giving their surviving children the love and support they need to cope with their loss. Children are deeply affected when a brother or sister dies, but their grief is often not fully appreciated (Lohan & Murphy, 2001–2002; Silverman, 2000). Siblings of children battling cancer, for example, may resent it if they are neglected by their parents, may be anxious about their own health, may feel guilty about some of the unsavory feelings of rivalry they have, and may feel pressure to replace the lost child in their parents' eyes (Adams & Deveau, 1987). One 12-year-old boy whose brother died described his experience this way: "My dad can't talk about it, and my mom cries a lot. It's really hard on them. I pretend I'm O.K. I usually just stay in my room" (Wass, 1991, p. 29). If siblings are isolated from their understandably upset parents or if their grief is not taken seriously, they may have an especially hard time recovering, whereas if their parents remain warm and supportive and encourage open discussion of feelings, they are likely to fare better (Applebaum & Burns, 1991; Graham-Pole et al., 1989).

Finally, grandparents also grieve following the death of a child, both for their grandchild and for their child, the bereaved parent. As one grandparent said, "It's like a double whammy!" (DeFrain, Jakub, & Mendoza, 1991–1992, p. 178). Grandparents are likely to feel guilty about surviving their grandchildren and helpless to protect their adult children from pain (Fry, 1997). Clearly, then, those who are attempting to help bereaved families need to include the whole family in their efforts.

The Loss of a Parent

Even if we escape the death of a child or spouse, the death of a parent is a normative life transition that most of us will experience. As noted already, some children experience long-lasting problems after the death of a parent. Fortunately, most of us do not have to face this event until we are in middle age. We are typically less emotionally dependent on our parents by then, and most of us are heavily invested in our own families. Moreover, we expect that our parents will die someday and have prepared ourselves, at least to some degree.

Perhaps for all of these reasons, adjusting to the death of a parent is usually not as difficult as adjusting to the death of a spouse or child (Leahy, 1992–1993). Yet it can be a turning point in an adult's life with effects on his identity and relationships with his spouse, children (who are grieving the loss of their grandparent), surviving parent, and siblings (Umberson, 2003). Adult children may feel vulnerable and alone in the world when their parents no longer stand between them and death, and they may redefine themselves to either take on the parent's qualities or reject them. Guilt about not doing enough for the parent who died is also common (Moss et al., 1993). These concerns take a toll: compared with adults who are not bereaved, adults who have lost a parent in the past 3 years have higher rates of psychological distress, alcohol use, and health problems (Umberson, 2003).

Challenges to the Grief Work Perspective

The view that has guided much of the research on bereavement we have described has come to be called the **grief work perspective**—the view that to cope adaptively with death, bereaved people must confront their loss, experience painful emotions, work through those emotions, and move toward a detachment from the deceased (Stroebe, 2001a). This view, which grew out of Freudian psychoanalytic theory, is widely held in our society, not only among therapists but among people in general, and it influences what we view as an abnormal reaction to death (Wortman & Silver, 2001). From the grief work perspective, either a chronic grief that lasts longer, is more intense than usual, or both, or an absence, inhibition, or delay of grief, in which the bereaved denies the loss and never seems to confront and express painful feelings, is viewed as "pathological" or "complicated" grief (see, for example, Raphael, 1983). This grief work perspective has now come under serious attack; questions have been raised about its assumptions that there is a right way to grieve, that bereaved people must experience intense grief to recover, and that they must sever their bonds with the deceased (Bonanno, 2004; Wortman & Silver, 2001).

First, cross-cultural studies reveal that there are many ways to grieve and suggest that the grief work model of bereavement may be culturally biased. An Egyptian mother may be conforming to her culture's norms of mourning if she sits alone, withdrawn and mute, for months or even years after a child's death. Likewise, a Balinese mother is following the rules of her culture if she is calm, composed, and even seemingly cheerful soon after a child's death (Wikan, 1988, 1991). We would be wrong to conclude, based on our own society's norms, that the Egyptian mother is suffering from chronic grief or the Balinese mother from absent or inhibited grief.

Second, there is surprisingly little support for the grief work perspective's assumption that bereaved individuals must confront their loss and experience painful emotions to cope successfully (Bonanno, 2004; Wortman & Silver, 2001). As you saw earlier, bereaved individuals who fail to show much emotional distress during the early months after the loss do not seem to pay for their lack of grief with a delayed grief reaction later—as the grief work model says they should. On the contrary, the individuals who adjust best to death are the resilient ones who display relatively little distress at any point in their bereavement, experience many positive emotions and thoughts, and manage to carry on with life despite their loss (Bonanno, 2004; Bonanno & Field, 2001).

Finally, the grief work view that we must break our bonds to the deceased to overcome our grief is being challenged. This view goes back to Sigmund Freud, who believed that bereaved people had to let go to invest their psychic energy elsewhere. By contrast, John Bowlby (1980) noticed that many bereaved individuals revise their internal working models of self and others and continue their relationships with their deceased loved ones on new terms (Bonanno & Kaltman, 1999; Noppe, 2000). Recent research supports Bowlby, suggesting that many bereaved individuals maintain their attachments indefinitely rather than severing those bonds, especially if they enjoyed a secure attachment before the death (Waskowic & Chartier, 2003). Bereavement rituals in some cultures (in Japan, for instance) are designed to ensure a continued bond between the living and the dead (Klass, 2001). Moreover, individuals who continue their bonds do not necessarily show poorer adjustment than those who do not, and some benefit from the continuing relationship (Field et al., 1999; Lohnes & Kalter, 1994).

Nigel Field and his colleagues (1999) have discovered that some forms of continuing attachment are healthier than others, however. They investigated whether continuing attachment to a deceased spouse was positively or negatively related to levels of grief symptoms among widows and widowers at 6 months, 14 months, and 25 months after their loss. It depended on the type of continuing attachment behavior displayed. Those who expressed their continuing attachment by having and sharing fond memories of the deceased and by sensing that their loved one was watching over and guiding

Is it pathological to maintain a relationship with a deceased parent for many years? Probably not. It is common practice in Japan to remember each morning during worship ancestors who have died, to leave them food and otherwise care for them, and to tell them about one's triumphs and disasters (Klass, 2001). Continuing attachment to rather than detachment from the deceased is normal in some cultural contexts.

them experienced relatively low levels of distress. By contrast, those who used their spouse's possessions to comfort themselves showed high levels of distress at the 6-month mark and little decrease in grief over the coming months. Continued obsession with the deceased is probably not healthy; in a follow-up to Field's study, maintaining a continuing bond with the deceased turned out to have more negative than positive effects 5 years after the death (Field, Gal-Oz, & Bonanno, 2003). Still, we should be cautious about labeling as abnormal individuals who sense the presence of a lost loved one and consult with him about important decisions years after a death.

So, norms for expressing grief vary widely across cultures; it is not clear that a person must experience emotional distress to adjust to a loss or that bereaved people who do not experience emotional distress will pay later with a delayed grief reaction; and people need not sever their attachment to the deceased to adjust to a loss. More fundamentally, researchers are now questioning the idea, embedded in the grief work model, that grief is a pathological process—like a disease that we catch, suffer from, and eventually get over (Bonanno, 2001). As you saw earlier, only about 15% of bereaved individuals experience complications of grief so severe that they can be described as pathological (Bonanno & Kaltman, 2000). What is more, it is common to experience positive emotions with the negative ones and to feel in the end that one has benefited from one's loss (Davis & Nolen-Hoeksema, 2001; Folkman &

Moskowitz, 2004; Harvey, 2001). Overall, we must conclude that grief takes many forms, involves positive and negative emotions, and is more complex and less pathological than the grief work model implies.

Who Copes and Who Succumbs?

Even if it is difficult to find the line between normal grief and pathological grief, we can still ask what risk and protective factors distinguish people who cope well with loss from people who cope poorly. Coping with bereavement is influenced by the individual's personal resources, the nature of the loss to be coped with, and the surrounding context of support and stressors.

Personal Resources

Just as some individuals are better able to cope with their own dying than others are, some are better equipped to handle the stresses of bereavement. Bowlby's attachment theory emphasizes that *early experiences in attachment relationships* influence the internal working models we form of self and other, how we later relate to others, and how we handle losses of relationships (Shaver & Tancredy, 2001; Noppe, 2000). If infants and young children receive loving and responsive care, they form internal working models of self and other that tell them that they are lovable and that other people can be trusted (see Chapter 14). Having a secure attachment style is associated with coping relatively well with the death of a loved one (Field et al., 2001; Waskowic & Chartier, 2003).

By contrast, infants or young children who receive inconsistent care or who suffer the loss of an important attachment figure are likely to develop an insecure attachment style and may have difficulty coping with loss later in life. They may, for example, develop a resistant (or ambivalent) style of attachment that leads them to overly depend on others and to display extreme and chronic grief and anxiety after a loss (Bowlby, 1980; Shaver & Tancredy, 2001). Or they may develop an avoidant attachment style. Recent research suggests that adaptation to loss is likely to be good if the individual is avoidant in the sense of being independent and does not need close relationships as much as most people do but that the grieving process is likely to be more difficult if the individual is both avoidant and anxious about relationships—that is, if she is afraid to get close to others for fear of being abandoned (Fraley & Bonanno, 2004).

Personality and coping style also influence how successfully people cope with death. For example, individuals who have difficulty coping tend to have low self-esteem (Lund et al., 1985–1986), to lack a sense that they are in control of their lives (Haas-Hawkings et al., 1985), and to be highly dependent (Bonanno et al., 2002). Many were experiencing psychological problems such as depression before they were bereaved (Bonanno, Wortman, & Nesse, 2004); many rely on ineffective coping strategies such as denial and escape through alcohol and drugs (Murphy, Johnson, & Lohan, 2003a). So, the enduring capacity of the individual to cope with life's problems is an important influence on bereavement outcomes.

The Nature of the Loss

Bereavement outcomes are also influenced by characteristics of the event with which the person must cope. The closeness of the person's *relationship to the deceased* is very important. Children grieve especially hard for parents to whom they were closely attached (Umberson & Chen, 1994), and spouses grieve especially hard for partners with whom they shared a common identity and on whom they were highly dependent (Carr et al., 2000; DeGarmo & Kitson, 1996). The *cause of death* can also influence bereavement outcomes. One reason the death of a child is so painful is that children's deaths are often the result of "senseless" and violent events such as car accidents and homicides.

The Context of Supports and Stressors

Finally, grief reactions are influenced positively by the presence of a strong social support system and negatively by additional life stressors (Lopata, 1996; Stroebe & Schut, 2001). Social support is crucial at all ages. It is especially important for the young child whose parent dies to have good substitute parenting (Raveis, Siegel, & Karus, 1999). Brothers and sisters can help each other cope (Hurd, 2002). Indeed, family members of all ages recover best when the family is cohesive and family members can share their emotions (Kissane et al., 1996; Traylor et al., 2003). Bereaved individuals indicate that they are helped most by family and friends who say they are sorry to hear of the loss, make themselves available to serve as confidants, and let bereaved individuals express painful feelings freely (Herkert, 2000; Lehman, Ellard, & Wortman, 1986). It often falls to the bereaved person to teach would-be supporters how best to be supportive because many of us have no idea what to do or say (Dyregrov, 2003–2004).

Just as social support helps the bereaved, additional stressors hurt. For example, outcomes tend to be poor for widows who must cope with financial problems after bereavement and for widowers who have difficulty managing household tasks without their wives (Lopata, 1996; Umberson, Wortman, & Kessler, 1992). Widows and widowers may have more than the

© Maggie Hallahan/CORBIS

Sensitive social support can make all the difference to the bereaved.

usual difficulty adjusting if they must also take on the challenges of caring single-handedly for young children, finding a new job, or moving (Parkes, 1996; Worden & Silverman, 1993).

By taking into account the person who has experienced a death, the nature of the death, and the context surrounding it, we can put together a profile of the individuals who are most likely to develop long-term problems after bereavement. These individuals have had an unfortunate history of interpersonal relationships, perhaps suffering the death of a parent when they were young or experiencing insecurity in their early attachments. They have had previous psychological problems and generally have difficulty coping effectively with adversity. The person who died is someone on whom they depended greatly, and the death was untimely and seemingly senseless. Finally, these high-risk individuals lack the kinds of social support that can aid them in overcoming their loss, and they are burdened by stresses in addition to the stress of bereavement.

Bereavement and Human Development

The grief work perspective on bereavement has tended to put the focus on the negative side of bereavement—on the damaging effects of loss and the need to "recover" from "symptoms" of grief. As you have seen, however, psychologists are coming to appreciate that bereavement and other life crises also have positive consequences and sometimes foster personal growth (Davis & Nolen-Hoeksema, 2001; Folkman & Moskowitz, 2004; Tedeschi & Calhoun, 2004). Granted, it can be a painful way to grow, and we could hardly recommend it as a plan for optimizing human development. Still, the literature on death and dying is filled with testimonials about the lessons that can be learned.

Many bereaved individuals believe that they have become stronger, wiser, more loving, and more religious people with a greater appreciation of life (Tedeschi & Calhoun, 2004). Many widows master new skills, become more independent, and emerge with new identities and higher self-esteem, especially those who depended heavily on their spouses and then discover that they can manage life on their own (Carr, 2004; Lopata, 1996). These testimonials make the point:

> A bereaved spouse: "I feel that [in] my present relationship I'm better able to be a real good friend, and I don't take things so personally." (Davis & Nolen-Hoeksema, 2001, p. 735)
>
> A widow, surprised by how successfully she had built a new and satisfying life: "I'm doing things I never thought I could do. I hate being alone but I have good friends and we care about each other. I'm even traveling. I enjoy my work. I never thought I'd hear myself say that I don't mind being single." (Silverman, 1981, p. 55)
>
> And a mother whose infant died: "Now I can survive anything." (DeFrain, Taylor, & Ernst, 1982, p. 57)

So perhaps it is by encountering tragedy that we learn to cope with tragedy, and perhaps it is by struggling to find meaning in death that we come to find meaning in life.

Summing Up

All deaths in the family have the potential to cause emotional damage and to perturb the family system, although many widows and widowers are resilient. The death of a child often takes a greater toll than the death of a parent. Recent research challenges the grief work perspective, which holds that there is a "normal" way to grieve and that it involves experiencing and working through painful emotions and breaking the bond to the deceased. Prolonged grief is especially likely among individuals who have insecure attachment styles or ineffective coping skills; who had close relationships with loved ones who died violently and senselessly; and who lack positive social support, face additional stressors, or both. Yet positive emotions and personal growth are common among the bereaved. ■

Taking the Sting Out of Death

Several efforts are under way to help children and adults who are dying or who are bereaved grapple with death and their feelings about it. Here is a sampling.

For the Dying

Dramatic changes in the care of dying people have occurred with the past few decades, thanks partly to the efforts of Elisabeth Kübler-Ross and others. Still, many signs suggest that hospital personnel continue to place much emphasis on curing terminally ill patients and keeping them alive and little on controlling their pain and allowing them to "die with dignity." Out of such concerns has arisen an approach to caring for the dying person that is intended to be more humane: the hospice.

A **hospice** is a program that supports dying people and their families through a philosophy of "caring" rather than "curing" (Connor, 2000; Saunders, 2002). One of the founders of the hospice movement and of St. Christopher's Hospice in London, Dr. Cicely Saunders (2002), puts it this way: "I remain committed to helping people find meaning in the end of life and not to helping them to a hastened death" (p. 289).

The hospice concept spread quickly to North America, where hospices have been established in most communities to serve individuals with cancer, AIDS, and other life-threatening diseases. In many hospice programs today, however, there is no care facility like St. Christopher's; instead, dying patients stay at home and are visited by hospice workers.

What makes hospice care different from hospital care? Whether hospice care is provided in a facility or at home, it entails these key features (Connor, 2000; Corr & Corr, 1992; Siebold, 1992):

1. The dying person and his family—not the "experts"—decide what support they need and want.

2. Attempts to cure the patient or prolong his life are deemphasized.
3. Pain control is emphasized.
4. The setting for care is as normal as possible (preferably the patient's own home or a homelike facility that does not have the sterile atmosphere of many hospital wards).
5. Bereavement counseling is provided to the family before and after the death.

Do dying patients and their families fare better when they spend their last days together receiving hospice care? Hospice leaders point to suggestive evidence that patients have less interest in physician-assisted suicide when they have access to hospice care and their pain is better controlled (Foley & Hendin, 2002). In one study, a third of individuals cared for by a home health care agency, nursing home, or hospital felt they received too little emotional support, whereas only about 20% of those receiving home hospice services felt this way (Teno et al., 2004). And an evaluation of hospice facility care, at-home hospice care, and conventional hospital care in Great Britain found that hospice patients spent more of their last days without pain, underwent fewer medical interventions and operations, and received nursing care that was more oriented to their emotional needs (Seale, 1991). Their families grieved as much as those of hospitalized patients but were more satisfied with the care they received (see also Teno et al., 2004). In still another study, spouses, parents, and other relatives of dying people who received hospice care displayed fewer symptoms of grief and greater well-being 1 to 2 years after the death than similar relatives who had coped with a death without benefit of hospice care (Ragow-O'Brien, Hayslip, & Guarnaccia, 2000).

© Gary Buss/Getty Images

Hospice care helps people live even while they are dying.

The hospice approach may not work for all, but for some it means an opportunity to die with dignity, free of pain and surrounded by loved ones. The next challenge may be to extend the hospice philosophy of caring rather than curing to children. Of children who die of cancer, half die in a hospital and many suffer from pain that is not adequately controlled, possibly because their doctors and parents cannot accept that the child is dying and so continue to treat the cancer aggressively (Wolfe et al., 2000; Stillion & Papadatou, 2002).

For the Bereaved

Most bereaved individuals do not need psychological interventions to help them cope with death; they deal with this normal life transition on their own and with support from significant others. At the same time, there are many options for bereaved individuals, ranging from counseling intended to prevent problems before they develop to interventions designed to treat serious psychological disorders precipitated by a loss (Kazak & Noll, 2004; Raphael, Minkov, & Dobson, 2001). Bereaved individuals at risk for depression—because of a history of losses, a history of depression or other psychological disorders, a lack of social support, or other factors—may benefit from therapy or counseling aimed at preventing them from becoming depressed (Murray et al., 2000; Zisook & Shuchter, 2001). And, like anyone with major depression, bereaved individuals who become seriously depressed can benefit from individual or group psychotherapy and antidepressant medication (see Chapter 16).

Because death takes place in a family context, a family systems approach and family therapy often make a good deal of sense, especially when children are involved (Kazak & Noll, 2004; Moore & Carr, 2000). Family therapy can help bereaved parents and children communicate more openly and share their grief. It can also enable parents to maintain the kind of warm and supportive parenting style that can be so important in facilitating their children's recovery.

Another approach to helping the bereaved that has proven popular is the mutual support or self-help group (Goodkin et al., 2001; Silverman, 2000; Zisook & Shuchter, 2001). One such program is Compassionate Friends, serving parents whose children have died. Other groups are aimed at widows and widowers. Parents without Partners, THEOS (They Help Each Other Spiritually), The Widowed Person's Service, and similar groups bring widows and widowers together to offer everything from practical advice on such matters as settling finances or finding a job to emotional support and friendship.

Bereavement support groups have also been designed for HIV-infected individuals who have experienced the AIDS-related deaths of partners, family members, and friends. Karl Goodkin and his colleagues (2001) have found that such groups can reduce the distress these people experience, help them adopt more effective coping strategies, and increase their use of social support. Moreover, the researchers were able to demonstrate that the intervention had significant positive effects on participants' neuroendocrine and immune system functioning and reduced the number of times they visited doctors, suggesting that support groups might have positive effects on health outcomes.

Participation in mutual support groups can be beneficial for bereaved parents, helping them find meaning in the death of their child (Murphy et al., 2003a). And, compared with widows who do not participate in support groups, participants tend to be less depressed and anxious, use less medication, and have a greater sense of well-being and self-esteem (Lieberman & Videka-Sherman, 1986). Perhaps this is because other bereaved people are in the best position to understand what a bereaved person is going through and to offer effective social support. One widow summed it up this way: "What's helpful? Why, people who are in the 'same boat.' Unless you've been there you just can't understand" (Bankoff, 1983, p. 230).

Summary Points

1. In defining death as a biological process, the Harvard definition of total brain death has been influential; many controversies surround issues of active and passive euthanasia and assisted suicide, and the social meanings of death vary widely.

2. The average life expectancy for a newborn in the United States has risen to 76½ years, higher than that in less developed countries. Death rates decline after infancy and rise after early adulthood as accidents give way to chronic diseases as the primary causes of death.

3. Programmed theories of aging hold that aging is governed by species heredity and individual genetic endowment, whereas damage theories of aging focus on an accumulation of random damage caused by destructive free radicals and other agents.

4. Elisabeth Kübler-Ross stimulated much concern for dying patients by describing five stages of dying, but, as Edwin Shneidman emphasized, the dying experience ever-changing emotions, depending on the course of their disease and on their personality.

5. Bereavement precipitates grief and mourning, which are expressed, according to the Parkes/Bowlby attachment model, in overlapping phases of numbness, yearning, disorganization and despair, and reorganization.

6. Infants may not comprehend death but clearly grieve, protesting and despairing after separations.

7. Children are curious about death and usually understand by age 5 to 7 that it is a final cessation of life processes that is irreversible and universal, later realizing that it is ultimately caused by internal biological changes. Terminally ill children often become very aware of their situation, and bereaved children often experience bodily symptoms, academic difficulties, and behavioral problems.

8. Adolescents understand death more abstractly and cope with dying and bereavement in ways that reflect the developmental themes of adolescence.

9. Widows and widowers experience many physical, emotional, and cognitive symptoms and are at increased risk of dying. The death of a child is often even more difficult for an adult to bear; the death of a parent, because it is expected, is often easier.

10. The grief work perspective has been challenged; what is normal depends on the cultural context, and many people display resilience, adjusting well by expressing few negative and many positive emotions after the death and by continuing rather than severing their attachments.

11. Intense and prolonged grief is especially likely among individuals who had painful early attachment experiences, who lack positive personality traits and coping skills, who had close relationships with individuals who died violently and senselessly, and who lack social support, face additional stressors, or both.

12. Successful efforts to take the sting out of death have included hospice programs for dying patients and their families and individual therapy, family therapy, and mutual support groups for the bereaved.

Critical Thinking

1. Look carefully at the five stages of dying that Elisabeth Kübler-Ross believes terminally ill patients experience and at the four phases of adjustment bereaved people experience according to Colin Murray Parkes and John Bowlby. What common themes do you see, and how do they differ?

2. Lucy (age 3), Lilly (age 9), and Lally (age 16) have all been diagnosed with cancer. They have been given chemotherapy and radiation treatments for several months but seem to be getting worse rather than better. Write a short monologue for each child conveying (a) how she understands death and (b) her major concerns and wishes based on what you know of normal development at her age.

3. Many people have misconceptions about what is normal and what is abnormal when it comes to grieving, as this chapter has illustrated. Identify three such misconceptions and, using relevant research, show why they are just that—misconceptions.

4. On what can proponents of assisted suicide and proponents of hospice care agree—and how do their views differ?

Key Terms

total brain death, 485
assisted suicide, 486
living will, 486
euthanasia, 487
life expectancy, 488
programmed theories of aging, 489
damage theories of aging, 489
maximum life span, 489
Hayflick limit, 490
telomere, 490
progeria, 490
free radical theory, 491
antioxidants, 491
caloric restriction, 492
denial, 492
bereavement, 495
grief, 495
mourning, 495
anticipatory grief, 495
Parkes/Bowlby attachment model of bereavement, 495
grief work perspective, 504
hospice, 507

Media Resources

Websites to Explore

Visit Our Website

For a chapter tutorial quiz and other useful features, visit the book's companion website at *http://psychology.wadsworth.com/sigelman_rider5e.* You can also connect directly to the following sites:

The End of Life: Exploring Death in America
The National Public Radio show *All Things Considered* aired a 6-month special starting in November 1997 on death. Its companion website has an archive of audio files and transcripts for each of the episodes, additional readings, and resources for exploring death from different angles.

Hospice
This site has good material on many death and dying topics, including articles about the hospice concept, talking to children about death, pain relief, and more.

Partnership for Caring
This website is a source of living wills and other advance directives for those who want to plan their dying experience.

Widows and Widowers
This website on coping with grief and loss, maintained by the American Association of Retired Persons (AARP), has useful guidance for bereaved people of all ages. The AARP's Widowed Persons Service provides support groups for widows and widowers.

Compassionate Friends
This site is for parents and others coping with the death of a child. It includes media stories on grief and the results of a survey of bereaved parents.

Supercentenarians
The Gerontology Research Group maintains a web page devoted to centenarians. It lists the names and profiles of "supercentenarians"—individuals who have lived to age 110 or older—worldwide; it also includes the photos of many.

Understanding the Data: Exercises on the Web

For additional insight on the data presented in this chapter, try the exercises for the following table and figure at *http://psychology.wadsworth.com/sigelman_rider5e:*

Table 17.1 Leading causes of death for different age groups in the Unites States

Figure 17.3 Depression symptom scores of five subgroups of elderly widows and widowers an average of 3 years before, 6 months after, and 18 months after the death of their spouse

Life-Span CD-ROM

Go to the Wadsworth Life-Span CD-ROM for further study of the concepts in this chapter. The CD-ROM includes narrated concept overviews, video clips, a multimedia glossary, and additional activities to expand your learning experience. For this chapter, check out the following clips, and others, in the video library:

VIDEO The Hayflick Limit

VIDEO The Hospice Approach

VIDEO Bereavement

DEVELOPMENTAL PsychologyNow™

Developmental PsychologyNow is a web-based, intelligent study system that provides a complete package of diagnostic quizzes, a personalized study plan, integrated multimedia elements, and learning modules. Check it out at *http://psychology.wadsworth.com/sigelman_rider5e/now.*

Fitting the Pieces Together

Major Trends in Development

Infants (Birth to Age 2)

Preschool Children (Ages 2 through 5)

School-Age Children (Ages 6 through 11)

Adolescents (Ages 12 through 19)

Young Adults (Ages 20 through 39)

Middle-Aged Adults (Ages 40 through 64)

Older Adults (Age 65 and Up)

Major Themes in Human Development

Nature and Nurture Truly Interact in Development

We Are Whole People throughout the Life Span

Development Proceeds in Multiple Directions

There Is Both Continuity and Discontinuity in Development

There Is Much Plasticity in Development

We Are Individuals, Becoming Even More Diverse with Age

We Develop in a Cultural and Historical Context

We Are Active in Our Own Development

Development Is a Lifelong Process

Development Is Best Viewed from Multiple Perspectives

Courtesy of Alice Kladnik

OUR SURVEY OF HUMAN DEVELOPMENT from conception to death, and of the many forces that influence it, is now complete. In this epilogue, our goal is to help you integrate what you have learned—to see the "big picture." We summarize significant trends in physical, cognitive, personal, and social aspects of development, age period by age period. We then pull together the major themes that have emerged from recent theory and research.

Major Trends in Development

Throughout this book, you have seen that each phase of the life span has distinct characteristics. Here, at the risk of oversimplifying, we offer portraits of the developing person in seven periods of life—sketches that show how the strands of development, intertwined, make a whole person.

Infants (Birth to Age 2)

What is most striking about infant development is the staggering speed with which babies acquire all the basic capacities that make us human. Because of orderly and rapid development before birth, a newborn starts life marvelously equipped to adapt to her environment using reflexes, to take in information through all of her senses, and to learn from and remember her experiences. The rapid growth of body and brain during the first 2 years after birth then transforms this neonate into a toddler who is walking, talking, and asserting a newfound sense of self.

As the cortical centers of the brain mature and become organized, and as infants gain sensory and motor experience, many automatic reflexes disappear and are replaced by voluntary motor behaviors. In a predictable sequence, infants sit, creep and crawl, and then walk independently, around 1 year of age; during their first year, they also perfect a pincer grasp and become better able to manipulate objects with their hands. As they become more able to make sense of the perceptual world, and as their motor skills advance, they explore the world around them more effectively—and actively contribute to their own cognitive development in the process.

As babies progress through Jean Piaget's sensorimotor period, they develop their minds through their own active efforts to perceive and act upon the world. They come to understand that objects have permanent existence, even when they are out of sight. They also acquire symbolic capacity—the ability to let one thing stand for another—which is central to intellectual activity throughout the remainder of the life span. By the end of the sensorimotor period, they can use symbols such as images to mentally devise solutions to problems before trying them. Meanwhile, their capacities to learn and remember are expanding, allowing them, toward the end of the first year, to recall events in the absence of cues and imitate actions after a delay and, by age 2, to deliberately reconstruct events that happened months earlier. After cooing and babbling, they will utter their first words at age 1 and form two-word sentences such as "Go car" by age 2. As Lev Vygotsky would remind us, these cognitive and linguistic breakthroughs grow out of the child's social interactions with parents and other guides.

As their cognitive capacities expand, infants become more aware of themselves as individuals. By 18 months, they

Courtesy Library of Congress

Throughout history, artists have tried to capture the nature of life-span development.

recognize themselves in the mirror and know that they are girls or boys. But infants are individuals from birth, each with a distinctive and genetically influenced temperament that serves as a foundation for later personality.

Infants' temperaments, with their parents' styles of interacting with them, influence how successfully they resolve Erik Erikson's first psychosocial conflict, that of trust versus mistrust, and whether they form secure, resistant, or avoidant attachments to their caregivers starting around 7 months. The parent–child attachment relationship dominates the social world of the infant and is a training ground for later social relationships, as theorized by John Bowlby and Mary Ainsworth. Cognitive advances and daily exchanges with attachment figures produce more sophisticated social skills that infants then apply in their at first clumsy encounters with peers. Equipped with the ability to perceive and act upon the environment, with impressive cognitive and linguistic capacities, with an awareness of self, and with internal working models of self and other derived from their experiences in attachment relationships, infants are ready to venture into a larger social world.

Preschool Children (Ages 2 through 5)

During the preschool years, 2-year-olds who toddle and teeter along and speak in two-word sentences become young children ready for formal schooling. As their brains continue to mature and as they gain motor experience, preschool children acquire the gross motor control they need to hop and catch balls and the fine motor skills they need to trace letters and use scissors.

During Piaget's preoperational stage of cognitive development, young children make wonderful use of their symbolic capacity, mastering all the basic rules of language (with the help of adults willing to converse with them) and joining other children in imaginative sessions of social pretend play. However, young children often have difficulty with problems that require logical thinking. They fail Piaget's tests of conservation, thinking that the juice poured from a stocky glass into a tall, narrow glass somehow becomes "more juice." They are egocentric at times, failing to appreciate differences between their own perspectives and those of other individuals and assuming that their listeners know what they know. They are distractible and lack some of the information-processing skills that allow older children to think about two or more aspects of a problem at once and to use strategies such as rehearsal and organization to learn and remember more efficiently.

Preschoolers' personalities continue to take shape as they struggle with Erikson's conflicts of autonomy versus shame and initiative versus guilt. If all goes well, they develop the confidence to assert themselves and to carry out bold plans, and their self-esteem is high. They learn a good deal about themselves and other people, developing a theory of mind that allows them to predict and explain human behavior in terms of mental states, although they still describe people largely in terms of physical characteristics and activities rather than inner qualities. Although relatively lacking in self-control, they increasingly become socialized to internalize and follow rules of morality. And in no time, they also learn what they must know to be a boy or a girl in their society.

Preschool children's attachments to their caregivers continue to be central in their social worlds, but they hone their social skills in interactions with peers, learning to take their playmates' perspectives, engage in cooperative play, and form friendships. Preschoolers are endlessly fascinating: charming and socially skilled but a bit egocentric, immensely curious and intellectually alive but sometimes illogical, here one moment but off on some new adventure the next.

School-Age Children (Ages 6 through 11)

Compared with preschool children, elementary school children seem considerably more self-controlled, serious, skilled, and logical. Their bodies grow slowly and steadily each year, and they continue to refine their motor skills and use their senses ever more intelligently by directing their attention where it most needs to be directed. As they enter Piaget's concrete operations stage, they become able to perform in their heads actions that previously had to be performed with their hands. They can mentally add, subtract, classify, and order objects; grasp conservation problems that fool preschoolers; and draw logical conclusions about the workings of the physical world. They master the fine points of the rules of language, use what Vygotsky called *private speech* (speech inside the head) as a tool in problem solving, and become better able to take the perspectives of their listeners in conversations. They acquire the memory strategies and other information-processing skills needed to do schoolwork. And, although their scores on intelligence tests can fluctuate from year to year, their IQs begin to predict fairly well their intellectual standing as adolescents or as adults.

The cognitive growth that occurs during the school years, combined with social experience, allows children to understand themselves and other people in terms of inner personality traits and underlying motives. School-age children work through Erikson's conflict of industry versus inferiority as they attempt to master new skills, compare themselves to their classmates, and absorb feedback about where they stand in their reading groups and where they finish in races. The unrealistically high self-esteem of the preschooler drops as children gain a more accurate view of their strengths and weaknesses. Most children also develop fairly consistent personalities, at least parts of which survive into adulthood.

School-age children also continue to learn about and conform to prevailing social standards regarding how boys and girls should behave, but their thinking is more flexible than that of preschoolers. Under the guidance of parents and teachers, and through their interactions with peers, children learn the values and moral standards of the society around them. Most are at Lawrence Kohlberg's level of preconventional morality, in which what matters most is whether their acts will be rewarded or punished.

The social world of school-age children is more extensive than that of infants and preschool children. Family life is still important, but more time is spent with peers—usually peers of the same sex—playing organized games and developing caring friendships, or chumships. Youngsters who are rejected by their peers and who do not have friends miss these important social learning opportunities and tend to become maladjusted adults. Teachers, coaches, TV characters, and sports stars also help children gain the skills and values they will need to do the serious work of adulthood.

Adolescents (Ages 12 through 19)

Adolescence, the passage between childhood and adulthood, is a time of substantial physical, cognitive, and social change. Adolescents adjusting to their growth spurt and to the sexual maturation of their bodies around 12 to 14 years are naturally preoccupied with their physical appearance and are often more upset by their misshapen noses or gargantuan feet than by any intellectual or character flaws they may possess. Puberty brings not only new physical capacities and unfamiliar sexual urges but also new, more adultlike relationships with members of the other sex and with parents.

Meanwhile, as the brain undergoes a growth spurt, particularly in the prefrontal areas of the cortex that are involved in planning and sustained attention, the mind undergoes its own metamorphosis. The child who could reason logically about real-world problems becomes the adolescent who can think systematically about worlds that do not even exist and ideas that contradict reality. When adolescents fully master Piaget's formal operations, they can formulate and test hypotheses to solve scientific problems and can grasp abstract theories and philosophies. These and other new cognitive capacities sometimes leave adolescents susceptible to adolescent egocentrism, confused about what to believe, painfully aware of gaps between what is and what should be, and rebellious when their parents or other authority figures are not "logical" enough for their tastes.

Cognitive gains also put adolescents in a position to think about themselves and other people in more sophisticated ways. Teenagers begin to describe themselves in more abstract terms, referring to their core values and philosophies of life. They are more introspective and self-aware than they were as children and can analyze themselves and other people to determine what makes them tick. By late adolescence, many can integrate their self-perceptions into a coherent sense of who they are, resolving Erikson's conflict of identity versus role confusion and charting careers and other life goals. Conventional moral reasoning is achieved as young adolescents first emphasize the importance of being a "good boy" or "good girl," as defined by parents and society, and later appreciate the need for law and order in the larger social system.

Partly because teenagers become more physically and cognitively mature, and partly because society demands that they prepare themselves for adult roles, social relationships undergo their own transformations during the adolescent years. The balance of power in the family shifts so that adolescents, although best served by an authoritative parenting style, increasingly participate in making decisions about their lives. Adolescents become more involved in peer activities, intimate friendships with same- and other-sex peers, and dating relationships, often showing heightened conformity to gender-role norms. Heightened conformity to peer influence gives many adolescents a brush or two with the law, but the peer group serves the useful function of helping children who depend heavily on their parents become adults who are less reliant on either parents or peers. Although about 20% of adolescents experience emotional storm and stress during this period of the life span, most teenagers emerge with impressive physical, intellectual, and social competencies and with at least preliminary notions of who they are and what they will become.

Young Adults (Ages 20 through 39)

The years of infancy, childhood, and adolescence are all a preparation for entry into adult life. Physiologically, young adults are at their peak; strength, endurance, reaction time, perceptual abilities, and sexual responsiveness are all optimal, even though the aging process is taking slight, and usually not even noticeable, tolls. Early adulthood is also a period of peak cognitive functioning. Some young adults will solidify and possibly expand upon their command of formal operational thought, especially in their areas of expertise. Most adults continue to be conventional moral reasoners, but about one in six begins to think at the level of postconventional morality, grasping the moral principles underlying society's rules and regulations. And, if they continue to use their minds, young adults will often improve on the IQ test scores they obtained as adolescents and gain expertise.

It is good that young adults are physically and intellectually capable, because they face many challenges. They must often continue to work on the adolescent task of identity formation, exploring different options before settling on a career direction. Meanwhile, they are likely to be working through Erikson's early-adult crisis of intimacy versus isolation, testing relationships, and, if all goes well, committing themselves to a partner. Young adults are changed and often stressed by marriage, new parenthood, and other events of the family life cycle; challenging work can expand their capacities but unemployment can threaten their self-esteem.

In view of the many life changes experienced by young adults, perhaps it is not surprising that this period is characterized by higher divorce rates and more stress-related mental health problems than the later adult years. However, for most young adults, this is also an exciting and productive time of life, a time for gaining expertise, independence, and confidence.

Middle-Aged Adults (Ages 40 through 64)

Middle adulthood often strikes as a more settled period than early adulthood, but it is not devoid of change. Gradual changes in the body's characteristics and capacities that began in the 20s and 30s may become noticeable. Gray hairs (or no hair), a shortness of breath after exercise, and a need for reading glasses or a louder TV proclaim that a person is aging. Women experience the changes of menopause around age 50; both men and women become more vulnerable to heart dis-

Courtesy of Alice Kladnik

☾ Alice at 6 months old. She was born July 9, 1906, in Holly, Michigan, to Gertrude Belle Wright and John Henry Alger.

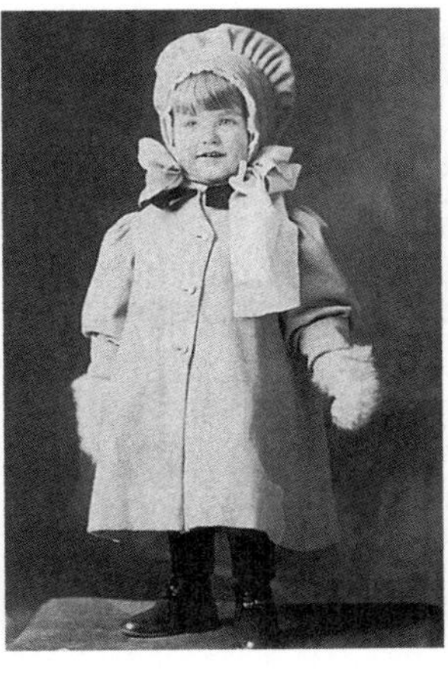

☾ As a 2-year-old, Alice was very active. One of her earliest memories is riding in a basket swing suspended from the living room ceiling.

☾ As a teenager, Alice loved sports. She played on a softball team and started playing tennis with her father at age 10. At 18, she was the first Women's State Tennis Champion in Wisconsin, a title she would earn twice. In college, she worked hard to help support her family through the Depression. Finally, she had to drop out of medical school. She continued taking night courses and met her future husband, whom she followed to California.

☾ Alice married in 1939 at age 33. She and her husband, George, traveled frequently and visited Catalina during the first year of their marriage. Three years later, they started a family. Alice worked as a manuscript typist for several well-known authors in Santa Barbara, California, and taught tennis to help support the family.

☾ At 45, Alice enjoyed outings with her three young children at Monterey, California. She was involved in her children's activities at home and school.

☾ Still active at 92, Alice plays tennis 3 days a week and is seen here flying a sailplane in the Santa Ynez Valley, California. She is also a Literacy Volunteer and knits cotton bandages for lepers through the Direct Relief Foundation. She reads voraciously and loves crossword puzzles. She sadly gave up playing bridge at age 90 because she was tired of being the "designated driver."

☾ At 80, Alice poses with her grown children and husband of 47 years in Santa Barbara, California.

☾ At 95, Alice is still active and continues to play weekly tennis matches. Here she is seen tending fruit trees in the orchard at her home.

ease, cancer, and other chronic illnesses. Yet most of the physical changes that middle-aged adults experience occur slowly and are not severe, giving people plenty of time to adjust to and compensate for them.

Meanwhile, although intellectual capacities generally are in top form, middle-aged adults gradually gain some intellectual capacities and lose others. They amass knowledge and often perform better than young adults on measures of crystallized intelligence (vocabulary or general information). Moreover, they build expertise that allows them to solve everyday problems effectively, and they reach peaks of creative achievement in their careers. Yet toward the end of middle adulthood, some individuals may feel that their memories are slipping or may begin to struggle with the sorts of unfamiliar problems that measure fluid intelligence.

Personalities that took form during childhood and that solidified during adolescence and early adulthood tend to persist into later adulthood, although significant change is possible. According to Erikson, middle-aged adults successfully resolve the conflict of generativity versus stagnation if they can invest their energies in nurturing the younger generation or in producing something of lasting value, but they may experience a sense of stagnation if they feel they have failed their children or are preoccupied with their own needs. Midlife crisis is quite rare. Indeed, after the nest empties and middle-aged adults are freed of major parenting responsibilities, they can enjoy their marriages, take pride in their grown children and grandchildren, contribute to their communities, and become more androgynous, expressing both their masculine and feminine sides.

Older Adults (Age 65 and Up)

The poet Robert Browning expressed a very positive image of late adulthood when he wrote: "Grow old along with me! The best is yet to be, the last of life for which the first was made." By contrast, William Shakespeare, in *As You Like It* (Act II, Scene 7), characterized the seventh and final age of life as "sec-

Summary of Physical, Cognitive, Personal, and Social Development across the Life Span

Period	Physical Development	Cognitive Development
Infant (Birth to 2 years)	Brain rapidly grows and is pruned; physical growth is rapid. Reflexes are followed by more voluntary motor control; walking occurs at 1 year. Functioning senses are available at birth; there is an early ability to understand sensory information.	Sensorimotor period: Through senses and actions, infants acquire symbolic capacity and object-permanence concept. Cooing and babbling are followed by one-word and two-word sentences. Learning capacity and recognition memory are present from birth; there are improvements in recall.
Preschool child (2 to 5 years)	Rapid brain development continues. Coordination and fine motor skills improve. Perceptual abilities are good; attention span is short.	Preoperational stage: Thought is guided by perceptions rather than logic. Symbolic capacity (language acquisition and pretend play) blossoms. There are some limits in information-processing capacity, use of memory strategies, and reasoning.
School-age child (6 to 11 years)	Physical growth is slow; motor skills gradually improve. Children have increased ability to control attention and use the senses intelligently.	Concrete operations stage: Logical actions occur in the head; children master conservation. They also master fine points of language; memory strategies and problem solving with concrete objects improve. IQs begin to stabilize.
Adolescent (12 to 19 years)	Adolescents experience a brain spurt, a growth spurt, and attainment of sexual maturity. Physical functioning improves. They are concerned with body image.	Formal operations stage: Hypothetical and abstract thought emerge; scientific problem solving begins. Attention and information-processing skills continue to improve, linked to brain growth spurt.
Young adult (20 to 39 years)	This is the time of peak functioning, but a gradual decline in physical and perceptual capacities begins.	Intellectual functioning is mostly stable, and peak expertise and creative achievement often occur. Fluid intelligence may begin to decline, but crystallized knowledge is maintained well.
Middle-aged adult (40 to 64 years)	Physical declines become noticeable (e.g., some loss of endurance, need for reading glasses). Chronic illness increases. Menopause and male andropause occur.	These adults develop sophisticated cognitive skills, especially in areas of expertise. There is the possibility of growth beyond formal thought and gains in knowledge.
Older adult (65 years and older)	Physical decline continues; more chronic disease, disability, and sensory impairment are common; and reaction time slows. But there is also continued plasticity and reorganization of the brain in response to intellectual stimulation.	Declines in cognition are common but not inevitable. Slower learning, memory problems, declines in IQ and problem solving occur, especially if skills are rarely exercised, but crystallized intelligence survives longer than fluid.

ond childishness and mere oblivion; sans teeth, sans eyes, sans taste, sans everything." The truth lies somewhere between the two: Old age brings some losses and declines in functioning, but it is also, for most, a period of continued growth and many satisfactions.

By the time adults are in their 60s and 70s, most of them have a physical impairment—a chronic disease, a disability, failing eyesight or hearing, or, at the least, a slower nervous system and slower reactions. Aging and disease, it seems, are inseparable. As they enter their 80s and 90s, more adults take longer to learn things, experience occasional memory lapses, or have difficulty solving novel problems. Although the odds of Alzheimer's disease increase relentlessly with age, only about 5% of elderly people have it or other forms of dementia. Most retain the knowledge that they have crystallized over a lifetime and the cognitive and linguistic skills that they practice every day.

Moreover, most adults adapt to physical and cognitive declines. They typically continue to carry out daily activities effectively, and they enjoy just as much self-esteem and life satisfaction as younger adults do. They do not crumble when facing life changes such as retirement or widowhood. They continue to lead active social lives, use their sophisticated social cognitive skills to understand other people and to engage in complex moral reasoning, and enjoy close ties with both family and friends. In the end, most are able to successfully resolve Erikson's conflict of integrity versus despair, finding meaning in their lives and coming to terms with the inevitability of death.

These, then, are the broad themes of later life. Yet what may be most striking of all about elderly adults is their immense diversity. Many older adults are healthy, active, and highly capable; others show signs of physical, sensory, or cognitive decline; still others suffer from Alzheimer's or other incapacitating diseases. Moreover, each adult carries into old age unique abilities, knowledge, personality traits, and values, and each will cope with the challenges of aging and dying in his own characteristic way.

Table 18.1 summarizes much of this information about physical, cognitive, personal, and social development within

Personal Development	Social Development
Infants acquire a sense of self, self-recognition, and early signs of theory of mind such as joint attention. They gain awareness of gender identity. Temperament becomes a basis for later personality. They undergo Erikson's conflict of trust versus mistrust.	These are social beings from birth. They are attached to a caregiver at 7 months; separation and stranger anxiety follow. They increase social skills with parents and peers and gain the capacity for simple pretend play. Theirs is a family-centered lifestyle.
Concrete, physical self-concept. A gender role is rapidly acquired. Children master the theory of mind concept that people can have false beliefs; they have an early conscience at 2 years but largely have a self-serving morality. There are conflicts of autonomy versus shame and initiative versus guilt.	Parent–child relationship is still central in the social world. Increased social cognitive abilities allow more cooperation with peers; social pretend play blossoms. First exposure to schooling occurs.
Self-concept includes psychological traits. Personality "gels." Strong gender typing occurs. Children have mostly preconventional morality centered on consequences for themselves. Much social comparison occurs when they are coping with the conflict of industry versus inferiority.	Involvement with same-sex peers increases; close chumships are formed. Role-taking skills advance. Play centers on organized games with rules. School and television are important socialization agents.
Adolescents have a more abstract and integrated self-concept. They adjust to sexuality and a gender role. Conventional moral reasoning reflects internalization of society's rules. They experience a conflict of identity versus role confusion.	Peak peer involvement and conformity occurs. More emotionally intimate friendships are followed by dating relationships. Parent–child relationship becomes more equal; autonomy increases. School and career exploration prepare them for adult roles.
Identity continues to be defined. Some shift from conventional to postconventional moral reasoning. There is increased confidence. Some experience a divergence of gender roles with new parenthood. Personality is fairly stable. They face a conflict of intimacy versus isolation.	Social networks continue to expand; romantic relationships form. Most establish families and assume roles as spouses and parents. Careers are launched; job switching is common. This is a period of much life change; there is a high risk of divorce and psychological problems.
Personality continues to be stable; for a minority, midlife questioning and androgyny shift. There may be a conflict of generativity versus stagnation.	The nest empties and the grandparent role is often added to existing roles. High responsibility is taken for younger and older generations. Career is more stable, and peak success is attained. Family and work roles dominate.
Most maintain their characteristic personality traits, self-esteem, and life satisfaction. Many grow as they resolve conflict of integrity versus despair.	Close ties to family and friends continue; loneliness is rare. Generally there is a smooth adjustment to retirement and continuity of social activities. For women especially, loss of spouse is normative and requires adjustment.

each period of the life span. This table can serve as a handy description of typical developmental changes. However, an understanding of human development is not complete without an understanding of some of the processes behind these changes.

Major Themes in Human Development

Another way in which to leave you with the big picture is to highlight some major generalizations about human development and the processes behind it. Many of these larger themes are incorporated in the life-span developmental perspective introduced in Chapter 1 (Baltes, 1987; Baltes, Lindenberger, & Staudinger, 1998); some represent stands on the developmental issues laid out in Chapter 2; and most have been echoed throughout this book. We leave you with the following thoughts.

Nature and Nurture Truly Interact in Development

The nature–nurture issue, which we have spotlighted throughout this book, has been largely resolved. It is clear that multiple causal forces, representing both nature and nurture and ranging from changes in cell chemistry to changes in the prevailing culture, conspire and interact to shape the course of human development. Biological and environmental influences jointly explain both universal developmental trends and individual differences in development. This is precisely the perspective taken by contextual and systems theories of development (such as Urie Bronfenbrenner's bioecological model, introduced in Chapter 1, or Gilbert Gottlieb's evolutionary–epigenetic systems perspective, introduced in Chapter 2).

Consider a universal accomplishment such as acquiring language. Biological maturation, guided by a specieswide genetic blueprint, clearly makes this achievement possible because no amount of stimulation from adults can make a 1-month-old speak sentences. Yet, even though an infant is maturationally ready, language skills will not be acquired without the input from the environment available in all societies—namely, opportunities to converse with speakers of the language. So it goes for many other developmental milestones: Little happens unless the individual is maturationally ready to learn and has the requisite learning experiences.

Why do individuals differ in, for example, their command of language skills? We could argue that it is because different people inherit different intellectual potentials, but we would also have to acknowledge that a genetic potential for high intelligence will never be realized if a child has no opportunities for intellectual stimulation. We could stress the importance of stimulation, but we would have to acknowledge that children with the genes for high intelligence are more likely to actively seek, elicit, and profit from such stimulation than children with limited genetic potential. In short, the experiences we have influence whether our genetic potentials are realized or not (gene–environment interactions), and the genes we inherit influence what experiences we seek and have and how we respond to them (gene–environment correlations). When there is goodness of fit between genetic predisposition and environment, nature and nurture work together in the person's favor.

The twin and adoption studies—and, more recently, molecular genetics studies—conducted by behavior geneticists also testify to the importance of both nature and nurture. Genetic differences among us help explain variation in virtually every human trait that has been studied, from hair color to verbal ability to depression proneness and social attitudes. Yet environmental factors count, particularly the unique (nonshared) experiences that make us different from our siblings. Depending on which aspect of human development we study, we may find that either heredity or environment is more influential, but we cannot escape the conclusion that development always reflects the ongoing, interacting, and ever fascinating contributions of both.

We Are Whole People throughout the Life Span

As our review of major developments in each life phase should make clear, it is the intermeshing of physical, cognitive, personal, and social development that gives each period of the life span—and each individual human—a distinctive and coherent quality. Thus, that 7-month-old infants become attached to their caregivers is not a milestone in social development divorced from other aspects of development. The maturation of sensory and motor abilities permits infants to crawl after their parents to maintain the proximity they desire, and their cognitive growth makes them aware that caregivers continue to exist when they leave the room (and therefore can be retrieved). The emergence of attachment bonds, in turn, affects development in other areas—for example, by providing toddlers with the security that allows them to explore the world around them and, in the process, develop their motor

© Myrleen Ferguson Cate/PhotoEdit

Advances in motor development open up possibilities for cognitive and social development.

skills and cognitive capacities. All the threads of development are interwoven in the whole developing person.

Development Proceeds in Multiple Directions

Chapter 5 introduced Heinz Werner's (1957) orthogenetic principle, which states that development proceeds from global states to states of increasing differentiation and integration of specific, differentiated states into coherent wholes. The orthogenetic principle is a useful way of summarizing many developmental trends. The single, undifferentiated cell formed at conception becomes billions of highly specialized cells (neurons, blood cells, and so on), all organized into functioning systems (such as the brain). The young infant flails its whole body as a unit (global response); the older child moves specific parts of the body on command (differentiation) and coordinates separate movements to ride a bike (integration). Similarly, young children describe other people's personalities in global terms ("He's nice" or "She's mean"); school-age children develop a more differentiated vocabulary of personality trait labels; and adolescents become true personality theorists, integrating all they have learned about their companions—contradictions included—into coherent theories about what makes these people tick.

Yet not all developmental change is a matter of acquiring more complex and organized behaviors or progressing toward some "mature" endpoint. As you have seen, human development involves gains and losses at every age and systematic changes that make us neither better nor worse than we were before but simply different. Thus, children who are gaining many academic learning skills are also losing some of their intrinsic motivation to learn as they progress through school, and older adults are losing mental speed but gaining knowledge, and sometimes even wisdom, that helps them compensate for slower information processing.

Paul Baltes has suggested that every gain may have its corresponding loss, and every loss its corresponding gain. Alice James, sister of pioneering psychologist William James and author Henry James, saw this even as her vision failed: "All loss is gain. Since I have become so near-sighted I see no dust or squalor, and therefore conceive of myself as living in splendor" (James cited in Baltes, Smith, & Staudinger, 1992, p. 158). We simply must abandon the tired view that human development consists of growth or improvement up to adulthood, stability into middle age, and decline in old age.

There Is Both Continuity and Discontinuity in Development

As you have seen throughout this book, developmentalists have long grappled with the issue of continuity versus discontinuity in human development. You should now appreciate the wisdom of staking out a middle ground on the continuity–discontinuity issue.

For example, research supports Piaget's claim that children progress through qualitatively different stages of cognitive development, but we now know that these advances in cognitive development are achieved gradually and occur faster in familiar than in less familiar domains of cognitive functioning (Flavell, Miller, & Miller, 1993). It seems that development often proceeds in a continuous, gradual manner that leads to stagelike discontinuities—qualitatively different performances that make us appreciate just how much growth has occurred.

Similarly, you have seen that some traits, including general intelligence and Big Five personality traits such as extraversion–introversion, carry over from childhood and become even more stable and consistent during adulthood. However, this continuity or consistency is imperfect, and there is ample room for change. A bright child may lose intellectual capacity if she is abused and neglected at home or attends inferior schools, and an introverted child may gain confidence and blossom into a more outgoing individual with the aid of supportive friends. Such discontinuity means that predicting the character of the adult from knowledge of the child is risky, even in the face of much continuity in development.

There Is Much Plasticity in Development

Repeatedly you have seen that humans of all ages are characterized by considerable plasticity—by a remarkable capacity to change in response to experience and to get off one developmental pathway and onto another. Thus, infants whose intellectual development is stunted by early malnutrition can catch up if they are given an adequate diet and enriching experiences. Adults not only learn new intellectual tricks but sprout new neural synapses and even new neurons in response to experience—evidence that the brain is plastic throughout the life span and that the first 3 years after birth are not the only years during which intellectual stimulation is important (Thompson & Nelson, 2001).

Evidence of plasticity and change in later life is especially heartening to those who want to foster healthy development. Contrary to what Sigmund Freud believed, early experiences rarely make or break us. Instead, there are opportunities throughout the life span—within limits—to undo the damage done by early traumas, to teach new skills, and to redirect lives along more fruitful paths. If adverse early experiences are followed by adverse later experiences, we can expect poor outcomes. But if potentially damaging early experiences are offset by favorable later experiences, we can expect developing humans to display considerable plasticity and resilience.

We Are Individuals, Becoming Even More Diverse with Age

In any human development textbook, there is a tendency to emphasize developmental phenomena shared by all or most individuals—to highlight the regularities and commonalities. We share a good deal with our fellow developing humans. But remember that each of us is truly one of a kind. Indeed, the diversity of developing humans is so great that it often seems impossible to generalize about them.

Individuality is apparent starting at birth if you look closely at each infant's temperament, daily rhythms, and rate of development. As people age, their individual genetic endowments express themselves more fully, and they increasingly accumulate their own unique histories of life experiences. The result? You can tell a good deal about an individual knowing that he is 2 weeks or 2 years old, whereas you know little about a person simply knowing that she is 25 or 65. Because diversity increases with age, elderly adults are the most diverse group of humans and therefore the age group you should work hardest to avoid stereotyping (Andrews, Clark & Luszcz, 2002; Morse, 1993).

We Develop in a Cultural and Historical Context

Repeatedly you have seen that humans are embedded in a sociocultural context that affects their development, a central theme in the sociocultural theory of Vygotsky and the bioecological theory of Bronfenbrenner (Bronfenbrenner & Morris, 1998; Vygotsky, 1978). Human development takes different forms in different cultures, socioeconomic groups, racial groups, and ethnic groups; human development in the 12th or 17th century was different from human development in the 20th century; and each person's development is influenced by social changes and historical events occurring during his lifetime.

We know, for example, that children reach puberty earlier and adults live longer now than they did a century ago. Today's cohorts of adults are also healthier and are functioning better intellectually and maintaining their intellectual capacities longer than adults who were born early in the 20th century and who received less education and poorer health care (Costa, 2002). Future cohorts of adults may maintain their physical and mental abilities even longer. Changes in the family and in men's and women's roles, technological and scientific breakthroughs such as the World Wide Web and the Human Genome Project, the terrorist attack on the World Trade Center and Pentagon and its aftermath, and significant historical events and social changes yet to take place may all make human development in the 21st century different from human development in the 20th century.

We develop in a cultural and historical context.

We Are Active in Our Own Development

Early developmental theorists tended to view humans as passively shaped by forces beyond their control. Sigmund Freud saw the developing child as driven by biological urges and molded by early experiences in the family; John Watson and other early learning theorists emphasized that human behavior is controlled by environmental stimuli. Jean Piaget did much to alter this image of developing humans by emphasizing how children actively explore the world around them and actively invent their own understandings, rather than merely absorbing lessons fed to them by adults. Piaget's insights about the developing child are firmly embedded in our assumptions about human development at all ages. Certainly we are affected by those around us and are sometimes the passive recipients of environmental influence. But just as certainly, we create our own environments, influence those around us, and, by doing so, contribute to our own development. It is this ongoing, dynamic transaction between an active person and a changing environment, each reciprocally influencing the other, that steers development.

Development Is a Lifelong Process

Developmentalists are more aware than ever of the importance of understanding links between earlier and later development, as illustrated by the emergence of the field of developmental psychopathology with its emphasis on the various pathways that can lead to normal or abnormal developmental outcomes. It is valuable to study infancy, adolescence, or any other developmental period. But it is more valuable to view behavior during any one phase of life from a life-span perspective. It helps to understand that the teenage girl who bickers with her parents in an effort to forge her own identity might not have the confidence to do so unless she had enjoyed a warm, secure attachment with them as an infant and child—and that this adolescent's quest for a separate identity and increased independence will ready her for intimacy and interdependence with another person. Because development is a process, it helps to know where it started and where it is heading.

Development Is Best Viewed from Multiple Perspectives

As this book testifies, many disciplines have something to contribute to a comprehensive understanding of human development, and we need them all. Geneticists, developmental biologists, neuroscientists, and other representatives of the biological sciences must help us understand the genes, hormones, and neural networks that guide human development and aging and how they both affect and are affected by environmental factors. Meanwhile, psychologists must help us understand the individual and his social relationships, and anthropologists, sociologists, historians, and economists must contribute their analyses of the changing sociocultural context in which that individual develops.

Multiple theories must also be brought to bear on the task of understanding human development. As we noted in Chapter 2, many developmental scientists are eclectics: They embrace several theories rather than feeling that they must select one and reject the rest. Psychoanalytic, social learning, cognitive developmental, and contextual and systems theories all have something important to say about how and why we change and remain the same as we age. We can thank stage theories for showing us that people all over the world develop along certain well-worn pathways and contextual theories and for adding that human development can take different directions depending on the day-to-day transactions between the maturing individual and the particular social world in which she is developing.

Often, it seems that the more you learn about a topic, the more you realize how much more there is to learn. This is certainly true of human development. As developmental scientists increasingly incorporate contextual assumptions into their thinking, they are asking new questions that might not have occurred to them in the past about how transactions between changing people and their changing environments play themselves out over the years. In the study of human development, then, there are always more questions than answers. We find this both a humbling and an inspiring thought. And we hope that you, too, feel both humbled and inspired as you complete your introduction to life-span human development. We hope that you are intrigued enough to observe more closely your own development and that of those around you—or even to take further course work. And we sincerely hope that you will use what you learn to steer your own and others' development in healthier directions.

Glossary

A, not B, error The tendency of 8- to 12-month-old infants to search for a hidden object in the place they last found it (A) rather than in its new hiding place (B).
ability grouping The practice in education of grouping students according to ability and educating them in classes with students of comparable academic or intellectual standing; also called ability tracking or simply tracking.
acceptance–responsiveness A dimension of parenting capturing the extent to which parents are supportive, sensitive to their children's needs, and willing to provide affection and praise when their children meet their expectations.
accommodation In Piaget's cognitive developmental theory, the process of modifying existing schemes to incorporate or adapt to new experiences. Contrast with *assimilation.* In vision, a change in the shape of the eye's lens to bring objects at differing distances into focus.
acquired immune deficiency syndrome (AIDS) The life-threatening disease in which the human immunodeficiency virus (HIV) destroys the immune system and makes victims susceptible to rare, so-called opportunistic, infections that eventually kill them. AIDS is transmitted through sexual activity, drug needle sharing, and from mother to child before or during birth.
activity A dimension of temperament that refers to the energy level of an individual.
activity–passivity issue The issue in developmental theory centering on whether humans are active contributors to their own development or are passively shaped by forces beyond their control.
activity theory A perspective holding that aging adults will find satisfaction to the extent that they maintain an active lifestyle. Contrast with *disengagement theory.*
adaptation In Piaget's cognitive developmental theory, a person's inborn tendency to adjust to the demands of the environment, consisting of the complementary processes of assimilation and accommodation.
adolescence The transitional period between childhood and adulthood that begins with puberty and ends when the individual has acquired adult competencies and responsibilities.
adolescent egocentrism A characteristic of adolescent thought that involves difficulty differentiating between the person's own thoughts and feelings and those of other people; evident in the personal fable and imaginary audience phenomena.
adolescent growth spurt The rapid increase in physical growth that occurs during adolescence.
age effects In developmental research, the effects of getting older or of developing. Contrast with *cohort effects* and *time of measurement effects.*
age grades Socially defined age groups or strata, each with different statuses, roles, privileges, and responsibilities in society.
age norms Expectations about what people should be doing or how they should behave at different points in the life span.
age of viability A point (around the 24th prenatal week) when a fetus may survive outside the uterus if the brain and respiratory system are well enough developed and if excellent medical care is available.
ageism Prejudice against elderly people.
agency An orientation toward individual action and achievement that emphasizes traits of dominance, independence, assertiveness, and competitiveness; considered masculine.
age-related macular degeneration Damage to cells in the retina responsible for central vision.
aging To most developmentalists, positive, negative, and neutral changes in the mature organism; different from *biological aging.*
alphabetic principle The idea that the letters in printed words represent the sounds in spoken words.
Alzheimer's disease A pathological condition of the nervous system that results in an irreversible loss of cognitive capacities; the leading cause of dementia in later life.
amniocentesis A method of extracting amniotic fluid from a pregnant woman so that fetal body cells within the fluid can be tested for chromosomal abnormalities and other genetic defects.
amnion A watertight membrane that surrounds the developing embryo, regulating its temperature and cushioning it against injuries.
amoral Lacking any sense of morality; without standards of right and wrong.
androgenized female A genetic female who was exposed to male sex hormones during the prenatal period and therefore developed malelike external genitals and some masculine behaviors.
androgens Male hormones that help trigger the adolescent growth spurt and the development of the male sex organs, secondary sex characteristics, and sexual motivation.
androgyny A gender-role orientation in which the person blends both positive masculine-stereotyped and positive feminine-stereotyped personality traits.
androgyny shift A psychological change that begins in midlife, when parenting responsibilities are over, in which both men and women retain their gender-typed qualities but add to them qualities traditionally associated with the other sex, thus becoming more androgynous.
andropause The slower and less-dramatic male counterpart of *menopause,* characterized by decreasing levels of testosterone and symptoms that include low libido, fatigue and lack of energy, erection problems, memory problems, and loss of pubic hair.
anorexia nervosa A life-threatening eating disorder characterized by failure to maintain a normal weight, a strong fear of weight gain, and a distorted body image; literally, "nervous lack of appetite."
anoxia A lack of sufficient oxygen to the brain that may result in neurological damage or death.
anticipatory grief Grieving before death for what is happening and for what lies ahead.
antioxidant Vitamins C, E, and similar substances that may increase longevity, although not for long, by inhibiting the free radical activity associated with oxidation and in turn preventing age-related diseases.

Apgar test A test routinely used to assess a newborn's heart rate, respiration, color, muscle tone, and reflexes immediately after birth and 5 minutes later; used to identify high-risk babies.
artificial insemination A method of conception that involves injecting sperm from a woman's partner or from a donor into the uterus.
Asperger syndrome An autistic spectrum disorder in which the child has normal or above-average intelligence, has good verbal skills, and wants to establish social relationships but has seriously deficient mind-reading and social skills.
assimilation Piaget's term for the process by which children interpret new experiences in terms of their existing schemata. Contrast with *accommodation.*
assisted reproduction technologies (ARTs) A range of methods used to help a couple conceive a child, from fertility drugs to in vitro fertilization.
assisted suicide Making available to individuals who wish to commit suicide the means by which they may do so, such as when a physician provides a terminally ill patient who wants to die with enough medication to overdose.
at risk Children who have a higher than normal chance of either short-term or long-term problems because of genetic defects, prenatal hazards, or perinatal damage.
attachment A strong affectional tie that binds a person to an intimate companion and is characterized by affection and a desire to maintain proximity.
attachment theory The theory of close relationships developed by Bowlby and Ainsworth and grounded in ethological theory (with psychoanalytic theory and cognitive theory); it says that close emotional bonds such as parent–child attachments are biologically based and contribute to species survival.
attention Focusing perception and cognition on something in particular.
attention deficit hyperactivity disorder (ADHD) A disorder characterized by attentional difficulties, impulsive behavior, and overactive or fidgety behavior.
authoritarian parenting A restrictive style of parenting combining high demandingness–control and low acceptance–responsiveness in which adults impose many rules, expect strict obedience, and often rely on power tactics rather than explanations to elicit compliance.
authoritative parenting A flexible style of parenting combining high demandingness–control and high acceptance–responsiveness in which adults lay down clear rules but also grant a fair amount of autonomy to their children and explain the rationale for their restrictions.
autism A pervasive and severe developmental disorder that begins in infancy and is characterized by such problems as an aversion to social contact, deviant communication or mutism, and repetitive, stereotyped behavior.
autobiographical memory Memory of everyday events that the individual has experienced.
automatization The process by which information processing becomes effortless and highly efficient as a result of continued practice or increased expertise.
autonomous morality The most mature Piagetian stage of morality in which rules are viewed as agreements between individuals that can be changed through a consensus of those individuals and in which the older child or adolescent pays more attention to intentions than to consequences in judging actions. Contrast with *heteronomous morality.*
autonomy The capacity to make decisions independently, serve as one's own source of emotional strength, and otherwise manage life tasks without being overdependent on other people; an important developmental task of adolescence.
autonomy versus shame and doubt The psychosocial conflict in which toddlers attempt to demonstrate their independence from and control over other people; second of Erikson's stages.
avoidant attachment An insecure infant–caregiver bond or other intimate relationship characterized by little separation anxiety and a tendency to avoid or ignore the attachment object upon reunion.
babbling An early form of vocalization that appears between 4 and 6 months of age and involves repeating consonant–vowel combinations such as "baba" or "dadada."
baby biographies Carefully recorded observations of the growth and development of children by their parents over a period; the first scientific investigations of development.
baby boom generation The huge generation of people born between 1946 (the close of World War II) and 1964.
beanpole family A multigenerational family structure characterized by many small generations.
behavioral genetics The scientific study of the extent to which genetic and environmental differences among individuals are responsible for differences among them in traits such as intelligence and personality.
behavioral inhibition A temperamental characteristic reflecting a person's tendency to withdraw from unfamiliar people and situations.
behaviorism A school of thinking in psychology that holds that conclusions about human development should be based on controlled observations of overt behavior rather than on speculation about unconscious motives or other unobservable phenomena; the philosophical underpinning of early theories of learning.
belief–desire psychology The theory of mind reflecting an understanding that people's desires and beliefs guide their behavior and that their beliefs are not always an accurate reflection of reality; evident by age 4. Contrast with *desire psychology.*
bereavement A state of loss that provides the occasion for grief and mourning.
beta-amyloid A toxic protein that injures neurons and is located in the senile plaques associated with Alzheimer's disease.
big-fish–little-pond effect The phenomenon in which a student's academic self-concept and performance are likely to be more positive in an academically unselective school than in a highly selective one with many high-achieving students.
Big Five The five major dimensions used to characterize people's personalities: neuroticism, extraversion, openness to experience, agreeableness, and conscientiousness.
bioecological model Bronfenbrenner's model of development that emphasizes the roles of both nature and nurture as the developing person interacts with a series of environmental systems (microsystem, mesosystem, exosystem, and macrosystem).
biological aging The deterioration of organisms that leads inevitably to their death.
blastocyst A hollow sphere of about 100 to 150 cells that the zygote forms by rapid cell division as it moves through the fallopian tube.
breech presentation A delivery in which the fetus emerges feet first or buttocks first rather than head first.
bulimia nervosa A life-threatening eating disorder characterized by recurrent eating binges followed by purging activities such as vomiting.
caloric restriction A technique demonstrated to extend the life span of laboratory animals involving a highly nutritious but severely calorie-restricted diet.
caregiver burden The psychological distress associated with providing care for someone with physical, cognitive, or both types of impairment.
carrier In genetics, individuals who possesses a recessive gene associated with a dis-

ease and who, although they do not have the disease, can transmit the gene for it to offspring.
case study method An in-depth examination of an individual that often involves compiling and analyzing information from a variety of sources such as observing, testing, and interviewing the person or people who know the individual.
cataracts A pathologic condition of the eye involving opacification (clouding) of the lens that can impair vision or cause blindness.
catch-up growth A phenomenon in which children who have experienced growth deficits will grow rapidly and catch up to the growth trajectory they are genetically programmed to follow.
categorical self A person's classification of the self along socially significant dimensions such as age and sex.
centenarian An individual who lives to be 100 years of age.
centration In Piaget's theory, the tendency to focus on only one aspect of a problem when two or more aspects are relevant.
cephalocaudal principle The principle that growth proceeds from the head (cephalic region) to the tail (caudal region).
cerebral cortex The convoluted outer covering of the brain involved in voluntary body movements, perception, and higher intellectual functions such as learning, thinking, and speaking.
cerebral palsy A neurological disability caused by anoxia that is associated with difficulty controlling muscle movements.
cesarean section A surgical procedure in which an incision is made in the mother's abdomen and uterus so that the baby can be removed through the abdomen.
child-directed speech Speech used by adults speaking with young children, it involves short, simple sentences spoken slowly and in a high-pitched voice, often with much repetition and with exaggerated emphasis on key words.
childhood amnesia A lack of memory for the early years of a person's life.
child effects model A model of family influence in which children are believed to influence their parents rather than vice versa.
chorion A membrane that surrounds the amnion and becomes attached to the uterine lining to gather nourishment for the embryo.
chorionic villus sampling An alternative to amniocentesis in which a catheter is inserted through the cervix to withdraw fetal cells from the chorion for prenatal testing to detect genetic defects.
chromosome A threadlike structure made up of genes; in humans, there are 46 chromosomes in the nucleus of each cell.
chromosome abnormalities Conditions in which a child has too few, too many, or incomplete chromosomes because of errors in the formation of sperm or ova.
chronosystem In Bronfenbrenner's bioecological approach, the system that captures the way changes in environmental systems, such as social trends and life events, are patterned over a person's lifetime.
chumship A close friendship with a peer of the same sex that emerges from age 9 to 12, according to Sullivan.
class inclusion The logical understanding that parts or subclasses are included in the whole class and that the whole is therefore greater than any of its parts.
classical conditioning A type of learning in which a stimulus that initially had no effect on the individual comes to elicit a response because of its association with a stimulus that already elicits the response.
clinical method An unstandardized interviewing procedure used by Piaget in which a child's response to each successive question (or problem) determines what the investigator will ask next.
clique A small friendship group that interacts frequently. See *crowd.*
cochlear implant A surgically implanted amplification device that stimulates the auditory nerve to provide the sensation of hearing to a deaf individual.
codominance In genetics, an instance in which two different but equally powerful genes produce a phenotype in which both genes are expressed.
coercive family environment A home in which family members are locked in power struggles, each trying to control the other through aggressive tactics such as threatening, yelling, and hitting.
cognition The activity of knowing and the processes through which knowledge is acquired (for example, attending, perceiving, remembering, and thinking).
cohabitation When two single adults live together as an unmarried couple.
cohort A group of people born at the same time; a particular generation of people.
cohort effects In cross-sectional research, the effects on findings that the different age groups (cohorts) being compared were born at different times and had different formative experiences. Contrast with *age effects* and *time of measurement effects.*
collectivist culture A culture in which people define themselves in terms of group memberships, give group goals higher priority than personal goals, and socialize children to seek group harmony. Contrast with *individualistic culture.*
communality An orientation that emphasizes the well-being of others and includes traits of emotionality and sensitivity to others; considered feminine.
comorbidity The co-occurrence of two or more psychiatric conditions in the same individual.
componential subtheory An aspect of Sternberg's triarchic theory of intelligence that focuses on the information-processing skills used to arrive at answers and their efficiency.
conception The moment of fertilization, when a sperm penetrates an ovum, forming a zygote.
concordance rate The percentage of cases in which a particular attribute is present for both members of a pair of people (for example, twins) if it is present for one member.
concrete operations stage Piaget's third stage of cognitive development, lasting from about age 7 to age 11, when children are acquiring logical operations and can reason effectively about real objects and experiences.
conditioned response A learned response to a stimulus that was not originally capable of producing the response.
conditioned stimulus An initially neutral stimulus that elicits a particular response after it is paired with an unconditioned stimulus that always elicits the response.
confidant A spouse, relative, or friend to whom a person feels emotionally close and with whom that person can share thoughts and feelings.
conformity The tendency to go along with the opinions or wishes of someone else or to yield to group pressures.
conservation The recognition that certain properties of an object or substance do not change when its appearance is altered in some superficial way.
constraint-seeking questions In the Twenty Questions task and similar hypothesis-testing tasks, questions that rule out more than one answer to narrow the field of possible choices rather than asking about only one hypothesis at a time.
constructivism The position taken by Piaget that children actively create their own understandings of the world from their experiences, as opposed to being born with innate ideas or being programmed by the environment.
contact comfort The pleasurable tactile sensations provided by a parent or a soft, terry cloth mother substitute; believed to foster attachments in infant monkeys and possibly humans.
contextual subtheory An aspect of Sternberg's triarchic theory of intelligence

that defines whether behavior is intelligent or unintelligent in terms of the sociocultural context in which it is displayed.
contextual systems theories Theories of development holding that changes over the life span arise from the ongoing interrelationship between a changing organism and a changing world.
continuity–discontinuity issue The debate among theorists about whether human development is best characterized as gradual and continuous or abrupt and stagelike.
contour The amount of light–dark transition or boundary area in a visual stimulus.
conventional morality Kohlberg's term for the third and fourth stages of moral reasoning in which societal values are internalized and judgments are based on a desire to gain approval or uphold law and social order.
convergent thinking Thinking that involves "converging" on the one best answer to a problem; what IQ tests measure. Contrast with *divergent thinking*.
cooing An early form of vocalization that involves repeating vowel-like sounds.
cooperative learning Procedures that involve assigning students, usually of different races or ability levels, to work teams that are reinforced for performing well as teams and that encourage cooperation among teammates.
correlation coefficient A measure, ranging from $+1.00$ to -1.00, of the extent to which two variables or attributes are systematically related to each other in either a positive or a negative way.
correlational method A research technique that involves determining whether two or more variables are related. It cannot indicate that one thing caused another, but it can suggest that a causal relationship exists or allow us to predict one characteristic from our knowledge of another.
creativity The ability to produce novel responses or works.
critical period A defined period in the development of an organism when it is particularly sensitive to certain environmental influences; outside this period, the same influences will have far less effect.
crossing over A process in which genetic material is exchanged between pairs of chromosomes during meiosis.
cross-modal perception The ability to use one sensory modality to identify a stimulus or a pattern of stimuli already familiar through another modality.
cross-sectional design A developmental research design in which different age groups are studied at the same point and compared.
crowd A network of heterosexual cliques that forms during adolescence and facilitates mixed-sex social activities. See *clique*.
crystallized intelligence Those aspects of intellectual functioning that involve using knowledge acquired through experience. Contrast with *fluid intelligence*.
cued recall memory Recollecting objects, events, or experiences in response to a hint or cue. Contrast with pure *recall memory* and *recognition memory*.
cultural–familial retardation Mental retardation that appears to be caused by some combination of low genetic potential and a poor family environment rather than by a specific biological cause. Contrast with *organic retardation*.
culture A system of meanings shared by a population of people and transmitted from one generation to the next.
culture bias The situation that arises in testing when one cultural or subcultural group is more familiar with test items than another group and therefore has an unfair advantage.
cumulative-deficit hypothesis The notion that impoverished environments inhibit intellectual growth and that these inhibiting effects accumulate over time.
cystic fibrosis A disease caused by a mutation that builds up sticky mucus in the lungs, makes breathing difficult, and shortens the lives of affected children.
damage theories of aging Theories that emphasize several haphazard processes that cause cells and organ systems to deteriorate. Contrast with *programmed theories of aging*.
dark adaptation The process by which the eyes become more sensitive to light over time as they remain in the dark.
decentration The ability to focus on two or more dimensions of a problem at one time.
decontextualization Separation of prior knowledge and beliefs from the demands of the task at hand.
decontextualized language Language that is not bound to the immediate conversational context and that is about past or remote events.
defense mechanisms Mechanisms used by the ego to defend itself against anxiety caused by conflict between the id's impulses and social demands.
deferred imitation The ability to imitate a novel act after a delay.
delirium A clouding of consciousness characterized by alternating periods of disorientation and coherence.
demandingness–control A dimension of parenting reflecting the extent to which parents as opposed to children exert control over decisions and set and enforce rules; also called permissiveness–restrictiveness.
dementia A progressive loss of cognitive capacities such as memory and judgment that affects some aging individuals and that has a variety of causes.
denial A defense mechanism in which anxiety-provoking thoughts are kept out of, or isolated from, conscious awareness.
dependent variable The aspect of behavior measured in an experiment and assumed to be under the control of, or dependent on, the independent variable.
depression See *major depressive disorder*.
desire psychology The earliest theory of mind: an understanding that desires guide behavior (for example, that people seek things they like and avoid things they hate). Contrast with *belief–desire psychology*.
development Systematic changes in the individual occurring between conception and death; such changes can be positive, negative, or neutral.
developmental norm The age at which half of a large group of infants or children master a skill or display a behavior; the average age for achieving a milestone in development.
developmental psychopathology A field of study concerned with the origins and course of maladaptive or psychopathological behavior.
developmental quotient (DQ) A numerical measure of an infant's performance on a developmental test relative to the performance of other infants the same age.
developmental stage A distinct phase within a larger sequence of development; a period characterized by a particular set of abilities, motives, behaviors, or emotions that occur together and form a coherent pattern.
diathesis–stress model The view that psychopathology results from the interaction of a person's predisposition to psychological problems and the experience of stressful events.
differentiation In brain development, the progressive diversification of cells that results in their taking on different characteristics and functions.
difficult temperament Characteristic mode of response in which the individual is irregular in habits and adapts slowly, often with vigorous protest, to changes in routine or new experiences. Contrast with *easy temperament* and *slow-to-warm-up temperament*.
diffusion status Identity status characterizing individuals who have not questioned who they are and have not committed themselves to an identity.
disengagement theory A perspective that holds that successful aging involves a mu-

tually satisfying withdrawal of the aging individual and society from each other. Contrast with *activity theory.*
disorganized–disoriented attachment An insecure infant–caregiver bond, common among abused children, that combines features of the resistant and avoidant attachment styles and is characterized by the infant's dazed response to reunion and confusion about whether to approach or avoid the caregiver.
divergent thinking Thinking that requires coming up with a variety of ideas or solutions to a problem when there is no one right answer. Contrast with *convergent thinking.*
dominant gene A relatively powerful gene that is expressed phenotypically and masks the effect of a less-powerful recessive gene.
double standard The view that sexual behavior appropriate for members of one gender is inappropriate for members of the other.
Down syndrome A chromosomal abnormality in which the child has inherited an extra 21st chromosome and is, as a result, mentally retarded; also called trisomy 21.
DSM-IV The fourth edition of the *Diagnostic and Statistical Manual of Mental Disorders,* which spells out defining features and symptoms for the range of psychological disorders.
dynamic assessment An approach to assessing intelligence that evaluates how well individuals learn new material when an examiner provides them with competent instruction.
dynamic systems approach A perspective on development applied to motor development, which proposes that more sophisticated patterns of motor behavior emerge over time through a "self-organizing" process in which children modify their motor behavior in adaptive ways on the basis of the sensory feedback they receive when they try different movements.
dyslexia Serious difficulties learning to read in children who have normal intellectual ability and no sensory impairments or emotional difficulties that could account for their learning problems.
easy temperament Characteristic mode of response in which the individual is even-tempered, content, and open and adaptable to new experiences. Contrast with *difficult temperament* and *slow-to-warm-up temperament.*
echolalia The repetition of sounds, such as when an autistic child parrots what someone else says.
eclectic In the context of science, an individual who recognizes that no single theory can explain everything but that each has something to contribute to our understanding.
ego Psychoanalytic term for the rational component of the personality.
egocentrism The tendency to view the world from the person's own perspective and fail to recognize that others may have different points of view.
elaboration A strategy for remembering that involves adding something to or creating meaningful links between the bits of information the person is trying to retain.
Electra complex Female version of the *Oedipus complex,* in which a 4- to 6-year-old girl is said to envy her father for possessing a penis and would choose him as a sex object in the hope of sharing this valuable organ that she lacks.
embryo See *embryonic period.*
embryonic period Second phase of prenatal development, lasting from the third through the eighth prenatal week, during which the major organs and anatomical structures begin to develop.
emergent literacy The developmental precursors of reading skills in young children, including knowledge, skills, and attributes that will facilitate the acquisition of reading competence.
emotion regulation The processes involved in initiating, maintaining, and altering emotional responses.
emotionality A dimension of temperament that refers to the tendency to be easily or intensely irritated by events.
empathy The vicarious experiencing of another person's feelings.
empiricist An individual whose approach to human development emphasizes the contribution of environmental factors; specifically, a person who believes that infants enter the world as blank slates and know nothing except what they learn through their senses. Contrast with *nativist.*
empty nest The term used to describe the family after the last child departs the household.
encoding The first step in learning and remembering something, it is the process of getting information into the information-processing system, or learning it, and organizing it in a form suitable for storing.
endocrine gland A type of gland that secretes chemicals called hormones directly into the bloodstream. Endocrine glands play critical roles in stimulating growth and regulating bodily functions.
environment Events or conditions outside the person that are presumed to influence and be influenced by the individual.
epigenetic process The process through which nature and nurture, genes and environment, jointly bring forth development in ways that are difficult to predict at the outset, according to Gottlieb's evolutionary–epigenetic systems perspective.
equity A balance of contributions and gains in a social relationship that results in neither partner feeling over- or underbenefited.
estrogen The female hormone responsible for the development of the breasts, the female sex organs, and secondary sex characteristics and for the beginning of menstrual cycles.
ethnic identity A sense of personal identification with the individual's ethnic group and its values and cultural traditions.
ethology A discipline and theoretical perspective that focuses on the evolved behavior of different species in their natural environments.
euthanasia Literally, "good death"; specifically, hastening, either actively or passively, the death of someone suffering from an incurable illness or injury.
evolutionary–epigenetic systems perspective Gottlieb's perspective that development is the product of complex interplays between nature and nurture, between interacting biological and environmental forces that form a larger system.
executive control processes Processes that direct and monitor the selection, organization, manipulation, and interpretation of information in the information-processing system, including executive functions.
executive dysfunction hypothesis View that autistic individuals are deficient in the executive functions that make it possible to plan, change flexibly from one course of action to another, inhibit actions already begun, and the like.
executive functions The planning and organizational functions that reside in the prefrontal cortex of the brain.
exosystem In Bronfenbrenner's bioecological approach, settings not experienced directly by individuals still influence their development (for example, effects of events at a parent's workplace on children's development).
expansion A conversational tactic used by adults in speaking to young children in which they respond to a child's utterance with a more grammatically complete expression of the same thought.
experiential subtheory An aspect of Sternberg's triarchic theory of intelligence that highlights the role of experience in intelligence and distinguishes between what is smart in response to novelty and what is smart in response to familiar tasks.
experiment A research strategy in which the investigator manipulates or alters some

aspect of a person's environment to measure its effect on the individual's behavior or development.
experimental control The holding of all other factors besides the independent variable in an experiment constant so that any changes in the dependent variable can be said to be caused by the manipulation of the independent variable.
explicit memory Memory that involves consciously recollecting the past. Contrast with *implicit memory.*
extended family household A family unit composed of parents and children living with other kin such as grandparents, aunts and uncles, cousins, or a combination of these. Compare with *nuclear family.*
externalizing problem Childhood behavioral problem that involves "undercontrolled" behavior such as aggression or acting out difficulties that disturb other people. Contrast with *internalizing problem.*
extinction The gradual weakening and disappearance of a learned response when it is no longer reinforced.
extreme male brain hypothesis Baron-Cohen's theory that individuals with autism have brains that are more masculine, or skilled at systematizing, than feminine, or skilled at empathizing.
eyewitness memory Remembering and reporting events the person has witnessed or experienced.
factor analysis A technique that identifies clusters of tasks or test items (called factors) that are highly correlated with one another and unrelated to other items.
failure to thrive A condition observed in infants who, because of either physical causes or emotional deprivation, are characterized by stunted growth, weight loss, and delays in cognitive and socioemotional development.
false belief task A research paradigm used to assess an important aspect of a theory of mind, mainly the understanding that people can hold incorrect beliefs and be influenced by them.
family life cycle The sequence of changes in family composition, roles, and relationships that occurs from the time people marry until they die.
family systems theory The conceptualization of the family as a whole consisting of interrelated parts, each of which affects and is affected by every other part, and each of which contributes to the functioning of the whole.
fetal alcohol syndrome (FAS) A group of symptoms commonly observed in the offspring of mothers who use alcohol heavily during pregnancy, including a small head, widely spaced eyes, and mental retardation.
fetal period The third phase of prenatal development, lasting from the ninth prenatal week until birth; during this period, the major organ systems begin to function effectively and the fetus grows rapidly.
fetus See *fetal period.*
filial responsibility Children's obligation to their parents.
fine motor skills Skills that involve precise movements of the hands and fingers or feet and toes. Contrast with *gross motor skills.*
fixation In psychoanalytic theory, a defense mechanism in which development is arrested and part of the libido remains tied to an early stage of development.
fluid intelligence Aspects of intelligence that involve actively thinking and reasoning to solve novel problems. Contrast with *crystallized intelligence.*
Flynn effect The rise in average IQ scores over the 20th century.
foreclosure status An identity status characterizing individuals who appear to have committed themselves to a life direction but who have adopted an identity prematurely, without much thought.
formal operations stage Piaget's fourth and final stage of cognitive development (from age 11 or 12), when the individual begins to think more rationally and systematically about abstract concepts and hypothetical ideas.
fragile X syndrome A chromosome abnormality in which one arm of the X chromosome is only barely connected to the rest of the chromosome; the most common hereditary cause of mental retardation.
fraternal twins Twins who are not identical and who result when a mother releases two ova at roughly the same time and each is fertilized by a different sperm.
free radical theory The theory of aging that views it as damage caused by free radicals, chemically unstable byproducts of metabolism that have an extra electron and react with other molecules to produce toxic substances that damage cells.
functional grammar An analysis of the semantic relations (meanings such as naming and locating) that children express in their earliest sentences.
fuzzy-trace theory The view that verbatim and general or gistlike accounts of an event are stored separately in memory.
gender consistency The stage of gender typing in which children realize that their sex is stable across situations or despite changes in activities or appearance.
gender identity Individuals' basic awareness that they are either a male or a female.
gender intensification A magnification of differences between males and females during adolescence associated with increased pressure to conform to traditional gender roles.
gender role A pattern of behaviors and traits that defines how to act the part of a female or a male in a particular society.
gender-role norms Society's expectations or standards concerning what males and females should be like and how they should behave.
gender-role stereotypes Overgeneralized and largely inaccurate beliefs about what males and females are like.
gender schema (plural: schemata) Organized sets of beliefs and expectations about males and females that guide information processing.
gender segregation The formation of separate boys' and girls' peer groups during childhood.
gender stability The stage of gender typing in which children realize that their sex remains the same over time.
gender typing The process by which children become aware of their gender and acquire the motives, values, and behaviors considered appropriate for members of their biological sex.
gene A functional unit of heredity made up of DNA and transmitted from generation to generation.
gene–environment correlation A systematic interrelationship between an individual's genes and that individual's environment; ways in which genes influence the kind of home environment provided by parents (passive gene–environment correlation), the social reactions to the individual (evocative gene–environment correlation), and the types of experiences the individual seeks (active gene–environment correlation).
gene–environment interaction The phenomenon in which the effects of people's genes depend on the kind of environment they experience and in which the effects of the environment depend on their genetic endowment.
gene therapy Interventions that involve substituting normal genes for the genes associated with a disease or disorder; otherwise altering a person's genetic makeup.
generativity versus stagnation The psychosocial conflict in which middle-aged adults must gain the sense that they have produced something that will outlive them and genuinely care for younger generations to avoid self-preoccupation; seventh of Erikson's stages.
genetic counseling A service designed to inform people about genetic conditions

they or their unborn children are at risk of inheriting.

genetic epistemology The study of how humans come to know reality and basic dimensions of it such as space, time, and causality; Piaget's field of interest.

genotype The genetic endowment that an individual inherits. Contrast with *phenotype.*

germinal period First phase of prenatal development, lasting about 2 weeks from conception until the developing organism becomes attached to the wall of the uterus.

gerontology The study of aging and old age.

giftedness The possession of unusually high general intellectual potential or of special abilities in such areas as creativity, mathematics, or the arts.

glaucoma A condition in which increased fluid pressure in the eye damages the optic nerve and causes progressive loss of peripheral vision and ultimately blindness.

goodness of fit The extent to which the child's temperament and the demands of the child's social environment are compatible or mesh, according to Thomas and Chess; more generally, a good match between person and environment.

grief The emotional response to loss. Contrast with *mourning.*

grief work perspective The view commonly held, but now challenged, that to cope adaptively with death bereaved people must confront their loss, experience painful emotions, work through these emotions, and move toward a detachment from the deceased.

gross motor skills Skills that involve large muscles and whole body or limb movements (for example, kicking the legs or drawing large circles). Contrast with *fine motor skills.*

growth The physical changes that occur from conception to maturity.

growth hormone Hormone produced by the pituitary gland that stimulates childhood physical growth and the adolescent growth spurt.

guided participation A process in which children learn by actively participating in culturally relevant activities with the aid and support of their parents and other knowledgeable individuals.

habituation A simple form of learning that involves learning not to respond to a repeated stimulus; learning to be bored by the familiar.

Hayflick limit The estimate that human cells can double only 50 times, plus or minus 10, and then will die.

hemophilia A deficiency in the blood's ability to clot. It is more common among males than females because it is associated with a sex-linked gene on the X chromosome.

heritability The amount of variability in a population on some trait dimension that is attributable to genetic differences among those individuals.

heteronomous morality A term meaning subject to authority and referring to the childhood beliefs that rules are handed down by authority figures and are sacred and unalterable and that wrongness should be judged on the basis of consequences rather than intentions; typical of children ages 6 to 10, according to Piaget. Contrast with *autonomous morality.*

holophrase A single-word utterance used by an infant that represents an entire sentence's worth of meaning.

Home Observation for Measurement of the Environment (HOME) inventory A widely used instrument that allows an observer to determine how intellectually stimulating or impoverished a home environment is.

horizontal décalage A term used by Piaget to characterize that different cognitive skills related to the same stage of cognitive development emerge at different times.

hormone replacement therapy (HRT) Taking estrogen and progestin to compensate for hormone loss because of menopause in women.

hospice A program that supports dying persons and their families through a philosophy of caring rather than curing, either in a facility or at home.

hot flash A sudden experience of warmth and sweating, often followed by a cold shiver, that occurs in a menopausal woman.

human agency Ways in which humans deliberately exercise cognitive control over their environments and lives, according to Bandura.

Human Genome Project A massive, government-sponsored effort to decipher the human genetic code.

Huntington's disease A genetic disease caused by a single, dominant gene that strikes in middle age to produce a deterioration of physical and mental abilities and premature death.

hyperactivity See *attention deficit hyperactivity disorder (ADHD).*

hypothesis A theoretical prediction about what will hold true if we observe a phenomenon.

hypothetical-deductive reasoning A form of problem solving in which a person starts with general or abstract ideas and deduces or traces their specific implications; "if–then" thinking.

id A psychoanalytic term for the inborn component of the personality that is driven by the instincts or selfish urges.

ideal self Idealized expectations of what one's attributes and personality should be like.

ideational fluency The most common measure of creativity; the sheer number of different, including novel, ideas that a person can generate.

identical twins Monozygotic twins who develop from a single zygote that later divides to form two genetically identical individuals.

identification Freud's term for the individual's tendency to emulate, or adopt the attitudes and behaviors of, another person, particularly the same-sex parent.

identity A self-definition or sense of who one is, where one is going, and how one fits into society.

identity achievement status An identity status characterizing individuals who have carefully thought through identity issues and made commitments or resolved their identity issues.

identity versus role confusion The psychosocial conflict in which adolescents must form a coherent self-definition or remain confused about their life directions; fifth of Erikson's stages.

imaginary audience A form of adolescent egocentrism that involves confusing one's own thoughts with the thoughts of a hypothesized audience for behavior and concluding that others share these preoccupations.

imaginary companion A play companion invented by a child in the preoperational stage who has developed the capacity for symbolic thought.

implicit memory Memory that occurs unintentionally and without consciousness or awareness. Contrast with *explicit memory.*

imprinting An innate form of learning in which the young of certain species will follow and become attached to moving objects (usually their mothers) during a critical period early in life.

in vitro fertilization (IVF) A method of conception in which fertilized eggs are transferred to a woman's uterus in the hopes that one will implant on the wall of the uterus.

inclusion The educational practice of integrating handicapped students into regular classrooms rather than placing them in segregated special education classes; also called mainstreaming.

incomplete dominance A condition in which a stronger gene fails to mask all the effects of a weaker partner gene; a phenotype results that is similar but not identical to the effect of the stronger gene.

independent variable The aspect of the environment that a researcher deliberately changes or manipulates in an experiment to see its effect on behavior; a causal variable. Contrast with *dependent variable.*
indirect effect The instance in which the relationship between two individuals in a family is modified by the behavior or attitudes of a third family member.
individualistic culture A culture in which individuals define themselves as individuals and put their own goals ahead of their group's goals, and one in which children are socialized to be independent and self-reliant. Contrast with *collectivist culture.*
induction A form of discipline that involves explaining why a child's behavior is wrong and should be changed by emphasizing its effects on other people.
industry versus inferiority The psychosocial conflict in which school-aged children must master important cognitive and social skills or feel incompetent; fourth of Erikson's stages.
infant states Coherent patterns of waking and sleeping evident in the fetus and young infant (for example, quiet sleep, active sleep, and active waking).
information-processing approach An approach to cognition that emphasizes the fundamental mental processes involved in attention, perception, memory, and decision making.
initiative versus guilt The psychosocial conflict in which preschool children must learn to initiate new activities and pursue bold plans or become self-critical; third of Erikson's stages.
instinct An inborn biological force assumed to motivate a particular response or class of responses.
integrity versus despair The psychosocial conflict in which elderly adults attempt to find a sense of meaning in their lives and to accept the inevitability of death; eighth of Erikson's stages.
intelligence quotient (IQ) A numerical measure of a person's performance on an intelligence test relative to the performance of other examinees of the same age, typically with a score of 100 defined as average.
internal working model In attachment theory, cognitive representation of self and other that children construct from their interactions with caregivers and that shape their expectations about relationships.
internalizing problem Childhood behavioral problem that represents an "overcontrolled" pattern of coping with difficulties and is expressed in anxiety, depression, and other forms of inner distress. Contrast with *externalizing problem.*
intimacy versus isolation The psychosocial conflict in which young adults must commit themselves to a shared identity with another person or remain aloof and unconnected to others; sixth of Erikson's stages.
intonation Variations in pitch, loudness, and timing when saying words or sentences.
intuitive theories Organized systems of knowledge, believed to be innate, that allow children to make sense of the world in areas such as physics and psychology.
joint attention The act of looking at the same object at the same time with someone else; a way in which infants share perceptual experiences with their caregivers.
karyotype A chromosomal portrait created by staining chromosomes, photographing them under a high-power microscope, and arranging them into a predetermined pattern.
Klinefelter syndrome A sex chromosome abnormality in which males inherit two or more X chromosomes (XXY or XXXY); these males fail to develop secondary sex characteristics and often show deficiencies on tests of verbal abilities.
knowledge base A person's existing information about a content area, significant for its influence on how well that individual can learn and remember.
Lamaze method Prepared childbirth in which parents attend classes and learn mental exercises and relaxation techniques to ease delivery.
language A symbolic system in which a limited number of signals can be combined according to rules to produce an infinite number of messages.
language acquisition device (LAD) A set of linguistic processing skills that nativists believe to be innate; presumably the LAD enables a child to infer the rules governing others' speech and then use these rules to produce language.
latchkey children Children who care for themselves after school with little or no adult supervision.
lateralization The specialization of the two hemispheres of the cerebral cortex of the brain.
learned helplessness orientation A tendency to avoid challenges and to cease trying in the face of failure primarily because of a tendency to attribute failure to lack of ability and therefore to believe that little can be done to improve the results. Contrast with *mastery orientation.*
learning A relatively permanent change in behavior (or behavioral potential) that results from a person's experiences or practice.
learning goal A goal adopted by learners in which they seek to learn new things so that they can improve their abilities. Contrast with *performance goal.*
libido Freud's term for the biological energy of the sex instinct.
life expectancy The average number of years a newborn baby can be expected to live; now 76.5 years in the United States.
life review Process in which elderly adults reflect on unresolved conflicts of the past and evaluate their lives; it may contribute to a sense of integrity and readiness for death.
life structure In Levinson's theory of adult development, an overall pattern of life that reflects the person's priorities and relationships.
life-span perspective A perspective that views development as a lifelong, multidirectional process that involves gain and loss, is characterized by considerable plasticity, is shaped by its historical–cultural context, has many causes, and is best viewed from a multidisciplinary perspective.
literacy The ability to use printed information to function in society, achieve goals, and develop potential.
living will A document in which people state in advance that they do not wish to have extraordinary medical procedures applied if they are hopelessly ill.
longitudinal design A developmental research design in which one group of subjects is studied repeatedly over months or years.
long-term memory Memory store in which information that has been examined and interpreted is stored relatively permanently.
looking-glass self The idea that a person's self-concept is largely a reflection of the ways in which other people respond to that person.
love withdrawal A form of discipline that involves withholding attention, affection, or approval after a child misbehaves.
macrosystem In Bronfenbrenner's bioecological approach, the larger cultural or subcultural context of development.
macular degeneration See *age-related macular degeneration.*
major depressive disorder An affective or mood disorder characterized by at least one episode of feeling profoundly sad and hopeless, losing interest in almost all activities, or both.
mastery motivation An intrinsic motive to master and control the environment evident early in infancy.
mastery orientation A tendency to thrive on challenges and persist in the face of failure because of healthy attributions that lead to the belief that increased effort will

pay off. Contrast with *learned helplessness orientation.*

maternal blood sampling A noninvasive method of prenatal diagnosis involving testing for substances in maternal blood; more recently, analysis of fetal cells that have slipped through the placenta into the mother's blood.

maturation Developmental changes that are biologically programmed by genes rather than caused primarily by learning, injury, illness, or some other life experience.

maximum life span A ceiling on the number of years that any member of a species lives; 120 years for humans.

mediation deficiency The initial stage of mastery of memory strategies in which children cannot spontaneously use or benefit from strategies even if they are taught to use them.

meiosis The process in which a germ cell divides, producing sperm or ova, each containing half of the parent cell's original complement of chromosomes; in humans, the products of meiosis normally contain 23 chromosomes.

menarche A female's first menstrual period.

menopause The ending of a woman's menstrual periods and reproductive capacity around age 51.

mental age A measure of intellectual development that reflects the level of age-graded problems that a child is able to solve; the age at which a child functions intellectually.

mental retardation Significant subaverage general intellectual functioning associated with impairments in adaptive behavior and manifested during the developmental period.

mesosystem In Bronfenbrenner's bioecological approach, interrelationships between microsystems or immediate environments (for example, ways in which events in the family affect a child's interactions at a day care center).

meta-analysis A research method in which the results of multiple studies addressing the same question are synthesized to produce overall conclusions.

metacognition Knowledge of the human mind and of the range of cognitive processes, including thinking about personal thought processes.

metalinguistic awareness Knowledge of language as a system.

metamemory A person's knowledge about memory and about monitoring and regulating memory processes.

method of loci A mnemonic technique that involves establishing a mental map of a familiar route and then creating images linking each item to be learned to a landmark along the route.

microsystem In Bronfenbrenner's bioecological approach, the immediate settings in which the person functions (for example, the family).

middle generation squeeze The phenomenon in which middle-aged adults sometimes experience heavy responsibilities for both the younger and the older generations in the family.

midlife crisis A period of major questioning, inner struggle, and re-evaluation hypothesized to occur in an adult's early 40s.

mild cognitive impairment A level of memory loss between normal loss with age and pathological loss from disease.

mitosis The process in which a cell duplicates its chromosomes and then divides into two genetically identical daughter cells.

modified extended family An arrangement in which nuclear families related by kinship maintain separate households but frequently interact rather than functioning in isolation.

molecular genetics The analysis of particular genes and their effects, including the identification of specific genes that influence particular traits and the comparison of animals or humans who have these specific genes and those who do not.

moral affect The emotional component of morality, including feelings of guilt, shame, and pride regarding one's conduct.

moral disengagement According to Bandura, the ability to avoid self condemnation when engaged in immoral behavior by justifying, minimizing, or blaming others for one's actions.

moral reasoning The cognitive component of morality; the thinking that occurs when people decide whether acts are right or wrong.

moral rules Standards of conduct that focus on the basic rights and privileges of individuals. Contrast with *social-conventional rules.*

morality The ability to distinguish right from wrong, to act on this distinction, and to experience pride when doing something right and to experience guilt or shame when doing something wrong. Morality has affective, cognitive, and behavioral components.

morality of care Gilligan's term for what she says is the dominant moral orientation of females, in which the individual emphasizes concern and responsibility for the welfare of other people rather than abstract rights. Contrast with *morality of justice.*

morality of justice Gilligan's term for what she says is the dominant moral orientation of males, in which moral dilemmas are viewed as inevitable conflicts between the rights of two or more parties that must be settled by law. Contrast with *morality of care.*

moratorium period A period of time in high school or college when young adults are relatively free of responsibilities and can experiment with different roles to find their identities.

moratorium status Identity status characterizing individuals who are experiencing an identity crisis or actively exploring identity issues but who have not yet achieved an identity.

morphology Rules governing the formation of words from sounds (for example, rules for forming plurals and past tenses).

mourning Culturally prescribed ways of displaying reactions to a loss. Contrast with *grief.*

mutation A change in the structure or arrangement of one or more genes that produces a new phenotype.

mutually responsive orientation A close, affectively positive, and cooperative relationship in which child and parent are attached to each other and are sensitive to each other's needs; a contributor to moral development.

myelin A fatty sheath that insulates neural axons and thereby speeds the transmission of neural impulses.

nativist An individual whose approach to human development emphasizes the contribution of genetic factors; specifically, a person who believes that infants enter the world equipped with knowledge that allows them to perceive a meaningful world from the start. Contrast with *empiricist.*

natural selection The evolutionary principle that individuals who have characteristics advantageous for survival in a particular environment are most likely to survive and reproduce. Over many generations, this process of "survival of the fittest" will lead to changes in a species and the development of new species.

naturalistic observation A research method in which the scientist observes people as they engage in common everyday activities in their natural habitats. Contrast with *structured observation.*

nature–nurture issue The debate over the relative importance of biological predispositions (nature) and environmental influences (nurture) as determinants of human development.

negative punishment The process in operant conditioning in which a response is weakened or made less probable when its consequence is the removal of a pleasant stimulus from the situation.

negative reinforcement The process in operant conditioning in which a response is strengthened or made more probable when its consequence is the removal of an unpleasant stimulus from the situation.

neglectful parenting A parenting style low in demandingness–control and low in acceptance–responsiveness; uninvolved parenting.

neonatal Pertaining to events or developments in the first month after birth.

neuron The basic unit of the nervous system; a nerve cell.

nonshared environmental influences Experiences unique to the individual that are not shared by other members of the family and that tend to make members of the same family different. Contrast with *shared environmental influences.*

normal distribution A symmetrical (bell-shaped) curve that describes the variability of characteristics within a population. Most people fall at or near the average score; there are relatively few high or low scores.

nuclear family A family unit consisting of husband–father, wife–mother, and at least one child. Compare with *extended family household.*

object permanence The understanding that objects continue to exist when they are no longer visible or otherwise detectable to the senses; fully mastered by the end of infancy.

observational learning Learning that results from observing the behavior of other people; emphasized in Bandura's social cognitive theory.

Oedipus complex Freud's term for the conflict that 4- to 6-year-old boys experience when they develop an incestuous desire for their mothers and a jealous and hostile rivalry with their fathers.

olfaction The sense of smell, made possible by sensory receptors in the nasal passage that react to chemical molecules in the air.

operant conditioning Also called instrumental conditioning, a form of learning in which freely emitted acts (or operants) become more or less probable depending on the consequences they produce.

organic retardation Mental retardation because of some identifiable biological cause associated with hereditary factors, diseases, or injuries. Contrast with *cultural–familial retardation.*

organization In Piaget's cognitive developmental theory, a person's inborn tendency to combine and integrate available schemes into more coherent and complex systems or bodies of knowledge; as a memory strategy, a technique that involves grouping or classifying stimuli into meaningful clusters.

organogenesis The process, occurring during the period of the embryo, in which every major organ takes shape in a primitive form.

orthogenetic principle Werner's principle that development proceeds from global and undifferentiated states toward more differentiated and integrated patterns of response.

osteoarthritis A joint problem among older adults resulting from a gradual deterioration of the cartilage that cushions the bones and keeps them from rubbing together.

osteoporosis A disease affecting older adults in which bone tissue is lost, leaving bones fragile and easily fractured.

overextension The young child's tendency to use a word to refer to a wider set of objects, actions, or events than adults do (for example, using the word *car* to refer to all motor vehicles). Contrast with *underextension.*

overregularization The overgeneralization of observed grammatical rules to irregular cases to which the rules do not apply (for example, saying *mouses* rather than *mice*).

parent effects model A model of family influence in which parents (particularly mothers) are believed to influence their children rather than vice versa.

parental imperative The notion that the demands of parenthood cause men and women to adopt distinct roles and psychological traits.

Parkes/Bowlby attachment model of bereavement Model of grieving describing four predominant reactions to loss of an attachment figure: numbness, yearning, disorganization and despair, and reorganization.

peer A social equal; a person who functions at a level of behavioral complexity similar to that of the self, often someone of similar age.

perception The interpretation of sensory input.

perceptual salience Phenomenon in which the most obvious features of an object or situation have disproportionate influence on the perceptions and thought of young children.

performance goal A goal adopted by learners in which they attempt to prove their ability rather than to improve it. Contrast with *learning goal.*

perinatal environment The environment surrounding birth.

perinatal period The period surrounding birth.

permissive parenting A lax style of parenting combining low demandingness–control and high acceptance–responsiveness in which adults love their children but make few demands on them and rarely attempt to control their behavior.

personal fable A form of adolescent egocentrism that involves thinking that oneself and one's thoughts and feelings are unique or special.

personality The organized combination of attributes, motives, values, and behaviors that is unique to each individual.

phenotype The way in which a person's genotype is expressed in observable or measurable characteristics.

phenylketonuria (PKU) A genetic disease in which the child is unable to metabolize phenylalanine; if left untreated, it soon causes hyperactivity and mental retardation.

phoneme One of the basic units of sound used in a particular spoken language.

phonological awareness The understanding that spoken words can be decomposed into some number of basic sound units, or phonemes; an important skill in learning to read.

phonology The sound system of a language and the rules for combining these sounds to produce meaningful units of speech.

pincer grasp A grasp in which the thumb is used in opposition to the fingers, enabling an infant to become more dexterous at lifting and manipulating objects.

pituitary gland The "master gland" located at the base of the brain that regulates the other endocrine glands and produces growth hormone.

placenta An organ, formed from the chorion and the lining of the uterus, that provides for the nourishment of the unborn child and the elimination of its metabolic wastes.

plasticity An openness of the brain cells (or of the organism as a whole) to positive and negative environmental influence; a capacity to change in response to experience.

polygenic trait A characteristic influenced by the action of many gene pairs rather than a single pair.

population A well-defined group that a researcher who studies a sample of individuals is interested in drawing conclusions about.

positive punishment The process in operant conditioning whereby a response is weakened when its consequence is an unpleasant event.

positive reinforcement The process in operant conditioning whereby a response is strengthened when its consequence is a pleasant event.

postconventional morality Kohlberg's term for the fifth and sixth stages of moral reasoning, in which moral judgments are based on a more abstract understanding of democratic social contracts or on universal principles of justice that have validity apart from the views of particular authority figures.

postformal thought Proposed stages of cognitive development that lie beyond formal operations.

postnatal depression An episode of severe, clinical depression lasting for months in a woman who has just given birth; to be contrasted with milder cases of the "baby blues," in which a new mother is tearful and moody in the first days after birth.

posttraumatic stress disorder A psychological disorder involving flashbacks to traumatizing events, nightmares, and feelings of helplessness and anxiety in the face of danger experienced by victims of extreme trauma such as soldiers in combat and sexually abused children.

power assertion A form of discipline that involves the use of superior power to administer spankings, withhold privileges, and so on.

pragmatics Rules specifying how language is to be used appropriately in different social contexts to achieve goals.

preconventional morality Kohlberg's term for the first two stages of moral reasoning, in which society's rules are not yet internalized and judgments are based on the punishing or rewarding consequences of an act.

preimplantation genetic diagnosis Prenatal diagnostic procedure in which a mother's eggs are fertilized in the laboratory using in vitro fertilization techniques, DNA tests are conducted on the first cells that result from mitosis of each fertilized egg, and only eggs that do not have chromosome abnormalities or genes associated with disorders are implanted in the uterus.

premenstrual syndrome (PMS) Several symptoms experienced shortly before each menstrual period that include having tender breasts, feeling bloated, and being irritable and moody.

premoral period According to Piaget, a period during the preschool years when children show little awareness or understanding of rules and cannot be considered to be moral beings.

prenatal environment The physical environment of the womb.

preoperational stage Piaget's second stage of cognitive development, lasting from about age 2 to age 7, when children think at a symbolic level but have not yet mastered logical operations.

presbycusis Problems of the aging ear, which commonly involve loss of sensitivity to high-frequency or high-pitched sounds.

presbyopia Problems of the aging eye, especially loss of near vision related to a decreased ability of the lens to accommodate to objects close to the eye.

pretend play Symbolic play in which one actor, object, or action symbolizes or stands for another.

private speech Nonsocial speech, or speech for the self, commonly used by preschoolers to guide their activities and believed by Vygotsky to be the forerunner of inner speech, or silent thinking in words.

problem solving The use of the information-processing system to achieve a goal or arrive at a decision.

production deficiency A phase in the mastery of memory strategies in which children can use strategies they are taught but cannot produce them on their own.

progeria A genetic disorder caused by a single dominant gene that makes victims age prematurely and die early.

programmed theories of aging Theories that emphasize the systematic genetic control of aging processes. Contrast with *damage theories of aging.*

prosocial behavior Positive actions toward other people such as helping and cooperating.

protective factors Factors such as personal resources and a supportive postnatal environment that work to prevent at-risk individuals from developing problems.

proximodistal principle In development, the principle that growth proceeds from the center of the body (or the proximal region) to the extremities (or the distal regions).

psychoanalytic theory The theoretical perspective associated with Freud and his followers that emphasizes unconscious motivations for behavior, conflicts within the personality, and stages of psychosexual development.

psychometric approach The research tradition that spawned standardized tests of intelligence and that views intelligence as a trait or a set of traits that can be measured and that varies from person to person.

psychosexual stages Freud's five stages of development, associated with biological maturation and shifts in the libido: oral, anal, phallic, latency, and genital.

psychosocial stages Erikson's eight stages of development (trust, autonomy, initiative, industry, identity, intimacy, generativity, and integrity), emphasizing social influences more and biological urges less than Freud's psychosexual stages.

puberty The point at which a person reaches sexual maturity and is physically capable of conceiving a child.

punishment Consequences that decrease the probability that an act will recur. See *positive punishment* and *negative punishment.*

quasi experiment An experiment-like study that evaluates the effects of different treatments but does not randomly assign individuals to treatment groups.

random assignment A technique in which research participants are placed in experimental conditions in an unbiased or random way so that the resulting groups are not systematically different.

random sample A sample formed by identifying all members of the larger population of interest and then selecting a portion of them in an unbiased or random way to participate in the study; a technique to ensure that the sample studied is representative or typical of the larger population of interest.

reaction time The interval between the presentation of a stimulus and a response to it.

recall memory Recollecting or actively retrieving objects, events, and experiences when examples or cues are not provided. Contrast with *cued recall memory* and *recognition memory.*

recessive gene A less powerful gene that is not expressed phenotypically when paired with a *dominant gene.*

reciprocal determinism The notion in social cognitive theory that the flow of influence between people and their environments is a two-way street; the environment may affect the person, but the person's characteristics and behavior will also influence the environment.

recognition memory Identifying an object or event as one that has been experienced before, such as when a person must select the correct answer from several options. Contrast with *cued recall memory* and *recall memory.*

reconstituted family A new family that forms after the remarriage of a single parent, sometimes involving the blending of two families into a new one.

reflex An unlearned and automatic response to a stimulus.

regression A defense mechanism that involves retreating to an earlier, less traumatic stage of development.

rehearsal A strategy for remembering that involves repeating the items the person is trying to retain.

reinforcement Consequences that increase the probability that an act will recur. See *positive reinforcement* and *negative reinforcement.*

relativistic thinking A form of postformal-operational thought in which it is understood that there are multiple ways of view-

ing a problem and that the solutions people arrive at will depend on their starting assumptions and perspective.
REM sleep A state of active, irregular sleep associated with dreaming; named for the rapid eye movements associated with it.
research ethics Standards of conduct that investigators are ethically bound to honor to protect their research participants from physical or psychological harm.
reserve capacity The ability of many organ systems to respond to demands for extraordinary output, such as when the heart and lungs work at maximal capacity.
resilience The self-righting or recuperative capacity that allows many children to recover from early disadvantages and return to a normal course of development.
resistant attachment An insecure infant–caregiver bond or other intimate relationship characterized by strong separation anxiety and a tendency to show ambivalent reactions to the attachment object upon reunion, seeking and yet resisting contact.
retinitis pigmentosa (RP) A group of hereditary disorders that involve gradual deterioration of the light-sensitive cells of the retina.
retrieval The process of retrieving information from long-term memory when it is needed.
reversibility In Piaget's theory, the ability to reverse or negate an action by mentally performing the opposite action.
rhythmic stereotypies Repetitive movements observed in infants shortly before a new motor skill emerges.
role reversal A switching of child and parent roles late in life such that the parent becomes dependent and the child becomes the caregiver.
role-taking skills The ability to assume other people's perspectives and understand their thoughts, feelings, and behaviors.
rubella A disease that has little effect on a pregnant woman but may cause several serious birth defects, such as blindness, deafness, and mental retardation, in unborn children exposed in the first 3 to 4 months of gestation; German measles.
rule assessment approach Siegler's approach to studying the development of problem solving that determines what information about a problem children take in and what rules they then formulate to account for this information.
sample The group of individuals chosen to be the subjects of a study.
savant syndrome The phenomenon in which extraordinary talent in a particular area is displayed by a person who is otherwise mentally retarded.
scheme (or schema; plural: schemes or schemata) A cognitive structure or organized pattern of action or thought used to deal with experiences.
schizophrenia A serious form of mental illness characterized by disturbances in logical thinking, emotional expression, and interpersonal behavior.
scientific method An attitude or value about the pursuit of knowledge that dictates that investigators must be objective and must allow their data to decide the merits of their theorizing.
script A mental representation of a typical sequence of actions related to an event that is created in memory and that then guides future behaviors in similar settings.
secular trend A trend in industrialized society toward earlier maturation and greater body size.
secure attachment An infant–caregiver bond or intimate relationship in which the individual welcomes close contact, uses the attachment object as a source of comfort, and dislikes but can manage separations.
secure base A point of safety, represented by an infant's attachment figure, that permits exploration of the environment.
selective attention Deliberately concentrating on one thing and ignoring something else.
selective breeding A method of studying genetic influence that involves deliberately determining whether a trait can be bred in animals through selective mating.
selective optimization with compensation The concept that older people cope with aging through a strategy that involves focusing on the skills most needed, practicing those skills, and developing ways to avoid the need for other skills.
self-concept People's perceptions of their unique attributes or traits.
self-conscious emotion A "secondary emotion" such as embarrassment or pride that requires an awareness of self unlikely to emerge until about 18 months of age.
self-esteem People's overall evaluation of their worth as based on an assessment of the qualities that make up the self-concept.
self-recognition The ability to recognize oneself in a mirror or photograph, which occurs in most infants by 18 to 24 months of age.
semantics The aspect of language centering on meanings.
semenarche A boy's first ejaculation.
sensation The process by which information is detected by the sensory receptors and transmitted to the brain; the starting point in perception.
sensorimotor stage Piaget's first stage of cognitive development, spanning the first 2 years of life, in which infants rely on their senses and motor behaviors in adapting to the world around them.
sensory register The first memory store in information processing in which stimuli are noticed and are briefly available for further processing.
sensory threshold The point at which low levels of stimulation can be detected.
separation anxiety A wary or fretful reaction that infants display when separated from their attachment objects.
sequential design A developmental research design that combines the cross-sectional approach and the longitudinal approach in a single study to compensate for the weaknesses of each.
seriation A logical operation that allows a person to mentally order a set of stimuli along a quantifiable dimension such as height or weight.
sex-linked characteristic An attribute determined by a gene that appears on one of the two types of sex chromosomes, usually the X chromosome.
sexual orientation A person's preference for sexual partners of the same or other sex, often characterized as primarily heterosexual, homosexual, or bisexual.
shared environmental influences Experiences that individuals living in the same home environment share and that work to make them similar. Contrast with *nonshared environmental influences.*
short-term memory The memory store in which limited amounts of information are temporarily held; called *working memory* when its active quality is being emphasized.
sibling rivalry A spirit of competition, jealousy, or resentment that may arise between two or more brothers or sisters.
sickle-cell disease A genetic blood disease in which red blood cells assume an unusual sickle shape and become inefficient at distributing oxygen throughout the body.
single gene-pair inheritance The genetic mechanism through which a characteristic is influenced by only one pair of genes, one gene from the mother and its partner from the father.
size constancy The tendency to perceive an object as the same size despite changes in its distance from the eyes.
slow-to-warm-up temperament A characteristic mode of response in which the individual is relatively inactive and moody and displays mild resistance to new routines and experiences but gradually adapts. Contrast with *easy temperament* and *difficult temperament.*

sociability A dimension of temperament that refers to the individual's degree of interest in and responsiveness to people.
social clock A personal sense of when things should be done in life and when the individual is ahead of or behind the schedule dictated by age norms.
social cognition Thinking about the thoughts, feelings, motives, and behavior of the self and other people.
social cognitive theory Bandura's social learning theory, which holds that children and adults can learn novel responses merely by observing the behavior of a model, making mental notes on what they have seen, and then using these mental representations to reproduce the model's behavior; more broadly, a theory emphasizing the importance of cognitive processing of social experiences.
social comparison The process of defining and evaluating the self through comparisons with other people.
social convoy The changing cadre of significant people who serve as sources of social support to the individual during the life span.
social learning theory See *social cognitive theory.*
social norm A socially defined expectation about how people should behave in particular social contexts.
social pretend play A form of play that involves both cooperation with playmates and pretend or symbolic activity.
social referencing Infants' monitoring of companions' emotional reactions in ambiguous situations and use of this information to decide how they should feel and behave.
social support The several forms of assistance from other people that bolster individuals and protect them from stress.
social-conventional rules Standards of conduct determined by social consensus that indicate what is appropriate within a particular social setting. Contrast with *moral rules.*
social-role hypothesis Eagly's view that gender-role stereotypes are created and maintained by differences in the roles that men and women play in society rather than being inherent in males and females.
sociocultural perspective Vygotsky's contextual theory of development, which maintains that cognitive development is shaped by the sociocultural context in which it occurs and grows out of children's social interactions with members of their culture.
socioeconomic status (SES) The position people hold in society based on such factors as income, education, occupational status, and the prestige of their neighborhoods.
socioemotional selectivity theory Carstensen's notion that our needs change as we grow older and that we actively choose to narrow our range of social partners to those who can best meet our emotional needs.
sociometric techniques Methods for determining who is well liked and popular and who is disliked or neglected in a group.
somatic symptoms Physical or bodily signs of emotional distress such as loss of appetite or disruption of normal sleep patterns.
species heredity The genetic endowment that members of a particular species have in common; a contributor to universal species traits and patterns of maturation.
spillover effects Events at work affect home life, and events at home carry over into the work place.
spirituality A search for ultimate meaning in life that may or may not be carried out in the context of religion.
static thought In Piaget's theory, the thought characteristic of the preoperational period that is fixed on end states rather than on the changes that transform one state into another. Contrast with *transformational thought.*
stem cell Undifferentiated, primitive cells that have the ability both to multiply and to differentiate into a variety of specific cells.
stereotype threat An individual's fear of being judged to have the qualities associated with negative stereotypes of his or her social group.
storage In information processing, the holding of information in the long-term memory store.
storm and stress Hall's term for the emotional ups and downs and rapid changes that he believed characterize adolescence.
stranger anxiety A wary or fretful reaction that infants often display when approached by an unfamiliar person.
Strange Situation A series of mildly stressful experiences involving the departure of the parent and exposure to a stranger to which infants are exposed to determine the quality of their attachments; developed by Ainsworth.
structured observation A research method in which scientists create special conditions designed to elicit the behavior of interest to achieve greater control over the conditions under which they gather behavioral data. Contrast with *naturalistic observation.*
successful intelligence Sternberg's concept that people are intelligent to the extent that they are able to succeed in life in their sociocultural context.
sudden infant death syndrome (SIDS) The death of a sleeping baby because of a failure of the respiratory system; linked to maternal smoking.
superego The psychoanalytic term for the component of the personality that consists of the individual's internalized moral standards.
surfactant A substance that aids breathing by preventing the air sacs of the lungs from sticking together.
symbolic capacity The capacity to use symbols such as words, images, or actions to represent or stand for objects and experiences; representational thought.
synapse The point at which the axon or dendrite of one neuron makes a connection with another neuron.
synchronized routine Harmonious, dance-like interaction between infant and caregiver in which each adjusts behavior in response to that of the other.
syntax Rules specifying how words can be combined to form meaningful sentences in a language.
syphilis A common sexually transmitted disease that may cross the placental barrier in the middle and later stages of pregnancy, causing miscarriage or serious birth defects.
systemize The brain's ability to analyze and explore how things work.
tabula rasa The idea that the mind of an infant is a "blank slate" and that all knowledge, abilities, behaviors, and motives are acquired through experience.
Tay-Sachs disease A genetic disease common among Jewish children that is caused by a pair of recessive genes and that results in a degeneration of the nervous system and death.
telegraphic speech Early sentences that consist primarily of content words and omit the less meaningful parts of speech such as articles, prepositions, pronouns, and auxiliary verbs.
telomere A stretch of DNA that forms the tip of a chromosome and that shortens after each cell division, possibly timing the death of cells.
temperament A genetically based pattern of tendencies to respond in predictable ways; building blocks of personality such as activity level, sociability, and emotionality.
teratogen Any disease, drug, or other environmental agent that can harm a developing fetus.
terminal drop A rapid decline in intellectual abilities that people within a few years of dying often experience.

test norms Standards of normal performance on psychometric instruments based on the average scores and range of scores obtained by a large, representative sample of test takers.
testosterone The most important of the male hormones, or androgens; essential for normal sexual development during the prenatal period and at puberty.
thalidomide A mild tranquilizer that, taken early in pregnancy, can produce a variety of malformations of the limbs, eyes, ears, and heart.
theory A set of concepts and propositions designed to organize, describe, and explain a set of observations.
theory of mind The understanding that people have mental states (feelings, desires, beliefs, intentions) and that these states underlie and help explain their behavior.
theory-of-mind hypothesis The theory that autism is rooted in a limited understanding of mental states and their role in human behavior—that individuals with autism lack a theory of mind.
time of measurement effects In developmental research, the effects on findings of historical events occurring when the data for a study are being collected (for example, psychological changes brought about by an economic depression rather than as a function of aging). Contrast with *age effects* and *cohort effects.*
total brain death An irreversible loss of functioning in the entire brain, both the higher centers of the cerebral cortex that are involved in thought and the lower centers of the brain that control basic life processes such as breathing.
transactional model A model of family influence in which parent and child are believed to influence each other reciprocally.
transformational grammar Rules of syntax that allow a person to transform declarative statements into questions, negatives, imperatives, and other kinds of sentences.
transformational thought In Piaget's theory, the ability to conceptualize transformations, or processes of change from one state to another, which appears in the stage of concrete operations. Contrast with *static thought.*
transitivity The ability to recognize the necessary or logical relations among elements in a serial order (for example, that if A is taller than B, and B is taller than C, then A must be taller than C).
triarchic theory of intelligence An information-processing theory of intelligence that emphasizes three aspects of intelligent behavior: the *context* in which people display intelligence, the previous *experience* they have with cognitive tasks, and the *information-processing components* they use to solve problems.
trust versus mistrust The psychosocial conflict of infancy in which infants must learn to trust others to meet their needs in order to trust themselves; first stage in Erikson's theory.
Turner syndrome A sex chromosome abnormality in which females inherit only one X chromosome (XO); they remain small in stature, fail to develop secondary sex characteristics, and may show some mental deficiencies.
ultrasound Method of examining physical organs by scanning them with sound waves—for example, scanning the womb and thereby producing a visual outline of the fetus to detect gross abnormalities.
umbilical cord A soft tube containing blood vessels that connects the embryo to the placenta and serves as a source of oxygen and nutrients and as a vehicle for the elimination of wastes.
unconditioned response The unlearned response elicited by an unconditioned stimulus.
unconditioned stimulus A stimulus that elicits a particular response without prior learning.
unconscious motivation Freud's term for feelings, experiences, and conflicts that influence a person's thinking and behavior even though they cannot be recalled.
underextension The young child's tendency to use general words to refer to a smaller set of objects, actions, or events than adults do (for example, using *candy* to refer only to mints). Contrast with *overextension.*
universality–context-specificity issue The debate over the extent to which developmental changes are common to everyone (universal, as in most stage theories) or different from person to person (particularistic).
utilization deficiency The third phase in mastery of memory strategies in which children fail to benefit from a memory strategy they are able to produce.
vascular dementia The deterioration of functioning and cognitive capacities caused by a series of minor strokes that cut off the blood supply to areas of the brain; also called multi-infarct dementia.
vicarious reinforcement In observational learning, the consequences experienced by models, because of their behavior, that affect the learner's likelihood of engaging in the behavior.
visual accommodation The ability of the lens of the eye to change shape to bring objects at different distances into focus.
visual acuity The ability to perceive detail in a visual stimulus.
visual cliff An elevated glass platform that creates an illusion of depth and is used to test the depth perception of infants.
vocabulary spurt A phenomenon occurring around 18 months of age when the pace of word learning quickens dramatically.
weak central coherence hypothesis A theory that autism is rooted in a focus on details and an inability to integrate perceptions, take into account the surrounding context, and see the "big picture" or form generalizations.
wisdom Exceptional insight or judgment regarding life's problems.
working memory A memory store, often referred to as a mental "scratch pad," that temporarily holds information when it is being actively operated upon; the active use of the short-term memory store.
X chromosome The longer of the two sex chromosomes; normal females have two X chromosomes, whereas normal males have only one.
Y chromosome The shorter of the two sex chromosomes; normal males have one Y chromosome, whereas females have none.
zone of proximal development Vygotsky's term for the difference between what a learner can accomplish independently and what a learner can accomplish with the guidance and encouragement of a more skilled partner.
zygote A single cell formed at conception from the union of a sperm and an ovum.

References

A

Aarons, S. J., & Jenkins, R. R. (2002). Sex, pregnancy, and contraception-related motivators and barriers among Latino and African-American youth in Washington, D.C. *Sex Education, 2,* 5–30.

Aber, J. L., Brown, J. L., & Jones, S. M. (2003). Developmental trajectories toward violence in middle childhood: Course, demographic differences, and response to school-based intervention. *Developmental Psychology, 39,* 324–348.

Ablard, K. E., & Mills, C. J. (1996). Implicit theories of intelligence and self-perceptions of academically talented adolescents and children. *Journal of Youth and Adolescence, 25,* 137–148.

Aboud, F. E., & Mendelson, M. J. (1996). Determinants of friendship selection and quality: Developmental perspectives. In W. M. Bukowski, A. F. Newcomb, & W. W. Hartup (Eds.), *The company they keep: Friendship in childhood and adolescence.* New York: Cambridge University Press.

Abraham, J. D., & Hansson, R. O. (1995). Successful aging at work: An applied study of selection, optimization, and compensation through impression management. *Journals of Gerontology: Psychological Sciences, 50,* P94–P103.

Abrams, R. A., & Christ, S. E. (2003). Motion onset captures attention. *Psychological Science, 14,* 427–432.

Achenbach, T. M. (1982). *Developmental psychopathology* (2nd ed.). New York: Wiley.

Achenbach, T. M., & Edelbrock, C. S. (1978). The classification of child psychopathology: A review and analysis of empirical efforts. *Psychological Bulletin, 85,* 1275–1301.

Achenbaum, W. A., & Bengtson, V. L. (1994). Re-engaging the disengagement theory of aging: On the history and assessment of theory development in gerontology. *Gerontologist, 34,* 756–763.

Achter, J. A., Benbow, C. P., & Lubinski, D. (1997). Rethinking multipotentiality among the intellectually gifted: A critical review and recommendations. *Gifted Child Quarterly, 41,* 5–15.

Ackermann-Liebrich, U., Voegeli, T., Gunter-Witt, K., Kunz, I., Zullig, M., Schindler, C., et al. (1996). Home versus hospital deliveries: Follow up study of matched pairs for procedures and outcome. *British Medical Journal, 313,* 1313–1318.

Acredolo, L., & Goodwyn, S. (1988). Symbolic gesturing in normal infants. *Child Development, 59,* 450–466.

Adam, E. K., Gunnar, M. R., & Tanaka, A. (2004). Adult attachment, parent emotion, and observed parenting behavior: Mediator and moderator models. *Child Development, 75,* 110–122.

Adams, C. (1991). Qualitative age differences in memory for text: A life-span developmental perspective. *Psychology and Aging, 6,* 323–336.

Adams, D. W., & Deveau, E. J. (1986). Helping dying adolescents: Needs and responses. In C. A. Corr & J. N. McNeil (Eds.), *Adolescence and death.* New York: Springer.

Adams, D. W., & Deveau, E. J. (1987). When a brother or sister is dying of cancer: The vulnerability of the adolescent sibling. *Death Studies, 11,* 279–295.

Adams, E. K., Nishimura, B., Merritt, R. K., & Melvin, C. (2003). Costs of poor birth outcomes among privately insured. *Journal of Health Care Finance, 29,* 11–26.

Adams, M. J. (1990). *Beginning to read: Learning and thinking about print.* Cambridge, MA: MIT Press.

Adams, M. J., Treiman, R., & Pressley, M. (1998). Reading, writing, and literacy. In I. E. Sigel & K. A. Renninger (Vol. Eds.), W. Damon (Editor-in-Chief), *Handbook of child psychology: Vol. 4. Child psychology in practice* (5th ed., pp. 275–355). New York: Wiley.

Adams, R. (2003, December 9). Baby's first pictures. *The Washington Post,* pp. F1, F5.

Adams, R., Maurer, D., & Davis, M. (1986). Newborns' discrimination of chromatic from achromatic stimuli. *Journal of Experimental Child Psychology, 41,* 267–281.

Adams, R. G. (1985–1986). Emotional closeness and physical distance between friends: Implications for elderly women living in age-segregated and age-integrated settings. *International Journal of Aging and Human Development, 22,* 55–76.

Adey, P. S., & Shayer, M. (1992). Accelerating the development of formal thinking in middle and high school students: II. Postproject effects on science achievement. *Journal of Research in Science Teaching, 29,* 81–92.

Adler, S. R., Fosket, J. R., Kagawa-Singer, M., McGraw, S. A., Wong-Kim, E., Gold, E., et al. (2000). Conceptualizing menopause and midlife: Chinese American and Chinese women in the U.S. *Maturitas, 35,* 11–23.

Adolph, K. E. (1997). Learning in the development of infant locomotion. *Monographs of the Society for Research in Child Development, 61* (Serial No. 251).

Adolph, K. E., & Avolio, A. M. (2000). Walking infants adapt locomotion to changing body dimensions. *Journal of Experimental Psychology: Human Perception and Performance, 26,* 1148–1166.

Agnew, R. (2003). An integrated theory of the adolescent peak in offending. *Youth & Society, 34,* 263–299.

Agnew, R., & Huguley, S. (1989). Adolescent violence toward parents. *Journal of Marriage and the Family, 51,* 699–711.

Aguiar, A., & Baillargeon, R. (1999). 2.5-month-old infants' reasoning about when objects should and should not be occluded. *Cognitive Psychology, 39,* 116–157.

Aguiar, A., & Baillargeon, R. (2002). Developments in young infants' reasoning about occluded objects. *Cognitive Psychology, 45,* 267–336.

Ainscough, C. E. (1990). Premenstrual emotional changes: A prospective study of symptomatology in normal women. *Journal of Psychosomatic Research, 34,* 35–45.

Ainsworth, M. D. S. (1973). The development of infant–mother attachment. In B. M. Caldwell & H. N. Ricciuti (Eds.), *Review of child development research* (Vol. 3). Chicago: University of Chicago Press.

Ainsworth, M. D. S. (1979). Attachment as related to mother–infant interaction. In J. G. Rosenblatt, R. A. Hinde, C. Beer, & M. Busnel (Eds.), *Advances in the study of behavior* (Vol. 9). New York: Academic Press.

Ainsworth, M. D. S. (1989). Attachments beyond infancy. *American Psychologist, 44,* 709–716.

Ainsworth, M. D. S., Blehar, M., Waters, E., & Wall, S. (1978). *Patterns of attachment.* Hillsdale, NJ: Erlbaum.

Ajrouch, K. J., Antonucci, T. C., & Janevic, M. R. (2001). Social networks among blacks and whites: The interaction between race and age. *Journals of Gerontology: Psychological Sciences and Social Sciences, 56,* S112–S118.

Akhtar, N., Jipson, J., & Callanan, M. A. (2001). Learning words through overhearing. *Child Development, 72,* 416–430.

Akiyama, H., Antonucci, T., Takahashi, K., & Langfahl, E. S. (2003). Negative interactions in close relationships across the life span. *Journals of Gerontology: Psychological Sciences and Social Sciences, 58,* P70–P79.

Albers, L. L. (1999). The duration of labor in healthy women. *Journal of Perinatology, 19,* 114–119.

Albert, R. S. (1996). Some reasons why childhood creativity often fails to make it past puberty into the real world. In M. A. Runco (Ed.), *Creativity from childhood through adulthood: The developmental issues.* San Francisco: Jossey-Bass.

Alexander, G. E., & Reiman, E. M. (2003). In M. F. Weiner & A. M. Lipton (Eds.), *The dementias: Diagnosis, treatment, and research.* Washington, D.C.: American Psychiatric Publishing.

Alfieri, T., Ruble, D. N., & Higgins, E. T. (1996). Gender stereotypes during adolescence: Developmental changes and the transition to junior high school. *Developmental Psychology, 32,* 1129–1137.

Allen, K. R., Blieszner, R., & Roberto, K. A. (2000). Families in the middle and later years: A review and critique of research in the 1990s. *Journal of Marriage and the Family, 62,* 911–926.

Allen, M. C., & Capute, A. J. (1986). Assessment of early auditory and visual abilities of extremely premature infants. *Developmental Medicine and Child Neurology, 28,* 458–466.

Allum, J. H., Greisiger, R., Straubhaar, S., & Carpenter, M. G. (2000). Auditory perception and speech identification in children with cochlear implants tested with the EARS protocol. *British Journal of Audiology, 34,* 293–303.

Almeida, D. M., & Horn, M. C. (2004). Is daily life more stressful during middle adulthood? In O. G. Brim, C. D. Ryff, & R. C. Kessler (Eds.), *How healthy are we? A national study of well-being at midlife.* Chicago: University of Chicago Press.

Almli, C. R., Ball, R. H., & Wheeler, M. E. (2001). Human fetal and neonatal movement patterns: Gender differences and fetal-to-neonatal continuity. *Developmental Psychobiology, 38,* 252–273.

Althaus, F. (2001). Levels of sexual experience among U.S. teenagers have declined for the first time in three decades. *Family Planning Perspectives, 33,* 180.

Alvarez, J. M., Ruble, D. N., & Bolger, N. (2001). Trait understanding or evaluative reasoning? An analysis of children's behavioral predictions. *Child Development, 72,* 1409–1425.

Amara, C. E., Rice, C. L., Coval, J. J., Paterson, D. H., Winter, E. M., & Cunningham, D. A. (2003). Allometric scaling of strength in an independently living population age 55–86 years. *American Journal of Human Biology, 15,* 48–60.

Amato, P. R. (1993). Children's adjustment to divorce: Theories, hypotheses, and empirical support. *Journal of Marriage and the Family, 55,* 23–38.

Amato, P. R. (1996). Explaining the intergenerational transmission of divorce. *Journal of Marriage and the Family, 58,* 628–640.

Amato, P. R. (2000). The consequences of divorce for adults and children. *Journal of Marriage and the Family, 62,* 1269–1287.

Amato, P. R. (2001). Children of divorce in the 1990s: An update of the Amato and Keith (1991) meta-analysis. *Journal of Family Psychology, 15,* 355–370.

Amato, P. R., Johnson, D. R., Booth, A., & Rogers, S. J. (2003). Continuity and change in marital quality between 1980 and 2000. *Journal of Marriage and the Family, 65,* 1–22.

Amato, P. R., & Sobolewski, J. M. (2004). The effects of divorce on fathers and children: Nonresidential fathers and stepfathers. In M. E. Lamb (Ed.), *The role of the father in child development* (4th ed.). Hoboken, NJ: John Wiley & Sons.

Ambert, A. (1992). *The effect of children on parents.* New York: Haworth.

American Academy of Pediatrics. (2000). Prevention and management of pain and stress in the neonate (RE9945). *Pediatrics, 105,* 454–461.

American Association on Mental Retardation. (2002). *Mental retardation: Definition, classification, and systems of supports* (10th ed.). Annapolis, MD: AAMR.

American Psychiatric Association. (1994). *Diagnostic and statistical manual of mental disorders* (4th ed.). Washington, DC: Author.

American Psychological Association. (1982). *Ethical principles in the conduct of research with human participants.* Washington, DC: Author.

Amini, S. B., Catalano, P. M., Dierker, L. J., & Mann, L. I. (1996). Births to teenagers: Trends and obstetric outcomes. *Obstetrics and Gynecology, 87,* 668–674.

Amstutz, D. D., & Sheared, V. (2000). The crisis in adult basic education. *Education and Urban Society, 32,* 155–166.

Anand, K. J., & Hickey, P. R. (1992). Halothane-morphine compared with high-dose sufentanil for anesthesia and postoperative analgesia in neonatal cardiac surgery. *New England Journal of Medicine, 326,* 1–9.

Anastasi, A. (1958). Heredity, environment, and the question, "how?" *Psychological Review, 65,* 197–208.

Anderman, E. M., & Midgley, C. (1997). Changes in achievement goal orientations, perceived academic competence, and grades across the transition to middle-level schools. *Contemporary Educational Psychology, 22,* 269–298.

Anderson, C. A., Berkowitz, L., Donnerstein, E., Huesmann, L. R., Johnson, J. D., Linz, D., et al. (2003). The influence of media violence on youth. *Psychological Science in the Public Interest, 4,* 81–110.

Anderson, C. A., & Bushman, B. J. (2002, March 29). The effects of media violence on society. *Science, 295,* 2377–2379.

Anderson, K. E., Lytton, H., & Romney, D. M. (1986). Mothers' interactions with normal and conduct-disordered boys: Who affects whom? *Developmental Psychology, 22,* 604–609.

Anderson, S. E., Dallal, G. E., & Must, A. (2003). Relative weight and race influence average age at menarche: Results from two nationally representative surveys of US girls studied 25 years apart. *Pediatrics, 111,* 844–854.

Andersson, A. M., Carlsen, E., Petersen, J. H., & Skakkebaek, N. E. (2003). Variation in levels of serum inhibin B, testosterone, estradiol, luteinizing hormone, follicle-stimulating hormone, and sex hormone-ginding globulin in monthly samples from healthy men during a 17-month period: Possible effects of seasons. *Journal of Clinical Endocrinology and Metabolism, 88,* 932–937.

Andrews, G., Clark, M., & Luszcz, M. (2002). Successful aging in the Australian Longitudinal Study of Aging: Applying the MacArthur model cross-nationally. *Journal of Social Issues, 58,* 749–765.

Andrews, G. J., Gavin, N., Begley, S., & Brodie, D. (2003). Assisting friendships, combating loneliness: Users' views on a "befriending" scheme. *Ageing & Society, 23,* 349–362.

Andrich, D., & Styles, I. (1994). Psychometric evidence of intellectual growth spurts in early adolescence. *Journal of Early Adolescence, 14,* 328–344.

Aneshensel, C. S., Pearlin, L. I., Mullan, J. T., Zarit, S. H., & Whitlatch, C. J. (1995). *Profiles in caregiving: The unexpected career.* San Diego: Academic Press.

Anglin, J. M. (1993). Vocabulary development: A morphological analysis. *Monographs of the Society for Research in Child Development, 58* (Serial No. 10).

Anisfeld, E., Casper, V., Nozyce, M., & Cunningham, N. (1990). Does infant carrying promote attachment? An experimental study of the effects of increased physical contact on the development of attachment. *Child Development, 61,* 1617–1627.

Anslow, P. (1998). Birth asphyxia. *European Journal of Radiology, 26,* 148–153.

Anstey, K. J., Hofer, S. M., & Luszcz, M. A. (2003). A latent growth curve analysis of late-life sensory and cognitive function over 8 years: Evidence for specific and common factors underlying change. *Psychology and Aging, 18,* 714–726.

Aoki, K. (1986). A stochastic model of gene-culture coevolution suggested by the "culture historical hypothesis" for the evolution of adult lactose absorption in humans. *Proceedings of the National Academy of Sciences, 83,* 2929–2933.

Apgar, V., & Beck, J. (1974). *Is my baby all right?* New York: Pocket Books.

Applebaum, D. R., & Burns, G. L. (1991). Unexpected childhood death: Posttraumatic stress disorder in surviving siblings and parents. *Journal of Clinical Child Psychology, 20,* 114–120.

Appollonio, I., Carabellese, C., Frattola, L., & Trabucchi, M. (1996). Effects of sensory aids on the quality of life and mortality of elderly people: A multivariate analysis. *Age and Ageing, 25,* 89–96.

Aquilino, W. S. (1991). Predicting parents' experiences with coresident adult children. *Journal of Family Issues, 12,* 323–342.

Aquilino, W. S. (1997). From adolescent to young adult: A prospective study of parent–child relations during the transition to adulthood. *Journal of Marriage and the Family, 59,* 670–686.

Aquino, K., & Reed, A. (2002). The self-importance of moral identity. *Journal of Personality & Social Psychology, 83,* 1423–1440.

Arana-Ward, M. (1997, May 11). As technology advances, a bitter debate divides the deaf. *The Washington Post,* p. A1.

Arber, S., & Ginn, J. (1991). *Gender and later life: A sociological analysis of resources and constraints.* London: Sage.

Arbona, C., & Power, T. G. (2003). Parental attachment, self-esteem, and antisocial behaviors among African American, European American, and Mexican American adolescents. *Journal of Counseling Psychology, 50,* 40–51.

Archer, J. (1991). The influence of testosterone on human aggression. *British Journal of Psychology, 82,* 1–28.

Archer, J. (1992). *Ethology and human development.* Hertfordshire, England: Harvester Wheatsheaf.

Archer, J. (1996). Sex differences in social behavior: Are the social role and evolutionary explanations compatible? *American Psychologist, 51,* 909–917.

Archer, S. L. (1982). The lower age boundaries of identity development. *Child Development, 53,* 1551–1556.

Archer, S. L. (1992). A feminist's approach to identity research. In G. R. Adams, T. P. Gullotta, & R. Montemayor (Eds.), *Adolescent identity formation: Vol. 4. Advances in adolescent development.* Newbury Park, CA: Sage.

Ardelt, M. (2000). Antecedents and effects of wisdom in old age. *Research on Aging, 22,* 360–394.

Ardelt, M., & Day, L. (2002). Parents, siblings, and peers: Close social relationships and adolescent deviance. *Journal of Early Adolescence, 22,* 310–349.

Arendt, R., Singer, L., Angelopoulos, J., Bass-Busdiecker, O., & Mascia, J. (1998). Sensorimotor development in cocaine-exposed infants. *Infant Behavior and Development, 21,* 627–640.

Ariès, P. (1962). *Centuries of childhood.* New York: Knopf.

Ariès, P. (1981). *The hour of our death* (H. Weaver, Trans.). New York: Knopf. (Original work published 1977).

Arking, R. (2004). Extending human longevity: A biological probability. In S. G. Post & R. H. Binstock (Eds.), *The fountain of youth: Cultural, scientific, and ethical perspectives on a biomedical goal.* New York: Oxford University Press.

Arlt, W., Callies, F., van Vlijmen, J. C., Koehler, I., Reincke, M., Bidlingmaier, M., Huebler, D., Oettel, M., Ernst, M., Schulte, H. M., & Allolio, B. (1999). Dehydroepiandrosterone replacement in women with adrenal insufficiency. *New England Journal of Medicine, 341,* 1013–1020.

Armor, D. J. (2001). On family size and intelligence. *American Psychologist, 56,* 521–522.

Armstrong, E. M. (2003). *Conceiving risk, bearing responsibility: Fetal alcohol syndrome and the diagnosis of moral disorder.* Baltimore, MD: The Johns Hopkins University Press.

Armstrong, P. I., & Crombie, G. (2000). Compromises in adolescents' occupational aspirations and expectations from grades 8 to 10. *Journal of Vocational Behavior, 56,* 82–98.

Arnett, J. J. (1995). Broad and narrow socialization: The family in the context of a cultural theory. *Journal of Marriage and the Family, 57,* 617–628.

Arnett, J. J. (1999). Adolescent storm and stress, reconsidered. *American Psychologist, 54,* 317–326.

Arnett, J. J. (2002). Developmental sources of crash risk in young drivers. *Injury Prevention, 8,* 7–13.

Arnett, J. J. (2000). Emerging adulthood: A theory of development from the late teens through the twenties. *American Psychologist, 55,* 469–480.

Aronson, J., Lustina, M. J., Good, C., Keough, K., Steele, C. M., & Brown, J. (1999). When white men can't do math: Necessary and sufficient factors in stereotype threat. *Journal of Experimental Social Psychology, 35,* 29–46.

Arroyo, C. G., & Zigler, E. (1995). Racial identity, academic achievement, and the psychological well-being of economically disadvantaged adolescents. *Journal of Personality and Social Psychology, 69,* 903–914.

Arseneault, L., Tremblay, R. E., Boulerice, B., & Saucier, J. (2002). Obstetrical complications and violent delinquency: Testing two developmental pathways. *Child Development, 73,* 496–508.

Asarnow, J. R., Jaycox, L. H., & Tompson, M. C. (2001). Depression in youth: Psychosocial interventions. *Journal of Clinical Child Psychology, 30,* 33–47.

Asbury, K., Dunn, J. F., Pike, A., & Plomin, R. (2003). Nonshared environmental influences on individual differences in early behavioral development: A monozygotic twin differences study. *Child Development, 74,* 933–943.

Asendorpf, J. B., & van Aken, A. G. (2003). Personality–relationship transaction in adolescence: Core versus surface personality characteristics. *Journal of Personality, 71,* 629–666.

Asendorpf, J. B., Warkentin, V., & Baudonnière, P. M. (1996). Self-awareness and other-awareness: 2. Mirror self-recognition, social contingency awareness, and synchronic imitation. *Developmental Psychology, 32,* 313–321.

Associated Press. (2003, November 21). Women earn 20% less than men, GAO finds. *The Washington Post,* p. E4.

Associated Press. (2004, January 18). Woman delivers daughter after dispute over C-section. *Sunday Patriot News* (Harrisburg, PA), p. B11.

Atchley, R. C. (1976). *The Sociology of retirement.* Cambridge, MA: Schenkman.

Athey, I. (1984). Contributions of play to development. In T. D. Yawkey & A. D. Pellegrini (Eds.), *Child's play: Developmental and applied.* Hillsdale, NJ: Erlbaum.

Atkinson, L., & Goldberg, S. (2004). Applications of attachment: The integration of developmental and clinical traditions. In L. Atkinson & S. Goldberg (Eds.), *Attachment issues in psychopathology and intervention.* Mahwah, NJ: Erlbaum.

Atkinson, R. C. & Shiffrin, R. M. (1968). Human memory: A proposed system and its control processes. In K. W. Spence & J. T. Spence (Eds.), *The psychology of learning and motiviation: Advances in research and theory (Vol. 2).* New York: Academic Press.

Au, R., Joung, P., Nicholas, M., Obler, L. K., Kass, R., & Albert, M. L. (1995). Naming ability across the adult life span. *Aging and Cognition, 2,* 300–311.

Austrian, S. G. (Ed) (2002). *Developmental theories through the life cycle.* New York: Columbia University.

Autti-Rämö, I. (2000). Twelve-year follow-up of children exposed to alcohol in utero. *Developmental Medicine & Child Neurology, 42,* 406–411.

Avellar, S., & Smock, P. J. (2003). Has the price of motherhood declined over time? A cross-cohort comparison of the motherhood wage penalty. *Journal of Marriage and Family, 65,* 597–607.

Avert (2004). *Preventing mother-to-child transmission of AIDS.* Available online: http://www.avert.org/motherchild.htm (retrieved September 2, 2004).

Avolio, B. J., & Sosik, J. J. (1999). A life-span framework for assessing the impact of work on white-collar workers. In S. L. Willis & J. D. Reid (Eds.), *Life in the middle: Psychological and social development in middle age.* San Diego: Academic Press.

Axinn, W. G., & Barber, J. S. (1997). Living arrangements and family formation attitudes in early adulthood. *Journal of Marriage and the Family, 59,* 595–561.

Aylward, G. P. (1997). *Infant and early childhood neuropsychology.* New York: Plenum.

Azmitia, M. (1992). Expertise, private speech, and the development of self-regulation. In R. M. Diaz & L. E. Berk (Eds.), *Private speech: From social interaction to self-regulation.* Hillsdale, NJ: Erlbaum.

B

Babikian, H. M., & Goldman, A. (1971). A study of teenage pregnancy. *American Journal of Psychiatry, 128,* 755–760.

Bacharach, V. R., & Baumeister, A. A. (1998). Direct and indirect effects of maternal intelligence, maternal age, income, and home environment on intelligence of preterm, low-birth-weight children. *Journal of Applied Developmental Psychology, 19,* 361–375.

Bachman, J. G., Safron, D. J., Sy, S. R., & Schulenberg, J. E. (2003). Wishing to work: New perspectives on how adolescents' part-time work intensity is linked to educational disengagement, substance use, and other problem behaviors. *International Journal of Behavioral Development, 27,* 301–315.

Baddeley, A. (1986). *Working memory.* Oxford: Oxford University Press.

Baddeley, A. (1992). Working memory. *Science, 255,* 556–559.

Badenes, L. V., Estevan, R. A. C., & Garcia Bacete, F. J. (2000). Theory of mind and peer rejection at school. *Social Development, 9,* 271–283.

Baek, H. (2002). A comparative study of moral development of Korean and British children. *Journal of Moral Education, 31,* 373–391.

Baer, J. (2002). Is family cohesion a risk or protective factor during adolescent development. *Journal of Marriage and the Family, 64,* 668–675.

Baer, J. S., Sampson, P. D., Barr, H. M., Connor, P. D., & Streissguth, A. P. (2003). A 21-year longitudinal analysis of the effects of prenatal alcohol exposure on young adult drinking. *Archives of General Psychiatry, 60,* 377–385.

Bahrick, H. P. (1984). Semantic memory content in permastore: Fifty years of memory for Spanish learned in high school. *Journal of Experimental Psychology: General, 113,* 1–29.

Bahrick, H. P., Bahrick, P. O., & Wittlinger, R. P. (1975). Fifty years of memory for names and faces: A cross-sectional approach. *Journal of Experimental Psychology: General, 104,* 54–75.

Bahrick, H. P., & Hall, L. K. (1991). Lifetime maintenance of high school mathematics content. *Journal of Experimental Psychology: General, 120,* 20–33.

Bahrick, L. E., & Pickens, J. N. (1995). Infant memory for object motion across a period of three months: Implications for a four-phase attention function. *Journal of Experimental Child Psychology, 59,* 343–371.

Bailey, A., Lecouteur, A., Gottesman, I., Bolton, P., Simonoff, E., Yuzda, E., et al. (1995). Autism as a strongly genetic disorder: Evidence from a British twin study. *Psychological Medicine, 25,* 63–77.

Bailey, C. E. (Ed.) (2000). *Children in therapy: Using the family as a resource.* New York: W. W. Norton.

Bailey, J. M., Bechtold, K. T., & Berenbaum, S. A. (2002). Who are tomboys and why should we study them? *Archives of Sexual Behavior, 31,* 333–341.

Bailey, J. M., Dunne, M. P., & Martin, N. G. (2000). Genetic and environmental influences on sexual orientation and its correlates in an Australian twin sample. *Journal of Personality and Social Psychology, 78,* 524–536.

Bailey, J. M., & Pillard, R. C. (1991). A genetic study of male sexual orientation. *Archives of General Psychiatry, 48,* 1089–1096.

Bailey, J. M., Pillard, R. C., Neale, M. C., & Agyei, Y. (1993). Heritable factors influence sexual orientation in women. *Archives of General Psychiatry, 50,* 217–223.

Baillargeon, R. (2002). The acquisition of physical knowledge in infancy: A summary in eight lessons. In U. Goswami (Ed.), *Blackwell handbook of child cognitive development* (pp. 47–83). Oxford: Blackwell.

Bajor, J. K., & Baltes, B. B. (2003). The relationship between selection optimization with compensation, conscientiousness, motivation, and performance. *Journal of Vocational Behavior, 63,* 347–367.

Baker, D. P., & Jones, D. P. (1992). Opportunity and performance: A sociological explanation for gender differences in academic mathematics. In J. Wrigley (Ed.), *Education and gender equality.* London: Falmer Press.

Baker, L., & Brown, A. L. (1984). Metacognitive skills and reading. In P. D. Pearson (Ed.), *A handbook of reading research.* New York: Longman.

Bakermans-Kranenburg, M. J., van IJzendoorn, M. H., & Juffer, F. (2003). Less is more: Meta-analyses of sensitivity and attachment interventions in early childhood. *Psychological Bulletin, 129,* 195–215.

Baker-Ward, L., Gordon, B. N., Ornstein, P. A., Larus, D. M., & Clubb, P. A. (1993). Young children's long-term retention of a pediatric examination. *Child Development, 64,* 1519–1533.

Baker-Ward, L., Ornstein, P. A., & Holden, D. J. (1984). The expression of memorization in early childhood. *Journal of Experimental Child Psychology, 37,* 555–575.

Baldwin, R. C. (2000). Poor prognosis of depression in elderly people: Causes and actions. *Annals of Medicine, 32,* 252–256.

Balk, D. E., & Corr, C. A. (2001). Bereavement during adolescence: A review of research. In M. S. Stroebe, R. O. Hansson, W. Stroebe, & H. Schut (Eds.), *Handbook of bereavement research: Consequences, coping, and care.* Washington, DC: American Psychological Association.

Baltes, P. B. (1987). Theoretical propositions of life-span developmental psychology: On the dynamics between growth and decline. *Developmental Psychology, 23,* 611–626.

Baltes, P. B., & Baltes, M. M. (1990). Psychological perspectives on successful aging: The model of selective optimization with compensation. In P. B. Baltes & M. M. Baltes (Eds.), *Successful aging: Perspectives from the behavioral sciences.* New York: Cambridge University Press.

Baltes, P. B., & Carstensen, L. L. (2003). The process of successful aging: Selection, optimization and compensation. In U. M. Staudinger & U. Lindenberger (Eds.), *Understanding human development: Dialogues with life-span psychology.* Dordecht, Netherlands: Kluwer Academic Press.

Baltes, P. B., & Freund, A. M. (2003). Human strengths as the orchestration of wisdom and selective optimization with compensation. In L. G. Aspinwall & U. M. Staudinger (Eds.), *A psychology of human strengths: Fundamental questions and future directions for a positive psychology.* Washington, DC: American Psychological Association.

Baltes, P. B. & Kliegl, R. (1992). Further testing of limits of cognitive plasticity: Negative age differences in a mnemonic skill are robust. *Developmental Psychology, 28,* 121–125.

Baltes, P. B., & Lindenberger, U. (1997). Emergence of a powerful connection between sensory and cognitive functions across the adult life span: A new window to the study of cognitive aging? *Psychology and Aging, 12,* 12–21.

Baltes, P. B., Lindenberger, U., & Staudinger, U. M. (1998). Life-span theory in developmental psychology. In R. M. Lerner (Vol. Ed.), W. Damon (Editor-in-Chief), *Handbook of child psychology: Vol. 1. Theoretical models of human development* (5th ed.). New York: Wiley.

Baltes, P. B., Reese, H. W., & Lipsitt, L. P. (1980). Life-span developmental psychology. *Annual Review of Psychology, 31,* 65–110.

Baltes, P. B., Smith, J., & Staudinger, U. M. (1992). Wisdom and successful aging. In T. B. Sonderegger (Ed.), *Nebraska Symposium on Motivation: Vol. 39. Psychology and aging.* Lincoln: University of Nebraska Press.

Baltes, P. B., & Staudinger, U. M. (2000). Wisdom: A metaheuristic (pragmatic) to orchestrate mind and virtue toward excellence. *American Psychologist, 55,* 122–136.

Baltes, P. B., Staudinger, U. M., Maercker, A., & Smith, J. (1995). People nominated as wise: A comparative study of wisdom-related knowledge. *Psychology and Aging, 10,* 155–166.

Bandura, A. (1965). Influence of models' reinforcement contingencies on the acquisition of imitative responses. *Journal of Personality and Social Psychology, 1,* 589–595.

Bandura, A. (1971). An analysis of modeling processes. In A. Bandura (Ed.), *Psychological modeling.* New York: Lieber-Atherton.

Bandura, A. (1977). *Social learning theory.* Englewood Cliffs, NJ: Prentice-Hall.

Bandura, A. (1986). *Social foundations of thought and action: A social cognitive theory.* Englewood Cliffs, NJ: Prentice-Hall.

Bandura, A. (1989). Social cognitive theory. In R. Vasta (Ed.), *Annals of child development: Vol. 6. Theories of child development: Revised formulations and current issues.* Greenwich, CT: JAI Press.

Bandura, A. (1991). Social cognitive theory of moral thought and action. In W. M. Kurtines & J. L. Gewirtz (Eds.), *Handbook of moral behavior and development: Vol. 1. Theory.* Hillsdale, NJ: Erlbaum.

Bandura, A. (2000). Social cognitive theory: An agentic perspective. *Annual Review of Psychology, 52,* 1–26.

Bandura, A. (2002). Selective moral disengagement in the exercise of moral agency. *Journal of Moral Education, 31,* 101–119.

Bandura, A., Caprara, G. V., Barbaranelli, C., Pastorelli, C., & Regalia, C. (2001). Sociocognitive self-regulatory mechanisms governing transgressive behavior. *Journal of Personality & Social Psychology, 80,* 125–135.

Banerjee, R., & Lintern, V. (2000). Boys will be boys: The effect of social evaluation concerns on gender-typing. *Social Development, 9,* 397–408.

Bank, L., Marlowe, J., Reid, J., Patterson, G., & Weinrott, M. (1991). A comparative evaluation of parent-training interventions for families of chronic delinquents. *Journal of Abnormal Child Psychology, 19,* 15–33.

Bankoff, E. A. (1983). Aged parents and their widowed daughters: A support relationship. *Journal of Gerontology, 38,* 226–230.

Banks, M. S., & Ginsburg, A. P. (1985). Infant visual preferences: A review and new theoretical treatment. In H. W. Reese (Ed.), *Advances in child development and behavior* (Vol. 19). Orlando, FL: Academic Press.

Banks, M. S. & Salapatek, P. (1983). Infant visual perception. In M. M. Haith & J. J. Campos (Eds.) & P. H. Mussen (Gen Ed.), *Handbook of child psychology: Vol 2. Infancy and developmental psychobiology* (4th ed.), New York: Wiley.

Banks, M. S., & Shannon, E. (1993). Spatial and chromatic visual efficiency in human neonates. In C. E. Granrud (Ed.), *Visual perception and cognition in infancy.* Hillsdale, NJ: Erlbaum.

Barack, J. A., Hodapp, R. M., & Zigler, E. (Eds.) (1998). *Handbook of mental retardation and development.* New York: Cambridge University Press.

Barash, D. P. (2002, May 24). Evolution, males, and violence. *The Chronicle of Higher Education,* pp. B7–B9.

Barber, B. L., Eccles, J. S., & Stone, M. R. (2001). Whatever happened to the jock, the brain, and the princess? Young adult pathways linked to adolescent activity involvement and social identity. *Journal of Adolescent Research, 16,* 429–455.

Barker, D. J. P. (1998). *Mothers, babies, and disease in later life* (2nd ed.). New York: Churchill Livingstone.

Barkley, R. A. (1997). Behavioral inhibition, sustained attention, and executive functions: Constructing a unifying theory of ADHD. *Psychological Bulletin, 121,* 65–94.

Barkley, R. A. (2000). Genetics of childhood disorders: XVII. ADHD, Part 1: The executive functions and ADHD. *Journal of the American Academy of Child and Adolescent Psychiatry, 39,* 1064–1068.

Barkley, R. A., Fischer, M., Edelbrock, C., & Smallish, L. (1991). The adolescent outcome of hyperactive children diagnosed by research criteria. Mother–child interactions, family conflicts and maternal psychopathology. *Journal of Child Psychology and Psychiatry and Allied Disciplines, 32,* 233–255.

Barling, J., Rogers, K. A., & Kelloway, E. K. (1995). Some effects of teenagers' part-time employment: The quantity and quality of work make the difference. *Journal of Organizational Behavior, 16,* 143–154.

Barnas, M. V., Pollina, L., & Cummings, E. M. (1991). Life-span attachment: Relations between attachment and socioemotional functioning in adult women. *Genetic, Social, and General Psychology Monographs, 117,* 175–202.

Barner, M. R. (1999). Sex-role stereotyping in FCC-mandated children's educational television. *Journal of Broadcasting & Electronic Media, 43,* 551–564.

Barnes, D. E., Yaffe, K., Satariano, W. A., & Tager, I. B. (2003). A longitudinal study of cardiorespiratory fitness and cognitive function in healthy older adults. *Journal of the American Geriatrics Society, 51,* 459–465.

Barnes, K. E. (1971). Preschool play norms: A replication. *Developmental Psychology, 5,* 99–103.

Barnett, R. C. (1994). Home-to-work spillover revisited: A study of full-time employed women in dual-earner couples. *Journal of Marriage and the Family, 56,* 647–656.

Barnett, R. C., Raudenbush, S. W., Brennan, R. T., & Pleck, J. H. (1995). Change in job and marital experiences and change in psychological distress: A longitudinal study of dual-earner couples. *Journal of Personality and Social Psychology, 69,* 839–850.

Barnett, W. S. (2002). Early childhood education. In A. Molnar (Ed.), *School reform proposals: The research evidence* (pp. 1–26). Greenwich, CT: Information Age Publishing.

Baron, N. S. (1992). Growing up with language: How children learn to talk. Reading, MA: Addison-Wesley.

Baron-Cohen, S. (1995). *Mindblindness: An essay on autism and theory of mind.* Cambridge, MA: MIT Press.

Baron-Cohen, S. (2000). Theory of mind and autism: A 15 year review. In S. Baron-Cohen, H. Tager-Flusberg, & D. J. Cohen (Eds.), *Understanding other minds: Perspectives from developmental cognitive neuroscience* (2nd ed.). Oxford: Oxford University Press.

Baron-Cohen, S. (2003). *The essential difference: The truth about the male and female brain.* New York: Basic Books.

Baron-Cohen, S., Leslie, A. M., & Frith, U. (1985). Does the autistic child have a "theory of mind"? *Cognition, 21,* 37–46.

Barr, H. M., & Streissguth, A. P. (1991). Caffeine use during pregnancy and child outcome: A 7-year prospective study. *Neurotoxicology and Teratology, 13,* 441–448.

Barr, R. G., Pantel, M. S., Young, S. N., Wright, J. H., Hendricks, L. A., & Gravel, R. (1999). The response of crying newborns to sucrose: Is it a "sweetness" effect? *Physiological Behavior, 66,* 409–417.

Barr, R., Dowden, A., & Hayne, H. (1996). Developmental changes in deferred imitation by 6- to 24-month-old infants. *Infant Behavior & Development, 19,* 159–170.

Barrett, M. (1995). Early lexical development. In P. Fletcher & B. MacWhinney (Eds.), *The handbook of child language* (pp. 362–392). Oxford: Blackwell.

Barrett, T. R., & Wright, M. (1981). Age-related facilitation in recall following semantic processing. *Journal of Gerontology, 36,* 194–199.

Bartels, M., Rietveld, M. J. H., van Baal, G. C. M., & Boomsma, D. I. (2002). Genetic and environmental influences on the development of intelligence. *Behavior Genetics, 32,* 237–249.

Bartholomew, K., & Horowitz, L. M. (1991). Attachment styles among young adults: A test of a four-category model. *Journal of Personality and Social Psychology, 61,* 226–244.

Bartlett, D. (1997). Primitive reflexes and early motor development. *Journal of Developmental and Behavioral Pediatrics, 18,* 151–157.

Baruch, R. (1967). The achievement motive in women: Implications for career development. *Journal of Personality and Social Psychology, 5,* 260–267.

Basseches, M. (1984). Dialectical thinking and adult development. Norwood, NJ: Ablex.

Bates, E., Marchman, V., Thal, D., Fenson, L., Dale, P., Reznick, J. S., et al. (1994). Developmental and stylistic variation in the composition of early vocabulary. *Journal of Child Language, 21,* 85–123.

Bates, E., O'Connell, B., & Shore, C. (1987). Language and communication in infancy. In J. D. Osofsky (Ed.), *Handbook of infant development* (2nd ed.). New York: Wiley.

Batshaw, M. L. (2002). *Children with disabilities* (5th ed.). Baltimore: Paul H. Brookes.

Bauchner, H. (1996). Failure to thrive. In R. E. Behrman, R. M. Kliegman, & A. M. Arvin (Eds.), *Nelson textbook of pediatrics* (15th ed.). Philadelphia: W. B. Saunders.

Bauer, P. J. (2004). Early memory development. In U. Goswami (Ed.), *Blackwell handbook of childhood cognitive development* (pp. 127–146). Malden, MA: Blackwell Publishing.

Bauer, P. J. (1996). What do infants recall of their lives? Memory for specific events by one- to two-year-olds. *American Psychologist, 51,* 29–41.

Bauer, P. J., Hertsgaard, L. A., & Wewerka, S. S. (1995). Effects of experience and reminding on long-term recall in infancy: Remembering not to forget. *Journal of Experimental Child Psychology, 59,* 260–298.

Bauer, P. J., Wenner, J. A., Dropik, P. L., & Wewerka, S. S. (2000). Parameters of remembering and forgetting in the transition from infancy to early childhood. *Monographs of the Society for Research in Child Development, 65* (Serial No. 263).

Baumrind, D. (1967). Child care practices anteceding three patterns of preschool behavior. *Genetic Psychology Monographs, 75,* 43–88.

Baumrind, D. (1977, March). *Socialization determinants of personal agency.* Paper presented at the biennial meeting of the Society for Research in Child Development, New Orleans.

Baumrind, D. (1991). Effective parenting during the early adolescent transition. In P. A. Cowan & M. Hetherington (Eds.), *Family transitions.* Hillsdale, NJ: Erlbaum.

Bauserman, R. (2002). Child adjustment in joint-custody versus sole-custody arrangements: A meta-analytic review. *Journal of Family Psychology, 16,* 91–102.

Baydar, N., & Brooks-Gunn, J. (1991). Effects of maternal employment and child-care arrangements on preschoolers' cognitive and behavioral outcomes: Evidence from the children of the National Longitudinal Survey of Youth. *Developmental Psychology, 27,* 932–945.

Bayley, N. (1993). *Bayley scales of infant development* (2nd ed.). San Antonio: Psychological Corporation.

Beal, C. R. (1990). The development of text evaluation and revision skills. *Child Development, 61,* 247–258.

Beal, C. R. (1994). *Boys and girls: The development of gender roles.* New York: McGraw-Hill.

Bear, M. F., Connors, B. W., & Paradiso, M. A. (2001). *Neuroscience: Exploring the brain* (2nd ed.). Philadelphia, PA. Lippincott, Williams & Wilkins.

Beautrais, A. L. (2003). Life course factors associated with suicidal behaviors in young people. *American Behavioral Scientist, 46,* 1137–1156.

Beck, C., Cody, M., Souder, E., Zhang, M. L., & Small, G. W. (2000). Dementia diagnostic guidelines: Methodologies, results, and implementation costs. *Journal of the American Geriatrics Society, 48,* 1195–1203.

Beck, M. (1994, January 17). How far should we push mother nature? *Newsweek,* 54–57.

Becker, A. E., Burwell, R. A., Herzog, D. B., Hamburg, P., & Gilman, S. E. (2002). Eating behaviours and attitudes following prolonged exposure to television among ethnic Fijian adolescent girls. *British Journal of Psychiatry, 180,* 509–514.

Beckwith, L., Cohen, S. E., & Hamilton, C. E. (1999). Maternal sensitivity during infancy and subsequent life events relate to attachment representation at early adulthood. *Developmental Psychology, 35,* 693–700.

Beckwith, L., Rozga, A., & Sigman, M. (2002). Maternal sensitivity and attachment in atypical groups. In R. V. Kail (Ed.), *Advances in child development and behavior* (Vol. 30). San Diego: Academic Press.

Bedford, V. H., & Volling, B. L. (2004). A dynamic ecological systems perspective on emotion regulation development within the sibling relationship context. In F. R. Lang & K. L. Fingerman (Eds.), *Growing together: Personal relationships across the life span.* Cambridge, UK: Cambridge University Press.

Bedford, V. H., Volling, B. L., & Avioli, P. M. (2000). Positive consequences of sibling conflict in childhood and adulthood. *International Journal of Aging and Human Development, 51,* 53–69.

Beehr, T. A., Glazer, S., Nielson, N. L., & Farmer, S. J. (2000). Work and nonwork predictors of employee's retirement age. *Journal of Vocational Behavior, 57,* 206–225.

Begley, S. (1998, September 7). The parent trap. *Newsweek,* 52–59.

Behrend, D. A., Rosengren, K., & Perlmutter, M. (1989). A new look at children's private speech: The effects of age, task difficulty, and parent presence. *International Journal of Behavioral Development, 12,* 305–320.

Beilin, H. (1992). Piaget's enduring contribution to developmental psychology. *Developmental Psychology, 28,* 191–204.

Beitchman, J. H., Zucker, K. J., Hood, J. E., daCosta, G. A., & Akman, D. (1991). A review of the short-term effects of child sexual abuse. *Child Abuse & Neglect, 15,* 537–556.

Bell, J. H., & Bromnick, R. D. (2003). The social reality of the imaginary audience: A grounded theory approach. *Adolescence, 38,* 205–219.

Bell, K. L., & Calkins, S. D. (2000). Relationships as inputs and outputs of emotion regulation. *Psychological Inquiry, 11,* 160–163.

Bellanti, C. J., Bierman, K. L., & Conduct Problems Prevention Research Group. (2000). Disentangling the impact of low cognitive ability and inattention on social behavior and peer relationships. *Journal of Clinical Child Psychology, 29,* 66–75.

Bellinger, D., Leviton, A., Waternaux, C., Needleman, H., & Rabinowitz, M. (1987). Longitudinal analyses of prenatal and postnatal lead exposure and early cognitive development. *New England Journal of Medicine, 316,* 1037–1043.

Bellugi, U. (1988). The acquisition of a spatial language. In F. S. Kessel (Ed.), *The development of language and language researchers: Essays in honor of Roger Brown.* Hillsdale, NJ: Erlbaum.

Belsky, J. (1981). Early human experience: A family perspective. *Developmental Psychology, 17,* 3–23.

Belsky, J., Jaffee, S. R., Caspi, A., Moffitt, T., & Silva, P. A. (2003). Intergenerational relationships in young adulthood and their life course, mental health, and personality correlates. *Journal of Family Psychology, 17,* 460–471.

Belsky, J., Jaffee, S., Hsieh, K., & Silva, P. A. (2001). Child-rearing antecedents of intergenerational relations in young adulthood: A prospective study. *Developmental Psychology, 37,* 801–813.

Belsky, J., Lang, M. E., & Rovine, M. (1985). Stability and change in marriage across the transition to parenthood: A second study. *Journal of Marriage and the Family, 47,* 855–865.

Belsky, J., & Rovine, M. J. (1988). Nonmaternal care in the first year of life and the security of infant–parent attachment. *Child Development, 59,* 157–167.

Belsky, J., Steinberg, L., & Draper, P. (1991). Childhood experience, interpersonal development, and reproductive strategy: An evolutionary theory of socialization. *Child Development, 62,* 647–670.

Bem, S. L. (1974). The measurement of psychological androgyny. *Journal of Consulting and Clinical Psychology, 42,* 155–162.

Bem, S. L. (1975). Sex-role adaptability: One consequence of psychological androgyny. *Journal of Personality and Social Psychology, 31,* 634–643.

Bem, S. L. (1978). Beyond androgyny: Some presumptuous prescriptions for a liberated sexual identity. In J. A. Sherman & F. L. Denmark (Eds.), *The psychology of women: Future directions in research.* New York: Psychological Dimensions.

Bem, S. L. (1989). Genital knowledge and gender constancy in preschool children. *Child Development, 60,* 649–662.

Bemporad, J. R. (1979). Adult recollections of a formerly autistic child. *Journal of Autism and Developmental Disorders, 9,* 179–197.

Benbow, C. P., & Arjmand, O. (1990). Predictors of high academic achievement in mathematics and science by mathematically talented students: A longitudinal study. *Journal of Educational Psychology, 82,* 430–441.

Benda, B. B., & DiBlasio, F. A. (1994). An integration of theory: Adolescent sexual contacts. *Journal of Youth and Adolescence, 23,* 403–420.

Benenson, J. F., Philippoussis, M., & Leeb, R. (1999). Sex differences in neonates' cuddliness. *Journal of Genetic Psychology, 160,* 332–342.

Benes, F. M. (1998). Human brain growth spans decades. *American Journal of Psychiatry, 155,* 1489.

Bengtson, V. L. (2001). Beyond the nuclear family: The increasing importance of multigenerational bonds. *Journal of Marriage and Family, 63,* 1–16.

Bengtson, V., Rosenthal, C., & Burton, L. (1990). Families and aging: Diversity and heterogeneity. In R. H. Binstock & L. K. George (Eds.), *Handbook of aging and the social sciences* (3rd ed.). San Diego: Academic Press.

Bengtson, V., Rosenthal, C., & Burton, L. (1996). Paradoxes of families and aging. In R. H. Binstock, L. K. George, V. W. Marshall, G. C. Myers, & J. H. Schulz (Eds.), *Handbook of aging and the social sciences* (4th ed.). San Diego: Academic Press.

Benjet, C., & Hernández-Guzmán, L. (2002). A short-term longitudinal study of pubertal change, gender, and psychological well-being of Mexican early adolescents. *Journal of Youth and Adolescence, 31,* 429–442.

Benjet, C., & Kazdin, A. E. (2003). Spanking children: The controversies, findings, and new directions. *Clinical Psychology Review, 23,* 197–224.

Benoit, D., & Coolbear, J. (2004). Disorders of attachment and failure to thrive. In L. Atkinson & S. Goldberg (Eds.), *Attachment issues in psychopathology and intervention.* Mahwah, NJ: Erlbaum.

Benoit, D., & Parker, K. C. (1994). Stability and transmission of attachment across three generations. *Child Development, 65,* 1444–1456.

Berg, C. A. (2000). Intellectual development in adulthood. In R. J. Sternberg (Ed.), *The handbook of intelligence* (pp. 117–137). New York: Cambridge University Press.

Berg, C. A., & Klaczynski, P. A. (1996). Practical intelligence and problem solving: Searching for perspectives. In F. Blanchard-Fields & T. M. Hess (Eds.), *Perspectives on cognitive change in adulthood and aging.* New York: McGraw-Hill.

Bergem, A. L. M., Engedal, K., & Kringlen, E. (1997). The role of heredity in late-onset Alzheimer disease and vascular dementia: A twin study. *Archives of General Psychiatry, 54,* 264–270.

Berger, A. S. (1993). *Dying and death in law and medicine: A forensic primer for health and legal professionals.* Westport, CT: Praeger.

Bering, J. M., & Bjorklund, D. F. (2004). The natural emergence of reasoning about the afterlife as a developmental regularity. *Developmental Psychology, 40,* 217–233.

Berk, L. E. (1992). Children's private speech: An overview of theory and the status of research. In R. M. Diaz & L. E. Berk (Eds.), *Private speech: From social interaction to self-regulation.* Hillsdale, NJ: Erlbaum.

Berk, L. E., & Landau, S. (1993). Private speech of learning disabled and normally achieving children in classroom academic and laboratory contexts. *Child Development, 64,* 556–571.

Berk, L. E., & Winsler, A. (1995). *Scaffolding children's learning: Vygotsky and early childhood education.* Washington, DC: National Association for the Education of Young Children.

Berkowitz, M. W., & Gibbs, J. C. (1983). Measuring the developmental features of moral discussion. *Merrill-Palmer Quarterly, 29,* 399–410.

Berman, A. L., & Jobes, D. A. (1991). *Adolescent suicide: Assessment and intervention.* Washington, DC: American Psychological Association.

Berman, W. H., & Sperling, M. B. (1991). Parental attachment and emotional distress in the transition to college. *Journal of Youth and Adolescence, 20,* 427–440.

Bernal, M. E., & Knight, G. P. (1997). Ethnic identity of Latino children. In J. G. Garcia & M. C. Zea (Eds.), *Psychological interventions and research with Latino populations.* Boston: Allyn & Bacon.

Berndt, T. J. (1979). Developmental changes in conforming to peers and parents. *Developmental Psychology, 15,* 608–616.

Berndt, T. J., & Murphy, L. M. (2002). Influences of friends and friendships: Myths, truths, and research recommendations. In R. V. Kail (Ed.), *Advances in child development and behavior* (Vol. 30). San Diego: Academic Press.

Berndt, T. J., & Perry, T. B. (1990). Distinctive features and effects of early adolescent friendships. In R. Montemayor, G. R. Adams, & T. P. Gullotta (Eds.), *From childhood to adolescence: A transitional period.* Newbury Park, CA: Sage.

Berntsen, D., & Rubin, D. (2002). Emotionally charged autobiographical memories across the life span: The recall of happy, sad, traumatic, and involuntary memories. *Psychology and Aging, 17,* 636–652.

Bernstein, A.C., & Cowan, P.A. (1975). Children's concepts of how people get babies. *Child Development,* 46, 77–91.

Berry, J. W., Poortinga, Y. H., Segall, M., & Dasen, P. R. (1992). *Cross-cultural psychology: research and applications.* Cambridge, England: Cambridge University Press.

Berson, E. L. (2000). Nutrition and retinal degenerations. *International Ophthalmology Clinic, 40,* 93–111.

Bertenthal, B. I., Campos, J. J., & Kermoian, R. (1994). An epigenetic perspective on the development of self-produced locomotion and its consequences. *Current Directions in Psychological Science, 3,* 140–145.

Bertenthal, B. I., & Fischer, K. W. (1978). Development of self-recognition in the infant. *Developmental Psychology, 14,* 44–50.

Bertenthal, B. I., & von Hofsten, C. (1998). Eye, head and trunk control: The foundation for manual development. *Neuroscience and Biobehavioral Reviews, 22,* 515–520.

Bertman, S. L. (1991). Children and death: Insights, hindsights, and illuminations. In D. Papadatou & C. Papadatos (Eds.), *Children and Death.* New York: Hemisphere.

Berzonsky, M. D., & Kuk, L. S. (2000). Identity status, identity processing style, and the transition to university. *Journal of Adolescent Research, 15,* 81–98.

Bess, F. H., & McConnell, F. E. (1981). *Audiology, education, and the hearing impaired child.* St. Louis: Mosby.

Best, D. L. (1993). Inducing children to generate mnemonic organizational strategies: An examination of long-term retention and materials. *Developmental Psychology, 29,* 324–336.

Best, D. L., & Williams, J. E. (1993). A cross-cultural viewpoint. In A. E. Beall & R. J. Sternberg (Eds.), *The psychology of gender* (pp. 215–248). New York: Guilford Press.

Beyer, S. (1995). Maternal employment and children's academic achievement: Parenting styles as mediating variable. *Developmental Review, 15,* 212–253.

Beyers, J. M., Bates, J. E., Pettit, G. S., & Dodge, K. A. (2003). Neighborhood structure, parenting processes, and the development of youths' externalizing behaviors: A multilevel analysis. *American Journal of Community Psychology, 31,* 35–53.

Beyers, W., Goossens, L., Vansant, I., & Moors, E. (2003). Structural model of autonomy in middle and late adolescence: Connectedness, separation, detachment, and agency. *Journal of Youth and Adolescence, 32,* 351–365.

Bianchi, S. M. (2000). Maternal employment and time with children: Dramatic change or surprising continuity? *Demography, 37,* 401–414.

Bianchi, S. M., Milkie, M. A., Sayer, L. C., & Robinson, J. P. (2000). Is anyone doing the housework? Trends in the gender division of household labor. *Social Forces, 79,* 191–228.

Biederman, I., Cooper, E. E., Fox, P. W., & Mahadevan, R. S. (1992). Unexceptional spatial memory in an exceptional memorist. *Journal of Experimental Psychology: Learning, Memory, and Cognition, 18,* 654–657.

Biederman, J., Faraone, S., Milberger, S., Guite, J., Mick, E., Chen, L., et al. (1996). A prospective 4-year follow-up study of attention deficit hyperactivity and related disorders. *Archives of General Psychiatry, 53,* 437–446.

Biederman, J., Milberger, S., Faraone, S. V., Kiely, K., Guite, J., Mick, E., et al. (1995). Family-environment risk factors for attention-deficit hyperactivity disorder: A test of Rutter's indicators of adversity. *Archives of General Psychiatry, 52,* 464–470.

Bierhoff, H., & Schmohr, M. (2003). Romantic and marital relationships. In F. R. Lang & K. L. Fingerman (Eds.), *Growing together. Personal relationships across the life span.* Cambridge, UK: Cambridge University Press.

Bigler, R. S., & Liben, L. S. (1990). The role of attitudes and interventions in gender-schematic processing. *Child Development, 61,* 1440–1452.

Billing, L., Eriksson, M., Jonsson, B., Steneroth, G., & Zetterstrom, R. (1994). The influence of environmental factors on behavioral problems in 8-year-old children exposed to amphetamine during fetal life. *Child Abuse and Neglect, 18,* 3–9.

Binstock, R. H. (2004). The search for prolongevity: A contentious pursuit. In S. G. Post & R. H. Binstock (Eds.), *The fountain of youth: Cultural, scientific, and ethical perspectives on a biomedical goal.* New York: Oxford University Press.

Birdsong, D. (1999). Introduction: Whys and why nots of the critical period hypothesis for second language acquisition. In D. Birdsong (Ed.), *Second language acquisition and the critical period hypothesis.* Mahwah, NJ: Erlbaum.

Birnbacher, R., Messerschmidt, & Pollak, A. P. (2002). Diagnosis and prevention of neural tube defects. *Current Opinion in Urology, 12,* 461–464.

Birren, J. E., Butler, R. N., Greenhouse, S. W., Sokoloff, L., & Yarrow, M. R. (Eds.). (1963). *Human aging: A biological and behavioral study.* Washington, DC: U.S. Government Printing Office.

Birren, J. E., & Fisher, L. M. (1995). Aging and speed of behavior: Possible consequences for psychological functioning. *Annual Review of Psychology, 46,* 329–353.

Bishop, J. A., & Cooke, L. M. (1975). Moths, melanism and clean air. *Scientific American, 232,* 90–99.

Bishop, J. E., & Waldholz, M. (1990). *Genome. The story of the most astonishing scientific adventure of our time: The attempt to map all the genes in the human body.* New York: Simon & Schuster.

Bivens, J. A., & Berk, L. E. (1990). A longitudinal study of the development of elementary school children's private speech. *Merrill-Palmer Quarterly, 36,* 443–463.

Bjork, J. M., Knutson, B., Fong, G. W., Caggiano, D. M., Bennett, S. M., & Hommer, D. W. (2004). Incentive-elicited brain activation in adolescents: Similarities and differences from young adults. *The Journal of Neuroscience, 24,* 1793–1802.

Bjork, R. A., & Bjork, E. L. (Eds.) (1998). *Memory.* New York: Academic Press.

Bjorklund, D. F. (1985). The role of conceptual knowledge in the development of organization in children's memory. In C. J. Brainerd & M. Pressley (Eds.), *Basic processes in memory development: Progress in cognitive development research.* New York: Springer-Verlag.

Bjorklund, D. F. (1995). *Children's thinking: Developmental function and individual differences.* Pacific Grove, CA: Brooks/Cole.

Bjorklund, D. F. (1997). In search of a metatheory for cognitive development (or, Piaget is dead and I don't feel so good myself). *Child Development, 68,* 144–148.

Bjorklund, D. F., Brown, R. D., & Bjorklund, B. R. (2002). Children's eyewitness memory: Changing reports and changing representations. In P. Graf & N. Ohta (Eds.), *Life-span development of human memory* (pp. 101–126). Cambridge, MA: Massachusetts Institute of Technology.

Bjorklund, D. F., Miller, P. H., Coyle, T. R., & Slawinski, J. L. (1997). Instructing children to use memory strategies: Evidence of utilization deficiencies in memory training studies. *Developmental Review, 17,* 411–441.

Bjorklund, D. F., & Pellegrini, A. D. (2002). *The origins of human nature.* Washington, DC: American Psychological Association.

Bjorkqvist, K. (1994). Sex differences in physical, verbal, and indirect aggression: A review of recent research. *Sex Roles, 30,* 177–188.

Black, J. E., Isaacs, K. R., & Greenough, W. T. (1991). Usual vs. successful aging: Some notes on experiential factors. *Neurobiology of Aging,* 12, 325–328.

Blackburn, J. A. (1984). The influence of personality, curriculum, and memory correlates on formal reasoning in young adults and elderly persons. *Journal of Gerontology, 39,* 207–209.

Blackburn, J. A., & Papalia, D. E. (1992). The study of adult cognition from a Piagetian perspective. In R. J. Sternberg & C. A. Berg (Eds.), *Intellectual development.* New York: Cambridge University Press.

Blair, R. J. R. (2003). Did Cain fail to represent the thoughts of Abel before he killed him? The relationship between theory of mind and aggression. In B. Repacholi & V. Slaughter (Eds.), *Individual differences in theory of mind: Implications for typical and atypical development.* New York: Psychology Press.

Blake, S. M., Simkin, L., Ledsky, R., Perkins, C., & Calabrese, J. M. (2001). Effects of a parent–child communications intervention on young adolescents' risk for early onset of sexual intercourse. *Family Planning Perspectives, 33,* 52–62.

Blakemore, J. E. O. (2003). Children's beliefs about violating gender norms: Boys shouldn't look like girls, and girls shouldn't act like boys. *Sex Roles, 49,* 411–420.

Blakemore, J. E. O., LaRue, A. A., & Olejnik, A. B. (1979). Sex-appropriate toy preference and the ability to conceptualize toys as sex-role related. *Developmental Psychology, 15,* 339–340.

Blanchard-Fields, F. (1986). Reasoning on social dilemmas varying in emotional saliency: An adult developmental perspective. *Psychology and Aging, 1,* 325–333.

Blanchard-Fields, F. (1996). Social cognitive development in adulthood and aging. In F. Blanchard-Fields & T. M. Hess (Eds.), *Perspectives on cognitive change in adulthood and aging.* New York: McGraw-Hill.

Blanchard-Fields, F., Chen, Y., & Norris, L. (1997). Everyday problem solving across the adult life span: Influence of domain specificity and cognitive appraisal. *Psychology and Aging, 12,* 684–693.

Blasi, A. (1980). Bridging moral cognition and moral action: A critical review of the literature. *Psychological Bulletin, 88,* 1–45.

Blatchford, P., Moriarty, V., Edmonds, S., & Martin, C. (2002). Relationships between class size and teaching: A multimethod analysis of English infant schools. *American Educational Research Journal, 39,* 101–132.

Blazer, D. G. (1993). *Depression in late life.* St. Louis: Mosby.

Blazer, D. G. (1996). Epidemiology of psychiatric disorders in late life. In E. W. Busse & D. G. Blazer (Eds.), *Textbook of geriatric psychiatry* (2nd ed.). Washington, DC: American Psychiatric Press.

Blazer, D. G. (2003). Depression in late life: Review and commentary. *Journal of Gerontology: Medical Sciences, 58A,* 249–265.

Blieszner, R., & Roberto, K. A. (2004). Friendship across the life span: Reciprocity in individual and relationship development. In F. R. Lang & K. L. Fingerman (Eds.), *Growing together: Personal relationships across the life span.* Cambridge, UK: Cambridge University Press.

Block, C. E. (2000). Dyadic and gender differences in perceptions of the grandparent–grandchild relationship. *International Journal of Aging and Human Development, 51,* 85–104.

Bloom, L. (1998). Language acquisition in its developmental context. In D. Kuhn & R. S. Siegler (Vol. Eds.), W. Damon (Editor-in-Chief), *Handbook of child psychology: Vol. 2. Cognition, perception, and language* (5th ed., pp. 309–370). New York: Wiley.

Bluebond-Langner, M. (1977). Meanings of death to children. In H. Feifel (Ed.), *New meanings of death.* New York: McGraw-Hill.

Blumberg, E. S. (2003). The lives and voices of highly sexual women. *The Journal of Sex Research, 40,* 146–157.

Bodkin, N. L., Alexander, T. M., Ortmeyer, H. K., Johnson, E., & Hansen, B. C. (2003). Morbidity and mortality in laboratory-maintained rhesus monkeys and effects of long-term dietary restriction. *Journal of Gerontology: Biological Sciences, 58A,* 212–219.

Bodnar, A. G., Oullette, M., Frolkis, M., Holt, S. E., Chiu, C., Morin, G. B., et al. (1998). Extension of life-span by introduction of telomerase into normal human cells. *Science, 279,* 349–352.

Bodrova, E., & Leong, D. J. (1996). *Tools of the mind: The Vygotskian approach to early childhood education.* Englewood Cliffs, NJ: Prentice Hall.

Bogenschneider, K. (1997). Parental involvement in adolescent schooling: A proximal process with transcontextual validity. *Journal of Marriage and the Family, 59,* 718–733.

Boggiano, A. K., & Katz, P. (1991). Maladaptive achievement patterns in students: The role of teachers' controlling strategies. *Journal of Social Issues, 47(4),* 35–51.

Bohannon, J. N., & Bonvillian, J. D. (2005). Theoretical approaches to language development. In J. Berko-Gleason (Ed.), *The development of language* (6th ed.). Needham Heights, MA: Allyn & Bacon.

Bohannon, J. N., & Stanowicz, L. (1988). The issue of negative evidence: Adult responses to children's language errors. *Developmental Psychology, 24,* 684–689.

Bohannon, J. R. (1990–1991). Grief responses of spouses following the death of a child: A longitudinal study. *Omega: Journal of Death and Dying, 22,* 109–121.

Boise, L., Camicioli, R., Morgan, D. L., Rose, J. H., & Congleton, L. (1999). Diagnosing dementia: Perspectives of primary care physicians. *Gerontologist, 39,* 457–464.

Boldizar, J. P. (1991). Assessing sex-typing and androgyny in children: The Children's sex-role inventory. *Developmental Psychology, 27,* 505–515.

Bolger, K. E., & Patterson, C. J. (2001). Developmental pathways from child maltreatment to peer rejection. *Child Development, 72,* 549–568.

Boll, T., Ferring, D., & Filipp, S. (2003). Perceived parental differential treatment in middle adulthood: Curvilinear relations with individuals' experienced relationship quality to sibling and parents. *Journal of Family Psychology, 17,* 472–487.

Boloh, Y., & Champaud, C. (1993). The past conditional verb form in French children: The role of semantics in late grammatical development. *Journal of Child Language, 20,* 169–189.

Bonanno, G. A. (2001). Introduction. New direction in bereavement research and theory. *American Behavioral Scientist, 44,* 718–725.

Bonanno, G. A. (2004). Loss, trauma, and human resilience: Have we underestimated the human capacity to thrive after extremely aversive events? *American Psychologist, 59,* 20–28.

Bonanno, G. A., & Field, N. P. (2001). Examining the delayed grief hypothesis across 5 years of bereavement. *American Behavioral Scientist, 44,* 798–816.

Bonanno, G. A., & Kaltman, S. (1999). Toward an integrative perspective on bereavement. *Psychological Bulletin, 125,* 760–776.

Bonanno, G. A., & Kaltman, S. (2000). The varieties of grief experience. *Clinical Psychology Review, 21,* 705–734.

Bonanno, G. A., Wortman, C. B., Lehman, D. R., Tweed, R. G., Haring, M., Sonnega, J., et al. (2002). Resilience to loss and chronic grief: A prospective study from preloss to 18 months postloss. *Journal of Personality and Social Psychology, 83,* 1150–1164.

Bonanno, G. A., Wortman, C. B., & Nesse, R. M. (2004). Prospective patterns of resilience and maladjustment during widowhood. *Psychology and Aging, 19,* 260–271.

Bongers, I. L., Koot, H. M., van der Ende, J., & Verhulst, F. C. (2003). The normative development of child and adolescent problem behavior. *Journal of Abnormal Psychology, 112,* 179–192.

Boodman, S. G. (1995, June 13). Researchers study obesity in children. *The Washington Post—Health,* pp. 10–15.

Boom, J., Brugman, D., & van der Heijden, P. G. M. (2001). Hierarchical structure of moral stages assessed by a sorting task. *Child Development, 72,* 535–548.

Booth, A., & Johnson, D. (1988). Premarital cohabitation and marital success. *Journal of Family Issues, 9,* 255–272.

Booth, W., & Snyder, D. (2001, March 7). Boy took gun from home. *The Washington Post,* pp. A1, A12.

Boothe, D., Sethna, B. W., & Stanley, J. C. (2000). Special educational opportunities for able high school students: A description of residential early-college-entrance programs. *Journal of Secondary Gifted Education, 26.*

Boris, N. W., & Zeanah, C. H. (1999). Disturbances and disorders of attachment in infancy: An overview. *Infant Mental Health Journal, 20,* 1–9.

Borkenau, P., Riemann, R., Angleitner, A., & Spinath, F. M. (2001). Genetic and environmental influences on observed personality: Evidence from the German Observational Study of Adult Twins. *Journal of Personality and Social Psychology, 80,* 655–668.

Bornstein, M. H. (1992). Perception across the lifespan. In M. H. Bornstein & M. E. Lamb (Eds.), *Developmental psychology: An advanced textbook* (3rd ed.). Hillsdale, NJ: Erlbaum.

Bornstein, M. H., & Bradley, R. H. (2003). *Socioeconomic status, parenting, and child development.* Mahwah, NJ: Erlbaum.

Bosacki, S. L. (2000). Theory of mind and self-concept in preadolescents: Links with gender and language. *Journal of Educational Psychology, 92,* 709–717.

Boston Retinal Implant Project. (2004). Available online http://www.bostonretinalimplant.org/ (retrieved September 8, 2004).

Botkin, D. R., Weeks, M. O., & Morris, J. E. (2000). Changing marriage role expectations: 1961–1996. *Sex Roles, 42,* 933–942.

Bouchard, T. J., Jr. (1984). Twins reared together and apart: What they tell us about human diversity. In S. W. Fox (Ed.), *Individuality and determinism: Chemical and biological bases.* New York: Plenum.

Bouchard, T. J., Jr., Lykken, D. T., McGue, M., Segal, N. L., & Tellegen, A. (1990). Sources of human psychological differences: The Minnesota Study of Twins Reared Apart. *Science, 250,* 223–228.

Bouchard, T. J., Jr., & McGue, M. (1981). Family studies of intelligence: A review. *Science, 212,* 1055–1059.

Bouchard, T. J., Jr., & Pedersen, N. (1999). Twins reared apart: Nature's double experiment. In M. C. LaBuda & E. L. Grigorenko (Eds.), *On the way to individuality: Methodological issues in behavioral genetics.* Commack, NY: Nova Science Publishers.

Bouldin, P., & Pratt, C. (1999). Characteristics of preschool and school-age children with imaginary companions. *The Journal of Genetic Psychology, 160,* 397–410.

Bowen, B. A. (1999). Four puzzles in adult literacy: Reflections on the national adult literacy survey. *Journal of Adolescent & Adult Literacy, 42,* 314–323.

Bower, T. G. R. (1982). *Development in infancy* (2nd ed.). San Francisco: W. H. Freeman.

Bower, T. G. R., Broughton, J. M., & Moore, M. K. (1970). The coordination of vision and tactile input in infancy. *Perception and Psychophysics, 8,* 51–53.

Bowlby, J. (1960). Separation anxiety. *International Journal of Psychoanalysis, 41,* 89–113.

Bowlby, J. (1969). *Attachment and loss: Vol. 1. Attachment.* New York: Basic Books.

Bowlby, J. (1973). *Attachment and loss: Vol. 2. Separation.* New York: Basic Books.

Bowlby, J. (1980). *Attachment and loss: Vol. 3. Loss, sadness and depression.* New York: Basic Books.

Bowlby, J. (1988). *A secure base: Parent–child attachment and healthy human development.* New York: Basic Books.

Boyce, P. M. (2003). Risk factors for postnatal depression: A review and risk factors in Australian populations. *Archives of Women's Mental Health, Supplement 2,* S43–S50.

Boykin-McElhaney, K., & Allen, J. P. (2001). Autonomy and adolescent social functioning: The moderating effect of risk. *Child Development, 72,* 220–235.

Bracey, J. R., Bamaca, M. Y., & Umana-Taylor, A.J. (2004). Examining ethnic identity and self-esteem among biracial and monoracial adolescents. *Journal of Youth and Adolescence,* 33, 123–132.

Brabeck, M. (1983). Moral judgment: Theory and research on differences between males and females. *Developmental Review, 3,* 274–291.

Brabyn, J. (2000). Visual function in the oldest old. Papers from the 15th Biennial Eye Research Seminar. New York: *Research to Prevent Blindness.* [Available online: http://www.rpbusa.org/new/pdf/jbrabyn1.pdf].

Bradbard, M. R., Martin, C. L., Endsley, R. C., & Halverson, C. F. (1986). Influence of sex stereotypes on children's exploration and memory: A competence versus performance distinction. *Developmental Psychology, 22,* 481–486.

Braddock, J. H., II, & McPartland, J. M. (1993). Education of early adolescents. *Review of Educational Research, 19,* 135–170.

Bradley, J. D. D., & Golden, C. J. (2001). Biological contributions to the presentation and understanding of attention-deficit/hyperactivity disorder: A review. *Clinical Psychology Review, 21,* 907–929.

Bradley, R. H., Caldwell, B. M., Rock, S. L., Ramey, C. T., Barnard, K. E., Gray, C., et al. (1989). Home environment and cognitive development in the first 3 years of life: A collaborative study involving six sites and three ethnic groups in North America. *Developmental Psychology, 25,* 217–235.

Bradley, R. H., Convyn, R. F., Burchinal, M., McAdoo, H. P., & Coll, C. G. (2001). The home environments of children in the United States, Part II: Relations with behavioral development through age thirteen. *Child Development, 72,* 1868–1886.

Bradley, R. H., & Corwyn, R. F. (2002). Socioeconomic status and child development. *Annual Review of Psychology, 53,* 371–399.

Bradley, R. H., Whiteside, L., Mundfrom, D. J., & Casey, P. H. (1994). Impact of the Infant Health and Development Program (IHDP) on the home environments of infants born prematurely and with low birth weight. *Journal of Educational Psychology, 86,* 531–541.

Brainerd, C. J., & Gordon, L. L. (1994). Development of verbatim and gist memory for numbers. *Developmental Psychology, 30,* 163–177.

Brainerd, C. J. & Reyna, V. F. (1993). Domains of fuzzy trace theory. In M. L. Howe & R. Pasnak (Ed.), *Emerging themes in cognitive development: Vol. 1. Foundations.* New York: Springer-Verlag.

Braithwaite, V. (2002). Reducing ageism. In T. D. Nelson (Ed.), *Ageism: Stereotyping and prejudice against older persons.* Cambridge, MA: The MIT Press.

Brandtstädter, J., & Greve, W. (1994). The aging self: Stabilizing and protective processes. *Developmental Review, 14,* 52–80.

Braver, E. R., & Trempel, R. E. (2004). Are older drivers actually at higher risk of involvement in collisions resulting in deaths or non-fatal injuries among their passengers and other road users? *Injury Prevention, 10,* 27–32.

Bray, N. W., Hersh, R. E., & Turner, L. A. (1985). Selective remembering during adolescence. *Developmental Psychology, 21,* 290–294.

Brazelton, T. B. (1979). Behavioral competence of the newborn infant. *Seminars in Perinatology, 3,* 35–44.

Breedlove, S. M. (1994). Sexual differentiation of the human nervous system. *Annual Review of Psychology, 45,* 389–418.

Bremner, J. D., & Narayan, M. (1998). The effects of stress on memory and the hippocampus throughout the life cycle: Implications for childhood development and aging. *Development and Psychopathology, 10,* 871–886.

Brendgen, M., Vitaro, F., & Bukowski, W. M. (2000). Deviant trends and early adolescents' emotional and behavioral adjustment. *Journal of Research on Adolescence, 10,* 173–189.

Brendgen, M., Vitaro, F., Doyle, A. B., Markiewicz, D., & Bukowski, W. M. (2002). Same-sex peer relations and romantic relationships during early adolescence: Interactive links to emotional, behavioral, and academic adjustment. *Merrill-Palmer Quarterly, 48,* 77–103.

Brent, S. B., Speece, M. W., Lin, C. G., Dong, Q., & Yang, C. M. (1996). The development of the concept of death among Chinese and U.S. children 3–17 years of age: From binary to "fuzzy" concepts? *Omega: Journal of Death and Dying, 33,* 67–83.

Bretherton, I. (1996). Internal working models of attachment relationships as related to resilient coping. In G. G. Noam, & K. W. Fischer (Eds.), *Development and vulnerability in close relationships.* Mahwah, NJ: Erlbaum.

Bretherton, I., & Beeghly, M. (1982). Talking about internal states: The acquisition of an explicit theory of mind. *Developmental Psychology, 18,* 906–921.

Bretherton, I., Stolberg, U., & Kreye, M. (1981). Engaging strangers in proximal interaction: Infants' social initiative. *Developmental Psychology, 17,* 746–755.

Bretz, R. D., & Judge, T. A. (1994). Person-organization fit and the theory of work adjustment: Implications for satisfaction, tenure, and career success. *Journal of Vocational Behavior, 44,* 32–54.

Brewster, K. L., & Padavic, I. (2000). Changes in gender-ideology, 1977–1996: The contributions of intracohort change and population turnover. *Journal of Marriage and the Family, 62,* 477–487.

Bridge, J. A., Day, N. L., Day, R., Richardson, G. A., Birmaher, B., & Brent, D. A. (2003). Major depressive disorder in adolescents exposed to a friend's suicide. *Journal of the American Academy of Child and Adolescent Psychiatry, 42,* 1294–1300.

Bridges, L. J., & Grolnick, W. J. (1995). The development of emotional self-regulation in infancy and early childhood. In N. Eisenberg (Ed.), *Social development: Vol. 15. Review of personality and social psychology.* Thousand Oaks, CA: Sage.

Brilleslijper-Kater, S. N., & Baartman, H. E. M. (2000). What do young children know about sex? Research on the sexual knowledge of children between the ages of 2 and 6 years. *Child Abuse Review, 9,* 166–182.

Broberg, A. G., Wessels, H., Lamb, M. E., & Hwang, C. P. (1997). Effects of day care on the development of cognitive abilities in 8-year-olds: A longitudinal study. *Developmental Psychology, 33,* 62–69.

Brody, E. B., & Brody, N. (1976). *Intelligence: Nature, determinants, and consequences.* New York: Academic Press.

Brody, E. M. (1985). Parent care as a normative family stress. *Gerontologist, 25,* 19–29.

Brody, E. M. (2004). *Women in the middle: Their parent care years* (2nd ed.). New York: Springer.

Brody, E. M., Litvin, S. J., Hoffman, C., & Kleban, M. H. (1992). Differential effects of daughters' marital status on their parent care experiences. *Gerontologist, 32,* 58–67.

Brody, G. H. (2003). Parental monitoring: Action and reaction. In A. C. Crouter, & A. Booth (Eds.), *Children's influence on family dynamics: The neglected side of family relationships.* Mahwah, NJ: Erlbaum.

Brody, G. H. (2004). Siblings' direct and indirect contributions to child development. *Current Directions in Psychological Science, 13,* 124–126.

Brody, G. H., & Shaffer, D. R. (1982). Contributions of parents and peers to children's moral socialization. *Developmental Review, 2,* 31–75.

Brody, G. H., & Stoneman, Z. (1996). A risk–amelioration model of sibling relationships: Conceptual underpinnings and preliminary findings. In G. H. Brody (Ed.), *Advances in applied developmental psychology: Vol. 10. Sibling relationships: Their causes and consequences.* Norwood, NJ: Ablex.

Brody, J. A., Grant, M. D., Frateschi, L. J., Miller, S. C., & Zhang, H. (2000). Reproductive longevity and increased life expectancy. *Age and Ageing, 29,* 75–78.

Brody, N. (1985). The validity of tests of intelligence. In B. B. Wolman (Ed.), *Handbook of intelligence.* New York: Wiley.

Broen, A. N., Moum, T., Bodtker, A. S., & Ekeberg, O. (2004). Psychological impact on women of miscarriage versus induced abortion: A 2-year follow-up study. *Psychosomatic Medicine, 66,* 265–271.

Bronfenbrenner, U. (1979). *The ecology of human development: Experiments by nature and design.* Cambridge, MA: Harvard University Press.

Bronfenbrenner, U. (1989). Ecological systems theory. In R. Vasta (Ed.), *Annals of child development: Vol. 6. Theories of child development: Revised formulations and current issues.* Greenwich, CT: JAI Press.

Bronfenbrenner, U., & Evans, G. W. (2000). Developmental science in the 21st century: Emerging questions, theoretical models, research designs and empirical findings. *Social Development, 9,* 115–125.

Bronfenbrenner, U., & Morris, P. A. (1998). The ecology of developmental processes. In R. M. Lerner (Vol. Ed.), W. Damon (Editor-in-Chief), *Handbook of child psychology: Vol. 1. Theoretical models of human development* (5th ed.). New York: Wiley.

Brookover, W., Beady, C., Flood, P., Schweitzer, J., & Wisenbaker, J. (1979). *School social systems and student achievement: Schools can make a difference.* New York: Praeger.

Brooks-Gunn, J., Britto, P. R., & Brady, C. (1999). Struggling to make ends meet: Poverty and child development. In M. E. Lamb (Ed.), *Parenting and child development in "nontraditional" families.* Mahwah, NJ: Erlbaum.

Brooks-Gunn, J., & Furstenberg, F. F., Jr. (1989). Long-term implications of fertility-related behavior and family formation on adolescent mothers and their children. In K. Kreppner & R. M. Lerner (Eds.), *Family systems and life-span development.* Hillsdale, NJ: Erlbaum.

Brooks-Gunn, J., Klebanov, P. K., & Duncan, G. J. (1996). Ethnic differences in children's intelligence test scores: Role of economic deprivation, home environment, and maternal characteristics. *Child Development, 67,* 396–408.

Brooks-Gunn, J., Klebanov, P. K., Liaw, F., & Spiker, D. (1993). Enhancing the development of low birth weight, premature infants: Changes in cognition and behavior over the first three years. *Child Development, 64,* 736–753.

Brooks-Gunn, J., & Lewis, M. (1981). Infant social perception: Responses to pictures of parents and strangers. *Developmental Psychology, 17,* 647–649.

Brown, A. L., & Smiley, S. S. (1978). The development of strategies for studying text. *Child Development, 49,* 1076–1088.

Brown, B. B. (1999). "You're going out with who?" Peer group influences on adolescent romantic relationships. In W. Furman, B. B. Brown, & C. Feiring (Eds.), *The development of romantic relationships in adolescence.* Cambridge, England: Cambridge University Press.

Brown, B. B., Feiring, C., & Furman, W. (1999). Missing the love boat. Why researchers have shied away from adolescent romance. In W. Furman, B. B. Brown, & C. Feiring (Eds.), *The development of romantic relationships in adolescence.* Cambridge, England: Cambridge University Press.

Brown, B. B., & Lohr, M. J. (1987). Peer-group affiliation and adolescent self-esteem: An integration of ego–identity and symbolic-interaction theories. *Journal of Personality and Social Psychology, 52,* 47–55.

Brown, B. B., Mory, M. S., & Kinney, D. (1994). Casting adolescent crowds in a relational perspective: Caricature, channel, and context. In R. Montemayor, G. R. Adams, & T. P. Gulotta (Eds.), *Personal relationships during adolescence.* Thousand Oaks, CA: Sage.

Brown, B. B., Mounts, N., Lamborn, S. D., & Steinberg, L. (1993). Parenting practices and peer group affiliation in adolescence. *Child Development, 64,* 467–482.

Brown, D. (2000, July 14). Drug preventing AIDS in infants. *The Washington Post,* p. A17.

Brown, D. (2000, June 12). New look at longevity offers disease insight. *The Washington Post,* p. A9.

Brown, D. (2000, March 26). Autism's new face. *The Washington Post,* pp. A1, A12.

Brown, J. L. (1964). States in newborn infants. *Merrill-Palmer Quarterly, 10,* 313–327.

Brown, R., Cazden, C., & Bellugi, U. (1969). The child's grammar from I to III. In J. P. Hill (Ed.), *Minnesota Symposia on child psychology* (Vol. 2). Minneapolis: University of Minnesota Press.

Brown, R., & Hanlon, C. (1970). Derivational complexity and order of acquisition. In J. R. Hayes (Ed.), *Cognition and the development of language.* New York: Wiley.

Brown, S. L. (2004). Family structure and child well-being: The significance of parental cohabitation. *Journal of Marriage and Family, 66,* 351–367.

Brown, S. M. (with contributions by J. G. Hay & H. Ostrer) (2003). *Essentials of medical genomics.* Hoboken, NJ: Wiley-Liss.

Brownell, C. A., & Carriger, M. S. (1990). Changes in cooperation and self/other differentiation during the second year. *Child Development, 61,* 1164–1174.

Bruck, M. (1990). Word recognition skills of adults with childhood diagnoses of dyslexia. *Developmental Psychology, 26,* 439–454.

Bruck, M. (1992). Persistence of dyslexics' phonological awareness deficits. *Developmental Psychology, 28,* 874–886.

Bruck, M., & Ceci, S. J. (1999). The suggestibility of children's memory. *Annual Review of Psychology, 50,* 419–439.

Bruer, J. T. (1999). The myth of the first three years: A new understanding of early brain development and lifelong learning. New York: Free Press.

Bruggeman, E. L., & Hart, K. J. (1996). Cheating, lying, and moral reasoning by religious and secular high school students. *Journal of Educational Research, 89,* 340–344.

Bruner, J. S. (1983). *Child's talk: Learning to use language.* New York: Norton.

Bruner, J. S. (1997). Celebrating divergence: Piaget and Vygotsky. *Human Development, 40,* 63–73.

Bryant, P. (1998). Sensitivity to onset and rhyme does predict young children's reading: A comment on Muter, Hulme, Snowling, and Taylor (1997). *Journal of Experimental Child Psychology, 71,* 39–44.

Bryant, W. K., & Zick, C. D. (1996). An examination of parent–child shared time. *Journal of Marriage and the Family, 58,* 227–237.

Bryson, K., & Casper, L. M. (1999). Coresident grandparents and grandchildren. *Current Population Reports, P23-P198.* Washington, D.C.: U.S. Census Bureau. Retrieved from http://purl.access.gpo.gov/GPO/LPS3174.

Buchanan, C. M., Eccles, J. S., & Becker, J. B. (1992). Are adolescents the victims of raging hormones? Evidence for activational effects of hormones on moods and behavior at adolescence. *Psychological Bulletin, 111,* 62–107.

Buchner, D. M. (1997). Preserving mobility in older adults. *Western Journal of Medicine, 167,* 258–264.

Buehler, C. A., Hogan, M. J., Robinson, B. E., & Levy, R. J. (1985–1986). The parental divorce transition: Divorce-related stressors and well-being. *Journal of Divorce, 9,* 61–81.

Bugental, D. B. (2001). *Parental cognitions as predictors of dyadic interaction with very young children.* Paper presented at the biennial meeting of the Society for Research in Child Development, Minneapolis, MN.

Bugental, D. B., & Beaulieu, D. A. (2003). A bio-social-cognitive approach to understanding and promoting the outcomes of children with medical and physical disorders. In R. V. Kail (Ed.), *Advances in child development and behavior* (Vol. 31). San Diego: Academic Press.

Bugental, D. B., Ellerson, P. C., Lin, E. K., Rainey, B., Kokotovic, A., & O'Hara, N. (2002). A cognitive approach to child abuse prevention. *Journal of Family Psychology, 16,* 243–258.

Buhrmester, D. (1996). Need fulfillment, interpersonal competence, and the developmental contexts of early adolescent friendship. In W. M. Bukowski, A. F. Newcomb, & W. W. Hartup (Eds.), *The company they keep: Friendship in childhood and adolescence.* Cambridge, England: Cambridge University Press.

Buhrmester, D., Camparo, L., Christensen, A., Gonzales, L. S., & Hinshaw, S. P. (1992). Mothers and fathers interacting in dyads and triads with normal and hyperactive sons. *Developmental Psychology, 28,* 500–509.

Buhrmester, D., & Furman, W. (1986). The changing functions of friends in childhood: A neo-Sullivanian perspective. In V. J. Derlega & B. A. Winstead (Eds.), *Friendship and social interaction.* New York: Springer-Verlag.

Buhrmester, D., & Furman, W. (1990). Perceptions of sibling relationships during middle childhood and adolescence. *Child Development, 61,* 1387–1398.

Buitelaar, J., Huizink, A. C., Mulder, E., de Medina, P., & Visser, G. (2003). Prenatal stress and cognitive development and temperament in infants. *Neurobiological Aging, 24* (Suppl. 1), S53–S60.

Bulanda, R. E. (2004). Paternal involvement with children: The influence of gender ideologies. *Journal of Marriage and Family, 66,* 40–45.

Bulcroft, R. A. (1991). The value of physical change in adolescence: Consequences for the parent–adolescent exchange relationship. *Journal of Youth and Adolescence, 20,* 89–105.

Bulik, C. M., Sullivan, P. F., Wade, T. D., & Kendler, K. S. (2000). Twin studies of eating disorders: A review. *International Journal of Eating Disorders, 27,* 1–20.

Burack, J. A., Enns, J. T., Iarocci, G., & Randolph, B. (2000). Age differences in visual search for compound patterns: Long- versus short-range grouping. *Developmental Psychology, 36,* 731–740.

Burchinal, M. R., Roberts, J. E., Riggins, R., Zeisel, S. A., Neebe, E., & Bryant, D. (2000). Relating quality of center-based child care to early cognitive and language development longitudinally. *Child Development, 71,* 339–357.

Burhans, K. K., & Dweck, C. S. (1995). Helplessness in early childhood: The role of contingent worth. *Child Development, 66,* 1719–1738.

Burn, S., O'Neil, A. K., & Nederend, S. (1996). Childhood tomboyishness and adult androgyny. *Sex Roles, 34,* 419–428.

Burns, G. W., & Bottino, P. J. (1989). *The science of genetics* (6th ed.). New York: Macmillan.

Burt, C. D. B., Kemp, S., & Conway, M. A. (2003). Themes, events, and episodes in autobiographical memory. *Memory & Cognition, 31,* 317–325.

Burton, L. M. (1990). Teenage childrearing as an alternative life-course strategy in multigenerational black families. *Human Nature, 1,* 123–143.

Burton, L. M. (1996a). Age norms, the timing of family role transitions, and intergenerational caregiving among aging African American women. *Gerontologist, 36,* 199–208.

Burton, L. M. (1996b). The timing of childbearing, family structure, and the role responsibilities of aging black women. In E. M. Hetherington & E. A. Blechman (Eds.), *Stress, coping, and resiliency in children and families.* Mahwah, NJ: Erlbaum.

Burton, R. V. (1963). The generality of honesty reconsidered. *Psychological Review, 70,* 481–499.

Burton, R. V. (1976). Honesty and dishonesty. In T. Lickona (Ed.), *Moral development and behavior.* New York: Holt, Rinehart & Winston.

Burton, R. V. (1984). A paradox in theories and research in moral development. In W. M. Kurtines & J. L. Gewirtz (Eds.), *Morality, moral behavior, and moral development.* New York: Wiley.

Bus, A. G., & van Ijzendoorn, M. H. (1999). Phonological awareness and early reading: A meta-analysis of experimental training studies. *Journal of Educational Psychology, 91,* 403–414.

Busch-Rossnagel, N. A. (1997). Mastery motivation in toddlers. *Infants and Young Children, 9,* 1–11.

Bushman, B. J., & Anderson, C. A. (2001). Media violence and the American public. Scientific facts versus media misinformation. *American Psychologist, 56,* 477–489.

Bushnell, E. M., & Boudreau, J. P. (1993). Motor development in the mind: The potential role of motor abilities as a determinant of aspects of perceptual development. *Child Development, 64,* 1005–1021.

Bushnell, E. W., & Baxt, C. (1999). Children's haptic and cross-modal recognition with familiar and unfamiliar objects. *Journal of Experimental Psychology: Human Perception and Performance, 25,* 1867–1881.

Buss, A. H., & Perry, M. (1992). The aggression question. *Journal of Personality and Social Psychology, 63,* 452–459.

Buss, A. H., & Plomin, R. (1984). *Temperament: Early developing personality traits.* Hillsdale, NJ: Erlbaum.

Buss, D. M. (1995). Psychological sex differences: Origins through sexual selection. *American Psychologist, 50,* 164–168.

Butcher, P. R., Kalverboer, A. F., & Geuze, R. H. (2000). Infants' shifts of gaze from a central to a peripheral stimulus: A longitudinal study of development between 6 and 26 weeks. *Infant Behavior & Development, 23,* 3–21.

Butler, R. (1990). The effects of mastery and competitive conditions on self-assessment at different ages. *Child Development, 61,* 201–210.

Butler, R. (1999). Information seeking and achievement motivation in middle childhood and adolescence: The role of conceptions of ability. *Developmental Psychology, 35,* 146–163.

Butler, R., & Ruzany, N. (1993). Age and socialization effects on the development of social comparison motives and normative ability assessment in kibbutz and urban children. *Child Development, 64,* 532–543.

Butler, R. N. (1963). The life review: An interpretation of reminiscence in the aged. *Psychiatry, 26,* 65–76.

Butters, M. A., Becker, J. L., Nebes, R. D., Zmuda, M. D., Mulsant, B. H., Pollock, B. G., et al. (2000). Changes in cognitive functioning following treatment of late-life depression. *American Journal of Psychiatry, 157,* 1949–1954.

Butters, M. A., Whyte, E. M., Nebes, R. D., Begley, A. E., Dew, M. A., Mulsant, B. H., et al. (2004). The nature and determinants of neuropsychological functioning in late-life depression. *Archives of General Psychiatry, 61,* 587–595.

Buysse, V., & Bailey, D. B. (1993). Behavioral and developmental outcomes in young children with disabilities in integrated and segregated settings: A review of comparative studies. *Journal of Special Education, 26,* 434–461.

Byne, W. (1994). The biological evidence challenged. *Scientific American, 270,* 50–55.

Byrnes, J. P. (1996). *Cognitive development and learning in instructional contexts.* Boston: Allyn & Bacon.

Byrne, B. (1998). The foundation of literacy: The child's acquisition of the alphabetic principle. East Sussex, UK: Psychology Press.

Byrnes, J. P., Miller, D. C., & Schafer, W. D. (1999). Gender differences in risk taking: A meta-analysis. *Psychological Bulletin, 125,* 367–383.

C

Cabrera, N. J., Tamis-LeMonda, C. S., Bradley, R. H., Hofferth, S., & Lamb, M. E. (2000). Fatherhood in the twenty-first century. *Child Development, 71,* 127–136.

Caddell, D. P., & Newton, R. R. (1995). Euthanasia: American attitudes toward the physician's role. *Social Science and Medicine, 40,* 1671–1681.

Cairns, R. B. (1998). The making of developmental psychology. In R. M. Lerner (Vol. Ed.), W. Damon (Editor-in-Chief), *Handbook of child psychology: Vol. 1. Theoretical models of human development* (5th ed.). New York: Wiley.

Caldera, Y. M., Huston, A. C., & O'Brien, M. (1989). Social interactions and play patterns of parents and toddlers with feminine, masculine, and neutral toys. *Child Development, 60,* 70–76.

Caldwell, B. M., & Bradley, R. H. (1984). *Manual for the home observation for measurement of the environment.* Little Rock: University of Arkansas.

Caldwell, P. (1996). Child survival: Physical vulnerability and resilience in adversity in the European past and the contemporary third world. *Social Science and Medicine, 43,* 609–619.

Call, K. T., Mortimer, J. T., & Shanahan, M. (1995). Helpfulness and the development of competence in adolescence. *Child Development, 66,* 129–138.

Camaioni, L. (2004). Early language. In G. Bremner & A. Fogel (Eds.), *Blackwell handbook of infant development* (pp. 404–426). Malden, MA: Blackwell Publishing.

Cameron, N., (2002). Human growth curve, canalization, and catch-up growth. In N. Cameron (Ed.), *Human growth and development* (pp. 19). New York: Academic Press.

Camp, C. J. (1989). World-knowledge systems. In L. W. Poon, D. C. Rubin, & B. A. Wilson (Eds.), *Everyday cognition in adulthood and late life.* Cambridge, England: Cambridge University Press.

Camp, C. J., Foss, J. W., O'Hanlon, A. M., & Stevens, A. B. (1996). Memory interventions for persons with dementia. *Applied Cognitive Psychology, 10,* 193–210.

Camp, C. J., & McKitrick, L. A. (1992). Memory interventions in Alzheimer's-type dementia populations: Methodological and theoretical issues. In R. L. West & J. D. Sinnott (Eds.), *Everyday memory and aging: Current research and methodology* (pp. 155–172). New York: Springer-Verlag.

Campbell, A., Shirley, L., & Caygill, L. (2002). Sex-typed preferences in three domains: Do two-year-olds need cognitive variables? *British Journal of Psychology, 93,* 203–217.

Campbell, F. A., Pungello, E. P., Miller-Johnson, S., Burchinal, M., & Ramey, C. T. (2001). The development of cognitive and academic abilities: Growth curves from an early childhood educational experiment. *Developmental Psychology, 37,* 231–242.

Campbell, F. A., & Ramey, C. T. (1994). Effects of early intervention on intellectual and academic achievement: A follow-up study of children from low-income families. *Child Development, 65,* 684–698.

Campbell, F. A., & Ramey, C. T. (1995). Cognitive and school outcomes for high-risk African-American students at middle adolescence: Positive effects of early intervention. *American Educational Research Journal, 32,* 743–772.

Campbell, V. A., Crews, J. E., Moriarty, D. G., Zack, M. M., & Blackman, D. K. (1999). Surveillance for sensory impairment, activity limitation, and health-related quality of life among older adults: United States, 1993–1997. *CDC MMWR Surveillance Summaries, 48 (SS08),* 131–156.

Campos, J. J., Bertenthal, B. I., & Kermoian, R. (1992). Early experience and emotional development: The emergence of wariness of heights. *Psychological Science, 3,* 61–64.

Campos, J. J., Langer, A., & Krowitz, A. (1970). Cardiac responses on the visual cliff in prelocomotor human infants. *Science, 170,* 196–197.

Canfield, R. L., Henderson, C. R., Cory-Slechta, D. A., Cox, C., Jusko, T. A., & Lanphaer, B. P. (2003). Intellectual impairment in children with blood lead concentrations below 10 microg per deciliter. *New England Journal of Medicine, 348,* 1517–1526.

Canfield, R. L., & Smith, E. G. (1996). Number-based expectations and sequential enumeration by 5-month-old infants. *Developmental Psychology, 32,* 269–279.

Cannon, M., Kendell, R., Susser, E., & Jones, P. (2003). Prenatal and perinatal risk factors for schizophrenia. In R. M. Murray, P. B. Jones, E. Susser, J. van Os, & M. Cannon (Eds.), *The epidemiology of schizophrenia.* Cambridge, UK: Cambridge University Press.

Cano, A., & Vivian, D. (2003). Are life stressors associated with marital violence? *Journal of Family Psychology, 17,* 302–314.

Cantor. N. L. (2001). Twenty-five years after Quinlan: A review of the jurisprudence of death and dying. *Journal of Law, Medicine, and Ethics, 29,* 182–196.

Capelli, C. A., Nakagawa, N., & Madden, C. M. (1990). How children understand sarcasm: The role of context and intonation. *Child Development, 61,* 1824–1841.

Caplan, L. J., & Schooler, C. (2001). Age effects on analogy-based memory for text. *Experimental Aging Research, 27,* 151–165.

Cardno, A., & Murray, R. M. (2003). The "classical" genetic epidemiology of schizophrenia. In R. M. Murray, P. B. Jones, E. Susser, J. van Os, & M. Cannon (Eds.), *The epidemiology of schizophrenia.* Cambridge, UK: Cambridge University Press.

Carlesimo, G. A., Mauri, M., Graceffa, A. M. S., Fadda, L., Loasses, A., Lorusso, S., et al. (1998). Memory performances in young, elderly, and very old healthy individuals versus patients with Alzheimer's disease: Evidence for discontinuity between normal and pathological aging. *Journal of Clinical and Experimental Neuropsychology, 20,* 14–29.

Carlson, V., Cicchetti, D., Barnett, D., & Braunwald, K. (1989). Disorganized/disoriented attachment relationships in maltreated infants. *Developmental Psychology, 25,* 525–531.

Carmichael, S. L., Shaw, G. M., Schaffer, D. M, Laurent, C., & Selvin, S. (2003). Dieting behaviors and risk of neural tube defects. *American Journal of Epidemiology, 158,* 1127–1131.

Caron, S. L., & Moskey, E. G. (2002). Changes over time in teenage sexual relationships: Comparing the high school class of 1950, 1975, and 2000. *Adolescence, 37,* 515–526.

Carpendale, J. I. M. (2000). Kohlberg and Piaget on stages and moral reasoning. *Developmental Review, 20,* 181–205.

Carpenter, M., Nagell, K., & Tomasello, M. (1998). Social cognition, joint attention, and communicative competence from 9 to 15 months of age. *Monographs of the Society for Research in Child Development, 63* (Serial No. 255).

Carr, D. (2004). Gender, preloss marital dependence, and older adults' adjustment to widowhood. *Journal of Marriage and Family, 66,* 220–235.

Carr, D., House, J. S., Kessler, R. C., Nesse, R. M., Sonnega, J., & Wortman, C. (2000). Marital quality and psychological adjustment to widowhood among older adults: A longitudinal analysis. *Journal of Gerontology: Social Sciences, 55,* S197–S207.

Carr, P. L., Ash, A. S., Friedman, R. H., Scaramucci, A., Barnett, R. C., Szalacha, L., et al. (1998). Relation of family responsibilities and gender to the productivity and career satisfaction of medical faculty. *Annals of Internal Medicine, 129,* 532–538.

Carrera, M., Kaye, J. W., Philliber, S., & West, E. (2000). Knowledge about reproduction, contraception, and sexually transmitted infections among young adolescents in American cities. *Social Policy, 30,* 41–50.

Carroll, J. B. (1993). *Human cognitive abilities: A survey of factor–analytic studies.* Cambridge, England: Cambridge University Press.

Carroll, J. M., Snowling, M. J., Hulme, C., & Stevenson, J. (2003). The development of phonological awareness in preschool children. *Developmental Psychology, 39,* 913–925.

Carstensen, L. L. (1992). Social and emotional patterns in adulthood: Support for socioemotional selectivity theory. *Psychology and Aging, 7,* 331–338.

Carstensen, L. L., Charles, S. T., Isaacowitz, D. M., & Kennedy, Q. (2003). Emotion and life-span personality development. In R. J. Davidson, K. R. Scherer, & H. H. Goldsmith (Eds.), *Handbook of affective sciences.* New York: Oxford University Press.

Carstensen, L. L., & Freund, A. M. (1994). Commentary: The resilience of the aging self. *Developmental Review, 14,* 81–92.

Carstensen, L. L., Levenson, R. W., & Gottman, J. M. (1995). Emotional behavior in long-term marriages. *Psychology and Aging, 10,* 140–149.

Carstensen, L. L., Pasupathi, M., Mayr, U., & Nesselroade, J. R. (2000). Emotional experience in everyday life across the adult life span. *Journal of Personality and Social Psychology, 79,* 644–655.

Carter, A. S., Briggs-Gowan, M. J., & Davis, N. O. (2004). Assessment of young children's social-emotional development and psychopathology: Recent advances and recommendations for practice. *Journal of Child Psychology and Psychiatry and Allied Disciplines, 45,* 109–134.

Carter, S. L. (1998). *Motor impairment associated with neurological injury in premature infants.* Available online: http://www.comeunity.com/disability/cerebral_palsy/cerebralpalsy.html (retrieved 9-1-2004).

Carver, K., Joyner, K., & Udry, J. R. (2003). National estimates of adolescent romantic relationships. In P. Florsheim (Ed.), *Adolescent romantic relations and sexual behavior:*

Theory, research, and practical implications. Mahwah, NJ: Erlbaum.

Casadesus, G., Perry, G., Joseph, J. A., & Smith, M. A. (2004). Eat less, eat better, and live longer: Does it work and is it worth it? The role of diet in aging and disease. In S. G. Post & R. H. Binstock (Eds.), *The fountain of youth: Cultural, scientific, and ethical perspectives on a biomedical goal.* New York: Oxford University Press.

Case, R. (1985). *Intellectual development: Birth to adulthood.* Orlando, FL: Academic Press.

Case, R. (1992). The role of the frontal lobes in the regulation of cognitive development. *Brain and Cognition, 20,* 51–73.

Case, R. (1998). The development of conceptual structures. In D. Kuhn & R. S. Siegler (Vol. Eds.), W. Damon (Editor-in-Chief), *Handbook of child psychology: Vol. 2. Cognition, perception, and language* (5th ed., pp. 745–800). New York: Wiley.

Casey, B. J., Giedd, J. N., & Thomas, K. M. (2000). Structural and functional brain development and its relation to cognitive development. *Biological Psychology, 54,* 241–257.

Casey, B. M., McIntire D. D., & Leveno, K. J. (2001). The continuing value of the Apgar score for the assessment of newborn infants. *New England Journal of Medicine, 344,* 467–471.

Caspi, A. (1998). Personality development across the life course. In R. M. Lerner (Vol. Ed.), W. Damon (Editor-in-Chief), *Handbook of child psychology: Vol. 1. Theoretical models of human development* (5th ed.). New York: Wiley.

Caspi, A. (2000). The child is father of man: Personality continues from childhood to adulthood. *Journal of Personality and Social Psychology, 78,* 158–172.

Caspi, A., Elder, G. H., Jr., & Bem, D. J. (1987). Moving against the world: Life-course patterns of explosive children. *Developmental Psychology, 23,* 308–313.

Caspi, A., Elder, G. H., Jr., & Bem, D. J. (1988). Moving away from the world: Life-course patterns of shy children. *Developmental Psychology, 24,* 824–831.

Caspi, A., Harrington, H., Milne, B., Amell, J. W., Theodore, R. F., & Moffitt, T. E. (2003). Children's behavioral styles at age 3 are linked to their adult personality traits at age 26. *Journal of Personality, 71,* 495–513.

Caspi, A., Herbener, E. S., & Ozer, D. J. (1992). Shared experiences and the similarity of personalities: A longitudinal study of married couples. *Journal of Personality and Social Psychology, 62,* 281–291.

Caspi, A., McClay, J., Moffitt, T., Mill, J., Martin, J., Craig, I. W., et al. (2002). Role of genotype in the cycle of violence in maltreated children. *Science, 297,* 851–854.

Caspi, A., Moffitt, T. E., Morgan, J., Rutter, M., Taylor, A., Arseneault, L., Tully, L., Jacobs, C., Kim-Cohen, J., & Polo-Tomas, M. (2004). Maternal expressed emotion predicts children's antisocial behavior problems: Using monozygotic-twin differences to identify environmental effects on behavioral development. *Developmental Psychology, 40,* 149–161.

Caspi, A., Moffitt, T. E., Newman, D. L., & Silva, P. A. (1996). Behavioral observations at age 3 years predict adult psychiatric disorders: Longitudinal evidence from a birth cohort. *Archives of General Psychiatry, 53,* 1033–1039.

Caspi, A., & Roberts, B. W. (2001). Personality development across the life course: The argument for change and continuity. *Psychological Inquiry, 12,* 49–66.

Caspi, A., Sugden, K., Moffitt, T. E., Taylor, A., Craig, I. W., Harrington, H., et al. (2003, July 18). Influence of life stress on depression: Moderation by a polymorphism in the 5-HTT gene. *Science, 301,* 386–389.

Cassia, V. M., Turati, C., & Simion, F. (2004). Can a nonspecific bias toward top-heavy patterns explain newborns' face preference? *Psychological Science, 15,* 379–383.

Cassidy, J., Ziv, Y., Mehta, T. G., & Feeney, B. C. (2003). Feedback seeking in children and adolescents: Associations with self-perceptions, attachment representations, and depression. *Child Development, 74,* 612–628.

Castro, A. (1999). Commentary: Increase in cesarean sections may reflect medical control not women's choice. *British Medical Journal, 319,* 1401–1402.

Cattell, R. B. (1963). Theory of fluid and crystallized intelligence: A critical experiment. *Journal of Educational Psychology, 54,* 1–22.

Cavanaugh, J. C. (1996). Memory self-efficacy as a moderation of memory change. In F. Blanchard-Fields & T. M. Hess (Eds.), *Perspectives on cognitive change in adulthood and aging.* New York: McGraw-Hill.

Cavanaugh, J. C., Grady, J. G., & Perlmutter, M. (1983). Forgetting and use of memory aids in 20 to 70 year olds' everyday life. *International Journal of Aging and Human Development, 17,* 113–122.

Ceci, S. J., & Bruck, M. (1998). Children's testimony: Applied and basic issues. In I. E. Sigel & K. A. Renninger (Vol. Eds.), W. Damon (Editor-in-Chief), *Handbook of child psychology: Vol. 4. Child psychology in practice* (5th ed., pp. 713–774). New York: Wiley.

Ceci, S. J., & Williams, W. M. (1997). Schooling, intelligence, and income. *American Psychologist, 52,* 1051–1058.

Centers for Disease Control. (1997). Youth risk behavior surveillance: National College Health Risk Behavior Survey—United States, 1995. *Morbidity and Mortality Weekly Reports, 46,* 1–56.

Centers for Disease Control. (2002). Adult weight (Chapter 5, p 48).

Cernoch, J. M., & Porter, R. H. (1985). Recognition of maternal axillary odors by infants. *Child Development, 56,* 1593–1598.

Chakrabarti, S., & Fombonne, E. (2001). Pervasive developmental disorders in preschool children. *Journal of the American Medical Association, 285,* 3093–3099.

Chall, J. S. (1967). *Learning to read: The great debate.* New York: McGraw-Hill.

Chandler, M., Fritz, A. S., & Hala, S. (1989). Small-scale deceit: Deception as a marker of two-, three-, and four-year-olds' early theories of mind. *Child Development, 60,* 1263–1277.

Chandler, M. J., Sokol, B. W., & Wainryb, C. (2000). Beliefs about truth and beliefs about rightness. *Child Development, 71,* 91–97.

Chandler, S., & Field, P. A. (1997). Becoming a father: First-time fathers' experience of labor and delivery. *Journal of Nurse-Midwifery, 42* 17–24.

Chao, R. K. (1994). Beyond parental control and authoritarian parenting style: Understanding Chinese parenting through the cultural notion of training. *Child Development, 65,* 1111–1119.

Chao, R. K. (2000). Cultural explanations for the role of parenting in the school success of Asian American children. In R. D. Taylor & M. C. Wang (Eds.), *Resilience across contexts: Family, work, culture, and community.* Mahwah, NJ: Erlbaum.

Chapman, A. R. (2004). The social and justice implications of extending the human life span. In S. G. Post & R. H. Binstock (Eds.), *The fountain of youth: Cultural, scientific, and ethical perspectives on a biomedical goal.* New York: Oxford University Press.

Chapman, L. L. (2000). Expectant fathers and labor epidurals. *American Journal of Maternity and Child Nursing, 25,* 133–138.

Chapman, M., & Lindenberger, U. (1988). Functions, operations, and décalage in the development of transitivity. *Developmental Psychology, 24,* 542–551.

Charles, S. T., Mather, M., & Carstensen, L. L. (2003). Aging and emotional memory: The forgettable nature of negative images for older adults. *Journal of Experimental Psychology: General, 132,* 310–324.

Charles, S. T., & Mavandadi, S. (2004). Social support and physical health across the life span: Socioemotional influences. In F. R. Lang & K. L. Fingerman (Eds.), *Growing together: Personal relationships across the life span.* Cambridge, UK: Cambridge University Press.

Charles, S. T., Reynolds, C. A., & Gatz, M. (2001). Age-related differences and change in positive and negative affect over 23 years. *Journal of Personality and Social Psychology, 80,* 136–151.

Charlesworth, W. R. (1992). Darwin and developmental psychology: Past and present. *Developmental Psychology, 28,* 5–16.

Charman, T. (2000). Theory of mind and the early diagnosis of autism. In S. Baron-Cohen, H. Tager-Flusberg, & D. J. Cohen (Eds.), *Understanding other minds. Perspectives from developmental cognitive neuroscience* (2nd ed.). Oxford: Oxford University Press.

Charney, D. S., Reynolds, C. F., Lewis, L., Lebowitz, B. D., Sunderland, T., Alexopoulos, G. S., et al. (2003). Depression and Bipolar Support Alliance consensus statement on the unmet needs in diagnosis and treatment of mood disorders in late life. *Archives of General Psychiatry, 60,* 664–672.

Chatoor, I., & Ganiban, J., (2004). The diagnostic assessment and classification of feeding disorders. In R. DelCarmen-Wiggins & A. Carter (Eds.), *Handbook of infant, toddler, and preschool mental health assessment.* New York: Oxford University Press.

Chavous, T. M., Bernat, D. H., Schmeelk-Cone, K., Caldwell, C. H., Kohn-Wood, L., & Zimmerman, M. A. (2003). Racial identity and academic attainment among African American adolescents. *Child Development, 74,* 1076–1090.

Chen, C., & Stevenson, H. W. (1995). Motivation and mathematics achievement: A comparative study of Asian-American, Caucasian-American, and East Asian high school students. *Child Development, 66,* 1214–1234.

Chen, D. (1996). Parent–infant communication: Early intervention for very young children with visual impairment or hearing loss. *Infants and Young Children, 9,* 1–12.

Chen, J. Q., & Gardner, H. (1997). Alternative assessment from a multiple intelligences theoretical perspective. In D. P. Flanagan, J.

Genshaft, & P. L. Harrison (Eds.), *Contemporary intellectual assessment: Theories, tests, and issues.* New York: Guilford.

Chen, X., Rubin, K. H., & Sun, Y. (1992). Social reputation in Chinese and Canadian children: A cross-cultural study. *Child Development, 63,* 1336–1343.

Chen, Z., & Siegler, R. S. (2000). Across the great divide: Bridging the gap between understanding of toddlers' and older children's thinking. *Monographs of the Society for Research in Child Development, 65* (Serial No. 261).

Cheng, A. K., Rubin, H. R., Powe, N. R., Mellon, M. K., Francis, H. W., & Niparko, J. K. (2000). Cost–utility analysis of the cochlear implant in children. *Journal of the American Medical Association, 284,* 850–856.

Cherlin, A. J., & Furstenberg, F. F., Jr. (1986). *The new American grandparent: A place in the family, a life apart.* New York: Basic Books.

Cherlin, A. J., Furstenberg, F. F., Jr., Chase-Lansdale, P. L., Kiernan, K. E., Robins, P. K., Morrison, D. R., et al. (1991). Longitudinal studies of effects of divorce on children in Great Britain and the United States. *Science, 252,* 1386–1389.

Cherry, K. E., & LeCompte, D. C. (1999). Age and individual differences influence prospective memory. *Psychology and Aging, 14,* 60–76.

Cherry, K. E., & Morton, M. R. (1989). Drug sensitivity in older adults: The role of physiologic and pharmacokinetic factors. *International Journal of Aging and Human Development, 28,* 159–174.

Cherry, K. E., & Smith, A. D. (1998). Normal memory aging. In M. Hersen & V. B. Van Hasselt (Eds.), *Handbook of clinical geropsychology* (pp. 87–110). New York: Plenum.

Chess, S., & Thomas, A. (1984). *Origins and evolution of behavior disorders: From infancy to early adult life.* New York: Brunner/Mazel.

Chess, S., & Thomas, A. (1999). *Goodness of fit: Clinical applications from infancy through adult life.* Ann Arbor, MI: Edwards Brothers.

Chi, M. T. H. (1978). Knowledge structures and memory development. In R. Siegler (Ed.), *Children's thinking: What develops?* Hillsdale, NJ: Erlbaum.

Chia, E. M., Wang, J. J., Rochtchina, E., Smith, W., Cumming, R. R., & Mitchell, P. (2004). Impact of bilateral visual impairment on health-related quality of life: The Blue Mountains Eye Study. *Investigations in Ophthalmology & Visual Science, 45,* 71–76.

Chipperfield, J. G., & Havens, B. (2001). Gender differences in the relationship between marital status transitions and life satisfaction in later life. *Journal of Gerontology: Psychological Sciences, 56B,* P176–P186.

Chiu, S., & Alexander, P. A. (2000). The motivational function of preschoolers' private speech. *Discourse Processes, 30,* 133–152.

Chochinov, H. M., & Schwartz., L. (2002). Depression and the will to live in the psychological landscape of terminally ill patients. In K. Foley, & H. Hendin (Eds.), *The case against assisted suicide: For the right to end-of-life care.* Baltimore: The Johns Hopkins Press.

Chochinov, H. M., Tataryn, D., Clinch, J. J., & Dudgeon, D. (1999). Will to live in terminally ill. *Lancet, 354,* 816–819.

Choi, J., & Silverman, I. (2003). Processes underlying sex differences in route-learning strategies in children and adolescents. *Personality and Individual Differences, 34,* 1153–1166.

Chomsky, N. (1968). *Language and mind.* New York: Harcourt Brace & World.

Chomsky, N. (1975). *Reflections on language.* New York: Pantheon Books.

Chomsky, N. (1995). *The minimalist program.* Cambridge: MIT Press.

Choudhury, N., & Gorman, K. S. (2000). The relationship between sustained attention and cognitive performance in 17–24-month old toddlers. *Infant and Child Development, 9,* 127–146.

Christensen, M., Emde, R., & Fleming, C. (2004). Cultural perspectives for assessing infants and young children. In R. DelCarmen-Wiggins & A. Carter (Eds.), *Handbook of infant, toddler, and preschool mental health assessment.* New York: Oxford University Press.

Christiansen, S. L., & Palkovitz, R. (1998). Exploring Erikson's psychosocial theory of development: Generativity and its relationship to parental identity, intimacy, and involvement with others. *Journal of Men's Studies, 7,* 133–156.

Christie, F. (2002). The development of abstraction in adolescence in subject English. In M. J. Schleppegrell & Colombi, M. C. (Eds.), *Developing advanced literacy in first and second languages: Meaning with power* (pp. 45–66). Mahwah, NJ: Lawrence Erlbaum Associates.

Christofalo, V. J. (1988). An overview of the theories of biological aging. In J. E. Birren & V. L. Bengtson (Eds.), *Emergent theories of aging.* New York: Springer.

Christopher, J. S., Nangle, D. W., & Hansen, D. J. (1993). Social-skills interventions with adolescents: Current issues and procedures. *Behavior Modification, 17,* 314–338.

Chumlea, W. C., Schubert, C. M., Roche, A. F., Kulin, H. E., Lee, P. A., Himes, J. H., et al. (2003). Age at menarche and racial comparisons in US girls. *Pediatrics, 111,* 110–113.

Cicchetti, D., & Rogosch, F. A. (2002). A developmental psychopathology perspective on adolescence. *Journal of Consulting and Clinical Psychology, 70,* 6–20.

Cicchetti, D., Rogosch, F. A., Maughan, A., Toth, S. L., & Bruce, J. (2003). False belief understanding in maltreated children. *Development & Psychopathology, 15,* 1067–1091.

Cicchetti, D., Toth, S. L., & Rogosch, F. A. (2004). Toddler–parent psychotherapy for depressed mothers and their offspring: Implications for attachment theory. In L. Atkinson & S. Goldberg (Eds.), *Attachment issues in psychopathology and intervention.* Mahwah, NJ: Erlbaum.

Cicirelli, V. G. (1982). Sibling influence throughout the life span. In M. E. Lamb & B. Sutton-Smith (Eds.), *Sibling relationships: Their nature and significance across the life-span.* Hillsdale, NJ: Erlbaum.

Cicirelli, V. G. (1991). Sibling relationships in adulthood. *Marriage and Family Review, 16,* 291–310.

Cicirelli, V. G. (1993). Attachment and obligation as daughters' motives for caregiving behavior and subsequent effect on subjective burden. *Psychology and Aging, 8,* 144–155.

Cicirelli, V. G. (1995). *Sibling relationships across the life span.* New York: Plenum.

Cillessen, A. H., & Bukowski, W. M. (Eds.). (2000). *New direction for child and adolescent development: No. 88. Recent advances in the measurement of acceptance and rejection in the peer system.* San Francisco, CA: Jossey-Bass.

Cillessen, A. H., Van IJzendoorn, H. W., Van Lieshout, C. F., & Hartup, W. W. (1992). Heterogeneity among peer-rejected boys: Subtypes and stabilities. *Child Development, 63,* 893–905.

Cipriani, N. (2002, Nov. 1). What kids should know when. *Parenting, 16,* 150.

Clark, D. C., Pynoos, R. S., & Goebel, A. E. (1994). Mechanisms and processes of adolescent bereavement. In R. J. Haggerty, L. R. Sherrod, N. Garmezy, & M. Rutter (Eds.), *Stress, risk, and resilience in children and adolescents: Processes, mechanisms, and interventions.* Cambridge, England: Cambridge University Press.

Clark, D. O., & Maddox, G. L. (1992). Racial and social correlates of age-related changes in functioning. *Journal of Gerontology: Social Sciences, 47,* S222–S232.

Clark, H. H., & Clark, E. V. (1977). *Psychology and language: An introduction to psycholinguistics.* New York: Harcourt Brace Jovanovich.

Clark, K. E., & Ladd, G. W. (2000). Connectedness and autonomy support in parent–child relationships: Links to children's socioemotional orientation and peer relationships. *Developmental Psychology, 36,* 485–498.

Clark, L. A., Kochanska, G., & Ready, R. (2000). Mother's personality and its interaction with child temperament as predictions of parenting behavior. *Journal of Personality and Social Psychology, 79,* 274–285.

Clark, L. A., Watson, D., & Reynolds, S. (1995). Diagnosis and classification of psychopathology: Challenges to the current system and future directions. *Annual Review of Psychology, 46,* 121–153.

Clark, W. R. (1999). *A means to an end: The biological basis of aging and death.* New York: Oxford University Press.

Clarke-Stewart, A. (1993). *Daycare* (rev. ed.) Cambridge, MA: Harvard University Press.

Clarke-Stewart, K. A. (1998). Reading with children. *Journal of Applied Developmental Psychology, 19,* 1–14.

Clarke-Stewart, K. A., Goossens, F. A., & Allhusen, V. D. (2001). Measuring infant-mother attachment: Is the strange situation enough? *Social Development, 10,* 143–169.

Clarkson, M. G., & Berg, W. K. (1983). Cardiac orienting and vowel discrimination in newborns: Crucial stimulation parameters. *Child Development, 54,* 162–171.

Cleckner-Smith, C. S., Doughty, A. S., & Grossman, J. A. (1998). Premenstrual symptoms: Prevalence and severity in an adolescent sample. *Journal of Adolescent Health, 22,* 403–408.

Cleiren, M. (1993). *Bereavement and adaptation: A comparative study of the aftermath of death.* Washington, D.C.: Hemisphere.

Cleveland, H. H. (2003). Disadvantaged neighborhoods and adolescent aggression: Behavioral genetic evidence of contextual effects. *Journal of Research on Adolescence, 13,* 211–238.

Cleveland, H. H., Jacobson, K. C., Lipinski, J. J., & Rowe, D. C. (2000). Genetic and shared environmental contributions to the relationship between the home environment and child and adolescent achievement. *Intelligence, 28,* 69–86.

Clyburn, L. D., Stones, M. J., Hadjistavropoulos, T., & Tuokko, H. (2000). Predicting caregiver burden and depression in Alzheimer's disease. *Journal of Gerontology: Social Sciences, 55B,* S2–S13.

Cnattingius, S., Signorell, L. B., Anneren, G., Clausson, B., Ekbom, A., Ljunger, E., et al. (2000). Caffeine intake and the risk of first-trimester spontaneous abortion. *New England Journal of Medicine, 343,* 1839–1945.

CNN News (2004, November 9). 56-year-old gives birth to twins. Retrieved online (January 15, 2005): http://www.cnn.com/2004/HEALTH/11/09/mom.56/

Coats, P. B., & Overman, S. J. (1992). Childhood play experiences of women in traditional and nontraditional professions. *Sex Roles, 26,* 261–271.

Cobb, R. W., & Coughlin, J. F. (1998). Are elderly drivers a road hazard? Problem definition and political impact. *Journal of Aging Studies, 12,* 411–420.

Cobliner, W. G. (1974). Pregnancy in the single adolescent girl: The role of cognitive functions. *Journal of Youth and Adolescence, 3,* 17–29.

Cohen, B. B., Friedman, D. J., Zhang, A., Trudeau, E. B., Walker, D. K., Anderka, M., et al. (1999). Impact of multiple births on low birth weight: Massachusetts, 1989–1996. *Morbidity & Mortality Weekly Report, 48,* 289–293.

Cohen, M. (1996). Preschoolers' practical thinking and problem solving: The acquisition of an optimal solution strategy. *Cognitive Development, 11,* 357–373.

Cohen, P., Kasen, S., Chen, H. N., Hartmark, C., & Gordon, K. (2003). Variations in patterns of developmental transitions in the emerging adulthood period. *Developmental Psychology, 39,* 657–669.

Coie, J. D., Dodge, K. A., & Coppotelli, H. (1982). Dimensions and types of social status: A cross-age perspective. *Developmental Psychology, 18,* 557–570.

Coie, J. D., Dodge, K. A., & Kupersmidt, J. B. (1990). Peer group behavior and social status. In S. R. Asher & J. D. Coie (Eds.), *Peer rejection in childhood.* Cambridge, England: Cambridge University Press.

Coie, J. D., Dodge, K. A., Terry, R., & Wright, V. (1991). The role of aggression in peer relations: An analysis of aggression episodes in boys' play groups. *Child Development, 62,* 812–826.

Coie, J. D., Lochman, J. E., Terry, R., & Hyman, C. (1992). Predicting early adolescent disorder from childhood aggression and peer rejection. *Journal of Consulting and Clinical Psychology, 60,* 783–792.

Colapinto, J. (1997, December 11). The true story of John Joan. *Rolling Stone,* 54–97.

Colapinto, J. (2000). *As nature made him: The boy who was raised as a girl.* New York: Harper Collins.

Colburn, D. (1996, September 24). Fetal alcohol babies face life of problems. *The Washington Post—Health,* p. 5.

Colburn, D. (2000, October 3). Wired for sound. *The Washington Post—Health,* 13–18.

Colby, A., & Kohlberg, L. (1987). *The measurement of moral judgment. Vol. 1: Theoretical foundations and research validation.* Cambridge, England: Cambridge University Press.

Colby, A., Kohlberg, L., Gibbs, J., & Lieberman, M. (1983). A longitudinal study of moral judgment. *Monographs of the Society for Research in Child Development, 48* (1–2, Serial No. 200).

Cole, D. A., Maxwell, S. E., Martin, J. M., Peeke, L. G., Seroczynski, A. D., Tram, J. M., et al. (2001). The development of multiple domains of child and adolescent self-concept: A cohort sequential longitudinal design. *Child Development, 72,* 1723–1746.

Cole, M. G. (2004). Delirium in elderly patients. *American Journal of Geriatric Psychiatry, 12,* 7–21.

Cole, P. M. (2003). The developmental course from child effects to child effectiveness. In A. C. Crouter, & A. Booth (Eds.), *Children's influence on family dynamics: The neglected side of family relationships.* Mahwah, NJ: Erlbaum.

Cole, P. M., Barrett, K. C., & Zahn-Waxler, C. (1992). Emotion displays in two-year-olds during mishaps. *Child Development, 63,* 314–324.

Cole, P. M., Martin, S. E., & Dennis, T. A. (2004). Emotion regulation as a scientific construct: Methodological challenges and directions for child development research. *Child Development, 75,* 317–333.

Cole, P. M., Michel, M. K., & Teti, L. O. (1994). The development of emotion regulation and dysregulation: A clinical perspective. In N. Fox (Ed.), *The development of emotion regulation: Biological and behavioral considerations. Monographs of the Society for Research in Child Development,* 59 (Nos. 2–3, Serial No. 240).

Cole, P. M., & Putnam, F. W. (1992). Effect of incest on self and social functioning: A developmental psychopathology perspective. *Journal of Consulting and Clinical Psychology, 60,* 174–184.

Cole, T. R. (1992). *The journey of life. A cultural history of aging in America.* Cambridge, England: Cambridge University Press.

Cole, W. (2003, Oct 6). School daze: When kids don't get enough sleep, bad things happen in class. *Time, 162,* A10.

Coleman, A. L., Stone, K., Ewing, S. K., Nevitt, M., Cummings, S., Cauley, J. A., et al. (2004). Higher risk of multiple falls among elderly women who lose visual acuity. *Ophthalmology, 111,* 857–862.

Coleman, J. (1961). *The adolescent society.* New York: Free Press.

Coles, L. S. (2004). Demography of human supercentenarians. *Journal of Gerontology: Biological Sciences, 59A,* 579–586.

Colin, V. (1996). *Human attachment.* New York: McGraw-Hill.

Colley, A., Griffiths, D., Hugh, M., Landers, K., & Jaggli, N. (1996). Childhood play and adolescent leisure preferences: Associations with gender typing and the presence of siblings. *Sex Roles, 35,* 233–245.

Collins, W. A. (2003). More than myth: The developmental significance of romantic relationships during adolescence. *Journal of Research on Adolescence, 13,* 1–24.

Collins, W. A., & Laursen, B. (2004). Changing relationships, changing youth: Interpersonal contexts of adolescent development. *Journal of Early Adolescence, 24,* 55–62.

Collins, W. A., Maccoby, E. E., Steinberg, L., Hetherington, E. M., & Bornstein, M. H. (2000). Contemporary research on parenting. The case for nature and nurture. *American Psychologist, 55,* 218–232.

Colón, A. R. (with P. A. Colón). (2001). *A history of children. A sociocultural survey across millennia.* Westport, CT: Greenwood Press.

Coltrane, S. (2000). Research on household labor: Modeling and measuring the social embeddedness of routine family work. *Journal of Marriage and the Family, 62,* 1208–1233.

Columbo, J. (1993). *Infant cognition: Predicting later intellectual functioning.* Newbury Park, CA: Sage.

Comer, J. P. (1997). *Waiting for a miracle: Why schools can't solve our problems—and how we can.* New York: Plume.

Committee on Adolescence. (1996). *Adolescent suicide* (Group for the Advancement of Psychiatry, Report No. 140). Washington, D.C.: American Psychiatric Press.

Commons, M. L., Richards, F. A., & Armon, C. (Eds.). (1984). *Beyond formal operations. Late adolescent and adult cognitive development.* New York: Praeger.

Compas, B. E., Connor-Smith, J. K., Saltzman, H., Thomsen, A. H., & Wadsworth, M. E. (2001). Coping with stress during childhood and adolescence: Problems, progress, and potential in theory and research. *Psychological Bulletin, 127,* 87–127.

Compian, L., Gowen, L. K., & Hayward, C. (2004). Peripubertal girls' romantic and platonic involvement with boys: Associations with body image and depression symptoms. *Journal of Research on Adolescence, 14,* 23–47.

Compton, K., Snyder, J., Schrepferman, L., Bank, L., & Shortt, J. W. (2003). The contribution of parents and siblings to antisocial and depressive behavior in adolescents: A double jeopardy coercion model. *Development & Psychopathology, 15,* 163–182.

Condon, J. T. (1993). The premenstrual syndrome: A twin study. *British Journal of Psychiatry, 162,* 481–486.

Condry, J., & Condry, S. (1976). Sex differences: A study in the eye of the beholder. *Child Development, 47,* 812–819.

Conduct Problems Prevention Research Group. (1999). Initial impact of the Fast Track Prevention Trial for Conduct Problems: I. The high risk sample. *Journal of Consulting and Clinical Psychology, 67,* 631–647.

Congdon, N., O'Colmain, B., Klaver, C. C., Klein, R., Munoz, B., Friedman, D. S., et al. (2004). Causes and prevalence of visual impairment among adults in the United States. *Archives of Ophthalmology, 122,* 477–485.

Conger, R. D., Conger, K. J., Elder, G. H., Jr., Lorenz, F. O., Simons, R. L., & Whitbeck, L. B. (1992). A family process model of economic hardship and adjustment of early adolescent boys. *Child Development, 63,* 526–541.

Conger, R. D., Cui, M., Bryant, C. M., & Elder, G. H., Jr. (2000). Competence in early adult romantic relationships: A developmental perspective on family influences. *Journal of Personality and Social Psychology, 79,* 224–237.

Conger, R. D., Neppl, T., Kim, K. J., & Scaramella, L. (2003). Angry and aggressive behavior across three generations: A prospective, longitudinal study of parents and children. *Journal of Abnormal Child Psychology, 31,* 143–160.

Conger, R. D., Patterson, G. R., & Ge, X. (1995). It takes two to replicate: A mediational model for the impact of parents' stress on adolescent adjustment. *Child Development, 66,* 80–97.

Conger, R. D., Wallace, L. E., Sun, Y., Simons, R. L., McLoyd, V. C., & Brody, G. H. (2002).

Economic pressure in African American families: A replication and extension of the family stress model. *Developmental Psychology, 38,* 179–193.

Connell, A. M., & Goodman, S. H. (2002). The association between psychopathology in fathers versus mothers and children's internalizing and externalizing behavior problems: A meta-analysis. *Psychological Bulletin, 128,* 746–773.

Connellan, J., Baron-Cohen, S., Wheelwright, S., Batki, A., & Ahluwalia, J. (2000). Sex differences in human neonatal social perception. *Infant Behavior and Development, 23,* 113–118.

Conner, K. A. (2000). *Continuing to care. Older Americans and their families.* New York: Falmer Press.

Connidis, I. A., & Davies, L. (1992). Confidants and companions: Choices in later life. *Journal of Gerontology: Social Sciences, 47,* S115–S122.

Connolly, J. A., & Doyle, A. B. (1984). Relation of social fantasy play to social competence in preschoolers. *Developmental Psychology, 20,* 797–806.

Connolly, J., Furman, W., & Konarski, R. (2000). The role of peers in the emergence of heterosexual romantic relationships in adolescence. *Child Development, 71,* 1395–1408.

Connor, M. (1998). A review of behavioral early intervention programs for children with autism. *Educational Psychology in Practice, 14,* 109–117.

Connor, S. R. (2000). Hospice care and the older person. In A. Tomer (Ed.), *Death attitudes and the older adult: Theories, concepts, and applications.* Philadelphia, PA: Brunner-Routledge.

Conrade, G., & Ho, R. (2001). Differential parenting styles for fathers and mothers: Differential treatment for sons and daughters. *Australian Journal of Psychology, 53,* 29–35.

Constantino, J. N., & Todd, R. D. (2003). Autistic traits in the general population: A twin study. *Archives of General Psychiatry, 60,* 524–530.

Conway, M., & Vartanian, L. R. (2000). A status account of gender stereotypes: Beyond communality and agency. *Sex Roles, 43,* 181–199.

Coohey, C., & Braun, N. (1997). Toward an integrated framework for understanding child physical abuse. *Child Abuse and Neglect, 21,* 1081–1094.

Cook, A. S., & Dworkin, D. S. (1992). *Helping the bereaved. Therapeutic interventions for children, adolescents, and adults.* New York: Basic Books.

Cook, B. G., & Semmel, M. I. (1999). Peer acceptance of included students with disabilities as a function of severity of disability and classroom composition. *Journal of Special Education, 33,* 50–61.

Cook, W. L. (2001). Interpersonal influence in family systems: A social relations model analysis. *Child Development, 72,* 1179–1197.

Cooley, C. H. (1902). *Human nature and the social order.* New York: Scribner's.

Cooney, T. M., & Smith, L. A. (1996). Young adults' relations with grandparents following recent parental divorce. *Journal of Gerontology: Social Sciences, 51B,* S91–S95.

Coontz, S. (2000a). Historical perspectives on family diversity. In D. H. Demo, K. R. Allen, & M. A. Fine (Eds.), *Handbook of family diversity.* New York: Oxford University Press.

Coontz, S. (2000b). Historical perspectives on family studies. *Journal of Marriage and the Family, 62,* 283–297.

Cooper, P. J., & Murray, L. (1998). Postnatal depression. *British Medical Journal, 316,* 1884–1886.

Cooper, R. P., Abraham, J., Berman, S., & Staska, M. (1997). The development of infants' preference for motherese. *Infant Behavior and Development, 20,* 477–488.

Coopersmith, S. (1967). *The antecedents of self-esteem.* San Francisco: W. H. Freeman.

Corcoran, J. (1999). Ecological factors associated with adolescent pregnancy: A review of the literature. *Adolescence, 34,* 603–619.

Cornelius, M. D., Goldschmidt, L., Day, N. L., & Larkby, C. (2002). Alcohol, tobacco and marijuana use among pregnant teenagers: 6-year follow-up of offspring growth effects. *Neurotoxicology & Teratology, 24,* 703–710.

Cornelius, S. W., & Caspi, A. (1987). Everyday problem solving in adulthood and old age. *Psychology and Aging, 2,* 144–153.

Corr, C. A. (1995). Entering into adolescent understanding of death. In E. A. Grollman (Ed.), *Bereaved children and teens.* Boston: Beacon Press.

Corr, C. A., & Corr, D. M. (1992). Children's hospice care. *Death Studies, 16,* 431–449.

Corwin, J., Loury, M., & Gilbert, A. N. (1995). Workplace, age, and sex as mediators of olfactory function: Data from the National Geographic Smell Survey. *Journals of Gerontology Series B: Psychological Sciences and Social Sciences, 50,* 179–186.

Costa, D. L. (2002). Changing chronic disease rates and long-term declines in functional limitation among older men. *Demography, 39,* 119–137.

Costello, E. J., Mustillo, S., Erkanli, A., Keeler, G., & Angold, A. (2003). Prevalence and development of psychiatric disorders in childhood and adolescence. *Archives of General Psychiatry, 60,* 837–844.

Cota-Robles, S. (2003, April). *Traditional Mexican cultural values and the reduced risk for delinquency: Acculturation, familism and parent–adolescent process.* Poster presented at the biennial meeting of the Society for Research in Child Development, Tampa, FL.

Cote, J. E., & Levine, C. (1988). A critical examination of the ego identity status paradigm. *Developmental Review, 8,* 147–184.

Courchesne, E., Carper, R., & Akshoomoff, N. (2003). Evidence of brain overgrowth in the first year of life in autism. *Journal of the American Medical Association, 290,* 337–344.

Courchesne E., Chisum, H. J., Townsend, J., Cowles, A., Covington, J., Egaas, B., et al. (2000). Normal brain development and aging: Quantitative analysis at in vivo MR imaging in healthy volunteers. *Radiology, 216,* 672–682.

Covington, M. V. (1998). *The will to learn.* New York: Cambridge University Press.

Covington, M. V. (2000). Goal theory, motivation, and school achievement: An integrative review. *Annual Review of Psychology, 51,* 171–200.

Cowan, C. P., & Cowan, P. A. (2000). *When partners become parents: The big life change for couples.* Mahwah, NJ: Erlbaum.

Cox, M. J., Owen, M. T., Henderson, V. K., & Margand, N. A. (1992). Prediction of infant-father and infant-mother attachment. *Developmental Psychology, 28,* 474–483.

Cox, M. J., Paley, B., Burchinal, M., & Payne, C. C. (1999). Marital perceptions and interactions across the transition to parenthood. *Journal of Marriage and the Family, 61,* 611–625.

Cox, S. M., Hopkins, J., & Hans, S. L. (2000). Attachment in preterm infants and their mothers: Neonatal risk status and maternal representations. *Infant Mental Health Journal, 21,* 464–480.

Cox, T. H., & Harquail, C. V. (1991). Career paths and career success in the early career stages of male and female MBAs. *Journal of Vocational Behavior, 39,* 54–75.

Coyle, T. R., & Bjorklund, D. F. (1996). The development of strategic memory: A modified microgenetic assessment of utilization deficiencies. *Cognitive Development, 11,* 295–314.

Coyne, J. C., & Whiffen, V. E. (1995). Issues in personality as diathesis for depression: The case of sociotropy dependency and autonomy self-criticism. *Psychological Bulletin, 118,* 358–378.

Crago, M. B., Allen, S. E., & Hough-Eyamir, W. P. (1997). Exploring innateness through cultural and linguistic variation. In M. Gopnik (Ed.), *The inheritance and innateness of grammars* (pp. 70–90). New York: Oxford University Press.

Crain, W. (2000). *Theories of development: Concepts and applications* (4th ed.). Upper Saddle River, NJ: Prentice Hall.

Crawford, M., & Popp, D. (2003). Sexual double standards: A review and methodological critique of two decades of research, *The Journal of Sex Research, 40,* 13–26.

Creasey, G., Kershaw, K., & Boston, A. (1999). Conflict management with friends and romantic partners: The role of attachment and negative mood regulation expectancies. *Journal of Youth and Adolescence, 28,* 523–543.

Cregger, M. E., & Rogers, W. A. (1998). Memory for activities for young, young-old, and old adults. *Experimental Aging Research, 24,* 195–201.

Creskoff, N., & Haas, A. (1999). Oral-motor skills and swallowing. In D. B. Kessler & P. Dawson (Eds.), *Failure to thrive and pediatric undernutrition: A transdisciplinary approach.* Baltimore, MD: Paul H. Brookes Publishing, Co.

Creusere, M. A. (1999). Theories of adults' understanding and use of irony and sarcasm: Applications to and evidence from research with children. *Developmental Review, 19,* 213–262.

Crews, F. (1996). The verdict on Freud [Review of *Freud evaluated: The completed arc*]. *Psychological Science, 7,* 63–68.

Crick, N. R., & Bigbee, M. (1998). Relational and overt forms of peer victimization: A multiinformant approach. *Journal of Consulting and Clinical Psychology, 66,* 337–347.

Crick, N. R., & Dodge, K. A. (1994). A review and reformulation of social information-processing mechanisms in children's social adjustment. *Psychological Bulletin, 115,* 74–101.

Crijnen, A. A. M., Achenbach, T. M., & Verhulst, F. C. (1997). Comparisons of problems reported by parents of children in 12 cultures: Total problems, externalizing, and internalizing. *Journal of the American Academy of Child and Adolescent Psychiatry, 36,* 1269–1277.

Criss, M. M., Pettit, G. S., Bates, J. E., Dodge, K. A., & Lapp, A. L. (2002). Family adversity, positive peer relationships, and children's externalizing behavior: A longitudinal perspective on risk and resilience. *Child Development, 73,* 1220–1237.

Cristofalo, V. J. (1996). Ten years later: What have we learned about human aging from studies of cell cultures? *Gerontologist, 36,* 737–741.

Crockenberg, S., & Leerkes, E. (2003). Infant negative emotionality, caregiving, and family relationships. In A. C. Crouter & A. Booth (Eds.), *Children's influence on family dynamics. The neglected side of family relationships.* Mahwah, NJ: Erlbaum.

Crockenberg, S., & Litman, C. (1991). Effects of maternal employment on maternal and two-year-old child behavior. *Child Development, 61,* 930–953.

Crockett, L. J., Bingham, C. R., Chopak, J. S., & Vicary, J. R. (1996). Timing of first sexual intercourse: The role of social control, social learning, and problem behavior. *Journal of Youth and Adolescence, 25,* 89–111.

Crooks, R., & Baur, K. (2004). *Our sexuality* (9th ed.). Pacific Grove, CA: Wadsworth.

Cross, S. E. (2000). What does it mean to "know thyself" in the United States and Japan? The cultural construction of the self. In T. J. Owens (Ed.), *Self and identity through the life course in cross-cultural perspective.* Stamford, CT: JAI Press.

Crouch, J. L., & Behl, L. E. (2001). Relationships among parental beliefs in corporal punishment, reported stress, and physical child abuse potential. *Child Abuse and Neglect, 25,* 413–419.

Crouter, A. C., & Booth, A. (Eds.) (2003). *Children's influence on family dynamics. The neglected side of family relationships.* Mahwah, NJ: Erlbaum.

Crouter, A. C., Manke, B. A., & McHale, S. M. (1995). The family context of gender intensification in early adolescence. *Child Development, 66,* 317–329.

Crowell, J. A., Fraley, R. C., & Shaver, P. R. (1999). Measurement of individual differences in adolescent and adult attachment. In J. Cassidy & P. R. Shaver (Eds.), *Handbook of attachment: Theory, research, and clinical applications.* New York: Guilford.

Crowell, J. A., Treboux, D., & Waters, E. (2002). Stability of attachment representations: The transition to marriage. *Developmental Psychology, 38,* 467–479.

Cruikshank, M. (2003). *Learning to be old. Gender, culture, and aging.* Lanham, MD: Rowman & Littlefield.

Csikszentmihalyi, M. (1996). *Creativity: Flow and the psychology of discovery and invention.* New York: HarperCollins.

Cumming, E., & Henry, W. E. (1961). *Growing old, the process of disengagement.* New York: Basic Books.

Cummings, E. M., Davies, P. T., & Campbell, S. B. (2000). *Developmental psychopathology and family process. Theory, research, and clinical implications.* New York: Guilford.

Cummings, S. M., Williams, M. M., & Ellis, R. A. (2003). Impact of an intergenerational program on 4th graders' attitudes toward elders and school behaviors. *Journal of Human Behavior in the Social Environment, 6,* 91–107.

Cunningham, D. A., Rechnitzer, P. A., Pearce, M. E., & Donner, A. P. (1982). Determinants of self-selected walking pace across ages 19 to 66. *Journal of Gerontology, 37,* 560–564.

Cunningham, H. (1996). The history of childhood. In C. P. Hwang, M. E. Lamb, & I. E. Sigel (Eds.), *Images of childhood.* Mahwah, NJ: Erlbaum.

Cytron, B. D. (1993). To honor the dead and comfort the mourners: Traditions in Judaism. In D. P. Irish, K. F. Lundquist, & V. J. Nelson (Eds.), *Ethnic variations in dying, death, and grief: Diversity in universality.* Washington, D.C.: Taylor & Francis.

Cytryn, L., & McKnew, D. H., Jr. (1996). *Growing up sad: Childhood depression and its treatment.* New York: W. W. Norton.

D

Dabbs, J. M., & Morris, R. (1990). Testosterone, social class, and antisocial behavior in a sample of 4462 men. *Psychological Science, 1,* 209–211.

Dahl, R. E. (1999). The consequences of insufficient sleep for adolescents: Links between sleep and emotional regulation. *Phi Delta Kappan, 80,* 354–359.

Dalton, D. S., Cruickshanks, K. J., Klein, B. E. K., Klein, R., Wiley, R. L., & Nondahl, D. M. (2004). The impact of hearing loss on quality of life in older adults. *Gerontologist, 43,* 661–668.

Damon, W. (1977). *The social world of the child.* San Francisco: Jossey-Bass.

Damon, W., & Hart, D. (1988). *Self-understanding in childhood and adolescence.* New York: Cambridge University Press.

Damon, W., & Hart, D. (1992). Self-understanding and its role in social and moral development. In M. H. Bornstein & M. E. Lamb (Eds.), *Developmental psychology: An advanced textbook.* Hillsdale, NJ: Erlbaum.

Daniluk, J. C. (1998). *Women's sexuality across the life span: Challenging myths, creating meanings.* New York: Guilford Press.

Darling, C. A., Davidson, J. K., & Passarello, L. C. (1992). The mystique of first intercourse among college youth: The role of partners, contraceptive practices, and psychological reactions. *Journal of Youth and Adolescence, 21,* 97–117.

Darling, N., & Steinberg, L. (1993). Parenting style as context: An integrative model. *Psychological Bulletin, 113,* 487–496.

Darwin, C. (1859). *The origin of species.* New York: Modern Library.

Darwin, C. A. (1877). A biographical sketch of an infant. *Mind, 2,* 285–294.

Darwish, D., Esquivel, G. B., Houtz, J. C., & Alfonso, V. C. (2001). Play and social skills in maltreated and non-maltreated preschoolers during peer interactions. *Child Abuse and Neglect, 25,* 13–31.

Davidson, R. G. (2002). *PDQ medical genetics.* Hamilton, ONT: B. C. Decker.

Davies, S. L., DiClemente, R. J., Wingood, G. M., Harrington, K. F., Crosby, R. A., & Sionean, C. (2003). Pregnancy desire among disadvantaged African American adolescent females. *American Journal of Health Behavior, 27,* 55–62.

Davis, C. G., & Nolen-Hoeksema, S. (2001). Loss and meaning: How do people make sense of loss? *American Behavioral Scientist, 44,* 726–741.

Dawson, G., & Ashman, S. B. (2000). On the origins of a vulnerability to depression: The influence of the early social environment on the development of psychobiological systems related to risk for affective disorder. In C. A. Nelson (Ed.), *Minnesota Symposium on Child Psychology: Vol. 31. The effects of early adversity on neurobehavioral development.* Mahwah, NJ: Erlbaum.

Dawson, T. L., & Gabrielian, S. (2003). Developing conceptions of authority and contract across the lifespan: Two perspectives. *Developmental Review, 23,* 162–218.

Day, K., & Jancar, J. (1994). Mental and physical health and ageing in mental handicap: A review. *Journal of Intellectual Disability Research, 38,* 241–256.

Day, N. L., Zuo, Y., Richardson, G. A., Goldschmidt, L., Larkby, C. A., & Cornelius, M. D. (1999). Prenatal alcohol use and offspring size at 10 years of age. *Alcoholism: Clinical & Experimental Research, 23,* 863–869.

Day, R. D., & Peterson, G. W. (1998). Predicting spanking of younger and older children by mothers and fathers. *Journal of Marriage & the Family, 60,* 79–92.

de Bode, S., & Curtiss, S. (2000). Language after hemispherectomy. *Brain Cognition, 43,* 135–138.

de Gaston, J. F., Jensen, L., & Weed, S. (1995). A closer look at adolescent sexual activity. *Journal of Youth and Adolescence, 24,* 465–479.

de Gaston, J. F., Weed, S., & Jensen, L. (1996). Understanding gender differences in adolescent sexuality. *Adolescence, 31,* 217–232.

de Jong-Gierveld, J. (1986). Loneliness and the degree of intimacy in interpersonal relationships. In R. Gilmour & S. Duck (Eds.), *The emerging field of personal relationships.* Hillsdale, NJ: Erlbaum.

de la Rochebrochard, E., & Thonneau, P. (2002). Paternal age and maternal age are risk factors for miscarriage: Results of a multicentre European study. *Human Reproduction, 17,* 1649–1656.

De Lisi, R., & Staudt, J. (1980). Individual differences in college students' performance on formal operations tasks. *Journal of Applied Developmental Psychology, 1,* 163–174.

de St. Aubin, E., McAdams, D. P., & Kim, T. (2004). The generative society: An introduction. In E. de St. Aubin, D. P. McAdams, & T. Kim (Eds.), *The generative society: Caring for future generations.* Washington, D.C.: American Psychological Association.

de Vries, B., & Walker, L. J. (1986). Moral reasoning and attitudes toward capital punishment. *Developmental Psychology, 22,* 509–513.

de Weerth, C., van Hees, Y., & Buitelaar, J. K. (2003). Prenatal maternal cortisol levels and infant behavior during the first 5 months. *Early Human Development, 74,* 139–151.

De Wolff, M. S., & van IJzendoorn, M. H. (1997). Sensitivity and attachment: A meta-analysis on parental antecedents of infant attachment. *Child Development, 68,* 571–591.

Deary, I. J., Whalley, L. J., & Starr, J. M. (2003). IQ at age 11 and longevity: Results from a follow up of the Scottish Mental Survey of 1932. In C. E. Finch, J. M. Robine, & Y. Christen (Eds.), *Brain and longevity: Perspectives in longevity* (pp. 153–164). Berlin, Germany: Springer.

Deater-Deckard, K. (2001). Recent research examining the role of peer relationships in the development of psychopathology. *Journal of Child Psychiatry and Allied Disciplines, 42,* 565–579.

Deater-Deckard, K., Dodge, K. A., Bates, J. E., & Pettit, G. S. (1996). Physical discipline among

African-American and European American mothers: Links to children's externalizing behaviors. *Developmental Psychology, 32,* 1065–1072.

Deaux, K., & Major, B. (1990). A social-psychological model of gender. In D. L. Rhode (Ed.), *Theoretical perspectives on sexual difference.* New Haven, CT: Yale University Press.

DeBusk, F. L. (1972). The Hutchinson-Gilford progeria syndrome: Report of 4 cases and review of the literature. *Journal of Pediatrics, 80,* 697–724.

DeCasper, A. J., & Fifer, W. P. (1980). Of human bonding: Newborns prefer their mothers' voices. *Science, 208,* 1174–1176.

DeCasper, A. J., & Spence, M. J. (1986). Prenatal maternal speech influences newborns' perception of speech sounds. *Infant Behavior and Development, 9,* 133–150.

Deci, E. L., Koestner, R., & Ryan, R. M. (1999). A meta-analytic review of experiments examining the effects of extrinsic rewards on intrinsic motivation. *Psychological Bulletin, 125,* 627–668.

Deci, E. L., & Ryan, R. M. (1992). The initiation and regulation of intrinsically motivated learning and achievement. In A. K. Boggiano & T. S. Pittman (Eds.), *Achievement and Motivation: A Social Developmental Perspective* (pp. 9–36). New York: Cambridge University Press.

DeFrain, J., Taylor, J., & Ernst, L. (1982). *Coping with sudden infant death.* Lexington, MA: Lexington Books.

DeFrain, J. D., Jakub, D. K., & Mendoza, B. L. (1991–1992). The psychological effects of sudden infant death on grandmothers and grandfathers. *Omega: Journal of Death and Dying, 24,* 165–182.

DeGarmo, D. S., & Kitson, G. C. (1996). Identity relevance and disruption as predictors of psychological distress for widowed and divorced women. *Journal of Marriage and the Family, 58,* 983–997.

DeLeire, T. C., & Kalil A. (2002). Good things come in threes: Single-parent multigenerational family structure and adolescent adjustment. *Demography, 39,* 393–413.

Delevati, N. M., & Bergamasco, N. H. P. (1999). Pain in the neonate: An analysis of facial movements and crying in response to nociceptive stimuli, *Infant Behavior and Development, 22,* 137–143.

DeLoache, J. S., Cassidy, D. J., & Brown, A. L. (1985). Precursors of mnemonic strategies in very young children's memory. *Child Development, 56,* 125–137.

DeLoache, J. S., Miller, K. F., & Pierroutsakos, S. L. (1998). Reasoning and problem solving. In D. Kuhn & R. Siegler (Vol. Eds.), W. Damon (Editor-in-Chief), *Handbook of child psychology: Vol. 2. Cognition, perception, and language* (5th ed., pp. 801–850). New York: Wiley.

Delsol, C., & Margolin, G. (2004). The role of family-of-origin violence in men's marital violence perpetration. *Clinical Psychology Review, 24,* 99–122.

DeMarie, D., & Ferron, J. (2003). Capacity, strategies, and metamemory: Tests of a three-factor model of memory development. *Journal of Experimental Child Psychology, 84,* 167–193.

DeMarie, D., Norman, A., & Abshier, D. W. (2000). Age and experience influence different verbal and nonverbal measures of children's scripts for the zoo. *Cognitive Development, 15,* 241–262.

DeMaris, A., & MacDonald, W. (1993). Premarital cohabitation and marital instability: A test of the unconventionality hypothesis. *Journal of Marriage and the Family, 55,* 399–407.

Demo, D. H., Allen, K. R., & Fine, M. A. (Eds.) (2000). *Handbook of family diversity.* New York: Oxford University Press.

Demo, D. H., & Cox, M. J. (2000). Families with young children: A review of research in the 1990s. *Journal of Marriage and the Family, 62,* 876–895.

Denney, N. W. (1980). Task demands and problem-solving strategies in middle-aged and older adults. *Journal of Gerontology, 35,* 559–564.

Denney, N. W. (1982). Aging and cognitive changes. In B. B. Wolman (Ed.), *Handbook of developmental psychology.* Englewood Cliffs, NJ: Prentice-Hall.

Denney, N. W. (1989). Everyday problem solving: Methodological issues, research findings, and a model. In L. W. Poon, D. C. Rubin, & B. A. Wilson (Eds.), *Everyday cognition in adulthood and late life.* Cambridge, England: Cambridge University Press.

Denney, N. W., & Pearce, K. A. (1989). A developmental study of practical problem solving in adults. *Psychology and Aging, 4,* 438–442.

Dennis, W. (1966). Creative productivity between the ages of 20 and 80 years. *Journal of Gerontology, 21,* 1–8.

DeRosier, M. E., & Thomas, J. M. (2003). Strengthening sociometric prediction: Scientific advances in the assessment of children's peer relations. *Child Development, 74,* 1379–1392.

DESAction. (2000). *Health risks and care for DES daughters.* Available online: http://www.desaction.org/ (retrieved 9-1-2004).

Descartes, R. (1965). La dioptrique. In R. J. Herrnstein & E. G. Boring (Eds.), *A sourcebook in the history of psychology.* Cambridge, MA: Harvard University Press. (Original work published 1638).

DesRosiers, F., Vrsalovic, W. T., Knauf, D. E., Vargas, M., & Busch-Rossnagel, N. A. (1999). Assessing the multiple dimensions of the self-concept of young children: A focus on Latinos. *Merrill-Palmer Quarterly, 45,* 543–566.

Deutsch, F. M. (1999). *Having it all: How equally shared parenting works.* Cambridge, MA: Harvard University Press.

Deutsch, F. M. (2001). Equally shared parenting. *Current Directions in Psychological Science, 10,* 25–28.

Devenny, D. A., Silverman, W. P., Hill, A. L., Jenkins, E., Sersen, E. A., & Wisniewski, K. E. (1996). Normal ageing in adults with Down's syndrome: A longitudinal study. *Journal of Intellectual Disability Research, 40,* 208–221.

Deveny, K. (2003, June 30). We're not in the mood. *Newsweek,* 40–46.

Devlin, B., Daniels, M., & Roeder, K. (1997). The heritability of IQ. *Nature, 388(6641),* 468–471.

DeVries, M. W. (1984). Temperament and infant mortality among the Masai of East Africa. *American Journal of Psychiatry, 141,* 1189–1194.

DeVries, R. (2000). Vygotsky, Piaget, and education: A reciprocal assimilation of theories and educational practices. *New Ideas in Psychology, 18,* 187–213.

Dewar, R. E., Kline, D. W., & Swanson, H. A. (1995). Age differences in the comprehension of traffic sign symbols. *Transportation Research Record, 1456,* 1–10.

Dews, S., Winner, E., Kaplan, J., Rosenblatt, E., Hunt, M., Lim, K., Mcgovern, A., Qualter, A., & Smarsh, B. (1996). Children's understanding of the meaning and functions of verbal irony. *Child Development, 67,* 3071–3085.

Diamond, L. M. (2003). What does sexual orientation orient? A biobehavioral model distinguishing romantic love and sexual desire. *Psychological Review, 110,* 173–192.

Diamond, M., & Sigmundson, H. K. (1997). Sex reassignment at birth: Long-term review and clinical implications. *Archives of Pediatric and Adolescent Medicine, 151,* 298–304.

Diaz, J. (1997). *How drugs influence behavior: A neuro-behavioral approach.* Upper Saddle River, NJ: Prentice-Hall.

Dick, D. M., Rose, R. J., Viken, R. J., & Kaprio, J. (2000). Pubertal timing and substance use: Associations between and within families across late adolescence. *Developmental Psychology, 36,* 180–189.

Dickson, F. C. (1995). The best is yet to be: Research on long-lasting marriages. In J. T. Wood & S. Duck (Eds.), *Under-studied relationships: Off the beaten track.* Thousand Oaks, CA: Sage.

Diekman, A. B., & Murnen, S. K. (2004). Learning to be little women and little men: The inequitable gender equality of nonsexist children's literature. *Sex Roles, 50,* 373–385.

Digman, J. M. (1990). Personality structure: Emergence of the 5-factor model. *Annual Review of Psychology, 41,* 417–440.

DiIorio, C., Dudley, W. N., Kelly, M., Soet, J. E., Mbwara, J., & Sharpe Potter, J. (2001). Social cognitive correlates of sexual experience and condom use among 13- through 15-year-old adolescents. *Journal of Adolescent Health, 29,* 208–216.

Dijkstra, I. C., & Stroebe, M. S. (1998). The impact of a child's death on parents: A myth (not yet) disproved? *Journal of Family Studies, 4,* 159–185.

DiLalla, L. F., Kagan, J., & Reznick, S. J. (1994). Genetic etiology of behavioral inhibition among 2-year-old children. *Infant Behavior and Development, 17,* 405–412.

Dilworth-Anderson, P., & Burton, L. M. (1996). Rethinking family development: Critical conceptual issues in the study of diverse groups. *Journal of Social and Personality Relationships, 13,* 325–334.

DiMatteo, M. R., Morton, S. C., Lepper, H. S., & Damush, T. M. (1996). Cesarean childbirth and psychosocial outcomes: A meta-analysis. *Health Psychology, 15,* 303–314.

Dimmock, P. W., Wyatt, K. M., Jones, P. W., & O'Brien, P. M. S. (2000). Efficacy of selective serotonin-reuptake inhibitors in premenstrual syndrome: A systematic review. *Lancet, 356,* 1131–1136.

Dinmore, I. (1997). Interdisciplinarity and integrative learning: An imperative for adult education. *Education, 117,* 452–468.

DiPietro, J. A., Costigan, K. A., & Gurewitsch, E. D. (2003). Fetal response to induced maternal stress. *Early Human Development, 74,* 125–138.

DiPietro, J. A., Hilton, S. C., Hawkins, M., Costigan, K. A., & Pressman, E. K. (2002). Maternal stress and affect influence fetal neurobehavioral development. *Developmental Psychology, 38,* 659–668.

DiPietro, J. A., Hodgson, D. M., Costigan, K. A., Hilton, S. C., & Johnson, T. R. B. (1996a). Fetal antecedents of infant temperament. *Child Development, 67,* 2568–2583.

DiPietro, J. A., Hodgson, D. M., Costigan, K. A., Hilton, S. C., & Johnson, T. R. B. (1996b). Fetal neurobehavioral development. *Child Development, 67,* 2553–2567.

Dishion, T. J., Andrews, D. W., & Crosby, L. (1995). Antisocial boys and their friends in adolescence: Relationship characteristics, quality, and interactional process. *Child Development, 66,* 139–151.

Dishion, T. J., McCord, J., & Poulin, F. (1999). When interventions harm: Peer groups and problem behavior. *American Psychologist, 54,* 755–764.

Dishion, T. J., Patterson, G. R., Stoolmiller, M., & Skinner, M. L. (1991). Family, school, and behavioral antecedents to early adolescent involvement with antisocial peers. *Developmental Psychology, 27,* 172–180.

Dittman, R. W., Kappes, M. E., & Kappes, M. H. (1992). Sexual behavior in adolescent and adult females with congenital adrenal hyperplasia. *Psychoneuroendocrinology, 17,* 153–170.

Division of Vital Statistics. (2004). *Infant mortality rates.* Hyattsville, MD: National Center for Health Statistics, Centers for Disease Control and Prevention, U.S. Department of Health and Human Services. Available online: http://www.cdc.gov/nchs/data/hus/tables/2001/01hus023.pdf (retrieved September 2, 2004).

Dixon, R. A. (1992). Contextual approaches to adult intellectual development. In R. J. Sternberg & C. A. Berg (Eds.), *Intellectual development.* New York: Cambridge University Press.

Dixon, R. A. (2003). Themes in the aging of intelligence: Robust decline with intriguing possibilities. In R. J. Sternberg, J. Lautrey, & T. I. Lubart (Eds.), *Models of intelligence: International perspectives* (pp. 151–167). Washington, D.C.: American Psychological Association.

Dodge, K. A. (1986). A social information processing model of social competence in children. In M. Perlmutter (Ed.), *Minnesota Symposia on Child Psychology* (Vol. 18). Hillsdale, NJ: Erlbaum.

Dodge, K. A. (1993). Social-cognitive mechanisms in the development of conduct disorder and depression. *Annual Review of Psychology, 44,* 559–584.

Dodge, K. A., Coie, J. D., Pettit, G. S., & Price, J. M. (1990). Peer status and aggression in boys' groups: Developmental and contextual analysis. *Child Development, 61,* 1289–1309.

Dodge, K. A., Lansford, J. E., Burks, V. S., Bates, J. W., Pettit, G. S., Fontaine, R., & Price, J. M. (2003). Peer rejection and social information-processing factors in the development of aggressive behavior problems in children. *Child Development, 74,* 374–393.

Dodge, K. A., & Pettit, G. S. (2003). A biopsychosocial model of the development of chronic conduct problems in adolescence. *Developmental Psychology, 39,* 349–371.

Dodge, K. A., & Price, J. M. (1994). On the relation between social information processing and socially competent behavior in early school-aged children. *Child Development, 65,* 1385–1397.

Dolen, L. S., & Bearison, D. J. (1982). Social interaction and social cognition in aging. *Human Development, 25,* 430–442.

Dominy, N. L., Johnson, W. B., & Koch, C. (2000). Perception of parental acceptance in women with binge-eating disorder. *Journal of Psychology, 134,* 23–36.

Domjan, M. J. (1993). *Principles of learning and behavior* (3rd ed.). Pacific Grove, CA: Brooks/Cole.

Dorn, L. D., Susman, E. J., & Ponirakis, A. (2003). Pubertal timing and adolescent adjustment and behavior: Conclusions vary by rater. *Journal of Youth and Adolescence, 32,* 157–167.

Dosoky, M., & Amoudi, F. (1997). Menarcheal age of school girls in the city of Jeddah, Saudia Arabia. *Journal of Obstetrics and Gynaecology, 17,* 195–198.

Doucette, A. (2002). Child and adolescent diagnosis: The need for a model-based approach. In L. E. Beutler & M. L. Malik (Eds.), *Rethinking the DSM: A psychological perspective.* Washington, D.C.: American Psychological Association.

Dougherty, T. M., & Haith, M. M. (1997). Infant expectations and reaction time as predictors of childhood speed of processing and IQ. *Developmental Psychology, 33,* 146–155.

Dowdney, L. (2000). Annotation: Childhood bereavement following parental death. *Journal of Child Psychology and Psychiatry and Allied Disciplines, 41,* 819–830.

Down syndrome prevalence at birth: United States, 1983–1990 (1994, August 26). *Mortality and Morbidity Weekly Reports, 43,* 617–622.

Downey, D. B. (2001). Number of siblings and intellectual development: The resource dilution explanation. *American Psychologist, 56,* 497–504.

Downey, D. B. (2002). Parental and family involvement in education. In A. Molnar (Ed.), *School reform proposals: The research evidence* (pp. 113–134). Greenwich, CT: Information Age Publishing.

Downey, D. B., & Condron, D. J. (2004). Playing well with others in kindergarten: The benefit of siblings at home. *Journal of Marriage and Family, 66,* 333–350.

Downey, J., Elkin, E. J., Ehrhardt, A. A., Meyer-Bahlburg, H. F., Bell, J. J., & Morishima, A. (1991). Cognitive ability and everyday functioning in women with Turner syndrome. *Journal of Learning Disabilities, 24,* 32–39.

Doyle, A. B., Brendgen, M., Markiewicz, D., & Kamkar, K. (2003). Family relationships as moderators of the association between romantic relationships and adjustment in early adolescence. *Journal of Early Adolescence, 23,* 316–340.

Doyle, A. B., Markiewicz, D., Brendgen, M., Lieberman, M., & Voss, K. (2000). Child attachment security and self-concept: Associations with mother and father attachment style and marital quality. *Merrill-Palmer Quarterly, 46,* 514–539.

Doyle, A. E., Biederman, J., Seidman, L. J., Weber, W., & Faraone, S. V. (2000). Diagnostic efficiency of neuropsychological test scores for discriminating boys with and without Attention Deficit-Hyperactivity Disorder. *Journal of Counseling and Clinical Psychology, 68,* 477–488.

Driskell, R. A., & Engelhardt, J. F. (2003). Current status of gene therapy for inherited lung diseases. *Annual Review of Physiology, 65,* 585–612.

Droege, K. L., & Stipek, D J. (1993). Children's use of dispositions to predict classmates' behavior. *Developmental Psychology, 29,* 646–654.

Dubas, J. S., Graber, J. A., & Petersen, A. C. (1991). The effects of pubertal development on achievement during adolescence. *American Journal of Education, 99,* 444–460.

Dublin, L. I., & Lotka, A. J. (1936). *Length of life. A study of the life table.* New York: Ronald Press.

Dumble, M., Gatza, C., Tyner, S., Venkatachalam, S., & Donehower, L. A. (2004). Insights into aging obtained from p53 mutant mouse models. *Annals of the New York Academy of Sciences, 1019,* 171–177.

Duncan, H., & Dick, T. (2000). Collaborative workshops and student academic performance in introductory college mathematics courses: A study of a Treisman model math excel program. *School Science and Mathematics, 100,* 365–373.

Duncan, R. M., & Pratt, M. W. (1997). Microgenetic change in the quantity and quality of preschoolers' private speech. *International Journal of Behavioral Development, 20,* 367.

Dunlosky, J., Kubat-Silman, A. K., & Hertzog, C. (2003). Training monitoring skills improves older adults' self-paced associative learning. *Psychology and Aging, 18,* 340–345.

Dunn, J. (1993). *Young children's close relationships. Beyond attachment.* Newbury Park, CA: Sage.

Dunn, J. (2003). Emotional development in early childhood: A social relationship perspective. In R. J. Davidson, K. R. Scherer, & H. H. Goldsmith (Eds.), *Handbook of affective sciences.* New York: Oxford University Press.

Dunn, J., Brown, J., Slomkowski, C., Tesla, C., & Youngblade, L. (1991). Young children's understanding of other people's feelings and beliefs: Individual differences and their antecedents. *Child Development, 62,* 1352–1366.

Dunn, J., Cutting, A. L., & Demetriou, H. (2000). Moral sensibility, understanding others, and children's friendship interactions in the preschool period. *British Journal of Developmental Psychology, 18,* 159–177.

Dunn, J., & Kendrick, C. (1982). *Siblings: Love, envy, and understanding.* Cambridge, MA: Harvard University Press.

Dunn, J., & Plomin, R. (1990). *Separate lives. Why siblings are so different.* New York: Basic Books.

Dunn, J., Slomkowski, C., & Beardsall, L. (1994). Sibling relationships from the preschool period through middle childhood and early adolescence. *Developmental Psychology, 30,* 315–324.

Dunne, M. P., Martin, N. G., Statham, D. J., Slutske, W. S., Dinwiddie, S. H., Bucholz, K. K., Madden, P. A. F., & Heath, A. C. (1997). Genetic and environmental contributions to variance in age at first sexual intercourse. *Psychological Science, 8,* 211–216.

Dunphy, D. C. (1963). The social structure of urban adolescent peer groups. *Sociometry, 26,* 230–246.

DuPaul, G. J., & Stoner, G. (2003). *ADHD in the schools. Assessment and intervention strategies* (2nd ed.). New York: Guilford.

Durik, A. M., Hyde, J. S., & Clark, R. (2000). Sequelae of cesarean and vaginal deliveries: Psychosocial outcomes for mothers and infants. *Developmental Psychology, 36,* 251–260.

Dustman, R. E., Emmerson, R. Y., Steinhaus, L. A., Shearer, D. E., & Dustman, T. J. (1992). The effects of videogame playing on neuropsychological performance of elderly individuals. *Journal of Gerontology, 47,* 168–171.

Dustman, R. E., Ruhling, R. O., Russell, E. M., Shearer, D. E., Bonekat, H. W., Shigeoka,

J. W., Wood, J. S., & Bradford, D. C. (1989). Neurobiology of aging. In A. C. Ostrow (Ed.), *Aging and motor behavior.* Indianapolis: Benchmark Press.

Duvall, E. M. (1977). *Marriage and family development* (5th ed.). Philadelphia: J. B. Lippincott.

Duyme, M., Dumaret, A., & Tomkiewicz, S. (1999). How can we boost IQs of "dull children"? A late adoption study. *Proceedings of the National Academy of Sciences of the United States of America, 96,* 8790–8794.

Dweck, C. S. (2002). The development of ability conceptions. In A. Wigfield & J. S. Eccles (Eds.), *Development of achievement motivation* (pp. 57–91). San Diego: Academic Press.

Dweck, C. S., & Leggett, E. L. (1988). A social-cognitive approach to motivation and personality. *Psychological Review, 95,* 256–273.

Dwyer, J. T., & Stone, E. J. (2000). Prevalence of marked overweight and obesity in a multiethnic pediatric population: Findings from the Child and Adolescent Trial for Cardiovascular Health (CATCH) study. *Journal of the American Dietetic Association, 100,* 1149–1155.

Dwyer, J. W., & Coward, R. T. (1991). A multivariate comparison of the involvement of adult sons versus daughters in the care of impaired parents. *Journal of Gerontology: Social Sciences, 46,* S259–S269.

Dyk, P. H., & Adams, G. R. (1990). Identity and intimacy: An initial investigation of three theoretical models using cross-lag panel correlations. *Journal of Youth and Adolescence, 19,* 91–110.

Dyregrov, K. (2003–2004). Micro-sociological analysis of social support following traumatic bereavement: Unhelpful and avoidant responses from the community. *Omega: Journal of Death and Dying, 48,* 23–44.

E

Eagly, A. H. (1987). *Sex differences in social behavior: A social-role interpretation.* Hillsdale, NJ: Erlbaum.

Eagly, A. H., & Steffen, V. J. (1986). Gender and aggressive behavior: A meta-analytic review of the social psychological literature. *Psychological Bulletin, 100,* 309–330.

Eagly, A. H., & Steffen, V. J. (2000). Gender differences stem from the distribution of women and men into social roles. In C. Stangor (Ed.), *Stereotypes and prejudice: Essential readings* (pp. 142–160). Philadelphia: Taylor & Francis.

Earles, J. L., & Kersten, A. W. (1999). Processing speed and adult age differences in activity memory. *Experimental Aging Research, 25,* 243–253.

Earles, J. L., & Salthouse, T. A. (1995). Interrelations of age, health, and speed. *Journal of Gerontology: Psychological Sciences and Social Sciences, 50,* 33–41.

Easterbrook, M. A., Kisilevsky, B. S., Muir, D. W., & Laplante, D. P. (1999). Newborns discriminate schematic faces from scrambled faces. *Canadian Journal of Experimental Psychology, 53,* 231–241.

Eaton, W. O., & Ritchot, K. F. M. (1995). Physical maturation and information-processing speed in middle childhood. *Developmental Psychology, 31,* 967–972.

Eaves, L., Martin, N., Heath, A., Schieken, R., Meyer, J., Silberg, J., Neale, M., & Corey, L. (1997). Age changes in the causes of individual differences in conservatism. *Behavior Genetics, 27,* 121–124.

Ebbeck, M. (1996). Parents' expectations and child rearing practices in Hong Kong. *Early Child Development and Care, 119,* 15–25.

Ebstein, R. P., Benjamin, J., & Belmaker, R. H. (2003). Behavioral genetics, genomics, and personality. In R. Plomin, J. C. DeFries, I. W. Craig, & P. McGuffin (Eds.), *Behavioral genetics in the postgenomic era.* Washington, D.C.: American Psychological Association.

Eccles, J. S., Jacobs, J. E., & Harold, R. D. (1990). Gender role stereotypes, expectancy effects, and parents' socialization of gender differences. *Journal of Social Issues, 46,* 183–201.

Eccles, J. S., Lord, S., & Midgley, C. (1991). What are we doing to early adolescents? The impact of educational contexts on early adolescents. *American Journal of Education, 99,* 521–542.

Eccles, J. S., Midgley, C., Wigfield, A., Buchanan, C. M., Reuman, D., Flanagan, C., & Mac Iver, D. (1993). Development during adolescence: The impact of stage–environment fit on young adolescents' experiences in schools and in families. *American Psychologist, 48,* 90–101.

Eccles, J., Wigfield, A., Harold, R. D., & Blumefeld, P. (1993). Age and gender differences in children's self- and task perceptions during elementary school. *Child Development, 64,* 830–847.

Eckenrode, J., Laird, M., & Doris, J. (1993). School performance and disciplinary problems among abused and neglected children. *Developmental Psychology, 29,* 53–62.

Eckerman, C. O., & Stein, M. R. (1990). How imitation begets imitation and toddlers' generation of games. *Developmental Psychology, 26,* 370–378.

Ecklund-Flores, L., & Turkewitz, G. (1996). Asymmetric headturning to speech and nonspeech in human newborns. *Developmental Psychobiology, 29,* 205–217.

Eddy, J. M., Leve, L. D., & Fagot, B. I. (2001). Coercive family processes: A replication and extension of Patterson's Coercion Model. *Aggressive Behavior, 27,* 14–25.

Eder, R. A. (1989). The emergent personologist: The structure and content of $3\frac{1}{2}$-, $5\frac{1}{2}$-, and $7\frac{1}{2}$-year-olds' concepts of themselves and other persons. *Child Development, 60,* 1218–1228.

Egeland, B. (1979). Preliminary results of a prospective study of the antecedents of child abuse. *International Journal of Child Abuse and Neglect, 3,* 269–278.

Egeland, B., & Carlson, E. A. (2004). Attachment and psychopathology. In L. Atkinson & S. Goldberg (Eds.), *Attachment issues in psychopathology and intervention.* Mahwah, NJ, Erlbaum.

Egeland, B., Jacobvitz, D., & Sroufe, L. A. (1988). Breaking the cycle of abuse. *Child Development, 59,* 1080–1088.

Egeland, B., Sroufe, L. A., & Erickson, M. (1983). The developmental consequences of different patterns of maltreatment. *International Journal of Child Abuse and Neglect, 7,* 459–469.

Ehrenberg, R. G., Brewer, D. J., Gamoran, A., & Willms, J. D. (2001). Class size and student achievement. *Psychological Science in the Public Interest, 2,* 1–30.

Ehrhardt, A. A. (1985). The psychobiology of gender. In A. S. Rossi (Ed.), *Gender and the life course.* New York: Aldine.

Ehrhardt, A. A., & Baker, S. W. (1974). Fetal androgens, human central nervous system differentiation, and behavioral sex differences. In R. C. Friedman, R. M. Rickard, & R. L. Van de Wiele (Eds.), *Sex differences in behavior.* New York: Wiley.

Ehri, L. C. (1999). Phases of development in learning to read words. In J. Oakhill & R. Beard (Eds.), *Reading development and the teaching of reading* (pp. 79–108). Oxford: Blackwell.

Ehrle, G. M. (2001). Grandchildren as moderator variables in the family, social, physiological, and intellectual development of grandparents who are raising them. In E. L. Grigorenko & R. J. Sternberg (Eds.), *Family environment and intellectual functioning: A life-span perspective.* Mahwah, NJ: Erlbaum.

Eichorn, D. H., Hunt, J. V., & Honzik, M. P. (1981). Experience, personality, and IQ: Adolescence to middle age. In D. H. Eichorn, J. A. Clausen, N. Haan, M. P. Honzik, & P. H. Mussen (Eds.), *Present and past in middle life.* New York: Academic Press.

Eimas, P. D. (1975a). Auditory and phonetic cues for speech: Discrimination of the (r-l) distinction by young infants. *Perception and Psychophysics, 18,* 341–347.

Eimas, P. D. (1975b). Speech perception in early infancy. In L. B. Cohen & P. Salapatek (Eds.), *Infant perception: From sensation to cognition.* New York: Academic Press.

Eimas, P. D. (1985). The perception of speech in early infancy. *Scientific American, 252,* 46–52.

Eisenberg, N. (2000). Emotion, regulation, and moral development. *Annual Review of Psychology, 51,* 665–697.

Eisenberg, N., Fabes, R. A., Guthrie, I. K., Murphy, B. C., Maszk, P., Holmgren, R., & Suh, K. (1996). The relations of regulation and emotionality to problem behavior in elementary school children. *Development and Psychopathology, 8,* 141–162.

Eisenberg, N., & Morris, A. S. (2002). Children's emotion-related regulation. In R. V. Kail (Ed.), *Advances in child development and behavior* (Vol. 30). San Diego: Academic Press.

Ekerdt, D. J., Bossé, R., & Levkoff, S. (1985). Empirical test for phases of retirement: Findings from the Normative Aging Study. *Journal of Gerontology, 40,* 95–101.

Ekerdt, D. J., Kosloski, K., & DeViney, S. (2000). The normative anticipation of retirement by older adults. *Research on Aging, 22,* 3–22.

Elbourne, D., & Wiseman, R. A. (2000). Types of intra-muscular opioids for maternal pain relief in labor. *Cochrane Database Systems Review 2000* (CD001237).

Elder, G. H., Jr. (1998). The life course as developmental theory. *Child Development, 69,* 1–12.

Elder, G. H., Jr., Liker, J. K., & Cross, C. E. (1984). Parent–child behavior in the Great Depression: Life course and intergenerational influences. In P. B. Baltes & O. G. Brim Jr. (Eds.), *Life-span development and behavior* (Vol. 6). Orlando, FL: Academic Press.

Elicker, J., Englund, M., & Sroufe, L. A. (1992). Predicting peer competence and peer relationships in childhood from early parent–child relationships. In R. D. Parke & G. W. Ladd (Eds.), *Family-peer relationships: Modes of linkage.* Hillsdale, NJ: Erlbaum.

Eliot, L. (1999). What's going on in there? How the brain and mind develop in the first five years of life. New York, NY: Bantam Books.

Elkind, D. (1967). Egocentrism in adolescence. *Child Development, 38,* 1025–1034.
Elkind, D. (1987). *Miseducation: Preschoolers at risk.* New York: Knopf.
Elkind, D. (1992, May/June). The future of childhood. Waaah!! Why kids have a lot to cry about. *Psychology Today,* 38–41, 80–81.
Elkind, D., & Bowen, R. (1979). Imaginary audience behavior in children and adolescents. *Developmental Psychology, 15,* 38–44.
Ella Galbraith Miller. Va. woman lived to 119. (2000, November 23). *The Washington Post,* B6.
Elliot, A. J., & Church, M. A. (1997). A hierarchical model of approach and avoidance achievement motivation. *Journal of Personality and Social Psychology, 72,* 218–232.
Elliot, A. J., & Reis, H. T. (2003). Attachment and exploration in adulthood. *Journal of Personality & Social Psychology, 85,* 317–331.
Elliott, D. S., & Ageton, S. S. (1980). Reconciling race and class differences in self-reported and official estimates of delinquency. *American Sociological Review, 45,* 95–110.
Elliott, E. S., & Dweck, C. S. (1988). Goals: An approach to motivation and achievement. *Journal of Personality and Social Psychology, 54,* 5–12.
Elliott, D. S., Williams, K. R., & Hamburg, B. (1998). An integrated approach to violence prevention. In D. S. Elliott, B. A. Hamburg, & K. R. Williams (Eds.), *Violence in American schools. A new perspective.* New York: Cambridge University Press.
Ellis, L., Ames, M. A., Peckham, W., & Burke, D. M. (1988). Sexual orientation in human offspring may be altered by severe emotional distress during pregnancy. *Journal of Sex Research, 25,* 152–157.
Ellis, B. J., Bates, J. E., Dodge, K. A., Fergusson, D. M., Horwood, L. J., Pettit, G. S., & Woodward, L. (2003). Does father absence place daughters at special risk for early sexual activity and teenage pregnancy? *Child Development, 74,* 801–821.
Ellis, B. J., & Garber, J. (2000). Psychosocial antecedents of variation in girls' pubertal timing: Maternal depression, stepfather presence, and marital and family stress. *Child Development, 71,* 485–501.
Ellis, S., Rogoff, B., & Cromer, C. C. (1981). Age segregation in children's social interactions. *Developmental Psychology, 17,* 399–407.
Ellison, P. T. (2002). Puberty. In N. Cameron (Ed.), *Human growth and development* (pp. 65–84). New York: Academic Press.
Ely, R. (1997). Language and literacy in the school years. In J. K. Gleason (Ed.), *The development of language* (4th ed.). Boston: Allyn & Bacon.
Ely, R. (2001). Language and literacy in the school years. In J. B. Gleason (Ed.), *The development of language* (5th ed.). Boston: Allyn & Bacon.
Ely, R. (2005). Language development in the school years. In J. B. Gleason (Ed.), *The development of language* (6th ed.). Boston: Allyn & Bacon.
Emanuel, E. J. (2001). Euthanasia: Where the Netherlands leads will the world follow? *British Medical Journal, 322,* 1376–1377.
Emde, R. N., Biringen, Z., Clyman, R. B., & Oppenheim, D. (1991). The moral self of infancy: Affective core and procedural knowledge. *Developmental Review, 11,* 251–270.
Emery, R. E. (1999). Post divorce family life for children. An overview of research and some implications for policy. In R. A. Thompson & P. R. Amato (Eds.), *The post divorce family. Children, parenting, & society.* Thousand Oaks, CA: Sage.
Emery, R. E., & Laumann-Billings, L. (1998). An overview of the nature, causes, and consequences of abusive family relationships: Toward differentiating maltreatment and violence. *American Psychologist, 53,* 121–135.
Emery, R. E., & Tuer, M. (1993). Parenting and the marital relationship. In T. Luster & L. Okagaki (Eds.), *Parenting. An ecological perspective.* Hillsdale, NJ: Erlbaum.
Emery, R. E., Laumann-Billings, L., Waldron, M. C., Sbarra, D. A., & Dillon, P. (2001). Child custody mediation and litigation: Custody, contact, and coparenting 12 years after initial dispute resolution. *Journal of Counseling and Clinical Psychology,* 69, 323–332.
England, P., Reid, L. L., & Kilbourne, B. S. (1996). The effect of the sex composition of jobs on starting wages in an organization: Findings from the NLSY. *Demography, 33,* 511–521.
Englander-Golden, P., Sonleitner, F. J., Whitmore, M. R., & Corbley, G. J. M. (1986). Social and menstrual cycles: Methodological and substantive findings. In V. L. Olesen & N. F. Woods (Eds.), *Culture, society, and menstruation.* Washington, D.C.: Hemisphere.
Engle, R. W., Tuholski, S. W., Laughlin, J. E., & Conway, A. R. A. (1999). Working memory, short-term memory and general fluid intelligence: A latent variable approach. *Journal of Experimental Psychology: General, 128,* 309–331.
Enoch, J. M., Werner, J. S., Haegerstrm-Portnoy, G., Lakshminarayanan, V., & Rynders, M. (1999). Forever young: Visual functions not affected or minimally affected by aging: A review. *Journal of Gerontology: Biological Sciences, 54A,* B336–B351.
Enright, R., Lapsley, D., & Shukla, D. (1979). Adolescent egocentrism in early and late adolescence. *Adolescence, 14,* 687–695.
Ensminger, M. E., & Slusarcick, A. L. (1992). Paths to high school graduation or dropout: A longitudinal study of a first-grade cohort. *Sociology of Education, 65,* 95–113.
Eppler, M. A. (1995). Development of manipulatory skills and the deployment of attention. *Infant Behavior & Development, 18,* 391–405.
Epstein, H. T. (2001). An outline of the role of brain in human cognitive development. *Brain and Cognition, 45,* 44–51.
Erber, J. T. (2005). *Aging and older adulthood.* Belmont, CA: Wadsworth.
Erdley, C. A., Loomis, C. C., Cain, K. M., & Dumas-Hines, F. (1997). Relations among children's social goals, implicit personality theories, and responses to social failure. *Developmental Psychology, 33,* 263–272.
Ericsson, K. A. (1996). The acquisition of expert performance: An introduction to some of the issues. In K. A. Ericsson (Ed.), *The road to excellence: The acquisition of expert performance in the arts and sciences, sports, and games.* Mahwah, NJ: Erlbaum.
Ericsson, K. A., & Charness, N. (1994). Expert performance: Its structure and acquisition. *American Psychologist, 49,* 725–747.
Ericsson, K. A., Chase, W. G., & Faloon, S. (1980). Acquisition of a memory skill. *Science, 208,* 1181–1182.
Ericsson, K. A., & Kintsch, W. (1995). Long-term working memory. *Psychological Review, 102,* 211–245.
Erikson, E. H. (1963). *Childhood and society* (2nd ed.). New York: Norton.
Erikson, E. H. (1968). *Identity: Youth and crisis.* New York: Norton.
Erikson, E. H. (1982). *The life cycle completed: A review.* New York: Norton.
Erikson, E. H., Erikson, J. M., & Kivnick, H. Q. (1986). *Vital involvement in old age.* New York: Norton.
Eriksson, M., Brown, W. T., Gordon, L. B., Glynn, M. W., Singer, J., Scott, L., Erdos, M. R., Robbins, C. M., Moses, T. Y., Berglund, P., Dutra, A., Pak, E., Durkin, S., Csoka, A. B., Boehnke, M., Glover, T. W., & Collins, F. S. (2003). Recurrent *de novo* point mutations in lamin A cause Hutchinson-Gilford progeria syndrome. *Nature, 423,* 239–298.
Ernst, M., Moolchan, E. T., & Robinson, M. L. (2001). Behavioral and neural consequences of prenatal exposure to nicotine. *Journal of the American Academy of Child and Adolescent Psychiatry, 40,* 630–641.
Escalona, S. (1968). *The roots of individuality: Normal patterns of individuality.* Chicago: Aldine.
Eskritt, M., & Lee, K. (2002). "Remember where you last saw that card": Children's production of external symbols as a memory aid. *Developmental Psychology, 38,* 254–266.
Espy, K. A., Molfese, V. J., & DiLalla, L. F. (2001). Effects of environmental measures on intelligence in young children: Growth curve modeling of longitudinal data. *Merrill-Palmer Quarterly, 47,* 42–73.
Essa, E. L., & Murray, C. I. (1994). Young children's understanding and experience with death. *Young Children, 49,* 74–81.
Etaugh, C., & Liss, M. B. (1992). Home, school, and playroom: Training grounds for adult gender roles. *Sex Roles, 26,* 129–147.
Evans, G. W. (2004). The environment of childhood poverty. *American Psychologist, 59,* 77–92.
Evans, J. R. (2001). Risk factors for age-related macular degeneration. *Progress in Retinal and Eye Research, 20,* 227.
Evans, J. R., Fletcher, A. E., Wormald, R. P., Ng, E. S., Stirling, S., Smeeth, L., Breeze, E., Bulpitt, C. J., Nunes, M., Jones, D., & Tulloch, A. (2002). Prevalence of visual impairment in people aged 75 years and older in Britain: Results from the MRC trial of assessment and management of older people in the community. *Ophthalmology,* 795–800.

F

Faber, C. E., & Grontved, A. M. (2000). Cochlear implantation and change in quality of life. *Acta Otolaryngology Supplement, 543,* 151–153.
Fabes, R. A., Eisenberg, N., & Miller, P. A. (1990). Maternal correlates of children's vicarious emotional responsiveness. *Developmental Psychology, 26,* 639–648.
Fabes, R. A., Martin, C. L., & Hanish, L. D. (2003). Young children's play qualities in same-, other-, and mixed-sex peer groups. *Child Development, 74,* 921–932.
Fagot, B. I. (1978). The influence of sex of child on parental reactions to toddler children. *Child Development, 49,* 459–465.
Fagot, B. I. (1985). Beyond the reinforcement principle: Another step toward understanding sex-role development. *Developmental Psychology, 21,* 1097–1104.

Fagot, B. I. (1997). Attachment, parenting, and peer interactions of toddler children. *Developmental Psychology, 33,* 489–499.

Fagot, B. I., & Kavanaugh, K. (1993). Parenting during the second year: Effects of children's age, sex, and attachment classification. *Child Development, 64,* 258–271.

Fagot, B. I., & Leinbach, M. D. (1989). The young child's gender schema: Environmental input, internal organization. *Child Development, 60,* 663–672.

Fagot, B. I., & Leinbach, M. D. (1993). Gender-role development in young children: From discrimination to labeling. *Developmental Review, 13,* 205–224.

Fagot, B. I., Leinbach, M. D., & Hagan, R. (1986). Gender labeling and the adoption of sex-typed behaviors. *Developmental Psychology, 22,* 440–443.

Fagot, B. I., Leinbach, M. D., & O'Boyle, C. (1992). Gender labeling, gender stereotyping, and parenting behaviors. *Developmental Psychology, 28,* 225–230.

Falcon, L. M., & Tucker, K. L. (2000). Prevalence and correlates of depressive symptoms among Hispanic elders in Massachusetts. *Journal of Gerontology: Social Sciences, 55,* S108–S116.

Fang, G., Fang, F., Keller, M., Edelstein, W., Kehle, T. J., & Bray, M. A. (2003). Social moral reasoning in Chinese children: A developmental study. *Psychology in the Schools, 40,* 125–138.

Fantz, R. L., & Fagan, J. F. (1975). Visual attention to size and number of pattern details by term and preterm infants during the first six months. *Child Development, 46,* 3–18.

Farber, N. (2003). *Adolescent pregnancy. Policy and prevention services.* New York: Springer.

Farmer, E. M. Z., Compton, S. N., Burns, B. J., & Robertson, E. (2002). Review of the evidence base for treatment of childhood psychopathology: Externalizing disorders. *Journal of Consulting and Clinical Psychology, 70,* 1267–1302.

Farver, J. A. M., & Lee-Shin, Y. (1997). Social pretend play in Korean and Anglo American preschoolers. *Child Development, 68,* 544–556.

Farver, J. A. M., Kim, Y. K., & Lee-Shin, Y. (2000). Within cultural differences: Examining individual differences in Korean American and European American preschoolers' social pretend play. *Journal of Cross-Cultural Psychology, 31,* 583–602.

Faulkner, D., Joiner, R., Littleton, K., Miell, D., & Thompson, L. (2000). The mediating effect of task presentation on collaboration and children's acquisition of scientific reasoning. *European Journal of Psychology of Education, 15,* 417–430.

Faulkner, K. W. (1997). Talking about death with a dying child. *American Journal of Nursing, 97,* 64, 66, 68–69.

Faust, M. A., & Glenzer, N. (2000). "I could read those parts over and over": Eighth graders rereading to enhance enjoyment and learning with literature. *Journal of Adolescent and Adult Literacy, 44,* 234–239.

Federal Interagency Forum on Aging-Related Statistics. (2000). *Older Americans 2000: Key indicators of well-being.* Available online: http://www.agingstats.gov/chartbook2000/healthstatus.html.

Feeney, J. A., & Noller, P. (1996). *Adult attachment.* Thousand Oaks, CA: Sage.

Feingold, A. (1988). Cognitive gender differences are disappearing. *American Psychologist, 43,* 95–103.

Feingold, A. (1992). Sex differences in variability in intellectual abilities: A new look at an old controversy. *Review of Educational Research, 62,* 61–84.

Feingold, A. (1994a). Gender differences in intellectual abilities: A cross-cultural perspective. *Sex Roles, 30,* 81–92.

Feingold, A. (1994b). Gender differences in personality: A meta-analysis. *Psychological Bulletin, 116,* 429–456.

Feinman, S. (1992). *Social referencing and the social construction of reality in infancy.* New York: Plenum.

Feiring, C. (1996). Concepts of romance in 15-year-old adolescents. *Journal of Research on Adolescence, 6,* 181–200.

Feiring, C. (1999). Other-sex friendship networks and the development of romantic relationships in adolescence. *Journal of Youth and Adolescence, 28,* 495–512.

Feldman, D. H. (1986). Nature's gambit: Child prodigies and the development of human potential. New York: Basic Books.

Feldman, D. H., & Fowler, R. C. (1997). The nature(s) of developmental change: Piaget, Vygotsky, and the transition process. *New Ideas in Psychology, 3,* 195–210.

Feldman, R. D. (1982). *Whatever happened to the Quiz Kids? Perils and profits of growing up gifted.* Chicago: Chicago Review Press.

Feldman, R., & Eidelman, A. I. (2003). Skin-to-skin contact (kangaroo care) accelerates autonomic and neurobehavioral maturation in preterm infants. *Developmental Medicine and Child Neurology, 45,* 274–281.

Feldman, R., Weller, A., Sirota, L., & Eidelman, A. (2003). Testing a family intervention hypothesis: The contribution of mother–infant skin-to-skin contact (kangaroo care) to family interaction, proximity, and touch. *Journal of Family Psychology, 17,* 94–107.

Feldman, S. S., Biringen, Z. C., & Nash, S. C. (1981). Fluctuations of sex-related self-attributions as a function of stage of family life cycle. *Developmental Psychology, 17,* 24–35.

Felton, B. J., & Berry, C. A. (1992). Do the sources of the urban elderly's social support determine its psychological consequences? *Psychology and Aging, 7,* 89–97.

Fenson, L., Dale, P. S., Reznick, J. S., Bates, E., Thal, D. J., & Pethick, S. J. (1994). Variability in early communicative development. *Monographs of the Society for Research in Child Development, 59* (Serial No. 242).

Ferbeyre, G., & Lowe, S. W. (2002). Ageing: The price of tumour suppression? *Nature, 415,* 26–27.

Fernald, A. (2004). Auditory development in infancy. In G. Bremner, & A. Fogel (Eds.), *Blackwell handbook of infant development* (pp. 35-70). Malden, MA: Blackwell Publishing.

Fernald, A., Taeschner, T., Dunn, J., Papousek, M., & Fukui, I. (1989). A cross-language study of prosodic modifications in mothers' and fathers' speech to preverbal infants. *Journal of Child Language, 16,* 477–501.

Feuerstein, R., Feuerstein, R., & Gross, S. (1997). The learning potential assessment device. In D. P. Flanagan, J. Genshaft, & P. L. Harrison (Eds.), *Contemporary intellectual assessment: Theories, tests, and issues.* New York: Guilford.

Field, D. (1981). Can preschool children really learn to conserve? *Child Development, 52,* 326–334.

Field, D., & Gueldner, S. H. (2001). The oldest-old: How do they differ from the old-old? *Journal of Gerontological Nursing, 27,* 20–27.

Field, D., & Millsap, R. E. (1991). Personality in advanced old age: Continuity or change? *Journal of Gerontology: Psychological Sciences, 46,* 299–308.

Field, J., Muir, D., Pilon, R., Sinclair, M., & Dodwell, P. (1980). Infants' orientation to lateral sounds from birth to three months. *Child Development, 51,* 295–298.

Field, N. P., Gal-Oz, E., & Bonanno, G. A. (2003). Continuing bonds and adjustment at 5 years after the death of a spouse. *Journal of Consulting and Clinical Psychology, 71,* 110–117.

Field, N. P., Nichols, C., Holen, A., & Horowitz, M. J. (1999). The relation of continuing attachment to adjustment in conjugal bereavement. *Journal of Consulting & Clinical Psychology, 67,* 212–218.

Field, N. P., Sturgen, S. E., Puryear, R., Hibbard, S., & Horowitz, M. J. (2001). Object relations as a predictor of adjustment in conjugal bereavement. *Development and Psychopathology, 13,* 399–412.

Field, T. M. (1987). Affective and interactive disturbances in infants. In J. D. Osofsky (Ed.), *Handbook of infant development* (2nd ed.). New York: Wiley.

Field, T. M. (1990). *Infancy.* Cambridge, MA: Harvard University Press.

Field, T. M. (1995a). Infants of depressed mothers. *Infant Behavior and Development, 18,* 1–13.

Field, T. M. (1995b). Massage therapy for infants and children. *Journal of Developmental and Behavioral Pediatrics, 16,* 105–111.

Fields, J. (2003). Children's living arrangements and characteristics: March 2002. *Current Population Reports, P20-547.* Washington, D.C.: U.S. Census Bureau. Available at: http://www.census.gov/prod/2003pubs/p20-547.pdf.

Fifer, W. P., Monk, C. E.,. & Grose-Fifer, J. (2004). Prenatal development and risk. In G. Bremner, & A. Fogel (Eds.), *Blackwell handbook of infant development* (pp. 505-542). Malden, MA: Blackwell Publishing.

Filipek, P. A., Accardo, P. J., Ashwal, S., & Baranek, G. T. (2000). Practice parameter: Screening and diagnosis of autism: Report of the Quality Standards Subcommittee of the American Academy of Neurology and the Child Neurology Society. *Neurology, 55,* 468–479.

Filipp, S. H. (1996). Motivation and emotion. In J. E. Birren, K. W. Schaie, R. P. Abeles, M. Gatz, & T. A. Salthouse (Eds.), *Handbook of the psychology of the aging* (4th ed.). San Diego: Academic Press.

Fincham, F. D. (2003). Marital conflict: Correlates, structure, and context. *Current Directions in Psychological Science, 12,* 23–27.

Fingerman, K. L., & Bermann, E. (2000). Applications of family systems theory to the study of adulthood. *International Journal of Aging and Human Development, 51,* 5–29.

Finitzo, T., Gunnarson, A. D., & Clark, J. L. (1990). Auditory deprivation and early conductive hearing loss from otitis media. *Topics in Language Disorders, 11,* 29–42.

Finkel, D., & McGue, M. (1998). Age differences in the nature and origin of individual differences in memory: A behavior genetic analysis. *International Journal of Aging and Human Development, 47,* 217–239.

Finkel, D., Pedersen, N. L., Reynolds, C. A., Berg, S., de Faire, U., & Svartengren, M. (2003a). Genetic and environmental influences on decline in biobehavioral markers of aging. *Behavior Genetics, 33,* 107–123.

Finkel, D., Reynolds, C. A., McArdle, J. J., Gatz, M., & Pedersen, N. L. (2003). Latent growth curve analyses of accelerating decline in cognitive abilities in late adulthood. *Developmental Psychology, 39,* 535–550.

Finkelhor, D., & Berliner, L. (1995). Research on the treatment of sexually abused children: A review and recommendations. *Journal of the American Academy of Child and Adolescent Psychiatry, 34,* 1408–1423.

Finkelhor, D., & Dziuba-Leatherman, J. (1994). Victimization of children. *American Psychologist, 49,* 173–183.

Finkelhor, D., Hotaling, G. T., Lewis, I. A., & Smith, C. (1989). Sexual abuse and its relationship to later sexual satisfaction, marital status, religion, and attitudes. *Journal of Interpersonal Violence, 4,* 379–399.

Finkelstein, J. A., & Schiffman, S. S. (1999). Workshop on taste and smell in the elderly: An overview. *Physiological Behavior, 66,* 173–176.

Finn, J. D. (2002). Class-size reduction in grades K–3. In A. Molnar (Ed.), *School reform proposals: The research evidence* (pp. 27–48). Greenwich, CT: Information Age Publishing.

Fisch, H., Hyun, G., Golder, R., Hensle, T. W., Olsson, C. A., & Liberson, G. L. (2003). The influence of paternal age on Down syndrome. *Journal of Urology, 169,* 2275–2278.

Fischer, C. S., & Phillips, S. L. (1982). Who is alone? Social characteristics of people with small networks. In L. A. Peplau & D. Perlman (Eds.), *Loneliness. A sourcebook of current theory, research and therapy.* New York: Wiley-Interscience.

Fischer, J. L., Sollie, D. L., Sorell, G. T., & Green, S. K. (1989). Marital status and career stage influences on social networks of young adults. *Journal of Marriage and the Family, 51,* 521–534.

Fischer, J. S. (2000, February 14). Best hope or broken promise? After a decade, gene therapy goes on trial. *U.S. News and World Report,* 46.

Fischer, K. W. (1980). A theory of cognitive development: The control and construction of hierarchies of skills. *Psychological Review, 87,* 477–531.

Fischer, K. W., Ayoub, C., Singh, I., Noam, G., Maraganore, A., & Raya, P. (1997). Psychopathology as adaptive development along distinctive pathways. *Development and Psychopathology, 9,* 749–779.

Fischer, K. W., & Bidell, T. (1991). Constraining nativist inferences about cognitive capacities. In S. Carey & Gelman (Eds.), *The epigenesis of mind: Essays on biology and cognition.* Hillsdale, NJ: Erlbaum.

Fischer, K. W., Kenny, S. L., & Pipp, S. L. (1990). How cognitive processes and environmental conditions organize discontinuities in the development of abstractions. In C. N. Alexander & E. J. Langer (Eds.), *Higher stages of human development: Perspectives on adult growth.* New York: Oxford Univeristy Press.

Fischer, R. B., Blazey, M. L., & Lipman, H. T. (1992). *Students of the third age.* New York: Macmillan.

Fischer, W. F. (1963). Sharing in pre-school children as a function of the amount and type of reinforcement. *Genetic Psychology Monographs, 68,* 215–245.

Fisher, C. B. (1999). Preparing successful proposals for Institutional Review Boards: Challenges and prospects for developmental scientists. *SRCD Newsletter, 42(2),* 7–9.

Fisher, C., & Tokura, H. (1996). Acoustic cues to grammatical structure in infant-directed speech: Cross-linguistic evidence. *Child Development, 67,* 3192–3218.

Fisher, E. P. (1992). The impact of play on development: A meta-analysis. *Play and Culture, 5,* 159–181.

Fisher, L., Ames, E. W., Chisholm, K., & Savoie, L. (1997). Problems reported by parents of Romanian orphans adopted to British Columbia. *International Journal of Behavioral Development, 20,* 67–82.

Fisher, S., & Greenberg, R. P. (1977). *The scientific credibility of Freud's theories and therapy.* New York: Basic Books.

Fitzgerald, J. M. (1999). Autobiographical memory and social cognition: Development of the remembered self in adulthood. In T. M. Hess & F. Blanchard-Fields (Eds.), *Social cognition and aging* (pp. 143–171). San Diego: Academic Press.

Fivush, R. (2002). Children's long-term memory of childhood events. In P. Graf & N. Ohta (Eds.), *Lifespan development of human memory* (pp. 83–100). Cambridge, MA: MIT Press.

Fivush, R., & Hammond, N. R. (1989). Time and again: Effects of repetition and retention interval on 2-year-olds' event recall. *Journal of Experimental Child Psychology, 47,* 259–273.

Fivush, R., Gray, J. T., & Fromhoff, F. A. (1987). Two-year-olds talk about the past. *Cognitive Development, 2,* 393–409.

Flaherty, J. H., & Morley, J. E. (2004). Delirium: A call to improve current standards of care. *Journal of Gerontology: Medical Sciences, 59A,* M341–M343.

Flaks, D. K., Ficher, I., Masterpasqua, F., & Joseph, G. (1995). Lesbians choosing motherhood: A comparative study of lesbian and heterosexual parents and their children. *Developmental Psychology, 31,* 105–114.

Flavell, J. H. (1963). *The developmental psychology of Jean Piaget.* New York: Van Nostrand Reinhold.

Flavell, J. H. (1985). *Cognitive development* (2nd ed.). Englewood Cliffs, NJ: Prentice Hall.

Flavell, J. H. (1996). Piaget's legacy. *Psychological Science, 7,* 200–203.

Flavell, J. H. (1999). Cognitive development: Children's knowledge about the mind. *Annual Review of Psychology, 50,* 21–45.

Flavell, J. H., Beach, D. R., & Chinsky, J. M. (1966). Spontaneous verbal rehearsal in a memory task as a function of age. *Child Development, 37,* 283–299.

Flavell, J. H., Everett, B. H., Croft, K., & Flavell, E. R. (1981). Young children's knowledge about visual perception: Further evidence for the level 1–level 2 distinction. *Developmental Psychology, 17,* 99–103.

Flavell, J. H., Miller, P. H., & Miller, S. A. (1993). *Cognitive development.* Englewood Cliffs, NJ: Prentice Hall.

Flavell, J. H., & Wellman, H. M. (1977). Metamemory. In R. V. Kail & J. W. Hagen (Eds.), *Perspectives on the development of memory and cognition.* Hillsdale, NJ: Erlbaum.

Fleeson, W. (2004). The quality of American life at the end of the century. In O. G. Brim, C. D. Ryff, & R. C. Kessler (Eds.), *How healthy are we? A national study of well-being at midlife.* Chicago: University of Chicago Press.

Fletcher, K. L., & Bray, N. W. (1996). External memory strategy use in preschool children. *Merrill-Palmer Quarterly, 42,* 379–396.

Fletcher, M. A., & Waxman, S. (2001, March 6). Boasts to friends went unbelieved. *The Washington Post,* A1, A4.

Flieller, A. (1999). Comparison of the development of formal thought in adolescent cohorts aged 10 to 15 years (1967–1996 and 1972–1993). *Developmental Psychology, 35,* 1048–1058.

Flint, M. (1982). Male and female menopause: A cultural put-on. In A. M. Voda, M. Dinnerstein, & S. R. O'Donnell (Eds.), *Changing perspectives on menopause.* Austin: University of Texas Press.

Florian, V., & Kravetz, S. (1985). Children's concepts of death. A cross-cultural comparison among Muslims, Druze, Christians, and Jews in Israel. *Journal of Cross-Cultural Psychology, 16,* 174–189.

Florsheim, P., Sumida, E., McCann, C., Winstanley, M., Fukui, R., Seefeldt, T., & Moore, D. (2003). The transition to parenthood among young African American and Latino couples: Relational predictors of risk for parental dysfunction. *Journal of Family Psychology, 17,* 65–79.

Flouri, E., & Buchanan, A. (2003). What predicts fathers' involvement with their children? A prospective study of intact families. *British Journal of Developmental Psychology, 21,* 81–97.

Floyd, M., & Scogin, F. (1997). Effects of memory training on the subjective memory functioning and mental health of older adults: A meta-analysis. *Psychology and Aging, 12,* 150–161.

Flum, H., & Blustein, D. L. (2000). Reinvigorating the study of vocational research. *Journal of Vocational Behavior, 56,* 380–404.

Flynn, C. P. (1994). Regional differences in attitudes toward corporal punishment. *Journal of Marriage and the Family, 56,* 314–324.

Flynn, J. R. (1987). Massive IQ gains in 14 nations: What IQ tests really measure. *Psychological Bulletin, 101,* 171–191.

Flynn, J. R. (1998). IQ gains over time: Toward finding the causes. In U. Neisser (Ed.), *The rising curve: Long-term gains in IQ and related measures.* Washington, D.C.: American Psychological Association.

Flynn, J. R. (1999). Search for justice: The discovery of IQ gains over time. *American Psychologist, 54,* 5–20.

Foley, K., & Hendin, H. (2002). Conclusion: Changing the culture. In K. Foley, & H. Hendin (Eds.), *The case against assisted suicide: For the right to end-of-life care.* Baltimore: The Johns Hopkins Press.

Folkman, S., & Moskowitz, J. T. (2004). Coping: Pitfalls and promise. *Annual Review of Psychology, 55,* 745–774.

Fonagy, P., & Target, M. (2000). The place of psychodynamic theory in developmental psychopathology. *Development and Psychopathology, 12,* 407–425.

Foorman, B. R. (1995). Research on "The Great Debate": Code-oriented versus whole language approaches to reading instruction. *School Psychology Review, 24,* 376–392.

Foorman, B. R., Francis, D. J., Fletcher, J. M., Schatschneider, C., & Mehta, P. (1998). The role of instruction in learning to read: Preventing reading failure in at-risk children. *Journal of Educational Psychology, 90,* 37–55.

Foos, P. W., & Sarno, S. J. (1998). Adult age differences in semantic and episodic memory. *Journal of Genetic Psychology, 159,* 297–312.

Ford, C. S., & Beach, F. A. (1951). *Patterns of sexual behavior.* New York: Harper & Row.

Ford, T., Goodman, R., & Meltzer, H. (2003). The British child and adolescent mental health survey 1999: The prevalence of DSM-IV disorders. *Journal of the American Academy of Child and Adolescent Psychiatry, 42,* 1203–1211.

Fordham, S., & Ogbu, J. U. (1986). Black students' school success: Coping with the "burden of 'acting white.'" *Urban Review, 18,* 176–206.

Forgatch, M. S., & DeGarmo, D. S. (1999). Parenting through change: An effective prevention program for single mothers. *Journal of Consulting and Clinical Psychology, 67,* 711–724.

Forrest, J. D., & Singh, S. (1990). The sexual and reproductive behavior of American women, 1982–1988. *Family Planning Perspectives, 22,* 206–214.

Forys, K., & Rider, E. (2000, April). *Factors influencing self-esteem during the transition from elementary to middle school.* Paper presented at the Annual Meeting of the Eastern Psychological Association, Baltimore.

Fowles, D. C., & Kochanska, G. (2000). Temperament as a moderator of pathways to conscience in children: The contribution of electrodermal activity. *Psychophysiology, 37,* 788–795.

Fox, B. (2001a). As times change: A review of trends in personal and family life. In B. J. Fox (Ed.), *Family patterns, gender relations* (2nd ed.). Don Mills, Ont.: Oxford University Press.

Fox, B. (2001b) Reproducing difference: Changes in the lives of partners becoming parents. In B. J. Fox (Ed.), *Family patterns, gender relations* (2nd ed.). Don Mills, Ont.: Oxford University Press.

Fox, N. A., Henderson, H. A., Rubin, K. H., Calkins, S. D., & Schmidt, L. A. (2001). Continuity and discontinuity of behavioral inhibition and exuberance: Psychophysiological and behavioral influences across the first four years of life. *Child Development, 72,* 1–21.

Fozard, J. L., & Gordon-Salant, T. (2001). Changes in vision and hearing with aging. In J. E. Birren & K. W. Schaie (Eds.), *Handbook of the psychology of aging, 5th ed* (pp. 241-266). San Diego: Academic Press.

Fraley, R. C. (2002). Attachment stability from infancy to adulthood: Meta-analysis and dynamic modeling of developmental mechanisms. *Personality and Social Psychology Review, 6,* 123–151.

Fraley, R. C., & Bonanno, G. A. (2004). Attachment and loss: A test of three competing models on the association between attachment-related avoidance and adaptation to bereavement. *Personality and Social Psychology Bulletin, 30,* 878–890.

Francis, K. L., & Spirduso, W. W. (2000). Age differences in the expression of manual asymmetry. *Experimental Aging Research, 26,* 169–180.

Frank, D. A., Augustyn, M., Knight, W. G., Pell, T., & Zuckerman, B. (2001). Growth, development, and behavior in early childhood following prenatal cocaine exposure: A systematic review. *The Journal of the American Medical Association, 285,* 1613–1625.

Frank, D. A., Brown, J., Johnson, S., & Cabral, H. (2002). Forgotten fathers: An exploratory study of mothers' report of drug and alcohol problems among fathers of urban newborns. *Neurotoxicology and Teratology, 24,* 339–347.

Frank, D. A., Jacobs, R. R., Beeghly, M., Augustyn, M., Bellinger, D., Cabral, H., & Heeren, T. (2002). Level of prenatal cocaine exposure and scores on the Bayley scales of infant development: Modifying effects of caregiver, early intervention, and birth weight. *Pediatrics, 110,* 1143–1152.

Frank, S. M., Raja, S. N., Bulcao, C., & Goldstein, D. S. (2000). Age-related thermoregulatory differences during core cooling in humans. *American Journal of Physiological Regulation, Integration, and Comparative Physiology, 279,* R349-354.

Frankel, V. (2003, Oct 1). Laugh it up! From peekaboo to jokes about you, what kids find funny age by age—and how to nurture their sense of humor. *Parenting, 17,* 122.

Frankenburg, W. K., Dodds, J. B., Archer, P., Shapiro, H., & Bresnick, B. (1992). The Denver II: A major revision and restandardization of the Denver Development Screening Test. *Pediatrics, 89,* 91–97.

Franklin, C., & Corcoran, J. (2000). Preventing adolescent pregnancy: A review of programs and practices. *Social Work, 45,* 40–52.

Franklin, M. B. (1995, April 25). New hope for osteoporosis sufferers? *The Washington Post—Health,* 8–9.

Fraser, M. W. (2004). The ecology of childhood: A multisystems perspective. In M. W. Fraser (Ed.), *Risk and resilience in childhood: An ecological perspective, 2nd ed.* (1-9). Washington, D. C. NASW Press.

Frawley, W. (1997). *Vygotsky and cognitive science: Language and the unification of the social and computational mind.* Cambridge, MA: Harvard University Press.

Fredriksen, K., Rhodes, J., Reddy, R., & Niobe, W. (2004). Sleepless in Chicago: Tracking the effects of adolescent sleep loss during the middle school years. *Child Development, 75,* 84–95.

Freedland, R. L., & Bertenthal, B. I. (1994). Developmental changes in interlimb coordination: Transition to hands-and-knees crawling. *Psychological Science, 5,* 26–32.

Freeman, S. F. N. (2000). Academic and social attainments of children with mental retardation in general education and special education settings. *Remedial and Special Education, 21,* 3–19.

Freid, V. M., Prager, K., MacKay, A. P., & Xia, H. (2003). *Health, United States, 2003, with Chartbook on trends in the health of Americans.* Hyattsville, MD: National Center for Health Statistics. Available at: http://www.cdc.gov/nchs/hus.htm.

French Pediatric HIV Infection Study Group, European Collaborative Study. (1997). Morbidity and mortality in European children vertically infected by HIV-1. *Journal of Acquired Immune Deficiency Syndrome Human Retrovirology, 14,* 442–450.

Fretts, R. C., & Usher, R. H. (1997). Causes of fetal death in women of advanced maternal age. *Obstetrics and Gynecology, 89,* 40–45.

Freud, S. (1930). *Three contributions to the theory of sex.* New York: Nervous and Mental Disease Publishing Company. (Original work published 1905).

Freud, S. (1933). *New introductory lectures in psychoanalysis.* New York: Norton.

Freud, S. (1960). *A general introduction to psychoanalysis.* New York: Washington Square Press. (Original work published 1935).

Freud, S. (1964). An outline of psychoanalysis. In J. Strachey (Ed.), *The standard edition of the complete psychological works of Sigmund Freud* (Vol. 23). London: Hogarth Press. (Original work published 1940).

Freund, A. M., & Baltes, P. B. (1998). Selection, optimization, and compensation as strategies of life management: Correlations with subjective indicators of successful aging. *Psychology and Aging, 13,* 531–543.

Freund, L. S. (1990). Maternal regulation of children's problem solving behavior and its impact on children's performance. *Child Development, 61,* 113-126.

Frey, K. S., & Ruble, D. N. (1985). What children say when the teacher is not around: Conflicting goals in social comparison and performance assessment in the classroom. *Journal of Personality and Social Psychology, 48,* 550–562.

Frey, K. S., & Ruble, D. N. (1992). Gender constancy and the cost of sex-typed behavior: A test of the conflict hypothesis. *Developmental Psychology, 28,* 714–721.

Fried, P. A., O'Connell, C. M., & Watkinson, B. (1992). 60- and 72-month follow-up of children prenatally exposed to marijuana, cigarettes, and alcohol: Cognitive and language assessment. *Developmental and Behavioral Pediatrics, 13,* 383–391.

Friedman, J. M., & Polifka, J. E. (1996). *The effects of drugs on the fetus and nursing infant: A handbook for health care professionals.* Baltimore: Johns Hopkins University Press.

Friedman, L. J. (1999). *Identity's architect: A biography of Erik H. Erikson.* New York: Scribner.

Friedrich, L. K., & Stein, A. H. (1973). Aggressive and prosocial television programs and the natural behavior of preschool children. *Monographs of the Society for Research in Child Development, 38* (4, Serial No. 51).

Frieske, D. A., & Park, D. C. (1999). Memory for news in young and old adults. *Psychology and Aging, 14,* 90–98.

Frieswijk, N., Buunk, B. P., Steverink, N., & Slaets, J. P. J. (2004). The effect of social comparison information on the life satisfaction of frail older persons. *Psychology and Aging, 19,* 183–190.

Frith, Uta. (2003). *Autism: Explaining the enigma* (2nd ed.). Malden, MA: Blackwell.

Frost, M. (2000). Ella Miller dies at age 119, *Rogersville Review.* Available at: http://www.grg.org/emiller.htm.

Fry, A. F., & Hale, S. (1996). Processing speed, working memory, and fluid intelligence: Evidence for a developmental cascade. *Psychological Science, 7,* 237–241.

Fry, C. L. (1985). Culture, behavior, and aging in the comparative perspective. In J. E. Birren & K. W. Schaie (Eds.), *Handbook of the psychology of aging* (2nd ed.). New York: Van Nostrand Reinhold.

Fry, C. L. (1999). Anthropological theories of age and aging. In V. L. Bengtson & K. W. Schaie (Eds.), *Handbook of theories of aging.* New York: Springer.

Fry, P. S. (1992). Major social theories of aging and their implications for counseling concepts and practice: A critical review. *Counseling Psychologist, 20,* 246–329.

Fry, P. S. (1997). Grandparents' reactions to the death of a grandchild: An exploratory factor analytic study. *Omega: Journal of Death and Dying, 35,* 119–140.

Fryauf-Bertschy, H., Tyler, R. S., Kelsay, D. M. R., Gantz, B. J., & Woodworth, G. G. (1997). Cochlear implant use by prelingually deafened children: The influence of age at implant and length of device use. *Journal of Speech, Language, and Hearing Research, 40,* 183–199.

Fuligni, A. J. (1998). Authority, autonomy, and parent–adolescent conflict and cohesion: A study of adolescents from Mexican, Chinese, Filipino, and European backgrounds. *Developmental Psychology, 34,* 782–792.

Fuligni, A. J., & Eccles, J. S. (1993). Perceived parent–child relationships and early adolescents' orientation toward peers. *Developmental Psychology, 29,* 622–632.

Fuligni, A. J., & Stevenson, H. W. (1995). Time use and mathematics achievement among American, Chinese, and Japanese high school students. *Child Development, 66,* 830–842.

Fullilove, R. E., & Treisman, E. M. (1990). Mathematics achievement among African American undergraduates at the University of California, Berkeley: An evaluation of the mathematics workshop. *Journal of Negro Education, 59,* 463–478.

Furman, E. (1984). Children's patterns in mourning the death of a loved one. In H. Wass & C. A. Corr (Eds.), *Childhood and death.* Washington, D.C.: Hemisphere.

Furman, W., & Buhrmester, D. (1992). Age and sex differences in perceptions of networks of personal relationships. *Child Development, 63,* 103–115.

Furman, W., & Shaffer, L. (2003) The role of romantic relationships in adolescent development. In P. Florsheim (Ed.), *Adolescent romantic relations and sexual behavior: Theory, research, and practical implications.* Mahwah, NJ: Erlbaum.

Furstenberg, F. F., Jr. (2000). The sociology of adolescence and youth in the 1990s: A critical commentary. *Journal of Marriage and the Family, 62,* 896–910.

Furstenberg, F. F., Jr. (2003). Teenage childbearing as a public issue and private concern. *Annual Review of Sociology, 29,* 23–29.

Furstenberg, F. F., Jr., Brooks-Gunn, J., & Chase-Lansdale, L. (1989). Teenage pregnancy and childbearing. *American Psychologist, 44,* 313–320.

Furstenberg, F. F., Jr., Brooks-Gunn, J., & Morgan, S. P. (1987). *Adolescent mothers in later life.* New York: Cambridge University Press.

Furstenberg, F. F., Jr., Lincoln, R., & Menken, J. (Eds.). (1981). *Teenage sexuality, pregnancy, and childbearing.* Philadelphia, PA: University of Pennsylvania Press.

G

Gable, S., & Lutz, S. (2000). Household, parent, and child contributions to childhood obesity. *Family Relations, 49,* 293–300.

Gabriel, K., Hofmann, C., Glavas, M., & Weinberg, J. (1998). The hormonal effects of alcohol use on the mother and fetus. *Alcohol Health & Research World, 22,* 170–177.

Gadsden, V. (1999). Black families in intergenerational and cultural perspective. In M. E. Lamb (Ed.), *Parenting and child development in "nontraditional" families.* Mahwah, NJ: Erlbaum.

Gage, J. D., & Kirk, R. (2002). First-time fathers: Perceptions of preparedness for fatherhood. *Canadian Journal of Nursing Research, 34,* 15–24.

Gagnon, M. D., Hersen, M., Kabacoff, R. I., & Vanhasselt, V. B. (1999). Interpersonal and psychological correlates of marital dissatisfaction in late life: A review. *Clinical Psychology Review, 19,* 359–378.

Galambos, N. L., Almeida, D. M., & Petersen, A. C. (1990). Masculinity, femininity, and sex role attitudes in early adolescence: Exploring gender intensification. *Child Development, 61,* 1905–1914.

Gall, T. L., Evans, D. R., & Howard, J. (1997). The retirement adjustment process: Changes in the well-being of male retirees across time. *Journals of Gerontology: Psychological Sciences, 52,* 110–117.

Gallagher, H. L., & Frith, C. D. (2003). Functional imaging of "theory of mind." *Trends in Cognitive Sciences, 7,* 77–83.

Gallagher, J. M., & Easley, J. A., Jr. (Eds.). (1978). *Knowledge and development: Vol. 2. Piaget and education.* New York: Plenum.

Gallagher, S. K., & Gerstel, N. (2001). Connections and constraints: The effects of children on caregiving. *Journal of Marriage and the Family, 63,* 265–275.

Gallo, L. C., Smith, T. W., & Ruiz, J. M. (2003). An interpersonal analysis of adult attachment style: Circumplex descriptions, recalled developmental experiences, self-representations, and interpersonal functioning in adulthood. *Journal of Personality, 71,* 141–181.

Gallup, G. G., Jr. (1979). Self-recognition in chimpanzees and man: A developmental and comparative perspective. In M. Lewis & L. A. Rosenblum (Eds.), *Genesis of behavior: Vol. 2. The child and its family.* New York: Plenum.

Gamé, F., Carchon, I., & Vital-Durand, F. (2003). The effect of stimulus attractiveness on visual tracking in 2- to 6-month-old infants. *Infant Behavior & Development, 26,* 135–150.

Gamoran, A., Porter, A. C., Smithson, J., & White, P. A. (1997). Upgrading high school mathematics instruction: Improving learning opportunities for low-achieving, low-income youth. *Educational Evaluation and Policy Analysis, 19,* 325–338.

Ganchrow, J. R., Steiner, J. E., & Daher, M. (1983). Neonatal facial expressions to different qualities and intensities of gustatory stimuli. *Infant Behavior and Development, 6,* 189–200.

Gandelman, R. (1992). *Psychobiology of behavioral development.* New York: Oxford University Press.

Gannon, L., & Ekstrom, B. (1993). Attitudes toward menopause: The influence of sociocultural paradigms. *Psychology of Women Quarterly, 17,* 275–288.

Garbarino, J. (1992). *Children and families in the social environment* (2nd ed.). New York: Aldine de Gruyter.

Garber, J. (1984). The developmental progression of depression in female children. In D. Cicchetti & K. Schneider-Rosen (Eds.), *Childhood depression* (New Directions for Child Development, No. 26). San Francisco: Jossey-Bass.

Garber, J., & Flynn, C. (2001). Vulnerability to depression in childhood and adolescence. In R. E. Ingram & J. M. Price (Eds.), *Vulnerability to psychopathology. Risk across the lifespan.* New York: Guilford.

Garcia, M. M., Shaw, D. S., Winslow, E. B., & Yaggi, K. E. (2000). Destructive sibling conflict and the development of conduct problems in young boys. *Developmental Psychology, 36,* 44–53.

Gard, M. C. E., & Freeman, C. P. (1996). The dismantling of a myth: A review of eating disorders and socioeconomic status. *International Journal of Eating Disorders, 20,* 1–12.

Gardner, H. (1985). *The mind's new science: A history of the cognitive revolution.* New York: Basic Books.

Gardner, H. (1993). *Frames of mind: The theory of multiple intelligences* [Tenth anniversary edition]. New York: Basic Books.

Gardner, H. (1999/2000). *Intelligence reframed: Multiple intelligences for the 21st century.* New York: Basic Books.

Gardner, H., Phelps, E., & Wolf, D. (1990). The roots of adult creativity in children's symbolic products. In C. N. Alexander & E. J. Langer (Eds.), *Higher stages of human development. Perspectives on adult growth.* New York: Oxford University Press.

Gardner, L. J. (1972). Deprivation dwarfism. *Scientific American, 227,* 76–82.

Garland, A., & Zigler, E. (1993). Adolescent suicide prevention: Current research and social policy implications. *American Psychologist, 48,* 169–182.

Garmezy, N. (1994). Reflections and commentary on risk, resilience, and development. In R. J. Haggerty, L. R. Sherrod, N. Garmezy, & M. Rutter (Eds.), *Stress, risk and resilience in children and adolescents: Processes, mechanisms, and interventions.* Cambridge, England: Cambridge University Press.

Garner, R. (1999, November 15). Failing at four. *New York Times Magazine, 26.*

Garvey, C. (1990). *Play* (enlarged ed.). Cambridge, MA: Harvard University Press.

Gathercole, S. E. (1998). The development of memory. *Journal of Child Psychology and Psychiatry and Allied Disciplines, 39,* 3-27.

Gatz, M., Svedberg, P., Pedersen, N. L., Mortimer, J. A., Berg, S., & Johansson, B. (2001). Education and the risk of Alzheimer's disease: Findings from the study of dementia in Swedish twins. *Journal of Gerontology: Psychological Sciences, 56B,* 292–300.

Gaugler, J. E., Davey, A., Pearlin, L. I., & Zarit, S. H. (2000). Modeling caregiver adaptation over time: The longitudinal impact of behavior problems. *Psychology and Aging, 15,* 437–450.

Gauvain, M., & Rogoff, B. (1989). Collaborative problem-solving and children's planning skills. *Developmental Psychology, 25,* 139–151.

Gauze, C., Bukowski, W. M., Aquanassee, J., & Sippola, L. K. (1996). Interactions between family environment and friendship and associations with self-perceived well-being during early adolescence. *Child Development, 67,* 2301–2316.

Gazzaniga, M. S. (1998). The split brain revisited. *Scientific American, 279,* 50–55.

Gazzaniga, M. S. (2000). Regional differences in cortical organization. *Science, 289,* 1887–1888.

Ge, X., Best, K. M., Conger, R. D., & Simons, R. L. (1996). Parenting behaviors and the occurrence and co-occurrence of adolescent depressive symptoms and conduct problems. *Developmental Psychology, 32,* 717–731.

Ge, X., Donnellan, M. B., & Harper, L. (2003). Are we finally ready to move beyond "nature vs. nurture"? In A. C. Crouter & A. Booth (Eds.), *Children's influence on family dynamics. The neglected side of family relationships.* Mahwah, NJ: Erlbaum.

Ge, X., Kim, I. J., Brody, G. H., Conger, R. D., Simons, R. L., Gibbons, F. X., & Cutrona, C. E. (2003). It's about timing and change: Pubertal transition effects on symptoms of major depression among African American youths. *Developmental Psychology, 39,* 430–439.

Ge, X., Lorenz, F. O., Conger, R. D., Elder, G. H., Jr., & Simons, R. L. (1994). Trajectories of stressful life events and depressive symptoms during adolescence. *Developmental Psychology, 30,* 467–483.

Geary, D. C. (2000). Evolution and proximate expression of human paternal investment. *Psychological Bulletin, 126,* 55–77.

Geithner, C. A., Satake, T., Woynarowska, B., & Malina, R. M. (1999). Adolescent spurts in body dimensions: Average and modal sequences. *American Journal of Human Biology, 11,* 287–295.

Geldart, S., Mondloch, C. J., Maurer, D., de Schonen, S., & Brent, H. P. (2002). The effect of early visual deprivation on the development of face processing, *Developmental Science, 5,* 490–501.

Gelman, R. (1972). The nature and development of early number concepts. In H. W. Reese (Ed.), *Advances in Child Development and Behavior* (Vol. 7). New York: Academic Press.

Gelman, R. (1978). Cognitive development. *Annual Review of Psychology, 29,* 297–332.

Gelman, S. A. (1996). Concepts and theories. In R. Gelman & T. K. Au (Eds.), *Perceptual and cognitive development.* San Diego: Academic Press.

Genc, M., & Ledger, W. J. (2000). Syphilis in pregnancy. *Sexual Transmission Information, 76,* 73–79.

German, P. S., Burton, L. C., Shapiro, S., Steinwachs, D. M., Tsuji, I., Paglia, M. J., & Damiano, A. M. (1995). Extended coverage for preventive services for the elderly: Response and results in a demonstration population. *American Journal of Public Health, 85,* 379–386.

Gershoff, E. T. (2002). Corporal punishment by parents and associated child behaviors and experiences: A meta-analytic and theoretical review. *Psychological Bulletin, 128,* 539–579.

Gest, S. D., Graham-Bermann, S. A., & Hartup, W. W. (2001). Peer experience: Common and unique features of number of friendships, social network centrality, and sociometric status. *Social Development, 10,* 23–40.

Getzels, J. W., & Jackson, P. W. (1962). Creativity and intelligence: Explorations with gifted children. New York: Wiley.

Ghetti, S., & Alexander, K. W. (2004). "If it happened, I would remember it": Strategic use of event memorability in the rejection of false autobiographical events. *Child Development, 75,* 542–560.

Giampaoli S. (2000). Epidemiology of major age-related diseases in women compared to men. *Aging, 12,* 93–105.

Giarrusso, R., Feng, D., Silverstein, M., & Bengtson, V. L. (2000). Self in the context of the family. In K. W. Schaie & J. Hendrick (Eds.), *The evolution of the aging self. The societal impact on the aging process.* New York: Springer.

Gibbs, J. C. (2003). *Moral development and reality: Beyond the theories of Kohlberg and Hoffman.* London, England: Sage Publications Ltd.

Gibson, E. J. (1988). Exploratory behavior in the development of perceiving, acting, and the acquiring of knowledge. *Annual Review of Psychology, 39,* 1–41.

Gibson, E. J., & Pick, A. D. (2000). *An ecological approach to perceptual learning and development.* New York: Oxford University Press.

Gibson, E. J., & Walk, R. D. (1960). The "visual cliff." *Scientific American, 202,* 64–71.

Gigy, L., & Kelly, J. B. (1992). Reasons for divorce: Perspectives of divorcing men and women. *Journal of Divorce and Remarriage, 18,* 169–187.

Gil, D. G. (1970). *Violence against children.* Cambridge, MA: Harvard University Press.

Gilbert, N. (1997). *Combating child abuse: International perspectives and trends.* New York: Oxford University Press.

Gilbert, W. M., Nesbitt, T. S., & Danielsen, B. (1999). Childbearing beyond age 40: Pregnancy outcomes in 24,302 cases. *Obstetrics and Gynecology, 93,* 9–14.

Gillberg, C., & Steffenburg, S. (1987). Outcome and prognostic factors in infantile autism and similar conditions: A population-based study of 46 cases followed through puberty. *Journal of Autism and Developmental Disorders, 17,* 273–287.

Gillick, M. R. (1998). *Tangled minds. Understanding Alzheimer's disease and other dementias.* New York: Penguin.

Gilligan, C. (1977). In a different voice: Women's conceptions of self and morality. *Harvard Educational Review, 47,* 481–517.

Gilligan, C. (1982). *In a different voice: Psychological theory and women's development.* Cambridge, MA: Harvard University Press.

Gilligan, C. (1993). Adolescent development reconsidered. In A. Garrod (Ed.), *Approaches to moral development: New research and emerging themes.* New York: Teachers College Press.

Gillis, J. R. (2003). The birth of the virtual child. A Victorian progeny. In W. Koops & M. Zuckerman. (Eds.), *Beyond the century of the child. Cultural history and developmental psychology.* Philadelphia: University of Pennsylvania Press.

Ginsburg, G. S., & Bronstein, P. (1993). Family factors related to children's intrinsic/extrinsic motivational orientation and academic performance. *Child Development, 64,* 1461–1474.

Ginzberg, E. (1972). Toward a theory of occupational choice: A restatement. *Vocational Guidance Quarterly, 20,* 169–176.

Ginzberg, E. (1984). Career development. In D. Brown, L. Brooks, & Associates (Eds.), *Career choice and development.* San Francisco: Jossey-Bass.

Giordano, P. C. (2003). Relationships in adolescence. *Annual Review of Sociology, 29,* 257–281.

Girard, C. (1993). Age, gender, and suicide: A cross-national analysis. *American Sociological Review, 58,* 553–574.

Glascock, J. (2001). Gender roles on prime-time network television: Demographics and behaviors. *Journal of Broadcasting & Electronic Media, 45,* 656–669.

Glaser, B. G., & Strauss, A. L. (1968). *Time for dying.* Chicago: Aldine.

Glaser, R., & Chi, M. T. H. (1988). Overview. In M. T. H. Chi, R. Glaser, & M. Farr (Eds.), *The nature of expertise.* Hillsdale, NJ: Erlbaum.

Glasgow, K. L., Dornbusch, S. M., Troyer, L., Steinberg, L., & Ritter, P. L. (1997). Parenting styles, adolescents' attributions, and educational outcomes in nine heterogeneous high schools. *Child Development, 68,* 507–529.

Glass, G. V. (2002a). Grouping students for instruction. In A. Molnar (Ed.), *School reform proposals: The research evidence* (pp. 95–112). Greenwich, CT: Information Age Publishing.

Glass, G. V. (2002b). Teacher characteristics. In A. Molnar (Ed.), *School reform proposals: The research evidence* (pp. 155–174). Greenwich, CT: Information Age Publishing.

Glass, G. V. (2002c). Time for school: Its duration and allocation. In A. Molnar (Ed.), *School reform proposals: The research evidence* (pp. 79–93). Greenwich, CT: Information Age Publishing.

Glass, G. V., McGaw, B., & Smith, M. L. (1981). *Meta-analysis in social research.* Beverly Hills, CA: Sage.

Gleason, T. R., Sebanc, A. M., & Hartup, W. W. (2000). Imaginary companions of preschool children. *Developmental Psychology, 36,* 419–428.

Gleaves, D. H., & Hernandez, E. (1999). Recent reformulations of Freud's development and abandonment of his seduction theory: Historical/scientific clarification or a continued assault on truth? *History of Psychology, 2,* 324–354.

Gleicher, N., Oleske, D. M., Tur-Kaspa, I. Vidali, A., & Karande, V. (2000). Reducing the risk of high-order multiple pregnancy after ovarian stimulation with gonadotropins. *New England Journal of Medicine, 343,* 2–7.

Glick, J. C. (1975). Cognitive development in cross-cultural perspective. In F. Horowitz (Ed.), *Review of child development research* (Vol. 1). Chicago: University of Chicago Press.

Glick, M., & Zigler, E. (1985). Self-image: A cognitive developmental approach. In R. L. Leahy (Ed.), *The Development of the self.* Orlando, FL: Academic Press.

Gloth, F. M. (2000). Geriatric pain: Factors that limit pain relief and increase complications. *Geriatrics, 55,* 51–54.

Glowinski, A. L., Madden, P. A. F., Bucholz, K. K., Lynskey, M. T., & Heath, A. C. (2003). Genetic epidemiology of self-reported lifetime DSM-IV major depressive disorder in a population-based twin sample of female adolescents. *Journal of Child Psychology and Psychiatry and Allied Disciplines, 44,* 988–996.

Gnepp, J., & Chilamkurti, C. (1988). Children's use of personality attributions to predict other people's emotional and behavioral reactions. *Child Development, 59,* 743–754.

Gold, E. B., Sternfeld, B., Kelsey, J. L., Brown, C., Mouton, C., Reame, N., Salamone, L., & Stellato, R. (2000). Relation of demographic and lifestyle factors to symptoms in a multiracial/ethnic population of women 40–55 years of age. *American Journal of Epidemiology, 152,* 463–473.

Goldberg, A. P., & Hagberg, J. M. (1990). Physical exercise in the elderly. In E. L. Schneider & J. W. Rowe (Eds.), *Handbook of the biology of aging* (3rd ed.). San Diego: Academic Press.

Goldberg, G. R., & Prentice, A. M. (1994). Maternal and fetal determinants of adult diseases. *Nutrition Reviews, 52,* 191–200.

Goldberg, S., Perrotta, M., Minde, K., & Corter, C. (1986). Maternal behavior and attachment in low–birth-weight twins and singletons. *Child Development, 57,* 34–46.

Goldberg, W. A., Greenberger, E., & Nagel, S. K. (1996). Employment and achievement: Mothers' work involvement in relation to children's achievement behaviors and mothers' parenting behaviors. *Child Development, 67,* 1512–1527.

Goldfarb, W. (1943). The effects of early institutional care on adolescent personality. *Journal of Experimental Education, 12,* 107–129.

Goldfarb, W. (1947). Variations in adolescent adjustment in institutionally reared children. *Journal of Orthopsychiatry, 17,* 449–457.

Goldfield, B. A., & Reznick, J. S. (1996). Measuring the vocabulary spurt: A reply to Mervis and Bertrand. *Journal of Child Language, 23,* 241–246.

Goldfield, B. A., & Snow, C. E. (2005). Individual differences in language acquisition. In J. B. Gleason (Ed.), *The development of language* (6th ed.). Boston: Allyn & Bacon.

Goldhaber, D. E. (2000). *Theories of human development. Integrative perspectives.* Mountain View, CA: Mayfield.

Goldsmith, H. H. (2003). Genetics of emotional development. In R. J. Davidson, K. R. Scherer, & H. H. Goldsmith (Eds.), *Handbook of affective sciences.* New York: Oxford University Press.

Goldwater, O. D., & Nutt, R. L. (1999). Teachers' and students' work-culture variables associated with positive school outcome. *Adolescence, 34,* 653–664.

Golombok, S., Cook, R., Bish, A., & Murray, C. (1995). Families created by the new reproductive technologies: Quality of parenting and social and emotional development of the children. *Child Development, 66,* 285–298.

Golombok, S., Perry, B., Burston, A., Murray, C., Mooney-Somers, J., Stevens, M., & Golding, J. (2003). Children with lesbian parents: A community study. *Developmental Psychology, 39,* 20–33.

Golub, M., Gorman, K., Grantham-McGregor, S., Levitsky, D., Schürch, B., Strupp, B., & Wachs, T. (1996). A reconceptualization of the effects of undernutrition on children's biological, psychosocial, and behavioral development. *Social Policy Report, Society for Research in Child Development, 10,* 1–21.

Good, C., Aronson, J., & Inzlicht, M. (2003). Improving adolescents' standardized test performance: An intervention to reduce the effects of stereotype threat. *Journal of Applied Developmental Psychology, 24,* 645–662.

Goodkin, K., Baldewicz, T. T., Blaney, N. T., Asthana, D., Kumar, M., Shapshak, P., Leeds, B., Burkhalter, J. E., Rigg, D., Tyll, M. D., Cohen, J., & Zheng, W. L. (2001). Physiological effects of bereavement and bereavement support group interventions. In M. S. Stroebe, & R. O. Hansson (Eds.), *Handbook of bereavement research: Consequences, coping, and care.* Washington, D.C.: American Psychological Association.

Goodman, S. H. (2002). Depression and early adverse experiences. In I. H. Gotlib & C. L. Hammen (Eds.), *Handbook of depression.* New York: Guilford.

Gopnik, A. (1996). The post-Piaget era. *Psychological Science, 7,* 221–225.

Gopnik, A., Capps, L., & Meltzoff, A. N. (2000). Early theories of mind: What the theory can tell us about autism. In S. Baron-Cohen, H. Tager-Flusberg, & D. J. Cohen (Eds.), *Understanding other minds. Perspectives from developmental cognitive neuroscience* (2nd ed.). Oxford: Oxford University Press.

Gopnik, A., & Choi, S. (1995). Names, relational words, and cognitive development in English and Korean speakers: Nouns are not always learned before verbs. In M. Tomasello & W. E. Merriman (Eds.), *Beyond names for things: Young children's acquisition of verbs* (pp. 83–90). Hillsdale, NJ: Erlbaum.

Gordon, B. N., Schroeder, C. S., & Abrams, J. M. (1990). Children's knowledge of sexuality: A comparison of sexually abused and nonabused children. *American Journal of Orthopsychiatry, 60,* 250–257.

Gordon, P. (1990). Learnability and feedback. *Developmental Psychology, 26,* 217–220.

Gordon, R. A. (2000). *Eating disorders. Anatomy of a social epidemic* (2nd ed.). Oxford, England: Blackwell.

Gorey, K. M. (2001). Early childhood education: A meta-analytic affirmation of the short- and long-term benefits of educational opportunity. *School Psychology Quarterly, 16,* 9-30.

Gorey, K. M., & Leslie, D. (1997). The prevalence of child sexual abuse: Integrative review adjustment for potential response and measurement bias. *Child Abuse and Neglect, 21,* 391–398.

Gorman, J., Leifer, M., & Grossman, G. (1993). Nonorganic failure to thrive: Maternal history and current maternal functioning. *Journal of Clinical Child Psychology, 22,* 327–336.

Gortmaker, S. L., Must, A., Sobol, A. M., Peterson, K., Colditz, G. A., & Dietz, W. H. (1996). Television viewing as a cause of increasing obesity among children in the United States. *Archives of Pediatric and Adolescent Medicine, 150,* 356–362.

Gosling, S. D., Rentfrow, P. J., & Swann, W. B. (2003). A very brief measure of the Big-Five personality domains. *Journal of Research in Personality, 37,* 504–528.

Gostin, L. O. (2001). National health information privacy: Regulations under the Health Insurance Portability and Accountability Act. *Journal of the American Medical Association, 23,* 3015–3021.

Goswami, U. (1999). Causal connections in beginning reading: The importance of rhyme. *Journal of Research in Reading, 22,* 217–241.

Gotlib, I. H., & Hammen, C. L. (1992). *Psychological aspects of depression. Toward a cognitive-interpersonal integration.* Chichester, England: John Wiley & Sons.

Gotlib, I. H., & Hammen, C. L. (2002). Introduction. In I. H. Gotlib & C. L. Hammen (Eds.), *Handbook of depression.* New York: Guilford.

Gott, M., & Hinchliff, S. (2003). How important is sex in later life? The views of older people. *Social Science & Medicine, 56,* 1617–1628.

Gottesman, I. I. (1991). *Schizophrenia genesis: The origins of madness.* New York: W. H. Freeman.

Gottfredson, L. S. (1996). Gottfredson's theory of circumscription and compromise. In D. Brown, L. Brooks, & Associates (Eds.), *Career choice and development* (3rd ed.). San Francisco: Jossey-Bass.

Gottfredson, L. S. (1997). Why g matters: The complexity of everyday life. *Intelligence, 24,* 79–132.

Gottfredson, L. S. (2002). G: Highly general and highly practical. In R. J. Sternberg & E. L.

Gottfredson, L. S. (2004). Intelligence: Is it the epidemiologists' elusive "fundamental cause" of social class inequalities in health? *Journal of Personality and Social Psychology, 86,* 174–199.

Gottfredson, L. S., & Deary, I. (2004). Intelligence predicts health and longevity, but why? *Current Directions in Psychological Science, 13,* 1–4.

Gottfried, A. E., Fleming, J. S., & Gottfried, A. W. (1998). Role of cognitively stimulating home environment in children's academic intrinsic motivation: A longitudinal study. *Child Development, 69,* 1448–1460.

Gottfried, A. W. (1984). Home environment and early cognitive development: Integration, meta-analyses, and conclusions. In A. W. Gottfried (Ed.), *Home environment and early cognitive development: Longitudinal research.* Orlando, FL: Academic Press.

Gottfried, A. W., & Gottfried, A. E. (1984). Home environment and cognitive development in young children of middle-socioeconomic-status families. In A. W. Gottfried (Ed.), *Home environment and early cognitive development: Longitudinal research.* Orlando, FL: Academic Press.

Gottfried, A. W., Gottfried, A. E., Bathurst, K., & Guerin, D. W. (1994). *Gifted IQ: Early developmental aspects: The Fullerton Longitudinal Study.* New York: Plenum.

Gottlieb, G. (1991). Experiential canalization of behavioral development: Theory. *Developmental Psychology, 27,* 4–13.

Gottlieb, G. (1992). *Individual development and evolution: The genesis of novel behavior.* New York: Oxford University Press.

Gottlieb, G. (1996). Commentary: A systems view of psychobiological development. In D. Magnussen (Ed.), *The lifespan development of individuals: Behavioral, neurological, and psychosocial perspectives—A synthesis.* Cambridge, England: Cambridge University Press.

Gottlieb, G. (2000). Environmental and behavioral influences on gene activity. *Current Directions in Psychological Science, 9,* 93–97.

Gottlieb, G. (2002). Developmental-behavioral initiation of evolutionary change. *Psychological Review, 109,* 211–218.

Gottlieb, G. (2003). On making behavioral genetics truly developmental. *Human Development, 46,* 337–355.

Gottlieb, G., Wahlsten, D., & Lickliter, R. (1998). The significance of biology for human development: A developmental psychobiological systems view. In R. M. Lerner (Vol. Ed.), William Damon (Editor-in-Chief), *Handbook of Child Psychology: Vol. 1. Theoretical Models of Human Development* (5th ed.). New York: Wiley.

Gottlieb, L. (2000). *Luring a child into this life: A Beng path for infant care* (Session on cultural differences in infant care). Presented at the International Society on Infant Studies Conference.

Gottman, J. M., & Levenson, R. W. (2000). The timing of divorce: Predicting when a couple will divorce over a 14-year period. *Journal of Marriage and the Family, 62,* 737–745.

Gottman, J. M., & Notarius, C. I. (2000). Decade review: Observing marital interaction. *Journal of Marriage and the Family, 62,* 927–947.

Gould, D. C., Petty, R., & Jacobs, H. S. (2000). The male menopause—does it exist? *British Medical Journal, 320,* 858–861.

Gould, M. S., Greenberg, T., Velting, D. M., & Shaffer, D. (2003). Youth suicide risk and preventive interventions: A review of the past

10 years. *Journal of the American Academy of Child and Adolescent Psychiatry, 42,* 386–405.

Gowers, S., & Bryant-Waugh, R. (2004). Management of child and adolescent eating disorders: The current evidence base and future directions. *Journal of Child Psychology and Psychiatry and Allied Disciplines, 45,* 63–83.

Graber, J. A., Lewinsohn, P. M., Seeley, J. R., & Brooks-Gunn, J. (1997). Is psychopathology associated with the timing of pubertal development? *Journal of the American Academy of Child and Adolescent Psychiatry, 36,* 1768–1776.

Graf, P., Squire, L. R., & Mandler, G. (1984). The information that amnesic patients do not forget. *Journal of Experimental Psychology: Learning, Memory, and Cognition, 10,* 164–178.

Graham, C. A., & Easterbrooks, M. A. (2000). School-aged children's vulnerability to depressive symptomatology: The role of attachment security, maternal depressive symptomatology, and economic risk. *Development and Psychopathology, 12,* 201–213.

Graham, N., Lindesay, J., Katona, C., Bertolote, J. M., Camus, V., Copeland, J. R. M., de Mendonca Lima, C. A., Gaillard, M., Nargeot, M. C. G., Gray, J., Jacobsson, L., Kingma, M., Kuhne, N., O'Loughlin, A., Rutz, W., Saraceno, B., Taintor, Z., & Wancata, J. (2003). Reducing stigma and discrimination against older people with mental disorders: A technical consensus statement. *International Journal of Geriatric Psychiatry, 18,* 670–678.

Graham-Pole, J., Wass, H., Eyberg, S., Chu, L., & Olejnik, S. (1989). Communicating with dying children and their siblings: A retrospective analysis. *Death Studies, 13,* 463–483.

Gralinski, J. H., & Kopp, C. B. (1993). Everyday rules for behavior: Mothers' requests to young children. *Developmental Psychology, 29,* 573–584.

Granic, I., Hollenstein, T., Dishion, T. J., & Patterson, G. R. (2003). Longitudinal analysis of flexibility and reorganization in early adolescence: A dynamic systems study of family interactions. *Developmental Psychology, 39,* 606–617.

Grant, K. E., Compas, B. E., Thurm, A. E., McMahon, S. D., & Gipson, P. Y. (2004). Stressors and child and adolescent psychopathology: Measurement issues and prospective effects. *Journal of Clinical Child and Adolescent Psychology, 33,* 412–425.

Gray, S. W., Ramsey, B. K., & Klaus, R. A. (1982). *From 3 to 20: The early training project.* Baltimore: University Park Press.

Gray, W. M., & Hudson, L. M. (1984). Formal operations and the imaginary audience. *Developmental Psychology, 20,* 619–627.

Gray-Little, B., & Carels, R. A. (1997). The effect of racial dissonance on academic self-esteem and achievement in elementary, junior high, and high school students. *Journal of Research on Adolescence, 7,* 109–131.

Gray-Little, B., & Hafdahl, A. R. (2000). Factors influencing racial comparisons of self-esteem: A quantitative review. *Psychological Bulletin, 126,* 26–54.

Grayson, D. A., Mackinnon, A., Jorm, A. F., Creasey, H., & Broe, G. A. (2000). Item bias in the Center for Epidemiologic Studies Depression Scale: Effects of physical disorders and disability in an elderly community sample. *Journal of Gerontology: Psychological Sciences, 55,* 273–282.

Grbich, C., Parker, D., & Maddocks, I. (2001). The emotions and coping strategies of caregivers of family members with a terminal cancer. *Journal of Palliative Care, 17,* 30–36.

Green, C. R. (2001). *Total memory workout: 8 easy steps to maximum memory fitness.* New York: Bantam Doubleday.

Green, J., & Goldwyn, R. (2002). Attachment disorganization and psychopathology: New findings in attachment research and their potential implications for developmental psychopathology in childhood. *Journal of Child Psychology and Psychiatry and Allied Disciplines, 43,* 835–846.

Green, R. (1987). *The "sissy boy syndrome" and the development of homosexuality.* New Haven, CT: Yale University Press.

Greenberger, E., & Steinberg, L. (1986). When teenagers work: The psychological and social costs of adolescent employment. New York: Basic Books.

Greenberger, E., O'Neil, R., & Nagel, S. K. (1994). Linking workplace and homeplace: Relations between the nature of adults' work and their parenting behaviors. *Developmental Psychology, 30,* 990–1002.

Greene, A. L., & Boxer, A. M. (1986). Daughters and sons as young adults: Restructuring the ties that bind. In N. Datan, A. L. Greene, & H. W. Reese (Eds.), *Life-span developmental psychology. Intergenerational relations.* Hillsdale, NJ: Erlbaum.

Greene, J. G. (1984). The social and psychological origins of the climacteric syndrome. Hants, England & Brookfield, VT: Gower.

Greene, K., Rubin, D. L., Hale, J. L., & Walters, L. H. (1996). The utility of understanding adolescent egocentrism in designing health promotion messages. *Health Communication, 8,* 131–152.

Greenfield, P. M., Keller, H., Fuligni, A., & Maynard, A. (2003). Cultural pathways through universal development. *Annual Review of Psychology, 54,* 461–490.

Greenfield, P. M., & Savage-Rumbaugh, E. S. (1993). Comparing communicative competence in child and chimp: The pragmatics of repetition. *Journal of Child Language, 20,* 1–26.

Greenhalgh, R., Slade, P., & Spiby, H. (2000). Fathers' coping style, antenatal preparation, and experiences of labor and the postpartum. *Birth, 27,* 177–184.

Greenough, W. T., Black, J. E., & Wallace, C. S. (1987). Experience and brain development. *Child Development, 58,* 539–559.

Greenspan, S. I. (1997). *The growth of the mind.* Reading, MA: Addison-Wesley.

Gregg, V., Gibbs, J. C., & Basinger, K. S. (1994). Patterns of developmental delay in moral judgment by male and female delinquents. *Merrill-Palmer Quarterly, 40,* 538–553.

Gresham, F. M., & MacMillan, D. L. (1998). Early intervention project: Can its claims be sustained and it effects replicated. *Journal of Autism and Developmental Disorders, 28,* 5–13.

Gressens, P., Laudenbach, V., & Marret, S. (2003). Mechanisms of action of tobacco smoke on the developing brain. *Journal of Gynecology, Obstetrics, and Biological Reproduction, 32,* IS30–IS32.

Grilo, C. M., & Pogue-Geile, M. F. (1991). The nature of environmental influences on weight and obesity: A behavior genetic analysis. *Psychological Bulletin, 110,* 520–537.

Grizenko, N., Zappitelli, M., Langevin, J. P., Hrychko, S., El-Messidi, A., Kaminester, D., Pawliuk, N., & Stepanian, M. T. (2000). Effectiveness of a social skills training program using self/other perspective-taking: A nine-month follow-up. *American Journal of Orthopsychiatry, 70,* 501–509.

Grober, E., & Kawas, C. (1997). Learning and retention in preclinical and early Alzheimer's disease. *Psychology and Aging, 12,* 183–188.

Grollman, E. A. (1995). Explaining death to young children: Some questions and answers. In E. A. Grollman (Ed.), *Bereaved children and teens.* Boston: Beacon Press.

Grolnick, W. S., Bridges, L. J., & Connell, J. P. (1996). Emotion regulation in two-year-olds: Strategies and emotional expression in four contexts. *Child Development, 67,* 928–941.

Grossberg, G. T., & Desai, A. K. (2003). Management of Alzheimer's disease. *Journal of Gerontology: Medical Sciences, 58A,* 331–353.

Grossman, A. W., Churchill, J. D., McKinney, B. C., Kodish, I. M., Otte, S. L., & Greenough, W. T. (2003). Experience effects on brain development: Possible contributions to psychopathology. *Journal of Child Psychology and Psychiatry and Allied Disciplines, 44,* 33–63.

Grossmann, K., Grossmann, K. E., Fremmer-Bombik, E., Kindler, H., Scheuerer-Englisch, H., & Zimmermann, P. (2002b). The uniqueness of the child-father attachment relationship: Fathers' sensitive and challenging play as a pivotal variable in a 16-year longitudinal study. *Social Development, 11,* 307–331.

Grossmann, K., Grossmann, K. E., Spangler, S., Suess, G., & Unzner, L. (1985). Maternal sensitivity and newborn responses as related to quality of attachment in Northern Germany. In I. Bretherton & E. Waters, *Growing points of attachment theory. Monographs of the Society for Research in Child Development,* 50 (1–2, Serial No. 209).

Grossmann, K. E., Grossmann, K., Winter, M., & Zimmermann, P. (2002a). Attachment relationships and appraisal of partnership: From early experience of sensitive support to later relationship representation. In L. Pulkkinen & A. Caspi (Eds.), *Paths to successful development: Personality in the life course.* Cambridge, UK: Cambridge University Press.

Grotevant, H. D., & Cooper, C. R. (1986). Individuation in family relations. A perspective on individual differences in the development of identity and role-taking skills in adolescence. *Human Development, 29,* 82–100.

Gruber-Baldini, A. L., Schaie, K. W., & Willis, S. L. (1995). Similarity in married couples: A longitudinal study of mental abilities and rigidity–flexibility. *Journal of Personality and Social Psychology, 69,* 191–203.

Grusec, J. E., Goodnow, J. J., & Kuczynski, L. (2000). New directions in analyses of parenting contributions to children's acquisition of values. *Child Development, 71,* 205–211.

Grusec, J. E., Kuczynski, L., Rushton, J. P., & Simutis, Z. (1979). Learning resistance to temptation through observation. *Developmental Psychology, 15,* 233–240.

Grych, J. H., & Fincham, F. D. (1992). Interventions for children of divorce: Toward greater integration of research and action. *Psychological Bulletin, 111,* 434–454.

Guay, F., Marsh, H. W., & Boivin, M. (2003). Academic self-concept and academic achievement: Developmental perspectives on their causal ordering. *Journal of Educational Psychology, 95,* 124–136.

Guerin, D. W., Gottfried, A. W., Oliver, P. H., & Thomas, C. W. (2003). *Temperament: Infancy through adolescence: The Fullerton Longitudinal Study.* New York: Kluwer Academic/Plenum Publishers.

Guerra, N. G., Huesmann, L. R., & Spindler, A. (2003). Community violence exposure, social cognition, and aggression among urban elementary school children. *Child Development, 74,* 1561–1576.

Guerra, N. G., & Slaby, R. G. (1990). Cognitive mediators of aggression in adolescent offenders: 2. Intervention. *Developmental Psychology, 26,* 269–277.

Guilford, J. P. (1967). *The nature of human intelligence.* New York: McGraw-Hill.

Guilford, J. P. (1988). Some changes in the structure-of-the-intellect model. *Educational and Psychological Measurement, 40,* 1–4.

Guinsburg, R., de Araujo Peres, C., Branco de Almeida, M. F., de Cassia Xavier Balda, R., Cassia Berenguel, R., Tonelotto, J., & Kopelman, B. I. (2000). Differences in pain expression between male and female newborn infants. *Pain, 85,* 127–133.

Gunnar, M. R. (1998). Quality of early care and buffering of neuroendocrine stress reactions: Potential effects on the developing human brain. *Preventive Medicine, 27,* 208–211.

Gunnar, M. R. (2000). Early adversity and the development of stress reactivity and regulation. In C. A. Nelson (Ed.), *Minnesota Symposium on Child Psychology: Vol. 31. The effects of early adversity on neurobehavioral development.* Mahwah, NJ: Erlbaum.

Gunnar, M. R., Bruce, J., & Grotevant, H. D. (2000). International adoption of institutionally reared children: Research and policy. *Development and Psychopathology, 12,* 677–693.

Guralnick, M. J. (Ed.). (1997). *The effectiveness of early intervention.* Baltimore: Brookes.

Gurland, B. (1991). Epidemiology of psychiatric disorders. In J. Sadavoy, L. W. Lazarus, & L. F. Jarvik (Eds.), *Comprehensive review of geriatric psychiatry.* Washington, D.C.: American Psychiatric Press.

Gurung, R. A. R., Taylor, S. E., & Seeman, T. E. (2003). Accounting for changes in social support among married older adults: Insights from the MacArthur Studies of Successful Aging. *Psychology and Aging, 18,* 487–496.

Gusella, J. F., Wexler, N. S., Conneally, P. M., Naylor, S. L., Anderson, M. A., Tanzi, R. E., Watkins, P. C., Ottina, K., Wallace, M. R., Sakaguchi, A. Y., Young, A. B., Shoulson, I., Bonilla, E., & Martin, J. B. (1983). A polymorphic DNA marker genetically linked to Huntington disease. *Nature, 306,* 234–238.

Guterl, F. (2002, November 11). What Freud got right. *Newsweek,* 50–51.

Gutman, L. M., Sameroff, A. J., & Cole, R. (2003). Academic growth curve trajectories from 1st grade to 12th grade: Effects of multiple social risk factors and preschool child factors. *Developmental Psychology, 39,* 777–790.

Gutman, L. M., Sameroff, A. J., & Eccles, J. S. (2002). The academic achievement of African American students during early adolescence: An examination of multiple risk, promotive, and protective factors. *American Journal of Community Psychology, 39,* 367–399.

Gutmann, D. (1987). *Reclaimed powers: Toward a new psychology of men and women in later life.* New York: Basic Books.

Gutmann, D. (1997). *The human elder in nature, culture, and society.* Boulder, CO: Westview.

Guttentag, R. E. (1985). Memory and aging: Implications for theories of memory development during childhood. *Developmental Review, 5,* 56–77.

Guttmacher, A. E., & Collins, F. S. (2003, September 4). Welcome to the genomic era. *New England Journal of Medicine, 349(10),* 996–998.

Guyer, B., Freedman, M. A., Strobino, D. M., & Sondik, E. J. (2000). Annual summary of vital statistics: Trends in the health of Americans during the 20th century. *Pediatrics, 106,* 1307–1317.

Guyer, B., Hoyert, D. L., Martin, J. A., Ventura, S. J., MacDorman, M. F., & Strobino, D. M. (1999). Annual summary of vital statistics—1998. *Pediatrics, 104,* 1229–1246.

H

Haan, N. (1981). Common dimensions of personality development: Early adolescence to middle life. In D. H. Eichorn, J. A. Clausen, N. Haan, M. P. Honzik, & P. H. Mussen (Eds.), *Present and past in middle life.* New York: Academic Press.

Haas-Hawkings, G., Sangster, S., Ziegler, M., & Reid, D. (1985). A study of relatively immediate adjustment to widowhood in later life. *International Journal of Women's Studies, 8,* 158–166.

Habek, D., Habek, J. C., Ivanisevic, M., & Djelmis, J. (2002). Fetal tobacco syndrome and perinatal outcome. *Fetal Diagnosis and Therapy, 17,* 367–371.

Haber, D. (1994). *Health promotion and aging.* New York: Springer.

Hack, M., & Fanaroff, A. A. (1999). Outcomes of children of extremely low birth weight and gestational age in the 1990's. *Early Human Development, 53,* 193–218.

Hack, M., Klein, N. C., & Taylor, H. G. (1995). Long-term developmental outcomes of low birth weight infants. *The Future of Children, 5,* 176–196.

Haddow, J. E., Palomaki, G. E., Allan, W. C., Williams, J. R., Knight, G. J., Gagnon, J., O'Heir, C. E., Mitchell, M. L., Hermos, R. J., Waisbren, S. E., Faix, J. D., & Klein, R. Z. (1999). Maternal thyroid deficiency during pregnancy and subsequent neuropsychological development of the child. *New England Journal of Medicine, 341,* 549–555.

Hagekull, B., & Bohlin, G. (1998). Preschool temperament and environmental factors related to the five-factor model of personality in middle childhood. *Merrill-Palmer Quarterly, 44,* 194–215.

Hagestad, G. O. (1985). Continuity and connectedness. In V. L. Bengtson & J. F. Robertson (Eds.), *Grandparenthood.* Beverly Hills, CA: Sage.

Hahn, C., & DiPietro, J. A. (2001). In vitro fertilization and the family: Quality of parenting, family functioning, and child psychosocial adjustment. *Developmental Psychology, 37,* 37–48.

Haight, W. L., Wong, X., Fung, H. H., Williams, K., & Mintz, J. (1999). Universal, developmental, and variable aspects of young children's play: A cross-cultural comparison of pretending at home. *Child Development, 70,* 1477–1488.

Hainline, L. (1998). The development of basic visual abilities. In A. Slater (Ed.), *Perceptual development: Visual, auditory and speech perception in infancy* (pp. 37-44). Hove, East Sussex, U.K.: Psychology Press.

Hainline, L., & Abramov, I. (1992). Assessing visual development: Is infant vision good enough? *Advances in Infancy Research, 7,* 39–102.

Haith, M. M., & Benson, J. B. (1998). Infant cognition. In D. Kuhn & R. S. Siegler (Vol. Eds.), W. Damon (Editor-in-Chief), *Handbook of child psychology: Vol. 2. Cognition, perception, and language* (5th ed., pp. 199–254). New York: Wiley.

Hajjar, I., Schumpert, J., Hirth, V., Wieland, D., & Eleazer, G. P. (2002). The impact of the use of statins on the prevalence of dementia and the progression of cognitive impairment. *Journal of Gerontology: Medical Sciences, 57A,* M414–M418.

Halford, G. S. (2004). Information-processing models of cognitive development. In U. Goswami (Ed.), *Blackwell handbook of childhood cognitive development* (pp. 555-574). Malden, MA: Blackwell Publishing.

Hall, C. S. (1954). *A primer of Freudian psychology.* New York: New American Library.

Hall, E. (2001). Babies, books and "impact": Problems and possibilities in the evaluation of a Bookstart project. *Educational Review, 53,* 57–64.

Hall, G. S. (1891). The contents of children's minds on entering school. *Pedagogical Seminary, 1,* 139–173.

Hall, G. S. (1904). *Adolescence* (2 vols.). New York: Appleton.

Hall, G. S. (1922). *Senescence: The last half of life.* New York: Appleton.

Hall, J. A., & Halberstadt, A. G. (1980). Masculinity and femininity in children: Development of the Children's Personal Attributes Questionnaire. *Developmental Psychology, 16,* 270–280.

Hall, J. G. (2000). Folic acid: The opportunity that still exists. *Canadian Medical Association Journal, 162,* 1571–1572.

Hall, W. G., Arnold, H. M., & Myers, K. P. (2000). The acquisition of an appetite. *Psychological Science, 11,* 101–105.

Hallgren, A., Kihlgren, M., Forslin, L., & Norberg, A. (1999). Swedish fathers' involvement in and experiences of childbirth preparation and childbirth. *Midwifery, 15,* 6–15.

Halligan, S. L., Herbert, J., Goodyer, I. M., & Murray, L. (2004). Exposure to postnatal depression predicts elevated cortisol in adolescent offspring. *Biological Psychiatry, 55,* 376–381.

Halpern, C. J. T., Udry, J. R., Suchindran, C., & Campbell, B. (2000). Adolescent males' willingness to report masturbation. *Journal of Sex Research* [Special Issue], *37,* 327–332.

Halpern, S. H., Leighton, B. L., Ohlsson A., Barrett, J. F., & Rice, A. (1998). Effect of epidural vs. parenteral opioid analgesia on the progress of labor: A meta-analysis. *Journal of the American Medical Association, 280,* 2105–2110.

Halverson, C. F., Havill, V. L., Deal, J., Baker, S. R., Victor, J. B., Pavlopoulous, V., Besevegis, E., & Wen, L. (2003). Personality structure as derived from parental ratings of free descriptions of children: The Inventory of Child Individual Differences. *Journal of Personality, 71,* 995–1026.

Hamilton, B. E., Martin, J. A., & Sutton, P. D. (2003). Births: Preliminary data for 2002. *National Vital Statistics Report, 51,* 1–20.

Hamilton, V. L., Blumenfeld, P. C., Akoh, H., & Miura, K. (1991). Group and gender in Japanese and American elementary classrooms. *Journal of Cross-Cultural Psychology, 22,* 317–346.

Hamm, J. V. (2000). Do birds of a feather flock together? The variable bases for African American, Asian American, and European American adolescents' selection of similar friends. *Developmental Psychology, 36,* 209–219.

Hanawalt, B. A. (2003). The child in the Middle Ages and Renaissance. In W. Koops & M. Zuckerman. (Eds.), *Beyond the century of the child. Cultural history and developmental psychology.* Philadelphia: University of Pennsylvania Press.

Hankin, J. R. (2002). Fetal alcohol syndrome prevention research. *Alcohol Research and Health, 26,* 58–65.

Hansen, D., Lou, H. C., & Olsen, J. (2001). Serious life events and congenital malformations: A national study with complete follow-up. *Obstetrical and Gynecological Survey, 56,* 68–69.

Hanson, M. J. (2003). Twenty-five years after early intervention: A follow-up of children with Down syndrome and their families. *Infants and Young Children, 16,* 354–365.

Hansson, R. O., DeKoekkoek, P. D., Neece, W. M., & Patterson, D. W. (1997). Successful aging at work: Annual review, 1992–1996: The older worker and transitions to retirement. *Journal of Vocational Behavior, 51,* 202–233.

Hanushek, E. A. (1997). Assessing the effects of school resources on student performance: An update. *Educational Evaluation and Policy Analysis, 19,* 141–164.

Hanushek, E. A. (1998). The evidence on class size: Occasional paper. ERIC: 443158.

Happé, F. G. E., & Frith, U. (1996a). The neuropsychology of autism. *Brain, 119,* 1377–1400.

Happé, F. G. E., & Frith, U. (1996b). Theory of mind and social impairment in children with conduct disorder. *British Journal of Developmental Psychology, 14,* 385–398.

Happé, F. G. E., Winner, E., & Brownell, H. (1998). The getting of wisdom: Theory of mind in old age. *Developmental Psychology, 34,* 358–362.

Hare, B., Call, J., & Tomasello, M. (2001). Do chimpanzees know what conspecifics know? *Animal Behavior, 61,* 139–151.

Harley, J. P., Ray, R. S., Tomasi, L., Eichman, P. L., Matthews, C. G., & Chun, R. (1978). Hyperkinesis and food additives: Testing the Feingold hypothesis. *Pediatrics, 61,* 818–828.

Harley, K., & Reese, E. (1999). Origins of autobiographical memory. *Developmental Psychology, 35,* 1338–1348.

Harlow, H. F., & Zimmerman, R. R. (1959). Affectional responses in the infant monkey. *Science, 130,* 421–432.

Harman, D. (2001). Aging: An overview. In S. C. Park, E. S. Hwang, H. Kim, & W. Park (Eds.), *Annals of the New York Academy of Sciences: Vol. 928. Molecular and cellular interactions in senescence.* New York: The New York Academy of Sciences.

Harman, S. M., & Talbert, G. B. (1985). Reproductive aging. In C. E. Finch & E. L. Schneider (Eds.), *Handbook of the biology of aging* (2nd ed.). New York: Van Nostrand Reinhold.

Harper, G., & Kember, D. (1986). Approaches to study of distance education students. *British Journal of Educational Technology, 17,* 211–212.

Harper, S. (1999). Building an intergenerational activity program for older adults: Implications for physical activity. *Journal of Physical Education, Recreation and Dance, 70,* 68–70.

Harrington, D. M., Block, J. H., & Block, J. (1987). Testing aspects of Carl Rogers's theory of creative environments: Child-rearing antecedents of creative potential in young adolescents. *Journal of Personality and Social Psychology, 52,* 851–856.

Harrington, L. C., Miller, D. A., McClain, C. J., & Paul, R. H. (1997). Vaginal birth after cesarean in a hospital-based birth center staffed by certified nurse-midwives. *Journal of Nurse-Midwifery, 42,* 304–307.

Harris, J. R. (1995). Where is the child's environment? A group socialization theory of development. *Psychological Review, 102,* 458–489.

Harris, J. R. (1998). *The nurture assumption. Why children turn out the way they do.* New York: Free Press.

Harris, J. R. (2000a). Context-specific learning, personality, and birth order. *Current Directions in Psychological Science, 9,* 174–177.

Harris, J. R. (2000b) Socialization, personality development, and the child's environments: Comment on Vandell (2000). *Developmental Psychology, 36,* 711–723.

Harris, J. R., Pedersen, N. L., McClearn, G. E., Plomin, R., & Nesselroade, J. R. (1992). Age differences in genetic and environmental influences for health from the Swedish Adoption/Twin Study of Aging. *Journal of Gerontology: Psychological Sciences, 47,* 213–220.

Harris, M. (1992). Language experience and early language development: From input to uptake. Hove, UK: Erlbaum.

Harris, P. L. (1989). *Children and emotion: The development of psychological understanding.* Oxford, England: Basil Blackwell.

Harris, P. L., & Kavanaugh, R. D. (1993). Young children's understanding of pretense. *Monographs of the Society for Research in Child Development, 58* (1, Serial No. 181).

Harris, T., & Bifulco, A. (1991). Loss of parent in childhood, attachment style, and depression in adulthood. In C. M. Parkes, J. Stevenson-Hinde, & P. Marris (Eds.), *Attachment across the life cycle.* London: Tavistock/Routledge.

Harrist, A. W., Zaia, A. F., Bates, J. E., Dodge, K. A., Pettit, G. S. (1997). Subtypes of social withdrawal in early childhood: Sociometric status and social-cognitive differences across four years. *Child Development, 68,* 278–294.

Hart, B., & Hilton, I. (1988). Dimensions of personality organization predictors of teenage pregnancy risk. *Journal of Personality Assessment, 52,* 116–132.

Hart, E. L., Lahey, B. B., Loeber, R., Applegate, B., & Frick, P. J. (1995). Developmental change in attention deficit hyperactivity disorder in boys: A four-year longitudinal study. *Journal of Abnormal Child Psychology, 23,* 729–749.

Hart, M. A., & Foster, S. N. (1997). Couples' attitudes toward childbirth participation: Relationship to evaluation of labor and delivery. *Journal of Perinatal & Neonatal Nursing, 11,* 10–20.

Harter, S. (1996). Historical roots of contemporary issues involving self-concept. In B. A. Bracken (Ed.), *Handbook of self-concept: Developmental, social, and clinical considerations.* New York: Wiley.

Harter, S. (1999). *The construction of the self. A developmental perspective.* New York: Guilford.

Harter, S. (2003). The development of self-representations during childhood and adolescence. In M. R. Leary & J. P. Tangney (Eds.), *Handbook of self and identity.* New York: Guilford.

Harter, S., & Monsour, A. (1992). Development analysis of conflict caused by opposing attributes in the adolescent self-portrait. *Developmental Psychology, 28,* 251–260.

Harter, S., & Pike, R. (1984). The pictorial scale of perceived competence and social acceptance for young children. *Child Development, 55,* 1969–1982.

Harter, S., & Whitesell, N. R., (2003). Beyond the debate: Why some adolescents report stable self-worth over time and situation, whereas others report changes in self-worth. *Journal of Personality, 71,* 1027–1058.

Hartshorne, H., & May, M. S. (1928–1930). *Studies in the nature of character: Vol. 1. Studies in deceit. Vol. 2. Studies in self-control. Vol. 3. Studies in the organization of character.* New York: Macmillan.

Hartup, W. W. (1996). The company they keep: Friendships and their developmental significance. *Child Development, 67,* 1–13.

Hartup, W. W., & Stevens, N. (1997). Friendships and adaptation in the life course. *Psychological Bulletin, 121,* 355–370.

Hartup, W. W., & van Lieshout, C. F. M. (1995). Personality development in social context. *Annual Review of Psychology, 46,* 655–687.

Harvey, J. H. (2001). The psychology of loss as a lens to a positive psychology. *American Behavioral Scientist, 44,* 817–837.

Harvey, J. H., & Fine, M. A. (2004). *Children of divorce. Stories of loss and growth.* Mahwah, NJ: Erlbaum.

Haskett, M. E., Johnson, C. A., & Miller, J. W. (1994). Individual differences in risk of child abuse by adolescent mothers: Assessment in the perinatal period. *Journal of Child Psychology and Psychiatry and Allied Disciplines, 35,* 461–476.

Hastings, P. D., Zahn-Waxler, C., Robinson, J., Usher, B., & Bridges, D. (2000). The development of concern for others in children with behavior problems. *Developmental Psychology, 36,* 531–546.

Hatfield, E., & Rapson, R. L. (2000). Love and attachment processes. In M. Lewis & J. M. Haviland-Jones (Eds.), *Handbook of emotions* (2nd ed.). New York: Guilford.

Hattie, J., Biggs, J., & Purdie, N. (1996). Effects of learning skills interventions on student learning: A meta-analysis. *Review of Educational Research, 66,* 99–136.

Haug, K., Irgens, L. M., Skjaerven, R., Markestad, T., Baste, V., & Schreuder, P. (2000). Maternal smoking and birthweight: Effect modification of period, maternal age and paternal smoking. *Acta Obstetric Gynecology Scandinavia, 79,* 485–489.

Haught, P. A., Hill, L. A., Nardi, A. H., & Walls, R. T. (2000). Perceived ability and level of education as predictors of traditional and practical adult problem solving. *Experimental Aging Research, 26,* 89–101.

Hausdorff, J. M., Levy, B. R., & Wei, J. Y. (1999). The power of ageism on physical function of older persons: Reversibility of age-related

gait changes. *Journal of the American Geriatrics Society, 47,* 1346–1349.
Havighurst, R. J., Neugarten, B. L., & Tobin, S. S. (1968). Disengagement and patterns of aging. In B. L. Neugarten (Ed.), *Middle age and aging.* Chicago: University of Chicago Press.
Hawley, R. S., & Mori, C. A. (1999). *The human genome. A user's guide.* San Diego: Academic Press.
Hay, D. F., Nash, A., & Pedersen, J. (1983). Interaction between six-month-old peers. *Child Development, 54,* 557–562.
Hay, D. F., Pawlby, S., Angold, A., Harold, G. T., & Sharp, D. (2003). Pathways to violence in the children of mothers who were depressed postpartum. *Developmental Psychology, 39,* 1083–1094.
Hay, J. G. (2003). Gene therapy. In S. M. Brown (with contributions by J. G. Hay & H. Ostrer). *Essentials of medical genomics.* Hoboken, NJ: Wiley-Liss.
Hayflick, L. (1976). The cell biology of human aging. *New England Journal of Medicine, 295,* 1302–1308.
Hayflick, L. (1994). *How and why we age.* New York: Ballantine.
Hayflick, L. (2004). "Anti-aging" is an oxymoron. *Journal of Gerontology: Biological Sciences, 59A,* 573–578.
Hayne, H. (2004). Infant memory development: Implications for childhood amnesia. *Developmental Review, 24,* 33–73.
Hayslip, B., & Hansson, R. (2003). Death awareness and adjustment across the life span. In C. D. Bryant (Ed.), *Handbook of death and dying.* Thousand Oaks, CA: Sage.
Hayward, C., Killen, J. D., Wilson, D. M., Hammer, L. D., Litt, I. F., Kraemer, H. C., Haydel, F., Varady, A., & Taylor, C. B. (1997). Psychiatric risk associated with early puberty in adolescent girls. *Journal of the American Academy of Child and Adolescent Psychiatry, 36,* 255–262.
Haywood, H. C., & Tzuriel, D. (2002). Applications and challenges in dynamic assessment. *Peabody Journal of Education, 77,* 40–63.
Hazan, C., & Shaver, P. (1987). Romantic love conceptualized as an attachment process. *Journal of Personality and Social Psychology, 52,* 511–524.
Hazan, C., & Shaver, P. (1990). Love and work: An attachment-theoretical perspective. *Journal of Personality and Social Psychology, 59,* 270–280.
Heaton, P., & Wallace, G. L. (2004). Annotation: The savant syndrome. *Journal of Child Psychology and Psychiatry, 45,* 899–911.
Heaton, T. B., Jacobson, C. K., & Holland, K. (1999). Persistence and change in decisions to remain childless. *Journal of Marriage and the Family, 61,* 531–539.
Hedlund, B., & Ebersole, P. (1983). A test of Levinson's midlife reevaluation. *Journal of Genetic Psychology, 143,* 189–192.
Heh, S. S. (2003). Relationship between social support and postnatal depression. *Kaohsiung Journal of Medical Science, 19,* 491–496.
Helderman, R. S. (2003, June 13). Inseparable sisters say a first goodbye. *The Washington Post,* B5.
Helgeson, V. S., & Mickelson, K. (2000). Coping with chronic illness among the elderly: Maintaining self-esteem. In S. B. Manuck, R. Jennings, B. S. Rabin, & A. Baum (Eds.), *Behavior, health, and aging.* Mahwah, NJ: Erlbaum.
Hellige, J. B. (1993). *Hemispheric asymmetry: What's right and what's left.* Cambridge, MA: Harvard University Press.
Hellstrom-Lindahl, E., & Nordberg, A. (2002). Smoking during pregnancy: A way to transfer addiction to the next generation? *Respiration, 69,* 289–293.
Helmreich, R. L., Sawin, L. L., & Carsrud, A. L. (1986). The honeymoon effect in job performance: Temporal increases in the predictive power of achievement motivation. *Journal of Applied Psychology, 71,* 185–188.
Helms, J. E. (1992). Why is there no study of cultural equivalence in standardized cognitive-ability testing? *American Psychologist, 47,* 1083–1101.
Helms, J. E. (1997). The triple quandary of race, culture, and social class in standardized cognitive ability testing. In D. P. Flanagan, J. Genshaft, & P. L. Harrison (Eds.), *Contemporary intellectual assessment: Theories, tests, and issues.* New York: Guilford.
Helson, R., Jones, C., & Kwan, V. S. Y. (2002). Personality change over 40 years of adulthood: Hierarchical linear modeling analyses of two longitudinal samples. *Journal of Personality and Social Psychology, 83,* 752–766.
Helwig, C. C., Zelazo, P. D., & Wilson, M. (2001). Children's judgments of psychological harm in normal and noncanonical situations. *Child Development, 72,* 66–81.
Henderson, J. E., & Goltzman, D. (Eds.). (2000). *The osteoporosis primer.* Cambridge, UK: Cambridge University Press.
Hendrie, H. C. (2001). Exploration of environmental and genetic risk factors for Alzheimer's disease: The value of cross-cultural studies. *Current Directions in Psychological Science, 10,* 98–101.
Henig, R. M. (2000). *The monk in the garden. The lost and found genius of Gregor Mendel, the father of genetics.* Boston, MA: Houghton Mifflin.
Henker, B., & Whalen, C. K. (1989). Hyperactivity and attention deficits. *American Psychologist, 44,* 216–223.
Henry, J. D., MacLeod, M. S., Phillips, L. H., & Crawford, J. R. (2004). A meta-analytic review of prospective memory and aging. *Psychology and Aging, 19,* 27–39.
Herbert, J., & Hayne, H. (2000). Memory retrieval by 18–30-month-olds: Age-related changes in representational flexibility. *Developmental Psychology, 36,* 473–484.
Herdt, G., & Davidson, J. (1988). The Sambia "turnim-man": Sociocultural and clinical aspects of gender formation in male pseudohermaphrodites with 5-alpha-reductase deficiency in Papua New Guinea. *Archives of Sexual Behavior, 17,* 33–56.
Herdt, G., & McClintock, M. (2000). The magical age of 10. *Archives of Sexual Behavior, 29,* 587–606.
Herkert, B. M. (2000). Communicating grief. *Omega: Journal of Death and Dying, 41,* 93–115.
Herman-Giddens, M. E., Slora, E. J., Wasserman, R. C., Bourdony, C. J., Bhapkar, M. V., Koch, G. G., & Hasemeier, C. M. (1997). Secondary sexual characteristics and menses in young girls seen in office practice: A study from the Pediatric Research in Office Settings network. *Pediatrics, 99,* 505–512.
Hermans, H. J., & Oles, P. K. (1999). Midlife crisis in men: Affective organization of personal meanings. *Human Relations, 52,* 1403–1426.
Hermelin, B. (with foreword by M. Rutter). (2001). *Bright splinters of the mind: A personal story of research with autistic savants. London:* Jessica Kingsley Publishers, Ltd.
Hernandez, D. J. (1997). Child development and the social demography of childhood. *Child Development, 68,* 149–169.
Herrnstein, R. J., & Murray, C. (1994). *The bell curve: Intelligence and class structure in American life.* New York: Free Press.
Hersch, P. (1998). *A tribe apart: A journey into the heart of American adolescence.* New York: Ballantine.
Hess, T. M. (1994). Social cognition in adulthood: Age-related changes in knowledge and processing mechanisms. *Developmental Review, 14,* 373–412.
Hess, T. M. (1999). Cognitive and knowledge-based influences on social representations. In T. M. Hess & F. Blanchard-Fields (Eds.), *Social cognition and aging.* San Diego: Academic Press.
Hess, T. M., & Pullen, S. M. (1996). Memory in context. In F. Blanchard-Fields & T. M. Hess (Eds.), *Perspectives on cognitive change in adulthood and aging.* New York: McGraw-Hill.
Hesse, E., & Main, M. (2000). Disorganized infant, child, and adult attachment: Collapse in behavioral and attentional strategies. *Journal of the American Psychoanalytic Association, 48,* 1097–1127.
Heston, L. L. (1970). The genetics of schizophrenia and schizoid disease. *Science, 167,* 249–256.
Heston, L. L., & White, J. A. (1991). *The vanishing mind: A practical guide to Alzheimer's disease and other dementias.* New York: W. H. Freeman.
Hetherington, E. M. (1981). Children and divorce. In R. W. Henderson (Ed.), *Parent–Child Interaction: Theory, Research and Prospects.* New York: Academic Press.
Hetherington, E. M. (1989). Coping with family transitions: Winners, losers, and survivors. *Child Development, 60,* 1–14.
Hetherington, E. M., Bridges, M., & Insabella, G. M. (1998). What matters? What does not? Five perspectives on the association between marital transitions and children's adjustment. *American Psychologist, 53,* 167–184.
Hetherington, E. M., Cox, M., & Cox, R. (1982). Effects of divorce on parents and children. In M. E. Lamb (Ed.), *Nontraditional families.* Hillsdale, NJ: Erlbaum.
Hetherington, E. M., & Frankie, G. (1967). Effect of parental dominance, warmth, and conflict on imitation in children. *Journal of Personality and Social Psychology, 6,* 119–125.
Hetherington, E. M., & Jodl, K. M. (1994). Stepfamilies as settings for child development. In A. Booth & J. Dunn (Eds.), *Stepfamilies: Who benefits? Who does not?* Hillsdale, NJ: Erlbaum.
Hetherington, E. M., & Kelly, J. (2002). *For better or for worse: Divorce reconsidered.* New York: Norton.
Hetherington, E. M., & Stanley-Hagen, M. (2000). Diversity among stepfamilies. In D. H. Demo, K. R. Allen, & M. A. Fine (Eds.), *Handbook of family diversity.* New York: Oxford University Press.
Hetu, R., & Fortin, M. (1995). Potential risk of hearing damage associated with exposure to

highly amplified music. *Journal of the American Academy of Audiology, 6,* 378–386.

Heyman, G. D.; Dweck, C. S., & Cain, K. M. (1992). Young children's vulnerability to self-blame and helplessness: Relationship to beliefs about goodness. *Child Development 63,* 401–415.

Hilgard, E. R., & Loftus, E. F. (1979). Effective interrogation of the eyewitness. *International Journal of Clinical and Experimental Psychology, 27,* 342–357.

Hill, E. L. (2004). Evaluating the theory of executive dysfunction in autism. *Developmental Review, 24,* 189–233.

Hill, J. B. & Haffner, W. H. J. (2002). Growth before birth. In M. L. Batshaw (Ed.), *Children with disabilities* (5th ed.). Baltimore: Paul H. Brookes.

Hill, J. P., & Lynch, M. E. (1983). The intensification of gender-related role expectations during early adolescence. In J. Brooks-Gunn & A. C. Petersen (Eds.), *Girls at puberty: Biological and psychosocial perspectives.* New York: Plenum.

Hill, N. E., & Craft, S. A. (2003). Parent–school involvement and school performance: Mediated pathways among socioeconomically comparable African American and Euro-American families. *Journal of Educational Psychology, 95,* 74–83.

Hill, N. E., & Taylor, L. C. (2004). Parent–school involvement and children's academic achievement: Pragmatics and issues. *Current Directions in Psychological Science, 13,* 161–164.

Hill, P. (1993). Recent advances in selected aspects of adolescent development. *Journal of Child Psychology and Psychiatry and Allied Disciplines, 34,* 69–99.

Hill, R., & Rodgers, R. H. (1964). The developmental approach. In H. Christensen (Ed.), *Handbook of marriage and the family.* Chicago: Rand-McNally.

Hill, S. D., & Tomlin, C. (1981). Self-recognition in retarded children. *Child Development, 52,* 145–150.

Hilton, N. Z., Harris, G. T., & Rice, M. E. (2000). The functions of aggression by male teenagers. *Journal of Personality and Social Psychology, 79,* 988–994.

Hinde, R. A. (1983). Ethology and child development. In M. M. Haith & J. J. Campos (Vol. Eds.), P. H. Mussen (Editor-in-Chief), *Handbook of Child Psychology: Vol. 2. Infancy and Developmental Psychobiology* (4th ed.). New York: Wiley.

Hine, T. (1999). *The rise and fall of the American teenager.* New York: Bard.

Hinton, J. (1975). The influence of previous personality on reactions to having terminal cancer. *Omega: Journal of Death and Dying, 6,* 95–111.

Hipwell, A. E., Goossens, F. A., Melhuish, E. C., & Kumar, R. (2000). Severe maternal psychopathology and infant–mother attachment. *Development and Psychopathology, 12,* 157–175.

Hirsch-Pasek, K., Golinkoff, R. M., & Hollich, G. (1999). Trends and transitions in language development: Looking for the missing piece. *Developmental Neuropsychology, 16,* 139–162.

Hobbs, F. B. (2001). The elderly population. U.S. Census Bureau [Online], http://www.census.gov/population/www/population/www/pop-profile/elderpop.html.

Hobbs, F. B. (with B. L. Damon). (1996). *65+ in the United States.* Washington, D.C.: U.S. Bureau of the Census.

Hock, E., Eberly, M., Bartle-Haring, S., Ellwanger, P., & Widaman, K. F. (2001). Separation anxiety in parents of adolescents: Theoretical significance and scale development. *Child Development, 72,* 284–298.

Hodges, J., & Tizard, B. (1989). IQ and behavioral adjustment of exinstitutional adolescents. *Journal of Child Psychology and Psychiatry, 30,* 53–75.

Hodgson, J. W., & Fischer, J. L. (1979). Sex differences in identity and intimacy development in college youth. *Journal of Youth and Adolescence, 8,* 37–50.

Hodnett, E. D., Gates, S., Hofmeyr, G. J., & Sakala, C. (2003). Continuous support for women during childbirth. *Cochrane Database System Review:* CD003766.

Hodnett, E. D., & Osborn, R. W. (1989). A randomized trial of the effects of monitrice support during labor: Mothers' views two to four weeks postpartum. *Birth, 16,* 177–183.

Hof, P., & Mobbs, C. (2001). *Functional neurobiology of aging.* Academic Press.

Hofer, S. M., Christensen, H., MacKinnon, A. J., Korten, A. E., Jorm, A. F., Henderson, A. S., & Easteal, S. (2002). Change in cognitive functioning associated with ApoE genotype in a community sample of older adults. *Psychology and Aging, 17,* 194–208.

Hoff, E. (2004). *Language development* (3rd ed.). Belmont, CA: Wadsworth.

Hoffman, K., Llagas, C., & Snyder, T. D. (2003). *Status and trends in the education of blacks.* National Center for Education Statistics, U. S. Department of Education.

Hoffman, L. W. (2000). Maternal employment: Effects of social context. In R. D. Taylor & M. C. Wang (Eds.), *Resilience across contexts: Family, work, culture, and community.* Mahwah, NJ: Erlbaum.

Hoffman, M. L. (1970). Moral development. In P. H. Mussen (Ed.), *Carmichael's manual of child psychology* (Vol. 2). New York: Wiley.

Hoffman, M. L. (2000). *Empathy and moral development: Implications for caring and justice.* Cambridge, UK: Cambridge University Press.

Hoffman, M., Levy-Shiff, R., & Malinski, D. (1996). Stress and adjustment in the transition to adolescence: Moderating effects of neuroticism and extroversion. *Journal of Youth and Adolescence, 25,* 161–175.

Hoffman, S. I., & Strauss, S. (1985). The development of children's concepts of death. *Death Studies, 9,* 469–482.

Hofstra, M. B., Van der Ende, J., & Verhulst, F. C. (2000). Continuity and change of psychopathology from childhood into adulthood. *Journal of the American Academy of Child & Adolescent Psychiatry, 39,* 850–858.

Hogan, D. P., & Park, J. M. (2000). Family factors and social support in the developmental outcomes of very low-birth weight children. *Clinical Perinatology, 27,* 433–459.

Hogan, D. P., Sun, R., & Cornwell, G. T. (2000). Sexual and fertility behaviors of American females aged 15–19 years: 1985, 1990, and 1995. *American Journal of Public Health, 90,* 1421–1425.

Holahan, A., & Costenbader, V. (2000). A comparison of developmental gains for preschool children with disabilities in inclusive and self-contained classrooms. *Topics in Early Childhood Special Education, 20, 224-235.*

Holahan, C., & Sears, R. (1995). *The gifted group in later maturity.* Stanford, CA: Stanford University Press.

Holden, G. W., & Miller, P. C. (1999). Enduring and different: A meta-analysis of the similarity in parents' child rearing. *Psychological Bulletin, 125, 223–254.*

Holland, J. L. (1985). *Making vocational choices: A theory of vocational personalities and work environments* (2nd ed.). Englewood Cliffs, NJ: Prentice-Hall.

Holley, J. (2004, Aug. 26). Psychiatrist, writer changed the view of death. *The Washington Post,* A1, A11.

Hollich, G. J., Hirsch-Pasek, K., & Golinkoff, R. M. (2000). Breaking the language barrier: An emergentist coalition model for the origins of word learning. *Monographs of the Society for Research in Child Development, 65* (No. 262).

Holliday, R. (2004). The close relationship between biological aging and age-associated pathologies in humans. *Journal of Gerontology: Biological Sciences, 59A,* 543–546.

Hollon, S. D., Thase, M. E., & Markowitz, J. C. (2002). Treatment and prevention of depression. *Psychological Science in the Public Interest, 3,* 39–77.

Holmbeck, G. N., Crossman, R. E., Wandrei, M. L., & Gasiewski, E. (1994). Cognitive development, egocentrism, self-esteem, and adolescent contraceptive knowledge, attitudes, and behavior. *Journal of Youth and Adolescence, 23,* 169–193.

Holmbeck, G. N., Greenley, R. N., & Franks, E. A. (2003). Developmental issues and considerations in research and practice. In A. E. Kazdin (Ed.), *Evidence-based psychotherapies for children and adolescents.* New York: Guilford Press.

Holowka, S., & Petitto, L. A. (2002). Left hemisphere cerebral specialization for babies while babbling. *Science, 297,* 1515.

Holt, C. L., & Ellis, J. B. (1998). Assessing the current validity of the Bem Sex-Role Inventory. *Sex Roles, 39,* 929–941.

Honey, K. L., Bennett, P., & Morgan, M. (2003). Predicting postnatal depression. *Journal of Affective Disorders, 76,* 201–210.

Honzik, M. P. (1983). Measuring mental abilities in infancy: The value and limitations. In M. Lewis (Ed.), *Origins of intelligence: Infancy and early childhood* (2nd ed.). New York: Plenum.

Hooker, K., & Siegler, I. C. (1993). Life goals, satisfaction, and self-rated health: Preliminary findings. *Experimental Aging Research, 19,* 97–110.

Hooper, F. H., Hooper, J. O., & Colbert, K. K. (1985). Personality and memory correlates of intellectual functioning in adulthood: Piagetian and psychometric assessments. *Human Development, 28,* 101–107.

Hopfer, C. J., Crowley, T. J., & Hewitt, J. K. (2003). Review of twin and adoption studies of adolescent substance use. *Journal of the American Academy of Child and Adolescent Psychiatry, 42,* 710–719.

Horiuchi, S., Finch, C. E., Mesle, F., & Vallin, J. (2003). Differential patterns of age-related mortality increase in middle age and old age. *Journal of Gerontology: Biological Sciences, 58A,* 495–507.

Horn, J. L., & Cattell, R. B. (1967). Age differences in fluid and crystallized intelligence. *Acta Psychologica, 26,* 107–129.

Horn, J. L., & Noll, J. (1997). Human cognitive capabilities: Gf-Gc theory. In D. P. Flanagan,

J. Genshaft, & P. L. Harrison (Eds.), *Contemporary intellectual assessment: Theories, tests, and issues.* New York: Guilford.

Hosaka, T. (1999, August 10). Don't come without it: Many states are requiring hospitals to screen newborns for hearing loss. *The Washington Post—Health,* 9.

Houston, D. M., Jusczyk, P. W., Kuijpers, C., Coolen, R., & Cutler, A. (2000). Cross-language word segmentation by 9-month-olds. *Psychonomics Bulletin Review, 7,* 504–509.

Houx, P. J., Vreeling, F. W., & Jolles, J. (1991). Rigorous health screening reduces age effect on memory scanning task. *Brain and Cognition, 15,* 246–260.

Howe, M. L. (2000). *The fate of early memories: Developmental science and the retention of childhood experiences.* Washington, D.C.: American Psychological Association.

Howe, M. L., & Courage, M. L. (1993). On resolving the enigma of infantile amnesia. *Psychological Bulletin, 113,* 305–326.

Howe, M. L., & Courage, M. L. (1997). The emergence and early development of autobiographical memory. *Psychological Review, 104,* 499–523.

Howe, M.L., & Courage, M.L. (2004). Demystifying the beginnings of memory. *Developmental Review, 24,* 1–5.

Howe, M. L., Courage, M. L., & Peterson, C. (1994). How can I remember when "I" wasn't there: Long-term retention of traumatic experiences and emergence of the cognitive self. *Consciousness and Cognition, 3,* 327–355.

Howe, N., Aquan-Assee, J., Bukowski, W. M., Rinaldi, C. M., & Lehoux, P. M. (2000). Sibling self-disclosure in early adolescence. *Merrill-Palmer Quarterly, 46,* 653–671.

Howe, N., & Ross, H. S. (1990). Socialization, perspective-taking, and the sibling relationship. *Developmental Psychology, 26,* 160–165.

Howes, C. (1988). Same- and cross-sex friends: Implications for interaction and social skills. *Early Childhood Research Quarterly, 3,* 21–37.

Howes, C. (1996). The earliest friendships. In W. M. Bukowski, A. F. Newcomb, & W. W. Hartup (Eds.), *The company they keep: Friendships in childhood and adolescence.* Cambridge, England: Cambridge University Press.

Howes, C., & Matheson, C. C. (1992). Sequences in the development of competent play with peers: Social and social pretend play. *Developmental Psychology, 28,* 961–974.

Howes, C., Phillips, D. A., & Whitebrook, M. (1992). Thresholds of quality: Implications for the social development of children in center-based child care. *Child Development, 63,* 449–460.

Howes, P., & Markman, H. J. (1989). Marital quality and child functioning: A longitudinal investigation. *Child Development, 60,* 1044–1051.

Howieson, D. B., Dame, A., Camicioli, R., Sexton, G., Payami, H., & Kaye, J. A. (1997). Cognitive markers preceding Alzheimer's dementia in the healthy oldest old. *Journal of the American Geriatrics Society, 45,* 584–589.

Howieson, N. (1981). A longitudinal study of creativity: 1965–1975. *Journal of Creative Behavior, 15,* 117–134.

Howlin, P, Mawhood, L., & Rutter, M. (2000). Autism and developmental receptive language disorder: A follow-up comparison in early adult life. II: Social, behavioral, and psychiatric outcomes. *Journal of Child Psychology and Psychiatry and Allied Disciplines, 41,* 561–578.

Hsu, L. K. G. (1990). *Eating disorders.* New York: Guilford Press.

Hubbard, J. A., Smithmyer, C. M., Ramsden, S. R., Parker, E. H., Flanagan, K. D., Dearing, K. F., Relyea, N., & Simons, R. F. (2002). Observational, physiological, and self-report measures of children's anger: Relations to reactive versus proactive aggression. *Child Development, 73,* 1101–1118.

Hubel, D. H., & Wiesel, T. N. (1970). The period of susceptibility to the physiological effects of unilateral eye-closure in kittens. *Journal of Physiology, 206,* 419–436.

Hudley, C., & Graham, S. (1993). An attributional intervention to reduce peer-directed aggression among African American boys. *Child Development, 64,* 124–138.

Huesmann, L. R., Moise-Titus, J., Podolski, C., & Eron, L. D. (2003). Longitudinal relations between children's exposure to TV violence and their aggressive and violent behavior in young adulthood: 1977–1992. *Developmental Psychology, 39,* 201–221.

Hughes, D., & Simpson, L. (1995). The role of social change in preventing low birth weight. *The Future of Children, 5,* 87–102.

Hughes, F. M., & Seta, C. E. (2003). Gender stereotypes: Children's perceptions of future compensatory behavior following violations of gender roles. *Sex Roles, 49,* 685–691.

Hultsch, D. F., Hammer, M., & Small, B. J. (1993). Age differences in cognitive performance in later life: Relationships to self-reported health and activity life style. *Journal of Gerontology: Psychological Sciences, 48,* 1–11.

Hunt, P., & Goetz, L. (1997). Research on inclusive educational programs, practices, and outcomes for students with severe disabilities. *Journal of Special Education, 31,* 3–29.

Hurd, L. C. (1999). "We're not old!" Older women's negotiation of aging and oldness. *Journal of Aging Studies, 13,* 419–439.

Hurd, R. C. (2002). Sibling support systems in childhood after a parent dies. *Omega: Journal of Death and Dying, 45,* 299–320.

Huston, A. C., Wright, J. C., Marquis, J., & Green, S. B. (1999). How young children spend their time: Television and other activities. *Developmental Psychology, 35,* 912–925.

Huston, M., & Schwartz, P. (1995). The relationships of lesbians and gay men. In J. T. Wood & S. Duck (Eds.), *Under-studied relationships: Off the beaten track.* Thousand Oaks, CA: Sage.

Huston, T. L., Caughlin, J. P., Houts, R. M., Smith, S. E., & George, L. J. (2001). The connubial crucible: Newlywed years as predictors of marital delight, distress, and divorce. *Journal of Personality and Social Psychology, 80,* 237–252.

Huston, T. L., McHale, S. M., & Crouter, A. C. (1986). When the honeymoon's over: Changes in the marriage relationship over the first year. In R. Gilmour & S. Duck (Eds.), *The emerging field of personal relationships.* Hillsdale, NJ: Erlbaum.

Hutchinson, K. E., Stallings, M., McGeary, J., & Bryan, A. (2004). Population stratification in the candidate gene study: Fatal threat or red herring? *Psychological Bulletin, 130,* 66–79.

Hyde, J. S. (1984). How large are gender differences in aggression? A developmental meta-analysis. *Developmental Psychology, 20,* 722–736.

Hyde, J. S., & DeLamater, J. (2003). *Understanding human sexuality (*8th ed.). New York: McGraw Hill.

Hyde, J. S., Fennema, E., & Lamon, S. J. (1990). Gender differences in mathematics performance: A meta-analysis. *Psychological Bulletin, 107,* 139–155.

Hyde, J. S., & Linn, M. C. (1988). Gender differences in verbal ability: A meta-analysis. *Psychological Bulletin, 104,* 53–69.

Hymel, S., McDougall, P., & Renshaw, P. (2002). Peer acceptance–rejection. In P. K. Smith & C. H. Hart (Eds.), *Blackwell handbook of childhood social development.* Malden, MA: Blackwell.

Hyson, M. C., Hirsch-Pasek, K., & Rescorla, L. (1989). *Academic environments in early childhood: Challenge or pressure?* Summary report to the Spencer Foundation.

I

Ialongo, N. S., Edelsohn, G., & Kellam, S. G. (2001). A further look at the prognostic power of young children's reports of depressed mood. *Child Development, 72,* 736–747.

Imel, S. (1996). Adult literacy education: Emerging directions in program development. ERIC Digest No. 179.

Imperato-McGinley, J., Peterson, R. E., Gautier, T., & Sturla, E. (1979). Androgens and the evolution of male gender identity among male pseudohermaphrodites with 5a-reductase deficiency. *New England Journal of Medicine, 300,* 1233–1237.

Ingoldsby, B. B., & Smith, S. (1995). *Families in multicultural perspective.* New York: Guilford.

Ingram, R. E., & Price, J. M. (2001). The role of vulnerability in understanding psychopathology. In R. E. Ingram & J. M. Price (Eds.), *Vulnerability to psychopathology. Risk across the lifespan.* New York: Guilford.

Ingrassia, M., & Springen, K. (1994, March 21). She's not baby Jessica anymore. *Newsweek, 123,* 60–66.

Inhelder, B. (1966). Cognitive development and its contribution to the diagnosis of some phenomena of mental deficiency. *Merrill-Palmer Quarterly, 12,* 299–319.

Inhelder, B., & Piaget, J. (1958). *The growth of logical thinking from childhood to adolescence: An essay on the construction of formal operational structures* (A. Parsons & S. Milgram, Trans.). New York: Basic Books.

Inhelder, B., & Piaget, J. (1964). Early growth of logic in the child: Classification and seriation. New York: Harper & Row.

International Human Genome Sequencing Consortium. (2001). Initial sequencing and analysis of the human genome. *Nature, 409,* 860–921.

Irwin, R. R. (1991). Reconceptualizing the nature of dialectical postformal operational thinking: The effects of affectively mediated social experiences. In J. D. Sinnott & J. C. Cavanaugh (Eds.), *Bridging paradigms: Positive development in adulthood and cognitive aging.* New York: Praeger.

Isabella, R. A. (1993). Origins of attachment: Maternal interactive behavior across the first year. *Child Development, 64,* 605–621.

Isabella, R. A., & Belsky, J. (1991). Interactional synchrony and the origins of infant-mother attachment: A replication study. *Child Development, 62,* 373–384.

Izard, C. E. (1982). *Measuring emotions in infants and children.* New York: Cambridge University Press.

Izard, C. E., & Ackerman, B. P. (2000). Motivational, organizational, and regulatory functions of discrete emotions. In M. Lewis & J. M. Haviland-Jones (Eds.), *Handbook of emotions* (2nd ed.). New York: Guilford.

J

Jacklin, C. N. (1989). Male and female: Issues of gender. *American Psychologist, 44,* 127–133.

Jacobs, J. E., & Klaczynski, P. A. (2002). The development of judgment and decision making during childhood and adolescence. *Current Directions in Psychological Science, 11,* 145–149.

Jacobs, J. E., Lanza, S., Osgood, D. W., Eccles, J. S., & Wigfield, A. (2002). Changes in children's self-competence and values: Gender and domain differences across grades one through twelve. *Child Development, 73,* 509–527.

Jacobs, S. C., Kosten, T. R., Kasl, S. V., Ostfeld, A. M., Berkman, L., & Charpentier, P. (1987–1988). Attachment theory and multiple dimensions of grief. *Omega: Journal of Death and Dying, 18,* 41–52.

Jacobsen, T., & Hofmann, V. (1997). Children's attachment representations: Longitudinal relations to school behavior and academic competency in middle childhood and adolescence. *Developmental Psychology, 33,* 703–710.

Jacobson, J. L., & Jacobson, S. W. (1999). Drinking moderately and pregnancy: Effects on child development. *Alcohol Research and Health, 25,* 25–30.

Jacobson, J. L., Jacobson, S. W., Sokol, R. J., Martier, S. S., Ager, J. W., & Kaplan-Estrin, M. G. (1993). Teratogenic effects of alcohol on infant development. *Alcoholism: Clinical and Experimental Research, 17,* 174–183.

Jacobson, S. W., Fein, G. G., Jacobson, J. L., Schwartz, P. M., & Dowler, J. K. (1984). Neonatal correlates of exposure to smoking, caffeine, and alcohol. *Infant Behavior and Development, 7,* 253–265.

Jacobvitz, D., & Sroufe, L. A. (1987). The early caregiver–child relationship and attention-deficit disorder with hyperactivity in kindergarten: A prospective study. *Child Development, 58,* 1496–1504.

Jaffe, J., Beebe, B., Feldstein, S., Crown, C. L., & Jasnow, M. D. (2001). Rhythms of dialogue in infancy: Coordinated timing in development. *Monographs of the Society for Research in Child Development, 66* (2, Serial No. 265).

Jaffee, S., & Hyde, J. S. (2000). Gender differences in moral orientation: A meta-analysis. *Psychological Bulletin, 126,* 703–726.

Jaffee, S. R., Moffitt, T. E., Caspi, A., & Taylor A. (2003). Life with (or without) father: The benefits of living with two biological parents depend on the father's antisocial behavior. *Child Development, 74,* 109–126.

Jagers, R. J., Bingham, K., & Hans, S. L. (1996). Socialization and social judgments among inner-city African-American kindergarteners. *Child Development, 67,* 140–150.

James, W. (1890). *Principles of psychology* (2 vols.). New York: Holt.

Jankowiak, W. R., & Fischer, E. F. (1992). A cross-cultural perspective on romantic love. *Ethnology, 31,* 149–155.

Janus, J. S., & Janus, C. L. (1993). *The Janus Report on Sexual Behavior.* New York: Wiley.

Jaquish, G. A., & Ripple, R. E. (1981). Cognitive creative abilities and self-esteem across the adult life-span. *Human Development, 24,* 110–119.

Jeffery, R., & Jeffery, P. M. (1993). Traditional birth attendants in rural north India: The social organization of childbearing. In S. Lindenbaum & M. Lock (Eds.), *Knowledge, power and practice: The anthropology of medicine and everyday life.* Berkeley: University of California Press.

Jenkins, J. M., & Astington, J. W. (1996). Cognitive factors and family structure associated with theory of mind development in young children. *Developmental Psychology, 32,* 70–78.

Jenkins, S. R. (1989). Longitudinal prediction of women's careers: Psychological, behavioral, and social–structural influences. *Journal of Vocational Behavior, 34,* 204–235.

Jennings, K. D., & Dietz, L. J. (2003). Mastery motivation and goal persistence in young children. In M. H. Bornstein & Davidson, L. (Eds.), *Well-being: positive development across the life course* (pp. 295–309). Mahwah, NJ: Lawrence Erlbaum.

Jensen, A. R. (1969). How much can we boost IQ and scholastic achievement? *Harvard Educational Review, 39,* 1–123.

Jensen, A. R. (1977). Cumulative deficit in the IQ of blacks in the rural South. *Developmental Psychology, 13,* 184–191.

Jensen, A. R. (1980). *Bias in mental testing.* New York: Free Press.

Jensen, A. R. (1990). Speed of information processing in a calculating prodigy. *Intelligence, 14,* 259–274.

Jensen, A. R. (1993). Why is reaction time correlated with psychometric *g*? *Current Directions in Psychological Science, 2,* 53–56.

Jensen, P. S. (2000). Current concepts and controversies in the diagnosis and treatment of attention-deficit/hyperactivity disorder. *Current Psychiatry Reports, 2,* 102–109.

Jensen, P. S., Bhatara, V. S., Vitiello, B., Hoagwood, K., Feil, M., & Burke, L. B. (1999). Psychoactive medication prescribing practices for U.S. children: Gaps between research and clinical practice. *Journal of the American Academy of Child and Adolescent Psychiatry, 38,* 557–565.

Jensen, P. S., Hinshaw, S. P., Swanson, J. M., Greenhill, L. L., Conners, C. K., Arnold, L. E., Abikoff, H. B., Elliott, G., Hechtman, L., Hoza, B., March, J. S., Newcorn, J. H., Severe, J. B., Vitiello, B., Wells, K., & Wigal, T. (2001). Findings from the NIMH Multimodal Treatment Study of ADHD (MTA): Implications and applications for primary care providers. *Journal of Developmental and Behavioral Pediatrics, 22,* 60–73.

Jessor, R. (Ed.) (1998). *New perspectives on adolescent risk behavior.* Cambridge, Eng: Cambridge University Press.

Jia, G., & Aaronson, D. (1999). Age differences in second language acquisition: The dominant language switch and maintenance hypothesis. In A. Greenhill, H. Littlefield, & C. Tano (Eds.), *Proceedings of the 23rd Annual Boston University Conference on Language Development* (pp. 301–312). Somerville, MA: Cascadilla Press.

Johanson, R. B., & Menon, B. K. (2000). Vacuum extraction versus forceps for assisted vaginal delivery. *Cochrane Database System Review,* 2:CD000224.

Johansson, B., Zarit, S. H., & Berg, S. (1992). Changes in cognitive functioning of the oldest old. *Journal of Gerontology: Psychological Sciences, 47,* P75–P80.

Johnson, C. L. (2000). Perspectives on American kinship in the later 1990s. *Journal of Marriage and the Family, 62,* 623–639.

Johnson, C. L., Stuckey, M. K., Lewis, L. D., & Schwartz, D. M. (1982). Bulimia: A descriptive survey of 316 cases. *International Journal of Eating Disorders, 2,* 3–16.

Johnson, C. L., & Troll, L. (1994). Constraints and facilitators to friendships in late life. *Gerontologist, 34,* 79–87.

Johnson, C. L., & Troll, L. (1996). Family structure and the timing of transitions from 70 to 103 years of age. *Journal of Marriage and the Family, 58,* 178–187.

Johnson, D. W., Johnson, R. T., & Maruyama, G. (1983). Interdependence and interpersonal attraction among heterogeneous and homogeneous individuals: A theoretical formulation and a meta-analysis of the research. *Review of Educational Research, 53,* 5–54.

Johnson, J., & Newport, E. (1989). Critical period effects in second language learning: The influence of maturational state on the acquisition of English as a second language. *Cognitive Psychology, 21,* 60–99.

Johnson, J. G., Cohen, P., Kasen, S., Smailes, E., & Brook, J. (2001). Association of maladaptive parental behavior with psychiatric disorder among parents and their offspring. *Archives of General Psychology, 58,* 453–460.

Johnson, M., & de Haan, M. (2001). Developing cortical specialization for visual-cognitive function: The case of face recognition. In J. L. McClelland & R. S. Siegler (Eds.), *Mechanisms of cognitive development: Behavioral and neural perspectives* (pp. 253–270). Mahwah, NJ: U Sum Associates Publishers.

Johnson, M. H. (1997). *Developmental cognitive neuroscience.* Cambridge, MA: Blackwell.

Johnson, M. P., & Ferraro, K. J. (2000). Research on domestic violence in the 1990s: Making distinctions. *Journal of Marriage and the Family, 62,* 948–963.

Johnson, S. P., & Aslin, R. N. (1995). Perception of object unity in 2-month-old infants. *Developmental Psychology, 31,* 739–745.

Johnson, S. P., Bremner, J. G., Slater, A. M., & Mason, U. (2000). The role of good form in young infants' perception of partly occluded objects. *Journal of Experimental Child Psychology, 76,* 1–25.

John-Steiner, V. (1992). Private speech among adults. In R. M. Diaz & L. E. Berk (Eds.), *Private speech: From social interaction to self-regulation.* Hillsdale, NJ: Erlbaum.

Johnston, F. E. (2002). Social and economic influences on growth and secular trends. In N. Cameron (Ed.), *Human growth and development* (pp. 197–211). New York: Academic Press.

Johnston, T. D., & Edwards, L. (2002). Genes, interactions, and the development of behavior. *Psychological Review, 109,* 26–34.

Johnston, T. D., & Gottlieb, G. (1990). Neophenogenesis: A developmental theory of phenotypic evolution. *Journal of Theoretical Biology, 147,* 471–496.

Joint Committee on Infant Hearing. (2000). Year 2000 position statement: Principles and guidelines for early hearing detection and intervention programs. *Pediatrics, 106,* 798–817.

Jones, C. J., & Meredith, W. (1996). Patterns of personality change across the life span. *Psychology and Aging, 11,* 57–65.

Jones, M. C. (1924). A laboratory study of fear: The case of Peter. *Pedagogical Seminary, 31,* 308–315.

Jones, M. C. (1965). Psychological correlates of somatic development. *Child Development, 56,* 899–911.

Jones, M., & Larson, E. (2003). Length of normal labor in women of Hispanic origin. *Journal of Midwifery, 48,* 2–9.

Jones, S. S. (1996). Imitation or exploration? Young infants' matching of adults' oral gestures. *Child Development, 67,* 1952–1969.

Jones, W. H., Hobbs, S. A., & Hockenbury, D. (1982). Loneliness and social skill deficits. *Journal of Personality and Social Psychology, 42,* 682–689.

Jordyn, M., & Byrd, M. (2003). The relationship between the living arrangements of university students and their identity development. *Adolescence, 38,* 267–278.

Joseph, R. M., & Tager-Flusberg, H. (2004). The relationship of theory of mind and executive functions to symptom type and severity in children with autism. *Development and Psychopathology, 16,* 137–155.

Judge, S. (2003). Developmental recovery and deficit in children adopted from Eastern European orphanages. *Child Psychiatry and Human Development, 34,* 49–62.

Judge, T. A., & Bono, J. E. (2001). Relationship of core self-evaluation traits—self-esteem, generalized self-efficacy, locus of control, and emotional stability—with job satisfaction and job performance: A meta-analysis. *Journal of Applied Psychology, 86,* 80–92.

Judy, B., & Nelson, E. S. (2000). Relationship between parents, peers, morality, and theft in an adolescent sample. *High School Journal, 83,* 31–42.

Jung, C. G. (1933). *Modern man in search of a soul* (W. S. Dell & C. F. Baynes, Trans.). New York: Harcourt, Brace.

Jungblut, P. R., Ostorne, J. A., Quigg, R. J., McNeal, M. A., Clauser, J., Muster, A. J., & McPherson, D. D. (2000). Echocardiographic Doppler evaluation of left ventricular diastolic filling in older, highly trained male endurance athletes. *Echocardiography, 17,* 7–16.

Juola, J. F., Koshino, H., Warner, C. B., McMickell, M., & Peterson, M. (2000). Automatic and voluntary control of attention in young and older adults. *American Journal of Psychology, 113,* 159–178.

Jusczyk, P. W. (1999). How infants begin to extract words from speech. *Trends in Cognitive Science, 3,* 323–328.

Jusczyk, P. W., Houston, D. M., & Newsome, M. (1999). The beginnings of word segmentation in English-learning infants. *Cognitive Psychology, 39,* 159–207.

Jussim, L., & Eccles, J. S. (1992). Teacher expectations II: Construction and reflection of student achievement. *Journal of Personality and Social Psychology, 63,* 947–961.

Justice, E. M., Bakerward, L., Gupta, S., & Jannings, L. R. (1997). Means to the goal of remembering: Developmental changes in awareness of strategy use–performance relations. *Journal of Experimental Child Psychology, 65,* 293–314.

K

Kacew, S. (1999). Effect of over-the-counter drugs on the unborn child: What is known and how should this influence prescribing? *Pediatric Drugs, 1,* 75–80.

Kagan, J. (1972). Do infants think? *Scientific American, 226,* 74–82.

Kagan, J. (1981). *The second year: The emergence of self-awareness.* Cambridge, MA: Harvard University Press.

Kagan, J. (1989). Temperamental contributions to social behavior. *American Psychologist, 44,* 668–674.

Kagan, J. (1994). *Galen's prophecy: Temperament in human nature.* New York: Basic Books.

Kagan, J. (1998). *Three seductive ideas.* Cambridge, MA: Harvard University Press.

Kagan, J. (2003). Biology, context, and developmental inquiry. *Annual Review of Psychology, 54,* 1–23.

Kahn, R. L., & Antonucci, T. C. (1980). Convoys over the life course: Attachment, roles, and social support. In P. B. Baltes & O. G. Brim Jr. (Eds.), *Life-span development and behavior* (Vol. 3). New York: Academic Press.

Kail, R. (1990). *The development of memory in children* (3rd ed.). New York: Freeman.

Kail, R. (1991). Developmental change in speed of processing during childhood and adolescence. *Psychological Bulletin, 109,* 490–501.

Kail, R., & Bisanz, J. (1992). The information-processing perspective on cognitive development in childhood and adolescence. In R. J. Sternberg & C. A. Berg (Eds.), *Intellectual development.* New York: Cambridge University Press.

Kail, R., & Salthouse, T. A. (1994). Processing speed as a mental capacity. *Acta Psychologica, 86,* 199–225.

Kakuma, R., duFort, G. G., Arsenault, L., Perrault, A., Platt, R. W., Monette, J., Moride, Y., & Wolfson, C. (2003). Delirium in older emergency department patients discharged home: Effect on survival. *Journal of the American Geriatrics Society, 51,* 443–450.

Kalmuss, D., Davidson, A., & Cushman, L. (1992). Parenting expectancies, experiences, and adjustment to parenthood: A test of the violated expectations framework. *Journal of Marriage and the Family, 54,* 516–526.

Kalter, N., Lohnes, K. L., Chasin, J., Cain, A. C., Dunning, S., & Rowan, J. (2002–2003). The adjustment of parentally bereaved children: I. Factors associated with short-term adjustment. *Omega: Journal of Death and Dying, 46,* 15–34.

Kaltiala-Heino, R., Marttunen, M., Rantanen, P., & Rimpela, M. (2003). Early puberty is associated with mental health problems in middle adolescence. *Social Science Medicine, 57,* 1055–1064.

Kameguchi, K., & Murphy-Shigematsu, S. (2001). Family psychology and family therapy in Japan. *American Psychologist, 56,* 65–70.

Kandel, E. R., & Jessell, T. (1991). Early experience and the fine tuning of synaptic connections. In E. R. Kandel, J. H. Schwartz, & T. Jessell (Eds.), *Principles of neural science* (3rd ed., pp. 945–958). Norwalk, CT: Appleton & Lange.

Kanner, L. (1943). Autistic disturbances of affective contact. *Nervous Child, 2,* 217–250.

Kant, I. (1958). *Critique of pure reason.* New York: Modern Library. (Original work published 1781).

Kaplan, A. S., & Murphy, G. L. (2000). Category learning with minimal prior knowledge. *Journal of Experimental Psychology: Learning, Memory, and Cognition, 26,* 829–845.

Kaplan, D. S., Damphousse, K. R., & Kaplan, H. B. (1994). Mental health implications of not graduating from high school. *Journal of Experimental Education, 62,* 105–123.

Kaplan, D. W., Feinstein, R. A., Fisher, M. M., Klein, J. D., Olmedo, L. F., Rome, E. S., & Yancy, S. (2001). Condom use by adolescents. *Pediatrics, 107,* 1463–1469.

Kaplan, H. I., & Sadock, B. J. (1998). *Synopsis of psychiatry: Behavioral sciences/clinical psychiatry* (8th ed.). Baltimore: Williams & Wilkens.

Kaplan, R. M., & Erickson, J. (2000). Quality adjusted life expectancy for men and women in the United States. In S. B. Manuck, R. Jennings, B. S. Rabin, & A. Baum (Eds.), *Behavior, health, and aging.* Mahwah, NJ: Erlbaum.

Karel, M. J., & Hinrichsen, G. (2000). Treatment of depression in late life: Psychotherapeutic interventions. *Clinical Psychology Review, 20,* 707–729.

Karraker, K. H., Vogel, D. A., & Lake, M. A. (1995). Parents' gender-stereotyped perceptions of newborns: The eye of the beholder revisited. *Sex Roles, 33,* 687–701.

Kart, C. S., Metress, E. K., & Metress, S. P. (1992). *Human aging and chronic disease.* Boston: Jones and Bartlett.

Kasl-Godley, J., & Gatz, M. (2000). Psychosocial interventions for individuals with dementia: An integration of theory, therapy, and a clinical understanding of dementia. *Clinical Psychology Review, 20,* 755–782.

Kaslow, N., Mintzer, M. B., Meadows, L. A., & Grabill, C. M. (2000). A family perspective on assessing and treating childhood depression. In C. E. Bailey (Ed.), *Children in therapy. Using the family as a resource.* New York: W. W. Norton.

Kastenbaum, R. (2000). *The psychology of death.* New York: Springer.

Kasworm, C. E., & Medina, R. A. (1990). Adult competence in everyday tasks: A cross-sectional secondary analysis. *Educational Gerontology, 16,* 27–48.

Katz, P. A. (1986). Modification of children's gender-stereotyped behavior: General issues and research considerations. *Sex Roles, 14,* 591–602.

Katz, P. A., & Walsh, P. V. (1991). Modification of children's gender-stereotyped behavior. *Child Development, 62,* 338–351.

Kaufman, A. S. (2001). WAIS-III IQs, Horn's theory, and generational changes from young adulthood to old age. *Intelligence, 29,* 131–167.

Kaufman, A. S., Kamphaus, R. W., & Kaufman, N. L. (1985). New directions in intelligence testing: The Kaufman Assessment Battery for Children (K-ABC). In B. B. Wolman (Ed.), *Handbook of intelligence.* New York: Wiley.

Kaufman, A. S., & Kaufman, N. L. (1997). The Kaufman Adolescent and Adult Intelligence Test. In D. P. Flanagan, J. L. Genshaft, & P. L. Harrison (Eds.), *Contemporary intellectual assessment: Theories, tests, and issues.* New York: Guilford.

Kaufman, A. S., & Kaufman, N. L. (2003). *KABC-II: Kaufman Assessment Battery for Children* (2nd ed.). Circle Pines, MN: AGS Publishing.

Kaufman, J., & Zigler, E. (1989). The intergenerational transmission of child abuse. In D. Cicchetti & V. Carlson (Eds.), *Child maltreatment. Theory and research on the causes and consequences of child abuse and neglect.* New York: Cambridge University Press.

Kaufman, R. H., Adam, E., Hatch, E. E., Noller, K., Herbst, A. L., Palmer, J. R., & Hoover, R. N. (2000). Continued follow-up of pregnancy outcomes in diethylstilbestrol-exposed offspring. *Obstetric Gynecology, 96,* 483–489.

Kaye, R. A. (1993). Sexuality in the later years. *Aging and Society, 13,* 415–426.

Kazak, A. E., & Noll, R. B. (2004). Child death from pediatric illness: Conceptualizing intervention from a family/systems and public health perspective. *Professional Psychology: Research and Practice, 35,* 219–226.

Kazdin, A. E. (2000). *Psychotherapy for children and adolescents : Directions for research and practice.* New York: Oxford University Press.

Kazdin, A. E. (2003). Psychotherapy for children and adolescents. *Annual Review of Psychology, 54,* 253–276.

Kean, A. W. G. (1937). The history of the criminal liability of children. *Law Quarterly Review, 3,* 364–370.

Keel, P. K., & Fulkerson, J. A. (2001). Vulnerability to eating disorders in childhood and adolescence. In R. E. Ingram & J. M. Price (Eds.), *Vulnerability to psychopathology. Risk across the lifespan.* New York: Guilford.

Keel, P. K., & Klump, K. L. (2003). Are eating disorders culture-bound syndromes? Implications for conceptualizing their etiology. *Psychological Bulletin, 129,* 747–769.

Keenan, T. (2003). Individual differences in theory of mind. The preschool years and beyond. In B. Repacholi & V. Slaughter (Eds.). *Individual differences in theory of mind: Implications for typical and atypical development.* New York: Psychology Press.

Keith, J. (1985). Age in anthropological research. In R. H. Binstock & E. Shanas (Eds.), *Handbook of aging and the social sciences* (2nd ed.). New York: Van Nostrand Reinhold.

Kelemen, W. L. (2000). Metamemory cues and monitoring accuracy: Judging what you know and what you will know. *Journal of Educational Psychology, 92,* 800–810.

Keller, B. B., & Bell, R. Q. (1979). Child effects on adult's method of eliciting altruistic behavior. *Child Development, 50,* 1004–1009.

Keller, H. (1954). *The story of my life.* New York: Doubleday.

Keller, H., & Scholmerich, A. (1987). Infant vocalizations and parental reactions during the first four months of life. *Developmental Psychology, 23,* 62–67.

Kelley-Buchanan, C. (1988). *Peace of mind during pregnancy: An A–Z guide to the substances that could affect your unborn baby.* New York: Facts on File.

Kellman, P. J., & Banks, M. S. (1998). Infant visual perception. In D. Kuhn & R. S. Siegler (Vol. Eds.), W. Damon (Editor-in-Chief), *Handbook of child psychology* (5th ed., pp. 103–146). New York: Wiley.

Kellman, P. J., & Spelke, E. S. (1983). Perception of partly occluded objects in infancy. *Cognitive Psychology, 15,* 483–524.

Kelsall, D. C., Shallop, J. K., & Burnelli, T. (1995). Cochlear implantation in the elderly. *American Journal of Otology, 16,* 609–615.

Kemler Nelson, D. G., Hirsch-Pasek, K., Jusczyk, P. W., & Cassidy, K. W. (1989). How the prosodic cues in motherese might assist in language learning. *Journal of Child Language, 16,* 55–68.

Kempe, R. S., & Kempe, C. H. (1978). *Child abuse.* Cambridge, MA: Harvard University Press.

Kempen, G. I., Ormel, J., Brilman, E. I., & Relyveld, J. (1997). Adaptive responses among Dutch elderly: The impact of eight chronic medical conditions on health-related quality of life. *American Journal of Public Health, 87,* 38–44.

Kemper, S. & Mitzner, T. L. (2001). Production and comprehension. In J. E. Birren & K. W. Schaie (Eds.), Handbook of the psychology of Aging, 5th ed.(pp.378-398). San Diego, CA: Academic Press.

Kemtes, K. A., & Kemper, S. (1997). Younger and older adults' on-line processing of syntactically ambiguous sentences. *Psychology and Aging, 12,* 362–371.

Kendall-Tackett, K. A., Williams, L. M., & Finkelhor, D. (1993). Impact of sexual abuse on children: A review and synthesis of recent empirical studies. *Psychological Bulletin, 113,* 164–180.

Kendig, H. L., Coles, R., Pittelkow, Y., & Wilson, S. (1988). Confidants and family structure in old age. *Journal of Gerontology: Social Sciences, 43,* S31–S40.

Kendler, K. S. (2003). Of genes and twins. *Psychological Medicine, 33,* 763–768.

Kendler, K. S., Gardner, C. O., & Prescott, C. A. (2002). Toward a comprehensive developmental model for major depression in women. *American Journal of Psychiatry, 159,* 1133–1145.

Kendler, K. S., Neale, M., Kessler, R., Heath, A., & Eaves, L. (1993). A twin study of recent life events and difficulties. *Archives of General Psychiatry, 50,* 789–796.

Kendler, K. S., Silberg, J. L., Neale, M. C., Kessler, R. C., Heath, A. C., & Eaves, L. J. (1992). Genetic and environmental factors in the aetiology of menstrual, premenstrual and neurotic symptoms: A population-based twin study. *Psychological Medicine, 22,* 85–100.

Keniston, K. (1970). Youth: A "new" stage of life. *American Scholar, 39,* 631–654.

Kennell, J., Klaus, M., McGrath, S., Robertson, S., & Hinkley, C. (1991). Continuous emotional support during labor in a US hospital: A randomized controlled trial. *Journal of the American Medical Association, 265,* 2197–2201.

Kenny, M. E. (1987). The extent and function of parental attachment among first-year college students. *Journal of Youth and Adolescence, 16,* 17–29.

Kenny, M. E., & Rice, K. G. (1995). Attachment to parents and adjustment in late adolescent college students: Current status, applications, and future considerations. *The Counseling Psychologist, 23,* 433–456.

Kent, A., & Waller, G. (2000). Childhood emotional abuse and eating psychopathology. *Clinical Psychology Review, 20,* 887–903.

Kenyon, B. L. (2001). Current research in children's conceptions of death: A critical review. *Omega: Journal of Death and Dying, 43,* 63–91.

Keough, J., & Sugden, D. (1985). *Movement skill development.* New York: Macmillan.

Kerka, S. (1995). Adult learner retention revisited. ERIC Clearinghouse on Adult, Career, and Vocational Education, Digest No. 166.

Kerns, K. A., Klepac, L., & Cole, A. K. (1996). Peer relationships and preadolescents' perceptions of security in the child-mother relationship. *Developmental Psychology, 32,* 457–466.

Kerr, M. A., Black, M. M., & Krishnakumar, A. (2000). Failure to thrive, maltreatment, and the behavior and development of 6-year-old children from low-income, urban families: A cumulative risk model. *Child Abuse and Neglect, 24,* 587–598.

Kerr, M., & Stattin, H. (2000). What parents know, how they know it, and several forms of adolescent adjustment: Further support for a reinterpretation of monitoring. *Developmental Psychology, 36,* 366–380.

Kerr, M., & Stattin, H. (2003). Parenting of adolescents: Action or reaction? In A. C. Crouter, & A. Booth (Eds.), *Children's influence on family dynamics: The neglected side of family relationships.* Mahwah, NJ: Erlbaum.

Kessen, W. (1975). *Childhood in China.* New Haven, CT: Yale University Press.

Kessler, R. C. (2000). Gender differences in major depression. Epidemiological finding through the world. In E. Frank (Ed.), *Gender and its effects on psychopathology.* Washington, D.C.: American Psychiatric Press.

Kessler, R. C., Avenevoli, S., & Merikangas, K. R. (2001). Mood disorders in children and adolescents: An epidemiologic perspective. *Biological Psychiatry, 49,* 1002–1014.

Kett, J. F. (1977). *Rites of passage. Adolescence in America 1790 to the present.* New York: Basic Books.

Kettlewell, H. B. D. (1959). Darwin's missing evidence. *Scientific American, 200 (3),* 48–53.

Key, S., & DeNoon, D. (1998, January 12). Statistics show fewer babies born with HIV. *AIDS Weekly Plus,* 21.

Keyes, C. L. M. (2002). The exchange of emotional support with age and its relationship with emotional well-being by age. *Journals of Gerontology: Psychological Sciences and Social Sciences, 57,* 518–525.

Kiecolt-Glaser, J. K., & Newton, T. L. (2001). Marriage and health: His and hers. *Psychological Bulletin, 127,* 472–503.

Kiesner, J., Dishion, T. J., & Poulin, F. (2001). A reinforcement model of conduct problems in children and adolescents: Advances in theory and intervention. In J. Hill & B. Maughan (Eds.), *Conduct disorders in childhood and adolescence.* New York: Cambridge University Press.

Kim, K., & Spelke, E. J. (1992). Infants' sensitivity to effects of gravity on visible object motion. *Journal of Experimental Psychology: Human Perception and Performance, 18,* 385–393.

Kimura, D. (1992). Sex differences in the brain. *Scientific American, 267,* 119–125.

King, A. C., Castro, C., Wilcox, S., Eyler, A. A., Sallis, J. F., & Brownson, R. C. (2000). Personal and environmental factors associated with physical inactivity among different racial-ethnic groups of U.S. middle-aged and older-aged women. *Health Psychology, 19,* 354–364.

Kingston, H. M. (2002). *ABC of clinical genetics.* London: BMJ Books.

Kinsella, K., & Gist, Y. J. (1998, October). Gender and aging. Mortality and health. *International Brief, IB/98-2.* Washington, D.C.: U.S. Census Bureau.

Kirby, D. (2002). Effective approaches to reducing adolescent unprotected sex, pregnancy, and childbearing. *Journal of Sex Research, 39,* 51–57.

Kirsch, I. S., Jungeblut, A., Jenkins, L., & Kolstad, A. (1993). *Adult literacy in America: A first look at the results of the National Adult Literacy Survey.* Washington, D.C.: National Center for Education Statistics.

Kisilevsky, B. S., & Muir, D. W. (1984). Neonatal habituation and dishabituation to tactile stimulation during sleep. *Developmental Psychology, 20,* 367–373.

Kisilevsky, B. S., Hains, S. M., Lee, K., Xie, X., Huang, H., Ye, H. H., Zhang, K., & Wang, Z. (2003). Effects of experience on fetal voice recognition. *Psychological Science, 14,* 220–224.

Kissane, D. W., Bloch, S., Onghena, P., McKenzie, D. P., Snyder, R. D., & Dowe, D. L. (1996). The Melbourne Family Grief Study, II: Psychosocial morbidity and grief in bereaved families. *American Journal of Psychiatry, 153,* 659–666.

Kitamura, C., & Burnham, D. (2003). Pitch and communicative intent in mother's speech: Adjustments for age and sex in the first year. *Infancy, 4,* 85–110.

Kitchener, K. S., King, P. M., Wood, P. K., & Davison, M. L. (1989). Sequentiality and consistency in the development of reflective judgment: A six-year longitudinal study. *Journal of Applied Developmental Psychology, 10,* 73–95.

Kitson, G. C. (1992). *Portrait of divorce: Adjustment to marital breakdown.* New York: Guilford.

Kitson, G. C. (2000). Adjustment to violent and natural deaths in later and earlier life for black and white widows. *Journal of Gerontology: Social Sciences, 55B,* S341–S351.

Kitson, G. C., Babri, K. B., & Roach, M. J. (1985). Who divorces and why. A review. *Journal of Family Issues, 6,* 255–293.

Kitzmann, K. M., Gaylord, N. K., Holt, A. R., & Kenny, E. D. (2003). Child witnesses to domestic violence: A meta-analytic review. *Journal of Consulting and Clinical Psychology, 71,* 339–352.

Klaczynski, P. A. (2000). Motivated scientific reasoning biases, epistemological beliefs, and theory polarization: A two-process approach to adolescent cognition. *Child Development, 71,* 1347–1366.

Klaczynski, P. A. (2001). Analytic and heuristic processing influences on adolescent reasoning and decision-making. *Child Development, 72,* 844–861.

Klaczynski, P. A., & Gordon, D. H. (1996a). Everyday statistical reasoning during adolescence and young adulthood: Motivational, general ability, and developmental influences. *Child Development, 67,* 2873–2892.

Klaczynski, P. A., & Gordon, D. H. (1996b). Self-serving influences on adolescents' evaluations of belief-relevant evidence. *Journal of Experimental Child Psychology, 62,* 317–339.

Klaczynski, P. A., & Narasimham, G. (1998). Development of scientific reasoning biases: Cognitive versus ego-protective explanations. *Developmental Psychology, 34,* 175–187.

Klapper, W., Parwaresch, R., & Krupp, G. (2001). Telomere biology in human aging and aging syndromes. *Mechanisms of Ageing and Development, 122,* 695–712.

Klass, D. (2001). Continuing bonds in the resolution of grief in Japan and North America. *American Behavioral Scientist, 44,* 742–763.

Klaus, H. M., & Kennell, J. H. (1976). *Maternal–infant bonding.* St. Louis: C. V. Mosby.

Klein, D. M., & White, J. M. (1996). *Family theories: An introduction.* Thousand Oaks, CA: Sage.

Klein, P. J., & Meltzoff, A. N. (1999). Long-term memory, forgetting, and deferred imitation in 12-month-old infants. *Developmental Science, 2,* 102–113.

Klein, R., Klein, B. E., Lee, K. E., Cruickshanks, K. J., & Chappell, R. J. (2001). Changes in visual acuity in a population over a 10-year period: The Beaver Dam Eye Study. *Ophthalmology, 108,* 1757–1766.

Klein, W. (1996). Language acquisition at different ages. In D. Magnusson (Ed.), *The lifespan development of individuals: Behavioral, neurobiological, and psychosocial perspectives: A synthesis.* Cambridge, England: Cambridge University Press.

Kleiner, C., & Lord, M. (1999, November 22). The cheating game. 'Everyone's doing it,' from grade school to graduate school. *U.S. News & World Report,* 54–66.

Kliegl, R., Smith, J., & Baltes, P. B. (1990). On the locus and process of magnification of age differences during mnemonic training. *Developmental Psychology, 26,* 894–904.

Klimes-Dougan, B., & Kistner, J. (1990). Physically abused preschoolers' responses to peers' distress. *Developmental Psychology, 26,* 599–602.

Klin, A., Chawarska, K., Rubin, E., & Volkmar F. (2004). Clinical assessment of young children at risk for autism. In R. DelCarmen-Wiggins & A. Carter (Eds.), *Handbook of infant, toddler, and preschool mental health assessment.* New York: Oxford University Press.

Kline, D. W., & Scialfa, C. T. (1996). Visual and auditory aging. In J. E. Birren & K. W. Schaie (Eds.), *Handbook of the psychology of aging* (4th ed.). San Diego: Academic Press.

Klineberg, O. (1963). Negro–white differences in intelligence test performance: A new look at an old problem. *American Psychologist, 18,* 198–203.

Kling, K. C., Hyde, J. S., Showers, C. J., & Buswell, B. N. (1999). Gender differences in self-esteem: A meta-analysis. *Psychological Bulletin, 125,* 470–500.

Kling, K. C., Ryff, C. D., Love, G., & Essex, M. (2003). Exploring the influence of personality on depressive symptoms and self-esteem across a significant life transition. *Journal of Personality and Social Psychology, 85,* 922–932.

Klinger, L. J., Hamilton, J. A., & Cantrell, P. J. (2001). Children's perceptions of aggressive and gender-specific content in toy commercials. *Social Behavior and Personality, 29,* 11–20.

Klitsch, M. (2002). Children with prenatal cocaine exposure have elevated risk of cognitive impairments at least until age two. *Perspectives on Sexual and Reproductive Health, 34,* 317–318.

Klump, K. L., McGue, M., & Iacono, W. G. (2003). Differential heritability of eating attitudes and behaviors in prepubertal versus pubertal twins. *International Journal of Eating Disorders, 33,* 287–292.

Knecht, S., Deppe, M., Drager, B., Bobe, L., Lohmann, H., Ringelstein, E., & Henningsen, H. (2000). Language lateralization in healthy right-handers. *Brain, 123,* 74–81.

Knight, G. P., Fabes, R. A., & Higgins, D. A. (1996). Concerns about drawing causal inferences from meta-analyses: An example in the study of gender differences in aggression. *Psychological Bulletin,* 119, 410–421.

Knight, J. A. (2000). The biochemistry of aging. *Advances in Clinical Chemistry, 35,* 1–62.

Kobak, R. R., Cole, H. E., Ferenz-Gilles, R., Fleming, W. S., & Gamble, W. (1993). Attachment and emotional regulation during mother–teen problem solving. A control theory analysis. *Child Development, 64,* 231–245.

Kobak, R. R., & Esposito, A. (2004). Levels of processing in parent–child relationships: Implications for clinical assessment and treatment. In L. Atkinson & S. Goldberg (Eds.), *Attachment issues in psychopathology and intervention.* Mahwah, NJ, Erlbaum.

Kochanska, G. (1993). Toward a synthesis of parental socialization and child temperament in early development of conscience. *Child Development, 64,* 325–347.

Kochanska, G. (1995). Children's temperament, mothers' discipline, and security of attachment: Multiple pathways to emerging internalization. *Child Development, 66,* 597–615.

Kochanska, G. (1997a). Multiple pathways to conscience for children with different temperaments: From toddlerhood to age 5. *Developmental Psychology, 33,* 228–240.

Kochanska, G. (1997b). Mutually responsive orientation between mothers and their young children: Implications for early socialization. *Child Development, 68,* 94–112.

Kochanska, G. (2001). Emotional development in children with different attachment histories: The first three years. *Child Development, 72,* 474–490.

Kochanska, G. (2002). Mutually responsive orientation between mothers and their young children: A context for the early development of conscience. *Current Directions in Psychological Science, 11(6),* 191–195.

Kochanska, G., Aksan, N., & Nichols, K. E. (2003). Maternal power assertion in discipline and moral discourse contexts: Commonalities, differences, and implications for children's moral conduct and cognition. *Developmental Psychology, 39,* 949–963.

Kochanska, G., Casey, R. J., & Fukumoto, A. (1995). Toddlers' sensitivity to standard violations. *Child Development, 66,* 643–656.

Kochanska, G., & Knaack, A. (2003). Effortful control as a personality characteristic of young children: Antecedents, correlates, and consequences. *Journal of Personality, 71,* 1087–1112.

Kochanska, G., Murray, K., Coy, K. C. (1997). Inhibitory control as a contributor to conscience in childhood: From toddler to early school age. *Child Development, 68,* 263–277.

Kodama, K., Mabuchi, K., & Shigematsu, I. (1996). A long-term cohort study of the atomic-bomb survivors. *Journal of Epidemiology, 6,* S95–S105.

Koegel, R. L., Koegel, L. K., & McNerney, E. K. (2001). Pivotal areas in intervention for autism. *Journal of Clinical Child Psychology, 30,* 19–32.

Koenen, K. C., Moffitt, T. E., Caspi, A., Taylor, A., & Purcell, S. (2003). Domestic violence is associated with environmental suppression of IQ in young children. *Development and Psychopathology, 15,* 297–311.

Koenig, A. L., Cicchetti, D., & Rogosch, F. A. (2000). Child compliance/noncompliance and maternal contributors to internalization in maltreating and nonmaltreating dyads. *Child Development, 71,* 1018–1032.

Koenig, A. L., Cicchetti, D., & Rogosch, F. A. (2004). Moral development: The association between maltreatment and young children's prosocial behaviors and moral transgressions. *Social Development, 13,* 97–106.

Koestner, R., Zuroff, D. C., & Powers, T. A. (1991). Family origins of adolescent self-criticism and its continuity into adulthood. *Journal of Abnormal Psychology,* 100, 191–197.

Koff, E., & Rierdan, J. (1995). Early adolescent girls' understanding of menstruation. *Women and Health, 22,* 1–19.

Kogan, N. (1983). Stylistic variation in childhood and adolescence: Creativity, metaphor, and cognitive styles. In J. H. Flavell & E. H. Markman (Eds.), *Handbook of child psychology: Vol. 3. Cognitive development* (4th ed.). New York: Wiley.

Kogan, S. M. (2004). Disclosing unwanted sexual experiences: Results from a national sample of adolescent women. *Child Abuse & Neglect, 28,* 147–165.

Kohl, G. O., Lengua, L. J., McMahon, R. J., & the Conduct Problems Prevention Research Group. (2000). Parent involvement in school: Conceptualizing multiple dimensions and their relations with family and demographic risk factors. *Journal of School Psychology, 38,* 501–523.

Kohlberg, L. (1963). The development of children's orientations toward a moral order: I. Sequence in the development of moral thought. *Vita Humana, 6,* 11–33.

Kohlberg, L. (1966a). A cognitive-developmental analysis of children's sex-role concepts and attitudes. In E. E. Maccoby (Ed.), *The development of sex differences.* Stanford, CA: Stanford University Press.

Kohlberg, L. (1966b). Cognitive stages and preschool education. *Human Development, 9,* 5–17.

Kohlberg, L. (1969). Stage and sequence: The cognitive developmental approach to socialization. In D. A. Goslin (Ed.), *Handbook of socialization theory and research.* Chicago: Rand McNally.

Kohlberg, L. (1975, June). The cognitive developmental approach to moral education. *Phi Delta Kappan,* 670–677.

Kohlberg, L. (1981). *Essays on moral development: Vol. 1. The philosophy of moral development.* San Francisco: Harper & Row.

Kohlberg, L. (1984). *Essays on moral development: Vol. 2. The psychology of moral development.* San Francisco: Harper & Row.

Kohlberg, L., Yaeger, J., & Hjertholm, E. (1968), Private speech: Four studies and a review of theories. *Child Development, 39,* 691–736.

Kohn, M. L. (1969). *Class and conformity: A study of values.* Homewood, IL: Dorsey Press.

Kohn, M. L., & Schooler, C. (1982). Job conditions and personality: A longitudinal assessment of their reciprocal effects. *American Journal of Sociology, 87,* 1257–1286.

Kojima, H. (2003). The history of children and youth in Japan. In W. Koops & M. Zuckerman. (Eds.), *Beyond the century of the child. Cultural history and developmental psychology.* Philadelphia: University of Pennsylvania Press.

Kolb, B., & Whishaw, I. Q. (2003). *Fundamentals of human neuropsychology* (5th ed.). New York: Worth.

Koller, H., Lawson, K., Rose, S. A., Wallace, I., & McCarton, C. (1997). Patterns of cognitive development in very low birth weight children during the first six years of life. *Pediatrics, 99,* 383–389.

Kolstad, V., & Aguiar, A. (1995, March). *Means–end sequences in young infants.* Paper presented at the biennial meeting of the Society for Research in Child Development, Indianapolis.

Konner, M. J. (1981). Evolution of human behavior development. In R. H. Munroe, R. L. Munroe, & B. B. Whiting (Eds.), *Handbook of cross-cultural human development.* New York: Garland STPM Press.

Koocher, G. P. (1973). Childhood, death, and cognitive development. *Developmental Psychology, 9,* 369–375.

Koocher, G. P. (1974). Talking with children about death. *American Journal of Orthopsychiatry, 44,* 404–411.

Koocher, G. P., & Keith-Spiegel, P. (1994). Scientific issues in psychosocial and educational research with children. In M. Grodin, & L. H. Glantz (Eds.), *Children as research subjects. Science, ethics, and law.* New York: Oxford University Press.

Koopmans-van Beinum, F. J., Clement, C. J., & van den Dikkenberg-Pot, I. (2001). Babbling and the lack of auditory speech perception: A matter of coordination? *Developmental Science, 4,* 61–70.

Koops, W. (2003). Imaging childhood. In W. Koops & M. Zuckerman. (Eds.), *Beyond the century of the child. Cultural history and developmental psychology.* Philadelphia: University of Pennsylvania Press.

Kopka, T. L. C., & Peng, S. S. (1993). *Adult education: Main reasons for participating.* Statistics in Brief NCES-93-451. Washington, D.C.: National Center for Education Statistics.

Kopp, C. B. (1989). Regulation of distress and negative emotions: A developmental view. *Developmental Psychology, 25,* 343–354.

Kopp, C. B., & Krakow, J. B. (1982). *The child: Development in a social context.* Reading, MA: Addison-Wesley.

Kopp, C. B., & Neufield, S. J. (2003). Emotional development during infancy. In R. J. Davidson, K. R. Scherer, & H. H. Goldsmith (Eds.), *Handbook of affective sciences.* New York: Oxford University Press.

Korbin, J. E. (2001). Context and meaning in neighborhood studies of children and families. In A. Booth, & A. C. Crouter (Eds.), *Does it take a village? Community effects on children, adolescents, and families.* Mahwah, NJ: Erlbaum.

Koriat, A., Goldsmith, M., & Pansky, A. (2000). Toward a psychology of memory accuracy. *Annual Review of Psychology, 51,* 481–538.

Korkman, M., Kettunen, S., & Autti-Rämö, I. (2003). Neurocognitive impairment in early adolescence following prenatal alcohol exposure of varying duration. *Neuropsychological Development Cognition (Section C: Child Neuropsychology), 9,* 117–128.

Kortenhaus, C. M., & Demarest, J. (1993). Gender role stereotyping in children's literature: An update. *Sex Roles, 28,* 219–232.

Kotimaa, A. J., Moilanen, I., Taanila, A., Ebeling, H., Smalley, S. L., McGough, J. J., Hartikainen, A. L., & Jarvelin, M. R. (2003). Maternal smoking and hyperactivity in 8-year-old children. *Journal of the American Academy of Child and Adolescent Psychiatry, 42,* 826–833.

Kotler, L. A., Cohen, P., Davies, M., Pine, D. S., & Walsh, B. T. (2001). Longitudinal relationships between childhood, adolescent, and adult eating disorders. *Journal of the American Academy of Child and Adolescent Psychiatry, 40,* 1434–1440.

Koutstaal, W., Schacter, D. L., Johnson, M. K., Angell, K. E., & Gross, M. S. (1998). Post-event review in older and younger adults: Improving memory accessibility of complex everyday events. *Psychology and Aging, 13,* 277–296.

Kovacs, D. M., Parker, J. G., & Hoffman, L. W. (1996). Behavioral, affective, and social correlates of involvement in cross-sex friendships in elementary school. *Child Development, 67,* 2269–2286.

Kovacs, M., & Goldston, D. (1991). Cognitive and social cognitive development of depressed children and adolescents. *Journal of the American Academy of Child and Adolescent Psychiatry, 30,* 388–392.

Kowal, A., Kramer, L., Krull, J. L., & Crick N. R. (2002). Children's perceptions of the fairness of parental preferential treatment and their socioemotional well-being. *Journal of Family Psychology, 16,* 297–306.

Kowalski, K. A. (2000). High-tech conception in the 21st century. *Current Health (Human Sexuality Supplement), 26,* 1–4.

Krafft, K. C., & Berk, L. E. (1998). Private speech in two preschools: Significance of open-ended activities and make-believe play for verbal self-regulation. *Early Childhood Research Quarterly, 13,* 637–658.

Krause, N. (1995). Negative interaction and satisfaction with social support among older adults. *Journal of Gerontology: Psychological Sciences, 50B,* 59–73.

Krause, N., & Rook, K. S. (2003). Negative interaction in late life: Issues in the stability and generalizability of conflict across relationships. *Journals of Gerontology: Psychological Sciences and Social Sciences, 58,* 88–99.

Krause, N., & Shaw, B. A. (2000). Role-specific feelings of control and mortality. *Psychology and Aging, 15,* 617–626.

Krebs, D. L., Denton, K., Wark, G., Couch, R., Racine, T., & Krebs, D. L. (2002). Interpersonal moral conflicts between couples: Effects of type of dilemma, role, and partner's judgments on level of moral reasoning and probability of resolution. *Journal of Adult Development, 9,* 307–316.

Kroger, J. (1996). Identity, regression and development. *Journal of Adolescence, 19,* 203–222.

Kroger, J. (1997). Gender and identity: The intersection of structure, content, and context. *Sex Roles, 36,* 747–770.

Krogh, K. M. (1985). Women's motives to achieve and to nurture in different life stages. *Sex Roles, 12,* 75–90.

Krucoff, C. (May 16, 2000). Good to the bone. *The Washington Post—Health,* 8.

Krueger, R. F., Markon, K. E., & Bouchard, T. J., Jr. (2003). The extended genotype: The heritability of personality accounts for the heritability of recalled family environments in twins reared apart. *Journal of Personality, 71,* 809–833.

Kruger, A. C. (1992). The effect of peer and adult–child transductive discussions on moral reasoning. *Merrill-Palmer Quarterly, 38,* 191–211.

Kruger, A. C., & Tomasello, M. (1986). Transactive discussions with peers and adults. *Developmental Psychology, 22,* 681–685.

Kübler-Ross, E. (1969). *On death and dying.* New York: Macmillan.

Kübler-Ross, E. (1974). *Questions and answers on death and dying.* New York: Macmillan.

Kuebli, J., & Fivush, R. (1994). Children's representation and recall of event alternatives. *Journal of Experimental Child Psychology, 58,* 25–45.

Kuehner, C. (2003). Gender differences in unipolar depression: An update of epidemiological findings and possible explanations. *Acta Psychiatrica Scandinavia, 108,* 163–174.

Kuhn, D. (1993). Connecting scientific and informal reasoning. *Merrill-Palmer Quarterly, 39,* 74–103.

Kuhn, D. (2000). Metacognitive development. *Current Directions in Psychological Science, 9,* 178–181.

Kulik, J. A., & Kulik, C. C. (1992). Meta-analytic findings on grouping programs. *Gifted Child Quarterly, 36,* 73–77.

Kuncel, N. R., Hezlett, S. A., & Ones, D. S. (2004). Academic performance, career potential, creativity, and job performance: Can one construct predict them all? *Journal of Personality and Social Psychology, 86,* 148–161.

Kurdek, L. A. (1991a). Correlates of relationship satisfaction in cohabiting gay and lesbian couples: Integration of contextual investment, and problem-solving models. *Journal of Personality and Social Psychology, 61,* 910–922.

Kurdek, L. A. (1991b). The relations between reported well-being and divorce history, availability of a proximate adult, and gender. *Journal of Marriage and the Family, 53,* 71–78.

Kurdek, L. A. (1995). Lesbian and gay couples. In A. R. Augelli & C. J. Patterson (Eds.), *Lesbian and gay identities over the life span: Psychological perspectives on personal, relational, and community processes.* New York: Oxford University Press.

Kurdek, L. A. (1999). The nature and predictors of the trajectory of change in marital quality for husbands and wives over the first 10 years of marriage. *Developmental Psychology, 35,* 1283–1296.

Kurdek, L. A., & Krile, D. (1982). A developmental analysis of the relation between peer acceptance and both interpersonal understanding and perceived social self-competence. *Child Development, 53,* 1485–1491.

Kwon, Y., & Lawson, A. (2000). Linking brain growth with the development of scientific reasoning ability and conceptual change during adolescence. *Journal of Research in Science Teaching, 37,* 44–62.

Kwong, M. J., Bartholomew, K., Henderson, A. J. Z., & Trinke, S. J. (2003). The intergenerational transmission of relationship violence. *Journal of Family Psychology, 17,* 288–301.

L

Labinowicz, E. (1980). *The Piaget primer.* Menlo Park, CA: Addison-Wesley.

Labouvie-Vief, G. (1985). Intelligence and cognition. In J. E. Birren & K. W. Schaie (Eds.), *Handbook of the psychology of aging* (2nd ed.). New York: Van Nostrand Reinhold.

Labouvie-Vief, G. (1992). A neo-Piagetian perspective on adult cognitive development. In R. J. Sternberg & C. A. Berg (Eds.), *Intellectual development.* New York: Cambridge University Press.

Labouvie-Vief, G., Adams, C., Hakim-Larson, J., & Hayden, M. (1983, April). *Contexts of logic: The growth of interpretation from preadolescence to mature adulthood.* Paper presented at the biennial meeting of the Society for Research in Child Development, Detroit.

Ladd, G. W. (1999). Peer relationships and social competence during early and middle childhood. *Annual Review of Psychology, 50,* 333–359.

Ladd, G. W., Buhs, E. S., & Seid, M. (2000). Children's initial sentiments about kindergarten: Is school liking an antecedent of early classroom participation and achievement? *Merrill-Palmer Quarterly, 46,* 255–279.

Ladd, G. W., & Troop-Gordon, W. (2003). The role of chronic peer difficulties in the development of children's psychological adjustment problems. *Child Development, 74,* 1344–1367.

Laflamme, D., Pomerleau, A., & Malcuit, G. (2002). A comparison of fathers' and mothers' involvement in childcare and stimulation behaviors during free-play with their infants at 9 and 15 months. *Sex Roles, 47,* 507–518.

Laible, D. J., Carlo G., & Raffaelli, M. (2000). The differential relations of parent and peer attachment to adolescent adjustment. *Journal of Youth and Adolescence, 29,* 45–183.

Laible, D. J., & Thompson, R. A. (2000). Mother–child discourse, attachment security, shared positive affect, and early conscience development. *Child Development, 71,* 1424–1440.

Laible, D. J., & Thompson, R. A. (2002). Mother–child conflict in the toddler years: Lessons in emotion, morality, and relationships. *Child Development, 73,* 1187–1203.

Lakatta, E. G. (1990). Heart and circulation. In E. L. Schneider & J. W. Rowe (Eds.), *Handbook of the biology of aging* (3rd ed.). San Diego: Academic Press.

Lamaze, F. (1958). *Painless childbirth: Psychoprophylactic method.* London: Burke.

Lamb, M. E., & Tamis-Lemonda, C. S. (2004). The role of the father: An introduction. In M. E. Lamb (Ed.), *The role of the father in child development* (4th ed.). Hoboken, NJ: John Wiley & Sons.

Lambert, S. R., & Drack, A. V. (1996). Infantile cataracts. *Survey of Ophthalmology, 40,* 427–458.

Lamborn, S. D., Mounts, N. S., Steinberg, L., & Dornbusch, S. M. (1991). Patterns of competence and adjustment among adolescents from authoritative, authoritarian, indulgent, and neglectful families. *Child Development, 62,* 1049–1065.

Lamborn, S. D., & Steinberg, L. (1993). Emotional autonomy redux: Revisiting Ryan and Lynch. *Child Development, 64,* 483–499.

Lampinen, P., Heikkinen, R., & Ruoppila, I. (2000). Changes in intensity of physical exercise as predictors of depressive symptoms among older adults: An eight-year follow-up. *Preventive Medicine, 30,* 371–380.

Lampl, M. (2002). Saltation and stasis. In N. Cameron (Ed.), *Human growth and development* (pp. 253–270). New York: Academic Press.

Lamy, P. P. (1986). The elderly and drug interactions. *Journal of the American Geriatrics Society, 34,* 586–592.

Landreth, G., & Homeyer, L. (1998). Play as the language of children's feelings. In D. P. Fromberg & D. Bergen (Eds.), *Play from birth to twelve and beyond.* New York: Garland.

Lane, M. A., Black, A., Handy, A., Tilmont, E. M., Ingram, D. K., & Roth, G. S. (2001). Caloric restriction in primates. In S. C. Park, E. S. Hwang, H. Kim, & W. Park (Eds.), *Annals of the New York Academy of Sciences: Vol. 928. Molecular and cellular interactions in senescence.* New York: The New York Academy of Sciences.

Lang, F. R., & Carstensen, L. L. (1994). Close emotional relationships in late life: Further support for proactive aging in the social domain. *Psychology and Aging, 9,* 315–324.

Lang, F. R., & Carstensen, L. L. (2002). Time counts: Future time perspective, goals, and social relationships. *Psychology and Aging, 17,* 125–139.

Lange, G., & Pierce, S. H. (1992). Memory-strategy learning and maintenance in preschool children. *Developmental Psychology, 28,* 453–462.

Langley-Evans, A. J., & Langley-Evans, S. C. (2003). Relationship between maternal nutrient intakes in early and late pregnancy and infants' weight and proportions at birth: Prospective cohort study. *Journal of Research in Social Health, 123,* 210–216.

Langlois, J. A., Keyl, P. M., Guralnik, J. M., Foley, D. J., Marottoli, R. A., & Wallace, R. B. (1997). Characteristics of older pedestrians who have difficulty crossing the street. *American Journal of Public Health, 87,* 393–397.

Lansford, J. E., Sherman, A. M., & Antonucci, T. C. (1998). Satisfaction with social networks: An examination of socioemotional selectivity theory across cohorts. *Psychology and Aging, 13,* 544–552.

Lanza, S. T., & Collins, L. M. (2002). Pubertal timing and the onset of substance use in females during early adolescence, *Prevention Science, 3,* 69–82.

Lapsley, D. K. (1996). *Moral psychology.* Boulder, CO: Westview.

Lapsley, D. K., Harwell, M. R., Olson, L. M., Flannery, D., & Quintana, S. M. (1984). Moral judgment, personality, and attitude toward authority in early and late adolescence. *Journal of Youth and Adolescence, 13,* 527–542.

Lapsley, D. K., Milstead, M., Quintana, S. M., Flannery, D., & Buss, R. R. (1986). Adolescent egocentrism and formal operations: Tests of a theoretical assumption. *Developmental Psychology, 22,* 800–807.

Lapsley, D. K., Rice, K. G., & FitzGerald, D. P. (1990). Adolescent attachment, identity, and adjustment to college: Implications for the continuity of adaptation hypothesis. *Journal of Counseling and Development, 68,* 561–565.

Larson, R. W., Richards, M. H., Moneta, G., Holmbeck, G., & Duckett, E. (1996). Changes in adolescents' daily interactions with their families from ages 10 to 18: Disengagement and transformation. *Developmental Psychology, 32,* 744–753.

Larson, R. W., & Verma, S. (1999). How children and adolescents spend time across the world: Work, play, and developmental opportunities. *Psychological Bulletin, 125,* 701–736.

Larsson, I. & Svedin, C. (2002). Sexual experiences in childhood: Young adults' recollections. *Archives of Sexual Behavior, 31,* 263-273.

Laumann, E. O., Gagnon, J. H., Michael, R. T., & Michaels, S. (1994). *The social organization of* sexuality: Sexual practices in the United States.* Chicago: University of Chicago Press.

Laumann, E. O., Paik, A., & Rosen, R. C. (1999). Sexual dysfunction in the United States: Prevalence and predictors. *Journal of the American Medical Association, 281,* 537–544.

Laurendeau-Bendavid, M. (1977). Culture, schooling, and cognitive development: A comparative study of children in French Canada and Rwanda. In P. R. Dasen (Ed.), *Piagetian psychology: Cross-cultural contributions* (pp. 123–168). New York: Gardner Press.

Laursen, B., & Williams, V. (2002). The role of ethnic identity in personality development. In L. Pulkkinen & A. Caspi (Eds.), *Paths to successful development. Personality in the life course.* Cambridge, UK: Cambridge University Press.

Lavan, H., & Johnson, J. G. (2002). The association between Axis I and II psychiatric symptoms and high-risk sexual behavior during adolescence. *Journal of Personality Disorders, 16,* 73–94.

Lavigne, J. V., Arend, R., Rosenbaum, D., Smith, A., Weissbluth, M., Binns, H. J., & Christoffel, K. K. (1999). Sleep and behavior problems among preschoolers. *Journal of Developmental and Behavioral Pediatrics, 20,* 164–169.

Law, K. L., Stroud, L. R., LaGasse, L. L., Niaura, R., Liu, J., & Lester, B. M. (2003). Smoking during pregnancy and newborn neurobehavior. *Pediatrics, 111,* 1318–1323.

Lawson, J., Baron-Cohen, S., & Wheelwright, S. (2004). Empathizing and systemizing in adults with and without Asperger syndrome. *Journal of Autism and Developmental Disorders, 34,* 301–310.

Lawton, M. P., Moss, M. S., Winter, L., & Hoffman, C. (2002). Motivation in later life: Personal projects and well-being. *Psychology and Aging, 17,* 539–547.

Lazar, I., & Darlington, R. (1982). Lasting effects of early education: A report from the Consortium for Longitudinal Studies. *Monographs of the Society for Research in Child Development, 47* (2–3, Serial No. 195).

Leahy, J. M. (1992–1993). A comparison of depression in women bereaved of a spouse, child, or a parent. *Omega: Journal of Death and Dying, 26,* 207–217.

Leaper, C. (1994). *Childhood gender segregation: Causes and consequences* (New Directions for Child Development, Vol. 65). San Francisco: Jossey-Bass.

Lee, C., Klopp, R. G., Weindruch, R., & Prolla, T. A. (1999). Gene expression profile of aging and its retardation by caloric restriction. *Science, 285,* 1390–1393.

Lee, S., Colditz, G., Berkman, L., & Kawachi, I. (2003). Caregiving to children and grandchildren and risk of coronary heart disease in women. *American Journal of Public Health, 93,* 1939–1944.

Lee, V. E., & Bryk, A. S. (1986). Effects of single-sex secondary schools on student achievement and attitudes. *Journal of Educational Psychology, 78,* 381–395.

Lee, V. E., Marks, H. M., & Byrd, T. (1994). Sexism in single-sex and coeducational independent secondary school classrooms. *Sociology of Education, 67,* 92–120.

Leeder, E. J. (2004). *The family in global perspective. A gendered journey.* Thousand Oaks, CA: Sage.

Lehman, D. R., Ellard, J. H., & Wortman, C. B. (1986). Social support for the bereaved: Recipients' and providers' perspectives on what is helpful. *Journal of Consulting and Clinical Psychology, 54,* 438–446.

Lehman, D. R., Wortman, C. B., & Williams, A. F. (1987). Long-term effects of losing a spouse or child in a motor vehicle crash. *Journal of Personality and Social Psychology, 52,* 218–231.

Lehman, H. C. (1953). *Age and achievement.* Princeton, NJ: Princeton University Press.

Leichtman, M. D., & Ceci, S. J. (1993). The problem of infantile amnesia: Lessons from fuzzy-trace theory. In M. L. Howe & R. Pasnak (Eds.), *Emerging themes in cognitive development: Vol. 1. Foundations.* New York: Springer-Verlag.

Leifer, B. P. (2003). Early diagnosis of Alzheimer's disease: clinical and economic benefits. *Journal of the American Geriatrics Society, 51,* S281–S288.

Lejarraga, H. (2002). Growth in infancy and childhood: A pediatric approach. In N. Cameron (Ed.), *Human growth and development* (pp. 21–44). New York: Academic Press.

Lemann, N. (1997, November). The reading wars. *Atlantic Monthly,* 128–134.

LeMare, L. J., & Rubin, K. H. (1987). Perspective taking and peer interaction: Structural and developmental analyses. *Child Development, 58,* 306–315.

Lemerise, E. A., & Arsenio, W. F. (2000). An integrated model of emotion processes and cognition in social information processing. *Child Development, 71,* 107–118.

Lempers, J. D., & Clark-Lempers, D. S. (1992). Young, middle and late adolescents' comparisons of the functional importance of five significant relationships. *Journal of Youth and Adolescence, 21,* 53–96.

Lenhart, J. (1999, September 7). Young Mr. Smith goes to college. *The Washington Post,* A1, A10.

Lenneberg, E. H. (1967). *Biological foundations of language.* New York: Wiley.

Leon, G. R., Gillum, B., Gillum, R., & Gouze, M. (1979). Personality stability and change over a 30-year period–middle age to old age. *Journal of Consulting and Clinical Psychology, 47,* 517–524.

Leonard, K. E., & Das Eiden, R. (2002). Cognitive functioning among infants of alcoholic fathers. *Drug and Alcohol Dependence, 67,* 139–147.

LePore, P. C., & Warren, J. R. (1997). A comparison of single-sex and coeducational Catholic secondary schooling: Evidence from the National Educational Longitudinal Study of 1988. *American Educational Research Journal, 34,* 485–511.

Lerner, J. V., & Noh, E. R. (2000). Maternal employment influences on early adolescent development: A contextual view. In R. D. Taylor & M. C. Wang (Eds.), *Resilience across contexts: Family, work, culture, and community.* Mahwah, NJ: Erlbaum.

Lerner, M. J., Somers, D. G., Reid, D., Chiriboga, D., & Tierney, M. (1991). Adult children as caregivers: Egocentric biases in judgments of sibling contributions. *Gerontologist, 31,* 746–755.

Lerner, R. M. (2003). What are SES effects effects of?: A developmental systems perspective. In M. H. Bornstein & R. H. Bradley (Eds.), *Socioeconomic status, parenting, and child development.* Mahwah, NJ: Erlbaum.

Lerner, R. M., & Kauffman, M. B. (1985). The concept of development in contextualism. *Developmental Review, 5,* 309–333.

Lesher, E. L., & Bergey, K. J. (1988). Bereaved elderly mothers: Changes in health, functional activities, family cohesion, and psychological well-being. *International Journal of Aging and Human Development, 26,* 81–90.

Leslie, A. M. (1994). ToMM, ToBy, and agency: Core architecture and domain specificity in cognition and culture. In L. Hirschfeld & S. Gelman (Eds.), *Mapping the mind: Domain specificity in cognition and culture.* New York: Cambridge University Press.

Lester, B. M., Kotelchuck, M., Spelke, E., Sellers, M. J., & Klein, R. E. (1974). Separation protest in Guatemalan infants: Cross-cultural and cognitive findings. *Developmental Psychology, 10,* 79–85.

Lester, D. (1994). Are there unique features of suicide in adults of different ages and developmental stages. *Omega: Journal of Death and Dying, 29,* 337–348.

Leung, A. K. C., & Robson, W. L. M. (1993). Childhood masturbation. *Clinical Pediatrics, 32,* 238–241.

LeVay, S. (1996). *Queer science: The use and abuse of research into homosexuality.* Cambridge, MA: MIT Press.

Leve, L. D., & Fagot, B. I. (1997). Gender-role socialization and discipline processes in one- and two-parent families. *Sex Roles, 36,* 1–21.

Levenkron, S. (2000). *Anatomy of anorexia.* New York: W. W. Norton.

Leventhal, T., & Brooks-Gunn, J. (2003). Moving on up: Neighborhood effects on children and families. In M. H. Bornstein & R. H. Bradley (Eds.), *Socioeconomic status, parenting, and child development.* Mahwah, NJ: Erlbaum.

Levinson, D. (1989). *Family violence in cross-cultural perspective.* Newbury Park, CA: Sage.

Levinson, D. J. (1986). A conception of adult development. *American Psychologist, 41,* 3–13.

Levinson, D. J. (in collaboration with J. D. Levinson) (1996). *The seasons of a woman's life.* New York: Alfred A. Knopf.

Levinson, D. J., Darrow, C. N., Klein, E. B., Levinson, M. H., & McKee, B. (1978). *The seasons of a man's life.* New York: Ballantine Books.

Levitt, M. J. (1991). Attachment and close relationships: A life-span perspective. In J. L. Gewirtz & W. M. Kurtines (Eds.), *Intersections with attachment.* Hillsdale, NJ: Erlbaum.

Levitt, M. J., Weber, R. A., & Guacci, N. (1993). Convoys of social support: An intergenerational analysis. *Psychology and Aging, 8,* 323–326.

Levy, B. (1996). Improving memory in old age through implicit self-stereotyping. *Journal of Personality and Social Psychology, 71,* 1092–1107.

Levy, B., & Langer, E. (1994). Aging free from negative stereotypes: Successful memory in China and among the American deaf. *Journal of Personality and Social Psychology, 66,* 989–997.

Levy, B. R. (2003). Mind matters: Cognitive and physical effects of aging self-stereotypes. *Journals of Gerontology: Psychological Sciences & Social Sciences, 58,* 203–211.

Levy, B. R., Slade, M. D., & Kasl, S. V. (2002). Longitudinal benefit of positive self-perceptions of aging on functional health. *Journals of Gerontology: Psychological Sciences and Social Sciences, 57,* 409–417.

Levy, G. D. (1999). Gender-typed and non-gender-typed category awareness in toddlers. *Sex Roles, 41,* 851–873.

Levy, G. D., Sadovsky, A. L., & Troseth, G. L. (2000). Aspects of young children's perceptions of gender-typed occupations. *Sex Roles, 42,* 993–1006.

Levy-Shiff, R. (1994). Individual and contextual correlates of marital change across the transition to parenthood. *Developmental Psychology, 30,* 591–601.

Lewandowsky, S., & Kirsner, K. (2000). Knowledge partitioning: Context-dependent use of expertise. *Memory & Cognition, 28,* 295–305.

Lewis, B. A., & Thompson, L. A. (1992). A study of developmental speech and language disorders in twins. *Journal of Speech and Hearing Research, 35,* 1086–1094.

Lewis, D. A., Sesack, S. R., Levey, A. I., & Rosenberg, D. R. (1998). Dopamine axons in primate prefrontal cortex: Specificity of distribution, synaptic targets, and development. *Advances in Pharmacology, 42,* 703–706.

Lewis, M. (2000). The emergence of human emotions. In M. Lewis & J. M. Haviland-Jones (Eds.), *Handbook of emotions* (2nd ed.). New York: Guilford.

Lewis, M., Alessandri, S. M., & Sullivan, M. W. (1990). Violation of expectancy, loss of control, and anger expressions in young infants. *Developmental Psychology, 26,* 745–751.

Lewis, M., & Brooks-Gunn, J. (1979). *Social cognition and the acquisition of self.* New York: Plenum.

Lewis, M., & Rosenblum, M. A. (1975). *Friendship and peer relations.* New York: Wiley.

Lewis, M., Sullivan, M. W., Stanger, C., & Weiss, M. (1989). Self-development and self-conscious emotions. *Child Development, 60,* 146–156.

Lewis, M., & Weinraub, M. (1979). Origins of early sex-role development. *Sex Roles, 5,* 135–153.

Lewis, P. G., & Lippman, J. G. (2004). *Helping children cope with the death of a parent. A guide for the first year.* Westport, CT: Praeger.

Lewontin, R. C. (1976). Race and intelligence. In N. J. Block & G. Dworkin (Eds.), *The IQ controversy.* New York: Pantheon.

Lewontin, R. C., Rose, S., & Kamin, L. J. (1984). *Not in our genes.* New York: Pantheon.

Leyendecker, B., & Lamb, M. E. (1999). Latino families. In M. E. Lamb (Ed.), *Parenting and child development in "nontraditional" families.* Mahwah, NJ: Erlbaum.

Li, D., Liu, L., & Odouli, R. (2003). Exposure to non-steroidal anti-inflammatory drugs during pregnancy and risk of miscarriage: Population based cohort study. *British Medical Journal, 327,* 368.

Li, K. Z. H., Lindenberger, U., Freund, A. M., & Baltes, P. B. (2001). Walking while memorizing: Age-related differences in compensatory behavior. *Psychological Science, 12,* 230–237.

Li, L. W., Seltzer, M. M., & Greenberg, J. S. (1999). Change in depressive symptoms among daughter caregivers: An 18-month longitudinal study, *Psychology and Aging, 14,* 206–219.

Li, S. (2003). Biocultural orchestration of developmental plasticity across levels: The interplay of biology and culture in shaping the mind and behavior across the life span. *Psychological Bulletin, 129,* 171–194.

Liben, L. S., & Signorella, M. L. (1993). Gender-schematic processing in children: The role of initial interpretations of stimuli. *Developmental Psychology, 29,* 141–149.

Lickliter, R., & Honeycutt, H. (2003). Developmental dynamics: Toward a biologically plausible evolutionary psychology. *Psychological Bulletin, 129,* 819–835.

Lidz, C. S. (1997). Dynamic assessment approaches. In D. P. Flanagan, J. Genshaft, & P. L. Harrison (Eds.), *Contemporary intellectual assessment: Theories, tests, and issues.* New York: Guilford.

Lidz, C. S., & Elliott, J. G. (Eds.). (2001). *Dynamic assessment: Prevailing models and applications.* Amsterdam: JAI/Elsevier Science.

Lidz, J., Waxman, S., & Freedman, J. (2003). What infants know about syntax but couldn't have learned: Experimental evidence for syntactic structure at 18 months. *Cognition, 89,* B65–B73.

Lie, E., & Newcombe, N. S. (1999). Elementary school children's explicit and implicit memory for faces of preschool classmates. *Developmental Psychology, 35,* 102–112.

Lieberman, A. F., Compton, N. C., Van Horn, P., & Ippen, C. G. (2003). *Losing a parent to death in the early years. Guidelines for the treatment of traumatic bereavement in infancy and early childhood.* Washington, D.C.: Zero to Three Press.

Lieberman, M. A., & Videka-Sherman, L. (1986). The impact of self-help groups on the mental health of widows and widowers. *American Journal of Orthopsychiatry, 56,* 435–449.

Lieven, E. V. M. (1994). Crosslinguistic and crosscultural aspects of language addressed to children. In C. Gallaway & B. J. Richards (Eds.), *Input and interaction in language acquisition.* Cambridge, England: Cambridge University Press.

Light, L. L. (1991). Memory and aging: Four hypotheses in search of data. *Annual Review of Psychology, 42,* 333–376.

Light, L. L., & LaVoie, D. (1993). Direct and indirect measures of memory in old age. In P. Graf & M. E. J. Masson (Eds.), *Implicit Memory: New Directions in Cognition, Development and Neuropsychology* (pp. 207–230). Hillsdale, NJ: Erlbaum.

Lillard, A. (1998). Ethno-psychologies: Cultural variations in theories of mind. *Psychological Bulletin, 123,* 3–32.

Lillard, A. (2001). Pretend play as twin earth: A social-cognitive analysis. *Developmental Review, 21,* 495–531.

Lillard, L. A., & Panis, C. W. A. (1996). Marital status and mortality: The role of health. *Demography, 33,* 313–327.

Lima, S. D., Hale, S., & Myerson, J. (1991). How general is general slowing? Evidence from the lexical domain. *Psychology and Aging, 6,* 416–425.

Lindegren, M. L., Byers, R. H., Thomas, P., Davis, S. F., Caldwell, B., Rogers, M., Gwinn, M., Ward, J. W., & Fleming, P. L. (1999). Trends in perinatal transmission of HIV/AIDS in the United States. *Journal of the American Medical Association, 282,* 531–538.

Lindenberger, U., & Baltes, P. B. (1994). Sensory functioning and intelligence in old age: A strong connection. *Psychology and Aging, 9,* 339–355.

Lindenberger, U., Marsiske, M., & Baltes, P. B. (2000). Memorizing while walking: Increase in dual-task costs from young adulthood to old age. *Psychology and Aging, 15,* 417–436.

Lindsey, E. W., & Mize, J. (2000). Parent–child physical and pretense play: Links to children's social competence. *Merrill-Palmer Quarterly, 46,* 565–591.

Linnet, K. M., Dalsgaard, S., Obel, C., Wisborg, K., Henriksen, T. B., Rodriguez, A., Kotimaa, A., Moilanen, I., Thomsen, P. H., Olsen, J., & Jarvelin, M. R. (2003). Maternal lifestyle factors in pregnancy risk of attention deficit hyperactivity disorder and associated behaviors: Review of the current evidence. *American Journal of Psychiatry, 160,* 1028–1040.

Lipsey, M. W., & Wilson, D. B. (2001). *Practical meta-analysis.* Thousand Oaks, CA: Sage.

Lipsitt, L. P. (1990). Learning processes in the human newborn: Sensitization, habituation and classical conditioning. *Annals of the New York Academy of Sciences, 608,* 113–127.

Lipton, A. M., & Weiner, M. F. (2003). Differential diagnosis. In M. F. Weiner & A. M. Lipton (Eds.), *The dementias. Diagnosis, treatment, and research.* Washington, D.C.: American Psychiatric Publishing.

Lipton, J. S., & Spelke, E. S. (2003). Origins of number sense. Large-number discrimination in human infants. *Psychological Science, 14,* 396–401.

Litwak, E. (1960). Geographic mobility and extended family cohesion. *American Sociological Review, 25,* 385–394.

Liu, C. (2003). Does quality of marital sex decline with duration? *Archives of Sexual Behavior, 32,* 55–60.

Livesley, W. J., & Bromley, D. B. (1973). *Person perception in childhood and adolescence.* London: Wiley.

Livson, F. B. (1976). Patterns of personality in middle-aged women: A longitudinal study. *International Journal of Aging and Human Development, 7,* 107–115.

Livson, F. B. (1981). Paths to psychological health in the middle years: Sex differences. In D. H. Eichorn, J. A. Clausen, N. Haan, M. P. Honzik, & P. H. Mussen (Eds.), *Present and past in middle life.* New York: Academic Press.

Lobel, M., DeVincent, C. J., Kaminer, A., & Meyer, B. A. (2000). The impact of prenatal maternal stress and optimistic disposition on birth outcomes in medically high-risk women. *Health Psychology, 19,* 544–553.

Lobel, T., Slone, M., & Winch, G. (1997). Masculinity, popularity, and self-esteem among Israeli preadolescent girls. *Sex Roles, 36,* 395–408.

Lock, A. (2004). Preverbal communication. In G. Bremner & A. Fogel (Eds.), *Blackwell handbook of infant development* (pp. 379–403). Malden, MA: Blackwell Publishing.

Lock, M. (1993). Encounters with aging: Mythologies of menopause in Japan and North America. Berkeley: University of California Press.

Locke, J. (1939). An essay concerning human understanding. In E. A. Burtt (Ed.), *The English philosophers from Bacon to Mill.* New York: Modern Library. (Original work published 1690).

Locke, J. L. (1997). A theory of neurolinguistic development. *Brain and Language, 58,* 265–326.

Lockhart, K. L., Chang, B., & Story, T. (2002). Young children's beliefs about the stability of traits: Protective optimism? *Child Development, 73,* 1408–1430.

Lockheed, M. E. (1986). Reshaping the social order: The case of gender segregation. *Sex Roles, 14,* 617–628.

Loeber, R., & Farrington, D. P. (2000). Young children who commit crime: Epidemiology, developmental origins, risk factors, early interventions, and policy implications. *Development and Psychopathology, 12,* 737–762.

Loehlin, J. C. (1985). Fitting heredity–environment models jointly to twin and adoption data from the California Psychological Inventory. *Behavior Genetics, 15,* 199–221.

Loehlin, J. C. (1992). *Genes and environment in personality development (Individual differences and development series, Vol. 2).* Newbury Park, CA: Sage.

Loehlin, J. C., Horn, J. M., & Willerman, L. (1997). Heredity, environment, and IQ in the Texas Adoption Project. In R. J. Sternberg & E. L. Grigorenko (Eds.), *Intelligence, heredity, and environment.* New York: Cambridge University Press.

Loehlin, J. C., McCrae, R. R., Costa, P. T., Jr., & John, O. P. (1998). Heritabilities of common and measure-specific components of the Big Five personality factors. *Journal of Research in Personality, 32,* 431–453.

Loewenstein, G., & Furstenberg, F. (1991). Is teenage sexual behavior rational? *Journal of Applied Social Psychology, 21,* 957–986.

Lohan, J. A., & Murphy, S. A. (2001–2002). Parents' perceptions of adolescent sibling grief responses after an adolescent or young adult child's sudden, violent death. *Omega: Journal of Death and Dying, 44,* 77–95.

Lohnes, K. L., & Kalter, N. (1994). Preventive intervention groups for parentally bereaved children. *American Journal of Orthopsychiatry, 64,* 594–603.

Lollis, S., Ross, H., & Leroux, L. (1996). An observational study of parents' socialization of moral orientation during sibling conflicts. *Merrill-Palmer Quarterly, 42,* 475–494.

Lonigan, C. J., Burgess, S. R., & Anthony, J. L. (2000). Development of emergent literacy and early reading skills in preschool children: Evidence from a latent-variable longitudinal study. *Developmental Psychology, 36(5),* 596–613.

Loovis, E. M., & Butterfield, S. A. (2000). Influence of age, sex, and balance on mature skipping by children in grades K–8. *Perceptual and Motor Skills, 90,* 974–978.

Lopata, H. Z. (1996). *Current widowhood: Myths and realities.* Thousand Oaks, CA: Sage.

Lopez, E. C. (1997). The cognitive assessment of limited English proficient and bilingual children. In D. P. Flanagan, J. Genshaft, & P. L. Harrison (Eds.), *Contemporary intellectual assessment: Theories, tests, and issues.* New York: Guilford.

Lopez, S. R., & Guarnaccia, P. J. J. (2000). Cultural psychopathology: Uncovering the social world of mental illness. *Annual Review of Psychology, 51,* 571–598.

Lorenz, J. M. (2000). Survival of the extremely preterm infant in North America in the 1990s. *Clinics in Perinatrology, 27,* 255–262.

Lorenz, K. Z. (1937). The companion in the bird's world. *Auk, 54,* 245–273.

Lorsbach, T. C., & Reimer, J. F. (1997). Developmental changes in the inhibition of previously relevant information. *Journal of Experimental Child Psychology, 64,* 317–342.

Lourenco, O., & Machado, A. (1996). In defense of Piaget's theory: A reply to 10 common criticisms. *Psychological Review, 103,* 143–164.

Lovaas, O. I. (1987). Behavioral treatment and normal educational and intellectual functioning in young autistic children. *Journal of Consulting and Clinical Psychology, 55,* 3–9.

Lovaas, O. I., & Smith, T. (2003). Early and intensive behavioral intervention in autism. In A. E. Kazdin & J. R. Weisz (Eds.), *Evidence-based psychotherapies for children and adolescents.* New York: Guilford.

Lovaas, O. I., Smith, T., & McEachin, J. J. (1989). Clarifying comments on the young autism study: Reply to Schopler, Short, and Mesibov. *Journal of Consulting and Clinical Psychology, 57,* 165–167.

Love, J. M., Harrison, L., Sagi-Schwartz, A., van IJzendoorn, M. H., Ross, C., Ungerer, J. A., Raikes, H., Brady-Smith, C., Boller, K., Brooks-Gunn, J., Constantine, J., Kisker, E. E., Paulsell, D., & Chazan-Cohen, R. (2003). Child care quality matters: How conclusions may vary with context. *Child Development, 74,* 1021–1033.

Luby, J. L. (2004). Affective disorders. In R. DelCarmen-Wiggins & A. Carter (Eds.), *Handbook of infant, toddler, and preschool mental health assessment.* New York: Oxford University Press.

Lueptow, L. B., Garovich-Szabo, L., & Lueptow, M. B. (2001). Social change and the persistence of sex typing: 1974–1997. *Social Forces, 80,* 1–36.

Luk, S. L. (1996). Cross-cultural aspects. In S. Sandberg (Ed.), *Hyperactivity disorders of childhood.* Cambridge, England: Cambridge University Press.

Lund, D. A., Dimond, M. F., Caserta, M. S., Johnson, R. J., Poulton, J. L., & Connelly, J. R. (1985–1986). Identifying elderly with coping difficulties after two years of bereavement. *Omega: Journal of Death and Dying, 16,* 213–224.

Lundy, B. L., Jones, N. A., Field, T., Nearing, G., Davalos, M., Pietro, P. A., Schanberg, S., & Kuhn, C. (1999). Prenatal depression effects on neonates. *Infant Behavior and Development, 22,* 119–129.

Luo, Y., Baillargeon, R., Brueckner, L., & Munakata, Y. (2003). Reasoning about a hidden object after a delay: Evidence for robust representations in 5-month-old infants. *Cognition, 88,* B23–B32.

Luria, A. (1987). *The Mind of a mnemonist.* MA: Harvard University Press.

Luster, T., & McAdoo, H. P. (1995). Factors related to self-esteem among African American youths: A secondary analysis of the High/Scope Perry Preschool data. *Journal of Research on Adolescence, 5,* 451–467.

Lustig, J. L., Wolchik, S. A., & Braver, S. L. (1992). Social support in chumships and adjustment in children of divorce. *American Journal of Community Psychology, 20,* 393–399.

Luszcz, M. A., Bryan, J., & Kent, P. (1997). Predicting episodic memory performance of very old men and women: Contributions from age, depression, activity, cognitive ability, and speed. *Psychology and Aging, 12,* 340–351.

Ly, D. H., Lockhart, D. J., Lerner, R. A., & Schultz, P. G. (2000). Mitotic misregulation and human aging. *Science, 287,* 2486–2492.

Lykken, D. T., Tellegen, A., & Iacono, W. G. (1982). EEG spectra in twins: Evidence for a neglected mechanism of genetic determination. *Physiological Psychology, 10,* 60–65.

Lyman, S., Ferguson, S. A., Braver, E. R. , & Williams, A. F. (2002). Older driver involvements in police reported crashes and fatal crashes: Trends and projections. *Injury Prevention, 8,* 116–120.

Lynch, M. P., Eilers, R. E., Oller, D. K., & Urbano, R. C. (1990). Innateness, experience, and music perception. *Psychological Science, 1,* 272–276.

Lynch, S. M., & George, L. K. (2002). Interlocking trajectories of loss-related events and depressive symptoms among elders. *Journal of Gerontology: Social Sciences, 57B,* S117–S125.

Lyonette, C., & Yardley, L. (2003). The influence on carer wellbeing of motivations to care for older people and the relationship with the care recipient. *Ageing & Society, 23,* 487–506.

Lyons-Ruth, K., Melnick, S., Bronfman, E., Sherry, S., & Llanas, L. (2004). Hostile-helpless relational models and disorganized attachment patterns between parents and their young children: Review of research and implications for clinical work. In L. Atkinson & S. Goldberg (Eds.), *Attachment issues in psychopathology and intervention.* Mahwah, NJ, Erlbaum.

Lyons-Ruth, K., Zeanah, C. H., & Benoit, D. (2003). Disorder and risk for disorder during infancy and toddlerhood. In E. J. Mash & R. A. Barkley (Eds.), *Child psychopathology* (2nd ed.). New York: Guilford Press.

Lytton, H. (1990). Child and parent effects in boys' conduct disorder: A reinterpretation. *Developmental Psychology, 26,* 683–697.

Lytton, H. (2000). Toward a model of family–environmental and child–biological influences on development. *Developmental Review, 20,* 150–179.

Lytton, H., & Romney, D. M. (1991). Parents' differential socialization of boys and girls: A meta-analysis. *Psychological Bulletin, 109,* 267–296.

M

Macario, A., Scibetta, W. C., Navarro, J., & Riley, E. (2000). Analgesia for labor pain: A cost model. *Anesthesiology, 92,* 643–645.

Maccoby, E. E. (1980). *Social development.* New York: Harcourt Brace Jovanovich.

Maccoby, E. E. (1998). *The two sexes: Growing up apart, coming together.* Cambridge, MA: Harvard University Press.

Maccoby, E. E. (2000). Parenting and its effects on children: On reading and misreading behavior genetics. *Annual Review of Psychology, 51,* 1–28.

Maccoby, E. E., & Jacklin, C. N. (1974). *The psychology of sex differences.* Stanford, CA: Stanford University Press.

Maccoby, E. E., & Jacklin, C. N. (1987). Gender segregation in childhood. In H. W. Reese (Ed.), *Advances in Child Development and Behavior* (Vol. 20). Orlando, FL: Academic Press.

Maccoby, E. E., & Martin, J. A. (1983). Socialization in the context of the family: Parent–child interaction. In E. M. Hetherington (Vol. Ed.), P. H. Mussen (Editor-in-Chief), *Handbook of child psychology: Vol. 4. Socialization, personality, and social development* (4th ed.). New York: Wiley.

MacDonald, C. D., & Cohen, R. (1995). Children's awareness of which peers like them and which peers dislike them. *Social Development, 4,* 182–193.

Mac Iver, D. J. & Reuman, D. A. (1988, April). *Decision-making in the classroom and early adolescents' valuing of mathematics.* Paper presented at the annual meeting of the American Educational Research Association, New Orleans.

Mac Iver, D. J., Reuman, D. A., & Main, S. R. (1995). Social structuring of the school: Studying what is, illuminating what could be. *Annual Review of Psychology, 46,* 375–400.

Mackey, R. A., & O'Brien, B. A. (1995). *Lasting marriages: Men and women growing together.* Westport, CT: Praeger.

MacLean, K. (2003). The impact of institutionalization on child development. *Development and Psychopathology, 15,* 853–884.

Macmillan, M. (1991). *Freud evaluated: The completed arc.* New York: Elsevier.

MacPhee, D., Fritz, J., & Miller-Heyl, J. (1996). Ethnic variations in personal social networks and parenting. *Child Development, 67,* 3278–3295.

MacPherson, S. E., Phillips, L. H., & Della Sala, S. (2002). Age, executive function and social decision making: A dorsolateral prefrontal theory of cognitive aging. *Psychology and Aging, 17,* 598–609.

Madden, D. J., Gottlob, L. R., & Allen, P. A. (1999). Adult age differences in visual search accuracy: Attentional guidance and target detectability. *Psychology and Aging, 14,* 683–694.

Madden, D. J., & Langley, L. K. (2003). Age-related changes in selective attention and perceptual load during visual search. *Psychology and Aging, 18,* 54–67.

Maddux, J. E. (2002). Self-efficacy: The power of believing you can. In C. R. Snyder & S. J. Lopez (Eds.), *Handbook of positive psychology* (pp. 277–287). New York: Oxford University Press.

Maehr, M., & Meyer, H. (1997). Understanding motivation and schooling: Where we've been, where we are, and where we need to go. *Educational Psychology Review, 9,* 371–409.

Maestripieri, D. (2001). Is there mother–infant bonding in primates? *Developmental Review, 21,* 93–120.

Magai, C., Cohen, C., Milburn, N., Thorpe, B., McPherson, R., & Peralta, D. (2001). Attachment styles in older European American and African American adults. *Journals of Gerontology: Psychological Sciences and Social Sciences, 56,* S28–S35.

Magnus, K., Diener, E., Fujita, F., & Payot, W. (1993). Extraversion and neuroticism as predictors of objective life events: A longitudinal analysis. *Journal of Personality and Social Psychology, 65,* 1046–1053.

Magnusson, D. (1995). Individual development: A holistic, integrated model. In P. Moen, & G. H. Elder Jr. (Eds.), *Examining lives in context: Perspectives on the ecology of human development.* Washington, D. C.: American Psychological Association.

Mahaffy, K. A., & Ward, S. K. (2002). The gendering of adolescents' childbearing and educational plans: Reciprocal effects and the influence of social context. *Sex Roles, 46,* 403–417.

Mahler, M. S., Pine, F., & Bergman, A. (1975). *The psychological birth of the infant.* New York: Basic Books.

Maiden, R. J., Peterson, S. A., Caya, M., & Hayslip, B. (2003). Personality changes in the old-old: A longitudinal study. *Journal of Adult Development, 10,* 31–39.

Maier, E. H., & Lachman, M. E. (2000). Consequences of early parental loss and separation for health and well-being in midlife. *International Journal of Behavioral Development, 24,* 183–189.

Main, M., & George, C. (1985). Responses of abused and disadvantaged toddlers to distress in agemates: A study in the day-care setting. *Developmental Psychology, 21,* 407–412.

Main, M., Kaplan, N., & Cassidy, J. (1985). Security in infancy, childhood, and adulthood: A move to the level of representation. In I. Bretherton & E. Waters (Eds.), Growing points in attachment theory and research. *Monographs of the Society for Research in Child Development, 50* (1–2, Serial No. 209), 66–106.

Main, M., & Solomon, J. (1990). Procedures for identifying infants as disorganized/disoriented during the Ainsworth Strange Situation. In M. T. Greenberg, D. Cicchetti, & E. M. Cummings (Eds.), *Attachment in the preschool years: Theory, research, and intervention.* Chicago: University of Chicago Press.

Main, M., & Weston, D. R. (1981). The quality of the toddler's relationship to mother and to father: Related to conflict and the readiness to establish new relationships. *Child Development, 52,* 932–940.

Maki, P. M., Zonderman, A. B., & Weingartner, H. (1999). Age differences in implicit memory, fragmented object identification, and category exemplar generation. *Psychology and Aging, 14,* 184–194.

Malatesta, C. Z., & Culver, L. C. (1984). Thematic and affective content in the lives of adult women. In C. Z. Malatesta & C. E. Izard (Eds.), *Emotion in adult development.* Beverly Hills, CA: Sage.

Malatesta, C. Z., Culver, C., Tesman, J. R., & Shepard, B. (1989). The development of emotion expression during the first two years of life. *Monographs of the Society for Research in Child Development, 54* (1–2, Serial No. 219).

Malatesta, C. Z., Grigoryev, P., Lamb, C., Albin, M., & Culver, C. (1986). Emotional socialization and expressive development in preterm and full-term infants. *Child Development, 57,* 316–330.

Malik, N. M., & Furman, W. (1993). Practitioner review: Problems in children's peer relations: What can the clinician do? *Journal of Child Psychology and Psychiatry, 34,* 1303–1326.

Malina, R. M., & Bouchard, C. (1991). *Growth, maturation, and physical activity.* Champaign, IL: Human Kinetics Academic.

Malinosky-Rummell, R., & Hansen, D. J. (1993). Long-term consequences of childhood physical abuse. *Psychological Bulletin, 114,* 68–79.

Malley-Morrison, K., & Hines, D. A. (2004). *Family violence in a cultural perspective. Defining, understanding, and combating abuse.* Thousand Oaks, CA: Sage.

Malmstrom, M., Sundquist, J., Bajekal, M., & Johansson, S. E. (1999). Ten-year trends in all-cause mortality and coronary heart disease mortality in socioeconomically diverse neighbourhoods. *Public Health, 113,* 279–284.

Mandoki, M. W., Sumner, G. S., Hoffman, R. P., & Riconda, D. L. (1991). A review of Klinefelter's syndrome in children and adolescents. *Journal of the American Academy of Child and Adolescent Psychiatry, 30,* 167–172.

Mangelsdorf, S. C. (1992). Developmental changes in infant-stranger interaction. *Infant Behavior and Development, 15,* 191–208.

Mangelsdorf, S. C., Gunnar, M., Kestenbaum, R., Lang, S., & Andreas, D. (1990). Infant proneness-to-distress temperament, maternal personality, and mother–infant attachment: Associations and goodness of fit. *Child Development, 61,* 820–831.

Mangelsdorf, S. C., Shapiro, J. R., & Marzolf, D. (1995). Developmental and temperamental differences in emotion regulation in infancy. *Child Development, 66,* 1817–1828.

Manset, G., & Semmel, M. I. (1997). Are inclusive programs for students with mild disabilities effective? A comparative review of model programs. *Journal of Special Education, 31,* 155–180.

Maraniss, D., Hull, A., & Schwartzman, P. (2001, September 30). The days after. *The Washington Post,* A1, A18.

Maratsos, M. (1998). The acquisition of grammar. In D. Kuhn & R. S. Siegler (Vol. Eds.), W. Damon (Editor-in-Chief), *Handbook of child psychology: Vol. 2. Cognition, perception, and language* (5th ed., pp. 421–466). New York: Wiley.

March of Dimes Birth Defects Foundation. (2003). *Prenatal statistics: Expenditures for perinatal care.* Available online: http://www.modimes.org/ (retrieved 9-1–04).

Marchant, G., Robinson, J., Anderson, U., & Schadewald, M. (1991). Analogical transfer and expertise in legal reasoning. *Organizational Behavior & Human Decision Making, 48,* 272–290.

Marcia, J. E. (1966). Development and validation of ego identity status. *Journal of Personality and Social Psychology, 3,* 551–558.

Marcon, R. A. (1999). Positive relationships between parent school involvement and public school inner-city preschoolers' development and academic performance. *School Psychology Review, 28,* 395–412.

Marcovitch, S., & Zelazo, D. (1999). The A-not-B error: Results from a logistic meta-analysis. *Child Development, 70,* 1297–1313.

Marcus, G. F., & Vijayan, S. (1999). Rule learning by seven-month-old infants. *Science, 283,* 77–80.

Marean, G. C., Werner, L. A., & Kuhl, P. K. (1992). Vowel categorization by very young infants. *Developmental Psychology, 28,* 396–405.

Margit, W., Vondracek, F. W., Capaldi, D. M., & Profeli, E. (2003). Childhood and adolescent predictors of early adult career pathways. *Journal of Vocational Behavior, 63,* 305–328.

Margolin, G., & Gordis, E. B. (2000). The effects of family and community violence on children. *Annual Review of Psychology, 51,* 445–479.

Marian, V., & Neisser, U. (2000). Language-dependent recall of autobiographical memories. *Journal of Experimental Psychology: General, 129,* 361–367.

Marini, Z., & Case, R. (1994). The development of abstract reasoning about the physical and social world. *Child Development, 65,* 147–159.

Markides, K. S., Boldt, J. S., & Ray, L. A. (1986). Sources of helping and intergenerational solidarity: A three-generations study of Mexican Americans. *Journal of Gerontology, 41,* 506–511.

Markman, E. M. (1989). *Categorization and naming in children.* Cambridge, MA: MIT Press.

Markstrom, C. A., & Iborra, A. (2003). Adolescent identity formation and rites of passage: The Navajo Kinaalda ceremony for girls. *Journal of Research on Adolescence, 13,* 399–425.

Markstrom-Adams, C. (1992). A consideration of intervening factors in adolescent identity formation. In G. R. Adams, T. P. Gullotta, & R. Montemayor (Eds.), *Adolescent identity formation* (Advances in Adolescent Development, Vol. 4). Newbury Park, CA: Sage.

Markstrom-Adams, C., & Adams, G. R. (1995). Gender, ethnic group, and grade differences in psychosocial functioning during middle adolescence. *Journal of Youth and Adolescence, 24,* 397–417.

Markus, H. R. (2004). Culture and personality: Brief for an arranged marriage. *Journal of Research in Personality, 38,* 75–83.

Markus, H. R., Mullally, P. R., & Kitayama, S. (1997). Self-ways: Diversity in modes of cultural participation. In U. Neisser & D. A. Jopling (Eds.), *The conceptual self in context. Culture, experience, self-understanding.* Cambridge, UK: Cambridge University Press.

Marschark, M. (1993). *Psychological development of deaf children.* New York: Oxford University Press.

Marsh, H. W. (1989). Effects of attending single-sex and coeducational high schools on achievement, attitudes, behaviors, and sex differences. *Journal of Educational Psychology, 81,* 70–85.

Marsh, H. W., & Ayotte, V. (2003). Do multiple dimensions of self-control become more differentiated with age? The differential distinctiveness hypothesis. *Journal of Educational Psychology, 95,* 687–706.

Marsh, H. W., Chessor, D., Craven, R., & Roche, L. (1995). The effect of gifted and talented programs on academic self-concept: The big fish strikes again. *American Educational Research Journal, 32,* 285–319.

Marsh, H. W., Craven, R., & Debus, R. (1999). Separation of competency and affect components of multiple dimensions of academic self-concept: A developmental perspective. *Merrill-Palmer Quarterly, 45,* 567–701.

Marsh, H. W., & Hau, K. (2003). Big fish-little pond effect on academic self-concept: A cross-cultural (26-country) test of the negative effects of academically selective schools. *American Psychologist, 58,* 364–376.

Marshall, S. (1995). Ethnic socialization of African American children: Implications for parenting, identity development, and academic achievement. *Journal of Youth and Adolescence, 24,* 377–396.

Marshall, W. A., & Tanner, J. M. (1970). Variation in the pattern of pubertal changes in boys, *Archives of Disease in Childhood, 45,* 13–23.

Marsiglio, W., Amato, P., Day, R. D., & Lamb, M. E. (2000). Scholarship on fatherhood in the 1990s and beyond. *Journal of Marriage and the Family, 62,* 1173–1191.

Marsiglio, W., & Donnelly, D. (1991). Sexual relations in later life: A national study of married persons. *Journals of Gerontology: Social Sciences, 46,* S338–S344.

Marsiske, M., & Willis, S. L. (1995). Dimensionality of everyday problem solving in older adults. *Psychology and Aging, 10,* 269–283.

Martin, C. L. (1990). Attitudes and expectations about children with nontraditional gender roles. *Sex Roles, 22,* 151–165.

Martin, C. L., & Fabes, R. A. (2001). The stability and consequences of young children's same-sex peer interactions. *Developmental Psychology, 37,* 431–446.

Martin, C. L., & Halverson, C. F., Jr. (1981). A schematic processing model of sex typing and stereotyping in children. *Child Development, 52,* 1119–1134.

Martin, C. L., & Halverson, C. F., Jr. (1983). The effects of sex-typing schemas on young children's memory. *Child Development, 54,* 563–574.

Martin, C. L., & Halverson, C. F., Jr. (1987). The roles of cognition in sex-roles and sex-typing. In D. B. Carter (Ed.), *Current conceptions of sex roles and sex-typing: Theory and research.* New York: Preager.

Martin, F. N., & Clark, J. G. (2002). *Introduction to audiology* (8th ed.). New York: Allyn & Bacon.

Martin, G. B., & Clark, R. D., III. (1982). Distress crying in neonates: Species and peer specificity. *Developmental Psychology, 18,* 3–9.

Martin, K. A. (1996). *Puberty, sexuality, and the self: Girls and boys at adolescence.* New York: Routledge.

Martin, M., Grunendahl, M., & Martin, P. (2001). Age differences in stress, social resources, and well-being in middle and old age. *Journal of Gerontology: Psychological Sciences, 56,* 214–222.

Martin, M. O., Mullis, I. V. S., Gonzales, E. J., Gregory, K. D., Smith, T. A., Chrostowski, S. J., Garder, R. A., & O'Connor, K. M. (2000). *TIMSS 1999 international science report: Findings from IEA's repeat of the third international mathematics and science study at the eighth grade.* Chestnut Hill, MA: Boston College.

Martlew, M., & Connolly, K. J. (1996). Human figure drawings by schooled and unschooled children in Papua New Guinea. *Child Development, 67,* 2743–2762.

Martorano, S. C. (1977). A developmental analysis of performance on Piaget's formal operations tasks. *Developmental Psychology, 13,* 666–672.

Masataka, N. (1996). Perception of motherese in a signed language by 6-month-old deaf infants. *Developmental Psychology, 32,* 874–879.

Masataka, N. (2000). The role of modality and input in the earliest stage of language acquisition: Studies of Japanese sign language. In C. Chamberlain, J. Morford, & Mayberry, R. I. (Eds.), *Language acquisition by eye* (pp. 3–24). Mahwah, NJ: Lawrence Erlbaum.

Massie, R. K., & Massie, S. (1975). *Journey.* New York: Knopf.

Masson, J. M. (1984). *The assault on truth: Freud's suppression of the seduction theory.* New York: Farrar, Straus, and Giroux.

Masten, A. S., & Reed, M. J. (2002). Resilience in development. In C. R. Snyder & S. J. Lopez (Eds.), *Handbook of positive psychology* (pp. 74–88). New York: Oxford University Press.

Masters, W. H., & Johnson, V. E. (1966). *Human sexual response.* Boston: Little, Brown.

Masters, W. H., & Johnson, V. E. (1970). *Human sexual inadequacy.* Boston: Little, Brown.

Masutomi, K., Yu, E. Y., Khurts, S., Ben-Porath, I., Currier, J. L., Metz, G. B., Brooks, M. W., Kaneko, S., Murakami, S., DeCaprio, J. A., Weinberg, R. A., Stewart, S. A., & Hahn, W. C. (2003). Telomerase maintains telomere structure in normal human cells. *Cell, 114,* 241–253.

Mathews, F., Youngman, L, & Neil, A. (2004). Maternal circulating nutrient concentrations in pregnancy: Implications for birth and placental weights of term infants. *American Journal of Clinical Nutrition, 79,* 103–110.

Mathews, J. (2003, Oct. 1). Not quite piling on the homework. *The Washington Post,* A1, A4.

Mattes, R. D. (2002). The chemical senses and nutrition in aging: Challenging old assumptions. *Journal of the American Dietetic Association, 102,* 192–196.

Matthews, K. A. (1992). Myths and realities of the menopause. *Psychosomatic Medicine, 54,* 1–9.

Matthews, K. A., Wing, R. R., Kuller, L. H., Meilahn, E. N., Kelsey, S. F., Costello, E. J., & Caggiula, A. W. (1990). Influences of natural menopause on psychological characteristics and symptoms of middle-aged healthy women. *Journal of Consulting and Clinical Psychology, 58,* 345–351.

Matthews, L. T., & Marwit, S. J. (2003–2004). Examining the assumptive world views of parents bereaved by accident, murder, and illness. *Omega: Journal of Death and Dying, 48,* 115–136.

Matusov, E., & Hayes, R. (2000). Sociocultural critique of Piaget and Vygotsky. *New Ideas in Psychology, 18,* 215–239.

Maughan, B. (2001). Conduct disorder in context. In J. Hill & B. Maughan (Eds.), *Conduct disorders in childhood and adolescence.* New York: Cambridge University Press.

Maughan, B., & Rutter, M. (2001). Antisocial children grown up. In J. Hill & B. Maughan (Eds.), *Conduct disorders in childhood and adolescence.* New York: Cambridge University Press.

Maurer, A. (1961). The child's knowledge of nonexistence. *Journal of Existential Psychiatry, 2,* 193–212.

Maurer, D., Lewis, T. L., Brent, H. P., & Levin, A. V. (1999). Rapid improvement in the acuity of infants after visual input. *Science, 286,* 108–110.

Maurer, D., & Maurer, C. (1988). *The world of the newborn.* New York: Basic Books.

Maurer, D., Stager, C. L., & Mondloch, C. J. (1999). Cross-modal transfer of shape is difficult to demonstrate in one-month-olds. *Child Development, 70,* 1047–1057.

Maxon, A. B., & Brackett, D. (1992). *The hearing-impaired child: Infancy through high school years.* Boston: Andover Medical Publishers.

Mayberry, R. I. (1994). The importance of childhood to language acquisition: Evidence from American Sign Language. In J. C. Goodman & H. C. Nusbaum (Eds.), *The development of speech perception: The transition from speech sounds to spoken words.* Cambridge, MA: MIT Press.

Mayberry, R. I., & Eichen, E. B. (1991). The long-lasting advantage of learning sign language in childhood: Another look at the critical period for language acquisition. *Journal of Memory and Language, 30,* 486–512.

Mayberry, R. I., Lock, E., & Kazmi, H. (2002). Linguistic ability and early language exposure. *Nature, 417,* 38.

Mayes, L. C., Feldman, R., Granger, R. H., Haynes, O. M., Bornstein, M. H., & Schottenfeld, R. (1997). The effects of polydrug use with and without cocaine on mother–infant interaction at 3 and 6 months. *Infant Behavior and Development, 20,* 489–502.

Mayeux, L., & Cillessen, A. H. N. (2003). Development of social problem solving in early childhood: Stability, change, and associations with social competence. *Journal of Genetic Psychology, 164,* 153–173.

Maylor, E. A., Moulson, J. M., Muncer, A. M., & Taylor, L. A. (2002). Does performance on theory of mind tasks decline in old age? *British Journal of Psychology, 93,* 465–485.
Maynard, A. E. (2002). Cultural teaching: The development of teaching skills in Maya sibling interactions. *Child Development, 73,* 969–982.
Mayseless, O., Danieli, R., & Sharabany, R. (1996). Adults' attachment patterns: Coping with separations. *Journal of Youth and Adolescence, 25,* 667–690.
Maziade, M., Caron, C., Côté, R., Merette, C., Bernier, H., Laplante, B., Boutin, P., & Thivierge, J. (1990). Psychiatric status of adolescents who had extreme temperaments at age 7. *American Journal of Psychiatry, 147,* 1531–1536.
McAdams, D. P., Hart, H. M., & Maruna, S. (1998). The anatomy of generativity. In D. P. McAdams & E. de St. Aubin (Eds.), *Generativity and adult development: How and why we care for the next generation.* Washington, D.C.: American Psychological Association.
McAdams, D. P., & Logan, R. L. (2004). What is generativity? In E. de St. Aubin, D. P. McAdams, & T. Kim (Eds.), *The generative society: Caring for future generations.* Washington, D.C.: American Psychological Association.
McAdams, P. P., de St. Aubin, E., & Logan, R. L. (1993). Generativity among young, middle, and older adults. *Psychology and Aging, 8,* 221–230.
McCall, R. B. (1977). Challenges to a science of developmental psychology. *Child Development, 48,* 333–344.
McCall, R. B. (1981). Nature–nurture and the two realms of development: A proposed integration with respect to mental development. *Child Development, 52,* 1–12.
McCall, R. B. (1983). A conceptual approach to early mental development. In M. Lewis (Ed.), *Origins of intelligence: Infancy and early childhood* (2nd ed.). New York: Plenum.
McCall, R. B., Applebaum, M. I., & Hogarty, P. S. (1973). Developmental changes in mental test performance. *Monographs of the Society for Research in Child Development, 38* (3, Serial No. 150).
McCall, R. B., & Carriger, M. S. (1993). A meta-analysis of infant habituation and recognition memory performance as predictors of later IQ. *Child Development, 64,* 57–79.
McCartney, K. (2003). On the meaning of models: A signal amidst the noise. In A. C. Crouter & A. Booth (Eds.), *Children's influence on family dynamics. The neglected side of family relationships.* Mahwah, NJ: Erlbaum.
McCartney, K., Harris, M. J., & Bernieri, F. (1990). Growing up and growing apart: A developmental meta-analysis of twin studies. *Psychological Bulletin, 107,* 226–237.
McCarton, C. M., Brooks-Gunn, J., Wallace, I. F., Bauer, C. R., Bennett, F. C., Bernbaum, J. C., Broyles, S., Casey, P. H., McCormick, M. C., Scott, D. T., Tyson, J., Tonascia, J., & Meinert, C. L. (1997). Results at age 8 years of early intervention for low-birth-weight premature infants. *Journal of the American Medical Association, 277,* 126–132.
McCaul, E. J., Donaldson, G. A., Coladarci, T., & Davis, W. E. (1992). Consequences of dropping out of school: Findings from high school and beyond. *Journal of Educational Research, 85,* 198–207.
McClintock, M. K., & Herdt, G. (1996). Rethinking puberty: The development of sexual attraction. *Current Directions in Psychological Science, 5,* 178–183.
McCloskey, L. A., Figueredo, A. J., & Koss, M. P. (1995). The effects of systematic family violence on children's mental health. *Child Development, 66,* 1239–1261.
McCormick, M. (1998). Mom's "BABY" vids sharpen new minds. *Billboard, 110,* 72–73.
McCrae, R. R. (2004). Human nature and culture: A trait perspective. *Journal of Research in Personality 38,* 3–14.
McCrae, R. R., Arenberg, D., & Costa, P. T., Jr. (1987). Declines in divergent thinking with age: Cross-sectional, longitudinal, and cross-sequential analyses. *Psychology and Aging, 2,* 130–137.
McCrae, R. R., & Costa, P. T., Jr. (2003). *Personality in adulthood: A five-factor theory perspective* (2nd ed.). New York: Guilford Press.
McCrae, R. R., Costa, P. T., Jr., Ostendorf, F., Angleitner, A., Hrebickova, M., Avia, M. D., Sanz, J., Sanchez-Bernardos, M. L., Kusdil, M. E., Woodfield, R., Saunders, P. R., & Smith, P. B. (2000). Nature over nurture: Temperament, personality, and life span development. *Journal of Personalty and Social Psychology, 78,* 173–186.
McCubbin, J. A., Lawson, E. J., Cox, S., Sherman, J. J., Norton, J. A., & Read, J. A. (1996). Prenatal maternal blood pressure response to stress predicts birth weight and gestational age: A preliminary study. *American Journal of Obstetrics and Gynecology, 175,* 706–712.
McCune, L., Vihman, M. M., Roug-Hellichius, L. Delery, D. B., & Gogate, L. L. (1996). Grunt communication in human infants *(Homo sapiens). Journal of Comparative Psychology, 110,* 27–27.
McDonald-Miszczak, L., Hertzog, C., & Hultsch, D. F. (1995). Stability and accuracy of metamemory in adulthood and aging: A longitudinal analysis. *Psychology and Aging, 10,* 553–564.
McFarlane, J. A., & Williams, T. M. (1990). The enigma of premenstrual syndrome. *Canadian Psychology, 31,* 95–108.
McGhee, P. E. (1979). *Humor: Its origin and development.* San Francisco: Freeman.
McGhee, P. E., & Chapman, A. J. (1980). *Children's humor.* London: Wiley.
McGhee-Bidlack, B. (1991). The development of noun definitions: A metalinguistic analysis. *Journal of Child Language, 18,* 417–434.
McGoldrick, M., Almeida, R., Hines, P. M., Garcia-Preto, N., Rosen, E., & Lee, E. (1991). Mourning in different cultures. In F. Walsh & M. McGoldrick (Eds.), *Living beyond loss: Death in the family.* New York: W. W. Norton.
McGrath, E. P., & Repetti, R. L. (2000). Mothers' and fathers' attitudes toward their children's academic performance and children's perceptions of their academic competence. *Journal of Youth and Adolescence, 29,* 713–723.
McGue, M., Bouchard, T. J., Jr., Iacono, W. G., & Lykken, D. T. (1993). Behavioral genetics of cognitive ability: A life-span perspective. In R. Plomin & G. E. McClearn (Eds.), *Nature, nurture, and psychology.* Washington, D.C.: American Psychological Association.
McGuire, S., Manke, B., Eftekhari, A., & Dunn, J. (2000). Children's perceptions of sibling conflict during middle childhood: Issues and sibling (dis)similarity. *Social Development, 9,* 173–190.
McHale, S. M., Updegraff, K. A., Helms-Erikson, H., & Crouter, A. C. (2001). Sibling influences on gender development in middle childhood and early adolescence: A longitudinal study. *Developmental Psychology, 37,* 115–125.
McHale, S. M., Updegraff, K. A., Jackson-Newsom, J., Tucker, C. J., & Crouter, A. C. (2000). When does parents' differential treatment have negative implications for siblings? *Social Development, 9,* 149–172.
McIntosh, G. C., Olshan, A. F., & Baird, P. A. (1995). Paternal age and the risk of birth defects in offspring. *Epidemiology, 6,* 282–288.
McKay, K. E., Halperin, J. M., Schwartz, S. T., & Sharma, V. (1994). Developmental analysis of three aspects of information processing: Sustained attention, selective attention, and response organization. *Developmental Neuropsychology, 10,* 121–132.
McKusick, V. A. (1990). *Mendelian inheritance in man* (9th ed.) Baltimore: Johns Hopkins Press.
McLanahan, S. S., & Sorensen, A. B. (1985). Life events and psychological well-being over the life course. In G. H. Elder Jr. (Ed.), *Life course dynamics: Trajectories and transitions, 1968–1980.* Ithaca, NY: Cornell University Press.
McLoyd, V. C. (1990). The impact of economic hardship on black families and children: Psychological distress, parenting, and socioemotional development. *Child Development, 61,* 311–346.
McLoyd, V. C., Cauce, A. M., Takeuchi, D., & Wilson, L. (2000). Marital processes and parental socialization in families of color: A decade review of research. *Journal of Marriage and the Family, 62,* 1070–1093.
McMaster, J., Pitts, M., & Poyah, G. (1997). The menopausal experiences of women in a developing country—There is a time for everything—To be a teenager, a mother and a granny. *Women and Health, 26,* 1–14.
McNeill, D. (1970). *The acquisition of language.* New York: Harper & Row.
Mead, G. H. (1934). *Mind, self, and society.* Chicago: University of Chicago Press.
Meadows-Orlans, K. P., & Orlans, H. (1990). Responses to loss of hearing in later life. In D. F. Moores & K. P. Meadows-Orlans, (Eds.), *Educational and developmental aspects of deafness.* Washington, D.C.: Gallaudet University Press.
Medina, J. J. (1996). *The clock of ages: Why we age—how we age—winding back the clock.* Cambridge, England: Cambridge University Press.
Medvedev, Z. A. (1991). The structural basis of aging. In F. C. Ludwig (Ed.), *Life span extension: Consequences and open questions.* New York: Springer.
Meeus, W., Iedema, J., Helsen, M., & Vollebergh, W. (1999). Patterns of adolescent identity development: Review of literature and longitudinal analysis. *Developmental Review, 19,* 419–461.
Mehan, H., Villaneueva, I., Hubbard, L., & Lintz, A. (1996). *Constructing school success: The consequences of untracking low-achieving students.* New York: Cambridge University Press.
Meier, R. P. (1991). Language acquisition by deaf children. *American Scientist, 79,* 69–70.

Meijer, J., & Elshout, J. J. (2001). The predictive and discriminant validity of the zone of proximal development. *British Journal of Educational Psychology, 71,* 93–113.

Meilman, P. W. (1979). Cross-sectional age changes in ego identity status during adolescence. *Developmental Psychology, 15,* 230–231.

Mekos, D., Hetherington, E. M., & Reiss, D. (1996). Sibling differences in problem behavior and parental treatment in nondivorced and remarried families. *Child Development, 67,* 2148–2165.

Mellinger, J. C., & Erdwins, C. J. (1985). Personality correlates of age and life roles in adult women. *Psychology of Women Quarterly, 9,* 503–514.

Meltzoff, A. N. (1988). Infant imitation and memory: Nine-month-olds in immediate and deferred tests. *Child Development, 59,* 216-225.

Meltzoff, A. N. (1995). What infant memory tells us about infantile amnesia: Long-term recall and deferred imitation. *Journal of Experimental Child Psychology, 59,* 497–515.

Meltzoff, A. N. (2004). Imitation as a mechanism of social cognition: Origins of empathy, theory of mind, and the representation of action. In U. Goswami (Ed.), *Blackwell handbook of childhood cognitive development* (pp. 6–25). Malden, MA: Blackwell Publishing.

Meltzoff, A. N., & Moore, M. K. (1977). Imitation of facial and manual gestures by human neonates. *Science, 198,* 75–78.

Meltzoff, A. N., & Moore, M. K. (1997). Explaining facial imitation: Theoretical model. *Early Development and Parenting, 6,* 179–192.

Memon, A., & Vartoukian, R. (1996). The effects of repeated questioning on young children's eyewitness testimony. *British Journal of Psychology, 87,* 403–415.

Menaghan, E. G., & Lieberman, M. A. (1986). Changes in depression following divorce: A panel study. *Journal of Marriage and the Family, 48,* 319–328.

Mennella, J. A., & Beauchamp, G. K. (2002). Flavor experiences during formula feeding are related to preferences during childhood. *Early Human Development, 68,* 71–82.

Mennella, J. A., Giffin, C. E., & Beauchamp, G. K. (2004). Flavor programming during infancy. *Pediatrics, 113,* 840–845.

Mennuti, M. T., & Driscoll, D. A. (2003). Screening for Down's syndrome: Too many choices? *New England Journal of Medicine, 349,* 1471–1473.

Ment, L. R., Vohr, B., Allan, W., Katz, K. H., Schneider, K. C., Westerveld, M., Duncan, C. C., & Makuch, R. W. (2003). Change in cognitive function over time in very low-birth-weight infants. *Journal of the American Medical Association, 289,* 705–711.

Meredith, P., & Noller, P. (2003). Attachment and infant difficultness in postnatal depression. *Journal of Family Issues, 24,* 668–686.

Merzenich, M. M., Jenkins, W. M., Johnston, P., Schreiner, C., Miller, S. L., & Tallal, P. (1996). Temporal processing deficits of language-learning impaired children ameliorated by training. *Science, 271,* 77–81.

Meschke, L. L., Bartholomae S., & Zentall, S. R. (2002). Adolescent sexuality and parent–adolescent processes: Promoting healthy teen choices. *Journal of Adolescent Health, 31,* 264–279.

Meschke, L. L., Zweig, J. M., Barber, B. L., & Eccles, J. S. (2000). Demographic, biological, psychological, and social predictors of the timing of first intercourse. *Journal of Research on Adolescence, 10,* 315–338.

Mesman, J., Bongers, I. L., & Koot, H. M. (2001). Preschool developmental pathways to preadolescent internalizing and externalizing problems. *Journal of Child Psychology and Psychiatry and Allied Disciplines, 42,* 679–689.

Messer, D. J., McCarthy, M. E., McQuiston, S., MacTurk, R. H., Yarrow, L. J., & Vietze, P. M. (1986). Relation between mastery behavior in infancy and competence in early childhood. *Developmental Psychology, 22,* 366–372.

Messinger-Rapport, B. J. (2003). Assessment and counseling of older drivers: A guide for primary care physicians. *Geriatrics, 58,* 16.

Metcalf, P., & Huntington, R. (1991). *Celebrations of death. The anthropology of mortuary ritual* (2nd ed.). Cambridge, England: Cambridge University Press.

Meydani, M. (2001). Nutrition interventions in aging and age-associated disease. In S. C. Park, E. S. Hwang, H. Kim, & W. Park (Eds.), *Annals of the New York Academy of Sciences: Vol. 928. Molecular and cellular interactions in senescence.* New York: The New York Academy of Sciences.

Meyer-Bahlburg, H. F. L., Dolezal, C., Baker, S. W., Carlson, A. D., Obeid, J. S., & New, M. I. (2004). Prenatal androgenization affects gender-related behavior but not gender identity in 5–12-year-old girls with congenital adrenal hyperplasia. *Archives of Sexual Behavior, 33,* 97–104.

Meyer-Bahlburg, H. F. L., Ehrhardt, A. A., Rosen, L. R., & Gruen, R. S. (1995). Prenatal estrogens and the development of homosexual orientation. *Developmental Psychology, 31,* 12–21.

Miceli, P. J., Goeke-Morey, M. C., Whitman, T. L., Kolberg, K. S., Miller-Loncar, C., & White, R. D. (2000). Brief report: Birth status, medical complications, and social environment: Individual differences in development of preterm, very low birth weight infants. *Journal of Pediatric Psychology, 25,* 353–358.

Mickelson, K. D., Kessler, R. C., & Shaver P. R. (1997). Adult attachment in a nationally representative sample. *Journal of Personality and Social Psychology, 73,* 1092–1106.

Midgley, C., Feldlaufer, H., & Eccles, J. S. (1989). Student/teacher relations and attitudes toward mathematics before and after the transition to junior high school. *Child Development, 60,* 981–992.

Midlarsky, E., Kahana, E., Corley, R., Nemeroff, R., & Schonbar, R. A. (1999). Altruistic moral judgment among older adults. *International Journal of Aging and Human Development, 49,* 27–41.

Mikulincer, M., & Shaver, P. R. (2003). The attachment behavioral system in adulthood: Activation, psychodynamics, and interpersonal processes. In M. P. Zanna (Eds.), *Advances in experimental social psychology* (*Vol. 35*). San Diego: Academic Press.

Milhausen, R. R., & Herold, E. S. (1999). Does the sexual double standard still exist: Perceptions of university women. *Journal of Sex Research, 36,* 361–368.

Milich, R., & Pelham, W. E. (1986). Effects of sugar ingestion on the classroom and playgroup behavior of attention deficit disordered boys. *Journal of Consulting and Clinical Psychology, 54,* 714–718.

Miller, A. (1985). A developmental study of the cognitive basis of performance impairment after failure. *Journal of Personality and Social Psychology, 49,* 529–538.

Miller, B. C. (2002). Family influences on adolescent sexual and contraceptive behavior. *Journal of Sex Research, 39,* 22–26.

Miller, J. A. (1995). Strictest diet avoids subtle detriments of PKU. *Bioscience, 45,* 244–245.

Miller, J. B., & Hoicowitz, T. (2004). Attachment contexts of adolescent friendship and romance. *Journal of Adolescence, 27,* 191–206.

Miller, N. B., Cowan, P. A., Cowan, C. P., Hetherington, E. M., & Clingempeel, W. G. (1993). Externalizing in preschoolers and early adolescents: A cross-study replication of a family model. *Developmental Psychology, 29,* 3–18.

Miller, P. H. (1990). The development of strategies of selective attention. In D. F. Bjorklund (Ed.), *Children's strategies: Contemporary views of cognitive development.* Hillsdale, NJ: Erlbaum.

Miller, P. H. (1994). Individual differences in children's strategic behavior: Utilization deficiencies. *Learning and Individual Differences, 6,* 285–307.

Miller, P. H. (2002). *Theories of developmental psychology* (4th ed.). New York: Worth.

Miller, P. H., & Seier, W. S. (1994). Strategy utilization deficiencies in children: When, where and why. In H. W. Reese (Ed.), *Advances in Child Development and Behavior* (Vol. *25,* pp. 107–156). New York: Academic Press.

Miller, P. H., & Weiss, M. G. (1981). Children's attention allocation, understanding of attention, and performance on the incidental learning task. *Child Development, 52,* 1183–1190.

Miller, R. A. (2004). Extending life: Scientific prospects and political obstacles. In S. G. Post & R. H. Binstock (Eds.), *The Fountain of Youth: Cultural, scientific, and ethical perspectives on a biomedical goal.* New York: Oxford University Press.

Miller, S. A. (1986). Parents' beliefs about their children's cognitive abilities. *Developmental Psychology, 22,* 276–284.

Miller-Johnson, S., Costanzo, P. R., Coie, J. D., Rose, M. R., Browne, D. C., & Johnson, C. (2003). Peer social structure and risk-taking behaviors among African American early adolescents. *Journal of Youth and Adolescence, 32,* 375–384.

Milos, G., Spindler, A., Schnyder, U., Martz, J., Hoek, H. W., & Willi, J. (2004). Incidence of severe anorexia nervosa in Switzerland: 40 years of development. *International Journal of Eating Disorders, 35,* 250–258.

Minard, K. L., Freudigman, K., & Thoman, E. B. (1999). Sleep rhythmicity in infants: Index of stress or maturation. *Behavioral Processes, 47,* 189–206.

Mingroni, M. A. (2004). The secular rise in IQ: Giving heterosis a closer look. *Intelligence, 32,* 65–83.

Miralt, G., Bearor, K., & Thomas, T. (2001–2002). Adult romantic attachment among women who experienced childhood maternal loss. *Omega: Journal of Death and Dying, 44,* 97–104.

Mischel, W. (1973). Toward a cognitive social learning reconceptualization of personality. *Psychological Review, 80,* 252–283.

Mischel, W., & Shoda, Y. (1995). A cognitive-affective system theory of personality: Reconceptualizing situations, dispositions, dynamics, and invariance in personality structure. *Psychological Review, 102,* 246–268.

Mishara, B. L. (1999). Synthesis of research and evidence on factors affecting the desire of terminally ill or seriously chronically ill persons to hasten death. *Omega: Journal of Death and Dying, 39,* 1–70.

Mitchell, D. B., & Bruss, P. J. (2003). Age differences in implicit memory: Conceptual, perceptual, or methodological? *Psychology and Aging, 18,* 807–822.

Mitchell, J. E., Baker, L. A., & Jacklin, C. N. (1989). Masculinity and femininity in twin children: Genetic and environmental factors. *Child Development, 60,* 1475–1485.

Mitchell, P. (1997). *Introduction to theory of mind: Children, autism, and apes.* London: Arnold.

Miyawaki, K., Strange, W., Verbrugge, R., Liberman, A. M., Jenkins, J. J., & Fujimura, D. (1975). An effect of linguistic experience: The discrimination of [r] and [l] by native speakers of Japanese and English. *Perception and Psychophysics, 18,* 331–340.

Modell, J., & Elder, G. H., Jr. (2002). Children develop in history: So what's new? In W. W. Hartup & R. A. Weinberg (Eds.), *Child psychology in retrospect and prospect. The Minnesota Symposium* (Vol. 32). Mahwah, NJ: Erlbaum.

Moen, P. (1992). *Women's two roles: A contemporary dilemma.* New York: Auburn House.

Moen, P., & Wethington, E. (1999). Midlife development in a life course context. In S. L. Willis & J. D. Reid (Eds.), *Life in the middle. Psychological and social development in middle age.* San Diego: Academic Press.

Moerk, E. L. (1989). The LAD was a lady and the tasks were ill-defined. *Developmental Psychology, 9,* 21–57.

Moffitt, T. E., & Caspi, A. (2001). Childhood predictors differentiate life-course persistent and adolescence-limited antisocial pathways among males and females. *Development and Psychopathology, 13,* 355–375.

Mohr, P. E., Feldman, J. J., Dunbar, J. L., McConkey-Robbins, A., Niparko, J. K., Rittenhouse, R. K., & Skinner, M. W. (2000). The societal costs of severe to profound hearing loss in the United States. *International Journal of Technology and Assessment of Health Care, 16,* 1120–1135.

Molfese, D. L. (2000). Predicting dyslexia at 8 years of age using neonatal brain responses. *Brain and Language, 72,* 238–245.

Molina, B. S. G., & Chassin, L. (1996). The parent–adolescent relationship at puberty: Hispanic ethnicity and parent alcoholism as moderators. *Developmental Psychology, 32,* 675–686.

Molinari, V. (1999). Using reminiscence and life review as natural therapeutic strategies in group therapy. In M. Duffy (Ed.), *Handbook of counseling and psychotherapy with older adults.* New York: Wiley.

Molinari, V., & Reichlin, R. E. (1984–1985). Life review reminiscence in the elderly: A review of the literature. *International Journal of Aging and Human Development, 20,* 81–92.

Moller, L. C., & Serbin, L. A. (1996). Antecedents of toddler gender segregation: Cognitive consonance, gender-typed toy preferences and behavioral compatibility. *Sex Roles, 35,* 445–460.

Money, J. (1985). Pediatric sexology and hermaphroditism. *Journal of Sex and Marital Therapy, 11,* 139–156.

Money, J. (1988). *Gay, straight, and in-between: The sexology of erotic orientation.* New York: Oxford University Press.

Money, J., & Ehrhardt, A. (1972). *Man and woman, boy and girl.* Baltimore: Johns Hopkins University Press.

Money, J., & Tucker, P. (1975). *Sexual signatures: On being a man or a woman.* Boston: Little, Brown.

Monk, C., Fifer, W. P., Myers, M. M., Sloan, R. P., Trien, L., & Hurtado, A. (2000). Maternal stress responses and anxiety during pregnancy: Effects on fetal heart rate. *Developmental Psychobiology, 36,* 67–77.

Montemayor, R., & Eisen, M. (1977). The development of self-conceptions from childhood to adolescence. *Developmental Psychology, 13,* 314–319.

Moore, E. G. J. (1986). Family socialization and the IQ test performance of traditionally and transracially adopted black children. *Developmental Psychology, 22,* 317–326.

Moore, M., & Carr, A. (2000). Depression and grief. In A. Carr (Ed.), *What works with children and adolescents?: A critical review of psychological interventions with children, adolescents, and their families.* Florence, KY: Taylor & Francis/Routledge.

Moore, M. K., & Meltzoff, A. N. (1999). New findings on object permanence: A developmental difference between two types of occlusion. *British Journal of Developmental Psychology, 17,* 563–584.

Moore, S. M. (1995). Girls' understanding and social constructions of menarche. *Journal of Adolescence, 18,* 87–104.

Moorehouse, M. J. (1991). Linking maternal employment patterns to mother–child activities and children's school competence. *Developmental Psychology, 27,* 295–303.

Moran, G. (2002). Williams reluctant to discuss past, future. SignOnSanDiego.com by the *Union-Tribune.* Available at: signonsandiego .com/news/metro/Santana/index.html.

Morelli, G. A., Rogoff, B., Oppenheim, D., & Goldsmith, D. (1992). Cultural variation in infants' sleeping arrangements: Questions of independence. *Developmental Psychology, 28,* 604–613.

Morgan, G. A., MacTurk, R. H., & Hrncir, E. J. (1995). Mastery motivation: Overview, definitions, and conceptual issues. In R. H. MacTurk & G. A. Morgan (Eds.), *Mastery motivation: Origins, conceptualizations, and applications.* Norwood, NJ: Ablex.

Morgan, G. A., & Ricciuti, H. N. (1969). Infants' responses to strangers during the first year. In B. M. Foss (Ed.), *Determinants of infant behavior* (Vol. 4). London: Methuen.

Morgan, M., Phillips, J. G., Bradshaw, J. L., Mattingley, J. B., Iansek, R., & Bradshaw, J. A. (1994). Age-related motor slowness: Simply strategic? *Journal of Gerontology, 49,* M133–M139.

Morin, R. (2003, January 9). Words matter. *The Washington Post,* B5.

Morinaga, Y., Frieze, I. H., & Ferligoj, A. (1993). Career plans and gender-role attitudes of college students in the United States, Japan, and Slovenia. *Sex Roles, 29,* 317–334.

Morizot, J., & Le Blanc, M. (2003). Continuity and change in personality traits from adolescence to midlife: A 25-year longitudinal study comparing representative and adjudicated men. *Journal of Personality, 71,* 705–755.

Morrell, R. W., Park, D. C., & Poon, L. W. (1989). Quality of instructions on prescription drug labels: Effects on memory and comprehension in young and old adults. *Gerontologist, 29,* 345–354.

Morris, J. (1999, October 18). Assessing children's toxic risks. *U.S. News & World Report,* 80.

Morris, J. C., Storandt, M., Miller, J. P., McKeel, D., Price, J. L., Rubin, E. H., & Berg, L. (2001). Mild cognitive impairment represents early-stage Alzheimer disease. *Archives of Neurology, 58,* 397–410.

Morrison, D. M. (1985). Adolescent contraceptive behavior: A review. *Psychological Bulletin, 98,* 538–568.

Morrison, D. R., & Coiro, M. J. (1999). Parental conflict and marital disruption: Do children benefit when high-conflict marriages are dissolved? *Journal of Marriage and the Family, 61,* 626–637.

Morrongiello, B. A., Fenwick, K. D., Hillier, L., & Chance, G. (1994). Sound localization in newborn human infants. *Developmental Psychobiology, 27,* 519–538.

Morrongiello, B. A., & Hogg, K. (2004). Mothers' reactions to children misbehaving in ways that can lead to injury: Implications for gender differences in children's risk taking and injuries. *Sex Roles, 50,* 1003–1118.

Morrow, D., Leirer, V., Altieri, P., & Fitzsimmons, C. (1994). When expertise reduces age differences in performance. *Psychology and Aging, 9,* 134–148.

Morse, C. A., Dudley, E., Guthrie, J., & Dennerstein, L. (1998). Relationships between premenstrual complaints and perimenopausal experiences. *Journal of Psychosomatic Obstetrics and Gynecology, 19,* 182–191.

Morse, C. K. (1993). Does variability increase with age? An archival study of cognitive measures. *Psychology and Aging, 8,* 156–164.

Mortimer, J. T., Finch, M. D., & Kumka, D. (1982). Persistence and change in development: The multidimensional self-concept. In P. B. Baltes & O. G. Brim Jr. (Eds.), *Life-span development and behavior* (Vol. 4). New York: Academic Press.

Mortimer, J. T., Finch, M. D., Ryu, S., Shanahan, M. J., & Call, K. T. (1996). The effects of work intensity on adolescent mental health, achievement, and behavioral adjustment: New evidence from a prospective study. *Child Development, 67,* 1243–1261.

Moshman, D. (1999). *Adolescent psychological development. Rationality, morality, and identity.* Mahwah, NJ: Erlbaum.

Moss, M. S., Moss, S. Z., Rubinstein, R., & Resch, N. (1993). Impact of elderly mother's death on middle age daughters. *International Journal of Aging and Human Development, 37,* 1–22.

Mroczek, D. K. (2004). Positive and negative affect at midlife. In O. G. Brim, C. D. Ryff, & R. C. Kessler (Eds.), *How healthy are we? A national study of well-being at midlife.* Chicago: University of Chicago Press.

Mueller, E., & Lucas, T. (1975). A developmental analysis of peer interactions among toddlers. In M. Lewis & L. Rosenblum (Eds.), *Friendship and peer relations.* New York: Wiley.

Mueller, E., & Vandell, D. (1979). Infant–infant interaction. In J. Osofsky (Ed.), *Handbook of infant development.* New York: Wiley.

Mulder, E. J., Robles de Medina, P. G., Huizink, A. C., Van den Bergh, B. R., Buitelaar, J. K., & Visser, G. H. (2002). Prenatal maternal stress: Effects on pregnancy and the (unborn) child. *Early Human Development, 70,* 3–14.

Mulsant, B. H., & Ganguli, M. (1999). Epidemiology and diagnosis of depression in late life. *Journal of Clinical Psychiatry, 60* (Suppl. 20), 9–15.

Munro, G., & Adams, G. R. (1977). Ego–identity formation in college students and working youth. *Developmental Psychology, 13,* 523–524.

Munroe, R. L., Hulefeld, R., Rodgers, J. M., Tomeo, D. L., & Yamazaki, S. K. (2000). Aggression among children in four cultures. *Cross-Cultural Research, 34,* 3–25.

Murnen, S. K., & Smolak, L. (1997). Femininity, masculinity and disordered eating: A meta-analytic review. *International Journal of Eating Disorders, 22,* 231–242.

Murphy, C. (1985). Cognitive and chemosensory influences on age-related changes in the ability to identify blended foods. *Journal of Gerontology, 40,* 47–52.

Murphy, C., Nordin, S., & Acosta, L. (1997). Odor learning, recall, and recognition memory in young and elderly adults. *Neuropsychology, 11,* 126–137.

Murphy, D. R., Craik, F. I. M., Li, K. Z. H., & Schneider, B. A. (2000). Comparing the effects of aging and background noise on short-term memory performance. *Psychology and Aging, 15,* 323–334.

Murphy, E. M. (2003). Being born female is dangerous for your health. *American Psychologist, 58,* 205–210.

Murphy, S. A., Johnson, C., & Lohan, J. (2003a). The effectiveness of coping resources and strategies used by bereaved parents 1 and 5 years after the violent deaths of their children. *Omega: Journal of Death and Dying, 47,* 25–44.

Murphy, S. A., Johnson, C., & Lohan, J. (2003b). Finding meaning in a child's violent death: A five-year prospective analysis of parents' personal narratives and empirical data. *Death Studies, 27,* 381–404.

Murphy, S. L. (2000). Deaths: Final data for 1998. *National Vital Statistics Report, 48,* 1–105.

Murray, J. A., Terry, D. J., Vance, J. C., Battistutta, D., & Connolly, Y. (2000). Effects of a program of intervention on parental distress following infant death. *Death Studies, 24,* 275–305.

Murray, L., Fiori-Cowley, A., Hooper, R., & Cooper, P. (1996). The impact of postnatal depression and associated adversity on early mother–infant interactions and later infant outcome. *Child Development, 67,* 2512–2526.

Murray, L., Sinclair, D., Cooper, P., Ducournau, P., Turner, P., & Stein, A. (1999). The socio-emotional development of 5-year-old children of postnatally depressed mothers. *Journal of Child Psychology and Psychiatry, 40,* 1259–1271.

Murray, M. P., Kory, R. C., & Clarkson, B. H. (1969). Walking patterns in healthy old men. *Journal of Gerontology, 24,* 169–178.

Murray, S. A., Grant, E., Grant, A., & Kendall, M. (2003). Dying from cancer in developed and developing countries: Lessons from two qualitative interview studies of patients and their carers. *British Medical Journal, 326,* 368–372.

Mussen, P. H., & Rutherford, E. (1963). Parent–child relations and parental personality in relation to young children's sex-role preferences. *Child Development, 34,* 589–607.

Must, A., Jacques, P. F., Dallal, G. E., Bajema, C. J., & Dietz, W. H. (1992). Long-term morbidity and mortality of overweight adolescents: A follow-up of the Harvard Growth Study of 1922 to 1935. *New England Journal of Medicine, 327,* 1350–1355.

Mwamwenda, T. S. (1999). Undergraduate and graduate students' combinatorial reasoning and formal operations. *Journal of Genetic Psychology, 160,* 503–506.

Mwamwenda, T. S., & Mwamwenda, B. A. (1989). Formal operational thought among African and Canadian college students. *Psychological Reports, 64,* 43–46.

Myers, J., Jusczyk, P. W., Nelson, D. G. K., Charles-Luce, J., Woodward, A. L., & Hirsch-Pasek, K. (1996). Infants' sensitivity to word boundaries in fluent speech. *Journal of Child Language, 23,* 1–30.

Myers, J. K., Weissman, M. M., Tischler, G. L., Holzer, C. E., III, Leaf, P. J., & Orvaschel, H. (1984). Six-month prevalence of psychiatric disorders in three communities. *Archives of General Psychiatry, 41,* 959–967.

Mylod, D. E., Whitman, T. L., & Borkowski, J. G. (1997). Predicting adolescent mothers' transition to adulthood. *Journal of Research on Adolescence, 7,* 457–478.

N

Nagumey, A. J., Reich, J. W., & Newsom, J. (2004). Gender moderates the effects of independence and dependence desires during the social support process. *Psychology and Aging, 19,* 215–218.

Naigles, L. G., & Gelman, S. A. (1995). Overextensions in comprehension and production revisited: Preferential-looking in a study of dog, cat, and cow. *Journal of Child Language, 22,* 19–46.

Najman, J. M., Vance, J. C., Boyle, F., Embleton, G., Foster, B., & Thearle, J. (1993). The impact of a child death on marital adjustment. *Social Science and Medicine, 37,* 1005–1010.

Najman, J. M., Williams, G. M., Nikles, J., Spence, S., Bor, W., O'Callaghan, M., Le Brocque, R., & Andersen, M. J. (2000). Mothers' mental illness and child behavior problems: Cause–effect association or observation bias? *Journal of the American Academy of Child and Adolescent Psychiatry, 39,* 592–602.

Nanez, J. E., & Yonas, A. (1994). Effects of luminance and texture motion on infant defensive reactions to optical collision. *Infant Behavior and Development, 17,* 165–174.

Nangle, D. W., Erdley, C. A., Newman, J. E., Mason, C. A., & Carpenter, E. M. (2003). Popularity, friendship quantity, and friendship quality: Interactive influences on children's loneliness and depression. *Journal of Clinical Child and Adolescent Psychology, 32,* 546–555.

Nash, A., & Hay, D. F. (2003). Social relations in infancy: Origins and evidence. *Human Development, 46,* 222–232.

National Academy of Sciences. (2000). *Sleep needs, patterns and difficulties of adolescents: Summary of a workshop.* Available online: http://www.nap.edu/openbook/030907177/html/3.html.

National Campaign to Prevent Teen Pregnancy. (2002). Available online: *www.teenpregnancy.org.*

National Center for Education Statistics. (1998). National Household Education Survey (NHES), "Adult Education Interview," 1991, 1995, 1999; Projections of Education Statistics to 2008 (NCES 98-016).

National Center for Education Statistics. (2001). *Dropout rates in the United States: 1999.* Available online: http://nces.ed.gov/pubs2001/dropout/HighSchoolRates3.asp.

National Center for Health Statistics. (2000a). Centers for Disease Control and Prevention growth charts. Available online: http://www.cdc.gov/growthcharts.

National Center for Health Statistics. (2000b). *Health, United States, 2000.* Hyattsville, MD: U.S. Department of Health and Human Services.

National Institute on Aging. (2000). *Progress report on Alzheimer's disease 2000. Taking the next steps* (NIH Publication No. 00-4859). Available at : www.alzheimers.org/pubs/prog00.htm.

National Institute on Aging & National Institute on Deafness and Other Communication Disorders. (1996). Hearing and older people. In L. M. Ross (Ed.), *Communication disorders sourcebook* (Vol. 11, pp. 183–184). Detroit: Omnigraphics.

National Institutes of Health. (1993, March 1–3). Consensus Statement on the Early Identification of Hearing Impairment in Infants and Young Children. In L. M. Ross (Ed.), *Communication disorders sourcebook* (Vol. 11, pp. 51–53). Detroit: Omnigraphics.

National Institutes of Health. (2000). Phenylketonuria (PKU): Screening and management. *NIH Consensus Statement 2000 October 16–18, 17(3),* 1–33.

National Institutes of Health. (2002). *Facts about postmenopausal hormonal therapy.* U.S. Department of Health and Human Services (NIH Publication No. 02-5200).

National Reading Panel. (1999). *Teaching children to read: An evidence-based assessment of the scientific literature on reading and its implications for reading instruction.* Washington, D.C.: National Institute of Child Health & Human Development.

National Research Council. (2001). *Preparing for an aging world: The case for cross-national research.* Panel on a Research Agenda and New Data for an Aging World, Community on Population and Committee on National Statistics, Division of Behavioral, Social Sciences and Education. Washington, D.C.: National Academy Press.

National Sleep Foundation. (2004). Adolescent sleep needs and patterns: Research report and resource guide. Washington, D.C.: Author.

Neale, M. C., & Martin, N. G. (1989). The effects of age, sex, and genotype on self-report drunkenness following a challenge dose of alcohol. *Behavior Genetics, 19,* 63–78.

Needham, A. (1999). The role of shape in 4-month-old infants' object segregation. *Infant Behavior and Development, 22,* 161–178.

Neiderhiser, J. M., Reiss, D., Pedersen, N. L., Lichtenstein, P., Spotts, E. L., Hansson, K., Cederblad, M., & Ellhammer, O. (2004).

Genetic and environmental influences on mothering of adolescents: A comparison of two samples. *Developmental Psychology, 40,* 335–351.

Neimark, E. D. (1975). Longitudinal development of formal operations thought. *Genetic Psychology Monographs, 91,* 171–225.

Neimark, E. D. (1979). Current status of formal operations research. *Human Development, 22,* 60–67.

Neisser, U. (2004). Memory development: New questions and old. *Developmental Review, 24,* 154–158.

Neisser, U., Boodoo, G., Bouchard, T. J., Jr., Boykin, A. W., Brody, N., Ceci, S. J., Halpern, D. F., Loehlin, J. C., Perloff, R., Sternberg, R. J., & Urbina, S. (1996). Intelligence: Knowns and unknowns. *American Psychologist, 51,* 77–101.

Nelson, C. A. & Luciana, M. (Eds.) (2001). *Handbook of developmental cognitive neuroscience.* MA: The MIT Press.

Nelson, G., Westhues, A., & MacLeod, J. (2003). A meta-analysis of longitudinal research on preschool prevention programs for children. *Prevention & Treatment, 6.* Available at http://journals.apa.org/prevention/volume6/toc-dec18-03.html.

Nelson, K. (1973). Structure and strategy in learning to talk. *Monographs of the Society for Research in Child Development, 38* (Serial No. 149).

Nelson, K. (1986). *Event knowledge: Structure and function in development.* Hillsdale, NJ: Erlbaum.

Nelson, K. (1997). Event representations then, now, and next. In P. W. van den Broek & P. J. Bauer (Eds.), *Developmental spans in event comprehension and representation: Bridging fictional and actual events* (pp. 1–26). Mahwah, NJ: Erlbaum.

Nelson, K., Hampson, J., & Shaw, L. K. (1993). Nouns in early lexicons: Evidence, explanations and implications. *Journal of Child Language, 20,* 61–84.

Nelson, K., & Hudson, J. (1988). Scripts and memory: Functional relationship in development. In F. E. Weinert & M. Perlmutter (Eds.), *Memory development: Universal changes and individual differences.* Hillsdale, NJ: Erlbaum.

Nelson, K., Skwerer, D. P., Goldman, S., Henseler, S., Presler, N., & Walkenfeld, F. F. (2003). Entering a community of minds: An experiential approach to "theory of mind." *Human Development, 46, 24–46.*

Nelson, S. A. (1980). Factors influencing young children's use of motives and outcomes as moral criteria. *Child Development, 51,* 823–829.

Nes, S. L. (2003). Using paired reading to enhance the fluency skills of less-skilled readers. *Reading Improvement, 40,* 179–193.

Nesse, R. M. (2000). Is depression an adaptation? *Archives of General Psychiatry, 57,* 14–20.

Nettelbeck, T., & Wilson, C. (2004). The Flynn effect: Smarter not faster. *Intelligence, 32,* 85–93.

Nettelbeck, T., & Young, R. (1996). Intelligence and savant syndrome: Is the whole greater than the sum of the fragments? *Intelligence, 22,* 49–68.

Neugarten, B. L. (1968). Adult personality: Toward a psychology of the life cycle. In B. L. Neugarten (Ed.), *Middle age and aging: A reader in social psychology.* Chicago: University of Chicago Press.

Neugarten, B. L., Moore, J. W., & Lowe, J. C. (1965). Age norms, age constraints, and adult socialization. *American Journal of Sociology, 70,* 710–717.

Neville, B., & Parke, R. D. (1997). Waiting for paternity: Interpersonal and contextual implications of the timing of fatherhood. *Sex Roles, 37,* 45–59.

Neville, H. J., Coffey, S. A., Lawson, D. S., Fischer, A., Emmorey, K., & Bellugi, U. (1997). Neural systems mediating American Sign Language: Effects of sensory experience and age of acquisition. *Brain and Language, 57,* 285–308.

Newell, A., & Simon, H. A. (1961). Computer simulation of human thinking. *Science, 134,* 2011–2017.

Newell, M. L. (2003). Antenatal and perinatal strategies to prevent mother-to-child transmission of HIV infection. *Transactions of the Royal Society of Tropical Medicine and Hygiene, 97,* 22–24.

Newman, C., Atkinson, J., & Braddick, O. (2001). The development of reaching and looking preferences in infants to objects of different sizes. *Developmental Psychology, 37,* 561–572.

Newport, E. L. (1991). Contrasting conceptions of the critical period for language. In S. Carey & R. Gelman (Eds.), *The epigenesis of mind: Essays on biology and cognition.* Hillsdale, NJ: Erlbaum.

Newsom, J. T., Nishishiba, M., Morgan, D. L., & Rook, K. S. (2003). The relative importance of three domains of positive and negative social exchanges: A longitudinal model with comparable measures. *Psychology and Aging, 18,* 746–754.

Newstead, A. H., Walden, J. G., Wood, R. C., & Gitter, A. J. (2000). A comparison of gait parameters in older adults with and without a history of falls during various gait tasks. *Physical Therapy, 80,* 49.

NICHD Early Child Care Research Network. (1997). The effects of infant child care on infant-mother attachment security: Results of the NICHD Study of Early Child Care. *Child Development, 68,* 860–879.

NICHD Early Child Care Research Network. (2001a). Child care and children's peer interaction at 24 and 36 months: The NICHD study of early child care. *Child Development, 72,* 1478–1500.

NICHD Early Child Care Research Network. (2001b). Child-care and family predictors of preschool attachment and stability from infancy. *Developmental Psychology, 37,* 847–862.

NICHD Early Child Care Research Network. (2002a). Early child care and children's development prior to school entry: Results from the NICHD Study of Early Child Care. *American Educational Research Journal, 39,* 133–164.

NICHD Early Child Care Research Network. (2002b). Parenting and family influences when children are in child care: Results from the NICHD Study of Early Child Care. In J. Borkowski, S. L. Ramey, & M. Bristol-Power (Eds.), *Parenting and the child's world: Influences on academic, intellectual, and social-emotional development. Monographs in parenting.* Mahwah, NJ: Lawrence Erlbaum Associates.

NICHD Early Child Care Research Network. (2003a). Does amount of time spent in child care predict socioemotional adjustment during the transition to kindergarten? *Child Development, 74,* 976–1005.

NICHD Early Child Care Research Network. (2003b). Does quality of child care affect child outcomes at age 4½? *Developmental Psychology, 39,* 451–469.

Nicholls, J. G., & Miller, A. T. (1984). Reasoning about the ability of self and others: A developmental study. *Child Development, 55,* 1990–1999.

Nichols, M. (1999). Clinging to life. *Maclean's, 112,* 66.

Nicolich, L. M. (1977). Beyond sensorimotor intelligence: Assessment of symbolic maturity through analysis of pretend play. *Merrill-Palmer Quarterly, 23,* 89–99.

Nielsen, M., Dissanayake, C., & Kashima, Y. (2003). A longitudinal investigation of self–other discrimination and the emergence of minor self-recognition. *Infant Behavior and Development, 26,* 213–226.

Niles, W. (1986). Effects of a moral development discussion group on delinquent and predelinquent boys. *Journal of Counseling Psychology, 33,* 45–51.

Nilsson, L., Adolfsson, R., Bäckman, L., Cruts, M., Edvardsson, H., Nyberg, L., & Van Broeckhoven, C. (2002). Memory development in adulthood and old age: The Betula prospective-cohort study. In P. Graf & N. Ohta (Eds.), *Lifespan development of human memory* (pp. 185–204). Cambridge, MA: Massachusetts Institute of Technology.

Nilsson, M., Perfilieva, E., Johansson, U., Orwar, O., & Eriksson, P. S. (1999). Enriched environment increases neurogenesis in the adult rat dentate gyrus and improves spatial memory. *Journal of Neurobiology, 39,* 569–578.

Nippold, M. A., Hegel, S. L., Sohlberg, M. M., & Schwarz, I. E. (1999). Defining abstract entities: Development in pre-adolescents, adolescents, and young adults. *Journal of Speech, Language, and Hearing Research, 42,* 473-481.

Nock, S. L., & Kingston, P. W. (1988). Time with children: The impact of couples' work-time commitment. *Social Forces, 67,* 59–85.

Nolen-Hoeksema, S. (1990). *Sex differences in depression.* Stanford, CA: Stanford University Press.

Nolen-Hoeksema, S. (2002). Gender differences in depression. In I. H. Gotlib & C. L. Hammen (Eds.), *Handbook of depression.* New York: Guilford.

Nolen-Hoeksema, S., & Ahrens, C. (2002). Age differences and similarities in the correlates of depressive symptoms. *Psychology and Aging, 17,* 116–124.

Nolen-Hoeksema, S., & Girgus, J. S. (1994). The emergence of gender differences in depression during adolescence. *Psychological Bulletin, 115,* 424–443.

Nomaguchi, K. M., & Milkie, M. A. (2003). Costs and rewards of children: The effects of becoming a parent on adults' lives. *Journal of Marriage and the Family, 65,* 356–374.

Noppe, I. C. (2000). Beyond broken bonds and broken hearts: The bonding of theories of attachment and grief. *Developmental Review, 20,* 514–538.

Noppe, I. C., & Noppe, L. D. (1997). Evolving meanings of death during early, middle, and later adolescence. *Death Studies, 21,* 253–275.

Noppe, L. D., & Noppe, I. C. (1996). Ambiguity in adolescent understandings of death. In C. A. Corr & D. E. Balk (Eds.), *Handbook of adolescent death and bereavement.* New York: Springer.

Nordin, S., Razani, L. J., Markison, S., & Murphy, C. (2003). Age-associated increases in intensity discrimination for taste. *Experimental Aging Research, 29,* 371–381.

Nordvik, H., & Amponsah, B. (1998). Gender differences in spatial abilities and spatial activity among university students in an egalitarian educational system. *Sex Roles, 38,* 1009–1023.

Nourhashemi, F., Gillette-Guyonnet, S., Andrieu, S., Ghisolfi, A., Ousset, P. J., Grandjean, H., Grand, A., Pous, J., Vellas, B., & Albarede, J. L. (2000). Alzheimer disease: Protective factors. *American Journal of Clinical Nutrition, 71,* 643s-649s.

Nowell, A., & Hedges, L. V. (1998). Trends in gender differences in academic achievement from 1960 to 1994: An analysis of differences in mean, variance, and extreme scores. *Sex Roles, 39,* 21–43.

Nsamenang, A. B. (1992). *Human development in cultural context: A third world perspective.* Newbury Park, CA: Sage.

Nucci, L., & Turiel, E. (1993). God's word, religious rules, and their relation to Christian and Jewish children's concepts of morality. *Child Development, 64,* 1475–1491.

Nucci, L. P. (2001). *Education in the moral domain.* Cambridge, UK: Cambridge University Press.

Nucci, L. P., & Nucci, M. S. (1982). Children's responses to moral and social conventional transgressions in free-play settings. *Child Development, 53,* 1337–1342.

Nyborg, H., & Jensen, A. R. (2001). Occupation and income related to psychometric *g. Intelligence, 29,* 45–55.

Nyborg, V. M, & Curry, J. F. (2003). The impact of perceived racism: Psychological symptoms among African American boys. *Journal of Clinical Child and Adolescent Psychology, 32,* 258–266.

Nydegger, C. N. (1986). Asymmetrical kin and the problematic son-in-law. In N. Datan, A. L. Greene, & H. W. Reese (Eds.), *Life-span developmental psychology. Intergenerational relations.* Hillsdale, NJ: Erlbaum.

O

Obler, L. K. (2005). Language in adulthood. In J. B. Gleason (Ed.), *The development of language* (6th ed.). Boston: Allyn & Bacon.

O'Brien, M. (1996). Child-rearing difficulties reported by parents of infants and toddlers. *Journal of Pediatric Psychology, 21,* 433–446.

O'Brien, M., Peyton, V., Mistry, R., Hruda, L., Jacobs, A., Caldera, Y., Huston, A., & Roy, C. (2000). Gender-role cognition in three-year-old boys and girls. *Sex Roles, 42,* 1007–1025.

Ochs, A. L., Newberry, J., Lenhardt, M. L., & Harkins, S. W. (1985). Neural and vestibular aging associated with falls. In J. E. Birren & K. W. Schaie (Eds.), *Handbook of the psychology of aging* (2nd ed.). New York: Van Nostrand Reinhold.

Ochs, E. (1982). Talking to children in western Samoa. *Language in Society, 11,* 77–104.

Ochse, R. (1990). *Before the gates of excellence: The determinants of creative genius.* Cambridge, England: Cambridge University Press.

O'Connor, B. P. (1995). Family and friend relationships among older and younger adults: Interaction motivation, mood, and quality. *International Journal of Aging and Human Development, 40,* 9–29.

O'Connor, B. P., & Nikolic, J. (1990). Identity development and formal operations as sources of adolescent egocentrism. *Journal of Youth and Adolescence, 19,* 149–158.

O'Connor, M. J., & Whaley, S. E. (2003). Alcohol use in pregnant low-income women. *Journal of Studies in Alcohol, 64,* 773–783.

O'Connor, T. G., Caspi, A., DeFries, J. C., & Plomin, R. (2000). Are associations between parental divorce and children's adjustment genetically mediated? An adoption study. *Developmental Psychology, 36,* 429–437.

O'Connor, T. G., Deater-Deckard, K., Fulker, D., Rutter, M., & Plomin, R. (1998). Genotype-environment correlations in late childhood and early adolescence: Antisocial behavioral problems and coercive parenting. *Developmental Psychology, 34,* 970–981.

O'Connor, T. G., Marvin, R. S., Rutter, M., Olrick, J. T., & Britner, P. A. (2003). Child–parent attachment following early institutional deprivation. *Development and Psychopathology, 15,* 19–38.

O'Dempsey, T. J. D. (1988). Traditional belief and practice among the Pokot people of Kenya with particular reference to mother and child health: 2. Mother and child health. *Annals of Tropical Pediatrics, 8,* 125.

Oden, M. H. (1968). The fulfillment of promise: 40-year follow-up of the Terman gifted group. *Genetic Psychology Monographs, 77,* 3–93.

Oden, S., & Asher, S. R. (1977). Coaching children in social skills for friendship making. *Child Development, 48,* 495–506.

O'Donnell, A. M., & O'Kelly, J. (1994). Learning from peers: Beyond the rhetoric of positive results. *Educational Psychology Review, 6,* 321–349.

O'Donnell, W. T., & Warren, S. T. (2002). A decade of molecular studies of fragile X syndrome. *Annual Review of Neuroscience, 25,* 315–338.

O'Donoghue, G. M., Nikolopoulos, T. P., & Archbold, S. M. (2000). Determinants of speech perception in children after cochlear implantation. *Lancet, 356,* 466–468.

Offer, D., & Schonert-Reichl, K. A. (1992). Debunking the myths of adolescence: Findings from recent research. *Journal of the American Academy of Child and Adolescent Psychiatry, 31,* 1003–1013.

Offer, D., Ostrov, E., & Howard, K. I. (1981). *The adolescent. A psychological self-portrait.* New York: Basic Books.

Ogbu, J. U. (1981). Origins of human competence: A cultural–ethological perspective. *Child Development, 52,* 413–429.

Ogbu, J. U. (1994). From cultural differences to differences in cultural frames of reference. In P. M. Greenfield & R. R. Cocking (Eds.), *Cross-cultural roots of minority child development.* Hillsdale, NJ: Erlbaum.

Ogbu, J. U. (2003). *Black American students in an affluent suburb: A study of academic disengagement.* Lawrence Erlbaum.

Ogletree, S. M., Martinez, C. N., Turner, T. R., & Mason, B. (2004). Pokemon: Exploring the role of gender. *Sex Roles, 50,* 851–859.

O'Grady, J. P., Pope, C. S., & Patel, S. S. (2000). Vacuum extraction in modern obstetric practice: A review and critique. *Current Opinion in Obstetric Gynecology, 12,* 475–480.

O'Halloran, C. M., & Altmaier, E. M. (1996). Awareness of death among children: Does a life-threatening illness alter the process of discovery? *Journal of Counseling and Development, 74,* 259–262.

Ohman, A., & Mineka, S. (2003). The malicious serpent: Snakes as a prototypical stimulus for an evolved module of fear. *Current Directions in Psychological Science, 12,* 5–9.

Okagaki, L. & Sternberg, R. J. (1993). Parental beliefs and children's school performance. *Child Development, 64,* 36-56.

Okami, P., Olmstead, R., & Abramson, P. R. (1997). Sexual experiences in early childhood: 18-year longitudinal data from the UCLA family lifestyles project. *Journal of Sex Research, 34,* 339–347.

Okie, S. (2001, May 8). Confronting Alzheimer's. Promising vaccine targets ravager of minds. *The Washington Post,* A1, A4.

Olds, D. L., Henderson, C. R., Jr., & Tatelbaum, R. (1994). Prevention of intellectual impairment in children of women who smoke cigarettes during pregnancy. *Pediatrics, 93,* 228–233.

Olfson, M., Shaffer, D., Marcus, S. C., & Greenberg, T. (2003). Relationship between antidepressant medication treatment and suicide in adolescents. *Archives of General Psychiatry, 60,* 978–982.

Oliver, E. I. (1995). The writing quality of seventh, ninth, and eleventh graders, and college freshmen: Does rhetorical specification in writing prompts make a difference? *Research in the Teaching of English, 29,* 422–450.

Olshan, A. F., Schnitzer, P. G., & Baird, P. A. (1994). Paternal age and the risk of congenital heart defects. *Teratology, 50,* 80–84.

Olshansky, S. J., & Carnes, B. A. (2004). In search of the holy grail of senescence. In S. G. Post & R. H. Binstock (Eds.), *The fountain of youth: Cultural, scientific, and ethical perspectives on a biomedical goal.* New York: Oxford University Press.

Olson, C. M. (2002). *Weight gain in pregnancy: A major factor in the development of obesity in childbearing women?* Cornell University. Available online: http://www.cce.cornell.edu/food/expfiles/topics/olson2/olson2overview.html.

Olson, J. M., Vernon, P. A., Harris, J. A., & Jang, K. L. (2001). The heritability of attitudes: A study of twins. *Journal of Personality and Social Psychology, 80,* 845–860.

Oltjenbruns, K. A. (2001). Developmental context of childhood: Grief and regrief phenomena. In M. S. Stroebe, R. O. Hansson, W. Stroebe, & H. Schut (Eds.), *Handbook of bereavement research. Consequences, coping, and care.* Washington, D.C.: American Psychological Association.

Oosterwegel, A., & Oppenheimer, L. (1993). *The self-system: Developmental changes between and within self-concepts.* Hillsdale, NJ: Erlbaum.

Oppenheim, D., Koren-Karie, M., & Sagi, A. (2001). Mothers' empathic understanding of their preschoolers' internal experience: Relations with early attachment. *International Journal of Behavior Development, 25,* 16–26.

Oppenheim, D., Sagi, A., & Lamb, M. E. (1988). Infant-adult attachments on the kibbutz and their relation to socioemotional development 4 years later. *Developmental Psychology, 24,* 427–433.

Orlofsky, J. L. (1993). Intimacy status: Theory and research. In J. E. Marcia, A. S. Waterman,

D. R. Matteson, S. L. Archer, & J. L. Orlofsky (Eds.), *Ego identity: A handbook for psychosocial research.* New York: Springer-Verlag.

Orobio de Castro, B., Veerman, J. W., Koops, W., Bosch, J. D., & Monshouwer, H. J. (2002). Hostile attribution of intent and aggressive behavior: A meta-analysis. *Child Development, 73,* 916–934.

Orth, L. C., & Martin, R. P. (1994). Interactive effects of student temperament and instruction method on classroom behavior and achievement. *Journal of School Psychology, 32,* 149–166.

Orvus, H., Nyirati, I., Hajdu, J., Pal, A., & Kovacs, L. (1999). Is adolescent pregnancy associated with adverse perinatal outcome? *Journal of Perinatal Medicine, 27,* 199–203.

Osterweis, M., Solomon, F., & Green, M. (Eds.). (1984). *Bereavement: Reactions, consequences, and care.* Washington, D.C.: National Academy Press.

Ostwald, S. K., Hepburn, K. W., Caron, W., Burns, T., & Mantell, R. (1999). Reducing caregiver burden: A randomized psychoeducational intervention for caregivers of persons with dementia, *Gerontologist, 39,* 299–309.

Owen, M. J., & O'Donovan, M. C. (2003). Schizophrenia and genetics. In R. Plomin, J. C. DeFries, I. W. Craig, & P. McGuffin (Eds.), *Behavioral genetics in the postgenomic era.* Washington, D.C.: American Psychological Association.

Owens, J., Spirito, A., McGuinn, M., & Nobile, C. (2000). Sleep habits and sleep disturbance in elementary school-aged children. *Journal of Developmental and Behavioral Pediatrics, 21,* 27–36.

Owsley, C., Ball, K., McGwin, G., Sloane, M. E., Roenker, D. L., White, M. F., & Overley, E. T. (1998). Visual processing impairment and risk of motor vehicle crash among older adults. *Journal of the American Medical Association, 279,* 1083–1088.

Oyserman, D., Coon, H. M., & Kemmelmeier, M. (2002). Rethinking individualism and collectivism: Evaluation of theoretical assumptions and meta-analyses. *Psychological Bulletin, 128,* 3–72.

Ozonoff, S. (1997). Components of executive function deficits in autism and other disorders. In J. Russel (Ed.), *Autism as an executive disorder.* Oxford: Oxford University Press.

P

Page, T. (1996, December 22). "Shine," brief candle. *The Washington Post,* G1, G10–G11.

Paikoff, R. L., & Brooks-Gunn, J. (1991). Do parent–child relationships change during puberty? *Psychological Bulletin, 110,* 47–66.

Palkovitz, R. (2002). *Involved fathering and men's adult development: Provisional balances.* Mahwah, NJ: Erlbaum.

Palmore, E. B., Burchett, B. M., Fillenbaum, G. G., George, L. K., & Wallman, L. M. (1985). *Retirement. Causes and consequences.* New York: Springer.

Pan, B. A. (2005). Semantic development. In J. B. Gleason (Ed.), *The development of language* (6th ed.). Boston: Allyn & Bacon.

Paneth, N. S. (1995). The problem of low birth weight. *The Future of Children, 5,* 19–34.

Parazzini, F., Luchini, L., La Vecchia, C., & Crosignani, P. G. (1993). Video display terminal use during pregnancy and reproductive outcomes: A meta-analysis. *Journal of Epidemiology and Community Health, 47,* 265–268.

Park, D. C., Morrell, R. W., Frieske, D., & Kincaid, D. (1992). Medication adherence behaviors in older adults: Effects of external cognitive supports. *Psychology and Aging, 7,* 252–256.

Parke, R. D. (1996). *Fatherhood.* Cambridge, MA: Harvard University Press.

Parke, R. D. (2004). Development in the family. *Annual Review of Psychology, 55,* 365–399.

Parke, R. D., Ornstein, P. A., Rieser, J. J., & Zahn-Waxler, C. (1994). The past as prologue: An overview of a century of developmental psychology. In R. D. Parke, P. A. Ornstein, J. J. Rieser, & C. Zahn-Waxler (Eds.), *A century of developmental psychology.* Washington, D.C.: American Psychological Association.

Parke, R. D., & Sawin, D. B. (1976). The father's role in infancy: A reevaluation. *Family Coordinator, 25,* 365–371.

Parker, F. L., Boak, A. Y., Griffin, K. W., Ripple, C., & Peay, L. (1999). Parent–child relationship, home learning environment, and school readiness. *School Psychology Review, 28,* 413–425.

Parkes, C. M. (1991). Attachment, bonding, and psychiatric problems after bereavement in adult life. In C. M. Parkes, J. Stevenson-Hinde, & P. Marris (Eds.), *Attachment across the life cycle.* London: Tavistock/Routledge.

Parkes, C. M. (1996). *Bereavement: Studies of grief in adult life* (3rd ed.). London: Routledge.

Parkes, C. M. (2000). Comments on Dennis Klass' article "Developing a cross-cultural model of grief." *Omega: Journal of Death and Dying, 41,* 323–326.

Parkes, C. M., & Weiss, R. S. (1983). *Recovery from bereavement.* New York: Basic Books.

Parkhurst, J. T., & Asher, S. R. (1992). Peer rejection in middle school: Subgroup differences in behavior, loneliness, and interpersonal concerns. *Developmental Psychology, 28,* 231–241.

Parnham, J. (2001). Lifelong learning: A model for increasing the participation of non-traditional adult learners. *Journal of Further and Higher Education, 25,* 57–65.

Parten, M. B. (1932). Social participation among preschool children. *Journal of Abnormal and Social Psychology, 27,* 243–269.

Pascalis, O., Deschonen, S., Morton, J., Deruelle, C., & Fabregrenet, M. (1995). Mother's face recognition by neonates: A replication and an extension. *Infant Behavior & Development, 18,* 79–85.

Passman, R. H. (1977). Providing attachment objects to facilitate learning and reduce distress: Effects of mothers and security blankets. *Developmental Psychology, 13,* 25–28.

Pasupathi, M., & Cartensen, L. L. (2003). Age and emotional experience during mutual reminiscing. *Psychology and Aging, 18,* 430–442.

Pasupathi, M., & Staudinger, U. M. (2001). Do advanced moral reasoners also show wisdom? Linking moral reasoning and wisdom-related knowledge and judgment. *International Journal of Behavioral Development, 25,* 401–415.

Pasupathi, M., Staudinger, U. M., & Baltes, P. B. (2001). Seeds of wisdom: Adolescents' knowledge and judgment about difficult life problems. *Developmental Psychology, 37,* 351–361.

Patel, D. R., Pratt, H. D., & Greydanus, D. E. (2003). Treatment of adolescents with anorexia nervosa. *Journal of Adolescent Research, 18,* 244–260.

Patterson C. J. (2004). Gay fathers. In M. E. Lamb (Ed.), *The role of the father in child development* (4th ed.). Hoboken, NJ: John Wiley & Sons.

Patterson, C. J., Kupersmidt, J. B., & Vaden, N. A. (1990). Income level, gender, ethnicity, and household composition as predictors of children's school-based competence. *Child Development, 61,* 485–494.

Patterson, G. R., DeBaryshe, B. D., & Ramsey, E. (1989). A developmental perspective on antisocial behavior. *American Psychologist, 44,* 329–335.

Patton, J. R. (2000). Educating students with mild mental retardation. *Focus on Autism and Other Developmental Disabilities, 15,* 80–89.

Paul, J. P. (1993). Childhood cross-gender behavior and adult homosexuality: The resurgence of biological models of sexuality. *Journal of Homosexuality, 24,* 41–54.

Pauli-Pott, U., Mertesacker, B., Bade, U., Haverkock, A., & Beckmann, D. (2003). Parental perceptions and infant temperament development. *Infant Behavior and Development, 26,* 27–48.

Pauli-Pott, U., Mertesacker, B., & Beckmann, D. (2004). Predicting the development of infant emotionality from maternal characteristics. *Development and Psychopathology, 16,* 19–42.

Paveza, G. J., Cohen, D., Eisdorfer, C., Freels, S., Semla, T., Ashford, J. W., Gorelick, P., Hirschman, R., Luchins, D., & Levy, P. (1992). Severe family violence and Alzheimer's disease: Prevalence and risk factors. *Gerontologist, 32,* 493–497.

Pearce, K. A., & Denney, N. W. (1984). A lifespan study of classification preference. *Journal of Gerontology, 39,* 458–464.

Pearlin, L. I. (1980). Life strains and psychological distress among adults. In N. J. Smelser & E. H. Erikson (Eds.), *Themes of work and love in adulthood.* Cambridge, MA: Harvard University Press.

Pears, K. C., & Moses, L. J. (2003). Demographics, parenting, and theory of mind in preschool children. *Social Development, 12,* 1–19.

Pearson, J. D., Morell, C. H., Gordon-Salant, S., Brant, L. J., Metter, E. J., Klein, L., & Fozard, J. L. (1995). Gender differences in a longitudinal study of age-associated hearing loss. *Journal of the Acoustical Society of America, 97,* 1196–1205.

Pearson, J. L. (2000). Preventing late life suicide: National Institutes of Health initiatives. *Omega: Journal of Death and Dying, 42,* 9–20.

Pedersen, N. L., McClearn, G. E., Plomin, R., & Friberg, L. (1985). Separated fraternal twins: Resemblance for cognitive abilities. *Behavior Genetics, 15,* 407–419.

Peeples, D. R., & Teller, D. Y. (1975). Color vision and brightness discrimination in two-month-old human infants. *Science, 189,* 1102–1103. *Physiology, 279,* R349–354.

Pegg, J. E., Werker, J. F., & McLeod, P. J. (1992). Preference for infant-directed over adult-directed speech: Evidence from 7-week-old infants. *Infant Behavior and Development, 15,* 325–345.

Pelham, W., Chacko, A., & Wymbs, B. (2004). Diagnostic and assessment issues in ADHD in the young child. In R. DelCarmen-Wiggins & A. Carter (Eds.), *Handbook of infant, toddler, and preschool mental health assessment.* New York: Oxford University Press.

Pellegrini, A. D. (1996). *Observing children in their natural worlds: A methodological primer.* Mahwah, NJ: Erlbaum.

Pellegrini, A. D., & Long, J. D. (2003). A sexual selection theory longitudinal analysis of sexual segregation and integration in early adolescence. *Journal of Experimental Child Psychology, 85,* 257–278.

Penner, S. G. (1987). Parental responses to grammatical and ungrammatical child utterances. *Child Development, 58,* 376–384.

Pennington, B. F. (2002). *The development of psychopathology. Nature and nurture.* New York: Guilford.

Pennisi, E. (2003, April 18). Reaching their goal early, sequencing labs celebrate. *Science, 300,* 409.

Pepper, S. C. (1942). *World hypotheses: A study in evidence.* Berkeley, CA: University of California Press.

Perez-Granados, D. R., & Callanan, M. A. (1997). Conversations with mothers and siblings: Young children's semantic and conceptual development. *Developmental Psychology, 33,* 120–134.

Perfetti, C. A. (1999). Cognitive research and the misconceptions of reading education. In J. Oakhill & R. Beard (Eds.), *Reading development and the teaching of reading* (pp. 42–58). Malden, MA: Blackwell.

Pericak-Vance, M. A. (2003). The genetics of autistic disorder. In R. Plomin, J. C. DeFries, I. W. Craig, & P. McGuffin (Eds.), *Behavioral genetics in the postgenomic era.* Washington, D.C.: American Psychological Association.

Perkins, D. (1996). Outsmarting IQ: The emerging science of learnable intelligence. New York: Free Press.

Perkins, H. W., & DeMeis, D. K. (1996). Gender and family effects on the "second-shift" domestic activity of college educated young adults. *Gender & Society, 10,* 78–93.

Perlmutter, M. (1986). A life-span view of memory. In P. B. Baltes, D. L. Featherman, & R. M. Lerner (Eds.), *Life-span development and behavior* (Vol. 7). Hillsdale, NJ: Erlbaum.

Perry, D. G., & Parke, R. D. (1975). Punishment and alternative response training as determinants of response inhibition in children. *Genetic Psychology Monographs, 91,* 257–279.

Perry, H. L. (1993). Mourning and funeral customs of African Americans. In D. P. Irish, K. F. Lundquist, & V. J. Nelson (Eds.), *Ethnic variations in dying, death, and grief: Diversity in universality.* Washington, D.C.: Taylor and Francis.

Perry, W. G., Jr. (1970). *Forms of intellectual and ethical development in the college years: A scheme.* New York: Holt, Rinehart & Winston.

Perry-Jenkins, M., Repetti, R. L., & Crouter, A. C. (2000). Work and family in the 1990s. *Journal of Marriage and the Family, 62,* 981–998.

Persson, G., & Svanborg, A. (1992). Marital coital activity in men at the age of 75: Relation to somatic, psychiatric, and social factors at the age of 70. *Journal of the American Geriatrics Society, 40,* 439–444.

Pesonen, A., Raeikkoenen, K., Keskivaara, P., & Keltikangas-Jaervinen, L. (2003). Difficult temperament in childhood and adulthood: Continuity from maternal perceptions to self-ratings over 17 years. *Personality and Individual Differences, 34,* 19–31.

Pessin, H., Rosenfeld, B., & Breitbart, W. (2002). Assessing psychological distress near the end of life. *American Behavioral Scientist, 46,* 357–372.

Peters, A. (2002). The effects of normal aging on myelin and nerve fibers: A review. *Journal of Neurocytology, 31,* 581–593.

Peters, A., & Liefbroer, A. C. (1997). Beyond marital status: Partner history and well-being in old age. *Journal of Marriage and the Family, 55,* 687–699.

Petersen, A., & Bunton, R. (2002). *The new genetics and the public's health.* London: Routledge.

Petersen, A. C., Compas, B. E., Brooks-Gunn, J., Stemmler, M., Ey, S., & Grant, K. E. (1993). Depression in adolescence. *American Psychologist, 48,* 155–168.

Petersen, R. C., Smith, G. E., Waring, S. C., & Ivnik, R. J. (1997). Aging, memory, and mild cognitive impairment. *International Psychogeriatrics, 65* (Supplement).

Petersen, R. C., Stevens, J. C., Ganguli, M., Tangalos, E. G., Cummings, J. L., & DeKosky, S. T. (2001). Early detection of dementia: Mild cognitive impairment. *Neurology, 56,* 1133-1142.

Peterson, B. E. (2002). Longitudinal analysis of midlife generativity, intergenerational roles, and caregiving. *Psychology and Aging, 17,* 161–168.

Peterson, C. C., Peterson, J. L., & Webb, J. (2000). Factors influencing the development of a theory of mind in blind children. *British Journal of Developmental Psychology, 18,* 431–447.

Peterson, C. C., & Rideout, R. (1998). Memory for medical emergencies experienced by 1 and 2-year-olds. *Developmental Psychology, 34,* 1059–1072.

Peterson, C. C., & Siegal, M. (1999). Representing inner worlds: Theory of mind in autistic, deaf, and normal hearing children. *Psychological Science, 10,* 126–129.

Peterson, C. C., & Siegal, M. (2002). Mind reading and moral awareness in popular and rejected preschoolers. *British Journal of Developmental Psychology, 20,* 205–224.

Peterson, C. C., & Slaughter, V. (2003). Opening windows into the mind: Mothers' preferences for mental state explanations and children's theory of mind. *Cognitive Development, 18,* 399–429.

Peterson, C. & Steen, T. A. (2002). Optimistic explanatory style. In C. R. Snyder & S. J. Lopez (Eds.) *Handbook of positive psychology* (pp. 244-256). New York: Oxford University Press.

Peterson, P. L. (1977). Interactive effects of student anxiety, achievement orientation, and teacher behavior on student achievement and attitude. *Journal of Educational Psychology, 69,* 779–792.

Petitto, L. A., & Marentette, P. F. (1991). Babbling in the manual mode: Evidence for the ontogeny of language. *Science, 251,* 1493–1496.

Phares, V. (1999). *"Poppa" psychology. The role of fathers in children's mental well-being.* Westport, CT: Praeger.

Phillips, M. (1997). What makes schools effective? A comparison of the relationships of communitarian climate and academic climate to mathematics achievement and attendance during middle school. *American Educational Research Journal, 34,* 633–662.

Phillips, S. D. (1982). Career exploration in adulthood. *Journal of Vocational Behavior, 20,* 129–140.

Phillips, T. M., & Pittman, J. F. (2003). Identity processes in poor adolescents: Exploring the linkages between economic disadvantage and the primary task of adolescence. *Identity, 3,* 115–129.

Phinney, J. S. (1993). A three-stage model of ethnic identity development in adolescence. In M. E. Bernal, & G. P. Knight (Eds.), *Ethnic identity: Formation and transmission among Hispanics and other minorities.* Albany, NY: State University of New York Press.

Phinney, J. S. (1996). When we talk about American ethnic groups, what do we mean? *American Psychologist, 51,* 918–927.

Phinney, J. S. (2000). Identity formation across cultures: The interaction of personal, societal, and historical change. *Human Development, 43,* 27–31.

Phipps, B. J. (1995). Career dreams of preadolescent students. *Journal of Career Development, 22,* 19–32.

Phipps, M. G., Blume, J. D., & DeMonner, S. M. (2002). Young maternal age associated with increased risk of postneonatal death. *Obstetrics and Gynecology, 100,* 481–486.

Piaget, J. (1926). *The child's conception of the world.* New York: Harcourt, Brace & World.

Piaget, J. (1950). *The psychology of intelligence.* New York: Harcourt Brace & World.

Piaget, J. (1952). *The origins of intelligence in children.* New York: International Universities Press.

Piaget, J. (1954). *The construction of reality in the child.* New York: Basic Books.

Piaget, J. (1965). *The moral judgment of the child.* New York: Free Press. (Original work published 1932).

Piaget, J. (1970). Piaget's theory. In P. H. Mussen (Ed.), *Carmichael's manual of child psychology* (Vol. 1). New York: Wiley.

Piaget, J. (1972). Intellectual evolution from adolescence to adulthood. *Human Development, 15,* 1–12.

Piaget, J. (1977). The role of action in the development of thinking. In W. F. Overton & J. M. Gallagher (Eds.), *Knowledge and development* (Vol. 1). New York: Plenum.

Piaget, J. (1985). *The equilibration of cognitive structures: The central problem of intellectual development* (T. Brown & K. J. Thampy, Trans.). Chicago: University of Chicago Press.

Piaget, J., & Inhelder, B. (1956). *The child's conception of space.* New York: Norton.

Piaget, J., & Inhelder, B. (1969). *The psychology of the child* (H. Weaver, Trans.). New York: Basic Books. (Original work published 1966).

Pianta, R., Egeland, B., & Erickson, M. F. (1989). The antecedents of maltreatment: Results of the Mother–child Interaction Research Project. In D. Ciccetti & V. Carlson (Eds.), *Child maltreatment: Theory and research on the causes and consequences of child abuse and neglect.* Cambridge, England: Cambridge University Press.

Pickens, J. (1994). Perception of auditory-visual distance relations by 5-month-old infants. *Developmental Psychology, 30,* 537–544.

Pickren, W. E. (2004). Fifty years on: Brown v. Board of Education and American psychology, 1954–2004: An introduction. *American Psychologist, 59,* 493–494.

Pigott, T. A. (2002). Anxiety disorders. In S. G. Kornstein & A. H. Clayton (Eds.), *Women's mental health: A comprehensive textbook* (pp. 195–221). New York: The Guilford Press.

Pilisuk, M., & Minkler, M. (1980). Supportive networks: Life ties for the elderly. *Journal of Social Issues, 36(2),* 95–116.

Pine, J. M. (1994). The language of primary caregivers. In C. Gallaway & B. J. Richards (Eds.), *Input and interaction in language acquisition.* Cambridge, England: Cambridge University Press.

Pinker, S. (2002). *The blank slate. The modern denial of human nature.* New York: Viking.

Pinquart, M., & Sorenson, S. (2000). Influences of socioeconomic status, social network, competence, or subjective competence in later life: A meta-analysis. *Psychology and Aging, 15,* 187–224.

Pinquart, M., & Sorensen, S. (2003). Associations of stressors and uplifts of caregiving with caregiver burden and depressive mood: A meta-analysis. *Journal of Gerontology: Psychological Sciences, 58B,* 112–128.

Pipp, S., Easterbrooks, M. A., & Harmon, R. J. (1992). The relation between attachment and knowledge of self and mother in one-year-old infants to three-year-old infants. *Child Development, 63,* 738–750.

Pitts, M., & Rahman, Q. (2001). Which behaviors constitute "having sex" among university students in the UK? *Archives of Sexual Behavior, 30,* 169–176.

Plassman, B. L., Havlik, R. J., Steffens, D. C., Helms, M. J., Newman, T. N., Drosdick, D., Phillips, C., Gau, B. A., Welsh-Bohmer, K. A., Burke, J. R., Guralnik, J. M., & Breitner, J. C. (2000). Documented head injury in early childhood and risk of Alzheimer's disease and other dementias. *Neurology, 55,* 1158–1166.

Pleck, J. H., & Masciadrelli, B. P. (2004). Paternal involvement by U.S. residential fathers: Levels, sources, and consequences. In M. E. Lamb (Ed.), *The role of the father in child development* (4th ed.). Hoboken, NJ: John Wiley & Sons.

Plomin, R. (1990). *Nature and nurture. An introduction to human behavioral genetics.* Pacific Grove, CA: Brooks/Cole.

Plomin, R., & Bergeman, C. S. (1991). The nature of nurture: Genetic influence on environmental measures. *Behavioral and Brain Sciences, 14,* 373–385.

Plomin, R., Corley, R., DeFries, J. C., & Fulker, D. W. (1990). Individual differences in television viewing in early childhood: Nature as well as nurture. *Psychological Science, 1,* 371–377.

Plomin, R., DeFries, J. C., & Loehlin, J. C. (1977). Genotype–environment interaction and correlation in the analysis of human behavior. *Psychological Bulletin, 84,* 309–322.

Plomin, R., DeFries, J. C., Craig, I. W., & McGuffin, P. (2003). Behavioral genetics. In R. Plomin, J. C. DeFries, I. W. Craig, & P. McGuffin (Eds.), *Behavioral genetics in the postgenomic era.* Washington, D.C.: American Psychological Association.

Plomin, R., DeFries, J. C., McClearn, G. E., & McGuffin, P. (2001). *Behavioral genetics* (4th ed.). New York: Worth.

Plomin, R., & McGuffin, P. (2003). Psychopathology in the postgenomic era. *Annual Review of Psychology, 54,* 205–228.

Plomin, R., Pedersen, N. L., McClearn, G. E., Nesselroade, J. R., & Bergeman, C. S. (1988). EAS temperaments during the last half of the life span: Twins reared apart and twins reared together. *Psychology and Aging, 3,* 43–50.

Plomin, R., & Spinath, F. M. (2004). Intelligence, genetics, genes, and genomics. *Journal of Personality and Social Psychology, 86,* 112–129.

Poehlmann, J., & Fiese, B. H. (2001). The interaction of maternal and infant vulnerabilities on developing attachment relationships. *Development and Psychopathology, 13,* 1–11.

Pollack, H., Lantz, P. M., & Fruhna, J. G. (2000). Maternal smoking and adverse birth outcomes among singletons and twins. *American Journal of Public Health, 90,* 395–400.

Pomerantz, E. M., Altermatt, E. R., & Saxon, J. L. (2002). Making the grade but feeling distressed: Gender differences in academic performance and internal distress. *Journal of Educational Psychology, 94,* 396–404.

Pomerantz, E. M., & Ruble, D. N. (1997). Distinguishing multiple dimensions of conceptions of ability: Implications for self-evaluation. *Child Development, 68,* 1165–1180.

Pomerantz, E. M., Ruble, D. N., Frey, K. S., & Grenlich, F. (1995). Meeting goals and confronting conflict: Children's changing perceptions of social comparison. *Child Development, 66,* 723–738.

Pomerantz, E. M., & Saxon, J. L. (2001). Conceptions of ability as stable and self-evaluative processes: A longitudinal examination. *Child Development, 72,* 152–173.

Pomerleau, A., Bolduc, D., Malcuit, G., & Cossette, L. (1990). Pink or blue: Environmental gender stereotypes in the first two years of life. *Sex Roles, 22,* 359–367.

Ponton, L. (2001). *The sex lives of teenagers: Revealing the secret world of adolescent boys and girls.* New York: Plume.

Poon, H. F., Calabrese, V., Scapagnini, G., & Butterfield, D. A. (2004). Free radicals: Key to brain aging and heme oxygenase as a cellular response to oxidative stress. *Journal of Gerontology: Medical Science, 59A,* 478–493.

Pope, S. K., Shue, V. M., & Beck, C. (2003). Will a healthy lifestyle help prevent Alzheimer's disease? *Annual Review of Public Health, 24,* 111–132.

Popelka, M. M., Cruickshanks, K. J., Wiley, T. L., Tweed, T. S., Klein, B. E., & Klein, R. (1998). Low prevalence of hearing aid use among older adults with hearing loss: The Epidemiology of Hearing Loss Study. *Journal of the American Geriatric Society, 46,* 1075-1078.

Porter, R. H. (1999). Olfaction and human kin recognition. *Genetica, 104,* 259–263.

Porter, R. H., Makin, J. W., Davis, L. B., & Christensen, K. M. (1992). Breast-fed infants respond to olfactory clues from their own mother and unfamiliar lactating females. *Infant Behavior and Development, 15,* 85–93.

Portes, A., & MacLeod, D. (1996). Educational progress of children of immigrants: The roles of class, ethnicity, and school context. *Sociology of Education, 69,* 255–275.

Posada, G., & Jacobs, A. (2001). Child-mother attachment relationships and culture. *American Psychologist, 56,* 821–822.

Posthuma, D., de Geus, E. J. C., & Boomsma, D. I. (2003). Genetic contributions to anatomical, behavioral, and neurophysiological indices of cognition. In R. Plomin, J. C. DeFries, I. W. Craig, & P. McGuffin (Eds.), *Behavioral genetics in the postgenomic era.* Washington, D.C.: American Psychological Association.

Poulin, F., & Boivin, M. (2000). The role of proactive and reactive aggression in the formation and development of boys' friendships. *Developmental Psychology, 36,* 233–240.

Poulin-Dubois, D., & Goodz, N. (2001). Language differentiation in bilingual infants: Evidence from babbling. In J. Cenoz & F. Genesee (Eds.) *Trends in bilingual acquisition* (pp. 95–106). Amsterdam: Netherlandsing Company.

Poulin-Dubois, D., Serbin, L. A., Eichstedt, J. A., Sen, M. G., & Beissel, C. F. (2002). Men don't put on make-up: Toddlers' knowledge of the gender stereotyping of household activities. *Social Development, 11,* 166–181.

Poulin-Dubois, D., Serbin, L. A., Kenyon, B., & Derbyshire, A. (1994). Infants' intermodal knowledge about gender. *Developmental Psychology, 30,* 436–442.

Powers, D. V., Thompson, L., Futterman, A., & Gallagher-Thompson, D. (2002). Depression in late life. Epidemiology, assessment, impact, and treatment. In I. H. Gotlib & C. L. Hammen (Eds.), *Handbook of depression.* New York: Guilford.

Powlishta, K. K. (2000). The effect of target age on the activation of gender stereotypes. *Sex Roles, 42,* 271–282.

Pratt, M. W., Diessner, R., Hunsberger, B., Pancer, S. M., & Savoy, K. (1991). Four pathways in the analysis of adult development and aging: Comparing analyses of reasoning about personal-life dilemmas. *Psychology and Aging, 4,* 666–675.

Pratt, M. W., Diessner, R., Pratt, A., Hunsberger, B., & Pancer, S. M. (1996). Moral and social reasoning and perspective taking in later life: A longitudinal study. *Psychology and Aging, 11,* 66–73.

Pratt, M. W., & Norris, J. E. (1999). Moral development in maturity. Life-span perspectives on the processes of successful aging. In T. M. Hess & F. Blanchard-Fields (Eds.), *Social cognition and aging.* San Diego: Academic Press.

Prebeg, Z., & Bralic, I. (2000). Changes in menarcheal age in girls exposed to war conditions. *American Journal of Human Biology, 12,* 503–508.

Pressley, M. (1983). Making meaningful materials easier to learn: Lessons from cognitive strategy research. In M. Pressley & J. R. Levin (Eds.), *Cognitive strategy research: Educational applications.* New York: Springer-Verlag.

Pressley, M., & Levin, J. R. (1980). The development of mental imagery retrieval. *Child Development, 51,* 558–560.

Pressley, M., Levin, J. R., & Ghatala, E. S. (1984). Memory strategy monitoring in adults and children. *Journal of Verbal Learning and Verbal Behavior, 23,* 270–288.

Price, D. W. W., & Goodman, G. S. (1990). Visiting the wizard: Children's memory for a recurring event. *Child Development, 61,* 664–680.

Prinstein, M. J., Meade, C. S., & Cohen, G. L. (2003). Adolescent oral sex, peer popularity, and perceptions of best friends' sexual behavior. *Journal of Pediatric Psychology, 28,* 243–249.

Proffitt, J. B., Coley, J. D., & Medin, D. L. (2000). Expertise and category-based induction. *Journal of Experimental Psychology: Learning, Memory, and Cognition, 26,* 811–828.

Pungello, E. P., & Kurtz-Costes, B. (1999). Why and how working women choose childcare: A review with a focus on infancy. *Developmental Review, 19,* 31–96.

Purifoy, F. E., Grodsky, A., & Giambra, L. M. (1992). The relationship of sexual daydreaming to sexual activity, sexual drive, and sexual attitudes for women across the life-span. *Archives of Sexual Behavior, 21,* 369–385.

Putallaz, M., & Wasserman, A. (1989). Children's naturalistic entry behavior and sociometric status: A developmental perspective. *Developmental Psychology, 25,* 297–305.

Putnam, F. W. (2003). Ten-year research update review: Child sexual abuse. *Journal of the American Academy of Child and Adolescent Psychiatry, 42,* 269–278.

Pyszczynski, T., Solomon, S., & Greenberg, J. (2003). *In the wake of 9/11: The psychology of terror.* Washington, D.C.: American Psychological Association.

Q

Quigley, B. A. (1997). Rethinking literacy education: The critical need for practice-based change. San Francisco: Jossey-Bass.

Quigley, B. A., & Uhland, R. L. (2000). Retaining adult learners in the first three critical weeks: A quasi-experimental model for use in ABE programs. *Adult Basic Education, 10,* 55–68.

Quill, T. E. (1993). *Death and dignity: Making choices and taking charge.* New York: W. W. Norton.

Quinsey, V. L. Skilling, T. A., Lalumiere, M. L., & Craig, W. M. (2004). *Juvenile delinquency. Understanding the origins of individual differences.* Washington, D.C.: American Psychological Association.

R

Rabbitt, P., Chetwynd, A., & McInnes, L. (2003). Do clever brains age more slowly? Further exploration of a nun result. *British Journal of Psychology, 94,* 63–71.

Rabiner, D. L., Keane, S. P., & MacKinnon-Lewis, C. (1993). Children's beliefs about familiar and unfamiliar peers in relation to their sociometric status. *Developmental Psychology, 29,* 236–243.

Ragland, D. R., Satariano, W. A., & MacLeod, K. E. (2004). Reasons given by older people for limitation or avoidance of driving. *Gerontologist, 44,* 237–244.

Ragow-O'Brien, D., Hayslip, B., & Guarnaccia, C. A. (2000). The impact of hospice on attitudes toward funerals and subsequent bereavement adjustment. *Omega: Journal of Death and Dying, 41,* 291–305.

Rahi, J. S., & Dezateux, C. (1999). National cross sectional study of detection of congenital and infantile cataract in the United Kingdom: Role of childhood screening and surveillance. *British Medical Journal, 318,* 362–365.

Rakoczy, H., Tomasello, M., & Striano, T. (2004). Young children know that trying is not pretending: A test of the "behaving-as-if" construal of children's early concept of pretense. *Developmental Psychology, 40,* 388–399.

Ramey, C. T., & Ramey, S. L. (1992). Effective early intervention. *Mental Retardation, 30,* 337–345.

Ramos, M., & Wilmoth, J. (2003). Social relationships and depressive symptoms among older adults in southern Brazil. *Journals of Gerontology: Psychological Sciences and Social Sciences, 58,* S253–S261.

Rando, T. A. (1986). A comprehensive analysis of anticipatory grief: Perspectives, processes, promises, and problems. In T. A. Rando (Ed.), *Loss and anticipatory grief.* Lexington, MA: Lexington Books.

Rando, T. A. (1991). Parental adjustment to the loss of a child. In D. Papadatou & C. Papadatos (Eds.), *Children and death.* New York: Hemisphere.

Raphael, B. (1983). *The anatomy of bereavement.* New York: Basic Books.

Raphael, B., Minkov, C., & Dobson, M. (2001). Psychotherapeutic and pharmacological intervention for bereaved persons. In M. S. Stroebe, & R. O. Hansson (Eds.), *Handbook of bereavement research: Consequences, coping, and care.* Washington, D.C.: American Psychological Association.

Rapkin, B. D., & Fischer, K. (1992). Personal goals of older adults: Issues in assessment and prediction. *Psychology and Aging, 7,* 127–137.

Ratcliffe, S. D., Byrd, J. E., & Sakornbut, E. L. (1996). *Handbook of pregnancy and perinatal care in family practice: Science and practice.* Philadelphia: Hanley & Belfus.

Raveis, V. H., Siegel, K., & Karus, D. (1999). Children's psychological distress following the death of a parent. *Journal of Youth & Adolescence, 28,* 165–180.

Raz, S., Goldstein, R., Hopkins, T. L., Lauterbach, M. D., Shah, F., Porter, C. L., Riggs, W. W., Magill, L. H., & Sander C. J. (1994). Sex differences in early vulnerability to cerebral injury and their neurodevelopmental implications. *Psychobiology, 22,* 244–253.

Redding, R. E., Harmon, R. J., & Morgan, G. A. (1990). Maternal depression and infants' mastery behaviors. *Infant Behavior and Development, 13,* 391–395.

Reder, L. M., Wible, C., & Martin, J. (1986). Differential memory changes with age: Exact retrieval versus plausible inference. *Journal of Experimental Psychology: Learning, Memory, and Cognition, 12,* 72–81.

Reed, R. (1996, Spring). Birthing fathers. *Mothering,* 50–55.

Reed, T., & Dick, D. M. (2003). Heritability and validity of healthy physical aging (wellness) in elderly male twins. *Twin Research, 6,* 227–234.

Reed, T., Dick, D. M., Uniacke, S. K., Foroud, T., & Nichols, W. C. (2004). Genome-wide scan for a healthy aging phenotype provides support for a locus near D4S1564 promoting healthy aging. *Journal of Gerontology, 59A,* 227–232.

Rees, M. (1993). Menarche when and why? *Lancet, 342,* 1375–1376.

Reese, H. W., & Overton, W. F. (1970). Models of development and theories of development. In L. R. Goulet & P. B. Baltes (Eds.), *Life-span developmental psychology: Research and theory.* New York: Academic Press.

Regier, D. A., Boyd, J. H., Burke, J. D., Rae, D. F., Myers, J. K., Kramer, M., Robins, L. N., George, L. K., Karno, M., & Locke, B. Z. (1988). One-month prevalence of mental disorders in the United States. *Archives of General Psychiatry, 45,* 977–986.

Reid, P. T., & Trotter, K. H. (1993). Children's self-presentations with infants: Gender and ethnic comparisons. *Sex Roles, 29,* 171–181.

Reid, T. R. (1993, January 16). 2 million accept duty of being 20. *The Washington Post,* A14, A24.

Reinherz, H. Z., Giaconia, R. M., Hauf, A. M. C., Wasserman, M. S., & Silverman, A. B. (1999). Major depression in the transition to adulthood: Risks and impairments. *Journal of Abnormal Psychology, 108,* 500–510.

Reis, H. T., Lin, Y., Bennett, M. E., & Nezlek, J. B. (1993). Change and consistency in social participation during early adulthood. *Developmental Psychology, 29,* 633–645.

Reis, O., & Youniss, J. (2004). Patterns of identity change and development in relationships with mothers and friends. *Journal of Adolescent Research, 19,* 31–44.

Reiss, D. (2003). Child effects on family systems: Behavioral genetic strategies. In A. C. Crouter & A. Booth (Eds.), *Children's influence on family dynamics. The neglected side of family relationships.* Mahwah, NJ: Erlbaum.

Reiss, D. (with J. M. Neiderhiser, E. M. Hetherington, & R. Plomin). (2000). *The relationship code. Deciphering genetic and social influences on adolescent development.* Cambridge, MA: Harvard University Press.

Reiss, D., & Neiderhiser, J. M. (2000). The interplay of genetic influences and social processes in developmental theory: Specific mechanisms are coming into view. *Development and Psychopathology, 12,* 357–374.

Reiss, S. (1994). Issues in defining mental retardation. *American Journal of Mental Retardation, 99,* 1-7.

Reitzes, D. C., & Mutran, E. J. (2004). Grandparenthood: Factors influencing frequency of grandparent–grandchildren contact and grandparent role satisfaction. *Journal of Gerontology: Social Sciences, 59B,* S9–S16.

Reker, G. T., Peacock, E. J., & Wong, P. T. P. (1987). Meaning and purpose in life and well-being: A life-span perspective. *Journal of Gerontology, 42,* 44–49.

Rempel, J. (1985). Childless elderly: What are they missing? *Journal of Marriage and the Family, 47,* 343–348.

Renzulli, J. S. (1998). The three-ring conception of giftedness. In S. M. Baum, S. M. Reis, & L. R. Maxfield (Eds.), *Nurturing the gifts and talents of primary grade students.* Mansfield Center, CT: Creative Learning Press.

Repacholi, B. M., & Gopnik, A. (1997). Early reasoning about desires: Evidence from 14- and 18-month-olds. *Developmental Psychology, 33,* 12–21.

Repacholi, B., Slaughter, V., Pritchard, M., & Gibbs, V. (2003). Theory of mind, Machiavellianism, and social functioning in childhood. In B. Repacholi & V. Slaughter (Eds.). *Individual differences in theory of mind: Implications for typical and atypical development.* New York: Psychology Press.

Resnick, S. M. (2000). One-year age changes in MRI brain volumes in older adults. *Cerebral Cortex, 10,* 464–472.

Resnick, S. M., Berenbaum, S. A., Gottesman, I. I., & Bouchard, T. J., Jr. (1986). Early hormonal influences on cognitive functioning in congenital adrenal hyperplasia. *Developmental Psychology, 22,* 191–198.

Rest, J., Narvaez, D., Bebeau, M. J., & Thoma, S. J. (1999). *Postconventional moral thinking. A neo-Kohlbergian approach.* Mahwah, NJ: Erlbaum.

Reuben, D. B., Walsh, K., Moore, A. A., Damesyn, M., & Greendale, G. A. (1998). Hearing loss in community-dwelling older persons: National prevalence data and identification using simple questions. *Journal of the American Geriatric Society, 46,* 1008–1011.

Reynolds, A. J., & Robertson, D. L. (2003). School-based early intervention and later child maltreatment in the Chicago Longitudinal Study. *Child Development, 74,* 3–26.

Reynolds, D. (1992). School effectiveness and school improvement: An updated review of the British literature. In D. Reynolds & P. Cuttance (Eds.), *School effectiveness: Research, policy, and practice.* London: Cassell.

Reynolds, T. (2003, October). Understanding emotion in abused children. *APS Observer, 16,* 1, 31–33.

Reznick, J. S., & Goldfield, B. A. (1992). Rapid change in lexical development in comprehension and production. *Developmental Psychology, 28,* 406–413.

Reznick, J. S., Kagan, J., Snidman, N., Gersten, M., Baak, K., & Rosenberg, A. (1986). Inhibited and uninhibited children: A follow-up study. *Child Development, 57,* 660–680.

Reznikoff, M., Domino, G., Bridges, C., & Honeyman, M. (1973). Creative abilities in identical and fraternal twins. *Behavior Genetics, 3,* 365–377.

Rhee, S. H., & Waldman, I. D. (2002). Genetic and environmental influences on antisocial behavior: A meta-analysis of twin and adoption studies. *Psychological Bulletin, 128,* 490–529.

Rhodes, S. R. (1983). Age-related differences in work attitudes and behavior: A review and conceptual analysis. *Psychological Bulletin, 93,* 328–367.

Rholes, W. S., Simpson, Jeffry A., Campbell, L., & Grich, J. (2001). Adult attachment and the transition to parenthood. *Journal of Personality and Social Psychology, 81,* 421–435.

Ricciardelli, L. A., & McCabe, M. P. (2001). Children's body image concerns and eating disturbance: A review of the literature. *Clinical Psychology Review, 21,* 325–344.

Rice, F., Harold, G. T., & Thapar, A. (2003). Negative life events as an account of age-related differences in the genetic aetiology of depression in childhood and adolescence. *Journal of Child Psychology and Psychiatry and Allied Disciplines, 44,* 977–987.

Richards, F. A., & Commons, M. L. (1990). Postformal cognitive-developmental theory and research: A review of its current status. In C. N. Alexander & E. J. Langer (Eds.), *Higher stages of human development: Perspectives on adult growth.* New York: Oxford University Press.

Richards, R. (1996). Beyond Piaget: Accepting divergent, chaotic, and creative thought. In M. A. Runco (Ed.), *Creativity from childhood through adulthood: The developmental issues.* San Francisco: Jossey-Bass.

Riddle, M. A., Kastelic, E. A., & Frosch, E. (2001). Pediatric psychopharmacology. *Journal of Child Psychology & Psychiatry, 42,* 73–90.

Riegel, K. F. (1973). Dialectic operations: The final period of cognitive development. *Human Development, 16,* 346–370.

Riegel, K. F. (1979). *Foundations of dialectical psychology.* New York: Academic Press.

Rieser, J., Yonas, A., & Wilkner, K. (1976). Radial localization of odors by human newborns. *Child Development, 47,* 856–859.

Rieser, P. & Underwood, L. E. (2004). *A guide to normal growth in children.* Available: http://www.andorrapediatrics.com/handouts/growth.html (retrieved 11/18/2004).

Riley, K. P., Snowdon, D. A., Saunders, A. M., Roses, A. D., Mortimer, J. A., & Nanayakkara, N. (2000). Cognitive function and apolipoprotein E in very old adults: Findings from the Nun Study. *Journal of Gerontology: Psychological Sciences & Social Sciences, 55B,* S69–S75.

Rilling, M. (2000). John Watson's paradoxical struggle to explain Freud. *American Psychologist, 55,* 301–312.

Rimm-Kaufman, S., & Pianta, R. C. (1999). Patterns of family–school contact in preschool and kindergarten. *School Psychology Review, 28,* 426–438.

Ringler, L. L., & Hayden, D. C. (2000). Adolescent bereavement and social support: Peer loss compared to other losses. *Journal of Adolescent Research, 15,* 209–230.

Riviere, J., & Lecuyer, R. (2003). The C-not-B error: A comparative study. *Cognitive Development, 18,* 285–297.

Roberto, K. A., & Scott, J. P. (1986). Equity considerations in the friendships of older adults. *Journal of Gerontology, 41,* 241–247.

Roberts, B. W., & Caspi, A. (2003). The cumulative continuity model of personality development: Striking a balance between continuity and change in personality traits across the life course. In U. M. Staudinger & U. Lindenberger (Eds.), *Understanding human development: Dialogues with life-span psychology.* Dordrecht, Netherlands: Kluwer Academic.

Roberts, B. W., & DelVecchio, W. F. (2000). The rank-order consistency of personality traits from childhood to old age: A quantitative review of longitudinal studies. *Psychological Bulletin, 126,* 3–25.

Roberts, B. W., & Robins, R. W. (2004). Person–environment fit and its implications for personality development: A longitudinal study. *Journal of Personality, 72,* 89–110.

Roberts, L. R., Sarigiani, P. A., Petersen, A. C., & Newman, J. L. (1990). Gender differences in the relationship between achievement and self image during early adolescence. *Journal of Early Adolescence, 10,* 159–175.

Robertson, N. R. C. (1993). *A manual of neonatal intensive care* (3rd ed.). London: Edward Arnold.

Robins, L. N., & Regier, D. A. (Eds.). (1991). *Psychiatric disorders in America. The Epidemiologic Catchment Area Study.* New York: The Free Press.

Robins, R. W., Caspi, A., & Moffitt, T. E. (2000). Two personalities, one relationship: Both partners' personality traits shape the quality of their relationship. *Journal of Personality and Social Psychology, 79,* 251–259.

Robins, R. W., Trzesniewski, K. H., Tracy, J. L., Gosling, S. D., & Potter, J. (2002). Global self-esteem across the life span. *Psychology and Aging, 17,* 423–434.

Robinson, C. C., & Morris, J. T. (1986). The gender-stereotyped nature of Christmas toys received by 36-, 48-, and 60-month-old children: A comparison between nonrequested vs. requested toys. *Sex Roles, 15,* 21–32.

Robinson, G. (1996). Cross-cultural perspectives on menopause. *Journal of Nervous and Mental Disease, 184,* 453–458.

Robinson, N. M., Abbott, R. D., Berninger, V. W., & Busse, J. (1996). The structure of abilities in mathematically precocious young children: Gender similarities and differences. *Journal of Educational Psychology, 88,* 341–352.

Robinson, N. M., & Janos, P. M. (1986). Psychological adjustment in a college-level program of marked academic acceleration. *Journal of Youth and Adolescence, 15,* 51–60.

Robinson, P. K. (1983). The sociological perspective. In R. B. Weg (Ed.), *Sexuality in the later years: Roles and behavior.* New York: Academic Press.

Roccella, M., & Testa, D. (2003). Fetal alcohol syndrome in developmental age: Neuropsychiatric aspects. *Minerva Pediatrics, 55,* 63–69.

Rochat, P., & Striano, T. (2000). Perceived self in infancy. *Infant Behavior and Development,* 23, 513–530.

Röcke, C., & Cherry, K. E. (2002). Death at the end of the 20th century: Individual processes and developmental tasks in old age. *International Journal of Aging and Human Development, 54,* 315–333.

Rodgers, J. L. (2001). What causes birth order–intelligence patterns? The admixture hypothesis, revived. *American Psychologist, 56,* 505–510.

Rodgers, J. L., Cleveland, H. H., van den Oord, E., & Rowe, D. C. (2000). Resolving the debate over birth order, family size, and intelligence. *American Psychologist, 55,* 599–612.

Rodier, P. M. (2000). The early origins of autism. *Scientific American, 282,* 56-63.

Rodin, J., & Langer, E. (1980). Aging labels: The decline of control and the fall of self-esteem. *Journal of Social Issues, 36,* 12–29.

Roenkae, A., & Pulkkinen, L. (1995). Accumulation of problems in social functioning in young adulthood: A developmental approach. *Journal of Personality and Social Psychology, 69,* 381–391.

Rogan, W. J., & Ware, J. H. (2003). Exposure to lead in children: How low is low enough? *New England Journal of Medicine, 384,* 1515–1516.

Rogers, M. T. (1986). *A comparative study of developmental traits of gifted and average children.* Unpublished doctoral dissertation, University of Denver.

Rogers, S. J., & May, D. C. (2003). Spillover between marital quality and job satisfaction: Long-term patterns and gender differences. *Journal of Marriage and the Family, 65,* 482–495.

Rogler, L. H. (2002). The case of the Great Depression and World War II. *American Psychologist, 57,* 1013–1023.

Rogoff, B. (1998). Cognition as a collaborative process. In D. Kuhn & R. S. Siegler (Vol. Eds.), W. Damon (Editor-in-Chief), *Handbook of child psychology: Cognition, perception, and language* (5th ed.). New York: Wiley.

Rogoff, B. (2003). *The cultural nature of human development.* New York: Oxford University Press.

Rogoff, B., Paradise, R., Arauz, R. M., Correa-Chavez, M., & Angelillo, C. (2003). Firsthand learning through intent participation. *Annual Review of Psychology, 54,* 175–203.

Roid, G. (2003). *Stanford-Binet Intelligence Scales* (5th ed.). Itasca, IL: Riverside Publishing.

Roizen, N. J., & Patterson, D. (2003). Down's syndrome. *Lancet, 361,* 1281–1289.

Rojewski, J. W., & Yang, B. (1997). Longitudinal analysis of select influences on adolescents' occupational aspirations. *Journal of Vocational Behavior, 51,* 375–410.

Rolater, S. (2000). One drink too many: Is there no safe level of alcohol consumption during

pregnancy? *American Journal of Nursing, 100,* 64–66.
Rollins, B. C., & Feldman, H. (1970). Marital satisfaction over the family life cycle. *Journal of Marriage and the Family, 32,* 20–28.
Rolls, B. J. (1999). Do chemosensory changes influence food intake in the elderly? *Physiological Behavior, 66,* 193–197.
Román, G. C. (2003). Neurological aspects of vascular dementia: Basic concepts, diagnosis, and management. In P. A. Lichtenberg, D. L. Murman, & A. M. Mellow (Eds.), *Handbook of dementia. Psychological, neurological, and psychiatric perspectives.* Hoboken, NJ: John Wiley & Sons.
Rook, K. S. (1984). Promoting social bonding. Strategies for helping the lonely and socially isolated. *American Psychologist, 39,* 1389–1407.
Rook, K. S. (1991). Facilitating friendship formation in late life: Puzzles and challenges. *American Journal of Community Psychology, 19,* 103–110.
Rose, R. J. (2002). How do adolescents select their friends? A behavior-genetic perspective. In L. Pulkkinen & A. Caspi (Eds.), *Paths to successful development: Personality in the life course.* Cambridge, UK: Cambridge University Press.
Rose, R. J., Viken, R. J., Dick, D. M., Bates, J. E., Pulkkinen, L., & Kaprio, J. (2003). It does take a village: Nonfamilial environments and children's behavior. *Psychological Science, 14,* 273–277.
Rose, S., & Maffulli, N. (1999). Hip fractures: An epidemiological review. *Bulletin of Joint Disease, 58,* 197–201.
Rose, S. A., & Feldman, J. F. (1997). Memory and speed: Their role in the relation of infant information processing to later IQ. *Child Development, 68,* 630–641.
Rose, S. A., Feldman, J. F., Futterweit, L. R., & Jankowski, J. J. (1997). Continuity in visual cognition memory: Infancy to 11 years. *Intelligence, 24,* 381–392.
Rose, S. A., Feldman, J. F., & Jankowski, J. J. (2003). Infant visual recognition memory: Independent contributions of speed and attention. *Developmental Psychology, 39,* 563–571.
Rose, S. A., Feldman, J. F., Wallace, I. F., & McCarton, C. (1989). Infant visual attention: Relation to birth status and developmental outcome during the first 5 years. *Developmental Psychology, 25,* 560–576.
Rosenberg, J. (2001). Exposure to multiple risk factors linked to delivery of underweight infants. *Family Planning Perspectives, 33,* 238.
Rosenberg, S. D., Rosenberg, H. J., & Farrell, M. P. (1999). The midlife crisis revisited. In S. L. Willis & J. D. Reid (Eds.), *Life in the middle. Psychological and social development in middle age.* San Diego: Academic Press.
Rosenblatt, P. C. (1993). Cross-cultural variation in the experience, expression, and understanding of grief. In D. P. Irish, K. F. Lundquist, & V. J. Nelson (Eds.), *Ethnic variations in dying, death, and grief: Diversity in universality.* Washington, D.C.: Taylor and Francis.
Rosenblatt, P. C. (2001). A social constructionist perspective on cultural differences in grief. In M. S. Stroebe, R. O. Hansson, W. Stroebe, & H. Schut (Eds.), *Handbook of bereavement research. Consequences, coping, and care.* Washington, D.C.: American Psychological Association.
Rosenfeld, R. G. (1997). Is growth hormone just a tall story? *Journal of Pediatrics, 130,* 172–174.
Rosenholtz, S. J., & Simpson, C. (1984). The formation of ability conceptions: Developmental trend or social construction? *Review of Educational Research, 54,* 31–63.
Rosenthal, P. A., & Rosenthal, S. (1984). Suicidal behavior by preschool children. *American Journal of Psychiatry, 141,* 520–525.
Rosenwasser, S. M., Lingenfelter, M., & Harrington, A. F. (1989). Nontraditional gender role portrayals on television and children's gender role perceptions. *Journal of Applied Developmental Psychology, 10,* 97–105.
Roskos, K. A., Christie, J. F., & Richgels, D. J. (2003, March). The essentials of early literacy instruction. *Young Children,* 52–60.
Ross, C. A., Miler, S. D., Bjornson, L., Reagor, P., Fraser, G. A., & Anderson, G. (1991). Abuse histories in 102 cases of multiple personality disorder. *Canadian Journal of Psychiatry, 36,* 97–101.
Ross, H. G., & Milgram, J. I. (1982). Important variables in adult sibling relationships: A qualitative study. In M. E. Lamb & B. Sutton-Smith (Eds.), *Sibling relationships: Their nature and significance across the lifespan.* Hillsdale, NJ: Erlbaum.
Ross, M., & Wilson, A. E. (2003). Autobiographical memory and conceptions of self: Getting better all the time. *Current Directions in Psychological Science, 12,* 66–69.
Ross, R. T., Begab, M. J., Dondis, E. H., Giampiccolo, J. S., Jr., & Meyers, C. E. (1985). *Lives of the mentally retarded: A forty-year follow-up study.* Stanford, CA: Stanford University Press.
Rossell, C. H., Armor, D. J., & Walberg, H. J. (Eds.) (2002). *School desegregation in the 21st century.* Westport, CT: Praeger.
Rosser, R. (1994). *Cognitive development: Psychological and biological perspectives.* Boston: Allyn & Bacon.
Roth, F. P., Speece, D. L., & Cooper, D. H. (2002). A longitudinal analysis of the connection between oral language and early reading. *Journal of Educational Research, 95,* 259–272.
Roth, P. L., Bevier, C. A., Switzer, F. S., & Schippmann, J. S. (1996). Meta-analyzing the relationship between grades and job performance. *Journal of Applied Psychology, 81,* 548–556.
Rothbart, M. K., Ahadi, S. A., & Evans, D. E. (2000). Temperament and personality: Origins and outcomes. *Journal of Personality and Social Psychology, 78,* 122–135.
Rothbaum, F., Weisz, J., Pott, M., Miyake, K., & Morelli, G. (2000). Attachment and culture: Security in the United States and Japan. *American Psychologist, 55,* 1093–1104.
Rothbaum, R., Pott, M., Azuma, H., Miyake, K., & Weisz, J. (2000). The development of close relationships in Japan and the United States: Paths of symbiotic harmony and generative tension. *Child Development, 71,* 1121–1142.
Rothberg, A. D., & Lits, B. (1991). Psychosocial support for maternal stress during pregnancy: Effect on birth weight. *American Journal of Obstetrics and Gynecology, 165,* 403–407.
Rotheram-Borus, M. J., Piacentini, J., Cantwell, C., Belin, T. R., & Song, J. W. (2000). The 18-month impact of an emergency room intervention for adolescent female suicide attempters. *Journal of Consulting and Clinical Psychology, 68,* 1081–1093.
Rothermund, K., & Brandtstädter, J. (2003a). Age stereotypes and self-views in later life: Evaluating rival assumptions. *International Journal of Behavioral Development, 27,* 549–554.
Rothermund, K., & Brandtstädter, J. (2003b). Coping with deficits and losses in later life: From compensatory action to accommodation. *Psychology and Aging, 18,* 896–905.
Rothermund, K., & Brandtstädter, J. (2003c). Depression in later life: Cross-sequential patterns and possible determinants. *Psychology and Aging, 18,* 80–90.
Rovee-Collier, C. (1997). Dissociations in infant memory: Rethinking the development of implicit and explicit memory. *Psychological Review, 104,* 467–498.
Rovee-Collier, C. (1999). The development of infant memory. *Current Directions in Psychological Science, 8,* 80–85.
Rovee-Collier, C. (2001). Information pick-up by infants: What is it, and how can we tell? *Journal of Experimental Child Psychology, 78,* 35–49.
Rovee-Collier, C., & Barr, R. (2004). Infant learning and memory. In G. Bremner & A. Fogel (Eds.), *Blackwell handbook of infant development* (pp. 139–168). Malden, MA: Blackwell Publishing.
Rovee-Collier, C., & Boller, K. (1995). Current theory and research on infant learning and memory: Application to early intervention. *Infants and Young Children, 7,* 1–12.
Rovner, S. (1994, March 29). An Alzheimer's journal. *The Washington Post—Health,* 12–15.
Rowe, D. C. (1994). *The limits of family influence: Genes, experience, and behavior.* New York: Guilford.
Rowe, D. C. (2003). Assessing genotype-environment interactions and correlations in the postgenomic era. In R. Plomin, J. C. DeFries, I. W. Craig, & P. McGuffin (Eds.), *Behavioral genetics in the postgenomic era.* Washington, D.C.: American Psychological Association.
Rowe, D. C., Almeida, D. M., & Jacobson, K. C. (1999). School context and genetic influences on aggression in adolescence. *Psychological Science, 10,* 277–280.
Rowe, D. C., & Jacobson, K. C. (1999). In the mainstream. Research in behavioral genetics. In R. A. Carson & M. A. Rothstein (Eds.), *Behavioral genetics. The clash of culture and biology.* Baltimore: Johns Hopkins University Press.
Rowe, D. C., Vesterdal, W. J., & Rodgers, J. L. (1999). Herrnstein's syllogism: Genetic and shared environmental influences on IQ, education, and income. *Intelligence, 26,* 405–423.
Rowe, J. W., & Kahn, R. L. (1998). *Successful aging.* New York: Pantheon.
Rowe, S. M., & Wertsch, J. V. (2004). Vygotsky's model of cognitive development. In U. Goswami (Ed.), *Blackwell handbook of childhood cognitive development* (pp. 538–554). Malden, MA: Blackwell Publishers.
Rubin, D. C. (2002). Autobiographical memory across the lifespan. In P. Graf & N. Ohta (Eds.), *Lifespan development of human memory* (pp. 159–184). Cambridge, MA: Massachusetts Institute of Technology.
Rubin, D. C., Rahhal, T. A., & Poon, L. W. (1998). Things learned in early adulthood are remembered best. *Memory and Cognition, 26,* 3–19.

Rubin, D. C., Wetzler, S. E., & Nebes, R. D. (1986). Autobiographical memory across the adult lifespan. In D. C. Rubin (Ed.), *Autobiographical memory* (pp. 202–221). Cambridge: Cambridge University Press.

Rubin, J. Z., Provenzano, F. J., & Luria, Z. (1974). The eye of the beholder: Parents' views on sex of newborns. *American Journal of Orthopsychiatry, 44,* 512–519.

Rubin, S. S., & Malkinson, R. (2001). Parental response to child loss across the life cycle: Clinical and research perspectives. In M. S. Stroebe, R. O. Hansson, W. Stroebe, & H. Schut (Eds.), *Handbook of bereavement research. Consequences, coping, and care.* Washington, D.C.: American Psychological Association.

Rubinow, D. R., & Schmidt, P. J. (1996). Androgens, brain, and behavior. *American Journal of Psychiatry, 153,* 974–984.

Rubinstein, R. L., Alexander, R. B., Goodman, M., & Luborsky, M. (1991). Key relationships of never married, childless older women: A cultural analysis. *Journal of Gerontology: Social Sciences, 46,* S270–S277.

Ruble, D. N. (1983). The development of comparison processes and their role in achievement-related self-socialization. In E. T. Higgins, D. N. Ruble, & W. W. Hartup (Eds.), *Social cognition and social development: A sociocultural perspective.* New York: Cambridge University Press.

Ruble, D. N., & Dweck, C. S. (1995). Self-conceptions, person conceptions, and their development. In N. Eisenberg (Ed.), *Social development.* Thousand Oaks, CA: Sage.

Ruble, D. N., Eisenberg, R., & Higgins, E. T. (1994). Developmental changes in achievement evaluation: Motivational implications of self–other differences. *Child Development, 65,* 1095–1110.

Ruble, D. N., & Martin, C. L. (1998). Gender development. In N. Eisenberg (Vol. Ed.), W. Damon (Editor-in-Chief), *Handbook of child psychology: Vol. 3. Social, emotional, and personality development* (5th ed., pp. 933–1016). New York: Wiley.

Ruchlin, H. S., & Lachs, M. S. (1999). Prevalence and correlates of exercise among older adults. *Journal of Applied Gerontology, 18,* 341–356.

Ruff, H. A., & Capozzoli, M. C. (2003). Development of attention and distractibility in the first 4 years of life. *Developmental Psychology, 39,* 877–890.

Ruff, H. A., & Lawson, K. R. (1990). Development of sustained, focused attention in young children during free play. *Developmental Psychology, 26,* 85–93.

Ruff, H. A., & Rothbart, M. K. (1996). *Attention in early development: Themes and variations.* New York: Oxford University Press.

Ruff, H. A., Saltarelli, L. M., Coppozzoli, M., & Dubiner, K. (1992). The differentiation of activity in infants' exploration of objects. *Developmental Psychology, 27,* 851–861.

Ruffman, T., Slade, L., Rowlandson, K., Rumsey, C., Garnham, A. (2003). How language relates to belief, desire, and emotion understanding. *Cognitive Development, 18,* 139–158.

Ruffman, T. K., & Olson, D. R. (1989). Children's ascriptions of knowledge to others. *Developmental Psychology, 25,* 601–606.

Ruggles, S. (1994). The origins of African-American family structure. *American Sociological Review, 59,* 136–151.

Runco, M. A. (1992). Children's divergent thinking and creative ideation. *Developmental Review, 12,* 233–264.

Russ, S. W. (1996). Development of creative processes in children. In M. A. Runco (Ed.), *Creativity from childhood through adulthood: The developmental issues.* San Francisco: Jossey-Bass.

Russel, S. T. (2002). Childhood developmental risk for teen childbearing in Britain. *Journal of Research on Adolescence, 12,* 305–324.

Russell, A., Aloa, V., Feder, T., Glover, A., Miller, H., & Palmer, G. (1998). Sex-based differences in parenting styles in a sample with preschool children. *Australian Journal of Psychology, 50,* 89–99.

Russell, R. J., & Wells, P. A. (1991). Personality similarity and quality of marriage. *Personality and Individual Differences, 12,* 407–412.

Rust, J., Golombok, S., Hines, M., Johnston, K., & Golding, J. (2000). The role of brothers and sisters in the gender development of preschool children. *Journal of Experimental Child Psychology, 77,* 292–303.

Ruth, J. E., & Coleman, P. (1996). Personality and aging: Coping and management of the self in later life. In J. E. Birren, K. W. Schaie, R. P. Abeles, M. Gatz, & T. A. Salthouse (Eds.), *Handbook of the psychology of aging* (4th ed.). San Diego: Academic Press.

Rutter, M. (1983). School effects on pupil progress: Research findings and policy implications. *Child Development, 54,* 1–29.

Rutter, M. (2000). Psychosocial influences: Critiques, findings, and research needs. *Development and Psychopathology, 12,* 375–405.

Rutter, M., & Maughan, B. (2002). School effectiveness findings 1979–2002. *Journal of School Psychology, 50,* 451–475.

Rutter, M., Maughan, B., Mortimore, P., Ouston, J., & Smith, A. (1979). *Fifteen thousand hours: Secondary schools and their effects on children.* Cambridge, MA: Harvard University Press.

Rutter, M., & O'Connor, T. G. (2004). Are there biological programming effects for psychological development? Findings from a study of Romanian adoptees. *Developmental Psychology, 40,* 81–94.

Rutter, M., & Sroufe, L. A. (2000). Developmental psychopathology: Concepts and challenges. *Development and Psychopathology, 12,* 265–296.

Ruusuvirta, T., Huotilainen, M., Fellman, V., & Naatanen, R. (2003). The newborn human brain binds sound features together. *Neuroreport, 14,* 2117–2119.

Ryan, R. M., & Kuczkowski, R. (1994). The imaginary audience, self-consciousness, and public individuation in adolescence. *Journal of Personality, 62,* 219–238.

Rybash, J. M. (1999). Aging and autobiographical memory: The long and bumpy road. *Journal of Adult Development, 6,* 1–10.

Ryff, C. D. (1991). Possible selves in adulthood and old age: A tale of shifting horizons. *Psychology and Aging, 6,* 286–295.

S

Saarni, C. (1999). *The development of emotional competence.* New York: Guilford Press.

Sabattini, L., & Leaper, C. (2004). The relation between mothers' and fathers' parenting styles and their division of labor in the home: Young adults' retrospective reports. *Sex Roles, 50,* 217–225.

Sackett, P. R., Hardison, C. M., & Cullen, M. J. (2004). On interpreting stereotype threat as accounting for African American-White differences on cognitive tests. *American Psychologist, 59,* 7–13.

Sacks, O. (1993, December 27). A neurologist's notebook: An anthropologist on Mars. *The New Yorker,* 106–125.

Sadeh, A., Gruber, R., & Raviv, A. (2003). The effects of sleep restriction and extension on school-age children: What a difference an hour makes. *Child Development, 74,* 444–455.

Sadeh, A., Raviv, A., & Gruber, R. (2000). Sleep patterns and sleep disruptions in school-age children. *Developmental Psychology, 36,* 291–300.

Sadker, M., & Sadker, D. (1994). *Failing at fairness: How America's schools cheat girls.* New York: Scribner's.

Sadler, T. W. (2004). *Langman's medical embryology* (9th ed.). Philadelphia: Lippincott, Williams, & Wilkins.

Sagall, R. J. (2003). Smoking and placental injury. *Pediatrics for Parents, 20,* 11.

Saigal, S., Hoult, L. A., Stoskopf, B. L., Rosenbaum, P. L., & Streiner, D. L. (2000). School difficulties at adolescence in a regional cohort of children who were extremely low birth weight. *Pediatrics, 105,* 325–331.

Salapatek, P. (1975). Pattern perception in early infancy. In L. B. Cohen & P. Salapatek (Eds.), *Infant perception: From sensation to cognition, Vol 1.* New York: Academic Press.

Salend, S. J. (1999). Facilitating friendships among diverse students. *Intervention in School and Clinic, 35,* 9–15.

Sales, B. D., & Folkman, S. (2000). *Ethics in research with human participants.* Washington, D.C.: American Psychological Association.

Salthouse, T. A. (1984). Effects of age and skill in typing. *Journal of Experimental Psychology: General, 113,* 345–371.

Salthouse, T. A. (1990). Cognitive competence and expertise in aging. In J. E. Birren & K. W. Schaie (Eds.), *The handbook of the psychology of aging* (3rd ed.). San Diego: Academic Press.

Salthouse, T. A. (1992). Why do adult age differences increase with task complexity? *Developmental Psychology, 28,* 905–918.

Salthouse, T. A. (1993). Speed and knowledge as determinants of adult age differences in verbal tasks. *Journal of Gerontology: Psychological Sciences, 48,* 29–36.

Salthouse, T. A. (1996). General and specific speed mediation of adult age differences in memory. *Journals of Gerontology: Psychological Sciences and Social Sciences, 51B,* 30–42.

Salthouse, T. A., Hancock, H. E., Meinz, E. J., & Hambrick, D. Z. (1996). Interrelations of age, visual acuity, and cognitive functioning. *Journals of Gerontology: Psychological Sciences and Social Sciences, 51,* 317–330.

Sameroff, A. (1975). Early influences on development: Fact or fancy? *Merrill-Palmer Quarterly, 21,* 263–294.

Sameroff, A. J. (2000). Developmental systems and psychopathology. *Development and Psychopathology, 12,* 297–312.

Sameroff, A. J., & Chandler, M. J. (1975). Reproductive risk and the continuum of caretaking casualty. In F. D. Horowitz, M. Hetherington, S. Scarr-Salapatek, & G. Siegel (Eds.), *Review of child development research* (Vol. 4). Chicago: University of Chicago Press.

Sameroff, A. J., Seifer, R., Baldwin, A., & Baldwin, C. (1993). Stability of intelligence from preschool to adolescence: The influence of social and family risk factors. *Child Development, 64,* 80–97.

Samson, M. M., Meeuwsen, I. B. A. E., Crowe, A., Dessens, J. A. G., Duursma, S. A., & Verhaar, H. J. J. (2000). Relationships between physical performance measures, age, height and body weight in healthy adults. *Age and Ageing, 29,* 235-242.

Samuels, S. C., & Davis, K. L. (2003). Advances in the treatment of Alzheimer's disease. In M. F. Weiner & A. M. Lipton (Eds.), *The dementias. Diagnosis, treatment, and research.* Washington, D.C.: American Psychiatric Publishing.

Samuelson, R. J. (2002, December 16). The "mature worker" glut. *Newsweek,* 55.

Samuolis, J., Layburn, K., & Schiaffino, K. M. (2001). Identity development and attachment to parents in college students. *Journal of Youth and Adolescence, 30,* 373–384.

Sanchez, L., Fristad, M., Weller, R. A., Weller, E. B., & Moye, J. (1994). Anxiety in acutely bereaved prepubertal children. *Annals of Clinical Psychiatry, 6,* 39–43.

Sanchez, L., & Thomson, E. (1997). Becoming mothers and fathers: Parenthood, gender, and the division of labor, *Gender & Society, 11,* 747–772.

Sander, C. J. (1994). Sex differences in early vulnerability to cerebral injury and their neurobehavioral implications. *Psychobiology, 22,* 244–253.

Sanders, C. M. (1979–1980). A comparison of adult bereavement in the death of a spouse, child and parent. *Omega: Journal of Death and Dying, 10,* 303–322.

Sanson, A., Hemphill, S. A., & Smart, D. (2004). Connections between temperament and social development: A review. *Social Development, 13,* 142–170.

Santor, D. A., Messervey, D., & Kusumakar, V. (2000). Measuring peer pressure, popularity, and conformity in adolescent boys and girls: Predicting school performance, sexual attitudes, and substance abuse. *Journal of Youth and Adolescence, 29,* 163–182.

Sargant, N., Field, J., Francis, H., Schuller, T., & Tuckett, A. (1997). *The learning divide.* Brighton, UK: National Organisation for Adult Learning.

Sarkisian, N., & Gerstel, N. (2004). Explaining the gender gap in help to parents: The importance of employment. *Journal of Marriage and Family, 66,* 431–451.

Sartor, C. E., & Youniss, J. (2002). The relationship between positive parental involvement and identity achievement during adolescence. *Adolescence, 37,* 221–234.

Sassler, S. (2004). The process of entering into cohabiting unions. *Journal of Marriage and Family, 66,* 491–505.

Saunders, C. (2002). A hospice perspective. In K. Foley, & H. Hendin (Eds.), *The case against assisted suicide: For the right to end-of-life care.* Baltimore: The Johns Hopkins Press.

Savin-Williams, R. C. (1995). An exploratory study of pubertal maturation timing and self-esteem among gay and bisexual male youths., *Developmental Psychology, 31,* 56-64.

Savin-Williams, R. C., & Esterberg, K. G. (2000). Lesbian, gay, and bisexual families. In D. H. Demo, K. R. Allen, & M. A. Fine (Eds.), *Handbook of family diversity.* New York: Oxford University Press.

Savin-Williams, R. C., & Ream, G. L. (2003). Sex variations in the disclosure to parents of same-sex attractions. *Journal of Family Psychology, 17,* 429–438.

Saxe, R., Carey, S., & Kanwisher, N. (2004). Understanding other minds: Linking developmental psychology and functional neuroimaging. *Annual Review of Psychology, 55,* 87–124.

Saxton, M. (1997). The contrast theory of negative input. *Journal of Child Language, 24,* 139–161.

Sayre, N. E., & Gallagher, J. D. (2001). *The young child and the environment.* Boston: Allyn & Bacon.

Scafidi, F. A., Field, T., & Schanberg, S. M. (1993). Factors that predict which preterm infants benefit most from massage therapy. *Journal of Developmental and Behavioral Pediatrics, 14,* 176–180.

Scarr, S., & Eisenberg, M. (1993). Child care research: Issues, perspectives, and results. *Annual Review of Psychology, 44,* 613–644.

Scarr, S., & McCartney, K. (1983). How people make their own environments: A theory of genotype→environment effects. *Child Development, 54,* 424–435.

Scarr, S., & Weinberg, R. A. (1978). The influence of family background on intellectual attainment. *American Sociological Review, 43,* 674–692.

Scarr, S., & Weinberg, R. A. (1983). The Minnesota adoption studies: Genetic differences and malleability. *Child Development, 54,* 260–267.

Schaal, B., Barlier, L., & Soussignan, R. (1998). Olfactory function in the human fetus: Evidence from selective neonatal responsiveness to the odor of amniotic fluid. *Behavioral Neuroscience, 112,* 1438-1449.

Schachar, R. J., Tannock, R., Cunningham, C., & Corkum, P. V. (1997). Behavioral, situational, and temporal effects of treatment of ADHD with methylphenidate. *Journal of the American Academy of Child and Adolescent Psychiatry, 36,* 754–763.

Schacter, D. L. (1996). *Searching for memory: The brain, the mind, and the past.* New York: Basic Books.

Schaefer, E. S. (1959). A circumplex model for maternal behavior. *Journal of Abnormal and Social Psychology, 59,* 226–235.

Schaffer, H. R. (2000). The early experience assumption: Past, present, and future. *International Journal of Behavior Development, 24,* 5–14.

Schaffer, H. R., & Emerson, P. E. (1964). The development of social attachments in infancy. *Monographs of the Society for Research in Child Development, 29* (3, Serial No. 94).

Schaie, K. W. (1983). The Seattle Longitudinal Study: A 21-year exploration of psychometric intelligence in adulthood. In K. W. Schaie (Ed.), *Longitudinal studies of adult psychological development.* New York: Guilford.

Schaie, K. W. (1989). The hazards of cognitive aging. *Gerontologist, 29,* 484–493.

Schaie, K. W. (1990). Intellectual development in adulthood. In J. E. Birren & K. W. Schaie (Eds.), *The handbook of the psychology of aging* (3rd ed.). San Diego: Academic Press.

Schaie, K. W. (1994). Developmental designs revisited. In S. H. Cohen & H. W. Reese (Eds.), *Life-span developmental psychology: Methodological contributions.* Hillsdale, NJ: Erlbaum.

Schaie, K. W. (1996). *Intellectual development in adulthood: The Seattle Longitudinal Study.* Cambridge, England: Cambridge University Press.

Schaie, K. W., & Parham, I. A. (1976). Stability of adult personality traits: Fact or fable? *Journal of Personality and Social Psychology, 34,* 146–158.

Schaie, K. W., & Willis, S. L. (1986). Can decline in adult intellectual functioning be reversed? *Developmental Psychology, 22,* 223–232.

Schalock, R. L., Holl, C., Elliott, B., & Ross, I. (1992). A longitudinal follow-up of graduates from a rural special education program. *Learning Disability Quarterly, 15,* 29–38.

Schank, R. C., & Abelson, R. P. (1977). *Scripts, plans, goals, and understanding.* Hillsdale, NJ: Erlbaum.

Scharf, M., Mayseless, O., & Kivenson-Baron, I. (2004). Adolescents' attachment representations and developmental tasks in emerging adulthood. *Developmental Psychology, 40,* 430–444.

Schell, L., & Knutsen, K. L. (2002). Environmental effects on growth. In N. Cameron (Ed.), *Human growth and development* (pp. 165–195). New York: Academic Press.

Schery, T. K., & Peters, M. L. (2003). Developing auditory learning in children with cochlear implants. *Topics in Language Disorders, 23,* 4–15.

Schiavi, R. C., Schreiner-Engel, P., White, D., & Mandeli, J. (1991). The relationship between pituitary-gonadal function and sexual behavior in healthy aging men. *Psychosomatic Medicine, 53,* 363–374.

Schieffelin, B. B. (1986). *How Kaluli children learn what to say, what to do, and how to feel.* New York: Cambridge University Press.

Schiff, A. R., & Knopf, I. J. (1985). The effect of task demands on attention allocation in children of different ages. *Child Development, 56,* 621–630.

Schiffman, H. R. (2000). *Sensation and perception* (5th ed.) New York: Wiley.

Schiffman, S. S. (1977). Food recognition by the elderly. *Journal of Gerontology, 32,* 586–592.

Schiffman, S. S. (1997). Taste and smell losses in normal aging and disease. *Journal of the American Medical Association, 278,* 1357–1362.

Schiffman, S. S., & Warwick, Z. S. (1993). Effect of flavor enhancement of foods for the elderly on nutritional status: Food intake, biochemical indices, and anthropometric measures. *Physiological Behavior, 53,* 395–402.

Schindl, M., Birner, P., Reingrabner, M., Joura, E., Husslein, P., & Langer, M. (2003). Elective cesarean section vs. spontaneous delivery: A comparative study of birth experience. *Acta Obstetrics and Gynecology of Scandinavia, 82,* 834–840.

Schmidt, F. L., & Hunter, J. E. (1998). The validity and utility of selection methods in personnel psychology: Practical and theoretical implications of 85 years of research findings. *Psychological Bulletin, 124,* 262–274.

Schmidt, F. L., & Hunter, J. E. (2004). General mental ability in the world of work: Occupational attainment and job performance. *Journal of Personality and Social Psychology, 86,* 162–173.

Schmidt, P. J., Nieman, L. K., Danaceau, M. A., Adams, L. F., & Rubinow, D. R. (1998). Differential behavioral effects of gonadal steroids in women with and in those without premenstrual syndrome. *New England Journal of Medicine, 338,* 209–216.

Schmitz, S., Saudino, K. J., Plomin, R., Fulker, D. W., & DeFries, J. C. (1996). Genetic and environmental influences on temperament in middle childhood: Analyses of teacher and tester ratings. *Child Development, 67,* 409–422.

Schneider, B. H., Atkinson, L., & Tardif, C. (2001). Child–parent attachment and children's peer relations: A quantitative review. *Developmental Psychology, 37,* 86–100.

Schneider, B. A., Daneman, M., Murphy, D. R., & See, S. K. (2000). Listening to discourse in distracting settings: The effects of aging. *Psychological Aging, 15,* 110–125.

Schneider, W. (2004). Memory development in childhood. In U. Goswami (Ed.), *Blackwell handbook of childhood cognitive development* (pp. 236–256)). Malden, MA: Blackwell Publishing.

Schneider, W., & Bjorklund, D. F. (1998). Memory. In D. Kuhn & R. S. Siegler (Vol. Eds.), W. Damon (Editor-in-Chief), *Handbook of child psychology: Vol. 2. Cognition, perception, and language* (5th ed., pp. 467–522). New York: Wiley.

Schneider, W., Bjorklund, D. F., & Maier-Bruckner, W. (1996). The effects of expertise and IQ on children's memory: When knowledge is, and when it is not enough. *International Journal of Behavioral Development, 19,* 773–796.

Schneider, W., Gruber, H., Gold, A., & Opwis, K. (1993). Chess expertise and memory for chess positions in children and adults. *Journal of Experimental Child Psychology, 56,* 328–349.

Schneider, W., & Pressley, M. (1997). *Memory development between two and 20* (2nd ed.). Mahwah, NJ: Erlbaum.

Schneider, W., & Sodian, B. (1988). Metamemory-memory behavior relationships in young children: Evidence from a memory-for-location task. *Journal of Experimental Child Psychology, 45,* 209–233.

Schneider, W., Roth, E., & Ennemoser, M. (2000). Training phonological skills and letter knowledge in children at risk for dyslexia: A comparison of three kindergarten intervention programs. *Journal of Educational Psychology, 92,* 284–295.

Schneider, W., Visé, M., Lockl, K., & Nelson, T. (2000). Developmental trends in children's memory monitoring: Evidence from a judgment-of-learning task. *Cognitive Development, 15,* 115–134.

Scholl, B. J., & Leslie, A. M. (2001). Minds, modules, and meta-analysis. *Child Development, 72,* 696–701.

Schonfeld, D. J., & Kappelman, M. (1990). The impact of school-based education on the young child's understanding of death. *Developmental and Behavioral Pediatrics, 11,* 247–252.

Schooler, C., Mulatu, M. S., & Oates, G. (1999). The continuing effects of substantively complex work on the intellectual functioning of older workers. *Psychology and Aging, 14,* 483–506.

Schott, J. M., & Rossor, M. N. (2003). The grasp and other primitive reflexes. *Journal of Neurology and Neurosurgical Psychiatry, 74,* 558–560.

Schuetze, P., & Zeskind, P. S. (1997). Relation between reported maternal caffeine consumption during pregnancy and neonatal state and heart rate. *Infant Behavior and Development, 20,* 559–562.

Schulz, R., & Aderman, D. (1974). Clinical research and the stages of dying. *Omega: Journal of Death and Dying, 5,* 137–143.

Schulz, R., & Beach, S. R. (1999). Caregiving as a risk factor for mortality: The caregiver health effects study. *Journal of the American Medical Association, 282,* 2215–2219.

Schulz, R., Belle, S. H., Czaja, S. J., Gitlin, L. N., Wisniewski, S. R., & Ory, M. G. (2003). Introduction to the special section on Resources for Enhancing Alzheimer's Caregiver Health (REACH). *Psychology and Aging, 18,* 357–360.

Schulz, R., Mendelsohn, A. B., Haley, W. E., Mahoney, D., Allen, R. S., Zhang, S., Thompson, L., & Belle, S. H. (2003). End-of-life care and the effects of bereavement on family caregivers of persons with dementia. *New England Journal of Medicine, 349,* 1936–1942.

Schulz, R., & Schlarb, J. (1987–1988). Two decades of research on dying: What do we know about the patient? *Omega: Journal of Death and Dying, 18,* 299–317.

Schunn, C. D., & Anderson, J. R. (1999). The generality/specificity of expertise in scientific reasoning. *Cognitive Science, 23,* 337–370.

Schwartz, C. E., Wright, C. I., Shin, L. M., Kagan, J., & Rauch, S. L. (2003). Inhibited and uninhibited infants "grown up": Adult amygdalar response to novelty. *Science, 300,* 1952–1953.

Schwitzgebel, E. (1999). Gradual belief change in children. *Human Development, 42,* 283–296.

Scialfa, C. T., Esau, S. P., & Joffe, K. M. (1998). Age, target–distracter similarity, and visual search. *Experimental Aging Research, 24,* 337–358.

Scott, K. D., Klaus, P. H., & Klaus, M. H. (1999). The obstetrical and postpartum benefits of continuous support during childbirth. *Journal of Women's Health and Gender Based Medicine, 8,* 1257–1264.

Scott, W. A., Scott, R., & McCabe, M. (1991). Family relationships and children's personality: A cross-cultural, cross-source comparison. *British Journal of Social Psychology, 30,* 1–20.

Scourfield, J., Rice, F., Thapar, A., Harold, G. T., Martin, N., & McGuffin, P. (2003). Depressive symptoms in children and adolescents: Changing etiological influences with development. *Journal of Child Psychology and Psychiatry and Allied Disciplines, 44,* 968–976.

Seale, C. (1991). A comparison of hospice and conventional care. *Social Science and Medicine, 32,* 147–152.

Sebald, H. (1986). Adolescents' shifting orientation toward parents and peers: A curvilinear trend over recent decades. *Journal of Marriage and the Family, 48,* 5–13.

Seccombe, K. (2000). Families in poverty in the 1990s: Trends, causes, consequences, and lessons learned. *Journal of Marriage and the Family, 62,* 1094–1113.

Segal, N. L. (2000). Virtual twins: New findings on within-family environmental influences on intelligence. *Journal of Educational Psychology, 92,* 442–448.

Segalowitz, S. J., Unsal, A., & Dywan, J. (1992). Cleverness and wisdom in 12-year-olds: Electrophysiological evidence for late maturation of the frontal lobe. *Developmental Neuropsychology, 8,* 279–298.

Seger, J. Y., & Thorstensson, A. (2000). Muscle strength and electromyogram in boys and girls followed through puberty. *European Journal of Applied Physiology, 81,* 54–61.

Seibert, S. E., & Kraimer, M. L. (2001). The five-factor model of personality and career success. *Journal of Vocational Behavior, 58,* 1–21.

Seiffge-Krenke, I. (1998). Adolescents' health: A developmental perspective. Mahwah, NJ: Erlbaum.

Seiffge-Krenke, I. (2003). Testing theories of romantic development from adolescence to young adulthood: Evidence of a developmental sequence. *International Journal of Behavioral Development, 27,* 519–531.

Seiffge-Krenke, I., & Stemmler, M. (2002). Factors contributing to gender differences in depressive symptoms: A test of three developmental models. *Journal of Youth and Adolescence, 31,* 405–417.

Selby, J. M., & Bradley, B. S. (2003). Infants in groups: A paradigm for the study of early social experience. *Human Development, 46,* 197–221.

Seleen, D. R. (1982). The congruence between actual and desired use of time by older adults: A predictor of life satisfaction. *Gerontologist, 22,* 95–99.

Selikowitz, M. (2004). *ADHD: The facts.* Oxford: Oxford University Press.

Selkoe, D. J. (1997). Alzheimer's disease: From genes to pathogenesis. *American Journal of Psychiatry, 154,* 1198.

Selman, R. L. (1976). Social cognitive understanding: A guide to educational and clinical experience. In T. Lickona (Ed.), *Moral development and behavior: Theory, research and social issues.* New York: Holt, Rinehart & Winston.

Selman, R. L. (1980). *The growth of interpersonal understanding.* New York: Academic Press.

Selman, R. L., Beardslee, W., Schultz, L. H., Krupa, M., & Podorefsky, D. (1986). Assessing adolescent interpersonal negotiation strategies: Toward the integration of structural and functional models. *Developmental Psychology, 22,* 450–459.

Seltzer, J. A. (2000). Families formed outside of marriage. *Journal of Marriage and the Family, 62,* 1247–1268.

Seltzer, M. M., & Li, L. W. (2000). The dynamics of caregiving: Transitions during a three-year prospective study, *Gerontologist, 40,* 165–178.

Senter, M. S., & Senter, R. (1997). Student outcomes and the adult learner. *Continuing Higher Education Review, 61,* 75–87.

Serbin, L. A., Poulin-Dubois, D., Colburne, K. A., Sen, M. G., & Eichstedt, J. A. (2001). Gender stereotyping in infancy: Visual preferences for and knowledge of gender-stereotyped toys in the second year. *International Journal of Behavioral Development, 25,* 7–15.

Serbin, L. A., Poulin-Dubois, D., & Eichstedt, J. A. (2002). Infants' response to gender-inconsistent events. *Infancy, 3,* 531–542.

Serbin, L. A., Powlishta, K. K., & Gulko, J. (1993). The development of sex typing in middle childhood. *Monographs of the Society for Research in Child Development, 58* (2, Serial No. 232).

Serbin, L. A., Tonick, I. J., & Sternglanz, S. H. (1977). Shaping cooperative cross-sex play. *Child Development, 48,* 924–929.

Settersten, R. A., Jr. (1998). A time to leave home and a time never to return? Age constraints on the living arrangements of young adults. *Social Forces, 76,* 1373–1400.

Shaffer, D., & Pfeffer, C. R. (2001). Practice parameters for the assessment and treatment of children and adolescents with suicidal behavior. *Journal of the American Academy of Child and Adolescent Psychiatry, 40,* 24S-51S.

Shaffer, D. R., Pegalis, L. J., & Cornell, D. P. (1992). Gender and self-disclosure revisited: Personal and contextual variations in self-disclosure to same-sex acquaintances. *Journal of Social Psychology, 132,* 307–315.

Shanahan, M. J. (2000). Pathways to adulthood in changing societies: Variability and mechanisms in life course perspective. *Annual Review of Sociology, 26,* 667–692.

Shanahan, M. J., Finch, M. D., Mortimer, J. T., & Ryu, S. (1991). Adolescent work experience and depressive affect. *Social Psychology Quarterly, 54,* 299–317.

Shapiro, E. R. (2001). Grief in interpersonal perspective: Theories and their implications. In M. S. Stroebe, R. O. Hansson, W. Stroebe, & H. Schut (Eds.), *Handbook of bereavement research. Consequences, coping, and care.* Washington, D.C.: American Psychological Association.

Sharabany, R., Gershoni, R., & Hofman, J. E. (1981). Girlfriend, boyfriend: Age and sex differences in intimate friendship. *Developmental Psychology, 17,* 800–808.

Sharpe, P. A., Jackson, K. L., White, C., Vaca, V. L., Hickey, T., Gu, J., & Otterness, C. (1997). Effects of a one-year physical activity intervention for older adults at congregate nutrition sites. *Gerontologist, 37,* 208–215.

Sharpe, T. M., Killen, J. D., Bryson, S. W., Shisslak, C. M., Estes, L. S., Gray, N., Crago, M., & Taylor, C. G. (1998). Attachment style and weight concerns in preadolescent and adolescent girls. *International Journal of Eating Disorders, 23,* 39–44.

Shaver, P. R., & Tancredy, C. M. (2001). Emotion, attachment, and bereavement: A conceptual commentary. In M. S. Stroebe, R. O. Hansson, W. Stroebe, & H. Schut (Eds.), *Handbook of bereavement research. Consequences, coping, and care.* Washington, D.C.: American Psychological Association.

Shaw, B. A., Krause, N., Chatters, L. M., Connell, C. M., & Ingersoll-Dayton, B. (2004). Emotional support from parents early in life, aging, and health. *Psychology and Aging, 19,* 4–12.

Shaw, C. (1997). The perimenopausal hot flash: Epidemiology, physiology, and treatment. *Nurse Practitioner, 22,* 55–66.

Shaywitz, S. E., Fletcher, J. M., Holahan, J. M., Shneider, A. E., Marchione, K. E., Stuebing, K. K., Francis, D. J., Pugh, K. R., & Shaywitz, B. A. (1999). Persistence of dyslexia: The Connecticut Longitudinal Study at Adolescence. *Pediatrics, 104,* 1351–1359.

Sheiner, E., Shoham-Vardi, I., Sheiner, E. K., Press, F., Hackmon-Ram, R., Mazor, M., & Katz, M. (2000). A comparison between the effectiveness of epidural analgesia and parenteral pethidine during labor. *Archives of Gynecology and Obstetrics, 263,* 95–98.

Shepard, R. J. (1997). Curricular physical activity and academic performance. *Pediatric Exercise Science, 9,* 113–126.

Shepard, R. N., & Metzler, J. (1971). Mental rotation of three-dimensional objects. *Science, 171,* 701–703.

Shepard, T. H. & Lemire, R. J. (2004). *Catalog of teratogenic agents* (11th ed.). Baltimore, MD: Johns Hopkins University Press.

Shih, M., Pittinsky, T. L., & Ambady, N. (1999). Stereotype susceptibility: Identity salience and shifts in quantitative performance. *Psychological Science, 10,* 80–83.

Shihadeh, A., & Al-Najdawi, W. (2001). Forceps or vacuum extraction: A comparison of maternal and neonatal morbidity. *Eastern Mediterranean Health, 7,* 106–114.

Shimamura, A. P., Berry, J. M., Mangels, J. A., Rusting, C. L., & Jurica, P. J. (1995). Memory and cognitive abilities in university professors: Evidence for successful aging. *Psychological Science, 6,* 271–277.

Shiner, R. L., Masten, A. S., & Roberts, J. M. (2003). Childhood personality foreshadows adult personality and life outcomes two decades later. *Journal of Personality, 71,* 1145–1170.

Ship, J. A., Pearson, J. D., Cruise, L. J., Brant, L. J., & Metter, E. J. (1996). Longitudinal changes in smell identification. *Journals of Gerontology: Biological Sciences and Medical Sciences, 51,* M86–M91.

Ship, J. A., & Weiffenbach, J. M. (1993). Age, gender, medical treatment, and medication effects on smell identification. *Journal of Gerontology, 48,* M26–M32.

Shneidman, E. S. (1973). *Deaths of man.* New York: Quadrangle.

Shneidman, E. S. (1980). *Voices of death.* New York: Harper & Row.

Shoda, Y., & Mischel, W. (2000). Reconciling contextualism with the core assumptions of personality psychology. *European Journal of Personality, 14,* 407–428.

Shonk, S. M., & Cicchetti, D. (2001). Maltreatment, competency deficits, and risk for academic and behavioral maladjustment. *Developmental Psychology, 37,* 3–17.

Short, E. J., Manos, M. J., Findling, R. L., & Schubel, E. A. (2004). A prospective study of stimulant response in preschool children: Insights from ROC analyses. *Journal of the American Academy of Child and Adolescent Psychiatry, 43,* 251–259.

Shuey, K., & Hardy, M. A. (2003). Assistance to aging parents and parents-in-law: Does lineage affect family allocation decisions? *Journal of Marriage and the Family, 65,* 418–431.

Shulman, S., & Ben-Artzi, E. (2003). Age-related differences in the transition from adolescence to adulthood and links with family relationships. *Journal of Adult Development, 10,* 217–226.

Shumway-Cook, A., Brauer, S., & Woollacott, M. (2000). Predicting the probability for falls in community-dwelling older adults using the timed up & go test. *Physical Therapy, 80,* 896–902.

Shurkin, J. N. (1992). *Terman's kids: The groundbreaking study of how the gifted grow up.* Boston: Little, Brown.

Shute, N. (2001, January 15). Children in anguish. A call for better treatment of kids' mental ills. *U.S. News & World Report,* 42.

Shute, N., Locy, T., & Pasternak, D. (2000, March 6). The perils of pills. *U.S. News & World Report,* 45–50.

Shweder, R. A., Goodnow, J., Hatano, G., LeVine, R., Markus, H., & Miller, P. (1998). The cultural psychology of development: One mind, many mentalities. In R. M. Lerner (Vol. Ed.), W. Damon (Editor-in-Chief), *Handbook of child psychology: Vol. 1. Theoretical models of human development* (5th ed.). New York: Wiley.

Shweder, R. A., Mahapatra, M., & Miller, J. G. (1990). Culture and moral development. In J. W. Stigler, R. A. Shweder, & G. Herdt (Eds.), *Cultural psychology. Essays on comparative human development.* Cambridge, England: Cambridge University Press.

Sibulesky, L., Hayes, K. C., Pronczuk, A., Weigel-DiFranco, C., Rosner, B., & Berson, E. L. (1999). Safety of <7500 RE (<25,000 IU) vitamin A daily in adults with retinitis pigmentosa. *American Journal of Clinical Nutrition, 69,* 656–663.

Siebold, C. (1992). *The hospice movement. Easing death's pains.* New York: Twayne Publishers.

Siegel, A. C., & Burton, R. V. (1999). Effects of baby walkers on motor and mental development in human infants. *Journal of Developmental and Behavioral Pediatrics, 20,* 355–361.

Siegler, I. C., & Brummett, B. H. (2000). Associations among NEO personality assessments and well-being at mid-life: Facet-level analyses. *Psychology and Aging, 15,* 710–714.

Siegler, R. S. (1981). Developmental sequences within and between concepts. *Monographs of the Society for Research in Child Development, 46* (2, Serial No. 189).

Siegler, R. S. (1989). Hazards of mental chronometry: An example from children's subtraction. *Journal of Educational Psychology, 81,* 497–506.

Siegler, R. S. (1996). *Emerging minds: The process of change in children's thinking.* New York: Oxford University Press.

Siegler, R. S. (2000). The rebirth of children's learning. *Child Development, 71,* 26–35.

Siegler, R. S., & Ellis, S. (1996). Piaget on childhood. *Psychological Science, 7,* 211–215.

Sieving, R. E., McNeely, C. S., & Blum, R. W. (2000). Maternal expectations, mother–child connectedness, and adolescent sexual debut. *Archives of Pediatrics and Adolescent Medicine, 154,* 809–816.

Sigelman, C. K., Carr, M. B., & Begley, N. L. (1986). Developmental changes in the influence of sex-role stereotypes on person perception. *Child Study Journal, 16,* 191–205.

Sigman, M., & Capps, L. (1997). *Children with autism. A developmental perspective.* Cambridge, MA: Harvard University Press.

Signorella, M. L., Bigler, R. S., & Liben, L. S. (1993). Developmental differences in children's gender schemata about others: A meta-analytic review. *Developmental Review, 13,* 147–183.

Signorella, M. L., Frieze, I. H., & Hershey, S. W. (1996). Single-sex versus mixed-sex classes and gender schemata in children and adolescents. *Psychology of Women Quarterly, 20,* 599–607.

Signorielli, N. (1990). Children, television, and gender roles. *Journal of Adolescent Health Care, 11,* 50–58.

Signorielli, N., & Kahlenberg, S. (2001). Television's world of work in the nineties. *Journal of Broadcasting and Electronic Media, 45,* 4–22.

Signorielli, N., & Lears, M. (1992). Children, television, and conceptions about chores: Attitudes and behaviors. *Sex Roles, 27,* 157–170.

Silverberg, S. B., & Steinberg, L. (1990). Psychological well-being of parents with early adolescent children. *Developmental Psychology, 26,* 658–666.

Silverman, I. W. (2003). Gender differences in resistance to temptation: Theories and evidence. *Developmental Review, 23,* 219–259.

Silverman, L. K., Chitwood, D. G., & Waters, J. L. (1986). Young gifted children: Can parents identify giftedness? *Topics in Early Childhood Special Education, 6,* 23–38.

Silverman, P. R. (1981). *Helping women cope with grief* (Sage Human Services Guide No. 25). Beverly Hills, CA: Sage.

Silverman, P. R. (2000). *Never too young to know. Death in children's lives.* New York: Oxford University Press.

Silverman, P. R., & Worden, J. W. (1993). Children's reactions to the death of a parent. In M. S. Stroebe, W. Stroebe, & R. O. Hansson (Eds.), *Handbook of bereavement. Theory, research, and intervention.* Cambridge, England: Cambridge University Press.

Silverstein, M., & Waite, L. J. (1993). Are blacks more likely than whites to receive and provide social support in middle and old age?—Yes, no, and maybe so. *Journal of Gerontology: Social Sciences, 48,* S212–S222.

Simcock, G., & Hayne, H. (2002). Breaking the barrier? Children fail to translate their preverbal memories into language. *Psychological Science, 13,* 225–231.

Simmons, R. G., & Blyth, D. A. (1987). *Moving into adolescence: The impact of pubertal change and school context.* New York: Hawthorne, Aldine de Gruyter.

Simmons, R. G., Burgeson, R., Carlton-Ford, S., & Blyth, D. A. (1987). The impact of cumulative change in early adolescence. *Child Development, 58,* 1220–1234.

Simon, H.A. (1995). The information-processing theory of mind. *American Psychologist, 50,* 507–508.

Simon, T. J. (1997). Reconceptualizing the origins of number knowledge: A "non-numerical" account. *Cognitive Development, 12,* 349–372.

Simon, T. J. (1999). The foundations of numerical thinking in a brain without numbers. *Trends in Cognitive Science, 3,* 363–365.

Simon, T. J., Hespos, S. J., & Rochat, P. (1995). Do infants understand simple arithmetic? A replication of Wynn (1992). *Cognitive Development, 10,* 253–269.

Simon, W., & Gagnon, J. (1998). Psychosexual development. *Society, 35,* 60–67.

Simonoff, E. (2001). Genetic influences on conduct disorder. In J. Hill & B. Maughan (Eds.), *Conduct disorders in childhood and adolescence.* New York: Cambridge University Press.

Simonoff, E., Bolton, P., & Rutter, M. (1996). Mental retardation: Genetic findings, clinical implications and research agenda. *Journal of Child Psychology and Psychiatry and Allied Disciplines, 37,* 259–280.

Simonton, D. K. (1984). *Genius, creativity, and leadership: Historiometric inquiries.* Cambridge, MA: Harvard University Press.

Simonton, D. K. (1990). Creativity in the later years: Optimistic prospects for achievement. *Gerontologist, 30,* 626–631.

Simonton, D. K. (1991). Career landmarks in science: Individual differences and interdisciplinary contrasts. *Developmental Psychology, 27,* 119–130.

Simonton, D. K. (1999). *Origins of genius: Darwinian perspectives on creativity.* New York: Oxford University Press.

Simpson, J. A., Rholes, W. S., Campbell, L., Tran, S., & Wilson, C. L. (2003). Adult attachment, the transition to parenthood, and depressive symptoms. *Journal of Personality and Social Psychology, 84,* 1172–1187.

Simpson, J. L., & Elias, S. (2003). *Genetics in obstetrics and gynecology.* Philadelphia, PA: Saunders.

Simpson, K. R., & Creehan, P. A. (1996). *Perinatal nursing.* Philadelphia: Lippincott-Raven.

Singer, D. G., & Singer, J. L. (1990). *The house of make-believe: Children's play and the developing imagination.* Cambridge, MA: Harvard University Press.

Singer, L. T., Arendt, R., Fagan, J., Minnes, S., Salvator, A., Bolek, T., & Becker, M. (1999). Neonatal visual information processing in cocaine-exposed and non-exposed infants. *Infant Behavior and Development, 22,* 1–15.

Singer, T., Lindenberger, U., & Baltes, P. B. (2003). Plasticity of memory for new learning in very old age: A story of major loss? *Psychology and Aging, 18,* 306–317.

Singer, T., Verhaeghen, P., Ghisletta, P., Lindenberger, U., & Baltes, P. B. (2003). The fate of cognition in very old age: Six-year longitudinal findings in the Berlin Aging Study (BASE). *Psychology and Aging, 18,* 318–331.

Singh, B., Berman, B. M., Simpson, R. L., & Annechild, A. (1998). Incidence of premenstrual syndrome and remedy usage: A national probability sample study. *Alternative Therapeutic Health Medicines, 4,* 75–79.

Singh, K., & Ozturk, M. (2000). Effect of part-time work on high school mathematics and science course taking. *Journal of Educational Research, 94,* 67–74.

Singh, S., & Darroch, J. E. (2000). Adolescent pregnancy and childbearing: Levels and trends in developed countries. *Family Planning Perspectives, 32,* 14–23.

Sinnott, J. (1996). The developmental approach: Postformal thought as adaptive intelligence. In F. Blanchard-Fields & T. M. Hess (Eds.), *Perspectives on cognitive change in adulthood and aging.* New York: McGraw-Hill.

Skinner, B. F. (1953). *Science and human behavior.* New York: Macmillan.

Skinner, B. F. (1957). *Verbal behavior.* New York: Appleton-Century-Crofts.

Skinner, B. F. (1983). Intellectual self-management in old age. *American Psychologist, 38,* 239–244.

Skolnick, A. (1986). Early attachment and personal relationships across the life course. In P. B. Baltes, D. L. Featherman, & R. M. Lerner (Eds.), *Life-span development and behavior* (Vol. 7). Hillsdale, NJ: Erlbaum.

Slaby, R. G., & Guerra, N. G. (1988). Cognitive mediators of aggression in adolescent offenders: 1. Assessment. *Developmental Psychology, 24,* 580–588.

Slater, A. (2004). Visual perception. In G. Bremner & A. Fogel (Eds.), *Blackwell handbook of infant development* (pp. 5–34). Malden, MA: Blackwell Publishing.

Slater, A., Mattock, A., & Brown, E. (1990). Size constancy at birth: Newborn infants' response to retinal and real size. *Journal of Experimental Child Psychology, 49,* 314–322.

Slater, C. L. (2003). Generativity versus stagnation: An elaboration of Erikson's adult stage of human development. *Journal of Adult Development, 10,* 53–65.

Slaughter, V., Jaakkola, R., & Carey, S. (1999). Constructing a coherent theory: Children's biological understanding of life and death. In M. Siegal & C. C. Peterson (Eds.), *Children's understanding of biology and health.* Cambridge, U.K.: Cambridge University Press.

Slaughter, V., & Lyons, M. (2003). Learning about life and death in early childhood. *Cognitive Psychology, 46,* 1–30.

Slavin, R. E. (1986). Cooperative learning: Engineering social psychology in the classroom. In R. S. Feldman (Ed.), *The social psychology of education: Current research and theory.* Cambridge: Cambridge University Press.

Slavkin, M., & Stright, A. D. (2000). Gender role differences in college students from one- and two-parent families. *Sex Roles, 42,* 23–37.

Sliwinski, M., & Buschke, H. (1999). Cross-sectional and longitudinal relationships among age, cognition, and processing speed. *Psychology and Aging, 14,* 18–33.

Sliwinski, M., Buschke, H., Kuslansky, G., Senior, G., & Scarisbrick, D. (1994). Proportional slowing and addition speed in old and young adults. *Psychology and Aging, 9,* 72–80.

Slobin, D. I. (1979). *Psycholinguistics* (2nd ed.). Glenview, IL: Scott, Foresman.

Slotkin, T. A. (1998). Fetal nicotine or cocaine exposure: Which one is worse? *Journal of Pharmacology and Experimental Therapy, 285,* 931–945.

Smagorinsky, P. (1995). The social construction of data: Methodological problems of investigating learning in the zone of proximal development. *Review of Educational Research, 65,* 191–212.

Small, S., & Memmo, M. (2004). Contemporary models of youth development and problem prevention: Toward an integration of terms, concepts, and models. *Family Relations, 53,* 3–11.

Smetana, J. G. (1981). Preschool children's conceptions of moral and social rules. *Child Development, 52,* 1333–1336.

Smetana, J. G. (2000). Middle-class African American adolescents' and parents' conceptions of parental authority and parenting practices: A longitudinal investigation. *Child Development, 71,* 1672–1686.

Smetana, J. G., Schlagman, N., & Adams, P. W. (1993). Preschool children's judgments about hypothetical and actual transgressions. *Child Development, 64,* 202–214.

Smith, A. D., & Earles, J. L. K. (1996). Memory changes in normal aging. In F. Blanchard-Fields & T. M. Hess (Eds.), *Perspectives on cognitive change in adulthood and aging.* New York: McGraw-Hill.

Smith, B., & Blass, E. M. (1996). Taste-mediated calming in premature, preterm, and full-term human infants. *Developmental Psychology, 32,* 1084–1089.

Smith, C. L., Calkins, S. D., Keane, S. P., Anastopoulos, A. D., & Shelton, T. L. (2004). Predicting stability and change in toddler behavior problems: Contributions of maternal behavior and child gender. *Developmental Psychology, 40,* 29–42.

Smith, G. E., Petersen, R. C., Ivnik, R. J., Malec, J. F., & Tangalos, E. G. (1996). Subjective memory complaints, psychological distress, and longitudinal change in objective memory performance. *Psychology and Aging, 11,* 272–279.

Smith, J., & Baltes, P. B. (1990). Wisdom-related knowledge: Age/cohort differences in response to life-planning problems. *Developmental Psychology, 26,* 494–505.

Smith, J. B. (1997). Effects of eighth-grade transition programs on high school retention and experiences. *Journal of Educational Research, 90,* 144–152.

Smith, K. E., Landry, S. H., & Swank, P. R. (2000). Does the content of mothers' verbal stimulation explain differences in children's development of verbal and nonverbal cognitive skills? *Journal of School Psychology, 38,* 27–49.

Smith, L. B., & Katz, D. B. (1996). Activity-dependent processes in perceptual and cognitive development. In R. Gelman & T. K. Au (Eds.), *Perceptual and cognitive development.* San Diego: Academic Press.

Smith, L. B., & Thelen, E. (1993). *A dynamic systems approach to development: Applications.* Cambridge, MA: MIT Press.

Smith, P. K. (1978). A longitudinal study of social participation in preschool children: Solitary and parallel play reexamined. *Developmental Psychology, 14,* 517–523.

Smith, P. K., & Daglish, L. (1977). Sex differences in parent and infant behavior in the home. *Child Development, 48,* 1250–1254.

Smith, T. W. (1991). Adult sexual behavior in 1989: Number of partners, frequency of intercourse and risk of AIDS. *Family Planning Perspectives, 23,* 102–107.

Smithmyer, C. M., Hubbard, J. A., & Simons, R. F. (2000). Proactive and reactive aggression in delinquent adolescents: Relations to aggression outcome expectancies. *Journal of Clinical Child Psychology, 29,* 86–93.

Smolak, L., & Levine, M. P. (1996). Adolescent transitions and the development of eating problems. In L. Smolak, M. P. Levine, & R. Striegel-Moore (Eds.), *The developmental psychopathology of eating disorders: Implications for research, prevention, and treatment.* Mahwah, NJ: Erlbaum.

Smoll, F. L., & Schutz, R. W. (1990). Quantifying gender differences in physical performance: A developmental perspective. *Developmental Psychology, 26,* 360–369.

Smotherman, W. P., & Robinson, S. R. (1996). The development of behavior before birth. *Developmental Psychology, 32,* 425–434.

Smyke, A. T., Dumitrescu, A., & Zeanah, C. H. (2002). Attachment disturbances in young children. I: The continuum of caretaking casualty. *Journal of the American Academy of Child and Adolescent Psychiatry, 41,* 972–982.

Snarey, J. R. (1985). Cross-cultural universality of social–moral development: A critical review of Kohlbergian research. *Psychological Bulletin, 97,* 202–232.

Sneed, C. D., Morisky, D. E., Rotheram-Borus, M. J., Ebin, V., Malotte, C. K., Lyde, M., & Gill, J. K. (2001). "Don't know" and "didn't think of it": Condom use at first intercourse by Latino adolescents. *AIDS Care, 13,* 303–308.

Snow, C. E., Arlman-Rupp, A., Hassing, Y., Jobse, J., Joosken, J., & Vorster, J. (1976). Mother's speech in three social classes. *Journal of Psycholinguistic Research, 5,* 1–20.

Snowdon, D. A. (1997). Aging and Alzheimer's disease: Lessons from the Nun Study. *Gerontologist, 37,* 150–156.

Society for Research in Child Development, Committee for Ethical Conduct in Child Development Research. (1990, Winter). SRCD ethical standards for research with children. *SRCD Newsletter,* 5–7.

Sodian, B. (1994). Early deception and the conceptual continuity claim. In C. Lewis & P. Mitchell (Eds.), *Children's early understanding of mind: Origins and development.* Hove, England: Erlbaum.

Somers-Smith, M. J. (1999). A place for the partner? Expectations and experiences of support during childbirth. *Midwifery, 15,* 101–108.

Somerville, S. C., Wellman, H. M., & Cultice, J. C. (1983). Young children's deliberate reminding. *Journal of Genetic Psychology, 143,* 87–96.

Sommers, M. S. (1997). Speech perception in older adults: The importance of speech-specific cognitive abilities. *Journal of the American Geriatrics Society, 45,* 633–637.

Somsen, R. J. M., van Klooster, B. J., van der Molen, M. W., van Leeuwen, H. M. P., & Licht, R. (1997). Growth spurts in brain maturation during middle childhood as indexed by EEG power spectra. *Biological Psychology, 44,* 187–209.

Son, L. K. (2004). Spacing one's study evidence for a metacognitive control strategy. *Journal of Experimental Psychology: Learning, Memory, and Cognition, 30,* 601–604.

Son, L. K., & Metcalfe, J. (2000). Metacognitive and control strategies in study-time allocation. *Journal of Experimental Psychology: Learning, Memory, and Cognition, 26,* 204–221.

Sorensen, L. C., & Borch, K. (1999). Neonatal asphyxia—prognosis based on clinical findings during delivery and the first day of life: A retrospective study of 54 newborn infants with asphyxia. *Ugeskr Laeger, 161,* 3094–3098.

Soriano, F. I., Rivera, L. M., Williams, K. J., Daley, S. P., & Reznik, V. M. (2004). Navigating between cultures: The role of culture in youth violence. *Journal of Adolescent Health, 34,* 169–176.

Sostek, A. M., Vietze, P., Zaslow, M., Kreiss, L., van der Waals, F., & Rubinstein, D. (1981). Social context in caregiver-infant interaction: A film study of Fais and the United States. In T. M. Field, A. M. Sostek, P. Vietze, & P. H. Liederman (Eds.), *Culture and early interactions.* Hillsdale, NJ: Erlbaum.

Span, P. (2000, August 27). Home alone. *The Washington Post Magazine,* 12–15, 24–25.

Sparling, P. B., O'Donnell, E. M., & Snow, T. K. (1998). The gender difference in distance running performance has plateaued: An analysis of world rankings from 1980 to 1996. *Medicine and Science in Sports and Exercise, 30,* 1725–1729.

Sparrow, S. S., & Davis, S. M. (2000). Recent advances in the assessment of intelligence and cognition. *Journal of Child Psychology and Psychiatry, 41,* 117–131.

Spear, L. P. (2000a). The adolescent brain and age-related behavioral manifestations. *Neuroscience and Biobehavioral Reviews, 24,* 417–463.

Spear, L. P. (2000b). Neurobehavioral changes in adolescence. *Current Directions in Psychological Science, 9,* 111–114.

Spearman, C. (1927). *The abilities of man.* New York: Macmillan.

Speece, M. W., & Brent, S. B. (1984). Children's understanding of death: A review of three components of a death concept. *Child Development, 55,* 1671–1686.

Speece, M. W., & Brent, S. B. (1992). The acquisition of a mature understanding of three components of the concept of death. *Death Studies, 16,* 211–229.

Spelke, E. S. (1990). Principles of object perception. *Cognitive Science, 14,* 29-56.

Spelke, E. S. (1994). Initial knowledge: Six suggestions. *Cognition, 50,* 431–445.

Spelke, E. S., Breinlinger, K., Macomber, J., & Jacobson, K. (1992). Origins of knowledge. *Psychological Review, 99,* 605–632.

Spelke, E. S., & Hermer, L. (1996). Early cognitive development: Objects and space. In R. Gelman & T. Fong (Eds.), *Handbook of perception and cognition* (2nd ed.). New York: Academic Press.

Spence, J. T. (1985). Achievement American style: The rewards and costs of individualism. *American Psychologist, 40,* 1285–1295.

Spence, J. T., & Hall, S. K. (1996). Children's gender-related self-perceptions, activity preferences, and occupational stereotypes: A test of three models of gender constructs. *Sex Roles, 35,* 659–691.

Spence, J. T., & Helmreich, R. L. (1978). *Masculinity and femininity: Their psychological dimensions, correlates, and antecedents.* Austin: University of Texas Press.

Spencer, M. B., & Markstrom-Adams, C. (1990). Identity processes among racial and ethnic minority children in America. *Child Development, 61,* 290–310.

Spencer, P. E. (1996). The association between language and symbolic play at two years: Evidence from deaf toddlers. *Child Development, 67,* 867–876.

Spiby, H., Henderson, B., Slade, P., Escott, D., & Fraser, R. B. (1999). Strategies for coping with labour: Does antenatal education translate into practice? *Journal of Advanced Nursing, 29,* 388–394.

Spilich, G. J., Vesonder, G. T., Chiesi, H. L., & Voss, J. F. (1979). Text processing of domain-related information for individuals with high and low domain knowledge. *Journal of Verbal Learning and Verbal Behavior, 18,* 275–290.

Spirduso, W. W., & MacRae, P. G. (1990). Motor performance and aging. In J. E. Birren & K. W. Schaie (Eds.), *Handbook of the psychology of aging* (3rd ed.). San Diego: Academic Press.

Spitz, R. A. (1946). Anaclitic depression: An inquiry into the genesis of psychiatric conditions in early childhood, II. *Psychoanalytic Study of the Child, 2,* 313–342.

Spokane, A. R., Meir, E. I., & Catalano, M. (2000). Person-environment congruence and Holland's theory: A review and reconsideration. *Journal of Vocational Behavior, 57,* 137–187.

Spraggins, R. E. (2003). Women and men in the United States: March 2002. *Current Population Reports, P20-544.* Washington, D.C.: U.S. Census Bureau. Available at: http://www.census.gov/prod/2003pubs/p20-544.pdf.

Sprang, G., & McNeil, J. (1995). *The many faces of bereavement.* New York: Brunner/Mazel.

Springen, K. (2004, January 26). The ancient art of making babies. *Newsweek,* 51.

Springer, S., & Deutsch, G. (1997). *Left brain, right brain: Perspectives from cognitive neuroscience* (5th ed.). New York: W. H. Freeman.

Squires, S. (1999, April 20). Midlife without the crisis. *The Washington Post—Health,* 20–24.

Suzman, R. M., Willis, D. P., & Manton, K. G. (Eds.). (1992). *The oldest old.* New York: Oxford University Press.

Sroufe, L. A. (1977). Wariness of strangers and the study of infant development. *Child Development, 48,* 1184–1199.

Sroufe, L. A. (1985). Attachment classification from the perspective of infant-caregiver relationships and infant temperament. *Child Development, 56,* 1–14.

Sroufe, L. A. (1996). *Emotional development: The organization of emotional life in the early years.* Cambridge, England: University of Cambridge Press.

Sroufe, L. A. (1997). Psychopathology as an outcome of development. *Development and Psychopathology, 9,* 251–268.

Sroufe, L. A., Bennett, C., Englund, M., Urban, J., & Shulman, S. (1993). The significance of gender boundaries in preadolescence: Contemporary correlates and antecedents of boundary violation and maintenance. *Child Development, 64,* 455–466.

Sroufe, L. A., & Rutter, M. (1984). The domain of developmental psychopathology. *Child Development, 55,* 17–29.

Sroufe, L. A., Waters, E., & Matas, L. (1974). Contextual determinants of infant affectional response. In M. Lewis & L. A. Rosenblum (Eds.), *The origins of fear.* New York: Wiley.

Staddon, J. E. R., & Cerutti, D. T. (2003). Operant conditioning. *Annual Review of Psychology, 54,* 115–144.

Stambrook, M., & Parker, K. C. H. (1987). The development of the concept of death in childhood: A review of the literature. *Merrill-Palmer Quarterly, 33,* 133–157.

Stams, G. J. J. M., Juffer, F., & van IJzendoorn, M. (2002). Maternal sensitivity, infant attachment, and temperament in early childhood predict adjustment in middle childhood: The case of adopted children and their biologically unrelated parents. *Developmental Psychology, 38,* 806–821.

Stanley, C., Murray, L., & Stein, A. (2004). The effect of postnatal depression on mother–infant interaction, infant response to the still-face perturbation, and performance on an instrumental learning task. *Development and Psychopathology, 16,* 1–18.

Stanovich, K. E. (1986). Matthew effects in reading: Some consequences of individual differences in the acquisition of literacy. *Reading Research Quarterly, 21,* 360–407.

Stanovich, K. E., & Stanovich, P. J. (1999). How research might inform the debate about early reading acquisition. In J. Oakhill & R. Beard (Eds.), *Reading development and the teaching of reading* (pp. 12–41). Oxford: Blackwell.

Stanovich, K. E., & West, R. F. (1997). Reasoning independently of prior belief and individual differences in actively open-minded thinking. *Journal of Educational Psychology, 89,* 342–357.

Starr, B. D., & Weiner, M. B. (1981). *The Starr-Weiner report on sex and sexuality in the mature years.* New York: Stein & Day.

State, M. W., Lombroso, P. J., Pauls, D. L., & Leckman, J. F. (2000). The genetics of childhood psychiatric disorders: A decade of progress. *Journal of the American Academy of Child and Adolescent Psychiatry, 39,* 946–962.

Staudinger, U. M., & Baltes, P. B. (1996). Interactive minds: A facilitative setting for wisdom-related performance? *Journal of Personality and Social Psychology, 71,* 746–762.

Staudinger, U. M., Smith, J., & Baltes, P. B. (1992). Wisdom-related knowledge in a life review task: Age differences and the role of professional specialization. *Psychology and Aging, 7,* 271–281.

Stearns, P. N. (2003). *Anxious parents: A history of modern childbearing in America.* New York: New York University Press.

Steele, C. M. (1997). A threat in the air: How stereotypes shape intellectual identity and performance. *American Psychologist, 52,* 613–629.

Steele, C. M. (1999). Thin ice: "Stereotype threat" and black college students. *Atlantic, 284,* 44–54.

Steele, C. M., & Aronson, J. (1995). Stereotype threat and the intellectual test performance of African Americans. *Journal of Personality and Social Psychology, 69,* 797–811.

Steenari, M., Vuontela, V., Paavonen, E. J., Carlson, S., Fjallberg, M., & Aronen, E. T. (2003). Working memory and sleep in 6- to 13-year-old schoolchildren. *Journal of the American Academy of Child and Adolescent Psychiatry, 42,* 85–92.

Steenland, K., Henley, J., & Thun, M. (2002). All-cause and cause-specific death rates by educational status for two million people in two American Cancer Society cohorts, 1959–1999. *American Journal of Epidemiology, 156,* 11–21.

Stefos, T. (2002). Amniocentesis. In F. A. Chervenak, A. Kurjak, & Z. Papp (Eds.), *The fetus as a patient.* New York: Parthenon.

Stein, J. H., & Reiser, L. W. (1994). A study of white middle-class adolescent boys' responses to "semenarche" (the first ejaculation). *Journal of Youth and Adolescence, 23,* 373–384.

Stein, Z. A., Susser, M. W., Saenger, G., & Marolla, F. (1975). *Famine and human development: The Dutch hunger winter of 1944–1945.* New York: Oxford University Press.

Steinberg, E. P., Holtz, P. M., Sullivan, E. M., & Villar, C. P. (1998). Profiling assisted reproductive technology: Outcomes and quality of infertility management. *Fertility and Sterility, 69,* 617–623.

Steinberg, L. (1989). Pubertal maturation and parent–adolescent distance: An evolutionary perspective. In G. R. Adams, R. Montemayor, & T. P. Gullotta (Eds.), *Advances in adolescent behavior and development* (pp. 71–97). Newbury Park, CA: Sage.

Steinberg, L. (2001). We know some things: Parent–adolescent relationships in retrospect and prospect. *Journal of Research on Adolescence, 11,* 1–19.

Steinberg, L. (2002). *Adolescence* (6th ed.). Boston: McGraw-Hill.

Steinberg, L., & Avenevoli, S. (2000). The role of context in the development of psychopathology: A conceptual framework and some speculative propositions. *Child Development, 71,* 66–74.

Steinberg, L., & Dornbusch, S. M. (1991). Negative correlates of part-time employment during adolescence: Replication and elaboration. *Developmental Psychology, 27,* 304–313.

Steinberg, L., Dornbusch, S. M., & Brown, B. B. (1992). Ethnic differences in adolescent achievement: An ecological perspective. *American Psychologist, 47,* 723–729.

Steinberg, L., Fegley, S., & Dornbusch, S. M. (1993). Negative impact of part-time work on adolescent adjustment: Evidence from a longitudinal study. *Developmental Psychology, 29,* 171–180.

Steinberg, L., & Silverberg, S. B. (1986). The vicissitudes of autonomy in early adolescence. *Child Development, 57,* 841–851.

Steiner, J. E. (1979). Human facial expressions in response to taste and smell stimulation. In H. W. Reese & L. P. Lipsitt (Eds.), *Advances in child development and behavior* (Vol. 13). New York: Academic Press.

Stelmach, G. E., & Nahom, A. (1992). Cognitive-motor abilities of the elderly driver. *Human Factors, 34,* 53–65.

Stemp, P. S., Turner, J., & Noh, S. (1986). Psychological distress in the postpartum period: The significance of social support. *Journal of Marriage and the Family, 48,* 271–277.

Stephan, W. G. (1978). School desegregation: An evaluation of the predictions made in Brown vs. Board of Education. *Psychological Bulletin, 85,* 217–238.

Stephens, M. A., Townsend, A. L., Martire, L. M., & Druley, J. A. (2001). Balancing parent care with other roles: Interrole conflict of adult daughter caregivers. *Journal of Gerontology: Psychological Sciences, 56B,* P24–34.

Stephens, M. A. P., & Franks, M. M. (1995). Spillover between daughters' roles as caregiver and wife: Interference or enhancement? *Journal of Gerontology: Psychological Sciences, 50B,* 9–17.

Stepp, L. S. (2001, November 2). Children's worries take new shape. *The Washington Post,* C1, C4.

Stern, D. (1977). *The first relationship: Infant and mother.* Cambridge, MA: Harvard University Press.

Stern, M., & Karraker, K. H. (1989). Sex stereotyping of infants: A review of gender labeling studies. *Sex Roles, 20,* 501–522.

Sternberg, R. J. (1985). *Beyond IQ: A triarchic theory of human intelligence.* Cambridge, MA: Cambridge University Press.

Sternberg, R. J. (1988). The triarchic mind: A new theory of human intelligence. New York: Viking.

Sternberg, R. J. (1992). Ability tests, measurements, and markets. *Journal of Educational Psychology, 84,* 134–140.

Sternberg, R. J. (1997). Educating intelligence: Infusing the triarchic theory into school instruction. In R. J. Sternberg & E.L. Grigorenko (Eds.), *Intelligence, heredity, and environment.* New York: Cambridge University Press.

Sternberg, R. J. (1999a). The theory of successful intelligence. *Review of General Psychology, 3,* 292–316.

Sternberg, R. J. (Ed.). (1999b). *Handbook of creativity.* New York: Cambridge University Press.

Sternberg, R. J. (2000). The concept of intelligence. In R. J. Sternberg (Ed.), *The handbook of intelligence* (pp. 3–15). New York: Cambridge University Press.

Sternberg, R. J. (2003). *Wisdom, intelligence, and creativity synthesized.* Cambridge, England: Cambridge University Press.

Sternberg, R. J. (2004). Culture and intelligence. *American Psychologist, 59,* 325–338.

Sternberg, R. J., Grigorenko, E. L., & Bundy, D. A. (2001). The predictive value of IQ. *Merrill-Palmer Quarterly, 47,* 1–41.

Sternberg, R. J., & Lubart, T. I. (1996). Investing in creativity. *American Psychologist, 51,* 677–688.

Sternberg, R. J., Wagner, R. K., Williams, W. M., & Horvath, J. A. (1995). Testing common sense. *American Psychologist, 50,* 912–927.

Stevens, D. P., & Truss, C. V. (1985). Stability and change in adult personality over 12 and 20 years. *Developmental Psychology, 21,* 568–584.

Stevens, G. (1999). Age at immigration and second language proficiency among foreign-born adults. *Language in Society, 28,* 555–578.

Stevens, M. M., & Dunsmore, J. C. (1996). Adolescents who are living with a life-threatening illness. In C. A. Corr & D. E. Balk (Eds.), *Handbook of adolescent death and bereavement.* New York: Springer.

Stevens, R. J., & Slavin, R. E. (1995). The cooperative elementary school: Effects on students' achievement, attitudes, and social relations. *American Educational Research Journal, 32,* 321–351.

Stevenson, H. W., Chen, C., & Lee, S. (1993). Mathematics achievement of Chinese, Japanese, and American children: Ten years later. *Science, 259,* 53–58.

Stevenson, H. W., & Lee, S. Y. (1990). Contexts of achievement: A study of American, Chinese, and Japanese children. *Monographs of the Society for Research in Child Development, 55* (1–2, Serial No. 221).

Stevenson, H. W., Lee, S. Y., & Stigler, J. W. (1986). Mathematics achievement of Chinese, Japanese, and American children. *Science, 231,* 693–699.

Stevenson, H. W., & Stigler, J. W. (1994). *The learning gap: Why our schools are failing and what we can learn from Japanese and Chinese education.* New York: Simon & Schuster.

Stevenson, H. W., Stigler, J. W., Lee, S. Y., Lucker, G. W., Litamura, S., & Hsu, C. (1985). Cognitive performance and academic achievement of Japanese, Chinese, and American children. *Child Development, 56,* 718–734.

Stevenson, M. B., VerHoeve, J. N., Roach, M. A., & Leavitt, L. A. (1986). The beginning of conversation. Early patterns of mother–infant vocal responsiveness. *Infant Behavior and Development, 9,* 423–440.

Stevenson, M. R., & Black, K. N. (1988). Paternal absence and sex-role development: A meta-analysis. *Child Development, 59,* 793–814.

Stewart, R. B., & Marvin, R. S. (1984). Sibling relations: The role of conceptual perspective-taking in the ontogeny of sibling caregiving. *Child Development, 55,* 1322–1332.

St. George, D. (2001, June 8). A child's unheeded cry for help. *The Washington Post,* A1, A20–A21.

St. George, I. M., Williams, S., & Silva, P. A. (1994). Body size and the menarche: The Dunedin study. *Journal of Adolescent Health, 15,* 573–576.

Stifter, C. (2003). Child effects on the family: An example of the extreme case and a question of methodology. In A. C. Crouter & A. Booth (Eds.), *Children's influence on family dynamics. The neglected side of family relationships.* Mahwah, NJ: Erlbaum.

Stigler, J. W., Lee, S. Y., & Stevenson, H. W. (1987). Mathematics classrooms in Japan, Taiwan, and the United States. *Child Development, 58,* 1272–1285.

Stillion, J. M., & McDowell, E. E. (1996). *Suicide across the life span: Premature exits* (2nd ed.). Washington, D.C.: Taylor & Francis.

Stillion, J. M., & Papadatou, D. (2002). Suffer the children: An examination of psychosocial issues in children and adolescents with terminal illness. *American Behavioral Scientist, 46,* 299–315.

Stine, E. A. L., Soederberg, L. M., & Morrow, D. G. (1996). Language and discourse processing through adulthood. In F. Blanchard-Fields & T. M. Hess (Eds.), *Perspectives on cognitive change in adulthood and aging.* New York: McGraw-Hill.

Stine-Morrow, E. A. L., Loveless, M. K., & Soederberg, L. M. (1996). Resource allocation in on-line reading by younger and older adults. *Psychology and Aging, 11,* 475–486.

Stipek, D., Gralinski, H., & Kopp, C. (1990). Self-concept development in the toddler years. *Developmental Psychology, 26,* 972–977.

Stipek, D. J. (1984). The development of achievement motivation. In R. Ames & C. Ames (Eds.), *Research on motivation in education* (Vol. 1). Orlando, FL: Academic Press.

Stipek, D. J., & Gralinski, J. H. (1996). Children's beliefs about intelligence and school performance. *Journal of Educational Psychology, 88,* 397–407.

Stipek, D. J., & Mac Iver, D. J. (1989). Developmental change in children's assessment of intellectual competence. *Child Development, 60,* 521–538.

Stipek, D. J., Feiler, R., Daniels, D., & Milburn, S. (1995). Effects of different instructional approaches on young children's achievement and motivation. *Child Development, 66,* 209–223.

Stipek, D. J., Recchia, A., & McClintic, S. (1992). Self-evaluation in young children. *Monographs of the Society for Research in Child Development, 57* (1, Serial No. 226).

Stith, S. M., Rosen, K. H., Middleton, K. A., Busch, A. L., Lundeberg, K., & Carlton, R. P. (2000). The intergenerational transmission of spouse abuse: A meta-analysis. *Journal of Marriage and the Family, 62,* 640–654.

St. James-Roberts, I., & Plewis, I. (1996). Individual differences, daily fluctuations, and developmental changes in amounts of waking, fussing, crying, feeding, and sleeping. *Child Development, 67,* 2527–2540.

Stoddart, T., & Turiel, E. (1985). Children's concepts of cross-gender activities. *Child Development, 56,* 1241–1252.

Stone, R. (1992). Can a father's exposure lead to illness in his children? *Science, 258,* 31.

Stones, M. J., & Kozma, A. (1985). Physical performance. In N. Charness (Ed.), *Aging and human performance.* Chichester, England & New York: Wiley.

Stoolmiller, M. (1999). Implications of the restricted range of family environments for estimates of heritability and nonshared environment in behavior-genetic adoption studies. *Psychological Bulletin, 125,* 392–409.

Storgaard, L., Bonde, J. P., Ernst, E., Spano, M., Andersen, C. Y., Frydenberg, M., & Olsen, J. (2003). Does smoking during pregnancy affect sons' sperm count? *Epidemiology, 14,* 278–286.

Stouthamer-Loeber, M. (1991). Young children's verbal misrepresentations of reality. In K. J. Rotenberg (Ed.), *Children's interpersonal trust.* New York: Springer-Verlag.

Stratton, K., Howe, C., & Battaglia, F. (Eds.). (1996). *Fetal alcohol syndrome: Diagnosis, epidemiology, prevention, and treatment.* Washington, DC: National Academy Press.

Straus, M. A., & Gelles, R. J. (1986). Societal change and change in family violence from 1975 to 1985 as revealed by two national surveys. *Journal of Marriage and the Family, 48,* 465–479.

Straus, M. A., & Gelles, R. J. (Edited with C. Smith). (1990). *Physical violence in American families. Risk factors and adaptations to violence in 8145 families.* New Brunswick, NJ: Transaction Publishers.

Strauss, V. (2001, May 8). No beating the problem of bullies. Stubborn, pervasive schoolyard behavior leaves long-term scars on perpetrators and victims. *The Washington Post,* A11.

Streissguth, A. P., Barr, H. M., Bookstein, F. L., Sampson, P. D., & Olson, H. C. (1999). The long-term neurocognitive consequences of prenatal alcohol exposure: A 14-year study. *Psychological Science, 10,* 186–190.

Streissguth, A. P., & Dehaene, P. (1993). Fetal alcohol syndrome in twins of alcoholic mothers: Concordance of diagnosis and IQ. *American Journal of Medical Genetics, 47,* 857–861.

Streissguth, A. P., Sampson, P. D., Barr, H. M., Bookstein, F. L., & Olson, H. C. (1994). The effects of prenatal exposure to alcohol and tobacco: Contributions from the Seattle Longitudinal Prospective Study and implications for public policy. In H. L. Needlebaum & D. Bellinger (Eds.), *Prenatal exposure to toxicants.* Baltimore: Johns Hopkins University Press.

Streri, A. (2003). Cross-modal recognition of shape from hand to eyes in human newborns. *Somatosensory Motor Research, 20,* 13–18.

Streri, A., & Gentaz, E. (2004). Cross-modal recognition of shape from hand to eyes and handedness in human newborns. *Neuropsychologia, 42,* 1365–1369.

Streri, A., & Pecheux, M. (1986). Vision-to-touch and touch-to-vision transfer of form in 5-month-old infants. *British Journal of Developmental Psychology, 4,* 161–167.

Strigini, P., Sansone, R., Carobbi, S., & Pierluigi, M. (1990). Radiation and Down's syndrome. *Nature, 347,* 717.

Stringer, J. S., Sinkala, M., Goldenberg, R. L., Kumwenda, R., Acosta, E. P., Aldrovandi, G. M., Stout, J. P., & Vermund, S. H. (2004). Universal nevirapine upon presentation in labor to prevent mother-to-child HIV transmission in high prevalence settings. *AIDS, 18,* 939-943.

Strober, M., Freeman, R., Lampert, C., Diamond, J., & Kaye, W. (2000). Controlled family study of anorexia nervosa and bulimia nervosa: Evidence of shared liability and transmission of partial syndromes. *American Journal of Psychiatry, 157,* 393–401.

Stroebe, M. (2001a). Bereavement research and theory: Retrospective and prospective. *American Behavioral Scientist, 44,* 854–865.

Stroebe, M. (2001b). Gender differences in adjustment to bereavement: An empirical and theoretical review. *Review of General Psychology, 5,* 62–83.

Stroebe, W., & Schut, H. (2001). Risk factors in bereavement outcome: A methodological and empirical review. In M. S. Stroebe, R. O. Hansson, W. Stroebe, & H. Schut (Eds.), *Handbook of bereavement research. Consequences, coping, and care.* Washington, D.C.: American Psychological Association.

Stumpf, H., & Stanley, J. C. (1996). Gender-related differences on the College Board's Advanced Placement and Achievement Tests, 1982–1992. *Journal of Educational Psychology, 88,* 353–364.

Sudhalter, V., & Braine, M. D. S. (1985). How does comprehension of passives develop? A comparison of actional and experiential verbs. *Journal of Child Language, 12,* 455–470.

Sugisawa, H., Shibata, H., Hougham, G. W., Sugihara, Y., & Liang, J. (2002). Impact of social ties on depressive symptoms in U.S. and Japanese elderly. *Journal of Social Issues, 58,* 785–804.

Suitor, J. J. (1991). Marital quality and satisfaction with the division of household labor across the family life cycle. *Journal of Marriage and the Family, 53,* 221–230.

Suitor, J. J., & Reavis, R. (1995). Football, fast cars, and cheerleading: Adolescent gender norms, 1978–1989. *Adolescence, 30,* 265–272.

Sullivan, H. S. (1953). *The interpersonal theory of psychiatry.* New York: Norton.

Sullivan, S., & Ruffman, T. (2004). Social understanding: How does it fare with advancing years? *British Journal of Psychology, 95,* 1–18.

Suomi, S. J. (1997). Long-term effects of different early rearing experiences on social, emotional and physiological development in nonhuman primates. In M. S. Kesheven & R. M. Murra (Eds.), *Neurodevelopmental models of adult psychopathology.* Cambridge, England: Cambridge University Press.

Suomi, S. J. (1999). Developmental trajectories, early experiences, and community consequences: Lessons from studies with rhesus monkeys. In D. P. Keating & C. Hertzman (Eds.), *Developmental health and the wealth of nations: Social, biological, and educational dynamics.* New York: Guilford.

Suomi, S. J., & Levine, S. (1998). Psychobiology of intergenerational effects of trauma: Evidence from animal studies. In Y. Danieli (Ed.), *International handbook of multigenerational legacies of trauma.* New York: Plenum.

Super, D. E., Savickas, M. L., & Super, C. M. (1996). The life-span, life-space approach to careers. In D. Brown, L. Brooks, & Associates (Eds.), *Career choice and development* (3rd ed.). San Francisco: Jossey-Bass.

Susser, M., & Stein, Z. (1994). Timing in prenatal nutrition: A reprise of the Dutch Famine Study. *Nutrition Reviews, 52,* 84–94.

Sutton-Brown, M., & Suchowersky, O. (2003). Clinical and research advances in Huntington's disease. *Canadian Journal of Neurological Sciences, 30* (Suppl. 1), S45.

Swanson, H. L. (1999). What develops in working memory? A life span perspective. *Developmental Psychology, 35,* 986–1000.

Swanson, K., Beckwith, L., & Howard, J. (2000). Intrusive caregiving and quality of attachment in prenatally drug-exposed toddlers and their primary caregivers. *Attachment and Human Development, 2,* 130–148.

Swarr, A. E., & Richards, M. H. (1996). Longitudinal effects of adolescent girls' pubertal development, perceptions of pubertal timing, and parental relations on eating problems. *Developmental Psychology, 32,* 636–646.

Symons, D. K., & Clark, S. E. (2000). A longitudinal study of mother–child relationships and theory of mind in the preschool period. *Social Development, 9,* 3–23.

Szinovacz, M., & Ekerdt, D. J. (1995). Families and retirement. In R. Blieszner & V. H. Bedford (Eds.), *Handbook of aging and the family.* Westport, CT: Greenwood.

Szinovacz, M. E., DeViney, S., & Atkinson, M. P. (1999). Effects of surrogate parenting on grandparents' well-being. *Journal of Gerontology: Social Sciences, 54B,* S376–S388.

Szkrybalo, J., & Ruble, D. N. (1999). "God made me a girl": Sex-category constancy judgments and explanations revisited. *Developmental Psychology, 35,* 392–402.

T

Taddio, A. (2002). Conditioning and hyperalgesia in newborns exposed to repeated heel lances, *Journal of the American Medical Association, 288,* 857–861.

Tafarodi, R. W., Lo, C., Yamaguchi, S., Lee, W. W., & Katsura, H. (2004). The inner self in three countries. *Journal of Cross-Cultural Psychology, 35,* 97–117.

Taft, L. B., & Nehrke, M. F. (1990). Reminiscence, life review, and ego integrity in nursing home residents. *International Journal of Aging and Human Development, 30,* 189–196.

Tager-Flusberg, H. (2000). Language and understanding minds: Connections in autism. In S. Baron-Cohen, H. Tager-Flusberg, & D. J. Cohen (Eds.), *Understanding other minds. Perspectives from developmental cognitive neuroscience* (2nd ed.). Oxford: Oxford University Press.

Tager-Flusberg, H. (2005). Morphology and syntax in the preschool years. In J. B. Gleason (Ed.), *The development of language* (6th ed.). Boston: Allyn & Bacon.

Takahashi, K. (1990). Are the key assumptions of the "Strange Situation" procedure universal? A view from Japanese research. *Human Development, 33,* 23–30.

Tallal, P., Miller, S. L., Bedi, G., Byma, G., Wang, X., Nagarajan, S. S., Schreiner, C., Jenkins, W. M., & Merzenich, M. M. (1996). Language comprehension in language-learning impaired children improved with acoustically modified speech. *Science, 271,* 81–84.

Tan, R. S., & Pu, S. J. (2004). Is it andropause? Recognizing androgen deficiency in aging men. *Postgraduate Medicine, 115,* 62–66.

Tan, U. & Tan, M. (1999). Incidences of asymmetries for the palmer grasp reflex in neonates and hand preference in adults. *Neuroreport: For Rapid Communication of Neuroscience Research, 10,* 3254-3256.

Tangney, J. P. (2003). Self-relevant emotions. In M. R. Leary & J. P. Tangney (Eds.), *Handbook of self and identity.* New York: Guilford.

Tanner, J. M. (1990). *Foetus into man: Physical growth from conception to maturity* (2nd ed.). Cambridge, MA: Harvard University Press.

Tanzi, R. E., & Parson, A. B. (2000). *Decoding darkness. The search for the genetic causes of Alzheimer's disease.* Cambridge, MA: Perseus Publishing.

Tardif, T., & Wellman, H. M. (2000). Acquisition of mental state language in Mandarin- and Cantonese-speaking children. *Developmental Psychology, 36,* 25–43.

Taylor, M. (1999). *Imaginary companions and the children who create them.* New York: Oxford University Press.

Taylor, M., & Carlson, S. M. (1997). The relation between individual differences in fantasy and theory of mind. *Child Development, 68,* 436–455.

Taylor, M., Cartwright, B. S., & Carlson, S. M. (1993). A developmental investigation of children's imaginary companions. *Developmental Psychology, 29,* 276–285.

Taylor, M., & Gelman, S. A. (1989). Incorporating new words into the lexicon: Preliminary evidence for language hierarchies in two-year-old children. *Child Development, 60,* 625–636.

Taylor, M. D., Frier, B. M., Gold, A. E., & Deary, I. J. (2003). Psychosocial factors and diabetes-related outcomes following diagnosis of Type 1 diabetes. *Diabetic Medicine, 20,* 135–146.

Taylor, M. G. (1996). The development of children's beliefs about social and biological aspects of gender differences. *Child Development, 67,* 1555–1571.

Taylor, M. R. (2003). Dealing with death: Western philosophical strategies. In C. D. Bryant (Ed.), *Handbook of death and dying.* Thousand Oaks, CA: Sage.

Taylor, R. D., Jacobson, L., Rodriquez, A. U., Dominguez, A., Cantic, R., Doney, J., Boccuti, A., Alejandro, J., & Tobon, C. (2000). Stressful experiences and the psychological functioning of African-American and Puerto Rican families and adolescents. In R. D. Taylor & M. C. Wang (Eds.), *Resilience across contexts: Family, work, culture, and community.* Mahwah, NJ: Erlbaum.

Taylor, R. E., & Richards, S. B. (1991). Patterns of intellectual differences of black, Hispanic, and white children. *Psychology in the Schools, 28,* 5–9.

Taylor, R. L. (2000). Diversity within African-American families. In D. H. Demo, K. R. Allen, & M. A. Fine (Eds.), *Handbook of family diversity.* New York: Oxford University Press.

Teachman, J. D. (2000). Diversity of family structure: Economic and social influences. In D. H. Demo, K. R. Allen, & M. A. Fine (Eds.), *Handbook of family diversity.* New York: Oxford University Press.

Teachman, J. D. (2002). Stability across cohorts in divorce risk factors. *Demography, 39,* 331–351.

Teachman, J. D. (2003). Premarital sex, premarital cohabitation and the risk of subsequent marital dissolution among women. *Journal of Marriage and the Family, 65,* 444–455.

Teachman, J. D. (2004). The childhood living arrangements of children and the characteristics of their marriages. *Journal of Family Issues, 25,* 86–111.

Tedeschi, R. G., & Calhoun, L. G. (2004). Posttraumatic growth: Conceptual foundations and empirical evidence. *Psychological Inquiry, 15,* 1–18.

Teeter, P. A. (1998). *Interventions for ADHD. Treatment in developmental context.* New York: Guilford.

Teicher, M. H., Anderson, C. M., Polcari, A., Glod, C. A., Maas, L. C., & Renshaw, P. F. (2000). Functional deficits in basal ganglia of children with attention-deficit/hyperactivity disorder shown with functional magnetic resonance imaging relaxometry. *Nature Medicine, 6,* 470–473.

Teichner, G., & Golden, C. J. (2000). The relationship of neuropsychological impairment to conduct disorder in adolescence: A conceptual review. *Aggression and Violent Behavior, 5,* 509–528.

Teixeira, J. M., Fisk, N. M., & Glover, V. (1999). Association between maternal anxiety in pregnancy and increased uterine artery resistance index: Cohort based study. *British Medical Journal, 318,* 153–157.

Temple, E., Poldrack, R. A., Protopapas, A., Nagarajan, S., Salz, T., Tallal, P., Merzenich, M. M., & Gabrieli, J. D. (2000). Disruption of the neural response to rapid acoustic stimuli in dyslexia: Evidence from functional MRI. *Proceedings of the National Academy of Science, 97,* 13907–13912.

Tenenbaum, H. R., & Leaper, C. (2003). Parent–child conversations about science: The socialization of gender inequities. *Developmental Psychology, 39,* 34–47.

Teno, J. M., Clarridge, B. R., Casey, V., Welch, L. C., Wetle, T., Shield, R., & Mor, V. (2004). Family perspectives on end-of-life care at the last place of care. *Journal of the American Medical Association, 291,* 88–93.

Terman, L. M. (1954). The discovery and encouragement of exceptional talent. *American Psychologist, 9,* 221–238.

Terry, R., & Coie, J. D. (1991). A comparison of methods for defining sociometric status among children. *Developmental Psychology, 27,* 867–880.

Teti, D. M., Sakin, J. W., Kucera, E., & Corns, K. M. (1996). And baby makes four: Predictors of attachment security among preschool-age firstborns during the transition to siblinghood. *Child Development, 67,* 579–596.

Thapar, A. (2003). Attention deficit hyperactivity disorder: New genetic findings, new directions. In R. Plomin, J. C. DeFries, I. W. Craig, & P. McGuffin (Eds.), *Behavioral genetics in the postgenomic era.* Washington, D.C.: American Psychological Association.

Tharinger, D. (1990). Impact of child sexual abuse on developing sexuality. *Professional Psychology: Research & Practice,* 21, 331–337.

Thelen, E. (1984). Learning to walk: Ecological demands and phylogenetic constraints. In L. P. Lipsitt & C. Rovee-Collier (Eds.), *Advances in infancy research* (Vol. 3). Norwood, NJ: Ablex.

Thelen, E. (1995). Motor development: A new synthesis. *American Psychologist, 50,* 79–95.

Thelen, E. (1996). The improvising infant: Learning about learning to move. In M. R. Merrens & G. G. Brannigan (Eds.). *The developmental psychologists: Research adventures across the life span* (pp. 21–35). McGraw-Hill.

Thelen, E., & Smith, L. B. (1994). *A dynamic systems approach to the development of cognition and action.* Cambridge, MA: MIT Press.

Thelen, M. H., Powell, A. L., Lawrence, C., & Kuhnert, M. E. (1992). Eating and body image concerns among children. *Journal of Clinical Child Psychology, 21,* 41–46.

Thiede, K. W., & Dunlosky, J. (1999). Toward a general model of self-regulated study: An analysis of selection of items for study and self-paced study time. *Journal of Experimental Psychology: Learning, Memory, and Cognition, 25,* 1024–1037.

Thoman, E. B., & Whitney, M. P. (1990). Behavioral states in infants: Individual differences and individual analyses. In J. Columbo & J. Fagen (Eds.), *Individual differences in infancy: Reliability, stability, prediction.* Hillsdale, NJ: Erlbaum.

Thomas, A., & Chess, S. (1986). The New York Longitudinal Study: From infancy to early adult life. In R. Plomin & J. Dunn (Eds.), *The study of temperament: Changes, continuities, and challenges.* Hillsdale, NJ: Erlbaum.

Thomas, F., Renaud, F., Benefice, E., de Meeus, T., & Guegan, J. (2001). International variability of ages at menarche and menopause: Patterns and main determinants. *Human Biology, 73,* 271.

Thomas, J. (1998, May 13). Concerns heighten as U.S. teens work increasing numbers of hours. *The New York Times.* Retrieved online (January 15, 2005): http://mbhs.bergtraum.k12.ny.us/cybereng/opinion3/working-teens.html

Thomas, J. R., Yan, J. H., & Stelmach, G. E. (2000). Movement substructures change as a function of practice in children and adults. *Journal of Experimental Child Psychology, 75,* 228–244.

Thompson A. M., & Smart, J. L. (1993). A prospective study of the development of laterality: Neonatal laterality in relation to perinatal factors and maternal behavior. *Cortex, 29,* 649–659.

Thompson, J. R., & Chapman, R. S. (1977). Who is "Daddy" revisited? The status of two-year-olds' overextended words in use and comprehension. *Journal of Child Language, 4,* 359–375.

Thompson, P. M., Giedd, J. N., Woods, R. P., MacDonald, D., Evans, A. C., & Toga, A. W. (2000). Growth patterns in the developing brain detected by using continuum mechanical tensor maps. *Nature, 404,* 190–193.

Thompson, R. A. (1994). Emotion regulation: A theme in search of definition. In N. A. Fox (Ed.), The development of emotion regulation: Biological and behavioral considerations. *Monographs of the Society for Research in Child Development, 59* (Nos. 2–3, Serial No. 240).

Thompson, R. A. (1998). Early sociopersonality development. In N. Eisenberg (Vol. Ed.), W. Damon (Editor-in-Chief), *Handbook of child psychology: Vol. 3. Social, emotional, and personality development.* New York: Wiley.

Thompson, R. A., & Amato, P. R. (1999). The post divorce family. An introduction to the issues. In R. A. Thompson & P. R. Amato (Eds.), *The post divorce family. Children, parenting, & society.* Thousand Oaks, CA: Sage.

Thompson, R. A., & Nelson, C. A. (2001). Developmental science and the media. Early brain development. *American Psychologist, 56,* 5–15.

Thompson, R. A., & Raikes, H. A. (2003). Toward the next quarter-century: Conceptual and methodological challenges for attachment theory. *Development and Psychopathology, 15,* 691–718.

Thompson, R.F. (1975). *Introduction to physiological psychology.* New York: Harper & Row.

Thompson, R. F. (2000). *The brain: An introduction to neuroscience* (3rd ed.). New York: Worth.

Thornberry, T. P., Freeman-Gallant, A., Lizotte, A. J., Krohn, M. D., & Smith, C. A. (2003). Linked lives: The intergenerational transmission of antisocial behavior. *Journal of Abnormal Child Psychology, 31,* 171–184.

Thorndike, R. L. (1997). The early history of intelligence testing. In D. P. Flanagan, J. L. Genshaft, & P. L. Harrison (Eds.), *Contemporary intellectual assessment: Theories, tests, and issues.* New York: Guilford.

Thorne, B. (1993). *Gender play: Girls and boys in school.* New Brunswick, NJ: Rutgers University Press.

Thorne, C., & Newell, M. (2000). Epidemiology of HIV infection in the newborn. *Early Human Development, 58,* 1–16.

Thurber, C. A. (1995). The experience and expression of homesickness in preadolescent and adolescent boys. *Child Development, 66,* 1162–1178.

Thurstone, L. L. (1938). *Primary mental abilities.* Chicago: University of Chicago Press.

Thurstone, L. L., & Thurstone, T. G. (1941). Factorial studies of intelligence. *Psychometric Monographs,* No. 2.

Thys-Jacobs, S. (2000). Micronutrients and the premenstrual syndrome: The case for calcium. *Journal of the American College of Nutrition, 19,* 220–227.

Tietjen, A. M., & Walker, L. J. (1985). Moral reasoning and leadership among men in a Papua New Guinea society. *Developmental Psychology, 21,* 982–992.

Timmer, E., Bode, C., & Dittmann-Kohli, F. (2003). Expectations of gains in the second half of life: A study of personal conceptions of enrichment in a lifespan perspective. *Ageing & Society, 23,* 3–24.

Tisak, M. S., & Tisak, J. (1990). Children's conceptions of parental authority, friendship, and sibling relations. *Merrill-Palmer Quarterly, 36,* 347–368.

Tomasello, M. (1999). The human adaptation for culture. *Annual Review of Anthropology, 28,* 502–529.

Tomasello, M., Call, J., & Hare, B. (2003). Chimpanzees understand psychological states: The question is which ones and to what extent. *Trends in Cognitive Sciences, 7,* 153–156.

Tomlinson-Keasey, C., & Keasey, C. B. (1974). The mediating role of cognitive development in moral judgment. *Child Development, 45,* 291–298.

Tomlinson-Keasey, C., & Little, T. D. (1990). Predicting educational attainment, occupational achievement, intellectual skill, and personal adjustment among gifted men and women. *Journal of Educational Psychology, 82,* 442–455.

Torrance, E. P. (1975). Creativity research in education: Still alive. In I. A. Taylor & J. W. Getzels (Eds.), *Perspectives in creativity.* Chicago: Aldine-Atherton.

Torrance, E. P. (1988). The nature of creativity as manifest in its testing. In R. J. Sternberg (Ed.), *The nature of creativity: Contemporary psychological perspectives.* Cambridge, England: Cambridge University Press.

Tousignant, M. (1995, November 17). The lesson of a lifetime: 2nd-graders thrill to 114-year-old Ella Miller's tales of growing up. *The Washington Post,* B1.

Tousignant, M. (1996, November 9). A seasoned voter speaks her mind: At 115 years old, Vienna woman says age of candidate is not an issue. *The Washington Post,* B5.

Trabasso, T. (1975). Representation, memory, and reasoning: How do we make transitive inferences? In A. D. Pick (Ed.), *Minnesota Symposia on Child Psychology* (Vol. 9). Minneapolis: University of Minnesota.

Tracy, J. L., Shaver, P. R., Albino, A. W., & Cooper, M. L. (2003). Attachment styles and adolescent sexuality. In P. Florsheim (Ed.), *Adolescent romantic relations and sexual be-*

havior: Theory, research, and practical implications. Mahwah, NJ: Erlbaum.

Trafford, A. (1996, March 26). The old gray-haired: They ain't what they used to be. *The Washington Post—Health,* 6.

Traylor, E. S., Hayslip, B. Jr., Kaminski, P. L., & York, C. (2003). Relationships between grief and family system characteristics: A cross lagged longitudinal analysis. *Death Studies, 27,* 575–601.

Treffert, D. A. (2000). *Extraordinary people: Understanding savant syndrome.* Available online: iUniverse.com.

Trehub, S. E., Schneider, B. A., Thorpe, L. A., & Judge, P. (1991). Observational measures of auditory sensitivity in early infancy. *Developmental Psychology, 27,* 40–49.

Treiman, R. (2000). The foundations of literacy. *Current Directions in Psychological Science, 9,* 89–92.

Treiman, R., & Broderick, V. (1998). What's in a name? Children's knowledge about the letters in their own names. *Journal of Experimental Child Psychology, 70,* 97–116.

Tremblay, M. S., Inman, J. W., & Willms, J. D. (2000). The relationship between physical activity, self-esteem, and academic achievement in 12-year-old children. *Pediatric Exercise Science, 12,* 312–323.

Tremblay, M. S., Pella, T., & Taylor, K. (1996). The quality and quantity of school-based physical education: A growing concern. *CAHPERD Journal, 62,* 4–7.

Tremblay, R. E. (2000). The development of aggressive behaviour during childhood: What have we learned in the past century? *International Journal of Behavioral Development. 24,* 129–141.

Trevethan, S. D., & Walker, L. J. (1989). Hypothetical versus real-life moral reasoning among psychopathic and delinquent youth. *Development and Psychopathology, 1,* 91–103.

Triandis, H. C. (1989). Self and social behavior in differing cultural contexts. *Psychological Review, 96,* 269–289.

Triandis, H. C. (1995). *Individualism and collectivism.* Boulder, CO: Westview Press.

Trickett, P. K., & Putnam, F. W. (1993). Impact of child sexual abuse on females: Toward a developmental, psychobiological integration. *Psychological Science, 4,* 81–87.

Tronick, E. Z. (1989). Emotions and emotional communication in infants. *American Psychologist, 44,* 112–119.

True, M. M., Pisani, L., & Oumar, F. (2001). Infant-mother attachment among the Dogon of Mali. *Child Development, 72,* 1451–1466.

Trueheart, C. (1997, August 5). Champion of longevity ends her reign at 122. *The Washington Post,* A1, A12.

Tryon, R. C. (1940). Genetic differences in maze learning in rats. *Yearbook of the National Society for Studies in Education, 39,* 111–119.

Trzesniewski, K. H., Donnellan, M. B., & Robins, R. W. (2003). Stability of self-esteem across the lifespan. *Journal of Personality and Social Psychology, 84,* 205–220.

Tucker, B. P. (1998). Deaf culture, cochlear implants, and elective disability. *Hastings Center Report, 28,* 6–14.

Tuckman, B. W. (1999). The effects of exercise on children and adolescents. In A. J. Goreczny & M. Hersen (Eds.), *Handbook of pediatric and adolescent health psychology* (pp. 275–286). Boston: Allyn & Bacon.

Turati, C. (2004). Why faces are not special to newborns: An alternative account of the face preference. *Current Directions in Psychological Science, 13,* 5–8.

Turiel, E. (1978). The development of concepts of social structure: Social convention. In J. Glick & A. Clarke-Stewart (Eds.), *The development of social understanding.* New York: Gardner Press.

Turiel, E. (1983). *The development of social knowledge. Morality and convention.* Cambridge, England: Cambridge University Press.

Turk-Charles, S., & Carstensen, L. L. (1999). The role of time in the setting of social goals across the life span. In T. M. Hess & F. Blanchard-Fields (Eds.), *Social cognition and aging.* San Diego: Academic Press.

Turkheimer, E. (1991). Individual and group differences in adoption studies of IQ. *Psychological Bulletin, 110,* 392–405.

Turkheimer, E. (2000). Three laws of behavior genetics and what they mean. *Current Directions in Psychological Science, 9,* 160–164.

Turkheimer, E., Haley, A., Waldron, M., D'Onofrio, B., & Gottesman, I. I. (2003). Socioeconomic status modifies heritability of IQ in young children. *Psychological Science, 14,* 623–628.

Turner, P. J., & Gervai, J. (1995). A multidimensional study of gender typing in preschool children and their parents: Personality, attitudes, preferences, behavior, and cultural differences. *Developmental Psychology, 31,* 759–772.

Turner, R. J., & Lloyd, D. A. (2004). Stress burden and the lifetime incidence of psychiatric disorder in young adults racial and ethnic contrasts. *Archives of General Psychiatry, 61,* 481–488.

Twenge, J. M. (1997). Changes in masculine and feminine traits over time: A meta-analysis. *Sex Roles, 36,* 305–325.

Twenge, J. M. (2000). The age of anxiety? Birth cohort change in anxiety and neuroticism, 1952–1993. *Journal of Personality and Social Psychology, 79,* 1007–1021.

Tyre, P. (2004, January 19). In a race against time. *Newsweek,* 62–66.

Tyson-Rawson, K. J. (1996). Adolescent responses to the death of a parent. In C. A. Corr & D. E. Balk (Eds.), *Handbook of adolescent death and bereavement.* New York: Springer.

U

Uchida, N., Fujita, K., & Katayama, T. (1999). Detection of vehicles on the other crossing path at an intersection: Visual search performance of elderly drivers. *Japanese Society of Automotive Engineers Review, 20,* 381.

Uchino, B. N., Cacioppo, J. T., & Keicolt-Glaser, J. K. (1996). The relationship between social support and physiological processes: A review with emphasis on underlying mechanisms and implications for health. *Psychological Bulletin, 119,* 488–531.

Udry, J. R., & Chantala, K. (2004). Masculinity–femininity guides sexual union formation in adolescents. *Personality and Social Psychology Bulletin, 30,* 44–55.

Uhlenberg, P., & de Jong-Gierveld, J. (2004). Age-segregation in later life: An examination of personal networks. *Ageing & Society, 24,* 5–28.

Umana-Taylor, A. J., Diversi, M., & Fine, M. A. (2002). Ethnic identity and self-esteem of Latino adolescents: Distinctions among the Latino populations. *Journal of Adolescent Research, 17,* 303–327.

Umberson, D. (1992). Relationships between adult children and their parents: Psychological consequences for both generations. *Journal of Marriage and the Family, 54,* 664–674.

Umberson, D. (2003). *Death of a parent: Transition to a new adult identity.* Cambridge, U.K.: Cambridge University Press.

Umberson, D., & Chen, M. D. (1994). Effects of a parent's death on adult children: Relationship salience and reaction to loss. *American Sociological Review, 59,* 152–168.

Umberson, D., & Slaten, E. (2000). Gender and intergenerational relationships. In D. H. Demo, K. R. Allen, & M. A. Fine (Eds.), *Handbook of family diversity.* New York: Oxford University Press.

Umberson, D., Wortman, C. B., & Kessler, R. C. (1992). Widowhood and depression: Explaining long-term gender differences in vulnerability. *Journal of Health and Social Behavior, 33,* 10–24.

Underwood, A. (2004, January 19). Now, reduce your risk of Alzheimer's. *Newsweek,* 72–73.

Unger, J. B., Molina, G. B., & Teran, L. (2000). Perceived consequences of teenage childbearing among adolescent girls in an urban sample. *Journal of Adolescent Health, 26,* 205–212.

Updegraff, K., & McHale, S. M., & Crouter, A. C. (1996). Gender roles in marriage: What do they mean for girls' and boys' school achievement? *Journal of Youth and Adolescence, 25,* 73–88.

Urofsky, M. I. (1993). *Letting go. Death, dying, and the law.* New York: Charles Scribner's Sons.

U.S. Agency for International Development. (2000, July). *New data shows tremendous impact of AIDS on developing world.* Available: http://www.usaid.gov/press/releases/2000/pr000710.html.

U.S. Census Bureau. (2000). *Statistical abstracts of the United States: 2000* (120th ed.). Washington, D.C.: Government Printing Office.

U.S. Census Bureau. (2003). *Statistical abstract of the United States: 2003* (123th ed.). Washington, D.C.: U.S. Government Printing Office.

U.S. Department of Education. (1997). Digest of Education Statistics, 1997. Washington, D.C.: National Center for Education Statistics.

U.S. Department of Health and Human Services, Administration for Children & Families. (2004). *Child maltreatment 2002. Reports from the states to the National Child Abuse and Neglect Data System.* Available at: http://www.acf.hhs.gov/programs/cb/publications/cmreports.htm.

U.S. Department of Labor, Bureau of Labor Statistics. (2001). *Highlights of women's earnings in 2000* (Report 952). Washington, D.C.: Author.

U.S. Department of Transportation. (1997). *Improving transportation for a maturing society.* Washington, D.C.: DOT-P10-97-01.

Usher, J. A., & Neisser, U. (1993). Childhood amnesia and the beginnings of memory for four early life events. *Journal of Experimental Psychology: General, 122,* 155–165.

V

Vaillant, G. E. (1977). *Adaptation to life.* Boston: Little, Brown.

Vaillant, G. E. (1983). Childhood environment and maturity of defense mechanisms. In D. Magnusson & V. L. Allen (Eds.), *Human development. An interactional perspective.* New York: Academic Press.

Vaillant, G. E., & Milofsky, E. (1980). Natural history of male psychological health. IX: Empirical evidence for Erikson's model of the life cycle. *American Journal of Psychiatry, 137,* 1348–1359.

Van Beurden, E., Zask, A., Barnett, L. M., & Dietrich, U. C. (2002). Fundamental movement skills—How do primary school children perform? The "Move it, Groove it" program in rural Australia. *Journal of Science and Medicine on Sport, 5,* 244–252.

Van Beveren, T. T., Little, B. B., & Spence, M. (2000). Effects of prenatal cocaine exposure and postnatal environment on child development. *American Journal of Human Biology, 12,* 417–428.

Vance, M. L., Mauras, N., & Wood, A. (1999). Growth hormone therapy in children and adults. *New England Journal of Medicine, 341,* 1206–1216.

Vandell, D. L. (2000). Parents, peer groups, and other socializing influences. *Developmental Psychology, 36,* 699–710.

Vandell, D. L., McCartney, K., Owen, M. T., Booth, C., & Clarke-Stewart, A. (2003). Variations in child care by grandparents during the first three years. *Journal of Marriage and the Family, 65,* 375–381.

Vandell, D. L., Wilson, K. S., & Buchanan, N. R. (1980). Peer interaction in the first year of life: An examination of its structure, content, and sensitivity to toys. *Child Development, 51,* 481–488.

van den Boom, D. C. (1995). Do first-year intervention effects endure? Follow-up during toddlerhood of a sample of Dutch irritable infants. *Child Development, 66,* 1798–1816.

van der Maas, H., & Jensen, B. R. J. (2003). What response times tell of children's behavior on the balance scale task. *Journal of Experimental Child Psychology, 85,* 141–177.

Van der Pols, J. C., Bates, C. J., McGraw, P. V., Thompson, J. R., Reacher, M., Prentice, A., & Finch, S. (2000). Visual acuity measurements in a national sample of British elderly people. *Ophthalmology, 84,* 165–170.

van Galen, G. P. (1993). Handwriting: A developmental perspective. In A. F. Kalverboer, B. Hopkins, & R. H. Geuze (Eds.), *Motor development in early and later childhood: Longitudinal approaches.* Cambridge, England: Cambridge University Press.

Van Giffen, K., & Haith, M. M. (1984). Infant visual response to Gestalt geometric forms. *Infant Behavior and Development, 7,* 335–346.

van Hoeken, D., Seidell, J., & Hoek, H. (2003). Epidemiology. In J. Treasure, U. Schmidt, & E. Van Furth (Eds.), *Handbook of eating disorders* (2nd ed.). Chicester, UK: Wiley.

van Hoof, A. (1999). The identity status field rereviewed: An update of unresolved and neglected issues with a view on some alternative approaches. *Developmental Review, 19,* 497–556.

van IJzendoorn, M. H. (1992). Intergenerational transmission of parenting: A review of studies in nonclinical populations. *Developmental Review, 12,* 76–99.

van IJzendoorn, M. H. (1995). Adult attachment representations, parental responsiveness, and infant attachment: A meta-analysis on the predictive validity of the Adult Attachment Interview. *Psychological Bulletin, 117,* 387–403.

van IJzendoorn, M. H., & Bakermans-Kranenburg, M. J. (1996). Attachment representations in mothers, fathers, adolescents, and clinical groups: A meta-analytic search for normative data. *Journal of Consulting and Clinical Psychology, 64,* 8–21.

van IJzendoorn, M. H., & DeWolff, M. S. (1997). In search of the absent father: Meta-analyses of infant-father attachment: A rejoinder to our discussants. *Child Development, 68,* 604–609.

van IJzendoorn, M. H., Goldberg, S., Kroonenberg, P. M., & Frenkel, O. J. (1992). The relative effects of maternal and child problems on the quality of attachment: A meta-analysis of attachment in clinical samples. *Child Development, 63,* 840–858.

van IJzendoorn, M. H., & Sagi, A. (1999). Cross-cultural patterns of attachment: Universal and contextual dimensions. In J. Cassidy & P. R. Shaver (Eds.), *Handbook of attachment.* New York: Guilford.

van IJzendoorn, M. H., Schuengel, C., & Bakermans-Kranenburg, M. J. (1999). Disorganized attachment in early childhood: Meta-analysis of precursors, concomitants, and sequelae. *Development and Psychopathology, 11,* 225–249.

van Kleeck, A., Gillam, R. B., Hamilton, L., & McGrath, C. (1997). The relationship between middle-class parents' book-sharing discussion and their preschooler's abstract language development. *Journal of Speech, Language, and Hearing Research, 40,* 1261–1271.

Van Laningham, J., Johnson, D., & Amato, P. (2001). Marital happiness, marital duration, and the U-shaped curve: Evidence from a five-wave panel study. *Social Forces, 79,* 1313–1341.

van Os, J., & Sham, P. (2003). Gene-environment correlation and interaction in schizophrenia. In R. M. Murray, P. B. Jones, E. Susser, J. van Os, & M. Cannon (Eds.), *The epidemiology of schizophrenia.* Cambridge, U.K.: Cambridge University Press.

Varea, C., Bernis, C., Montero, P., Arias, S., Barroso, A., & Gonzalez, B. (2000). Secular trend and intrapopulational variation in age of menopause in Spanish women. *Journal of Biosocial Science, 32,* 383–393.

Varendi, H., Christensson, K., Porter, R. H., & Winberg, J. (1998). Soothing effect of amniotic fluid smell in newborn infants. *Early Human Development, 51,* 47–55.

Vartanian, L. R., & Powlishta, K. K. (1996). A longitudinal examination of the social-cognitive foundations of adolescent egocentrism. *Journal of Early Adolescence, 16,* 157–178.

Vaughn, B. E., Azria, M. R., Krzysik, L., Caya, L. R., Bost, K. K., Newell, W., & Kazura, K. L. (2000). Friendship and social competence in a sample of preschool children attending head start. *Developmental Psychology, 36,* 326–338.

Vaughn, B. E., Lefever, G. B., Seifer, R., & Barglow, P. (1989). Attachment behavior, attachment security, and temperament during infancy. *Child Development, 60,* 728–737.

Vazsonyi, A. T., Hibbert, J. R., & Snider, J. B. (2003). Exotic enterprise no more? Adolescent reports of family and parenting processes from youth in four countries. *Journal of Research on Adolescence, 13,* 129–160.

Vedantum, S. (2004, September 14). FDA confirms antidepressants raise children's suicide risk. *Washington Post,* A1, A16.

Veenstra-Vanderweele, J., & Cook, E. H. (2003). Genetics of childhood disorders: XLVI. Autism, part 5: Genetics of autism. *Journal of the American Academy of Child and Adolescent Psychiatry, 42,* 116–118.

Vellutino, F. R. (1991). Introduction to three studies on reading acquisition: Convergent findings on theoretical foundations of code-oriented versus whole language approaches to reading instruction. *Journal of Educational Psychology, 83,* 437–443.

Vellutino, F. R., Scanlon, D. M., Sipay, E. R., & Small, S. G. (1996). Cognitive profiles of difficult-to-remediate and readily remediated poor readers: Early intervention as a vehicle for distinguishing between cognitive and experiential deficits as basic causes of specific reading disability. *Journal of Educational Psychology, 88,* 601–638.

Ventura, S., Martin, J., Curtin, S., Menacker, F., & Hamilton, B. E. (2001). Births: Final data for 1999. *National Vital Statistics Report, 49,* 1–100.

Verghese, J., Lipton, R. B., Katz, M. J., Hall, C. B., Derby, C. A., Kuslansky, G., Ambrose, A. F., Sliwinski, M., & Buschke, H. (2003). Leisure activities and the risk of dementia in the elderly. *New England Journal of Medicine, 348,* 2508–2516.

Verhaeghen, P. (2003). Aging and vocabulary scores: A meta-analysis. *Psychology and Aging, 18,* 332–339.

Verhaeghen, P., & Marcoen, A. (1996). On the mechanisms of plasticity in young and older adults after instruction in the method of loci: Evidence for an amplification model. *Psychology and Aging, 11,* 164–178.

Vermeulen, A. (2000). Andropause. *Maturitas, 15,* 5–15.

Veroff, J., Reuman, D., & Feld, S. (1984). Motives in American men and women across the adult life span. *Developmental Psychology, 20,* 1142–1158.

Verquer, M. L., Beehr, T. A., & Wagner, S. H. (2003). A meta-analysis of relations between person-organization fit and work attitudes. *Journal of Vocational Behavior, 63,* 473–489.

Verrillo, R. T., & Verrillo, V. (1985). Sensory and perceptual performance. In N. Charness (Ed.), *Aging and human performance.* Chichester, England: Wiley.

Verschueren, K., Buyck, P., & Marcoen, A. (2001). Self-representations and socioemotional competence in young children: A 3-year longitudinal study. *Developmental Psychology, 37,* 126–134.

Vinden, P. G., & Astington, J. W. (2000). Culture and understanding other minds. In S. Baron-Cohen, H. Tager-Flusberg, & D. J. Cohen (Eds.), *Understanding other minds. Perspectives from developmental cognitive neuroscience* (2nd ed.). Oxford: Oxford University Press.

Viner, R. (2002). Splitting hairs: Is puberty getting earlier in girls? *Archives of Disease in Childhood, 86,* 6–8.

Vining, E. P. G., Freeman, J. M., Pillas, D. J., Uematsu, S., Carson, B. S., Brandt, J., Boatman, D., Pulsifer, M. B., & Zuckerberg,

A., (1997). Why would you remove half a brain? The outcome of 58 children after hemispherectomy—the Johns Hopkins experience: 1968 to 1996. *Pediatrics, 100,* 163–171.

Vink, T., Hinney, A., van Elburg, A. A., van Goozen, S. H., Sandkuji, L. A., Sinke, R. J., Herpertz-Dahlmann, B. M., Hebebrand, J., Remschmidt, H., van Engeland, H., & Adan, R. A. (2001). Association between an agouti-related protein gene polymorphism and anorexia nervosa. *Molecular Psychiatry, 6,* 325–328.

Vita, A. J., Terry, R. B., Hubert, H. B., & Fries, J. F. (1998). Aging, health risks, and cumulative disability. *New England Journal of Medicine, 338,* 1035–1041.

Vobejda, B. (1998, May 28). Traditional families hold on. Statistics show a slackening of 1970s, '80s social trends. *The Washington Post,* A2.

Vobejda, B., & Havemann, J. (1997, May 2). Teenagers less sexually active in U.S. *The Washington Post,* A1, A12.

Volkmar, F. R. (2001). Pharmacological interventions in autism: Theoretical and practical issues. *Journal of Clinical Child Psychology, 30,* 80–87.

Volkmar, F. R., Lord, C., Bailey, A., Schultz, R. T., & Klin, A. (2004). Autism and pervasive developmental disorders. *Journal of Child Psychology and Psychiatry and Allied Disciplines, 45,* 135–170.

Vondra, J., & Belsky, J. (1993). Developmental origins of parenting: Personality and relationship factors. In T. Luster & L. Okagaki (Eds.), *Parenting. An ecological perspective.* Hillsdale, NJ: Erlbaum.

von Hofsten, C. (1993). Studying the development of goal-directed behavior. In A. F. Kalverboer, B. Hopkins, & R. H. Geuze (Eds.), *Motor development in early and later childhood: Longitudinal approaches.* Cambridge, England: Cambridge University Press.

Vorhees, C. V., & Mollnow, E. (1987). Behavioral teratogenesis: Long-term influences on behavior from early exposure to environmental agents. In J. D. Osofsky (Ed.), *Handbook of infant development* (2nd ed.). New York: Wiley.

Voyer, D., Voyer, S., & Bryden, M. P. (1995). Magnitude of sex differences in spatial abilities: A meta-analysis and consideration of critical variables. *Psychological Bulletin, 117,* 250–270.

Vurpillot, E. (1968). The development of scanning strategies and their relation to visual differentiation. *Journal of Experimental Child Psychology, 6,* 632–650.

Vygotsky, L. S. (1962). *Thought and language* (E. Hanfmann & G. Vakar, Eds. & Trans.). Cambridge, MA: MIT Press. (Original work published 1934).

Vygotsky, L. S. (1978). *Mind in society: The development of higher mental processes* (M. Cole, V. John-Steiner, S. Scribner, & E. Souberman, Eds.). Cambridge, MA: Harvard University Press. (Original work published 1930, 1933, 1935).

W

Wachs, T. D. (1995). Relation of mild-to-moderate malnutrition to human development: Correlational studies. *Journal of Nutrition Supplement, 125,* 2245S–2254S.

Wachs, T. D. (2000). *Necessary but not sufficient. The respective roles of single and multiple influences on individual development.* Washington, D.C.: American Psychological Association.

Wade, B., & Moore, M. (1998). An early start with books: Literacy and mathematical evidence from a longitudinal study. *Educational Review, 50,* 135–145.

Waechter, E. H. (1984). Dying children. Patterns of coping. In H. Wass & C. A. Corr (Eds.), *Childhood and death.* Washington, D.C.: Hemisphere.

Wagner, E. H., LaCroix, A. Z., Buchner, D. M., & Larson, E. B. (1992). Effects of physical activity on health status in older adults. I. Observational studies. *Annual Review of Public Health, 13,* 451–468.

Wahl, H., & Kruse, A. (2003). Psychological gerontology in Germany: Recent findings and social implications. *Ageing & Society, 23,* 131–163.

Wahlberg, K. E., Wynne, L. C., Oja, H., Keskitalo, P., Pykalainen, L., Lahti, I., Moring, J., Naarala, M., Sorri, A., Seitamaa, M., Laksy, K., Kolassa, J., & Tienari, P. (1997). Gene-environment interaction in vulnerability to schizophrenia: Findings from the Finnish Adoptive Family Study of Schizophrenia. *American Journal of Psychiatry, 154,* 355–362.

Waite, L. J., & Gallagher, M. (2000). *The case for marriage. Why married people are happier, healthier, and better off financially.* New York: Doubleday.

Wakeley, A., Rivera, S., & Langer, J. (2000). Can young infants add and subtract? *Child Development, 71,* 1525–1534.

Waldenström, U., Borg, I., Olsson, B., Sköld, M., & Wall, S. (1996). The childbirth experience: A study of 295 new mothers. *Birth, 23,* 144–153.

Walford, R. L. (1983). *Maximum life span.* New York: Norton.

Walford, R. L., Mock, D., Verdery, R., & MacCallum, T. (2002). Calorie restriction in Biosphere 2: Alterations in the physiologic, hematologic, hormonal, and biochemical parameters in humans restricted for a 2-year period. *Journal of Gerontology, 57A,* B211–B224.

Walker, L. J. (1980). Cognitive and perspective-taking prerequisites of moral development. *Child Development, 51,* 131–139.

Walker, L. J. (2004). Gus in the gap: Bridging the judgment-action gap in moral reasoning. In D. K. Lapsley & D. Narvaez (Eds.), *Moral development, self, and identity.* Mahwah, NJ: Erlbaum.

Walker, L. J., Hennig, K. H., & Krettenauer, T. (2000). Parent and peer contexts for children's moral reasoning development. *Child Development, 71,* 1033–1048.

Walker, L. J., & Taylor, J. H. (1991). Family interactions and the development of moral reasoning. *Child Development, 62,* 264–283.

Walker-Andrews, A. S. (1997). Infants' perception of expressive behaviors: Differentiation of multimodal information. *Psychological Bulletin, 121,* 437–456.

Wallace, P. S., & Whishaw, I. Q. (2003). Independent digit movements and precision grip patterns in 1–5-month-old human infants: Hand-babbling, including vacuous then self-directed hand and digit movements, precedes targeted reaching. *Neuropsychologia, 41,* 1912–1918.

Wallach, M. A. & Kogan, N. (1965). *Thinking in young children.* New York: Holt, Rinehart & Winston.

Wallander, J. L., & Hubert, N. C. (1985). Long-term prognosis for children with attention deficit disorder with hyperactivity (ADD/H). In B. B. Lahey & A. E. Kazdin (Eds.), *Advances in clinical child psychology* (Vol. 8). New York: Plenum.

Wallen, K. (1996). Nature needs nurture: The interaction of hormonal and social influences on the development of behavioral sex differences in rhesus monkeys. *Hormones and Behavior, 30,* 364–378.

Wallerstein, J. S., Lewis, J. M., & Blakeslee, S. (2000). *The unexpected legacy of divorce: A 25-year landmark study.* New York: Hyperion.

Walls, R. T. (2000). Vocational cognition: Accuracy of 3rd-, 6th-, 9th-, and 12th-grade students. *Journal of Vocational Behavior, 56,* 137–144.

Walsh, C. (2000). The life and legacy of Lawrence Kohlberg. *Society, 37,* 36–41.

Walsh, C. E. (2003). Gene therapy progress and prospects: Gene therapy for the hemophilias. *Gene Therapy, 10,* 999–1003.

Walster, E., Walster, G. W., & Berscheid, E. (1978). *Equity: Theory and research.* Boston: Allyn & Bacon.

Wang, H. Y., & Amato, P. R. (2000). Predictors of divorce adjustment: Stressors, resources, and definitions. *Journal of Marriage and the Family, 62,* 655–668.

Wang, M. C., Haertel, G. D., & Walberg, H. J. (1993). Toward a knowledge base for school learning. *Review of Educational Research,* 63, 249–294.

Wang, Q. (2004). Cultural self-constructions: Autobiographical memory and self-description in European American and Chinese children. *Developmental Psychology, 40,* 3–15.

Ward, C. D., & Cooper, R. P. (1999). A lack of evidence in 4-month-old human infants for paternal voice preference. *Developmental Psychobiology, 35,* 49–59.

Ward, M. J., Lee, S. S., & Lipper, E. G. (2000). Failure to thrive is associated with disorganized infant–mother attachment and unresolved maternal attachment. *Infant Mental Health Journal, 21,* 428–442.

Ward, R., & Spitze, G. (1992). Consequences of parent–adult child coresidence. *Journal of Family Issues, 13,* 533–572.

Ward, R., & Spitze, G. (2004). Marital implications of parent–adult child coresidence: A longitudinal view. *Journal of Gerontology: Social Sciences, 59B,* S2–S8.

Wardle, J., & Watters, R. (2004). Sociocultural influences on attitudes to weight and eating: Results of a natural experiment. *International Journal of Eating Disorders, 35,* 589–596.

Warin, J. (2000). The attainment of self-consistency through gender in young children. *Sex Roles, 42,* 209–231.

Wark, G. R., & Krebs, D. L. (1996). Gender and dilemma differences in real-life moral judgment. *Developmental Psychology, 32,* 220–230.

Warr, P. (1992). Age and occupational well-being. *Psychology and Aging, 7,* 37–45.

Warren, J. R., LePore, P. C., & Mare, R. D. (2000). Employment during high school: Consequences for students' grades in academic courses. *American Educational Research Journal, 37,* 943–970.

Waskowic, T. D., & Chartier, B. M. (2003). Attachment and the experience of grief following the loss of a spouse. *Omega: Journal of Death and Dying, 47,* 77–91.

Wass, H. (1991). Helping children cope with death. In D. Papadatou & C. Papadatos (Eds.), *Children and death.* New York: Hemisphere.

Waterman, A. S. (1982). Identity development from adolescence to adulthood: An extension of theory and a review of research. *Developmental Psychology, 18,* 341–358.

Waterman, A. S. (1992). Identity as an aspect of optimal psychological functioning. In G. R. Adams, T. P. Gullotta, & R. Montemayor (Eds.), *Adolescent identity formation* (Advances in Adolescent Development, Vol. 4). Newbury Park, CA: Sage.

Waters, E., Merrick, S., Treboux, D., Crowell, J., & Albersheim, L. (2000). Attachment security in infancy and early adulthood: A twenty-year longitudinal study. *Child Development, 71,* 684–689.

Waters, E., Wippman, J., & Sroufe, L. A. (1979). Attachment, positive affect, and competence in the peer group: Two studies in construct validation. *Child Development, 50,* 821–829.

Watson, J. B. (1913). Psychology as the behaviorist views it. *Psychological Review, 20,* 158–177.

Watson, J. B. (1925). *Behaviorism.* New York: Norton.

Watson, J. B., & Raynor, R. (1920). Conditioned emotional reactions. *Journal of Experimental Psychology, 3,* 1–14.

Waxman, S. R., & Hatch, T. (1992). Beyond the basics: Preschool children label objects flexibly at multiple hierarchical levels. *Journal of Child Language, 19,* 153–166.

Wayne, A. J., & Youngs, P. (2003). Teacher characteristics and student achievement gains: A review. *Review of Educational Research, 73,* 89–122.

Webster, J. D. (1998). Attachment styles, reminiscence functions, and happiness in young and elderly adults. *Journal of Aging Studies, 12,* 315–330.

Webster, J. D., & Haight, B. K. (Eds.) (2002). *Critical advances in reminiscence work: From theory to application.* New York: Springer.

Webster, J. D., & McCall, M. E. (1999). Reminiscence functions across adulthood: A replication and extension. *Journal of Adult Development, 6,* 73–85.

Wechsler, D. (1991). *Manual, WISC-III: Wechsler Intelligence Scale for Children–Third Edition.* San Antonio, TX: Psychological Corporation.

Wechsler, D. (1997). *Wechsler Adult Intelligence Scale* (3rd ed.). San Antonio: Harcourt.

Wechsler, D. (2002). *Wechsler Preschool and Primary Scale of Intelligence* (3rd ed.). The Psychological Corporation.

Wehner, J. M., & Balogh, S. A. (2003). Genetic studies of learning and memory in mouse models. In R. Plomin, J. C. DeFries, I. W. Craig, & P. McGuffin (Eds.), *Behavioral genetics in the postgenomic era.* Washington, D.C.: American Psychological Association.

Weiffenbach, J. M., Cowart, B. J., & Baum, B. J. (1986). Taste intensity perception in aging. *Journal of Gerontology, 41,* 460–468.

Weinberg, R. A., Scarr, S., & Waldman, I. D. (1992). The Minnesota transracial adoption study: A follow-up of IQ test performance at adolescence. *Intelligence, 16,* 117–135.

Weinert, F. E., & Hany, E. A. (2003). The stability of individual differences in intellectual development: Empirical evidence, theoretical problems, and new research questions. In R. J. Sternberg, J. Lautrey, & T. I. Lubart (Eds.), *Models of intelligence: International perspectives* (pp. 169–181). Washington, D.C.: American Psychological Association.

Weinert, F. E., & Schneider, W. (1999). *Individual development from 3 to 12: Findings from the Munich Longitudinal Study.* Cambridge, England: Cambridge University Press.

Weinfield, N. S., Sroufe, L. A., & Egeland, B. (2000). Attachment from infancy to early adulthood in a high-risk sample: Continuity, discontinuity, and their correlates. *Child Development, 71,* 695–702.

Weinfield, N. S., Sroufe, L. A., Egeland, B., & Carlson, E. A. (1999). The nature of individual differences in infant-caregiver attachment. In J. Cassidy & P. R. Shaver (Eds.), *Handbook of attachment: Theory, research, and clinical applications.* New York: Guilford.

Weinraub, M., & Lewis, M. (1977). The determinants of children's responses to separation. *Monographs of the Society for Research in Child Development,* (4, Serial No. 172).

Weisberg, P. (1963). Social and nonsocial conditioning of infant vocalization. *Child Development, 34,* 377–388.

Weisfeld, G. E., & Woodward, L. (2004). Current evolutionary perspectives on adolescent romantic relations and sexuality. *Journal of the American Academy of Child and Adolescent Psychiatry, 43,* 11–19.

Weisner, T. S., & Gallimore, R. (1977). My brother's keeper: Child and sibling caretaking. *Current Anthropology, 18,* 169–190.

Weiss, B., & Garber, J. (2003). Developmental differences in the phenomenology of depression. *Development and Psychopathology, 15,* 403–430.

Weiss, G., & Hechtman, L. T. (1993). *Hyperactive children grown up* (2nd ed.). New York: Guilford.

Weiss, L. H., & Schwarz, J. C. (1996). The relationship between parenting types and older adolescents' personality, academic achievement, adjustment, and substance use. *Child Development, 67,* 2101–2114.

Weiss, R. (2000, May 23). For DNA, a defining moment. With code revealed, challenge will be to find its meaning and uses. *The Washington Post,* A1, A16–A17.

Weiss, R. (2003a, February 28). Dream unmet 50 years after DNA milestone. *The Washington Post,* A1, A10.

Weiss, R. (2003b, April 15). Genome Project completed. *The Washington Post,* A6.

Weiss, R., & Gillis, J. (2000, June 27). DNA-mapping milestone heralded. *The Washington Post,* A1, A12–A13.

Weisz, J. R., McCarty, C. A., Eastman, K. L., Chaiyasit, W., & Suwanlert, S. (1997). Developmental psychopathology and culture: Ten lessons from Thailand. In S. S. Luthar, J. A. Burack, D. Cicchetti, & J. R. Weisz (Eds.). *Developmental psychopathology: Perspectives on adjustment, risk and disorder.* Cambridge, England: Cambridge University Press.

Weisz, J. R., & Weiss, B. (1993). *Effects of psychotherapy with children and adolescents* (Vol. 27, Developmental Clinical Psychology and Psychiatry Series). Newbury Park, CA: Sage.

Weizman, A. O., & Snow, C. E. (2001). Lexical input as related to children's vocabulary acquisition: Effects of sophisticated exposure and support for meaning. *Developmental Psychology, 37,* 265–279.

Wellman, H. M. (1990). *The child's theory of mind.* Cambridge, MA: MIT Press.

Wellman, H. M., & Bartsch, K. (1994). Before belief: Children's early psychological theory. In C. Lewis & P. Mitchell (Eds.), *Children's early understanding of mind: Origins and development.* Hove, England: Erlbaum.

Wellman, H. M., & Gelman, S. A. (1992). Cognitive development: Foundational theories of core domains. *Annual Review of Psychology, 43,* 337–375.

Wellman, H. M., & Lagattuta, K. H. (2000). Developing understandings of mind. In S. Baron-Cohen, H. Tager-Flusberg, & D. J. Cohen (Eds.), *Understanding other minds. Perspectives from developmental cognitive neuroscience* (2nd ed.). Oxford: Oxford University Press.

Wellman, H. M., & Liu, D. (2004). Scaling of theory-of-mind-tasks. *Child Development, 75,* 523–541.

Wellman, H. M., Cross, D., & Watson, J. (2001). Meta-analysis of theory-of-mind development: The truth about false-belief. *Child Development, 72,* 655–684.

Wellman, H. M., Phillips, A. T., & Rodriguez, T. (2000). Young children's understanding of perception, desire, and emotion. *Child Development, 71,* 895–912.

Wender, P. H. (1995). *Attention-deficit hyperactivity disorder in adults.* New York: Oxford University Press.

Wenglinsky, H. (1998). Finance equalization and within-school equity: The relationship between education spending and the social distribution of achievement. *Educational Evaluation and Policy Analysis, 20,* 269–283.

Wentz, E., Gillberg, C., Gillberg, I. C., & Rastam, M. (2001). Ten-year follow-up of adolescent-onset anorexia nervosa: Psychiatric disorders and overall functioning scales. *Journal of Child Psychology and Psychiatry and Allied Disciplines, 42,* 613–622.

Wentzel, K. R. (1988). Gender differences in math and English achievement: A longitudinal study. *Sex Roles, 18,* 691–699.

Wentzel, K. R. (2003). Sociometric status and adjustment in middle school: A longitudinal study. *Journal of Early Adolescence, 23,* 5–28.

Werker, J. F., & Desjardins, R. N. (1995). Listening to speech in the first year of life: Experiential influences on phoneme perception. *Current Directions in Psychological Science, 4,* 76–81.

Werker, J. F., Gilbert, J. H. V., Humphrey, K., & Tees, R. C. (1981). Developmental aspects of cross-language speech perception. *Child Development, 52,* 349–355.

Werner, E. E. (1989a). Children of the Garden Island. *Scientific American, 260,* 106–111.

Werner, E. E. (1989b). High-risk children in young adulthood: A longitudinal study from birth to 32 years. *American Journal of Orthopsychiatry, 59,* 72–81.

Werner, E. E., & Smith, R. S. (1982). *Vulnerable but invincible: A longitudinal study of resilient children and youth.* New York: McGraw-Hill.

Werner, E. E., & Smith, R. S. (1992). *Overcoming the odds: High risk children from birth to adulthood.* Ithaca, NY: Cornell University Press.

Werner, E. E., & Smith, R. S. (2001). *Journeys from childhood to midlife: Risk, resilience, and recovery.* Ithaca, NY: Cornell University Press.

Werner, H. (1957). The concept of development from a comparative and organismic point of view. In D. B. Harris (Ed.), *The concept of de-*

velopment: An issue in the study of human behavior. Minneapolis: University of Minnesota Press.
Werth, J. L., Jr., Blevins, D., Toussaint, K. L., & Durham, M. R. (2002). The influence of cultural diversity on end-of-life care and decisions. *American Behavioral Scientist, 46,* 204–219.
West, R. L., Crook, T. H., & Barron, K. L. (1992). Everyday memory performance across the life span: Effects of age and noncognitive individual differences. *Psychology and Aging, 7,* 72–82.
Weyandt, L. L. (2001). *An ADHD primer.* Boston: Allyn & Bacon.
Whalen, C. K., Henker, B., Buhrmester, D., Hinshaw, S. P., Huber, A., & Laski, K. (1989). Does stimulant medication improve the peer status of hyperactive children? *Journal of Consulting and Clinical Psychology, 57,* 545–549.
Whalley, L., & Deary, I. J. (2001). Longitudinal cohort study of childhood IQ and survival up to age 76. *British Medical Journal, 322,* 819–824.
Whipp, B. J., & Ward, S. A. (1992). Will women soon outrun men? *Nature, 355,* 25.
Whipple, E. E., & Richey, C. A. (1997). Crossing the line from physical discipline to child abuse: How much is too much? *Child Abuse and Neglect, 21,* 431–444.
Whitbeck, L. B., Hoyt, D. R., Simons, R. L., Conger, R. D., Elder, G. H., Jr., Lorenz, F. O., & Huck, S. (1992). Intergenerational continuity of parental rejection and depressed affect. *Journal of Personality and Social Psychology, 63,* 1036–1045.
Whitbourne, S. K. (2001). *Adult development and aging: Biopsychosocial perspectives.* New York: Wiley.
Whitbourne, S. K. (2004). *Adult development and aging: Biopsychosocial perspectives.* New York: Wiley.
Whitbourne, S. K., & Tesch, S. A. (1985). A comparison of identity and intimacy statuses in college students and alumni. *Developmental Psychology, 21,* 1039–1044.
White, K., Speisman, J. C., & Costos, D. (1983). Young adults and their parents: Individuation to mutuality. In H. D. Grotevant & C. R. Cooper (Eds.), *Adolescent development in the family* (New Directions for Child Development, No. 22). San Francisco: Jossey-Bass.
White, L., & Edwards, J. N. (1990). Emptying the nest and parental well-being: An analysis of national panel data. *American Sociological Review, 55,* 235–242.
White, L., & Rogers, S. J. (1997). Strong support but uneasy relationships: Coresidence and adult children's relationships with their parents. *Journal of Marriage and the Family, 59,* 62–76.
White, L., & Rogers, S. J. (2000). Economic circumstances and family outcomes: A review of the 1990s. *Journal of Marriage and the Family, 62,* 1035–1051.
White, S. H., & Pillemer, D. B. (1979). Childhood amnesia and the development of a socially accessible memory system. In J. F. Kihlstrom & F. J. Evans (Eds.), *Functional disorders of memory.* Hillsdale, NJ: Erlbaum.
Whitebread, D. (1999). Interactions between children's metacognitive abilities, working memory capacity, strategies and performance during problem-solving. *European Journal of Psychology of Education, 14,* 489–507.
Whitehead, B. D., & Popenoe, D. (2003). *The state of the unions. The social health of marriage in America 2003. Essay: Marriage and children: Coming together again?* The National Marriage Project, Rutgers University. Available from: http://marriage.rutgers.edu/Publications/Print/PrintSOOU2003.htm.
Whitehurst, G. J., & Lonigan, C. J. (1998). Child development and emergent literacy. *Child Development, 69,* 848–872.
Whitehurst, G. J., & Valdez-Menchaca, M. C. (1988). What is the role of reinforcement in early language acquisition? *Child Development, 59,* 430–440.
Whiting, B. B., & Edwards, C. P. (1988). *Children of different worlds: The formation of social behavior.* Cambridge, MA: Harvard University Press.
Wickens, A. P. (1998). *The causes of aging.* Amsterdam: Harwood Academic Publishers.
Wideroe, M., Vik, T., Jacobsen, G., & Bakketeig, L. S. (2003). Does maternal smoking during pregnancy cause childhood overweight? *Paediatric Perinatology Epidemiology, 17,* 171–179.
Widmayer, S., & Field, T. (1980). Effects of Brazelton demonstrations on early interactions of preterm infants and their teen-age mothers. *Infant Behavior and Development, 3,* 79–89.
Widmer, E. D., Treas, J., & Newcomb, R. (1998). Attitudes toward nonmarital sex in 24 countries. *Journal of Sex Research, 35,* 349–358.
Wiehe, V. R. (1996). *Working with child abuse and neglect.* Thousand Oaks, CA: Sage.
Wigfield, A., Eccles, J. S., Yoon, K. S., & Harold, R. D. (1997). Change in children's competence beliefs and subjective task values across the elementary school years: A 3-year study. *Journal of Educational Psychology, 89,* 451–469.
Wiggins, S., Whyte, P., Huggins, M., Adam, S., Theilmann, J., Bloch, M., Sheps, S. B., Schechter, M. T., Hayden, M. R. (1992). The psychological consequences of predictive testing for Huntington's disease. *New England Journal of Medicine, 327,* 1401–1405.
Wikan, U. (1988). Bereavement and loss in two Muslim communities: Egypt and Bali compared. *Social Science and Medicine, 27,* 451–460.
Wikan, U. (1991). *Managing turbulent hearts.* Chicago: University of Chicago Press.
Wilbur, J., Miller, A., & Montgomery, A. (1995). The influence of demographic characteristics, menopausal status, and symptoms on women's attitudes toward menopause. *Women and Health, 23,* 19–39.
Wilcock, A., Kobayashi, L., & Murray, I. (1997). Twenty-five years of obstetric patient satisfaction in North America: A review of the literature. *Journal of Perinatal and Neonatal Nursing, 10,* 36–47.
Wilcox, S., Evenson, K. R., Aragaki, A., Wassertheil-Smoller, S., Mouton, C. P., & Loevinger, B. L. (2003). The effects of widowhood on physical and mental health, health behaviors, and health outcomes: The Women's Health Initiative. *Health Psychology, 22,* 513–522.
Wildes, J. E., Emery, R. E., & Simons, A. D. (2001). The roles of ethnicity and culture in the development of eating disturbance and body dissatisfaction: A meta-analytic review. *Clinical Psychology Review, 21,* 521–551.
Wilks, J. (1986). The relative importance of parents and friends in adolescent decision making. *Journal of Youth and Adolescence, 15,* 323–334.
Willats, P. (1990). Development of problem solving strategies in infancy. In D. F. Bjorklund (Ed.), *Children's strategies.* Hillsdale, NJ: Erlbaum.
Williams, A. F., & Carsten, O. (1989). Driver age and crash involvement. *American Journal of Public Health,* 326–327.
Williams, J. (2003). Dementia and genetics. In R. Plomin, J. C. DeFries, I. W. Craig, & P. McGuffin (Eds.), *Behavioral genetics in the postgenomic era.* Washington, D.C.: American Psychological Association.
Williams, J. E., & Best, D. L. (1990). *Measuring sex stereotypes: A multination study* (rev. ed.). Newbury Park, CA: Sage.
Williams, J. M., & Currie, C. (2000). Self-esteem and physical development in early adolescence: Pubertal timing and body image. *Journal of Early Adolescence, 20,* 129–149.
Williams, K. C. (1996). Piagetian principles: Simple and effective application. *Journal of Intellectual Disability Research, 40,* 110–119.
Williams, M. E. (1995). *The American Geriatrics Society's complete guide to aging and health.* New York: Harmony Books.
Williams, M. R. (2000, September 27). Teen recklessness linked to still-developing brains. *Charleston Gazette.*
Williams, M. V., Baker, D. W., Parker, R. M., & Nurss, J. R. (1998). Relationship of functional health literacy to patients' knowledge of their chronic disease. *Archives of Internal Medicine, 158,* 166–172.
Williams, P. T. (1997). Evidence for the incompatibility of age-neutral overweight and age-neutral physical activity standards from runners. *American Journal of Clinical Nutrition, 65,* 1391–1396.
Willis, S. L., & Schaie, K. W. (1999). Intellectual functioning in midlife. In S. L. Willis & J. D. Reid (Eds.), *Life in the middle. Psychological and social development in middle age.* San Diego: Academic Press.
Wilmoth, J. R., Deegan, L. J., Lundstrom, H., & Horiuchi, S. (2000). Increase of maximum life-span in Sweden, 1861–1999. *Science,* 289, 2366–2368.
Wilson, A. E., Smith, M. D., Ross, H. S., & Ross, M. (2004). Young children's personal accounts of their sibling disputes. *Merrill-Palmer Quarterly, 50,* 39–60.
Wilson, G. T. (1994). Behavioral treatment of childhood obesity: Theoretical and practical implications. *Health Psychology, 13,* 371–372.
Wilson, G. T., Becker, C. B., & Heffernan, K. (2003). Eating disorders. In E. J. Mash & R. A. Barkley, (Eds.), *Child psychopathology* (2nd ed.). New York: Guilford Press.
Wilson, R. (2003, December 5). How babies alter careers for academics. *The Chronicle of Higher Education,* A1, A6–A8.
Wilson, R. S. (1978). Synchronies in mental development: An epigenetic perspective. *Science, 202,* 939–948.
Wilson, R. S. (1983). The Louisville twin study: Developmental synchronies in behavior. *Child Development, 54,* 298–316.
Wilson, S. J., Lipsey, M. W., & Derzon, J. H. (2003). The effects of school-based intervention programs on aggressive behavior: A meta-analysis. *Journal of Consulting and Clinical Psychology, 71,* 136–149.
Windle, R. C., & Windle, M. (1997). An investigation of adolescents' substance use behav-

iors, depressed affect, and suicidal behaviors. *Journal of Child Psychology and Psychiatry and Allied Disciplines, 38,* 921–929.

Wineberg, H., & Werth, J. L. Jr. (2003). Physician-assisted suicide in Oregon: What are the key factors? *Death Studies, 27,* 501–518.

Wingfield, A., Poon, L. W., Lombardi, L., & Lowe, D. (1985). Speed of processing in normal aging: Effects of speech rate, linguistic structure, and processing time. *Journal of Gerontology, 40,* 579–595.

Wink, P., & Dillon, M. (2002). Spiritual development across the adult life course: Findings from a longitudinal study. *Journal of Adult Development, 9,* 79–94.

Wink, P., & Dillon, M. (2003). Religiousness, spirituality, and psychosocial functioning in late adulthood: findings from a longitudinal study. *Psychology and Aging, 18,* 916–924.

Wink, P., & Helson, R. (1993). Personality change in women and their partners. *Journal of Personality and Social Psychology, 65,* 597–605.

Winkler, I., Kushnerenko, E., Horvath, J., Ceponiene, R., Fellman, V., Huotilainen, M., Naatanen, R., & Sussman, E. (2003). Newborn infants can organize the auditory world. *Proceedings of the National Academy of Sciences, 100,* 11812–11815.

Winn, H. N., & Hobbins, J. C. (Eds.). (2000). *Clinical maternal-fetal medicine.* London: Parthenon.

Winner, E. (1996). *Gifted children: Myths and realities.* New York: Basic Books.

Winsler, A., Carlton, M. P., & Barry, M. J. (2000). Age-related changes in preschool children's systematic use of private speech in a natural setting. *Journal of Child Language, 27,* 665–687.

Winterich, J. A., & Umberson, D. (1999). How women experience menopause: The importance of context. *Journal of Women and Aging, 11,* 57.

Wisborg, K., Kesmodel, U., Henriksen, T. B., Olsen, S. F., & Secher, N. J. (2000). A prospective study of smoking during pregnancy and SIDS. *Archives of Disease in Childhood, 83,* 203–206.

Witt, S. (1997). Parental influence on children's socialization to gender roles. *Adolescence, 32,* 253–259.

Wlodkowski, R. J. (1999). *Enhancing adult motivation to learn : A comprehensive guide for teaching all adults.* San Francisco: Jossey-Bass Higher and Adult Education Series.

Wolchik, S. A., West, S. G., Sandler, I. N., Tein, J. Y., Coatsworth, D., Lengua, L., Weiss, L., Anderson, E. R., Greene, S. M., & Griffin, W. A. (2000). An experimental evaluation of theory-based mother and mother–child programs for children of divorce. *Journal of Consulting and Clinical Psychology, 68,* 843–856.

Wolf, R. S. (2000). Elder abuse. In V. B. Van Hasselt & M. Hersen (Eds.), *Aggression and violence: An introductory text.* Needham Heights, MA: Allyn & Bacon.

Wolfe, J., Grier, H. E., Klar, N., Levin, S. B., Ellenbogen, J. M., Salem-Schatz, S., Emanuel, E. J., & Weeks, J. C. (2000). Symptoms and suffering at the end of life in children with cancer. *New England Journal of Medicine, 342,* 326–333.

Wolfe, R., Morrow, J., & Fredrickson, B. L. (1996). Mood disorders in older adults. In L. L. Carstensen, B. A. Edelstein, & L. Dornbrand (Eds.), *The practical handbook of clinical gerontology.* Thousand Oaks, CA: Sage.

Wolfe, W. S., Campbell, C. C., Frongillo, E. A., Haas, J. D., & Melnik, T. A. (1994). Overweight schoolchildren in New York State: Prevalence and characteristics. *American Journal of Public Health, 84,* 807–813.

Wolff, P. H. (1963). Observations on the early development of smiling. In B. M. Foss (Ed.), *Determinants of infant behavior* (Vol. 2). London: Methuen.

Wolfner, G. D., & Gelles, R. J. (1993). A profile of violence toward children: A national study. *Child Abuse and Neglect, 17,* 197–212.

Wolfson, A. R., & Carskadon, M. A. (1998). Sleep schedules and daytime functioning in adolescents. *Child Development, 69,* 875–998.

Women's Health Initiative. (2004). *The estrogen-plus-progestin study.* Available online: http://www.nhlbi.nih.gov/whi/estro_pro.htm (retrieved September 9, 2004).

Wong, C. A., Eccles, J. S., & Sameroff, A. (2003). The influence of ethnic discrimination and ethnic identification on African American adolescents' school and socioemotional adjustment. *Journal of Personality, 71,* 1197–1232.

Wong, P. T. P., & Watt, L. M. (1991). What types of reminiscence are associated with successful aging? *Psychology and Aging, 6,* 272–279.

Wood, E., Desmarais, S., & Gugula, S. (2002). The impact of parenting experience on gender stereotyped toy play of children. *Sex Roles, 47,* 39–49.

Woodhill, B. M., & Samuels, C. A. (2003). Positive and negative androgyny and their relationship with psychological health and well-being. *Sex Roles, 49,* 555–565.

Woodhill, B. M., & Samuels, C. A. (2004). Desirable and undesirable androgyny: A prescription for the twenty-first century. *Journal of Gender Studies, 13,* 15–28.

Woodward, A. L., & Markman, E. M. (1998). Early word learning. In D. Kuhn & R. S. Siegler (Vol. Eds.), W. Damon (Editor-in-Chief), *Handbook of child psychology: Vol. 2. Cognition, perception, and language* (5th ed., pp. 371–420). New York: Wiley.

Woodward, L., Fergusson, D. M., & Belsky, J. (2000). Timing of parental separation and attachment to parents in adolescence: Results of a prospective study from birth to age 16. *Journal of Marriage and the Family, 62,* 162–174.

Woolfe, T., Want, S. C., & Siegal, M. (2002). Signposts to development: Theory of mind in deaf children. *Child Development, 73,* 768–778.

Worchel, F. F., Copeland, D. R., & Barker, D. G. (1987). Control-related coping strategies in pediatric oncology patients. *Journal of Pediatric Psychology, 12,* 25–38.

Worden, J. W., & Silverman, P. R. (1996). Parental death and the adjustment of school-age children. *Omega: Journal of Death and Dying, 33,* 91–102.

Worden, J. W., & Silverman, P. S. (1993). Grief and depression in newly widowed parents with school-age children. *Omega: Journal of Death and Dying, 27,* 251–261.

Worfolk, J. B. (2000). Heat waves: Their impact on the health of elders. *Geriatric Nursing, 21,* 70–77.

Worthen, L. T., & Yeatts, D. E. (2000–2001). Assisted suicide: Factors affecting public attitudes. *Omega: Journal of Death and Dying, 42,* 115–135.

Wortman, C. B., & Silver, R. C. (2001). The myths of coping with loss revisited. In M. S. Stroebe, R. O. Hansson, W. Stroebe, & H. Schut (Eds.), *Handbook of bereavement research. Consequences, coping, and care.* Washington, D.C.: American Psychological Association.

Wright, C., & Birks, E. (2000). Risk factors for failure to thrive: A population based survey. *Child: Care, Health, and Development, 26,* 5–16.

Wright, K. (2000). Thalidomide is back. *Discover, 21,* 31–33.

Wrosch, C., Schulz, R., & Heckhausen, J. (2004). Health stresses and depressive symptomatology in the elderly: A control-process approach. *Current Directions in Psychological Science, 13,* 17–20.

Wu, C. Y., Yu, T. J., & Chen, M. J. (2000). Age related testosterone level changes and male andropause syndrome. *Changgeng Yi Xue Za Zhi [Chinese Medical Journal], 23,* 348–353.

Wu, T., Mendola, P., & Buck, G. M. (2002). Ethnic differences in the presence of secondary sex characteristics and menarche among US girls: The Third National Health and Nutrition Examination Survey, 1988–1994. *Pediatrics, 110,* 752–757.

Wyly, M. V. (1997). *Infant assessment.* Boulder, CO: Westview.

Wynn, K. (1992). Addition and subtraction by human infants. *Nature, 358,* 749–750.

Y

Yaffe, K., Barnes, D., Nevitt, M., Lui, L., & Covinsky, K. (2001). A prospective study of physical activity and cognitive decline in elderly women. *Archives of Internal Medicine, 161,* 1703–1708.

Yan, B., & Arlin, P. K. (1995). Nonabsolute/relativistic thinking: A common factor underlying models of postformal reasoning? *Journal of Adult Development, 2,* 223–240.

Yan, J. H., Thomas, J. R., & Stelmach, G. E. (1998). Aging and rapid aiming arm movement control. *Experimental Aging Research, 24,* 155–168.

Yan, J. H., Thomas, J. R., Stelmach, G. E., & Thomas, K. T. (2000). Developmental features of rapid aiming arm movements across the lifespan. *Journal of Motor Behavior, 32,* 121–140.

Yang, Y. H., Kim, S. H., & Jung, J. E. (2002). Prenatal diagnosis of fetal cells in maternal blood by comparative genomic hybridization. In F. A. Chervenak, A. Kurjak, & Z. Papp (Eds.), *The fetus as a patient.* New York: Parthenon.

Yanowitz, K. L., & Weathers, K. J. (2004). Do boys and girls act differently in the classroom? A content analysis of student characters in educational psychology textbooks. *Sex Roles, 51,* 101–107.

Yashin, A. I., Iachine, I. A., & Harris, J. R. (1999). Half of the variation in susceptibility to mortality is genetic: Findings from Swedish twin survival data. *Behavior Genetics, 29,* 11–19.

Yeates, K. O., MacPhee, D., Campbell, F. A., & Ramey, C. T. (1983). Maternal IQ and home environment as determinants of early childhood intellectual competence: A developmental analysis. *Developmental Psychology, 19,* 731–739.

Yeates, K. O., & Selman, R. L. (1989). Social competence in the schools: Toward an integrative developmental model for intervention. *Developmental Review, 9,* 64–100.

Yeh, H., & Lempers, J. D. (2004). Perceived sibling relationships and adolescent development. *Journal of Youth and Adolescence, 33,* 133–147.

Yendovitskaya, T. V. (1971). Development of attention. In A. V. Zaporozhets & D. B. Elkonin (Eds.), *The psychology of preschool children.* Cambridge, MA: MIT Press.

Yirmiya, N., Solomonica-Levy, D., Shulman, C., & Pilowsky, T. (1996). Theory of mind abilities in individuals with autism, Down syndrome, and mental retardation of unknown etiology: The role of age and intelligence. *Journal of Child Psychology and Psychiatry and Allied Disciplines, 37,* 1003–1014.

Youn, G. Y., Knight, B. G., Jeong, H. S., & Benton, D. (1999). Differences in familism values and caregiving outcomes among Korean, Korean American, and White American dementia caregivers. *Psychology and Aging, 14,* 355–364.

Young, W. C., Goy, R. W., & Phoenix, C. H. (1964). Hormones and sexual behavior. *Science, 143,* 212–218.

Youngblade, L. M., & Dunn, J. (1995). Individual differences in young children's pretend play with mother and sibling: Links to relationships and understanding of other people's feelings and beliefs. *Child Development, 66,* 1472–1492.

Youniss, J. (1980). *Parents and peers in social development. A Sullivan–Piaget perspective.* Chicago: University of Chicago Press.

Yuill, N. (1993). Understanding of personality and dispositions. In M. Bennett (Ed.), *The development of social cognition: The child as psychologist.* New York: Guilford.

Yussen, S. R., & Levy, V. M. (1975). Developmental changes in predicting one's own memory span of short-term memory. *Journal of Experimental Child Psychology, 19,* 502–508.

Z

Zahn-Waxler, C., Friedman, R. J., Cole, P. M., Mizuta, I., & Himura, N. (1996). Japanese and United States preschool children's responses to conflict and distress. *Child Development, 67,* 2462–2477.

Zahn-Waxler, C., Radke-Yarrow, M., & King, R. A. (1979). Child rearing and children's prosocial initiations toward victims of distress. *Child Development, 50,* 319–330.

Zahn-Waxler, C., Radke-Yarrow, M., Wagner, E., & Chapman, M. (1992). Development of concern for others. *Developmental Psychology, 28,* 126–136.

Zajac, R., & Hayne, H. (2003). I don't think that's what really happened: The effect of cross-examination on the accuracy of children's reports. *Journal of Experimental Psychology: Applied, 9,* 187–195.

Zajonc, R. B. (1976, April 16). Family configuration and intelligence. *Science, 192,* 227–236.

Zajonc, R. B. (2001a). Birth order debate resolved? *American Psychologist, 56,* 522–523.

Zajonc, R. B. (2001b). The family dynamics of intellectual development. *American Psychologist, 56,* 490–496.

Zander, L., & Chamberlain, G. (1999). Place of birth. *British Medical Journal, 318,* 721.

Zaporozhets, A. V. (1965). The development of perception in the preschool child. *Monographs of the Society for Research in Child Development, 30* (2, Serial No. 100), 82–101.

Zaslow, M. (1980). Relationships among peers in kibbutz toddler groups. *Child Psychiatry and Human Development, 10,* 178–189.

Zeanah, C. H. (2000). Disturbances of attachment in young children adopted from institutions. *Journal of Developmental and Behavioral Pediatrics, 21,* 230–236.

Zeanah, C. H., Boris, N. W., & Scheeringa, M. S. (1997). Psychopathology in infancy. *Journal of Child Psychology and Psychiatry and Allied Disciplines, 38,* 81–99.

Zemel, B. (2002). Body composition during growth and development. In N. Cameron (Ed.), *Human growth and development* (pp. 271–293). New York: Academic Press.

Zhang, L. (2002). Thinking styles and cognitive development. *Journal of Genetic Psychology, 163,* 179–195.

Zick, C. D., & Holden, K. (2000). An assessment of the wealth holdings of recent widows. *Journal of Gerontology: Social Sciences, 55,* S90–S97.

Zigler, E. (1995). Can we "cure" mild mental retardation among individuals in the lower socioeconomic stratum? *American Journal of Public Health, 85,* 302–304.

Zigler, E., Abelson, W. D., Trickett, P. K., & Seitz, V. (1982). Is an intervention program necessary to improve economically disadvantaged children's IQ scores? *Child Development, 53,* 340–348.

Zigler, E., & Hodapp, R. M. (1991). Behavioral functioning in individuals with mental retardation. *Annual Review of Psychology, 42,* 29–50.

Zimmer-Gembeck, M. J. (1999). Stability, change and individual differences in involvement with friends and romantic partners among adolescent females. *Journal of Youth and Adolescence, 28,* 419–438.

Zimprich, D., & Martin, M. (2002). Can longitudinal changes in processing speed explain longitudinal age changes in fluid intelligence? *Psychology and Aging, 17,* 690–695.

Zisook, S., & Shuchter, S. R. (2001). Treatment of the depressions of bereavement. *American Behavioral Scientist, 44,* 782–797.

Zucker, A. N., Ostrove, J. M., & Stewart, A. J. (2002). College-educated women's personality development in adulthood: Perceptions and age differences. *Psychology and Aging, 17,* 236–244.

Zunzunegui, M. V., Alvarado, B. E., DelSer, T., & Otero, A. (2003). Social networks, social integration, and social engagement determine cognitive decline in community-dwelling Spanish older adults. *Journals of Gerontology: Psychological Sciences and Social Sciences, 58,* S93–S100.

Name Index

D

E

H

I

J

K

L

M

N

Q

R

S

T

U

X

Y

Z

Subject Index

E

F

G